FLAVIUS JOSEPHUS

VOLUME 7B

JUDEAN ANTIQUITIES 15

FLAVIUS JOSEPHUS

TRANSLATION AND COMMENTARY

EDITED BY

STEVE MASON

VOLUME 7B

JUDEAN ANTIQUITIES 15

TRANSLATION AND COMMENTARY

BY

JAN WILLEM VAN HENTEN

BRILL
LEIDEN · BOSTON
2014

Library of Congress Cataloging-in-Publication Data

Josephus, Flavius, author.
 [Antiquitates Judaicae. Liber 15. English]
 Judean antiquities 15 : translation and commentary / by Jan Willem Van Henten.
   p. cm. -- (Flavius Josephus translation and commentary ; Volume 7b)
 Includes bibliographical references and index.
 Summary: "In Antiquities 15 Josephus offers an account of the Judean kingdom ruled by Herod the Great (37-4 BCE). The commentary interprets his narrative in detail and identifies historical considerations that arise in the course of such analysis"--Provided by publisher.
 ISBN 978-90-04-26302-4 (hardback : alk. paper) 1. Jews--History--168 B.C.-135 A.D. 2. Herod I, King of Judea, 73 B.C.-4 B.C. 3. Jews--Kings and rulers--Biography. I. Henten, J. W. van, translator, author of commentary. II. Title.
 DS122.3.J6713 2014
 933.05092--dc23
                           2013040510

ISBN 978-90-04-26302-4

Copyright 2014 by Koninklijke Brill NV, Leiden, The Netherlands.
Koninklijke Brill NV incorporates the imprints Brill, Global Oriental, Hotei Publishing,
IDC Publishers and Martinus Nijhoff Publishers.

All rights reserved. No part of this publication may be reproduced, translated, stored in
a retrieval system, or transmitted in any form or by any means, electronic, mechanical,
photocopying, recording or otherwise, without prior written permission from the publisher.

Authorization to photocopy items for internal or personal use is granted by Koninklijke Brill NV
provided that the appropriate fees are paid directly to The Copyright Clearance Center,
222 Rosewood Drive, Suite 910, Danvers, MA 01923, USA.
Fees are subject to change.

This book is printed on acid-free paper.

PRINTED BY DRUKKERIJ WILCO B.V. - AMERSFOORT, THE NETHERLANDS

CONTENTS

List of Maps	vii
Series Preface: The Brill Josephus Project	ix
Preface and Acknowledgements	xiii
Abbreviations and Sigla	xvii
Summary of Antiquities 15	1
Text and Commentary	3
Bibliography	327
Bibliography of Primary Sources	345
Index of Ancient Texts	355
Index of Ancient Persons and Places	381
Index of Modern Authors	393

LIST OF MAPS

Map of Judea xv

Map of Caesarea Maritima xxxiv

Map of Herodean Temple precinct xxxv

Drawing of Herodean Temple complex xxxvi

SERIES PREFACE

THE BRILL JOSEPHUS PROJECT

Flavius Josephus (37–ca. 100 CE) was born Joseph son of Mattathyahu, a priestly aristocrat in Judea. During the early stages of the war against Rome (66-74 CE), he found himself leading a part of the defense in Galilee, but by the spring of 67, his territory overrun, he had surrendered under circumstances that would furnish grounds for endless accusation. Taken to Rome by the Flavian conquerors, he spent the balance of his life writing about the war, Judean history and culture, and his own career. He composed four works in thirty volumes.

If Josephus boasts about the unique importance of his work (*War* 1.1-3; *Ant*. 1.1-4) in the fashion of ancient historians, few of his modern readers could disagree with him. By the accidents of history, his narratives have become the indispensable source for all scholarly study of Judea from about 200 BCE to 75 CE. Our analysis of other texts and of the physical remains unearthed by archaeology must occur in dialogue with Josephus' stories, the only comprehensive and connected accounts of the period. This does not make Josephus reliable. It is only that historians of the period must try to understand and explain his evidence where it exists.

Although Josephus' name has been known continuously through nearly two millennia, and he has been cited extensively in support of any number of agendas, his writings have not always been valued as compositions. Readers have tended to look beyond them to the underlying historical facts or to Josephus' sources. Concentrated study in the standard academic forms—journals, scholarly seminars, or indeed commentaries devoted to Josephus—have been lacking. The past few decades, however, have witnessed the birth and rapid growth of "Josephus studies" in the proper sense. Signs of the new environment include all the vehicles and tools that were absent before, as well as K. H. Rengstorf's *Complete Concordance* (1983), Louis Feldman's annotated bibliographies, and a proliferation of Josephus-related dissertations. The time is right, therefore, for the first comprehensive English commentary to Josephus.

The commentary format is ancient, and even in antiquity commentators differed in their aims and methods. Philo's goals were not those of the author of Qumran's *Commentary on Nahum* or of the Christian writer Origen. In order to assist the reader of this series, the Brill Project team would like to explain our general aims and principles. Our most basic premise is that we do not intend to provide the last word: an exhaustive exegesis of this rich corpus. Rather, since no commentary yet exists in English, we hope simply to provide a resource that will serve as an invitation to further exploration. Although we began with the mandate to prepare a commentary alone, we soon realized that a new translation would be helpful. Keeping another existing translation at hand would have been cumbersome for the reader. And since we must comment on particular Greek words and phrases, we would have been implicitly challenging such existing translations at every turn. Given that we needed to prepare a working translation for the commentary in any case, it seemed wisest to include something like that with the commentary as a point of reference. A few words about the translation, then, are in order.

Granted that every translation is an interpretation, one can still imagine a spectrum of options. For example, the translator may set out to follow the contours of the original language more expressly or to place greater emphasis on idiomatic phrasing in the target language. There is much to be said for both of these options and for each interim stop in the spectrum. Accuracy is not a single, stable criterion in such choices, for one might gain precision in one respect (e.g., for a single word or form) only at the cost of accuracy elsewhere (e.g., in the sentence). Homer's epic poems provide a famous example of the problem: Does one render them in English dactylic hexameter, in looser verse, or even in prose to better convey the sense? One simply needs to make choices.

In our case, the course was suggested by the constraints of the commentary. If we were preparing a stand-alone translation for independent reading, we might have made other choices. Certainly if Josephus had been an Athenian poet, other considerations might have weighed more heavily. But Greek was his second or third language. His narratives are not great literature, and they vary in quality considerably from one part to another. Since the commentary bases itself upon his particular Greek words and phrases, it seemed necessary in this case that we produce a translation to reflect the patterns of the Greek as closely as possible. We can tolerate somewhat less clarity in our translation, where the Greek is ambiguous, because we intend it to be read with the commentary.

We happily confess our admiration for the Loeb translation, which has been the standard for some time, begun by Henry St. John Thackeray in the 1920s and completed by our colleague on the Brill Project (responsible for *Ant.* 1-4) Louis H. Feldman in 1965. For us to undertake a new translation implies no criticism of the Loeb. The older sections of it are somewhat dated now but it still reads well, often brilliantly. The chief problem with the Loeb for our purpose is only that it does not suit the needs of the commentator. Like most translations, it makes idiomatic English the highest virtue. It renders terms that Josephus frequently uses by different English equivalents for variety's sake; it often injects explanatory items to enhance the narrative flow; it collapses two or more Greek clauses into a single English clause; it alters the parts of speech with considerable freedom; and it tends to homogenize Josephus' changing style to a single, elevated English level.

Since we have undertaken to annotate words and phrases, we have required a different sort of foundation. Our goal has been to render individual Greek words with as much consistency as the context will allow, to preserve the parts of speech, letting adjectives be adjectives and participles be participles, to preserve phrases and clauses intact, and thus to reflect something of the particular stylistic level and tone of each section.

Needless to say, even a determined literalness must yield to the ultimate commandment of basic readability in English. Cases in which we have relinquished any effort to represent the Greek precisely include Josephus' preference for serial aorist-participle clauses. Given the frequency of complicated sentences in Josephus, as among most of his contemporaries, we have dealt quite freely with such clauses. We have often broken a series into separate sentences and also varied the translation of the form, thus: "After X had done Y," "When [or Once] X had occurred," and so on. Again, although in a very few cases Josephus' "historical present" may find a passable parallel in colloquial English, we have generally substituted a past tense. Thus we have not pursued literalness at all costs, but have sought it where it seemed feasible.

In the case of Josephus' personal names, we have used the familiar English equivalent where it is close to his Greek form. Where his version differs significantly from the one familiar to Western readers, or where he varies his form within the same narrative, we have represented his Greek spelling in Roman characters. That is because his unusual forms may be of interest to some readers, and Latin transliteration is most familiar to English readers. In such cases we have supplied the familiar English equivalent for reference in square brackets within the text or in a footnote. Similarly, we keep Josephus' units of measurement and titles, giving modern equivalents in the notes.

We do not pretend that this effort at literalness is always more accurate than an ostensibly freer rendering, since translation is such a complex phenomenon. Further, we have not always been able to realize our aims. Ultimately, the reader who cares deeply about the Greek text will want to read the Greek. But we have endeavored to provide a translation that permits us to discuss what is happening in the Greek with all of its problems, for the reader of our commentary.

The commentary aims at a balance between what one might, for convenience, call historical and literary issues. "Literary" here includes matters most pertinent to the interpretation of the text itself. "Historical" covers matters related to the hypothetical reconstruction of a reality outside the text. This does not mean that we are pursuing historical problems for themselves. Rather, aware that most readers will be interested in such questions we reflect on the ways in which the text has been used and might be used in such reconstructions. For example: How Josephus presented the causes of the war against Rome is a literary problem, in the sense that we need first to understand this question as part of his overall narrative (and in light of sources, parallels, themes, and rhetorical devices) whereas recovering the actual causes of the war is the task of historical reconstruction. Again, understanding Josephus' portraits of the Essenes is a matter for the interpreter of the text, whereas reconstructing the real Essenes and their possible relationship to Qumraners or other groups is for the historian—who may indeed be the same person, wearing a different hat. These are not hermetically sealed operations, of course, for we are always aware of one while doing the other, but some such classification helps us to remain aware of the discrete tasks before us and their different criteria.

On the literary side: to assist the reader who is interested in recovering some sense of what Josephus might have expected his first audience to understand, we have tried to observe some ways in which each part of his narrative relates to the whole. We point out apparently charged words and phrases in the narratives, which may also occur in such significant contexts as the prologues, speeches, and editorial asides. We look for parallels in some of the famous texts of the time, whether philosophical, historical, or dramatic, and whether Greco-Roman, Jewish, or Christian. We observe set pieces (*topoi*) and other rhetorical effects. Even apparently mundane but habitual features of Josephus' language and style are noted. Where puzzling language appears, we discuss possible explanations: rhetorical artifice, multiple editions, unassimilated vestiges of sources, the influence of a literary collaborator, and manuscript corruption.

A basic literary problem is the content of the text itself. Although we decided against preparing a new Greek edition as part of the project, we have paid close attention to textual problems in translation and commentary. The translation works mainly from Benedictus Niese's *editio maior*, since it remains the standard complete text with reasonably full apparatus. But since Niese's printed text is very conservative and often implausible, we have taken note of both the significant variants in Niese's own critical apparatus and other modern reconstructions where they are available. These include: the Loeb Greek text, the Michel-Bauernfeind edition of the *Judean War*, the current Münster project directed by Folker Siegert for Josephus's later works, and the ongoing French project led by Étienne Nodet. We have felt no particular loyalty to Niese's text where these others have proposed better readings.

Under the "historical" rubric fall a variety of subcategories. Most important perhaps are the impressive archaeological finds of recent decades in places mentioned by Josephus: building sites, coins, pottery, implements, inscriptions, and other items of material culture. Reading his stories of Masada or Herodium or Gamala is greatly enriched by observation of these newly identified sites, while in return, his narrative throws light on the history of those places. The commentary attempts to include systematic reference to the relevant archaeology. Other major historical categories include the problems of Josephus' own biography, his social context in Rome, and the historical reconstruction of persons, places, events, and social conditions mentioned by him. These issues can only be explored by reference to outside texts and material evidence for the conditions of life in the time of Josephus' narratives. Alongside questions of interpretation, therefore, we routinely discuss such problems as they appear in particular passages.

In preparing a commentary on such a vast corpus, it is a challenge to achieve proportion. Some stretches of narrative naturally call for more comment than others, and yet the aesthetics of publication requires a measure of balance. This commitment to a degree of symmetry (cf. *Ant.* 1.7) has required us to avoid too-lengthy discussion of famous passages, such as those on Jesus or the Essenes, while giving due attention to easily neglected sections.

A different kind of challenge is posed by the coming together of a dozen or more independent scholars for such a collegial enterprise. Uniformity is not among our goals. Committees do not create good translations or commentaries. We have striven rather for an appropriate balance between overall coherence and individual scholarly insight—the animating principle of humanistic scholarship. The simple Greek word *Ioudaios* affords an example of the diversity among us. Just as scholars in general differ as to whether the English "Judean" or "Jew" comes closest to what an ancient Greek or Roman heard in this word, so also our team members differ. Some of us have opted for "Judean" as a standard; some use both terms, depending upon the immediate context; and others use "Jew" almost exclusively. For the modern translator, as for Josephus himself, any particular phrase is part of an integrated world of discourse; to coerce agreement on any such point would violate that world. We hope that our readers will benefit from the range of expertise and perspective represented in these volumes. Nevertheless, wherever we can—for example, in representing certain semantic ranges in Greek by agreed equivalents in English—we strive for broad consistency.

It remains for the team members to thank some central players in the creation of this work, *amici* in scholarship whose names do not otherwise appear. First, many scholars in Josephan studies and related fields have offered encouragement at every step. Though we cannot name them all, we express our debt to those who are reading our work in progress, without thereby implicating them in its faults. They include David M. Goldenberg, Erich Gruen, Gohei Hata, Donna Runnalls, and Pieter van der Horst. Second, we are grateful to the editorial staff at Brill for initiating this project and seeing it through so professionally. In the early years, Elisabeth Erdman, Elisabeth Venekamp, Job Lisman, Sam Bruinsma, Jan-Peter Wissink, Anita Roodnat, and Ivo Romein provided constant encouragement as the first volumes appeared, even as we announced unavoidable delays with much of the publishing schedule. More recently, Loes Schouten and Mattie Kuiper have absorbed these delays with enormous grace, working with us patiently, flexibly and with unflagging professionalism to ensure the success of this important project.

Finally, in addition to expressing the group's thanks to these fine representatives of a distinguished publishing house (not least in Josephus-related publication) I am pleased to record my personal gratitude to the various agencies and institutions that have made possible my work as editor and contributor, alongside other demands on my time. These include: York University, my former academic home, for its remarkable support (including my appointment as Canada Research Chair in Greco-Roman Cultural Interaction, 2003–2011); the Social Sciences and Humanities Research Council of Canada (SSHRC) for funding throughout the project; the Killam Foundation of Canada, for a two-year leave fellowship in 2001-2003; All Souls College and Wolfson College, Oxford, for visiting fellowships during the Killam leave; The Alexander von Humboldt Stiftung, for a research award in 2013 that permitted a year in Berlin; the University of Groningen and its Qumran Institute for the Dirk Smilde fellowship in early 2014; and my current academic home, the University of Aberdeen, for allowing me to take up these research opportunities.

Steve Mason, The University of Aberdeen
General Editor, Brill Josephus Project

PREFACE AND ACKNOWLEDGEMENTS

This volume concerns part of Josephus' report about Herod the Great, the King of Judah who is probably best known among non-Jews. Herod's fame is mostly negative; his reputation was damaged once and for all by the story of the birth of Jesus Christ in Matthew's Gospel. Matthew presents Herod as the counterpart of Jesus, because he murdered all the children two years old or under in and around Bethlehem in order to prevent the birth of the new king (Matt 2:16). Josephus devotes about half of the first book of his *Jewish War* to the rule of Herod and his *Jewish Antiquities* offer an even more elaborate description of Herod's period in books 14-17. Herod's portraits in both of Josephus' works differ, and the overall picture is clearly more negative in *Antiquities*.

At the instigation of Mark Antony, Herod was appointed King of Judea, Galilee and Perea by the Roman Senate in 40 BCE (Josephus, *War* 1.281-285; *Ant.* 14.379-389). Before that he had made a profound impression on the Romans as governor of Galilee, where he put down a revolt of Hezekiah and his fellow-brigands. Although we will never know the precise motives of the Romans to prefer Herod as king over one of the Hasmonean rulers, it is plausible that under the circumstances Herod appeared to the Romans to be the most likely candidate to serve as a so-called friendly king who would guarantee peace and order at the fringe of their territories. In fact, it took Herod several years to capture his territory with the support of the Romans, but from 37 (or 36) BCE until 4 BCE he actually was king of Judea and other territories. *Antiquities* 15 starts when Herod is in control of Judea. The book deals with the history of his reign from the capture of Jerusalem to the expansion and renovation of the Jerusalem Temple (set in Herod's 18th regnal year, which is usually dated in 20-19 BCE).

The focus of this commentary is a contextual reading of Josephus' narrative about Herod, i.e., an attempt to understand the meaning of Josephus' text by linking it to plausible contexts of his Jewish and Graeco-Roman readers. I will discuss the content of Josephus' story and compare it with the Herod report in *War*, and also deal with the way he tells that story. Therefore, in addition to explaining the content I will analyze the vocabulary, style, and composition of Josephus' report. In addition to this, I apply a narratological approach whenever this seems useful, basically following the guidelines of the Studies in Ancient Greek Narrative series edited by Irene de Jong and others.[1]

This volume's designation as "7b" implies that the original numbering of the series had to be adapted in order to accommodate the large size of some of the volumes. Originally all four books that deal with Herod the Great (*Judean Antiquities* 14-17) were planned for one volume, but the size of the commentary on book 15 already makes this plan unrealistic. I am grateful to Louise Schouten from Brill, who agreed to publish this section as a separate volume.

I gladly acknowledge several institutions and many individuals who helped me to complete this volume. Most of the draft translation was prepared at Yarnton Manor, where I had a fellowship for the first semester of 2004. A considerable part of the commentary was written during a second half sabbatical in 2008 at the Netherlands Institute for Advanced Study at Wassenaar, which facilitated a small research group on Josephus that also included Daniel Schwartz and Joseph Patrich from the Hebrew University. The Institute for Culture and History and the Amsterdam School for Cultural Analysis financed many smaller trips, which allowed me to present and discuss draft sections of the commentary during scholarly meetings. A series of meetings with Joseph Sievers and Anthony Forte from the Pontifical Biblical Institute at Rome, who prepare the translation of and commentary on Judean War 1 (which runs partly parallel with Anti-

---

[1] See the introductions to I.J.F. de Jong, R. Nünlist & A. Bowie (eds), *Narrators, Narratees and Narratives in Ancient Greek Literature* (Leiden: Brill, 2004); I.J.F. de Jong & R. Nünlist (eds), *Time in Ancient Greek Literature* (Leiden: Brill, 2007); I.J.F. de Jong (ed.), *Space in Ancient Greek Literature* (Leiden: Brill, 2012).

quities 14-17), was extremely useful. I also thank my own university, the University of Amsterdam, for enabling me to work with three research assistants and a researcher for certain periods. Luuk Huitink, Rogier Oranje, Emma England and Bieke Mahieu provided bibliographies and notes on specific issues, or checked sections of my translation and corrected my bibliographies on primary and secondary sources. I also thank Rachel Hachlili for help in archaeological matters and Gaia Lembi for information on *Antiquities* 14. Shaye Cohen and Jonathan Price kindly responded to difficult queries. I greatly benefitted from the expertise of my co-fellows, Daniel Schwartz and Joseph Patrich, not only during our period at the NIAS but also afterwards. My former Amsterdam colleague Omert Schrier gave most helpful advice concerning text-critical issues. Luuk Huitink and Bieke Mahieu provided invaluable support. Luuk helped me to better understand some of the peculiarities of Josephus' style of historiography, and Bieke meticulously corrected the last draft version of the entire work. Peter Nagel helped me out with the preparation of the indices. I owe warmest thanks to Steve Mason, who gracefully edited the entire manuscript, also making many helpful suggestions for alternative translations. Finally I warmly thank Louise Schouten and Mattie Kuiper from Brill Academic Publishers, for their efficient and very kind support during various stages of the manuscript.

Jan Willem van Henten, University of Amsterdam/ Stellenbosch University

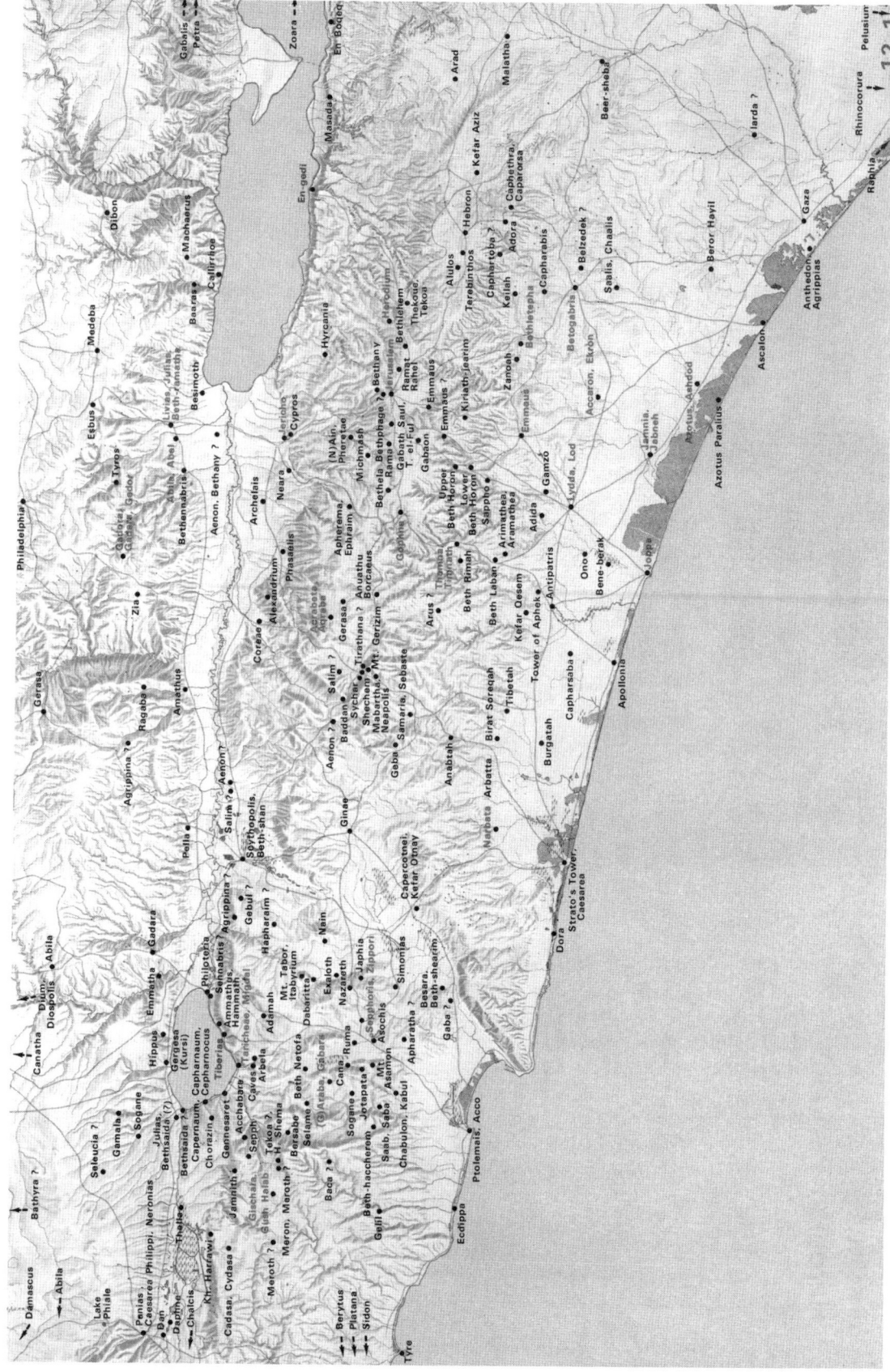

Courtesy of Richard Cleave, of Rohr Productions (Nicosia, Cyprus), from his *Student Map Manual: Historical Geography of the Bible Lands* (Jerusalem: Pictorial Archive, 1979).

ABBREVIATIONS AND SIGLA

Greek and Latin Authors

Achilles Tatius 2nd c. CE
(Leucippe et Clitophon)

Adamantius 5th c. CE
Physiogn.   *Physiognomonica*

Aelian 235 CE
Nat. an.   *De natura animalium*

Aelius Aristides 181 CE
Achill.   *Legatio ad Achillem = Oratio* 52 (Dindorf)/16 (Behr)
Ars rhet.   *Ars rhetorica*
Conc.   *De concordia ad civitates Asiaticas = Oratio* 42 (Dindorf)/23 (Behr)
Dem.   *Adversus Demosthenem de immunitate = Oratio* 53 (Dindorf)/absent (Behr)
Iov.   *In Iovem = Oratio* 1 (Dindorf)/43 (Behr)
Leuctr.   *Orationes Leuctricae = Orationes* 33-37 (Dindorf)/11-15 (Behr)
Pan. Cyz.   *Panegyrica in laudem Cyzici = Oratio* 16 (Dindorf)/27 (Behr)
Plat.   *Ad Platonem pro quattuor viris = Oratio* 46 (Dindorf)/3 (Behr)
Plat. rhet.   *Ad Platonem pro rhetorica = Oratio* 15 (Dindorf)/2 (Behr)
Reg.   *In regem = Oratio* 9 (Dindorf)/35 (Behr)
Roma   *De urbe Roma = Oratio* 14 (Dindorf)/26 (Behr)
Sacri serm.   *Sacri sermones = Orationes* 23-28 (Dindorf)/47-52 (Behr)

Aeschines 314 BCE
Ep.   *Epistulae*
Tim.   *In Timarchum*

Aeschylus ca. 455 BCE
Ag.   *Agamemnon*
Fragm.   *Fragmenta*
Pers.   *Persae*
Prom.   *Prometheus vinctus*
Suppl.   *Supplices*

Aesop 564 BCE
(Fabulae)

Agatharchides 2nd c. BCE
Mar. Erythr.   *De mari Erythraeo*

Alexander of Aphrodisias 200 CE
Comm. Top.   *In Aristotelis Topicorum libros octo commentaria*

Anaximenes of Lampsacus 320 BCE
(Ars rhetorica)

Andocides 390 BCE
Red.   *De reditu*

Antiphon 411 BCE
Caed. Her.   *De caede Herodis*

Aphthonius 2nd half 4th c. CE
(Progymnasmata)

Apollonius of Rhodes 3rd c. BCE
Arg.   *Argonautica*

Appian 160 CE
Bell. civ.   *Bella civilia*
Hist. rom.   *Historia romana*

Aristophanes 386 BCE
Av.   *Aves*
Eq.   *Equites*
Thesm.   *Thesmophoriazusae*
Vesp.   *Vespae*

Aristotle 322 BCE
Ath. pol.   *Athenaion politeia*
Cael.   *De caelo*
De an.   *De anima*
Eth. Eud.   *Ethica Eudemia*
Eth. Nic.   *Ethica Nicomachea*
Fragm.   *Fragmenta*
Hist. an.   *Historia animalium*
Mir. ausc.   *De mirabilibus auscultationibus*
Phys.   *Physica*
Physiogn.   *Physiognomonica*
Pol.   *Politica*
Probl.   *Problemata*
Rhet.   *Rhetorica*
Thesm.   *Thesmophoriazusae*
Top.   *Topica*
Virt. vit.   *De virtutibus et vitiis*

Arrian 175 CE
Anab.   *Anabasis*
Hist. succ. Alex.   *Historia successorum Alexandri*
Ind.   *Indica*

Aspasius 150 CE
(In Aristotelis Ethica Nicomachea)

Athanasius 373 CE
Syn.   *De synodis Arimini in Italia et Seleuciae in Isauria*
Vit. Anton.   *Vita Antonii*

Athenaeus 230 CE
(Deipnosophistae)

Basil of Caesarea 379 CE
Hom. Ps.   *Homiliae super Psalmos*

Calpurnius Siculus 2nd half 1st c. CE
(Eclogae)

Cassius Dio 235 CE
(Historia romana)

Chariton 1st/2nd c. CE
(De Chaerea et Callirhoe)

Cicero 43 BCE
Att.	*Epistulae ad Atticum*
De or.	*De oratore*
Leg.	*De legibus*
Off.	*De officiis*
Part. or.	*Partitiones oratoriae*
Phil.	*Orationes philippicae*
Pis.	*In Pisonem*
Rab. Perd.	*Pro Rabirio Perduellionis Reo*
Re publ.	*De re publica*
Tusc.	*Tusculanae disputations*

Clement of Alexandria 215 CE
Ecl.	*Eclogae propheticae*
Exh. Graec.	*Exhortatio ad Graecos*
Paed.	*Paedagogus*
Strom.	*Stromata*

Constantine Porphyrogenitus 959 CE
Legat.	*De legationibus Romanorum ad Gentes*
Virt. vit.	*De virtutibus et vitiis*

Cornutus 1st c. CE
(De natura deorum)

Damascius after 538 CE
Vit. Isid.	*Vita Isidori*

Demosthenes 322 BCE
Cor.	*De corona*
Erot.	*Eroticus*
Exord.	*Exordia*
Or.	*Orationes*
Pant.	*Contra Pantaenetum*
Phil. 1-4	*Philippica I-IV*

Didymus the Blind 398 CE
Fragm. Ps.	*Fragmenta in Psalmos*
Gen.	*In Genesim*

Dinarch 291 BCE
Aristog.	*In Aristogitonem*
Demosth.	*In Demosthenem*
Fragm.	*Fragmenta*
Phil.	*In Philoclem*

Dio Chrysostom 120 CE
(Orationes)

Diodorus 21 BCE
(Bibliotheca historica)

Diogenes Laertius early 3rd c. CE
(De vita et moribus philosophorum)

Dionysius of Halicarnassus after 7 BCE
Ant. rom.	*Antiquitates romanae*
Ars rhet.	*Ars rhetorica*
Comp.	*De compositione verborum*
Dem.	*De Demosthene*
Pomp.	*Epistula ad Pompeium Geminum*

Dionysius Periegetes 2nd c. CE
(Orbis descriptio)

Epictetus 135 CE
Diatr.	*Diatribae*
Ench.	*Enchiridion*

Epiphanius 403 CE
Haer.	*Adversus haereses*

Erotianus 1st c. CE
(Fragmenta)

Eunapius 5th c. CE
Fragm.	*Fragmenta*

Euripides 406 BCE
Alc.	*Alcestis*
Andr.	*Andromache*
Bacch.	*Bacchae*
Fragm.	*Fragmenta*
Heracl.	*Heraclidae*
Hipp.	*Hippolytus*
Ion	*Ion*
Iph. aul.	*Iphigenia aulidensis*
Iph. taur.	*Iphigenia taurica*
Med.	*Medea*
Orest.	*Orestes*
Phoen.	*Phoenissae*
Rhes.	*Rhesus*
Suppl.	*Supplices*

Eusebius 339 CE
Chron.	*Chronicon*
Comm. Isa.	*Commentarius in Isaiam*
Comm. Ps.	*Commentarius in Psalmos*
Dem. ev.	*Demonstratio evangelica*
Gen. elem. intr.	*Generalis elementaria introductio*
Hist. eccl.	*Historia ecclesiastica*

Onom.	*Onomasticon*
Passio mart. Aeg.	*Passio sanctorum decem martyrum Aegyptiorum*
Praep. ev.	*Praeparatio evangelica*
Vit. Const.	*Vita Constantini*

Eustathius of Thessalonica 12th c. CE
Od.	*Commentarii ad Homeri Odysseam*

Eutecnius 3rd-5th c. CE
(Paraphrasis in Nicandri Theriaca*)*

Eutropius 370 CE
(Breviarium historiae Romanae)

Florus early 2nd c. CE
(Epitomae)

Galen 199/217 CE
Alim. facult.	*De alimentorum facultatibus*
Bile	*De atra bile*
Diff. resp.	*De difficultate respirationis*
Glauc.	*Ad Glauconem de methodo medendi*
Hipp. aphor.	*In Hippocratis aphorismos commentarii VII*
Hipp. epid.	*In Hippocratis librum VI epidemiarum commentarii VI*
Meth. med.	*De methodo medendi*
Plac. Hipp. Plat.	*De placitis Hippocratis et Platonis libri IX*
Praes. puls.	*De praesagitione ex pulsibus*
Prop. an.	*De propriorum animi cuiuslibet affectuum dignotione et curatione*
Prot.	*Protrepticus*
Reb. suc.	*De rebus boni malique suci*
San. tuend.	*De sanitate tuenda*
Temperam.	*De temperamentis*
Usu part.	*De usu partium corporis humani*

George Hamartolus 9th c. CE
Chron.	*Chronicon*
Chron. brev.	*Chronicon breve*

George Syncellus after 810 CE
(Chronographia)

Gorgias 376 BCE
Fragm.	*Fragmenta*

Gregory of Nazianzus 389 or 390 CE
Fun. or.	*Funebris oratio in patrem (Oratio 18)*
Laud. Athan.	*In laudem Athanasii (Oratio 21)*

Gregory of Nyssa 395 CE
Apol. Hex.	*Apologia in Hexaemeron*
Cant. cant.	*In Canticum canticorum*
Ep.	*Epistulae*
Eun.	*Contra Eunomium*
Hom. opif.	*De hominis opificio*
Inscr. Ps.	*In inscriptiones Psalmorum*

Orat. cons. Pulch.	*Oratio consolatoria in Pulcheriam*
Sanct. pasch.	*In sanctum pascha*
Vit. Macr.	*Vita sanctae Macrinae*
Vit. Mos.	*De vita Mosis*

Hecataeus of Abdera 4th c. BCE
(Fragmenta)

Heliodorus 3rd c. CE
(Aethiopica)

Hermogenes 2nd half 2nd c. CE
Inv.	*De inventione*
Stat.	*De statibus*

Herodian 240 CE
(*Ab excessu divi Marci*)

Herodotus 425 BCE
(Historiae)

Heron 70 CE
Diop.	*Dioptra*
Pneum.	*Pneumatica*

Hesiod 700 BCE
Fragm. astr.	*Fragmenta astronomica*

Hieronymus of Cardia 4th/3rd c. BCE
(Fragmenta)

Hippocrates 370 BCE
Art. rep.	*De articulis reponendis*
Ep.	*Epistulae*

Hippolytus 235 CE
Haer.	*Refutatio omnium haeresium*

Historia Augusta 4th c. CE
Hadr.	*Hadrianus*

Homer 8th/7th c. BCE
Il.	*Ilias*
Od.	*Odyssea*

Horace 8 BCE
Carm.	*Carmina*

Hyperides 322 BCE
Eux.	*Oratio pro Euxenippo*

Isaeus 340 BCE
(Orationes)

ABBREVIATIONS AND SIGLA   XXIII

Isocrates 338 BCE
Aeginet.   *Aegineticus*
Antid.   *Antidosis*
Archid.   *Archidamus*
Areop.   *Areopagiticus*
Bus.   *Busiris*
Callim.   *In Callimachum*
Demon.   *Ad Demonicum*
Ep.   *Epistulae*
Euth.   *In Euthynum*
Hel. enc.   *Helenae encomium*
Nic.   *Nicocles*
Pac.   *De pace*
Panath.   *Panathenaicus*
Paneg.   *Panegyricus*
Phil.   *Philippus*
Plat.   *Plataicus*

John Chrysostom 407 CE
Bab. Iul.   *De sancto Babyla contra Iulianum et gentiles*
Comm. Isa.   *Commentarius in Isaiam*
Dav.   *De Davide et Saule*
Ecl.   *Eclogae I-XLVIII ex diversis homiliis*
Exp. Ps.   *Expositiones in Psalmos*
Fat. prov.   *De fato et providentia*
Fragm. Jer.   *Fragmenta in Jeremiam*
Hom. 2 Cor.   *Homiliae in epistulam II ad Corinthios*
Hom. Eph.   *Homiliae in epistulam ad Ephesios*
Hom. Gal.   *Homiliae in epistulam ad Galatas*
Hom. Gen.   *Homiliae in Genesim*
Hom. Isa. 6:1   *In illud: Vidi Dominum*
Hom. Jo.   *Homiliae in Joannem*
Hom. Matt.   *Homiliae in Matthaeum*
Hom. Rom.   *Homiliae in epistulam ad Romanos*
Hom. 2 Tim.   *Homiliae in epistulam II ad Timotheum*
Meretr.   *De meretrici*
Oppugn.   *Adversus oppugnatores vitae monasticae*
Stag.   *Ad Stagirium a daemone vexatum*

John of Damascus 749 CE
Vit. Barl. Joas.   *Vita Barlaam et Joasaph*

John Philoponus 570 CE
Aet. mund.   *De aeternitate mundi contra Proclum*

Josephus
Ant.   *De antiquitatibus judaicis*
Apion   *Contra Apionem*
Life   *Vita*
War   *De bello judaico*

Julian 363 CE
Cyn. ind.   *Adversus cynicos indoctos* = Oratio 9 (Budé)/6 (Wright)
Euseb. laud.   *In Eusebiae laudem* = Oratio 2 (Budé)/3 (Wright)
Regn.   *De regno* = Oratio 3 (Budé)/2 (Wright)

Justin end 2nd/early 3rd c. CE
Epit.   *Epitoma historiarum Philippicarum Pompeii Trogi*

Justin 165 CE
Apol.   *Apologia*
Dial.   *Dialogus cum Tryphone*

Libanius 394 CE
Decl.   *Declamationes*
Ep.   *Epistulae*
Or.   *Orationes*
Prog.   *Progymnasmata*

Livy 17 CE
(*Ab urbe condita*)
Epit.   *Epitomae*

Lucan 65 CE
(*Pharsalia*)

Lucian after 180 CE
Alex.   *Alexander (Pseudomantis)*
Anach.   *Anacharsis*
Bis acc.   *Bis accusatus*
Cal.   *Calumniae non temere credendum*
Dial. d.   *Dialogi deorum*
Dial. mort.   *Dialogi mortuorum*
Dom.   *De domo*
Fug.   *Fugitivi*
Hermot.   *Hermotimus (De sectis)*
Hist. conscr.   *Quomodo historia conscribenda sit*
Ind.   *Adversus indoctum*
Jupp. trag.   *Juppiter tragoedus*
Laps.   *Pro lapsu inter salutandum*
Merc. cond.   *De mercede conductis*
Nav.   *Navigium*
Peregr.   *De morte Peregrini*
Phal.   *Phalaris*
Prom. es   *Prometheus es in verbis*
Rhet. praec.   *Rhetorum praeceptor*
Symp.   *Symposium*
Tox.   *Toxaris*

Lycurgus of Athens 323 BCE
(*Contra Leocratem*)

Lysias 380 BCE
(*Orationes*)

Marcus Aurelius 180 CE
(*Meditationes*)

Menander 291 BCE
Fragm.   *Fragmenta*
Mis.   *Misumenus*

Michael Attaliates 11th c. CE
Hist. *Historia*

Michael Psellus 1078 (or 1096) CE
Chron. *Chronographia*

Nicephorus Gregoras 1360 CE
Hist. rom. *Historia romana*

Nicolaus of Damascus beginning 1st c. CE
(Fragmenta)

Nonnus 4th/5th c. CE
Dion. *Dionysiaca*

Olympiodorus the Younger 570 CE
Alcib. *In Platonis Alcibiadem commentarii*

Onosander 1st c. CE
(Strategicus)

Oppian of Corycus 2nd half 2nd c. CE
(Halieutica)

Origen 253/254 CE
Comm. Matt. *Commentarium in evangelium Matthaei*
Exp. Prov. *Expositio in Proverbia*

Orosius 420 CE
(Historiae adversus paganos)

Parthenius of Nicaea 14 CE
(Erotica pathemata)

Pausanias 2nd c. CE
(Graeciae descriptio)

Philo 45 CE
Abr. *De Abrahamo*
Aet. *De aeternitate mundi*
Agr. *De agricultura*
Cher. *De cherubim*
Conf. *De confusione linguarum*
Congr. *De congressu eruditionis gratia*
Contempl. *De vita contemplativa*
Decal. *De decalogo*
Det. *Quod deterius potiori insidari soleat*
Ebr. *De ebrietate*
Flacc. *In Flaccum*
Fug. *De fuga et inventione*
Gig. *De gigantibus*
Her. *Quis rerum divinarum heres sit*
Hyp. *Hypothetica*
Ios. *De Iosepho*
Leg. *Legum allegoriae*

Legat.	*Legatio ad Gaium*
Mos.	*De vita Mosis*
Mut.	*De mutatione nominum*
Opif.	*De opificio mundi*
Plant.	*De plantatione*
Post.	*De posteritate Caini*
Praem.	*De praemiis et poenis*
Prob.	*Quod omnis probus liber sit*
Prov.	*De providentia*
QG	*Quaestiones et solutiones in Genesin*
Sacr.	*De sacrificiis Abelis et Caini*
Sobr.	*De sobrietate*
Somn.	*De somniis*
Spec.	*De specialibus legibus*
Virt.	*De virtutibus*

Philo of Byblos 141 CE
Verb. sign.	*De diversis verborum significationibus*

Philochorus ca. 261 BCE
(Fragmenta)

Philodamus 335/325 BCE
(Paean in Dionysum)

Philodemus 40 or 35 BCE
Mus.	*De musica*

Philostratus ca. 2nd half 3rd c. CE
Imag.	*Imagines*
Vit. Apoll.	*Vita Apollonii*
Vit. soph.	*Vitae sophistarum*

Photius 898 CE
Bibl.	*Bibliotheca*

Plato 347 BCE
Alc. mai.	*Alcibiades maior*
Apol.	*Apologia*
Crit.	*Critias*
Def.	*Definitiones*
Gorg.	*Gorgias*
Ion	*Ion*
Leg.	*Leges*
Lys.	*Lysis*
Menex.	*Menexenus*
Phaed.	*Phaedo*
Phaedr.	*Phaedrus*
Phileb.	*Philebus*
Pol.	*Politicus*
Resp.	*Respublica*
Symp.	*Symposium*

Pliny the Elder 79 CE
(Naturalis historia)

Plutarch 125 CE

Aem.	*Aemilius Paulus*
Ages.	*Agesilaus*
Agis	*Agis*
Alc.	*Alcibiades*
Alex.	*Alexander*
Alex. fort.	*De Alexandri magni fortuna aut virtute*
Amat.	*Amatorius*
Amat. narr.	*Amatoriae narrationes*
Amic. mult.	*De amicorum multitudine*
An seni	*An seni respublica gerenda sit*
Ant.	*Antonius*
Apoph. lac.	*Apophthegmata laconica*
Arat.	*Aratus*
Arist.	*Aristides*
Art.	*Artaxerxes*
Brut.	*Brutus*
Caes.	*Caesar*
Cam.	*Camillus*
Cat. Min.	*Cato Minor*
Cic.	*Cicero*
Cim.	*Cimon*
Cleom.	*Cleomenes*
Cohib. ira	*De cohibenda ira*
Comm. not.	*De communibus notitiis adversus Stoicos*
Comp. Demetr. Ant.	*Comparatio Demetrii et Antonii*
Coni. praec.	*Coniugalia praecepta*
Cons. Apoll.	*Consolatio ad Apollonium*
Cor.	*Marcius Coriolanus*
Crass.	*Crassus*
Def. orac.	*De defectu oraculorum*
Dem.	*Demosthenes*
Demetr.	*Demetrius*
Dion	*Dion*
Fab.	*Fabius Maximus*
Fat.	*De fato*
Flam.	*Titus Flaminus*
Fort. Rom.	*De fortuna Romanorum*
Fragm.	*Fragmenta*
Frat. amor.	*De fraterno amore*
Galb.	*Galba*
Gen. Socr.	*De genio Socratis*
Inim. util.	*De capienda ex inimicis utilitate*
Is. Os.	*De Iside et Osiride*
Laud.	*De laude ipsius*
Lib. ed.	*De liberis educandis*
Luc.	*Lucullus*
Lyc.	*Lycurgus*
Lys.	*Lysander*
Mar.	*Caius Marius*
Marc.	*Marcellus*
Mor.	*Moralia*
Mulier. virt.	*Mulierum virtutes*
Nic.	*Nicias*
Num.	*Numa*

Oth.	*Otho*
Par. min.	*Parallela minora*
Pel.	*Pelopidas*
Per.	*Pericles*
Phil.	*Philopoemen*
Phoc.	*Phocion*
Pomp.	*Pompeius*
Praec. ger. rei publ.	*Praecepta gerendae rei publicae*
Prov. Alex.	*De proverbiis Alexandrinorum*
Publ.	*Publicola*
Pyrrh.	*Pyrrhus*
Pyth. or.	*De Pythiae oraculis*
Quaest. conv.	*Quaestiones convivales*
Quaest. plat.	*Quaestiones platonicae*
Quom. adul.	*Quomodo adulator ab amico internoscatur*
Reg. imp. apophth.	*Regum et imperatorum apophthegmata*
Rom.	*Romulus*
Sert.	*Sertorius*
Sol.	*Solon*
Soll. an.	*De sollertia animalium*
Stoic. rep.	*De Stoicorum repugnantis*
Suav. viv.	*Non posse suaviter vivi secundum Epicurum*
Sull.	*Sulla*
Symp.	*Symposium*
Them.	*Themistocles*
Tim.	*Timoleon*
Tranq. an.	*De tranquillitate animi*
Virt. vit.	*De virtute et vitio*
Vit. pud.	*De vitioso pudore*

Polyaenus 2nd c. CE
(Strategemata)

Polybius 120 BCE
(Historiae)

Posidonius 51 BCE
(Fragmenta)

Procopius 565 CE
Aed.	*De aedificiis*
Bell.	*De bellis*

Propertius shortly after 15 BCE
(Elegiae)

Pseudo-Apollodorus 2nd c. CE
(Bibliotheca)

Pseudo-Callisthenes 3rd c. CE
(Historia Alexandri Magni)

Pseudo-Clement 3rd c. CE
Hom.	*Homiliae*

Pseudo-Galen
Def. med.   *Definitiones medicae*
Intr.   *Introductio seu medicus*

Pseudo-Hecataeus 2nd c. BCE-1st c. CE

Pseudo-Ignatius late 4th c. CE
Ep.   *Epistulae*

Pseudo-Justin 3rd/4th c. CE
Orat. gent.   *Oratio ad gentiles*
Quaest. resp.   *Quaestiones et responsiones ad orthodoxos*

Pseudo-Lucian
Am.   *Amores*
Charid.   *Charidemus*

Pseudo-Plutarch 2nd/3rd c. CE
Hom.   *De Homero*

Pseudo-Seneca late 1st c. CE
Oct.   *Octavia*

Pseudo-Socrates 2nd/3rd c. CE
Ep.   *Epistulae*

Sappho 580-570 BCE
(Fragmenta)

Seneca the Younger 65 CE
Ep.   *Ad Lucilium epistulae morales*
Mal. bell. civ.   *De malo belli civilis*

Sextus Empiricus 210 CE
Math.   *Adversus mathematicos*

Simplicius 560 CE
Comm. Epict.   *Commentarius in Epicteti enchiridion*

Socrates of Constantinople 5th c. CE
(Historia ecclesiastica)

Sopater 4th/5th c. CE
Quaest. div.   *Quaestionum divisio*

Sophocles winter 406/405 BCE
Aj.   *Ajax*
Ant.   *Antigone*
El.   *Electra*
Fragm.   *Fragmenta*
Oed. tyr.   *Oedipus tyrannus*

Sozomen 450 CE
(Historia ecclesiastica)

Statius 96 CE
Theb. *Thebais*

Stobaeus 5th c. CE
(Anthologium)

Strabo 24 CE
(Geographica)

Suetonius 150 CE
Aug. *Divus Augustus*
Jul. *Divus Julius*
Nero *Nero*
Tib. *Tiberius*
Vit. *Vitellius*

Synesius 414 CE
Catast. *Catastases*
Ep. *Epistulae*

Tacitus 117 CE
Ann. *Annales*
Dial. *Dialogus de oratoribus*
Hist. *Historiae*

Theocritus 3rd c. BCE
(Idyllia)

Theodoretus 460 CE
Hist. eccl. *Historia ecclesiastica*
Int. Dan. *Interpretatio in Danielem*
Int. ep. Paul. *Interpretatio in XIV epistulas sancti Pauli*
Int. proph. min. *Interpretatio in XII prophetas minors*
Quaest. Regn. Paral. *Quaestiones in libros Regnorum et Paralipomenon*

Theognis 6th c. BCE
(Elegiae)

Theophrastus 287 BCE
Char. *Characteres*

Theophylact Simocatta 7th c. CE
(Historiae)

Theopompus 4th c. BCE
(Fragmenta)

Thucydides 400 BCE
(Historia belli Peloponnesiaci)

Velleius Paterculus 31 CE
(Historiae romanae)

Virgil 19 BCE
Ecl. *Eclogae*

Vitruvius 1st c. BCE
(De architectura)

Xenophon 355 BCE

Ages.	*Agesilaus*
Anab.	*Anabasis*
Cyn.	*Cynegeticus*
Cyr.	*Cyropaedia*
Hell.	*Hellenica*
Mem.	*Memorabilia*
Oec.	*Oeconomicus*
Symp.	*Symposium*
Vect.	*De vectigalibus*

Xenophon of Ephesus 2nd/3rd c. CE
(Ephesiaca)

Anthology and fragments

Anth. Lat.	*Anthologia Latina*
FGH	*Die Fragmente der griechischen Historiker*

Old Testament Pseudepigrapha

As. Mos.	Assumption of Moses
Jub.	*Jubilees*
Let. Aris.	*Letter of Aristeas*
3 Macc	*3 Maccabees*
4 Macc	*4 Maccabees*
Sib. Or.	*Sibylline Oracles*

Rabbinic Literature

b.	*Babylonian Talmud*
m.	*Mishnah*
t.	*Tosefta*
y.	*Jerusalem Talmud*
'Abot	*'Abot*
'Arak.	*'Arakin*
B. Bat.	*Baba Batra*
Ber.	*Berakot*
Giṭ.	*Giṭṭin*
Ḥag.	*Ḥagigah*
Ḥul.	*Ḥullin*
Kel.	*Kelim*
Mid.	*Middot*
Parah	*Parah*
Roš Haš.	*Roš Haššanah*
Šabb.	*Šabbat*
Sanh.	*Sanhedrin*
Šeqal.	*Šeqalim*
Soṭ.	*Soṭah*
Ta'an.	*Ta'anit*
Zebaḥ.	*Zebaḥim*

'Abot R. Nat.	*'Abot de Rabbi Nathan*
Lam. Rab.	*Lamentations Rabbah*
Sifra Lev.	*Sifra to Leviticus*
Sifre Num.	*Sifre to Numbers*

Anonymous early Christian writings

Acts Apoll.	*Acts of Apollonius*
Acts Eupl.	*Acts of Euplus*
Mart. Pol.	*Martyrdom of Polycarp*

Documents from the Judean Desert

5/6Hev	Documents from Nahal Hever
XHev/Se	Documents from Nahal Hever/Seiyal
1QS	Qumran: Community Rule

Inscriptions and papyri

BGU	*Aegyptische Urkunden aus den Königlichen (later Staatlichen) Museen zu Berlin, Griechische Urkunden*
CIA	*Corpus inscriptionum Atticarum*
CIG	*Corpus inscriptionum Graecarum*
CIIP	*Corpus Inscriptionum Iudaeae/Palaestinae*
CIJ	*Corpus inscriptionum Judaicarum*
IG	*Inscriptiones Graecae*
IGR	*Inscriptiones Graecae ad res Romanas pertinentes*
IJO	*Inscriptiones Judaicae Orientis*
ILS	*Inscriptiones Latinae selectae*
Inscr. It.	*Inscriptiones Italiae*
JIGRE	*Jewish Inscriptions of Graeco-Roman Egypt*
OGIS	*Orientis Graeci inscriptiones selectae*
Res gest. divi Aug.	*Res gestae divi Augusti*
SB	*Sammelbuch griechischer Urkunden aus Ägypten*
SEG	*Supplementum epigraphicum Graecum*
SIG	*Sylloge inscriptionum Graecarum*

Coins

BMC	*Catalogue of the Greek Coins in the British Museum*

Dictionaries, grammars and editions

Bauer-Aland	Bauer, W., and B. Aland, *Wörterbuch zum Neuen Testament*. 6th edn. Berlin: de Gruyter, 1988.
BJP	Brill Josephus Project. Mason, S., H. Chapman, L. H. Feldman, C. T. Begg, P. Spilsbury, J. M. G. Barclay, A. Forte, and J. Sievers. *Josephus: Judean War (Books 1–2), Judean Antiquities (Books 1–10), Life of Josephus, and Against Apion*. Flavius Josephus: Translation and Commentary 1ab, 3, 4, 5, 9, 10. Leiden: Brill, 2000-**forthcoming**.
GELS	Lust, J., E. Eynikel, and K. Hauspie (1992-96). *A Greek-English Lexicon of the Septuagint*. 2 vols. Stuttgart: Deutsche Bibelgesellschaft.
Jastrow	Jastrow, M. (1886-1903). *A Dictionary of the Targumim, the Talmud Babli and Yerushalmi, and the Midrashic Literature*. 2 vols. London: Luzac.

KBL	Koehler, L., W. Baumgartner, and J. J. Stamm. *Hebräisches und aramäisches Lexikon zum Alten Testament*, 3rd edn. 4 vols. Leiden: Brill, 1967-1990.
LSJ	Liddell, H. G., R. Scott, and H. S. Jones, *A Greek-English Lexicon*, revised 9th edn. Oxford: Oxford University Press, 1983.
LXX	Septuagint
Marcus	Marcus, R. (1933). *Josephus in Nine [Ten] Volumes*, vol. 7: *Jewish Antiquities, Books XII-XIV*. LCL 365. Cambridge, Mass.: Harvard University Press.
Marcus-Wikgren	Marcus, R. and A. Wikgren (1963). *Josephus in Nine [Ten] Volumes*, vol. 8: *Jewish Antiquities, Books XV-XVII*. LCL 410. Cambridge, Mass.: Harvard University Press.
Meijer-Wes	Meijer, F. and M. A. Wes (1996-98). *Flavius Josephus: De oude geschiedenis van de Joden*. 3 vols. Ambo-Klassiek. Baarn: Ambo.
Michel-Bauernfeind	Michel, O. and O. Bauernfeind (1962-69). *Flavius Josephus: De bello judaico, der jüdische Krieg: Griechisch und Deutsch*. 3 vols. in 4 (vol. 1: revised edn.). Munich: Kösel.
MS(S)	Manuscript(s)
MT	Masoretic text
NETS	Pietersma, A., B. G. Wright, et al. (2007). *A New English Translation of the Septuagint and the Other Greek Translations Traditionally Included under that Title*. Oxford: Oxford University Press.
NRSV	*The Holy Bible: New Revised Standard Version: Containing the Old and New Testaments with the Apocryphal/Deuterocanonical Books*. Translated by the Division of Christian Education of the National Council of the Churches of Christ in the United States of America. Nashville, Tenn.: Nelson, 1989.
Niese	Niese, B. (1885-95). *Flavii Iosephi opera: Edidit et apparatu critico instruxit Benedictus Niese*. 7 vols. Berlin: Weidmann. [volume 3 referred to in commentary]
Niese minor	Niese, B. (1888-95). *Flavii Iosephi opera: Recognovit Benedictus Niese*. 6 vols. Berlin: Weidmann. [volume 3 referred to in commentary]
OLD	Glare, P. G. W., ed. (1968-82). *Oxford Latin Dictionary*. Oxford: Clarendon.
PG	Patrologia Graeca
*PIR*²	Groag, E., A. Stein, L. Petersen et al. (1933-2009). *Prosopographia Imperii Romani saec. I. II. III.*, 2nd edn. 8 vols. in 13. Berlin: de Gruyter.
Rengstorf	Rengstorf, K. H. et al. (1973-83). *A Complete Concordance to Flavius Josephus*. 4 vols. Leiden: Brill.
Schürer-Vermes	Schürer, E. (1973-87). *The History of the Jewish People in the Age of Jesus Christ (175 B.C.–A.D. 135)*. 3 vols. in 4. Revised by G. Vermes et al. Edinburgh: T&T Clark.

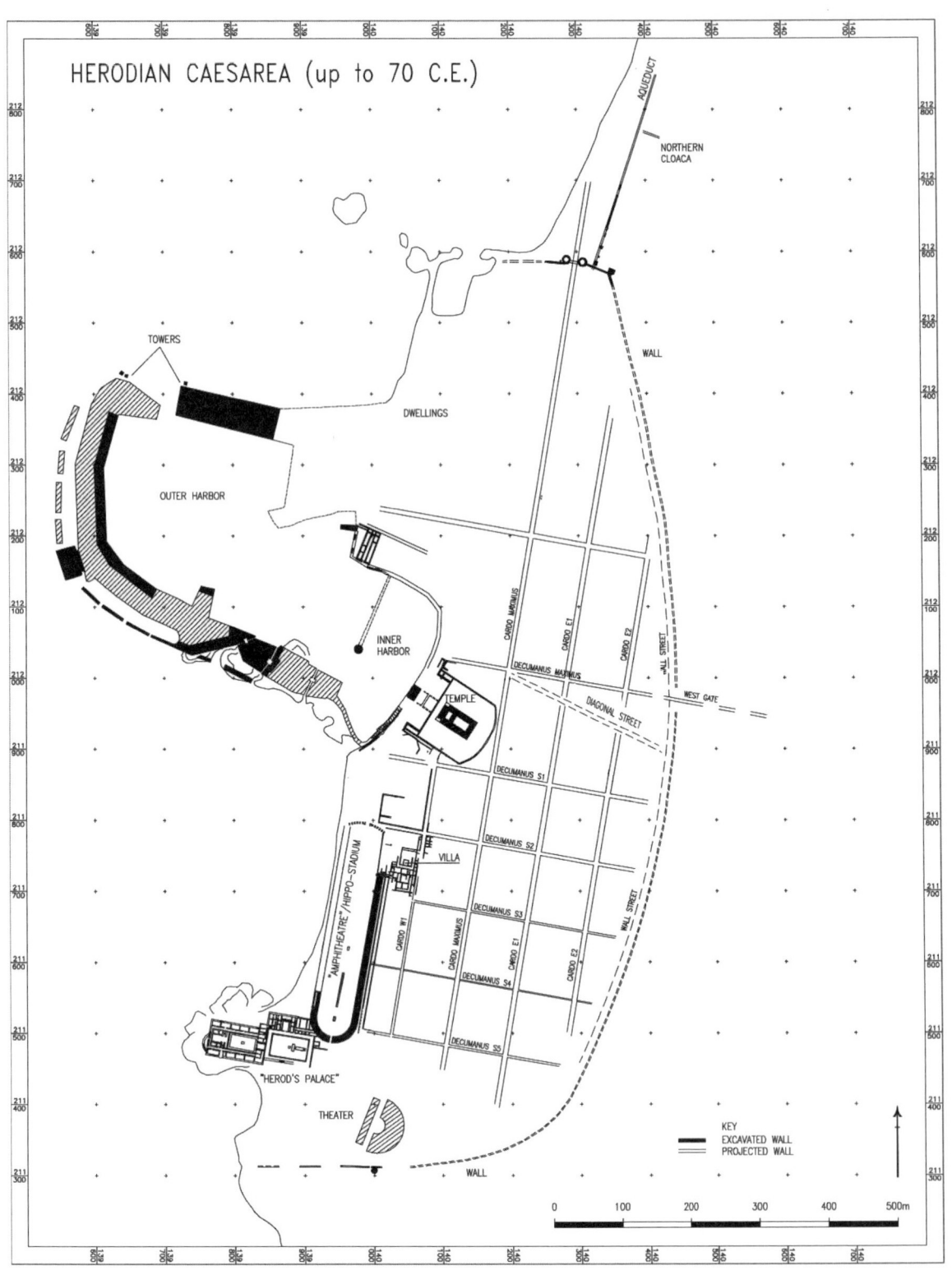

Map of Caesarea Maritima: Courtesy of Prof. Joseph Patrich, Jerusalem.

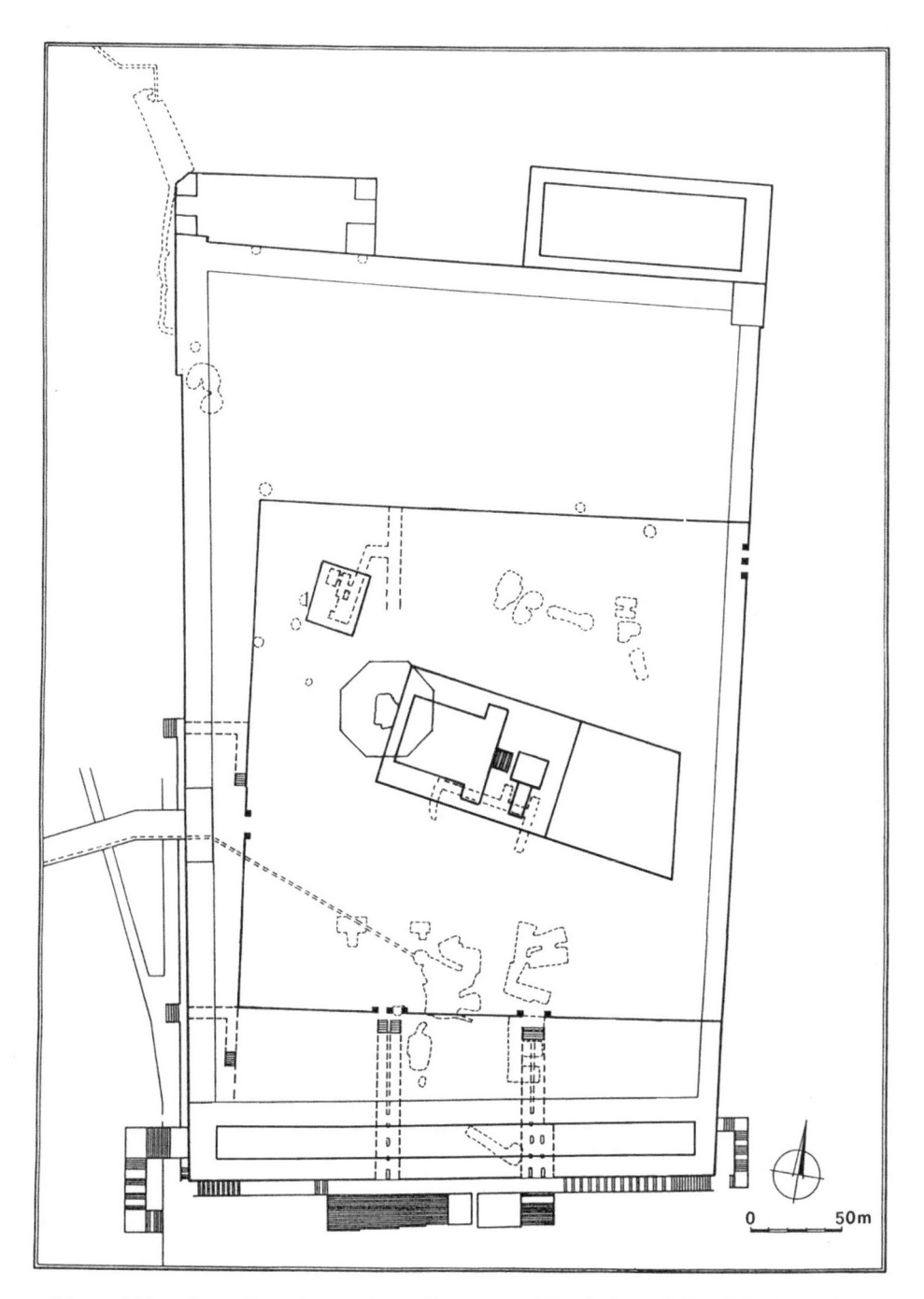

Map of Herodean Temple precinct: Courtesy of Prof. Joseph Patrich, Jerusalem.

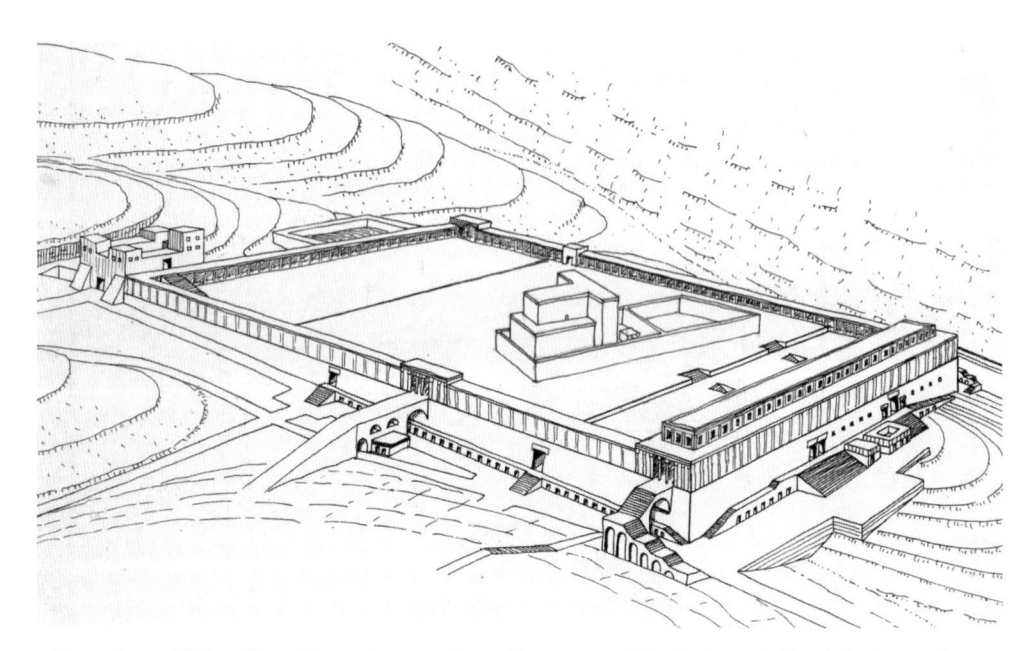

Drawing of Herodean Temple complex: Courtesy of Prof. Joseph Patrich, Jerusalem.

JOSEPHUS, *ANTIQUITIES 15*

SUMMARY OF ANTIQUITIES 15

Book 15 deals with the history of Herod the Great's reign from the capture of Jerusalem (usually dated to 37 BCE) until the expansion and renovation of the Jerusalem Temple complex (set in Herod's 18th regnal year, which is usually dated to 20-19 BCE). The beginning (15.1-4, about the capture of Jerusalem) and end of the book (15.421-425, about the completion of the Jerusalem Temple) are clearly marked, and the main part is a coherent narrative about Herod's rule between these major events. The introduction (15.1-4) characterizes Herod as a harsh ruler and refers to the king's supporters and enemies. After that a brief section lists Herod's first measures in Jerusalem (15.5-7), and likewise presents him negatively (see Laqueur 1920 for an analysis of the changes in the portrait of Herod from *War* to *Ant.*). The narrative continues with brief references to the execution of Antigonus (15.8-11)—Herod's main opponent in book 14—and the report of the return to Jerusalem of Hyrcanus II (15.12-22), one of Herod's Hasmonean predecessors.

With the introduction of Alexandra, Herod's mother-in-law (15.23), starts a series of episodes in which women at the court figure prominently. Alexandra acts as a successful lobbyist for her son Aristobulus III in order to get the High Priesthood for him (15.23-49). Herod quickly has the young High Priest killed in one of the royal swimming pools at Jericho (15.50-56), which triggers more intrigues from the side of Alexandra, who approaches Cleopatra VII for help. Herod has to travel abroad in order to give to Mark Antony an account of Aristobulus III's death (15.64), which leads to a complicated situation at the court, culminating in Herod's sister Salome's accusation that Herod's Hasmonean wife Mariamme had been committing adultery with her caretaker Joseph during the king's absence (15.57-87). In 15.88-103 Josephus focuses upon Cleopatra VII, who acts as a dangerous enemy and tries to take over Herod's kingdom.

During the preamble of the Battle of Actium (31 BCE; 15.109, 121), the decisive contest between Antony and Octavian, Herod has several military conflicts with "the Arabs" (i.e., the Nabateans; 15.104-160), which are triggered by the unwillingness of the Nabatean king to pay a sum of money to Herod (15.107). Herod's hard-won victory and his elaborate commander speech (15.127-146) present a very positive image of the king.

The outcome of Actium with Octavian-Augustus as new leader of Rome is a serious threat for Herod (as stated in 15.161) because the king had supported Octavian's opponent. Herod is successful in acquiring Octavian's patronage (15.161-201). His move over to Octavian as patron forms the context of two other episodes: the tragic death of Hyrcanus II, of which Josephus presents two versions (both in 15.164-182), and Mariamme and Alexandra's stay at the desert fortress Alexandrium during Herod's journey to Octavian (15.185-187). The second episode is brief but important for the subsequent narrative. It hints at a further intimate relationship of Mariamme with her caretaker, which is strongly reminiscent of 15.65-87 (about Mariamme's 'affaire' with Joseph). Crucial to both passages is Herod's secret order to kill his wife if something would happen to him (15.186; cf. 15.65, 69). The aftermath of Mariamme's stay at Alexandrium—with the queen's knowledge about the secret order—leads to her downfall and execution through a cluster of dramatic events (15.202-231), with the most prominent women (Mariamme and Alexandra, as well as Salome and Cyprus, Herod's sister and mother) at each other's throats. Alexandra tries to save herself at the expense of her daughter (15.232-239), and Herod first suffers greatly because of Mariamme's death and then falls ill (15.240-246).

The section 15.247-266 again focuses upon plots against Herod, with Alexandra's final attempt (15.247-251) and the betrayal by Costobar and other friends (15.252-266), which includes a subsection about the Sons of Baba (15.260-266). All these opponents are executed. *Ant.* 15.267 highlights Herod's transgressions of Jewish practices and introduces the episode of Herod's foundation of quadrennial games in Jerusalem and the response of the Jerusalemites to this initiative (15.267-291). A brief description of Herod's building projects (15.292-298) is connected with the previous section about the festival in Jerusalem (see 15.291). It presents Herod's fortifications in the light of the security situation in the kingdom and of the tendency of the Jewish population to revolt against their king (15.295).

Ant. 15.299-316, set in Herod's 13th regnal year (probably 25-24 BCE), reports disasters: a drought resulting in illnesses and famine among the population (15.299-304), which are countered successfully by Herod (15.305-316). *Ant.* 15.317-325 offers a cluster of brief reports about various events set in the same period, including the building of the fortress of Herodium (15.323-325). The next section (15.326-341) first focuses upon Herod's benefactions outside his kingdom (15.326-330), highlighting once more the king's violation of Jewish practices (15.328-329). It continues with a detailed description of the building of the harbor city of Caesarea Maritima (15.331-341).

A brief note about Herod's sons Alexander and Aristobulus being sent to Rome (15.342-343; the sons are prominent figures in book 16) forms the transition to a cluster of events focusing on a local ruler near the northern border of Herod's kingdom, named Zenodorus (15.343-364). The section starts with Zenodorus' attack on the inhabitants of Damascus and Augustus' transfer of his territories (Trachonitis, Batanea, and Auranitis) to Herod (15.343-349). *Ant.* 15.350-353 reports Herod's conflict with the Gadarenes, in which Zenodorus plays a prominent role. *Ant.* 15.354-364 concerns Augustus' grant of Zenodorus' dominion to Herod, the ruler's death, as well as Herod's building of a temple near Paneion (in Zenodorus' territory). *Ant.* 15.365 switches to Herod's tax reduction, which is connected to the massive opposition to his rule and an introduction of an oath of loyalty (15.365-371). The story about the Essene Manaemus' prediction that Herod would become king (15.372-379) explains why Herod decided to exempt the Essenes from the obligation of the oath.

The final section (15.380-400), set in Herod's 18th regnal year, deals with Herod's renovation of the Jerusalem Temple, including a brief speech by Herod (15.382-387). The description of the building activities goes hand in hand with a description of the Temple complex from various viewpoints (15.390-403, 410-420). *Ant.* 15.403-409 offers an excursus on the Antonia Fortress on the north side of the Temple as the location where the priestly robes were kept. A note about the completion of the renovation of the Temple and subsequent celebrations ends the book (15.421-425).

A synthesis of Josephus' presentation of Herod in *Antiquities* will be given in the excursus following 17.199.

Flashbacks and flashforwards in Ant. *15.1-4*

The beginning of book 15 (15.1-4) conveys a complex cluster of flashbacks (*analepses*) and flashforwards (*prolepses*), which suggests to the reader a rather critical interpretation of the subsequent events of Herod's reign. After these introductory paragraphs Josephus begins the narrative about Herod's rule in 15.5, as the marker "at that time" indicates. The narrative function of 15.1-4 in the larger context implies three points about Herod's rule: (1) the *analepses* to events narrated in book 14 help to explain that Herod had important supporters as well as enemies; (2) both the *prolepses* and *analepses* suggest that Herod was a harsh ruler; and (3) the combination of the announcement of the punishment of Hyrcanus II and the members of the court (see 15.4) with the note that God fulfilled Samaias/Pollio's words (see 15.3) implies that the events during Herod's rule followed a divine scenario. Two members of the Hasmonean dynasty, Antigonus and Hyrcanus II (see 15.1, 4), figure prominently in 15.1-22 (about the beginning of Herod's rule in Jerusalem). The first was Herod's main competitor for the throne; the second returns in this section from Babylon to the royal court in Jerusalem. Herod's mother-in-law Alexandra figures as a further important opponent since she acted as a lobbyist for her son Aristobulus III, though she is only introduced in 15.23.

BOOK FIFTEEN

(1.1) 1 How Sossius[1] and Herod[2] captured Jerusalem[3] by force,[4] and in addition how they took Antigonus captive,[5] have been explained in our previous book.[6] Now we shall speak about the things that followed those events.[7]

Introduction of book 15.

2 After Herod had obtained[8] the rule over all Judea,[9] he gave prominence to all those

Herod in power. War 1.358

---

[1] The manuscripts mention Sossius (Σόσσιος), but Josephus no doubt refers to Gaius Sosius, one of Mark Antony's commanders. He assisted Herod in the siege of Jerusalem (37 or perhaps 36 BCE), as Josephus narrates in book 14 (*Ant.* 14.468-488). One wonders whether the order of the names is deliberate here, implying that Herod helped Sosius and not the other way around, as the *War* report suggests (but cf. *War* 1.353-357; 5.408-409 and esp. 6.436; see Sievers/Forte in BJP 1a 1.327, noting that Seneca the Elder and Tacitus suggest that Sosius captured Jerusalem and received the honor for it). *Ant.* 14.447 states that Antony ordered Sosius to assist Herod; *Ant.* 15.5 only mentions Herod in connection with the capture of Jerusalem. Sosius celebrated a triumph for this victory (see 15.8 with the note to "triumphant procession").

Sosius was *consul designatus* in 36 BCE but could not take up his office because of his military service in the East as Mark Antony's lieutenant. He became consul in 32 BCE (Huzar 1978: 140, 142-43, 164, 175, 206). See also *War* 1.19; *Ant.* 14.176; Broughton 1951-1986: 2.393, 397-398, 402; 3.200; Bartels 2001.

[2] Herod is the main character of *Ant.* 15.1-17.199 (Landau 2006: 115-85), which narrative is part of a long section that starts in 14.158, with the note about Herod's appointment as commander of Galilee by his father Antipater. The Herod narrative of *Antiquities* is not only much more elaborate than the parallel section in *War* but frequently also more negative about Herod. This already becomes apparent in the first episode in Galilee (*Ant.* 14.158-184; cf. *War* 1.203-215), during which Herod crushed Ezekias and his fellow brigands. *Antiquities* suggests that Herod had a violent and bold character and that he had the ambition to rule as a tyrant (14.165). This motif is absent from *War* (see the excursus on Herod's image at the end of the Herod narrative of *Antiquities*).

[3] Literally "Hierosolyma." Josephus almost always uses the name Ἱεροσόλυμα instead of Ἱερουσαλήμ ("Jerusalem"; but see *Apion* 1.179 with Barclay's comments in BJP 10 1.179), contrary to the LXX, which uses the second name predominantly. In the New Testament both names are common.

[4] The successful siege of Jerusalem by Herod and Sosius is described in *Ant.* 14.468-488. On the date of the capture, see 15.7 with notes.

[5] Antigonus was of Hasmonean descent and a son of Aristobulus II (Schürer-Vermes 1.281-86). He was Herod's major competitor for the throne. The struggle between the Hasmoneans and Herod's family starts in *Antiquities* in 14.140 with the report of Antigonus' appeal to Julius Caesar about Hyrcanus II and Antipater's usurpation. Subsequently, Antigonus assembled an army and invaded Judea but was driven out by Herod (14.297-300). Antigonus struck back by making an agreement with the Parthians, who then held sway over the area. Several skirmishes between Antigonus and Herod followed, but in the end the Parthians gained control over Jerusalem. They captured Hyrcanus and Phasael, handed them over to Antigonus, and also delivered the city to him (14.330-369). Herod went to Rome to gain support, where he was appointed king and Antigonus declared an enemy of Rome (14.379-389). In the meantime Antigonus was besieging Herod's relatives at Masada (14.390). Herod rescued them, captured Joppa, and afterwards marched against Antigonus in Jerusalem (14.394-401). Antigonus' surrender to Sosius is described in 14.481.

[6] This refers to book 14 and very briefly summarizes the last events narrated there (see the notes to *Ant.* 15.1; for a list of other internal cross-references in Josephus, see Drüner 1896: 82-94). With the cross-reference here Josephus highlights Sosius and Herod's capture of Jerusalem as a *caesura*. The capture in combination with the transition to book 15 suggests that from now on Herod was in control of Judea (as already implied in *Ant.* 15.2-3), which matches the contents of books 15-17, describing Herod's actual rule. Josephus basically presents the Herod story in a chronological order (van Henten and Huitink: 2007).

[7] The reading of MSS PVF (τὰ δ' ἐκείνης συνεχῆ, Niese 333) implies "the main issues of that book" instead of "the things that followed those events," which hardly makes sense. Josephus not only refers back in *Ant.* 15.1 to events narrated in book 14, but he also announces a report about subsequent events (see Rengstorf *s.v.* συνεχής and the preceding note).

[8] An alternative literal translation would be "When Herod had been granted …," which would emphasize

Pollio and Samaias rewarded.

of the city's population[10] who were being loyal to him while he was still a commoner,[11] whereas he did not fail to take vengeance upon all those who had taken the side of his opponents[12] and he punished them day after day.[13] **3** Pollio the Pharisee and Samaias, his

---

that Herod's power was dependent on the Romans and match the situation after Herod's appointment as king in 40 BCE (see the next note). The context implies, however, that Josephus refers to the situation after the capture of Jerusalem.

[9] "All Judea" implies that with the capture of Jerusalem and the knocking out of his competitor Antigonus (cf. *Ant.* 14.469) Herod had become ruler over the entire region. Herod's Judean territory comprised the ethnarchy of Hyrcanus II, to which other areas were added later. It consisted roughly of the territories west from the Jordan and the Dead Sea, consisting of the coastal area from around Jamnia and Joppa to the fortress of Alexandrium in the northeast and the fortress of Herodium in the southeast. It was bordered by Samaria in the north and by Idumea in the south (Buchheim 1960: 66-67; Stern 1974b: 221 with n. 2; Möller and Schmitt 1976: 202-03; see for maps Avi-Yonah in Stern 1974b: 228-29; Mittmann and Schmitt 2001: map B V 16.2). On the name Judea, see Goodblatt 1998: 12.

In addition to Judea, Herod's kingdom bestowed upon him by the Romans in 40 BCE (*War* 1.281-285; *Ant.* 14.379-389) comprised Idumea, Perea, and Galilee. Richardson [1996: 131-52] offers a convenient survey of the expansion of Herod's kingdom.

[10] The Greek combination of κατὰ τὴν πόλιν and πλῆθος echoes vocabulary in *War* 1.358. Schalit (2001: 491 n. 1129) interprets "gave prominence to" to mean that Herod literally bought the support of the population. The reward for Herod's supporters is, however, only indicated in general terms (see also the next note). Cohen (1979: 53-58) offers a survey of the correspondences between *War* 1 and *Ant.* 15-16 as well as their dependence on possible sources. In the Herod narrative of *Antiquities* τὸ πλῆθος ("the population") frequently refers to the Jewish population of Herod's kingdom or to the Jewish people (e.g., 15.50, 52, 183, 263-264, 280, 284, 368). Sometimes τὸ πλῆθος, which occurs more than 500 times in Josephus, has a depreciatory meaning ("mob, multitude, horde, throng, rabble," more or less equivalent to the Latin *vulgus*; see Mason in BJP 1b on 2.1, 9, also 15.183 with the note to "cause the rabble to revolt" and 15.231 with the note to "disturbances of the masses").

[11] The translation is based on the reading ἰδιωτεύοντος of E. The reading of most of the Greek MSS (ἰδιωτεύοντες) implies a different translation: "he promoted all of the city's population, who were commoners and still loyal to him." The genitive singular reading of E makes more sense: Josephus refers to Herod as a commoner (ἰδιώτης, Rengstorf *s.v.*) in *War* 1.209,

387, 432, 665; *Ant.* 14.169, 403, 489, 491; 15.367, 374; 16.78; 17.20 (according to the *editio princeps*); 17.192 (cf. ἰδιωτεύω ["be a commoner"] in *Ant.* 15.17; 16.78).

Depending on the preferred reading, the passage either refers to the group of commoners in Jerusalem that remained loyal to Herod while he was competing with Antigonus (cf. the references to Pollio and Samaias in *Ant.* 15.3 and to the people's loyalty to Antigonus in 15.8), or to a period before Herod's appointment as king by the Romans. The first interpretation implies that the passage highlights the role of Jerusalem's commoners during Herod's struggle for power. They can be contrasted with the Hasmoneans and their supporters, who must have objected against the transfer of the kingdom to somebody outside of the royal family (and even of Idumean descent). The reading of E (also followed by Marcus-Wikgren 2; Richardson 1996: 161) focuses on Herod's attitude towards those persons who had supported him in his early years. It is plausible that Herod rewarded them generously (see also *Ant.* 15.3 and *War* 1.358, which state that Herod conferred honors upon them). Schalit (2001: 315-16, 479-81) identifies this group of Herod's supporters with the "Herodians" mentioned in the New Testament (Matt 22:16; Mark 3:6; 12:13), arguing that they belonged to various social groups. Josephus elsewhere suggests that Herod's initial generous attitude changed during his rule. Later Herod would have acted more and more like a tyrant capable of executing persons, whether loyal to him or not, at random (*Ant.* 16.4; 17.159; cf. *War* 2.86; van Henten 2011b).

[12] I.e., those who had taken the side of Antigonus, who is mentioned in *Ant.* 15.1. Josephus does not specify who Antigonus' supporters were. They are Herod's major enemies in the last part of book 14 (see the commentary on 15.1). *Ant.* 15.6 also concerns their punishment. The parallel passage of *War* (1.358) briefly reports that Antigonus' supporters were executed. The flashbacks in *Ant.* 15.3-4 suggest that Herod would have all the members of the council (Greek συνέδριον; see 15.173 with the note about Herod's council)—except Samaias/Pollio—killed. Schalit (2001: 98-100) takes the connection between 15.2 and 15.3-4 as a starting point and argues that Herod's enemies included the remaining members of the Hasmonean family, most members of the council, the greatest part of the Jerusalem aristocracy, and a section of the common people, which, in his view, was strongly influenced by the Pharisees (cf. Schürer-Vermes 1.296). The note about the punishment of Antigonus' supporters may anticipate—in combination

student,[14] were particularly honored[15] by him; for when Jerusalem was besieged, these men advised the citizens to admit Herod,[16] and now they received their reward for this.[17]

---

with other information in the introduction of book 15—later (severe) punishments of enemies. In that case the passage would refer to the execution of Antigonus' group as well as later opponents, whose execution is reported in the subsequent narrative. This reading would match the narrative function of 15.1-4 (see the end of the summary of *Antiquities* 15 above). Later punishments are reported in 15.164-179, 365-366, 368-369.

The phrase ὅσοι ... τἀκείνου φρονοῦντες ("all those who had taken his side"; φρονέω plus a personal pronoun in the genitive means "stand on someone's side," Rengstorf *s.v.*) is reminiscent of *War* 1.358 (τοὺς τὰ αὐτοῦ φρονήσαντας; cf. *Ant.* 13.28), also referring to supporters of Antigonus. *War* 1.319, 358 call Antigonus' group Ἀντιγόνειοι.

[13] The punishment "day after day" characterizes Herod as a severe ruler for his own subjects. Schalit (2001: 99-100, 258-60) argues that Herod's enemies lost their possessions, including their lands (which is suggested by a concluding remark in *Ant.* 17.305; see its commentary). Herod's punishment may have been severe, but several reports are transmitted about rulers who captured a city and destroyed all, or at least a part, of the leadership and/or the population. Striking examples concern Rome, first with the proscriptions of Sulla in 82-81 BCE (Cassius Dio 33.109.12-21) and later in 43-42 BCE, when Octavian, Mark Antony, and Lepidus were consolidating their triumvirate (Plutarch, *Sull.* 31.1-33.2; Suetonius, *Aug.* 27; Appian, *Bell. civ.* 4.1-51; Cassius Dio 47.1-13). Cases outside Rome include the bloody fate of Corinth in 146 BCE, when the entire adult male population was killed by the Romans (Pausanias 7.16.8; for other examples, see Harris 1979: 52, 263-64).

[14] Pollio is also mentioned in *Ant.* 15.4, 370; Samaias in 14.172, 175; 15.370 (Schalit 1968: 98, 105, and 2001: 768-71). Samaias is mentioned alone, as a member of the council, in *Ant.* 14.172, 175. Pollio does not occur in book 14; he is mentioned here for the first time, and this together with Samaias (as in 15.370; Mason 1991: 261-63). In both passages Pollio is identified as a Pharisee (for Josephus' references to the Pharisees, see Mason 1991). Samaias is consistently presented as Pollio's student: *Ant.* 15.4 focuses upon Pollio as the more important scholar, and when the two appear as a duo in Josephus' narrative Pollio is mentioned first (here as well as in 15.370). A combination of the references to Samaias in book 14 and the information about Pollio and Samaias in book 15 implies that prominent Pharisees supported Herod despite their criticism (see also the last note to this paragraph). Sievers (1997) questions whether Samaias was a Pharisee; being a student of a Pharisee doesn't necessarily mean being a Pharisee.

Samaias/Pollio's motive for supporting Herod is apparently that Herod acted as leader of the Jews with God's consent (see 15.4 and the next notes; cf. Mason 1991: 262-63). Scholars have often assumed that both were Pharisees and identified them with one of the famous pairs of rabbinic sages: Shemaya and Avtalyon (*m. 'Abot* 1.10-11), or Shammai and Hillel (*m. 'Abot* 1.12-15; Schürer-Vermes 1.296; 2.262-67; Mason 1991: 262 n. 18; Schalit 2001: 768-71).

The reference to Pollio and Samaias in *Ant.* 15.3 is part of a flashback to events narrated in book 14. Jewish leaders were opposing Herod (or more precisely Antipater and his sons, Herod being one of them) and warned Hyrcanus II against Herod (14.163-167). These opponents recalled Herod's unlawful execution of Ezekias and his fellow bandits without permission from the council and Hyrcanus (14.167). Their accusations (14.165, 167-168, 171) and the daily appeals in the Temple by the mothers of the murdered men made Hyrcanus put Herod on trial (14.168-178). In 14.177 Josephus notes that the members of the council intended to execute Herod, which implies that they agreed with the Jewish leaders. This trial is the context of Samaias' prediction about Herod killing all members of the council, including Hyrcanus but except himself (14.174-175). Samaias' prediction is taken up in 15.4. It did come true according to a proleptic remark in 14.175 referring to the time when Herod had assumed royal power (see also the next notes). Hyrcanus' end is described in 15.164-179. The deaths of the council members are not mentioned explicitly but are probably implied in 15.2-4.

[15] The Greek echoes *Ant.* 14.176, concerning Samaias (see the next note).

[16] The analeptic remark refers to the episode of Herod's trial in Jerusalem (see the note to Samaias and Pollio at the beginning of the paragraph). Josephus' description of the trial includes a brief passage in which he notes that Samaias was the only member of the council standing in Herod's favor (*Ant.* 14.176). *Ant.* 14.176 refers to the siege of Jerusalem by Sosius and Herod, reported later in book 14 (see 15.1 with the note to "captured Jerusalem"), during which Samaias—and not Pollio and Samaias as stated here—would have advised Jerusalem's population to admit Herod. The Greek vocabulary of 14.176 is partly echoed here, but Josephus does not repeat Herod's role of executing the divine punishment for the people's sins as motive for Samaias' advice (Schalit 2001: 96-97). *Ant.* 15.3 (like

4 When Herod was once being tried on a capital charge,[18] this Pollio[19] made a prediction. He reproached Hyrcanus[20] and the judges, saying that if Herod escaped with his life he would punish all of them.[21] And this happened after some time[22] because God fulfilled his [Pollio's] words.[23]

Herod in need of money. Gift to Antony and punishment of opponents. War 1.358

(1.2) 5 At that time,[24] when he had taken hold of Jerusalem, he [Herod] brought together

---

War 1.293, 358) indicates that not all Jerusalemites opposed Herod, contrary to what Josephus sometimes suggests (see the commentary on 15.274). Stern (1974b: 226) suggests that Samaias/Pollio's motive was to prevent a useless bloodshed after the situation had become desperate for Herod's opponents.

[17] Obviously, Herod's capture of Jerusalem is the moment to reward Pollio and Samaias for their advice; Herod was finally in the position to offer such a reward. Josephus does not elaborate on what the reward included. Mason (1991: 263-64) argues that Pollio and Samaias belong to the enemy camp in Josephus' narrative despite Herod's reward (see also *Ant.* 15.370).

[18] The brief excursus about Pollio in *Ant.* 15.4 is an implicit flashback of Herod's trial (14.168-177) despite the fact that Samaias is mentioned there instead of Pollio (parallel account in *War* 1.210-211; references to Samaias in *Ant.* 14.172, 175, and to Herod in *War* 1.210-211; *Ant.* 14.173-174; note the occurrence of the key phrase κρίνομαι ["be on trial"] in *Ant.* 14.172; 15.4; cf. *War* 1.210). The discrepancy concerning Samaias being mentioned alone in *Ant.* 14.172-176 and together with Pollio in 15.3-4 remains a problem; it might be explained by the assumption that the reference to both of them in 15.370 caused Josephus to incorporate a double reference in 15.3-4.

Josephus seems to hint here at Samaias' speech during Herod's trial (*Ant.* 14.172-174). Samaias criticized Herod for appearing at the court with his soldiers, clothed in purple, and for showing contempt for the Law, but he also blamed Hyrcanus and the council members for allowing Herod such a great freedom.

[19] The Greek Epitome (E) and the Latin version read Σαμαῖος ("Samaias"), Σαμέας or *Sameas* ("Sameas," Niese 333). This is probably a correction because it harmonizes the text with the report of *Ant.* 14.172-176, focusing upon Samaias only. The major Greek MSS read Πολλίων ("Pollio"), which is the *lectio difficilior* and is also supported by Josephus' note in 15.370, again indicating that Pollio was more prominent than Samaias (Marcus-Wikgren 3 n. *b*; Mason 1991: 262 n. 19; differently Schalit 2001: 768).

[20] I.e., Hyrcanus II (see *Ant.* 15.11 with commentary).

[21] This line also refers to Samaias' speech during Herod's trial (*Ant.* 14.174). The speech included a prediction of the future punishment of Hyrcanus and the council members: "Be assured, however, that God is great, and this man [i.e., Herod] whom you now wish to release for Hyrcanus' sake, will one day punish you [i.e., the members of the council] and the king [i.e., Hyrcanus] as well" (*Ant.* 14.174, transl. Marcus). The verb ἐπεξέρχομαι can mean "proceed against, attack, prosecute, punish" (Plutarch, *Caes.* 69; LSJ *s.v.* 2). Josephus' reference to the statement of Samaias/Pollio is ambiguous because Hyrcanus and the council are criticized ("He reproached Hyrcanus ..."), implying that they should have convicted and executed Herod. At the same time Josephus suggests in *Ant.* 14.174 ("And he was not mistaken in either part of his prediction," transl. Marcus) and here ("And this happened after some time, because God fulfilled his words") that God made Samaias/Pollio's prediction come true. Schalit (2001: 99-100) takes Josephus' note that all members of the council were killed as an overstatement and concludes that Herod executed those who were part of the Jerusalem aristocracy. He further assumes that the 45 prominent members of Antigonus' party (*Ant.* 15.6) belonged to the council but warns against calculations of the actual number of the council members.

[22] This concerns the punishment of Herod's opponents and confirms the prediction by Samaias/Pollio (see the previous note).

[23] This phrase and *Ant.* 14.174 (see the note to "he would punish all of them" in this paragraph) suggest that the chain of events was in accordance with God's will: Herod could act as leader of the Jews because of God's support. Josephus states this explicitly in the brief story about the Essene Manaemus, who predicted Herod's future (15.373-378). God's fulfillment of Samaias/Pollio's statement also indicates a special bond between God and these two men as persons entitled to receive divine revelations.

[24] This somewhat unusual chronological marker (ἐν δὲ τῷ τότε) occurs six times in Josephus. All occurrences fall in books 15-16 of *Antiquities* (15.5, 220; 16.134, 160, 180, 359). Elsewhere in Greek literature the expression occurs rarely without a corresponding noun (but see, e.g., Andocides, *Red.* 14.5; Plutarch, *Arat.* 9.7). In other passages a noun like χρόνῳ is added (e.g. Plutarch, *Cam.* 2.7; *Alex.* 49.3; see also Plato, *Leg.* 699c; *Menex.* 237e; *Phaedr.* 241a; Philo, *Prob.* 142). The chronological marker introduces Josephus' list of Herod's first measures in Jerusalem (*Ant.* 15.5-7), which clearly presents the king from a negative perspective, like the introduction of the book (15.1-4).

all the precious items[25] in the kingdom, even making those who were wealthy destitute.[26] After collecting a massive amount of silver and gold,[27] he presented all this as a gift to Antony[28] and the friends around him.[29] **6** He killed forty-five of the most prominent men

---

[25] The word κόσμος, here translated with "precious items," has many different meanings in Josephus, ranging from "orderly state" (e.g., communities, armies) to "fancy dress" (e.g., jewelry, official robes; Rengstorf *s.v.*). Richardson (1996: 161) and Schalit (2001: 100) argue that Herod collected money and possessions from his wealthy Jerusalem opponents. Marcus-Wikgren 4-5 n. *b*) suggest that κόσμος refers here to equipment or (military) gear, which might be supported by other passages (e.g., *Ant.* 13.308; 17.198). However, this is improbable for 15.5 because of the context, which refers to silver and gold as well as to a gift to Mark Antony and his friends, who would not have been pleased with used gear. The word is used with a similar meaning in the parallel passage of *War* (1.358).

[26] Josephus' report (paralleled by *War* 1.358) here and elsewhere implies that Herod was always in great need of money owing to his lavish gifts to patrons, military expeditions, building activities, and donations to foreign states. On Herod's opening of David's tomb to take money stored there, see *Ant.* 7.394; 16.179-181; on his buildings in cities outside the kingdom, *War* 1.422-425; about the expropriations conducted by Herod to fund these gifts, *Ant.* 17.305-308. There is no doubt that Herod's financial needs were great (surveys in Gabba 1990; Udoh 2005: 113-206). The question remains whether Herod actually exploited his Jewish subjects in order to finance his ambitious projects, as several scholars have argued (for a critical discussion and further references, see Pastor 2003). Josephus' information about Herod may well be biased in this respect. His note here that even those with many resources became destitute emphasizes the harshness of Herod's actions in collecting valuables and may indeed suggest that Herod exploited the Judeans (see also *Ant.* 15.7). However, Josephus usually ignores the benefits of Herod's activities for the Jews, although his enthusiastic description of Herod's activities in *Antiquities* and *War* 1, often without his complaint as narrator, might give the impression that Herod was a great anchor of Jewish stability, and therefore good for Judea. Most of his building projects concerned Jewish areas and must have provided work for thousands of craftsmen (Pastor 2003: 162-63). A verdict concerning Herod's harshness as a ruler depends much on one's criteria about good rulership and one's values in general, because Josephus' evidence does not tell us much about the nitty gritty of Herod's dealings with his people. See also *Ant.* 17.305, 307, with commentaries.

[27] Several scholars conclude that Herod also confiscated land from Jewish landowners and turned it into royal land or re-allocated it to Gentiles (Freyne 1980: 164; Gabba 1990: 162; Schalit 2001: 258-60). Pastor (2003: 154-160) counters this view and argues (1) that Herod took over the royal land from the Hasmoneans (including the areas of Jericho, Ein Gedi, and other portions of the Jordan Valley), (2) that he allocated land to loyal Jewish and non-Jewish supporters, family members, and military settlers (*War* 1.403, 485; 2.69; 3.36; *Ant.* 15.294, 296; 16.285; 17.23-25, 147, 289), (3) that Jewish freeholders continued to exist in Judea, and (4) that Herod allotted to Jews sections of royal land outside the Jewish areas (e.g., in Trachonitis and Batanea; see *Ant.* 15.343).

[28] Herod's second deed after capturing Jerusalem was to reward his patron (similarly in the parallel passage of *War* [1.358]). Other gifts to Mark Antony are reported in *Ant.* 14.490; 15.75, 132 (see also *War* 1.242; *Ant.* 14.303, 326-327, 381-382; 15.19 with notes; Udoh 2005: 143). Mark Antony, one of the triumvirs after Julius Caesar's death and the most powerful Roman official in the East in this period (Buchheim 1960; Huzar 1978; Halfmann 2011), was Herod's main patron from *Ant.* 14.303 onward (Halfmann 2011: 120), in which passage he decided, in Rome, to support Herod's cause. Herod moved over to Octavian after Mark Antony and Cleopatra had lost the Battle of Actium in 31 BCE (*Ant.* 15.161, 183–201). The mutually beneficial relationship between Herod and Mark Antony corresponded in several ways to the king's later relationship with Marcus Agrippa (Braund 1984: 82-83).

Mark Antony is mainly mentioned in *War* and *Antiquities* in connection with Herod, who was one of the major friendly kings of the Romans. In both works Josephus emphasizes, in different tones, that Antony subjected himself to Cleopatra (e.g., *War* 1.359-363; *Ant.* 15.63-65). Josephus implies, therefore, that Herod had to compete with Cleopatra for Antony's favors (van Henten 2005a). The first reference to Mark Antony in *War* is 1.118 (for further references, see Sievers/Forte in BJP 1a 1.162; Huzar 1978: 162-68, 213).

Herod's official status was *rex sociusque et amicus* ("king, ally, and friend") of the Romans, as is apparent from Josephus' report of Herod's appointment as king (*Ant.* 14.379-389; Braund 1984: 23-25). As a friendly king of the Romans, Herod's power was largely based on Mark Antony's policy and support (see also Livy, *Epit.* 128; Tacitus, *Hist.* 5.9; Appian, *Bell. civ.* 5.75; Eusebius, *Hist. eccl.* 1.7.12; Orosius 6.18.24, and in general,

of Antigonus' faction[30] after stationing guards at the gates of the walls, so that nothing would be taken outside together with the corpses.[31] They searched the dead bodies, and all the silver, gold, or other valuable items found were brought to the king. There was no end to their miseries.[32] **7** For, on the one hand, the greed of a master who needed

---

Braund 1984; Braund 1988; Jacobson 2001b). There are important parallels between Herod and other friendly kings of the Romans: he was a commoner who took over the power from a well-established local royal dynasty, as King Polemon of Pontus, King Amyntas of Galatia, and King Archelaus of Cappadocia did. Like Herod, these kings were supported by Mark Antony because of their outstanding qualities as leaders and organizers (Buchheim 1960: 51-53, 56, 58-59). The relationship between Antony and local client rulers was mutually beneficial (Braund 1984: 82). Braund also emphasizes that "the exchange of gifts and favors was at the very heart of friendly relationships in antiquity" (p. 59). Antony benefited from his clients' financial, material, and military support during his campaigns against the Parthians. Friendly kings usually did not pay tribute to Rome, but they were to contribute troops and resources when Rome required. Their kingdoms functioned as buffers against external enemies and as a protection against pirates and bandits (cf. *War* 1.204-205, 389-390; *Ant.* 14.159-160; 15.344-348; Braund 1984: 66, 91, 184; for Antony's policy in the East and his relations with client rulers, see Syme 1939: 259-75; Magie 1950: 1.433-36; Buchheim 1960: 11-83; Huzar 1978: 148-68, and for further references, Kienast 1999: 455 n. 12). The passages about Herod's journey to Octavian after the Battle of Actium (*War* 1.386-397; *Ant.* 15.187-201) also provide information about Herod's relationships with Antony and Octavian.

[29] "The friends" (οἱ περὶ αὐτὸν φίλοι and similar expressions) of a ruler or an official is a formulaic expression, which is also found in the LXX (e.g., 1 Macc 10:20; cf. 1 Chr 27:33; Esth 6:13; *4 Macc.* 12.8; Stählin 1974: 147-48, 154-55). Hellenistic rulers had a close circle of "friends" around them, who were not necessarily officials; they had a personal relationship with the ruler and enjoyed a privileged status. They also provided services on behalf of the ruler (Bickerman 1938: 40-48; Herman 1980-81; Badian 1996; Jacobson 2001b: 31; Schalit 2001: 405). Roman administrators used to be accompanied already in the Republican period by their "friends" on missions and during their terms in the provinces (Kienast 1999: 308). In *Ant.* 17.301 Josephus reports that Augustus assembled a council of his friends and prominent Romans in the Temple of Apollo in Rome to decide about the rule of the Herodians. Most *amici* of Roman rulers were magistrates or pro-magistrates belonging to the senatorial or equestrian orders (Kienast 1999: 180-81, 308-09).

Several passages in Josephus refer to a circle of "friends" of Herod (see *Ant.* 15.31, about Herod convening a meeting of friends in order to accuse Alexandra; cf. 15.98, 100, 173; 17.46). Shaw (1993: 196-98) argues that Josephus presents Herod's family as those expected to be his most important circle of support (on the political significance of personal relationships, see Shaw 1995: 357-90).

[30] For Antigonus taken captive see *Ant.* 15.1 with the note to "they took Antigonus captive." The reference to a party or group (αἵρεσις) of Antigonus is without parallels. Josephus uses the same word for the "philosophical" groups described by him (Pharisees, Sadducees, Essenes, and The Fourth Philosophy; e.g., *War* 2.119, 162; Mason in BJP 1b on 2.118-119). The parallel passage of *War* (1.358) simply states that Antigonus' group was killed. The information here that only 45 of the most prominent supporters were killed is more plausible. There is no compelling argument for identifying these persons with the council members referred to in *Ant.* 15.4, though it is possible that both passages concern the same persons.

[31] The context shows that these guards at the city gates mainly have an economic function. Jewish burial customs implied that corpses had to be brought outside of the town or its walls (Hachlili 2005: 1). *M. B. Bat.* 2.9 defines the minimum distance between the cemetery and the last house of the town as 50 cubits. The complex verb συνεκκομίζω (one further occurrence in Josephus in *Ant.* 6.5) here means "carry outside together with a corpse." Josephus uses ἐκκομίζω once in a funerary context with the meaning "carry a corpse outside": in *War* 5.567 (LSJ *s.v.* 2; cf. Luke 7:12). The transport of corpses outside of a city was a well-known escape route for people (cf. *Ant.* 15.46) as well as valuables, as Herod's measure here implies.

[32] This stock phrase functions as introduction of Josephus' comment that concludes the list of Herod's first deeds in Jerusalem (*Ant.* 15.5-7). For similar phrases with πέρας plus κακῶν or κινδύνων and a negation in Josephus, see 15.208; 16.237, and especially 16.299 (cf. *War* 7.157; *Ant.* 16.161). Josephus echoes vocabulary from Greek tragedies (see, e.g., Euripides, *Andr.* 1216 ἄτεκνος ἔρημος οὐκ ἔχων πέρας κακῶν ["Childless and bereft, with no limit set to misfortune ..."], expressed by Peleus after the death of his grandson Neoptolemus], also Aeschylus, *Pers.* 632; *Orest.* 511; cf. Dionysius, *Ant. rom.* 7.14.4; Plutarch, *Sull.* 31.1-2; Synesius, *Catast.* 2.6; Suda *s.v.*).

[money]³³ plundered them.³⁴ On the other hand, the sabbatical year necessitated that the land rest fallow.³⁵ For this happened to be the case at that time.³⁶ To sow the land in such a year is forbidden to us.

8 When Antony had received Antigonus as prisoner,³⁷ he decided to keep him bound until his triumphal procession,³⁸ but when he heard that the [Jewish] nation³⁹ was rebelling⁴⁰

Execution of Antigonus.
War *1.357*

---

³³ The greed of rulers (cf. *War* 1.358) is a *topos* of wicked tyrants (van Henten 2011b). Josephus' comments in *Ant.* 15.6-7 combine three hints associating Herod with tyrants: his tyrannical behavior, his greed, and the transgression of the Law. Landau (2006: 165) also connects "greediness" to the perverted exercise of power, which is exemplified by the image of Cleopatra in *Antiquities* (see the commentary on 15.88-93).

³⁴ This general statement explains the continuous disasters mentioned in the previous sentence and links up with Josephus' more precise information in *Ant.* 15.5.

³⁵ Josephus suggests that the effects of Herod's supposed greed were enhanced by the fact that the king's capture of Jerusalem coincided with a sabbatical year, as already stated in *Ant.* 14.475 (see the commentary on that passage). In 3.281 he explains this Jewish custom, based on biblical Law (Exod 23:11; Lev 25:4-7), of leaving agricultural land fallow every 7 years (Feldman in BJP 3 on 3.281; see also *War* 1.60; *Ant.* 11.343). Tacitus mentions this custom in one of his well-known anti-Jewish passages: "They say that they first chose to rest on the seventh day because that day ended their toils; but after time they were led by the charms of indolence to give over the seventh year as well to inactivity. (*Hist.* 5.4, transl. Moore)." Josephus' references to sabbatical years imply that the Judeans observed this custom during Herod's rule and sometimes suffered severely as a consequence (see *Ant.* 14.475; Richardson 1996: 222, 236).

³⁶ This links up with Josephus' reference to the sabbatical year in *Ant.* 14.475 (see the previous note). Both references are missing in the parallel report of *War*. Most scholars conclude that the siege of Jerusalem took place in the summer of 37 BCE (e.g., Otto 1913: 31; van Bruggen 1978: 13-14; Schürer-Vermes 1.284-87; Schalit 2001: 766-68). The most important reasons for that date are Josephus' notes that the capture of Jerusalem took place in the third year after Herod's appointment as king in Rome (*War* 1.343; *Ant.* 14.465) and during the consulship of Marcus Agrippa and Caninius Gallus (*Ant.* 14.487, in 37 BCE). This date of summer 37 BCE is problematic in combination with the reference to the sabbatical year, which ran from the month of Tishri (September/October) in one year to the same month in the next (see *m. Roš Haš.* 1.1; Zuckerman 1866). Dating the capture to the summer of 37 BCE implies a sabbatical year running from the autumn of 38 BCE to the autumn of 37 BCE, while the sabbatical year probably ran from 37 to 36 BCE (see the calculations by Wacholder 1973: 189; Richardson 1996: 236 n. 69; the sabbatical years during Herod's rule were 37/36, 30/29, 23/22 BCE, etc.). Mahieu (2012: 60-99) concludes that the capture took place in 36 BCE, which is plausible to her because she assumes that Herod took advantage of the food shortages caused by the sabbatical year (p. 62). Marcus (196-97 n. *a*, concerning *Ant.* 12.378, 694-695) and Marcus-Wikgren (5 n. *e*) argue that Josephus is making only a loose connection between the siege and the sabbatical year. Schürer-Vermes (1.18-19, following North) call for caution concerning Josephus' references to sabbatical years because they do not always match other chronological data. It is difficult to decide between the years 37 and 36 BCE because there is conflicting evidence and the danger of a circular argument: Josephus has been used heavily for calculating the sabbatical cycles.

³⁷ Although Josephus' formulation is ambiguous and could be interpreted to mean that Mark Antony had personally taken Antigonus captive, Josephus elsewhere explains that Antigonus surrendered to Sosius (*Ant.* 14.481; 15.1 notes that he was taken captive by Sosius and Herod). *War* 1.357 and *Ant.* 14.488 report that Sosius brought Antigonus as a prisoner to Antony (in the winter of 37 BCE, Marcus 701 n. *c*), and *Ant.* 15.8 may refer back to 14.488.

³⁸ This triumphal procession (Latin *triumphus*, which is taken over from the Greek θρίαμβος, LSJ *s.v.* II) by Mark Antony remains unspecified. Josephus probably refers to a triumphal march in Rome that Antony had planned for the future. Halfmann (2011: 144 with n. 6) connects it with Sosius' triumphant procession in Rome on September 3, 34 BCE (*Inscr. It.* 13 no. 1 ll. 86-87, 342-343 in Degrassi 1954: 110). It might refer to Antony's celebration in Athens in 38 BCE, which commemorated the victory of his commander Publius Ventidius Bassus over the Parthians (Huzar 1978: 174; Fündling 2003 with references), though this predates the capture of Antigonus and was not a triumph. Displaying representatives of a defeated people, or leaders of an opposing force, during a triumphal procession was common practice, as Titus' triumphal arch in Rome shows (*War* 6.418, 434; 7.36, 118, 138, 147, 154; Braund 1984: 169-171 with n. 59; Künzl 1988: 42-44, 75-77). The captive leaders of the opponents were usually

and continued to be loyal to Antigonus out of hatred for Herod,[41] he decided to behead him with an axe[42] in Antioch.[43] **9** For the Jews could hardly be kept quiet in another way.[44] Strabo of Cappadocia confirms my words and says as follows:[45] "Antony beheaded

---

executed during the ritual of the procession (*War* 7.153-154; Versnel 1970: 95).

[39] See *Ant.* 15.15 with the note to "the Jewish nation" (ἔθνος) and 15.179.

[40] The verb νεωτερίζω ("make innovations, rebel") and the related noun νεωτερισμός ("attempt to change, rebellion") occur frequently in Josephus, always with a negative connotation (e.g., *War* 1.4, 202, 224, 320; 2.5, 8, 224-225; *Ant.* 11.323; 14.157, 450; *Ant.* 15.30, 291; 16.135; 18.92; 20.7, 117, 133). There are several further hints in *Antiquities* at possible revolts of the Jewish people against Herod (e.g. 15.424; cf. *War* 1.303; see van Henten 2011d).

The motive for executing Antigonus according to the report in *Ant.* 14 is far more plausible than Josephus' note here (with Schalit 2001: 692), which perhaps echoes Josephus' previous hint at a revolt in Judea (*Ant.* 14.450). The note does, however, anticipate the information found in Strabo's quotation (15.9-10; cf. also 15.30, which mentions both the possibility of revolt and the hope for a Hasmonean king—in connection with Aristobulus III). The Latin version of *Antiquities* includes an addition to 15.8, referring to Herod's bribing of Mark Antony.

The parallel passage of *War* (1.358) does not mention a rebellion of the Jewish people, and the previous passage about Antigonus' capture attests a different motive: Herod feared that Antigonus would plead his own cause, or that of his sons, before the Senate and therefore offered a large sum to Mark Antony for executing his competitor (*Ant.* 14.489-490).

[41] The people's hatred for Herod makes sense in the light of Josephus' information in *Ant.* 15.1-7, mentioning Herod's severe punishment of opponents (15.2, 6) and his greed (15.7); yet the parallel report of *War* lacks a reference to this hatred (see *War* 1.357-358). *Antiquities* refers once again to the hatred in 15.10 (see also 15.286). These two nearby references, without parallels in *War*, suggest that Herod's portrait is more complex in *Antiquities*. They tie in with other small details that together create an image of Herod as a wicked tyrant (see also the notes concerning Herod at 15.1-2, 7).

[42] Antigonus' execution with an axe (see also *Ant.* 15.9) seems very severe for a royal person. Nevertheless, Plutarch, *Ant.* 36 confirms it (Pelling 1988: 219; cf. also Cassius Dio 49.22.6). The harsh punishment may be explained by Antigonus' taking the side of the Parthians, Rome's arch-enemies (though *Ant.* 15.9-10 offers another explanation). The parallel account of *War* (1.357) mentions the same punishment for Antigonus (without Antioch as its location). It offers a similar explanation for the execution and adds depreciating information about Antigonus' character: "Befitting his meanness (ἀγέννεια), it was an axe that felled this man [i.e., Antigonus], who clung to life up to the end with a vain hope" (trans. Sievers/Forte in BJP 1a 1.357). The "vain hope" probably hints at a kingship under Parthian suzerainty. Stern (1974-84: 1.285) assumes that the addition is dependent on Nicolaus of Damascus' pro-Herod report. *Ant.* 14.490 describes Antigonus' death at Mark Antony's orders in very general terms. Cassius Dio 49.22.6 reports Antigonus' death differently: "… but Antigonus he [i.e., Antony] bound to a cross and flogged—a punishment no other king had suffered at the hand of the Romans—and afterwards he slew him" (trans. Cary). For further references concerning Antigonus' death, see Stern 1974-84: 1.285, and for details about capital punishment through beheading with an axe, the commentary by Sievers/Forte in BJP 1a on 1.185, 357. The verb πελεκίζω ("behead with an axe," Rengstorf s.v.) also occurs in *Ant.* 14.39; 15.9; 20.117 (cf. Polybius 1.7.12; 11.30.2; Diodorus 19.101; 32.26; 36.2; 38/39.8; Strabo, 16.2.18; Josephus, *War* 1.185; Plutarch, *Ant.* 67; *Publ.* 7.6; Rev 20:4).

[43] Antioch on the Orontes was a temporary residence for Mark Antony. Cassius Dio (48.54.7) reports that Antony, after parting from his wife Octavia and his children in Corfu, returned to Syria in the autumn of 37 BCE and spent the winter with Cleopatra in Antioch (Huzar 1978: 160-64; Halfmann 2011: 147). Antioch had been Syria's capital since 64 BCE, when Pompey organized the new province of Syria and settled the fate of the city (Downey 1961: 144). *War* 1.243 reports that the unsuccessful Jewish delegation that protested before Antony against Herod and his brother Phasael in 41 BCE had a hearing at Daphne near Antioch (cf. *Ant.* 14.324-325).

[44] The explanation indicates that Mark Antony executed Antigonus to set an example to the Jews, which links up with the hint at a rebellion of the Jews given in *Ant.* 15.8. The passage further suggests that Antigonus, as a member of the Hasmonean dynasty, still enjoyed strong support from the Judeans (cf. 14.450). It also implies that the brutal execution of Antigonus was effective. Nevertheless, the narrative informs us later that remaining Hasmoneans, as well as part of the Judean population, kept hoping for a change of rule (e.g., 15.30).

[45] Josephus uses a quotation of Strabo (see below) as confirmation of his own report (Landau 2006: 165). This is remarkable if we assume (with Stern 1974-84: 1.284) that Josephus' note in *Ant.* 15.8 is a paraphrase of

Antigonus the Jew, who had been brought to Antioch, with an axe.[46] He had a reputation for being the first Roman who decided to behead a king with an axe[47] since he believed that he probably could not change the opinions of the Jews in another way so that they would accept Herod,[48] who had been appointed in Antigonus' place.[49] For even if they were put to torture,[50] they would not submit and proclaim him king;[51] **10** so highly did they

---

Strabo's information in 15.9-10. Strabo's quote is missing in the parallel account of *War*, apart from a reference to Antigonus' execution by an axe (1.357). Josephus' use of Strabo as corroboration adds emphasis to the Jews' great dislike of Herod, which is the main point of Strabo's explanation for Antigonus' execution (see the notes to *Ant.* 15.9-10).

Strabo of Amaseia (64/63 BCE-after 23 CE) was a famous polymath and writer, who is paraphrased and quoted explicitly by Josephus (*Ant.* 13.284-287, 319, 345; 14.34-36, 66-68, 104, 111-118, 138-139; 15.8-10; *Apion* 2.83-84; Stern 1974-84: 1.261-85). Josephus usually introduces him as simply "Strabo" or as "Strabo the Cappadocian" (Στράβων ὁ Καππάδοξ, *Ant.* 13.286; 14.35, 104, 111; 15.9; *Apion* 2.84). Josephus' quotation in *Ant.* 15.9-10 (see *FGH* 91 F 18; Stern 1974-84: 1.283-85) is one of the 19 fragments that remain from Strabo's *Historica hypomnemata*, intended as a continuation of Polybius' history, with a survey of the history of the Greeks until 145/144 BCE, and an extensive history of the Graeco-Roman world up to Octavian's capture of Alexandria in 30 BCE.

[46] This matches the information in *Ant.* 15.8.

[47] See *Ant.* 15.8 with the note to "axe." The formulation here implies that Strabo says that Antony seems to have been the first who executed someone with an axe (cf. Plutarch, *Ant.* 36.4, who states that he was the first). Strabo and Josephus focus on the innovation of this type of execution and the main point of the passage seems to be that this brutal form of execution was both unprecedented and an unmistakable signal by Mark Antony for the Judean Jews (as the continuation of the narrative suggests): they should be sensible and accept Herod as their ruler. Antigonus' brother Alexander faced the same form of execution, also in Antioch (see also the note to "Alexander" at *Ant.* 15.23). He was executed in 49/48 BCE by the proconsul and governor of Syria, Q. Caecilius Metellus Pius Scipio Nasica, whose son-in-law Pompey had ordered the execution (*War* 1.185; *Ant.* 14.125; cf. *Ant.* 14.73; Cassius Dio 41.18.1).

[48] Strabo's explanation for Antigonus' execution (see the preceding notes) further clarifies Josephus' information in *Ant.* 15.8. Stern (1976: 1131) argues, referring to 14.481, that Josephus' main Herod narrative is based upon Nicolaus of Damascus, who attempted to belittle Antigonus (for a survey of the discussion about Josephus' use of Nicolaus, see Landau 2006: 23-28). In Stern's opinion, Strabo presented Antigonus as a leader who was well-respected by the Jews and much preferred to Herod. Schalit (2001: 692) argues that Strabo's fragment puts more responsibility on Mark Antony for the execution, with the result that Herod could be blamed less. There seems indeed to be a shift in Josephus' information about who was responsible for Antigonus' death: if we connect the execution with Herod's gift of money (*Ant.* 15.5), Antony may have beheaded Antigonus as a favor to Herod; *Ant.* 15.9 suggests that Antony himself decided to execute Antigonus (because of the risk of a Jewish rebellion and the great support for Antigonus). Schalit also suggests that Strabo's fragment originally derived from Octavian's circle, which had a keen interest in blackening Antony and demonstrating his barbarian character (see also Syme 1939: 104-05). However, Antigonus was an enemy of the state, which implies that Antony's reputation hardly suffered from the Hasmonean's execution.

Antigonus' execution served Herod well; the continuation of the narrative describes how Herod himself succeeded in eliminating Alexandra's son Aristobulus, another Hasmonean who could have claimed the throne because of his royal descent (*Ant.* 15.49-56). This implies that Herod's plan was to have possible Hasmonean rivals killed.

[49] Herod's appointment as king by the Romans is described in *War* 1.281-285; *Ant.* 14.379-389.

[50] The statement is clearly an exaggeration, which, however, legitimates the harsh action against Antigonus and suggests at the same time that the Judeans were strongly against Herod as their ruler. It links up with the double references to the hatred that they felt for Herod (*Ant.* 15.8, 10). The Greek vocabulary (βασανιζόμενοι ... ὑπέμειναν) associates the attitude of the Judean Jews with noble death, which is a common motif in Josephus (van Henten 2007a; for similar vocabulary, cf. *4 Macc.* 9.6; 16.1; 17.7, 10, 23; *Acts Eupl.* 2.2; Eusebius, *Hist. eccl.* 4.15; John Chrysostom, *Hom. Gal.* [PG 61.629]). The extremely negative image of Herod in Strabo's quotation matches Josephus' negative portrayal of the king in *Antiquities*, which casts doubt on the reliability of the quotation.

[51] Richardson (1996: 161) suggests that Josephus refrains from using the title King for Herod until *Ant.* 15.39, whereas he would use this title in *War* already in

Return of Hyrcanus II from Babylonia to Judea.

think[52] of their former king.[53] [Antony] therefore thought that the shame would diminish their memory of him somewhat[54] and diminish their hatred of Herod[55] as well." That is what Strabo writes.

(2.1) 11 When Hyrcanus the High Priest[56]—he was a captive among the Parthians[57]—learned that Herod had gained possession of the kingdom, he came to Herod,[58] after having been released from captivity in the following way.[59] **12** When Barzaphanes and Pacorus,

---

an earlier period, i.e., starting from the moment Herod took a bath at Isana (1.340-341). This is not entirely correct since Josephus already calls Herod a king in isolated references that anticipate the Herod narrative of *Antiquities* (7.394; 13.357; 14.9, 121) as well as in the first part of that narrative (14.280, 382, 385, 430, 442, 455, 465, 469). Similarly, *War* already calls Herod a king before 1.340-341 (see 1.64, 87, 156, 181, 225, 282, 284, 320; I owe these references to Prof. Joseph Sievers [Rome]).

[52] Josephus also uses this vocabulary (μέγα φρονέω) in *War* 7.383; *Ant.* 3.83; 4.100; 6.298; 7.301; 17.41; 20.176; *Life* 17, 43, 52; *Apion* 1.99; 2.136, 286 (see also μεγαλοφρονέω with the meaning "be high-minded" in *Ant.* 5.221; 19.219; *Apion* 2.30, or "be confident, think highly of" in *Ant.* 5.221; 19.219, 328; *Apion* 2.30; Rengstorf *s.v.* μεγαλοφρονέω and φρονέω).

[53] This confirms the very positive image of Antigonus in Strabo's quotation, which is almost the opposite of the last lines about Antigonus in *War* (1.357; see *Ant.* 15.8 with the note to "prisoner"; Stern 1974b: 226). From the Roman perspective Antigonus did not deserve any respect because he had rejected the Senate's appointment of Herod and formed a pact with the Parthians (*Ant.* 14.403-404, 469, 489).

[54] The transmitted text is corrupt. Niese (334) notes that there is a lacuna and suggests to read μὲν τὴν ἀξίωσιν ("[the memory of] his reputation ..."). The addition of τι by Gutschmid or μέν τι by Richards and Shutt (followed by Marcus-Wikgren 6; see also Rengstorf *s.v.* ἀξίωσις) implies the addition of "somewhat" in the translation and seems to be the easiest solution for creating an acceptable Greek text (cf. *Ant.* 4.62 μειῶσαι τι τῆς Μωυσέος μεγαλαυχίας "moderate somewhat the arrogance of Moyses," trans. Feldman in BJP 3 4.62). In line with the "honor and shame" values of ancient society (Knoche 1934; Neyrey 1998), Antigonus' shameful execution must have had a devastating effect upon his memory for anybody, apart from, perhaps, his supporters.

[55] See *Ant.* 15.8 with the note to "hatred for Herod" and 15.10 with the note to "torture."

[56] Josephus' narrative now switches to a new section (*Ant.* 15.12-22, without a parallel report in *War*) about another Hasmonean, Hyrcanus II, who was—with interruptions (see 15.12 with the note to "Parthians")—High Priest from ca. 76 until 40 BCE, when he became unfit for the office because of a mutilation (*War* 1.269-270; *Ant.* 14.365-366; 15.181). His mother, Salome Alexandra, appointed him High Priest after the death of her husband Alexander Janneus (*War* 1.109; *Ant.* 13.408). Pompey re-appointed him as High Priest in 63 BCE and also made him the ruler of the Jewish people (*War* 1.153; *Ant.* 14.73; 20.244). In reward for his support against Pompey, Julius Caesar confirmed his High Priesthood and appointed him ethnarch in 47 BCE (*War* 1.194; *Ant.* 14.137, 143-144, 190-195; Schürer-Vermes 1.271-72). Hyrcanus II is a key person from *Ant.* 14.4 onward. For further discussions of Hyrcanus, see Schürer-Vermes 1.229, 232-42, 267-86, 297, 301; Kasher 1988: 108-25.

[57] This introductory remark is taken up again a few lines later. Hyrcanus was living in exile in Babylon after his capture by the Parthians in 40 BCE (see 15.12). The Parthian kings were the only rulers who could withstand the Romans in that period. They countered Crassus' attack at the Battle of Carrhae in 53 BCE and not only defeated him, but also captured the Roman standards and took many prisoners (Mattern-Parkes 2003). Augustus managed to retrieve the standards and the remaining prisoners in 20 BCE, following a peace treaty with Phraates IV. When the balance of power in the East changed after the murder of Julius Caesar, the Parthians undertook a campaign against Mark Antony and Octavian. They managed to capture Syria (in 40 BCE) and large parts of Asia Minor (Cassius Dio 48.24; Buchheim 1960: 11, 74-79; Ziegler 1964: 34-47; Colledge 1967: 37-46; Schürer-Vermes 1.278-79).

[58] While Herod may have considered Hyrcanus II, despite his old age, a competitor because of his Hasmonean lineage (see *Ant.* 15.20), Hyrcanus may have had good reasons to assume that he would be treated well by Herod (as Josephus points out in 15.16): Antigonus was their mutual enemy, Hyrcanus had previously formed a pact with Herod's father Antipater, and Herod was married to Hyrcanus' granddaughter Mariamme (Schürer 1973-1987: 1.234-35).

[59] The formula concludes the transitional passage of *Ant.* 15.11 and leads up to the story of Hyrcanus' return to Jerusalem (15.12-22), which is partly based on information already narrated in book 14. For the expression τρόπῳ τοιούτῳ ("in the following way") in similar introductions of a new section focusing upon a different character, see *Ant.* 9.141; 14.448.

the commanders of the Parthians,[60] had taken captive Hyrcanus—who was first High Priest and then king[61]—and Herod's brother Phasael,[62] they wanted to bring them to Parthia.[63] **13** But Phasael could not bear the disgrace of being in bonds[64] and considered a glorious death

---

[60] The story about Hyrcanus II's return starts with a flashback (which becomes explicit in *Ant.* 15.13) about the Parthian interference in Judea in 40 BCE. The technique of starting a report of a new episode with a flashback of a related former event can already be observed in Herodotus (Rood 2007: 126). This previous episode is described in detail in *Ant.* 14.330-369 (paralleled by *War* 1.248-273). Barzaphanes and Pacorus are mentioned together in *Ant.* 14.330, in which passage Pacorus is identified as a son of the Parthian king (i.e., King Orodes, who was a son of Phraates III and Parthian king in 57-37 BCE; Orodes is not named in 14.330) and Barzaphanes as a Parthian satrap. Niese (334) reads Βαζαφράνης (as in 14.330), but the reading Βαρζαφράνης is to be preferred (Schürer-Vermes 1.279 n. 46). Pacorus fell in Syria in 38 BCE during a battle against Mark Antony's general P. Ventidius (for further details, see Strabo 16.1.28; Justin *Epit.* 42 prol.; 42.4.5-13; Ziegler 1964: 34-35; Colledge 1967: 43-44; Huzar 1978: 138-39, 162-64, 173-74; Rajak 2001: 273-297; and the commentary on *Ant.* 14.330). Josephus' double narrative of the Parthian interference with the Judeans, however, mentions a different Pacorus, a royal cupbearer who was in charge of the Parthian detachment sent to Judea (*War* 1.249; *Ant.* 14.333, 339). Since Josephus calls both Barzaphranes and Pacorus commanders, Pacorus the cupbearer is most probably meant here.

[61] For references about Hyrcanus' High Priesthood, see the first note to *Ant.* 15.11. When Queen Salome Alexandra died in 67 BCE, Hyrcanus was, as her eldest son, the legitimate successor (14.11, 42). A struggle for the political power arose between Hyrcanus (supported by Herod's father Antipater) and Hyrcanus' younger brother Aristobulus II, soon after the queen's death (Schürer-Vermes 1.233-42). It is uncertain whether Hyrcanus remained High Priest between 67 and 63 BCE (cf. *Ant.* 14.6-7 with 14.41, 97; 20.244). His High Priesthood was confirmed after Pompey's intervention in 63 BCE, on which occasion he also became the political leader of the Jewish people (*War* 1.153; *Ant.* 14.73; 20.244). Gabinius apparently deprived Hyrcanus of his political powers when he divided the Jewish territory into five districts (*War* 1.169-170; *Ant.* 14.90-91; Schürer-Vermes 1.267-68). Julius Caesar confirmed his High Priesthood in 47 BCE (*Ant.* 14.143-144). In spite of the fact that Hyrcanus was officially not a king (*Ant.* 20.244), the Judean Jews may have considered him to be so (see *Ant.* 14.157, 172; Marcus 523 n. *f*, 532 n. *a*).

[62] Josephus reports that Hyrcanus II and Phasael went to the camp of Barzaphanes on a diplomatic mission after Antigonus had proposed to engage Pacorus (the royal cupbearer and commander, see *Ant.* 15.12 with the note to "Parthians") to end the combat over Jerusalem (*War* 1.254-255; *Ant.* 14.337-342). The proposal turned out to be a trap, and Hyrcanus and Phasael ended up as prisoners in the Parthian camp (*War* 1.254, 256-260; *Ant.* 14.340, 342-348).

[63] The imperfect ἀνῆγον ("they wanted to bring ...") here is taken as conative leading up to the brief reference to Phasael's noble death in *Ant.* 15.13. Only Hyrcanus was taken to Parthia (*War* 1.273).

[64] Here begins a short, explicit flashback (see the last part of the paragraph) about the heroic death of Herod's brother Phasael, narrated in *War* 1.271-272; *Ant.* 14.367-369. Both passages use noble-death vocabulary (van Henten 2007a) and report two versions: according to the first version Phasael killed himself by dashing his head against a rock; according to the second he only wounded himself by this act, after which a physician killed him. Phasael's act must have appealed to many Roman readers, who admired a self-chosen death in order to escape the enemy. Velleius Paterculus praises such a self-killing in connection with the defeat of the Romans in the Battle of the Teutoburg Forest against the Germans in 9 CE. He writes: "When the Germans were venting their rage upon their captives, an heroic act was performed by Caldus Caelius, a young man worthy in every way of his long line of ancestors, who, seizing a section of the chain with which he was bound, brought it down with such force upon his own head as to cause his instant death, both his brains and his blood gushing from the wound" (2.120, transl. Shipley). Publius Quintilius Varus, the Roman general, also committed suicide, by running himself through with his sword (2.119). Julius Africanus reports (in Georgius Syncellus [ed. Dindorf 1.581]) that Phasael died during a combat (ἐν τῇ μάχῃ ἀναιρεῖται). Kokkinos (1998: 159 n. 19) argues that this note derives from Justus of Tiberias. Phasael's choice to prefer death to a shameful execution by the enemy links up with other self-chosen deaths in Josephus in order to escape slavery or execution (see *War* 7.334, 336, 341, 372, 386, as well as *War* 1.311; 2.475; 5.458; 6.186-187, 280; *Ant.* 14.429; cf. also *War* 3.380; *Life* 137-138 for the opposite view). Similar expressions about the shame of being in chains can be found in John Chrysostom, *Hom. 2 Tim.* (PG 62.607-608).

better than all life.⁶⁵ So he became his own murderer,⁶⁶ as I have said before.⁶⁷ **(2.2) 14** When Hyrcanus had been brought [to Parthia], Phraates, the king of the Parthians,⁶⁸ treated him very reasonably⁶⁹ because he had already heard about the eminence of his noble ancestry.⁷⁰ Therefore he released him from his bonds⁷¹ and allowed him to settle in

---

⁶⁵ The noble-death vocabulary echoes Josephus' two reports of Phasael's death, but with a different touch. Josephus here uses an explicit formula that Phasael opted for a glorious death (πάσης δὲ ζωῆς κρείττονα τὸν μετὰ δόξης ἡγούμενος θάνατον), which reminds one of the self-chosen death of the old Maccabean martyr Eleazar, who refused Antiochus IV's order to eat swine's flesh (although there are no close correspondences with Josephus' vocabulary): "But he [i.e., Eleazar] preferred a glorious death to a life of defilement and walked out of his own accord towards the drum" (2 Macc 6:19; cf. 2 Macc 7:2; *4 Macc.* 9.1; 16.24; Philo, *Virt.* 32; Josephus, *Ant.* 18.59; van Henten 1997: 97-108). For similar phrases with a hint at immortality (ἀθανασία)—which word is missing here, but the notion is implied by the glory for Phasael after his death— cf. *War* 1.58; 2.151 (see Mason in BJP 1b on *War* 2.151).

⁶⁶ The formulation is unique in Josephus. The combination of the verb φονεύω and a reflexive pronoun indicating "self-murdering" further occurs in Justin, *Apol.* 2.4.1, 3; Lucian, *Dial. mort.* 23.1; Cassius Dio 2.11.19. It focuses upon Phasael murdering himself and perhaps conveys the narrator's veiled criticism of Phasael's act. Josephus is ambiguous about self-killings by Jews, even if they are heroic (van Henten 2007a). See *Ant.* 7.228-230, concerning David's councillor Achitophel's self-killing: Josephus comments that Achitophel had become his own judge (δικαστὴν αὑτῷ γενόμενον, 7.229), which is explained by the context: Achitophel did not wait for David's punishment. The comment may also suggest that Achitophel disregarded God's judgment (cf. *War* 3.369-379). Josephus also comments upon the self-sacrifice of Eleazar Avaran (*War* 1.41-45; *Ant.* 12.373-374), one of the five Maccabean brothers who tried to kill the Seleucid king, seated on an elephant, in the Battle of Beth-Zechariah (in 162 BCE), south of Jerusalem. The report in *War* is quite critical about Eleazar's attempt, despite the noble-death vocabulary (1.43 θέμενος εὐκλείας ἐν δευτέρῳ τὸ ζῆν; 1.44 λαμπροῦ κατορθώματος). In 1.44 Josephus highlights the negative result of the audacious act: "In fact, the elephant driver was a commoner; yet even if he had happened to be Antiochus, the daring fighter would have accomplished nothing more than to appear to have chosen death for the single prospect of a brilliant heroic action" (trans. Sievers/Forte in BJP 1a on *War* 1.44). See also Josephus' criticism of killing oneself in *War* 3.362, at the beginning of his famous speech at Jotapata-Yodfat (*War* 3.361-382).

⁶⁷ The formula (cf. *Ant.* 9.112; 12.158) makes the preceding narratorial *analepsis* explicit (van Henten and Huitink 2007).

⁶⁸ This is the first reference in *Antiquities* to Phraates, King of the Parthians (see also *Ant.* 15.18-19; 18.39-42; Schalit 1968: 125). It must concern Phraates IV, who murdered his father Orodes and his 29 brothers in 37 BCE and was king of Parthia in 37-2 BCE. Mark Antony occupied the Parthian city of Phraaspa as a base for his actions against him in 36-34 BCE. Phraates had to flee to the Scythians soon thereafter because the usurper Tiridates had conquered the throne. Phraates retrieved the throne in 25 BCE and established a peaceful co-existence with the Romans in 20 BCE (Justin, *Epit.* 42.5.11). Augustus sent to Phraates a slave woman called Musa, who married the king and gave birth to Phraatakes ("Little Phraates"). She had her husband killed in 2 BCE and put her son on the throne (Colledge 1967: 46-47; Dabrowa 1989: 311-14; Schottky 2000: 960). Josephus pays no attention to the change of rule in Parthia or to the consequences for Parthia of Herod's victory over Antigonus, whose regime had been restored by the Parthians (*War* 1.269; *Ant.* 14.340, 365).

⁶⁹ The passage about Hyrcanus II's stay in Parthian territory (*Ant.* 15.14-20) may be partly based upon a separate tradition. It echoes Josephus' description of the Judean king Jehoiachin-Jechoniah's release in Babylon by King Evil-Merodach (562-560 BCE) in the 37th year of Jehoiachin's exile (*Ant.* 10.229-230; cf. 2 Kgs 25:27-30; Jer 52:31-34).

⁷⁰ Josephus also refers to the noble (and royal) descent (εὐγένεια) of the Hasmoneans in *War* 1.435, 449, 458, 468, 522; *Ant.* 15.73, 210, 236; 16.192; *Life* 2 (with respect to his own Hasmonean descent) (Mason in BJP 9 on 6).

⁷¹ Similar vocabulary appears in *Ant.* 10.229 ('Ιεχονίαν τῶν δεσμῶν ἀφείς) and 17.145. The first of these passages is significant because it concerns the Judean king Jehoiachin (see the note to "reasonably" at this paragraph). The brief note about Hyrcanus' period spent among the Parthians shows a striking analogy to the fate of King Jehoiachin: Jehoiachin was taken to Babylon by Nebuchadnezzar in 597 BCE, with the royal family and the elite (2 Kgs 24:1-17; 2 Chr 36:9-10; Josephus, *Ant.* 10.97-102), kept into custody (*Ant.* 10.102), and released after 37 years of exile (Begg 2000: 523-31). Josephus states that Jehoiachin had a kind and just character (*Ant.* 10.100). Biblical passages indicate that King Evil-Merodach (Akkadian name: Amel-

Babylon,[72] where also a great number of Jews was living.[73] **15** These honored him as High Priest and king,[74] as did the entire nation of the Jews[75] that inhabited the region as far as the Euphrates.[76] He was content with these things.[77] **16** When he learned that Herod had

---

Marduk) considered Jehoiachin as one of his closest friends. He gave him many presents and positioned him above the other kings in Babylonia (*Ant.* 10.229, which is based upon 2 Kgs 25:28; Jer 52:32 "He [i.e., Evil-Merodach] spoke kindly to him, and gave him a seat above the other seats of the kings who were with him in Babylon").

War 1.434 adds to the information in *Ant.* 15.14 by stating that Hyrcanus' fellow Jews had asked to release him (Rajak 2001: 277). Ziegler (1964: 17-18) states that the Parthian kings treated foreign rulers with respect and friendliness even after having defeated them.

[72] Babylon (Βαβυλών) is here the name of the region equivalent to Babylonia (Βαβυλωνία; cf. Diodorus 17.67.3; Schalit 1968: 23). Josephus probably refers to the fertile plain along and between the Euphrates and Tigris south of present-day Baghdad. The area included the cities of Babylon, Seleucia on the Tigris, and Ctesiphon. The Babylonians lived together there with, among others, Syrians, Arabs, Macedonians, Greeks, Armenians, and Jews (Neusner 1969: 1-3; Stern 1974a: 170). Marcus-Wikgren (9 n. *c*) suggest that the precise location was not far from Seleucia on the Tigris, where a large Jewish community lived (*Ant.* 18.372-377; see also the next note).

Ancient authors refer to various regions with the name Babylon, including the territory of the Achaemenid satrapy of Babylonia. Herodotus included the Assyrian lowland in "Babylonia" (e.g., 1.178). During the Seleucid and Parthian rules Babylonia continued to be an administrative unit.

[73] From the Babylonian captivity onward Jews were living in Babylonia (see *Ant.* 11.22, 74, 122, 388; 12.149; 15.39; 17.24, 26; 18.310-379; 20.34). Josephus mentions Seleucia on the Tigris (see the previous note), Ctesiphon, a city near Seleucia (18.377-378), Nehardea (18.310-313, 379), Nisibis (18.379), and Charax Spasini (20.34) as locations where Jews were living. Nehardea on the Euphrates was a major Jewish centre in the rabbinic period (Neusner 1969: 10-15; Stern 1974a: 170-79; Oppenheimer 1983; Schürer-Vermes 3.5-9; see also Gafni 1997: 52-57, about how the ancient local roots became an identity marker for the Babylonian Jews in late antiquity). See also *Ant.* 11.132-133; 15.39.

[74] Hyrcanus had held both offices in the past (see *Ant.* 15.12 with notes). He had become unfit for the High Priesthood after his mutilation by Antigonus (15.17). Josephus implies that the Jews east of the Jordan treated Hyrcanus as if he were a king and High Priest (cf. 14.162, about Antipater being honored as a king by the Jewish people). Josephus does not inform us why the Babylonian Jews did so, apart from the remark at the beginning of the paragraph that they liked Hyrcanus very much. Hyrcanus may still have had considerable resources and it is plausible that there was some sort of a patron-client relation between Hyrcanus and the Babylonian Jews. If so, there were several reasons to treat him as the leader of the Jewish community in Babylonia since he could act as a *trait d'union* between the community and the Parthian administration. Hyrcanus was a representative person of royal descent, and apparently well-received at the Parthian court (see the previous notes).

[75] The term τὸ Ἰουδαίων ἔθνος ("the nation of the Jews"; also *War* 2.197; 7.423; *Ant.* 11.123, 184, 270, 303, 340; 12.6, 136, 357, 412, 417; 13.1, 48, 127, 143, 166; 14.196, 212, 248, 306, 320; 15.179, 384; 16.56, 158; 17.162, 330; 19.278, 284, 309) is an ethnic identity marker (Rengstorf *s.v.*; cf. 2 Macc 10:8; 11:25, 27). The word ἔθνος is, among other things, a common formal political designation of a nation in Classical and Hellenistic Greek passages (Bickerman 1938: 164), which was also used for Jews living in Judea-Israel and the Diaspora (see, e.g., Philo, *Spec.* 2.163; *Virt.* 212). Piattelli (1971: 251, 304) states on the basis of Josephus (*Ant.* 14.114, 117-118) that neither the internal organization nor the territory of Judea determined the identity of the Jewish ἔθνος. The term refers to a nation—with its own practices and values—which was recognized by other states.

[76] Apparently, Hyrcanus acted as leader of the Jewish communities in Babylonia and in the region between the Jordan and the Euphrates. The second area included the Jews of Dura-Europos on the Euphrates (Schürer-Vermes 3.10-13 with references).

[77] The brief note about Hyrcanus' view of his own position matches Josephus' characterization of him as naive, unambitious, and indecisive (*Ant.* 14.165; 15.165; cf. *War* 1.109, 203, 210-213, 234, 433-434; *Ant.* 13.407-408; 14.13, 158, 179-180; 15.182). The continuation of the narrative matches this picture: Hyrcanus falls for vague expectations of an improvement in his position with Herod's assistance (*Ant.* 15.16). A clever politician would surely have been suspicious about Herod's promises of a shared kingdom (15.18) and about his gifts (15.19). The expression ἀγαπητός with ἐστι and a dative

taken hold of the kingdom,[78] he gave way to new hopes[79] since he had been close with him from the beginning onward[80] and expected that his favor would be remembered;[81] for he [Hyrcanus] had rescued him [Herod] from the danger to be punished when he stood trial[82] and was going to receive the death penalty.[83] So he addressed[84] the Jews,[85] being eager to go to him [Herod].[86] **17** But they tried to keep him there[87] and asked him to stay.[88] They

---

referring to a person means "be content" (LSJ *s.v.* ἀγαπητός I.2, with a reference to *War* 5.438 offering the meaning "be acquiesced in [as the least in a choice of evils]"). For similar vocabulary, see Josephus, *War* 2.54; Hyperides, *Eux.* 30; Dionysius, *Ant. rom.* 8.71.5; Basil of Caesarea, *Hom. Ps.* (PG 29.485).

[78] See *Ant.* 15.2 with notes. For the fixed expression of παραλαμβάνω with τὴν βασιλείαν ("take over the throne"), see 15.254. The narrative about Hyrcanus' return to Judea first focuses upon Hyrcanus' perspective and then switches to Herod's (15.18).

[79] This statement as well as *Ant.* 15.18 ("he yearned to leave") does not match the image of Hyrcanus as an indecisive person that Josephus presents elsewhere (see the last note at 15.16). The verb ἀντιμεταχωρέω (meaning literally "go away to the other side") is usually interpreted metaphorically (LSJ *s.v.* here suggests "make room for new [hope]"). The literal meaning of the verb would make sense as well, although it makes the continuation of the sentence more difficult. An alternative translation would be "he attempted to change his location in hopes (of a better situation)," as suggested to me by Prof. Steve Mason. The rare verb is a *hapax legomenon* in Josephus. It further occurs in Heron, *Pneum.* 2.26 (1st cent. CE) and several times in Eustathius of Thessalonica (12th cent. CE).

[80] The phrase φιλοστόργως διακείμενος ("he was close with ...") is elliptic. Combinations of διάκειμαι and φιλοστόργως usually go with πρός plus a person in the accusative (see Josephus, *Ant.* 7.43 πρὸς τὸν Ἀβεννῆρον φιλοστόργως διακείμενον; Plutarch, *Fab.* 21.2 φιλοστόργως διακειμένην πρὸς αὐτόν; for similar vocabulary, see Diodorus 19.33.1; John Chrysostom, *Hom. Matt.* [PG 58.471]). Hyrcanus' first encounter with Herod in both *War* and *Antiquities* concerns Herod's trial in Jerusalem. The details about Hyrcanus' treatment of Herod during this trial vary (see *War* 1.210-211; *Ant.* 14.168-178), and both reports are ambiguous. According to *War*, Hyrcanus took the initiative to bring Herod to trial but released him after messengers from Sextus Julius Caesar had arrived. The brief report ends with "But he [i.e., Hyrcanus], eager for other reasons, namely that he loved Herod (ἠγάπα γὰρ Ἡρώδην), acquitted him" (trans. Sievers/Forte in BJP 1a 1.211). *Antiquities* notes that prominent Jews persuaded Hyrcanus to bring Herod to court (14.168), but that a letter from Sextus Caesar gave him a pretext to let Herod go "because he loved him as a son" (14.170). *Ant.* 14.177 adds that Hyrcanus postponed the trial by a day in order to let Herod escape. It seems that Josephus' statements about Hyrcanus' role contradict each other: *War* 1.211 and *Ant.* 14.170 (cf. 14.182) imply that Hyrcanus acquitted Herod, possibly at the order of Sextus Caesar; *Ant.* 14.177 suggests that Hyrcanus only had the trial adjourned. Buchheim (1960: 62) argues that the pro-Roman Herod survived the trial only because of Sextus Caesar's intervention (see also Sullivan 1977: 296-354).

[81] The phrase leads up to the reason given in the continuation of the narrative and also evokes the curiosity of the reader as to whether or not Herod is going to reward Hyrcanus. The noun χάρις ("grace, favor") is the key word in this passage. It is repeated in *Ant.* 15.17-18. On returning favors, see also 15.19. Marcus-Wikgren (9 n. *d*) note that χάριτος ἀπομνησθήσεσθαι echoes Thucydides 1.137.2 (χάριν ἀπομνήσεσθαι). This vocabulary, however, is not restricted to Josephus (see also *Ant.* 19.225) and Thucydides (e.g., Euripides, *Alc.* 299; Plutarch, *Fragm.* 157 line 51 [ed. Sandbach 96]; Aelius Aristides, *Leuctr.* 2.43 [ed. Dindorf 1.659]; Aelian, *Nat. an.* 8.22 χάριτος ἀπομνησθῆναι; Libanius, *Ep.* 99.3). The present formula is also found in Antony's letter to Tyre (Josephus, *Ant.* 14.315).

[82] Herod's trial, described in book 14, has already been referred to in *Ant.* 15.4 (see the relevant notes to that paragraph and 15.16 with the note to "from the beginning onward").

[83] This also refers to Herod's trial. The vocabulary of *Ant.* 15.16 echoes that of 15.4 and that of the report of the trial in book 14 (cf. κρινόμενον in 15.16 with κατακρίνωμεν in 14.173 and κρινομένου in 15.4; θανάτῳ in 15.16 with θανάτῳ in 15.4; τοῦ κινδύνου in 15.16 with τὸν κίνδυνον in 14.177).

[84] Phrases with προσφέρω plus λόγους as object ("address," Rengstorf *s.v.* προσφέρω) also occur in *War* 7.301; *Ant.* 2.42, 45; 6.209; 11.322; 14.60; 15.249; 16.210, 224, 323-324 (cf. *Ant.* 15.175, and see also Thucydides 1.57.5; 3.4.2; Philo, *Ios.* 40; Plutarch, *Brut.* 52).

[85] I.e., the Jews in Babylon (see *Ant.* 15.15).

[86] Hyrcanus apparently had high hopes for Herod's support, but Josephus' formulation ("[he] expected that his favor would be remembered ...") indicates that it was uncertain whether Hyrcanus' expectations would be fulfilled. The end of *Ant.* 15.17 also suggests to the reader that the outcome could be very different from what Hyrcanus expected.

talked about their services [to him] as well as their honors [for him],[89] and said that none of the honors for High Priests and kings would lack him because of their acting[90] and, more importantly, that he could not enjoy these [honors] over there[91] because of the mutilation of his body,[92] which he had suffered from Antigonus.[93] [They also said that] kings do not return the favors[94] in the same way as they had received them while they were still commoners[95] because fortune[96] changes them in no small measure.[97] **(2.3) 18** Even though they offered these things for his advantage, Hyrcanus had a yearning to leave.[98] Herod wrote to him[99] and urged him to appeal to Phraates as well as the Jews there not to

---

[87] An alternative translation would be "they were fond (of him)" (LSJ *s.v.* περιέχω III.2). Rengstorf (*s.v.*) offers "want to keep" as meaning for the passage. The imperfect (περιείχοντο) may be interpreted as a conative.

[88] The negative response to Hyrcanus' speech by the Babylonian Jews is elaborated in the subsequent lines, which imply that Hyrcanus had to be satisfied with the position he was enjoying among the Babylonian Jews and that they were skeptical about his prospects. The latter point is argued with a general statement about the changeability of the attitude of kings towards their subjects, especially if they are of common descent, as Herod was. The narrative may hint at Hyrcanus' sad fate in Jerusalem (*Ant.* 15.165-178) and it implies that Hyrcanus was naive in deciding to return to Jerusalem (see also 15.18). *War* 1.434 states in plain language that Hyrcanus would not have been executed if he had listened to his Babylonian fellow-Jews.

[89] The Babylonian Jews apparently provided Hyrcanus with unspecified services and honored him as a king and High Priest (as already stated in *Ant.* 15.15), although he was no longer qualified for the High Priesthood because of his mutilation, as the continuation of the narrative indicates (see also 15.11 with the note to "Hyrcanus the High Priest").

[90] See *Ant.* 15.15.

[91] I.e., in Judea (see *Ant.* 15.16).

[92] Antigonus mutilated Hyrcanus when the latter was in Jerusalem as a captive of the Parthians. According to *War* 1.270 Antigonus bit off Hyrcanus' ears, but *Ant.* 14.366 tells that he cut them off. The phrase κατὰ λώβην ("because of the mutilation") echoes the verb λωβάομαι ("mutilate") used in *War* 1.270; *Ant.* 14.366. Lev 21:17-18 states that mutilated priests (including mutilation of their faces) are unfit for fulfilling the priestly duties.

[93] See the previous note as well as *Ant.* 15.1 with the note to Antigonus.

[94] The truism expressed in the last part of *Ant.* 15.17 anticipates in a veiled way Herod's reaction to Hyrcanus' return. Landau (2006: 165) notes that the passage includes a recurring theme in the *Antiquities* narrative about Herod: that change of fortune is inevitable and has grave consequences (see also *Ant.* 17.192). The phrase χάριν/ χάριτας ἀποδίδωμι (see also 19.225) is common (e.g., Isocrates, *Phil.* 36.1; *Plat.* 1.3; Demosthenes, *Or.* 45.78; 53.13; Plutarch, *Flam.* 12.7).

[95] See *Ant.* 15.2 with the note to "commoner."

[96] The Greek word τύχη can mean, among other things, "fortune, fate, deity" (Rengstorf *s.v.*). It is often ambiguous in Josephus because God determines humankind's fate in Josephus' opinion. Eleazar ben Yair, e.g., argues that the Masada suicide was the fate destined by God for the remaining rebels (*War* 7.324-325, 330-336; cf. 7.358-359; Brighton 2009: 105-31). Josephus explicitly states that God is responsible for the successive events in Herod's life (see *Ant.* 15.4 with the note to "God fulfilled [Pollio's] words"; about τύχη in Josephus, see Lindner 1974: 46-47, 89-94; Landau 2006: 165, 175-76). Cf. Thucydides, who refers to fortune (τυχή) in a rather loose way; it means hardly more than good luck in several passages (2.87.2-3; 7.67.4; 7.68.1). The noun τυχή also occurs frequently in Polybius (e.g., 3.63.4; 15.10.5; Pédech 1964: 278), who influenced Josephus heavily (Eckstein 1990).

[97] The translation is based on the reading οὐκ ὀλίγως of MSS PFA¹V and Marcus-Wikgren (10). Niese (335) reads with MSS LA²M οὐκ ἀλόγως ("not unaccountably"). The idea that ancient rulers repaid those who had helped them achieve power is common, and Josephus implies that Claudius repaid Agrippa I for his indispensable aid in Claudius' accession by making him king (see Mason in BJP 1b on *War* 2.206-215). Nevertheless, I have found no close ancient parallels for the vocabulary of Josephus' generalizing statement about kings returning favors they had received before becoming a king.

[98] The statement is surprising in the light of Hyrcanus' image elsewhere in Josephus (see *Ant.* 15.15 with the note to "He was content with these things"). The reason for Hyrcanus' yearning must be the hopes expressed in 15.16. The phrase πόθον ἔχω ("yearn," also 10.75) is common in Greek literature (Herodotus 3.67; Euripides, *Iph. aul.* 431; *Orest.* 189; Dionysius, *Ant. rom.* 5.36.3; 10.19.1; Philo, *Somn.* 2.150; Plutarch, *Ant.* 68.4).

[99] On the basis of the information in *Ant.* 15.16 one would expect that Hyrcanus would have written to Herod with a request to be allowed to return to Jerusalem, but that is not what Josephus reports. Herod apparently had

begrudge him[100] the power of a shared kingdom.[101] For now was the time for him [Herod][102] to repay the favors[103] he had enjoyed, both by having been supported by him [Hyrcanus] and having escaped with his life,[104] and for Hyrcanus to receive [his reward].[105] **19** He wrote such things to Hyrcanus and sent his envoy Saramallas[106] to Phraates with a considerable number of gifts,[107] so that he [Phraates] would not prevent him [Herod] from bestowing favors upon his benefactor[108] with the same kindness as was shown to him.[109]

---

heard of Hyrcanus' wish and seized the occasion by writing to the former High Priest.

The focus of the narrative switches to Herod, and the letter to Hyrcanus referred to (see also 15.19) prepares Phraates and the Babylonian Jews for Hyrcanus' departure and motivates why it would be important for Hyrcanus to return to Judea. The continuation of the narrative points out that Herod's actual motives for persuading Hyrcanus to return were very different from what the letter mentioned implies. *Ant.* 15.20 explains that Herod considered Hyrcanus a competitor for the throne, and thus had to be eliminated or at least put under his direct control (Schalit 2001: 696). Otto (1913: 36) and Stern (1974b: 230) suggest an additional motive: Mark Antony may have urged Herod to bring over Hyrcanus because the former High Priest's presence in the Parthian territory was a potential danger to Roman interests. In case of a new conflict with Rome, the Parthians could have used Hyrcanus for raising Jewish support.

[100] The "him" (i.e., Hyrcanus) remains implicit in the Greek text. The verb φθονέω plus a personal dative means "envy, resent, deny" (LSJ *s.v.* I.2-3; Rengstorf *s.v.*; see Josephus, *War* 1.463; *Ant.* 1.248; 4.41, 131).

[101] The passage implies some form of participation in the rule of the kingdom, not necessarily sharing the rule, as a related passage about Herod's brother Pheroras shows (*Ant.* 16.195, with similar vocabulary: "[Herod …] had given him a share in the power of the kingdom [δυνάμει δὲ καὶ κοινωνὸν ἔχειν τῆς βασιλείας] …"). This interpretation is confirmed by a parallel passage of *War* (1.483), which states that Pheroras shared all the royal honors with Herod except the diadem (ὃς πάσης μὲν ἐκοινώνει τῆς βασιλείας πλὴν διαδήματος).

[102] The Greek (εἶναι καιρὸν αὐτῷ μὲν ... ἐκείνῳ δὲ) implies that it was time for both Herod (αὐτῷ) and Hyrcanus (ἐκείνῳ) to act.

[103] This links up with *Ant.* 15.16, concerning Hyrcanus' expectation to be rewarded for his favors to Herod. The fixed expression for returning favors (ἐκτίνω χάριν/ χάριτας) also occurs in Euripides, *Orest.* 453; Plato, *Menex.* 242c; *Resp.* 338b; Josephus, *Ant.* 2.262; Dio Chrysostom 75.6; Pausanias 5.16.4; 9.11.4; Plutarch, *Phoc.* 7.5; *Sull.* 32.2.

[104] The phrase again refers to Hyrcanus' role during Herod's trial, which is here formulated in unambiguously positive terms. See *Ant.* 15.4, 16 with notes.

[105] Herod plays the game well and anticipates Hyrcanus' expectation that his previous favors to Herod would be returned.

[106] This is probably the Saramallas mentioned in *War* 1.259; *Ant.* 14.345. He is characterized as the richest person of the Syrians and was the man who informed Ophellius of the Parthians' plan about Phasael (*War* 1.259; *Ant.* 14.345). The fact that Herod chose him as an envoy to Phraates implies that Saramallas had a good relationship with the Parthians.

Buchheim (1960: 65-66) suggests that Saramallas came from the coastal city of Tyre or had, at least, close connections with that city. Tyre was friendly to the Parthians and preferred the Jews to be under foreign rule, which would explain why Saramallas assisted Phasael only to a certain extent. Schalit (2001: 78, 687-89) argues that Saramallas was a Nabatean because his name was Nabatean, deriving from an expression meaning "Shara (= Dushara) is god." Dushara was the supreme Nabatean god. It is plausible that there were close connections between Herod's Idumean family and the Nabatean elite. Stern (1974b: 230) states that Saramallas was a friend of Herod's family.

[107] The Greek of the passage includes several phrases commonly used in connection with the practice of benefaction (see the next notes). Bestowing gifts upon (future) benefactors was common practice in ancient society (see *Ant.* 15.5 with the note to "gift to Antony"; Danker 1982; Joubert 2000). It demonstrated one's loyalty to the benefactor. Returning an important favor is also what one would expect in the patronage system at the court of a friendly king (see *Ant.* 12.206; 15.233). Herod frequently applied this practice (*War* 1.238, 274, 356, 393, 423, 425, 456, 483, 511-512, 530, 646; 2.100; *Ant.* 14.486; 15.5, 103, 196, 271, 327; 16.16, 18, 128, 132, 269, 301, 309, 355; 17.53, 173). He also presented himself as a great benefactor (see, e.g., *Ant.* 15.196).

[108] I.e., Hyrcanus. The noun εὐεργέτης ("benefactor") also occurs in *War* 1.215, 388 (Antony as Herod's benefactor), 530; 2.538, 607; 3.459; 4.113; 5.536; 7.71; *Ant.* 2.136 (Joseph as his brothers' benefactor); 4.187; 11.278 (Mordecai as the king's benefactor and savior); 12.206, 261; 13.214 (the Hasmonean Simon as the Jews' benefactor); 14.253 (Hyrcanus II as benefactor of everybody), 257 (the Romans as benefactors of humankind); 15.190, 233; 16.98 (Augustus as benefactor of Herod and his sons), 212 (Herod as Pheroras'

20 However, his eagerness did not spring from this motive: he feared that upheavals[110] would take place, with good reason,[111] because he himself was ruling while he did not deserve it.[112] He was eager to get control over[113] Hyrcanus or even get him out of the way[114] altogether. For this is what he achieved later.[115]

(2.4) 21 Yet, when he [Hyrcanus] arrived—after he had allowed himself to be persuaded,[116] the Parthian [king] had let him go, and the Jews had supplied money[117]—

Hyrcanus treated well by Herod. Appointment of Ananel as High Priest.

---

benefactor); 17.45, 243; 20.254; *Life* 244, 259 (both concerning Josephus himself; on euergetism in general and in Jewish contexts, see Sorek 2010).

[109] I.e., Herod. Josephus' phrase suggests that a favor and the response to it would ideally match each other (Berthelot 2003: 330). The verb φιλανθρωπεύομαι ("do someone a kindness, show oneself humane in something," Rengstorf *s.v.*) occurs once elsewhere in Josephus (*Ant.* 13.47).

[110] The plural of μεταβολή ("change") can have a political connotation (LSJ *s.v.* II.3; Rengstorf *s.v.*; cf. *War* 1.23; 2.113; 4.231; 7.65; *Ant.* 1.13; 15.264; *Life* 87), as it probably does here. The context implies that the word hints at political changes.

[111] The translation follows the reading εὐλόγων of the Greek MSS, which is confirmed by E and the Latin version (with Marcus-Wikgren 10). Rengstorf (*s.v.*) further offers "according to reason, plausibly" as meanings for εὔλογος. Niese (336) proposes to read ἀλόγων ("out of irrational grounds"; cf. his reading οὐκ ἀλόγως in *Ant.* 15.17; see the last note at 15.17). This conjecture is unnecessary.

[112] The phrase μὴ κατ' ἀξίαν can have several nuances, including "not rightfully" (Rengstorf *s.v.*) and "undeservedly" (LSJ *s.v.* ἀξία 3). This motive is highly implausible because Herod was the legal king of the Jews, appointed by the Romans (see *Ant.* 15.1 with the note to "captive"), and at this stage in full control of the country. Josephus' remark perhaps discloses his own view that Herod was not the legitimate king and that the Judean Jews continually tried to revolt against Herod (for this motif, which is especially important in *Antiquities*, see van Henten 2011d).

[113] The paragraph suggests that controlling or even eliminating Hyrcanus as a possible competitor was Herod's real motive for inviting the former High Priest over (see also *Ant.* 15.21). Neusner (1969: 37-38) argues that Hyrcanus' claim to the throne could only have been endorsed with the military help of the Parthians. For the phrase ὑποχείριον ἔχω referring to a person ("get someone into/have someone in one's power," Rengstorf *s.v.*), see *Ant.* 15.98, 248; *Life* 387, also Thucydides 3.11; Lycurgus of Athens 115; Polybius 1.21.8; Plutarch, *Mor.* 475a [*Tranq. an.*].

[114] The fixed expression ἐκποδὼν ποιεῖσθαι plus a personal object ("get someone out of the way") occurs 15 times in Josephus and—apart from one exception (*Life* 189)—only in *Antiquities* (6.63; 10.94, 252; 13.187, 335; 14.12, 281; 15.20, 49, 77, 183, 231, 369; 16.257). Seven occurrences are part of the Herod narrative. The continuation of that narrative implies that the phrase functions as a euphemism for having someone murdered (see also 13.187; 14.281; 15.49, 77, 183, 231, 369; 16.257). In 15.183 the same phrase is used in a reference to Hyrcanus' death, reported in the preceding narrative.

[115] Josephus briefly anticipates his report about Hyrcanus' death (*Ant.* 15.164-182).

[116] The note is surprising since the previous information about Hyrcanus suggests that he was eager to go to Jerusalem. The continuation of the narrative also differs from the preceding paragraphs about Hyrcanus and presents Herod in a much more positive light if one focuses upon his actions only. These apparent contradictions may be explained by Josephus' tendency to create complex and rounded characters in *Ant.* as well as *War*. He presents Saul, for example, as an extreme sinner—deserving of divine punishment—and at the same time as the greatest, toughest and most virtuous man whoever lived (further examples in Mason's introductory essay to BJP 3 [p. xxxii].

Several details suggest that Herod really did his best to return Hyrcanus' favors to him. Nevertheless, the verb ἐξαπατάω ("deceive") and the end of *Ant.* 15.21 match the picture of Herod presented in 15.16-20: Herod's intention was to eliminate Hyrcanus. The ambiguity may be explained by assuming that Josephus adapted and expanded the information found in his source (possibly Nicolaus of Damascus; see the note to "Herod" at 15.9); yet Josephus' rewriting of the data prevents us from pointing out where this source appears in the relevant paragraphs. Cf. also *Ant.* 15.370, about Herod trying to persuade the group around Pollio and Samaias to take an oath of loyalty to him.

The reading συμπεπεισμένος ("after he had allowed himself to be persuaded") of MSS LAMWE is, as *lectio difficilior*, to be preferred to πεπεισμένος ("after he had been persuaded"), which Niese (336) reads with MSS PFV (Marcus-Wikgren [10] read συμπεπεισμένος). The simplex πεπεισμένος occurs frequently in Josephus (e.g., *Ant.* 16.304; Rengstorf *s.v.*), which may have caused a copyist to omit the συμ–.

[117] Josephus does not explain the purpose of the

Herod received him with all honor and assigned him the first place in the assemblies.[118] He deceived him during banquets[119] by having him recline before the others,[120] by calling him "father,"[121] and by contriving in many ways that his plot should remain unsuspected.[122] **22** He[123] also tried to make other arrangements[124] to the benefit of his rule, but the outcome

---

money. One could think of a sum to pay the transfer to Jerusalem or to compensate Phraates. The detail that Babylonian Jews provided the money is confusing in the light of Josephus' information in *Ant.* 15.17 that they advised Hyrcanus against travelling to Jerusalem. One wonders why they would have provided money if they were urging Hyrcanus to stay. Moreover, the previous paragraph clearly states that Herod provided Phraates with gifts, which may imply that he gave the money. Nevertheless, it is certainly imaginable that the Babylonian Jews provided the money out of respect for Hyrcanus in spite of the fact that they wanted him to stay.

[118] *Ant.* 15.31 mentions a council of Herod's friends, and *Ant.* 16.305 refers to assemblies of Herod (without specification). The context implies political gatherings, to which assemblies of Herod's friends certainly belonged (see the last note at 15.5). Hyrcanus' status apparently was that of Herod's most important friend (cf. *War* 1.515, 532; *Ant.* 12.17; 13.85, 146).

[119] This perhaps already anticipates the questions that would lead up to Herod's accusation against Hyrcanus II during a banquet (*Ant.* 15.175-176; for references to banquets at Herod's court, see 15.175; 16.305, and for a description of lavish banquets [*sumposia*] for the elite, Garnsey 1999: 113-31). Banquets belonged to the usual social activities at the courts of Hellenistic rulers (Garnsey 1999: 131; Vössing 2004: 92-186).

[120] Herod apparently gave Hyrcanus the first place during banquets, which must have been a great honor, although it remains unclear whether it concerns the very first place (i.e. the place before Herod himself) or the first place after the king (see Vössing 2004: 126, who prefers the first interpretation). The verb προκατακλίνω ("assign the first place on the reclining couch [during a banquet]") occurs once elsewhere in Josephus, concerning Samuel sitting in front of his guests (*Ant.* 6.48; cf. also 20.61, which together with ἑστίασις ["banquet"] refers to the Parthian king Artabanus' receiving the highest honors at the court of Izates, the king of Adiabene). Cf. the verb verb ὑποκατακλίνω "to have one's place at the foot of the table" (Rengstorf *s.v.*) in 12.210 and ἡ πρώτη ἀνάκλισις "the first couch, the first place at the table" in *Let. Aris.* 187.

[121] "Father" is here an honorary title that may be connected to Hyrcanus' favors to Herod (for similar honorary titles in Josephus, see *Ant.* 12.148; 13.127, which latter passage is based on 1 Macc 11:32). The elder Razis, who killed himself in Jerusalem in a heroic way (2 Macc 14:37-46), is called "father of the Jews" (πατὴρ τῶν Ἰουδαίων) because of his goodwill to his fellow Jews (van Henten 1997: 205-07). The title father is also common in non-Jewish contexts (e.g., Dionysius, *Ant. rom.* 12.1.8; Plutarch, *Cam.* 10.6; *Pel.* 33.1; *Sull.* 34.1; Herodian 2.2.9.3). Roman readers were familiar with honorary titles consisting of "father" and various additions, such as *parens/pater patriae*. They were honorary rewards for military persons who had saved others (though they were later applied in other contexts as well). M. Manlius Capitolinus received the title *parens plebis romanae* ("father of the Roman people") for paying the debt of a *centurio* (Livy 6.14.5). Cicero attributes the titles *pater patriae* ("father of the fatherland") and *parens rei publicae* ("father of the republic") to Gaius Marius (*Rab. Perd.* 10.27). Julius Caesar styled himself as *pater patriae* (Suetonius, *Jul.* 76.1), a title which was first given to Cicero by the Roman people at the instigation of Cato (Plutarch, *Cic.* 23.5; Cicero himself mentions that the title was attributed to him by Q. Lutatius Catulus in the Senate: *Pis.* 3.6; Alföldi 1978: 47, 81-82). Similar titles in Greek are transmitted from the 1st cent. CE onward (Mason 1974: 74). Jewish inscriptions (e.g., *CIJ* nos. 88, 93, 319, 494, 508-510, 535, 537) attest to the honorary title πατὴρ συναγωγῆς ("father of the synagogue," Lüderitz 1983: 142; van der Horst 1991: 93-94).

[122] This second hint at Herod's murderous intention concerning Hyrcanus (see also *Ant.* 15.20) emphasizes Herod's wickedness and is keeping the reader in suspense. Only much later in the narrative does Herod succeed in removing Hyrcanus from the court (15.164-182). Josephus uses similar vocabulary (τὸ ἀνύποπτον τῆς ἐπιβουλῆς ... πράγμασιν ... ἀτόποις) in connection with Joab's treacherous murder of Abner (7.34).

[123] This paragraph forms the transition between the section about Herod's dealings with Hyrcanus (*Ant.* 15.11-22) and the section in which his mother-in-law Alexandra is a prominent character (15.23-49).

[124] Josephus does not specify the arrangements made by Herod, but one can easily think of all kinds of projects that would strengthen Herod's rule, including strategic appointments. The Greek may, however, hint at secret actions. Niese (336) reads ὑποκαθίστατο with the majority of the Greek MSS. E reads ἀποκαθίσταται ("restored"). The Latin version attests *disponebat* ("put in order," fol. 164 *recto* of the Cologne edition of 1524). The verb ὑποκαθίσταμαι is a *hapax legomenon* in Josephus. Rengstorf (*s.v.*) suggests as possible translations

for him was that disagreements also arose among persons within his household.¹²⁵ For he avoided appointing one of the distinguished priests as High Priest of God¹²⁶ and sent for a rather obscure¹²⁷ priest from Babylon,¹²⁸ with the name Ananel,¹²⁹ and gave him the High Priesthood.

(2.5) 23 Immediately, Alexandra¹³⁰ could not bear this insulting treatment.¹³¹ She was

Alexandra II lobbies for her son Aristobulus III.
War *1.437-440*

"set in motion, practice." The prefix ὑπό can express a notion of secrecy (LSJ s.v. F.III), which fits the context very well. In that case the Greek phrase can be translated as "made other secret arrangements ...." This interpretation was suggested to me by Omert J. Schrier (Amsterdam).

¹²⁵ Conflicts within Herod's household are a recurring motif in the Herod section of *Antiquities* (van Henten 2011d: 243-50). Josephus refers to disagreements or even rebellions within Herod's family (*Ant.* 16.66, 84) as well as to disorders (15.40, 202; 16.75, 229, 300; see also *War* 1.483, 488, 516, 530; *Ant.* 15.42, 218; 16.188-189, 209; 17.142, and *Ant.* 14.491 about the decline of the Hasmonean family). After Hyrcanus II's return from Babylonia, all remaining members of the Hasmonean family were living at Herod's court: Hyrcanus II, his daughter Alexandra, his granddaughter Mariamme, and his grandson Aristobulus III. These Hasmoneans figure prominently in the subsequent narrative and are all killed under Herod's orders (*Ant.* 15.55, 173, 176, 229-236, 251). Herod's two sons by Mariamme, Alexander and Aristobulus, suffer a similar fate, as book 16 describes in detail. Josephus contrasts Herod's success in his administration and external affairs with the very unfortunate events in his family (e.g., 16.75-77). *War* 1.431-673 offers a coherent description of the disastrous history of Herod's family, including the execution of Mariamme's sons Alexander and Aristobulus as well as Antipater. *War* highlights Herod's misfortune in connection with the disastrous fate of his sons (1.622, 646-647, 665; cf. *Ant.* 17.94-95). The Herod narrative of *Antiquities* intermingles the events of Herod's rule with the history of his family. The conflict described in the following section focuses upon Herod's mother-in-law Alexandra (15.23-87).

¹²⁶ The translation follows the reading τινα τῶν ἐπισήμων ... ἀρχιερέα of Niese (336). The reading τῶν οἰκείων τινά ... ἀρχιερέα of MSS LAMWE implies a local person as High Priest and may anticipate the reference to Aristobulus III in *Ant.* 15.23. Before Anael's appointment (see below), the office of High Priest had been held by a member of the Hasmonean family, starting with Alexander Balas' appointment of Jonathan in the autumn of 153/152 BCE (1 Macc 10:15-21; Josephus, *Ant.* 13.43-46). Herod's change of policy is conspicuous, and Josephus tells us of Herod's motive, to avoid appointing a distinguished Jerusalemite, but he does not spell out the significance of this choice. It is plausible that Herod's fear of possible competitors for the throne (see *Ant.* 15.1-2, 18-19 with notes) was the main reason. The High Priest could easily be considered to be the leader of the Jewish people, as the passages about Jonathan's appointment imply.

¹²⁷ This note about the relatively humble origin (ἱερέα τῶν ἀσημοτέρων, which contrasts τινα τῶν ἐπισήμων ... ἀρχιερέα; see the previous note) of Anael (see the next note) does not evoke his descent from a family of High Priests, which is mentioned in the subsequent reference to him (*Ant.* 15.40-41). Josephus' information about Anael's origin here is connected with a distinction between local, distinguished High Priests (i.e., Hasmoneans) and foreign, less distinguished High Priests (cf. the contrast ἀσημοτέρων/ἐπισήμων). This is in any case part of Alexandra's criticism about Herod's appointment (15.23-24). From Alexandra's perspective any candidate other than her son Aristobulus III was of humble origin. Josephus' remarks about Anael's descent in 15.40-41 seem more plausible than the note here because the credits of a non-Hasmonean High Priest should have been convincing for Herod's subjects (Richardson 1996: 162 n. 45; differently Otto 1913: 38; Schürer-Vermes 1.297; cf. Schalit 2001: 101, 694; Rajak 2001: 274).

¹²⁸ See *Ant.* 15.14 with notes for references about the Babylonian Jews, and 15.40 about Anael's family.

¹²⁹ Anael ('Ανάνηλος) is mentioned again in *Ant.* 15.34, 40-41, 56. 15.56 reports that he was re-installed as High Priest after the death of Aristobulus III. There is no reference to him in *War*. *M. Parah* 3.5 mentions "Hanamel the Egyptian" as one of the three post-Hasmonean High Priests during whose office a red heifer was burned (cf. Num 19). He may be identical with Anael in *Ant.* 15. In that case Hanamel's surname "the Egyptian" is probably a mistake, which may have been caused by the fact that other Herodian High Priests were of Egyptian origin (Neusner 1969: 37-38 with n. 2; Schürer-Vermes 2.229; Schalit 2001: 101, 693-95, who argues that Anael was living in Jerusalem before his appointment). Richardson (1996: 243 with n. 13) argues on the basis of the co-incidence of the end of Anael's second term as High Priest and the death of Hyrcanus II in 30 BCE that Anael would have been a friend and "client" of Hyrcanus II.

¹³⁰ The paragraph introduces Alexandra II, Herod's mother-in-law, in the *Antiquities* narrative. Three Hasmonean women with the name Alexandra figure in

the daughter of Hyrcanus[132] and the wife of Alexander,[133] the son of King Aristobulus.[134] She had children by Alexander;[135] one was very handsome[136] and called Aristobulus,[137] the other was Mariamme, who was living in wedlock with Herod[138] and strikingly beautiful.[139]

24 She was upset and took the disgrace of her son badly[140]—that somebody summoned

---

Josephus: Alexander Janneus' wife Salome Alexandra, who succeeded her husband on the throne (*War* 1.107; *Ant.* 13.320); Alexandra II, the daughter of Hyrcanus II; and Alexandra III, a sister of Antigonus II, who married Philippion, the son of Ptolemy, King of Chalcis, who became king himself after murdering his father (*War* 1.186; *Ant.* 14.126; Kokkinos 1998: 114-15).

Alexandra II is one of the key persons in *Ant.* 15, until her execution (15.247-252). She figures as one of Herod's major opponents at the court, who is continuously scheming against the king. She acts as a lobbyist for her son Aristobulus III and hopes, at a certain stage, even to take over the throne herself (15.23-38, 42, 45-46, 247-249). After Aristobulus' death she aims at arranging the throne for her daughter, father, grandchildren (15.73, 87, 167-170). Schalit (2001: 131) considers Alexandra to have been Herod's most determined enemy within the Hasmonean family. For explicit references to her, see 15.23, 25, 27, 31, 42, 47, 53, 58, 62-63, 69, 72, 80, 87, 166, 169, 183, 185, 202, 232, 247, 249, 250-251. She is not mentioned at all in *War* (Ilan 1999: 108).

[131] This remark can be interpreted in two ways: Herod intended to treat Alexandra in an insulting way, or his treatment was insulting in Alexandra's opinion. The second interpretation seems to be supported by Alexandra's statement in *Ant.* 15.36.

For similar phrases of φέρω with ἐπήρεια as object, see Diodorus 16.41 and especially John Chrysostom (e.g., *Hom. Gen.* [PG 54.491.43; 54.516.66]; *Hom. Matt.* [PG 58.594.52]; *Stag.* [PG 47.451, 466]).

[132] Josephus introduces Alexandra before describing her anger in detail. *Ant.* 15.166 notes in passing that she was Hyrcanus II's daughter (see also *War* 1.241).

[133] Alexandra was a widow; her husband Alexander, a brother of Antigonus II, was executed by Pompey in 49/48 BCE (see *Ant.* 15.9 with the note to "axe"). When Pompey, after his intervention in Judea in 63 BCE, was bringing Aristobulus II and his children (including Alexander; see the next notes) to Rome as prisoners of war, Alexander escaped (*War* 1.157-158; *Ant.* 14.77-79). His unsuccessful attempts to take over Hyrcanus' power by force were countered by the Romans (*War* 1.160-168, 175-178; *Ant.* 14.82-89, 98-102; Schürer-Vermes 1.267-270).

[134] Alexander's father was Aristobulus II (*War* 1.158, 160, 176, 241, 344, 432), who took over the throne and the High Priesthood from his brother Hyrcanus II in 67 BCE (references in Schürer-Vermes 1.233-42).

[135] Kokkinos (1998: 114 n. 98) argues that Alexandra and Alexander married in 55 BCE in Ascalon. They had 3 children: Mariamme I, an unnamed daughter who married Herod's brother Pheroras (*War* 1.483), and Jonathan-Aristobulus III (see the next notes).

[136] The meaning "spring time" of the noun ὥρα (also "[youthful] beauty, elegance") developed into "bloom of youth, beauty" (LSJ *s.v.* B.II; see also *Ant.* 15.29).

[137] Josephus mentions Aristobulus III's age twice: according to *Ant.* 15.29 he was 16 before he became High Priest, while *Ant.* 15.51 notes that he was 17 when he was installed as High Priest (see also *Ant.* 15.56 about Aristobulus' age when he died: "... being not entirely eighteen years old"). Kokkinos (1998: 114 n. 98) calculates that Aristobulus was born in 52/51 BCE. Aristobulus is called Jonathan in *War* 1.437.

[138] Herod married Mariamme I in Samaria in 37 BCE during an interval in his siege of Jerusalem (*War* 1.344; *Ant.* 14.467), when she was about 17 (assuming that Mariamme was born in 54 BCE; Schürer-Vermes 1.283-84; Schalit 2001: 566 n. 4; Kokkinos 1998: 114 nn. 98-99 argues that Mariamme was born in 53 BCE). She had been betrothed to Herod in 42 BCE (*War* 1.241; *Ant.* 14.300; further discussion and references in Ilan 1999: 105-15).

[139] The expression εὐμορφίᾳ διάσημον ("strikingly beautiful") is without parallels in ancient sources and emphasizes Mariamme's exceptional beauty. Josephus stresses her beauty in *Antiquities* (see also 15.25, 67, 237), but he hardly does this in the parallel narratives of *War*. The motif was perhaps added to enhance the novelistic character.

The Greek noun εὐμορφία ("[physical] beauty," Rengstorf *s.v.*) occurs 14 times elsewhere in *Antiquities*. It refers mostly to biblical persons: 1.162 (Sara); 2.41 (Joseph), 231 (Moses); 4.129 (the daughters of Madian); 5.276 (Manoah's wife); 6.158 and 160 (Samuel), 167 (David); 10.186 (Daniel and his companions); 11.197 (the young women brought to the Persian king). In 4 cases it does not: 8.184 (Solomon's horses); 15.66-67 (Mariamme); 18.40 (the wife of the Parthian king Phraates IV). It occurs only twice in *War*: 1.477 (referring to all of Herod's wives) and 2.57 (about the royal slave Simon).

[140] Alexandra's anger is understandable given that her son, Aristobulus III, was the logical candidate for the succession of his grandfather Hyrcanus II as High Priest (see the next note). The section of *Ant.* 15.23-41

from abroad was really thought worthy of the High Priesthood while he was around.[141] So she wrote to Cleopatra,[142] with the assistance of some musician who helped her to manage

---

revealingly describes the role of a mother at a royal court as a broker of a son's interest. Alexandra's trouble about her son's disgrace (τὴν ἀτιμίαν τοῦ παιδός) echoes Aeschylus, *Pers*. 847, in which passage Xerxes' mother Atossa laments her son's disgrace following his defeats in Greece. Josephus' phrase is ironic if it is read as an anticipation of the proposal that Dellius is making to Alexandra in *Ant*. 15.26 because παῖς ("boy") is the common term for the junior partner in a homosexual relationship (see 15.29 with the note to "sixteen").

The combination of φέρω with χαλεπῶς ("take badly") is quite common in Josephus (but only in *Antiquities*: 2.210; 5.58, 137; 6.35; 7.5, 300; 9.231; 11.174; 13.77; 15.203, 210, 223, 365; 16.342; 18.202; Rengstorf [*s.v.* χαλεπός] gives "be ill humored/annoyed/displeased/troubled" as meanings).

[141] Whether Herod's appointment of Anael as High Priest was really a disgrace with respect to the members of the Hasmonean family is debatable given that Aristobulus was still very young at the time: he was probably born in 52/51 BCE (see *Ant*. 15.23 with the note to "Aristobulus") and appointed High Priest in 36 or 35 BCE (see 15.39-41 with notes). *Ant*. 15.29, which is chronologically set before Aristobulus' appointment as High Priest, mentions in passing that he was 16. There was no official minimum age in the Hellenistic period for acting as High Priest, but it is highly probable that the age limit for priestly service in the Temple also applied to High Priests. The lowest limit mentioned in the Bible is 20 years (1 Chr 23:24, 27; 31:17; Ezra 3:8), with 25 (Num 8:24) or 30 years (Num 4:3, 23, 30, 35, 39, 43, 47; 1 Chr 23:3) as alternatives. Rabbinic passages (*t. Zebaḥ*. 11.6; *b. Ḥul*. 24ab) mention having reached manhood as criterion. Qumran passages imply that the age of 30 was the lowest limit for holding major priestly offices (1Q28a 1.8-15; CD 14.6-9; Schürer-Vermes 2.243-44; Schalit 2001: 101-02 with n. 18). Several scholars argue that priests under the age of 20 did not participate in the sacrificial services in the Temple (Baumann 1983: 169; Schalit *l.c.*). If the biblical mimimum age of 20 was taken seriously in Herod's time, the king must have faced a dilemma: he could not appoint Aristobulus, but he could not leave the High Priesthood vacant either. A realistic wish from Alexandra's perspective would have been the appointment of an elderly priest as a transitory figure. For the combination ἀξιοῦμαι τῆς ἀρχιερωσύνης ("be thought worthy of the High Priesthood"), cf. *War* 1.199; *Ant*. 19.314.

[142] Cleopatra apparently functioned as a contact person for Alexandra in order to get access to Antony. This is the first reference to Cleopatra in *Ant*. 15. Cleopatra VII (70/69-30 BCE) was the last Ptolemaic ruler of Egypt (51-30 BCE). She partly restored the immense territory of the Ptolemaic empire of the 3rd cent. BCE by using unorthodox partnerships with 2 powerful Romans, Julius Caesar and Mark Antony (Huzar 1978: 167; Hölbl 1994: 217-18). Josephus renders the opinion of Herod's friends that Cleopatra was the woman with the highest status (ἀξίωμα) in this period (*Ant*. 15.101), which may well have been true (Mayer-Schärtel 1995: 86). Roman authors murdered her character from the year 33 BCE onward (when the split between Antony and Octavian had become definitive) and even more so after her and Antony's defeat at Actium in 31 BCE. Appian (*Bell. civ*. 5.9) reports how Cleopatra winded Antony around her little finger and had her way "regardless of laws, human or divine" (trans. White), including having her sister Arsinoe killed secretly (Mayer-Schärtel 1995: 76-77).

Josephus is one of the most negative ancient sources about Cleopatra. In—mainly brief—references to the queen in *War* he suggests that Cleopatra ruined Antony, which is very much in line with her portrait in the Roman sources. Cleopatra and Herod appear as natural enemies in *War*; both were strongly dependent on Antony's favors (cf. *Ant*. 15.75; Grant 1972: 139-41, 158-60; Huzar 1978: 167-68). In *Antiquities* Josephus goes beyond the usual contempt for Cleopatra's sexual immorality, greed, and perverted hunger for power, and in *Apion* 2.56-61 he offers a condensed list of Cleopatra's crimes and portrays her as the ultimately wicked foreign ruler (for further references and a discussion of the differences between Cleopatra's image in *War* and *Antiquities*, see van Henten 2005a). Huzar (1978: 244) argues that Josephus' very negative portrayal of the queen was influenced by Nicolaus of Damascus. *War* 1.243 notes that Antony was already "enslaved by his love for Cleopatra" (Ἀντώνιον ἤδη τῷ Κλεοπάτρας ἔρωτι δεδουλωμένον, trans. Sievers/Forte in BJP 1a 1.243; cf. *Ant*. 14.324 "she laid her hands on him by love [δι' ἔρωτος αὐτὸν ἐκεχείρωτο]," trans. Marcus) when he met her in Cilicia (Southeast Turkey). Josephus is not very specific about the time and location of this meeting (it took place at Tarsus in 41 BCE on Antony's initiative). Plutarch (*Ant*. 26) describes it as an impressive and very successful seduction of Antony by Cleopatra on her golden barge (cf. Appian, *Bell.civ*. 5.8; Cassius Dio 48.24.2). Buchheim (1960: 23, 25) argues convincingly that Antony considered it crucial to secure the indispensable support

the delivery of the letter,[143] to request from Antony the High Priesthood for her son.[144]

(2.6) 25 Antony responded rather indifferently,[145] but when his friend Dellius[146] came to Judea for some business[147] and saw Aristobulus he was impressed by his elegance.[148] He admired the tall stature and beauty of the boy, and no less the beauty of Mariamme, who

---

of the queen before implementing his policy for Syria, a region that was looked upon by the Egyptians as their *hinterland*. It was wise to do that in Asia Minor, i.e., before entering Syrian territory. This implies that his motives to meet in Tarsus were strategic and political. Roman authors indicate that Antony fell in love with the queen only several years later, in 36 BCE (Livy, *Epit.* 130) or 34 BCE (Velleius Paterculus 2.82.3-4), though Huzar (1978: 32) suggests that Antony may already have fallen in love with her during Gabinius' campaign against the Alexandrians in support of Ptolemy XI Auletes (in 56 BCE), when she was only 14 years old (Cicero, *Phil.* 2.48; Strabo 12.3.34; 17.1.11; Plutarch, *Ant.* 3.5-6; Appian, *Bell. civ.* 5.8; Cassius Dio 39.58). Other authors (such as Josephus) suggest that Antony became Cleopatra's slave (Florus 21.11; Plutarch, *Ant.* 25.1; 28.1; 36.1; 37.4; Appian, *Bell. civ.* 4.38; Cassius Dio 48.22-27; Becher 1966: 64-65); yet Huzar (1978: 155) concludes: "... despite the tales of illicit passion told by his contractors, Antony was ruled by his head, not his heart."

In the light of Josephus' suggestion that Antony was strongly dependent on Cleopatra, Alexandra's attempt to use Cleopatra as an intermediary to influence Antony was a very smart move.

[143] There was no postal service for private individuals in antiquity; the transport of letters depended on the assistance of relatives and acquaintances, and—especially for confidential messages—of trusted slaves (White 1986: 214-16; Bagnall and Cribiore 2006: 37-40). Augustus founded a postal service for messages that concerned the Roman state, the *cursus publicus* (Suetonius, *Aug.* 49; Pflaum 1940: 210-45; Eck 1995: 88-110). The couriers (*tabellarii*) could also carry messages that were strictly speaking no state post and sometimes take private letters for a fee. Businessmen and passing strangers—like musicians and other artists (in order to perform at courts and during festivals; see *Ant.* 15.269-270)—were also convenient persons for delivering letters since they were traveling a lot. For other references to the secret correspondence between Alexandra and Cleopatra, see 15.31, 45-46, 62-63, and for Josephus' vocabulary concerning letters (besides γράμματα also ἐπιστολή), Olson 2010: 74, 173.

[144] Antony's presence in Egypt implies that Alexandra's request was made at the end of 36 BCE at the earliest (Buchheim 1960: 84; Schürer-Vermes 1.252). Josephus' description suggests the existence of a complicated web of competing aristocratic persons, who were all dependent on Antony as the ultimate *patronus*. They could use Cleopatra as broker by entering into a client relationship with her. Costobar used such a strategy when he defected from Herod (*Ant.* 15.256-258; Huzar 1978: 156-57).

[145] The brief section *Ant.* 15.25-31, introduced by this note, presupposes that the reader knows about Antony's bad reputation concerning love affairs and sex (see the notes at 15.28-29).

[146] Several Greek MSS read here and in *Ant.* 15.27 Γελλαῖος; the Latin version offers *Gellius*. The reading Δέλλιος ("Dellius") is certain, though. Dellius is mentioned in *War* 1.290 as Antony's representative (parallel report in *Ant.* 14.394, in which passage his name is given as Bdel[l]ius). Quintus Dellius was famous for switching patrons at the right moment. He became close with Antony in 42 BCE but went over to Octavian shortly before the Battle of Actium in 31 BCE. He fulfilled several confidential missions for Antony and delivered Antony's invitation to Cleopatra to meet at Tarsus (in 41 BCE). Cassius Dio (49.39) calls Dellius a favorite (παιδικά) of Antony, which could imply a sexual relationship (Marcus-Wikgren 14 n. *a*; Dover 1978: 16, 85). Richardson (1996: 162) takes Josephus' account to be "almost farcical" because Dellius would have been Antony's lover while Antony did not act because he was afraid of Cleopatra (further references and discussions in Broughton 1951-86: 2.559; Buchheim 1960: 23-24, 90-91; Huzar 1978: 153, 165, 182, 201-02, 217, 228, 243-44; Sievers 1989).

[147] Josephus does not specify Dellius' business in Judea and there is no parallel report in *War*. It is plausible, though, that it concerned a diplomatic mission ordered by Antony (see the preceding note). Mahieu (2012: 347-348) argues that Dellius' visit took place in the post-Sabbatical year Tishri 36/35 BC and that it was connected with a tax which the Jews were expected to pay to Antony.

[148] The Greek phrase ἠγάσθη τῆς ὥρας echoes the vocabulary of *Ant.* 15.23 (see the note to "very handsome"). Codex V reads ἠράσθη instead of ἠγάσθη, which suggests that Dellius passionately desired the beauty of Aristobulus, implying a much more active role. Josephus' phrase is rare, although it does occur elsewhere (Pseudo-Lucian, *Charid.* 16.4-5; Philostratus, *Imag.* 1.17.2).

was living in wedlock with the king.[149] It was clear that he believed Alexandra was somebody blessed with beautiful children.[150] **26** When she had a word with him, he persuaded her to have portraits painted of both of them and send these over to Antony.[151] For once he saw those, she would not fail to obtain anything[152] she asked.[153] **27** Alexandra was excited about these words and sent the portraits to Antony. And Dellius talked of marvels[154] saying that it seemed to him that the children were the offspring of some god rather than of human beings.[155] This was undertaken by him in order to draw Antony into

---

[149] The phrase repeats Josephus' information of *Ant.* 15.23 about Herod's marriage with Mariamme I. The repetition emphasizes that it would have been problematic for Antony to start an affair with Mariamme, which anticipates Antony's response to Dellius' proposal (15.28).

[150] The noun καλλίπαις ("blessed with beautiful children") occurs only once in Josephus (for other occurrences, see Aeschylus, *Ag.* 762; Euripides, *Heracl.* 839; Plato, *Phaedr.* 261a; Philodamus 7; 4 Macc 16:10; Plutarch, *Mor.* [*Quaest. plat.*] 1001a; Galen, *Hipp. epid.* 6 [ed. Kühn 17b.145.14]). The phrase links up with the mention of the exceptional beauty of Aristobulus and Mariamme (*Ant.* 15.23, 27). It may also hint at the tragic fates of Alexandra and her children narrated later in *Ant.* 15: Alexandra and her children all died at Herod's order. Several parallel occurrences of καλλίπαις highlight the misfortunes of parents with beautiful children: e.g., Euripides (*Heracl.* 830-842) dramatically depicts the misfortune of Heracles, who killed his own children. 4 Maccabees' praise for the mother of the Maccabean martyrs, who watched her 7 sons dying during horrible tortures, includes a passage that formulates what the mother could have thought: "Alas, I who had so many and beautiful children (ὦ ἡ πολύπαις καὶ καλλίπαις ἐγώ) am a widow and alone, with many sorrows" (4 Macc 16:10, trans. *NRSV*).

[151] *War* 1.439 does not mention Alexandra and reports that Herod's mother and sister accused Mariamme of sending her portrait to Antony in Egypt. Schalit (2001: 104-07) argues that the *Antiquities* version of the "portrait story" (cf. *War* 1.439-440) is highly improbable. A famous papyrus text from the 2nd cent. CE implies that sending over portraits was a rather common practice in antiquity: *BGU* (2 no. 423) transmits a letter for the home front from an Egyptian sailor called Apion. He writes from Misenum (near Naples, Italy) to his father Epimachus in Philadelphia (Fayum, Egypt) and states: "I have sent through Euctemon a portrait of myself" (ll. 21-22). This also presupposes that artists skilled to make such portraits were readily available at Misenum (for an English translation of the papyrus and references, see White 1986: 159-60). It is significant that Alexandra apparently did not bother about the 2nd commandment, which forbids Jews to make images of living creatures (see *Ant.* 15.276 with the note to "images [of human persons]").

[152] The reading οὐδενὸς ἀθετήσειν of MSS FV (Niese 337) implies a slightly different meaning: "would not be denied anything." Ernesti's conjecture οὐδενὸς ἀτυχήσειν ("would not fail anything") is supported by many parallel phrases (e.g., Xenophon, *Hell.* 3.1.22; Dionysius, *Ant. rom.* 6.40.1; Plutarch, *Alex.* 29.9; *Lys.* 5.4) but is unnecessary.

[153] The passage may be ambiguous. Josephus presents Dellius' plan as the means to realize Alexandra's strategy, but the reader may wonder whether Dellius himself had different things in mind when he did his proposal to Alexandra. This may be implied by *Ant.* 15.27 (see the note to "sexual pleasures").

[154] *Ant.* 15.28 presupposes that Dellius was still in Judea, which implies that he sent a message to Antony together with the portraits. Letters frequently accompanied the sending of goods (Bagnall and Cribiore 2006: 39). Josephus emphasizes that Dellius is exaggerating the beauty of Mariamme and Aristobulus with, possibly, a depreciating tone.

The verb τερατεύομαι ("talk marvels," LSJ *s.v.*; "assert something extravagant," Rengstorf *s.v.*) occurs twice elsewhere in Josephus, with a negative connotation (*War* 1.526; 6.200; cf. 3 Macc 1:14). The noun τερατεία can also have a pejorative meaning in Josephus: "trickery, imposture" (*War* 1.495, 630, Rengstorf *s.v.*; cf. 6.297).

[155] Dellius' statement reads like a conventional statement presenting beautiful children as potential attractive sexual partners by hinting at their divine origin, though close literary parallels are rare. A fragment from Sappho expresses the feelings of a woman observing a man and a woman in love with that man: "He seems to me to be equal to gods, that man who is sitting facing you and hearing your sweet voice close by, and your lovely laugh. That, I swear, set my heart fluttering in my breast ..." (Sappho 31, trans. Dover 1978: 177). The equation to the gods probably indicates great beauty and strength, which implies that the statement of the woman expresses despair: she cannot compete with the man (Dover 1978: 178). The exceptional beauty of Mariamme and Aristobulus added to their attractiveness as sexual partners (Dover 1978: 69-70).

The motif of a divine origin of a human child is rare

sexual pleasures.[156] **28** But Antony feared summoning the girl, who was married to Herod,[157] and he wanted to avoid that any slander being passed on to Cleopatra because of such an affair.[158] So he commanded [Dellius] to send the son in a respectable way, adding "if it is no burden."[159]

---

in a Jewish context, but it does occur in Isaiah's famous prophecy in 9:6 ("For a child has been born for us, a son is given to us; authority rests upon his shoulders; and he is named Wonderful Counselor, Mighty God, Everlasting Father, Prince of Peace), which is alluded to in Luke's story of the annunciation (Luke 1:32). Several early Jewish writings attribute divine properties to Moses (Meeks 1968; van Henten 2006). The motif is prominent in Virgil's famous fourth *Ecloge*: "… now a new generation descends from heaven on high. Only do you, pure Lucina, smile on the birth of the child, under whom the iron brood shall at last cease and a golden race spring up throughout the world! Your own Apollo now is king!" (ll. 7-10); "… dear offspring of the gods, mighty seed of a Jupiter to be!" (l. 49; transl. Fairclough). These lines have frequently been interpreted as a veiled reference to the later emperor Augustus (Beaujeu 1982: 191-93), but Slater (1912) already argued convincingly that Virgil composed the poem in ca. 40 BCE in honor of the marriage between Antony and Octavia.

[156] Sexual relationships between high Roman officials and members of the family of a client king were a commonplace (Braund 1984: 179 with references; cf. also *Ant.* 15.97, about Herod and Cleopatra). Josephus makes Dellius' motive explicit here, although the benefit for Dellius himself is not indicated. It is plausible, though, that providing Antony with one or even two junior lovers would bring some profit to him. Josephus frequently uses the verb πραγματεύομαι ("undertake, bring about," Rengstorf *s.v.*) for bringing about something bad or objectionable: poisoning (*War* 1.583), rebellion (*War* 2.259, 283, 318; *Ant.* 11.27), or transgression of the Jewish laws (*Ant.* 17.151; see also *War* 2.594; *Ant.* 15.33). The passage presupposes Antony's bad reputation concerning love affairs. He was known for his fondness of love affairs with men and women, drinking bouts, gambling and for having huge debts (Cicero, *Phil.* 2.18, 56, 58, 63, 67-68, 76-77; Plutarch, *Ant.* 2.3; 4.4; 29.1; 33.3; *Dem.* 1.7; *Mor.* [*Fort. Rom.*] 319f; Huzar 1978: 24, 55-56, 65-66, 99, 154, 168, 190-91, 237, 246, 254; Buchheim 1960: 56, 103; Langlands 2006: 305-15).

Josephus must have abhorred Dellius' plan since he claimed not to seek sexual pleasures, as other passages imply. He was very much against extramarital sexual relationships, in line with the biblical laws (e.g., *Apion* 2.199-204). Like Philo and several other Jewish authors from the Second Temple period he supported the view that a marriage has to be focused upon running the household and upon procreation (*Ant.* 1.247; 3.274; *Apion* 2.199; Satlow 2001: 14-16). The famous story about Joseph and Mrs. Potiphar (Gen 39) sets the example (*Ant.* 2.39-61). Joseph functions as a model figure, who exemplifies the virtue of self-control (σωφροσύνη). In one of his responses to Mrs. Potiphar he argues that marital fidelity is much more important than the temporary pleasure of satisfying one's lust (*Ant.* 2.51-52; Feldman in BJP 3 on *Ant.* 2.51-52).

[157] Josephus does not inform us of Antony's response to the portraits, but the episode presupposes the extraordinary beauty of Alexandra's children. There were obvious reasons for Antony not to summon Mariamme to Egypt, which had to do with Herod as much as with Cleopatra (see the next note). Mariamme was a Hasmonean princess married to the current king of Judea (see *Ant.* 15.23), who was one of Antony's most important friends (see 15.5 with the note to "Antony" and 15.77). Starting an affair with Mariamme would have taxed Herod's loyalty if not turned him into an enemy.

[158] Cleopatra's response to Antony's advances to Mariamme would be rather predictable: she would surely not tolerate a lover of Antony as competitor. Other passages in Josephus suggest that slander transmitted to Cleopatra was a powerful tool for eliminating an opponent of her. *Ant.* 15.77 reports about a letter from Herod to his home front, in which he refers to Cleopatra's accusations against him (which were motivated by her strategy to take over his kingdom). *War* 1.359-361, 365 suggest in more general terms that Cleopatra applied this strategy to high-ranking officials in Syria as well as to the kings of Judea and Arabia (see also 1.439-440, on Cleopatra's involvement in the deaths of King Lysanias of Chalcis and the Nabatean king Malichus I [cf. *Ant.* 15.92], and 15.48, 65, 97). Malichus of Nabatea was also one of Antony's client kings, but he had been previously punished by Ventidius for siding with the Parthians and was later punished again for his hostile attitude towards Herod. Cassius Dio (49.32.5) confirms that Antony gave portions of Malichus' land to Cleopatra and her children (Huzar 1978: 160).

[159] The expression is almost comical (for a close parallel, see Olympiodorus the Younger, *Alcib.* 61.23: εἰ μὴ εἴη τοῦτο βαρύ [ed. Westerink 41]). The phrase perhaps hints at Dellius' dependence on Antony as *patronus* and ridicules this relationship, or, more plausibly, at Dellius' delight in accompanying the handsome Aristobulus to Egypt.

BOOK FIFTEEN

29 When these matters were reported to Herod,[160] he decided that it was unsafe[161] to send Aristobulus, who was at that time very handsome[162]—he was just sixteen[163] and from an eminent family,—to Antony, for he was more powerful than any other Roman at that time[164] and prepared to use him for erotic diversion[165] and to obtain his pleasures undisguised[166] because of his power.[167] **30** So he [Herod] wrote in reply[168] that in the event

Herod refuses to send Aristobulus to Antony. Conflict with Alexandra.

---

[160] Josephus does not inform us directly how Herod got to know this. One can think of spies at Herod's court, whose role is highlighted elsewhere in Josephus (*War* 1.492; *Ant.* 16.236), or of some sort of correspondence between Herod and Dellius or Antony. The latter possibility is confirmed by *Ant.* 15.30, which passage mentions a response by Herod to Antony.

[161] At first glance there seems to be a discrepancy between this statement and other indications that Herod would be glad when Aristobulus—as one of his possible competitors—would be out of his way (cf. *Ant.* 15.23-38, 42, 45-46). Nevertheless, Josephus' narrative shows that there were important reasons for Herod to prevent Aristobulus' trip to Egypt. Aristobulus was Herod's brother-in-law and of royal descent. It would have been a big shame for Herod's family if this young man became a lover of Antony (see 15.27 with the note to "sexual pleasures"), or even of Antony and Dellius. Parents tried to protect young men from relationships with senior men (Plato, *Symp.* 183cd; cf. Aristophanes, *Av.* 137-142).

[162] The phrase ὥρᾳ κάλλιστον ὄντα ("very handsome") repeats the vocabulary of *Ant.* 15.23, also referring to Aristobulus (similar vocabulary is found in Aristophanes, *Av.* 1724; Xenophon, *Anab.* 4.6.8; Aeschines, *Tim.* 134.6; 158.11-12; Plutarch, *Cleom.* 37.7).

[163] Aristobulus' young age was an additional reason for not letting him go: he could not protect himself well enough and was all the more attractive as a junior sexual partner. The noun παῖς ("boy") is the common word for the 'passive' partner in such a relationship. Xenophon (*Anab.* 7.4.7) refers to such a "boy" who had just reached maturity (Dover 1978: 86): "There was a certain Episthenes of Olynthus who was a lover of boys (παιδεραστής), and upon seeing a handsome boy (παῖδα καλὸν), just in the bloom of youth and carrying a light shield, on the point of being put to death, he ran up to Xenophon and besought him to come to the rescue of a handsome lad" (trans. Brownson).

[164] Antony formed with Lepidus and Octavian the 2nd triumvirate, which basically ruled the Roman state in 42-37 BCE. He was the most powerful Roman administrator in the East in the period from the division of the Roman territory at the Treaty of Brundisium in 40 BCE until Octavian's victory at the Battle of Actium in 31 BCE (Huzar 1978: 138).

[165] The passage explicitly states Antony's lively interest in sexual entertainment, which was already presupposed in *Ant.* 15.25-27 (for his reputation in sexual contacts with males and females, see 15.27 with the note to "sexual pleasures"). Josephus' comments about Antony's relationship with Cleopatra suggest that sexual love (ἔρως) was important from the very beginning and that Antony was enslaved by the queen (see 15.24 with the note to "Cleopatra" and 15.93, 101).

[166] An alternative translation of ἀπαρακάλυπτος would be "without feeling shame" (Rengstorf *s.v.*). The phrase also occurs in *Ant.* 15.97 (referring to Cleopatra) and in 16.375.

[167] Elite men apparently had the privilege to indulge in sexual relationships that were not openly acceptable for others. They could also afford to choose the female partners they wanted, as is apparent from the passage that describes Herod's marriage with Mariamme II. After the death of Mariamme I, Herod managed to arrange another marriage with the most beautiful woman that lived in Judea in those days (*Ant.* 15.319-322). Her name was also Mariamme. Interestingly, Josephus connects this arrangement to Herod's power: he indicates that Herod was capable of simply forcing the woman to live with him, but reports at the same time that Herod decided to strike a deal with her father, appointing him High Priest. Josephus writes: "Yet, he [i.e., Herod] rejected the thought of accomplishing everything *by using his power*, suspecting, which was true, that he would be accused of using force as well as tyrannical behavior, and considered it better to marry the maiden" (15.321, italics added).

Some women could afford to withstand elite men or even take the initiative in finding sexual partners. Cleopatra was one of the very few women who may have allowed themselves a liberal attitude in finding sexual partners (see 15.96-103), although it is not certain that she actually took this liberty. The relationship between Antony and Cleopatra, which started with Antony's invitation of her to Tarsus in 41 BCE, must have been wanted by Cleopatra as well. It lasted for about 10 years (Cicero, *Att.* 14.20.2; Strabo 17.1.11; Josephus, *War* 1.243; *Ant.* 14.324; Plutarch, *Ant.* 25-28; Suetonius, *Aug.* 17.5; *Jul.* 50.1-2; 52.1-3; Appian, *Bell. civ.* 5.8; Cassius Dio 48.24.2; Socrates of Rhodes in Athenaeus 4.29; Huzar 1978: 153-54; van Henten 2005a: 114) and Cleopatra married Antony according to Egyptian customs in 35 BCE or somewhat later (Buchheim 1960: 88 with n. 213).

the young man would merely leave the country, everything would become filled with[169] war and disorder,[170] because the Jews had hoped for a change of government[171] and a new regime[172] with a different king.[173] **(2.7) 31** After offering Antony his excuses with these [arguments], he decided not to leave the boy and Alexandra entirely without honor,[174] especially because his wife Mariamme[175] had slickly pressed him[176] to give her brother the High Priesthood.[177] He also believed that it was to his advantage, since it would be impossible for Aristobulus to go abroad when he had been rewarded with the honor.[178] Therefore he met with his friends[179] and strongly accused Alexandra.[180]

---

[168] This suggests that Antony put a request to Herod (directly or through Dellius). It implies that Herod was in a position that forced him to balance on the tight rope: although he may have liked that Aristobulus was out of the way, he could not allow Alexandra to proceed with her plan because the risk that the boy would become Antony's sexual partner was unacceptable (see *Ant.* 15.29 with the note to "unsafe"). He could not afford either to endanger his relationship with Antony, and had to find an excuse that was acceptable.

[169] Reading ἀναπλησθήσεται ("be filled with," perhaps "be infected with," LSJ *s.v.* ἀναπίμπλημι II.2) with Niese (337).

[170] Other Josephan passages referring to Judea filled with war and/or rebellion include *War* 2.65, 265; *Ant.* 18.9. Rebellion (ταραχή), whether internal or external, is a *leitmotiv* in *War* and is presented as an important cause of the war against Rome (e.g., 4.137, 318; 5.356-357). The theme is also prominent in *Antiquities*, already in the report about the revolt of Korah, Dathan, and Abiram (Num 16; *Ant.* 4.11-62; see also *War* 1.245; 2.29, 170, 175-176; 3.308; *Ant.* 3.43; 14.100; 15.33, 231, 286, 293-295, 326, 353; *Life* 422). Josephus suggests that Herod used the Jews' reputation of being a rebellious people to avoid Aristobulus' journey to Antony, which implies that Herod highlighted his peacekeeping task as Rome's friendly king, which role Antony could not question.

[171] For μεταβολή with the meaning "political change" (Rengstorf *s.v.*), see, e.g., *War* 1.5, 171, 270; 2.113; *Ant.* 1.13; 15.163, 166, 264; 17.346-347; 18.9; *Life* 36.

[172] For the rebellion motif, see *Ant.* 15.8 with the note to "rebelling." For νεωτερισμός ("uprising, revolutionary intention," Rengstorf *s.v.*), see *War* 2.259; *Ant.* 15.353, 424; 17.289, 314; 19.327; 20.106, 113, 133; *Life* 17, 23, 56, 184. *War* 1.171, 335; 2.224-225 and *Ant.* 20.106-107 suggest in several ways that the Jews were inclined to rebel.

[173] Hyrcanus II and Aristobulus III were both of Hasmonean descent and obvious candidates for replacing Herod. Although Herod's motive as described by Josephus is pragmatic, it implies that Herod was at least thinking about potential competitors. Elsewhere Josephus is much more explicit about this and indicates that Herod aimed at having his possible competitors killed (see *Ant.* 15.49; about Hyrcanus II, see 15.20, 164). That Herod refers to competitors in his correspondence with Antony is ironical, but it matches his role as Rome's friendly king who had to keep peace in Judea.

[174] The verb ἀτιμάζω ("exclude from honor," Rengstorf *s.v.*) echoes the noun ἀτιμία ("disgrace") in *Ant.* 15.24 (cf. 16.84, 195).

[175] See *Ant.* 15.23 with the note to "Mariamme."

[176] The combination of ἔγκειμαι ("press") with λιπαρῶς ("slickly, oily, brilliantly, easily," LSJ *s.v.*; Rengstorf *s.v.*) is quite rare in ancient literature, but it occurs 4 times in Josephus (*War* 7.108; *Ant.* 1.56; 16.13; cf. *Ant.* 4.107; see also Philo, *Cher.* 48; *QG* 4.202; Petit 1978: 205). Rengstorf (*s.v.*) suggests another meaning: "beseeching persistently/constantly/earnestly." See also *Ant.* 15.205 about Mariamme and Alexandra's paying court to Soemus in order to find out about Herod's secret instructions.

[177] Aristobulus III was the obvious candidate for the High Priesthood—also because his grandfather Hyrcanus II had become unfit for it—though he was very young (see *Ant.* 15.23 with the note to "Aristobulus"; 15.24 with the note to "around"; and 15.11 with the note to "High Priest"). The combination of ἀποδίδωμι and τὴν ἀρχιερωσύνην ("offer the High Priesthood") also occurs in 20.244, concerning Hyrcanus II.

[178] The obvious advantage for Herod was that the High Priesthood would be a very good reason to stop Antony, or Dellius, from trying to get Aristobulus to Egypt (Stern 1974b: 231). An additional advantage was that the office implied that the boy would basically stay in Jerusalem, i.e., in Herod's environment (although occasional trips outside of Judea of a High Priest are attested in primary sources; Schalit 2001: 109 with n. 43). Schalit (2001: 108-09, 771-72) argues that Herod aimed from the beginning at removing Aristobulus as a possible competitor. The appointment as High Priest would have been part of this long-term strategy.

[179] About the friends of a ruler, see *Ant.* 15.5 with the note to "friends." Possibly, Herod's council of friends was partly similar to an emperor's council, which was a flexible group: it consisted of members from the senatorial and equestrian classes; the specific membership depended on the occasion (Kienast 1999: 181). Such councils were also involved in Augustus' decision to

BOOK FIFTEEN

32 He said that she secretly plotted against the throne[181] and was arranging, through Cleopatra,[182] that he would be deprived of his rule[183] and that the young man would receive the government[184] instead of him through Antony.[185] **33** It was not right that she wanted[186] these matters because it would imply that her daughter would be stripped of[187] her current honor.[188] It would bring about disorder[189] for the kingdom, which he had obtained after a lot of suffering[190] and by undergoing extraordinary dangers.[191] **34** He truly did not call to

---

divide Herod's kingdom in 3 regions following the king's death (*War* 2.25, 85, 93; *Ant.* 17.229, 301, 318). The meeting of the king's friends allowed Herod to consult them, but it also made Herod's accusation of Alexandra official and hence obviously functioned as legitimation of the king's future dealings with his mother-in-law. Herod used to organize meetings with officials when he was accusing someone of a capital crime (see *Ant.* 15.174-178 on Hyrcanus' accusation; 15.229 on Mariamme's; 16.361-369 on Alexander and Aristobulus'; 16.393 on that of military commanders; 17.93 on Antipater's trial; and 17.161-167 on a meeting of Jewish officials, which led to the execution of Mathias and several of his companions; see also Schalit 2001: 405).

[180] The line functions as introduction of Josephus' report about a meeting of Herod with his friends (*Ant.* 15.32-38), which opens with Herod accusing Alexandra (15.31-34). Alexandra defends herself directly after the accusation (15.35-38). Herod then drops the accusation and offers Aristobulus the High Priesthood, and the meeting ultimately leads to a reconciliation between Herod and Alexandra (15.38).

[181] With this general first point Herod's accusation of Alexandra before the king's friends starts. The next points specify the accusation, which is presented in indirect speech. The issue of Alexandra's secretly plotting (κρύφα ἐπιβουλεῦσαι; cf. *War* 1.263) against the throne seems to be an exaggeration at first glance; yet her interference with Herod's appointment of the High Priest (*Ant.* 15.22, 24) concerned a matter of crucial importance for the Jewish state. Although the continuation of the narrative specifies Herod's accusation of Alexandra, this general charge already implies that Alexandra committed high treason, which no doubt meant that she deserved the death penalty.

[182] Alexandra's choice of Cleopatra as her secret lobbyist was really dangerous for Herod since Cleopatra was his most powerful opponent. Cleopatra and Herod were natural enemies because both of them were dependent on Antony and had to compete for his favors (see *Ant.* 15.24 with the note to "Cleopatra"). Cleopatra tried many times to get favors from Antony, who was extremely generous to her. He did not always give in, especially if her wishes did not match his or Rome's interests (15.76; Huzar 1978: 254; Schalit 2001: 120). She did, however, receive several grants, and both *War* and *Antiquities* suggest that one of her strategies was to have kings who were dependent on Rome removed and take over their territories (*War* 1.359-362, 365; *Ant.* 15.75-79, 88-103, 110 with notes).

[183] Here Herod's accusation goes much further than Alexandra's arranging the High Priesthood for her son (*Ant.* 15.24). Herod himself may have exaggerated the scope of Alexandra's rebellious attempt during the interrogation, or Josephus may have made it up. It is nonetheless conceivable that Alexandra aimed for a restoration of Hasmonean rule, with her son as the new king, despite the fact that her daughter was married with Herod. Further on Josephus notes that Alexandra hoped for a change of government (15.42, 73, 166, 183).

[184] The plural τὰ πράγματα ("the matters," here translated with "the government") frequently has a political meaning in Josephus and sometimes refers to the government or administration of Judea (e.g., *War* 1.50, 85, 209; *Ant.* 15.68, 183-184, 264, 323; Rengstorf *s.v.*; see also *Ant.* 15.109, 189, in which similar phrases refer to the government of the Roman Republic; cf. Latin *res publica*).

[185] Cleopatra could only realize Alexandra's plan if Antony granted it to her as a favor.

[186] Reading βούλεσθαι with Niese (338). Several MSS read βεβουλεῦσθαι ("had planned"). The first section of the paragraph fits well the indirect speech in which Herod's accusation is formulated, though there are no close parallels in other discourses in Josephus (but cf. *Ant.* 16.94) or other sources.

[187] The rare verb συναποστερέω ("[help to] strip/ cheat," LSJ *s.v.*; Rengstorf *s.v.*) is a *hapax legomenon* in Josephus.

[188] Alexandra's daughter Mariamme was the queen (see *Ant.* 15.23), and Herod would most probably have ended his marriage with her if Alexandra was successful with her plan. Marriages of kings and high officials frequently extended and strengthened networks of useful relations among the powerful; a change of the political situation could lead to the dissolution of such marriages.

[189] For the motif of disorder, see *Ant.* 15.22 with the note to "within his household" and van Henten 2011d.

[190] Note the alliteration in the phrase πολλὰ πονήσαντος. The combination of the adverbial πολλά ("a lot") and the verb πονέω ("work hard, suffer") also occurs in *Life* 11 (Mason in BJP 9 on 11). It is a

mind the things Alexandra had done[192] in an unbecoming way, nor would he recoil from being just to them.[193] He even said that he offered the High Priesthood now to her son. He had appointed Ananel before[194] because Aristobulus was after all still a young boy.[195] **35** He said these things not without consideration but exactly as he deemed fit,[196] because he was especially concerned about deceiving the women[197] and the friends called to their help.[198] Alexandra was deeply moved by her happiness about this unexpected [outcome] as well as by her fear of being under suspicion.[199] So she defended herself with tears.[200]

36 As for the [High] Priesthood, she said that she had zealously pursued every possible

---

conventional phrase in non-Jewish Greek literature (e.g., Homer, *Il.* 9.348; Ctesias *FGH* 688 1b.2.4; Aristophanes, *Vesp.* 685; Xenophon, *Cyr.* 7.2.11; *Oec.* 8.21; Aristotle, *Rhet.* 1363 a3; Diodorus 2.2.4; 17.99.6; Plutarch, *Cam.* 8.1; *Pomp.* 29.5; Diogenes Laertius 5.72).

[191] This is a further conventional motif in Greek literature (Lysias 2.43). In *Ant.* 16.94 Herod uses a similar argument during the accusation of his sons before Caesar: "How was it possible and right that they did not allow him to be master over a realm that he had acquired after many hardships and dangers?" The combination of references to hardships as well as dangers is conventional too in Greek literature, from the late 1st cent. BCE onward (see, e.g., Dionysius, *Ant. rom.* 3.9.4).

Josephus elsewhere uses the aorist participle of τυγχάνω ("happen to be at") with the negation οὐ and the article to highlight the extraordinary character of persons, things, or events (see *War* 4.90; *Ant.* 2.120; 6.292; 7.44; 15.380; *Apion* 2.46; LSJ *s.v.* A.I.2b; Rengstorf *s.v.*).

[192] By stating that he was not going to talk about Alexandra's deeds, Herod drew attention to them. Although Josephus does not present Herod's statement in direct speech, the passage is related to a well-known figure of speech, *praeteritio* (i.e., stating something by saying that one is not going to mention it), which is sometimes used in an ironic way (Lausberg 1998: 393-94; see also the next note).

[193] Herod presents himself as a just person, which is ironic in the perspective of other Josephan passages, especially in *Antiquities*, which emphasize his lack of justice: 15.375-376 (Manaemus' prediction); 16.376 (the soldier Tiro's criticism of Herod; cf. *War* 1.544); and 16.404 (with Josephus' own comment concluding the narrative of book 16: "In his later [period] he also showed that he did not even keep away from all those remaining behind whom he considered his dearest. In their case justice caused that those who perished were less pitied for, but his cruelty remained the same because he did not even spare them. But we shall deal with them in detail when we relate the next section [of our report]," my trans.).

The continuation of the narrative in book 15 suggests that Herod was considerate of Alexandra and Aristobulus' honor, but it is doubtful whether that was a matter of justice: Alexandra had behaved very badly, as she herself admits (15.35), but Herod tempers justice with mercy.

[194] For the verb προκαθίστημι ("appoint previously, etc."), see *Ant.* 15.381 with the note to "preparing them beforehand."

[195] The statement concludes Josephus' rendering of Herod's speech. For Ananel's appointment, see *Ant.* 15.22; on Herod's possible motives for this appointment and Aristobulus' age—also in connection with the High Priesthood—15.24 with the note to "he was around" and 15.29, 51 with notes. Strikingly, the accusation of Alexandra leads, in fact, to Herod's decision to let her have her way, which implies that there were limits to his power. Alexandra and Aristobulus' sister, Mariamme, exerted considerable pressure on Herod (see 15.31 and 15.35 with the plural "the women"; cf. also 15.202).

[196] Josephus' own comment follows upon Herod's speech and suggests that the king manipulated the chain of the events in detail.

[197] This remark suggests that Herod was clever as well as perfidious, and very much capable of working on a long-term strategy, all the more so because one of these women was his spouse. Josephus, whose statements are often not really flattering for women (Sievers 1989; Mayer-Schärtel 1995; Ilan 1999: 85-97; Brenner 2003), sometimes portrays women deceiving men (e.g., *War* 2.249; *Ant.* 8.211).

[198] The passage indicates that Alexandra and Mariamme were capable of forming a faction at the court that included "friends"—which term probably has the technical meaning of "friends of the king," i.e., influential persons at the court (see *Ant.* 15.5 with the note to "the friends around him" and 15.185, 202-203, 206, 213, 231).

[199] The passage attributes mixed feelings to Alexandra during her accusation. Being under Herod's suspicion (ὑποψία) was a dangerous position (*War* 1.493; *Ant.* 16.108, 236, 315; cf. *War* 1.538, 561, 584, 612; *Ant.* 15.42, 44, 221, 265; 16.11, 125, 210, 251). *Antiquities* highlights Herod's boundless suspicion as one of his tyrannical traits (van Henten 2011b).

[200] Josephus' note in the introduction of Alexandra's defense—like Herod's given in indirect speech—that she

option because of the shameful situation.[201] However, concerning the kingdom, she was not making any attempt upon it,[202] nor did she want to take it even if it came her way.[203] And now her honor was sufficient since the office would be held by Aristobulus. Safety for her entire family would be the result because he was more capable than others to rule.[204] **37** Now, she said, being overwhelmed by his [Herod's] benefactions,[205] she would accept the honor for her son and be obedient in every respect.[206] She also asked to be excused if she, because of her kin and frankness,[207] had done something rash out of indignation over her unworthy treatment.[208] **38** This way they addressed each other.[209] They even gave [each other] assurances[210]—more eagerly than quickly[211]—and they reconciled

---

was in tears underlines this dramatic moment in the narrative and may also characterize her as a woman who knows the impact of an appeal to the audience's emotions. Her emotional behavior immediately before her daughter Mariamme's execution (*Ant.* 15.232-234) was counter-productive (cf. 15.58).

[201] Alexandra sticks to her claim that her son Aristobulus was entitled to receive the high priestly office (*Ant.* 15.24) and presents it twice in this passage as a matter of honor (cf. 15.23), which is in keeping with the cultural code of "honor and shame" in ancient society (Neyrey 1998). The noun ἀδοξία ("disgrace, disdain," Rengstorf *s.v.*) also occurs in 15.210, referring to Mariamme I.

[202] This counters Herod's accusation of Alexandra as reported in *Ant.* 15.32 (cf. 15.42). It would have been suicide, of course, if Alexandra admitted in public that her strategy was to have her son on the throne instead of Herod. Cf. 15.73, where Josephus suggests that she was aiming for the throne even after the death of her son.

[203] This detail is ironic in light of Alexandra's attempts to revolt and to take over the throne (see *Ant.* 15.23 with the note to "Alexandra").

[204] The statement is perfectly understandable since it is coming from a proud mother, but it is highly ironic in the larger context of the narrative because Aristobulus would soon die, being still young. He even died (*Ant.* 15.50-56) before Mariamme, Hyrcanus, and Alexandra herself were executed (15.172-182, 231-237, 251).

[205] This is again ironic since Alexandra got her objectives from Herod and not from Antony (see *Ant.* 15.24). At the same time these almost ridiculously polite words reflect what one would expect to hear from a civilized and important person at the court. In the light of the context there may even be some reason for gratitude on the part of Alexandra since she had asked Herod's rival Cleopatra for help. From this perspective Herod's decision not to punish her as well as his transfer of the High Priesthood to Alexandra's son were benevolent acts. For other benefactions of Herod, see *War* 1.284, 293, 632; *Ant.* 16.24-25, 140, 146, 150, 159.

[206] This statement is ironic because Alexandra's actual behavior is far from being obedient in every respect (see *Ant.* 15.23 with the note to "Alexandra"). She calls on Cleopatra for help on 2 further occasions (15.45, 62).

[207] These words express a remarkable amount of self-knowledge in the light of the comments by others, including the narrator, that Alexandra (as well as her daughter Mariamme; see *Ant.* 15.238) acted as an arrogant woman, who allowed herself great liberties and freedom of speech (παρρησία), which were legitimated in her view because of her Hasmonean descent (*War* 1.437; cf. *Ant.* 15.44, 85, 210, 212, 236, 238). Mariamme's sons Alexander and Aristobulus IV (*War* 1.445-449, 468, 522; *Ant.* 16.192, 399) displayed similar behavior (see especially *War* 1.468: "They, however, given their high birth, said whatever was on their mind," trans. Sievers/Forte in BJP 1a 1.468). Alexander's spouse Glaphyra, the daughter of King Archelaus of Cappadocia, measures up to Alexandra and Mariamme's haughtiness (*War* 1.476; *Ant.* 16.193).

[208] The noun ἀναξιοπάθεια is rare in Josephus. LSJ (*s.v.*) mention the passage and offer "unworthy treatment" or "indignation (about such treatment)" as meanings. Rengstorf (*s.v.*) gives "indignation (at unreasonable demands)" (see also *Ant.* 15.283; 18.47). In 15.44 the verb ἀναξιοπαθέω ("be/grow indignant about/at") again refers to Alexandra. The verb occurs once elsewhere in Josephus, referring to Glaphyra (16.193; see also the preceding note and 15.23-24, 36 about "honor" as Alexandra's main motive).

[209] With this note Josephus starts his conclusion of the brief trial scene (consisting of speeches by Herod and Alexandra). The verb ὁμιλέω can mean "converse with, speak" (e.g., *Ant.* 11.159, 260) but has in this forensic context the more official meaning of "address" (LSJ *s.v.* III.3).

[210] The phrase ἐν δεξιαῖς is highly unusual in Greek literature. Niese (339) reads ἐπί instead of ἐν and proposes to add a verbal form (γενόμενοι), which makes sense, although it is not strictly necessary since Josephus uses the plural δεξιαῖς with the preposition ἐπί without a verbal form in *Ant.* 17.284: "He [i.e., one of Athronges' brothers] surrendered to Archelaus, after making a pledge (ἐπὶ δεξιαῖς) and receiving a guarantee of his personal safety in the name of God" (my trans.). The

Appointment of Aristobulus III as High Priest. War 1.437

themselves.[212] All suspicion, so they thought,[213] had been taken away.

(3.1) 39 King Herod immediately took away the High Priesthood from Ananel,[214] who was, as we said before,[215] not from the country but from the Jews who had settled beyond the Euphrates.[216] For many[217] tens of thousands of this people had been sent away to Babylonia. **40** Ananel was from there, being from a high priestly family.[218] He had been treated with respect by Herod before, according to custom.[219] [Herod] honored this man[220] when he took hold of the kingdom, but he deposed him again—in order to stop the dissent in his family[221]—by committing an unlawful act,[222] for never was anyone deprived of this honor once he had received it.[223] **41** Yet Antiochus Epiphanes was the first who broke the

---

plural δεξιαί from δεξιά ("right hand") can mean "assurances, pledges" (LSJ *s.v.* 2; see also *War* 4.96; *Ant.* 14.7).

[211] The expression σπουδαιότερον ἢ θᾶττον ("more eagerly than quickly" [implying they were keen but it took some time] or "more carefully than quickly") has no parallels in ancient Greek literature. Niese (339) conjectures that the word order should be changed: "more quickly than carefully," which suits the context well because the continuation of the paragraph already raises doubt whether the settlement will last for long. Several other translators propose "with greater enthusiasm than before" (Marcus-Wikgren 18 n. *b*; Meijer-Wes 3.156; see also the next note).

[212] The translation is supported by the Latin version (Niese 339; see also Thackeray and Marcus 1930-55: 8). The imperfect διελύοντο can also be interpreted as an *imperfectum de conatu*: "they tried to reconcile themselves" (cf. Theophrastus, *Char.* 12.13). An alternative translation would be "and broke up their meeting."

[213] With this brief note Josephus focuses the attention on the issue of Alexandra and Herod's suspicion of each other, anticipating further occasions on which this suspicion would crop up again (see *Ant.* 15.42 with the note to "suspicion").

[214] This decision was taken at the beginning of 35 BCE at the earliest (Schürer-Vermes 1.288 n. 3, 297).

[215] Cross-references in Josephus frequently do not specify the previous passages. Here it concerns *Ant.* 15.22, about Ananel's appointment. For similar expressions that indicate cross-references, see, e.g., *War* 7.253; *Ant.* 1.135, 203; 4.311; 9.28; 10.150; 13.62, 256; 14.467; 15.240.

[216] Concerning the Jews living in Babylonia, see *Ant.* 15.14 with notes.

[217] Literally Josephus writes "not a few tens of thousands." He frequently applies the figure of *litotes*, i.e., making a statement by indicating the negative of its opposite, which emphasizes something by understating it (e.g., "not small" = "quite big"). See, e.g., *Ant.* 3.299; 8.378; 9.165; 11.312; 13.60; 15.150-151, 169, 171, 271, 307.

[218] A previous passage about Ananel (*Ant.* 15.22) suggests a quite different status of his family ("a rather obscure priest from Babylon"). The information given here seems more plausible.

[219] The phrase κατὰ συνήθειαν ("according to custom") probably refers to the normal way (cf. *Ant.* 2.11) of treating people of high priestly ancestry, which was quickly nullified by the fact that when Herod's personal family situation imposed itself he had no qualms about violating these customary manners. Another but less plausible interpretation, translating "according to his [Herod's] habit," focuses on Herod's way of dealing with persons of high priestly ancestry. This reading would be remarkable in the light of Josephus' usually negative portrayal of the king and draws attention to the possibility that Herod's image in *Antiquities* is the result of Josephus' own negative interpretation of the person Herod as well as of his rule (van Henten 2011b).

[220] For τιμάω ("honor, esteem highly") with Herod as subject, see *Ant.* 15.372 with the note to "honor."

[221] The disorder in Herod's household is a recurring motif in the Herod section of *Antiquities* (see 15.22 with the note to "within his household"). The remark links up with the earlier information about Alexandra and Mariamme's efforts to have Aristobulus appointed High Priest (see 15.23-24, 31).

[222] The comment must reflect Josephus' own voice as narrator because Alexandra, Mariamme, and Aristobulus clearly did not bother about Ananel's dismissal. Josephus points out several times that Herod transgressed the Jewish laws with particular decisions (e.g., *Ant.* 15.272-290; 17.148-164, 304). The continuation of the narrative elaborates this accusation.

[223] Josephus presents the removal as an unlawful deed because the High Priesthood was apparently an appointment for life (Schürer-Vermes 1.297). The exceptions mentioned in *Ant.* 15.41, however, show that similar decisions had already been taken. They suggest that the power of the ruler was the decisive factor. Josephus does not mention any biblical passage that indicates that the High Priesthood was an office to be held until death. Yet a lifelong appointment seems self-

law[224] by removing Jesus[225] and appointing his brother Onias;[226] the second was Aristobulus, who removed his brother Hyrcanus;[227] and the third was Herod, who transferred the office to the boy Aristobulus.[228]

(3.2) 42 At that time he [Herod] thought he had taken care of the matters of his family.[229] Yet he truly did not remain without suspicion[230] for a long time, as is likely in a case of reconciliation,[231] because he had reason to fear[232] that Alexandra, with the things undertaken

Conflict with Alexandra, who tries to flee with her son.

---

evident because of the hereditary character of the High Priesthood, which was adopted by the Hasmoneans. Herod put this tradition to an end: he, his successor Archelaus, as well as the Roman governors dismissed several High Priests and clearly did not consider an appointment for life as standard practice (Schürer-Vermes 2.228, 232-33). Richardson (1996: 163 n. 50) argues that the degree of Herod's offense depends on the legitimacy of Ananel's appointment (whether or not he was from a high priestly family) and the validity of Aristobulus (he may have been too young for the High Priesthood; see 15.24 with the note to "he was around").

[224] The Seleucid king Antiochus IV (175-164 BCE) is presented as the archenemy of the Jewish people in 1, 2, and 4 Maccabees (1 Macc 1; 2 Macc 4:7-9:29; 4 Macc 4:15-17:24) as well as in other ancient Jewish sources (see, e.g., Dan 7:8, 11, 20-21, 24-26; 8:9-12, 23-25; 11:21-45; Josephus, *Ant.* 12.234-361; Mörkholm 1966; Lebram 1975; van Henten 1993). For concise surveys of Antiochus' policy in Judea, see Schürer-Vermes 1.146-62; Gera 1998: 141-61. That Antiochus was a forerunner of Herod in connection with the dismissal of High Priests adds to the negative appreciation of Herod in *Antiquities*.

[225] Jesus is named Jason in 2 Maccabees, which is the primary source about this High Priest (2 Macc 4:7-5:10). He received the high priestly office from Antiochus IV shortly after Antiochus had succeeded his brother Seleucus IV in 175 BCE. He had promised the king 440 talents of silver (2 Macc 4:8) in order to take over the office from his brother Onias III (Schürer-Vermes 1.148-50). Josephus (*Ant.* 12.237) states that Jason received the High Priesthood from Antiochus after Onias had died, which does not match the information given in 2 Macc 4.

[226] Onias is identical with the High Priest Menelaus mentioned in 2 Macc 4:23-5:15; 11:29; 13:1-8. He could take over the High Priesthood from Jason because he offered 300 talents of silver more than Jason did (2 Macc 4:23-24). Josephus states that he was a brother of Jason and another Onias (Onias III), and that he changed his name to Menelaus (*Ant.* 12.238-239; 20.235).

[227] This refers to Aristobulus II, who was involved in a power-struggle with his elder brother Hyrcanus II. The latter had been appointed High Priest by their mother, Queen Salome Alexandra (see *Ant.* 15.12 with the note to "High Priest and then king").

[228] I.e., Aristobulus III (see *Ant.* 15.34, 39-40, and cf. *War* 1.437). The year of his appointment was 37/36 or 36/35 BCE. If Josephus' order of the events is correct and we assume that Dellius' proposal to Alexandra (*Ant.* 15.25-28) made sense only when Antony was in Egypt, then the appointment took place after the end of 36 BCE, which implies that the Festival of Tabernacles (celebrated in the month of Tishri) during which Aristobulus acted as High Priest (15.50-51) was the festival of 35 BCE. Buchheim (1960: 116-17) assumes, however, that Josephus was not well informed about Antony's periods in Egypt and opts for (Tishri) 36 BCE on the basis of the chronological framework of *Antiquities*, which is reliable in his opinion (contrary to the presentation in *War*). Schalit (2001: 111-12 with n. 48) argues for the turn of the Jewish year 37/36 BCE, which is the early fall of 36 BCE, i.e., about the same period as the one argued for by Buchheim.

[229] For the motif of disturbances within Herod's family (cf. *Ant.* 15.40), see 15.22 with the note to "household."

[230] Herod's suspicion (ὑποψία) is a recurring motif in the *Antiquities* narrative about his reign (see 15.35 with the note to "suspicion" as well as 15.183 concerning Alexandra; 15.210 concerning Mariamme; 15.258 concerning Costobar; 16.223 concerning Syllaeus and Salome; and last but not least 16.90, 108, 119, 324, 334 concerning Herod's sons). For ἀνύποπτος ("unsuspected, without suspicion," Rengstorf *s.v.*) in the Herod narrative of *Antiquities*, see 15.21, 258; 16.82, 119 (cf. *War* 1.604).

[231] Josephus' note may reflect a truism ("people remain suspicious after a reconciliation"; for other truisms, see *Ant.* 15.353 with the note to "rejoice most"), although it also makes sense in connection with the continuing story of Herod's relationships with his mother-in-law and with his wife (van Henten 2010). The noun διαλλαγή ("change, reconciliation," LSJ *s.v.*) occurs in 15.211 in connection with Herod's relationship with Mariamme, highlighting the short duration of Herod's reconciliation with her (see also *War* 1.454, 456, 465, 511, 513; *Ant.* 16.128, 131, 309, 367 about Herod's reconciliations with his sons Alexander and Aristobulus IV).

[232] For the rare combination of the verb ἀξιόω ("expect, etc.") and the infinitive δεδοικέναι ("fear"), see Heliodorus, *Aeth.* 8.11.4; Libanius, *Decl.* 48.1.39; *Prog.* 9.7.28.

by her already, would aim for a political change[233] if she received the opportunity.[234] **43** Therefore he ordered her to stay in the palace[235] and do nothing on her own authority. The guards were careful that nothing escaped [their] notice,[236] not even what she did in her daily life.[237] **44** All these things made her furious,[238] little by little, and produced hatred.[239] For being full of female thoughts[240] she grew indignant about her unworthy treatment[241] based on suspicion.[242] She thought that anything was better than being deprived of her freedom[243] and living on in an apparently honorable position[244] but, in fact, in slavery and fear. **45** So she sent a message to Cleopatra,[245] in which she lamented endlessly and incited her to help her as much as she could. And she [Cleopatra] ordered her to secretly escape to Egypt to her, with her son.[246] **46** This seemed a good idea [to Alexandra][247] and she

---

[233] The Greek νεώτερα πράγματα implies that Herod feared that Alexandra would aim for a rebellion when she had the opportunity (cf. *War* 5.152; *Ant.* 14.327; 15.8 [with the note to "rebelling"], 30 [with notes]; 17.2; 19.91; 20.109; *Life* 36, 70, 87, 391). For the vocabulary, see Xenophon, *Hell.* 5.2.9; Isocrates, *Areop.* 59; Diodorus 15.77; LSJ *s.v.* νεώτερος II.2.

[234] The phrase καιρὸν λαμβάνω ("seize the occasion, receive the opportunity") is common in Classical and Hellenistic Greek (see, e.g., Euripides, *Ion* 659; Thucydides 6.86.4; 2 Macc 14:5; Josephus, *War* 1.527; *Ant.* 4.10; 13.135; 15.213; Plutarch, *Arat.* 33.3).

[235] Josephus does not specify the palace. One could also translate "her palace," but a special palace for Alexandra is nowhere mentioned. The phrase could refer to any of the Herodian palaces or fortresses, though the Hasmonean palace in Jerusalem used by Herod (see *Ant.* 15.71 with the note to "the palace") or one of the Herodian palaces at Jericho would be most plausible (descriptions and references in Netzer 2001). In these cases Alexandra would have been staying close to Herod most of the time.

[236] For a similar expression of the verb λανθάνω ("escape [notice]," Rengstorf *s.v.*) followed by the negation οὐδέ, see *Ant.* 15.277, in which passage Herod is the object ("it did not escape Herod's notice").

[237] The information is remarkable in connection with the previous sentences. Alexandra's situation comes close to house arrest, which puts Josephus' description of the reconciliation between Herod and his mother-in-law in a different perspective. The passage suggests that there was some punishment of her, and that Herod's treatment shows the king's serious suspicion that she would undermine his rule. At the same time Josephus' characterization of Alexandra as a determined and independent aristocratic woman (see the next paragraph and Schalit 2001: 110) implies that the treatment was asking for trouble, as the continuation of the narrative shows.

[238] Josephus also uses the verb ἐξαγριόω ("make/be wild") in the description of Herod at the end of his life (see *Ant.* 17.148 with notes).

[239] With Niese (340), who reads ἐπέφυετο ("originated …," Rengstorf *s.v.*) with MSS PFV. MSS LAMWE read ὑπέφυετο ("caused [hatred] to grow in secret," Marcus-Wikgren 22 n. *a*).

[240] Josephus' vocabulary suggests his view that women had a special mindset (φρόνημα γυναικεῖον), which caused Alexandra to be incapable of controlling her emotions (cf., however, *Ant.* 15.59-60). See also 15.69, 168, 218 and 15.235-237 with notes, and on Josephus' not always favorable portrayal of women in general, 15.35 with the note to "deceiving the women."

[241] See *Ant.* 15.37 with the note to "unworthy treatment." The noun ἐπιμέλεια ("care, supervision," Rengstorf *s.v.*) can have a negative connotation, as it does here. Ironically, *Ant.* 15.44 links up with Alexandra's excuse offered to Herod in 15.37 for acting rashly out of indignation.

[242] See *Ant.* 15.35, 42 with the notes to "suspicion."

[243] The phrase τῆς παρρησίας στερομένη also recalls *Ant.* 15.37 (see the note to "frankness"), which contains the noun παρρησία ("freedom [of speech/to act]"). For similar phrases, see Demosthenes, *Or.* 3.32; 7.1; 45.79; 59.28; Diodorus 1.78.2, 9; 34-35.26.1.

[244] For honor and shame as important motives for Alexandra's acts, see *Ant.* 15.23-24, 31, 36.

[245] History repeats itself: Alexandra wrote for the first time to Cleopatra in *Ant.* 15.24.

[246] Josephus does not inform us about Cleopatra's motive for the advice. It would have ended up in a similar result as Dellius' earlier plan (*Ant.* 15.27): a transfer of the young Aristobulus to Egypt. In light of Josephus' depiction of Cleopatra's behavior in *Antiquities* (see van Henten 2005a) one can easily imagine that the queen's purpose was to weaken Herod's position. Even if the plan failed, the outcome would plausibly be that Herod had become further alienated from his mother-in-law and brother-in-law, which would enhance the dissension within the family.

[247] Alexandra's decision does not seem plausible, which raises doubt about the reliability of the whole story about her attempt to escape. The flight of Alexandra and her son would no doubt jeopardize Aristobulus' role

contrived[248] the following plan. She had two coffins prepared for her as if for a burial of dead bodies. She put herself and her son in these and ordered those servants who knew about it to bring them out of the city during the night.[249] From there they had a road to the sea and a ship was lying ready,[250] in which they would sail to Egypt. **47** Alexandra's servant Aesopus[251] reported this to Sabbion,[252] one of her friends,[253] by a slip of the tongue,[254] on the assumption that he knew about it. Now Sabbion had previously been an enemy of Herod because he was considered to be one of those who had plotted against Antipater with poison.[255] When he learned about the plan, he thought he could change Herod's hatred into the [sort of] kindness that follows upon the disclosure of information,[256] and he told the king in full about Alexandra's plot. **48** Herod allowed the plot to proceed until it was carried out and he caught them in the act[257] of fleeing. He remitted her mistake and did not dare to arrange something harsh, even though this was badly wanted by him.[258] He thought

---

as High Priest. Had the plan succeeded, she and her son would have lived as exiles in Egypt without much prospect of a return to Jerusalem. Perhaps Alexandra thought that Cleopatra could work something out for her, but the larger context implies that Cleopatra mainly pursued her own interests. The plan would also have made Mariamme's position complicated: she would have ended up in a loyalty conflict between faithfulness to her husband on the one hand and to her mother and brother on the other hand. Alexandra's decision only makes sense if she also arranged for Herod's murder, but Josephus does not inform us of such a plan. Schalit (2001: 110) considers the core of the story to be historical.

[248] The rare verb τεχνάζω ("use art/cunning," LSJ *s.v.* II; Rengstorf *s.v.*) also has a negative connotation in *Ant.* 18.85.

[249] Josephus' report about Alexandra's plan to leave with her son for Egypt in 2 coffins recalls the Jewish funerary custom of burying outside a town or city (see *Ant.* 15.6 with the note to "with the corpses"). The plan resembles the famous tradition about Rabbi Yohanan ben Zakkai leaving Jerusalem in a coffin during the war against Rome. The story is found in the 2 versions of the *Avot of Rabbi Nathan* (*'Abot R. Nat.* a 4.1.2 and *'Abot R. Nat.* b 6), in the Babylonian Talmud (*b. Giṭ.* 56b), and in *Lam. Rab.* 1.5 (detailed discussion and further references in Neusner 1962; 1970).

[250] Josephus' geographical information is rather vague; the obvious route was to travel to the harbor city of Joppa-Jafo and embark there.

[251] The name Aesopus (Αἴσωπος) occurs only once in Josephus (Schalit 1968: 6). It is a well-known Greek name; a collection of fables was attributed to a slave with that name (see already Herodotus 2.134; further references in Luzzato and Wittenburg 1996). It is unclear whether Aesopus was a Jewish servant. His name is not incorporated by Ilan 2002.

[252] The rare Greek name Sabbion (Σαββίων) is a *hapax legomenon* in Josephus (Schalit 1968: 104; Fraser and Matthews 1987-2010: 1.400). A variant of this name (i.e., Σαβ[β]ίωνος) is transmitted in an inscription on a sarcophagus from Nablus (probably 2nd cent. CE, Ilan 2002: 305).

[253] "Friend" here probably has the social-political meaning of somebody belonging to the inner circle of influential persons of a ruler or high official (see *Ant.* 15.5 with the note to "the friends around him"), which is confirmed by the context and implies that Sabbion belonged to Alexandra's faction before he took Herod's side.

[254] The translation follows LSJ (*s.v.* προπίπτω II.2). Rengstorf (*s.v.*) proposes to translate "when he met him accidentally."

[255] This is a flashback that refers to the murder of Herod's father Antipater at the instigation of a Nabatean called Malichus, who acts as Antipater's main opponent in *War* 1.220-237. Herod's father was poisoned (*War* 1.226; *Ant.* 14.281; Schürer-Vermes 1.277). The Greek of Josephus' phrase echoes, with ἐπιβουλευσάντων ("those who plotted against") and φαρμακείαν ("poison"), the vocabulary of *War* 1.223, 226; *Ant.* 14.277, 281. Sabbion is not mentioned in *War* 1.226; *Ant.* 14.281. The continuation of the narrative suggests that Herod considered Sabbion to have been part of the plot against his father.

[256] Josephus reports in *Ant.* 15.170 about Dositheus' betrayal of Hyrcanus II to Herod; Dositheus would also have hoped that the king would reward him (Kokkinos 1998: 151). Stern (1974b: 271) argues that important supporters of the Hasmonean cause went over to Herod because he had become much more powerful.

[257] Cf. *Ant.* 16.213, concerning Pheroras. For vocabulary similar to ἐπ' αὐτοφώρῳ ("in the act") combined with λαμβάνω or complex forms of that verb, see Euripides, *Ion* 1214; Plato, *Resp.* 359c; Lysias 13.85; Isocrates, *Callim.* 53; Demosthenes, *Or.* 19.132; 45.59, 70; Dinarchus, *Demosth.* 77; Achilles Tatius 7.11.1.

[258] Josephus distinguishes between Herod's personal thoughts and his actual behavior towards Alexandra and

that Cleopatra, out of hatred towards him,[259] would not bear to receive the blame. So, rather, he showed enough magnanimity[260] to pardon them out of kindness.[261] **49** Yet it was evident to him that in any possible way he had to get the young man out of his way.[262] But to escape being noticed it seemed more credible not to do that quickly, or as a follow-up to these events.[263]

Murder of Aristobulus III at Jericho.
War 1.437

(3.3) 50 When the Festival of Tabernacles[264] was at hand[265]—this festival is observed

---

Aristobulus, which highlights the king's shrewdness (see also *Ant.* 15.49). Niese (340) reads βουλομένῳ ἦν αὐτῷ, following Hudson's conjecture. Marcus-Wikgren (24 n. *a*) state that the expression was already used by Thucydides (2.3.2). However, the reading βουλόμενον ἦν αὐτῷ transmitted by the MSS and E is also supported by a parallel in Thucydides (5.65.3; see also Athenaeus 2.10.100; 9.56.31).

[259] Fear for Cleopatra's hatred is also mentioned as Herod's motive in *Ant.* 15.106. Otto (1913: 42) and Schalit (2001: 110 n. 47) argue that such a fear cannot have been the reason for pardoning Alexandra. Schalit suggests that killing mother and son simultaneously would have been counter-productive for Herod. Richardson (1996: 163 n. 52) states that Josephus' note suggests a serious breach in the relationship between Herod and Cleopatra. However, it is plausible that Herod and Cleopatra had become enemies starting from the moment Herod's position as King of Judea was secure (see 15.24 with the note to "Cleopatra").

[260] The noun μεγαλοψυχία can have several nuances: "greatness of mind, magnanimity, generosity, liberality" (Rengstorf *s.v.*). The word occurs several times in the Herod narrative of *Antiquities* (and not at all in *War*), and most of the passages highlight it as an important feature of Herod's character: *Ant.* 15.48 (referring to Herod's magnanimity towards Alexandra); 15.196 (concerning Herod's very generous reception of Octavian and his army); 15.237 (referring to Mariamme); and 16.140-141 (concerning Herod's generosity towards Octavian and Marcus Agrippa). In 16.153 Josephus mentions μεγαλοψυχία as one of Herod's central characteristics (cf. *War* 1.554; *Ant.* 15.316). See also the related adjective μεγαλόψυχος ("high-minded, magnanimous, liberal," Rengstorf *s.v.*), which is used in *War* 1.422 in connection with Herod's building activities and in 1.554 in connection with Antipater's generosity (interpreted negatively) towards Octavian's friends. It occurs several times in the Herod narrative of *Antiquities*: in 15.316 it concerns Herod's character; in 15.326-328 his generosity towards foreign cities and his Roman patrons, as well as his behavior as king; and in 15.356 his magnanimity towards foreigners (cf. 16.25 concerning Marcus Agrippa). For the combination of ἐμφαίνω and μεγαλοψυχία as object ("show magnanimity"), see 15.196 and Polybius 30.17.4.

[261] Having made up his mind, Herod apparently realized that the only serious option was to pardon both, which he did in a large-hearted way according to Josephus' description (cf. Hyrcanus II, who's reasonableness or kindness [ἐπιείκεια] is emphasized several times by Josephus: *Ant.* 14.13; 15.165, 177, 182).

[262] The statement anticipates the murder of Aristobulus, which is narrated in *Ant.* 15.50-56. The phrase ἐκποδὼν ποιεῖσθαι ("get [someone] out of one's way," meaning "have someone murdered") also occurs in 15.20, concerning Hyrcanus II, who was ultimately executed at Herod's orders (see 15.20 with the note to "get him out of the way" at 15.20). For similar vocabulary, see Xenophon, *Anab.* 1.6.9; *Hell.* 2.3.16; Isocrates, *Antid.* 175; Arrian, *Anab.* 1.25.5; Cassius Dio 61.7.2. The association with the passage about Hyrcanus II in *Ant.* 15.20 is strengthened by the repetition of παντάπασιν ("in any possible way").

[263] Josephus' vocabulary is rather vague here, but the implication is clear: Herod apparently realized that having Aristobulus murdered immediately after the attempt to escape for Egypt would make it obvious that he was behind the young man's death (Schalit 2001: 113). Nevertheless, Josephus' sequence of the events suggests that Aristobulus was murdered soon afterwards (see *Ant.* 15.50-56). The brief report about Aristobulus' death in *War* 1.437 strongly suggests that he was killed directly after his installation as High Priest.

[264] The Festival of Tabernacles (further references in *War* 2.515; *Ant.* 4.209; 8.100, 123; 11.77, 154; 13.46, 241, 304, 372) is one of the main Jewish holidays and is described in the Bible (Exod 23:16; 34:22; Lev 23:41-43). It is celebrated during 8 days in the month of Tishri (15-22 Tishri), in the autumn. In the periods of the First and Second Temples it functioned as a festival of pilgrimage during which the Jews from abroad were coming to Jerusalem. The crowds gathered in the Temple precinct in order to participate in the festivities (Safrai 1976: 875). Characteristic practices are the setting up of booths as temporary residences and carrying palm-fronds (as described in *Ant.* 13.372). If Aristobulus was appointed in 35 BCE (see 15.41 with the note to "Aristobulus"), it concerns the Festival of Tabernacles of the year 35 BCE (with Schürer-Vermes 1.297; Buchheim [1960: 116-17] argues for 36 BCE).

[265] The translation follows the reading ἐνστάσης of

by us with special care[266]—he let these days pass.[267] He himself and the rest of the people participated in the festivities.[268] Nevertheless, exactly because of such occasions, his jealousy[269]—which visibly provoked him—made him move and push on with his plan. **51** For when the young man Aristobulus,[270] having reached his seventeenth year,[271] went up to the altar[272] according to the Law to fulfill the sacrifices,[273] wearing the outfit of the High Priests[274] and executing the rites connected with the event, he looked extraordinary handsome[275] and taller than most youths of his age. Yet it was his dignity connected with his descent[276] that particularly showed itself in his appearance. **52** An eager desire arose

---

MSS LAMWE, which is confirmed by 2 parallel passages (*Ant.* 4.209; 13.46; cf. 13.304). Niese (341) reads ἐπεχούσης ("was being celebrated") with MS P.

[266] When a Jewish festival or another Jewish practice is mentioned, Josephus frequently interrupts his narrative with a parenthesis in which he briefly explains the relevant festival or practice (see, e.g., *Ant.* 14.25; 17.254; 20.106). This habit indicates that non-Jewish readers were important for Josephus (further discussion in Mason 1998). Here Josephus merely notes that the Festival of Tabernacles was well observed by the Jews (cf. 8.100).

[267] This remark is ironic in the light of the information in *Ant.* 15.49 that Herod's strategy was to wait long enough with his measures against Aristobulus in order that the public would not connect the High Priest's death with the attempt to escape to Egypt (related in 15.45-48). Herod was apparently impatient.

[268] This detail confirms that Herod observed Jewish religious practices, at least when he was in Jerusalem (van Henten 2008b)—although the continuation of the narrative immediately blackens the king again.

[269] The next paragraphs indicate that Herod was envious of Aristobulus for several reasons. The king's jealousy is a recurring motif in both of Josephus' Herod narratives (*War* 1.463, 633-634; *Ant.* 15.66-67, 82, 164; 16.248).

[270] Aristobulus is also called a young man (μειράκιον) in *Ant.* 15.30, 32, 49, 53, 55. The same noun is frequently used for Herod and Mariamme's 2 sons, Alexander and Aristobulus IV (see 16.7, 68-69, 71, 78, etc.).

[271] That Aristobulus was 17 when he received the high priestly office is confirmed by the parallel passage of *War* (1.437). The transfer of the High Priesthood to Aristobulus probably took place in the fall of 35 BCE (see *Ant.* 15.41 with the note to "Aristobulus" and 15.50 with the note to "Festival of Tabernacles").

[272] This phrase introduces the report about Aristobulus' first actual performance as High Priest (Schalit 2001: 111). The parallel passage in *War* (1.437) briefly reports that Aristobulus put on the sacred vestments and approached the altar during a festive assembly of the people. The ordination procedure of Aaron and his sons as High Priests is described in great detail in Exod 29:1-37, 43-46, and their actual ordination in Lev 8-9 (see also Josephus' rendering of these passages in *Ant.* 3.188-192, 204-207). Josephus does not explicitly refer to the ritual of Aristobulus' installation, and there are no close parallels between *Ant.* 15.51 and LXX Exod 29; LXX Lev 8-9. However, the response of the people present at Aristobulus' first public appearance as High Priest (15.52) renders it plausible that 15.51 refers to his installation.

[273] The ordination procedure described in Exod 29:1-37, 43-46 is interrupted by a brief description of the daily sacrifices in the Temple (29:38-42): a lamb, flour mixed with beaten oil, and wine in the morning; a lamb, grain, and wine in the evening. It is possible that Josephus hints at this passage with "the Law" (the noun θῦμα ["sacrifice"] also occurs in LXX Exod 29:28; cf. *Ant.* 6.101; 14.477), though the reference might also concern the extensive section about sacrifices and the installation of Aaron and his sons in Lev 1-9. For further discussion and references about the daily sacrifices in the Temple, see Schürer-Vermes 2.292-308.

[274] Similar vocabulary in *Ant.* 3.178. The High Priest wore a very special and costly outfit, including a breastpiece and the so-called ephod (see the extensive description in Exod 28). *Antiquities* (3.159-187, 214-218) offers a detailed discussion of the vestments of the High Priest and their symbolic meanings (see the notes of Feldman in BJP 3).

[275] Aristobulus' handsomeness is also highlighted in *Ant.* 15.23, 29. Josephus' apt phrase (κάλλει τε κάλλιστος καὶ) is a nice example of alliteration (for other examples of alliterations with k, see *War* 2.68, 76; *Ant.* 15.339; *Apion* 2.35, 175).

[276] Josephus emphasizes here and elsewhere that the members of the Hasmonean dynasty distinguished themselves from other Jews by the "noblesse" that came with their royal descent (ἀξίωμα can mean "dignity, status, rank," Rengstorf *s.v.*). This motif is articulated in 3 ways: (1) the noble descent is clearly apparent from the exceptional beauty of—at least some of—the Hasmoneans, such as Aristobulus III and his sister Mariamme (e.g., *Ant.* 15.23, 25-29, 237; see also 16.7); (2) their aristocratic origin meant that they they would not tolerate being criticized or dominated by others, and

among the people to show its sympathy for him.²⁷⁷ Also, they had a clear memory of the deeds of his grandfather, Aristobulus.²⁷⁸ Being overwhelmed, their feelings gradually became evident; they were glad and confused at the same time.²⁷⁹ They uttered best wishes for him, interspersed with prayers,²⁸⁰ so that the sympathy of the crowd became manifest. The acknowledgment of their feelings²⁸¹ seemed rather untimely in connection to the kingdom.²⁸² **53** In the light of all these things²⁸³ Herod decided to carry out the plan that he had for the young man.²⁸⁴ When the festival was over, he [the young man] was entertained at a party²⁸⁵ in Jericho.²⁸⁶ Alexandra was their hostess.²⁸⁷ Herod treated the

---

that they would speak their minds, even if that would be clearly counter-productive (cf. several passages about Mariamme; see 15.238 with the note to "license of tongue"); and (3) the descent had consequences for the honor and shame code since the royal Hasmoneans were hypersensitive toward infringements on their honor and status, as Alexandra's responses to Herod's actions show (15.23, 36-37, 44-45).

²⁷⁷ This passage introduces the elaborate description of the Jewish people's emotional response to Aristobulus' public performance. It suggests, like Herod's motive for not sending Aristobulus over to Antony (see *Ant.* 15.30), that the young man enjoyed considerable support (see also 15.167; 16.7, 234; 17.330). Two reasons seem obvious for this support. First, Aristobulus was a young and very promising member of the dynasty that had previously ruled the people. The association with his grandfather in the continuation of the narrative supports this interpretation. The Hasmoneans still had powerful supporters at Herod's court (see 15.47 with the note to "Sabbion"). The second reason concerns the obvious antipathy for Herod. It is not explicitly mentioned here, though probably presupposed, since it is a main thread in the Herod narrative of *Antiquities*.

²⁷⁸ Papponomy (i.e., to be named after one's grandfather) was rather common in high priestly families in the Persian and Hellenistic periods (Scolnic 1999). Aristobulus' grandfather was Aristobulus II, who took over the High Priesthood from Hyrcanus II in 67 BCE (see *Ant.* 15.12 with the note to "High Priest and then king").

²⁷⁹ The people's mixed feelings are easily explainable in the light of Herod's sensitivity about possible competitors (see *Ant.* 15.1-2, 18-20 with notes) and his suspicious character (see 15.35, 42 with the notes to "suspicion"). The last part of the paragraph implies that too much sympathy and support for Aristobulus would backfire. The parallel passage in *War* (1.437) briefly notes that the crowd burst out into tears when Aristobulus approached the altar.

²⁸⁰ The best wishes and prayers suggest a role for the people during Aristobulus' installation ceremony (see *Ant.* 15.51 with the note to "went up to the altar"). This would be more or less in line with the description of the ordination of Aaron and his sons (Lev 8:3-5; 9:3-24), although these biblical sections do not describe good wishes and prayers of the people; they refer to the crowd's reaction after divine fire had consumed the sacrifices: "Fire came out from the Lord and consumed the burnt offering and the fat on the altar; and when all the people saw it, they shouted and fell on their faces" (9:24).

²⁸¹ The translation follows the reading τὴν ὧν πεπόνθεσαν ὁμολογίαν of Niese (341). MSS LAMW read εὖ πεπόνθεισαν ("[the acknowledgment of] the benefits they had received") instead of πεπόνθεσαν.

²⁸² Marcus-Wikgren (27) propose a different translation: "and their acknowledgment of their emotions seemed too impulsive in view of their having a king" (similarly Meijer-Wes 3.158). The point of Josephus' comment that concludes the description of the people's response to Aristobulus' ordination seems to be that its affectionate welcoming of Aristobulus as new High Priest was excessive and could easily be interpreted as an indication that the young man would also be most welcome as new king, which was dangerous since the Jews had a king who would stick to his power (this is also suggested by Josephus' reference to Herod's jealousy in *Ant.* 15.50). For another hint about Aristobulus' possible future rulership of the Jews, see 15.30.

²⁸³ It is obvious that the warm support for Aristobulus at his installation as High Priest would arouse Herod's jealousy (see *Ant.* 15.50 with the note to "his jealousy") and strengthen the king's feelings that this competitor had to be eliminated.

²⁸⁴ Herod's plan is already indicated in *Ant.* 15.49.

²⁸⁵ The verb ἑστιάω can mean "entertain, give a feast" (LSJ *s.v.*, here passive, "he/they were given a feast"). See also *Ant.* 17.200, on Archelaus' entertaining the Jewish people after Herod's death, and 15.21, referring to banquets at Herod's court. The brief parallel report of *War* (1.437) does not mention Alexandra's party in Jericho.

²⁸⁶ There was a complex of palaces in Jericho, partly built by the Hasmoneans and partly by Herod (Jericho was his regular winter residence). It was located at the end of Wadi Qelt, about 2 km south of the old city (Möller and Schmitt 1976: 101; Tsafrir, Di Segni, and

young man amicably[288] and he lured him to drink[289] without fear,[290] being ready to play with him[291] and please him by acting as a young man.[292] **54** Because the particular climate of this place happens to be rather hot,[293] after having assembled they[294] soon went outside for a stroll and stood next to the swimming pools.[295] The pools near the courtyard happened to be large,[296] and they[297] cooled themselves off from the extreme heat of midday.[298] **55** At first they watched those of the servants and friends[299] who were swimming, and next the

---

Green 1994: 143-44; Netzer 1996; 1999; and 2001).

[287] Richardson (1996: 164) concludes on the basis of the Greek text that Herod had allowed Alexandra to retain the Hasmonean palace at Jericho. This is not warranted by Josephus' vocabulary, which only implies that Alexandra acted as hostess in Jericho; in which palace this was remains unspecified.

[288] Cf. *Ant.* 16.61, on Marcus Agrippa's friendly attitude towards Herod.

[289] The translation follows the reading εἰς ... πότον ("to drink," perhaps "to a drinking-bout"; cf. *Ant.* 15.241) of Niese (341), attested by MS P and the Latin version. The majority of the Greek MSS reads εἰς ... τόπον ("to a place"). Niese's reading should be preferred since it is the more difficult one. The occurrence of τόπος in the next paragraph may have caused copyists to change πότον to τόπον. The noun πότος frequently indicates the drinking of wine (LSJ *s.v.* II.1). Hence the narrative may hint at the obvious strategy of luring someone to drink a lot before murdering him. Cf. the famous story about Judith's seduction of Holophernes, who is decapitated after drinking an enormous quantity of wine (Jdt 12:10-13:10; note the word πότος in 12:10; 13:1).

[290] This detail is ironic in the light of Aristobulus' way of dying at nightfall on that same day (see *Ant.* 15.55). It also keeps the reader in suspense because the association of drinking and fear makes one wonder at this stage whether Aristobulus is going to be poisoned (cf. Marcus-Wikgren 27 n. *d*). The passage anticipates Aristobulus' death through a hint at the danger of being poisoned. The reader learns only afterwards that the cause of death was drowning instead of poisoning.

[291] The verb συμπαίζω ("play/sport with," LSJ *s.v.*) is a *hapax legomenon* in Josephus. Cf. the allusion to playing a game in the description of Aristobulus' murder (*Ant.* 15.55).

[292] The only other occurrence of νεανιεύομαι ("act as a young man," LSJ *s.v.*) in Josephus appears in *War* 4.263. Herod's companionable attitude towards Aristobulus (κεχαρισμένως "pleasing [him]"; cf. *Ant.* 15.238) seems to be part of his strategy to lure the young man into a situation that would make it easy to kill him. At the same time this kind of behavior seems self-evident for a king when sons or other young male relatives are in his company (see also 16.315).

[293] Because of its unique location close to the Dead Sea in the Jordan Valley, more than 250 m below sea level, the climate in Jericho is very mild, even in winter. The annual average temperature in Jericho between 1994 and 2004 was 23.3 °C (http://edoc.hu-berlin.de/dissertationen/al-jawabreh-amer-2005-11-25/HTML/chapter2, consulted on 17 April, 2007). In winter the temperature is usually much lower, but even then it can easily reach 25 °C in the early afternoon on a nice day.

[294] Josephus doesn't specify the subject, but because of the context (see "after having assembled" further on in the sentence) it is plausible that it concerns a group of guests including Herod and Aristobulus.

[295] The noun κολυμβήθρα ("pond, swimming pool," Rengstorf *s.v.*) also occurs in the parallel passage of *War* (1.437; see also 5.145, 467-468).

[296] The Hasmonean and Herodian palaces at Jericho had several pools, including large ones for swimming and other water activities (Netzer 2001: 50-139, 299-342). It is not easy to determine the exact location of Aristobulus' death. Herod's first palace—constructed in ca. 35 BCE—included 2 units with baths but no swimming pools. The much more magnificent second and third Herodian palaces did include swimming pools, but they were built long after Aristobulus' death, in ca. 25 and 15 BCE respectively (Netzer 1999: 32-55; 2006: 45). Since Alexandra is mentioned as hostess of the party (*Ant.* 15.53), we may safely assume that Aristobulus was drowned in one of the swimming pools of the Hasmonean palaces, which remained intact until an earthquake in 31 BCE (Netzer 2001: 73, 303-06; 2006: 10, 43). The location concerned may be the twin pools that were part of the Hasmonean twin palaces. These pools, which survived the earthquake, were later turned by Herod into one big pool of 32 x 18 m and included in his second palace. This pool was surrounded by a garden. Josephus' vague description seems to match the twin pools best.

[297] Josephus switches the subject from the pools to an unspecified group of guests including Herod and Aristobulus.

[298] Ancient authors attest that noon is the hottest moment of the day (see, e.g., Aristotle, *Probl.* 939b; Diodorus 14.70.6; Galen, *Temperam.* [ed. Kühn 1.528.5]).

[299] On Herod's friends, see *Ant.* 15.5 with the note to "the friends around him."

young man was persuaded[300] [to swim] as well, also by Herod's urging.[301] When it was getting dark,[302] some of his friends, who were ordered to do this,[303] kept pressing him down and immersing him while he was swimming—as if playing a game[304]—and they did not let him come up until[305] they had completely choked the life out of him.[306] **56** In this way Aristobulus was killed,[307] being not entirely[308] eighteen years old.[309] He had held the High Priesthood for a year,[310] which [office] Ananel got back again for himself.[311]

---

[300] The verb προάγω can mean "induce, persuade" (LSJ s.v. I.4).

[301] Herod's involvement in the murder of Aristobulus becomes clear by the little pieces of information dropped by Josephus at several occasions (see the hint at Aristobulus' fear in *Ant.* 15.53; the vague reference to Herod's order to his friends in the next sentence; and Alexandra's conclusion described in 15.58). Willrich (1929: 51-52) argues that Aristobulus' death was an accident, but Schürer-Vermes (1.297) and Schalit (2001: 112-13) claim that Herod murdered the young High Priest. Baumann (1983: 176-78) considers both options possible.

[302] The verb ἐπέχω ("hold [out]") with σκότος ("darkness") as subject means "come on" (LSJ s.v. VI.2; cf. Aristotle, *Mir. ausc.* 842a). *War* 1.437 briefly notes that Aristobulus was brought to Jericho during the night.

[303] The parallel passage in *War* (1.437) reports that Aristobulus was plunged in a pool by "the Gauls" (see the note to "choked the life out of him" below) "according to instructions." Despite the vagueness of Josephus' formulation it is obvious in *War* that Herod ordered Aristobulus' death. Otto (1913: 42) and Richardson (1996: 164 n. 54) prefer *Antiquities* as the more reliable report.

[304] Cf. the vocabulary in *Ant.* 15.53.

[305] For the phrase "they did not let go … until" (οὐκ ἀνῆκαν ἕως), cf. *Ant.* 18.246, about Herodias manipulating Herod Antipas until she was successful.

[306] The parallel passage in *War* (1.437) reports that Aristobulus was drowned (βαπτιζόμενος, LSJ s.v. 1; cf. βαπτίζοντες in *Ant.* 15.55) by "the Gauls." These Gauls were most probably part of the 400 Gauls from Cleopatra's bodyguard whom Herod received from Octavian in 31 BCE after the Battle of Actium (*War* 1.396-397; *Ant.* 15.215, 217 with the notes to "Gauls" and "who were Cleopatra's body-guards"). If so, the reference to the Gauls in *War* 1.437 must be an anachronism (Michel-Bauernfeind 1.420 n. 212; Richardson 1996: 164 n. 54). Ilan (1998: 232-34) argues that the *Antiquities* report about Aristobulus' death is based on Nicolaus of Damascus: Nicolaus would have suggested that it was an accident and Josephus would have reworked Nicolaus' report, emphasizing that Herod caused Aristobulus' death because he wanted to eliminate all the Hasmoneans who could be considered to be his competitors.

[307] This remark concludes the brief report about Aristobulus' death. Josephus does not add any comment about Aristobulus' person or office, as he usually does when relating deaths of kings or High Priests (see, e.g., *Ant.* 15.179-182 about Hyrcanus II; 17.191-192 about Herod). The lack of such a comment may result from the short period Aristobulus was in office.

[308] Following Niese (342), who reads οὐ πάντα ("not entirely") with MSS PF and E. This reading is also given by Photius in the section—with excerpts from Josephus' *Antiquities*—that focuses on Herod (Codex 238). The reading τὰ πάντα ("just/all together [eighteen]," LSJ s.v. πᾶς D II.4) with MSS LAMW (followed by Marcus-Wikgren 28) is paralleled by *Ant.* 4.84, referring to Aaron's death: βιοὺς δὲ ἔτη τὰ πάντα τρία πρὸς τοῖς εἴκοσι καὶ ἑκατόν "having lived altogether one hundred and twenty-three years" (trans. Feldman in BJP 3; see also 2.196).

[309] Depending on the reading of the preceding passage (see the previous note), Aristobulus died when he was 17 or 18 years old. Both ages match the other chronological data about Aristobulus' life given in *Antiquities* (15.29, 41, 51). His age implies—together with Josephus' reference to one year of high priestly service—that Aristobulus died at the end of 35 BCE at the earliest. Since a party at Jericho would make most sense in the winter season (see 15.53 with the note to "Jericho"), it is plausible that Aristobulus died in the winter of 35/34 BCE, though the autumn of 35 BCE (after the Feast of Tabernacles) and the early spring of 34 BCE (as argued by Mahieu 2012: 184) are certainly possible as well. Kokkinos (1998: 212 with n. 19) states that Aristobulus died in late 35 BCE. Schalit (2001: 111-12 with nn. 36 and 48) calculates that he died about one year earlier.

[310] This seems to be an inclusive way of calculating since the actual period must have been less than a year: it concerns the interval between Aristobulus' installation in 35 BCE and his death in the winter of 35/34 BCE (or possibly late fall 35–early spring 34 BCE). Mahieu (2012: 184) argues that Aristobulus served an entire year as High Priest (early 35–spring 34 BCE). The combination of κατέχω and ἀρχιερωσύνην ("hold the High Priesthood") also occurs in *Ant.* 12.434; 20.237; cf. 14.199.

[311] For the High Priest Ananel, see *Ant.* 15.22, 40 with notes.

(3.4) 57 When the accident was reported[312] to the women,[313] there was an immediate turn to[314] mourning and uncontrollable grief over the dead body laid out for burial.[315] By the time the news spread around,[316] the city also grieved exceedingly;[317] every family appropriated the misfortune as if it had not happened to a stranger.[318] **58** Alexandra was most touched[319] because she understood the ins and outs of the death.[320] On the one hand she felt the pain more[321] since she knew how it had been done, on the other hand she knew that it was necessary to persevere since she expected greater disasters.[322] **59** Frequently she would come to the point of drawing a line across her life[323] by her own hands,[324] but she

Mourning for Aristobulus III.

---

[312] The phrase ἐξαγγελθέντος τοῦ πάθους ("when the accident was reported") occurs with slight variations in Herodotus 5.95.6; Plutarch, *Agis* 21.1. The noun πάθος can mean "accident, calamity" (LSJ *s.v.* I.1-2).

[313] Josephus does not specify which women. The 2 women who were close relatives of Aristobulus were his sister Mariamme I and his mother Alexandra. *Ant.* 15.58 focalizes Alexandra; *War* 1.437 and *Ant.* 15.222 report Mariamme's criticism of Herod for murdering her brother and grandfather. Yet, instead of Alexandra and Mariamme, the passage perhaps refers to an anonymous group of keening women, who usually began their lamentations in the house of the deceased. Sir 38:16-17 indicates that keening over a deceased person after the burial lasted 1 or 2 days, but the traditional period of mourning became 7 days (Kraemer 2000: 15-16; Hachlili 2005: 481-82).

[314] The phrase εὐθὺς ... ἐκ μεταβολῆς ("by a sudden change") is rare but paralleled by Diodorus 14.76; Appian, *Hist. rom.* 8.16.1.

[315] Cf. Josephus' more elaborate descriptions of Herod's burial in *War* 1.670-673; *Ant.* 17.196-199 (cf. *War* 3.435-437; *Apion* 2.205). Josephus' vocabulary links up with a custom (the *prothesis*) known from fourth-century-BCE Athens that a body was laid out in a house in order to be greeted by relatives and friends. Burial had to take place before sunrise on the day following the laying out of the body (Hachlili 2005: 482).

[316] The phrase "when the news spread around" (τοῦ λόγου διαδοθέντος) is conventional (see, e.g., Polybius 36.7.4; Diodorus 20.66).

[317] Cf. *Ant.* 15.52 on the crowd's response to Aristobulus' first appearance as High Priest. The verb ὑπεραλγέω ("grieve exceedingly," LSJ *s.v.* 2) is a *hapax legomenon* in Josephus. The words ἡ πόλις ὑπερήλγει ("the city grieved exceedingly") are paralleled by Heliodorus 4.21.3.

[318] This statement almost seems a euphemism in the light of the strong support from the Jerusalem crowd for Aristobulus (see *Ant.* 15.52 as well as the preceding sentence in 15.57); yet it makes sense against the background of a distinction between private and public mournings. Thus in *War* 3.435-437 Josephus briefly describes the mourning after the fall of Jotapata-Yodfat, which took place per family for all the deceased except Josephus (who was supposed to have died); for the commander Josephus there was a public mourning (Michel-Bauernfeind 1.462).

[319] Ironically, the expression μᾶλλον ἐκπαθής ("most touched") reoccurs in *Ant.* 16.208, this time referring to Herod.

[320] Readers are left in the dark about how Alexandra knew the details of Aristobulus' death. The description of the murder in *Ant.* 15.55 indicates that the young man was drowned when it was getting dark, which implies that only persons who stood near the edge of the swimming pool could have seen something. Alexandra must have been well informed at Herod's court and very much aware of the king's capacity of taking drastic measures, which renders it plausible that she realized the cause of Aristobulus' death by intuition.

[321] Alexandra is focalized in this passage. The statement summarizes her view about the death of her son Aristobulus. In *War* the narrative continues with Mariamme's response to Aristobulus' death (1.438; Richardson 1996: 164).

Here and in the next paragraph Josephus describes Alexandra's conflicting emotions and thoughts, which is a significant aspect of Josephus' characterizations of the main figures of the Herodian narrative in *Antiquities*. The depiction of Herod being torn apart by feelings of love and hatred towards Mariamme is the most dramatic example (*Ant.* 15.211-212).

[322] The "greater disasters" anticipate the later executions of Mariamme and Alexandra (*Ant.* 15.202-251).

[323] Niese (342) follows Wesseling's conjecture in Diodorus 1.41. His reading of περιγράψασθαι τὸν βίον ("end her life") may even be supported by the Latin version of *Ant.* 15.59. However, the reading παραγράψασθαι τὸν βίον ("draw a line across her life") of the Greek MSS makes sense, such that the conjecture is unnecessary. The verb παραγράφω can mean "draw a line across, cancel" (LSJ *s.v.* II.5).

[324] Hyrcanus from the family of the Tobiads killed himself with his own hands (*Ant.* 12.236). The noun αὐτοχειρίᾳ ("murder perpetrated by one's own hand,"

held back nevertheless, in case she would during her lifetime be able to help[325] the one who had been killed treacherously and lawlessly.[326] For this reason she was all the more motivated[327] to live on. She assumed that showing no suspicion[328] at all about the premeditated murder of her son[329] was sufficient to give her an opportunity for revenge.[330] **60** So Alexandra controlled[331] her suspicion.

Herod plausibly tried to take away[332] the impression of all outsiders that the death of the boy had happened on purpose.[333] He not only practiced all the usual acts of mourning, but also gave way to tears[334] and even conveyed the sincere confusion of his feelings.[335] Perhaps his emotion overpowered him when he saw [Aristobulus'] youth and beauty,[336] even though the death of the boy was meant to be for his own safety. Yet it was clear that he busied himself with these things to defend himself. **61** Nevertheless, he displayed all

---

LSJ *s.v.* αὐτοχειρία II; Rengstorf *s.v.*) has an adverbial meaning elsewhere too (e.g., Diodorus 15.54; Photius, *Bibl.* 57). On suicide in Josephus, see van Henten 2007a.

[325] The rare verb προσαρκέω ("help," Rengstorf *s.v.*), which originated in Greek tragedies (references in LSJ *s.v.*), occurs 3 times in Josephus, all in *Ant.* 15 (see 15.63, 301).

[326] The phrase τῷ ἀνόμως διεφθαρμένῳ ("the one who had been killed lawlessly") is paralleled by Isocrates, *Plat.* 52.5.

[327] MSS LAMW read παρεκράτει (from the verb παρακρατέω, meaning, among other things, "retain," LSJ *s.v.*), which reading probably corrupts the more original reading παρεκρότει (followed by Niese 342; from the rare verb παρακροτέω ["incite, encourage"]). The latter verb occurs relatively frequently in *War* (1.380, 617; 2.264; 3.153, 239, 484, etc.; Rengstorf *s.v.*).

[328] Concerning Herod's suspicions, see *Ant.* 15.22, 42, and on Alexandra's fear of being under suspicion, 15.35 (cf. 15.38, 44). The expression ὑποψίαν ἐνδίδωμι ("yield/show suspicion") also occurs in Plato, *Leg.* 887e; Plutarch, *Alc.* 6.2; Galen, *Praes. puls.* (ed. Kühn 9.218).

[329] According to Josephus Alexandra knew that Herod was responsible for the death of her son (see *Ant.* 15.58, 62), which matches Josephus' own presentation in 15.49. Cf. Josephus' presentation of Herod's treatment of Hyrcanus II in 15.21, which also includes the noun ἐπιβουλή ("plot, treachery"; see 15.21 with the note to "to keep the plot unsuspected"). Hyrcanus was apparently unaware of Herod's ultimate plan.

[330] Alexandra's strategy was apparently to await her chances. Her revenge could have come with a change of government, for which she aimed according to *Ant.* 15.32, 42. The noun εὐκαιρία ("right moment, suitable time, opportunity") occurs 6 times in the Herod narrative of *Antiquities* (15.59, 315, 327, 366; 16.301) and only once elsewhere in Josephus (18.54; Rengstorf *s.v.*).

[331] The expression ἐγκρατῶς φέρω (literally "bear with self-control"; cf. *Ant.* 15.219, about Herod) is conventional (see, e.g., Menander, *Fragm.* 556; Appian, *Hist. rom.* 12.11.73; Dio Chrysostom 29.22). The virtue of ἐγκράτεια ("self-control") was a well-known ideal in Hellenistic philosophy (Chadwick 1962) and was also incorporated in Hellenistic Jewish ethics (see, e.g., 4 Macc 5:34; Philo, *Spec.* 1.149). A description of the Essenes in *War* emphasizes the importance of this virtue for them (2.120, 138).

[332] Josephus' suggestion that Herod tried to give outsiders the impression that Aristobulus' death was an accident is ambiguous. Herod's participation in the mourning shows the king's strong emotional involvement, though it was (according to Josephus) at the same time part of his attempt to dupe the outsiders. The imperfect ἀπεσκευάζετο ("tried to take away") should be taken as an *imperfectum de conatu* (Meijer-Wes 3.159), particularly since Josephus indicates at the end of the paragraph that the attempt failed.

[333] The repetition of πρόνοια ("foreknowledge, purpose") echoes Alexandra's thoughts about Herod's involvement in the death of her son.

[334] For a similar expression (δάκρυσιν ... χρώμενον), see *Ant.* 17.106, on Antipater (cf. Gregory of Nyssa, *Inscr. Ps.* [ed. McDonough 5.78]; Theodoretus, *Int. proph. min.* [PG 81.1645]).

[335] The noun ψυχή probably indicates here one's self or personality as the center of emotions, desires, and affections (LSJ *s.v.* IV.1), which is an interpretation supported by the continuation of the narrative. Herod appears as a complex character: on the one hand he does not hesitate to eliminate a possible competitor when an occasion presents itself,; on the other hand he is deeply moved by the death of his young brother-in-law. The expression σύγχυσις τῆς ψυχῆς ("sincere confusion of his feelings") is repeated in *Ant.* 16.75, also referring to Herod. There are only a few parallels, in scholia and patristic sources (John of Damascus, *Vit. Barl. Joas.* 324.10; Eustathius of Thessalonica, *Od.* 4.716 [ed. Stallbaum 1.189]).

[336] The reference to Aristobulus' beauty echoes similar vocabulary in *Ant.* 15.23, 25, 29, 51, and adds to the dramatization of his death.

the more[337] extravagance with the carrying out of the corpse,[338] made a lot of the preparation of the grave,[339] arranged plenty of fragrances for embalmment,[340] and buried him together with a lot of valuable items,[341] so that he drove out the pain of the women's suffering[342] and assuaged them for this part.[343]

(3.5) 62 Alexandra, however, was not won over by any of these actions.[344] The memory of the evil deed kept causing her more and more pain[345] and made her querulous[346] and contentious.[347] So she wrote to Cleopatra[348] about Herod's plot[349] and the murder of her son.

Herod has to explain Aristobulus' death before Antony.

---

[337] The phrase μᾶλλον ἐπεδείξατο ("he displayed all the more ...") is paralleled by Demosthenes, *Or.* 61.13.

[338] Herod's sumptuous arrangements for the funeral and burial place of Aristobulus correspond to the royal status of the young man and the king's tendency to spare no expenses for important public events (see, e.g., *Ant.* 15.268-274). The noun ἐκφορά ("carrying out of a corpse," LSJ *s.v.*) is a *hapax legomenon* in Josephus (cf. *War* 4.330 τοὺς νεκροὺς ἐκφοροῦντες "carrying the corpses outside").

[339] Josephus does not indicate the location of Aristobulus' grave. It may have been close to Jerusalem or Jericho, i.e., the 2 cities where the Hasmonean family was usually staying. Rengstorf (*s.v.*) considers the possibility that θήκη ("grave, tomb, burial place") means "burial" here.

[340] Josephus uses the same noun in connection with the tabernacle and sacrifices (*Ant.* 3.103; 8.101-102; cf. LXX 1 Chr 6:34). Here θυμίαμα may refer to fragrances for the anointment or embalmment of Aristobulus' body (LSJ *s.v.* 2), or to spices sprinkled on the body (Rengstorf *s.v.*; cf. Matt 26:12; Mark 14:8). The fragrances could consist of incense or spices (ἀρώματα; cf. *War* 1.673; *Ant.* 17.199 concerning Herod's funeral) in dry or liquid forms, such as myrrh or aloes (cf. John 19:39). Rabbinic passages suggest that the purified body was sprinkled with perfume before it was wrapped in shrouds (*m. Šabb.* 23.5; *b. Sanh.* 48b; cf. John 19:40 "They took the body of Jesus and wrapped it with the spices [μετὰ τῶν ἀρωμάτων] in linen cloths, according to the burial custom of the Jews"). New Testament passages indicate, in connection with Jesus' death, that fragrances were sprinkled on the corpse in the grave (Mark 16:1; Luke 23:56-24:1; *m. Šabb.* 8.1; Brown 1994: 2.1256-64; Kraemer 2000: 20-22). Sometimes spices and perfumes were left behind in order to keep a nice odor in the tomb or to slow down the body's decomposition. *Unguentaria* (i.e., small bottles that contained fragrances) have been frequently found in tombs from the Second Temple period (Hachlili 2005: 383-85, 444, 460, 480).

[341] An alternative translation would be "ornaments," but the most probable interpretation is that the phrase refers to costly items that were buried together with Aristobulus' corpse. Artefacts were frequently buried with a deceased person. They usually consisted of personal belongings and items of everyday use. Occasionally, objects were produced to be put in the grave, which probably was also the case for Aristobulus' burial. Grave goods from Jewish burial sites include pottery, glass, wood, iron objects, leather, textiles, and coins (Hachlili 2005: 375-446). The verb συγκαταθάπτω ("bury together with") is a *hapax legomenon* in Josephus.

[342] The expression ἐκπλῆξαι τὸ λυπηρόν echoes a comforting phrase about recreation after work found in Pericles' famous funeral oration for the fallen Athenian soldiers (Thucydides 2.34-46): "... we have ... homes fitted out with good taste and elegance; and the delight we each day find in these things drives away sadness (τὸ λυπηρὸν ἐκπλήσσει)" (2.38, trans. Smith; see Marcus-Wikgren 31 n. *b*).

[343] Herod's taking care of Aristobulus' funeral in lavish style must have left nothing to complain about; yet to those who were aware of his involvement in the High Priest's death, it must have caused bitter feelings, as the continuation of the narrative—by focusing on Alexandra—shows.

[344] The sentence links up with *Ant.* 15.58-59, about Alexandra's reaction to Aristobulus' death. She knew that Herod was responsible for her son's death and had set her mind on revenge. For similar phrases of ἡττάω ("overcome") with οὐδέν ("nothing") as subject and a person as object, see Cornutus, *Nat. d.* 9 (ed. Lang 10.16); Philostratus, *Vit. Apoll.* 3.22.21.

[345] The expression παρέχουσα τὴν ὀδύνην ("causing [her] pain") is conventional (see, e.g., Philo, *QG* 1.41; Galen, *Bile* [ed. Kühn 5.120-121]; *Glauc.* [ed. Kühn 11.112]; Eutecnius [ed. Gualandri p. 60]).

[346] The adjective ὀδυρτικός ("complaining, querulous," Rengstorf *s.v.*) is a *hapax legomenon* in Josephus. It is rather rare and occurs for the first time in Aristotle, *Rhet.* 1390a (cf. *Fragm.* 1.82 [ed. Rose 86]; *Pol.* 1340a; see also Plutarch, *Mor.* [*Amat.*] 751a; Adamantius, *Physiogn.* 2.28 [ed. Foerster 1.380]).

[347] The combination of being "querulous" and "contentious" characterizes Alexandra in a most negative way. The adjective φιλόνεικος ("contentious") is frequently used in a pejorative sense (LSJ *s.v.* φιλόνικος 1). Rengstorf (*s.v.*) gives the meaning "embittered" for this passage. The word re-occurs in *Ant.* 15.166, 168 in connection with other references to Alexandra, and in

63 Since she [Cleopatra][350] had been eager for a long time to help her with her request and felt pity for Alexandra's mishaps,[351] she made the entire thing her own business.[352] She did not give up urging[353] Antony to punish [the person responsible for] the murder of the boy.[354] For it was not right that Herod, who was king thanks to him [Antony][355] over a territory that in no way belonged to him [Herod],[356] displayed such unlawfulness to the ones who were real kings.[357] **64** Antony was persuaded by these words[358] and sent for Herod when he had set out for Laodicea,[359] ordering [him] to come and clear himself of[360] the accusation

---

15.237 in a reference to Mariamme (cf. *War* 2.267; 4.132; *Ant.* 15.156, 290; 16.252; *Apion* 1.160).

[348] This is the third time that Alexandra is turning to Cleopatra for help (for Alexandra's earlier requests to the queen, see *Ant.* 15.24, 45; cf. 15.167-168).

[349] See also *Ant.* 15.59, 64, and for similar letters reporting a plot and anticipating a punishment for the plotter, *War* 2.616; *Ant.* 13.107.

[350] About Cleopatra, see *Ant.* 15.24 with the note to "Cleopatra."

[351] For similar vocabulary (οἰκτείρω plus ἀτυχία as object, "lament ... misfortune"), see Diodorus 13.24.

[352] Josephus does not elaborate on the apparently close relationship between Alexandra and Cleopatra (cf. *Ant.* 15.24, 45-46). The energetic way in which Cleopatra presents Alexandra's case is perfectly understandable as part of her strategy to take over Rome's client kingdoms situated in Egypt's neighborhood (see 15.28 with the note to "such an affair"). Alexandra's accusation of Herod for having murdered a Hasmonean prince who was also the High Priest was a very serious one, and Cleopatra's support of this accusation before Antony must have seriously endangered Herod's position. Alexandra and Cleopatra shared the same goal of getting rid of Herod, but the aftermath of Herod's removal was speculated on in very different ways: Alexandra was hoping for a restoration of the Hasmonean rule, while Cleopatra for a take-over of the Judean kingdom (Buchheim 1960: 68-71).

[353] The reading ἐρεθίζουσα ("provoking") given by E (Niese 343) is even more negative about Cleopatra's effort to make Antony punish Herod.

[354] The noun παῖς ("child, son, boy") links up with earlier references to Aristobulus as a boy (*Ant.* 15.28, 31, 34, 41, 60; cf. 15.23-24, 27) and dramatizes the murderous act. It may also echo Josephus' earlier hint at an eventual sexual relationship between Antony and Aristobulus (see 15.29 with the note to "very handsome").

[355] Cleverly Cleopatra emphasizes Antony's responsibility for Herod's appointment as king (for references to the appointment, see *Ant.* 15.2 with the note to "all Judea").

[356] The phrase τῆς οὐδὲν προσηκούσης ἀρχῆς ("over a territory that in no way belonged to him") probably means that Cleopatra was arguing that Herod was not entitled to be the king of Judea because he was not of Hasmonean descent (cf. *Ant.* 15.2 with the note to "commoner"). Becher (1966: 67) notes that Cleopatra's contempt for Herod as a self-made king of non-Judean origin is obvious. Another explanation for Cleopatra's point is that she was arguing that Judea belonged to her territory (see Schalit 2001: 113 and *Ant.* 15.24 with the note to "Cleopatra"). Such a claim could be supported by the fact that the Ptolemaic kings controlled Judea until Antiochus III's victory over the Egyptian army at Paneas in 198 BCE (Schürer-Vermes 2.89).

For a similar phrase with a participle of προσήκω plus οὐδέν, cf. Plutarch, *Comp. Demetr. Ant.* 1.2 concerning Mark Antony: "... and yet Antony had the courage to seek the power of Caesar (τήν Καίσαρος ... ἀρχήν), to which his birth gave him no claim (οὐδὲν αὐτῷ κατὰ γένος προσήκουσαν)" (trans. Perrin; cf. Plato, *Gorg.* 471a).

[357] The passage hints at Aristobulus' royal descent (see also *Ant.* 15.51 with the note to "descent"). For the expression "real king" (ὄντως βασιλεύς), see Plato, *Alc. mai.* 122a; *Pol.* 276e; Philo, *Somn.* 2.99; Clement of Alexandria, *Paed.* 3.12.

[358] Although Cleopatra called upon Antony to punish Herod for having murdered Aristobulus, Antony only ordered Herod to render account for his actions, which shows that he did not slavishly obey the queen in all matters (cf. *War* 1.243, and see *Ant.* 15.24 with the note to "Cleopatra"). For vocabulary similar to τούτοις ἀναπειθόμενος, see *War* 2.183; *Ant.* 15.355.

[359] Antony's trip to Laodicea on the Syrian coast was connected with a second campaign against the Parthians, in 35 BCE (Plutarch, *Ant.* 53.7; Dio Cassius 49.39.3; Buchheim 1960: 71). Several scholars assume that Herod met Antony at Laodicea (e.g., Stern 1974b: 232; Richardson 1996: 218; Schalit 2001: 113-20), but Josephus only indicates that Herod was invited to visit Antony after the latter had taken off (ἐστάλη) for Laodicea. *Ant.* 15.74 implies that Cleopatra was with Antony when Herod came over. Hence Herod may have met Antony while he was on his way to Laodicea, possibly still in Egypt.

[360] The translation is based on the reading ἀποδύσασθαι ("take off, clear oneself of") of MS P (Marcus-Wikgren 32). Niese (343) reads ἀπολύσασθαι ("refute")

concerning Aristobulus. For, he wrote,³⁶¹ if the plot had happened through him, he had not acted rightly.³⁶² **65** Since Herod was afraid of the accusation and Cleopatra's hostility³⁶³—because she did not cease working to develop Antony's enmity towards him³⁶⁴—he decided to obey, for there was nothing else he could do.³⁶⁵ So he left his uncle Joseph³⁶⁶ behind as the caretaker of the kingdom³⁶⁷ and his affairs there, and also secretly instructed him to kill Mariamme immediately³⁶⁸ if something happened to him while he was with Antony.

Herod's caretaker Joseph reveals the king's secret instruction.
War 1.441-442

---

with most of the other MSS. The one reading could have easily led to the other owing to a change of δ to λ, or vice versa. Yet the infinitive ἀποδύσασθαι is also attested in *Ant.* 11.223, and the verb ἀποδύω in 4.83; 10.11; 11.234; 13.84, 220; 19.295. The infinitive ἀπολύσασθαι is absent from Josephus (but cf. ἀπολύσεσθαι in *War* 1.539). The verb ἀπολύω occurs much more frequently in Josephus (ca. 150 times), which renders it probable that the less obvious reading ἀποδύσασθαι was replaced by ἀπολύσασθαι.

³⁶¹ The transition to indirect speech suggests that Antony had sent a messenger and/or a letter to Herod (Schalit 2001: 113).

³⁶² This passage is ambiguous: Antony seems to take it for granted that Aristobulus was murdered (this is implied by the use of ἐπιβουλή ["plot"]; see *Ant.* 15.21 with the note to "that his plot should remain unsuspected") but leaves open the possibility that Herod was not involved. Yet the conclusion that Aristobulus was murdered would basically have implied that Herod had ordered it because he clearly had a good motive for getting rid of the youngster. Hence Herod's rule was in serious danger, as the next paragraph confirms.

³⁶³ The reference to Cleopatra's hostility towards Herod links up with the content of the previous passage. Cleopatra's repeated support of Alexandra (*Ant.* 15.28, 45, 62; cf. 15.32) was clearly directed against Herod. The noun δυσμένεια ("hostility") also occurs in *War* 1.362 in a reference to Cleopatra: Herod mollified her during her visit to Judea by showering her with large gifts (cf. *Ant.* 15.96-103).

³⁶⁴ Josephus implies that Antony was the key to Cleopatra's success. Unfortunately for her Antony did not always give in (see also *Ant.* 15.64 with the note to "persuaded by these words").

³⁶⁵ Had Herod disregarded Antony's order, he would undoubtedly have lost the goodwill of his patron, which would have been fatal for his position as one of Rome's friendly kings (see *Ant.* 15.5 with the note to "Antony").

³⁶⁶ Other passages seem to contradict that Joseph was Herod's uncle: *War* 1.441 and *Ant.* 15.81 note that Joseph was the husband of Herod's sister Salome and *Ant.* 15.169 implies that Josephus was unaware of Joseph being Herod's uncle. Several scholars argue, therefore, that the Greek τὸν θεῖον ("his uncle"; cf. *War* 1.475, 483; *Ant.* 11.261; 12.387) is a mistake and that the original text may have read τὸν πενθερόν ("his brother-in-law," Marcus-Wikgren 33 n. *d*; Mayer-Schärtel 1995: 207). Schalit (2001: 116) states that Joseph was both Herod's uncle and his brother-in-law. Günther (2005: 112) claims that Joseph was the youngest brother of Herod's father, Antipater, and Herod's brother-in-law after he had been married to Dositheus' sister (see also Kokkinos 1998: 151; about Dositheus, see *Ant.* 15.169 with the note to "Dositheus was a relative of Joseph").

³⁶⁷ For a similar expression in Josephus, see *Ant.* 20.31 concerning the kingdom of Adiabene (τινα τῆς ἀρχῆς ἐπίτροπον).

³⁶⁸ This puzzling and cruel command is unfolded in the next paragraphs, including Joseph's explanation of the instruction to Mariamme (*Ant.* 15.69). Otto (1913: 8, 51) argues that the section about Herod's instruction for Joseph in connection with his journey to Antony and its aftermath (15.65-87; parallel report in *War* 1.441-443) is a doublet of the king's instructions for Joseph and Soemus connected with his trip to Octavian (*Ant.* 15.183-187). On the analogies and differences between the two reports, see 15.236 with the note to "her last moments."

Herod apparently had serious doubts whether he would get away with the accusation of having murdered Aristobulus (*Ant.* 15.67; Schalit 2001: 113, 116). The instruction is also motivated by the king's great affection for his wife, and his fear that somebody would court her after his death (15.66). This fear is associated with Antony (15.67) as well as with Cleopatra's malign influence upon Antony (Richardson 1996: 164). *Ant.* 15.82 also suggests that Herod could not bear the thought of a rival courting Mariamme. The parallel passage in *War* (1.441-443) explains Herod's motive differently. Joseph revealed the secret to Mariamme "… out of a desire to give proof to the woman of the king's love for her, since not even in death could he endure to be separated from her" (1.441, trans. Sievers/Forte in BJP 1a; see also 1.442 and *Ant.* 15.69).

Herod's order seems unprecedented in Jewish and Graeco-Roman traditions (but cf. Plutarch on the suicides of Antony and Cleopatra; see 15.69 with the note to "be separated from her through death"). To a certain extent it reminds one of the Indian practice of *sati*: widows are burned or buried alive together with their dead husbands in order to be with them in the afterlife (Hawley 1994). Cf. also the line of thinking shown by Achilles, who

66 For, he said, he felt great affection for[369] his wife[370] and feared the outrage[371] that somebody else would court her[372] after his death because of her physical attractiveness. **67** All this indicated Antony's desire for the woman[373] since he happened to have heard accidentally[374] of her delicate appearance[375] long before. After Herod had given these instructions, he left to meet Antony, having uncertain hopes about the entire affair.[376]

(3.6) 68 While Joseph was dealing with the administration of the affairs of the kingdom,[377] he was, both for this reason and because of the respect he had to pay to her

---

regards it as Agamemnon's monumental *hybris* against him that Agamemnon has taken his prize woman, Briseis (Homer, *Il.* 1.203, 214). Kasher (2007: 119 with n. 40) offers a psychological explanation and argues that Herod's behavior reveals a paranoid personality disorder that is reminiscent of the so-called "Othello syndrome."

The expression παραχρῆμα ἀνελεῖν ("kill immediately") is repeated in *Ant.* 17.142, about Herod's decision concerning Antipater.

[369] The vocabulary in this passage is extremely rare. The words ἔχειν φιλοστόργως πρός plus a personal object ("feeling great affection for ...") is paralleled by *Ant.* 4.135, about the seduction of Israelite youth by Midianite women (Feldman 1993). See also *Ant.* 15.68, 70, 83, 222 (the latter passage refers to Herod's affection [φιλοστοργία] for Mariamme).

[370] Josephus emphasizes Herod's love for Mariamme several times (see, e.g., *Ant.* 15.82, 207, 222).

[371] Josephus does not specify against whom outrageous acts would be directed. One could assume that Herod's fear was inspired by the thought that suitors could commit acts of insolence with Mariamme, but it is more plausible that the outrage concerns Herod and his reputation, In that case Josephus implies that it was unbearable for Herod that other men would have a relationship with Mariamme after his death (cf. what Homer relates in connection with Penelope's suitors when Odysseus was away [LSJ *s.v.* ὕβρις I.1 with references]. Roman readers may have interpreted Herod's fear in the light of the *univira* ideal that a widow would never marry again (Funke 1965-66; Kötting 1973; Lightman and Zeisel 1977; Kienast 1999: 167; about Jewish practices concerning divorce and remarriage, see *Ant.* 15.259 with notes, also 17.352). The verb δείδω ("fear") with ὕβρις ("insolence, outrage") as object also occurs in Libanius, *Prog.* 7.4.8.

[372] The verb σπουδάζω in the passive voice can mean "be courted" (LSJ *s.v.* II.2; Rengstorf *s.v.*). In *Ant.* 15.40 the same passive verb means "be treated with respect" (LSJ *s.v.* II.2).

[373] Josephus' explanation of Herod's order to Joseph continues. The close connection between *Ant.* 15.66 (describing a statement by Herod) and 15.67 implies that the reference to Antony's desire for Mariamme is not a comment by Josephus: it should be understood from Herod's perspective, elaborating the king's remarks in 15.66. The expression ἡ ἄνθρωπος ("the woman") occurs several times in Josephus. It can refer to a specific woman (e.g., *Ant.* 5.329; 15.212 concerning Mariamme I; 18.72, 349, 351), sometimes with a negative connotation (see *War* 1.111, concerning the Hasmonean Queen Salome Alexandra; 1.571 and 578, about the slave woman whom Pheroras was living with; *Ant.* 17.34 (plural), about Pheroras' wife, mother, and sister; see also *Ant.* 16.194, 198; 18.40; Rengstorf *s.v.*). The combination of the verb ἐμφαίνω ("display, indicate") and ὁρμή ("impulse, desire [for]") as its object is rare, though it does occur a few times in ancient Greek passages (Polybius 3.44.13; Pseudo-Callisthenes recension b 1.13 [ed. van Thiel 1974: 18]).

[374] Scholars have proposed several emendations because the words "have heard accidentally" would contradict Josephus' earlier report about Antony getting to know the beautiful Mariamme (*Ant.* 15.23-28). Naber's conjecture προακηκοώς ("had previously heard"; Naber 1888-96: 3.xl, 322) is supported by a parallel phrase in Aesop (199). His as well as Niese's proposal (γὰρ ἀκηκοώς "for he had heard," Niese 344) would solve the contradiction between 15.23-28 and 15.67. However, the reading παρακηκοώς ("he happened to have heard accidentally") of the Greek MSS makes sense if one reads the passage with Herod as focalizer (see the preceding note): the discrepancy is absent if one assumes that Josephus puts into words Herod's feelings about what Antony could do to Mariamme after his own death, when there would no longer be any restraint to approach her. How Antony had heard about Mariamme was unimportant for Herod in this situation.

[375] The repetition of εὐμορφία ("beauty of form, appearance"—the noun also occurs in *Ant.* 15.66) emphasizes Mariamme's beauty and echoes the first reference to Mariamme (15.23).

[376] For phrases with ἐλπίς ("hope")—or related words—and τῶν ὅλων ("all matters, altogether") plus preposition, see *Ant.* 2.237, 280; 3.11; 5.38.

[377] Joseph was taking care of the kingdom on Herod's instructions (*Ant.* 15.65). Similar vocabulary in 16.1 (cf. 16.21).

as the queen,[378] continuously conversing[379] with Mariamme concerning the handling of the affairs. He kept initiating[380] continuous talks about Herod's loyalty and affection[381] for her. **69** When they ridiculed[382] his words in the way women usually do,[383] especially Alexandra,[384] Joseph took great pains[385] to point out the king's feelings. He was even led on to tell the details concerning his instruction,[386] making assurances[387] that [Herod] could not live without her,[388] nor consent to be separated from her through death[389] if he would suffer

---

[378] About Mariamme's marriage to Herod, see *Ant.* 15.23 with the note to "living in wedlock with Herod."

[379] The rare expression συνεχὲς ἐντυγχάνων ("continuously conversing") is paralleled by *Ant.* 1.330 (see also Pseudo-Lucian, *Am.* 6).

[380] There are slight differences among the readings of the Greek MSS. The translation is based on the reading καθίει (following MS M and the correction in MS A, with Niese 344), which can be interpreted as an imperfect with durative nuance from the verb καθίημι ("let fall, set in motion"). The same verbal form is found in *War* 1.411, 470; *Ant.* 3.53; 14.423. The reading καθίεις (the present participle of the same verb καθίημι; cf. *Ant.* 15.334, in which case most MSS read καθίεις) may have resulted from an assimilation to the first character (i.e., σ-) of the following word συνεχές. The reading καθίει εἰς of E (followed by Marcus-Wikgren 34) may be a correction of the reading καθίει since καθίημι is frequently followed by the preposition εἰς (LSJ *s.v.* 2-3).

[381] For Herod's affection (φιλοστοργία) for Mariamme, see *Ant.* 15.66 with the note to "affection for" and 15.84. The combination of εὔνοια and φιλοστοργία ("loyalty and affection") is conventional (for other passages in Josephus, see *Ant.* 4.273; 8.193; 16.21; cf. Polybius 22.20; Plutarch, *Mor.* [*Frat. amor.*] 489c; John Chrysostom, *Dav.* [PG 54.687]; *Hom. Jo.* [PG 59.469]).

[382] There is one further occurrence of the rare verb ἐξειρωνεύομαι ("ridicule," LSJ *s.v.*; Rengstorf *s.v.*) in Josephus: *Ant.* 15.219, which concerns Mariamme.

[383] The adverb γυναικείως (literally "womanly," Rengstorf *s.v.*) suggests that women are capable of a typical kind of sarcasm. Remarks in the margin contribute to the stereotypical and negative image of women in Josephus (see also the next paragraph and the *adagium* "women cannot be trusted" of which Alexander accuses his wife Glaphyra in her dream, *Ant.* 17.352). Further discussion in Sievers 1989; Mayer-Schärtel 1995: 358-74; Brenner 2003.

[384] In *Ant.* 15.68 Josephus mentions only Mariamme as Joseph's conversation partner, but the narrative implies that mother and daughter again operated as a pair (cf. 15.31). The continuation of the sentence focuses on Alexandra, suggesting that she took the lead in ridiculing Joseph.

[385] Joseph's great efforts to persuade the women are comical and tragic at the same time: the women's reaction is the opposite of what he seems to have expected, and his attempt ultimately leads to his own execution (*Ant.* 15.87). The verb ὑπερσπουδάζω ("be over-jealous," Rengstorf *s.v.*) is a *hapax legomenon* in Josephus.

[386] This refers to Herod's secret order to Joseph (*Ant.* 15.65).

[387] The phrase πίστιν ποιέω ("make assurances, pledge," LSJ *s.v.* πίστις II.1; Lindsay 1993) is conventional (cf. Philo, *Decal.* 172; *Spec.* 1.70). It is highly ambiguous in this context because the narratees may wonder whether Joseph's confession reveals the opposite of what he tries to convince Mariamme and Alexandra of. This is indeed the conclusion to which the women come according to the next paragraph.

[388] I.e., Mariamme. The romantic cliché is rather cynical in light of Herod's order. For similar vocabulary (οὐ χωρὶς αὐτοῦ ζῆν δύναται), see Stobaeus 4.19.47 concerning Diogenes (cf. Plutarch, *Mor.* [*Inim. util.*] 86e).

[389] The phrase θανάτῳ διαζευχθῆναι ("be separated [from her] through death"; cf. Gregory of Nyssa, *Vit. Macr.* 35.20 [ed. Maraval 256]; Theodoretus, *Int. ep. Paul.* [PG 82.273]) echoes Josephus' vocabulary in the parallel passage of *War* (1.441): "Joseph, however, revealed the secret not at all out of malice, but rather out of a desire to give proof to the woman of the king's love for her, since not even in death could he endure to be separated from her (ὡς οὐδὲ ἀποθανὼν αὐτῆς ὑπομένοι διαζευχθῆναι)" (trans. Sievers/Forte in BJP 1a).

It is interesting to compare Herod's case with the idea elaborated by Plutarch in connection with the suicides of Antony and Cleopatra described in the *Life of Antony*: a marital relationship should be prolonged in death, burial, and afterlife. When Antony was making preparations for his suicide, after he had lost his final battle at Alexandria and had heard about Cleopatra's apparent suicide, he said: "O Cleopatra, I am not grieved to be bereft of thee, for I shall straightway join thee; but I am grieved that such an imperator as I am has found to be inferior to a woman" (*Ant.* 76.3, trans. Perrin). After this statement he drove his sword through his belly and died considerably later, after he had been brought to Cleopatra in her tomb (*Ant.* 76-77). Cleopatra committed suicide after having poured libations for Antony and having embraced his

something terrible.³⁹⁰ That was what Joseph said. **70** Yet the women,³⁹¹ as was to be expected,³⁹² did not grasp³⁹³ the affection³⁹⁴ of Herod's disposition to them but the cruelty of it: if he should die, they would not escape destruction and a tyrannical death.³⁹⁵ So they considered the deeper sense of what was said to be cruel.³⁹⁶

(3.7) 71 At this time³⁹⁷ a story turned up in the city of the Jerusalemites that Antony

---

urn, during which she said: "Do not expect other honours or libations; these are the last from Cleopatra the captive. For though in life nothing could part us from each other, in death we are likely to change places; thou, the Roman, lying buried here, while I the hapless woman, lie in Italy, and get only so much of thy country as my portion. But if indeed there is any might or power in the gods of that country (for the gods of this country have betrayed us), do not abandon thine own wife while she lives, nor permit a triumph to be celebrated over thyself in my person, but hide and bury me here with thyself, since out of all my innumerable ills not one is so great and dreadful as this short time I have lived apart from thee (σοῦ χωρὶς ἔζησα)" (*Ant.* 84.3-4, trans. Perrin). The Society of Partners in Death (ἡ συναποθανουμένων ἐκάλουν), a drinking and feasting society founded by Antony and Cleopatra after the Battle of Actium (*Ant.* 71), hints at their simultaneous death as well. Plutarch briefly reports that Antony and Cleopatra were buried together (*Ant.* 86; further discussion and references in Brenk 1992a: 4393-4402; 1992b: 163, 165, 172). The comparison with Plutarch's description highlights Herod's self-centered and brutal thinking according to Josephus' presentation: he pre-empts any volition on Mariamme's part, by ordering her death. In case he died, Mariamme had to die as well, as if she were his property.

³⁹⁰ The conjunction εἰ ("if") and the verb πάσχω ("suffer") echo the vocabulary of *Ant.* 15.65.

³⁹¹ The phrasing of the last short sentence of *Ant.* 15.69 and of the beginning of the first sentence of this paragraph highlights (cf. μὲν ... δέ) the contrast between Joseph's attempt to persuade the women of Herod's love for Mariamme and the women's interpretation of his words.

³⁹² Josephus' brief comment may focus on Alexandra and Mariamme's common sense that Herod's instruction was obviously cruel. The comment may also have a negative nuance, suggesting that women usually focus on the negative aspects of something (cf. Josephus' phrase "in the way women usually do" [*Ant.* 15.69] and its relevant note).

The phrase ὡς εἰκός ("as was to be expected") is used 15 times in Josephus, and the distribution is telling: 2 occurrences in War (3.1, 504), and the other 13 occurrences concern *Ant.*; of those 13, 10 are in the Herod narrative in *Ant.* 15-16, the next occurrence coming already in the next section (15.71; see also 7.44; 15.130, 167, 168, 209, 234; 16.286, 306; 19.293; 20.94). The words are not evenly distributed in *Ant.* 15-16; 4 of the 10 occurrences are in 2 clusters (15.70-71 and 15.167-68). In *War*, by contrast, Josephus uses this fixed phrase only twice (*War* 3.1, 504), preferring other forms such as ὡς ἔοικε(ν): *War* 1.392, 593, 609; 5.154, 558; 7.359, as also in *Apion* 2.124 (in his own voice). These data might imply that Josephus took over this vocabulary from a source (Nicolaus of Damascus), but repeating vocabulary in close proximity is typical of Josephus' style elsewhere (see Shutt [1961:74-5] and Mason's introduction to *Life* in BJP 9 [pp. li-liii]).

³⁹³ The translation follows the reading προλαμβάνουσαι (literally "assuming in advance") with Niese (344). The alternative reading προσλαμβάνουσαι ("believing") of MSS LAMW (supported by the Latin version) is the easier and therefore the secondary reading, which simply evolved from the other reading by the addition of an σ after προ-.

³⁹⁴ The vocabulary (φιλόστοργον "affection") echoes that of *Ant.* 15.66, 68.

³⁹⁵ "A tyrannical death" probably means a death caused by a tyrant, which implies that Mariamme and Alexandra associate Herod's decision with that of a cruel tyrant. The passage is part of a cluster of brief hints in *Antiquities* at Herod ruling and behaving like a tyrant (see also *Ant.* 14.165; 15.7-8, 222, 321, 353-354; 16.4, 363; 17.66-67, 148, 164, 304-314; van Henten 2011b). In the parallel passage of *War* (1.441-443) there is no hint whatsoever that Herod was a tyrant.

³⁹⁶ The follow-up of Mariamme and Alexandra's response to Joseph's disclosure is described in *Ant.* 15.74-87. The narrative first continues with the story about the rumor of Herod's death (15.71-73), set in the same period (see the next note). The parallel passage in *War* mentions Herod's return and then reports Mariamme's response to Herod's boasting of his love for her in rather cynical terms (1.442), after which the narrative describes in an extremely brief way that Herod lost control of himself because of his anger and jealousy and that he immediately ordered the executions of both Mariamme and Joseph (1.443; cf. *Ant.* 15.85-87, 223-239). *War* sets Mariamme's execution within Antony's rule (1.441), but that raises questions (see *Ant.* 15.236-237 with notes and Richardson 1996: 218 n. 8).

³⁹⁷ This expression (ἐν δὲ τούτῳ) is one of Josephus' formulae to introduce a parallel story that is synchronized

had tortured and killed him [Herod].[398] It came from those who hated Herod.[399] This rumor troubled all of the people in the palace,[400] as was to be expected,[401] but especially the women. **72** Alexandra tried to persuade Joseph to leave the palace with them[402] and flee for refuge to the troops[403] of the Roman legion[404] that were under the command of Julius.[405] (They were camping near the city at that time in order to protect the monarchy.)[406] **73** For

---

with a previous story (*War* 1.261, 288, 309; 2.55, 284, 533; 3.414; 4.440, 550, 570, 633; 5.460; 6.149, 229; *Ant.* 13.330, 353; 14.29, 86, 418; 15.88, 121; 17.79, 206, 264; 18.109; 19.24, 158; van Henten and Huitink 2007: 225-27). It is probably a short hand version of ἐν δὲ τούτῳ τῷ καιρῷ (*Ant.* 16.6) or ἐν τούτῳ τῷ χρόνῳ (12.156; cf. 19.360), having the same meaning. The new story here is, however, closely related with the previous one because Herod's death implied that Mariamme had to be executed (see 15.65, 69), such that the situation became very dangerous for the women.

[398] The context implies that execution would have been Herod's punishment if Antony had declared him guilty of Aristobulus' murder (see especially *Ant.* 15.65-66), which is not self-evident, because killing off rivals even in one's family was quite common among rulers, not least among the Romans. The point of the rumor, torture followed by execution, is highly implausible from this perspective. Herod's father Antipater was a Roman citizen (*Ant.* 14.137), and Herod had inherited the Roman citizenship. Roman citizens were not tortured during the Late Republic and Early Empire, except in cases of high treason (Garnsey 1970: 141-47).

[399] This statement implies that the rumor was false, which the continuation of the narrative confirms. About Herod's possible enemies, see *Ant.* 15.2 with the note to "his opponents."

[400] The context implies that it must concern a palace of Herod in Jerusalem. This was probably the Hasmonean royal palace, which Herod used before he constructed his own splendid palace to the west of the Temple Mount (see *Ant.* 15.248 with notes and Mahieu 2012: 158-165 about the date of construction of this palace). See also 15.43 with the note to "the palace" and 15.247 with the note to "the citadels in the city." Josephus describes Herod's own palace in *War* 5.176-181 (further discussion in Netzer 2006: 129-32).

[401] Obviously the consternation about the death of the king must have been great among the members of the family, the king's friends, and the other persons at the court since the consequences of a change of government would be enormous (cf. *Ant.* 15.24, 57; 17.184).

[402] This is an extraordinary request in light of Joseph's double task: Joseph not only replaced Herod as supreme administrator of the kingdom, but was also the supervisor of the 2 women (Schalit 2001: 119). Alexandra's proposal was extremely risky from the perspective of Herod's secret order and is only plausible if one assumes that Joseph had taken the side of the women (as argued by Wellhausen 1914: 319-20, who assumes that Joseph was executed by Herod for this reason). However, Otto (1913: 41-42) argues that it is plausible that Joseph remained loyal to Herod and that the safest option for the women was indeed to flee to the Romans (see the next notes) because there was still severe opposition to Herod as king. He also argues that Alexandra and Mariamme would have maintained the friendly relationship with the Romans after Herod's death (see also Schalit 2001: 117-18 and 15.73 with the note to "some disturbance"). There was no immediate need to flee if Joseph had taken the side of the women since he would not have executed Herod's order in that case. All in all, the story about the rumor of Herod's death and the response by Alexandra raises several questions about its plausibility. Nevertheless, Schalit (2001: 116-19) considers the tradition to be authentic and assumes that there were disturbances directed against Herod and the Romans. In that case, Joseph would have done the right thing by bringing the women to the Roman legion.

[403] An alternative translation would be "to the standards" (Marcus-Wikgren 35; Meijer-Wes 3.161) because σημεῖον can mean "signal for battle, flag, standard" in addition to a body of soldiers (LSJ *s.v.* 3 and 4b).

[404] A Roman legion was apparently stationed in or near Jerusalem, probably in order to support Herod in his early years as friendly king, when his position was not completely secure (Otto 1913: 41-42; Stern 1974b: 227; Shatzman 1991: 168; Schalit 2001: 117-19).

[405] Niese (345) reads ἡγουμένου υἱοῦ ἰούδα with MSS PF and marginal readings in MSS AM, which implies a translation like "under the command of a son of Juda." This reading would strenghten the motive for Alexandra and Mariamme's decision to flee to the Roman troops: they would be even safer under the wings of a Jewish commander of the troops. However, it is extremely unlikely that a Jew was the commander of a Roman legion. The reading ἡγουμένου Ἰουλίου ("under the command of Julius") of MSS LAMW (supported by the Latin version) is therefore to be preferred. There is no further information about this Julius (Marcus-Wikgren 36 n. *b*).

[406] Braund (1984: 94) refers to the anonymous work *Bellum Alexandrinum* (33) and notes that a Roman

Letter from Herod reports about his visit to Antony.

because of this [plan],[407] she said, they would in the first place remain safer—because the Romans were friendly to them[408]—in case some disturbance[409] would occur in connection to the palace.[410] In the second place they would get everything they had hoped for[411] if Antony saw Mariamme,[412] and through him they would receive the rule again[413] and not lack anything that is expected for persons of royal birth.[414]

(3.8) 74 While they were busy with these thoughts, a letter[415] from Herod arrived about everything.[416] It countered the rumor as well as what had been spoken of before.[417] **75** For when he had come to Antony,[418] he quickly won him over with the gifts[419] from Jerusalem he was carrying with him, and also quickly changed his opinion during meetings,[420] such

---

garrison could function as a check on friendly kings. Shatzman (1991: 168) argues that the legion was stationed near Jerusalem in order to secure Herod's kingdom against the antagonism his rule provoked (see also the note to "leave the palace with them" above).

[407] Niese (345; followed by Marcus-Wikgren 36) conjectures διὰ γὰρ τούτου ("for through this [force]"), but this is unnecessary since the reading διὰ γὰρ τοῦτο ("for on this account") of the MSS is common (LSJ *s.v.* διά B III.2).

[408] Obviously the Roman legion would protect the members of the family of the friendly king (see *Ant.* 15.72 with the note to "protect the monarchy").

[409] The noun ταραχή ("disturbance") echoes the verb ἐτάραξεν ("troubled") found in *Ant.* 15.71. Josephus does not specify the disturbance, but it is plausibly related to Herod's enemies who were responsible for spreading the rumor about Herod's death (see 15.71 with the note to "those who hated Herod").

[410] In addition to "court" and "court yard" αὐλή sometimes means "palace" (Rengstorf *s.v.*; see, e.g., *Ant.* 15.292; Mark 14:54; 15:16).

[411] This passage and its continuation indicate again that Alexandra had the ambition to end Herod's rule and restore the Hasmonean house as ruler of the Judean kingdom (see also *Ant.* 15.32, 42, 47, and cf. 15.35). This could imply that Joseph was involved in the planned coup, which would explain his execution (15.87; see also 15.72 with the note to "leave the palace with them").

[412] Like *Ant.* 15.68 this passage reminds one of 15.26-28, about Dellius' proposal to Alexandra to send portraits of Aristobulus and Mariamme over to Antony (note the repetition of θεασαμένου ["if he would see"] with Antony as subject, 15.26, 73). *Ant.* 15.28 implies that Antony had already seen Mariamme's portrait.

[413] Taking away the throne from Herod (similar vocabulary in *Ant.* 16.295 concerning Syllaeus) implied a restoration of the Hasmonean rule.

[414] This concluding statement confirms Alexandra's previous remark and may also be connected with her repeated complaint that Herod did not treat her family the way its royal status required (see *Ant.* 15.23-24, 44-45, 62).

[415] The plural τὰ γράμματα can have several meanings, including "the documents," "the scriptures," "the correspondence," but also "the letter" in the singular (Rengstorf *s.v.* γράμμα). The latter meaning seems most plausible in the context here.

[416] Josephus' rendering of this letter (*Ant.* 15.74-79) focuses on Herod's acquittal and the relationship with his patron Antony. In 15.79 the letter anticipates Herod's complicated power struggle with Cleopatra, which is an important theme in the subsequent narrative. The letter, therefore, fits the narrative context well; at the same time it marks a switch of perspective: Herod can be taken as the main focalizer in 15.74-79, instead of Alexandra, who is the main focalizer in the previous section (15.62-73).

[417] The passage refers to *Ant.* 15.71 through the repetition of φήμη ("rumor"). The reading προλαληθέντων ("[the things] stated before," Niese 345) is without parallel in Josephus; yet it links up with λόγος ("story") in 15.71. The variant reading προληφθέντων ("anticipated") of MSS LAMW is also found (though in different grammatical cases) in *War* 4.385; 5.79. It is the *lectio facilior* and can easily have evolved from προλαληθέντων by contraction (λαλη—λη) and the addition of a φ.

[418] For the possible location of this meeting, see *Ant.* 15.64 with the note to "Laodicea." The continuation of the narrative implies that Cleopatra was also present.

[419] This is what one would expect of a friendly king; repetitive gifts were an important dimension in the relationship between a friendly king and his patron, especially at moments when it was appropriate to confirm the relationship (see *Ant.* 15.5 with the note to "a gift to Antony"). It is plausible that Antony acquitted Herod not because he thought that the king was innocent, but because Herod did what a friendly king was supposed to do: maintaining order and providing significant gifts to his patron (Braund 1984: 67).

[420] With the repetition of ταχύ ("quickly") Josephus emphasizes that Herod was successful in his mission soon after his arrival. He indicates 2 strategies used by Herod: gifts (see the previous note) and personal contact during meetings. The latter means links up with other

BOOK FIFTEEN 53

that [Antony] would not think sternly about him. Cleopatra's words[421] meant little in comparison to the favors[422] coming from Herod. **76** For Antony said that it was not appropriate to demand of a king public examinations[423] concerning the events of his rule since in that case he would not be a king at all.[424] People who give offices and deem persons worthy of authority should allow them to use it.[425] At the same time he said to Cleopatra that it would be better for her if she did not interfere[426] in the matters of governance.[427] **77** Herod wrote about these things and went over the other honors he had received from Antony in great detail. He was a partner in [Antony's] juridical decisions[428] and feasted with him every day.[429] He also wrote that[430] he had gained these honors despite Cleopatra's giving him a hard time with her accusations against him.[431] Cleopatra desired his country and demanded that his kingdom would be added to hers,[432] zealously pursuing

---

passages in which Josephus describes how Herod made an extremely good impression on his superiors (see, e.g., *War* 1.282; *Ant.* 15.187-194).

[421] The passage refers to Cleopatra's accusation of Herod in *Ant.* 15.63 (see also 15.65, 77, 97-98).

[422] The noun θεραπεία means "favor" or "paying court" here and in *War* 1.554 (which also refers to gifts); *Ant.* 15.199, 204, 328 (LSJ *s.v.* I.2).

[423] A relationship between a friendly king and his Roman patron was not only based on mutual beneficiality, but also on mutual trust (πίστις) and loyalty (εὔνοια), as the section on Herod's meeting with Octavian after the Battle of Actium and the follow-up of this meeting points out (15.187-201; see especially 15.193-194, 201 with notes). The particular relationship between Herod and Augustus remained intact as long as the king did not exceed his authority, which he did in Augustus' opinion when he launched a punitive expedition against the Nabateans (16.271-293).

Since there was no conclusive evidence that Herod was responsible for Aristobulus' murder, Antony could easily acquit Herod. Cf. *War* 1.361, in which passage Josephus states (though the precise context is unclear because of the Greek) that in response to Cleopatra's plan to have Herod and the Nabatean king Malichus killed Antony "thought that it would be a sacrilege to kill respectable men and kings of such importance ..." (trans. Sievers/Forte in BJP 1a).

The word εὔθυνα ("account") is a *hapax legomenon* in Josephus.

[424] This is implicit criticism of Cleopatra; a little farther along in the paragraph Antony explicitly indicates that Cleopatra should not interfere in the matters of Herod's kingdom.

[425] The sentence basically repeats the preceding statement but with a positive formulation, which is a rhetorical device of repetition (Lausberg 1998: 372-73, 376-77).

[426] The verb πολυπραγμονέω ("be busy about many things," or pejoratively "meddle in state affairs, intrigue," LSJ *s.v.* 2b) occurs 11 times in Josephus and only in *Antiquities* (e.g., 15.165, 285; 16.96).

[427] The passage suggests once again that Cleopatra did not always succeed in getting from Antony what she wanted (see also the previous paragraph with notes). It might also imply that the queen had better not interfere in Antony's political and administrative affairs, which, perhaps, reflects a criticism of Cleopatra from a Roman perspective by assuming that Cleopatra ruined Antony because she interfered to much in his affairs. It is, however, also possible to interpret the words "the matters of governance" as a refererence only to the matters of Herod's kingdom. In any case, Antony closely co-operated with Cleopatra in several of his endeavors and needed her military support, especially when his relationship with Octavian became openly hostile (Buchheim 1960: 22-25, 37-38, 68-74, 85-97).

[428] Hudson's conjecture συνθακῶν ("sit with, be a partner in," LSJ *s.v.* συνθακέω) is taken over by Niese (346). LSJ (*s.v.* συνθωκέω) notes that the reading συνθωκῶν given by MSS FAM has the same meaning as συνθακῶν. The reading συνθηκῶν ("conventions, treaties," the genitive plural of συνθήκη, LSJ *s.v.*), attested by MSS PLWE, must have resulted from a scribal error, which is easily understandable given that this form is much more common in Greek literature and occurs 7 times in Josephus. The rare participle συνθακῶν occurs in Euripides (*Heraclidae* 994) in a different context.

[429] Feasting together and participating in a Roman official's judicial decisions were part of the activities of a ruler's friends (see *Ant.* 15.5 with the note to "the friends around him" and 15.31; about banquets of Hellenistic rulers and Roman emperors in general, see Vössing 2004). Having a banquet was one of the ways a ruler could reward a friendly king (Braund 1984: 83).

[430] Most MSS (supported by the Latin version) read ὅμως ("all the same, nevertheless") instead of ὅπως as introduction of this indirect speech (Niese 346).

[431] The Greek echoes *Ant.* 15.28. On Cleopatra's accusations, see also 15.63, 75 with notes.

[432] Buchheim (1960: 71) argues that Cleopatra

every possible means to get him out of the way.[433] **78** Nevertheless, finding that Antony was just, he did not expect any further unpleasantness[434] and he even expected to come home soon,[435] after having received the confirmation from him[436] that his benevolence[437] towards his throne and the matters of his kingdom had become [even] stronger.[438] **79** And Cleopatra could no longer cherish any hope of satisfying her greed,[439] since Antony had given her Coele-Syria[440] instead of what she had asked for.[441] In this way he had assuaged her and at the same time finished the conversations she kept on having with him about Judea.[442]

---

requested Judea and Nabatea from Antony in 36 BCE and that he refused because she had already received several territories in 37 BCE (see *Ant.* 15.79, 94-95 with notes). This and Josephus' other reports of Cleopatra's interferences with Judean politics (15.32, 45, 48, 62-63) imply that the queen was consistently trying to incorporate Judea in her territory, although this is the first explicit statement that Cleopatra wanted to take over Judea from Herod (see also 15.79, 88, 92).

[433] *Ant.* 15.97-98 hints at Cleopatra's strategy to have Herod executed on the accusation of having raped her. For the expression ἐκποδὼν ποιεῖσθαι ("get [someone] out of the way"), see 15.20 with the note to "get him out of the way," also 15.231 with the note to "out of the way."

[434] For the combination of προσδοκάω ("expect") and δυσχερές ("unpleasant"), cf. *Ant.* 15.238.

[435] The phrase introduces the conclusion of the letter, which focuses on additional information about Antony and Cleopatra, who were the key persons during Herod's trip.

[436] I.e., Antony.

[437] The noun εὔνοια can also mean "loyalty" in connection with a close relationship between a patron and his client (see *Ant.* 15.193 with the note to "loyalty to him").

[438] The expression βεβαιοτέραν τὴν εὔνοιαν ("his benevolence ... had become stronger") is paralleled by Isocrates, *Demon.* 36.

[439] The Greek in *Ant.* 15.79 is ambiguous and can be translated by "hope for a greater advantage" or "hope of satisfying her greediness." The latter translation matches Josephus' depiction of Cleopatra in other passages (see, e.g., 15.89-90, and for the queen's alleged greediness, 15.90).

[440] The name "Coele-Syria" ("Hollow Syria") is ambiguous because in Herod's time it refers to different areas, including the kingdom of Chalcis (see *Ant.* 15.92 with the note to "Lysanias, the son of Ptolemy") and the region between Mt Lebanon and the Anti-Lebanon, which traditionally carried the name "Hollow Syria" (e.g., Strabo, *Geogr.* 16.2.16). Coele-Syria can also refer to all of southern Syria, including Judea, from the Libanon/Bekaa Valley to the south. The Ptolemies and Seleucids used this name for the contested region of southern Syria (Polybius 5.34.5; 5.42.5-9; 86.1-7; 8.17.11; 16.22a.2; 23.2.4; 28.1.1-5). Strabo, in fact, mentions two meanings: the Bekaa Valley (properly, see above) or all of the south (referring also to the Jordan and Lake Gennesareth, 16.2.16). He adds that many people divide all of Syria (i.e., the Phoenician and Palestinian coasts with their *hinterland*) into 3 areas: those of the Syrians, the Phoenicians (on the coast), and Coele-Syria, with 4 ethnic groups (Judeans, Gazans, Azotians and Idumeans, Strabo, *Geogr.* 16.2.21-3.1). Josephus (*War* 1.155-157) says that Pompey took away the Hasmonean-conquered cities from Coele-Syria and gave them back. These cities (reading the opening of 1.155 as a topic sentence for the whole paragraph) are all of the internal and coastal cities of southern Syria. "Coele-Syria" sometimes refers to the Decapolis area and the Hauran region (see *Ant.* 15.112). Schalit (2001: 775-77) and Buchheim (1960: 100-01 n. 28) argue that Josephus usually intends the latter region, which may have included the city of Damascus (see also Bickerman 1947; Kasher 1988: 144; Richardson 1996: 70 n. 74; Nodet 2005: 139, and for the later period, Millar 1993b: 121-23).

The *Antiquities* narrative differs from Josephus' presentation in *War* because 15.79 may imply that there had already been a grant of territories (i.e., "Coele-Syria") by Antony to Cleopatra before the region of Jericho and the cities between the river Eleutherus and Egypt were granted to the queen (*War* 1.361, paralleled by *Ant.* 15.95-96) and that Antony had tried to satisfy Cleopatra by giving her Coele-Syria instead of Judea. If there actually was a separate first grant to Cleopatra, it may have concerned the kingdom of Chalcis (Marcus-Wikgren 38 n. *a*; cf. Richardson 1996: 165 n. 62), or the kingdom of Chalcis with the Decapolis and Damascus (Schalit 2001: 775). For further discussion and references, see *Ant.* 15.92-96 with notes.

[441] The context clearly implies that Cleopatra wanted to get the kingdom of Judea from Antony (see *Ant.* 15.77 "... Cleopatra desired his country ..." and the end of this paragraph).

[442] See *Ant.* 15.63, 77, 92.

(3.9) 80 When this letter was delivered,[443] they [the women][444] stopped the effort they were making to flee and take refuge with the Romans[445] because they believed Herod was dead.[446] However, their [former] plan did not remain a secret.[447] For when the king returned to Judea, after he had escorted Antony to the Parthians,[448] his sister Salome[449] and his mother[450] immediately indicated to him the intention[451] Alexandra and her associates[452] had harbored. **81** Salome also gave an account against her husband Joseph,[453] accusing[454] him

Return of Herod. Salome accuses Joseph of being intimate with Mariamme.
War 1.442-443

---

[443] A similar phrase (τῶν γραμμάτων ... ἀπενεχθέντων) is found in *Ant.* 16.358 (see the note to "letter") concerning Augustus' letter about Herod's options for dealing with his sons Alexander and Aristobulus IV.

[444] The continuation of the sentence clearly refers to Alexandra and Mariamme I (cf. *Ant.* 15.72).

[445] The vocabulary echoes that of *Ant.* 15.72 (see the previous note), although close parallels are absent.

[446] This links up with the rumor that Antony had killed Herod (*Ant.* 15.71).

[447] The rare combination of the verb λανθάνω ("escape notice") and προαίρεσις ("plan") also occurs in *Ant.* 13.8, 176, but there προαίρεσις is object instead of subject (see also Polybius 3.11.1, 12.5).

[448] Escorting Antony or Octavian for part of their campaigns was an obvious tribute from Herod as friendly king (see also *Ant.* 15.199-201, and cf. 15.96, 168). Antony undertook a campaign against the Parthians in 36 BCE (Halfmann 2011: 153-61) because he wanted to get back the Roman standards and captives that the Parthians had been keeping since their victory over Crassus in 53 BCE (Plutarch, *Ant.* 37.2; Cassius Dio 49.24.5; Buchheim 1960: 39). The Armenian king Artabazes-Artavasdes, who may have played a double role during Antony's attempt to retrieve the standards, advised him to take a northern route through Media. Antony followed up this advice, but the journey turned out to be a disaster: Antony's baggage train with heavy siege instruments was captured by the Parthians, and his offer of a peace treaty to the Parthian king Phraates IV was rejected. Thanks to his great military skills Antony still managed to retreat and save two thirds of his army, but his reputation of being invincible was ruined forever (Ziegler 1964: 35-36; Huzar 1978: 175-79). In 35 BCE Antony prepared for a new campaign against Parthia (see *Ant.* 15.64 with the note to "Laodicea"), but he did not carry it through. In 34 BCE he launched a campaign against Armenia (see 15.96 with the note to "Armenia").

[449] Salome is mentioned ca. 40 times as Herod's sister in Josephus (explicitly in *War* 1.441, 443, 566, 646, 660; *Ant.* 15.223, 254; 16.8; 17.93, 147, 175, 189, 220; 18.31). She appears to have been extremely well-informed and did not hesitate to enlighten Herod if that would suit her (*War* 1.570, 573; *Ant.* 17.38, 44). Josephus characterizes her as a companion most loyal to Herod (Mayer-Schärtel 1995: 193) and a shrewd schemer against Mariamme and her sons (*War* 1.446, 475-480, 483, 534; *Ant.* 15.81, 223, 231; 16.8, 66-74, 193, 201-205; cf. *War* 1.641-644; *Ant.* 16.226; 17.38, 137-140, 142, 220). Schalit (2001: 571) concludes on the basis of Josephus' portrayal of Salome that she actually was a most hateful and unscrupulously murderous person. For further references about Salome, see Kokkinos 1998: 177-205; Ilan 1999: 115-26.

[450] Apparently Salome and Herod's mother Cyprus (see *Ant.* 15.184 with the note to "his mother Cyprus") had found out about Alexandra and Mariamme's plan, which implies not only that the court was a kind of snake pit, but also that there were 2 factions among the women at the court: "Hasmoneans" around Alexandra and Mariamme (cf. the reference to "Alexandra and her associates" [οἱ περὶ τὴν Ἀλεξάνδραν] further on in this paragraph), and "Herodians," whose most prominent members must have been Salome and Cyprus (van Henten 2010).

[451] The rare combination of ἀποσημαίνω ("indicate") with διάνοια ("thought, purpose") as object occurs 3 times elsewhere in Josephus (*Ant.* 17.186, 344; 18.302).

[452] For references on Alexandra's role as intrigante, see *Ant.* 15.23 with the note to "Alexandra."

[453] *War* 1.443 reports a similar accusation (though Joseph is first described in rather positive terms; see 1.441): Herod assumes that Joseph had seduced Mariamme.

Niese (346) indicates that there is a lacuna in the Greek text here: Joseph has been mentioned several times in the preceding narrative (*Ant.* 15.65-73; see 15.65 with the note to "his uncle Joseph"), but—apart from 14.122; 15.80—Salome has not. This absence raises the question what had happened such that Salome accused her husband. The continuation of the narrative helps to resolve this (although the reader should be aware that Josephus' hints may be biased and that he may even have invented the entire story; see 15.87 with the note to "he ordered Joseph to be killed"): even if Joseph had had no sexual relationship with Mariamme (see the next note), he obviously had become too intimate with her for Salome's taste, as she considered Mariamme and the other Hasmoneans to be her enemies (see also 15.80 with the note to "his sister Salome"). Mayer-Schärtel (1995: 195-96) argues that Salome's accusation of Joseph served Herod's political interests: Joseph's

of continuing to see[455] Mariamme. And she said these things because she had been angry with her[456] for a long time; for she [Mariamme] showed a great arrogance[457] in their hostilities and kept reproaching[458] their low birth.[459] **82** Herod was always hot-headed[460] about Mariamme and loved her terribly.[461] So immediately he was greatly disturbed[462] and could not bear having a rival.[463] Yet he continued to control himself[464] not to do anything

---

guilt enabled the accusation against Mariamme.

[454] The order of the events is different in *War*: Herod finds out about the close relationship between Joseph and Mariamme through the latter (1.442; likewise *Ant.* 15.85-87), and only afterwards Salome seizes the opportunity to launch her accusations against Mariamme and Joseph (1.443). Here Salome accuses only Joseph, her husband.

Other references to accusations by Salome including the noun διαβολή ("slander, [false] accusation," Rengstorf *s.v.*) or the verb διαβάλλω ("accuse, reproach, speak slanderously," Rengstorf *s.v.*) are found in *War* 1.443; *Ant.* 15.213. See also *Ant.* 15.229 with the note to "in line with the slanders."

[455] The verb συγγίγνομαι followed by a reference to a woman is ambiguous: it can simply mean "see/converse with a woman," but it can also have the sexual connotation of "have intercourse with" (LSJ *s.v.* II.1 and 3; Rengstorf *s.v.*). The latter reading is supported by the continuation of the narrative (*Ant.* 15.86-87). This would imply that Joseph and Mariamme had committed adultery, which is a capital crime according to the Law (Exod 20:14; Lev 20:10; Deut 5:28; 22:20-30), with stoning as the usual punishment (Lev 20:10; Ezek 16:38-40; cf. John 8:5, and also *War* 1.438-439 about Salome and Cyprus accusing Mariamme of adultery). The combination of διατελέω with a participle ("continue to ...") is common, but the participle should be in the present tense (Rijksbaron 2002: 112; see the reading of E) instead of the aorist.

[456] The phrase χαλεπῶς ἔχειν πρός plus a personal object ("be angry with/hostile to," Rengstorf *s.v.*) also occurs in *Ant.* 7.186; 13.195; 14.404; 16.267.

[457] Salome's criticism of Mariamme matches Josephus' characterization of Mariamme (see *Ant.* 15.237-238 with notes). The phrase φρόνημα μεῖζον ("proud spirit"), here with a pejorative connotation, also occurs in Euripides, *Suppl.* 862; Xenophon, *Anab.* 3.1.22; Dionysius, *Ant. rom.* 7.34.1; 19.18.7; Philo, *Ios.* 4; *Somn.* 1.140; Plutarch, *Lys.* 18.2.

[458] The verb ἐξονειδίζω ("reproach") occurs once elsewhere in Josephus (*War* 6.124).

[459] Actually, Herod and Salome's father Antipater was one of the most prominent persons in Judea, and their mother Cyprus descended from a distinguished Nabatean family, possibly even the royal family (Kokkinos 1998: 95 with n. 37). The decisive point for Mariamme and her mother Alexandra, as presented by Josephus, was that Herod and Salome were born as commoners (see *Ant.* 15.2 with the note to "commoner"), while Mariamme and her mother descended from the Hasmonaean royal family (cf. 15.220 with the note to "their low birth," the only other Josephan passage in which the noun δυσγένεια ["low birth"] occurs, Rengstorf *s.v.*). This theme seems to be connected with the motif of Alexandra attempting to replace Herod by a Hasmonaean ruler (see 15.32, 42, 62-63, 73).

[460] Cf. the characterization of Jeroboam as a hot-headed youth (φύσει θερμὸς ὢν νεανίας) in *Ant.* 8.209 (see also *War* 4.292; 5.491).

[461] This is one of several passages in *Antiquities* that highlight Herod's exceptional passion (ἔρως) for Mariamme (see also 15.65, 69, 204, 207, 209, 211, 214, 218, 238). *Ant.* 15.82-87 depicts this period in Herod and Mariamme's relationship in intimate and dramatic terms. *Ant.* 15.84 suggests that their love was mutual. For similar phrases with ἐρωτικῶς ("amorous"), see *Ant.* 1.337 (concerning Sikimon-Shechem's love for Dinah; Gen 34); 2.41 (about Mrs. Potiphar's love for Joseph; Gen 39); 11.195 (about Artaxerxes' love for Aste-Vashti; Esth 1); 12.162 (about Joseph the Tobiad's fondness of money). See also 15.84, 319.

[462] Herod's consternation is understandable in light of his passion for Mariamme (see the preceding note). The king's response to Salome and his mother's accusation against Mariamme ("he was greatly disturbed," ἐξετετάρακτο) is similar to his reaction in the much shorter *War* report (1.438-440): "This struck Herod like a thunderbolt and perturbed him (ἐτάραξεν) ..." (1.440, trans. Sievers/Forte in BJP 1a). Herod responds in a comparable way to Pheroras and Salome's accusation against his sons Aristobulus and Alexander that they would not leave their mother's execution unavenged (*Ant.* 16.75; cf. 16.78). For similar phrases with ταράσσω and related vocabulary referring to Herod, see *War* 1.328; *Ant.* 15.210, 223-224; 16.197, 208, 259, 261, 265, 385, and also *Ant.* 16.363 (ἀταρακτήσας). See also 15.24 referring to Alexandra, and 15.235 referring to Mariamme (and 15.71, 277). In both of Josephus' Herod narratives expressions with (ἐκ-)ταράσσω ("trouble, disturb") and related words occur, with the majority in *Antiquities*.

[463] This point links up with Herod's order to Joseph (see *Ant.* 15.65). *War* reports Salome and Cyprus' accusation against Mariamme directly before the narrative

rash[465] because of his love. With intense emotions, and provoked by his jealousy,[466] he questioned Mariamme in private about her affair with Joseph.[467] **83** She denied [the accusation] under oath and applied[468] every method that could help a woman who has not done anything wrong[469] to defend herself. So he let himself be persuaded bit by bit, and his angry mood changed.[470] Overcome by affection[471] for his wife, he even apologized[472] for having believed what he thought he had heard, and he offered many thanks[473] for her propriety.[474] **84** He kept recapitulating what love and affection[475] he felt for her. So, finally,

---

about Herod's trip to Antony and his order to Joseph. Herod is shocked by this accusation "because his passion made him jealous" (διὰ τὸν ἔρωτα ζηλοτύπως ἔχοντα, 1.440, trans. Sievers/Forte in BJP 1a). A little farther on, *War* uses the noun ζηλοτυπία in a sentence that reports the king's reaction to Salome's accusation of both Mariamme and Joseph: "Then, driven mad with sheer jealousy (ὑπ' ἀκράτου ζηλοτυπίας ἐκμανείς), he [i.e., Herod] ordered both of them to be put to death immediately" (1.443, trans. Sievers/Forte in BJP 1a). About ζηλοτυπία referring to the jealousy of husbands, see *Ant.* 3.271; 15.213 (also referring to Herod); 16.207; 20.149 (cf. 5.277 and Chariton 4.4.9; Achilles Tatius 6.11; Dio Chrystom 61.12).

[464] MSS LW read ἐπικρατούμενος δέει ("controlled himself for fear"; cf. *Ant.* 15.87 ἐκράτησεν ἑαυτοῦ) instead of ἐπικρατούμενος δ' ἀεὶ (literally "but he continuously controlled himself," Niese 346). Moments of severe anger occur earlier in the Herod narratives of both *War* and *Antiquities* (*War* 1.212, 214, 252, 320, 484, 507, 526, 565, 571, 654-655; *Ant.* 14.180, 436; 15.83, 211, 214, 229; 16.90, 199-200, 262, 366; 17.50, 69, 83, 191). The 2 works show, apart from a few exceptions (e.g., *War* 1.443; *Ant.* 15.299), that the king was usually capable of controlling and concealing his anger (see, e.g., *War* 1.320, 484; *Ant.* 17.50, 83; van Henten 2011b).

[465] *Ant.* 15.177 contains a similar phrase with προπετές and ποιέω ("do [something] rash"), concerning Hyrcanus II.

[466] See the note to "could not bear having a rival" above. The Greek (τῷ ζήλῳ παρωξυμμένος) may allude to Deut 32:19 (= Odes 2:19): "And the Lord saw it and was jealous (ἐζήλωσεν), and he was provoked (παρωξύνθη) on account of the wrath of his sons and daughters" (trans. *NETS*).

[467] See the next note on the different endings of this story in *War* and *Antiquities*.

[468] Literally "counted up everything." The verb καταλογίζομαι ("count up, calculate, present," Rengstorf *s.v.*) also occurs in *Ant.* 15.177 (in a similar context); 16.69, 75. Contrary to the parallel passage of *War* (1.443), in which Herod immediately gives orders to execute Mariamme and Joseph, the *Antiquities* narrative provides space for Mariamme's defense (for the probable date of Mariamme's death, see 15.237 with the note to "died this way" and van Henten 2010: 159-73).

[469] Josephus' vocabulary is slightly ambiguous because the abstract formulation leaves room for the interpretation that Mariamme had committed adultery. Nevertheless, the overall picture of Mariamme is positive: she defends herself as well as she can, and manages to persuade Herod, which is also a victory over Salome, who clearly tries to destroy Mariamme according to *Antiquities* (see, e.g., 15.80-81; van Henten 2010).

[470] This fits in with the general picture about Herod managing to control his anger (see *Ant.* 15.82 with the note to "controlled himself"; differently 15.211). Compare with the very different presentation in *War* 1.443.

[471] On Herod's affection (φιλοστοργία) for Mariamme, see *Ant.* 15.66 with the note to "great affection for" and 15.68 with the note to "loyalty and affection." For the combination of φιλοστοργία and a passive voice of ἡττάομαι ("be overcome"), see John Chrysostom, *Hom. Gen.* (PG 54.467).

[472] Mariamme's defense is so successful that Herod and his wife almost reverse roles: the verb ἀπολογεῖσθαι ("apologize") links up with the noun ἀπολογία ("defense") a few lines earlier (i.e., "defend herself"), referring to Mariamme.

[473] The phrase χάριν ὁμολογέω ("offer thanks, express gratitude," Rengstorf *s.v.*) is common in ancient Greek writings, also in Josephus (*Ant.* 2.162; 5.13, 30; 8.112; 9.270; 15.83; 16.61; 17.201; *Life* 143).

[474] The rare expression κοσμιότης means "proper behavior, decorum" in connection with sexual behavior (LSJ *s.v.*; Rengstorf *s.v.*; Mayer-Schärtel 1995: 191). It is usually associated with σωφροσύνη ("self-control," Plato, *Alc. mai.* 122c; *Gorg.* 508a; Philo, *Fug.* 33, 154; *Ios.* 40; *Somn.* 1.124; *Spec.* 3.51; Josephus, *Ant.* 2.59) and sometimes also with εὐταξία ("discipline," Diogenes Laertius 7.126).

[475] The combination of στοργή ("love") and εὔνοια ("goodwill, affection") also occurs in *Ant.* 4.134, which is part of the speech of the Midianite women to the Israelite young men who were seduced by them (Num 25). See also *Ant.* 15.68 with the note to "loyalty and affection," and for στοργή referring to the relationship between Herod and his sons Alexander and Aristobulus, *War* 1.460, 465, 473.

as is usual among persons who love each other,[476] they burst into tears[477] and clung to each other with great eagerness. **85** But since the king continued to give more pledges [of his love] and was dragging on about his own disposition towards her,[478] Mariamme said:[479] "The thing about the order was not the decision of a lover:[480] that if the lover should suffer something bad through Antony, I should perish as well, having no guilt."[481] **86** When these words came to his ears,[482] the king got into a state of violent indignation[483] and immediately let her go out of his hands. He cried out and tore his hair[484] with his hands, saying that he had clear and damning evidence[485] of Joseph's sexual relationship with her.[486] **87** For he [Joseph] would not have told[487] her this, which he had heard in private,[488] if a great trust had not grown[489] between them. Being in such a state he [Herod] almost killed[490] his wife but, overcome by his love for her,[491] he mastered his own impulse[492] and persevered,[493] with

---

[476] See *Ant.* 15.82 with the note to "loved her terribly."

[477] Forms of the verb πίπτω ("fall, burst"), or its compounds, in combination with the expression εἰς δάκρυα ("into tears") are very rare (cf. Libanius, *Decl.* 36.1.38), although 3 such occurrences are found in Josephus (see also *Ant.* 2.109 about Joseph, and 5.292 about Samson's wife).

[478] The shorter reading ἀεὶ δὲ καὶ μᾶλλον τοῦ βασιλέως πιστουμένου τὴν αὑτοῦ διάθεσιν of MSS PFV (followed by Niese 347) implies a translation like "But since the king continued to give more pledges of his disposition towards her." The reading ἀεὶ δὲ καὶ μᾶλλον τοῦ βασιλέως πιστουμένου καὶ ἐπὶ τὴν αὑτοῦ διάθεσιν ἕλκοντος of MSS LAMWE (followed by the present translation) seems to be the more difficult and therefore the preferable reading.

[479] Josephus' description indicates that Mariamme seized the opportunity to be honest with Herod; she told him what had bothered her so much since his trip to Antony. Although Herod's behavior almost invited this kind of frankness, which is supposed to be self-evident for lovers (cf. Mariamme's following statement), it apparently turned out badly for her, as the continuation of the narrative shows.

[480] The beginning of Mariamme's statement (οὐ φιλοῦντος ... τό) suggests that Herod did exactly what a lover is not supposed to do. A passage in Chariton's famous novel *Chaereas and Callirhoe* (4.4.9) reflects the truism that jealousy is typical of a lover: Ἀλλὰ ἐζηλοτύπησα. Τοῦτο ἴδιόν ἐστι φιλοῦντος ("You say I was jealous. That is not unusual of a lover," trans. Goold; see also Cassius Dio 41.27.2). For other cases of φιλοῦντος as a substantivated participle meaning "lover," see Plato, *Lys.* 212b-c; Achilles Tatius 2.37.7.

[481] This phrase echoes previous passages about Herod's order to kill Mariamme if he was executed by Antony (see *Ant.* 15.69 εἰ πάσχοι τι [cf. 15.65]; 15.70 χαλεπόν; 15.65 ὑπ' Ἀντωνίου).

[482] The conjecture προπεσόντος (followed by Niese 347) implies a translation such as: "when (these words) were presented." However, it has no parallels and is unnecessary: the reading attested by the MSS (προσπεσόντος τοῦ λόγου "when these words came to his ears," LSJ *s.v.* προσπίπτω II.5) is perfectly understandable and is confirmed by other passages in which the verb has a similar meaning (e.g., Plutarch, *Brut.* 15.9; *Phil.* 12.3).

[483] The verb περιπαθέω ("be greatly excited," Rengstorf *s.v.*) is a *hapax legomenon* in Josephus.

[484] Herod's reaction may seem theatrical, but the continuation of the narrative implies that Salome's severe accusation of adultery (see *Ant.* 15.81 with notes) had become convincing to Herod. For the verb (ἐπι-) δράττομαι used for tearing one's hair as a gesture to show one's horror, see Menander, *Mis.* 322; Josephus, *Ant.* 16.216; Libanius, *Decl.* 51.1.16.

[485] For the rare expression φώριον ἔχειν ("have damning evidence," LSJ *s.v.* φώριον), cf. Nonnus, *Dion.* 8.332; 13.385. Concerning περιφανές ("clear"), cf. *Ant.* 15.93, 235.

[486] The noun κοινωνία can mean "association, fellowship," but it can also refer to sexual intercourse, as is implied here and in *Ant.* 15.228 (also referring to Mariamme, LSJ *s.v.* II; Rengstorf *s.v.*).

[487] For the verb ἐξεῖπον with the connotation "disclose confidential meaning," see *Ant.* 15.205; 19.112; *Life* 204.

[488] This refers to Herod's secret order to Joseph (*Ant.* 15.64, paralleled by *War* 1.441).

[489] The noun πίστις ("trust," Rengstorf *s.v.*; Lindsay 1993: 78) refers here to an intimate relationship between lovers that presupposes full mutual trust.

[490] The expression ὀλίγου ... ἀπέκτεινε ("he almost killed ...") occurs with slight differences 3 times in Cassius Dio (39.63; 62.29; 68.11).

[491] Mariamme is once again saved by Herod's exceptional love for her. For references concerning Herod's love for Mariamme, see *Ant.* 15.83 with the note to "overcome by affection" (note also the variation in Josephus' vocabulary: cf. ἡττώμενος τῆς περὶ τὴν γυναῖκα φιλοστοργίας in 15.83 with νικώμενος τῷ πρὸς αὐτὴν ἔρωτι in 15.87).

[492] The Greek echoes *Ant.* 15.82 ("he ... controlled himself").

[493] The verb διακαρτερέω ("endure, bear") in

pain and difficulty. However, he ordered Joseph to be killed[494] without even coming into his [Herod's] sight;[495] Alexandra he chained and put in custody as the cause of all this.[496]

(4.1) 88 In these days[497] the situation in Syria[498] was also in disarray,[499] since Cleopatra did not leave Antony with any option but to attack everybody,[500] for she had persuaded

Cleopatra manipulates Antony, who grants her several territories.
War 1.359-361; 439-440
Apion 2.56-61

Josephus usually implies the enduring of suffering (*War* 6.280, 318; *Ant.* 6.370; 16.379) or torture (*Ant.* 16.315, 389). Here it indicates Herod's great emotional pain because he believes, according to *Antiquities*, Salome's accusation on the basis of Mariamme's statement (15.85). Nevertheless, the king decides to be merciful to his wife. Herod's emotional suffering can also be understood in the light of Josephus' hints at the king's jealousy (*Ant.* 15.65, 70; this is explicit in the parallel passage of *War* [1.443]).

[494] Otto (1913: 8-9 n. **, building on von Destinon 1882: 113 n. 1) considers the entire passage of *Ant.* 15.65-87 (paralleled by *War* 1.441-443) to be fictitious. He suggests that it concerns an adapted duplicate of the closely related story about Alexandra and Mariamme being put up in the Fortress Alexandrium, which ultimately led to Mariamme's death (*Ant.* 15.185-186, 202-236). The duplicate would result from the fact that Josephus depended on 2 sources for Mariamme's death: an anonymous source, which set it erroneously in 35/34 BCE; and Nicolaus of Damascus, who correctly placed it in 29 BCE. For a comparison of both passages, see *Ant.* 15.236 with the note to "her last moments." Sandmel (1967: 164-65 n. 5), Schürer-Vermes (1.302-03 n. 49), and Schalit (2001: 115-16, 135 n. 127) reject Otto's argument; Baumann (1983: 183) and Günther (2005: 109) support it. Schalit (*l.c.*) argues that both stories about Herod's journey abroad and a secret order to kill Mariamme in case he would not return are historical and that the correspondences between the two accounts result from the similar ways in which Herod responded to the dangerous situations during which he had to defend himself before his Roman patron abroad (first before Antony and later before Octavian). He situates the events narrated in *War* 1.441-443; *Ant.* 15.65-87 in 35 BCE and also argues that Herod seriously feared for his life when he entered his journey to Mark Antony in 35 BCE. Richardson (1996: 218-20) partly follows Otto and suggests that Josephus fabricated *Ant.* 15.65-87 in order to explain Herod's motive for the execution of Joseph (see 15.65 with the note to "kill Mariamme immediately").

[495] For phrases parallel to ἔρχομαι εἰς ὄψιν, see Euripides, *Iph. taur.* 902; Diodorus 32.10; Plutarch, *Ant.* 72.3; *Cic.* 31.3.

[496] The punishment of Alexandra is surprising at first glance: if Salome's accusation was accurate, Herod had much more reason to blame his wife Mariamme than her mother. The conclusion of the parallel narrative of *War*, ending with the executions of both Joseph and Mariamme (1.443), supports that reasoning. The narrative of *Antiquities*, however, leaves Alexandra to carry the can more than once (see also 15.31-32, 42-43). Mariamme and Alexandra cooperate in several actions directed against Herod (15.26-27, 31, 35, 80), but Alexandra usually takes the initiative (15.24, 69, 72-73). The adjective παραίτιος means literally "being in part the cause of something" (LSJ *s.v.*; Rengstorf *s.v.*; see also *Ant.* 4.208, 464; 10.126; 15.152).

[497] This formula (ἐν δὲ τούτῳ) of Josephus introduces a new section of the narrative that focuses upon Cleopatra (*Ant.* 15.88-103), but chronologically this episode is set in about the same period as the events told in the preceding section. Sometimes the formula commences a parallel story when Josephus is working with several story lines and moves from one to the other by transferring to another location (see 15.71 with the note to "In this time").

[498] While the previous section focuses on Herod and his family within a Judean context, Josephus moves now to Syria, although Herod and Judea are still playing a role (e.g., *Ant.* 15.96). In this new episode (15.88-160) Cleopatra plays a key role (see the next 2 notes).

Syria probably refers here to the region of Syria and not the Roman province with that name (Schalit 1968: 116; Möller and Schmitt 1976: 178-80). This region roughly bordered on the Mediterranean Sea to the west, the Amanus and Taurus Mountains to the northwest, and the River Euphrates to the east. Palestine and Phoenicia were frequently included, though also differentiated from it (see 15.79 with the note to "Coele-Syria"). Pompey founded the Roman province of Syria in 64 BCE, with Antioch as its capital. Judea, Iturea, the Nabatean kingdom, and the Decapolis were connected with the province through various relationships and with various degrees of autonomy (Lifshitz 1977; Rey-Coquais 1978; Millar 1993b: 32-39; Kennedy 1996; Klengel and Ruprechtsberger 2001).

[499] The disarray in Syria (ταραχὰς εἶχεν) does not mean rebellion (cf. *Ant.* 15.30 with notes), but is clearly linked to Cleopatra as an evil person able to manipulate Antony according to her own interests and to undermine the authority of local rulers, including Herod.

[500] This overstatement indicates that Josephus immediately characterizes the queen in a negative way (cf. *War* 1.359). For a list of Cleopatra's crimes, see *Ant.* 15.89-91, and for further references, 15.24 with the note to "Cleopatra."

him to remove everyone's powers and give them to her.[501] And she prevailed in most things because of his passion for her.[502] **89** Taking pleasure in her greedy character,[503] she left no

---

[501] Cleopatra's strategy is laid out clearly with a few words: Josephus suggests that Cleopatra focused on Rome's friendly kings in Egypt's periphery (e.g., Judea, Syria, and the Nabatean territories) and wanted them to be removed in order to become the ruler of their territories (Kasher 1988: 131-33). The parallel passage of *War* (1.359-361) indicates that this policy implied that the kings had to be murdered. In *Ant.* 15.88-103 Josephus expands *War*'s rather compact passage about Cleopatra's murderous attitude towards Antony's friendly kings and also changes the sequence of the events somewhat. He highlights Cleopatra's attempt to have Herod murdered (15.97) and emphasizes in this way that Cleopatra aimed for Herod's death and territory (cf. 15.92; this motif is anticipated in 15.77, 79). *Ant.* 15.88 links up with these passages by noting that Cleopatra kept pressing Antony to give her the dominions (δυναστείας) of neighboring rulers after murdering them and that Antony gave in to her in most cases out of his passion for her (see the next note). *War* 1.361, however, notes that Antony refrained from killing these rulers but did take away parts of their territories. It may also indicate that Cleopatra ended these rulers' status as Antony's "friends" (τὸ δὲ τούτων ἔγγιον φίλους διεκρούσατο; see *Ant.* 15.5 with the note to "the friends around him"), although Schalit (2001: 774) argues that these words in *War* are corrupt. The *Antiquities* narrative not only reports Cleopatra's actions against Antony's friendly kings (15.92-95), but also implies that Antony never gave the main territories of Herod and the Nabatean king Malichus I (see 15.107 with the note to "the Arab") to Cleopatra; such behavior would not have matched Antony's general policy concerning the friendly kingdoms (see 15.5 with the note to "Antony"). The obvious reason for Antony's attitude towards Herod and Malichus is the support that he received from them, e.g., during his wars against the Parthians and Armenians (Halfmann 2011: 175, 200).

[502] Josephus suggests that Antony was instrumental for Cleopatra to implement her strategies. The claim that Cleopatra manipulated Antony by taking advantage of his passion (ἐπιθυμία) for her is also found in *War* 1.359; *Ant.* 15.93. The latter passage also refers to a sexual relationship and Cleopatra's use of drugs in order to manipulate Antony. *Ant.* 15.88 is slightly milder than its parallel passage of *War* (1.359) because it notes that Cleopatra did not succeed to have all her wishes fulfilled, while *War* states in plain language that Antony was already corrupted by his love for Cleopatra (ἤδη γὰρ Ἀντώνιος τῷ Κλεοπάτρας ἔρωτι διεφθαρμένος). The key noun in *War* (ἔρως "love") is absent in *Ant.* 15.88; however, the passages share a second key word (ἐπιθυμία "desire, passion"). Velleius Paterculus (2.85.6) and Seneca the Younger (*Ep.* 83.25) emphasize that Antony's love for Cleopatra ruined him, which view was more or less the official one at Rome after Octavian's victory at Actium (Becher 1966: 62; Huzar 1978: 245-46).

[503] With the expression φύσει, which literally means "by nature/character" (cf. *Ant.* 13.319 concerning Aristobulus I and 15.237 concerning Mariamme), Josephus starts a description of Cleopatra's character in a brief excursus (15.89-91), which surpasses the parallel comment of *War* (1.359) with regard to its repetitive negative vocabulary and devastating characterization of Cleopatra.

In the context of the characterization of someone (e.g., in a eulogy) the noun φύσει and related expressions can refer to a person's physical characteristics (e.g., Achilles Tatius 1.6.2; 2.17.3) as well his or her inner (i.e., psychological and moral) traits (e.g., Chariton 1.4.5; 2.3.3; 2.5.2; 2.6.4). Ancient authors dealing with the theory of rhetoric indicate that the qualities indicated by phrases with φύσει are inherent and should be distinguished from characteristics that are the result of one's descent, social environment, peers, and education, which goes back to the sophists' distinction between *physis* and *nomos* (De Temmerman 2006: 94-98).

Although an explicit characterization of Cleopatra is missing in *War*, several traits highlighted in *Antiquities* are already present: *War* 1.360 emphasizes Cleopatra's greed (πλεονεξία), specified as greed for more territories. The motif of Cleopatra's greediness (see also *Ant.* 15.90 and, possibly, 15.79) may have been partly inspired by reports about her desperate attempts to collect whatever money she could lay her hands on after the devastating defeat at Actium, by executing wealthy Egyptians, confiscating their possessions, and plundering temples (Cassius Dio 51.5.4). In *Apion* 2.58 Josephus accuses the queen of pillaging her ancestral gods and her forefathers' sepulchers; these minor additions of *paternosque* and *progenitorum* make her image even worse than that in *Antiquities* because they imply that Cleopatra turned into an enemy of her own people. Becher (1966: 68, following Reinach) assumes that Josephus' exaggerated reproach in *Apion* 2.58 originates in the bitterness of the Alexandrian Jews about Cleopatra's aggressive behavior towards them (cf. 2.59-60). Josephus' statements about the queen in *Antiquities* and *Apion* match the stereotypic image of the godless tyrant (Lebram 1975; van Henten 2005a; see also *Ant.* 15.91).

unlawful deed undone.[504] She had first killed[505] her brother with poison when he was fifteen years old[506] because she knew that he would get the throne. On account of Antony's [assistance] she had her sister Arsinoe killed when she, as a suppliant, was visiting the temple of Artemis in Ephesus.[507] **90** Temples and tombs were violated for the sake of money[508] if there was any hope of finding it. No sacred place seemed so inviolable to her that it could not be stripped of its valuables; no secular place[509] would be exempt from undergoing anything unlawful whatsoever, provided that it enhanced the wealth[510] fed by this wicked female's greediness. **91** In short, nothing at all was sufficient for this woman,[511]

---

[504] The queen's unlawfulness (παρανομία) is highlighted again and specified in *Ant.* 15.90 (παρενομήθησαν). The statement is paralleled by the first item in the catalogue of Cleopatra's crimes (*Apion* 2.56-61): *cui nihil omnino iniustitiae et malorum operum defuit* ("who was steeped in every kind of injustice and criminal activity …," Barclay in BJP 10 on *Apion* 2.57; van Henten 2005a: 128-32).

[505] *War* 1.359-361 (cf. 1.440) refers to Cleopatra's murderous intentions, with 1.359 noting—in general terms—that the queen murdered all her remaining relatives (which fact is elaborated in *Antiquities*). *Apion* 2.57 refers to Cleopatra's crimes against her husbands. The rare verb προαναιρέω ("take away before, kill first," Rengstorf *s.v.*) also occurs in *Ant.* 14.344; 15.192 (referring to Cleopatra as object); 20.149.

[506] The general statement about Cleopatra murdering her relatives in *War* 1.359 is elaborated here with specific information: the note that Cleopatra's brother Ptolemy XIV was poisoned is not attested elsewhere (Becher 1966: 64; *Apion* 2.58 states more generally that Cleopatra murdered her brother). Ptolemy XIV was not only Cleopatra's younger brother but also her husband according to Cassius Dio 42.44 (Hölbl 1994: 212 with n. 71).

[507] See also *Apion* 2.57-58 and Appian, *Bell. civ.* 5.1.9, which (wrongly) gives Milete—also referring to the temple of Artemis Leucophryene (which was located at Magnesia on the Meander)—instead of Ephesus as the location of Arsinoe's death (Marcus-Wikgren 44 n. *a*; Huzar 1978: 154; Hölbl 1994: 216). Buchheim (1960: 25) argues that killing Arsinoe and a few other opponents of Cleopatra was a very small price for Antony for gaining the huge support of Egypt and its queen.

The Greek virgin goddess Artemis was associated with Ephesus in mythological traditions about her birth. Artemis' mother Leto had to flee for Hera, the jealous spouse of Zeus, who was the father of the twins Artemis and Apollo. Leto gave birth to Artemis in Ortygia or "Quails' Land," which was located near Ephesus according to certain traditions. Artemis was widely venerated in Asia Minor, and her most prominent local cult was at Ephesus. Her sanctuary there, built by Chersiphron and his son Metagenes in 356 BCE (Strabo 14.1.22), was counted among the Seven Wonders of the World. It functioned as a place of asylum. Augustus reduced the area for asylum seekers because the place attracted too many criminals (Strabo 14.1.23; Mussies 1999: 91-94).

[508] Cleopatra's greed for money is exemplified by her robbing of temples and tombs. This trait, which is paralleled by *Apion* 2.58, belongs to the tyrannical stereotype (see 15.89 with the note to "her greedy character"): rulers with a very bad reputation like Cambyses, Antiochus IV, and Nero were famous for robbing temples (concerning Antiochus IV, see 1 Macc 6:1-4; 2 Macc 1:13-16; 9:2). Nero in particular was characterized as enemy of the gods because of his temple robberies (Pseudo-Seneca, *Oct.* 239; Tacitus, *Ann.* 15.45; Suetonius, *Nero* 32.4; Cassius Dio 63.11.3-4; van Henten 1993: 228-35, 242; 2000). For the expression χρημάτων ἕνεκεν ("for the sake of money"), see Aristotle, *Eth. Eud.* 1216a; Dio Chrysostom 74.24; Eusebius, *Comm. Isa.* 1.92.85 (ed. Ziegler 180); John Chrysostom, *Exp. Ps.* (PG 55.297.58).

[509] Josephus' parallel statements concerning sacred and secular spaces highlight that nothing was safe from Cleopatra's wicked acts and attempts to enrich herself, which ties in with the opening remarks of *Ant.* 15.89.

[510] Several scholars assume that there is a lacuna in the Greek text, which is sometimes filled with the addition of a verb (e.g., ἀρκέσειν "satisfy," in accordance with the Latin version, as conjectured by Richards and Shutt 1939: 173, and followed by Marcus-Wikgren 44). However, the text transmitted by the MSS (Niese 348) makes sense and there is no reason for adapting it. The extensive quotation of this section in Constantine Porphyrogenitus (*Virt. vit.* [ed. Roos 2.1.82]) also lacks a verb.

[511] An interesting passage in Herodian associates the phrase "nothing at all was sufficient (οὐδὲν αὔταρκες)" with tyranny: "Plenty of money cannot offer sufficient protection against the lack of self-control of a tyrant (οὔτε γὰρ χρημάτων πλῆθος οὐδὲν αὔταρκες πρὸς τυραννίδος ἀκρασίαν), nor can body-guards protect a ruler sufficiently if the subjects are not loyal to him" (1.4.4, my trans.).

who was extravagant and also a slave to her desires.[512] Everything imaginable fell short of the things she was craving for.[513] For these very reasons she was always pressing Antony to take things away from the others and give them to her as favors.[514] When she was passing through Syria with him,[515] she kept scheming about how she could acquire it.[516] **92** Therefore, she accused Lysanias, the son of Ptolemy,[517] of bringing in the help of the Parthians against the interest of the state[518] and had him killed.[519] And she kept asking

---

[512] About the key noun ἐπιθυμία ("passion, lust, desire"), see *Ant.* 15.88 with the note to "his passion for her," and about Cleopatra's own lust, 15.97 with notes. Horace (*Carm.* 1.37.7-10) highlights Cleopatra's lust: "plotting ruin 'gainst the Capitol and destruction for the empire, with her polluted crew of creatures foul with lust" (trans. Bennett). Landau (2006: 121-22) notes that the themes of Cleopatra's greed and Antony's weakness (because of his passion for her) recur later in *Antiquities* in connection with Herod (see 15.219).

[513] The Greek text is enigmatic and open to several interpretations, but the implication might be that the queen was not qualified to be a ruler because she was intemperate and lacked self-control, which would match Josephus' criticism of the queen elsewhere in *Antiquities* and *Apion* (van Henten 2005a).

[514] This dovetails with *Ant.* 15.88 about Cleopatra using Antony to take over territories of other rulers (cf. the repetition of ἀφαιρούμενον in 15.88, 91). These 2 lines enfold Josephus' brief excursus about Cleopatra's character (15.89-91).

[515] This phrase introduces Cleopatra's interferences with local rulers in the region of Syria (see *Ant.* 15.88 with the note to "remove everyone's powers and give them to her"). Cleopatra's journey through Syria (cf. 15.96) might provide a clue to the date of the events narrated in 15.92-103, although 2 caveats should be taken into account. First, Cleopatra may have accompanied Antony several times when he was traveling from Alexandria to Antioch (the capital of the Roman province of Syria): Josephus relates that she escorted Antony up to the Euphrates River when he was on his way to Armenia (15.96, which trip may be set in 34 BCE; see the note to "war against Armenia"), but the queen may have also accompanied him when he marched to Laodicea (15.64, which journey may be situated in 35 BCE). Second, in 15.92-103, which passage should be situated in different periods (see the notes to 15.94-96), Josephus may have clustered cognate traditions about the extensions of Cleopatra's territory.

[516] I.e., Syria's regions, as the continuation of the narrative implies.

[517] In ca. 41 BCE Lysanias succeeded his father Ptolemy, the son of Mennaeus, as ruler of Chalcis, a city between Mt Lebanon and the Anti-Lebanon (Jebel Lubnan al-Sharqi) in the Plain of Massyas (Bekaa Valley), south of Damascus. A certain Monicas, an ancestor of Lysanias, founded the principality of Chalcis. Several sources attesting to Monicas imply a setting of ca. 85 BCE. Antony probably appointed Lysanias king of Chalcis in the fall of 39 BCE (Cassius Dio 49.32.5; Buchheim 1960: 19). Lysanias was also appointed king of the Itureans (49.32.5; about the Itureans, see *Ant.* 15.185 with the note to "the Iturean") because he was expected to control the robber gangs from this region (Strabo 16.2.18). He supported Antigonus against Hyrcanus II during the Parthian intervention in Syria and Judea (*War* 1.248; *Ant.* 14.330). The rulers of Chalcis were natural competitors of the rulers of Judea because they had a great interest in the fertile region of Gaulanitis, northeast of the Sea of Galilee, which belonged to Judea in certain periods (cf. *Ant.* 13.396; Buchheim 1960: 15-20).

[518] This was a most serious accusation because the Parthians were Antony's greatest enemy in this period (see *Ant.* 15.11 with the note to "the Parthians"). Buchheim (1960: 19) considers this accusation to be a fabrication because, when Antony appointed Lysanias king of Chalcis, it must have been well known that Lysanias had been a supporter of the Parthian cause and Antony nevertheless made this appointment. However, Cleopatra's accusation as given here may refer to a later period in which Lysanias was again siding with the Parthians. There may also have been other reasons for Lysanias' execution, which were probably connected with his rule as Antony's friendly king. Lysanias may, e.g., not have lived up to his promise to keep the robbers in the region under control (see the previous note). One out of several possible dates for Lysanias' death is connected with Antony's campaign against the Parthians in 36 BCE (see the next note).

[519] The tenor of *Ant.* 15.92 ("and she kept asking …") implies an analogy between Lysanias' territory and those of Herod and the Nabatean king, which suggests that Lysanias' death was followed by Antony's gift of Lysanias' territory to Cleopatra. This gift is not mentioned in *War*, but confirmed by inscriptions and coins (Buchheim 1960: 69; see also Strabo 14.5.3; 14.6.6; Plutarch, *Ant.* 35.5-36.2). Lysanias' death is mentioned in passing in *War* 1.439-440 together with the death of the Nabatean king Malichus I (see also *Ant.* 15.344). *War* indicates that both of them died because of Cleopatra's

Antony for Judea and the territory of the Arabs,[520] and requested that he remove the kings from these territories.[521] **93** As for Antony, he was totally overcome by this woman,[522] such that it seemed that he obeyed Cleopatra's every desire, not only because of their intimate sexual relationship,[523] but also because she drugged him.[524] Yet her wrong-doing was so conspicuous that he was ashamed[525] of becoming so obedient that he would commit the greatest crimes.[526] **94** So in order not to deny [her] entirely, but also not to look bad in his

---

"cleverness" (δεινότης, possibly a *double entendre*) and that Herod feared for his life as well. Cassius Dio (49.32.5) mentions that Lysanias was executed by Antony and does not connect his death to Cleopatra. In line with this, Roller (1998: 202 n. 14) argues that Josephus' remark that Cleopatra was responsible for Lysanias' death is improbable (differently Reinhold 1933: 64; Schürer-Vermes 1.565). Lysanias died either in the 16th year of Cleopatra (September 37-August 36 BCE; Cassius Dio 49.32.4-5) or in 34 BCE (according to a specific reconstruction of the chronological context of the gift referred to in *Ant.* 15.95; see the notes to this paragraph and Schürer-Vermes 1.253, 288-89 with n. 5, 565). Buchheim (1960: 19) prefers the first date and specifies it: Lysanias would have been killed during the spring of 36 BCE at the latest since Antony was busy with his campaign against the Parthians in the summer of 36 BCE.

[520] I.e., the territory of the Nabateans or part of it (Hackl, Jacobs, and Weber 2010: 43; cf. *Ant.* 15.79, in which passage Coele-Syria is mentioned: Antony had given Cleopatra Coele-Syria instead of what she had been asking for). The Nabatean kingdom consisted of a large territory running from the Southern Hauran (east of the Decapolis and with Bostra as its main city; Nabateans had settled south of the east-west line of Salkhad-Bostra-Der'a, but it is doubtful whether they formed the majority of the population; see Shatzman 1991: 279-81; Hackl, Jenni, and Schneider 2003: 497) to the mountainous region of the Northern Hedjaz (east of the Red Sea). The Nabateans also settled across the Northern Negev Desert (almost up to the Mediterranean Sea) and in the Sinai Desert. The famous city of Petra was their capital, although the main area of the Nabatean settlement lay north of Petra, in the fertile plains of Moab (Millar 1993b: 387-408).

[521] Literally "from them," i.e., Judea and the territory of the Nabateans.

The reference to the death of the Nabatean king Malichus I in the parallel passage of *War* (1.440) is probably a mistake: other sources show that Malichus outlived Cleopatra and that he ruled from the early fifties to ca. 30 BCE (Richardson 1996: 165 n. 62; Mahieu 2012: 129-32, however, argues for Malichus' death in March/April 30 BCE, which is before Cleopatra's death in August 30 BCE; see also *Ant.* 15.107 with the note to "the Arab"). Josephus may have corrected this mistake in *Antiquities*.

[522] The verb ἡττάομαι ("being overcome [by a woman/the beauty of a woman]") is also used in *Ant.* 7.130, in which case it refers to David falling for Beethsabe-Bathsheba (cf. 15.205). *War* 1.359 makes a similar statement about Antony: "For Antony was entirely overcome by his passion for her (ἥττων ἦν ἐν πᾶσιν τῆς ἐπιθυμίας)" (trans. BHP 1a). *Apion* 2.58 implies Antony's dependence on Cleopatra, but formulates this in a bluntly negative way: "[... she] corrupted Antony by her sexual charms (*Antoniumque corrumpens amatoriis rebus*) ..." (Barclay in BJP 10 on 2.58). See also *Ant.* 15.88 with notes about Josephus' characterization of Antony and Cleopatra's relationship (cf. also Appian, *Hist. rom.* 12.16.112 concerning Mithridates of Pontus, who "yielded only to pleasures with women," trans. White).

[523] The Greek word ὁμιλία is ambiguous because it can mean "company, conversation" (cf. *Ant.* 1.45; 2.62; 5.191; 15.68, 75, also *War* 1.442; *Ant.* 2.41; 4.134; 7.344; 18.69, 74) as well as "sexual intercourse" (LSJ *s.v.*). The context implies here that it refers to Cleopatra's sexual relationship with Antony (see also *Ant.* 15.97 about Cleopatra's attempt to have sex with Herod).

[524] Cleopatra's use of drugs (φαρμάκοι) or sorcery in her attempts to seduce men is well known from other sources. Her success with males was attributed to her beauty in later sources only; the motif of her exceptional beauty occurs for the first time in Lucan's *Pharsalia* (further references in Becher 1966: 108-10).

[525] The rare verb ἐκδυσωπέω ("put [someone] to shame," LSJ *s.v.*) also occurs in *War* 1.51.

[526] This passage implies that Antony realized that being obedient to Cleopatra meant that he would be as bad as she, and as such he—as a character in the narrative—endorses Josephus' very negative view of Cleopatra (see *Ant.* 15.24 with the note to "Cleopatra"). Josephus suggests that Antony's shame made him control himself at least to a certain extent, which is perhaps true. However, it is plausible that Antony's policy with respect to the kings who were his "friends" was determined chiefly by the criterion of advantage to him and Rome (see 15.5 with the note to "the friends around him" and 15.75-76 with notes).

Cleopatra tries to seduce Herod, who considers murdering her.
War 1.361-362

public actions by bringing about everything she ordered, he removed bits of the territories of each [king] and presented her with them.[527] **95** He also gave her the cities between the River Eleutherus[528] and Egypt,[529] except for Tyre and Sidon,[530] knowing that they had been free since the time of their ancestors,[531] although she strongly insisted that they would be given to her.

(4.2) 96 After receiving these gifts and escorting Antony—who was waging war against Armenia[532]—as far as the Euphrates,[533] Cleopatra turned back and arrived at Apamea and

---

[527] Cf. *War* 1.361: "Reacting sensibly against at least one part of her orders, Antony thought that it would be a sacrilege to kill respectable men and kings of such importance" (trans. BHP 1a). Both *War* 1.361 and the statement here imply that Cleopatra's strategy (cf. *Ant.* 15.88 with the note to "remove everyone's powers and give them to her") partly succeeded.

[528] The River Eleutherus (currently *Nahr el-Kebir*), in northern Syria, between Orthosia and Tripoli (Strabo 16.2.12-15), was considered to be the boundary between Seleucia and Coele-Syria (16.2.12). A river with the same name is mentioned in 1 Macc 11:7; 12:30, but it is uncertain whether these references concern the relevant river (Abel 1949: 203, 226). Ptolemy I Soter captured the coast of Syria up to the River Eleutherus (Diodorus 20.113.1-2), and the river seems to have been the border between the Ptolemaic and the Seleucid parts of Syria for most of the 3rd cent. BCE (Hölbl 1994: 24, 43). The passage here, therefore, may suggest that it was Cleopatra's goal to reestablish the early boundaries of the Ptolemaic Empire (cf. Halfmann 2011, who argues that this was Antony's aim).

[529] The parallel phrase of *War* (1.361) is slightly different: "… he gave … her … all the cities this side of the River Eleutherus …" (trans. BHP 1a). Cassius Dio (49.32.4-5) and Plutarch (*Ant.* 36) confirm a huge grant of territories to Cleopatra, in 37 (or 36) BCE, but they refer to Phoenicia instead of the cities between the River Eleutherus and Egypt. The date of 37 BCE is adhered to by Buchheim (1960: 68-74), Grant (1972: 240), and Hölbl (1994: 217; see also the gift mentioned in *Ant.* 15.96, which should be dated in 34 BCE). Schalit (2001: 777) identifies "Phoenicia" (mentioned by Dio and Plutarch) with the cities between the Eleutherus and Egypt referred to by Josephus, which is not entirely accurate because Dio (49.32.4-5), contrary to Plutarch, refers not merely to Phoenicia but to "large parts of Phoenicia and Palestine." Dio's phrase may equal Josephus' reference, which would mean that Josephus and Dio refer to basically the same coastal area that extended from Gaza in the south (see *Ant.* 15.96 with the note to "the areas in Arabia that were given to her") to the River Eleutherus in the north. Buchheim (1960: 73) argues that the grants of the coastal region as well as Chalcis (*Ant.* 15.92) were further motivated by Antony's strategy to build up a large fleet against Octavian with Cleopatra's help.

[530] Similarly in the parallel passage of *War* (1.361), but the explanation for this exception is only given in *Antiquities*.

[531] Tyre and Sidon had become autonomous cities in 126/125 BCE, under Seleucid rule, and remained semi-autonomous under the Romans because they were their allies (Udoh 2005: 146 with references). They were not exempt from Roman jurisdiction. Tyre's special status is apparent from its mint: the city minted silver shekels and half-shekels from 126/125 BCE until 58/59 CE. The Tyrian shekel was the standard currency in which dues to the Jerusalem Temple were paid (Millar 1993b: 285-89).

[532] In the parallel passage of *War* (1.362-363) Josephus refers twice to the Parthians: when Antony was launching a campaign against them and at Antony's return from the campaign. *Antiquities* correctly mentions Armenia and reports later that the Armenian king Artabazes-Artavasdes was taken prisoner of war during the campaign (15.104), which was launched in 34 BCE (Halfmann 2011: 169-72). Schalit (2001: 774) argues that *War* rightly names Parthia, and refers in this connection to Dio's note in 49.33.3 that Antony tried to fool the Armenian king by pretending that he was marching out against the Parthians. During the late Roman Republic 2 regions were called Armenia. Lesser Armenia (*Armenia inferior*) was a small region to the northeast of Asia Minor, west of the Euphrates and south of the Black Sea and the Pontic Mountains. The Romans removed it from the territory of King Tigranes II of Armenia in 66 BCE; it either became an autonomous territory or part of one of the Roman provinces in Asia Minor. Greater Armenia (*Armenia maior*) was a client kingdom in this period, either in the Roman or the Parthian sphere of influence. This was a much larger area, north of Mesopotamia and south of the Caucasian Mountains (Mitford 1980; Schottky 1989; Brentjes 1997). For Antony's campaign against Armenia, see Buchheim (1960: 90-91), Bengtson (1974: 21-41), Huzar (1978: 179-82), and Halfmann (2011: 162-76).

[533] I.e., to the border of Syria and the Roman sphere of influence (see *Ant.* 15.88 with the note to "Syria").

Damascus.[534] Next, she passed by Judea, where Herod met her[535] and leased from her the areas in Arabia that had been given to her,[536] as well as the public revenues from the area of Jericho.[537] This country produces balsam,[538] which is the costliest of the products there[539]

---

[534] Both cities belonged to the Roman province of Syria. The order of these 2 names (also in the parallel account of *War* [1.362]) may imply that Cleopatra traveled from north to south: Apamea was located near the River Orontes in northern Syria, more than 200 km north of Damascus. Damascus had various rulers in the 1st cent. BCE (see *War* 1.103, 115; *Ant.* 13.392, 418) and became part of the Roman province of Syria after its occupation by Pompey's legates (*War* 1.127; *Ant.* 14.29). The city may have belonged to Cleopatra's territory from 37 to 32 BCE, as coins from 37/36 and 33/32 BCE bearing the images of Antony and Cleopatra suggest (Schürer-Vermes 2.129; Schalit 2001: 120-21, 775-76)—although these coins may also express that there was merely a special relationship between Damascus and Cleopatra (as suggested by Andrew Meadows in Walker and Higgs 2001: 234-35). There is no explicit reference that Antony gave Damascus to Cleopatra, but it is plausible that he did so (with Schalit 2001: 776). The queen must have had a good reason for traveling from the Euphrates to Damascus. The continuation of the narrative refers to economic transactions. A plausible scenario is that Cleopatra went to Damascus to take note of her business affairs after the city had been given to her by Antony, although there is no conclusive evidence for this.

[535] Josephus does not specify the place, but one could think of Jerusalem or Jericho since Herod would probably meet the queen in one of his palaces in these cities. In comparison to the brief parallel narrative of *War* (1.362) Josephus greatly expands the episode of Cleopatra's visit to Judea in *Antiquities* (15.96-103; cf. 15.106-107).

[536] A region from "Arabia" (i.e., the Nabatean kingdom, Schalit 1968: 14; Millar 1993a: 33; see also *Ant.* 15.92 with the note to "the territory of the Arabs" and 15.111 with the note to "Arabia") that Cleopatra probably received was the enclave at the southeastern section of the Dead Sea, where bitumen was produced (Hieronymus of Cardia, *FGH* 154 F 5; Diodorus 2.48.6; 2.98.1-2). In *Antiquities* (cf. the parallel account of *War* [1.361-362]) Josephus seems to date Antony's grant of the territories near the Dead Sea to Cleopatra in 34 BCE since he connects it with Antony's campaign against Parthia, which took place in 34 BCE (see the note to "war against Armenia" above and 15.104). The setting implies that this gift should be distinguished from Antony's grant in 37 BCE, referred to by Plutarch and Porphyrius (see 15.95 with notes and Eusebius, *Chron.* [ed. Schoene 1.170]).

Schalit (2001: 773-77) argues that there were probably 3 successive grants to Cleopatra: a first one (in 37 or perhaps 36 BCE) consisted of the kingdom of Chalcis, Coele-Syria (see *Ant.* 15.79), Cilicia, Cyprus, and the cities between the Eleutherus and Egypt (see 15.95); a second one (in 35 BCE) of Gaza; and a third one (in 34 BCE) of Jericho and certain Nabatean areas. The separate grant of Gaza becomes improbable if one assumes that the geographical references in Josephus and Dio are correct and that Plutarch's account is deficient. In that case Gaza was probably part of the coastal area included in Antony's grant of 37 (or 36) BCE (with Shatzman 1991: 287). *Ant.* 15.254 implies that Gaza originally belonged to Herod's territory since it states that Herod appointed Costobarus as governor of Gaza in 40 BCE (Jones 1937: 271 with n. 57). *Ant.* 15.217 indicates that Gaza was taken away from Herod and given to Cleopatra (i.e., by Antony), and returned to Herod by Octavian in the autumn of 30 BCE (Schürer-Vermes 1.289); it does not refer to a separate gift of Gaza to Cleopatra. Huzar (1978: 167) suggests that Herod lost Gaza and Joppa in 36 BCE as a result of Costobar's scheming with Cleopatra. Stern (1974b: 306-07) mentions Gaza, Samaria, and Joppa as cities that may have been removed from Herod's territory. The gifts of Samaria and Joppa are possible, but they are not mentioned explicitly in the relevant passages (cf. Buchheim 1960: 68-74; Becher 1966: 40-41; Schürer-Vermes 1.298-300).

[537] The parallel passage of *War* (1.361) mentions "the palm-grove of Jericho where the balsam-tree grows" as one of the territories received by Cleopatra. In *Antiquities* Josephus expands the information about Herod leasing back the territories within "Arabia" given to Cleopatra (15.96, 106-107, 132). *Ant.* 15.107 implies that Herod acted as an intermediary between Cleopatra and the Nabatean king Malichus I, who had to pay Herod 200 talents, most probably for the lease of these territories or part of them. Strabo does not mention Jericho in his reports about Antony's gifts to Cleopatra, but he does mention Korakesion and Amaxia (14.5.3), and also recalls that Cleopatra owned the island Elaiussa (14.5.6).

[538] Diodorus (2.48.9; 19.98), Strabo (16.2.41), and Plutarch (*Ant.* 36.3) praise the balsam from the region of Jericho. Balsam was used for cosmetic purposes and as a medicine against headache and eyesight problems (on the balsam plantations, see also *War* 4.469; *Ant.* 8.174, and for the cultivation of both balsam and dates in the region of Jericho, Schürer-Vermes 1.298-300 with n. 36). Niese (349) conjectures ὀποβάλσαμον ("the juice of the

and grows only there, as well as many excellent date-palms.⁵⁴⁰ **97** Being in this region and meeting Herod frequently, she kept trying to have sex with the king.⁵⁴¹ By nature⁵⁴² she enjoyed these pleasures without disguise.⁵⁴³ Perhaps she did experience some erotic desire for him, or, what is more plausible, she was secretly preparing for⁵⁴⁴ an outrageous act, supposedly done to her, to be the beginning of a trap.⁵⁴⁵ Overall, she kept presenting herself

---

balsam-tree") instead of βάλσαμον ("balsam-tree," Rengstorf *s.v.*) because ὀποβάλσαμον also occurs in a related passage about Jericho (*Ant.* 14.54). However, this conjecture is unnecessary since βάλσαμον can also refer to the fragrant oil coming from the balsam-trees (LSJ *s.v.* I.2).

⁵³⁹ The costly products from the area of Jericho (apart from balsam also dates) as well as the bitumen from the Dead Sea yielded huge profits (Schalit 2001: 261; on these products see also *War* 4.468-481; *Ant.* 14.54). The revenues of the lease of this region must have been a considerable contribution to Cleopatra's enormous wealth at the end of her life (Cassius Dio 51.15.4). Richardson (1996: 166) calculates that the amount that Herod had to pay to Cleopatra equaled half of his income of the year 4 BCE.

⁵⁴⁰ The Greek φοῖνιξ means, i.a., "date-palm" (*Phoenix dactylifera*, LSJ *s.v.* II) and "date" (Rengstorf *s.v.*, referring to *Ant.* 10.190). Marcus-Wikgren and Meijer-Wes translate "palm trees."

⁵⁴¹ Josephus considerably expands the information given in *War* 1.362 about Cleopatra's visit to Judea (*Ant.* 15.97-103). Otto (1913: 47) and Schalit (2001: 121) consider it entirely possible that Cleopatra really tried to seduce Herod since she was famous for doing such things. Cleopatra's relationships with Caesar and Antony were well known, and her unsuccessful attempt to seduce Octavian after the Battle of Actium was reported widely (e.g., Florus 2.21.9; Cassius Dio 51.12; Becher 1966: 34; Huzar 1978: 227)—although this last attempt to seduce a powerful man may have been fictitious, part of a trend to present her as a woman who used sex to push her plans through. Josephus' portrait of the queen in *Antiquities* matches this trend to portray Cleopatra in a very negative light (see also the next notes). If she really did try to seduce Herod, one would expect Josephus to have included the episode already in *War*. Grant (1972: 159-60) and Günther (2005: 105-06) argue that both Cleopatra's attempt to seduce Herod and the king's plan to murder her (see *Ant.* 15.98) are unhistorical since both deeds would have made Antony extremely angry. Huzar (1978: 167 n. 46) considers Cleopatra's attempt to seduce Herod to be highly implausible. If the story is fictitious indeed, it may have derived either from Herod's memoirs or from Josephus himself (Herod's memoirs were incorporated in *Antiquities* according to *Ant.* 15.174; see

Otto 1913: 46; Schalit 2001: 121). Whether or not Herod invented the story, it definitely turns him into a friend of the Roman people in the perspective of Cleopatra and Antony's defeat at Actium. On the narrative level, the story anticipates the advice that Herod, during his meeting with Octavian, claimed to have previously given to Antony, namely to kill Cleopatra (*Ant.* 15.191-192; cf. *War* 1.389-390. *Ant.* 15.101 hints at a similar advice). The story about Cleopatra's attempt to seduce Herod and Herod's plan to murder her could, therefore, also be Josephus' invention: he may have taken the report of Herod's discussion with Octavian after Actium (*War* 1.389-390; *Ant.* 15.191-192) as point of departure for another, fictitious, story about Cleopatra, i.e., that she attempted to have sex with Herod and have him executed afterwards.

The noun συνουσία can mean "company, banquet, gathering," and it sometimes refers to intercourse with a sexual connotation (LSJ *s.v.* I.4; Rengstorf *s.v.*; see Philo, *Leg.* 3.156; Josephus, *War* 1.489; *Ant.* 3.78, 275; 5.307; 6.236; *Apion* 2.234).

⁵⁴² Josephus' description of Cleopatra's attempt to seduce Herod links up with his brief characterization of the queen in *Ant.* 15.89-91 through the repetition of "by nature" (φύσει; see 15.89 with the note to "character"). Together, the 2 passages depict Cleopatra as a most dangerous killer queen.

⁵⁴³ See *Ant.* 15.29 with the notes to "erotic diversion" and "undisguised" concerning Antony. The statement here about Cleopatra lines up with suggestions by other authors that sexual pleasure was a goal in itself for her. Propertius (3.11.39) and Pliny the Elder (9.58.119) characterize her as a whoring queen (*regina meretrix*; see also Lucan 10.358-360, 369-370, 374-375; Becher 1966: 181-82; Wyke 2009). Grant (1972: XVII) links up with this negative portrayal and states that Cleopatra's sexuality dominated her character. He seems to be not critical enough of his sources, but his view matches the tenor of Josephus' portrait of the queen in *Antiquities*.

⁵⁴⁴ The other occurrence (*Ant.* 16.10) of the rare verb ὑποκατασκευάζω ("prepare beforehand/secretly") in Josephus is also part of the Herod narrative.

⁵⁴⁵ Josephus is highly ambiguous about Cleopatra's motive to start a sexual relationship with Herod (cf. Richardson 1996: 166). Her meeting with the king clearly concerns business (*Ant.* 15.96), but Josephus

as having been overcome by desire.⁵⁴⁶ **98** For a long time Herod had not really been well-disposed to Cleopatra,⁵⁴⁷ knowing that she was difficult to everybody.⁵⁴⁸ But at that time he thought it fitting to hate her, if she would go this far for the sake of licentiousness,⁵⁴⁹ and to pre-empt her in exacting vengeance if she attempted such things,⁵⁵⁰ setting a trap with others.⁵⁵¹ So he rejected her words⁵⁵² and held counsel with his friends⁵⁵³ in order to kill her while he had her in his power.⁵⁵⁴ **99** He said that he would take away⁵⁵⁵ many evils from everyone to whom she had already been a burden⁵⁵⁶ and was expected to be so in the

---

suggests that she used to enjoy sexual pleasures during such occasions. He also hints at Cleopatra's being attracted to Herod but suggests at the same time that the attempt to have sex with him was likely a trap, which would imply that Cleopatra unscrupulously used sex as a means to realize her political goals. Josephus' suggestion of intimacies planned by Cleopatra as a set-up to a framed accusation of sexual harassment by Herod matches the very negative portrayal of Cleopatra elsewhere in *Antiquities*. One can imagine well that such a trap would be effective with Antony and might have resulted in the gift of Herod's kingdom to Cleopatra.

⁵⁴⁶ The Greek with the infinitive verb ἡττῆσθαι echoes *Ant.* 15.93, concerning Antony's being overcome by Cleopatra (see also 15.242 with the note to "overcome by his passion").

⁵⁴⁷ Both *War* and *Antiquities* suggest that Herod and Cleopatra were competitors and that the queen consistently tried to take over the territories of Antony's client rulers (*War* 1.359-360, 365; *Ant.* 15.77, 92-93). *Antiquities* adds to this point that Cleopatra was involved in Alexandra's plot against Herod (15.32), that she hated the king (15.48), and that she tried to have him punished for the murder of Aristobulus III (15.63, 65, 75). Herod's hostility towards Cleopatra is understandable in the light of these passages (see also the next note).

⁵⁴⁸ This general motive (cf. *Ant.* 15.88) hardly legitimates the decision to kill the queen. Herod had certainly better reasons for having Cleopatra murdered, as Josephus points out elsewhere (see the previous note). However, the motive fits Josephus' negative portrayal of Cleopatra in *Antiquities*.

⁵⁴⁹ Enjoying sexual pleasures during a business trip must hardly have been something special for powerful men (see *Ant.* 15.29 with the note to "because of his power"). Antony was famous for having love affairs when he was abroad (see 15.27 with notes). For women, of course, such behavior was unacceptable, as Herod's response implies (see also 15.99, 102). Herod's reaction to Cleopatra's attempt as presented by Josephus matches Josephus' own avowed standards (see 15.27 with the note to "sexual pleasures"), and her portrait in *Antiquities* confirms Josephus' distrust of women in general (Mayer-Schärtel 1995: 184-91, also 15.35 with the note to "deceiving the women"). His writings imply that promiscuous behavior by women was a horror for him and he may have advocated the *univira* ideal for women (about this ideal that women should not remarry, see 15.66 with the note to "the outrage" and 17.352).

⁵⁵⁰ Josephus' long-winded wording implies that, if Cleopatra aimed at trapping Herod, the king preferred to punish her in advance.

⁵⁵¹ Bekker's conjecture ἐνεδρεύουσα ("placing in ambush") is followed by Niese (349) but unnecessarily. The reading συνεδρεύουσα of the Greek MSS makes sense because the verb συνεδρεύω ("sit in council") can also mean "lie in ambush together" (LSJ *s.v.* II). This verb is less common than ἐνεδρεύω ("lie in wait, set a trap") in Josephus; however, it still occurs 5 times elsewhere in Josephus (*War* 4.213; *Ant.* 13.364; 16.244; 17.90, 93), although with different meanings. Although Josephus does not mention Cleopatra's helpers, it is plausible to assume that she needed assistance for laying a trap for Herod.

⁵⁵² Phrases similar to τοὺς μὲν λόγους αὐτῆς διεκρούσατο ("he rejected her words") are found otherwise only in Late Antique Greek passages (Libanius, *Or.* 54.75; Procopius, *Bell.* 6.8.7).

⁵⁵³ About Herod's friends and their meetings with the king, see *Ant.* 15.5 with the note to "the friends around him."

⁵⁵⁴ Several scholars argue that both Cleopatra's attempt to seduce Herod and the king's plan to murder her are most likely fictitious (see *Ant.* 15.97 with the note to "have sex with the king"). For the expression ὑποχείριον ἔχω ("having [someone] in one's power"), see 15.20 with the note to "get control over."

⁵⁵⁵ *Ant.* 15.99 briefly renders Herod's motivation for his plan to have Cleopatra murdered. *Ant.* 15.100-103 continues with Josephus' paraphrase of Herod's friends' response. Josephus' rendering of the friends' advice starts and ends with paraphrases of their statements (15.100, 103) and presents the crux of their words in indirect speech (15.101-102).

The infinitive ἀπαλλάξειν indicates a transition to indirect speech here.

⁵⁵⁶ The Greek of the first part of Herod's motivation echoes the negative statement about Cleopatra in *Ant.* 15.98 ("knowing that she was difficult to everybody") via the repetitions of χαλεπή ("difficult") and ἅπαντας

future. At the same time it was even better for Antony,[557] for she would not even be faithful to him, if some occasion or need should occupy him so much that he had to ask for [her support in] these matters.[558] **100** His friends prevented him from planning[559] this. In the first place they pointed out that it was not worthwhile to take upon himself the most obvious danger by committing this weighty deed.[560] So they urged and even begged[561] him not to undertake anything out of rashness.[562] **101** For Antony would not bear this patiently,[563] they said, not even if someone were to point out what was his advantage right in front of his eyes,[564] since the thought that he was deprived of her through violence and treachery would inflame his love more.[565] Nothing reasonable would appear in his [Herod's] defense because, on the one hand, the attempt would have occurred against a woman who held the greatest honor of all women at that time;[566] on the other hand, the advantage [of

---

("everybody"). Herod set himself up as the protector of the public interest, although he clearly had important personal reasons to get rid of the queen (see 15.98 with notes).

[557] This motive connects Herod's plan with his speech before Octavian (*Ant.* 15.191-192), in which he recalls that he had advised Antony to kill Cleopatra (see 15.97 with the note to "have sex with the king"). For Josephus' characterization of the relationship between Antony and Cleopatra, see 15.88, 93 with notes.

[558] An alternative translation for "that he had to ask for [her support in] these matters" (τοιούτων δεησόμενον) is "and he needed such things." Herod suggests here that Cleopatra had no problem in being disloyal to her partner and patron Antony if that served her self-interest, which corresponds well with Josephus very negative portrayal of the queen (see *Ant.* 15.93-94, 97 with notes and van Henten 2005a; about the trustworthiness of Herod's point, see 15.29 with the note to "because of his power").

[559] MSS FLVW read βουλόμενον ("wishing") instead of Niese's βουλευόμενον ("planning," 350), but this does not make sense in the context. The reading βουλόμενον may easily have resulted from the omission of the characters (-ευ- of the reading βουλευόμενον. Significantly, Herod allows himself to be persuaded by his friends. There is not any trace of tyrannical behavior in this passage; in *Antiquities* such behavior only becomes prominent at the end of Herod's rule (van Henten 2011b).

[560] It is obvious that the least Antony would do in case Cleopatra died in Judea was demand an account from Herod (cf. *Ant.* 15.64). He might have held the king responsible for the queen's death, as the elaboration of the friends' advice in 15.101 indicates.

[561] For phrases similar to ἐγκείμενοι καὶ δεόμενοι, see *War* 7.108.

[562] In *Antiquities* the noun προπέτεια ("rashness," Rengstorf *s.v.*) only occurs in the section about Herod. Josephus repeatedly uses it in connection with Herod's attitude towards his wife Mariamme and their sons Alexander and Aristobulus (*Ant.* 15.223; 16.254-255, 263; cf. 15.230, 290; 16.252, 262). Nevertheless, Herod does control himself, at least at this stage of the narrative (cf. 16.263; see also 15.230 with the note to "not to kill her hastily in this way"). Here Herod's friends withhold him from doing something rash without thinking about the consequences.

[563] In *Ant.* 15.101 Josephus switches to indirect speech again, focusing on Antony's probable reaction to a murder of Cleopatra (as presented from the perspective of Herod's friends).

[564] This hypothetical reference to advice given to Mark Antony that killing Cleopatra would be to his benefit may hint at *Ant.* 15.191-192, in which passage Herod claims before Octavian that he had given Antony the advice to kill Cleopatra. Following up this advice would have enabled Antony to keep his power and come to an agreement with Octavian (see also 15.97 with the note to "have sex with the king"). For phrases similar to τὸ συμφέρον στήσειε πρὸ τῶν ὀμμάτων, see Libanius, *Or.* 60.11; John Chrysostom, *Bab. Iul.* 112; and also *Ant.* 15.192.

[565] The first of the 3 arguments put forward by Herod's friends is that Antony is desperately in love with Cleopatra. This echoes earlier passages about Antony and Cleopatra (*Ant.* 15.88, 93) and implies that killing Cleopatra would only increase his love. Such an emotional response is confirmed by Herod's own behavior after the death of his wife Mariamme (15.240-246). For the verb ὑπεκκαίω with τὸν ἔρωτα as object ("inflame someone's love," Rengstorf *s.v.*), cf. Charito 1.3.7. The verb occurs once elsewhere in Josephus (*War* 1.480).

[566] The second point made by the friends, i.e., that Cleopatra is the most important woman in this period, may in fact be accurate (see *Ant.* 15.24 with the note to "Cleopatra"). See also Josephus' statement that Mariamme surpassed all women because of her beauty and dignity of manners (15.237). The expression μέγιστον ἀξίωμα ("greatest honor, highest reputation") is quite common (see, e.g., Thucydides 4.18; Plato, *Leg.*

killing her]—if anyone would think it was an advantage—would show at the same time his[567] stubbornness and condemnation of Antony's behavior.[568] **102** From these arguments it was evident[569] that the future of his[570] rule and his family[571] would be full of great and never-ending disasters, while it was possible to get away from the lapse that Cleopatra was encouraging him to make[572] and handle the situation like a gentleman.[573] **103** By frightening[574] him with such a consideration and by intimating[575] the probable danger, they stopped him from making the attempt. He conciliated Cleopatra with presents[576] and escorted her to Egypt.[577]

(4.3) 104 After Antony had captured[578] Armenia,[579] he sent off Artabazes, Tigranes' son,[580] as a captive to Egypt[581] together with his sons.[582] He presented them as a gift to

Antony sends the Armenian king Artabazes as a gift to Cleopatra.
War *1.363*

690b; Diodorus 12.79; 14.31; 15.78; Plutarch, *Fab.* 17.4; *Rom.* 13.6).

[567] I.e., Herod's.

[568] The third argument of the friends is that the potential advantage of killing Cleopatra will never outweigh Antony's conclusion that Herod has been disloyal to his patron.

[569] Literally "it was not uncertain/unclear that" (οὐκ ἄδηλον). It is a case of *litotes*, a figure of speech that Josephus uses frequently (see, e.g., *War* 1.241; *Life* 1; Mason in BJP 9 on 1; see also *Ant.* 15.39 with the note to "many").

[570] I.e., Herod's. The king's friends now focus on the probable outcome for Herod in case Cleopatra would be killed.

[571] Both Herod's rule and his family are mentioned, which matches an important feature of *Antiquities*' Herod narrative: in *Antiquities* Josephus intermingles the history of Herod's rule with the events within his family, in contrast to the presentation in *War*. *War* relates the dramatic history about Herod's family in one coherent section (1.431-673), which especially highlights the deteriorating relationship between Herod and his sons by Mariamme. *Antiquities* reports how Herod strengthened his power step by step with the help of his Roman patrons after the capture of Jerusalem. Already at the beginning of *Antiquities* 15, immediately after the capture, Josephus focuses on conflicts within Herod's family by highlighting the discontent of Herod's mother-in-law Alexandra and her attempts to undermine the king's rule (see 15.23 with the note to "Alexandra").

[572] This statement obviously refers to Cleopatra's proposal reported in *Ant.* 15.97. It disqualifies it as a lapse from Herod's perspective, which might be surprising in the light of the conventional images of male rulers. The lapse is, however, perfectly understandable if we assume that it reflects Josephus' own point of view (see also 15.98 with the note to "out of licentiousness").

[573] An alternative translation for τίθεσθαι τὸν καιρόν is suggested by Rengstorf (*s.v.* καιρός): "seize the opportunity." This translation seems less probable than the one given above because of the subsequent adverb εὐσχημόνως, which can mean, i.a., "honorably, worthily" (Rengstorf *s.v.*) and "like a gentleman" (LSJ *s.v.* εὐσχημων II.1). Cf. *Ant.* 16.101; *Life* 32.

[574] The verb δεδίττομαι ("frighten," Rengstorf *s.v.*) occurs once elsewhere in Josephus (*War* 4.224).

[575] The verb παραδηλόω ("intimate, mention in passing," Rengstorf *s.v.*) occurs 5 times in Josephus (apart from *War* 4.124 only in *Antiquities*: 12.357; 15.103, 372, 409).

[576] Herod acts in this way as one of Cleopatra's friends in business and politics who were dependent on her (about this meaning of "friends," see *Ant.* 15.5 with the note to "the friends around him"). For other combinations of θεραπεύω ("pay court to, conciliate," Rengstorf *s.v.*) and δωρεαῖς/δώροις, see 5.189; 15.205; 20.205.

[577] In *Ant.* 15.103 Josephus matches the parallel account of *War* again. *War* 1.362 is also brief but notes more specifically that Herod escorted Cleopatra to Pelusium (in Egypt, east of the eastern Nile Delta) and that he treated her with the highest respect. *Ant.* 15.103 echoes part of the vocabulary of *War* 1.362 through the verbs προπέμπω ("escort," Rengstorf *s.v.*) and θεραπεύω ("conciliate").

[578] The translation is based on the reading λαβών (Niese 350). MSS PF read ἀναλαβών ("recaptured").

[579] This note links up with *Ant.* 15.96 (see the note to "war against Armenia") about Antony's campaign against Armenia, in 34 BCE.

[580] I.e., the Armenian king Artabazes-Artavasdes II. He ruled from ca. 55 to 34 BCE (see *Ant.* 15.105) and died in ca. 30 BCE. His father was Tigranes the Great (95-55 BCE). Cleopatra executed him after the Battle of Actium (Strabo 11.14.15; Cassius Dio 51.5.5; Buchheim 1960: 81-83; Huss 2001: 738-40; see also the next note).

[581] Antony had taken Artabazes-Artavasdes II prisoner of war (cf. *Ant.* 15.96 with the note to "war against Armenia"). He trapped the king in the Roman camp, supposedly because Artabazes-Artavasdes had betrayed him during his campaign against Parthia in 36 BCE (Plutarch, *Comp. Demetr. Ant.* 5.2; Buchheim 1960: 82-83). Artabazes-Artavasdes accompanied Antony as

Cleopatra along with all the valuables of the kingdom,[583] which he had taken from it. **105** Artaxias, the eldest of Artabazes' sons,[584] having escaped at that time, became king of Armenia.[585] Archelaus[586] and Nero Caesar[587] expelled him[588] and brought Tigranes, his

---

hostage during the journey through his kingdom in order to allow Antony access to Armenian treasuries. Antony put him in silver chains, when the Parthians appointed his son Artaxias king (cf. *Ant.* 15.105), and took him to Alexandria (Strabo 11.13.4; 11.14.15; Tacitus, *Ann.* 2.3; Plutarch, *Ant.* 50.4; 53.6; Cassius Dio 49.39.3-40.4; 49.44.2). On the connections between Rome and Armenia in this period, see Chaumon 1976.

[582] This passage expands on the parallel passage of *War* (1.363), which only mentions the Armenian king as captive and does not refer to the sons of Artabazes-Artavasdes (likewise Plutarch, *Ant.* 50.4).

The translation follows the reading σὺν τοῖς παισί of MSS FAMV. MS P reads σὺν τοῖς παισὶ σατράπαις ("together with his children-satraps," which is the text given by Niese [353] and which is supported by the Latin version); MS W and E attest a corrected reading (σὺν τοῖς παισὶ καὶ σατράπαις ["together with his children and satraps"], which is the text given by Marcus-Wikgren 50). The readings with the word σατράπαις ("satraps") may derive from a scribal error, which evolved from the word παισί, which shares 4 characters with σατράπαις. The information that Antony brought not only the king but also his sons to Alexandria is confirmed by Cassius Dio, who also mentions Artabazes-Artavasdes' wife in this connection but no satraps (49.40.2-3; cf. 51.16.2; Buchheim 1960: 90-91; Becher 1966: 29; Chaumont 1976: 72-73). *War* 1.363 mentions, in addition to Artabazes-Artavasdes, money and booty from Armenia as Antony's presents to Cleopatra (see the next note). Denarius coins with the portraits of Antony and Cleopatra from 32/31 BCE proclaim Armenia's complete defeat with the legend *Armenia devicta* (Sydenham 1952: 194 no. 1210; Goodman 1997: 245-46).

[583] This passage may be an allusion to Antony's mock triumphal procession in Alexandria: Antony entered Alexandria as *Neos Dionysos* and presented the Armenian king Artabazes-Artavasdes, in golden chains, together with the king's family to Cleopatra (Cassius Dio 49.40.3-4; Buchheim 1960: 74; Huzar 1978: 182; despite certain analogies, this procession was, of course, not an official triumphal procession, it took place outside Rome and was not granted by the Senate). One day later the well-known scene in the gymnasium of Alexandria took place, during which Antony declared Cleopatra "Queen of Kings" (*regina regum*) and divided the territories in the East in a new way. Ptolemy Caesarion was recognized by Antony as Julius Caesar and Cleopatra's son and appointed as Cleopatra's co-ruler. He was called "King of Kings" (Plutarch, *Ant.* 54.5-6; Cassius Dio 49.41.1-6). Both actions were part of Antony's preparations for a new campaign against Parthia (Kienast 1999: 61, 63).

[584] Artaxias II (also called Artaxes or Artashes) was the eldest son of Artabazes-Artavasdes II and king of Armenia from 34 to 20 BCE, when he lost the support of his fellow Armenians (Cassius Dio 49.39.6-40.1; see also the next notes and *Ant.* 15.104 with the note to "Artabazes, Tigranes' son").

[585] During Antony's campaign in Armenia, Artaxias fled to the Parthian king Phraates IV, who put him on the throne of Armenia (Cassius Dio 49.40.2). Artaxias killed the Roman garrison troops that had stayed behind in Armenia (Cassius Dio 51.16.2; Chaumont 1976: 73-75).

[586] King Archelaus of Cappadocia is meant here, one of Antony's friendly kings (Sullivan 1980: 1149-61). Antony supported him starting from 41 BCE and made him king of Cappadocia in 36 BCE. Archelaus received Lesser Armenia, certain regions of Rough Cilicia, and the Cilician coast in 20 BCE (see the next note).

[587] Josephus refers to the future emperor Tiberius and makes a chronological jump (i.e., from 34 to 20 BCE, Sullivan 1980: 1155). Tiberius' official name was Tiberius Claudius Nero (Kienast 1996: 76).

[588] Armenian envoys to Augustus in 20 BCE requested Artaxias' deposition and the appointment of Artaxias' brother Tigranes as king. Augustus agreed and sent Tiberius off with an army to Armenia. When Tiberius arrived, relatives had already murdered Artaxias (*Res gest. divi Aug.* 27; Velleius Paterculus 2.94, who refers to Artabazes-Artavasdes instead of Tigranes as the new Armenian king; Tacitus, *Ann.* 2.3; Suetonius, *Tib.* 9.1; Cassius Dio 54.9.4-5; Chaumont 1976: 74-75; Kienast 1999: 343), which implies that Josephus' remark is not entirely correct (as noted by Marcus-Wikgren 51 n. *f*). The Parthian king Phraates IV accepted Tiberius' intervention in Armenia because of the peace treaty concluded between the Romans and Parthians in the same year (see *Ant.* 15.11 with the note to "the Parthians").

[589] Tigranes III was king of Armenia from 20 to 8 BCE. He was a son of Artabazes-Artavasdes II (see *Ant.* 15.104 with the note to "Artabazes, Tigranes' son") and a brother of Artaxias II (see the previous note; *Res gest. divi Aug.* 27; Tacitus, *Ann.* 2.3). He was living in Rome when the Armenian embassy arrived with the request that he would become king instead of his brother (Cassius Dio 54.9.4-5).

younger brother,[589] to rule the kingdom. These things, however, happened later.[590]

(4.4) 106 Now, as for the duties[591] that Herod had to pay [Cleopatra] for the land given [to her] by Antony,[592] he was obeying the contract[593] because he considered it unsafe[594] to give Cleopatra a reason for hating him.[595] **107** The Arab,[596] however, whose tribute Herod had taken upon himself,[597] kept supplying the two hundred talents[598] to Herod for some

Herod pays duties to Cleopatra. Fights two battles against "the Arab".
War *1.362; 364-369*

---

[590] This formula (ταῦτα μὲν οὖν ἐν ὑστέρῳ) indicates that the last events reported in *Ant.* 15.105 fall outside Josephus' chronological framework for this section of the Herod narrative, which is set before the Battle of Actium (in 31 BCE; see 15.109), although Josephus usually presents the events in their chronological order (van Henten and Huitink 2007). Landau (2006: 122) calls 15.104-105 a short external *prolepsis*, meaning that the Armenian succession is not narrated elsewhere in Josephus. For a similar formula in Josephus, see 18.194 (cf. 15.20). The formulae with ὕστερον in *War* 5.445; *Ant.* 20.48 also point to later events, but they include cross-references to later passages in Josephus.

[591] The noun φόρος ("tax, tribute, duty," Rengstorf *s.v.*) does not necessarily mean "tribute"; it can denote various kinds of payments (Braund 1984: 63-64; Udoh 2005: 142).

[592] "The land given" most probably concerns the territories mentioned in *Ant.* 15.96, given to Cleopatra (i.e., areas in Arabia and Jericho; cf. *War* 1.362 "... [Herod] ... rented the lands that had been torn from his kingdom," trans. Sievers/Forte in BJP 1a). This gift led to Cleopatra's visit of Herod and to Herod's lease of Nabatean territories (cf. *Ant.* 15.107, which implies that Herod provided surety for the Nabatean king) and the region of Jericho (15.96). Josephus does not specify here the amount of money involved in the leases of these territories, which may have been 200 or 400 talents, depending on the passages on which the interpretation is based. The account of *War* (1.362) reports that Herod leased back the territories that Antony had taken away for an annual sum of 200 talents; *Ant.* 15.132 implies a sum of 400 talents: "... I gave two hundred talents and also became the guarantor for two hundred [more], which went to her [i.e., Cleopatra] as collector ...." Richardson (1996: 166 with nn. 70 and 74) argues that the annual sum that Herod had to pay to Cleopatra was 200 and not 400 talents and that *Ant.* 15.106-107 implies that Herod had to pay 200 talents all in all; this would mean that Herod got Jericho for free since he received 200 talents from the Nabatean king Malichus (as 15.107 indicates). Shatzman (1991: 287), Schalit (2001: 121), and Udoh (2005: 145-48) argue that Herod had to pay 400 talents (200 plus 200 because he was surety for the 200 talents from Malichus). Huzar (1978: 167) mentions an even higher amount of 1200 talents, but she does not explain her calculation.

[593] *Ant.* 15.106-160 frequently presents the events from the king's perspective and offers a rather positive portrait of him.

The adjective δίκαιος ("just, legal") implies here that Herod fulfilled the obligations that the lease contract implied (LSJ *s.v.* I.2; see also *Ant.* 15.108), which means that the land in question was that under lease from Cleopatra.

[594] The expression (οὐκ) ἀσφαλές plus ἡγέομαι ("consider [un]safe") is common in ancient literature (e.g., Xenophon, *Cyr.* 7.2.29; Demosthenes, *Or.* 24.165; Philo, *Mos.* 2.247; Polyaenus 5.19.1) and also occurs in Josephus (*War* 3.451, 457; 4.33; *Ant.* 15.164).

[595] Cleopatra was a most dangerous opponent for Herod (see *Ant.* 15.24 with the note to "Cleopatra"). If her attitude towards Herod turned into hatred, he would definitely be in trouble. The brief parallel passage of *War* (1.362) suggests that Herod behaved as if he was Cleopatra's friendly king by trying to mollify her hostility (δυσμένειαν; cf. *Ant.* 15.65) with huge presents and leasing back the territories that Antony had taken away from him.

[596] This short-hand title (cf. *War* 1.159, 274, 278; *Ant.* 15.172; 16.224; 20.78) most probably refers to the Nabatean king Malichus I. He is mentioned in *Ant.* 14.370 as "Malchus [or Malichus with MS P], the king of the Arabs" (Hackl, Jenni, and Schneider 2003: 42-44; see Schalit 2001: 749-50 about the Nabatean name Malichus). Malichus outlived Cleopatra; he ruled from the early fifties to ca. 30 BCE (Richardson 1996: 165 n. 62; Mahieu 2012: 129-32 argues for his death in March/April 30 BCE; Retsö 2003: 371-73 argues for a rule from ca. 58 to ca. 28 BCE).

Greek and Roman authors apply the name "Arabs" to a variety of ethnic groups, but Josephus frequently attaches it to the Nabateans (Millar 1993a). The context here confirms the reference to the Nabatean king (see also *Ant.* 15.96 with the note to "the areas in Arabia that were given to her"). Retsö (2003:371-91) distinguishes the Arabs from the Nabateans, arguing that the Arabs acted as a kind of military elite on behalf of the Nabateans.

[597] The translation is based on Niese's conjecture of ἐπιδεξαμένου ("[Herod] had taken upon himself," 351). The reading ἐπιδειξαμένου ("[Herod] had displayed for himself") of most of the Greek MSS does not make sense and is easily explainable as a corruption of Niese's conjectured reading.

The Nabatean king probably subleased from Herod

time, but he became malicious afterwards and slow with his payments.[599] Parts of the account he would settle barely, if it all, and not even these did he wish to give with no strings attached.[600] **(5.1) 108** Because [the Arab][601] acted unfairly[602] in this way and in the end no longer wanted to do anything that was lawfully agreed upon,[603] Herod was ready to attack him, though he took the Roman war[604] as an occasion for a delay.[605] **109** For the

---

the Nabatean territories given to Cleopatra (Richardson 1996: 166; Schalit 2001: 121; see *Ant.* 15.106 with the note to "for the land given by Antony"). Herod stood, in any case, surety for the lease of the Nabatean territories (see 15.132 with the note to "became the guarantor for two hundred [more]"; Stern 1974b: 232; Smallwood 1976: 67; Kasher 1988: 136; Hackl, Jenni, and Schneider 2003: 43, 502). Shatzman (1991: 288-90) concludes on the basis of Plutarch's note (*Ant.* 36.2) about the Nabatean territory given to Cleopatra (i.e., the part of Arabia that inclines toward the outer sea) that it concerned the Nabatean land east-northeast of the Dead Sea.

[598] The noun τάλαντον ("talent") originally referred to weigh-scales and later became a standard weight: the Attic talent weighed ca. 26 kg/57 lb of gold or silver, and the Aeginetic talent ca. 38 kg/84 lb. The talent was worth 6,000 drachmas (Mason in BJP 1b on *War* 2.50). In *Ant.* 17.146, 189-190, 321-323 Josephus suggests that a Judean talent was worth 10,000 Attic drachmas.

The amount of 200 talents for Malichus' lease and the total sum of 400 talents for Herod's lease (i.e., Jericho plus Nabatean territories) are extremely high. The 200 talents for the Nabatean territory may be explained by the profitable bitumen industry at the Dead Sea, which was a major source of income for the Nabateans, second only to the spice trade (Shatzman 1991: 288). The amount of 200 talents is the same as the sum mentioned in connection with Herod's lease of the area of Jericho taken from his own kingdom (*Ant.* 15.96—*War* 1.362 does not specify this territory). In *Ant.* 17.318 (paralleled by *War* 2.95) Josephus indicates that an annual tax revenue of 200 talents was collected from all of Galilee and Perea (Sievers/Forte in BJP 1a on 1.362).

[599] The implication of Malichus' being in default seems to be that Herod had to make up the amount out of his own pocket (on Herod's being surety for Malichus towards Cleopatra, see *Ant.* 15.106 with the note to "for the land given by Antony"). *War* 1.220-222 reports a similar situation for Herod's father Antipater, who coordinated contributions to Cassius: the passage mentions slow payments and refers in this connection to a certain Malichus, who is further otherwise unknown (Schürer-Vermes 1.277). In *Antiquities* Josephus transfers this episode to Herod's period (14.370). Cassius almost executed this Malichus because of his sluggish payment, which Antipater prevented by appeasing Cassius with 100 talents (Shatzman 1991: 286-87).

[600] This translation of ἀζήμιως is uncertain. Marcus-Wikgren (53) translate "without withholding part of it" (cf. Rengstorf *s.v.* ἀζήμιος, who gives "without curtailment/inflicting loss/causing damage" as meanings); Thackeray and Marcus (1930-55: 1.10) and LSJ (*s.v.* ἀζήμιος I.1) propose "not without fraud." The adjective ἀζήμιος occurs once in Josephus, in the context of military actions meaning "without inflicting loss" (see *Ant.* 15.120 with the note to "inflict severe losses upon").

[601] The sentence presupposes "the Arab," mentioned in *Ant.* 15.107, as subject. Josephus does not explicitly refer to the Nabatean king Malichus I, but the context implies that Herod wanted to attack this king because of his inadmissible behavior (see the next note, and about Malichus I, 15.92 with the note to "the territory of the Arabs" and 15.107 with the note to "the Arab"). For a survey of the relationships between the Nabateans and Herod and his relatives, see Shatzman 1991: 277-309.

[602] The first words of this paragraph refer to the last part of *Ant.* 15.107 and introduce the motivation for Herod's military actions against the Nabateans, on which the long section of 15.108-160 focuses. The elaborate and well-composed commander speech in 15.127-146 constitutes its central part. From a narratological perspective the entire section can be characterized as a 'scene': the pace of the narrative slows down and Josephus offers elaborate scenic descriptions (about scenes in ancient Greek narratives, see de Jong 2007: 11-12); he quotes Herod's entire speech and describes the battle's beginning and outcome in great detail (*Ant.* 15.147-159; cf. *War* 1.380-385). By contrast, the main combat is summarized very briefly in general terms (*Ant.* 15.151). The verb ἀγνωμονέω ("act unfairly") also occurs in 16.283, 285, 353, which passages also refer to Nabateans.

[603] The repetition of δίκαιος ("just, lawful") in *Ant.* 15.106, 108 highlights the contrast between Herod and the Nabatean king (see also 15.106 with the note to "he was obeying the contract"): contrary to Herod, Malichus I did not fulfill his obligation. Syllaeus, another Nabatean leader, later behaves in a similar way (16.282).

[604] Josephus specifies this war in *Ant.* 15.109 (see the next note). Herod's patron Antony was one of its protagonists, which explains Herod's postponement of the campaign against King Malichus.

[605] This detail suggests that Herod acted as a respon-

Battle of Actium,[606] which actually took place in the hundred and eighty-seventh Olympiad,[607] was anticipated. Caesar[608] was about to contend with Antony for the

---

sible and loyal friendly king since it was to be expected that his patron Antony would need his support in the conflict with Octavian. It is surprising that Antony rejected Herod's military aid (*Ant.* 15.110).

Kasher (1988: 138-41, 146-47) argues that the conflict between Herod and the Nabateans, which was complex and led to several battles, must have started quite some time before the Battle of Actium and that it actually lasted from the summer of 32 to the summer of 31 BCE.

[606] The Battle of Actium (in 31 BCE, also mentioned in *Ant.* 15.121, 161) was officially a battle against the foreign queen Cleopatra (Dio 50.6), but in fact the decisive battle between Octavian and Antony. Their relationship had deteriorated considerably in the preceding years, especially after Antony had divorced his wife Octavia, Octavian's sister (in May 32 BCE). Antony stationed his camp near Actium, which was located at the entrance of the Ambracian Gulf (also called "Gulf of Arta"), a large enclosed gulf along the Ionian coast of northwest Greece. The sea battle took place on 2 September 31 BCE and changed the political scene considerably (Hölbl 1994: 222-27; Kienast 1999: 63-77; Halfmann 2011: 198-229). Octavian commemorated his triumph over Antony and Cleopatra intensely: he founded a new Greek city north of Actium, at the location where his army was stationed (i.e., northwest of the Ambracian Gulf). Its name Nicopolis (officially *Actia Nicopolis*) alluded to Octavian's victory. The victory was also highlighted by a monument and votive inscriptions for Mars and Neptunus at the Michalitsi Hill (Kienast 1999: 78-79, 242, 433-34, 445, 458-59, 461-63, 469). The so-called Actian Games were organized every 4 years in Nicopolis and kept the memory of Octavian's victory alive. They were probably founded on 2 September 27 BCE (Strabo 7.325; Cassius Dio 41.1; Marcus-Wikgren 262 n. *a*). Octavian erected impressive memorials near the site of the battle (Suetonius, *Aug.* 18.2) and gave the existing local Actian Games an isolympic status. Political leaders in other districts organized similar games in honor of Octavian and sometimes even claimed a same status for them, calling them *isaktia* (Otto 1913: 64-65; Pleket 1975: 67; Schalit 2001: 370-71). Gurval (1995: 65-81) offers a survey of the *Aktia* celebrated throughout the empire. Finally, a new era, called "Actiad," also recalled Octavian's victory (*War* 1.398; *Ant.* 18.26; Mahieu 2012: 134). Part of Actium's aftermath was that Octavian decided to work with several of the friendly kings who had cooperated with Antony, including Herod (see *War* 1.386-397; *Ant.* 15.187-201, 215-218). Other references to the Battle of Actium in *Antiquities* are rather similar to the phrase used here (τῆς ἐπ' Ἀκτίῳ μάχης; cf. 15.121, 161, 191). Josephus uses another formula in *War* 1.364: τοῦ δ' Ἀκτιακοῦ πολέμου ("the War of Actium"; cf. 1.370, 386, 388).

[607] The calendar based on the 4-yearly cycle of the Olympic Games started according to tradition with the first games in the summer of 776 BCE. The 187th Olympiad lasted from the summer of 32 to the summer of 28 BCE (for further references to the Olympiads, see *Ant.* 12.248, 321; 13.236; 14.4, 66, 389, 487; 16.136; *Apion* 1.184-185; 2.17). Other historians also use this calendar, but Josephus' references are particularly significant because he frequently combines Olympiads with other dating references (van Henten and Huitink 2007). Lämmer (1974: 110-11, 130-35) suggests that Josephus means the first year of an Olympiad if the year is not specified (as in this passage). *Ant.* 15.109, however, does not support this hypothesis since the passage implies the 2nd year of the relevant Olympiad (i.e., the year summer 31-summer 30 BCE).

[608] "Caesar" (Καῖσαρ; Latin *Caesar*) was originally the surname (*cognomen*) of the *gens* Julia, especially of Julius Caesar. The name refers here to Octavian (63 BCE-14 CE), who was the adopted son of Julius Caesar (see below). For Octavian "Caesar" was a family name, on which he relied heavily in his early years. For the later Julio-Claudians, likewise, the Caesar name was familial, all of them had a connection to Julius Caesar. Later on, especially since the Flavians, "Caesar" became a title of the emperor (LSJ *s.v.*). Octavian-Augustus was scrupulously careful not to accept other titles than that of *princeps* ("the most eminent, leader," see below; cf. his *Res Gestae*). He even declined Caesar's title "dictator." In spite of the fact that he had arranged for a *de facto* monarchy, Augustus emphasized in his statements that he was a true Republican leader. Later Roman authors like Cassius Dio, however, considered Augustus to be the first emperor (Kienast 1999: 204-12).

This is the first reference to Octavian in *Ant.* 15 (for further references, see Schalit 1968: 69-70). Octavian was the son of C. Octavius and Atia and adopted by Julius Caesar. Caesar's testament designated Octavian as his most important heir in 44 BCE. Together with Mark Antony, Octavian defeated Julius Caesar's murderers in 42 BCE. The Roman territories were divided between Octavian, Antony, and Lepidus during the Treaty of Brundisium in 40 BCE: Antony received authority over the East, Octavian over the West, and Lepidus over North-Africa. Octavian's power increased during the 2nd half of 30s at the expense of Antony, and the Battle of

Commonwealth.[609] Herod, whose country had already yielded abundant crops[610] for him for a long time, such that revenues and resources were gained,[611] enrolled an auxiliary force for Antony[612] and equipped it most carefully with armaments. **110** Antony, however, said that he did not at all need Herod's allied force[613] and commanded him to attack[614] the Arab, for he had heard about his [the Arab's] treachery[615] from Herod as well as from Cleopatra.[616] Actually, Cleopatra had requested this, thinking that it would be good for her if the one would suffer badly from the other.[617]

Actium (see the note to this battle above) brought about the decisive defeat of Antony and Cleopatra. On 16 January 27 BCE Octavian accepted the (well-prepared) proposal of the Senate to become the *princeps* (i.e., leader) of Rome. From this date onward his name switched to Augustus (further discussion and references in Kienast 1996: 61-68; 1999).

[609] For the decisive character of the Battle of Actium, see the notes to "Battle of Actium" and "Caesar" at this paragraph. On τὰ πράγματα meaning "government" or "administration," (here of the Romans), see *Ant.* 15.32 with the note to "the government" and cf. *War* 1.109, 111, 120, in which passages τῶν ὅλων is used with a similar meaning.

[610] The rare verb εὐβοτέομαι (literally "furnish good pasture," LSJ *s.v.*; Rengstorf *s.v.*) is a *hapax legomenon* in Josephus. Josephus hints here at Herod's income from the tax on agricultural produce (Udoh 2005: 162; see *Ant.* 15.303 with the note to "the revenues he received from the land").

[611] Several alternative readings have been proposed (Niese 351; Marcus-Wikgren 52), but the transmitted text (προσόδων καὶ δυνάμεως εὑρημένων) is perfectly understandable if one interprets εὑρημένων as "were gained" (LSJ *s.v.* εὑρίσκω IV).

Herod had been ruling over Judea for about 6 years, and Josephus does not give indications elsewhere that Judea prospered at this stage of Herod's rule (cf. *Ant.* 15.5). Antony's gift of Jericho and the coastal region to Cleopatra (15.94-96) must have reduced Herod's income. Nevertheless, Josephus indicates that Herod's means were considerable, and he emphasizes several times that the king tried hard to impress his patrons with gifts and services (e.g., 15.5, 75, 103, 200-201).

[612] Supporting one's patron with auxiliary troops during a campaign was an obvious task for a friendly king (see *Ant.* 15.5 with the note to "the friends around him"; about auxiliary forces during the Early Empire, see Holder 1980).

[613] In *Ant.* 15.189 Herod recalls during his meeting with Octavian on the island of Rhodes in 30 BCE that he had sent money and grain to Antony in order to support him in his campaign against Octavian. The parallel passage of *War* (1.388) mentions military aid and countless supplies of grain. In *Antiquities* Josephus implies that Antony's refusal of Herod's military support, which seems unplausible, was the result of Cleopatra's advice to him (see the continuation of this paragraph).

[614] Antony commands Herod to do what the king already intended to do (according to *Ant.* 15.108). In the next lines, however, Josephus presents Herod's campaign against the Nabateans as the result of Cleopatra's devilish scheming. That Antony actually ordered Herod to attack another friendly king of the Romans within Antony's sphere of influence when a major confrontation with Octavian was at hand is far from plausible (see also the next notes).

The infinitive ἐπεξελθεῖν ("attack") echoes *Ant.* 15.108 ("Herod was ready to attack him [ἐπεξελευσόμενος]").

[615] On Malichus I's negligent payment to Herod, see *Ant.* 15.107-108. Josephus uses a much stronger word here to characterize the Nabatean king's negligence (ἀπιστία "treachery"), which is echoed by ἀπίστως ("treacherously") in Herod's commander speech (15.130).

[616] This statement makes sense from Herod's perspective but not from that of Cleopatra, who would have received the money of Malichus' lease anyway since Herod acted as guarantor (see *Ant.* 15.107 with the note to "whose payment Herod had taken upon himself" and 15.132 with the note to "became the guarantor for two hundred [more]"; differently *War* 1.365). The continuation of the paragraph offers another motive for Cleopatra's complaint to Antony (see the next note).

[617] This remark links up with previous passages in the Herod narrative of *Antiquities*, which suggest that Cleopatra tried to take over Herod's or Malichus' kingdom, in line with her overall strategy to take over the territories of Antony's friendly kings living near Egypt (see 15.77, 92-93 with notes; Schalit 2001: 122). The passage implies that Cleopatra at this stage succeeded in persuading Antony with her cunning plan (see also 15.111), although this is implausible in the setting of the preparations for the Battle of Actium (as implied by 15.107-108) because it would have weakened Antony's power: a military conflict between Herod and Malichus would prevent them from sending auxiliary soldiers to Antony (Kasher 1988: 136-37). The parallel passage of *War* (1.365) points to a similar strategy of

111 When these things were said to him by Antony, Herod turned back and kept his army together,[618] such that he could invade Arabia[619] immediately. After a cavalry and an infantry force[620] had been equipped, he came to Diospolis,[621] where the Arabs met him in battle, since the preparation for his war had not escaped their notice.[622] A fierce battle took place,[623]

Cleopatra and suggests that she would get "Arabia" (i.e., the Nabatean kingdom; see the next note) if Herod defeated Malichus, and Judea if Herod was defeated by the Nabateans.

Once again Josephus presents Cleopatra as a wicked person who manipulated Antony time and again. Becher (1966: 67-68) argues that Josephus' description of Cleopatra's successful strategy of keeping Herod away from supporting Antony is trustworthy since it matches similar actions by her. Kasher (1988: 134-48) argues differently and concludes—on the basis of the discrepancy between *Ant.* 15.108 and 15.110 (see 15.108 with the note to "an occasion for a delay") and the implausibility of the preparations for the Battle of Actium as the setting of Josephus' report about Herod's conflict with the Nabateans—that Herod had realized beforehand that he had nothing to gain from joining forces with Antony at Actium; Herod would have started his campaign against the Nabateans in order to loosen his ties with Antony without detaching himself from him and to open the door for a new relationship as a friendly king of Octavian, Antony's opponent. His interpretation implies that Josephus' report is tendentious because it takes away the blame from Herod for starting a war against the Nabateans and focuses on Cleopatra as the evil genius instead (cf. Günther 2005: 126). A further possible reason for Cleopatra's interference appears in contemporary sources: Cleopatra may have wanted to play the first fiddle in supporting Antony in his decisive battle against Octavian (Grant 1972: 196). Cleopatra's role during this battle has been much discussed by ancient authors, and several of them suggest that Octavian's opponent was actually Cleopatra rather than Antony (Becher 1966: 32, 75-77, 108-10, 182-83; Huzar 1978: 237).

[618] This remark could suggest that Herod kept the auxiliary forces which he had collected for Antony's campaign standing by (cf. *War* 1.388), but this does not fit the context (see *Ant.* 15.110 and the previous note).

[619] "Arabia" refers to the Nabatean kingdom (see *Ant.* 15.96 with the note to "the areas in Arabia that were given to her"). The continuation of the narrative (supported by *War* 1.366) suggests that Herod's campaign was directed against the region north of Southern Hauran. For discussions of the military conflicts between Herod and the Nabateans before Actium, see Kasher 1988: 131-51; Shatzman 1991: 284-91. The Greek phrase εἰς τὴν Ἀραβίαν ἐμβαλῶν ("invading Arabia") also occurs in *War* 1.159, in a different context.

[620] *War* 1.366 only mentions that Herod levied a large cavalry force. Shatzman (1991: 170-216) offers a detailed discussion of Herod's army, which comprised 2 categories of soldiers: (1) men who received plots of land from the king for which they had to render military services in return (see *Ant.* 15.294-295; 17.24-28), and (2) troop soldiers of the king's standing army (see also 17.198-199). The bulk of the army consisted of Jews (Shatzman 1991: 186).

[621] Diospolis was the Greek name later given to the city of Lod by Septimius Severus (Kaplan 1977: 753; Tsafrir, Di Segni, and Green 1994: 171). That cannot be the reference here, since Lod was located near the Mediterranean coast, southeast of Joppe-Jafo. Most scholars assume that the original reference is to Dion (cf. *War* 1.132; *Ant.* 13.393; 14.47), one of the Decapolis cities, located ca. 40 km east of the Sea of Galilee (Marcus-Wikgren 54 n. *a*; Möller and Schmitt 1976: 82-83; Kasher 1988: 145; Shatzman 1991: 289-90; Schalit 2001: 122; Hackl, Jenni, and Schneider 2003: 497). This would fit the preceding reference to Arabia because Dion was near to the Nabatean kingdom and probably included Nabatean inhabitants. The city was captured by Alexander Janneus and later taken away again from the Judean territory by Pompey (Möller and Schmitt 1976: 82).

[622] This detail is missing in the parallel passage of *War* (1.366). It is plausible that the Nabateans were reckoning with a punitive expedition by Herod. One can even imagine that Cleopatra had informed them, since such a revelation would suit her plan (*Ant.* 15.110).

[623] The Greek μάχης καρτερᾶς γενομένης ("a fierce battle took place") echoes the vocabulary in the parallel passage of *War* (1.366; note καρτερᾶς ["fierce"] in *Ant.* 15.111 and καρτερῶς in *War* 1.366). The phrase μάχης καρτερᾶς γενομένης is a fixed expression in Josephus (*War* 1.101; *Ant.* 1.175; 5.66; 6.368; 8.383; 12.409; *Life* 327). The combination μάχη καρτερά ("fierce battle") is common since Thucydides (e.g., 4.43; 4.96; cf. Diodorus 3.54.7; 11.7.1; 11.74.3; Plutarch, *Alc.* 31.5; *Fab.* 11.5; *Rom.* 18.6) and frequently occurs in Josephus (e.g., *War* 2.47; 3.302; 6.74; *Ant.* 7.13; 8.383; 15.151; 17.258).

[624] This passage also echoes *War* 1.366 (cf. ἐκράτησαν in *Ant.* 15.111 with ἐκράτησέν in *War* 1.366 ["they/he were/was victorious"]), but the contents differ slightly: in *War* Josephus notes that Herod was victorious, while here he uses a plural verb with "the Jews" as subject. The section of *Ant.* 15.111-160 (paralleling *War* 1.366-385) reports 3 battles between Herod and the Nabateans:

and the Jews were victorious.[624] **112** After this battle a large army of Arabs assembled in Canata.[625] This is a region in Coele-Syria.[626] Herod went there too because he had heard about it beforehand, and led the greatest part of the force that he had against them. After approaching them, he decided to camp at a good [location],[627] putting up a palisade,[628] such that he could position himself to fight at his convenience. **113** When he was arranging these things, the crowd of the Jews[629] shouted that he should stop delaying and march against the Arabs. They were also eager because they believed that they were well positioned for battle.[630] Most eager were all those who had been victorious in the first

---

(1) a first battle at Diospolis, during which Herod was victorious (15.111); (2) a second one near Canata, which ended in a massacre for the Jews (15.112-119); and (3) a final one, which resulted in an overwhelming victory for Herod (15.147-160). A major part of this section consists of Herod's commander speech immediately before the third battle (15.127-146).

[625] Reading Κάνατα with Niese (352). Scholars have identified Κάνατα with Canata (Kenat in biblical passages), ca. 30 km east of Dion. MSS LAMW (supported by the Latin version) read Κανᾶ ("Cana"), but this reading must be corrupt: Cana lies west of the Sea of Galilee and does not fit with the geographical area where Herod's conflicts with the Nabateans took place (see *Ant.* 15.111 with the notes to "Arabia" and "Diospolis"). The parallel passage of *War* (1.366-367) reads Κάναθα (Canatha), which either refers to a city even further east in the Hauran Mountains (currently El-Qanawat, one of the Decapolis cities; Schalit 2001: 122, 697-98; Hackl, Jenni, and Schneider 2003: 200; Schalit [1968: 71] argues that the names Κάναθα and Κάνατα refer to the same location), or to a region that is not exactly known but probably consists of the city of Soada-Suweida and its neighborhood (west of the Hauran Mountains). All 3 locations (i.e., Kenat, El-Qanawat, and the area of Soada-Suweida) lay near to the important Nabatean city of Bostra, and the Nabateans probably formed a significant proportion of the population at those settlements, though not the majority (see 15.111 with the note to "Arabia"). An argument in favor of the third location may be that Josephus refers to a region, and not to a city or town, in the next sentence. For further discussion of this reference, see Möller and Schmitt 1976: 118-20; Schreckenberg 1977: 132-35; Kasher 1988: 144-45; Shatzman 1991: 289-90; Schalit 2001: 697-98.

[626] This statement confirms that the reference to Cana (see the previous note) cannot be correct. "Coele-Syria" can refer to several regions, which sometimes include the area of the Decapolis (see *Ant.* 15.79 with the note to "Coele-Syria"). If Josephus' previous reference concerns Canata or Canatha, then "Coele-Syria" refers here to the southern part of Syria, east of the Jordan River (Kasher 1988: 143-44).

[627] Reading ἐν καλῷ ("at a good [location]") with Niese (352), which seems to be a fixed expression, applicable to various contexts and rather common in the sense of siting a military camp (see LSJ *s.v.* καλός II; cf. Thucydides 5.59.4; 60.2; Sophocles, *El.* 384; Aristophanes, *Thesm.* 292; Xenophon, *Hell.* 21.2.25; 4.3.5; 6.2.9; *Ages.* 2.3; Plato, *Resp.* 571b; common in Dionysius and Plutarch, 5 occurrences in Josephus). Sometimes a noun like χωρίῳ ("place") is added (cf. the phrase καταστρατοπεδεύω ἐν καλῷ χωρίῳ ["encamp at a good location"] in Plutarch, *Mor.* [*Reg. imp. apophth.*] 790b; similarly *Mor.* [*An seni*] 178a). The MSS LAMW read Κανᾶ ("Cana"). Schreckenberg (1977: 132-35) conjectures ἐν καθαρῷ (sc. τόπῳ; "in the open country"), which is a Homeric phrase. Josephus' phrase στρατοπεδεύεσθαι ἐν καλῷ [χωρίῳ] is paralleled by Michael Psellus, *Chron.* 4.44.

[628] For similar expressions with βάλλεσθαι and χάραξ as object ("put up a palisade") in Josephus, see *Ant.* 20.86; *Life* 214, 395. The parallel passage of *War* (1.367) is formulated differently: "Herod ... gave the order to pitch a fortified camp (στρατόπεδον τειχίζειν) ..." (trans. Sievers/Forte in BJP 1a).

[629] For further occurrences of τὸ πλῆθος (cf. *Ant.* 15.2 with the note to "the city's population") together with τῶν Ἰουδαίων (meaning "the crowd of the Jews"), see *War* 1.335, 347; 2.342, 485; 3.151, 471; 5.489; 7.49, 300; *Ant.* 11.67; 13.353; 15.14; 16.27; 17.254, 301; 18.123; 20.7, 120, 133; *Apion* 1.313 (and *Ant.* 15.114, 126). The parallel passage of *War* (1.367) refers to the crowd of Herod's soldiers but distinguishes sharply between Herod, who tried to conduct the war most prudently, and the soldiers, who did not obey him (cf. 1.375), such that the soldiers were partly to be blamed for the subsequent defeat. The *Antiquities* report is less critical about Herod's soldiers and suggests that the king tried to make the best out of the situation.

[630] The eagerness of the soldiers to enter into battle evolves, according to Josephus' presentation, out of their assessment of the situations of both armies before the battle. A promising point of departure motivates soldiers to fight and is a common topic in commander speeches

battle⁶³¹ and had not [even] permitted the enemy to come to blows with them.⁶³² **114** While they were making noise and displaying every kind of zeal, the king, therefore, decided to make full use of the eagerness of the multitude.⁶³³ He proclaimed that he was not inferior in bravery⁶³⁴ to them. He was the first one in arms and took the lead,⁶³⁵ all of them following him in their usual positions.⁶³⁶ **115** Consternation immediately fell on the Arabs;⁶³⁷ for they offered resistance for a while,⁶³⁸ but as soon as they saw that the Jews were unbeatable⁶³⁹ and full of spirit,⁶⁴⁰ most of them retreated⁶⁴¹ and fled.⁶⁴² They would even have been beaten, had Athenio not inflicted defeat upon Herod and the Jews.⁶⁴³ **116** For he was a

---

before a battle. Being well-prepared and having a well-ordered formation were part of this rhetoric (van Henten 2005b: 193-95).

⁶³¹ This is again a well-known motif in passages describing the assessment of a situation before a battle (see the previous note). The Greek phrase τὴν πρώτην μάχην νενικήκεσαν ("had been victorious in the first battle") echoes τῇ προτέρᾳ νίκῃ ("by their recent victory") in the parallel passage of *War* (1.367).

⁶³² The expression εἰς χεῖρας ἔρχομαι with a dative construction referring to other persons meaning "come to blows with" is common and occurs already in Thucydides (e.g., 4.96; 7.44; LSJ *s.v.* χείρ II.6d). The passage highlights the greatness of the Jews' victory in their first battle against the Nabateans.

⁶³³ The vocabulary of *Ant.* 15.113 is here repeated in several phrases. Herod's decision to make use of his soldiers' eagerness differs from the information in *War* 1.367, 369 that Herod's soldiers disobeyed him (see also *Ant.* 15.119 with the note to "to get help").

⁶³⁴ The noun ἀρετή ("virtue, excellence, bravery") may be variously interpreted, depending on the context and the person characterized by this term (Finkelberg 2002). It occurs with several meanings in the Herod narrative of *Antiquities* (14.446; 15.114, 146; 16.247, 382; 17.13, 29-30, 44, 49, 54, 60, 75, 100-102, 107, 116, 118, 124, 129-130, 149, 152-153, 158, 171, 181). Here, in a military context, it concerns "bravery" (see also *War* 1.332; *Ant.* 14.446; 15.146).

⁶³⁵ In line with the Greek ideal of military commanders, Herod goes ahead of his soldiers and leads the way to the enemy (see, e.g., Xenophon, *Anab.* 6.5; Diodorus 17.57.6; cf. 2 Macc 8:23; 11:7; Josephus, *War* 3.483-484; *Ant.* 7.390). As a final touch of encouragement after delivering his commander speech the Spartan commander Brasidas sets the example to his soldiers by entering battle first (Thucydides 5.9.6, 10; 5.10.1).

⁶³⁶ The noun τέλος sometimes means "army unit, position" (Rengstorf *s.v.*; Shatzman 1991: 158, 207).

⁶³⁷ The well-organized attack of the Jewish army immediately leads to consternation among the enemy soldiers, which suggests, together with subsequent statements in this paragraph, that a fast Jewish victory was to be expected. The expression ἔκπληξις ἐμπίπτει ("consternation fell on") is typical for Josephus (see *War* 3.1; 5.547 and cf. 5.472) and also occurs a few times elsewhere (Thucydides 4.34.2; Dionysius, *Ant. rom.* 6.47.1; Philostratus, *Vit. soph.* 516).

⁶³⁸ The phrase ἀντιστάντες εἰς ὀλίγον ("they offered resistance for a while") has a close parallel in Lucian, *Dial. d.* 22.1.

⁶³⁹ The invincibility of the Jews is an important motif in 2 Maccabees, which book emphasizes that the Jews were unbeatable because of the support of their God (van Henten 1997: 153-56, 194-95). Thus the Greek commander Lysias states after his failure to capture Beth-Zur: "As he was not without intelligence, he pondered over the defeat that had befallen him, and realized that the Hebrews were invincible because the mighty God fought on their side ..." (2 Macc 11:13). Josephus also uses the word ἄμαχος ("invincible") in a passage about the high priest Ananus, who knew that the Romans were invincible and therefore was looking for ways to end the conflict with them safely (*War* 4.320).

⁶⁴⁰ The phrase μεστός φρονήματος ("full of spirit"; similarly *War* 1.602) is common in contemporary Greek authors (e.g., Plutarch, *Ages.* 29.4; *Brut.* 13.4; Philo, *Legat.* 62; *Virt.* 3). The word φρόνημα occurs several times in Herod's commander speech of *War* (1.376, 378; see also *Ant.* 15.128, 139; cf. *War* 1.387; *Ant.* 15.126).

⁶⁴¹ Niese (352) and Marcus-Wikgren (56) read ἐγκλίναντες ("bending in, fleeing"), following Bekker's conjecture. However, the reading ἐκκλίναντες ("bending out, retreating") of most MSS makes sense: it can mean "giving ground, retreating" (LSJ *s.v.* ἐκκλίνω II.1; see also *Ant.* 15.152 with the note to "had retreated").

⁶⁴² The imperfect verbal form ἔφευγον ("they fled") should be interpreted as an immediative imperfect, indicating that the Nabateans fled straight away (about such imperfects, see Rijksbaron 2002: 17-18).

⁶⁴³ Athenio was one of Cleopatra's generals (*Ant.* 15.116, 139; he is also mentioned in *War* 1.367, 369, 375). His intervention against the Jews in the second battle (*Ant.* 15.115-117, 140) matches Cleopatra's plan for Herod and the Nabatean king (see *War* 1.365, 440; *Ant.* 15.77, 92-93, 110). The parallel passage in *War*

general of Cleopatra⁶⁴⁴ in that area⁶⁴⁵ and hostile towards Herod.⁶⁴⁶ He was watching for the outcome, for which he was well-prepared.⁶⁴⁷ He had decided to remain inactive⁶⁴⁸ as long as the Arabs performed brilliantly.⁶⁴⁹ In case they should lose, which actually did happen, [he had decided] to attack the Jews⁶⁵⁰ with [the troops] formed of his own men⁶⁵¹ and those who had joined him from the region.⁶⁵² **117** At that time he unexpectedly fell⁶⁵³ upon them [the Jews], who had become weary and were thinking themselves victorious;⁶⁵⁴

(1.369) highlights Athenio's treacherous role. The passage here already reveals that his interference would have a decisive impact on the battle, which resulted in a massacre for the Jews (*Ant.* 15.117-119; cf. *War* 1.368-369; further discussion in Kasher 1988: 138-41, 144-48).

⁶⁴⁴ The Greek οὗτος γὰρ ὢν στρατηγὸς Κλεοπάτρας is close to Josephus' introductory information about Athenio in *War* 1.367. The noun στρατηγός means "general" or "commander" here, as it does in several other passages in Josephus (e.g., *War* 1.47; *Ant.* 13.43; Rengstorf *s.v.*; see also the next note).

⁶⁴⁵ This detail is missing in the parallel report of *War* (1.367). The Greek is elliptical and open to several interpretations: an alternative translation is "in charge of her forces there" (cf. Marcus-Wikgren 57; Meijer-Wes 3.167), in which case the ἐπί plus the genitive would express Athenio's control over the men mentioned (see Luraghi 2003: 311), but this reading seems less probable in the light of the continuation of the narrative. Athenio may have been in the area to control territories that belonged to Cleopatra: Chalcis and, possibly, Damascus (see *Ant.* 15.92 with the note to "Lysanias, the son of Ptolemy" and 15.96 with the note to "Damascus"). Shatzman (1991: 290) argues that Athenio was both a commander of Cleopatra and a governor of the region.

⁶⁴⁶ Athenio was apparently obeying Cleopatra's orders. Interestingly, Herod characterizes him later in his speech (see *Ant.* 15.139-140) in similar terms as Josephus characterizes Cleopatra. Josephus does not report that Athenio intervened in the third battle (15.126-159), which is surprising since Athenio's strategy implies that he would unceasingly prevent a victory by Herod (see also the next notes). Kasher (1988: 139-40, 148, building on Joseph Klausner's reading of the passage [1949-1951: 4.22-3 with footnote 39]) offers two possible explanations for this detail: (1) Athenio had left the region before the third battle in order to assist Cleopatra at the Battle of Actium (which implies that Herod's conflict with the Nabateans started before Actium), or (2) Athenio's double game, as described in this paragraph, was invented by someone at Herod's court, who rewrote the history of the conflict for 2 purposes, namely: to put even more blame on Cleopatra and to conceal that Herod had started the war at his own initiative (and thus had exceeded his authority as a friendly ruler since he had not asked Antony for permission). Kasher (1988: 140-41) considers the second explanation to be more plausible because Cleopatra could only have sent Athenio with Antony's consent and such a consent is only imaginable if Herod had exceeded his authority. However, on the basis of Josephus' text it remains complicated to discern what Athenio actually did.

The Greek διάφορος plus a dative ("hostile towards [Herod]") repeats the vocabulary of *War* 1.367 about Athenio.

⁶⁴⁷ The Greek οὐκ ἀπαρασκεύως (literally "not without preparation") expresses a *litotes* and is echoed a few lines later in the same paragraph through the participle παρεσκευασμένος ("prepared").

⁶⁴⁸ The expression ἡσυχίαν ἄγειν ("remain inactive") is quite common in Greek literature (e.g., Thucydides 5.94; Euripides, *Andr.* 143; Plutarch, *Pel.* 11.4; *Publ.* 4.5).

⁶⁴⁹ For phrases similar to δρασάντων τι λαμπρὸν ("performing brilliantly"), see Diodorus 15.86.3; Plutarch, *Cim.* 19.4.

⁶⁵⁰ Athenio's strategy is not mentioned in the parallel account of *War* (1.367-368). It matches Cleopatra's policy towards Antony's client kings in the region (see *Ant.* 15.115 with the note to "defeat upon Herod and the Jews"). It implies that Herod had to be defeated, either by the Nabateans or by Athenio himself.

⁶⁵¹ The Greek remains vague here because it fails to specify whether Athenio's men were regular soldiers. They were plausibly mercenaries.

⁶⁵² Since Athenio had occasional local fighters at his disposal he may have been violating the rules of just war; one could only put trained soldiers into action (see *Ant.* 15.135 with the note to "justified"). *War* 1.367 states unambiguously that Athenio dispatched the inhabitants of Canatha against Herod. Given that these local fighters were Herod's enemies an identification of these fighters as Nabateans is plausible but at the same time at odds with the fact that the Nabateans had settled mostly further south in this region (i.e., south of the line of Salkhad-Bostra-Der'a; see *Ant.* 15.111 with the note to "Arabia" and 15.112 with the note to "Canata").

⁶⁵³ The combination of ἐπιπίπτω ("fall upon") and ἀπροσδοκήτως ("unexpectedly") also occurs in Diodorus 15.40.2; 19.37.2; Josephus, *Life* 253; cf. Procopius, *Aed.* 4.9.8; *Bell.* 1.15.23; 1.24.1.

⁶⁵⁴ Athenio apparently chose the right moment to

he slaughtered a great number of them.⁶⁵⁵ For, because the Jews had exhausted⁶⁵⁶ their eagerness with respect to their known⁶⁵⁷ enemies and were enjoying their victory without fear, they were quickly defeated by the attackers. They suffered many blows on rocky terrain that was unsuited for cavalry,⁶⁵⁸ where the attackers had more experience.⁶⁵⁹ **118** While they⁶⁶⁰ were faring badly,⁶⁶¹ the Arabs regained their strength. After their return they immediately killed those who had been routed already. Those who died perished in all sorts of ways, and only a few⁶⁶² of those who escaped took refuge in the camp.⁶⁶³ **119** In despair over the outcome of the battle, King Herod rode off⁶⁶⁴ to get help.⁶⁶⁵ But in spite of his haste, he was not fast enough in bringing help, and the camp of the Jews was

---

attack: when the morale of the Jewish troops could be expected to be low (as the continuation of the narrative further explains). The combination of κάμνω ("exert oneself, be exhausted/hard-pressed," Rengstorf *s.v.*) and νικάω ("be victorious") also occurs in Thucydides 2.51.5.

⁶⁵⁵ In the parallel report of *War* (1.368) Athenio's attack also brings the turning point, but the slaughter of the Jews is attributed to the Nabateans.

The phrase πολὺν ἐποίει φόνον ("he slaughtered") has many parallels in Diodorus (e.g., 11.10.2; 11.80.5; 12.79.5; 15.65.2; 15.91.5; 16.12.2; 17.12.5; see also Plutarch, *Luc.* 17.1).

⁶⁵⁶ The verb ἐκδαπανάω (literally "expend," Rengstorf *s.v.*) is a *hapax legomenon* in Josephus.

⁶⁵⁷ The translation is based on Niese's reading of ὁμολογουμένους, which is attested by the MSS (Niese 353). Marcus-Wikgren (56) and Rengstorf (*s.v.* ὁμολογέω) follow Naber's conjecture of ὁμολογουμένως ("in the open"; Naber 1888-96: 3.xli, 330), the resulting phrase of which (τοὺς ὁμολογουμένως ἐχθρούς) is paralleled by Demosthenes *Or.* 14.11. Nevertheless the transmitted text can be maintained since it makes sense in the light of fair behavior in warfare. From the context it is apparent that Herod had a conflict with the Nabateans that was to be settled during a combat. Athenio interfered in the conflict, which act was unfair and treacherous from Herod's perspective: decent warfare required that proper procedures were met and that the war was officially declared beforehand (see *Ant.* 15.135 with the note to "justified"). Herod elaborates this point of view in his commander speech (15.139-140). Moreover, the word ἐχθρός ("enemy") with an attributive participle of ὁμολογέω ("agree, declare"), as read by the MSS, also occurs in Polybius 2.45.3; Philo, *Flacc.* 146; Herodian 3.5.8; 7.10.1.

⁶⁵⁸ The information in *War* 1.368 is slightly different: "... the Arabs turned around, and concentrating their forces on a rocky and difficult terrain, they put Herod's troops to flight and inflicted a huge massacre on them" (trans. Sievers/Forte in BJP 1a). The vocabulary in *Antiquities* suggests that the fact that Herod's cavalry could not be properly brought into action was an important factor in the defeat of the Jews. *War* 1.366 reports that Herod had formed a strong cavalry force in preparation of his campaign against the Nabateans.

⁶⁵⁹ At least part of Athenio's army consisted of local combatants (*Ant.* 15.116).

The last 9 words of this paragraph are a striking example of alliteration, which figure of speech occurs regularly within this paragraph (with *k*, *l*, and *p* as the leading consonant sounds). The alliteration emphasizes the massacre of the Jews caused by Athenio's interference (for other significant cases of alliteration, see *War* 2.359; 6.337, 343, 345; *Ant.* 15.151).

⁶⁶⁰ I.e., the Jews, who are mentioned explicitly in *Ant.* 15.117.

⁶⁶¹ The combination of κακῶς ("badly") and πάσχω ("suffer") is common already in Thucydides (1.38, 86, 122; 5.23, 47; see also Euripides, *Ion* 1330; *Med.* 280; *Rhes.* 473; Xenophon, *Anab.* 3.3.12; 5.2.2; 7.7.16; Plutarch, *Alc.* 25.2; *Arist.* 14.2; *Cor.* 33.6). Josephus uses it only in *Antiquities* (4.299; 13.231; 15.111, 345; 16.47, 161).

⁶⁶² The Greek οὐ πολλοί ("only a few," literally "not many"; see also *Ant.* 6.170; 13.431; *Apion* 1.5) is another example of *litotes*.

⁶⁶³ In *War* 1.368 the location of the camp is specified as Ormiza, which lay west of Canata (if it can be identified with El-Mezra'). The second part of *Ant.* 15.118 features alliteration again, with *p* as the leading consonant sound (see also 15.117 with the note to "took refuge in the camp").

⁶⁶⁴ The rare verb ἀφιππάζομαι ("ride off") also occurs in *Ant.* 14.345; 18.49.

⁶⁶⁵ The parallel passage of *War* (1.369) has similar vocabulary (βοήθειαν ἄγων). The *War* report attributes Herod's defeat to the disobedience of his lieutenants, who had forced a rash battle upon Herod and had provided Athenio the opportunity to interfere, which exonerates Herod from the blame of the defeat. This detail is missing in *Antiquities* (cf. also 15.114 with *War* 1.367, 369).

taken.[666] The Arabs were exceedingly[667] fortunate in unexpectedly winning a victory[668]—which they were very much in need of—and in destroying a large force of the enemy. **120** From this time on Herod adopted bandit-style attacks[669] and ravaged the territory of the Arabs at many locations,[670] inflicting harm on them with his raids. He camped in the mountains[671] and ceased entirely from fighting with them in the open.[672] He continued to inflict severe losses upon[673] them by his perseverance[674] and diligence, and took care of his soldiers[675] by remedying his failure in every possible way.[676]

Earthquake in Judea. Attack by the Arabs. War 1.370-371

(5.2) 121 In the meantime, when the Battle of Actium took place between Caesar and Antony,[677] in the seventh year of Herod's reign,[678] there was an earthquake in Judea[679] the

---

[666] *War* 1.368-369 also reports this but with different vocabulary.

[667] The Greek phrase οὐδὲ μετρίως (literally "not moderately") is a case of *litotes* that occurs frequently in Josephus (*War* 2.631; *Ant.* 6.349; 15.194, 276; 16.81, 230, 294; 19.221; 20.83, 109; *Life* 289, 371; *Apion* 1.243; 2.8).

[668] The expression ἐκ παραλόγου ("unexpectedly," Rengstorf *s.v.*) also occurs in *War* 7.212 (MS P) and *Ant.* 6.282. *Ant.* 6.116 expresses the motif of an unexpected victory by King Saul with παραλόγως ("unexpectedly"; see also Diodorus 20.13.3; Appian, *Hist. rom.* 11.7.37, and cf. παράλογος in Josephus, *War* 5.291). See also the beginning of Herod's commander speech in *War* 1.373: "The fear which is now taking hold of you seems to me to be entirely unreasonable (παραλογώτατα)" (trans. Sievers/Forte in BJP 1a).

[669] The context implies that Herod switched from standard open warfare between armies to the "bandit" (cf. the Greek: λῃστείαις ἐχρῆτο) or guerrilla mode of retreating to the hills, launching sudden raids and avoiding direct confrontation. For a similar combination of λῃστείαις plus χράομαι ("resort to banditry"), see *Ant.* 14.471.

[670] The Greek τὰ πολλὰ κατατρέχων τὴν τῶν Ἀράβων is slightly elliptic and presupposes an additional word like χώραν ("territory"), which is found in the briefer parallel report of *War* (1.369). For combinations of κατατρέχω ("ravage") and χώραν in Josephus, see *War* 1.304; 2.62, 505; 3.431; 7.9; *Ant.* 11.161 (cf. Diodorus 22.8.1; 36.7.2). Josephus also uses the verb κατατρέχω in the parallel passage of *War* (1.369).

[671] Niese (353) reads ἐπὶ τῶν ὅρων ("on the borders"); MSS FAME (supported by the Latin version) read ἐπὶ τῶν ὀρῶν ("in the mountains"; for a similar case, see *Ant.* 9.38). The latter reading seems preferable and is followed, among others, by Marcus-Wikgren (58) and Meijer-Wes (3.168). It matches the type of territory of the Hauran, where Herod had confronted the Nabateans before (see 15.111 with the note to "Arabia"; for other occurrences of ἐπὶ τῶν ὀρῶν in Josephus, see *War* 1.300; *Ant.* 8.279; 14.409). *Ant.* 15.121 presupposes that Herod was staying outside of Judea in this period.

[672] This suggests that Herod's military force was too weak in this period to confront the Nabatean army directly (Shatzman 1991: 290).

[673] This is a case of *litotes* (literally "not without inflicting loss"; see *Ant.* 15.107 with the note to "not without curtailment" and cf. Galen, *Usu part.* [ed. Kühn 3.660]).

[674] The noun συνέχεια ("perseverance," Rengstorf *s.v.*) is a *hapax legomenon* in Josephus.

[675] Niese minor (283) notes that there is a lacuna in the Greek text after φιλοπόνῳ ("by diligence"). However, the transmitted Greek text makes sense. For other combinations of τῶν οἰκείων ("his own [soldiers]") and ἐπιμελέομαι ("take care"), see, e.g., Xenophon, *Cyr.* 4.5.39; Isocrates, *Bus.* 29.5; Plutarch, *Cic.* 44.7.

[676] The parallel report of *War* (1.369) also notes the result of these raids by Herod, but it focuses on the emotional impact on the Nabateans: "However, he [i.e., Herod] in turn, avenged himself on the Arabs by constantly devastating their land with raids, so that they could often bewail loudly their single victory" (trans. Sievers/Forte in BJP 1a).

The last lines of *Ant.* 15.120 attest a further case of alliteration, with *p* as the leading consonant sound.

[677] About the Battle of Actium (in 31 BCE), see *Ant.* 15.109 with the note to "the Battle of Actium."

[678] The determination of this 7th year is complicated for several reasons: the years of Herod's rule may be counted from his appointment as king in 40 BCE (see *Ant.* 15.2 with the note to "the rule over all Judea") or from his capture of Jerusalem in 37 BCE (or 36, as several scholars argue). It is further dependent on whether the 1st year of Herod's rule was counted as his accession year or as his first full regnal year, and on whether a new regnal year started in the spring (i.e., on 1 Nisan) or in the fall (i.e., on 1 Tishri). If 37/36 BCE is taken as Herod's 1st regnal year, the 7th year would be 31/30 BCE (either 1 Nisan 31–1 Nisan 30 BCE or 1 Tishri 31–1 Tishri 30 BCE). Otto (1913: 46), Marcus-Wikgren (58-59), Schürer-Vermes (1.289, 301), Kasher (1988: 138), and Schalit (2001: 122 with n. 98) date the earthquake to the spring of 31 BCE. In the parallel passage of *War* (1.370) Josephus connects the earthquake

likes of which had not been seen before.[680] It caused great losses[681] among the livestock in the country-side. **122** About 30,000 human beings[682] perished under their collapsed houses.[683] Yet the army, which was staying in the open air,[684] was unharmed by this disaster.[685] **123** When the Arabs learned of this and when all of those who tried to cajole the hearers' hatred[686] reported an account of the events to them that went beyond the truth, they got carried away.[687] They thought that, with the land of the enemy in ruins and its people killed,[688] there was nothing left to oppose them.[689] **124** They arrested the envoys of the Jews[690]—who had come to make peace[691] in the aftermath of the events—,[692] killed

---

with Herod's 7th year, the peak of the War of Actium, and the early spring. For a detailed discussion of the chronology of Herod's rule, see Mahieu 2012.

[679] The parallel account of *War* (1.370) includes similar vocabulary (ἡ γῆ σεισθεῖσα) but does not refer to Judea.

[680] This detail is absent in *War* 1.370. Landau (2006: 156) notes that descriptions of unusual natural phenomena (enhancing the drama of the narrative) occur more frequently in *Antiquities* than in *War* and that they sometimes anticipate reports about human misconduct or highlight the connection between human sins and divine punishment. This is not the case here, but the introduction of the parallel report of *War* (1.370) does suggest that the earthquake was a divine intervention: a "heaven-sent calamity" (συμφορὰ δαιμόνιος).

[681] The MSS offer various readings (Niese 354), which, however, in most cases hardly affect the meaning of the passage. For vocabulary similar to φθόρον ἐποίησεν ("it caused [great] losses"), see Plato, *Pol.* 273a (about a great earthquake causing a new destruction [ποιῶν ἄλλην αὖ φθοράν] of all sorts of living creatures); Dionysius, *Ant. rom.* 5.59.4 (about a famine causing great losses among human beings [πολὺν φθόρον ἀνθρώπων ἐποίησεν]); 7.68.2.

[682] *War* 1.370 provides similar information.

[683] This detail is missing in the parallel report in *War* (1.370). Landau (2006: 156) notes that the description in *Antiquities* is more detailed than in the parallel version of *War*: both reports describe the earthquake's impact on cattle and humans, but the *Antiquities* narrative is more dramatic through its additional note "the likes of which had not been seen before" (15.121) and the reference to humans who died in the ruins of their houses.

[684] The nouns στρατιωτικόν ("army") and ὕπαιθρος ("open country/air") also occur in the parallel account of *War* (1.370).

[685] This is similar to the report in *War* 1.370. Josephus' vocabulary (οὐδὲν ὑπὸ τοῦ πάθους κατεβλάβη "was unharmed by this disaster") echoes that of *War* 1.370 (ἀβλαβές "[escaped] unharmed").

[686] Josephus' vocabulary is tantalizingly vague or even subtle. The object of the hatred is not indicated; it is plausible that the Jews are meant (thus *War* 1.2; 2.478,

502; 5.556; 6.263; 7.50 and *Ant.* 18.371 explicitly refer to hatred towards the Jews), particularly Herod and his soldiers. Josephus does not specify either who the hearers of the report are. If the immediate context is taken into account, those hating the Jews could be the Arabs (who are already mentioned in the first part of the sentence), or Cleopatra, or Athenio, or both. One can also think of a reference to hatred towards the Jews in general since Josephus' formulations are imprecise and exaggeration is a common feature of ancient anti-Jewish statements (for detailed discussions see Sevenster 1975; Schäfer 1997). In *War* 1.371 Josephus only mentions the Arabs (i.e., the Nabateans) as the ones who received the rumor about the earthquake and points to the fact that such rumors tend to become more dramatic: "… at this moment rumor, which always adds something more grievous to miseries in the spreading of a story, stirred the Arabs to greater boldness" (trans. Sievers/Forte in BJP 1a).

[687] The expression μεῖζον φρονέω literally means "have over-high thoughts" (LSJ *s.v.* φρονέω II.2b). The phrase occurs again in Herod's commander speech, also referring to the Nabateans (*Ant.* 15.143).

[688] This phrase echoes *Ant.* 15.122 (cf. the repetition of χώρα and φθόρον/διεφθορότων), but it offers variation as well (note the reference to the loss among livestock [κτηνῶν] in 15.121 and to the loss of humans [τῶν ἀνθρώπων] here).

[689] *War* 1.371 roughly expresses the same in different wordings. For the combination of ἀντίπαλος ("adversary, belonging to the opposite party") and καταλείπω ("leave behind"), see Dionysius, *Ant. rom.* 3.63.1; Julian, *Regn.* 6.15 (ed. Bidez 1.1.124).

[690] The issue of the Nabateans' treatment of Herod's envoys is taken up in the king's commander speech (*Ant.* 15.136-137, 146).

[691] The translation is based on the longer reading (γεγενημένοις εἰρήνην ποιησόμενοι) attested by almost all of the ancient textual witnesses. Niese (354) follows the shorter text of MS L (γεγενημένοις). The combination of εἰρήνην ("peace") and ποιοῦμαι ("make") occurs once elsewhere in Josephus (*War* 4.320).

[692] This parenthesis explains the mission of the envoys, who have not been mentioned before. The parallel report of *War* (1.371) also mentions the envoys

them,[693] and advanced to their camp with great eagerness.[694] **125** The Jews did not expect their attack,[695] and being in this desperate situation,[696] with respect to their misfortunes,[697] they gave up altogether.[698] They felt their situation was utterly hopeless,[699] for there was hope neither for receiving a fair treatment[700] after being defeated[701] in their battles, nor for getting help since their situation at home was in such a bad state.[702]

Herod's commander speech.
War *1.372-379*

126 While they were in this situation,[703] the king led the commanders on, tried to persuade them with a speech,[704] and attempted[705] to lift their sunken spirits.[706] First he

---

at this stage (see also *War* 1.378; *Ant.* 15.136). Kasher (1988: 139-41) argues that Herod had previously sent still other envoys in order to declare war on the Nabateans (which is not mentioned in *Ant.* 15.110). The participle τὰ γεγενημένα can mean "event" (Rengstorf *s.v.* γίγνομαι) or "past" (LSJ *s.v.* γίγνομαι I.3).

[693] Killing the envoys of the enemy was considered to be a terrible crime by the Greeks and the Romans (Herodotus 5.18-21; 7.136.2; Thucydides 4.98.7; Plato, *Leg.* 941a; Livy 4.58.6; 8.6.7; 10.12.2-3). Envoys were protected by law and had immunity. A murder of envoys justified a war against those who had killed them (Albert 1980: 18; Mantovani 1990: 44; see also *Ant.* 14.346).

[694] For vocabulary similar to μετὰ πάσης προθυμίας ἐχώρουν ("they advanced with great eagerness"), see Dionysius, *Ant. rom.* 6.38.2; 6.63.3; 9.9.9; cf. Plutarch, *Sull.* 9.3; Appian, *Bell. civ.* 5.4.33.

[695] An alternative translation would be "did not withstand ..." (Marcus-Wikgren 61; Meijer-Wes 3.168). The verb ἐκδέχομαι can mean "expect" as well as "sustain" (Rengstorf *s.v.*). The combination of ἔφοδος ("attack"; see also *War* 1.373; *Ant.* 15.139) and ἐκδέχομαι occurs once elsewhere in Josephus (*War* 4.86) and apart from that only in medieval Greek literature (Michael Attaliates, *Hist.* [ed. Bekker 25.2, 32.19], 11th cent.; Nicephorus Gregoras, *Hist. rom.* [ed. Schopen and Bekker 1.200.22], 14th cent.).

[696] The combination of ἀθύμως ("fainthearted, desperate") and διάκειμαι ("being in a certain state") also occurs in *Ant.* 3.5, which passage refers to the Israelites in the desert (see Exod 15; for similar vocabulary, see Isocrates, *Callim.* 60.2; *Paneg.* 93.1; Polyaenus 4.9.3). The phrase echoes part of the vocabulary of the introduction of Herod's speech in *War* 1.373: "It was indeed natural to lose heart (ἀθυμεῖν εἰκὸς ἦν) in the face of heaven-sent calamities ..." (trans. Sievers/Forte in BJP 1a).

[697] The more elaborate report in *Antiquities* repeats the noun συμφοραί ("misfortunes") of *War* 1.372.

[698] *War* 1.372 notes that the Jews were discouraged because of the continuous misfortunes. *Antiquities* describes their situation in more dramatic terms. For vocabulary similar to προΐεντο τὰ πράγματα, see Plutarch, *Per.* 33.7; Aelius Aristides, *Ars rhet.* 2.13.1.

[699] The noun ἀπόγνωσις ("despair") echoes the description of Herod's assessment of the situation after the Jewish defeat during the second battle against the Nabateans (*Ant.* 15.119): "In despair (ἀπεγνωκώς) over the outcome of the battle ...."

[700] The noun ἰσοτιμία usually means "equality of privilege" in ancient literature (LSJ *s.v.*), but here it must refer to the outcome of the military conflict for both parties. Rengstorf (*s.v.*) hesitantly gives "equal standing (in battle)" as meaning for this passage. The phrase also occurs in *Ant.* 16.98, in which case it indicates equality in a legal context. In 16.193 it refers to equality of social status. Cf. *War* 2.487 (a variant reading; see Mason in BJP 1b on 2.487); *Ant.* 7.284; 19.317.

[701] The verb προηττάω ("defeat beforehand," Rengstorf *s.v.*) is a *hapax legomenon* in Josephus.

[702] See Josephus' description of this situation in *Ant.* 15.121-122.

[703] This phrase forms the transition to the introduction of Herod's elaborate commander speech (*Ant.* 15.127-146, paralleling *War* 1.373-379) before the third battle against the Nabateans (*Ant.* 15.147-160 and *War* 1.380-385). The speech comes at a dramatic point in the narrative, and the narrator greatly slows down the pace of the narrative (van Henten and Huitink 2007: 227-28).

[704] The speech that follows in *Antiquities* (15.127-146) is much more elaborate than its counterpart in *War* (1.373-379): the vocabulary and rhetorical style are embellished, and the composition is much more sophisticated (on speeches in general in Josephus, see Runnalls 1971; 1997; Villalba i Varneda 1986: 89-117; Landau 2006: 134-56; Mason 2011). Research on ancient Greek historiography reveals that speeches serve several functions: apart from highlighting certain interpretations of the events, they can mark a dramatic climax in the narrative (e.g., Moses' speech at the end of his life in *Ant.* 4.177-193; Attridge 1976: 77-78), point out the underlying motives of a main character, or have an aetiological function, e.g., explaining the causes of the events following the speech (Villalba i Varneda 1986: 101-03, 107, referring to Herod's commander speech in *War* 1.373-379). Runnalls (1997: 738) claims that Josephus not only uses speeches as a means to present his own theological evaluation of certain events but also as a stylistic tool to elaborate the personality of his narrative's characters. The latter function is especially

stirred up[707] some of the braver men and encouraged them.[708] Then he also dared to address the crowd. He had been hesitant about this before, since he was afraid that they would treat him badly[709] because of their mishaps. So he incited the crowd[710] and spoke these words to them:[711]

---

relevant for Herod's commander speech because it presents Herod in a very positive light.

It is, of course, possible that Herod actually gave a speech of encouragement before this battle against the Arabs and that Josephus (or somebody else) tried to catch the tenor of his words, as Thucydides tried in the commander speeches reported by him (see below), but there is no way to reconstruct the original speech. Mantovani (1990: 95) argues that Josephus based himself on a source that contained the speech, possibly Herod's memoirs (see *Ant.* 15.174). However, we do not possess any source that transmitted the speech; only Josephus' earlier version (*War* 1.373-379) has been transmitted to us. Hackl, Jenni, and Schneider (2003: 502) argue that either Nicolaus of Damascus or Josephus himself invented the speech. Grant (1970: 258) states that Josephus fabricated speeches with particular lavishness (see also Villalba i Varneda 1986: 90-92; differently Collomb 1947). There are pros and cons concerning the hypothesis that Josephus himself played a major role in the composition of the speech in *Antiquities*. The very positive image of Herod in the speech may, at first glance, not go well with Josephus' own explicit comments about Herod, which are often negative. The speech's well-polished composition, its persuasive rhetoric, and its content contribute significantly to the image of Herod as the ideal commander who successfully encourages his soldiers. However, this may still reflect Josephus' own view if we assume that he constructed Herod as a person with a complex character (see *Ant.* 15.21 with the note to "he had allowed himself to be persuaded"), who was successful in several ways (i.e., as military commander and builder) but failing in other respects (e.g. controlling his family and treating his Jewish subjects). The smooth transition from speech to narrative and vice versa, and the strong cohesion between the speech's content and its narrative context imply that its vocabulary and argumentation are Josephus' own creation (cf. Runnalls 1971: 10-11 about the speeches in *War*).

The *Antiquities* version of Herod's speech includes many rhetorical *topoi* of commander speeches from the Classical period (van Henten 2005b). Josephus (or another author who was responsible for the composition of the speech) no doubt was familiar with the well-known Greek and Roman custom of commanders giving a speech of encouragement before a major battle. This habit triggered various fictitious speeches made up by historians: e.g., Herodotus' speeches set in the mouth of key players of historical narratives are a device to present to the audience specific views and assessments of the events reported (Lendle 1992: 53-63); Thucydides incorporates speeches in his report of the Peloponnesian War and admits in his famous "methodological chapter" (1.22.1) that he freely invented his orators' phrases and, different from Herodotus, that he attempts to catch the tenor of the speeches in order to offer a balanced and correct presentation of the events and even to present what the speakers ought to have said on particular occasions (Leimbach 1985: 9-14; Lendle 1992: 85-87; Rood 1998: 39-46). In the Roman period Cassius Dio follows the practice of inventing speeches, which started with Herodotus (Lendle 1992: 255).

[705] The participle πειρώμενος ("attempting") is the only word that corresponds with the vocabulary of the much shorter introduction of Herod's speech in the parallel report of *War* (1.372 ἐπειρᾶτο ["tried to"]).

[706] The expression πεπτωκότα τὰ φρονήματα ("sunken spirits") is characteristic for Josephus. Similar phrases refer to Jews who had lost confidence and to Josephus himself in his role as commander (*War* 3.130, 142; see also *War* 1.376; *Ant.* 15.128, 139 in Herod's commander speeches). Like Herod in *Ant.* 15.126 Josephus encourages his soldiers in *War* 3.142.

[707] The verb προδιακινέω (literally "set previously in motion," Rengstorf *s.v.*) is a *hapax legomenon* in Josephus.

[708] The reason that Herod approached the braver soldiers first is explained in the continuation of the paragraph, which highlights that the situation was precarious and that Herod had to act with caution (similarly Eleazar ben Yair in his first speech, *War* 7.322). He apparently made use of a vanguard to persuade the other soldiers (cf. Xenophon, *Anab.* 3.1.37, who points out that the officers had to take responsibility for the common soldiers). The distinction between the elite and the common soldiers is absent in the parallel report of *War* (1.372). For similar combinations of παραθαρσύνω ("encourage") and παρακαλέω ("incite") further on in this paragraph, see Aesop 3.1; Xenophon, *Cyr.* 7.1.18; Plutarch, *Cat. Min.* 21.1; *Cor.* 8.5; *Pomp.* 30.3.

[709] The subject and object are not explicit here in the reading of the MSS (μὴ καὶ χαλεπῷ χρήσηται, Niese 354): Josephus may refer to the multitude of soldiers or to Herod, although the latter is less plausible and implies a translation like "he would be too tough on them."

[710] The composition, vocabulary, and motifs indicate

(5.3) 127[712] "I am in no way unaware, men,[713] that we have experienced many adversities[714] in this period in our undertakings, and that it is not likely that even those who excel most in bravery[715] would keep their courage[716] under such circumstances. **128** But since we are compelled to fight,[717] and nothing that has happened is so [serious] that it cannot be amended by a single well-executed action, I have deliberately chosen to

---

that Herod's speech of encouragement is a typical commander speech before a battle to enhance the soldiers' motivation to fight (Leimbach 1985: 15 and the note to "a speech" above). The key word παρακαλέω ("incite") in the introduction (see also *Ant.* 15.128) also indicates that the delivery is a commander speech. This kind of speech is sometimes called a παρακλητικός λόγος ("hortatory speech," Polybius 12.25i.3; cf. 23.2.9; 28.4.1; Dionysius, *Ant. rom.* 4.26; LXX Zech 1:13; Leimbach 1985: 14; van Henten 2005b: 186-87).

[711] Commander speeches belong to one of the 3 major types of speech according to ancient theories of rhetoric, to deliberative speech (*genos sumbouleutikon*, Runnalls 1997: 742-46; for this type of speech, see Aristotle, *Rhet.* 1.3.3 1358b; Lausberg 1998: 32-33, 97-103). Other deliberative speeches in Josephus are Moses' speech at the end of his life (*Ant.* 4.177-193), Ananus' speech against the Zealots (*War* 4.162-192), Josephus' own speeches in *War* 5.376-419; 6.99-110, and Eleazar's 2 speeches at Masada (*War* 7.323-388). There are some features in Herod's speech that belong to forensic speech, another main type of speech (see Herod's accusations against the Arabs and his statements connected with just war in *Ant.* 15.130-145). Overlaps between deliberative and forensic speech are common (Lausberg 1998: 97).

Herod's call upon his soldiers' courage, which is partly repeated at the speech's end, supports the assumption that the speech belongs to the genre of commander speeches (for this genre, see Luschnat 1942; Leimbach 1985, and for conventional motifs in commander speeches, van Henten 2005b). The vocabulary typical of such speeches includes ἀνδραγαθία (*Ant.* 15.127, 140, 146; cf. *War* 1.376), θαρρέω (*Ant.* 15.127, 143; cf. *War* 1.374), ἀνδρεία (*Ant.* 15.138; cf. *War* 1.379), and τόλμα (*Ant.* 15.142). The continuation of the narrative in *Ant.* 15.147 also matches the genre of a commander speech: the soldiers regained their self-confidence and triumphed over the Arabs (15.147-160).

Moses' brief speech (*Ant.* 3.43-46), Titus' commander speeches (*War* 3.472-484; 6.33-53), and Vespasian's speech (*War* 4.39-48) are also speeches of encouragement. They concern matters of war and peace, which is one of the 5 subjects of deliberative speech discussed by Aristotle (*Rhet.* 1.4.7-9 1359b-1360a).

[712] Herod's commander speech (see *Ant.* 15.126 with the note to "a speech") in 15.127-146 is composed in 4 sections, in line with Aristotle's view of the composition of speeches (*Rhet.* 3.13.4 1414b, also Cicero, *Part. or.* 27): (1) introduction (*exordium*, *Ant.* 15.127-128); (2) statement (*propositio*, 15.129); (3) proof (*argumentatio*, 15.130-145); and (4) conclusion (*peroratio* with *recapitulatio* and *affectus*, 15.146; Runnalls 1997: 746-47). Villalba i Varneda (1986: 108) proposes a composition in 3 sections: (1) introduction (15.127-129); (2) corpus of the speech (15.130-143); and (3) conclusions (15.144-146). The parallel speech of the *War* (1.373-379) has a rather loose composition.

[713] Herod's introduction of his speech uses a common formula to call for attention (οὐκ ἀγνοῶ μέν, ὦ ἄνδρες, "I am in no way unaware, men, ..."); see Demosthenes, *Or.* 16.3; 23.90; 39.27; Aeschines, *Tim.* 4.1; Dinarch, *Fragm.* 19.1; Dio Chrysostom 34.1; Lucian, *Bis acc.* 20; Hermogenes, *Inv.* 1.1 (ed. Rabe 99.16); cf. 2 Cor 1:8; 2:11; 1 Thess 4:13. On "men", qualified in various ways, cf. Josephus, *War* 3.472 ("It is well for me to remind you, men. ..."); 6.328; 7.323; *Ant.* 3.189; 6.20; 8.227; 11.169 ("You know, men..."); 15.382 ("To speak about my other deeds in connection to the throne, my fellow countrymen, is, I assume, superfluous").

[714] In *Antiquities* Herod's introduction first mentions the adversities of his soldiers and the fact that it is unusual to remain brave in such circumstances, and secondly that the combat is unavoidable (15.128). In *War* Herod starts his speech differently, by referring to the fear of his men, which was unjustified and cowardly because they had been attacked by humans and not by a heavenly force (1.373). The noun ἐναντίωμα ("obstacle," Rengstorf *s.v.*) is a *hapax legomenon* in Josephus.

[715] The noun ἀνδραγαθία ("bravery") also occurs in the parallel speech of *War* (1.376, explicitly referring to the Jews) and further on in the speech in *Antiquities* (15.140, 146; cf. also 15.160). The combination of ἀνδραγαθία and διαφέρω ("stand out") also occurs in Demosthenes, *Or.* 61.39.

[716] The Greek θαρρεῖν εἰκός ("it is not likely that ... keep courage") echoes a phrase from the introduction of Herod's speech in *War* 1.373 (see *Ant.* 15.125 with the note to "being in this desperate situation").

[717] Polybius (2.7.7) offers vocabulary similar to ἐπειδὴ κατεπείγει τὸ πολεμεῖν. Herod's observation that it is necessary to fight the battle is taken up again in the body of the speech (see *Ant.* 15.135).

encourage you and instruct you[718] at the same time how you can be true to your proud designs.[719] **129** But first, concerning the fighting of the war, I want to show that it is right[720] that we fight it,[721] since we were forced into it by the insolence of our opponents.[722] For if you understand this, it will be the greatest cause of your eagerness [to fight].[723] I will next show that there is nothing to fear[724] in our present situation and that we have the greatest prospects for winning.[725]

---

[718] Josephus indicates that Herod has a double intention with his speech: "I have deliberately chosen to encourage you and instruct you ... (παρακαλέσαι ... καὶ διδάξαι)." For the first aim, see *Ant.* 15.126 with the note to "he incited the crowd." The second aim, instruction, is not a hollow phrase here because Herod does instruct his soldiers about the enemy and their own situation (15.130-45; cf. *War* 1.374-376), which functions as support of his encouragement. Other commander speeches show that such a twofold purpose is conventional. The Spartan commander and politician Brasidas starts his speech in Thucydides 4.126 with a phrase that indicates his intention to encourage and instruct: "Did I not suspect, men of Peloponnesus, that you are in a state of panic because you have been left alone, and because your assailants are barbarous and numerous, I should not offer you instruction combined with encouragement (οὐκ ἂν ὁμοίως διδαχὴν ἅμα τῇ παρακελεύσει ἐποιούμην). But as it is, in view of our abandonment by our allies and of the multitude of our opponents, I shall try by a brief reminder and by advice to impress upon you the most important considerations" (trans. Smith). The instruction in commander speeches concerns the part of speech that analyses the situation, the location of the battle, the enemy's army, etc. (Luschnat 1942: 71-72, 107-09). The analysis of the situation allows for the choice of the best strategy in the given circumstances. The commander's clarifications of the situation and his strategy show his intentions (cf. Thucydides 5.8.4-5.9.10). It is obvious that all this information, if presented persuasively, could be a major ground for the soldiers' encouragement (cf. 2.87.7).

[719] The translation follows Dindorf's conjecture, which is also read by Niese (355). The noun φρονήματα probably means "spirits" in *Ant.* 15.126 (see the note to "lift their sunken spirits"), but the combination with the verb ἐμμένω ("abide in/by") requires a different meaning; "proud designs" is given by LSJ (*s.v.* φρόνημα II.1).

[720] For Herod's argumentation in connection with just war, see *Ant.* 15.135 with the note to "justified."

[721] *Ant.* 15.129 concerns the brief second section of Herod's speech, i.e., the statement (about the main composition of the speech, see the first note to 15.127). The statement in 15.129 concisely formulates the speech's 2 main points (cf. the Greek πρῶτον μὲν ... μετὰ δέ), anticipating Herod's proof for both of them (βούλομαι ἐπιδεῖξαι ... μετὰ δέ τοῦτο δεῖξαι). The 2 main topics are: (1) the battle that has to be fought is just (δικαίως πολεμεῖν) and necessary (ἠναγκασμένοι, 15.130-137/138; see 15.135 with the notes to "justified" and "necessary"), and (2) there is no reason for fear and the soldiers' prospects for victory are great (15.138/139-145).

[722] This statement anticipates the accusation that the Nabateans had killed Herod's envoys (see *Ant.* 15.124 with the note to "killed them," also 15.135-136). It is obvious that one has to defend oneself against an attack by an enemy, especially if its behavior is an act of ὕβρις ("insolence, outrage"). Such an accusation is launched several times at the Athenians in earlier Greek commander speeches (e.g., Thucydides 2.11.7-9; 4.92.1-2, 7) because they threatened the liberty of the other Greek states—in short, the freedom of all Hellas—in their strive for supremacy in the Greek world (e.g., 4.92.7; 5.9.1, 9; see Leimbach 1985: 90). Dionysius' commander speeches (e.g., 3.23.6-21; 6.6-9; 9.9) point at outrageous acts by the enemy preceding the battle (e.g., the way the war was announced or embassies were treated) with the stock phrase ἡ ὕβρις τῶν πολεμίων ("the enemy's outrageous act"). Publius Postumius (*Ant. rom.* 5.44.2) calls the Sabines' unannounced incursion into Roman territory an intolerable outrageous act. In 5.45.1 the Romans receive a very insolent and arrogant embassy from them (παρὰ τῶν πολεμίων πρεσβεία πολλὴν ὕβριν ἐχούσῃ; see also Fabius' opening words in Polybius 9.9).

[723] This phrase concludes the first point of Herod's statement, focusing upon the violation of the just war conventions by the Nabateans.

[724] The translation follows the reading δεινὸν οὐδέν ἐστιν of Niese (355). The reading δεινῶν ... of most MSS may be caused by the adaptation of δεινὸν to the genitive plural of the preceding τῶν and perhaps be translated as "that the fearful things for us are nothing." The phrase δεινὸν οὐδέν ἐστιν is a fixed expression (see, e.g., Demosthenes, *Or.* 11.19; Plutarch, *Mor.* [*Quom. adul.*] 57e; Lucian, *Jupp. trag.* 1). Josephus frequently uses the singular δεινόν with οὐδέν or μηδέν (*War* 3.202; *Ant.* 1.59; 6.316; 7.79; 10.96, 161, 258, 260; 11.327; 12.395, 403). The plural genitive occurs once elsewhere with οὐδέν and ἐστιν (John Chrysostom, *Fat. prov.* [PG 50.751.38]).

[725] Herod's second major point focuses on the situation of his soldiers. It is repeated several times in his

130 I will start with[726] the first point[727] and thus make you witnesses to what I say.[728]

---

speech: there is no serious reason to be frightened, and the prospects for a victory (τὸ νικᾶν) are great (the word ἐλπίς ["hope, prospect"] is also highlighted by Herod in *Ant.* 15.140, 143 as well as in the parallel speech of *War* [1.373]; cf. *Ant.* 15.150, 153). Thucydides (6.68.2) and Dionysius (*Ant. rom.* 9.9.6-7) have statements with ἐλπίς anticipating the outcome of a battle. Such statements are especially common in Polybius (e.g., 1.49.10; 3.64.4; 15.2.3) and in Josephus' *Antiquities* (e.g., 6.26; 9.16; 12.300).

Josephus seems to follow the convention, already found in Thucydides (see *Ant.* 15.128 with the note to "instruct you"), that speeches of encouragement before a battle focus on a discussion of the specific circumstances and the opportunities offered by this situation. This requires an analysis of the battle's location and the specifics and capabilities of both armies (number, experience, courage, and discipline), with their advantages and disadvantages, as well as a discussion of past performances (cf. Aristotle, *Rhet.* 1.4 1359b-1360a). In the Thucydidean speeches commanders frequently analyze the circumstances, like the battle's location and the opportunities it provides, the qualities of both armies, their experience and former successes, and the particularities of the enemy's condition. The Peloponnesian commanders encourage their soldiers in 2.87 before a naval battle, after Athens' earlier triumph over them in the summer of 429 BCE on the high sea, by listing their advantages: "You have the advantage, both in number of ships and in fighting close to the land, which is friendly to us, and you are supported by hoplites; and victory is generally on the side of those who are the more numerous and better prepared. There is accordingly not a single reason that we can find why we should fail ..." (2.87.6-7, trans. Smith; cf. 4.10.3-5; 6.68.3; Polybius 3.54.2-4; 3.111.1-11; 15.10.1). Polybius adheres to Thucydides' principle that commander speeches should address the circumstances: "... addressed them in words suitable to the occasion ... (παρακαλέσαντες αὐτοὺς τὰ πρέποντα τῷ καιρῷ)" (1.32.8, trans. Paton; cf. 1.45.3; 1.60.5; 2.64.1; 3.71.8; 4.80.15; 5.53.6; 11.11.2). The speeches in Thucydides sometimes also reveal the strategy that obviously resulted from the analysis, which also helped to encourage the soldiers (Luschnat 1942: 113, 117). The tenor of most Thucydidean commander speeches is that fear for the enemies—whether because of their huge force, former defeats against them, or difficult circumstances—should change into courage and high spirits through the commander's encouragements and instructions, and consequently lead to triumph (Thucydides 4.10.1-5; 6.68.3; Luschnat 1942: 35-37; Leimbach 1985: 58, 62, 80).

In comparison to the arsenal of arguments linked to the particular military situation found in earlier Greek commander speeches, Herod's speech is rather vague about the circumstances of the future battle against the Nabateans. He does not spend a word on the battle's location, which is unclear anyway in *Antiquities* (see 15.147-148 with notes), but he does offer a brief comparison of both armies after discussing the Nabateans' outrageous acts against the Jews (15.138) and also turns the soldiers' adversities into an advantage (15.142). In the parallel speech of *War* (1.373-379) Herod focuses more on the circumstances for his soldiers. For similar phrases of ἐλπίς plus ἔχω ("have prospects") and νικάω ("win") or νίκη ("victory"), see *Ant.* 12.300; 13.93, also Thucydides 6.68; Anaximenes of Lampsacus 8.14; Dionysius, *Ant. rom.* 9.16; Polybius 3.64.4; 16.32.2; Lucian, *Cal.* 12; Athenaeus 1.29.

[726] The expression ἄρξομαι δ' ("I will start with") is conventional; it projects the beginning to the future, and enhances the audience's eager expectation in this way (Pfeijffer 1999: 33; cf. Dionysius, *Comp.* 20.145 [ed. Usener and Radermacher 6.94]).

[727] The body of the speech—the proof—perfectly matches this summary of the content (*Ant.* 15.129). Its first topic (15.130-137) elaborates Herod's statement that the battle is just and necessary, obviously because of the behavior of the enemy. The section includes a double *narratio* in order to support Herod's point: *Ant.* 15.131-134 lists the reprehensible deeds of the Nabateans and *Ant.* 15.136 mentions their outrageous killing of the Jewish envoys. Herod's second major topic focuses on the soldiers' own situation. It starts in 15.138 or 15.139 (see the notes to these paragraphs). Herod's points in this section are: (1) he and his soldiers were victorious in the previous battles up to the moment Athenio entered the battlefield in a treacherous way (15.139-140); (2) if the enemies are courageous, this should be an extra motivation to beat them (15.141); (3) the earthquake caused less damage than the Nabateans are thinking, which should be taken as an advantage (15.142-143); and (4) God will be on their side (15.144-146). For the last 2 points, cf. the parallel version of *War* (1.373).

[728] Herod's proof calls upon the soldiers' own experiences by making them witnesses. It takes off with a list of the wicked deeds of the Nabateans (see the next note). Hannibal encouraged his soldiers in one of his commander speeches by calling upon the testimony of their own eyes that they had succeeded in crossing the river Po and that the allies were ready to help them (Polybius 3.44.11).

For the combination of ποιέω with μάρτυς and persons as objects ("make someone a witness"), see *Ant.*

For I suppose you know of the lawlessness of the Arabs[729] and how treacherously they deal with everyone else,[730] as is the custom of a barbarous[731] people that also lacks any notion of God.[732] Of course, the main reason that they were hostile to us was greed[733] and

---

6.230 (God) and 16.106 (Caesar), also Dinarch, *Demosth.* 86; Cassius Dio 50.18.1.

[729] Josephus here lists the wicked deeds of the Nabateans (see also *Ant.* 15.107 with notes). Most of his accusations are taken up again in the speech's narrative sections. About the Nabateans' lawlessness (παρανομία), see 15.136, 140, 156.

[730] The unfaithfulness of the Nabateans (ἀπίστως διακειμένων) is also referred to in *Ant.* 15.110, 130, 132, 134, 140.

[731] The phrase τὸ βάρβαρον means "the barbarians" here (Rengstorf *s.v.* βάρβαρος). In Classical Greek sources the meaning of βάρβαρος developed from "not speaking Greek" (cf. βαρβαρίζω in Herodotus 2.57; LSJ *s.v.*) into "non-Greek" (see also *Ant.* 15.136 with the note to "Greeks and barbarians"), frequently with a pejorative meaning (Lévy 1984: 5-14). The adjective βάρβαρος can also mean "uncivilized, cruel, savage," especially in Hellenistic passages (Windisch 1964: 548). The antagonism between Greeks ("Ελληνες) and non-Greeks (βάρβαροι) occurs time and again in reports about the wars of the Greeks against the Persians in the 5th cent. BCE (the *locus classicus* is Herodotus 8.142.5; Mantovani 1990: 21-23). Frequently this opposition implies a value judgment: the Greeks are supposed to be civilized and the non-Greeks not; they are barbarians. Brasidas hints at such a binary opposition at the beginning of his speech of encouragement by calling the Macedonian enemies barbarians and by arguing that there is no reason to fear them because they are barbarians (Thucydides 4.126.1; Leimbach 1985: 80 and see 15.128 with the note to "instruct you").

Elsewhere in Josephus (οἱ) βάρβαροι refers to non-Israelites or non-Jews: the Midianites (*Ant.* 2.263), non-Jewish inhabitants east of the Jordan (12.222), and the Parthians (*War* 1.264, 268). The latter passage implies a pejorative meaning; Josephus highlights the unreliability or disloyalty (ἀπιστία) of the Parthians. He seems to exclude the Jews from the βάρβαροι in these passages, as he does here in Herod's speech (Windisch 1964: 550). The meaning "non-Greek" is also found in *War* 1.5-6 (Rajak 2001: 275).

From a Jewish perspective the Nabateans were foreigners, of course, but the pejorative meaning "barbarians" is clearly presupposed because Herod summarizes their wicked deeds in this paragraph. Herod's qualification of the Nabateans as barbarians underpins his criticism of them. The presentation of the enemies as barbarians may imply that the Jews, as the counterpart of the barbarians, are associated with the Greeks or the civilized, which suggests that Josephus may have re-interpreted the binary opposition Greeks versus non-Greeks/barbarians as Israelites/Jews versus non-Israelites/non-Jews/barbarians. Other Hellenistic-Jewish passages also show a re-interpretation of the opposition Greeks versus non-Greeks/barbarians from a Jewish insider perspective. In 2 Macc 2:21 "the barbarian hordes (τὰ βάρβαρα πλήθη)" refer to the troops of the Seleucid king against whom Judas the Maccabee and his soldiers had fought (see also 10:4). Nevertheless, the epitomist of 2 Maccabees does not suggest a complete reversal of roles (cf. Gruen 2001: 84-85), which would turn the Greeks into the barbarians and the Jews into the civilized. 2 Macc 4:25, referring to the High Priest Menelaus, indicates that individual Jews can also be characterized as barbarian persons: "After receiving the king's orders he [i.e., Menelaus] returned, possessing no qualification for the high priesthood, but having the hot temper of a cruel tyrant (θυμοὺς δὲ ὠμοῦ τυράννου) and the rage of a savage wild beast (καὶ θηρὸς βαρβάρου ὀργὰς ἔχων)." Apparently, one's uncivilized and savage deeds imply, in the perspective of 2 Maccabees, that one is a "barbarian" and do not refer to one's ethnic identity (see also LXX Ps 113:1 [= MT 114:1]; 2 Macc 5:22; 13:9; 15:2; the next note; and van Henten 2011a).

[732] Herod's association of the Nabateans with a barbarian people (see the preceding note) is elaborated with the statement that they did not have a conception of God (ἀνεννόητον θεοῦ). The word ἀνεννόητος ("without any notion of," Rengstorf *s.v.*) is a *hapax legomenon* in Josephus. Herod's reasoning indicates that having knowledge of the God of Israel or not is a principle difference between the Jews and the Nabateans. This underpins the negative associations associated with the word βάρβαρος and offers an additional explanation of the wicked behavior of the Nabateans. It also anticipates another point in Herod's speech, namely that the Jews have the support of the God of Israel and the Nabateans do not (*Ant.* 15.144-146). LXX Ps 113:1 offers a close parallel to Herod's statement. The psalm praises God for bringing Israel miraculously to the promised land: "Hallelouiah. At Israel's exodus from Egypt, of Jacob's house from a barbarian people (ἐκ λαοῦ βαρβάρου), Judea became his holy precinct, Israel his seat of authority" (trans. *NETS*). The beginning of this psalm constructs a binary opposition between the Israelites/Jews and a foreign people, i.e., Egypt. It presupposes that the Israelites are superior because they are being

jealousy;[734] they were waiting to make a sudden attack[735] in our confused state. **131** But why do I have to say much [more]?[736] When they were in danger of being deprived of their self-government[737] and becoming subject to Cleopatra,[738] was there anyone else who freed them from their fear?[739] For it was because of my friendship with Antony[740] and his

---

supported by their God. The inferiority of the Egyptians remains implicit in the psalm; their barbaric deeds are not highlighted, while the deeds of the Nabateans are in *Ant*. 15.130. The binary opposition of Israel and Egypt nevertheless suggests that βάρβαρος also has a pejorative connotation in LXX Ps 113:1 (van Henten 2011a).

[733] The Nabateans' greed (πλεονεξία) is taken up again in *Ant*. 15.134 (with 2 occurrences of the verb κερδαίνω ["making profit"]).

[734] The jealousy (φθόνος) of the Nabateans is not mentioned again. Landau (2006: 138) suggests that the reference to the Nabateans' greed and jealousy is ironic because both traits are characteristic of Herod's own behavior (cf. *Ant*. 15.89, 91 about Cleopatra).

[735] Herod blames the Nabateans for starting a war unannounced (cf. *War* 1.269; 2.30; *Apion* 1.318), which can be connected with the topic of just war. According to Graeco-Roman passages starting a war unannounced was a clear violation of the obligation to fight a war in a fair way. In Herodotus 5.81.2 such a war (ἀκήρυκτος πόλεμος) is seen as a crime (cf. Polybius 5.42.2; Josephus, *War* 1.269; 2.30; *Apion* 1.318; Mantovani 1990: 60-70, 94, also *Ant*. 15.135 with the note to "justified"). The Nabateans' treacherous behavior is taken up again in *Ant*. 15.140-142. The phrase ἐξ ὑπογύου ("suddenly," Rengstorf *s.v.*) is a *hapax legomenon* in Josephus. The parallel passage of *War* (1.375) focuses upon Athenio's attack, which is referred to in *Ant*. 15.139.

[736] Deliberative speech can include narrative sections (*narrationes*) that underpin the speaker's argumentation (Aristotle, *Rhet*. 3.16.11 1417b). The first *narratio* of Herod's speech (*Ant*. 15.131-134) concerns the lawless deeds of the Nabateans. It is introduced by the rhetorical formula "But why do I have to say much [more]?" (καὶ τὰ μὲν πολλὰ τί δεῖ λέγειν;). Exactly the same phrase is found in Demosthenes, *Or*. 37.12 (also in a *narratio*). Phrases like τί δεῖ λέγειν; can indicate a transition (e.g., Thucydides 1.73.2; Dionysius, *Ant. rom.* 10.6). The formula here suggests that there is no need to say more about these wicked Nabateans, although it functions as the introductory phrase for a whole list of accusations. This function reminds one of the figure of speech of *praeteritio* (i.e., stating something by saying that one is not going to mention it; Lausberg 1998: 393-94).

In the next paragraphs Herod briefly describes his own benefactions toward the Nabateans: they benefited from his friendship with Antony (*Ant*. 15.132) and from his taking care of Cleopatra's greedy attempts to take over territories from both kingdoms (15.131, 133). Yet they returned his friendship with treachery (15.133-134). Injustice done by the enemy (15.131-134) was an important reason for justifying a war against them. Greek commander speeches frequently justify a war by recalling the enemy's unjust acts. In Thucydides the Syracusan commander Gylippus justifies a war against the Athenians before a naval battle (413 BCE). Revenge was called for because Athens was attempting to enslave all Sicily and would, if successful, commit all kinds of outrages against the Sicilians, even against wives and children (7.68.1-3; cf. 1.86.2-3). The speech of the Spartan king Archidamus also refers to improper behavior of the Athenians (2.11.7-9).

[737] The Nabateans did run the risk of losing their autonomy because of Cleopatra's strategy to take over the Nabatean and Judean kingdoms, as Josephus indicates in a previous passage (see *Ant*. 15.110 with the note to "it would be good for her if the one would suffer badly from the other"). The phrase τῆς οἰκείας ἀρχῆς ἐκπεσεῖν ("being deprived of their self-government") occurs several times in Eusebius (*Praep. ev*. 5.20.10; 5.21.1, 3).

[738] The implication of the passage is probably that the Nabateans would have been ruled directly by Cleopatra, which matches the previous phrase. However, the verb δουλεύω ("be a subject/slave of") may have a double entendre and also hint at Cleopatra's evil character. Being a slave of Cleopatra could have frightening consequences (see *Ant*. 15.89-91 with notes, also *War* 1.243, which passage suggests that Antony was enslaved by Cleopatra).

[739] Herod may hint here at his role as intermediary between Cleopatra and the Nabateans, which prevented the queen from becoming the ruler of the Nabateans (see the continuation of this *narratio*). *War* 1.373 briefly refers to God's vengeance on the Nabateans. The motif of fear in *War* concerns the Jewish soldiers. For a similar phrase with τοῦ δέους and ἀπαλλάσσω ("free from fear"), see *Ant*. 2.133, also Isocrates, *Phil*. 111; Demosthenes, *Or*. 21.129; Dio Chrysostom 6.43; Appian, *Hist. rom*. 7.52.

[740] Herod refers to his close relationship with his patron Antony, which was the basis for his successful rule (similar phrases in *Ant*. 15.162, 183; see 15.162 with the note to "because of his close friendship with Antony," also *War* 1.386). The friendship motif (expressed by the words φίλοι and πίστις) returns in *Ant*. 15.133-134.

favorable disposition towards us that they did not suffer irreparable harm.[741] That man[742] was on his guard not to undertake anything that could raise our suspicion.[743] **132** Nevertheless, when he wanted to grant Cleopatra certain parts of both our realms,[744] it was I who took care of this too. By providing many gifts from my own possessions[745] I attained security for both of us,[746] and I myself took care of all the costs.[747] That is, I gave[748] two hundred talents and also became the guarantor for two hundred [more],[749] which went to her[750] as collector. We have been robbed by them of this [money].[751] **133** And, indeed, it was not right[752] for the Jews to pay tribute to any one at all, nor to give up a part of their land. But if, in fact, [they had to pay tribute,] then [it should] not [be] for those whom we ourselves have saved.[753] Nor should the Arabs, after having made an agreement with us,[754] wrong us[755] by depriving us of what they initially thought a great concession and favor,[756]

---

[741] Phrases like (μηδὲ) ἀνήκεστόν (τι) παθεῖν ("[not] suffer [something] fatal") occur several times in Josephus (*War* 3.480; *Ant.* 15.145, 197; cf. *War* 1.121; 2.233, 320; 6.123; *Ant.* 18.359). Thucydides uses the phrase already in 3.39.8 (see also Demosthenes, *Or.* 54.5; Diodorus 17.15.2; Dionysius, *Dem.* 12; Philo, *Conf.* 13; *Legat.* 109; *Spec.* 3.166; 4.173; Athenaeus 6.89).

[742] I.e., Antony.

[743] The phrase hints at Antony's role as Herod's patron, but the formulation is platitudinous. As a matter of fact, Cleopatra's interference in the Nabatean and Judean affairs must have made Herod very suspicious; the queen was a formidable competitor for him (van Henten 2005a).

[744] This refers to Antony's grant of Judean and Nabatean territories to Cleopatra, reported in *Ant.* 15.96, 106 (see the notes to these paragraphs).

[745] Although providing gifts to a patron was the obvious thing to do to obtain a favor, it is doubtful whether Herod actually did this in connection with the lease of these territories. Josephus does not report such gifts in the report about the deal with Cleopatra (*Ant.* 15.106-107). On the other hand, it is certainly possible that Herod had to bribe Antony first in order to be able to make the deal with Cleopatra.

[746] The main point of Herod's reasoning is that he did his utmost to prevent Cleopatra from directly ruling over the territories granted to her by Antony—not only the Judean part of it, but also the Nabatean section. The obvious response by the Nabateans would have been gratefulness to Herod and compliance with the deal, but this did not happen, as the continuation of the *narratio* points out. This point leads up to Herod's accusation that the Nabateans cheated him (*Ant.* 15.132-134). The combination of πορίζω and ἀσφαλές or ἀσφάλεια ("attain security") also occurs in *War* 1.567, 623; *Ant.* 2.220; 8.13 (see also Philo, *Spec.* 1.75; Arrian, *Anab.* 7.9.4).

[747] This links up with the previous phrase ("from my own possessions") and highlights Herod's own financial sacrifices for establishing the deal with Cleopatra.

[748] MSS PFLW read διδούς ("by giving," Niese 356).

[749] The actual amount of talents involved in the tripartite deal with Cleopatra is debated, but the passage may mean that Herod paid 200 talents for his own lease of Judean territories from Cleopatra and also acted as guarantor (ἐγγυητής; see also *Ant.* 14.81) of the 200 talents for the lease of the Nabatean territories by the Nabatean king (see 15.106-107 with the note to "which Herod had to pay for the land given by Antony").

[750] Josephus' phrase is elliptic here, but the context implies that the revenues went to Cleopatra. MSS LAMW add γῇ ("to the land") after μὲν, which does not make sense, but may have evolved from the assumption of copyists that the article τῇ need to be followed by a noun.

[751] See *Ant.* 15.107-108 about King Malichus' violation of the deal concerning the lease, which made Herod decide to go to war.

[752] Herod's complicated argument, starting with ἄξιον ἦν ("it was [not] right"), makes 2 statements about what was not right: (1) the Jews had to pay tribute and give up part of their territory (to Cleopatra), and (2) the Nabateans did not keep the agreement with Herod. The first statement is connected with another statement, which follows upon the assumption that the first one was wrong: if there was a reason for the Jews to pay tribute, it should not have been on behalf of those who had already been helped by Herod.

[753] Herod has just explained his great help to the Nabateans in *Ant.* 15.132.

[754] I.e., the financial deal about the lease of the Nabatean territory (see the previous paragraph).

[755] Herod takes up the injustice (ἀδικεῖν) of the Nabateans in the next paragraphs in order to make his point that the war against them is just (see *Ant.* 15.135 with the note to "justified").

[756] The Greek is elliptic and open to more than one interpretation. The noun ἔντευξις is translated with "concession," as suggested by Rengstorf (*s.v.*), but it can also mean "request" or "appeal" here (cf. *Ant.* 15.79). The phrase τὴν ἀρχήν is interpreted as an adverbial

given that we were not enemies but friends.[757] **134** For, indeed, if there is room for observing the bond of trust[758] even with one's greatest enemies, it must be most strictly applied to one's friends.[759] But no! This is not the case with these people, who firmly believe that making profit in any way is best[760] and that doing wrong is not liable to punishment, provided that[761] they profit from it. **135** So is there still any question[762] for you as to whether these wrongdoers ought to be punished, when God too wants this[763] and always[764] commands us[765] to hate insolence and wrongdoing?[766] Especially as we are

---

expression meaning "at first" (LSJ *s.v.* ἀρχή 1c; Rengstorf *s.v.*).

[757] The statement highlights the treachery of the Nabateans. In the next paragraph Herod elaborates that friendship implies that friends are faithful to each other. This argument is based on Herod's initially friendly relationship with the Nabateans, also because of his father's connections with the Nabateans and the fact that his mother, Cyprus, descended from a prominent Nabatean family (*War* 1.181; Kokkinos 1998: 95). The financial help provided by Herod to the Nabateans is proof of this relationship of friendship, which required from the Nabateans that they would treat Herod as a friend. Herod's aid matches earlier transactions by Herod's father Antipater (see *War* 1.220-222 and *Ant.* 15.107 with the note to "slow with his payments"). About the phrase ἀδικεῖν ... ἀποστεροῦντας ... φίλους ("doing wrong by robbing friends"), cf. 1 Cor 6:8 "But you yourselves wrong and defraud—and believers at that (ἀλλὰ ὑμεῖς ἀδικεῖτε καὶ ἀποστερεῖτε καὶ τοῦτο ἀδελφούς)."

[758] Another difficult rhetorical statement, which partly repeats the vocabulary of *Ant.* 15.133, elaborates what trust or faithfulness (πίστις) and friendship should imply (see the next note) and highlights the treachery of the Nabateans by contrast. It leads to the preliminary conclusion that the criminal acts of the Nabateans have to be punished (see also *Apion* 2.207, in which passage Josephus emphasizes that friendship implies absolute trust; Barclay in BJP 10 on *Apion* 2.207). Lindsay (1993: 95) connects Josephus' vocabulary to the formula πίστιν τηρεῖν in 2 Tim 4:7, meaning "to remain faithful/loyal." The phrase τόπον ἔχειν can mean, i.a., "have a place, have room for" (LSJ *s.v.* τόπος I.2); Rengstorf (*s.v.*) suggests "be respected" as a possible meaning here (see also *War* 4.434; *Ant.* 15.158).

[759] This repeats, again with emphasis, Herod's point of *Ant.* 15.133 that the Nabateans violated the conventions for relations between friends. Friendship is an important ideal in ancient Greek and Roman societies: in Classical Greece friendship concerns societal as well as private reciprocal relations, which implies that both sides were aiming for the happiness or benefit of the other (Aristotle, *Eth. Nic.* 8.1-2 1155a-1156a). In Hellenistic and Roman times the focus is upon personal relationships. That friends are just and faithful towards and equal to each other is self-evident (Aristotle, *Eth. Nic.* 9.2 1168b; see also Plutarch's treatises *De amicorum multitudine* and *De fraterno amore*; further references in Treu 1972: 418-25; Klauck 1992: 98-101; Scholtissek 2004: 415-25). The motif of faithfulness among friends is prominent in Greek literature (e.g., Diodorus 10.17.2; Lucian, *Tox.* 41; Klauck 1992: 98) and also implied by biblical passages: friends are equated to brothers (Deut 13:7; Ps 35:14; cf. Lev 19:18); in emergency situations friends deserve loyalty and solidarity (1 Sam 20:8; 2 Sam 16:16-17). Trust and friendship are a common collocation in Josephus (Mason in BJP 1b on 2.257).

[760] Aiming for profit obviously goes against the ethics of friendship referred to in Herod's previous statement. This is Herod's second reference to the greed of the Nabateans (see *Ant.* 15.130, which mentions πλεονεξία ["greed"] in this connection). Herod repeats the verb κερδαίνω ("make profit") in this sentence and emphasizes in this way the Nabateans' unscrupulousness, which is apparent from the point elaborated in the previous paragraphs: they received the yield from the land leased from Cleopatra but did not keep their deal with Herod, which implies that they leased the land for free and that Herod, being guarantor, had to make up for that.

[761] The introduction of the conditional phrase by εἰ μόνον ("provided that") instead of the usual εἰ (γε) turns the condition into an exclusive or necessary one ("if only"; Wakker 1994: 340).

[762] MS P (Niese 356) reads ἐπιζήτησις ("desire," Rengstorf *s.v.*).

[763] That the punishment of the Nabateans is wanted by God as well follows from the continuation of the sentence. It is also indicated in the parallel speech of *War* (1.373). Josephus uses vocabulary similar to τοῦ θεοῦ βουλομένου in *Ant.* 1.229; 3.45; 4.288 (cf. 1.223; LXX 1 Sam 2:25).

[764] Niese (356) conjectures καὶ τοῦ νόμου ("and the Law [commands ...])," which improves the sentence but is unnecessary (see the next note).

[765] God is intended as the subject of the participle παραγγέλλοντος ("commanding [us]"), although there are no close parallels in Josephus to support this reading. Josephus refers to God's commandments in *Ant.* 1.41 (τοῖς τοῦ θεοῦ παραγγέλμασιν; Feldman in BJP 3 on

conducting a war that is not only justified[767] but even necessary?[768] **136** For that which is

---

Ant. 1.41). Acts 17:30 has God as the subject of the verb παραγγέλλω ("command"): "While God (ὁ θεός) has overlooked the times of human ignorance, now he commands (παραγγέλλει) all people everywhere to repent."

[766] The statement "God ... always commands us to hate insolence and wrongdoing (μισεῖν τὴν ὕβριν καὶ τὴν ἀδικίαν)" is perhaps an allusion to LXX Prov 8:13: "The fear of the Lord hates injustice, also outrage (φόβος κυρίου μισεῖ ἀδικίαν, ὕβριν) and arrogance, and the ways of the wicked (trans. *NETS*, slightly adapted)." If so, the passage from Proverbs was probably interpreted as a statement that persons faithful to God should hate wrongdoing, outrage, etc., by acting against it and punishing the perpetrators. The implication would be that Herod and his soldiers would have God's approval during their punishment of the Nabateans. For a further occurrence of μισέω plus ἀδικία in Josephus, see *Ant.* 3.274 (cf. *War* 2.139; Jdt 5:17 "And as long as they [i.e., the Israelites] did not sin in the sight of their God, good fortune was with them, for with them is a God who hates iniquity [θεὸς μισῶν ἀδικίαν]," trans. *NETS*; LXX Ps 118:128, 163; LXX Prov 28:16; LXX Isa 33:15).

[767] Here Herod formulates one of his main points, already hinted at in *Ant.* 15.128: the battle is just as well as necessary (οὐ μόνον δίκαιον ἀλλὰ καὶ ἀναγκαῖον πόλεμον, 15.134-135). Many words in the speech highlight the first point that the war is justified (ἄδικος ["unjust"]: 15.134, 146; ἀδικέω ["do wrong"]: 15.134, 144; ἀδικία ["injustice"]: 15.135, 140; δίκαιος ["just"]: 15.135, 137, 138, 145-146; δικαίως ["rightly"]: 15.129). This vocabulary is absent in the parallel version of *War* (1.373-379). The *Antiquities* version of Herod's commander speech is, as a matter of fact, the most elaborate passage dealing with just war in Josephus. It seems to be based on a combination of biblical notions of holy war commanded by God (see the note to "God too wants this" above and 15.136 with notes) and Graeco-Roman traditions concerning just war (Mantovani 1990: 86). Herod emphasizes time and again that another battle against the Nabateans is called for because it would be a justified war (15.129, 135, 138, 145-146).

Ancient historians frequently report about just and unjust causes for the many wars fought in antiquity, whether in their attempt to reconstruct the events as precisely as possible, or to legitimate wars afterwards. In the case of the Romans the theory of just war is even used in advance as a pretext to start a war (cf. the examples in Dionysius mentioned below). From Thucydides onwards the theme of just war appears in commander speeches and other passages with a rather fixed vocabulary (key words: πόλεμος ["war"] with δίκαιος ["just"], ὅσιος ["holy"], or ἱερός ["holy"] and the Latin equivalents *bellum iustum* ["just war"] or *bellum pium* ["holy war"]; Albert 1980; Clavadetscher-Thürlemann 1985; Mantovani 1990). At the outbreak of the war between the Athenians and Spartans (in 431 BCE), the Spartan king Archidamus points out to his soldiers that the battle against Athens is "right" (δίκαιος, perhaps "obligatory") for 2 reasons: 1) faithfulness to the reputation of the Peloponnesians and their allies' ancestors, and 2) the unusual acts of Athens against other Greeks by attacking their lands and destroying them (Thucydides 2.11.2, 7-9; Leimbach 1985: 19-20, 33). Some 50 years previously Mardonius urged the Persian king Xerxes to continue his war against Greece by indicating the outrageous acts against the Persians by the Athenians, which was calling for revenge (Herodotus 7.5, 9). Dionysius often uses *bellum iustum* vocabulary in his description of Rome's early history. A striking example is Tullus' declaration of war on the Albans because of their breaking a treaty: "I declare against the Albans the war that is both necessary and just (τὸν ἀναγκαῖόν τε καὶ δίκαιον πόλεμον)" (*Ant. rom.* 3.3.6, trans. Cary). In 8.2-5 Marcius warns Tullus not to attack Rome immediately, but to establish deliberately a righteous and just ground for the war (αἰτίαν ... δεῖν εὐσεβῆ καὶ δικαίαν ἐνστήσασθαι τοῦ πολεμοῦ, 8.2.2) because of the gods; his advice is to let the Romans break the treaty first. In 5.5.4 Collatinus advises the consuls not to keep the possessions of the expelled tyrants because that could give them a just reason to begin a war (πρόφασιν πολέμου δικαίαν).

Coherent theoretical reflections about just war start only with Cicero (*Off.* 1.20-23, 34-36, 80-81; 2.26-27; *Re publ.* 2.31; 3.35; Albert 1980: 20-25; Ramage 2001), although he builds on arguments brought forward in previous statements about the issue whether a war is just or not. A justified cause for a war could be based on religious, philosophical, or juridical reasons. Religious grounds for launching a just war could exist of outrageous deeds (acts of ὕβρις) against deities (like the desecration of their temples), unjust and godless acts against relatives (violation of blood ties), and internal wars (violating kinship relations, alliances, or the political bodies of states). A philosophical reason could be that the strong have a right to fight inferiors, e.g., animals or barbarians. Juridical grounds were most important and included the right to defend oneself against an enemy attack or to help an ally, the right to take revenge on the enemy for outrageous deeds, as well as the right to free oneself from tyranny or foreign oppressors (Albert 1980: 17-18; Mantovani 1990: 1-84).

Just war requires that a proper procedure is met

agreed upon as being most lawless by both Greeks and barbarians[769] is what they did to our envoys;[770] namely, they cut their throats. The Greeks actually have declared their envoys to be sacred and immune,[771] and we have learned the most beautiful of our doctrines

---

before declaring the war. According to Greek traditions the procedure includes in any case a formal declaration presented by envoys (Oehler 1921: 355). Roman sacral law (*ius fetiale*) prescribes several steps of the procedure for Romans: a consultation of the senate, a decision by the people, and the transference of the decision by priestly envoys (Albert 1980: 12-16). In the Republican period the priestly role of the *fetiales* declined and was taken over by envoys from the senate (Albert 1980: 15; Mantovani 1990: 60-61). A justified war has to be fought in a just manner: both sides have to fight the war with fairness, nobleness, avoidance of cunning and guile, and with only trained soldiers (Clavadetscher-Thürlemann 1985: 104-26; Mantovani 1990: 70-79). Of course, the remarks above reflect the ideal situation and handbooks on warfare and examples transmitted to us, from Caesar's *Gallic War* through Frontinus' stratagems, imply a very different picture concerning the Romans: warfare was all about deception, cunning, and guile (cf. Josephus in *War* 3). For the Romans a just war may have been, in fact, (a) a justified war, undertaken from some perceived iniuria—in other words the unique right to save face and maintain Rome's absolute supremacy; (b) a proper war, i.e., a war done the proper way with the usual rituals, and not a civil war or a provincial rebellion (Mattern-Parkes 2003).

Several other passages in Josephus touch upon the theme of justified war. The victory of the Israelites over the Ethiopians is attributed to the Israelites being just and holy (ὅτι δικαίους καὶ ὁσίους ἑαυτοὺς παρέσχον, *Ant.* 8.295). God prevented the battle between Rehoboam and Jeroboam (1 Kgs 15:6) on the ground that it is not just to fight somebody of the same kin: "He was, however, prevented by God, via a prophet, from undertaking the campaign; for he said that it was not just to wage war on one's compatriots (οὐ γὰρ εἶναι δίκαιον τοὺς ὁμοφύλους πολεμεῖν) and that these things, namely the revolt of the crowd, was in accord with God's intent ..." (*Ant.* 8.223; trans. Begg in BJP 5). See also *War* 2.399, 582; *Ant.* 8.280; 14.63; *Life* 22, and cf. Eleazar's speech at Masada referring to a just contest (ἀγὼν δίκαιος, *War* 7.355).

[768] Herod's statement that the battle against the Nabateans is necessary seems to be closely related to his just war argument; the Nabateans absolutely have to be punished (see also the motif of necessity in Josephus' own speech at Yodfat [*War* 3.361] and Eleazar's Masada speeches [*War* 7.330, 352, 358, 380, 382, 387]; Runnalls 1971: 261; Lindner 1972: 35-37). Thucydides' com-

mander speeches refer a few times to necessity (ἀνάγκη), indicating that the battles cannot be avoided in the circumstances at hand, or that specific strategies are forced upon the army because of the circumstances (4.10.1; 6.68.4; 7.62.4; 7.77.5; Luschnat 1942: 35-36, 76-77, 133; Leimbach 1985: 97).

[769] For the reference to "barbarians" (meaning "non-Greeks" here), see *Ant.* 15.130 with the note to "barbarous." Herod mentions Greeks and non-Greeks together ("Ελληνες καὶ βάρβαροι), which are the 2 categories of humankind from a Greek perspective. The implication is that it is self-evident that envoys have immunity (see the next notes). Landau (2006: 138) considers this reference to Greeks and barbarians to be a commonplace, referring to Thucydides 1.1 and *War* 1.1, in which passages the wars that are going to be described are considered to be the greatest disasters known to both Greeks and non-Greeks. The combination Ἕλληνες καὶ βάρβαροι also occurs in *Ant.* 1.93, 107; *Apion* 1.58, 161, as a reference to Greek and non-Greek authors.

[770] The slaughtering of the Jewish envoys is Herod's main accusation in the second *narratio* of Herod's speech (*Ant.* 15.136-137; cf. *War* 1.378). It is highlighted as a huge sacrilege among Greeks and non-Greeks (see also *Ant.* 15.124 with the note to "killed them"), which screams for revenge (cf. *War* 1.378). It leads up to an additional argument for a victorious outcome, God's support (*Ant.* 15.138, 144-146). Another case of just war because of maltreatment of envoys is found in *Ant.* 7.119-120, in which passage David takes revenge upon the Ammonites because their king shaved off half of the envoys' beards and cut off half of their garments. It is remarkable that Herod, later in the narrative, when the Nabateans send envoys to the king after their defeat, does not repeat their unjust act (15.155). In this light the detail of the Nabateans' murdering the Jewish envoys gains even more significance and makes Herod look even more favorable.

[771] Envoys were protected by longstanding conventions or by law. Killing them was a terrible crime (see *Ant.* 15.124 with the note to "killed them"). In the continuation of his argument Herod seems to suggest that the Jews, who are here counted among the barbarians, have divine laws transmitted to them that forbid them to kill envoys, but this argument is hardly made explicit. In the parallel speech of *War* (1.378) Herod refers in this connection to the law that is in force for all humans (τὸν πάντων ἀνθρώπων νόμον). The noun νόμος has the

and the most holy of our laws through God's messengers.[772] For this name[773] makes[774] God known to humans and is able to reconcile enemies with each other.[775] **137** What greater sacrilege[776] could take place than[777] that of killing envoys who [came to] hold discussions about a just arrangement?[778] How could they[779] still enjoy peaceful lives[780] or be successful

---

meaning of a universal law as the basis of humankind's morality in this passage, which seems to be a unique case in Josephus (Schröder 1996: 50). Herodotus mentions that the Spartans did not receive good omens for a long time because they had killed the envoys of the Persian king Darius (7.133-137; cf. Diodorus 33.5.4; 36.15.1-2).

[772] This is a remarkable passage for various reasons. On the basis of the foregoing statements one would expect that Herod would mention the Jewish equivalent of regulations concerning the immunity of envoys. However, he could not do that because specific regulations concerning envoys are missing in the Jewish laws circulating at that period. This probably explains why Herod refers to the laws of the Jews in a vague and general way. Although this point hardly contributes to his argument, he highlights, in Josephus' presentation, these laws in superlatives: "most beautiful" and "most holy." This connects well with Josephus' presentation of the Jewish laws elsewhere (e.g., *Apion* 2.175 with similar superlative qualifications). Herod's statement perhaps also anticipates his later point about God's support during the battle (*Ant.* 15.138, 144-146).

The noun ἄγγελος ("messenger") is ambiguous here because it can refer to human as well as heavenly messengers (i.e., angels; Rengstorf *s.v.*). Both interpretations have been defended in scholarly literature (Marcus-Wikgren 66 n. *a*; Najman 2000: 313, 318, with references). If the phrase refers to human messengers, one can think of prophets (cf. *Apion* 1.37; Davies 1954), High Priests (Walton 1955), or perhaps a vague reference to Moses as the one who was God's intermediary in revealing the Law to Israel (Exod 24:12; 31:18; 34:1-2, also 2 Macc 7:30). Jewish and New Testament parallels render it more probable that the passage hints at heavenly messengers, either a heavenly Moses (4Q377 2.ii; *Sifre Num.* [ed. Horovitz 101]; Najman 2000: 318-19, 331-32; van Henten 2003), or angels (*Jub.* 1.27, 29; 2.1 [the angel of God's presence instructs Moses with the words about the creation]; Philo, *Somn.* 1.141-142; Acts 7:53; Gal 3:19, referring to the angels as well as to Moses, without mentioning him: "... it [i.e., the Law] was ordained through angels by a mediator"; esp. Heb 1:4–2:16 (2:2); Najman 2000). For the plural δόγματα ("decrees") referring to Jewish laws revealed by God, see also *Apion* 1.42, which mentions God's decrees (θεοῦ δόγματα), probably the laws of the Pentateuch (Barclay in BJP 10 on 1.42). For a rather different combination of δόγματα and νόμοι ("laws"), see *Ant.* 17.159.

[773] Instead of the usual meaning "name" the word ὄνομα perhaps means "phrase" (LSJ *s.v.* V) or "category" (Bauer-Aland *s.v.* II) here, but the translation "category" would presuppose a philosophical context, which is absent. Herod is valuing the treasured and protected name of "messenger" before his troops. His reasoning is that messengers among nations must be sacrosanct just as the messengers who brought the laws were sacred and inviolate. The name refers to the heavenly messengers mentioned in the preceding sentence. The angels (or perhaps Moses; see the previous note) reveal the divine to humans (see also *Ant.* 15.425, in which passage the genitive τοῦ θεοῦ after ἐμφανείας should be interpreted as a subjective genitive: "the other manifestations of God").

[774] With Niese (356), who reads ἄγει ("makes") instead of the infinitive ἄγειν (attested in MSS LMW and as a correction in MS A), which is dependent on δύναται ("can ... make").

[775] A literal translation is "enemies with enemies"; the repetition gives emphasis. Josephus still focuses on the function of the messengers mentioned previously, but the passage perhaps presupposes a shift from supernatural to human messengers (as Omert J. Schrier, Amsterdam, communicated to me). Obviously human envoys can help to reconcile enemies. Such a role could, however, also be fulfilled by supernatural messengers. The passage may also hint at Moses' role as mediator and intercessor on behalf of Israel (possibly as heavenly messenger), cf. *As. Mos.* 11.14, 17; 12.6; 1Q22 iv.1; 2Q21 1; 4Q368 1; 4Q374 7; 4Q378 26; 4Q393 3; 4Q504 1.ii.7-11.

[776] The noun ἀσέβημα ("sacrilege," Rengstorf *s.v.*) perhaps echoes the use of the adjective ἀσεβής ("godless") in the parallel speech of *War* (1.376), although Josephus also often uses parallel terminology in *War* and *Antiquities* in rather different ways.

[777] The rhetorical phrase introduced by ποῖον οὖν μεῖζον ("what greater ...") returns to the accusation of the killing of the Jewish envoys (*Ant.* 15.136) and embellishes this accusation with rhetorical means.

[778] *Ant.* 15.124 notes that the mission of the envoys was to discuss the conclusion of peace with the Nabateans, which negotiation is part of the conventions connected with just war (see 15.135 with the note to "justified"). The combination of διαλέγομαι ("discuss") and τοῦ δικαίου/τῶν δικαίων ("just matter[s]") also

in war[781] when such things have been done by them?[782] To me this seems utterly impossible. **138** At this point someone will perhaps say:[783] "Although holiness and justice are with us,[784] they happen to be more courageous[785] or more numerous."[786] But, first of all, you

---

occurs in Isocrates, *Archid.* 39; Demosthenes, *Or.* 56.12; Dionysius, *Ant. rom.* 7.66.5; Plutarch, *Alc.* 14.7; Athenaeus 13.92.

[779] The formula πῶς δ' ἂν δύναιτο introduces a rhetorical question emphasizing the impossibility of the issue stated (LSJ *s.v.* πῶς II; cf. similar formulas in Plato, *Gorg.* 467a; Philo, *Agr.* 22; *Decal.* 112; *Ebr.* 199; Plutarch, *Mor.* [*Apophth. lac.*] 230f; *Pyrrh.* 11.2; Athenaeus 2.1.159; Acts 8:31).

[780] The verb εὐσταθέω ("find/enjoy peace," Rengstorf *s.v.*) is a *hapax legomenon* in Josephus. About a peaceful life, cf. Pseudo-Lucian, *Am.* 43.1; Clement of Alexandria, *Strom.* 4.25.161.

[781] The phrase περὶ τὸν πόλεμον εὐτυχεῖν ("be successful in war"; cf. *Ant.* 12.339 τῆς ἐν τοῖς πολέμοις εὐτυχίας "good fortune in war") perhaps echoes a phrase in Thucydides (1.120 ὅ τε ἐν πολέμῳ εὐτυχίᾳ "good fortune in war"; see also Herodotus 1.171; Xenophon, *Cyn.* 12.8).

[782] Herod obviously refers to the killing of his envoys (*Ant.* 15.124, 136-137).

[783] It is not entirely clear where the section about the second major topic of the speech, which concerns Herod's comparison between his own soldiers and the enemy (see the next note), starts. It is either with this rhetoric formula—pointing at an anonymous voice (ἴσως τοίνυν ἐρεῖ τις "someone will perhaps say," de Jong 1987)—or with the formula "Let us also look at our own situation" (*Ant.* 15.139). Both can be interpreted as the transition to the second issue (i.e., the soldiers' own situation), but the first option seems more probable because Herod starts his comparison between his own soldiers and the enemy already in 15.138, as the continuation of the sentence indicates.

[784] This is the first point of Herod's comparison of his own soldiers' situation with that of the enemy. Herod first briefly refers to divine support and justice on the Jews' side in contrast with the Nabateans' courage and multitude. In the next paragraphs he elaborates this as well as 4 other points: (1) Herod and his soldiers were victorious in earlier battles (*Ant.* 15.139-140) until Athenio entered the battlefield (15.140); (2) even if the enemy is courageous, which is not the case, this should be an extra motivation to beat them (15.141); (3) the earthquake caused less damage than the Nabateans think, which should be seen as an advantage (15.142-143); and (4) God will be on the side of the Jews (15.144-145). Herod briefly refers to the fourth point here. The mention of "justice" links up with the earlier points connected with just war (see 15.135 with the note to "justified").

The noun ὅσιον ("holiness") plus μεθ' ἡμῶν ("with us") hints at God's support to the Jewish soldiers, which is elaborated in the subsequent sentences as well as in 15.144-145. The phrase is a Greek variant of the Hebrew phrase *'immānû 'Ēl* ("El [i.e., God] is with us"), which is also attested as a name (Immanuel, Isa 7:14). It expresses God's promise of protection (Ps 46:4-7, 11; cf. Isa 8:9-10). The usual Greek rendering of this name is ὁ θεός ἡμῶν (ἐστι) μεθ' ἡμῶν ("our God [is] with us"): LXX 1 Kgs 8:57; LXX 2 Chr 32:8; Jdt 13:11; Matt 1:23 (cf. LXX Isa 8:8; Justin, *Apol.* 1.33.1, also Josephus, *War* 2.390-391; 5.380, 382, 386, 389, 403-404; 6.99-100; *Ant.* 3.45-46; 8.282, about God as divine ally).

[785] This phrase anticipates Herod's discussion of the enemies' courage (*Ant.* 15.140). Herod refers to the irresistible courage (ἀνδρεία) of his own soldiers in the conclusion of the parallel speech of *War* (1.379; cf. 1.373 and the next note).

[786] Being "more numerous" (see also πλῆθος ["number"] further on in this paragraph) builds on a common place in Greek commander speeches as well as on a motif in the Bible. It is twice associated with courage (ἀνδρεία) in this passage, in a chiastic order (ἀνδρειότεροι … πλείους / πλῆθος … ἀνδρεία). In the events connected with the Battle of Thermopylae Herodotus time and again contrasts multitude and courage with experience: in the Persian council Mardonius first convinces Xerxes that there is no risk in attacking Greece because of the multitude of the army (7.9). Next Herodotus offers a marvelous speech by Artabanus, who strongly advises Xerxes not to attack the Greeks. Artabanus combines the importance of divine support with the observation that the bigger army does not necessarily win: "You see how the god (ὁ θεός) smites with his thunderbolt creatures of greatness more than common, nor suffers them to display their pride …. Thus a numerous host is destroyed by one that is lesser, the god of his jealousy sending panic fear or thunderbolt among them, whereby they do unworthily perish …" (7.10, trans. Godley). In his discussion with Demaratus, however, Xerxes keeps putting his trust in his army's multitude, whereas Demaratus stresses the Spartans' excellence in battle (7.101-105). Thucydides' speeches also raise the matter of the number of enemy soldiers. Before the naval battle near Naupactus against the Spartans (in 429 BCE), the Athenian commander Phormio discusses the multitude of the Peleponnesian forces (2.89; cf. 4.12) but does not consider it to be a

ought not to say this.[787] For those who have justice with them [also] have God with them,[788] and wherever God is present, there are also numbers and courage.[789] **139** Let us also look

---

reason for fear. Referring to the earlier enemies' defeats and Athens' triumphs he points out that the greater army nevertheless lost because of lack of experience (ἀπειρία) and courage (ἀτολμία, 2.89.7; Leimbach 1985: 52). The Athenian commander Nicias counters the great number of enemy soldiers and their expectation to triumph because of their majority, with the quality and experience of the fighters of Athens (6.68; cf. 2.87.6; 7.61.3; Luschnat 1942: 60-61, 133). Dionysius (*Ant. rom.* 6.8.1) contrasts multitude and valor in one of his elaborate commander speeches: "... all wars are won, not by the forces which are larger in numbers (οἱ πλείους τοῖς ἀριθμοῖς), but by those which are superior in valour (οἱ κρείττους ἀρετῇ)" (trans. Cary). Biblical and early Jewish passages sometimes emphasize that because the Israelites or Jews had courage and the support of God they were victorious despite the huge number of enemy soldiers (Judg 7; 1 Sam 14:6; Jdt 9:11; 1 Macc 3:18; Josephus, *Ant.* 1.178, 313; 4.296-297; 8.280, 293; 12.290-291, 307, 409; see also the last note to this paragraph).

Herod's argument about the number of the enemy troops is absent in the parallel speech of *War* (1.373-379).

[787] This formula introduces Herod's refutation of a hypothetical counterargument (uttered by an anonymous person; see the first note to this paragraph).

[788] Herod's first reaction to the reasoning of his hypothetical opponent follows from his argumentation that the war against the Nabateans is just, which implies that God will support the Jews (*Ant.* 15.130, 136, 144-146). Landau (2006: 138-39) notes that God will turn his back on Herod when he acts in unjust ways, as books 16-17 of *Antiquities* describe.

[789] Herod's second refutation builds on his argument about courage (ἀνδρεία) and numbers in the preceding sentences, and links up with biblical and other passages that suggest that the help of God is decisive for the outcome of a battle (see also the note to "more numerous" above). The Hebrew Bible, as well as additional passages in the LXX, frequently refers to divine support during battles and even presents wars as being authorized by God (e.g., 1 Sam 17:47; 18:17). Deuteronomy 20 renders God's laws concerning warfare. In the sections of *Antiquities* that offer paraphrases of the Bible Josephus frequently builds on the biblical notion of holy war and also incorporates the just war vocabulary in several passages in which it is absent in the Hebrew Bible and the LXX (Mantovani 1990: 86).

In Herod's speech God's help is closely related to the just war theme (*Ant.* 15.137-138, 144-146). This argument builds on motifs in older Greek commander speeches, which clearly indicate that divine support is guaranteed if a war is just. Divine support is an important presupposition in Graeco-Roman descriptions of just war because only soldiers who are fighting for a just cause are entitled to get divine support (Livy 21.10.9; Mantovani 1990: ix, 4-6). The Beotian commander Pagondas points out a central notion of just war in his speech found in Thucydides 4.92. He elaborates the outrageous acts of the Beotians' neighbors, the Athenians, who were destroying their country and occupying their sanctuary (4.92.1-2, 7). The support of the deity of the occupied sanctuary was certain in the Beotian war of defense against the Athenians: "Trusting that the god whose sanctuary they have impiously fortified and now occupy will be on our side, and relying on the sacrifices, which appear to be propitious to us, who have offered them, ..." (4.92.7, trans. Smith). Polybius' report of Hannibal's speech before the decisive battle at Cannae (in 216 BCE) starts in plain language with a double thanksgiving (3.111.1-10): one to the gods who granted the earlier victories over the Romans, and one to himself because he compelled the Romans to fight at Cannae. His past performance rhetoric is combined with the prospect of the unheard victory, mastering Italy, but the triumph over the Romans is ultimately dependent on the will of the gods, as the last words of the speech indicate: "Therefore no more words are wanted, but deeds; for if it be the will of the gods (θεῶν βουλομένων) I am confident that I [i.e., Hannibal] shall fulfill my promises forthwith" (3.111.10, trans. Paton). God's support during military conflicts is also essential according to other speeches in Josephus (the speech of Agrippa II in *War* 2.346-401, esp. 2.388-391; of Titus in 3.472-484, esp. 3.484; Ananus' speech against the Zealots in 4.163-192, esp. 4.190-191; Josephus' own speech in 5.362-419, esp. 5.367-369, 376-378, 401-414; Eleazar ben Yair's speech in 7.323-336, 341-388, esp. 7.318-319, 327-332, 358-359; Lindner 1972: 28; Villalba i Varneda 1986: 93-101, 105). Apart from hints that God "has cast bait to the Arabs so as to deliver them to our vengeance and have them punished" (1.373, trans. Sievers/Forte in BJP 1a), and that the Nabateans soon will be punished (1.378), the parallel speech of *War* does not discuss God's interference, but it does focus upon the courage of Herod's soldiers with the phrase ἄνανδρος ("unmanly," 1.373).

at our own situation.⁷⁹⁰ We won the first battle.⁷⁹¹ When we came to blows in the second,⁷⁹² they did not even hold out against us but fled immediately, unable to withstand⁷⁹³ our attack and our high spirit.⁷⁹⁴ But even though we were victorious, Athenio attacked us⁷⁹⁵ and started a war without declaring it.⁷⁹⁶ **140** Was this [a proof of] their bravery⁷⁹⁷ or a second [example] of [their] lawlessness and treachery?⁷⁹⁸ So why are we discouraged⁷⁹⁹ about matters for which we should have the highest hopes?⁸⁰⁰ And how is it that we are terrified⁸⁰¹ by such [men] who, whenever they fight honestly, are always defeated⁸⁰² and, whenever they are believed to win, succeed by means of depravity?⁸⁰³ **141** However, should someone consider them heroic,⁸⁰⁴ how could one not be driven even more by this very [thought]?⁸⁰⁵

---

⁷⁹⁰ The formula ἵνα δὲ καὶ τὰ καθ' ἑαυτοὺς ἐξετάσωμεν introduces Herod's main point in this section: the circumstances of his own soldiers compared to those of the opponents (see also *War* 1.373-374 and *Ant.* 15.138 with the note to "someone will perhaps say").

The situation before the battle is an important factor in Thucydides' commander speeches, which are set in the history of the wars between Athens and Sparta (Luschnat 1942; Leimbach 1985; for the commanders' analysis of the battle's circumstances in Thucydides, see 15.128 with the note to "instruct you").

⁷⁹¹ Herod first briefly looks back at the earlier battles against the Nabateans, which are reported in *Ant.* 15.111-119. Past performances by one's own army as well as by the enemy's soldiers are a major reason for encouragement in commander speeches (e.g., Thucydides 2.89.2, 5, 9; 3.111.1-10; 4.95.3).

⁷⁹² The second battle against the Nabateans is reported in *Ant.* 15.112-119. The verb συμβάλλω ("come to blows," Rengstorf *s.v.*) also occurs in Josephus' report of the third battle against the Nabateans in *War* (1.380).

⁷⁹³ This statement links up with *Ant.* 15.115, in which passage the verb φεύγω ("flee") is used as well (see also 15.151). The verb ἀντέχω ("withstand") also occurs in the report of the third battle in *War* (1.383).

⁷⁹⁴ About φρονήματα ("spirit"), see *Ant.* 15.126 with the note to "lift their sunken spirits."

⁷⁹⁵ The accusation connects with the description of Athenio's interference in *Ant.* 15.115-117, and the indicative aorist ἐπέθετο ("attacked") repeats the present infinitive ἐπιτίθεσθαι of 15.116. Herod's formulation highlights the unfairness of Athenio's act, which is elaborated in the next phrase.

⁷⁹⁶ The accusation is already hinted at in *Ant.* 15.117 and implied by Herod's repeated arguments about just war. Starting a war without declaring it through envoys violates the conventions of just war (see 15.135 with the note to "justified"). The phrase ἀκήρυκτος πόλεμος ("undeclared war") is common in ancient Greek literature (e.g., Herodotus 5.81; Josephus, *War* 1.269; 2.30; *Apion* 1.318; cf. with a metaphorical meaning, Philo, *Fug.* 114, also *Mut.* 60; Plutarch, *Mor.* [*Mulier. virt.*] 253f; [*Suav. viv.*] 1095f; Cassius Dio 46.35.5).

⁷⁹⁷ See *Ant.* 15.127 with the note to "courage" and 15.138 with the note to "courageous."

⁷⁹⁸ This is the first of a series of rhetorical questions in this paragraph (cf. *Ant.* 15.137). Herod highlights Athenio's lawless behavior here, which associates him with the character of his mistress Cleopatra (see 15.89 with the note to "her greedy character"). The second example of lawlessness refers to the unexpected and undeclared attack by Athenio (see the preceding note), who is apparently directly associated with the Nabateans here. The first example must be the Nabatean violation of the deal about the lease of their land (15.107-108). The noun ἐνέδρα ("treachery, ambush") also occurs in the parallel speech of *War* (1.375) in a reference to Athenio.

⁷⁹⁹ The phrase ἔλαττον φρονέω ("be poor-spirited/discouraged, humble oneself," Rengstorf *s.v.* φρονέω) is also found in Isocrates, *Panath.* 47, 167; Demosthenes, *Or.* 13.34; Aelius Aristides, *Achill.* (ed. Dindorf 2.606).

⁸⁰⁰ See *Ant.* 15.129 with the note to "the greatest prospects for winning."

⁸⁰¹ The verb καταπλήσσομαι ("be terrified") also occurs in the introduction of Herod's speech in *War* (1.372; see also *Ant.* 15.142).

⁸⁰² Herod makes the same observation twice in 2 analogously formulated statements (ὅταν μὲν ... ὅταν δε "whenever ... whenever"), first focusing upon fair warfare by the Nabateans and its consequences, and next highlighting their treacherous fighting and its results, albeit in a chiastic order. The outcome of the 2 previous battles supports Herod's point (cf. *Ant.* 15.111-119).

⁸⁰³ This is the third passage in Herod's speech that suggests that the Nabateans had violated the laws of war (see also *Ant.* 15.130, 136). About ἀδικία ("injustice, depravity") in connection with the Nabateans, see 15.135 with the note to "hate insolence and wrongdoing."

⁸⁰⁴ The rhetorical question is ironic at the same time because Herod argues elsewhere that the Nabateans had acted treacherously with Athenio's sudden attack (see *Ant.* 15.140 with the note to "lawlessness and treachery"; about irony in Josephus, see Mason 2005). The introduction of the subordinate clause by the counterfactual conditional εἰ καί ("even if ...") implies that it concerns

For bravery[806] has nothing to do with attacking those who are weaker, but with being able to defeat[807] even those who are stronger. **142** If[808] our own[809] sufferings[810] and the events of the earthquake[811] should terrify anyone,[812] let him first of all keep in mind[813] that the very same is also deceiving the Arabs,[814] who think that what has happened [to us] is more

---

a concessive conditional clause: conceding the possibility that the Nabateans had been fighting heroically, which they have not ... (Wakker 1994: 329-32).

Glory is a dominant theme in speeches and reports concerning warfare (e.g., the funeral orations for Athens' soldiers fallen in war; Loraux 1981). The motif is also prominent in commander speeches. In Polybius' report of Publius Scipio's speech of encouragement before his soldiers before the battle against Hannibal at the Ticinus (in 218 BCE), Scipio highlights the glorious reputation of the Roman fatherland and the deeds of their ancestors (3.64.2). A speech by his son Publius Cornelius Scipio Africanus before the battle against Hannibal at Zama in 202 BCE offers a cluster of commonplaces (15.10.1-7; 15.11.6-13), including heroic fighting. Scipio reminds his soldiers of earlier victories, encourages them to fight in a manner worthy of the glorious tradition of their country, but also warns for the disgrace of flight or falling into the hands of the enemy (15.10.1-4). He suggests that the soldiers' choice was dead simple, "triumph or die" (νικᾶν ἢ θνήσκειν, 15.10.5; cf. 3.63.4).

[805] Herod's point is very clear, as explained in the continuation of this paragraph. His soldiers had to fight bravely in any case: if the Nabateans would be fighting heroically, this should be taken as an encouragement to fight even more bravely, in line with established values of the battlefield (see the preceding note). In *War* 1.373 Herod also hints at courage and glory as the attitudes expected of his soldiers.

[806] Courage is a central motif in commander speeches. It is sometimes associated with skill and experience. Nicias, e.g., concludes a commander speech with a beautiful statement: "For her sake, if anyone surpasses another in skill or in courage (εὐψυχίᾳ), he will never find a better occasion for displaying them, at once for his own advantage and for the salvation of us all" (Thucydides 7.64.2, trans. Smith). In 2.87.3-5 a commander argues that in a battle courage is much more important than experience and skill (Luschnat 1942: 24-25, 27, 75, 114-15, 132-34).

[807] The verb κρατέω ("have power, prevail, be victorious") occurs several times in the parallel speech of *War*: "One could learn this from personal experience: in the first battle, being conquerors, the enemy conquered us (κρατούντων ἐκράτησαν), and now in all likelihood they are going to be defeated, even though they thought they would be victorious (κρατήσειν)" (1.374, trans. Sievers/Forte in BJP 1a; see also 1.377).

[808] The conditional εἰ δέ with a verb in the present indicative introduces a neutral condition, which does not indicate whether the state of affairs will be realized or not. Herod's point bears on the actual situation of Herod's men, which matches this type of conditional phrases (Wakker 1994: 125-30; see also the next notes).

[809] The adjective οἰκεῖος ("[our] own") also occurs in *War* 1.373, 374, but not in close parallels to the speech in *Antiquities* (cf. 15.128, 131, 143).

[810] The phrase hints at the crushing defeat against the Nabateans because of Athenio's intervention (*Ant.* 15.116-118) and perhaps also at the earthquake (15.121-122; note the repetition of the noun πάθος ["suffering, disaster"] in 15.122, 142; cf. πάθη τινά in 15.144).

[811] See the report about the earthquake in *Ant.* 15.121-122. Herod also discusses the earthquake in the parallel speech of *War* (1.373, 377).

[812] The verbal form καταπλήττεται ("[should] terrify"), which MSS LAMW attest (likewise the marginal reading καταπλήττει in MS A; Niese 357) links up with the form καταπλαγείημεν ("we are terrified") in *Ant.* 15.140 (see the note to "we are terrified"). Niese (357) proposes reading κατέπληξε ["has terrified"]). The difference in meaning of the readings is small.

[813] Xenophon (*Mem.* 4.8.1; *Vect.* 5.5.4) offers similar vocabulary. In Thucydides some of the commander speeches also recall a defeat. In 2.87.1-7 the commanders argue that insufficient preparations, inexperience, or misadventure can lead to a defeat, but they add that having the proper courage (ἀνδρεία) can prevent another defeat. The soldiers should learn from their mistakes in the past, such that future battles will turn out well. Paulus Aemilius addresses his soldiers' recent mishaps (τῶν νεωστὶ γεγονότων συμπτωμάτων) in a speech before the battle against Hannibal at Cannae (3.108.3-3.109.13). His discussion of the causes for the misfortune of his soldiers (ignorance, haste, and bad visibility, 3.108.3-9) is the upbeat for his argument that the circumstances for the next battle are exactly the opposite of the soldiers' former situation, such that a victory is self-evident (3.108.10-3.109.5; see also *War* 1.377-378).

[814] The point takes up part of Herod's introduction in the parallel speech of *War* (1.373), in which Herod suggests that God has sent the earthquake as bait to the Nabateans so as to deliver them to the vengeance of the Jews.

serious than it really is,[815] and secondly, that it is not appropriate that the same cause should lead them to audacity and us to cowardice.[816] **143** For these men get their bravery[817] not from any personal competence but from their hope that we are already hard-pressed by our misfortunes.[818] And by going after them we will deprive them of their arrogance[819] and ourselves take up the fight against soldiers who no longer have courage.[820] **144** For we have not been so severely afflicted,[821] nor is what has happened an indication of God's wrath,[822] as some believe. But these events are rather mishaps and misfortunes.[823] And if they are brought about in accordance with God's will,[824] it is clear that[825] they have also

---

[815] In this way Herod uses the misfortunes as a springboard for his argument that the prospects for the upcoming battle are great. He turns a disadvantage into an advantage with his argumentation (see also *Ant.* 15.143-144), which is a rhetorical strategy that earlier commanders also apply in their speeches. Brasidas deals with the issue of the larger number of enemy forces in a way characteristic for ancient Spartans. He constructs an analogy between the situation of the battle at hand and the Spartan oligarchic rule. The great number of enemy soldiers should not be frightening because the Spartans know out of their own experience that it is not the multitude that is ruling over the few but the minority over the majority, and that the minority's power is based on nothing else other than military success (Thucydides 4.126.2). Brasidas applies in this way the rhetorical strategy of turning real advantages of the enemy into merely seeming advantages (Luschnat 1942: 59; Leimbach 1985: 79-80). The paragraph also connects with *Ant.* 15.123, about the exaggeration of the impact of the earthquake (cf. the repetition of ἀλήθεια in 15.123, 142).

[816] The second point of Herod's argument that counters the feelings about the misfortune of the Jews is entirely logical though artificial as well because the response to mishaps is foremost emotional, as Josephus' description of the defeat and the aftermath of the earthquake (*Ant.* 15.117-118, 123) also indicates.

[817] The phrase τὸ εὔψυχον ("[their] bravery") already occurs in *Ant.* 15.141 with respect to the Nabateans.

[818] Herod's phrase links up with the conditional subordinate clause in *Ant.* 15.142, with which he started this point of his argument. The verb κάμνω ("exert oneself, be exhausted/hard-pressed") also occurs in the report about the defeat of the Jews during the second battle against the Nabateans (15.117). For similar vocabulary, cf. Thucydides 2.51.5.

[819] The phrase μεῖζον φρονέω also occurs in *Ant.* 15.123 (see the note to "they got carried away"), in which passage Josephus describes the Nabatean state of mind after their victory over the Jews. Herod's statement here may hint at that paragraph.

[820] This statement, which turns around the Nabateans' state of mind after their victory (cf. *Ant.* 15.123-124, 142), seems wishful thinking from Herod's side at this stage, although it may also form the transition to Herod's next argument, God's support (15.144-146), and by way of anticipation hint already at the Nabateans losing their courage because of the divine support for the Jews.

[821] Herod's statement is a further example of turning a disadvantage into an advantage (see *Ant.* 15.142 with the note to "who think that things are more serious than they really are"). The verb κακόω ("harm") also occurs in 15.115, 120, 158.

[822] The assumption that a military defeat is caused by divine anger matches Graeco-Roman as well as Jewish religious beliefs (e.g., 1 Sam 15:1-9 together with 1 Sam 28:18, and Josephus, *Ant.* 5.256). Josephus' argument about God's support (15.144-146; see also 15.138 with the note to "have God with them") can be summarized in 3 points: (1) if the mishaps to the Jews happened in accordance with God's will, God's attitude to the Jews has changed by now because the Jews have been punished enough (15.144); (2) God will support the Jews this time because God knows it concerns a just war (15.145; cf. 15.146); and (3) a clear sign of God's changed attitude is the fact that all soldiers have been spared during the earthquake (15.145).

[823] In the parallel speech of *War* (1.377) Herod argues that disturbances of the elements are a natural phenomenon. The noun σύμπτωμα ("mishap, misfortune") further occurs in Josephus only in *War* 4.287; *Ant.* 3.267. The combination of σύμπτωμα and πάθος ("suffering, misfortune") is also found in Aristotle, *Top.* 126b; Plutarch, *Mor.* [*Pyth. orac.*] 399a; [*Quaest. conv.*] 719c.

[824] The conditional phrase of Herod, introduced by εἰ and followed by an indicative perfect (Wakker 1994: 125 n. 4), suggests that the events have indeed taken place with God's consent, which is a *leitmotiv* in *War* as well as *Antiquities* (Lindner 1972: 93, 142-50). The expression ἡ τοῦ θεοῦ γνώμη ("the will of God") and related phrases occur frequently in Josephus (*War* 7.327, 358; *Ant.* 1.14, 112, 255; 2.209, 223, 283, 309; 3.16-17, 315; 4.110; 5.107; 8.4). For similar vocabulary, see Justin, *Dial.* 95.2; Pseudo-Ignatius, *Ep.* 8.4.1; George Hamartolus, *Chron.* 1.16 (ed. de Boor 29).

[825] The phrase δῆλον ὡς ("it is clear that …") anticipates the words δεδήλωκεν αὐτός ("he [i.e., God] himself has made it clear that …," *Ant.* 15.145).

ceased according to his will[826] because [God] is satisfied by the events.[827] For if he had wanted to do even more harm,[828] he would not have changed his mind.[829] **145** He wishes this war to be carried out effectively[830] and he also knows that it is just.[831] For although some have been killed in the earthquake throughout the country,[832] nobody under arms has suffered any harm.[833] Rather, all of you have been spared.[834] God has made it clear[835] that, even if[836] you—together with the entire population[837] and your children and wives—waged war, the net result would be that you would not have suffered any irreparable harm.[838]

---

[826] The parallelism in the formulation (κατὰ θεοῦ γνώμην ... κατὰ τὴν ἐκείνου γνώμην) puts emphasis on Herod's argument.

[827] The logic of the argument remains implicit, but from the perspective of Jewish religious beliefs—which reckon with God's intervention in history—the reasoning would be that, if the mishaps were caused by God, they must have been his punishment for disobedience to him from the side of the Jews. Such disobedience is absent in the immediate context of Herod's commander speech in *Antiquities* and, although *War* (1.369) states that the disobedience of Herod's lieutenants had forced a rash battle upon him, the parallel passage of *War* is also silent about unfaithfulness to God. This shows that Herod's argument is purely artificial here. Nevertheless, if the mishaps were caused by God as punishment, the obvious conclusion would be that this punishment would be temporary, as indicated in, e.g., 2 Macc 6:12-16; 7:18, 32-33 (van Henten 1997: 136-40).

A speech by the Athenian commander Hippias (Thucydides 7.77) offers an interesting parallel to Herod's argument in *Ant.* 15.140-144. Looking back at the Athenians' unfortunate defeat against the Syracusans, Hippias notes that it would not be right to give up hope because of the recent mishaps and present sufferings: "... you should still have hope—in the past men have been saved from even worse straits than these—and not blame yourselves too much either for your reverses or for your present unmerited miseries" (7.77.1, trans. Smith). He continues by constructing an analogy between his own life and conduct towards gods and humans and those of his soldiers, concluding that there is no reason for giving up hope (ἐλπίς) despite the terrifying mishaps (7.77.2-3). He also argues that the enemy was successful because fortune was on his side, but that this will change because the Athenians have been punished enough (7.77.3; Luschnat 1942: 104).

[828] The Greek is ambiguous because of the verb ἀδικέω ("harm, sin"), which Herod uses in previous statements in connection with the Nabateans (see *Ant.* 15.133-135). The verb probably has a different nuance here, like "visit upon" (Rengstorf *s.v.*); otherwise Herod would hint at God's injustice.

[829] The verb μεταβάλλω can mean, i.a., "change one's mind/purpose" or "change sides" (LSJ *s.v.* B III.2).

The latter meaning would be possible here as well. *Ant.* 15.145 offers the explanation for Herod's statement.

[830] In *Antiquities* Josephus refers several times to God's intervention by stating that God was willing something (1.114; 2.333, 348; 5.200, 226; 7.373; 18.119 [concerning the destruction of Herod Antipas' army, which in the opinion of the Jews was God's punishment for the execution of John the Baptist]). The combination of πόλεμος ("war") and the passive voice of ἐνεργέω ("be actively carried out," LSJ *s.v.* II) also occurs in Polybius 1.13.5 (cf. 7.5.8); Heliodorus 1.30.3.

[831] Herod returns to his earlier point that the war is just (see especially *Ant.* 15.135), which implies that God will support the Jews (see also 15.130, 136, 138).

[832] In *Ant.* 15.122 Josephus describes the human casualties caused by the earthquake.

[833] The double negation in οὐδεὶς οὐδὲν ἔπαθεν ("nobody suffered any harm") is emphatic (Blass, Debrunner, and Rehkopf: 1976: 359 par. 431.2). For very similar phrases, see Xenophon, *Anab.* 1.8.20; Josephus, *Ant.* 10.92; John Chrysostom, *Hom. Matt.* (PG 58.544).

[834] Herod's repetition of his previous statement in positive terms again adds emphasis and leads to a climax: the point he is making in the next phrase. The fact that none of the soldiers was killed during the earthquake is proof for Herod that God will support the Jewish soldiers in the final battle against the Nabateans.

[835] The phrase φανερὸν ποίεω ("make clear") occurs about 20 times in Josephus but nowhere else with God as subject.

[836] The conditional subordinate clause introduced by κἂν εἰ ("even if"), followed by an indicative verb, indicates a possible state of affairs (Kühner and Gerth 1898-1904: 2.2.488), which is, however, extremely unlikely. Herod maximizes his point by adding this possibility, which also aims at an emotional effect on his soldiers because of the reference to their wives and children (similarly Eleazar ben Yair in his second Masada speech, *War* 7.386-387; Runnalls 1971: 255).

[837] The word πανδημεί ("with the entire population, universally, publically," Rengstorf *s.v.*) is very common in Thucydides (e.g., 1.73.4; 1.90.3). It also occurs in *Ant.* 6.377; 11.75; *Life* 290.

[838] The phrase μηδὲν ἀνήκεστον παθεῖν ("not suffer any irreparable harm"; cf. *War* 3.480; *Ant.* 15.197) is

146 Taking these things to heart[839] and also, what is more important, that you have God as [your] protector[840] at every moment, go forth with justified bravery[841] against those who are unjust to friendship,[842] untrustworthy in battle,[843] sacrilegious to envoys,[844] and always inferior to your excellence."[845]

Defeat of the Arabs.
War 1.380-385

(5.4) 147 When they heard these words, the Jews became much more courageous with regard to the battle.[846] After Herod had performed the sacrifices according to the customs,[847]

---

common in ancient Greek literature (e.g., Thucydides 3.39.8; Polybius 4.18.11; 15.1.8; Diodorus 17.15.2; Dionysius, *Dem.* 12; Philo, *Conf.* 13; *Legat.* 109; *Spec.* 3.166; 4.173).

[839] The conclusion of Herod's speech is extremely brief and offers hardly more than a *staccato* summary of the major points. It starts with the last point of the second section, God's help, in a chiastic arrangement. It emphasizes again the enemy's treachery and notes at the end that the Nabateans always have been inferior to Herod's soldiers during previous battles. According to Aristotle (*Rhet.* 3.19.1 1419b) a conclusion of a deliberative speech has 4 functions: (1) disposing the hearer favorably toward the speaker und unfavorably toward the opponent, (2) amplifying and depreciating, (3) exciting the hearer's emotions, and (4) recapitulation (Runnalls 1997: 748-49). Apart from the amplification Aristotle's 4 functions are covered by Herod's conclusion of his speech. Villalba i Varneda (1986: 108) argues that the conclusion of the speech exists of *Ant.* 15.144-146 instead of 15.146.

For phrases similar to ταῦτα ἐνθυμηθέντες ("taking these things to heart"), see Xenophon, *Anab.* 2.5.15; 3.1.24; *Cyr.* 4.1.5; Demosthenes, *Or.* 47.33; 48.9; Dionysius, *Ant. rom.* 9.58.2; *Dem.* 52; Matt 1:20.

[840] This passage summarizes Herod's argument about God's support (*Ant.* 15.144-146), but Herod subtly adds "at every moment." God's support during impending battles is also anticipated in other pre-battle speeches: Abiah's speech in *Ant.* 8.279-280 and Judas Maccabaeus' in 12.307; cf. Eleazar ben Yair's first speech before the collective suicide at Massada (*War* 7.323-336). For other phrases about God with προΐσταμαι ("protect, act as leader," Rengstorf *s.v.*) in Josephus, see *Ant.* 4.6; 6.187 (in David's speech against Goliath, paraphrasing 1 Sam 17:45-47); 18.288; cf. also John Chrysostom, *Exp. Ps.* (PG 55.179).

[841] This connects with Herod's remarks about bravery (ἀνδραγαθία) in *Ant.* 15.127, 140 (see also 15.138, 141, 143).

[842] The phrase ἀδίκους ... φιλίαν recalls Herod's arguments about just war and friendship, and echoes the vocabulary connected with these motifs (see *Ant.* 15.133-135 with notes).

[843] Here Herod uses vocabulary that has not been applied earlier in his speech, which shows, together with other phrases, that his conclusion not only summarizes his argument but also rephrases it at the same time through variations of the vocabulary. The adjective ἄσπονδος ("implacable, untrustworthy," Rengstorf *s.v.*) also occurs in *Ant.* 4.264; 15.220 and echoes a phrase in the parallel speech of *War* (1.378) that presents the Jews as avengers of the treachery (τιμωροὶ τῶν παρεσπονδημένων) of the Nabateans, which refers to their murder of the Jewish envoys.

[844] This refers to Herod's argument about the murder of his envoys by the Nabateans (*Ant.* 15.136-137). The Greek ἀνοσίους ("unholy, sacrilegious") echoes ὅσιον ("holy," *Ant.* 15.138).

[845] With this final phrase about the superiority of his soldiers Herod returns to the theme of the analysis of the circumstances, which is common in commander speeches and should enhance the soldiers' motivation to fight (see *Ant.* 15.129 with the note to "we have the greatest prospects for winning"). The combination of ἡττάομαι ("being inferior") and ἀρετή ("virtue, excellence") in the genitive also occurs in Plutarch, *Cam.* 10.7; *Dion* 47.1; *Publ.* 17.4; *Mor.* (*Laud.*) 542f; Aelius Aristides, *Plat.* 177 (ed. Dindorf 2.237).

[846] This sentence forms the transition between Herod's commander speech and the report about Herod's third battle against the Nabateans (*Ant.* 15.147-160). It implies that Herod's speech was very successful in raising the spirits of the soldiers. The report about the battle (15.147-160) is matched by *War* 1.380-385, which passage is briefer and offers a more dramatic description of the events and the emotions of the persons involved. The narrative of 15.147-160 mostly elaborates the increasing distress of the Nabateans, culminating in a definitive defeat (15.159).

Josephus does not give a date for the third battle. The preparation of another army against the Nabateans must have taken up considerable time, but the continuation of the narrative in 15.161 (cf. 15.109) implies that this battle also took place before Actium (about Kasher's argument that the chronology of Josephus' report about Herod's conflict with the Nabateans is implausible, see 15.108 with the note to "an occasion for a delay"). For the phrase τὰς ψυχὰς ἀμείνους ἐγένοντο (literally "began to be in better spirits"), cf. Plutarch, *Arist.* 16.4; Lucian, *Anach.* 23.

[847] This note is surprising because there is hardly

he quickly took them with him[848] and led them against the Arabs, after they had crossed the River Jordan.[849] **148** He encamped near the enemy,[850] but it seemed wise to him to seize the fortress[851] that was lying in between [both camps].[852] For in this way he would have the advantage: he would be able to join the battle faster[853] and, if he needed to delay the battle, he would have provided himself with a fortified camp.[854] **149** But because the Arabs

---

evidence from the Second Temple period that there was a convention of sacrificing to God outside the Temple before entering a battle. Sacrifices outside of the Temple complex were even strictly forbidden (Michel-Bauernfeind 1.416 n. 171). It was conventional to pray (e.g., 2 Chr 20:5-22; 1 Macc 3:44, 46; 2 Macc 8:2-4) and sometimes also to fast (2 Chr 20:5-22; 1 Macc 3:47) before a battle. A priestly blessing could also be part of the preparation for a battle (Deut 20:2-4; frequently in Qumran passages: 1QM 8.6; 16.4-5; 17.10; 18.6; 19.12; 4Q285). However, biblical passages that refer to the period before the building of the First Temple do suggest that a burnt-offering was offered before battle (Judg 20:26; 1 Sam 7:8, 10; 13:9-12; cf. Jephtha's vow in Judg 11:30-31, which may echo this practice). Marcus-Wikgren (71 n. *a*) suggest that Herod asked the priests to enact a sacrifice in the Jerusalem Temple, which is possible though not very plausible in the context, which implies that the army and Herod were in the field (*Ant.* 15.122, 124-126, but see the note to "after they had crossed the River Jordan" below). Moreover, *War* 1.380 clearly states that Herod himself performed the sacrifice. Josephus' note about the sacrifice would have been quite obvious for Greek and Roman readers, for whom a sacrifice before battle was a well-known practice, either to placate the gods, or to find out whether there was divine approval for the battle (e.g., Livy 8.9.1; Jameson 1991; Parker 2000; cf. Michel-Bauernfeind 1.416 n. 171, who suggest that Josephus adopted his report here for non-Jewish readers).

[848] Herod took the Jewish soldiers (i.e., "the Jews" of the previous sentence) with him. The verb ἀναλαμβάνω also occurs in *Ant.* 15.126, 132, 143. Here it means "take (troops) with one" (LSJ *s.v.* 1; cf. Polybius 10.9.6).

[849] This note implies an ellipsis in Josephus' narrative (similarly in the parallel narrative of *War* [1.380]). The geographic information suggests that the upcoming battle took place within or near the territory of the Nabateans (*Ant.* 15.122-126), i.e., east of the River Jordan (as is also implied by *War* 1.380). The note presupposes that Herod had previously returned to Judea, where he may have prepared his army for the third battle against the Nabateans. Yet such information is not provided by Josephus.

Antiquities does not mention the location of this final battle. *War* 1.380 indicates that it took place near Philadelphia, a city of the Decapolis since 63 BCE (currently mod. Amman). The distance between Canata, the location of the second battle (*Ant.* 15.112), and Philadelphia is about 100 km. Philadelphia had a considerable number of Nabatean inhabitants (Hackl, Jenni, and Schneider 2003: 133, 200). The distance between Canata and Philadelphia was perhaps the reason for Josephus to leave out the reference to this place in *Antiquities*. The phrase κατὰ τὰ νομιζόμενα ποιήσας ("performed ... according to the customs") is paralleled by Cassius Dio 53.1.1 (cf. *Ant.* 14.260).

[850] This corresponds with *War* 1.380, which passage also has the verb στρατοπεδεύω ("encamp").

[851] The phrase φρούριον καταλαμβάνω ("seize a fortress") already occurs in Thucydides 4.113 (see also Diodorus 15.40.5; Josephus, *War* 2.484; 7.192). The verb καταλαμβάνω also occurs in the parallel passage of *War* (1.380).

[852] If the reference to Philadelphia in *War* 1.380 is correct, the fortress mentioned in *Antiquities* may have been located west of Philadelphia. Kasher (1988: 148 n. 41) and Hackl, Jenni, and Schneider (2003: 505) suggest that it may have been one of the fortresses of the Heshbon area, which lies ca. 20 km southwest of Philadelphia. The city of Heshbon was located on top of a mountain range overlooking the southern part of the Jordan Valley (Netzer 2006: 227). This would fit in with Josephus' additional information in *War* 1.381 that the fortified place was located on a hill. Josephus later includes Heshbon among Herod's fortresses and fortified cities (*Ant.* 15.294). *War* also mentions the fortress and adds that Herod fired missiles from a distance in order to capture it.

[853] In *War* 1.380 Josephus formulates it slightly differently: "... in the hope of engaging them in combat quickly" (trans. Sievers/Forte in BJP 1a).

[854] Hackl, Jenni, and Schneider (2003: 505) indicate that the Greek text of the last sentence of *Ant.* 15.148 and that of the first sentence of 15.149 is corrupt, but they may be mistaken. The last sentence of 15.148 is a long-winded statement, and the transmitted Greek text (with slight differences in the MSS) is perfectly understandable (see also 15.149 with the note to "more soldiers were coming to blows from either side"). The possession of the fortress would offer a double advantage to Herod: he could prepare a quick attack in a relatively safe environment, and he would be protected in the case that the battle needed to be delayed. The adjective

planned the same thing,[855] a conflict started concerning this place. First there was only a discharge of light weapons,[856] but after a while more and more soldiers were coming to blows from either side[857] until those from the Arab side were defeated and withdrew.[858] **150** This immediately and significantly[859] raised the hopes of the Jews.[860] When [Herod] noticed[861] that their[862] troops wanted[863] anything other than to engage in battle, he attempted to tear down their palisade[864] even more boldly and to advance[865] in attack against their

---

ἐρυμνός ("fortified") echoes the related noun ἔρυμα ("fortified place") of *War* 1.380.

[855] The advantage of the fortress (see the preceding note) must have been obvious to the Nabateans as well, who apparently did not control it. Josephus does not tell who controlled the fortress at that time. Yet this does not need to be an omission by him because the fortress could also have been unoccupied.

[856] The noun ἀκροβολισμός ("discharge of light weapons") echoes the verb ἀκροβολίζομαι ("fight with light weapons," Rengstorf *s.v.*) in the parallel passage of *War* (1.380).

[857] The translation follows the text of Niese (359), which is attested by MSS PF and the Latin version. The longer reading ἀμφοτέρων ἔπιπτον of MSS LAMWE ("[they were coming to blows and more and more soldiers] fell from either side") is easier to understand and therefore probably an attempt to improve the shorter reading. Niese notes that the Greek text of the entire paragraph is difficult to make sense of. Marcus-Wikgren (73 n. *a*) state that the transmitted Greek text of the last sentence of *Ant.* 15.149 and that of the first sentence of 15.150 is probably corrupt.

[858] The defeat of the Nabateans implies that Herod got hold of the fortified place. In *War* Josephus reports more specifically that the Nabateans had sent forth some men in order to secure the place and that Herod's soldiers prevented this (1.380-381).

The transmitted Greek text (ἡττηθέντες οἱ παρὰ τῶν Ἀράβων ἀπεχώρουν, Niese 359) does make sense (see also the preceding note) and is paralleled by a passage in Xenophon's *Anabasis*: ὅτε ἐκ τῆς Ἑλλάδος ἡττηθεὶς τῇ μάχῃ ἀπεχώρει ("he [i.e., Xerxes] retreated from Greece after having lost in the battle," 1.2.9, quoted in Aelius Aristides, *Ars rhet.* 2.13.21).

[859] The phrase οὐ μικρόν (literally "not a little") is a case of *litotes*. Occurrences of a *litotes* with μικρός ("small, little") are common in Josephus, especially in the Herod narrative of *Antiquities* (11.312; 12.312; 14.71; 15.150, 169, 206, 213, 271, 356; 16.84, 130, 188; cf. *War* 1.574; 3.34; *Apion* 2.40). For the combination of μικρός and ἐλπίς ("hope"), see *Ant.* 15.232 with the note to "little hope of not receiving a similar [treatment] from Herod."

[860] Dindorf (1845: 588) concludes that something is left out after ἐγεγόνει ("led to, raised"). This may indeed be the case because there are serious text-critical problems in the next sentence (see the subsequent notes). The Greek text needs minor adaptations in order to make sense. Niese (359) proposes to reconstruct the text on the basis of the Greek parallel passage of *War* (1.381).

[861] The accusative case of the participle ἐννοούμενον ("noticing") does not match the rest of the sentence. Hudson's proposal (1720: 675, followed by Marcus-Wikgren 72) to change it to the nominative is helpful. In that case the participle phrase would concern Herod, which fits the continuation of the sentence. For a further combination of ἐννοέω ("notice") and δύναμις ("power, army") as object, see Herodian 7.9.4. MS W reads ἕτοιμον ("ready") instead of ἐννοούμενον. Niese (359) proposes to read Ἔλθεμον, i.e., the Nabatean commander Elthemus (mentioned in *War* 1.381).

[862] Most MSS read αὐτῶν ("their"), which, given the context, should refer to the Nabateans, despite the fact that the Greek implies that the Jews are referred to. MSS PF read αὐτοῦ ("his"), which would refer to Herod.

[863] The translation follows the Greek βουλομένην ("wanting," modifying δύναμιν), conjectured by Ernesti (1795: 128). The reading of the Greek MSS (βουλόμενος, Niese 359) presupposes Herod as subject, which runs against the purport of the subsequent narrative. A copyist may have missed the connection between βουλομένην and δύναμιν and changed it into βουλόμενος, assuming that the participle refers to Herod (though there are no traces of such an adaptation in the textual evidence). The parallel narrative of *War* (1.381) confirms that the Nabateans tried to avoid the combat.

[864] For vocabulary similar to τὸν χάρακα διασπᾶν, see Polybius 1.17.13; 3.102.4; Plutarch, *Ant.* 18.6. Cf. also the related phrase χαράκωμα ("camp, palisade," Rengstorf *s.v.*) in *War* 1.381 (Herod demolished the Nabatean camp).

[865] In *War* 1.381-382 Josephus describes Herod's actions as well as the attitude of the Nabatean opponents in much more dramatic terms: "Every day he [i.e., Herod] led out his troops (προάγων τὴν δύναμιν), lined them up for battle (εἰς μάχην παρετάσσετο), and provoked the Arabs [to combat]. But when no one came out—for a terrible fear overtook them and, even more than his troops, their general Elthemus was paralyzed by fright—he [i.e., Herod] came forth and demolished their camp" (trans. Sievers/Forte in BJP 1a). Elthemus (see

camp. For when [the Arabs] were forced out by these [maneuvers], they proceeded in a disorderly[866] fashion, without any enthusiasm[867] or hope of victory.[868] **151** Nevertheless, they[869] fought hand to hand[870] since they were in the majority[871] and were forced to fight[872] boldly out of necessity.[873] A fierce battle[874] started and a great number fell[875] on both sides. Finally the Arabs were routed and started to flee.[876] **152** There was such a great slaughter[877] of those who had retreated[878] that they were not only killed by the enemy, but also because they aggravated their own misfortunes:[879] they were trampled under foot[880] because of their

---

the commentary on *War* 1.381) is not mentioned in *Antiquities*. The participle προσάγων ("advancing") in this paragraph can be linked with προάγων in the parallel passage of *War* (1.381, "led out his troops"). The vocabulary of *Ant.* 15.150 also shares the nouns δύναμις ("troops"; see the note to "troops wanted" above) and μάχη ("battle") with *War* 1.381. However, δύναμις refers to Herod's army in *War* 1.381 (being the object of προάγων), but in *Ant.* 15.150 it probably refers to the Nabatean troops. This is one of the examples of Josephus applying related vocabulary in the parallel passages of the Herod narratives in *War* and *Antiquities* with different meanings, or different persons or things referred to.

[866] The adjective ἄτακτος ("without order") occurs again in *Ant.* 15.152. It is paralleled by *War* 1.382, which passage also refers to the disorder of the Nabatean troops.

[867] The word προθυμία here means "enthusiasm" or "eagerness to fight." It also occurs in the parallel narrative of *War* (1.382).

[868] For the combination of ἐλπίς ("hope, prospect"), ἔχω ("have"), and νικάω ("win"; cf. the related noun νίκη in *War* 1.382), see *Ant.* 15.129 with the note to "we have the greatest prospects for winning."

[869] I.e., the Nabateans.

[870] The phrase εἰς χεῖρας ἰέναι ("engage in hand-to-hand combat," Rengstorf *s.v.* εἶμι; see also *Ant.* 14.474) echoes εἰς χεῖρας ἔρχεσθαι in 15.149. Both phrases are common in Greek passages from the Early Imperial Age (frequently in Appian, Arrian, and Cassius Dio, also Lucian, *Anach.* 25; *Hermot.* 49; *Symp.* 35).

[871] Having a larger number of fighters (here formulated as πλείους ὄντες) was, of course, an important motivation for soldiers during combats, but it did not guarantee victory. This detail (paralleled by *War* 1.382 but in different words: πλήθει μὲν οὖν τῶν Ἰουδαίων περιῆσαν) recalls *Ant.* 15.138 in Herod's commander speech (see the note to "more numerous").

[872] The verb στρατηγέω (here in the passive voice: "be led by," Rengstorf *s.v.*) also occurs in *War* 1.379, with a different meaning: "be commander."

[873] Herod's maneuvers, narrated in *Ant.* 15.150, forced the Nabateans to confront his troops in battle. *War* 1.382 makes a similar statement with different vocabulary. About the motif of necessity during war, see *Ant.* 15.135 with the note to "necessary." The phrase ὑπὸ τῆς ἀνάγκης ("out of necessity") echoes συναναγκασθέντες ("being compelled") in *War* 1.382.

[874] The expression μάχη καρτερά ("fierce battle") is common from Thucydides onward (4.43, 96; cf. Diodorus 3.54.7; 11.7.1; 11.74.3; Plutarch, *Alc.* 31.5; *Fab.* 11.5; *Rom.* 18.6). It occurs frequently in Josephus (e.g., *War* 2.47; 3.302; 6.74; *Ant.* 7.13; 8.383; 17.258; see also *Ant.* 15.111 with the note to "a fierce battle took place").

[875] *Ant.* 15.151 shares the verb πίπτω ("fall," referring to Nabatean victims) with the parallel passage in *War* (1.383).

[876] In *War* 1.383 Josephus formulates it slightly differently: "But when they turned their backs, many were slain ..." (trans. Sievers/Forte in BJP 1a). The last lines of the paragraph include cases of alliteration, with *t* as the leading consonant sound. For vocabulary very similar to τέλος τραπέντες ... ἔφευγον ("finally they were routed and started to flee"), see Polybius 4.71.11.

[877] The translation is based on the reading τοσοῦτος φόνος attested by MSS LAMW (cf. the Latin version: *plurima mors* "great slaughter"). Niese (359) follows the shorter reading φόνος ("killing") of MSS PF. The shorter reading is perhaps more original, but it may also derive from the omission of τοσοῦτος (a case of *homoioteleuton*). The parallel text of *War* (1.383) reads οὐ πολὺς ἦν αὐτῶν φόνος ("there was not a great number of casualties"). This reading should not be taken as evidence for the shorter reading of *Antiquities* because Josephus frequently varies his vocabulary and changes its meaning in *Antiquities* in cases where the text is paralleled by *War* (see 15.150 with the note to "to advance").

[878] Niese (359) and Marcus-Wikgren (72) read ἐγκλινάντων ("bending in, fleeing," conjectured by Bekker) instead of ἐκκλινάντων ("bending out, retreating," attested by the Greek MSS). The conjecture is unnecessary since the transmitted Greek text makes sense (see *Ant.* 15.115 with the note to "retreated"). The participle ἐκκλινάντων is also attested in Dionysius, *Ant. rom.* 5.46.4 ("And now, as both their wings gave way [τῶν κεράτων ἀμφοτέρων ... ἐκκλινάντων], the Sabines were utterly routed," trans. Cary).

[879] For παραίτιος ("being partly the cause of") in Josephus, see *Ant.* 15.87 with the note to "she was involved in all of this." For phrases parallel to παραιτίους

large numbers[881] and disorderly movement, and they fell upon their own weapons.[882] At least 5,000 of them[883] perished.[884] **153** The rest of the crowd managed to take refuge within the palisade,[885] but their hope of being saved[886] was not secure because of their lack of provisions,[887] especially water.[888] **154** The Jews pursued them but were not able to enter at the same time as them.[889] Yet they settled around the palisade and kept watch closely;[890] they prevented those who would come to their aid from entering, and those who wanted to take flight from departing.[891]

(5.5) 155 So under such circumstances the Arabs sent envoys[892] to Herod, first to discuss a settlement.[893] Next they simply asked to obtain safe conduct[894] for the time being. For

---

γίνεσθαι τῶν κακῶν, see Polybius 9.34.4; 18.41.3.

[880] Josephus' vocabulary (σφίσιν αὐτοῖς ... συμπατουμένων) here is close to that of the parallel passage of *War* (1.383 ὑπὸ σφῶν αὐτῶν συμπατούμενοι "... being trampled on by their own men ...," trans. Sievers/Forte in BJP 1a).

[881] See *Ant.* 15.151 with the note to "they were in the majority." The word πλῆθος ("large numbers") also occurs in *War* 1.383-384.

[882] The content of this sentence matches the parallel passage of *War* (1.383), which is phrased in different terms. *Antiquities* is much more elaborate. Diodorus (17.12.5) describes a similar scene, in which Thebans fighting against Alexander the Great fall in a chaotic situation and are killed by their own weapons. The noun ὅπλα ("weapons") also occurs in the parallel passage of *War* (1.383), but in a different context.

[883] The phrase πεντακισχίλιοι γοῦν ("at least 5,000") is matched exactly by *War* 1.383.

[884] The formula ἐγένοντο νεκροί (literally "became dead bodies") with a number indicates the amount of casualties in a battle (e.g., Plutarch, *Marc.* 26.4; 29.9; *Nic.* 21.11). Josephus' formulation in *War* 1.383 is different: "In any case, 5,000 fell in their flight (ἔπεσον ἐν τῇ τροπῇ)" (trans. BJP 1a).

[885] This refers to the remaining Nabatean soldiers. The Greek vocabulary at the beginning of the sentence (τὸ δ' ἄλλο πλῆθος ἔφθη) is very close to that of *War* 1.383 (τὸ δὲ λοιπὸν πλῆθος ἔφθη "the rest of the crowd managed"). The second part of the sentence is also close to *War* 1.383, though ἔφθη ("managed [to]") is followed by an infinitive in *Antiquities* (συμφυγεῖν "find refuge"; cf. 15.118), and by a participle in *War* (συνωσθέν "finding shelter"). The phrase εἰς τὸ χαράκωμα ("within the palisade/camp") of *War* 1.383 is repeated in *Ant.* 15.153 (see also 15.150 with the note to "their palisade").

[886] The passage partly repeats the statement at the end of *Ant.* 15.150 (see the note to "hope of victory"). Phrases like ἔχω τὴν ἐλπίδα τῆς σωτηρίας ("having hope of being saved") are common from Thucydides onward (1.65; 4.96 [τινα εἶχον ἐλπίδα σωτηρίας]; 8.53; e.g., Demosthenes, *Or.* 15.2; 25.5; 49.46; Philo, *QG* 4.198; Plutarch, *Ant.* 7.5).

[887] This detail is absent in the parallel passage of *War* (1.383). The expression ἀπορίᾳ τῶν ἐπιτηδείων ("because of their lack of provisions") is perhaps a Thucydean phrase, taken up by later authors (Thucydides 7.80, 83; Plutarch, *Pomp.* 19.6; Arrian, *Anab.* 1.12.10; Cassius Dio 46.36.2; cf. Josephus, *War* 1.349).

[888] The information matches the parallel passage of *War* (1.383-384), but in that report Josephus describes the consequences of the lack of water in much more dramatic terms: "... thirst and the scarcity of water defeated them first .... Parched from thirst, [the Arabs] came forth in crowds and handed themselves over willingly to the Judeans" (trans. Sievers/Forte in BJP 1a). See also *Ant.* 15.155 with the note to "they were urgently in need of water."

[889] *War* 1.383 only notes that Herod surrounded and besieged the Nabateans in their camp.

[890] See the preceding note. Josephus slightly altered the meaning and also used different vocabulary in the *Antiquities* report.

[891] The second part of the sentence has a parallel structure: 2 sub clauses with participle constructions in the accusative are dependent on the *verbum finitum* εἶργον at the end of the clause; one is combined with εἰσόδου ("entrance, entering"), the other with ἐξόδου ("exit, departing"). Nevertheless, this adds no substantial information to the shorter parallel report of *War* (1.383).

[892] The report in *War* 1.384 is briefer than that in *Antiquities*. They share the verb πρεσβεύω in the middle voice ("send envoys, be an envoy," Rengstorf *s.v.*). That the Nabateans were forced to send envoys to Herod is ironical in the light of their previous murder of Herod's envoys (*Ant.* 15.124).

[893] The settlement probably concerns the ransom hinted at in *Ant.* 15.156.

[894] The noun ἄδεια can mean, i.a., "indemnity, amnesty, security, safe conduct" (Thackeray and Marcus 1930-55: 7; Rengstorf *s.v.*). Since the Nabateans were negotiating for a temporary arrangement, "safe conduct" seems to fit best; it would allow the Nabateans to leave their camp and fetch water. For other combinations of ἀξιόω ("ask for") and ἄδεια as object, see Plutarch, *Alc.* 23.1; Philo, *Flacc.* 40; cf. Dionysius, *Ant. rom.* 5.4.1.

they were urgently in need of water[895] and would agree to anything.[896] **156** But Herod did not allow envoys or a ransom for those captured,[897] or any other reasonable solution.[898] He was eager to avenge[899] the lawless acts of the Arabs committed against them [the Jews].[900] Being compelled, especially because of their thirst,[901] they came forward and surrendered themselves[902] to be led away in chains.[903] **157** In five days a multitude[904] of 4,000 was captured[905] in this way.[906] On the sixth day[907] all the others decided to come out[908] and to approach the enemy in a warlike manner.[909] If[910] they were bound to suffer some kind of disaster, they chose to attack rather than be ingloriously[911] annihilated[912] in small groups.

---

[895] As noted already (see *Ant.* 15.153 with the note to "especially water"), Josephus' vocabulary in this section of *Antiquities* is less dramatic than that in the parallel version of *War* (see 1.384). The substantive δίψος ("thirst") occurs in both passages. The phrase τὸ δίψος ἤπειγε (literally "the thirst was pressing") echoes προκατήπειγεν ἡ δίψα ("the thirst defeated them first") in *War* 1.383.

[896] For vocabulary very similar to πᾶν ὁτιοῦν ὑφιστάμενοι, see Pseudo-Lucian, *Charid.* 4; Eusebius, *Passio mart. Aeg.* (PG 20.1533); Sopater, *Quaest. div.* (ed. Walz 8.309).

[897] The parallel passage of *War* (1.384) is more specific: the Nabateans offer 500 talents as redemption money, which is a huge sum (cf. the sum of 200 talents that the Nabateans had to pay to Herod in *Ant.* 15.107). The word λύτρα ("ransom") also occurs in the parallel passage of *War* (1.384). The verb ἁλίσκομαι ("be captured/overcome") also occurs in that parallel passage, although in a different context.

[898] This phrase and the next passage are not matched by the parallel report of *War*, which briefly states that Herod treated the Nabatean envoys arrogantly and assailed them all the more after their offer of the ransom (*War* 1.384; see the preceding note).

[899] Herod's eagerness is perfectly understandable in the light of what the Nabateans had done to his envoys (see *Ant.* 15.124 with notes). His punishment of the Nabateans is very severe. Nevertheless, he does not retaliate by murdering the Nabatean envoys; that would have made him as wicked as the Nabateans according to one of his statements in his commander speech (see *Ant.* 15.136).

[900] The passage refers to the murder of Herod's envoys by the Nabateans following the second battle (*Ant.* 15.124), which killing is called a lawless act in Herod's commander speech (15.136; cf. 15.130, 140).

[901] This third reference to the Nabateans being in urgent need of water (cf. *Ant.* 15.153, 155) leads to a climax: their decision to leave the camp.

[902] The parallel report of *War* (1.384) has a similar note, including the verb ἐγχειρίζω ("surrender"), which is also used here.

[903] The phrase ἄγειν καὶ δεῖν is a *hendiadys* ("to be led away and to be enchained"). E and MS L read δή instead of δεῖν, which should be combined with the preceding καὶ as the beginning of the next sentence. The combination καὶ δή expresses emphasis: "and what is more" (LSJ *s.v.* δή III.4). Niese (360) concludes that καὶ δή may be the correct reading. However, this reading can easily have evolved out of ἄγειν καὶ δεῖν if a scribe missed the *hendiadys*, while a change the other way around is very unlikely. The verb δέω ("bind, chain") also occurs in the parallel passage of *War* (1.384), which is an additional indication that καὶ δεῖν is probably the more original reading.

[904] The word πλῆθος ("multitude") is also used in *War* 1.384, in a slightly different way.

[905] The aorist ἑάλωσαν repeats ἡλωκότων (*Ant.* 15.156). Both forms derive from the verb ἁλίσκομαι ("be captured"). *War* 1.384 has δεθῆναι ("be put in chains"; cf. the preceding note).

[906] The Greek closely follows the parallel passage of *War* (1.384), though Josephus adds a few words here.

[907] Similarly *War* 1.384.

[908] Niese (360) and Marcus-Wikgren (74) follow the reading ἐξιέναι of E. The Greek MSS read ἐξεῖναι (i.e., the aorist infinitive of ἐξίημι, "send out"), which perhaps makes sense if it is interpreted in an intransitive way ("discharge themselves," LSJ *s.v.* I.2).

[909] The phrase πολέμου νόμῳ can mean "according to the law of war" (*War* 2.90; 5.332; 6.239, 353; *Ant.* 1.315; 6.9; 12.273; 14.304, and perhaps 9.58) or "in a warlike manner, fighting" (*War* 3.363; 4.260, 388; Rengstorf *s.v.* νόμος; for similar phrases in other authors before and after Josephus, see BJP 1b 2.90).

[910] MSS PF and E read καὶ εἰ ("[even] if"), which reading is followed by Niese (360), while MSS LAMW read the slightly weaker concessive conditional εἰ καί. The difference between the 2 conditionals is not great; καὶ εἰ is sometimes used for extraordinary or extreme cases (Wakker 1994: 335-36), which fits the current passage.

[911] The preference of the remaining Nabateans to die nobly on the battlefield by the hand of enemy soldiers rather than to be taken captive and executed matches Greek and Roman values about dying honorably. Herodotus recounts, e.g., how Croesus, the extremely

158 Determined to do this[913] they came out of the palisade but did not endure in the battle[914] in any way. For, afflicted in body and soul,[915] they had no strength[916] to fight vigorously.[917] So they considered it profitable to die[918] and a misfortune to live on.[919] About 7,000[920] of them fell in that terrible[921] battle. **159** Having suffered such a blow[922] their self-confidence, which had been previously so great, was lost.[923] However, since they admired Herod's

---

rich king of Lydia, interviewed the famous Athenian lawgiver Solon and asked him who was the happiest person on earth. Solon proposed the Athenian Tellus because of the prosperity of his city, his 5 sons, his wealth and, above all, his noble death during battle (1.30). World famous is a line of Horace: *dulce et decorum pro patria mori* ("It is sweet and appropriate to die for the fatherland," *Carm.* 3.2.13, my trans.); cf. 3.19.2; 4.9.51-52), which also glorifies death on the battlefield. Josephus expresses the ideal of noble death well in his speech at Yodfat: "… 'It is honourable to die in war': yes, but according to the law of war, that is to say by the hand of the conqueror" (*War* 3.363, trans. Thackeray; for a discussion of noble death in Josephus, see van Henten 2007a). The motif of noble death is absent in the parallel report of *War* (1.384); Josephus simply notes that the remaining Nabateans came forth for combat on the sixth day, out of desperation. For vocabulary similar to ἀδόξως ("ingloriously") and αἱρέω ("choose," in the middle voice) in connection with the noble death motif, see Alexander of Aphrodisias, *Comm. Top.* (ed. Wallies 225).

[912] The verb διαφθείρω ("destroy, annihilate") also occurs in the parallel report of *War* (1.383).

[913] An alternative translation is "After this decision …." The participle γνόντες ("being determined, having decided") echoes διέγνωσαν ("they decided") in *Ant.* 15.156.

[914] The substantive μάχη ("battle"; cf. *Ant.* 15.147-148, 150-151) also occurs in the parallel report of *War* (1.384; cf. 1.381-382).

[915] Phrases with σῶμα ("body") and ψυχή ("soul, life") frequently express that a person's entire being is involved in an action or experience. 2 Macc 14:37 states concerning the Jewish elder Razis that he had most zealously risked body and soul for the Jewish cause (cf. 7:37; 15:30). Such phrases are also common in Josephus (*War* 2.136, 476, 580; 3.102, 212, 362, 378; 5.368; 6.81; *Ant.* 15.190, 251), and Josephus' expression κεκακωμένοι καὶ τὰς ψυχὰς καὶ τὰ σώματα ("afflicted in body and soul") has a close parallel in Plutarch, *Per.* 34.5 (see also Josephus, *Ant.* 15.251 ψυχῇ καὶ σώματι κεκακωμένος ["afflicted in body and soul"] and cf. Philo, *Spec.* 3.23; 4.100).

[916] The phrase τόπον ἔχειν literally means "have room (for)" (see *Ant.* 15.134 with the note to "room for observing the bond of trust").

[917] The phrase λαμπρῶς ἀγωνίσασθαι ("fight vigorously"; see also *Ant.* 6.370; 12.409) is common vocabulary in descriptions of heroic fighting and noble death, especially during battle (see, e.g., Diodorus 2.45.5; 11.32.2; Plutarch, *Alex.* 32.4; *Demetr.* 29.3; Appian, *Hist. rom.* 7.30; Dionysius, *Ant. rom.* 9.67.6; 10.30.8).

[918] For the Nabateans preferring to die rather than live on in misery, see *Ant.* 15.157 with the note to "ingloriously." Josephus' remark (κέρδος δ' εἰ θνήσκοιεν) recalls Electra's statements in Sophocles: "For when mortals are involved in ruin, what does the man whose death is delayed gain by the time (θνήσκειν ὁ μέλλων τοῦ χρόνου κέρδος φέροι;)?" (*El.* 1486; trans. Lloyd-Jones), which implies that death is better to follow quickly.

[919] Rengstorf (*s.v.* συμφορά) gives "regard as a misfortune" as meaning for the phrase ἐν συμφορᾷ ποιεῖσθαι. Cf. Eleazar ben Yair's statement in his second speech at Masada—before the collective suicide of him and his fellow rebels—which closely corresponds to the vocabulary here: "… life, not death, is man's misfortune (ὅτι συμφορὰ τὸ ζῆν ἐστιν ἀνθρώποις, οὐχὶ θάνατος)" (*War* 7.343, trans. Thackeray).

[920] This number is also given in the parallel passage of *War* (1.384), but E reads 6,000.

[921] The translation follows the reading τῇ καρτερᾷ μάχῃ conjectured by Marcus-Wikgren (74). The readings τῇ προτέρᾳ μάχῃ ("the former battle") and τῇ προτεραιᾷ μάχῃ ("the day before the battle [?]," Niese 360) do not make sense in the context; the Greek text is probably corrupt. The reading proposed by Marcus-Wikgren is a good guess: the combination of μάχη ("battle") and καρτερός ("strong, fierce") is common and also occurs in *War* 1.101.

[922] Josephus also uses the noun πληγή ("blow") in the parallel passage of *War* (1.385), though in a different way: "Having punished Arabia by such a fierce blow …" (trans. Sievers/Forte in BJP 1a).

[923] The parallel passage also includes a phrase with φρόνημα, which has a slightly different meaning: "… having crushed the spirit of its people [i.e., the people of Arabia] …" (*War* 1.385, trans. Sievers/Forte in BJP 1a). While *War* is making a concluding statement, *Antiquities* may be ironic here. It refers to an earlier situation, which most probably concerns the period following Athenio's defeat of the Jews (*Ant.* 15.123-125), during which the Nabateans killed Herod's envoys and advanced to the

generalship[924] under unfortunate circumstances, they gave in to him in all respects and acclaimed him patron of their people.[925] **160** And Herod considered it appropriate to look upon his accomplishments as highly successful.[926] He returned home after having earned huge praise[927] because of this act of courage.[928]

(6.1) 161 So when everything else went well for him[929] and he had become invulnerable

Herod's rule endangered after the Battle of Actium.
War *1.386-387*

---

camp of the Jews with great eagerness (15.124). The combination of ἀφαιρεῖσθαι ("be deprived of") and φρονήματος ("spirit, self-confidence") also occurs in 16.293.

[924] Rengstorf (*s.v.*) gives "talent as a field-commander, generalship" as meanings for στρατηγιά. For phrases of θαυμάζω ("admire") with στρατηγία as object, see Plutarch, *Phil.* 10.8; Libanius, *Decl.* 12.2.38; cf. Diodorus 4.53.7; 15.91.7; 17.30.2.

[925] An alternative translation is "ruler of their nation" (suggested by Negev 1977: 544; cf. *War* 1.633). The term προστάτης can mean, i.a., "leader, ruler, protector" (Rengstorf *s.v.*; see *Ant.* 14.157, 444, and cf. 15.313 with the note to "left behind without receiving appropriate help"). *War* 1.385 shares the title προστάτης and the noun ἔθνος ("people," referring to the Nabateans) with *Ant.* 15.159.

Momigliano (1934: 325 with n. 2), Smallwood (1976: 67-68 with n. 20), and Shatzman (1991: 291) conclude that it is unclear what προστάτης exactly means here (see also Otto 1913: 47), although Momigliano mentions the possibility that Herod imposed some kind of protectorate on the Nabateans. Kasher (1988: 148 n. 42) argues that a political meaning, which would imply some sort of rule by Herod over the Nabatean people, is highly improbable. The continuation of the narrative does not indicate any change in the political situation for the Nabateans and presupposes that King Malichus was sitting firmly in the saddle (see 15.167). Kasher argues that those Nabateans who were defeated by Herod and were allowed to escape expressed their gratitude by giving him this title (cf. *OGIS* no. 415, a dedicatory inscription from Si'a, near Canatha, in which Herod is called "master"; translation and references in Richardson 1996: 206-07). However, even if it concerns only an honorary title, the narrative still raises questions. Josephus does not refer to a Nabatean leader who was involved in the decision to give him the title, nor does he write about a settlement, which must have followed upon the Nabatean defeat. Herod's motive for starting the campaign against the Nabateans was their reluctance in paying back the lease for the territories given to Cleopatra (15.107-108), which involved King Malichus, who is not mentioned at all in this section. If Herod really had won a definitive victory against the Nabateans, he would certainly have made an arrangement that the Nabateans were to pay back their debt to him, which probably would have included severe sanctions in case they failed to do so. Herod's appointment as ruler or protector of the Nabateans (*War* 1.385; *Ant.* 15.159) seems, therefore, rather implausible. It may well be an invention depicting Herod as a military genius, highlighted by a (fictitious) appointment by his enemies. Otto (1913: 47, 90) takes this possibility into account but also considers the option that the Nabateans gave Herod this title (with its meaning still being unclear). Richardson (1996: 67 n. 57) considers it unlikely that the Nabateans appointed Herod as ruler or protector because it is not confirmed elsewhere. If the acclamation by the Nabateans is fictitious indeed, it is plausible that Josephus did not invent it since he is more inclined to blacken Herod than to enhance the king's glory in *Antiquities*. The detail perhaps derives from Herod's memoranda (*Ant.* 15.174) or from Nicolaus of Damascus. Shatzman (1991: 291) argues that Octavian's victory at Actium weakened the position both of Herod and the Nabatean king Malichus because they had supported Antony. Both rulers had good reasons for coming to an agreement in his opinion. Mahieu (2012: 129-31) argues differently that Malichus died in the battle against Herod and that the Nabateans accepted Herod as their ruler.

[926] The parallel report of *War* (1.385) lacks this passage, which focalizes Herod and emphasizes his feelings of pride about his military success. The noun εὐημέρημα ("good fortune, success," Rengstorf *s.v.*) is a *hapax legomenon* in Josephus (cf. *Ant.* 15.210).

[927] The narrator confirms Herod's military success with this short statement that the king earned a great reputation because of his final victory over the Nabateans. The note concludes the section about the military conflicts with the Nabateans before Actium. The phrase μέγα ἀξίωμα ("huge praise") also occurs in Strabo 10.1.11; Plutarch, *Sert.* 10.1 (cf. John Chrysostom, *Oppugn.* [PG 47.344]).

[928] The key noun ἀνδραγαθία ("courage, bravery") is repeated several times in the narrative about the Nabatean conflicts (see *Ant.* 15.127 with the note to "bravery").

[929] The formula is a transition to the next section about the consequences of the Battle of Actium for Herod (*Ant.* 15.161-193), in which the end of Hyrcanus

to attacks in every way,⁹³⁰ danger fell upon him,⁹³¹ which caused a crisis for his entire rule;⁹³² Caesar⁹³³ had triumphed over Antony in the Battle of Actium.⁹³⁴ **162** For at that time the situation was hopeless⁹³⁵ for Herod and his entourage,⁹³⁶ enemies and friends alike:⁹³⁷ it was unlikely that he would remain unpunished⁹³⁸ on account of his close friendship with Antony.⁹³⁹ **163** Thus his friends lost their hope⁹⁴⁰ for him, while those who were hostile [to

---

II is embedded (15.164-182). The phrase καλῶς ἔχειν ("go/be/do well") occurs frequently in Josephus (e.g., 15.76; 16.117, 355; 17.153, 354; Rengstorf s.v. ἔχω).

⁹³⁰ This may be an overstatement because Herod decided to build several fortresses to enhance the security of his kingdom (*Ant.* 15.192-198). Josephus' remark creates a contrast with the next statement and enhances the drama in this way. The adjective δυσεπιχείρητος ("hard to attack," Rengstorf s.v.) occurs once elsewhere in Josephus (*War* 4.162).

⁹³¹ The word κίνδυνος ("danger") also occurs in the parallel narrative of *War* (1.387), but with a different comment: in *War* Josephus reports that Octavian's victory at Actium worried Herod and that he decided to confront the danger.

⁹³² The Greek phrase τῶν ὅλων with the political meaning "(his) entire rule" (Rengstorf s.v. ὅλος) also occurs in the parallel narrative of *War* (1.386). Niese (361) reads κρίσιν ἐξάγων ("bringing forth a crisis") with MS P, while most MSS read κρίσιν ἐπάγων ("causing a crisis"). The latter reading is perhaps preferable since the combination of κρίσις and ἐπάγω is attested in other writings (Aphthonius 4.7; Diodorus 36.15.1; Justin, *Dial.* 39.2), while the combination of κρίσις and ἐξάγω is not. For the meaning "crisis" (i.e., a decisive event or issue) of κρίσις, see LSJ s.v. III; Rengstorf s.v.

⁹³³ I.e., Octavian (see *Ant.* 15.109 with the note to "Caesar").

⁹³⁴ For the battle and its aftermath, see *Ant.* 15.109 with the note to "the Battle of Actium" (also *Ant.* 15.121, 190).

⁹³⁵ The phrase ἀπέγνωστο ... τὰ πράγματα ("the situation was hopeless") is paralleled by a few later passages: John Chrysostom, *Fragm. Jer.* (PG 64.904); *Hom. Gen.* (PG 53.301); Eutropius 9.9.

⁹³⁶ The phrase οἱ περὶ αὐτόν sometimes refers to the entourage of a ruler (*War* 1.359, 515; *Ant.* 15.5, 168, 284; 16.238, 346), of which "the friends" are the nucleus (*War* 1.515 referring to Herod; *Ant.* 15.5 referring to Antony; 15.168 referring to Hyrcanus). About Herod's friends, see *Ant.* 15.5 with the note to "the friends around him" and 15.31 with the note to "his friends."

⁹³⁷ In the next paragraph Josephus elaborates the response of Herod's friends and enemies to the new political situation. This is absent in the parallel passage of *War* (1.386-387), which focuses on Herod's own response to Antony's defeat.

The friends may refer to the inner circle of important persons who were close to the king and were consulted by him on important matters of the government (see the preceding note). The Greek suggests that the enemies were also part of Herod's entourage, which is confirmed by other passages; especially Herod's mother-in-law Alexandra schemed against him (for references, see *Ant.* 15.23 with the note to "Alexandra," also 15.166).

Josephus' remark about friends and enemies also prepares for the story about the end of Hyrcanus (15.164-182), which interrupts the narrative about the aftermath of Actium. The way this story is embedded makes Hyrcanus appear like one of Herod's enemies (see also 15.165).

⁹³⁸ The phrase ἀτιμώρητος μένειν ("remain unpunished") also occurs in *Ant.* 16.116.

⁹³⁹ About the close patron-client relationship between Antony and Herod, see *Ant.* 15.5 (with the note to "the friends around him"), 131, 183, 189, 409; 18.92. Herod's father, Antipater, was already a friend of Antony (*War* 1.281). Herod himself stated before Octavian that "he had had an extraordinary friendship with Antony (φιλίαν αὐτῷ γενέσθαι μεγίστην πρὸς Ἀντώνιον)" (*Ant.* 15.189; cf. also 15.183).

Josephus points out in *War* that Herod's close friendship with Antony was the reason for the king's worries, which led to his decision to make a journey to Rhodes to meet Octavian (1.386-387). *War* 1.386 indicates that Octavian did not consider Antony to be definitively defeated as long as Herod remained loyal to him, which suggests that Herod was Antony's tower of strength. This overstatement (Cleopatra was Antony's mainstay in this period; see Becher 1966: 32, 75-77, 108-10, 182-83), highlighting Herod's status as *intimus* of Antony, is missing in *Antiquities*. Yet in both reports Herod emphasizes that he did not abandon Antony after Actium (*War* 1.388; *Ant.* 15.190).

⁹⁴⁰ The vocabulary links up with the beginning of *Ant.* 15.162 through the repetition of φίλοις ("friends") and the noun ἀπόγνωσις ("abandonment [of hope], desperate situation," Rengstorf s.v.), which echoes the verb ἀπογινώσκω ("dismiss, abandon [hope])." For other combinations of ἀπόγνωσις and ἐλπίς ("hope"), see Philo, *Mut.* 222; *Spec.* 3.6.

him][941] outwardly appeared to be friendly with [him],[942] but secretly they greatly enjoyed their feeling that they would get a change for the better.[943] **164** Herod himself,[944] seeing that Hyrcanus was the only person left of a royal rank,[945] thought it would be better to prevent him from being a hindrance[946] any longer. If he[947] would stay alive and escape the danger,[948] he considered it to be the safest option[949] not to have a man who was more worthy[950] of obtaining the throne than himself[951] waiting and watching[952] in such difficult

---

[941] Niese (361) reads ἐχθρῶς ("hostile") with MSS PFV and E. The reading ἐχθρωδῶς ("hostilely disposed," Rengstorf s.v. ἐχθρώδης), attested by MSS LAMW, occurs once elsewhere in Josephus (*War* 1.475). The phrase ἐχθρωδῶς ἔχειν τινι ("be hostile to someone") is a fixed expression (LSJ s.v. ἐχθρώδης). The reading of MSS LAMW may therefore be preferable.

[942] The verb συνάγω in the passive voice may mean "be friends with" (cf. LSJ s.v. I.5).

[943] Josephus' phrase is a polite way of saying that Herod's reign would end. For μεταβολή with the meaning "political change," see *Ant.* 15.30 with the note to "a change of government," also 15.20 with the note to "political changes" and 15.166. For vocabulary similar to ἀμείνονος ... τῆς μεταβολῆς, see Aristotle, *Fragm.* 1.20 (ed. Rose 36); Philo, *Aet.* 33; *Praem.* 115; *QG* 2.41; *Spec.* 2.249; *Virt.* 183; Josephus, *Ant.* 16.359; Clement of Alexandria, *Strom.* 2.19.97.

[944] Josephus' focus switches back to Herod, who apparently realized that Hyrcanus was the last remaining possible competitor of Hasmonean descent. The switch is surprising because one would expect—on the basis of the information in the preceding paragraphs—that the king would do something about his weak position following Antony's defeat. This is indeed what Josephus reports in the parallel narrative of *War* (1.386-387). Nevertheless, with the reference to Herod's enemies in *Ant.* 15.162-163, Josephus prepares for a digression about Hyrcanus (15.165-178), which is without a parallel in *War*.

[945] Hyrcanus was of Hasmonean descent (see *Ant.* 15.11 with the note to "Hyrcanus the High Priest"). *Ant.* 15.18-21 reports how Herod successfully persuaded Hyrcanus to return to Judea (see also 15.12-17). In 15.18 Josephus notes that Herod promised to share his kingdom with Hyrcanus. *Ant.* 15.164-182 is connected with 15.18-21 because Josephus anticipates Herod's actions against Hyrcanus (narrated in 15.164-182) in 15.20 (see also the next note). For phrases similar to ἐπ' ἀξιώματος βασιλικοῦ ("of a royal rank"), see Plutarch, *Cor.* 22.1; *Mor.* (*Mulier. virt.*) 255a; Lucian, *Laps.* 11; Herodian 2.5.5. Marcus-Wikgren (11 n. *e*) refer to von Destinon (1882: 110), who argues that 2 sources have been combined in this passage: Nicolaus of Damascus, and an anonymous writer hostile to Herod.

[946] In the subsequent narrative Josephus offers 2 reports of the events that led to Herod's order to execute Hyrcanus (*Ant.* 15.165-173 and 15.174-176). Josephus claims in connection with the second report that Hyrcanus was innocent (15.177), which puts the blame fully on Herod.

The phrase μηκέτ' ἐμποδὼν ἐᾶν ("prevent [him] from being a hindrance," Rengstorf s.v. ἐάω) echoes ἐκποδὼν ποιεῖσθαι ("get [someone] out of the way"), used in 15.20 referring to Herod and Hyrcanus (see also 15.183 with the note to "out of the way").

[947] I.e., Herod (see also the next note). Josephus describes here—by taking Herod's perspective—what the king intended to do with Hyrcanus in the cases of Octavian's 2 plausible decisions (being allowed to continue to be a friendly king of the Romans or being punished for his loyalty to Mark Antony; cf. the construction of the Greek sentence with εἰ μὲν ... εἰ δὲ ...).

[948] Herod is implied as the subject of this passage, which refers to his dangerous new situation after Octavian's victory at Actium (see *Ant.* 15.161-163 and the next note).

[949] The passage introduces Herod's motivation for eliminating Hyrcanus as a possible competitor in case Herod would remain king.

Josephus suggests time and again that Herod consistently worked on removing all competitors (*Ant.* 14.469, 489-490; 15.1, 8 on Antigonus; 15.23-38, 42, 45-46, 53, 55 on Aristobulus III; 15.73, 87, 167-170, 247-249 on Alexandra; 15.20 on Hyrcanus). Vogel (2002: 106) argues that the threatening situation after Actium formed Herod's main motivation for eliminating Hyrcanus, who was the most important member of the Hasmonean house and had already been High Priest and ruler of Judea during several periods (see 15.11-12 and 15.176 with the notes to "fabricated them maliciously" and "own methods"). Günther (2005: 111) ascribes the motivation to the anti-Herodian report of 15.174-176.

[950] Niese (361) reads ἀξιώτερον ("more worthy") with E. The Greek MSS read ἀξιολογώτερον ("more important").

[951] I.e., Herod. The passage echoes a detail of *Ant.* 15.18-21, where Josephus writes that Herod himself was "ruling while he did not deserve it" (15.20 with the note

Alexandra persuades Hyrcanus to flee to Malchus. Death of Hyrcanus.

times for him. If he[953] should suffer something because of Caesar, he desired, out of envy,[954] to kill the only other person who might get the throne.[955]

(6.2) 165 While these thoughts were going through his mind,[956] something was presented to him by his enemies.[957] For Hyrcanus did not think then, or at any other time, to meddle in state affairs[958] or start a rebellion,[959] given his reasonable character.[960] He yielded to fortune to love everything that was happening on its account.[961] **166** But Alexandra was quarrelsome[962] and strongly hoping for a political change.[963] She had discussions with her father:[964] that he should not allow for Herod's lawless behavior[965] against their[966] family forever and also that he should make a start in bringing their hopes for the future onto

---

to this phrase). On Hyrcanus' descent, see 15.11 with the note to "Hyrcanus the High Priest".

[952] The verb ἐφορμέω ("lie in wait") occurs once elsewhere in Josephus (*War* 1.278), in which case it means "lie at anchor" (Rengstorf *s.v.*). Here it suggests that Hyrcanus was waiting for a chance to gain the throne. This was dangerous for Herod given his insecure situation after Actium, as the continuation of the narrative indicates.

[953] I.e., Herod (see the note to "If he" above).

[954] Herod's jealousy is a recurring motif in *Antiquities* (see 15.50 with the note to "his jealousy").

[955] At this stage Herod had eliminated most of the other possible competitors. Apart from Hyrcanus only Alexandra was still alive (see *Ant.* 15.167-170, especially 15.166 with the note to "strongly hoping for a political change").

[956] The phrase δι' ἐννοίας ἔχω ("think") is a fixed expression in Josephus (*Ant.* 3.307; 16.89; *Life* 227, 282).

[957] Josephus' reference concerns the group of enemies mentioned in *Ant.* 15.162-163, although in the lines just before the enemy refers only to Hyrcanus. The narrative continues with Hyrcanus as well as his daughter Alexandra as key persons next to Herod. This implies once again that Hyrcanus is presented as an enemy of Herod, despite the fact that he had not undertaken anything against Herod so far.

[958] The verb πολυπραγμονέω ("meddle in state affairs") clearly has a negative connotation here (LSJ *s.v.* 2b; see also *Ant.* 15.182).

[959] The phrase νεωτέρων ἅπτεσθαι ("start a rebellion") is connected with the verb νεωτερίζω ("rebel") and the noun νεωτερισμός ("rebellion, revolt"; see *Ant.* 15.8, 30, 42 with the note to "aim for a political change"). Philostratus (*Vit. Apoll.* 8.7) offers a close parallel.

[960] Hyrcanus' "reasonableness" or "generosity" (ἐπιείκεια, Rengstorf *s.v.*; cf. the related adjective ἐπιεικής "reasonable, kind") was proverbial (see *Ant.* 14.13; 15.177, 182). Virtues closely related to ἐπιείκεια are self-control, prudence (σωφροσύνη; cf. 7.391), and moderation-modesty (μετριότης; cf. 6.263). Josephus describes Hyrcanus' character in the flashback following the report of Hyrcanus' death (15.177-178). Josephus also characterizes Aristobulus I as a reasonable person (φύσει δ' ἐπιεικεῖ). This is confirmed by a statement of Timagenes, attested by Strabo, which highlights Aristobulus' ἐπιείκεια (*Ant.* 13.319).

The substantive τρόπος can mean "way of life, habit" in references to persons (LSJ *s.v.* III) as well as "character" (Rengstorf *s.v.*). For phrases similar to ἐπιεικείᾳ τρόπου ("his reasonable character [or habit]," see Hecataeus of Abdera (*FGH* 264 F 25; Demosthenes, *Or.* 36.59; Polybius 5.10.1; Diodorus 1.54.2; Lucian, *Alex.* 61; Aelius Aristides, *Ars rhet.* 2.3.4; *Reg.* (ed. Dindorf 1.106); Julian, *Euseb. laud.* 1.46 (ed. Bidez 74).

[961] Hyrcanus' submission to what fortune (τύχη; see *Ant.* 15.17 with the note to "fortune") had in store for him characterizes him as a passive and weak person, which matches his image elsewhere in Josephus (see 14.13; 15.15 with the note to "He was content with these things," also 15.177-178 with notes).

[962] Josephus' characterization of Alexandra here corresponds to the way she is presented elsewhere in *Antiquities* (see 15.23 with the note to "Alexandra"). Josephus suggests in 15.42, while he focalizes Herod, that Alexandra would aim for a political change (νεωτέρων πραγμάτων; see also the note to "start a rebellion" in 15.165) if she had the opportunity. The adjective φιλόνεικος ("contentious, quarrelsome") echoes 15.62. Rengstorf (*s.v.*) suggests "ambitious, fond of rule" as meanings for φιλόνεικος in 15.166, 168.

[963] For μεταβολή meaning "political change," see *Ant.* 15.30 with the note to "change of government," also 15.163 as well as 15.42, 167, 183, referring to Alexandra.

[964] I.e., Hyrcanus (see *War* 1.241; *Ant.* 15.23).

[965] Herod is associated with lawlessness (παρανομία) elsewhere in Josephus: *War* 2.84, 86; *Ant.* 15.40, 63 (a complaint formulated by Alexandra), 243; 16.4, 185; 17.168, 304 (van Henten 2011b).

[966] MS A (first corrector) and MSS VW read τὸν αὐτὸν οἶκον ("the same family") instead of τὸν αὐτῶν οἶκον ("their family," Niese 361).

safer ground again.⁹⁶⁷ **167** And she begged him to write about these matters to Malchus,⁹⁶⁸ who was the ruler of the Arabs,⁹⁶⁹ to receive [the two of] them⁹⁷⁰ and bring them into safety. For having left secretly they would, if the things concerning Herod should turn out the way they were likely to do in view of Caesar's hostility to him,⁹⁷¹ be the only ones to receive the throne,⁹⁷² because of their birth⁹⁷³ and the support of the masses for them.⁹⁷⁴ **168** In spite of her pleading for these things, Hyrcanus kept rejecting⁹⁷⁵ her arguments. But since she had a contentious⁹⁷⁶ and womanly⁹⁷⁷ character and did not stop, night or day, always discussing⁹⁷⁸ these matters, particularly Herod's plot against them,⁹⁷⁹ he was finally persuaded⁹⁸⁰ to give a letter to Dositheus, one of his friends.⁹⁸¹ In the letter it was arranged

---

⁹⁶⁷ Josephus' phrase is a long-winded way of saying that Alexandra was hoping that the Hasmonean dynasty (cf. the reference to their family; see the preceding note) could regain the throne. He indicates several times that this was Alexandra's ultimate goal (*Ant.* 15.22, 24, 32, 42, 73; cf. 15.36, 183).

⁹⁶⁸ This is most probably the Nabatean king Malichus I (early fifties-ca. 30 BCE), who is referred to in *Ant.* 15.107 (see the note to "The Arab") and 15.108.

Alexandra applied the strategy to ask a friendly ruler for assistance several times in the preceding narrative (see her letters to Cleopatra, *Ant.* 15.24, 32, 45, 62).

⁹⁶⁹ The longer reading τῷ τὴν ἀραβαρχίαν ἔχοντι ("having the rule over Arabia"), attested by MSS LAMW, is preferable since it is the *lectio difficilior*. MSS VE read τῷ τὴν Ἀραβιάν ἔχοντι ("holding Arabia"), which is also attested by the Latin version (Niese 362). The word ἀραβαρχία ("rule over the Arabs," LSJ *s.v.* and Suppl.; Rengstorf *s.v.*; Retsö 2003: 373) is a *hapax legomenon* in Josephus.

⁹⁷⁰ Niese (362) reads αὐτόν ("him") with MSS PFV, but this does not match the continuation of the narrative, which implies that both Hyrcanus and Alexandra would travel to Malichus.

⁹⁷¹ Cf. Josephus' brief report about the plausible consequences of Octavian's victory at Actium for Herod (*Ant.* 15.161-163).

⁹⁷² The combination of ἀπολαμβάνω ("receive") with ἀρχή ("throne") also occurs in *Ant.* 10.216; 17.327; 20.64.

⁹⁷³ Hyrcanus and his daughter Alexandra belonged to the Hasmonean house, which had ruled Judea until Herod became king in 40/37 BCE (see *Ant.* 15.1-2 with notes).

⁹⁷⁴ There is no direct reference to a warm support of the masses for Hyrcanus and Alexandra. Yet Josephus' report about the inauguration of the young Jonathan-Aristobulus III as High Priest suggests that he definitely enjoyed the sympathy of the crowd (*Ant.* 15.51-52). The phrase τὴν εὔνοιαν τῶν ὄχλων ("the support [or sympathy] of the crowd") also occurs in 15.52 in regard with Aristobulus III (cf. 7.196 concerning Absalom).

⁹⁷⁵ The verb διωθέω ("reject," Rengstorf *s.v.*) occurs once elsewhere in Josephus (*War* 4.604).

⁹⁷⁶ The adjective φιλόνεικον ("contentious," perhaps "ambituous"—with Rengstorf *s.v.* φιλόνεικος) repeats φιλόνεικος in *Ant.* 15.62, 166 (likewise referring to Alexandra; see 15.166 with the note to "quarrelsome").

⁹⁷⁷ The adjective γυναικεῖος ("womanly") recalls 2 earlier passages about Alexandra (*Ant.* 15.44 and 15.69). The combination with φιλόνεικος (15.166, 168) implies that γυναικεῖος is used pejoratively here, which matches Josephus' consistently negative characterization of Alexandra (see 15.166 and 15.23 with the note to "Alexandra").

⁹⁷⁸ Josephus adds emphasis with a double formulation, first negatively and then positively: "did *not stop—night or day* (καὶ μήτε νύκτα μήθ' ἡμέραν ἀπολειπομένης)—*always* (ἀλλ' ἀεὶ) discussing." For a close parallel of a participle of ἀπολείπω plus μήτε νύκτα μήθ'ἡμέραν ("not stopping, night or day"), see Plutarch, *Mor.* (*Soll. an.*) 981a.

⁹⁷⁹ Josephus' phrase about Alexandra repeats his earlier information that Alexandra wrote to Cleopatra about Herod's plot against her son Aristobulus III (*Ant.* 15.62; cf. 15.59, 64). Since Josephus refers twice to Herod's scheming against Hyrcanus (15.21, 174), the tenor of the narrative confirms Alexandra's complaint about Herod, which is ironic in the light of Josephus' negative characterization of her.

⁹⁸⁰ Josephus' report suggests in this way that Hyrcanus was basically innocent, but the fact that he finally gave in to his daughter—or agreed on a compromise with her—implies that he was weak and rather naïve because he did not realize what the consequences of such a letter could be if Herod found out about it (see *Ant.* 15.173).

⁹⁸¹ It is not immediately clear to whom the pronoun "his" refers: either Malichus or Hyrcanus. The continuation of the narrative renders Hyrcanus more probable (see *Ant.* 15.170), which implies that Dositheus was one of Hyrcanus' friends and, as a consequence, that Hyrcanus had his own circle of friends at Herod's court (about "friends," see 15.162 with the note to "his entourage").

Dositheus is also mentioned in 15.169, 170, 252, 260. The name Dositheus is attested in an inscription from Marissa (*SEG* 8 no. 253b), and Josephus refers to another

that the Arab[982] would send to him [Hyrcanus][983] some horsemen who would pick them up and escort them to Lake Asphaltitis.[984] This lake is 300 *stadia*[985] away from Jerusalem's border.[986] **169** [Hyrcanus][987] trusted Dositheus because he was paying court to him and Alexandra[988] and had significant reasons[989] for feeling ill-will towards Herod: Dositheus was a relative of Joseph,[990] whom Herod had killed,[991] and a brother[992] of those who had been murdered earlier[993] in Tyre by Antony.[994] **170** These reasons truly did not[995] induce[996]

---

[981] Dositheus in 13.260 (Kokkinos 1998: 152). Otto (1913: 86) argues that Dositheus was Jewish but of Idumean ethnic origin (see also Richardson 1996: 222).

[982] I.e., the Nabatean king Malichus I (see *Ant.* 15.167 with the note to "Malchus").

[983] The context presupposes that both Hyrcanus and Alexandra would travel to Malichus (see *Ant.* 15.167).

[984] This is the Greek name for the Dead Sea, the lowest point of the Jordan Rift Valley. Josephus refers about 20 times to this "lake" (references in Schalit 1968: 19; Tsafrir, Di Segni, and Green 1994: 179) and offers a description of the Dead Sea in *War* 4.476-485. He briefly refers to the production of asphalt (which explains the origin of the lake's Greek name) and notes that asphalt was used as a sealing device for ship skins and as an ingredient for medicine (*War* 4.480-481, also Diodorus 2.48; 19.98-9; Strabo 16.2.42-43; Tacitus, *Hist.* 5.15.71-2; Möller and Schmitt 1976: 27). The journey of Hyrcanus and Alexandra to King Malichus most probably implied that they would travel to the Nabatean capital Petra, south of the Dead Sea. In that case the obvious route would be via the Dead Sea (see the next note).

[985] According to several scholars the ancient length standard of the *stadion* (στάδιον) equals ca. 185 m, which is based on the length of the Roman *stadium* (which roughly equals 400 Roman cubits; LSJ *s.v.*; Simons 1952: 395 n. 1). The actual length of a *stadion* is often not clear (see the notes by Mason at BJP 9: 64). If Josephus follows the Roman standard, 300 *stadia* would be ca. 55 km.

[986] The distance between the northern Dead Sea and Jerusalem was ca. 30 km, which means that the Latin version (Niese 362), reading *ducentis* ("200" = ca. 37 km), is probably a correction taking the northern end of the Dead Sea as point of departure. The modern road trip from Jerusalem to the northern Dead Sea, which is similar to the ancient one, is about 39+ km. If Josephus' estimation of 300 stades is based upon the ancient road system, implying a trip from Jerusalem to Jericho through Wadi Kelt and then along the western shore of the Dead Sea, the distance of 300 stades implies a location roughly halfway the west side of the Dead Sea. The journey to Petra was perhaps planned along the road via Masada, Zoara (south of the Dead Sea), Wadi Hasa, Khirbet Tannur, and Khirbet Dharih (Villeneuve and al-Muheisen 2003: 83-84).

[987] Literally "He."

[988] This behavior is obvious in the light of Dositheus' being a friend of Hyrcanus (see *Ant.* 15.168). The verb θεραπεύω ("pay one's court [to]," Rengstorf *s.v.*) with a person as object frequently occurs in Josephus (5.189; 14.393; 15.205; 16.157; 17.33; 18.188, 294, 339; 19.66).

[989] This is another case of *litotes* in Josephus. It leads up to Josephus' explanation of Dositheus' antipathy for Herod. The phrase οὐ μικρὰς αἰτίας ἔχοντος (literally "having no small reason [for]") has a close parallel in Isaeus 10.20.

[990] This is probably the Joseph whom Herod appointed as substitute during his trip to Antony. Joseph had to kill Mariamme in case Herod would not return from this trip (*Ant.* 15.65). Stern (1982: 44-45) argues that Joseph was a brother of Dositheus. However, this interpretation does not seem to be supported by the precise Greek formulation of Josephus (referring to a "relative" [συγγενὴς ἦν]; about Joseph, see *Ant.* 15.65 with the note to "his uncle Joseph").

[991] Joseph was executed after Herod's return from his trip to Antony because Herod believed Joseph had become too intimate with his wife Mariamme I (*Ant.* 15.87).

[992] In the Greek the word for brother (ἀδελφός) stands at the end, which emphasizes the close relationship between Dositheus and this (or these) relative(s) (see the next 2 notes).

[993] Several Greek MSS read πρότερος ("the first/earlier") instead of πρότερον ("before," Niese 362, who suggests that the reading πρότερος [attested by MSS LAMW and the Latin version] may derive from a personal name). The name could be even Πρότερος ("Proteros"). Osborne and Byrne (1994: 383) list one person with this name, from the 3rd cent. BCE.

[994] Josephus' information is slightly elliptic: the text probably implies that one of the persons who were killed by Antony in Tyre was a brother of Dositheus. Josephus describes that killing of a group of opponents of Antony in *Ant.* 14.327-329 (paralleled by *War* 1.245-247).

[995] The introduction of the sentence by οὐ μήν ("truly not") emphasizes the contrast with the preceding sentence (Wakker 1997: 223). Although Herod was responsible for the execution of a relative (i.e., Joseph) and indirectly for the death of a brother, Dositheus apparently decided to place his hope in the king. Günther (2005: 113) surmises that he acted as a double agent, using a forged letter from King Malichus in order to

Dositheus to serve[997] Hyrcanus trustfully. He preferred the things he could expect from the king to those from Hyrcanus,[998] and so he delivered the letter to Herod.[999] **171** Herod was content with his loyalty and encouraged him to assist him[1000] even more with this matter by giving the letter to Malchus, after rolling it up and sealing it,[1001] and also by taking hold of Malchus' letter.[1002] For it would be very important[1003] that he also knew Malchus' opinion.[1004] **172** After Dositheus had rendered this service willingly,[1005] the Arab[1006] wrote in answer that he would receive Hyrcanus, everybody who accompanied him,[1007] as well

---

discredit Hyrcanus and Alexandra (see also *Ant.* 15.176 with the note to "ordered for the man to be strangled").

[996] Niese (362) conjectures ἐνήγαγε ταῦτα ("these things led on"), but the text transmitted by the MSS (ἐπήγαγε ταῦτα "these things induced") makes sense and is paralleled by Arrian, *Anab.* 7.21.6: Ταῦτα ἀπαγγελθέντα ἐπήγαγεν Ἀλέξανδρον (literally "These matters having become known induced Alexander to"). The verb ἐπάγω followed by an infinitive can mean "induce (to)" (Rengstorf *s.v.*; see also *Ant.* 15.174).

[997] Half of the 12 occurrences of ὑπηρεσία ("service") in Josephus are found in the Herod narrative of *Antiquities* (15.170, 199, 201, 273; 16.97, 184).

[998] This implies that Dositheus went for realistic politics and that he estimated his prospects better by serving Herod. If so, he must have switched from Hyrcanus' circle of friends (see *Ant.* 15.168 with the note to "Dositheus, one of his friends") to Herod's friends. Obviously he would have expected a generous reward, but Josephus does not inform us about that (cf. 15.171). Kokkinos (1998: 151) explains Dositheus' move by the assumption that, following the execution of Joseph, Herod had established a closer relationship with Dositheus by marrying Joseph's daughter, who would have been Dositheus' niece.

[999] For the content of the letter, see *Ant.* 15.168.

[1000] The verb προσυπουργέω ("do an additional service," Rengstorf *s.v.*) is a *hapax legomenon* in Josephus.

[1001] Rolling up and sealing a letter was a standard practice (White 1986: 213-14). The verb πτύσσω ("fold, roll up") occurs once elsewhere in Josephus (*Ant.* 10.16; Rengstorf *s.v.*). The verb κατασημαίνομαι ("seal [up]," Rengstorf *s.v.*) also occurs in 4.64; 17.222.

[1002] The Greek probably means that Hyrcanus would receive a letter as a response from Malichus, although the plural τὰ γράμματα can mean that Malichus would write several letters (Rengstorf *s.v.* γράμμα). In *Ant.* 15.173 Josephus clearly refers to one letter from Malichus, but in 15.175, which is part of the second version about Hyrcanus' end, he mentions letters in a general way (τινας ἐπιστολάς).

Schalit (2001: 252 n. 359 and 698-99) argues that it is highly implausible that Hyrcanus would have written to Malichus; Herod himself would have fabricated the letters of Hyrcanus and Malichus in order to be able to present evidence for Hyrcanus' conviction. This implies that a charge that was fabricated by Herod underlies the first report about Hyrcanus' death, something which Josephus points out in connection with the second tradition about this death (see *Ant.* 15.174).

[1003] The phrase οὐ μικρὸν τὸ διάφορον (literally "not a small difference") is a case of *litotes* (cf. Aelius Aristides, *Plat.* [ed. Dindorf 2.158, 245]; Heliodorus 5.10.2; Gregory of Nazianzus, *Laud. Athan.* [PG 35.1109]).

[1004] Hyrcanus' leaving Herod's court after having returned to it from Babylon (*Ant.* 15.12-21) could have serious implications for Herod. It is plausible that Malichus was aware of this and that Herod would have strongly disliked a decision by the Nabatean king to support Hyrcanus' case. Malichus had previously had a serious conflict with Herod about the lease of Cleopatra's territories, which led to Herod's campaign against the Nabateans (15.107-108). In this light, the best option for Malichus was to refuse Hyrcanus' request in order to keep a good relationship with Herod. The continuation of the narrative suggests, however, that Malichus did not do so (see 15.177 about Josephus' own assessment of the reliability of the first report about Hyrcanus' death and 15.176 with the note to "ordered for the man to be strangled" for a discussion of both versions and their trustworthiness).

[1005] The participle ὑπουργήσαντος ("rendering a service") echoes προσυπουργῆσαι in *Ant.* 15.171. The word may have a negative connotation like the parallel expression in *Mart. Pol.* 13.1, which refers to the Jews gladly assisting in building Polycarp's pyre. For the phrase προθύμως ὑπουργέω ("render a service willingly"), see Josephus, *Ant.* 3.7; Plutarch, *Crass.* 5.2; *Mor.* (*Vit. pud.*) 534a; Gregory of Nazianzus, *Fun. or.* (PG 35.1016).

[1006] I.e., King Malichus (see *Ant.* 15.168).

[1007] This could imply Hyrcanus' relatives as well as his friends (see the reference to Dositheus as a friend of Hyrcanus in *Ant.* 15.168).

as all those Jews who were on his side.[1008] He[1009] would send an armed force that would escort them safely,[1010] and they would lack none of the things [Hyrcanus][1011] would ask for.[1012] **173** When Herod also received this[1013] letter, he immediately sent for[1014] Hyrcanus, and interrogated him about the arrangement[1015] made between him and Malchus. Since Hyrcanus[1016] denied this,[1017] he slew[1018] the man after showing the letters to the council.[1019]

[1008] This detail implies that Hyrcanus represented a Hasmonean faction that opposed Herod's role. It also suggests that Malichus was happy to support the opposition against Herod. The situation implied by Malichus' letter presents Hyrcanus' role in a different light than Josephus' own remarks, which point out that the former High Priest was never involved in rebellious activities (see *Ant.* 15.165, 177). Josephus emphasizes, on the other hand, that Alexandra had been disloyal to Herod before (15.22, 24, 32, 42, 73), and it is Alexandra who takes the initiative to write to the Nabatean king (15.167).

The verb φρονέω plus a noun in the accusative and a person in the genitive can mean "stand on somebody's side" (7.204; 12.392; 13.4, 377; LSJ *s.v.* II.2c; Rengstorf *s.v.*).

[1009] The Arab, i.e., Malichus.

[1010] If the journey aimed for Petra (see *Ant.* 15.168 with the note to "escort them to Lake Asphaltitis"), an armed escort would be necessary because the route to Petra was obvious and Herod could easily send a force to pursue Hyrcanus' group. The phrase μετ᾽ ἀσφαλείας κομίζω ("transport/escort safely") also occurs in Plutarch, *Aem.* 12.1.

[1011] Literally "he."

[1012] MSS AMW read ἠξίουν ("they asked for") instead of ἠξίου ("he asked for," Niese 363). The first reading seems to be an attempt to harmonize the subject with the preceding "them" (αὐτούς) and is, therefore, an adaptation of the second, more original reading.

[1013] The Greek καὶ ταύτην ("also this") presupposes an earlier letter, i.e., the letter by Hyrcanus given to Herod by Dositheus (*Ant.* 15.170).

[1014] The rare combination of εὐθύς ("immediately") and μεταπέμπω ("send for, summon") occurs from Thucydides onward (4.100.1; Xenophon, *Anab.* 7.1.20; Plutarch, *Ages.* 32.5).

[1015] The continuation of the narrative presupposes that this interrogation took place during a meeting of Herod's council (see the note to "the council" below). The plural of συνθήκη can have the stronger meaning "treaty" here, which is very common (LSJ *s.v.* II.2). In that case Hyrcanus and Malichus would have established a pact against Herod.

[1016] Literally "he."

[1017] Hyrcanus' denial does not match the information found in *Ant.* 15.168 that Hyrcanus gave to Dositheus a letter for Malichus. By itself the Greek here allows for a reading that Hyrcanus was honest about his denial because the substantive συνθῆκαι ("arrangement, treaty"), which Josephus uses a few words before, is ambiguous (see the note to "the arrangement" above).

[1018] The verb διαχειρίζω ("have in hands") can also mean "slay" in the middle voice (LSJ *s.v.* II). The reading διεχρήσατο, attested by MS W (Niese 363), probably has only a slightly different meaning: διαχράομαι means "kill, execute" (Rengstorf *s.v.*).

[1019] The letter from Hyrcanus to Malichus and Malichus' reply (*Ant.* 15.168, 172) obviously formed the evidence for Hyrcanus' conviction by the council. The narrative implies that Herod usually convened his council when he planned to execute somebody (cf. 16.357; 17.46, 93). He acted as prosecutor as well as supreme judge of such councils, which usually consisted of his friends and relatives (Schalit 2001: 252). Mariamme I was sent to death after a meeting of the council (15.229-231; see 15.229 with the note to "having gathered the persons who were most close to him"). Further examples concern the trial of those responsible for the demolition of a golden eagle at the Temple (*War* 1.654; *Ant.* 17.160-164) and that of his sons Alexander and Aristobulus IV in Beirut (*War* 1.538; cf. *Ant.* 16.356-357, 361, and also *War* 1.556; *Ant.* 16.62; 17.46, 93). When Herod thought about killing Cleopatra during her visit to Judea, on which occasion she tried to seduce Herod (*Ant.* 15.88-103), he consulted his friends, who prevented him from murdering the queen (15.98-103). See also Herod's own trial before Hyrcanus because he had executed brigands without organizing a trial first (14.168-178 and 15.3 with the note to "Pollio the Pharisee and Samaias, his student"). Kasher (2007: 158) qualifies Hyrcanus' trial as a "show trial" and even draws an analogy with Stalin's notorious trials.

Herod's council should be distinguished from the later Sanhedrin, which was also dealing with capital offences, as reflected in the Gospels (cf. *Ant.* 14.167, 175). The Sanhedrin operated on the basis of the Pentateuchal legislation (Deut 1:16-17; 19:15-21; cf. Num 35:30; Deut 17:2-8; John 7:51). Rabbinic interpretations of the requirements for trying capital cases are found in, e.g., *m. Sanh.* 4:1-5:5 (Brown 1994: 1.357-64; McLaren 1991: 74-79; Richardson 1996: 111; Levine 1998: 87-90).

(6.3) 174 We write these things[1020] such as they are contained in the memoranda of King Herod.[1021] But the other sources do not agree with these things.[1022] For they suggest that Herod did not bring charges against [Hyrcanus] on such grounds but rather fabricated them maliciously[1023] in order to kill Hyrcanus according to [Herod's][1024] own methods.[1025] **175** For they write as follows:[1026] "He addressed Hyrcanus at a certain banquet,[1027] giving him no ground for suspicion whatsoever,[1028] [asking him] whether he had received letters[1029]

[1020] Josephus' formula introduces an alternative account by stating that his report so far followed a specific source. Landau (2006: 129-30) argues that presenting 2 versions of a report confirms the authority and credibility of a historian (see on historiographical authority in general Marincola 1997). Josephus may follow here the historiographical practice of Herodotus, who considered it important to pass on more than one tradition about an event, even if the reports conflict each other or the reliability of one of them is to be distrusted. Herodotus would sometimes indicate in a personal comment what the most trustworthy version was (e.g., 1.1-5; Lendle 1992: 44-45; cf. Josephus' comment about the first tradition about Hyrcanus' death in 15.178). Another example of 2 versions of a certain event in Josephus concerns Phasael's death (see *War* 1.271-272; *Ant.* 14.367-369).

[1021] The word ὑπόμνημα can mean "note, record, chronicle" (e.g., *Ant.* 7.110, 293; 10.5, 55; 11.94, 208; Rengstorf *s.v.*). It is frequently used in the plural and perhaps means "memoirs" here, as several scholars suggest (e.g., Kokkinos 1998: 124). Richardson (1996: 169) concludes that at least part of 15.163-173 derives from Herod's memoirs. Josephus does refer to "records of the king(s)" (ὑπομνήματα, 11.94, 98, 248; cf. 11.104), but he does not specify that these royal archives concern memoirs. In 11.248 he mentions "the records of the kings who were before him and those of his own deeds" (trans. Marcus) in connection with the king Artaxerxes of the Esther story (see also 2 Macc 2:13 about Nehemiah's "memoirs" [ὑπομνηματισμοί]; van Henten 1997: 49-50). Josephus also refers to the ὑπομνήματα of the emperor, i.e., the diary-like notes or reminders (*Life* 342, 358; *Apion* 1.56; BJP 9 342, with references). The suggestion by Kokkinos (1998: 124) that Herod followed the examples of the memories of Augustus and Marcus Agrippa is problematic since the date of Marcus Agrippa's lost autobiography is unknown (Reinhold 1933: 142; cf. Roddaz 1984: 570, who suggests 23-21 BCE but acknowledges that this is only a guess). Augustus' *Res gestae* were published in 14 CE (for references, see Kienast 1999: 210-11, 263), while the chronological setting of Josephus' reference to Herod's memoranda is 31-30 BCE (*Ant.* 15.161). If Herod did indeed write his own memoirs, their language was most probably Greek, which Herod could have learned at Hyrcanus' court in Jerusalem (Hengel 1989: 35-36), or at Marissa or Ascalon (Kokkinos 1998: 124).

[1022] Josephus uses the verb συμφωνέω ("agree," Rengstorf *s.v.*) in a technical way, which implies in the current context agreement (or not) with a historical report (see also *Ant.* 1.107; 8.55; *Apion* 1.17, 144; 2.15). In *Ant.* 15.9-10 Josephus refers to Strabo as his source about Hyrcanus.

[1023] The phrase ἐξ ἐπιβουλῆς ("treacherously" or "with malicious intent," Rengstorf *s.v.* ἐπιβουλή) is a fixed expression in Josephus, also for the treacherous murder of persons (*War* 7.448; *Ant.* 8.307; 13.228; 20.74, 239). The death of Aristobulus III (*Ant.* 15.50-56), orchestrated by Herod, would fit this category very well (see also the note to "no ground for suspicion whatsoever" below about the repetition of vocabulary from 15.21, including the noun ἐπιβουλῆς).

[1024] Literally "his."

[1025] This suggests that execution was Herod's usual way of getting rid of competitors or other persons dangerous to him (see also the note to "fabricated them maliciously" above). MSS LAMW read κατὰ τὸν αὐτὸν τρόπον ("according to the same method"), which does not make sense in the context.

[1026] For introductory formulae of a quoted document or report similar to γράφουσι οὕτως ("they write as follows"), see *Ant.* 12.148; *Apion* 1.208, 237.

[1027] Participating in a banquet basically implied pleasure and entertainment (cf. *Ant.* 15.77 about Herod's stay with Antony; Garnsey 1999: 128-31; see also 15.21 with the notes to "banquets" and "recline before the others"). Herod's question during the presumably pleasant atmosphere at the banquet therefore highlights the king's wickedness (see also the next note).

[1028] This matches Josephus' earlier passage about Hyrcanus (*Ant.* 15.21), in which he describes how Herod treated Hyrcanus better than everybody else but also notes that "He [i.e., Herod] deceived him [i.e., Hyrcanus] during banquets by having him recline before the others, by calling him "father," and by contriving in many ways that his plot should remain unsuspected (τὸ τῆς ἐπιβουλῆς ἀνύποπτον πραγματευόμενος)." Note also the similarities of the vocabulary in 15.21 and 15.174-175: ὑποψίας ("suspicion") in 15.175 echoes ἀνύποπτον

from Malchus.[1030] When he conceded[1031] that he had received written greetings,[1032] **176** Herod asked him in return whether he had also received a present.[1033] [When Hyrcanus said that] he had received only four riding animals[1034] sent by [Malchus], Herod referred to this as a charge of[1035] taking bribes and treason,[1036] and ordered for the man to be strangled."[1037] **177** As proof that his life came to such an end[1038] without doing anything

---

in 15.21; ἐπιβουλή ("plot") occurs in 15.21 and 15.174.

[1029] The plural "letters" is perhaps significant because it differs in detail from what Josephus describes in *Ant.* 15.168, 171-173, mentioning a letter from Hyrcanus to Malichus and a letter from Malichus to Hyrcanus. *Ant.* 15.171 allows for a reading that Malichus sent several letters to Hyrcanus (see the note to "Malchus' letter"), but this reading is hardly plausible because *Ant.* 15.173 refers to 1 specific letter from Malichus (ταύτην τὴν ἐπιστολήν).

[1030] In the Greek the article before Malichus' name catches the eye because he has been mentioned several times previously already. The article, therefore, may emphasize the active participation of the Nabatean king in Hyrcanus' plan, or his prominent role (for a discussion of such a usage of the article, see Rijksbaron 2001: 16-18).

[1031] This is a clear contrast with the first version of the report, in which Hyrcanus denies having made arrangements with Malichus (*Ant.* 15.173).

[1032] The adjective προσαγορευτικός ("of address/greetings," LSJ *s.v.*) is a *hapax legomenon* in Josephus, and the extremely rare combination προσαγορευτικὰ γράμματα probably means "written greetings," as Rengstorf (*s.v.* προσαγορευτικός) suggests. This implies that there was no arrangement about a journey from Jerusalem to Petra or another Nabatean city in contradistinction to the first version of the report (*Ant.* 15.168).

[1033] Herod's first question may still seem innocent, but the second one clearly indicates that his interrogation of Hyrcanus was leading to an accusation of treason. Herod's questions also imply that Malichus, instead of Hyrcanus, was taking the initiative, and this, in turn, presupposes that Malichus aimed at harming Herod's position by using Hyrcanus as a tool.

[1034] The adjective ἀναβατικός ("[animal] used for riding," Rengstorf *s.v.*) is a *hapax legomenon* in Josephus. Josephus' rather general vocabulary perhaps refers to horses or mules fit for riding (cf. LSJ *s.v.* κτῆνος 2).

[1035] The verb ἐπαναφέρω (here meaning "to derive criminal charges from") occurs once elsewhere in Josephus (*Ant.* 3.72, with the meaning "bring before one," Rengstorf *s.v.*).

[1036] The combination of δωροδοκία ("bribe, bribery") and προδοσία ("treason") occurs in Josephus only here (for other combinations of these words, cf. Dinarch, *Aristog.* 22; *Phil.* 19; Appian, *Hist. rom.* 11.7.40; Arrian, *Hist. succ. Alex.* 1.15 [transmitted by Photius; see *FGH* 156 F 9]). Herod's double accusation is extremely severe since the letter only concerns greetings and the relatively innocent gift of 4 riding animals. The background of a possible rebellious act is missing in this second report (cf. *Ant.* 15.166, 172).

[1037] The verb ἀπάγχω ("strangle") occurs once elsewhere in Josephus (*Ant.* 12.256). MS P reads ἀπαγεῖν and MSS FAV ἀπαγαγεῖν; both readings imply that Hyrcanus was led away to be executed (cf. *occidi* in the Latin version; Rengstorf *s.v.* ἀπάγω).

Herod's sons Alexander and Aristobulus IV were also killed by strangling (*Ant.* 16.394). Strangling was one of the 4 types of capital punishment according to the rabbinic law (*m. Sanh.* 11.1). Yet treason or bribery are not mentioned among the crimes listed for this capital punishment (Marcus-Wikgren 84-85 n. *a*).

The 2 versions of the account of Hyrcanus' death both end with Hyrcanus' accusation by Herod and the old man's execution, but their content and their description of the role of the key persons differ in several ways. Let us focus on the content first. According to the first version (*Ant.* 15.165-173) Alexandra manipulated Hyrcanus to approach the Nabatean king Malichus in order to ask him for a safe haven for the time that Herod would still be on the throne, so that they could take over after Herod's death (15.167). Hyrcanus wrote a letter and gave it to Dositheus, who revealed the letter as well as Malichus' response to Herod. When Hyrcanus was interrogated by Herod, he denied (which is understandable since he was relying on Dositheus' faithfulness to him). When Hyrcanus was confronted with the 2 letters during a meeting of Herod's council (15.173), he was convicted; his treason had become obvious. Although Alexandra was (at least indirectly) responsible for Hyrcanus' death (15.166), the execution seems justified in this report because Hyrcanus participated in a rebellious initiative (Günther 2005: 111).

The second version (15.174-176) immediately states that Herod fabricated the charges against Hyrcanus (15.174). The king set a trap for the old Hyrcanus during a banquet and turned the meal into an interrogation with deadly consequences (15.175-176). This version mentions letters (a plural) from Malichus but does not refer to a letter from Hyrcanus, nor to a journey to Malichus. It does not refer to Alexandra, Dositheus, or Herod's council either. Hyrcanus admitted having received a letter and a few animals from Malichus, and Herod used this for sentencing Hyrcanus to death. This version specifies the type of execution: Hyrcanus was strangled (15.176; cf. 15.173).

The roles of the persons involved also differ in both reports. The first version focuses on Herod's enemies (15.165), which implies that Hyrcanus, who is mentioned next, was one of them. However, *Ant.* 15.165 emphasizes that Hyrcanus did not want to engage in a rebellious act against Herod; his daughter Alexandra did do so (15.166). Nevertheless, Hyrcanus could have resisted Alexandra but he did not, which confirms his weak character (cf. 15.177). Malichus was more than happy to assist Hyrcanus and Alexandra, and the detail about "all those Jews who were on his [i.e., Hyrcanus'] side" (15.172) shows that he was fully aware of the fact that the journey to him was part of a scenario to bring back the Hasmonean rule in Judea. The first version, therefore, in the beginning presents Hyrcanus as a victim of Alexandra's and Malichus' strategies against Herod, but in the end as a participant in the plan. In the second version Hyrcanus does not seem to have done much wrong, and he is acting in good faith during Herod's interrogation. Alexandra is mentioned in the first version only and her behavior is very much in line with what Josephus writes elsewhere about her, including her attempts to end Herod's rule (see 15.166). Malichus' role is more active in the second version, but the connection with a rebellious move against Herod is absent. A crucial difference between the 2 versions is that Herod's role is much more negative in the second: he is the evil genius, while Alexandra plays that role in the first. Moreover, in the first version Hyrcanus' death penalty seems justified; in the second the contact between Hyrcanus and Malichus seems to be rather innocent, and the verdict for the old man is extremely harsh. The second version, therefore, links up with Josephus' earlier remark that Herod clearly wanted Hyrcanus dead and would use the opportunity to arrange this when he could (15.20-21; cf. 15.164). If we can assume that the first version derives from a source—as 15.174 suggests,—this source seems to serve Herod's interests well: the blame is put on Alexandra and Hyrcanus, and Hyrcanus is rightly executed. It is plausible that the second version, which puts the blame entirely on Herod, flowed from Josephus' own pen. Its extremely negative image of Herod corresponds with Josephus' view about Herod in *Antiquities* (van Henten 2011b).

Scholars have different opinions about the reliability of the two versions. Grant (1971: 90-92) tends to accept the first version as reliable, but Jones (1938: 58) concludes that the second is plausible. Otto (1913: 49-50), Kasher (1988: 149-50), and Schalit (2001: 124-26, 133-35, 252 n. 359, 698-99) try to reconstruct what actually happened. Otto and Schalit argue that Herod's long-term strategy was to eliminate every male member of the Hasmonean family in order to secure the position of his own dynasty (cf. *Ant.* 15.186). This policy became urgent when Herod was to visit Octavian after Actium (Schürer-Vermes 1.301). Herod therefore fabricated letters ascribed to Hyrcanus and Malichus in order to convict Hyrcanus during a show process. Otto and Schalit consider Hyrcanus and Alexandra's intended trip to Malichus to be highly unlikely because they would have been at the center of power had Octavian executed Herod, and could have taken over the throne immediately. As an additional argument for the implausibility of the first version they note that Alexandra was not executed together with Hyrcanus (see also Richardson 1996: 170; Günther 2005: 113, and cf. *Ant.* 15.183). Kasher (1988: 150) adds that Malichus could not have been a military threat to Herod after the Nabatean defeat (15.147-160), and he and Schalit (2001: 698-99) argue that Herod's fabrication of the evidence against Hyrcanus (i.e., the letter from Hyrcanus to Malichus and that from Malichus to Hyrcanus) was inspired on the earlier journey of Hyrcanus to the Nabatean king Aretas at the advice of Herod's father, Antipater (*Ant.* 14.14-19). Richardson (1996: 170) points out that the second version is partly based on data from the first. He qualifies the second as "an intentionally alternative explanation."

A critical reading shows that both versions are tendentious: the first exonerates Herod from killing Hyrcanus without juridical grounds, and the second takes away all blame from Hyrcanus. It is plausible that Herod wanted Hyrcanus to be out of the way before the crucial visit to Octavian, as Otto and Schalit argue (see above, also Kasher 1988: 149; Kasher [2007: 156-59] explains Herod's "obsessive fear of anyone of Hasmonean extraction" by the king's paranoid personality). The first version provides a perfect legitimation of Hyrcanus' execution from Herod's perspective. Josephus' information that the first version derives from Herod's memoranda may, therefore, be correct. In that case we would have to reckon with at least 2 distortions of the events: Herod probably forged the evidence with the help of Dositheus given that the journey to Malichus is highly implausible, and *Ant.* 15.166 (about Alexandra as the instigator) must have been added later (cf. a similar note about Alexandra after Hyrcanus' death in 15.183) because otherwise she would have been executed with Hyrcanus. The second version may have been an invention by Josephus, with the purpose of highlighting once again Herod's wicked character.

[1038] The phrase τέλει περιπίπτω ("come to an end")

wrong, they claim[1039] that his character was reasonable[1040] and that he had demonstrated no boldness nor rashness,[1041] either in his youth or in the period he held the throne himself;[1042] even in that period he had handed over most matters of the administration to Antipater.[1043] **178** At that time[1044] his age[1045] happened to be somewhat more than eighty.[1046] He knew that Herod ruled with full security[1047] and even then crossed the Euphrates[1048] to be totally under his authority, leaving those on the other side behind, who held him in honor.[1049] That he

---

also occurs in Sextus Empiricus, *Math.* 5.91.

[1039] The subject of καταλογίζονται ("they claim") is not specified. One possibility is that this connects with Herod's memoranda, which would imply that the author(s) or editor(s) of these memoranda are meant. However, this does not match the justified death penalty for Hyrcanus according to the first version (*Ant.* 15.173). It therefore seems much more probable that the "they" links up with the anonymous reference to other sources in 15.174.

[1040] The phrase τὴν ἐπιείκειαν τοῦ τρόπου ("the reasonableness of his character") repeats a closely similar phrase in *Ant.* 15.165, also referring to Hyrcanus (see the note to "because of his reasonable character," also 15.182 and, as a contrast, 15.174 [about Herod]).

[1041] About the conventional association of a person's character and his or her deeds in obituaries, see Landau 2006: 128. The combination of θράσος ("boldness") and προπέτεια ("rashness") also occurs in Philo, *Legat.* 262; *QG* 4.52; *Spec.* 3.66 (cf. also *Ant.* 15.100 with the note to "rashness," about Herod).

[1042] Hyrcanus was High Priest from ca. 76 to 40 BCE, and he was appointed as ruler of Judea by Pompey in 63 BCE and by Julius Caesar in 47 BCE (for references, see *Ant.* 15.11 with the note to "Hyrcanus the High Priest" and 15.180 with the notes to "Pompey" and "received back all of his honors").

[1043] Josephus' narrative suggests that Hyrcanus was very much dependent on Herod's father, Antipater (see especially *Ant.* 14.165, also 13.407; 14.8, 16, 37, 80, 99, 127, 131, 141, 276; Schürer-Vermes 1.275-77).

[1044] Josephus switches here from his anonymous informants to his own comments, focusing upon Hyrcanus' old age and his return to Judea, which is relevant for the argument that Hyrcanus did not act against Herod (see *Ant.* 15.174). *Ant.* 15.179-182 provides more information about Hyrcanus in a second and longer flashback.

[1045] Whether more than 80 or 81, the number does not fit in with the date of Hyrcanus' parents' marriage, which must have been after ca. 103 BCE (Otto 1913: 52; Wellhausen 1914: 307 n. 2; Marcus-Wikgren 85 n. *c*; Kokkinos 1998: 212 n. 20; Schalit 2001: 124). If the setting of the relevant marriage and the numbers 80 or 81 were both correct, the period referred to would be 23-22 BCE, which is not shortly after Actium (31 BCE).

Richardson (1996: 169 n. 89) proposes 71 as Hyrcanus' age.

[1046] The Greek text attested by the MSS is corrupt. MSS LAMWE, followed by Naber (1888-96: 3.XLIII) and Marcus-Wikgren (84), read ἑνός ("one") instead of ἐντῶ ("within"), which is read by MSS PF (followed by Niese 363). The reading ἑνός cannot be correct: the genitive cannot go with πλείω because in that case the remaining part of the clause is left hanging; it cannot function as a modifier of πλείω either—implying that Hyrcanus would be 81 (as several scholars assume on the basis of the reading ἑνός)—because that would require a *dativus mensurae* (ἑνί). The reading ἑνός perhaps results from a corruption because of an exchange of Ω and ΟΣ, which could easily happen in Greek uncials (see van Groningen 1967: 34, 44, 54). Niese's reading ἐντῶ does not make sense. One could conjecture that the text originally read ἐνίοις, which implies "some (years) more than eighty." Photius (†891 CE), who summarized and paraphrased Josephus, offers a starting point for an alternative reconstruction of the original reading (as was suggested to me by Omert J. Schrier). He writes in codex 238 of the *Bibliotheca*: ἀνεῖλεν ἄνδρα ὑπὲρ τὰ π' ἔτη ἐνιαυτῷ ἑνί ... βεβιωκότα "He killed the man before he became eighty-one years old ..." (trans. Henry). Photius' words ἐνιαυτῷ ἑνί may be taken from Josephus' text. If so, a copyist of a predecessor of MSS PF (reading ἐντῶ) may have contracted the words ἐνιαυτῷ ἑνί on account of the same beginning of both words, resulting in ἐντῶ.

[1047] Josephus' second point is anachronistic if one connects it with Herod's situation after Actium, which was extremely dangerous (see *Ant.* 15.161-163; cf. also 15.291, with similar vocabulary). However, the point is presented as a flashback concerning Hyrcanus, which focuses upon his decision to return to Judea (which is narrated in 15.11-21, especially 15.11, 16). The flashback supports Josephus' argument that Hyrcanus had no plans whatsoever to participate in a rebellion against Herod.

[1048] The Euphrates is also mentioned in the story about Hyrcanus' return to Judea (*Ant.* 15.15).

[1049] In *Ant.* 15.17 Josephus writes that the Babylonian Jews asked Hyrcanus to stay with them and that they honored him as king and High Priest. The participle τιμῶντας ("holding him in honor") echoes τὰς τιμὰς ("the honors") in 15.17.

would attempt something[1050] and start a rebellion[1051] is totally unconvincing[1052] and against his nature,[1053] but these charges were brought about as a pretext by Herod.[1054]

(6.4) 179 This happened to be the end of Hyrcanus' life,[1055] after he had experienced complex and changing[1056] fortunes in his lifetime.[1057] For immediately at the beginning of his mother Alexandra's rule he was appointed High Priest of the Jewish people,[1058] and he held this office for nine years.[1059] **180** Having taken over the throne[1060] when his mother died,[1061] he held it for three months[1062] and was deprived of it by his brother, Aristobulus.[1063]

[1050] The structure of the Greek sentence, with several infinitives, links up with Josephus' rendering of the view of his anonymous informants in *Ant.* 15.177. The expression ἐγχειρεῖν ... τι ("undertake something") has the connotation of rebellious activities (cf. 15.42, at which instance the same verb is used in connection with Alexandra's behavior; see also 15.166 with the note to "hoping for a political change").

[1051] The phrase καινοτέρων ἅπτεσθαι ("start a rebellion") is a variant of νεωτέρων ἅπτεσθαι in *Ant.* 15.165, also referring to Hyrcanus.

[1052] For parallel phrases of πάντων ἀπιθανώτατον ("totally unconvincing"), see Sextus Empiricus, *Math.* 1.268; Eusebius, *Gen. elem. intr.* 4.1 (ed. Gaisford 167).

[1053] Josephus describes Hyrcanus' character in the immediate context of this passage in *Ant.* 15.165, 177, 182 (for further references, see 15.165 with the notes to "his reasonable character" and "He consented to fortune to love everything that was happening on its account"). For φύσις indicating someone's nature or character, see Rengstorf *s.v.* and *Ant.* 15.89 with the note to "her greedy character."

[1054] With this statement Josephus returns to his introduction of the second version about Hyrcanus' end, which highlights Herod's fabrication of the accusation against Hyrcanus (*Ant.* 15.174).

[1055] *Ant.* 15.179-182 is connected with 15.178, and both passages together form the flashback about Hyrcanus as a person and as a leader of the Jews. Such brief *analepses* in cases where an important character "leaves the stage" (i.e., dies) are typical for Josephus, Arrian, and Herodian (van Henten and Huitink 2007: 222). These obituaries briefly repeat the character's previous actions, and often include qualifying statements. The formula τοῦτο τὸ τέλος τοῦ βίου plus a personal name and a verb also occurs in *Apion* 2.144, to indicate the end of Apion's life (cf. *Ant.* 6.378 about Saul; 13.433 about Salome Alexandra).

[1056] The combination ποικίλος καὶ πολύτροπος ("complex and changing") also occurs in *Ant.* 10.142, concerning God's nature.

[1057] The phrase functions as the introduction to Josephus' flashback about the life of Hyrcanus, who had, indeed, been through a lot, as the continuation of the narrative points out.

[1058] Hyrcanus' mother, Queen Salome Alexandra, appointed him High Priest after the death of her husband, Alexander Janneus, in 76 BCE (*War* 1.109; *Ant.* 13.408; for further references, see *Ant.* 15.11 with the note to "Hyrcanus the High Priest"). For ἔθνος referring to the Jewish people, see *Ant.* 15.15 with the note to "the entire nation of the Jews."

[1059] The note presupposes that Hyrcanus' High Priesthood lasted as long as Salome Alexandra ruled as queen (76-67 BCE). This matches Josephus' information that both Hyrcanus' office and that of Salome Alexandra were held for 9 years (*Ant.* 20.242; cf. 15.179 ἔτεσιν ἐννέα τὴν τιμὴν κατέσχεν "held this office for nine years", referring to Hyrcanus, with 20.242 αὐτὴ δὲ τὴν βασιλείαν ἔτη ἐννέα κατασχοῦσα "she held the throne for nine years"). Salome Alexandra probably died in 67 BCE (Schürer-Vermes 1.200-01, 232). It is uncertain whether Hyrcanus remained High Priest between 67 and 63 BCE (cf. *Ant.* 14.6-7 with 14.41, 97 and 20.244). Hyrcanus was in any case restored as High Priest by Pompey and again by Caesar (see 15.180 with notes). Concerning the phrase ἀρχιερεὺς καταστάς ("he was appointed High Priest"), see 20.242, which passage notes that Alexander Janneus entrusted the appointment of the High Priest (καταστῆσαι τὸν ἀρχιερατευσόμενον) to his wife Salome Alexandra.

[1060] *War* 1.120 states that Hyrcanus was appointed king by Salome Alexandra. The phrase παραλαμβάνω τὴν βασιλείαν ("take over the throne") occurs 29 times in Josephus, but only once in *War* (1.479). It is used in various political contexts (e.g., *Ant.* 8.2; 11.21; 12.11; 15.254; 16.92; 17.95). In 14.4 (only in MSS PF) it is used in connection with Hyrcanus himself.

[1061] I.e., Salome Alexandra (see *Ant.* 15.179 with notes).

[1062] This information is connected with *Ant.* 14.4 (about Hyrcanus' royal office), but the chronological information is different: it does not mention the 3 months period of Hyrcanus' rule as king. The phrase κατέχω (τὴν βασιλείαν) ("holding/obtaining [the throne]") also occurs in 15.11, referring to Herod, and in 20.242, referring to Salome Alexandra.

[1063] *War* 1.120-122 and *Ant.* 14.4-8 describe more elaborately how Aristobulus II took over the throne from Hyrcanus after a combat near Jericho.

He was brought in again by Pompey,[1064] received back all of his honors,[1065] and continued to be among them [the Jews][1066] for forty years.[1067] **181** Removed from office for the second time[1068] by Antigonus[1069] and having been mutilated in his body,[1070] he was taken captive by the Parthians.[1071] After some time he returned from there to his country,[1072] because of the hopes given[1073] to him by Herod,[1074] of which, contrary to his expectation,[1075] nothing

---

[1064] Pompey re-appointed Hyrcanus as High Priest in 63 BCE (*War* 1.153; *Ant.* 14.73; 20.244). The adverb αὖθις ("again") echoes *War* 1.153.

[1065] Pompey also appointed Hyrcanus as ruler (ethnarch) of the Jewish people (*Ant.* 20.244). Julius Caesar rewarded Hyrcanus in 47 BCE—for his support against Pompey—with the confirmation of his High Priesthood and his re-appointment as ethnarch (*War* 1.194; *Ant.* 14.137, 151, 191-192, 194, 197, 199-200, 211, 226, 314).

[1066] This is a tentative translation, assuming that the "them" (reading διετέλεσεν ἐν αὐτοῖς with Niese 364 and most of the Greek MSS) refers to the Jews in Judea. MSS PF read ἐνιαυτοῖς ("years"), which is redundant (cf. ἔτη "years," a few words earlier). Marcus-Wikgren (86) read ἐν αὐταῖς (see already Thackeray and Marcus 1930-55: 163), which results in a smooth meaning of the text ("continued to have them [i.e., the honors; literally: "he continued in them"] for forty years"), but this reading is not supported by any extant textual witness. Thackeray and Marcus (1930-55: 163) give the meaning "to continue in a certain state" for διατελέω ἐν. Cf. the related phrase διατελέω ἐπί in *Ant.* 16.199, which probably means "remain with [the first woman]" (Rengstorf *s.v.* διατελέω).

[1067] The number 40 is well attested by the transmitted MSS but does not match the other data concerning Hyrcanus' life or career (the period of 63-40 BCE makes up 23 years; in *Ant.* 20.245 Josephus states that Hyrcanus ruled for 24 years; Udoh 2005: 127 with n. 58). Josephus' remark about Hyrcanus being more than 80 years old is wrong as well (see 15.178 with the note to "more than eighty"). The 40 years should perhaps be taken as a round figure symbolizing a long period; cf. the 40 days of rain that brought the Flood (Gen 7:4; Josephus, *Ant.* 1.89), Israel's period of 40 years in the desert following the Exodus (*Ant.* 3.32; 5.21; etc.), and Moses being with God on the mountain for 40 days (Exod 24:18; Josephus, *Ant.* 3.95). Richardson (1996: n. 98) argues that the number derives from a source favorable to Hyrcanus, which wanted to indicate that Hyrcanus was the legitimate king of the Jews from 67 BCE onward. Kasher (2007: 156 n. 3) argues that the period of 40 years matches the period between Hyrcanus' nomination as king and High Priest in 76 BCE and his return from Babylon in 36 BCE. The different number found in the list of High Priests (*Ant.* 20.245) fits the data much better. It states that Hyrcanus ruled for 9 years during the first period (76-67 BCE; see 15.179 with the note to "for nine years") and for an additional 24 years during the second (63-40 BCE; see also 15.181).

[1068] On Hyrcanus' first removal from office (67 BCE), see *Ant.* 15.180.

[1069] This remark is connected with Josephus' earlier reports that Antigonus (see *Ant.* 15.1 with the note to "Antigonus captive") took the rule over from Hyrcanus with the assistance of the Parthians in 40 BCE (*War* 1.248-249, 269, 273; *Ant.* 14.331-332, 340, 365, 379; 20.245).

[1070] This information links up with Josephus' reports in *War* 1.270 and *Ant.* 14.366 (see also *Ant.* 15.17). In *War* 1.270 Josephus states that Antigonus bit off Hyrcanus' ears, and in *Ant.* 14.366 that he cut them off. The verb λωβάομαι ("mutilate") is also used in *War* 1.270; *Ant.* 14.366 (cf. 15.17 κατὰ λώβην "because of the mutilation," also referring to Hyrcanus). For parallel phrases of λωβάομαι in the passive voice with σῶμα ("body"), see Josephus, *Apion* 1.234, 253, 273; Pausanias 1.5.4; Aelian, *Nat. an.* 3.1; Herodian 8.8.7.

[1071] The Parthians had caught Hyrcanus, together with Herod's brother Phasael (*War* 1.269; *Ant.* 14.365), and carried him away in chains to Parthia (*War* 1.273). The vocabulary here partly repeats Josephus' previous information that Hyrcanus was held by the Parthians as a captive (*Ant.* 15.11 ἦν δὲ παρὰ Πάρθοις αἰχμάλωτος; see also 14.379 and 15.12 with the note to "the commanders of the Parthians").

[1072] *Ant.* 15.11-21 reports Hyrcanus' return to Judea. MSS LA¹MVW read εἰς τὴν οἰκίαν ("to his house/family"), which is a case of *itacism* (οἰκίαν–οἰκείαν); εἰς τὴν οἰκείαν ("to his own") is the more original reading (with Niese [364]). Philo (*Abr.* 62) offers a close parallel concerning Abraham: εἰς τὴν οἰκείαν ἐπανίων ("returning ... to his home," trans. Colson; cf. Diodorus 20.25.4).

[1073] The variant reading προσγενομένας of MSS PFV ("happened," Niese 364) hardly results in a different meaning of the passage.

[1074] The report about Hyrcanus' return in *Ant.* 15.11-21 formulates it slightly differently: "... he [i.e., Hyrcanus] gave way to new hopes ..." (15.16). The phrase is motivated by Hyrcanus' awareness that Herod had taken over the rule from Antigonus, Hyrcanus' former enemy. *Ant.* 15.18 narrates that Herod persuaded Hyrcanus to

actually happened, after he had endured many calamities in his life.[1076] What was most annoying was, as I have told before,[1077] that he did not come to a worthy end[1078] in his old age.[1079] **182** He seemed to be reasonable[1080] and moderate[1081] in all matters and to handle most parts of his rule through administrators.[1082] He was not skilled for a job that dealt with many things,[1083] nor for being in charge of a kingdom.[1084] And it happened to Antipater and Herod[1085] to proceed as far as they did because of that man's [Hyrcanus] reasonableness.[1086] So finally he met such an end from them, which was neither just nor pious.[1087]

---

return by assuring that he would be rewarded by him for his favors.

[1075] The phrase κατὰ προσδοκίαν also occurs in *Ant.* 15.302; 16.264. It echoes προσδοκῶν ("expecting") in 15.16 (also referring to Hyrcanus). Herod, in fact, treated Hyrcanus very well after his return (15.21). Nevertheless, Josephus' comments as narrator in 15.20-21 imply that Hyrcanus' decision to return would ultimately lead to his ruin.

[1076] The remark suggests that Hyrcanus deserved to be treated well after the long life of sufferings that Josephus had just been summarizing (*Ant.* 15.178-181). This prepares the reader for the concluding remark (see the next note). The expression πολυπάθεια ("suffering of many afflictions," Rengstorf *s.v.*) is a *hapax legomenon* in Josephus.

[1077] Josephus' cross-reference probably focuses upon the second version of Hyrcanus' end (*Ant.* 15.174-176), in which Herod is clearly the evil genius who wants the old Hasmonean ruler dead.

[1078] The addition of τοιούτου ("such") in MSS LAMW (Niese 364) probably derives from τοιούτου τέλους ("such end") at the end of the next paragraph.

[1079] Dying in a way worthy of one's old age is a common motif in laudatory passages of ancient literature—also in Hellenistic-Jewish writings, as 2 Macc 6:23-28 (about the 90 years old martyr Eleazar) shows. Eleazar was very keen on dying in a way that was "worthy of his years" and "worthy of his old age" (van Henten 1997: 226-30). Josephus implies Herod's evil, in not allowing Hyrcanus to die a death worthy of his age.

[1080] *Ant.* 15.182 offers Josephus' final assessment of Hyrcanus as a person and as a ruler of the Jews, whereby mostly repeating previous remarks about Hyrcanus. Hyrcanus' reasonableness (ἐπιεικής) is also highlighted in 14.13; 15.165, 177 (ἐπιείκεια; see 15.165 with the note to "because of his reasonable character").

[1081] The combination of ἐπιεικής ("reasonableness") and μετριότης ("moderation, modesty"—related to the adjective μέτριος ["moderate"], Rengstorf *s.v.*) is obvious since both virtues are closely related (see *Ant.* 15.165 with the note to "because of his reasonable character," and for similar combinations, 6.263; Lucian, *Rhet. praec.* 15).

[1082] This remark links up with the previous statement about Antipater taking care of most matters of state during Hyrcanus' rule (*Ant.* 15.177). The substantive διοικηταῖς ("administrators") echoes διοίκησιν ("administration") of 15.177.

[1083] The word πολυπράγμων ("being busy about many things," Rengstorf *s.v.*) is a *hapax legomenon* in Josephus. It repeats πολυπραγμονέω ("be busy with state affairs," probably with a negative connotation) of *Ant.* 15.165, which also refers to Hyrcanus. Cf. 14.13 referring to Hyrcanus' lack of political ambition (τὸ ἄπραγμον).

[1084] This repeats in different words the previous remark about leaving the matters of state to administrators (see also *War* 1.109; *Ant.* 14.13, 165; 15.15 with the note to "He was content with these things").

[1085] The remark is very similar to the accusation of prominent Jews before Hyrcanus that Antipater and his sons were usurping Hyrcanus' royal power (*Ant.* 14.165). About Antipater, see 15.177 with the note to "Antipater."

[1086] The phrase repeats ἐπιεικής ("reasonable") at the beginning of the sentence.

[1087] This remark about Hyrcanus' unworthy death connects with the final point of the previous paragraph, which also focuses upon Hyrcanus' death. The repetition of the vocabulary (especially the repetition of τέλος ["end, death"] in *Ant.* 15.181-182; cf. 15.168, 177, 179) adds emphasis, such that Josephus' criticism of Herod cannot be missed.

The pair (neither) just—(nor) pious (οὔτε δίκαιον οὔτ' εὐσεβές) occurs several times in books 7 and 8 of *Antiquities*, mostly in references to Solomon's rule (7.338, 341, 356, 374, 384; Mason 1991: 85-89, 132-55). It implies just rule towards the citizens and a pious attitude towards God (explicitly so in 7.384). By way of contrast Josephus uses the same pair in 8.300 in the negative assessment of King Baasha's rule. In the perspective of these passages *Ant.* 15.182 implies that Herod did not act as a good ruler by executing the old Hyrcanus. The combination of piety and justice frequently occurs in ancient Greek literature (e.g., Diodorus [4.18.3; 6.8.1] refers to persons who distinguish themselves by these 2 virtues). At the same time the pair also echoes the vocabulary of just war (*bellum iustum*; see *Ant.* 8.280 and 15.135 with the note to "justified"). The expression may, therefore, also be interpreted from

Herod travels to Caesar. Secret instructions for Joseph and Soemus.

(6.5) 183 And when Herod had indeed put Hyrcanus out of the way,[1088] he hurried towards Caesar.[1089] Since he could not hope for anything good concerning the future of his affairs, because of his friendship with Antony,[1090] he held Alexandra under the suspicion[1091] that she would take advantage of the situation,[1092] cause the rabble to revolt,[1093] and bring the affairs of the kingdom into disorder.[1094] **184** He put his brother Pheroras[1095] in charge of everything[1096] and accommodated his mother Cyprus,[1097] his sister, and all his children[1098]

---

a Roman perspective; Josephus' phrase can easily be translated into Latin (*nec iustum nec pium*). The implication would again be that Herod did not act as a sensible ruler should do.

The adjective *pius* (equivalent to εὐσεβής ["pious"]) and its corresponding virtue *pietas* express the proper attitude ("duty, devotion") towards relatives, gods (and deceased parents), and the state. One of Cicero's various definitions of *pietas* is "love justice and duty (*iustitiam cole et pietatem*), which are indeed strictly due to parents and kinsmen, but most of all to the fatherland" (*Re publ.* 6.16, trans. Keyes; the combination of *iustitia* and *pietas* also occurs on Augustus' shield of honor put up in the Curia Julia (about *pietas*, see Wagenvoort 1980: 1-20; about Augustus' shield of honor, Kienast 1999: 95-98). The adjective *pius* was also an epithet of several emperors (LSJ *s.v.* εὐσεβής I.2). Schwartz (1994: 220) notes that in Josephus' estimation the fate of Hyrcanus was unjust and unfair but nevertheless what reasonable people would have expected given Hyrcanus' incapability to rule.

[1088] This sub-clause is part of the introduction to the narrative about Herod's journey to Octavian (*Ant.* 15.183-198), which had been interrupted by the section about the end of Hyrcanus (see 15.161-163 and 15.164-182). The beginning and end of the digression about Hyrcanus are marked by the words ἐμποδών ("hindrance," 15.164) and ἐκποδών ("out of the way," 15.183). About the combination ἐκποδών ποιεῖσθαι plus a personal object ("get someone out of the way"), see 15.20 with the note to "get him out of the way." The repetition in 15.183 recalls Josephus' remark in 15.20 that Herod aimed at trying to get Hyrcanus out of the way and succeeded in doing so.

[1089] This information links up with the stage of the narrative in *Ant.* 15.161, concerning the consequences of Octavian's victory at Actium in 31 BCE (cf. *War* 1.386-387).

[1090] The phrase ἐκ τῆς γενομένης αὐτῷ πρὸς Ἀντώνιον φιλίας partly repeats τοσαύτης αὐτῷ φιλίας πρὸς Ἀντώνιον γεγενημένης in *Ant.* 15.162 (see the note to "because of his close friendship with Antony"). The motif also occurs in *War* 1.386 ("because of his friendship with Antony") but with different Greek words.

[1091] Josephus already reports in *Ant.* 15.42 (see the note to "he truly did not remain without suspicion") that Herod held his mother-in-law under suspicion. The phrase ὕποπτον ἔχω ("hold [someone] under suspicion") also occurs in Philo, *Prov.* 2.26; Josephus, *Ant.* 7.213; Eusebius, *Praep. ev.* 8.14.26.

[1092] The phrase τῷ καιρῷ συνεπιθεμένη ("taking advantage of the situation") in connection with rebellion has a close parallel in Diodorus 20.33.7; cf. 14.40.3; 20.104.3.

[1093] On τὸ πλῆθος having a depreciatory meaning ("mob, throng, rabble"), see *Ant.* 15.2 with the note to "the city's population." For the association of the mob with rebellion, see already 8.223 (τῆς τοῦ πλήθους ἀποστάσεως γεγενημένης; cf. 15.183 τό τε πλῆθος ἀποστήσῃ καὶ στασιάσῃ τὰ περὶ τὴν βασιλείαν πράγματα) about the rebellion of the Israelites against King Rehoboam (1 Kgs 12:18-19), and 15.292.

[1094] On Alexandra's attempts to start a rebellion and cause the return of the Hasmonean rule, see *Ant.* 15.166 with notes. In the light of the preceding narrative it is surprising that Alexandra was not executed with Hyrcanus; she was the instigator according to the first version of the report about Hyrcanus' death (see 15.166).

[1095] Herod's parents, Antipater and Cyprus, had 5 children: 4 sons (Herod, Phasael, Pheroras, and Joseph) and 1 daughter (*War* 1.181; *Ant.* 14.121). Pheroras was the youngest son. He was born in ca. 65 BCE. Scholars differ about the date of his death (Kokkinos [1998: 171-72 with n. 84 and 210] argues for 7 BCE; Schürer-Vermes [1.294] for 5 BCE; and Mahieu [2012: 269] for "after 5 February 2 BC"). For references concerning Pheroras in Josephus, see Schalit 1968: 123, and for a survey of Pheroras' life, Kokkinos 1998: 164-75, 186-89, 210-13.

[1096] Pheroras acted as caretaker of the kingdom, as Joseph had done during Herod's journey to Antony (*Ant.* 15.65).

[1097] Herod's mother's family was part of the Nabatean aristocracy and probably related to the Nabatean/Arabian royal house (*War* 1.181; *Ant.* 14.121; Kokkinos 1998: 95-96; Retsö 2003: 374).

[1098] The words γενεά plus πᾶσα/ἅπασα can indicate the entire family (*War* 2.38, 476; *Ant.* 2.173; 6.255; 7.328; 8.309), but they sometimes particularly refer to its descendants, i.e., Herod's children (cf. *War* 1.473; Rengstorf *s.v.* γενεά).

in Masada.[1099] He gave [Pheroras] instructions to take care of the matters of the kingdom,[1100] if he[1101] should hear that anything bad had happened to him.[1102] **185** He accommodated his wife Mariamme[1103] with her mother Alexandra[1104] in Alexandrium,[1105] since in view of the dispute that obtained with his sister and her mother,[1106] living in the same place was impossible.[1107] He left the administrator[1108] Joseph[1109] and the Iturean[1110] Soemus[1111] in charge

---

[1099] In *War* 7.285 Josephus reports that the Hasmonean ruler Jonathan (161-142 BCE) made a fortress out of the inaccessible hill on the western shore of the Dead Sea and called it Masada. Schalit (2001: 343-44) and Möller and Schmitt (1976: 135) argue that Alexander Janneus (103-76 BCE) built Masada. Herod fortified the place and built a palace (*War* 7.286-294; he actually built 2 palaces at Masada). During the war against the Parthians he used Masada as a safe haven for his family (*Ant.* 14.358, 361, 390, 396-397, 400, 413).

Large-scale excavations have been undertaken at Masada, which has been a Unesco World Heritage site since 2001 (further references in Möller and Schmitt 1976: 134-35; Tsafrir, Di Segni, and Green 1994: 180; Schalit 2001: 343-56; Netzer 2006: 17-41).

The variant readings Μεσάδοις (MSS FAW) and Μεσσάδοις (MS M; Niese 265) are probably simply variant spellings (*a* exchanged for *e*). There is a slight possibility that they derive from the identification with another place, called Mesada, which is located ca. 40 km east of the northern tip of the Dead Sea (if the identification with Qasr el-Mushetta, where an Umayyad castle is located, is correct; Sauvaget 1939: 31-35).

[1100] Cf. *Ant.* 15.65, 68, about Joseph as caretaker during Herod's trip to Antony.

[1101] I.e., Pheroras.

[1102] Josephus' phrase is rather general. Herod takes important steps that clearly reckon with the worst case scenario, i.e., that he would be arrested or even executed by Octavian (see *Ant.* 15.184, 186). About Masada as a refuge for Herod's family, see 15.184 with the note to "Masada." Herod's measures for the period that he would be away on his trip to Octavian (15.184-186) are absent in the parallel narrative of *War* (cf. 1.386-387). There is a close analogy with the secret instructions to Joseph to kill Mariamme in case Herod would not return from his journey to Antony (*Ant.* 15.65).

[1103] For Mariamme, see *Ant.* 15.23 with the notes to "Mariamme, who was living in wedlock with Herod" and "strikingly beautiful."

[1104] Mother and daughter side with each other several times in *Antiquities*. In 15.31 Mariamme persuades Herod to support the case of her mother and to appoint her brother Aristobulus III High Priest. In 15.68-70 both women operate together in finding out Herod's secret instructions to Joseph (see also 15.202-203 and the next note).

[1105] Alexandrium (Ἀλεξανδρεῖον) was a Hasmonean fortress (*War* 1.134; *Ant.* 13.417; 14.49; etc.) expanded by Pheroras (*War* 1.308; *Ant.* 14.419). It was located in the mountains of Acrabetene (East Samaria), overlooking the Jordan Valley, about 35 km north of the Dead Sea. The Arabic name of the location is Qarn Sartaba. Remains of a peristyle court from the Herodian period suggest that the fortress was a palace in Herod's days (Möller and Schmitt 1976: 12; Tsafrir, Di Segni, and Green 1994: 60-61; Netzer 2006: 204-06).

[1106] This is one of Josephus' hints at competing women factions in Herod's court (see also *Ant.* 15.35 with the note to "the friends called to their help" and 15.239 with the note to "hostile towards her"). The passage may anticipate 15.213, where Salome and Cyprus—Herod's sister and mother—are spreading slanders about Mariamme. Salome's accusation of adultery brings about Mariamme's execution (15.223-231). Earlier in the narrative Salome accuses her husband Joseph of adultery with Mariamme, in retaliation for the latter's hostile attitude and her reproaching of Salome's low birth (15.81). The phrase ἐν διαφορᾷ τῇ ("considering her hostile attitude") may echo κατὰ τὰς διαφοράς ("in their hostilities," 15.81), which also refers to Mariamme and Salome. Otto (1913: 50) suggests that Herod already distrusted Mariamme at this stage and that this was an additional reason to separate her from her sons. Schalit (2001: 133-35) also emphasizes that Herod had additional motives for separating his wife and mother-in-law from the rest of the family. This seems plausible, especially since the secret instructions concerned both Mariamme and Alexandra. Herod must have been keen on minimizing the chances for the Hasmonean house to regain the throne.

[1107] The Greek sentence has a sandwich structure with an embedded parenthesis starting with δυνατὸν γὰρ οὐκ ἦν ("for it was impossible"). The parenthesis explains the reason, formulated in the main clause, for Herod's measures concerning the women.

[1108] The translation follows the reading ταμίαν ("administrator, steward") found in MSS LAMW and read by Marcus-Wikgren (88; see also Rengstorf *s.v.* ταμίας). The MSS attest to various related readings. Niese (365) reads ταμιαίαν with MSS PV and suggests that Joseph's surname or father's name lies hidden behind this Greek word (see also Schalit 1968: 68, 118, and 2001: 135, who builds on Niese's suggestion and considers ταμιαίαν to be a corruption of Γαλιλαῖον ["the Galilean"], which could easily have happened in

of them.[1112] They had been the men most faithful to him from the beginning,[1113] and now they were left behind to guard the women under the pretext of honor.[1114] **186** There were indeed instructions for them[1115] to kill[1116] both women immediately, if they should learn

---

uncial manuscripts, cf. ΤΑΜΙΑΙΑΝ with ΓΑΛΙΛΑΙΟΝ). Otto (1913: 50) takes ταμιαίαν to be a case of dittography and considers ταμίαν to be the original reading. I did not find other occurrences of ταμιαίαν, which supports the view that this word is a corruption. The reading ταμίαν makes sense and is also attested elsewhere in Josephus (*Ant.* 2.120, 124; cf. *War* 1.627; 2.135; *Ant.* 14.198, 219, 221). *Ant.* 2.120, 124 refer to the steward of the biblical Joseph.

[1109] This Joseph is not mentioned elsewhere in Josephus. He is perhaps identical with the Joseph mentioned in *Ant.* 15.65, who is fulfilling a similar role. It is striking that Joseph does not appear later on together with Soemus (see, e.g., 15.205, 228). Otto (1913: 50) explains Joseph's disappearance by the assumption that, in contrast to Soemus, he did not betray Herod and that there was nothing more to tell about him.

[1110] "Iturean" (Ἰτουραῖος) is the name of an ethnic group mainly living in the mountainous region of Lebanon (Lebanon, Anti-Lebanon, and perhaps the slopes of Mount Hermon), as Strabo (16.2.10, 18-20) suggests. The kings of Chalcis (see *Ant.* 15.92) were supposed to control the robbers operating from these areas. The name Iturean is often associated with the Biblical name Jetur, who is one of Ishmael's sons (Gen 25:15; 1 Chron 5:19). The Hasmonean king Aristobulus I campaigned against the Itureans and conquered part of their territory (*Ant.* 13.318-319). The Itureans were known as good soldiers; Antony had a bodyguard of Itureans (Cicero, *Phil.* 2.19, 112; 13.18). Further discussion in Schürer-Vermes 1.561-65; Millar 1993b: 35-36, 273-74, 310-11, 506; Aliquot 1999-2003; Myers 2010).

[1111] Soemus is also mentioned in *Ant.* 15.204-205, 216, 227-229 in connection with his task to take care of Mariamme. He was apparently the army officer responsible for guarding the fortress (*Ant.* 15.204; Kasher 1988: 151, who suggests that Soemus belonged to the military unit recruited by Herod on Mount Lebanon [*War* 1.329; *Ant.* 14.352]). Kokkinos (1998: 114) claims that Soemus was a son of King Ptolemy of Chalcis and the Hasmonean princess Alexandra III, but this is not supported by the sources.

[1112] Richards and Shutt (1939: 173) suggest ἐπ' αὐταῖς instead of ἐπ' αὐτῶν ("[in charge] of them," i.e., the women). The MS tradition is divided: MSS LV and the *editio princeps* have a singular form of the personal pronoun ("him" or "it," probably the fortress; Niese 365).

[1113] Two similar phrases about Soemus' loyalty (*Ant.* 15.205, 228) will follow in the narrative leading up to Mariamme's death. The slight variations among these phrases enhance the readers' suspense: in 15.185 Josephus writes that Joseph and Soemus were Herod's most faithful men from the beginning on (πιστοτάτους ἐξ ἀρχῆς); in 15.205 he states that Soemus was trustworthy at the beginning (κατὰ τὰς ἀρχὰς πιστός); and in 15.228, looking back, that he was "at all other times most faithful (πιστότατος) to him and the monarchy" (cf. *War* 1.441 about Joseph being faithful to Herod [πιστὸς ἦν] and favorably disposed because of his marriage to Herod's sister Salome, and *Ant.* 16.180, 255 about faithful friends of Herod). Herod needed his most trustworthy men for the delicate task of guarding Mariamme and her mother.

[1114] The phrase probably means that Joseph and Soemus were supposed to stay with the women because of their royal status (see *Ant.* 15.23), which may have been true in a certain way (see below). Günther (2005: 113) argues that the stay at Alexandrium was meant as a punishment for Mariamme and Alexandra. However, in the next paragraph Josephus reveals another reason for guarding the women.

Herod's motivation for their separation from the rest of the family may have been more complex than the hostilities between the factions of the women mentioned in 15.185. Though Herod's jealousy concerning Mariamme is not mentioned here (cf. 15.66), one can easily imagine it was an important motive in this situation as well (as Schalit [2001: 133-34] does). Moreover, the continuation in 15.186 suggests that Herod was also very much concerned about securing the kingdom for his sons, which implies that he saw himself as the founder of a royal dynasty. Mariamme and Alexandra were a threat to this (cf. 15.166, 183) because they opted for a return of the Hasmonean rule. They therefore had to be killed immediately after his death (Otto 1913: 50-51; Schalit 2001: 133-35). Otto also notes that Mariamme's separation from her children demonstrates Herod's distrust.

[1115] The parallel narrative of *War* (1.441) reports that Joseph received similar secret instructions (κρύφα ἐντολάς) from Herod (see also *Ant.* 15.65, 69 on Salome's husband Joseph).

[1116] The verb μεταχειρίζομαι can mean "do away with, kill" (LSJ *s.v.* 5b). The variant reading διαχειρίσασθαι of E has the same meaning. Both verbs are occurring several times in Josephus (Rengstorf *s.v.* διαχειρίζω and μεταχειρίζομαι).

anything bad had happened to him,[1117] and to do everything possible to secure the kingdom[1118] for his sons together with his brother Pheroras.[1119]

(6.6) 187 Having given these instructions,[1120] he hastened to Rhodes[1121] to meet[1122] Caesar.[1123] When he entered the city's harbor,[1124] he removed his diadem[1125] but did not take off[1126] any other sign of his rank.[1127] And when he was permitted to converse with [Caesar] upon meeting him,[1128] he demonstrated to an even greater degree his enormous pride[1129] 188 by turning neither to supplications,[1130] which is customary in such circumstances, nor

Successful meeting with Caesar at Rhodes.
War 1.387-393

[1117] The phrase repeats *Ant.* 15.184: "... if he would hear anything bad ..." (repetition of τι ... δυσχερές; see the note to "hear anything bad had happened to him").

[1118] This phrase clearly indicates that Herod reckoned with his execution by Octavian. The combination of διατηρέω ("preserve, secure") and τὴν βασιλείαν ("the throne") also occurs in *Ant.* 10.223; *Apion* 1.138; cf. Plutarch, *Mor.* (*Apoph. lac.*) 216e.

[1119] Pheroras was instructed to be Herod's caretaker during the king's absence (*Ant.* 15.184). Kokkinos (1998: 165-66) connects *War* 1.483-484 about Pheroras' position (e.g., sharing all royal honors with Herod except the diadem, having a personal income of 100 talents, and marrying the sister of Herod's wife Mariamme; cf. *Ant.* 15.362) with Herod's trip to Octavian and argues that Pheroras' position became much more prominent from this period onward.

[1120] With this transitional phrase Josephus returns to the main point in the section, i.e., Herod's trip to Octavian (*Ant.* 15.161, 183, 187-193).

[1121] When he was on his way to Rome in 40 BCE Herod had been forced to go ashore at Rhodes owing to a heavy storm (*War* 1.280; *Ant.* 14.377) and had assisted in its restoration projects (*Ant.* 14.378, following Rhodes' brutal punishment by Cassius in 42 BCE).

[1122] Josephus uses exactly the same phrase ἠπείγετο συντυχεῖν plus dative ("he hastened to meet") in *Ant.* 16.16, concerning Herod's journey to Marcus Agrippa.

[1123] The parallel narrative of *War* (1.387) also states that Octavian was staying at Rhodes at that time. Octavian spent the winter of 31/30 BCE at Samos but had to return to Rome in order to stamp out a rebellion of his veterans. Thereafter he went to Greece in the spring of 30 BCE and travelled to Asia Minor, via Rhodes, in order to prepare for his campaign against Egypt. Syria was the point of departure for the actual campaign (see *Ant.* 15.198). Herod met Octavian on his way to Egypt during the spring of 30 BCE (Kienast 1999: 71-72; Mahieu 2012: 94 n. 11).

[1124] Josephus does not specify the location. It must have been Lindus, Rhodes' most important city. Lindus had a natural harbor (Hiller von Gaertringen 1931: 746). For a description of Rhodes in the 2nd and 1st cent. BCE, see Strabo 14.2.10-12.

[1125] This matches the parallel account of *War* (1.387), which shares the noun διάδημα ("diadem") with *Ant.* 15.187. The diadem reflected Herod's status as king. This aspect is apparent from 20.244: Pompey confirmed Hyrcanus II's status as ruler of the Jews but did not allow him to wear a diadem. Herod's gesture made clear that it was Octavian's authority to decide whether or not to confirm Herod in his rule as King of Judea (cf. 17.202 concerning Archelaus, who refrained from accepting the title king and the diadem from the army because his rule had not yet been confirmed by Octavian).

[1126] The verb ὑφίημι ("lay aside, let go," Rengstorf *s.v.*) also occurs in *Ant.* 5.171; 15.287.

[1127] This detail differs from *War*, which states that Herod approached Octavian "in the attire and appearance of an ordinary person" (1.387, trans. BJP 1a).

[1128] The phrase κοινωνέω λόγου (literally "take part in a discussion") means "converse with someone" here (Rengstorf *s.v.* κοινωνέω). The vocabulary that is additional to that of the parallel report of *War* (1.387) is repetitive. The noun συντυχίαν ("meeting") repeats συντυχεῖν ("meet") a few lines earlier; the aorist ἠξιώθη ("permitted, considered worthy") repeats ἀξιώματος ("dignity, sign of rank").

[1129] The parallel report of *War* (1.387) states more briefly that Herod approached Octavian "with the high-mindedness of a king (τὸ δὲ φρόνημα βασιλεύς)" (trans. Sievers/Forte in BJP 1a). In *Antiquities* Josephus embellishes the description of Herod's attitude before Octavian by enhancing the degree in which Herod holds on to his self-awareness and pride. The substantive μεγαλεῖον ("greatness," Rengstorf *s.v.*) also occurs in *Ant.* 8.49; *Apion* 2.157.

[1130] The composition of the first part of this paragraph (which is not found in *War*) is highly rhetorical because of the similarities in the structure of the sentence (οὔτε ... ὡς—οὔτε ... ὡς) and alliteration (with *k*, *s*, *t*, and *p* as the recurring consonant sounds).

The readings ἰκεσίας (MSS FVE and the excerpts) and ἰκετείας (MSS LAMW) have the same meaning: "supplications" (Rengstorf *s.v.* ἰκεσία and ἰκετεία). The combination of τρέπω ("turn") and εἰς ἰκεσίας/ ἰκετείας/ ἰκεσίαν/ ἰκετείαν occurs frequently (2 Macc 12:42; Posidonius 102a.15; Diodorus 33.5.3; Dionysius, *Ant.*

to a request,[1131] as in the case of a transgression,[1132] but he gave an account of his deeds in [such] a way that he could not adequately be punished.[1133] **189** For he told Caesar that[1134] he had had an extraordinary friendship with Antony[1135] and had done everything in his power[1136] so that the Commonwealth would fall to him.[1137] [He said that] he had not participated in the campaign[1138] because of the diversions by the Arabs,[1139] but [that] he had sent him both money and grain.[1140] **190** And this benefaction was more moderate than what

---

rom. 3.54; 8.17; Josephus, *Ant.* 5.256; Cassius Dio 238). In Diodorus 33.5.3 and Dionysius, *Ant. rom.* 4.52; 6.77; 11.40 a more elaborate formula is found, which is close to Josephus' phrase here: εἰς ἱκεσίας καὶ δεήσεις τρέπεσθαι ("turn to supplications and petitions").

[1131] The phrase δέησιν προτείνω means "bring a request" here (Rengstorf *s.v.* προτείνω; cf. John Chrysostom, *Hom. Isa. 6:1* 1.2.32 [ed. Dumortier 52]).

[1132] Supplications is what one would expect in this delicate situation (cf. Haman's supplications to Queen Esther in order to pardon his offences, *Ant.* 11.265).

[1133] Josephus perhaps already anticipates the positive outcome for Herod. The parallel report of *War* (1.387) simply states: "Then, without concealing the truth, he spoke openly" (trans. Sievers/Forte in BJP 1a). Herod first gives a survey of his acts as Antony's loyal friend (*Ant.* 15.189-192; cf. *War* 1.388-390) and then moves on to his possible position under Octavian (*Ant.* 15.193; cf. *War* 1.390).

The rare adverb ἀνυποτιμήτως also occurs in *Ant.* 16.27 (cf. -τος in 15.265; 16.402). Its meaning is uncertain: LSJ (*s.v.* ἀνυποτίμητος) gives "that cannot adequately be punished"; Rengstorf (*s.v.*) gives "without fear of punishment, unpunished, exempt from punishment, without excuse" as possible meanings. Cocceius conjectures ἀνεπιτιμήτως ("not to be censured, unpunished," Niese 365), which word does not occur elsewhere in Josephus. The Latin version reads *sine dubitatione*, which is the equivalent of ἀνυποστόλως ("fearlessly") according to Richards and Shutt (1939: 173; Rengstorf [*s.v.*] proposes "undisguised, openly"). This adverb also occurs in *Ant.* 16.69. Both conjectures are unnecessary because the MS tradition is largely univocal and ἀνυποτιμήτως is also attested elsewhere in Josephus (see above). The text makes sense if the meaning given by LSJ is correct.

[1134] The parallel report of *War* (1.388-390) offers Herod's words to Octavian in direct speech. *Antiquities* starts with indirect speech (15.189-191) and switches to direct speech when Herod mentions Cleopatra (15.192-193). The switch puts emphasis on the last part of Herod's speech, focusing on Antony and Cleopatra.

[1135] The phrase repeats *Ant.* 15.162 (see the note to "because of his close friendship with Antony") and 15.183. In the parallel account of *War* Herod discusses the motif of friendship in 1.390. For φιλία ("friendship"), see also *Ant.* 15.193, and for φίλος ("friend"), 15.190.

[1136] The phrase κατὰ (τὴν) δύναμιν ("according to one's ability") is a common expression in Josephus (*Ant.* 3.102, 108, 206; 15.45, 422). It echoes κατὰ τὸ δυνατόν ("as much as possible") in the parallel passage of *War* (1.388).

[1137] The phrase τὰ πράγματα can mean "power, government, administration, etc." (see *Ant.* 15.32 with the note to "the government"). Here it concerns the Commonwealth (*res publica*), i.e., the rule of the Roman Republic (as in 15.109, which passage refers to the Battle of Actium as a contest over the Roman government). Herod had been a very loyal supporter of his patron Antony (see 15.5 with the note to "Antony"), but he did not participate in the battle, as Herod subsequently explains. In *War* 1.388 Herod states that he had devoted himself to Antony in everything because Antony had made him King of Judea (*War* 1.281-285; *Ant.* 14.379-389).

[1138] Instead of στρατεία ("campaign") Josephus uses the closely related noun στρατία ("army") in the parallel report of *War* (1.389), which is more specific: "I promised him [i.e., Antony], once he killed her [i.e., Cleopatra; see *Ant.* 15.191], money, walls for his safety, an army (στρατιὰν), and myself as an ally in war against you" (trans. Sievers/Forte in BJP 1a). The phrase (τῆς) στρατείας κοινωνέω ("participate in the campaign") also occurs in Dionysius, *Ant. rom.* 6.29.1; Plutarch, *Dion* 22.4; Athenaeus 5.55; cf. Diodorus 32.15.7. *War* 1.389 uses the similar noun κοινωνός: he promised himself as "an ally in war against you (κοινωνὸν τοῦ πρὸς σὲ πολέμου)." The motif of Herod's alliance is already taken up in 1.388.

[1139] The parallel account of *War* (1.388) reports the same in different words. The "diversions" of the Nabateans are narrated in *Ant.* 15.108-110 (see the notes to these paragraphs and Kasher 1988: 137). The noun περιολκή can mean "diversion" in a context of war (LSJ *s.v.* II; Rengstorf [*s.v.*] gives "prevention, hindrance" as meanings). It is a *hapax legomenon* in Josephus.

[1140] The parallel report of *War* (1.388) mentions countless supplies of grain (σίτου πολλὰς μυριάδας) as well as military aid (συμμαχία). The grain probably derived from the direct tax on agricultural produce (Udoh 2005: 162).

was appropriate for him to get.[1141] For when a person agrees[1142] to be somebody's friend and realizes that that person is his benefactor,[1143] he must always put himself on the line, risking[1144] his life, body, and resources.[1145] In this his behavior was less than noble.[1146] But this he knew,[1147] at least, that he had acted in a noble fashion[1148] in not abandoning Antony[1149] after he had been defeated in the Battle of Actium[1150] **191** and in not transferring his

---

[1141] In the parallel account of *War* Josephus emphasizes the open-handedness of Herod's benefaction (see the preceding note), but in *Antiquities* he relativizes it and thus introduces the motif of friendship, discussed in the next sentences.

[1142] The participle ὁμολογοῦντα ("agreeing") recalls ὁμολογῶ ("I admit") in the parallel account of *War* (1.388), but the meaning is different.

[1143] The noun εὐεργέτης ("benefactor") is also used in *War* 1.388 in a reference to Antony (see *Ant.* 15.5 and 15.19 with the notes to "a gift to Antony" and "a considerable number of gifts," and 15.193, in which passage Herod returns to this motif).

[1144] The verb συγκινδυνεύω (literally "share someone's danger with him") also occurs in *War* 3.69; 5.283, 419 (Rengstorf *s.v.*; cf. Aristotle, *Rhet.* 1368b; Isocrates, *Hel. enc.* 20; Dionysius, *Ant. rom.* 6.76.1; 10.16.3). The verb is related to the theme of friendship found in Epictetus, *Ench.* 32.3 (and Simplicius, *Comm. Epict.* [ed. Dübner 110-11]).

[1145] The crux of a sound friendship in ancient Greek society was the principle of reciprocity (Blundell 1989: 28-31). One had to support one's friends as much as one could, especially in times of trouble (e.g., Euripides, *Orest.* 727-728; Plato, *Crit.* 44b-45a). Loyalty and faithfulness were important values in friendship ethics (e.g., Theognis 416, 529-530, 811-813, 1151-1152; Blundell 1989: 34-38; Konstan 1997: 56-59). These values remain relevant in the Hellenistic and Early Roman periods for political friends of a ruler (Treu 1972; Gehrke and von Reibnitz 1998). The noun περιουσία ("surplus, wealth") is here added to the common combination of σῶμα ("body") and ψυχή ("soul, life"; see *Ant.* 15.158 with the note to "afflicted in body and soul").

[1146] The phrase ἔλαττον ἢ καλῶς εἶχεν ἀναστραφείς ("his behavior was less than noble") suggests that Herod's performance did not match the standard of friendship; the norm would have been expressed by phrases with ἀναστρέφω ("act") or ἀναστροφή ("behavior, way of life") plus καλῶς ("nobly") and related words (e.g., 2 Macc 6:23; Heb 13:18; Jas 3:13; Clement of Alexandria, *Strom.* 3.11.75; 4.7.46). The statement prepares Octavian for an exceptional example of noble behavior towards friends or patrons (see the next note).

[1147] Niese (366) does not provide punctuation for the second half of the sentence and suggests that the relative pronoun ὧν is corrupt. The structure becomes clear if we assume that ἀλλ' ("but") interrupts the argumentation by moving over to a new perspective on the theme of Herod's friendship with Antony. For a discussion of various types of ἀλλά as discursive interruption, see Basset 1997: 83-89. Plato offers an interesting parallel of ἀλλά with the verb σύνοιδα: Ion says to Socrates: "I cannot gainsay you on that, Socrates, *but this I know* about myself (ἀλλ' ἐκεῖνο ἐμαυτῷ σύνοιδα): that I excel all humans in speaking on Homer ..." (*Ion* 533c, trans. Lamb, adapted; my italics).

[1148] The phrase καλῶς ποιέω ("act nobly, etc.") is very common (e.g., Thucydides 8.37; Plutarch, *Ages.* 9.4; *Phoc.* 27.2; Luke 6:27).

[1149] This is ironic since abandoning Antony is exactly what Herod does during the meeting with Octavian; Antony was still alive (see the next note).

The verb καταλείπω ("abandon") is also used in the parallel account of *War* (1.388).

[1150] Herod argues that remaining faithful to a patron whose situation was desperate was a noble act. In *War* 1.388 Herod makes a similar claim (cf. also Josephus' suggestion in 1.386 that Octavian did not consider Antony to be definitively defeated as long as Herod remained loyal to him). Antony's situation after Actium was hopeless. He had to withdraw to Egypt. Octavian came after him from the East, while Cornelius Gallus, Octavian's future commander of Africa, approached him from the West. Antony attempted to fight a final battle before the gates of Alexandria on 1 August 30 BCE, but his fleet and cavalry deserted. He committed suicide and died in Cleopatra's arms (Plutarch, *Ant.* 74-77; Cassius Dio 51.10; Hölbl 1994: 223-24; Kienast 1999: 71-72). Here Josephus perhaps hints at Cleopatra's treacherous behavior during the Battle of Actium (cf. *Apion* 2.59) or at her attempt to switch camps upon the defeat (cf. Cassius Dio 51.8.6-7; 51.9.5; 51.10.6-9; van Henten 2005a: 130-31). If so, Herod's loyalty to Antony after Actium would stand out even more, though it is plausible that Herod switched camps soon after Antony's defeat (see *Ant.* 15.195 with the note to "every kind of willingness").

expectation[1151] at a time when fortune was clearly passing over to somebody else.[1152] But he took care that he was, if not a worthy fellow-combatant,[1153] then at least a most competent[1154] adviser[1155] of Antony, indicating that the only way[1156] for him to be saved and not be removed from political life [1157] was by putting Cleopatra out of the way.[1158] **192** "For," he said,[1159] "if she had been put out of the way[1160] beforehand, [Antony] would have been able[1161] to maintain his rule[1162] and would have found it easier to come to an

---

[1151] The verb συμμεταβαίνω ("pass over together," Rengstorf s.v.) is a *hapax legomenon* in Josephus. The verb is partly repeated a few words later by the participle μεταβαινούσης ("passing over"). Cf. the parallel report of *War* (1.390), in which Herod places his hope of safety on his renowned loyalty as a friend.

[1152] The statement suggests that Herod was fully aware that Antony's situation was hopeless after Actium (see *Ant.* 15.190 with the note to "defeated in the Battle of Actium"), which makes his enduring loyalty to his patron impressive. Concerning the combination μεταβαίνω plus τύχη ("fortune passes over"), cf. *War* 2.360. For τύχη, see *Ant.* 15.17 with the note to "fortune." In *War* 1.390 Herod states in plain words that God granted Octavian victory and also: "I am defeated together with Antony and, in conjunction with his fortune (μετὰ τῆς ἐκείνου τύχης), I lay down my diadem" (trans. Sievers/Forte in BJP 1a).

[1153] The noun συναγωνιστής ("fellow-fighter") occurs once elsewhere in Josephus, likewise in the Herod narrative of *Antiquities* (16.22; Rengstorf s.v.).

[1154] The translation follows the reading δεξιώτατον ("most competent"), supported by MSS PFV and E and followed by Niese (366). The alternative reading ἀξιώτατον ("most worthy") may have resulted from a scribal adaptation triggered by the previous word ἀξιόχρεων ("outstanding").

[1155] The combination of συναγωνιστής ("fellow-fighter") and σύμβουλος ("adviser") is conventional (see Isocrates, *Ep.* 8.7; Philo, *Somn.* 1.111-112; Josephus, *Ant.* 16.22 [about Herod towards Marcus Agrippa]; Cassius Dio 42.13.2; Hippolytus, *Haer.* 9.7.2). In *War* 1.389 Herod expresses the same thought in different words, while σύμβουλος ("adviser") also occurs.

[1156] The conjecture κἄν of Niese (366), indicating the possible—but not realized—consequences of the condition, is unnecessary. The double καί (followed by the infinitives), attested by the MSS, adds emphasis ("not only ... but also").

[1157] The phrase partly repeats *Ant.* 15.189, in which passage Herod suggests that Antony would have gained the rule over the Romans with Herod's help ("so that the Commonwealth would fall to him"; cf. τὰ πράγματα in 15.189 with τῶν πραγμάτων in 15.191).

[1158] Cleverly Herod puts the blame on Cleopatra, which matches a trend in Roman sources about Antony and Cleopatra, clearly blackening Cleopatra (e.g., Velleius Paterculus 2.85.6; Lucan 10.358-360, 369-370, 374-375; Pliny the Elder 9.119; Becher 1966: 32, 63-68, 75-77, 108-10, 182-83; Zanker 1988: 58-60). Antony was never declared an enemy of state by the Romans (Kasher 1988: 135). In the parallel report of *War* (1.389) Herod also states that he had advised Antony to kill Cleopatra: "I told him that the death of Cleopatra was the only remedy (μίαν ... διόρθωσιν) for his misfortunes" (trans. BJP 1a; the word μίαν is shared with *Ant.* 15.191).

Otto (1913: 47) argues that Herod's speech derives from his memoirs and that the king probably made a statement about his advice to kill Cleopatra as an attempt to show his loyalty to the Roman people. However, Josephus usually crafts speeches (see *Ant.* 15.126 with the note to "a speech"), which may imply that this point—like most other information in speeches—flowed out of his own pen. This interpretation is supported by the observation that Herod's blaming of Cleopatra links up with Josephus' suggestion that Antony's deeds resulted out of his love for Cleopatra (*War* 1.243), whereas this was only partly true. An additional reason for doubting the historicity of this point is that it matches the very negative assessment of Cleopatra in Roman sources, which obviously date from after Herod's meeting with Octavian (see also *Ant.* 15.96-103 about Cleopatra's visit to Herod and Herod's rejected plan to murder her, which report perhaps anticipates Herod's reference to his advice to kill Cleopatra). Schalit (2001: 127-29) argues that the detail may be historical since it would demonstrate that serving the interests of Rome was Herod's most important goal, already when being Antony's client. Schalit further thinks that Herod had not given this advice to Antony and that Octavian most probably did not believe him.

[1159] At this point Josephus switches to direct speech, which highlights the crucial role of Cleopatra in Antony's ruin (see the preceding note).

[1160] The verb προαναιρέω ("put out of the way," Rengstorf s.v.) occurs 3 times elswhere in Josephus, and only in *Antiquities*: 14.344; 15.89 (with Cleopatra as subject); 20.149.

[1161] The verb ὕπειμι ("be possible," Rengstorf s.v.) is a *hapax legomenon* in Josephus (but cf. the variant reading in *Ant.* 14.81).

[1162] This is the third time in his speech that Herod refers to the possibility that Antony would have been able to retain his power or even to become the sole ruler

agreement with you rather than be enemies.[1163] But, unprofitably for him—and fortunately for you[1164]—he did not seriously consider any of these [options], and he preferred[1165] to disregard this advice.[1166] **193** So, if you condemn in accordance with your anger towards Antony[1167] also my goodwill [towards him], there is no way I could deny what I have done.[1168] I am not ashamed[1169] to publicly state my loyalty to him.[1170] Yet if you, in disregarding the personal aspect,[1171] carefully look at what kind of person I am to my benefactors and what kind of friend I am,[1172] you will have the possibility of knowing me through what has already happened.[1173] For, with a [mere] change of name,[1174] the solid

---

of Rome (see the repetitions of phrases with πράγματα ["government, rule, power"] in *Ant*. 15.189, 191-192).

[1163] The implicit point at the background of this statement is probably that Antony would have acted much more sensibly had he not been under the bad influence of Cleopatra, who was apparently able to manipulate him because of his love for her (*War* 1.243, 359; *Ant*. 14.324; 15.88, 93, 101). The motif is explicit in the parallel report of *War* (1.389-390): "... his passionate love for Cleopatra ... stopped up his ears" (trans. Sievers/Forte in BJP 1a).

[1164] The parallelism consisting of 2 adverbial phrases followed by a personal pronoun in the dative, emphasizing the contrast between Antony and Octavian, adds to Herod's rhetoric. Both adverbs stand out in Josephus' vocabulary: ἀλυσιτελῶς ("unprofitably," Rengstorf *s.v.* ἀλυσιτελής) occurs once elsewhere (*Ant*. 16.224, as an adjective), and συμφερόντως ("fortunately," Rengstorf *s.v.*: "for the benefit of") is a *hapax legomenon*.

[1165] The verb προτιμάω (here "prefer," Rengstorf *s.v.*) also occurs in *Ant*. 15.209.

[1166] The noun ἀβουλία (literally "ill-advisedness"; cf. *Ant*. 2.163; 13.173; 17.108) may be a double entendre, stating that Antony refused to follow Herod's counsel and hinting at Cleopatra's wicked advice for him, either in general or during the Battle of Actium. In *Apion* 2.59 Josephus emphasizes that Cleopatra deserted Antony during the battle (van Henten 2005a: 131; see also *War* 1.390).

[1167] This passage introduces a turn in Herod's speech by focusing on the king's future under the new regime of Octavian. Herod cleverly first formulates Octavian's presumptive response to his speech in order to prepare for 2 related points that may change Octavian's mind: 1) Herod's frankness about his loyalty to Antony, and 2) the recall of the motif of friendship by way of analogy, which turns his friendship with Antony into a powerful argument that he could also be a most loyal friend to Octavian. Octavian's anger is mentioned in *War* 1.393, in connection with Antony's friend Alexas (see *Ant*. 15.197).

[1168] Herod thus kills 2 birds with 1 stone: he demonstrates his frankness and his pride about his loyalty to Antony, and he offers a new perspective by focusing upon the deeds from which Antony had benefited so much (cf. the repetition of πράσσω in *Ant*. 15.188-189, 193: τῶν πεπραγμένων, πρᾶξαι, and τῶν πεπραγμένων).

[1169] The verb ἀπαξιόω ("be ashamed," Rengstorf *s.v.*) occurs once elsewhere in Josephus (*Ant*. 18.47).

[1170] Here the substantive εὔνοια expresses the loyalty of a client to his patron and vice versa (see its repetition in *Ant*. 15.194, concerning Octavian's attitude towards Herod). Herod refers to the close friendship between him and Antony (see 15.78 and 15.189 with the note to "extraordinary friendship with Antony"). The noun also implies goodwill towards each other as well as mutual benefactions, gifts, and favors (Shaw 1993: 185-89).

[1171] Rengstorf (*s.v.* πρόσωπον) gives "disregard the person (i.e., to look at the matter itself)" as meaning for the rare phrase τὸ πρόσωπον ἀνελών (but adds a question mark). This may be correct, though the phrase can refer to Herod's personal involvement, i.e., his relationship with Antony, as well as to Antony himself. The latter is more probable given Herod's hint at a change of names later on in this paragraph. It is unlikely that the phrase refers to Herod since Herod's argument builds exactly on the way he acts in the context of a friendship.

[1172] This is the main point of Herod's argument: his behavior as a friend of Antony (which includes his role as friendly king). The topic has been raised before in Herod's impressive speech (see *Ant*. 15.189-190 with notes). The phrase ποῖος φίλος ἐξετάζοις ("examine ... what kind of friend") echoes the final statement in the *War* version of Herod's speech (1.390): "... assuming that it will be asked (ἐξετασθήσεσθαι) not whose friend, but what kind of friend (ποταπὸς φίλος), I have been" (trans. BJP 1a).

[1173] Herod invites Octavian to reflect upon Herod's relationship with Antony by way of analogy. The survey of his acts as a friend of Antony (*Ant*. 15.189-192; cf. *War* 1.388-390) aims to show that Herod could be a very loyal and useful friend of Octavian as well.

[1174] I.e., Octavian's name instead of Antony's.

[1175] Phrases with φιλία ("friendship") and βέβαιος/βεβαίως ("solid") are common from Thucydides onward (e.g., 2.7.3; 3.10.1; Plato, *Menex*. 244a; *Symp*. 182c, 209c; Isocrates, *Nic*. 54; Diodorus 3.7.2; 13.32.5;

friendship[1175] can—as far as I am concerned[1176]—remain no less distinguished."[1177]

(6.7) 194 By saying this and by showing his total[1178] independence of spirit,[1179] he very much[1180] attracted Caesar, who was magnanimous and generous,[1181] so that the grounds for the accusations[1182] by this time resulted in [Caesar's] benevolence to him.[1183] **195** And [Caesar] returned the diadem to him,[1184] urging him to behave[1185] towards him in no less a [loyal] way than he had previously done towards Antony.[1186] He treated him with every

---

15.30.5; Plutarch, *Mor*. [*Amic. mult.*] 93c). The phrase τὸ βέβαιον plus genitive perhaps echoes Thucydides 2.89 (cf. Marcus-Wikgren 92 n. *a*).

[1176] Here the argument on the basis of analogy (see above) becomes explicit (cf. also the continuation of the sentence: "no less distinguished"). Herod suggests that he will be as loyal to Octavian as he has been to Antony. At the same time his formulation remains careful, focusing only on his side of the relationship and leaving it to Octavian to decide whether or not such a new relationship should be established. The phrase ἐν ἡμῖν expresses Herod's involvement ("in my hands, within my reach," LSJ *s.v.* ἐν A I.6).

[1177] The verb εὐδοκιμέω means "be distinguished" here (LSJ *s.v.* 1).

[1178] The word παράπαν ("altogether") appears once elsewhere in Josephus (*Apion* 1.199). The combination of παράπαν and ἐμφαίνω ("show altogether") also occurs in Philo, *Conf.* 69; Cassius Dio 12.43.25.

[1179] The phrase summarizes well Herod's attitude in his speech to Octavian. Rengstorf (*s.v.* ἐλευθέριος) suggests several meanings for τὸ ἐλευθέριον: "magnanimity, liberality, frankness" (with the latter being given as meaning here). Philo's *Every Good Man is Free* offers a detailed discussion of the concept of freedom of spirit, an ideal of several Hellenistic philosophical schools. The Jewish Essenes exemplify it. It is also highlighted by non-Jews belonging to Hellenistic philosophical schools, e.g., the Cynic philosopher Diogenes of Sinope (Philo, *Prob.* 121-124, also 63, 113, 143; cf. Aristotle, *Physiogn.* 809b, 811a; Dionysius, *Ant. rom.* 6.38.2; 6.42.1).

[1180] This is a free rendition of the *litotes* "not moderately," which frequently occurs in Josephus (*War* 2.631; *Ant.* 15.276; 16.81, 230, 294; 20.83, 109; *Life* 313, 371; *Apion* 1.243; 2.8).

[1181] The adjective φιλότιμος (literally "loving honor") means "magnanimous" here according to Rengstorf (*s.v.*), though the word could also express Octavian's admiration for Herod's frank and noble performance and mean "loving distinction." This interpretation matches Octavian's statement in *War* 1.391 that he was envisioning "the most brilliant hopes (λαμπροτάτας ἐλπίδας ἔχω) in your [e.g., Herod's] high-mindedness (τοῦ σοῦ φρονήματος)" (trans. BJP 1a). Rengstorf (*s.v.*) gives "generous" as meaning for λαμπρός, which adjective can also mean "brilliant" (cf. *War* 1.391; see above). Both φιλότιμος and λαμπρός appear together as adverbs in *Ant.* 9.59, 272.

[1182] This appears to be rhetoric and may derive from Herod's memoirs or from Josephus himself: there is no reference whatsoever to accusations against Herod in the preceding narrative. The passage implies that Herod's analogy about friendship persuaded Octavian. The noun σύστασις ("beginning, basis," Rengstorf *s.v.*) is a *hapax legomenon* in Josephus, but it does also occur in the summary of book 1 of *Antiquities*, in which case it refers to the beginning of the world (Sievers 2007: 281).

[1183] Herod's friendship with Antony could have led to a charge against him (see the preceding note) but leads instead to the opposite result: another friendship, this time with Octavian. About εὔνοια, see *Ant.* 15.193. Octavian probably considered the possible benefits on the basis of the king's previous performance and realized that Herod was the best person to act as friendly king of the Romans in Judea (Baumann 1983: 194-95): Herod had been successful so far, and there was no alternative candidate to rule over Judea (Stern 1974b: 234-35). Octavian continued Antony's policy of relying on client kingdoms in the East. Herod was not the only friendly king appointed by Antony who was maintained by Octavian: King Archelaus of Cappadocia, King Amyntas of Galatia, and King Polemon of Pontus also remained in office (Buchheim 1960: 56, 59).

[1184] I.e., Herod. The gesture links up with *Ant.* 15.187, which passage reports that Herod removed his diadem (see the note to "he removed the diadem" and cf. *War* 1.393).

[1185] The parallel passage of *War* (1.391-392) gives Octavian's response in direct speech.

[1186] Interestingly, Octavian's call applies the analogy between the friendship of Herod and Antony and the one of Herod and himself, on which Herod had been focusing (*Ant.* 15.189-193). The analogy is highlighted by a parallel structure with a repetition of περί as well as by alliteration (with *p* as the main consonant sound). The verb φαίνομαι means "appear/prove to be" here (Rengstorf *s.v.* φαίνω). In *War* 1.391 Octavian acknowledges that Herod was a defender of friendship.

[1187] The phrase διὰ τιμῆς ἄγω (τινα) ("honor [someone]") is a fixed expression (Aeschylus, *Fragm.* 9A 68 [ed. Mette 24]; Josephus, *Ant.* 5.185; 20.182; *Life*

honor,[1187] adding that Didius[1188] had written[1189] that Herod had assisted him in the matters of the gladiators with every kind of willingness.[1190]

196 Having been honored by such a reception[1191] and seeing, beyond his expectations,[1192] that the throne was more secure for him[1193] than in the beginning[1194]—through Caesar's gift[1195] and the Romans' decree[1196] which Caesar had composed to make things secure for him[1197]—[Herod] escorted Caesar towards Egypt.[1198] He gave him[1199] and his friends more

Herod returns home and receives Caesar with royal service.
War 1.394-395

273, 414; Appian, *Bell. civ.* 3.11.80; Lucian, *Fug.* 3.11; *Prom. es* 4; Aelian, *Nat. an.* 10.16; Synesius, *Ep.* 29 line 3 [ed. Hercher 652]; LSJ *s.v.* ἄγω V).

[1188] Several names have been transmitted by the MSS. Niese (367) offers with MS P καταιδιος as reading (cf. MSS FV) but conjectures καὶ Δίδιος ("and Didius"). This matches Hudson's earlier conjecture Κύιντος Δίδιος ("Quintus Didius"), based on a passage in Cassius Dio (51.7), which probably explains the background of Josephus' information. MSS LAMW read Καπίδιος ("Capidius"), which does not make sense since there is no Roman official attested with that name. The readings of the MSS, as well as the name Ventidius given by the parallel passage of *War* (Βεντίδιος, 1.392), may all go back to the name Didius (note the similar ending -ιδιος of all the readings). Octavian appointed Quintus Didius governor of Syria briefly after the Battle of Actium. Didius helped Octavian with the final elimination of Antony: he persuaded the Nabateans to destroy the fleet of Antony and Cleopatra on the Red Sea, prevented a group of Antony's gladiators from assisting Antony after Actium (Kasher 1988: 141-42), and helped them to settle at Daphne near Antioch (Cassius Dio 51.7).

[1189] In *War* 1.392 the Greek MSS attest to the name Ventidius in connection with this message written to Octavian (see the previous note).

[1190] The statement presupposes that Herod helped Quintus Didius in blocking the road to Antony's gladiators, though Cassius Dio does not confirm this (51.7; Marcus-Wikgren 93 n. *c*). If the detail is reliable, it implies that Herod decided to switch camps before the journey to Rhodes. A passage in Plutarch (*Ant.* 71) suggests that Herod went over to Octavian soon after Actium. Kasher (1988: 134-48) argues that Herod was aiming at a change already before Actium (see *Ant.* 15.110 with the note to "if the one would suffer badly from the other"). *War* 1.392 is slightly more specific by referring to military assistance (συμμαχία) from Herod.

[1191] For phrases similar to ἀποδοχῆς ἠξιωμένος ("having been granted a reception"), see Diodorus 15.81.4; Diogenes Laertius 9.24. It echoes the parallel passage of *War* (1.391), in which Octavian says that Herod was "worthy of (ἄξιος ... εἶ) ruling over many people" (trans. Sievers/Forte in BJP 1a). The noun ἀποδόχη ("reception") occurs in Josephus exclusively in *Antiquities* (6.347; 12.94; 18.274).

[1192] The expression παρ' ἐλπίδας ("beyond [his] expectations") frequently occurs in *Antiquities* (e.g., 1.236; 2.57, 193; 4.8; 5.359), while the singular παρ' ἐλπίδα is common in *War* (e.g., 1.34, 123, 192, but cf. the plural in 6.57).

[1193] In the parallel passage of *War* (1.391) Octavian states the same in fewer words: "... stay safe and rule now with more security (βασίλευε νῦν βεβαιότερον)" (trans. Sievers/Forte in BJP 1a). The word βέβαιος ("solid, secure") is repeated in the next sub clause (see *Ant.* 15.193 and *War* 1.391-392).

[1194] The passage refers in a very abstract way to Herod's appointment as king by the Romans in 40 BCE (*War* 1.281-285; *Ant.* 14.379-389). The phrase ἐξ ὑπαρχῆς ("in/from the beginning," LSJ *s.v.* ὑπαρχή II) occurs once elsewhere in Josephus (*Ant.* 15.316; Rengstorf *s.v.* ὑπαρχή, who suggests "anew" as meaning). The adverb πάλιν ("again, in turn") is redundant in clauses that concern a return to an earlier situation (Blass, Debrunner, and Rehkopf 1976: 413-14).

[1195] Cf. Braund 1984: 27: "Gifts were often conferred upon kings together with recognition." The phrase δόσει Καίσαρος ("through Caesar's gift") is additional to the vocabulary in the parallel passage of *War* (1.392). It forms a parallelism with δόγματι Ῥωμαίων (see the next note), which perhaps echoes Herod's first appointment as king: Antony took the initiative to that appointment, and it was ratified by the Senate in a decree (*War* 1.283-285; *Ant.* 14.382, 385-386, 388-389).

[1196] Instead of by a decree (δόγμα) of the Romans, *War* 1.392-393 reports that Octavian made public the confirmation of Herod's kingdom by means of a proper decree (δόγματι). The extremely positive note of the decree in *War* ("... having placed the diadem on him, he [i.e., Caesar] made known this privilege by a decree, in which he spoke magnanimously and at length in praise of the man ...," 1.393, trans. Sievers/Forte in BJP 1a) is absent in *Antiquities*, which fits the latter's more critical trend about Herod.

[1197] The parallel passage of *War* (1.391) also has the adjective βέβαιος (see the note to "more secure for him" above), which refers to the written confirmation of Herod's rule. Stern (1974b: 237) and Schalit (2001: 147) suggest that the earlier ratification of Herod's rule by the Roman Senate was renewed by Octavian.

[1198] Herod had provided a similar service to Antony

presents than he could afford,[1200] displaying every kind of generosity.[1201] **197** He also asked for Alexas,[1202] one of Antony's intimates, to suffer nothing fatal,[1203] but he did not obtain this because Caesar was already bound by an oath.[1204] **198** And he returned again to Judea,[1205] with more honor and freedom of action.[1206] He caused consternation[1207] among those who had expected the opposite.[1208] He always seemed to gain in splendor[1209] when he came out of the dangers,[1210] in line with God's favor.[1211] So[1212] he straightaway dealt with

---

upon his visit to him when Antony was marching against the Parthians (see *Ant.* 15.80 with the note to "he had escorted Antony to the Parthians," also 15.198).

[1199] I.e., Octavian.

[1200] This is the self-evident expression of gratitude to one's patron by a friendly king (see *Ant.* 15.5 with the note to "Antony" about Herod giving presents to Antony and his friends). Here Josephus emphasizes that Herod went beyond his resources (δωρησάμενος ὑπὲρ δύναμιν). This subtle criticism is absent in *War* 1.393, which simply states that Herod placated Octavian with gifts (δώροις ἐπιμειλιξάμενος). The expression ὑπὲρ δύναμιν ("beyond [his] strength/resources") again occurs in *Ant.* 16.154 in a reference to Herod (see also *War* 1.173, 328; *Ant.* 18.291-292).

[1201] The phrase (πᾶσαν) ἐμφαίνων μεγαλοψυχίαν repeats *Ant.* 15.48 (see the note to "he showed the magnanimity") about Herod's magnanimity towards Alexandra, who had tried to escape with her son. Here Josephus uses even stronger language by adding πᾶσαν ("every").

[1202] The Greek MSS and the Latin version read Ἀλέξανδρον-*Alexandrum* ("Alexander"), but in the parallel passage of *War* (1.393) the Greek MSS read Ἀλέξαν ("Alexas," Niese 367). It is much more probable that the shorter and less well-known name Ἀλέξαν resulted into Ἀλέξανδρον because of a scribal misunderstanding than that Ἀλέξανδρον was abbreviated into Ἀλέξαν. It is therefore likely that the name Alexas is original (Niese 377; Marcus-Wikgren 94; Schalit 1968: 8). Alexas was apparently a close friend (συνήθης) of Mark Antony. Plutarch (*Ant.* 72) notes that Alexas was sent to Herod in order to persuade the king to remain faithful to Antony, but that he betrayed Antony and went to Octavian while relying on Herod. He was later executed by Octavian. *War* 1.393 depicts Alexas as a "friend" of Antony (about Antony's friends, see *Ant.* 15.5 with the note to "the friends around him").

[1203] For the phrase μηδὲν ἀνήκεστόν παθεῖν ("suffer nothing fatal"), see *Ant.* 15.131 with the note to "suffer irreparable harm."

[1204] The parallel report of *War* (1.393) gives a different reason for Octavian's refusal to meet Herod's request. It highlights Octavian's angriness because of many grievous reproaches against Alexas. *Antiquities* presents Octavian's decision in a more positive light.

[1205] This phrase marks the end of Josephus' report about Herod's meeting with Octavian; cf. the similar conclusion of the narrative about a meeting of Herod and 2 of his sons with Octavian in *Ant.* 16.130 (concluding 16.90-129).

[1206] Once again Herod survived a serious crisis and came out well. His journey to Antony in order to account for the death of Aristobulus III (*Ant.* 15.63-80) had also ended very well: Antony granted him several honors (15.77). The nouns παρρησία (here meaning "freedom of," Rengstorf *s.v.*; cf. 15.44) and τιμή ("honor") also appear as a pair in 15.44 (concerning Alexandra).

[1207] The verb παρέχω ("procure, cause, etc.") with ἔκπληξις ("consternation") as object is common from Thucydides onward (e.g., 4.55.3; 6.70.1; 6.98.2; Diodorus 14.72.5; Josephus, *Ant.* 2.83; 7.157; Plutarch, *Cam.* 3.3; *Pyrrh.* 18.1; Arrian, *Anab.* 1.9.2; 6.3.4).

[1208] This remark focuses on Herod's opponents, who had been very doubtful about a positive outcome for Herod following the Roman change of power. Previously Josephus has indicated that Herod's enemies were hoping for political change (see *Ant.* 15.162-163). In this light it is obvious that they were very disappointed with the result of Herod's visit to Octavian (cf. 15.166 about Alexandra's hope that Herod would be replaced as king). The verb προσδοκάω ("expect") plus (τὰ) ἐναντία ("[the] opposite") also occurs in *Ant.* 6.233; cf. Appian, *Bell. civ.* 2.17.120.

[1209] The noun λαμπρότερον ("more splendor") echoes λαμπροτάτας/λαμπρόν ("[most] brilliant, generous") in *War* 1.391; *Ant.* 15.194.

[1210] The passage formulates a *leitmotiv* of the Herod narrative in *Antiquities*: Herod was very successful as ruler of the Jews because of God's support (see also the next note). As a result the king escaped serious dangers several times (see 14.177 concerning Herod's trial in Jerusalem and 14.455 on the collapse of a house in which Herod was staying; Josephus comments that this rescue made everybody believe that Herod was a favorite of God [Ἡρώδην εἶναι θεοφιλῆ] since he had escaped such a great and unexpected danger [μέγαν οὕτω καὶ παράδοξον διαφυγόντα κίνδυνον]). The verb προσεπικτάομαι ("gain even more," Rengstorf *s.v.*) is a *hapax legomenon* in Josephus.

[1211] God as determining factor is a major motif in *Antiquities* (van Henten and Huitink 2007: 219-21). The

the reception for Caesar,[1213] who was about to invade Egypt from Syria.[1214] **199** And when he [Caesar] arrived,[1215] he [Herod] received him in Ptolemais[1216] with every royal service.[1217] He provided welcoming gifts to his army and abundant provisions.[1218] He was even counted among his [Caesar's] most loyal friends.[1219] When [Caesar] was mustering his soldiers, he [Herod] was riding together with him.[1220] He received [Caesar] and his friends in 150

Manaemus episode (15.373-379, absent in *War*) elaborates the theme of God supporting Herod.

The noun εὐμένεια ("goodwill, favor") in reference to God also occurs in *Ant.* 1.111; 2.291; 3.46; 5.213; 8.119, 297 (cf. Lucian, *Merc. cond.* 1). In *Ant.* 16.104 it concerns Herod's and Octavian's attitudes towards Herod's sons Alexander and Aristobulus IV.

[1212] MSS PVFE add μέν ("then").

[1213] There seems to be an inconsistency in the narrative flow: Josephus has already very briefly reported in *Ant.* 15.196 that Herod escorted Octavian on his way to Egypt. In 15.198 the geographical focus changes to Judea, and Herod's opponents at home are the focalizers of the first part of the paragraph (see the note to "those who had expected the opposite" above). Now the focus is again on Octavian and his expedition to Egypt. In 15.202 Josephus definitely switches to the situation in the Judean kingdom (in fact, to Herod's family matters). The noun ὑποδοχή ("reception, entertainment") echoes ἀποδοχή ("reception, approval") in 15.196 (referring to Herod), which may highlight the reciprocal aspect of the new relationship between Herod and Octavian. Octavian's reception is elaborated in 15.199.

[1214] The parallel narrative of *War* (1.394) also presupposes that Octavian marched to Egypt coming from Syria. About Octavian's invasion of Egypt, see *Ant.* 15.187 with the note to "Caesar" and 15.190 with the note to "defeated in the Battle of Actium."

The variant reading ἐμβαλεῖν, attested by MSS LAMW and the excerpts for εἰσβαλεῖν (Niese 367), hardly makes a difference since both εἰσβάλλω and ἐμβάλλω probably mean "invade" here (Rengstorf *s.v.*).

[1215] The context implies that Octavian arrived at the border of Herod's territory. Cf. *Ant.* 15.21 about Hyrcanus II's return to Judea, in which passage the phrase ἐπειδὴ παρῆν ("when he arrived") is also used.

[1216] Ptolemais (Πτολεμαΐς) is the Hellenistic name of the city of Acco, on the Phoenician coast. Ptolemy II Philadelphus refounded the city and gave it a new name (Möller and Schmitt 1976: 156-57; Tsafrir, Di Segni, and Green 1994: 204-05). Antony granted Ptolemais and other coastal cities to Cleopatra (see *Ant.* 15.95 with the notes to "the cities between the River Eleutherus and Egypt"). Octavian apparently marched along the coastal road from Syria to the south. Herod picked him up in Ptolemais, when Octavian was near Herod's kingdom (see the map in Tsafrir, Di Segni, and Green 1994: 12). *War* 1.394 also mentions Ptolemais, though not that Herod picked up Octavian. Octavian seems to have taken the same route on returning from Egypt (*Ant.* 15.218, which refers to Antioch in Syria).

[1217] MSS PFVE and the excerpts read πάσῃ τῇ βασιλικῇ τιμῇ ("with every royal honor") instead of πάσῃ τῇ βασιλικῇ θεραπείᾳ ("with every royal service," Niese 367). The variant reading is paralleled by Herodian 7.10.5, Niese's reading by Sozomen 9.8.5. The change from the less common word θεραπείᾳ to τιμῇ is more obvious than the alternative change. Moreover, τιμῇ may have slipped into the textual tradition because of the preceding phrase πλείονι τιμῇ (*Ant.* 15.198; cf. *War* 1.396).

The verb δέχομαι ("receive") and the adjectives βασιλικός ("royal") and πᾶς ("every") also occur in the parallel passage of *War* (1.394, παντὶ τῷ βασιλικῷ πλούτῳ δεξάμενος "received him ... with all royal luxuries," trans. Sievers/Forte in BJP 1a).

[1218] Herod's services to Octavian and his soldiers belong to the conventional favors of a client towards his patron (see *Ant.* 15.5 with the note to "Antony"; 15.80, and cf. *War* 1.175 on Antipater's assistance to Gabinius, who was on the way to Egypt). Tigranes made similar contributions to Pompey's troops (Plutarch, *Pomp.* 33.5; Braund 1984: 80 with n. 48). Yet some of Herod's services mentioned in *Ant.* 15.199-200 clearly stand out. The phrase τῶν ἐπιτηδείων ἀφθονία ("abundance of supplies/provisions") is common (e.g., Diodorus 14.21.6; 17.65.2; Philo, *Decal.* 16; *Det.* 113; *Spec.* 2.158; Josephus, *War* 1.299, 304; 7.277; *Ant.* 1.181; Herodian 8.5.3). *Ant.* 1.181 also mentions ξένια ("hospitable reception, gifts") together with abundant provisions, in connection with Melchizedek's reception of Abraham's army (cf. *War* 6.615; *Ant.* 14.131). The parallel passage of *War* (1.395) mentions ὕδωρ ἄφθονον ("plenty of water") and states that Herod took care that Octavian's army did not lack any supplies (οὐδὲ ἔστιν ὅ τι τῶν ἐπιτηδείων ἐνεδέησεν τῇ δυνάμει).

[1219] The superlative εὐνούστατος ("most loyal") expresses Herod's attitude towards Octavian, though Octavian apparently also considered Herod to be a most loyal "friend." The passive form of ἐξετάζω means "be counted" here (Rengstorf *s.v.*) and echoes the noun ἐξέτασις ("examination, muster") in the parallel passage of *War* (1.394), though with a clearly different meaning (see the next note).

[1220] This passage closely parallels *War* 1.394, which states that Herod was riding at Octavian's side when

apartments,[1221] all furnished with great extravagance and plenty of service.[1222] **200** He also provided the supplies of pressing matters for them when they were crossing the desert,[1223] so that neither wine nor water,[1224] which was much needed by the soldiers,[1225] would be lacking. He gave to Caesar himself truly 800 talents[1226] and led everyone form the view [1227] that the services he was displaying were much bigger and more splendid than the kingdom[1228] he really controlled.[1229] **201** This brought him [Caesar] all the more to trust[1230]

Octavian was reviewing his troops near Ptolemais. *War* 1.394 shares several words with *Ant*. 15.199: συνιππάζομαι ("ride at someone's side," with one further occurrence in Josephus: *Ant*. 16.314; Rengstorf *s.v.*), δύναμις ("force," in the plural in *Antiquities*), and ἐξετάζω ("be counted")/ἐξέτασις ("muster"; see the previous note). The verb ἐκτάττω ("muster [troops for review or battle]," Rengstorf *s.v.*) also occurs in *War* 5.349; *Ant*. 3.50; 4.68 (in a variant reading).

[1221] The Greek text is probably corrupt: the noun ἀνδράσιν (the dative plural of ἀνήρ ["man"]) does not fit the context (see also the next note). Hudson's conjecture ἀνδρῶσιν ("residences, apartments," the dative plural of ἀνδρών ["hall/room/residence for men," Rengstorf *s.v.*]; cf. *War* 2.503; *Ant*. 5.177; 16.164) is helpful. It is inspired by the Latin version *domibus* ("houses") and taken over by Niese (367). Nevertheless, one or more words seem to be missing. The text cannot be corrected on the basis of the parallel report of *War* because the detail is missing in *War* 1.394-395. A hundred and fifty apartments, even if they had only one room, is a huge number and does not seem very realistic if one compares this with what we know about the sizes of Herod's buildings, including his palaces (Netzer 2006: 3-201). *War* 1.394 reports a much more modest (and more plausible) reception of Octavian: "... he entertained (εἰστίασεν) him and all his friends with a banquet" (trans. Sievers/Forte in BJP 1a).

[1222] If the reading ἀνδράσιν ("men"; see the preceding note) is correct, this part of the sentence could be translated as "with hundred and fifty men, all trained to provide extravagant and plenty service." The verb ἀσκέω can mean "equip, furnish" as well as "train, exercise" (Rengstorf *s.v.*). The substantive πλοῦτος ("riches, wealth") is the only noun that also occurs in the parallel account of *War* (1.394).

[1223] Similar information is found in the parallel passage of *War* (1.395), which refers to Pelusium. The route from the Palestinian coast to Egypt, i.e., from Raphia to Pelusium (at the edge of the northeastern Nile Delta, *War* 1.175; cf. Cassius Dio 51.9.5-6), was notoriously difficult (*War* 4.608-610; Plutarch, *Ant*. 3) because it included a passage through the northwest of the Negev Desert and the north of the Sinai Desert. The shortage of water is highlighted by the adjective ἄνυδρος (literally "without/short on water," Rengstorf *s.v.*; the word also occurs in *War* 1.395), which is echoed by ὕδωρ ("water") in the next sub-clause (cf. *War* 1.395).

There were several Roman roads from the east to Pelusium, including one going north of Lake Serbonitis via Mount Casius (for further details, see the map of Eretz Israel and the Sinai during the Hellenistic, Roman, and Byzantine periods in Tsafrir, Di Segni, and Green 1994).

[1224] The phrase μήτε οἴνου μήτε ὕδατος ("wine nor water") is not necessarily rhetorical (although wine is not mentioned in the parallel account of *War* [1.394-395]). Wine (either *aceta*, sour wine, or *vinum*, vintage wine) was part of the regular diet of the Roman soldiers, which further consisted of bread, water, meat, oil, vegetables, and salt (Davies 1971; Roth 1999: 18-44). Wine was usually mixed with water. Josephus' reference to wine is perhaps inspired by *War* 1.394, about concerning Herod's entertaining of the regular soldiers (a passage absent in *Antiquities*): "... he also gave the rest of the army everything for a feast" (trans. BJP 1a).

[1225] *Antiquities* shares the noun στρατιώταις ("soldiers") with the parallel account of *War* (1.395).

[1226] The enormous gift (compare the sum of, probably, 200 talents for Herod's lease of territories from Cleopatra found in *Ant*. 15.106-107) is not mentioned in *War* 1.394-395.

[1227] *Antiquities* shares the verb παρίστημι ("supply, cause, put in an appearance") with the parallel passage of *War* (1.395). The phrase ἔννοιαν λαβεῖν ("form an idea/a design," LSJ *s.v.* ἔννοια I.2) is common (e.g., Euripides, *Hipp*. 1027; Polybius 1.57.2; Philo, *Somn*. 1.68; Plutarch, *Mor*. [*Quaest. plat.*] 1010a; [*Comm. not.*] 1072b).

[1228] The noun βασιλεία ("kingdom") also occurs in the parallel passage of *War* (1.395).

[1229] *War* 1.395 expresses the same impression in different words and in a negative formulation (cf. "much too small" in *War* with "much bigger" in *Ant*. 15.200): "The thought forced itself both upon Caesar himself and his soldiers that Herod's realm was much too small in comparison with what he had provided them" (trans. Sievers/Forte in BJP 1a). Another slight difference is the reference to the focalizers: "Caesar himself and his soldiers" in *War*, and "all" in *Antiquities*. As usual Josephus embellishes the parallel material from *War* in *Antiquities*. This is apparent from the addition "more

his loyalty and enthusiasm.[1231] He [Herod] gained the most for himself[1232] by adapting his generosity[1233] to the needs of the situation.[1234] And when they[1235] returned from Egypt,[1236] he displayed nothing less by way of service[1237] than the first time.[1238]

(7.1) 202 Yet, when he came to the kingdom that time,[1239] he found on his arrival that

Crisis in Herod's family.

---

splendid." For a similar statement, see *Ant.* 16.141 (in connection with the festivities after the completion of Caesarea Maritima).

[1230] The noun πίστις means "faith (or trust) in something" here, i.e., faith in Herod's loyalty and devotion to Octavian (cf. Josephus' use of πίστις in *Ant.* 15.87; 17.246; 19.58; Lindsay 1993: 78, 99).

[1231] The substantive προθυμία ("willingness, eagerness") can have several nuances (Rengstorf *s.v.*); "personal affection" would be a further meaning fitting the context. The nouns εὔνοια ("loyalty") and προθυμία also occur as a pair in *Ant.* 6.82; 8.57; 17.195 (cf. Demosthenes, *Or.* 18.286, 312; Polybius 2.50.3; Dionysius, *Ant. rom.* 10.16.4; Plutarch, *Brut.* 39.1; *Caes.* 16.1; *Dion* 10.4; Herodian 6.8.8).

[1232] For the phrase πλεῖστον ἠνέγκατο ("he gained the most for himself"), cf. Plutarch, *Ant.* 22.5, and see LSJ *s.v.* φέρω A.VI.3.

[1233] About μεγαλοψυχία ("generosity, magnanimity") as a central characteristic of Herod, see *Ant.* 15.48 with the note to "the magnanimity."

[1234] This concluding statement by the narrator implies high praise for Herod: it highlights the king's generosity once elsewhere (cf. *Ant.* 15.199-200) and adds that he was prudent since he applied this virtue on a scale that matched the circumstances. Combining this with the information given in the context, the result is that Herod was wise to reward Octavian in an extremely generous way. This is basically confirmed by the tenor of the Herod narrative in *Antiquities*. The meeting at Rhodes was crucial for the continuation of Herod's rule, and the grandiose services as Herod's response to Octavian's establishment of the client relationship later turned out to be a very good investment.

[1235] I.e., Caesar and his friends, or Caesar and his soldiers (see *Ant.* 15.200 and the next note).

[1236] This anticipates Josephus' report about the aftermath of Octavian's campaign to Egypt (*Ant.* 15.215-218). It presupposes that Octavian's army again took the coastal road to Syria (cf. 15.218). Octavian turned Egypt into a special Roman province, administrated by a prefect (Hölbl 1994: 223-27; Kienast 1999: 72-74).

Josephus does not write about Octavian's invasion of Egypt and his elimination of Antony and Cleopatra, which are described in detail in Plutarch's *Life of Antony* (74-87; cf. Cassius Dio 51.4-17; see also *Ant.* 15.187 with the note to "Caesar" and 15.190 with the note to "defeated in the Battle of Actium"). In *Ant.* 15.217 he indicates the consequences of Octavian's victory over Antony and Cleopatra for Herod (cf. *War* 1.396).

[1237] The plural ὑπηρεσίας ("services") repeats the same noun (in the singular) of *Ant.* 15.199, which emphasizes that Herod's services during Octavian's return trip fully matched those of the first reception (15.198-200).

[1238] The parallel account of *War* (1.395) reports the same in fewer words. The verb ἐπάνειμι ("return") also occurs in 1.395. Cf. also τῶν πρώτων οὐδὲν ("nothing less than the first time") with πρῶτον ("for the first time") in connection with Herod's reception of Octavian's troops described in *War* 1.394.

[1239] *Ant.* 15.202-252 focuses mainly on 2 Hasmonean women in Herod's family and their interaction with Herod and Salome: Herod's wife Mariamme and his mother-in-law Alexandra (for references, see 15.23 with the notes to "Alexandra" and "Mariamme, who was living in wedlock with Herod"). The 2 women are almost depicted as each other's opposites: Mariamme controls herself up to the very end, while Alexandra exceeds all limits with her self-centered and hysterical behavior. *Ant.* 15.202-239 offers a dramatic report that starts with a flashback concerning Mariamme and Alexandra's stay in the Fortress Alexandrium (15.202-208) and ends with Mariamme's death (15.231-237).

Schalit (2001: 132, 575-88) characterizes the style of the section as tragic history (p. 577) since it focuses on the feelings and emotions of the main characters, depicting dramatic events in graphic terms that evoke the sympathy of the readers, with Mariamme's suffering as principle topic (cf. Kasher 2007: 165, who argues that the tragic-pathetic rhetorical style does not necessarily imply that the account is unreliable). Schalit further argues that the section derives from Nicolaus of Damascus (cf. *Ant.* 16.185), who had in his opinion a great liking for rhetoric and tragic-pathetic historiography. When Schalit originally wrote his history of Herod (Hebrew original appeared in 1960, the first German edition in 1969), many scholars were taking it for granted that a genre called tragic history existed, a view which is nowadays almost universally rejected (Fromentin 2001; Marincola 2003; Baron 2012: 202-31). Nevertheless, Josephus puts great emphasis on the psychological

his family was in disorder[1240] and that his wife Mariamme and her mother Alexandra were angry.[1241] **203** For they believed, as was to be suspected,[1242] that they were brought under in that estate[1243] not for their personal safety,[1244] but for being held to be kept in custody, without having any authority over anybody, neither over others nor over themselves,[1245] which they were taking badly.[1246] **204** Mariamme assumed that the king's love[1247] was masquerade[1248] and just an attempt to deception for his own advantage.[1249] She was embittered[1250] by the thought that, if he [Herod] should suffer something terrible,[1251] she

---

aspects of his characters' responses to the dramatic developments in this section. Another typical aspect of this section is that the narrator focuses on different characters in rapid succession.

Ant. 15.202 connects with 15.183-186, which passage describes the measures taken by Herod before meeting Octavian in Rhodes. The noun βασιλεία also refers to Herod's kingdom in 15.183, 186.

[1240] The verb καταλαμβάνω ("capture, find") means "find on arrival" here (LSJ *s.v.* II.2). It also goes with οἰκίαν/οἰκίας as object plus a predicate in *War* 1.302; *Life* 376. Trouble in Herod's family is a recurring motif in the Herod narrative of *Antiquities* (see 16.75, 300 and 15.22 with the note to "disagreements also arose among persons within his household").

[1241] Mariamme and Alexandra had been put up at Alexandrium, while the rest of Herod's family had been brought to Masada (*Ant.* 15.184-185). Mariamme was thus separated from her sons Alexander and Aristobulus IV. The next paragraph explains the angriness of both women. The phrase χαλεπῶς ἔχειν ("be angry/hostile," Rengstorf *s.v.* χαλεπός) is common in *Antiquities* (4.262; 7.186; 13.195, 236; 15.75, 81; 16.267, 276).

[1242] The separation from the rest of Herod's family could easily make Mariamme and Alexandra suspicious since they had good reasons to fear Herod's measures according to the preceding narrative. Alexandra had been frustrated when Herod did not appoint her son Jonathan-Aristobulus III High Priest (*Ant.* 15.24, 31, 35) and, after Herod had given in, she had been confronted with his death (15.55-56). She knew that Herod was responsible for her son's death (15.58-60) but did not reveal her suspicion (ἐγκρατῶς ἔφερε τὴν ὑποψίαν, 15.60). Her 3 attempts to flee from the court—twice with one of her children—demonstrate her suspicion towards Herod (15.46, 72, 166-168). The death of the old Hyrcanus II (15.165-182), a further member of the Hasmonean dynasty, must have added to the distrust of both ladies. Mariamme had become very cautious because of Herod's order to have her killed in case he would not return from his journey to Antony (15.65, 70, 85, 204). Joseph, who had had to take care of both ladies, had ultimately been executed (15.80-87). Alexandra was held responsible for these troubles and had been kept in chains for a while (15.87).

[1243] I.e., Alexandrium (see *Ant.* 15.185).

[1244] *Ant.* 15.185 states that the womens' honor (i.e., their royal status) was the pretext for separating them from the rest of Herod's family. The underlying motive was probably that they were to be killed if Herod died, in order to secure the continuation of the Herodian dynasty (see 15.185 with the note to "they were left behind to guard the women under the pretext of honor"). The noun σῶμα means "person" here (LSJ *s.v.* II.2; Rengstorf *s.v.*).

[1245] The isolated situation at Alexandrium must have aggravated Mariamme and Alexandra, who were used to a *prima donna* role at Herod's court (although they may have had a small domestic staff at the fortress). Joseph and Soemus were clearly in charge, which explains the strategy of Mariamme and Alexandra to win both men over (*Ant.* 15.204-205).

[1246] For the expression χαλεπῶς ἔφερον ("they were taking it badly"), see *Ant.* 15.24 with the note to "took the disgrace of her son badly." The repetition of χαλεπῶς (see the previous note) emphasizes Mariamme and Alexandra's annoyance.

[1247] About Herod's love for Mariamme, see *Ant.* 15.82 with the note to "loved her terribly."

[1248] This assumption was grounded in Herod's former order to Joseph to kill Mariamme (*Ant.* 15.65; see the note to "suffered something terrible" below). Mariamme's response to this order, during an intimate moment with her husband, states that it could not have come from someone who loved her: "… [it] was not the decision of a *lover*: that if the lover would suffer something bad through Antony, I should perish as well, having no guilt" (15.85).

[1249] A few other passages in both versions of the Herod narrative suggest that Herod arranged certain things for the advantage of himself or his rule (see *War* 1.458, 465; *Ant.* 15.22, 31, 164; 17.123).

[1250] The verb ἄχθομαι ("be embittered/sad/grieved," Rengstorf *s.v.*) occurs frequently in the Herod section of *Antiquities* (15.210-211, 235, 349; 16.72, 85, 88, 195, 219, 248, 279, 305, 356).

[1251] The phrase εἰ πάσχοι τι δεινὸν ἐκεῖνος ("if Herod [literally "that person"] would suffer something terrible") recalls Herod's order to Joseph to kill Mariamme in case he would not return from his journey

had no hope of surviving[1252] because of him.[1253] She recalled[1254] the orders given to Joseph,[1255] and therefore she was already paying court[1256] to her guards,[1257] especially Soemus;[1258] she understood that he was in charge of everything.[1259] **205** Soemus was trustworthy at the beginning,[1260] neglecting none of the things Herod had commanded him to do.[1261] But because the women were trying to win him over in a rather slick way,[1262] with words as well as gifts,[1263] he had already started to yield[1264] slightly. Finally he made known[1265] the king's commands,[1266] especially because he did not expect[1267] that [Herod] would return with the same authority.[1268] **206** In this way[1269] he assumed[1270] that he would please the

---

to Mark Antony (*Ant.* 15.65; see 15.69 εἰ πάσχοι τι δεινόν and cf. 15.65 εἰ πάθοι τι παρ' Ἀντωνίῳ; 15.85 εἰ πάσχοι τι χαλεπὸν ὑπ'Ἀντωνίου).

[1252] This phrase also connects with Herod's order to Joseph (*Ant.* 15.65, 69, 85), although here there are no verbal echoes.

[1253] Mariamme's fate was linked to Herod's. She raises the possibility that Herod could die and, as a consequence, she as well. Concerning Herod's possible motives for these instructions, see *Ant.* 15.65 with the note to "secretly instructed him to kill Mariamme immediately."

[1254] The verb ἀναμνημονεύω ("remember, recall," Rengstorf *s.v.*) is a *hapax legomenon* in Josephus.

[1255] This passage echoes the 2 references to Herod's instruction for Joseph (*Ant.* 15.69 τὰ περὶ τὴν ἐντολὴν εἰπεῖν; 15.85 τὸ κατὰ τὴν ἐντολήν). Here the connection with the instruction for Joseph becomes explicit. Mariamme seems to draw an analogy between her situation during and following Herod's journey to Antony (15.64-80) and that during the one to Octavian (15.184-201). She does not know yet the content of the instruction to Soemus at this stage of the narrative, but her intuition is right: the instructions were identical, apart from the fact that this time both she and her mother were to be killed (15.208).

[1256] The phrase διὰ θεραπείας ἔχω ("pay court") is paralleled by Pausanias 4.10.6.

[1257] During Herod's journey to Antony, Mariamme and Alexandra also had tried to manipulate the person who was taking care of them (i.e., Joseph), but they had ridiculed him and induced him to reveal the instructions, particularly Alexandra (*Ant.* 15.68-69). Here the focus is on Mariamme (15.204-208), who uses a clearly different strategy by paying court to Soemus.

[1258] Soemus is mentioned for the first time in *Ant.* 15.185 (see the note to "Soemus").

[1259] Cf. *Ant.* 15.375 about Manaemus, who "knew everything (τὸ πᾶν ἐπιστάμενος)."

[1260] The adjective πιστός ("faithful, trustworthy") and the expression κατὰ τὰς ἀρχάς ("at the beginning") recall *Ant.* 15.185 about Joseph and Soemus as "the most faithful men to him from the beginning on (πιστοτάτους μέν ἐξ ἀρχῆς γενομένους αὐτῷ)," although here it concerns only Soemus (Joseph is not mentioned again after 15.185; see 15.185 with the note to "Joseph").

[1261] This phrase suggests that Soemus had received various instructions, although the passage that describes these instructions restricts them to the women (*Ant.* 15.185-187).

[1262] An alternative translation for λιπαρέστερον is "most persistently" (see *Ant.* 15.31 with the note to "had slickly pressed him"). The verb ἐκθεραπεύω ("court someone," Rengstorf *s.v.*) occurs once elsewhere in Josephus, referring to the Spartan Eurycles (16.303).

[1263] Cf. King David, who summoned Jonathan's son Mephibosheth and invited him to eat together every day. The boy thanked David for these "words and gifts" (*Ant.* 7.114-115).

[1264] Josephus also uses the verb ἡττάομαι ("be overpowered by, yield to") in connection to men giving in to women in *Ant.* 15.83 (Herod and Mariamme); 15.93 (Antony and Cleopatra); 16.197, 227 (Pheroras and the slave woman); 16.206 (Herod and Glaphyra, according to an accusation by Salome and Pheroras).

[1265] For this meaning of ἐξεῖπον, see *Ant.* 15.87 with the note to "told."

[1266] Soemus' unfaithfulness to Herod recalls Joseph's disclosure of Herod's instructions to Mariamme and Alexandra (*Ant.* 15.69), although verbal echoes are absent.

[1267] This passage echoes *Ant.* 15.163 about the pessimistic expectations of Herod's friends concerning Herod's prospects after Octavian's victory at Actium (cf. ἐλπίσας with τῶν κατ' αὐτὸν ἐλπίδων in 15.163). Soemus distinguishes himself from the friends, however, by moving over to other patrons who could serve his interests better, as the next paragraph explains. Soemus' motivation for revealing Herod's instructions is described in detail in 15.205-207.

[1268] This phrase is euphemistic: if Octavian did not accept Herod as client king of Judea, he probably would expell or even execute him, as happened with Alexas, another close friend of Mark Antony (see *Ant.* 15.197 with the note to "Alexas").

[1269] Richards and Shutt (1937: 174) propose to read εἰ δὲ μή ("otherwise") instead of ἐν ᾧ (Niese 369). Their conjecture may be supported by the Latin version (*sed*

women much[1271] and all the more escape the danger[1272] from him [Herod].[1273] It was likely that the women would not lose their superior status,[1274] but would receive[1275] an even higher [position] by way of compensation,[1276] either[1277] by becoming queen[1278] or by becoming close to the ruler.[1279] **207** What no less buoyed [Soemus'] hope[1280] was that, even if Herod returned after having arranged everything as he intended,[1281] he would not be able to deny his wife anything she wanted.[1282] For [Soemus][1283] knew that the king's love for Mariamme[1284] was beyond description.[1285] These [thoughts][1286] led him[1287] to report the orders.[1288]

---

et) and improve the Greek, but it remains a guess and unnecessary.

[1270] The verb ὑπελάμβανεν ("he assumed") repeats the same verb of *Ant.* 15.204, with Mariamme as subject.

[1271] Soemus' decision to reveal Herod's instructions implies that he switched patrons (see *Ant.* 15.205 with the note to "Soemus was trustworthy at the beginning"). The expression οὐ μικρά ("a lot," literally "not a little") is a case of *litotes*.

[1272] The verb ἐκφεύγω ("escape") followed by τὸν κίνδυνον ("the danger") is a fixed expression in Josephus (*Ant.* 2.346; 6.220, 245).

[1273] At that moment there was no danger coming from Herod yet, but the situation was likely to become dangerous for Herod's friends in case Octavian would not reconfirm the king's rule.

[1274] Mariamme and Alexandra were prominent members not only of the royal house but also of the Hasmonean dynasty (see *Ant.* 15.23 with notes). This status would remain if Herod was deposed, such that they could be involved in the succession of the throne. The noun ἀξίωμα means "dignity, prestige, rank" here (Rengstorf *s.v.*). Josephus uses the word only in connection with women of royal status (Mayer-Schärtel 1995: 57-59, 86; see *Ant.* 15.101 about Cleopatra and cf. 15.51 about Aristobulus III; 15.164 about Hyrcanus II; 15.187 about Herod).

[1275] The Greek text is corrupt and clearly wrong. Niese (369) reads ἕξειν ἤ ("would get either"), which may underly the reading ἕξειν εἰ of MS P (ἕξειν εἰ may have evolved out of ἕξειν ἤ through *iotacism*). Most Greek MSS read ἐξεῖναι ("send out, discharge"). Dindorf conjectures ἐξιέναι ("go out, quit"). However, the majority reading and Dindorf's conjecture do not make sense.

[1276] Josephus does not indicate the ground for this compensation, but the context suggests that it would concern support to activities causing the end of Herod's rule (see also the note above to "lose their superior status").

[1277] The translation follows Niese minor (295), who conjectures ἤ ("either") based on the reading (ἕξειν) εἰ attested by MS P (Niese 369; see the note to "would get" above).

[1278] Niese (369) conjectures βασιλευσούσας ("becoming queen") instead of βασιλευούσας ("being queen"). The reading βασιλευσούσας makes more sense in the immediate context. As a matter of fact, Mariamme was queen at this moment. A change of power might have made Alexandra the new queen, something she may have hoped for (cf. *Ant.* 15.183 and 15.166 with the note to "bringing their hopes for the future into safer ground again").

[1279] The king referred to is Herod's successor, although it is difficult to imagine who that would be. The passage implies that Mariamme and Alexandra would remain prominent members at the court of the new king. The phrase occurs once elsewhere in Josephus, in a reference about himself: "... we descend from a family that is close to the kings who descend from Asmonaeus (ὄντες ἀγχοῦ τῶν ἐξ Ἀσαμωναίου βασιλέων) ..." (*Ant.* 16.187, my trans.).

[1280] Soemus apparently also counted with the less probable option that Herod would return unharmed from his journey to Octavian, as the continuation of the narrative shows. The verb ἐπελπίζω ("cause to hope, be hopeful," Rengstorf *s.v.*) occurs a few more times in *Antiquities* (8.205; 13.329; 15.353) and is also found in Thucydides (8.1.1; 8.54.1, Marcus-Wikgren 99 n. *a*) and later writings (e.g., Pausanias 1.13.9; 4.26.3; Appian, *Bell. civ.* 1.7.55; 2.3.16; Cassius Dio 19.18.13 [ed. Boissevain 1.285 l.19]; 41.11.1; 48.11.1; 54.11.4).

[1281] The expression κατὰ νοῦν ("as he intended," Rengstorf *s.v.* νοῦς) is a fixed phrase in Josephus.

[1282] Cf. *Ant.* 15.31, which passage reports Mariamme's successful appeal to Herod to appoint her brother Jonathan-Aristobulus III High Priest.

[1283] Literally "he."

[1284] Herod's exceptional love for Mariamme is also highlighted in *Ant.* 15.82 (see the note to "loved her terribly") and was apparently common knowledge at the king's court. Josephus suggests that Soemus calculated to be safe if he would have at least Mariamme's support since she was able to protect him because of her influence over the king (see also 15.210).

[1285] The expression μείζονα λόγου ("beyond description, exceedingly great") and closely related phrases also occur in *War* 5.189; *Ant.* 1.7; 5.350; 8.97; 15.316 (Rengstorf *s.v.* λόγος).

208 Mariamme was shocked to hear [this];[1289] she wondered whether there would be no end to the dangers coming to her from Herod.[1290] Being upset,[1291] she prayed that he would receive nothing like considerate treatment,[1292] judging it very hard to endure[1293] living with him if he received [such treatment].[1294] And this [state of mind] she plainly revealed later,[1295] because she did not conceal any of her[1296] feelings.[1297]

[1286] MSS LAMW read ταῦτ' ἦν τά ("these were the") instead of ταῦτα ("these [things or thoughts]," Niese 369; for other cases of lipography, see van Groningen 1967: 54).

[1287] Marcus-Wikgren (98) read (ταῦτ' ἦν τά) προσελκύσαντα ("[it was these considerations that] induced [him]") with MS M, which may be the original reading. The verb προσέλκω does not occur elsewhere in Josephus (Rengstorf s.v.). The other Greek MSS read προσεκλύσαντα (Niese 369), which may derive from the reading attested by MS M via a transposition of κ and λ. This majority reading in any case cannot be right: the extremely rare verb προσεκλύω ("relax, weaken the more," LSJ s.v., giving Plutarch, *Mor.* [*Coni. praec.*] 143d as a further occurrence) does not occur elsewhere in Josephus and the meanings given by LSJ hardly fit the context here.

[1288] This passage concludes the description of Soemus' motives for disclosing Herod's instructions (*Ant.* 15.205-207).

[1289] Whether there is an object connected with ἤκουσεν ("heard") depends on the text proposed for *Ant.* 15.207 (see the note to "these [thoughts]"). The text given by Niese (369) implies that ταῦτα προσεκλύσαντα is the object of ἤκουσεν, which may be translated as "Mariamme was shocked by hearing that he gave these [thoughts] for reporting the instructions." However, it is much more plausible that Mariamme was shocked about the instructions rather than about Soemus' motives, which supports the reading of MS M in 15.207. Rengstorf (s.v. χαλεπός) gives "be shocked by hearing" as meaning for the phrase χαλεπῶς ἀκούειν (cf. the opposite phrase ἡδέως ἤκουσεν ["he welcomed the news"] in 6.197 concerning Saul; cf. 5.194).

[1290] The phrase τῶν ἐξ Ἡρώδης κινδύνων ("the dangers coming from Herod") repeats τὸν ἀπ' αὐτοῦ κίνδυνον in *Ant.* 15.206 concerning the possible dangers for Soemus caused by Herod. This is ironic since Soemus assumed that he was safe as long as he had Mariamme's support. As a matter of fact, the preceding narrative mentions the secret instructions for Joseph during Herod's journey to Antony as the only threat to Mariamme from Herod (15.65). The phrase may also hint at Mariamme's dreadful fate that follows upon this episode (15.231-237).

The phrase μηδὲν πέρας ... τῶν ... κινδύνων is a variant of the conventional expression πέρας (τε) κακῶν (οὐδὲν ἦν) (see 15.6 with the note to "no end to their miseries").

[1291] The phrase χαλεπῶς διάκειμαι ("be shocked/upset/displeased/sulk," Rengstorf s.v. χαλεπός) also occurs in *Ant.* 7.163; 12.327; 16.389 and in Diodorus 11.2.2; 12.46.4; 13.65.2; Pseudo-Callisthenes recension a 2.8.2 (ed. Kroll 74); Plutarch, *Per.* 35.3; *Them.* 29.1.

[1292] An alternative translation is "no fair terms at all." Both meanings of ἴσος may be influenced by the meanings of the Latin equivalent *aequus* ("fair, just, reasonable," OLD s.v. 6). Rengstorf (s.v. ἴσος) suggests "the appropriate things" as meaning for τῶν ἴσων. For other combinations of τὰ ἴσα and τυγχάνω ("receive"), see Isocrates, *Callim.* 50.3; Diodorus 3.64.4; 8.7.6; Plutarch, *Lyc.* 7.3; Aelius Aristides, *Plat. rhet.* [ed. Dindorf 2.65]. This passage hinting at Herod's possible failure to persuade Octavian to maintain him as ruler depicts Mariamme as a resentful woman. Her reaction is understandable, however: Herod's instruction was extremely harsh; there is no evidence that any other ruler from the Graeco-Roman period took similar measures (see *Ant.* 15.65 with the note to "instructed him to kill Mariamme immediately").

[1293] The adjective δυσύποιστος ("intolerable," Rengstorf s.v.) is a *hapax legomenon* in Josephus.

[1294] The expression εἰ τύχοι ("if he would receive") is elliptical, but the meaning is clear because of the repetition of τυγχάνω ("receive").

[1295] This phrase anticipates Mariamme's reaction to Herod's return from his trip to Octavian (*Ant.* 15.210-211) and concludes, together with the subsequent phrase, the flashback of 15.202-208. The reading δὲ ἔδειξε ("but she showed") of MSS LAMW (cf. E) is probably a corruption of διέδειξε ("she revealed plainly," Rengstorf s.v. διαδείκνυμι), attested by MSS PFV (Niese 369), because δέ does not fit the structure of the sentence.

[1296] Marcus-Wikgren (100) read καθ' αὑτήν ("concerning herself") with Dindorf's conjecture, which matches the context very well and would result in a translation like "(did not conceal any of) her inner (feelings)." Most MSS read κατ' αὐτήν ("concerning her," Niese 369), which perhaps derives from καθ' αὑτήν owing to a scribal error. MS W reads κατ' αὐτόν ("concerning him [i.e., Herod])."

Relationship between Mariamme and Herod deteriorates.

(7.2) 209 So Herod[1298] was tremendously fortunate,[1299] more than he had hoped for.[1300] After he had sailed home,[1301] he told the good news—as was usual[1302]—first to his wife.[1303] He embraced her, honoring her alone[1304] specially,[1305] because of his love[1306] and the intimacy[1307] he felt for her. **210** When he reported to her about his success,[1308] she did not happen to be glad but rather took it badly,[1309] nor could she conceal her feelings.[1310] On the contrary, she groaned[1311] in response to his embrace,[1312] out of disdain[1313] and her superior nobility.[1314] She

---

[1297] This motif is taken up again in *Ant.* 15.210.

[1298] Via a brief transitional formula (ὁ μὲν γὰρ ...) Josephus focuses again on Herod, who is mentioned explicitly in *Ant.* 15.208. There is also a chronological transition: Josephus turns here to the description of Mariamme's response to Herod's visit to Octavian (15.209-212). For the explanatory function of γάρ ("so") preceded by μέν, focusing on Herod as one of the persons mentioned in the preceding sentence, see Denniston 1954: 67.

[1299] The verb εὐτυχέω ("be fortunate") is used again in *Ant.* 15.218, in a flashback of Herod's marriage with Mariamme. Herod's successful visit to Octavian is described in 15.187-198. His success as a ruler is a recurring motif in the Herod narrative of *Antiquities* (see 15.361, 377; 16.77).

[1300] The expression παρ' ἐλπίδας ("beyond [his] expectations") repeats *Ant.* 15.196 (see the note to "beyond his expectations"), referring to Herod's expectations about his journey to Octavian, and echoes 15.183 (μηδὲν ἐλπίσαι) about the same trip.

[1301] The verb καταπλέω ("sail, land, enter a harbor") also occurs in *Ant.* 15.187, concerning Herod's voyage to Rhodes.

[1302] For the phrase ὡς εἰκός ("as was usual"), see *Ant.* 15.70 with the note to "as was to be expected."

[1303] Interestingly, the previous episode of Herod's journey to Mark Antony does not confirm this picture: it ends with a letter from Herod to the women, reporting Herod's success (*Ant.* 15.74-80). Upon Herod's return his sister and mother immediately inform him of Alexandra's former plan to flee with Mariamme to the Roman legion nearby (15.72, 80-81).

[1304] This confirms Herod's intimate relationship with Mariamme and her unique status (cf. *Ant.* 15.207 on Soemus' calculation based upon Mariamme's special relationship with Herod). For expressions similar to μόνην ἐκ πάντων ("her alone"), cf. 9.96; 16.22.

[1305] The verb προτιμάω ("honor above others, esteem very highly," Rengstorf *s.v.*) also occurs in *Ant.* 15.170 (concerning Dositheus); 15.361 (concerning Octavian's appreciation of Herod). For the meaning "prefer," see 15.192.

[1306] About Herod's love for Mariamme, see *Ant.* 15.82 with the note to "loved her terribly."

[1307] The noun συνήθεια ("intercourse," Rengstorf *s.v.*) means "intimate relationship" here, which may have a sexual connotation (cf. *Ant.* 15.97 concerning Cleopatra; see also 15.240 with the note to "the king's desire was inflamed even more"; 16.237, 302; and 15.238 with the note to "not pleasing the king" about the relationship between Herod and Mariamme). In 15.240 the word again occurs together with ἔρως ("love"; cf. Diodorus 32.10.9; Cassius Dio 56.7.2).

[1308] The noun εὐημερία ("good fortune, fortunate result," Rengstorf *s.v.*) is a *hapax legomenon* in Josephus.

[1309] The phrase χαλεπῶς φέρω ("take [it] badly") is a fixed expression in Josephus (see *Ant.* 15.24 with the note to "took the disgrace of her son badly"). Josephus uses the phrase 3 times in reference to Mariamme (15.203 [referring to both Mariamme and Alexandra], 210, 223).

[1310] This phrase repeats ἐπικρυψαμένη τοῦ πάθους ("concealing [her] feelings") of *Ant.* 15.208.

[1311] The verb ἀναστένω ("give a groan, sigh audibly," Rengstorf *s.v.*) is a *hapax legomenon* in Josephus. Note the alliteration with *s* as the prominent consonant sound in the sub-clause.

[1312] With Rengstorf (*s.v.* ἀσπασμός). The noun ἀσπασμός (with "greeting" as usual meaning) occurs once elsewhere in Josephus (*War* 2.323).

[1313] Most MSS read ἀδοξίας ("disdain, disgrace," Rengstorf *s.v.* ἀδοξία; Niese 370), but MS F reads εὐδοξίας ("renown, esteem"), which is probably a case of *homoioarkton* (εὐ-; cf. the next noun εὐγενείας). The reading ἀξίας ("dignity"), attested by MS M and E, is also secondary (-δο- has been erased). The noun ἀδοξία occurs elsewhere in Josephus (*Ant.* 5.360; 15.36; 16.321; 18.47), and ἀδοξίας is the *lectio difficilior* (Schalit [2001: 576] offers a different view, with several alternative readings).

Josephus first notes that Mariamme held Herod in contempt because of his secret instruction and then refers to her feelings of superiority caused by her royal descent.

[1314] The noun εὐγένεια ("nobility of birth," Rengstorf *s.v.*) is a recurring motif in passages about members of the Hasmonean family: *Ant.* 15.37 (Alexandra); 15.73 (Mariamme and Alexandra; cf. 15.36 on Alexandra and Aristobulus III); 15.236 (Mariamme); and *War* 1.449, 468, 522; *Ant.* 16.192 (Mariamme's sons Alexander and Aristobulus IV; cf. *War* 1.475-476 about Glaphyra). In several of these passages, including the present one, the noun εὐγένεια also implies a specific elitist attitude, which was mostly taken as an admirable matter in ancient

indicated that she was grieved by his reports rather than merely being happy with him,[1315] so that not only suspicion[1316] but also evident facts[1317] troubled Herod.[1318] **211** For he was dismayed,[1319] seeing his wife's unreasonable[1320] hatred of him unconcealed.[1321] He was grieved by the matter[1322] but, being unable[1323] to bear up against his love,[1324] he did not stick to his [feelings of] anger or forgiveness;[1325] he constantly moved from the one to the other,[1326] suffering great distress in either case.[1327] **212** So when he was left in a state

---

society (cf. Rengstorf s.v., who also gives the meaning "aristocratic mentality" for εὐγένεια; see also Josephus' description of Mariamme's death and her "obituary" in *Ant.* 15.235-239).

[1315] These phrases repeat a preceding sub-clause of this paragraph (cf. συγχαίρειν—χαίρειν and διηγήμασιν—διηγουμένου), which is all the more striking because some of the phrases are rare: the verb συγχαίρω ("rejoice with, congratulate," Rengstorf s.v.) occurs once elsewhere in Josephus (*Ant.* 8.50), as does the noun διήγημα ("report, story," *War* 1.1). Mariamme's disgust with Herod's behavior is strongly emphasized by this vocabulary.

[1316] Josephus' formulation suggests that suspicion had become second nature to Herod. About Herod's suspicion as a recurring motif, see *Ant.* 15.35 with the note to "being under suspicion" and 15.42 with the note to "he truly did not remain without suspicion."

[1317] These facts most probably refer to Mariamme's attitude towards Herod at his return, which was an unmistakable signal, as the next sentence explains. Here the situation appears to be extremely painful for Herod because the obvious thing to do after his successful trip was to celebrate with his beloved wife.

[1318] For Herod's being troubled by unpleasant tidings about the misbehavior of people close to him, see *Ant.* 15.82 with the note to "immediately he was greatly disturbed." The verb ἐπιταράττω ("trouble," Rengstorf s.v.) occurs once elsewhere in Josephus (13.410).

[1319] The verb ἀδημονέω ("be dismayed/worried") occurs once elswhere in Josephus, likewise in the Herod narrative of *Antiquities* (15.388).

[1320] If the word παράλογος means "unreasonable" here (cf. Rengstorf s.v.), it indicates a strong disqualification by Herod of his wife's behavior. A less negative translation would be "unexpected" (see also *Ant.* 15.119 with the note to "unexpectedly winning a victory").

[1321] This statement further explains Herod's being troubled by the response of his wife (*Ant.* 15.210). Herod is focalized and the continuation of the narrative shows his agony of doubt about what to do with Mariamme (15.211-212). Such glimpses into his feelings are rare in the Herod narrative (Landau 2006: 166).

[1322] For a similar construction of a passive voice of φέρω with τῷ πράγματι ("being devastated by the matter"), cf. Cassius Dio 36.38.3.

[1323] The verb ἀδυνατέω ("be unable"; cf. Rengstorf s.v.) occurs once elsewhere in Josephus (*Ant.* 6.371).

[1324] The contrast between Mariamme's hatred of Herod and Herod's love for her is also apparent from the parallel passage of *War* (1.436): "For Mariamme's hatred for him (τοσοῦτον γὰρ ἦν μῖσος εἰς αὐτόν τῆς Μαριάμμης) was as great as his passionate love for her (πρὸς αὐτὴν ἔρως)" (trans. Sievers/Forte in BJP 1a).

The noun ἔρως ("[sexual] love, passion") is a key word in this section of the Herod narrative (see *Ant.* 15.204, 207, 209, 211, 214, 218, 238, and about Herod's love for Mariamme, 15.82 with the note to "loved her terribly"). For other phrases of φέρω ("bear up against, stand firm to") with ἔρως ("love") as object, see Parthenius of Nicaea 23.1; Lucian, *Nav.* 43.6; Xenophon of Ephesus 4.5.4.

[1325] Josephus makes the same statement twice: negatively in this passage and positively in the next sub-clause. For a related combination of ὀργή ("anger") and διαλλαγή ("reconciliation, pardon"), cf. Plutarch, *Dion* 16.3.

[1326] The presentation of Herod as being torn apart by 2 competing powerful emotions, love and hate (see also *Ant.* 15.212 and cf. 15.208 which still focuses on Herod's love for Mariamme), is characteristic of his image in *Antiquities*.

Kasher (2007: 13) analyzes the Herod narratives from a psychological perspective and argues, by applying the *Diagnostic and Statistical Manual of Mental Disorders* (DSM), that Herod suffered from a paranoid personality disorder. Herod's behavior is indeed reminiscent of the type of mental disorder described in DSM as "borderline personality disorder," which is characterized by (1) impulsive or unpredictable acts, (2) unstable and intense interpersonal relationships, (3) inappropriate, intense anger or lack of control of anger, (4) identity disturbance, (5) affective instability, (6) intolerance of being alone, (7) physically self-damaging acts, and (8) chronic feelings of emptiness or boredom. The question remains, however, whether these characteristics are representative of the historical Herod or rather reflect stereotypes articulated by Josephus or one of his sources. It is problematic to apply modern psychological assessments, which are based on contemporary conditions, to ancient monarchs and emperors. Many ancient rulers would fit the characteristics pointed out by Kasher in connection with Herod.

between hate[1328] and love,[1329] being often ready to punish[1330] her for her arrogance,[1331] he was becoming too weak to remove the woman[1332] by killing her[1333] because he was crushed by his emotions.[1334] In short,[1335] he would gladly have punished Mariamme but feared that unintentionally[1336] he would exact more punishment from him[-self than from her][1337] if she died.[1338]

(7.3) 213 When his sister and mother noticed[1339] that he felt this way about Mariamme, they thought they had an excellent opportunity[1340] to [act upon][1341] their feelings of hatred

---

For an expression similar to ἀπὸ θατέρου μεταβαίνω εἰς θάτερον ("moving from the one to the other"), see John Philoponus, *Aet. mund.* (ἐκ θατέρου εἰς θάτερον μεταβαίνειν, ed. Rabe 357).

[1327] For other combinations of πολλὴν ἀπορίαν with ἔχω ("suffer great distress"), cf. Antiphon, *Caed. Her.* 65; Lysias 19.1; Aristotle, *De an.* 432b; *Phys.* 189b; *Pol.* 1284b; Arrian, *Anab.* 4.17.5.

[1328] Niese (370) reads στυγεῖν ("hate, abhor," Rengstorf *s.v.* στυγέω) with MSS LAMW. The reading δυστυχεῖν ("suffer") of MSS PFV and E may derive from a scribal lapse, switching to a related and more common verb. The verb στυγέω does occur a few more times in Josephus (*War* 5.413; *Ant.* 16.203; *Apion* 2.199).

[1329] The parallelism in στυγεῖν καὶ στέργειν is another argument for the authenticity of the reading στυγεῖν (see the previous note). Both verbs echo the key words μῖσος ("hatred") and ἔρως ("love") of *Ant.* 15.211 and emphasize again that Herod was torn by these 2 emotions. Both verbs occur in Philo, *Sobr.* 23, which comments on Deut 21:15 (about a man who has 2 wives, the one beloved and the other disliked): "... we declare that in the beloved wife we have a figure of pleasure and in the hated wife a figure of prudence" (trans. Colson and Whitaker).

[1330] The adjective ἕτοιμος followed by the middle voice of an infinitive of ἀμύνω ("being prepared to punish/fight/protect," Rengstorf *s.v.*) may echo Thucydean vocabulary (see 4.73.2; cf. Appian, *Bell. civ.* 2.20.145).

[1331] Mariamme's arrogance (ὑπερηφανία), a characteristic she apparently shares with her mother, is a recurring motif in the Herod narrative of *Antiquities* (see 15.37 with the note to "frankness").

[1332] The expression ἡ ἄνθρωπος ("the woman") may have a depreciating connotation in this context (see *Ant.* 15.67 about Cleopatra with the note to "the woman"). Cf. 15.231, again about Mariamme but with a different connotation.

[1333] The verb μεθίστημι means "remove by killing" here (cf. *Ant.* 4.48; 18.147, 352; LSJ *s.v.* II.2; Rengstorf *s.v.*). *Ant.* 18.352 (about the poisoning of Asineus) offers a close parallel, having τὸν ἄνθρωπον ("the man") as object of the verb.

[1334] The noun ψυχή refers here to Herod's conscious self, or his personality as the center of his emotions (LSJ *s.v.* IV). Rengstorf (*s.v.*) suggests "be already captivated (by love)" as meaning for the passive voice of προκαταλαμβάνω.

[1335] The focus switches from Herod to the narrator. The concluding comment that follows is even more negative than the description of Herod's feelings in *Ant.* 15.211-212 because it highlights Herod's self-interest as his most important motive for not executing Mariamme.

[1336] This detail is ironical: it suggests that it was not Herod's intention to have his wife killed. When he ultimately did have her executed, his fear was realized (*Ant.* 15.229-247). For λανθάνω with verbs that express acting ("[doing something] without knowing or guessing [it]"), see Rengstorf *s.v.*

[1337] The phrase is elliptical. Niese (370) reads παρ' αὐτοῦ ("from him") with MSS PF, but Marcus-Wikgren (100) read παρ' αὐτῆς ("from her"—or "upon her," as they translate). The combination of εἰσπράττω plus τιμωρίαν and παρά ("exact payment/punishment from [someone])" is conventional (e.g., Demosthenes, *Or.* 35.44; Xenophon of Ephesus 2.1.2, also Josephus, *War* 4.415).

[1338] Josephus' comment not only highlights the wickedness of Herod's reasoning but also anticipates the king's grief and illness following Mariamme's execution (see *Ant.* 15.240-246).

[1339] Herod's sister Salome and his mother Cyprus also acted as a tandem during the aftermath of Herod's journey to Mark Antony (*Ant.* 15.65). Immediately upon Herod's return they revealed Mariamme and Alexandra's former plan to flee to the Roman legion nearby (15.80), and Salome accused her husband Joseph of having a sexual relationship with Mariamme (15.81; see also *War* 1.438; *Ant.* 15.220, 239, 258 as well as 15.184-185 about the different fortified places where Mariamme and Alexandra on the one hand and the rest of Herod's family—including Salome and Cyprus—on the other hand were brought under during Herod's journey to Octavian).

[1340] Kasher (2007: 166) suggests that Salome and Cyprus were much aware of Herod's impulsive and tempestuous character so they deliberately tried to provoke him in order to cause an outburst of insanity during which he would execute Mariamme. For the verb

towards Mariamme.¹³⁴² In order to provoke Herod¹³⁴³ they kept talking a lot about slanderous things,¹³⁴⁴ which could at the same time develop his hatred and jealousy.¹³⁴⁵ **214** And he did not listen to such stories without pleasure,¹³⁴⁶ nor did he dare¹³⁴⁷ to do something against her by putting trust into the stories.¹³⁴⁸ Nevertheless, his attitude towards her continued to become more hostile,¹³⁴⁹ and his passion kindled in turn,¹³⁵⁰ while she did not conceal her disposition [towards him].¹³⁵¹ He continuously switched¹³⁵² from love to

---

λαμβάνω with καιρός as object ("receive the opportunity"), see *Ant.* 15.42 with the note to "received the opportunity."

¹³⁴¹ The Greek text is elliptical, but the context makes clear that Salome and Cyprus were eager to undertake actions that would harm Mariamme.

¹³⁴² The noun μῖσος ("hatred") also occurs in connection with Mariamme hating Herod in *War* 1.436; *Ant.* 15.211 (cf. 15.44 about Alexandra's hatred for Herod). About the 2 female factions at Herod's court, one led by Salome and Cyprus and the other by Alexandra and Mariamme, see 15.80 with the note to "his mother." The Hasmonean women hated not only Herod (15.211) but also his mother and sister (15.220), and Josephus' report indicates that this hatred was mutual.

¹³⁴³ The verb παροξύνω ("incite, provoke, make angry," Rengstorf *s.v.*) also has Herod as object in *Ant.* 16.89, 308 (both about arousing Herod's anger against his sons); cf. 17.64. The verb also occurs in 15.82, about the aftermath of Herod's journey to Antony (see the note to "provoked by his jealousy").

¹³⁴⁴ Niese (370) reads οὐ μικρῶς, which is a case of *litotes* (literally "not a little"). Marcus-Wikgren (102) read οὐ μικραῖς (διαβολαῖς) with MSS VE, which implies a slightly different translation: "(talking about) serious (causes for suspicion)" (see also *War* 1.443; *Ant.* 15.81 about Salome's accusations against her husband Joseph; the latter passage includes the noun διαβολή, which can mean "slander" as well as "[false] accusation," Rengstorf *s.v.*).

¹³⁴⁵ This passage is reminiscent of the aftermath of Herod's journey to Mark Antony, during which Salome accused Joseph of having committed adultery with Mariamme (*Ant.* 15.81-82), which charge immediately triggered Herod's jealousy. The noun ζηλοτυπία ("jealousy," Rengstorf *s.v.*) also occurs in 15.82; for the recurring motif of Herod's jealousy, see 15.50 with the note to "jealousy" and 15.82 with the note to "could not bear having a rival." Herod's hatred (μῖσος) of Mariamme is not mentioned in 15.81-87 (about Joseph's adultery with Mariamme), which suggests that the relationship between Herod and Mariamme is deteriorating here, as the next paragraph states explicitly (see also 15.212).

¹³⁴⁶ This is a further nuance of Herod's complex and wicked character. The reason for Herod's pleasure is not given, but the readers may think of Herod's suspicion, which is emphasized several times elsewhere in *Antiquities* (see *Ant.* 15.35 and 15.42 with the notes to "suspicion"). In line with this motif it is imaginable that Herod was glad that his assumptions concerning his wife, which had been triggered because of the affair with Joseph (15.81-87), were confirmed. The combination of ἀκούω and ἀηδῶς ("listen ... without pleasure") is common (e.g., Demosthenes, *Exord.* 33.2; Plutarch, *Sull.* 35.5; Chariton 5.8.6; Cassius Dio 44.45.5).

¹³⁴⁷ The verb ἀποθαρρέω ("dare," Rengstorf *s.v.*) is a *hapax legomenon* in Josephus.

¹³⁴⁸ This statement reflects Herod's deeply ambiguous attitude towards Mariamme as described by Josephus (*Ant.* 15.211-212). The verb πιστεύω ("believe, trust," Rengstorf *s.v.*) also occurs in the related passage of 15.81-87, in which Herod even apologizes for "having believed what he thought he had heard" (15.83; cf. the noun πίστις ["trust"] in 15.87). Compared to this earlier episode Herod's present relationship with Mariamme is worse: he is trusting slanderous accusations against his wife.

¹³⁴⁹ Josephus states here explicitly what several preceding details had already been hinting at. The imperfect tense εἶχεν ("had/continued to become") implies that this was an ongoing process.

¹³⁵⁰ The noun πάθος is repeated several times in this section and also occurs in related passages, but with various nuances (Rengstorf *s.v.*). In *Ant.* 15.208, 210 it indicates Mariamme's inner feelings, but here and in 15.242 it refers to Herod's passion for Mariamme (cf. 15.82 about the aftermath of Herod's journey to Antony, in which case πάθος indicates Herod's intense emotions; the word occurs twice in the parallel passage of *War* [*War* 1.443-444], indicating Herod's anger). Herod's passion for Mariamme fired up again after her death (*Ant.* 15.242).

The verb ἀντεκκαίω ("kindle in turn," LSJ *s.v.*; Rengstorf [*s.v.*] gives "be set ablaze against" as meaning) is found only here in all of ancient and medieval Greek literature (so the TLG). Josephus uses the simpler and much more common form ἐκκαίω at *War* 1.436 in a comparable but more general statement, contrasting Herod's passion for Mariamme with her contempt for him.

¹³⁵¹ This statement connects with Josephus' earlier description of Mariamme's feelings about Herod in *Ant.*

Herod meets Caesar and receives grant. War 1.396-397

anger.[1353] **215** Something fatal would even[1354] have been done[1355] without delay, but Caesar was now reported to have won the war[1356] and hold Egypt following Antony's and Cleopatra's deaths.[1357] [Herod] hastened to meet Caesar[1358] and left the matters of his family as they were.[1359] **216** As he was leaving,[1360] Mariamme brought Soemus[1361] forward.[1362] She expressed great gratitude[1363] for his care[1364] and requested some kind of

---

15.208, 210 (note the correspondence between ἀποκρυπτομένης τὴν διάθεσιν "[not] conceal her disposition" and ἐπικρύπτεσθαι with τὸ πάθος "[not] conceal her feelings" in 15.208, 210).

[1352] This statement connects with the description of Herod's deeply ambiguous feelings about Mariamme and his agony in *Ant.* 15.211-212 (see, e.g., the beginning of 15.212).

MSS LAMWE read μεταβάλλοντος ("change," Rengstorf *s.v.* μεταβάλλω) instead of μεταλαμβάνοντος ("switch, change," Rengstorf *s.v.* μεταλαμβάνω; Niese 370; for a similar variant reading, see 11.173). It is difficult to decide which reading is the more original; the reading μεταβάλλοντος is, however, likely a corruption of μεταλαμβάνοντος. The meaning of both participles is basically the same.

[1353] This final clause summarizes the very different feelings of both spouses (cf. the construction with τῆς μὲν … τοῦ δέ) and repeats previous statements (see the preceding notes).

[1354] The conjunction κἂν is a *crasis* of καὶ ἄν and functions as a more intense form of καί ("even," LSJ *s.v.*).

[1355] The vague formulation adds suspense. The context suggest Mariamme's execution (*Ant.* 15.230-231) as the fatal event intended (cf. 16.356 in connection with Herod's punishment of his sons by Mariamme: Octavian advises Herod "not to accomplish anything incurable [μηδὲν ἀνήκεστον διαπράττεσθαι]," my trans.). Cf. Procopius, *Bell.* 2.4.21 and see *Ant.* 15.131 with the note to "irreparable harm."

[1356] The first part of this sub-clause connects with the previous report about Octavian's victory at Actium (*Ant.* 15.161), but here the final scene of Octavian's victory is meant: his capture of Egypt (see the next note).

[1357] Antony committed suicide after a disastrous final battle before the gates of Alexandria on 1 August 30 BCE. Cleopatra committed suicide following her failure to persuade Octavian to enter into a partnership with her. Octavian turned Egypt into a Roman province (Plutarch, *Ant.* 75-86; Cassius Dio 51.6-17; see *Ant.* 15.190 with the note to "defeated in the Battle of Actium" and 15.201 with the note to "returned from Egypt"). The deaths of Antony and Cleopatra and Octavian's capture of Egypt are also reported in the parallel passage of *War* (1.396).

[1358] The meeting took place in Egypt (*Ant.* 15.217), most probably in the early autumn of 30 BCE (shortly after 1 August; cf. the preceding note and Herod's haste to meet Octavian). Herod attempted to be a model of loyalty to his new patron (see 15.201). Josephus characteristically describes Herod's visits of his patrons by emphasizing the king's haste (cf. ἐπείγω ["be eager, haste"] in 15.187; 16.91 concerning visits to Octavian and in 16.12 concerning a visit to Marcus Agrippa). *Ant.* 15.201 mentions Herod's support to Octavian and his army during their return trip from Egypt.

[1359] Herod apparently considered Octavian's affairs to be the most important; they clearly overrule his family concerns. The phrase τὰ περὶ τὴν οἰκίαν ("the matters of his family") also occurs in *Ant.* 15.22, 42; 16.300. The troubles within Herod's family mentioned in 15.202 concentrate here on Herod's relationship with Mariamme, which thread will be taken up again in 15.218.

[1360] The story implies that Mariamme chose this moment deliberately because Herod was pressed for time (see the note to "hastened to meet Caesar" above), such that he likely would give in quickly to a request from his wife. This behavior matches her smart and successful pleading for the appointment of her brother as High Priest (see *Ant.* 15.31 "… not in the least because his wife Mariamme had slickly pressed him …" with the note to "had slickly pressed him"). Mariamme's request was successful (15.217).

[1361] Together with the administrator Joseph, Soemus was responsible for guarding Mariamme and Alexandra at Alexandrium (see *Ant.* 15.185 with the note to "Soemus").

[1362] Niese (371) reads the future participle παραστησομένη with MSS PF (expressing an intention: "in order to") instead of the aorist participle παραστησαμένη of MSS LAMVWE (read by Marcus-Wikgren 102). The future participle is the *lectio difficilior*, but it is hardly compatible with the other information mentioned in this clause, which is not at all situated in the future (cf. Rijksbaron 2002: 33; the future participle παραστησόμενος in *Ant.* 12.243 indicates the intention of the actor). The aorist participle is, therefore, preferable. The reading παραστησομένη may result from a scribal lapse changing α incidentally to ο. The verb παρίστημι probably means "introduce, bring forward" here (Rengstorf *s.v.*). The Latin version reads *commendans* ("commended," Niese 371; cf. LSJ *s.v.* C I.2 "commend," referring to this passage).

[1363] For the common phrase χάριν ὁμολογέω ("express

ruling position[1365] for him from the king. **217** And indeed he obtained this honor.[1366]

When Herod arrived in Egypt,[1367] he spoke to[1368] Caesar with greater frankness,[1369] as someone who was by this time a friend.[1370] [Herod] was honored with the greatest favors.[1371] For he [Caesar] gave him[1372] 400 of the Gauls[1373] who were Cleopatra's body-guards[1374] as

---

gratitude"), see *Ant.* 15.83 with the note to "he offered many thanks."

[1364] The word ἐπιμέλεια ("care") is more positive than the term φρουρεῖν ("guard") used to indicate Soemus' task in *Ant.* 15.185 (see 15.44 with the note to "care"). This may be in line with Mariamme's attempt to get a favor from Herod. The noun therefore probably has a positive meaning here, although it can have a negative connotation (as it does in 15.44 concerning Alexandra).

[1365] The word μεριδαρχία ("governorship," Rengstorf *s.v.*) is a *hapax legomenon* in Josephus, and before him attested only in LXX 1 Esdras (1:5, 12; 5:4; 8:28). The related noun μεριδάρχης ("governor") occurs twice in a reference to a high Seleucid official named Apollonius (*Ant.* 12.261, 264), but the name of Apollonius' district is not explicitly given. Stern (1974b: 250) suggests that the "meridarchies" are identical with the regions of Idumea, Judea, Samaria, Galilee, and Perea. Schalit (2001: 214 n. 252) argues that the district meant must have been outside Judea since Soemus was an Iturean. Yet we can only speculate about the name and size of Soemus' district. The point of the passage seems to be to present Soemus' grant of office as an indistinct token extracted from Herod.

[1366] This simple remark indicates that Mariamme's request reported in *Ant.* 15.216 was successful, which is remarkable in the light of Herod's highly ambiguous attitude towards his wife described in the preceding paragraphs. Josephus perhaps contrasts the vague and presumably relatively small honor for Soemus with the huge grant Herod receives from Octavian according to this passage.

Phrases with τυγχάνω ("receive") and (τῆς) τιμῆς ("honor, office, etc.," Rengstorf *s.v.* τιμή) as object occur frequently in Josephus (e.g., *Ant.* 2.128; 5.199; 11.244, 254, 280; cf. 3.188 on Aaron and the high priestly office). In *War* 1.396 Josephus refers to "additional honors" for Herod with a plural of τιμή.

[1367] Herod must have marched towards Octavian in Egypt after hearing the news about the final victory over Antony and Cleopatra; and met him somewhere on the route (possibly in Pelusium because that was an obvious place to halt) or in Alexandria. The parallel account of *War* (1.395-397) only mentions Herod's services during Octavian's return from Egypt in a general way.

[1368] The expression εἰς λόγους ἐλθεῖν/ἀφικνεῖσθαι ("discuss, speak with," Rengstorf *s.v.* λόγος) is a fixed phrase in Josephus (*Ant.* 1.285; 13.282).

[1369] Speaking with frankness (παρρησία, Rengstorf *s.v.*) to Octavian was apparently part of Herod's personal relationship with Octavian as one of his friends (see the next note). This new relationship of frankness (παρρησία, Rengstorf *s.v.*) is confirmed by *Ant.* 16.293, which states that later it became temporarily impossible, when Herod had damaged the relationship by his actions against the Nabateans.

[1370] This note refers to Herod's meeting with Octavian in Rhodes, where he was installed as one of Octavian's friends (*Ant.* 15.195-196, 199; see 15.5 with the note to "the friends around him," concerning political friendship relationships), and echoes earlier statements about his friendship with Octavian (see 15.195 on Octavian's treating Herod with every honor, and 15.199 on Herod's being counted among Octavian's most loyal friends). The note also introduces Octavian's huge grants to Herod described in the remaining part of the paragraph.

[1371] The phrase μεγίστων ἠξιώθη ("he was honored with the greatest favors/rewarded with the greatest honors") is a fixed expression (e.g., Isocrates, *Aeginet.* 37; Diodorus 15.56.3; Josephus, *Ant.* 13.411; Lucian, *Dial. mort.* 25.2; Appian, *Hist. rom.* 2.9.1).

[1372] The verb ἐδωρήσατο ("he gave [him]") occurs also in the parallel account of *War* (1.397), at the end of which a motivation is given for Octavian's generous grants to Herod: "And nothing drove him so much to grant these favors as the magnanimity of their beneficiary" (trans. Sievers/Forte in BJP 1a).

[1373] *War* 1.397 adds that the 400 Gauls were given to Herod as a bodyguard.

[1374] Josephus formulates it slightly differently in the parallel passage of *War* (1.397) but also uses the verb δορυφορέω ("protect, form the bodyguard," Rengstorf *s.v.*). It was usual practice to recruit foreign elite troops (e.g., Germans or Gauls) as bodyguards because such mercenaries were motivated by receiving good pay and not by local political ideology. Therefore, they were considered to be much more reliable than indigenous soldiers (Goldsworthy 1996: 71). Various ethnic groups of soldiers are mentioned in connection with Herod's funeral procession (*War* 1.672; *Ant.* 17.198). Josephus also lists Gauls there (Γαλάται in *War*; τὸ Γαλατικόν in *Ant.*) but distinguishes them from the bodyguards (οἱ δορυφόροι; cf. *War* 1.437 on the Gauls who were responsible for the death of Aristobulus III).

Relationship between Mariamme and Herod further deteriorates.
War 1.436-437

a present and returned the land to him that had been taken away by her.[1375] He also added[1376] Gadara,[1377] Hippus,[1378] and Samaria[1379] to the kingdom, as well as Gaza,[1380] Anthedon,[1381] Joppa,[1382] and Straton's Tower[1383] in the coastal region.[1384]

[1375] This information is also given in the parallel account of *War* (1.396-397), partly with other words (the noun χώρα ["land"] occurs in both passages). See *Ant.* 15.95-96 on Antony's gift of the coastal cities between the River Eleutherus and Egypt and the region of Jericho to Cleopatra (see the notes to "the cities between the River Eleutherus" and "and Egypt"; also Otto 1913: 48-49; Kienast 1999: 75-76).

[1376] The verb προσέθηκε plus τῇ βασιλείᾳ ("he [i.e., Octavian] added to his kingdom") also occurs in the parallel account of *War* (1.396-397). The remaining part of the paragraph is, apart from a few variations, similar to *War* 1.396, in which passage the same geographical references are given.

[1377] Gadara (currently Umm Qais) was one of the free cities of the Decapolis (Pliny the Elder 5.16.74), located on a hill south of the River Yarmuk, ca. 10 km southeast of Lake Gennesaret. The city was captured by Alexander Janneus and later removed from Judean territory by Pompey. After Herod's death it became a free city again (Möller and Schmitt 1976: 59; Schürer-Vermes 2.132-36; see also *Ant.* 15.351-359 on Herod's relationship with the Gadarenes).

[1378] Hippus was a further city of the Decapolis (Pliny the Elder 5.15.71; 5.16.74, who refers to the name Hippo). Its location was ca. 3 km east of Lake Gennesaret. Like Gadara the city was captured by Alexander Janneus and liberated again by Pompey (Möller and Schmitt 1976: 110; Schürer-Vermes 2.130-02; Tsafrir, Di Segni, and Green 1994: 147). Augustus removed the cities of Gadara (see the preceding note), Hippus, and Gaza from the Herodian territory when Herod was succeeded by Archelaus as ruler of Judea (see *War* 2.97). In *War* 2.97 Josephus specifies that Archelaus received only an ethnarchy based in Jerusalem (and not Galilee or Perea, nor the Golan), i.e., Idumea, Judea, and Samaria. The only *poleis* connected with this were Jerusalem, Sebaste, Caesarea, and Joppa. The other Greek cities mentioned in this passage (Gaza, Gadara and Hippus) were removed from what Herod had governed and attached to the Province of Syria.

[1379] The city of Samaria (renamed Sebaste by Herod, *War* 1.403; *Ant.* 15.246, 392), located ca. 11 km northwest of Mount Gerizim and ca. 50 km north of Jerusalem, was turned into a Macedonian colony by Alexander the Great or Perdiccas. The sons of John Hyrcanus captured it in ca. 107 BCE, and Pompey separated it again from the Judean territory. Since Samaria was part of Herod's territory before Antony's grants to Cleopatra (see *War* 1.213, 229, 302, 344; *Ant.* 14.284, 411, 413, 467), Octavian apparently returned Samaria to Herod in 30 BCE (Schalit 2001: 130, 161-62; further references in Udoh 2005: 141 n. 139). Otto (1913: 49, 55) argues that Octavian's grant of Samaria means that he abolished the tribute that Herod previously had had to pay for Samaria (cf. Appian, *Bell. civ.* 5.75).

[1380] Gaza, the southern-most coastal city of Judea, was a Greek city (*War* 2.97; *Ant.* 17.320) and originally not part of the Judean territory. It was a transit port for merchandise coming from South Arabia. Alexander Janneus conquered and destroyed the city following a siege of a year, Pompey liberated it, and Gabinius rebuilt it together with various other cities, including Samaria and Anthedon (*Ant.* 14.88; Möller and Schmitt 1976: 61-62; Schürer-Vermes 2.98-103; Tsafrir, Di Segni, and Green 1994: 129-31). Gaza most probably belonged to Herod's territory (as Samaria did; see the preceding note) before Antony's grant of the coastal cities to Cleopatra, which is supported by Herod's appointment of Costobarus as governor of Idumea and Gaza (*Ant.* 15.260). Gaza was probably included in Antony's grant of the coastal area to Cleopatra in 37(36) BCE, although Schalit (2001: 773-77) considers the possibility that there had been a separate grant of Gaza to Cleopatra (see *Ant.* 15.96 with the note to "the areas in Arabia that had been given to her").

[1381] Anthedon is located a few km north of Gaza. Herod restored it and renamed it Agrippias or Agrippeum in honor of Marcus Agrippa (*War* 1.118, 416; *Ant.* 13.357; Möller and Schmitt 1976: 17; Schürer-Vermes 2.104; Tsafrir, Di Segni, and Green 1994: 63).

[1382] The Greek harbor city of Joppa (currently Yafo, south of Tel-Aviv), from which agricultural products from its *hinterland* were exported, was turned into a Jewish city by the Hasmonean ruler Simon. Pompey separated the city from Judean territory (*Ant.* 14.76). Julius Caesar returned it to the Jews (*Ant.* 14.205). It was part of Herod's territory before Antony's grant of the coastal region to Cleopatra (15.95), although Schürer-Vermes (2.113) is hesitant about this (further references in Möller and Schmitt 1976: 105; Schürer-Vermes 2.110-14; Tsafrir, Di Segni, and Green 1994: 152-53).

[1383] The origin of Straton's Tower is debated. The previously common view that the city was founded by a Sidonian king named Straton in the Persian period is contested on the basis of the Louvre Caesarea Cup, a 4th-cent. CE commemorative bronze cup that presents the city's foundation legend in 3 scenes implying that Straton's Tower was founded by the Greeks (one of them being called Straton) in the 3rd cent. BCE (Patrich 2007:

(7.4) 218 And attaining these things he [Herod] became even more illustrious.[1385] He escorted Caesar[1386] in the direction of Antioch.[1387] Having returned home[1388] he thought[1389] that as much as his situation increased in fortune[1390] through external means,[1391] he suffered from his family affairs,[1392] and especially those concerning his marriage,[1393] in which he

---

95-100). Straton's Tower is located on the coast, ca. 35 km south of the current city of Haifa. It was handed over to Alexander Janneus, but Pompey separated it again from the Judean territory. Josephus refers to it for the first time in *War* 1.77 (further references in Schalit 1968: 116). Herod built a new city at the location of Straton's Tower in honor of Octavian-Augustus and named it Caesarea Sebaste (Καισάρεια Σεβαστή; *Ant.* 15.293, 339). Levine (1975: 12) points out that the city was in disrepair before Herod decided to rebuild it (cf. Möller and Schmitt 1976: 114-15; Schürer-Vermes 2.115-18; Tsafrir, Di Segni, and Green 1994: 94-96).

[1384] The last 4 cities mentioned in this list are part of the coastal area of Palestine. The word παράλιος ("situated by the sea, coastal region," Rengstorf *s.v.*) is used in the plural in the parallel passage of *War* (1.396), with the same meaning. Octavian also enhanced the territory of King Archelaus of Cappadocia (Strabo 12.1.4; Cassius Dio 54.9.2; Buchheim 1960: 56).

[1385] Octavian's grants obviously increased Herod's prestige, not at least because they happened within a year after Herod had become Octavian's friend in the spring of 30 BCE (*Ant.* 15.195-196, 199; about the date, see 15.187 with the note to "Caesar"). The connection with Herod's visit to Octavian may be also apparent from the fact that the same adjective λαμπρός ("brilliant, magnificent, illustrious, generous, etc.," Rengstorf *s.v.*) is used in the description of this meeting in connection with Octavian (15.194). The parallel passage of *War* (1.391) even uses it in Octavian's phrases about Herod (see 15.194 with the note to "magnanimous and generous"). The word also occurs in 15.198 (ὡς ἀεὶ τὸ λαμπρότερον ... προσεπικτώμενος "he always seemed to gain in splendor when he came out of the dangers") and 15.200 (about Herod's services to Octavian being "much bigger and more splendid [λαμπρότερα] than the kingdom").

[1386] Herod had escorted Octavian before (*Ant.* 15.196, 199-201), as he had previously done for his patron Antony (see 15.80 with the note to "he had escorted Antony to the Parthians" about escorting as one of the services of a client king).

[1387] This connects with *Ant.* 15.201 (see the note to "returned from Egypt") about Herod's services to Octavian and his army on their return from Egypt. Since Antioch is most probably Antioch on the Orontes, the capital of Syria (see 15.8 with the note to "Antioch"), Octavian apparently returned along the same route as the one he had taken to Egypt (see also 15.199 with the note to "Ptolemais").

[1388] With this formula Josephus returns to the main theme of the episode: the domestic troubles, with the focus on Mariamme (Landau 2006: 167). For a similar transition with ἐπανελθών, cf. *Ant.* 16.276 "After Herod had returned from Rome, he learned that ..." (my trans.).

[1389] Herod, the subject of "he thought," is the focalizer again (cf. *Ant.* 15.211-212).

[1390] Herod draws a parallel by contrast, making an analogy between the increasing success in external affairs (i.e., as a ruler) and the increasing problems within his family, which matches Josephus' own opinion about the king (see the next note).

For a similar phrase to ἐπιδίδωμι εἰς ("provide, increase") with εὐδαιμονίαν ("fortune, prosperity, well-being," Rengstorf *s.v.* εὐδαιμονία) as object, see *War* 7.74 on the reception of Vespasian by the Romans.

[1391] Although Josephus presents this reasoning through the perspective of Herod, the contrast between Herod's success as a ruler and the tremendous troubles connected with his family and private life is, in fact, one of the recurring motifs of the Herod narrative in *Antiquities* (van Henten 2011d: 243-50). *Ant.* 16.76-77 (cf. 16.150-151, 156-159) also expresses this theme and questions whether it had been right to buy such great success in external matters at the price of the disasters at home (here too Josephus uses the words τὰ πράγματα ["his matters/situation"] and ἔξωθεν ["external"]).

[1392] On the troubles in Herod's family, see *Ant.* 15.202 with the note to "his family was in disorder" and the preceding note.

[1393] The marital relationship between Herod and Mariamme, on which this section focuses, apparently had gone through several crises already: Dellius' proposal to send Mariamme's portrait over to Antony, which was embraced by Alexandra, may have caused a temporary alienation and certainly had serious consequences for Herod's relationship with his mother-in-law (*Ant.* 15.26-33; cf. 15.73); Herod's secret orders to Joseph during his journey to Antony had a devastating effect on Mariamme (15.65-87); and the similar procedure during Herod's journey to Octavian turned Mariamme's love into hatred (15.185, 202-215). Herod himself switched between deep feelings of love and anger (e.g., 15.211-212, 214), and Josephus suggests several times that the king was thinking of killing his wife (15.87, 212, 215).

seemed to have been rather fortunate before.[1394] For the passion[1395] he rightly[1396] felt for Mariamme was greater than any [passion] recorded.[1397] **219** She was prudent in most things[1398] and also faithful to him,[1399] but she had something womanly[1400] and difficult[1401] about her by nature.[1402] She took full advantage[1403] of the fact that he was enslaved by his

---

[1394] Josephus does not explicitly report about Herod's previous happiness with Mariamme, but there are 2 indications for this: (1) Herod derived tremendous prestige from his marriage with Mariamme since she was not only of royal (i.e., Hasmonean) descent but also extremely beautiful (see *Ant.* 15.23 with the note to "strikingly beautiful"), and (2) Josephus repeats that Herod madly loved his wife (see 15.82 with the note to "loved her terribly" and 15.211 with the note to "his love").

[1395] About Herod's love for Mariamme, see the previous note.

[1396] Herod had good reasons for loving Mariamme (see the note to "have been rather fortunate before" above). The expression μετὰ τοῦ δικαίου is an adverbial phrase equivalent to δικαίως ("lawfully, rightly, justly," LSJ *s.v.* δίκαιος B I.2).

[1397] The complicated formulation ἔρωτα ... οὐδενὸς ἐλάττω τῶν ἱστορουμένων ἐπεπόνθει ("the love ... was greater than any [love] recorded" or "the love ... was greater than [the love] of anybody on record") may be corrupt (cf. Marcus-Wikgren 104-05). Nevertheless, there is a related expression in Philodemus, *Mus.* 36 (ed. Kemke 108): τῶν ἱστορουμένων οὐδενὸς ἧττον πολυπράγμων ("the most industrious person on record," my trans.; LSJ *s.v.* ἱστορέω II). The plural τῶν ἱστορουμένων is ambiguous: it can be neutral or masculine/feminine and therefore refer to things or persons (cf. Rengstorf *s.v.* ἱστορέω, who prefers the second option).

[1398] Josephus briefly interrupts the narrative flow with a characterization of Mariamme (see also *Ant.* 15.237-239). The first key word, σώφρων ("prudent, wise"), is the most important virtue of a prudent ruler, as the Joseph story in *Antiquities* exemplifies (2.9-200, especially 2.48, 50, 56, 69, 138; Feldman 1992, in contrast to Josephus' depiction of Cleopatra in 15.89-91; van Henten 2005a). Several other women in Josephus also exemplify this virtue (Mrs. Potiphar, from the perspective of her husband, *Ant.* 2.59; Nabal's wife [cf. 1 Sam 25], *Ant.* 6.296; the wise old woman [2 Sam 20:16], *Ant.* 7.289; Paulina, *Ant.* 18.66, 73; Antonia, *Ant.* 18.180). In some of these passages the word σώφρων probably has a sexual connotation, indicating self-control in a context of improper sexual contacts and/or faithfulness to one's partner (2.59; cf. 2.48, 50, 56, 69; 18.73). This connotation may also be present here, especially if the larger context is taken into account (cf. Salome's accusation against Joseph and Mariamme in 15.81 and the slanderous remarks by Salome and Cyprus concerning Mariamme in 15.213; see also the next note).

[1399] Mariamme's faithfulness probably should not be taken in a general sense since Alexandra and Mariamme's attempt to flee to the Roman legion—after they had become aware of Herod's secret instructions for Joseph to kill Mariamme (*Ant.* 15.65)—was a clear case of disloyalty (15.72-73). The adjective πιστή ("faithful") can have a sexual connotation (Mayer-Schärtel 1995: 230-31), which would in this case imply that Salome's accusations and slander about Mariamme's adulterous behavior (see the preceding note) were unwarranted. Alexander's accusation of his wife Glaphyra is a parallel that supports a sexual interpretation of πιστή: Glaphyra was unfaithful to him (referring to women who cannot be trusted, ἄπιστα) by having entered into relationships with other men (*Ant.* 17.352).

[1400] The word γυναικεῖος/-ως ("pertaining to women," Rengstorf *s.v.*) already occurs in the Herod narrative in *Ant.* 15.44, 69, the first time in a reference to Alexandra and the second time referring to both Mariamme and Alexandra (with the emphasis on Alexandra). The 2 passages are far from flattering and express various aspects of typically female behavior (see 15.44 with the note to "full of female thoughts").

[1401] Mariamme's difficult character (see also *Ant.* 15.220, 237-238) becomes apparent in her arrogance, highlighted already in the description of the aftermath of Herod's visit to Antony (15.81), as well as in her frankness of speech (see 15.238 with the note to "license of tongue"; cf. *War* 1.437).

The expression χαλεπός/-ῶς is a key word in this section (15.202-203, 208 [twice], 210, 219, 223). See also χαλεπῶς ἐχούσας ("they were angry," 15.202 with the note to "were angry") and χαλεπῶς ἔφερον ("they were taking it badly," 15.203 with the note to "which they were taking badly") concerning Mariamme and Alexandra's response to Herod's decision to lodge and guard them in Alexandrium apart from the rest of the family (15.185, 203-204). A similar phrase (χαλεπῶς διέκειτο "she was annoyed") concerns Mariamme alone (15.208).

[1402] The phrase ἐκ φύσεως is here synonymous with φύσει ("by nature, according to one's character," Rengstorf *s.v.* φύσις). It implies that the statements in this passage concern Mariamme's character. For similar phrases concerning the characters of Cleopatra, Hyrcanus, and Herod, see respectively *Ant.* 15.89 (with the note to "greedy character"), 15.178 (with the note to

desire,[1404] not taking into account at certain moments that somebody else was king and ruler over her.[1405] Many times she treated him insolently,[1406] but he bore that with self-control[1407] and superiority, although he was being ridiculed.[1408] **220** She openly[1409] treated his mother and sister[1410] most scornfully because of their low birth[1411] and reviled them,[1412] such that, while there had already been dissension and implacable hatred[1413] among the

"against his nature"), and 17.304 (with the note to "his character").

[1403] Niese (371) reads ἱκανῶς ἐντρυφῶσα with most MSS, which can be translated in several ways because ἐντρυφάω (which is a *hapax legomenon* in Josephus) can be interpreted as "treat haughtily" (Rengstorf *s.v.* ἐντρυφάω), "delight in" (LSJ *s.v.* I), or "(ab-)use at pleasure" (LSJ *s.v.* III). Instead of ἱκανῶς MSS LW and a marginal reading of MS A have ἀνικάνως ("insufficiently, not capable, being dissatisfied with everything," LSJ *s.v.*), which only seems to go with the third meaning of ἐντρυφάω: "she made insufficiently use of."

[1404] This phrase echoes passages about Antony and Cleopatra being enslaved by love (ἔρως) or passion/desire (ἐπιθυμία): Antony was "enslaved by his passionate love for Cleopatra (τῷ Κλεοπάτρας ἔρωτι δεδουλωμένον)" (*War* 1.243, trans. Sievers/Forte in BJP 1a); Cleopatra herself was "a slave to her desires (δουλευούσῃ ταῖς ἐπιθυμίαις)" (*Ant.* 15.91; see also 15.88, 93 [with the note to "he was totally overcome by this woman"], 97, 131, and van Henten 2005a: 114-15). Landau (2006: 167) emphasizes, however, that the analogy between Mariamme and Cleopatra is only partial.

[1405] This criticism is connected with Josephus' earlier remarks about Mariamme's difficult character: her arrogance (because of her royal descent; see the note to "difficult" above) and frankness of speech (*Ant.* 15.238). The latter characteristic is related to what Josephus seems to criticize here: Mariamme "did not know her place"; she sometimes forgot that Herod was not only her husband but also the king. Mariamme could even not keep her opinion to herself when expressing it was to her disadvantage (cf. 15.85-86, 210; differently Alexandra according to 15.60). In this light τῷ καιρῷ probably means "at the right time/moment" (cf. Rengstorf *s.v.* καιρός).

The verb συγκαταλογίζομαι ("take into account," Rengstorf *s.v.*) occurs once elsewhere in Josephus (16.96).

[1406] The phrase ὑβριστικῶς προσηνέχθη ("she treated [him] insolently/arrogantly") elaborates a further aspect of Mariamme's difficult character. For related vocabulary, see Diodorus 16.41.2; 34/35.2.36; Plutarch, *Mor.* (*Mulier. virt.*) 259a. Mariamme's arrogance towards Herod matches her and her mother's behavior towards Herod's relatives (see *Ant.* 15.37, 44).

[1407] This is one of the passages that suggest that Herod was capable of controlling his emotions if he wanted to (van Henten 2008a: 202-03). Josephus uses the same phrase ἐγκρατῶς ἔφερε ("bore with self-control") in *Ant.* 15.60 (see the note to "Alexandra controlled") concerning Alexandra's self-control with respect to her suspicions about her son's death.

[1408] The rare compound ἐξειρωνεύομαι ("ridicule, being ridiculed") occurs once elsewhere in Josephus, in connection with Alexandra and Mariamme's attempt to worm Herod's secret instructions out of Joseph (see *Ant.* 15.69).

[1409] Apparently Mariamme insulted Herod's mother and sister even in public (ἀναφανδόν —"openly"; cf. the same adverb in *Ant.* 16.73 concerning Mariamme's sons Alexander and Aristobulus), which is a further indication of Mariamme's lack of self-control (see 15.219 with notes).

[1410] On the antagonistic relationship between Herod's mother Cyprus and sister Salome on the one hand, and Mariamme and Alexandra on the other hand, see *Ant.* 15.81, 213, the continuation of the narrative below and the following notes.

[1411] The noun δυσγένεια ("low birth") partly repeats *Ant.* 15.81 (see the note to "their low birth"), concerning Mariamme's reproaching the low birth of Salome's family. Here Josephus uses the verb διαχλευάζω ("scoff at, ridicule," Rengstorf *s.v.*; cf. *War* 2.281; 4.338; *Ant.* 9.265 [variant reading]), with δυσγένειαν as object, instead of ἐξονειδίζω ("reproach"). *War* 1.437-438 suggests that in addition to his mother and sister Mariamme also reproached Herod himself for having Hyrcanus II and Aristobulus III murdered: "It was for this reason that Mariamme upbraided (ὠνείδιζεν) Herod, and insulted his sister and mother with disgraceful reproaches (δειναῖς ἐξύβραζεν λοιδορίαις)" (trans. Sievers/Forte in BJP 1a).

[1412] The same phrase κακῶς λέγω ("revile, ridicule," Rengstorf *s.v.* λέγω) is used in *Ant.* 16.72 concerning Salome reviling Mariamme as well as her sons (cf. also *Apion* 1.318).

[1413] Dissension (στασίς) and hatred (μῖσος) are words that fit the previous descriptions of the relationship between the 2 camps of women (i.e., Hasmonean versus

women, there were rather serious slanders[1414] too that time. **221** The nurturing of his suspicion[1415] extended over a period of a year,[1416] from the time that Herod had returned from Caesar.[1417] Finally, however, what had been managed[1418] for a rather long period exploded[1419] with the following event as a catalyst.[1420]

222 When the king was lying down to rest at noon,[1421] he called for Mariamme[1422] out of the affection he always felt for her.[1423] She did come in but did not lie down,[1424] although

---

Herodian) very well (see *Ant.* 15.80-81, 184-185, 213 [in which passage μῖσος is used] and cf. 15.23-24, 35-38, 44). For the rare expression μῖσος ἄσπονδον ("implacable hatred"), cf. Sozomen 5.22.2. The adjective ἄσπονδος ("implacable, untrustworthy") also occurs in *Ant.* 4.264; 15.146 (see the note to "untrustworthy in battle").

[1414] The expression διαβολὰς μείζονας ("rather serious slanders") connects with Salome's slanderous accusation (διαβολή) against her husband Joseph (and, in fact, also against Mariamme, *Ant.* 15.81), as well as with Cyprus and Salome's manifold slander about Mariamme (οὐ μικραῖς διαβολαῖς, 15.213).

[1415] Josephus frequently refers to Herod's suspicion (see *Ant.* 15.42 with the note to "suspicion"). Being under his suspicion was dangerous for the person involved (15.35 with the note to "suspicion").

[1416] Mariamme was apparently in an extremely dangerous situation because of Cyprus and Salome's slander. It is obvious that both ladies could do a lot of damage to Mariamme's reputation in the course of a year, but the period of a year also suggests that Herod was capable of controlling himself from taking rash decisions (see *Ant.* 15.219).

[1417] Josephus' remark is ambiguous because the preceding paragraphs reports 2 visits of Herod to Octavian and 2 returns: (1) the visit to Rhodes after Actium (*Ant.* 15.187-197), followed by a reference to Herod's return (15.198), and (2) Herod's meeting with Octavian in Egypt, after the final victory over Mark Antony and Cleopatra (15.215-218), followed by a reference to Herod's return home (15.218). There are 2 further references to a return from a trip to Octavian (15.202, 209), which probably both concern the first visit. That visit took place in the spring of 30 BCE (see 15.187 with the note to "Caesar"), the second probably in the early autumn of that same year (see 15.215 with the note to "hold Egypt following Antony's and Cleopatra's deaths"). It is plausible that the second visit (15.215-218) is meant in 15.221 (differently Otto 1913: 51) because it is described in the immediate context. In that case "the period of a year" would extend from the early autumn of 30 BCE until the early autumn of 29 BCE. If the first visit is meant, which remains possible, the period would be the spring of 30 BCE—the spring of 29 BCE.

[1418] The meaning of the passive voice of the rare verb προοικονομέω ("arrange before," LSJ *s.v.*, or "take precautions," Rengstorf *s.v.*; cf. *War* 7.279; *Ant.* 2.87) is uncertain here. Rengstorf (*s.v.*) suggests "be kept previously under control" as meaning (although with a question mark added). LSJ (*s.v.*) give "be so arranged."

[1419] The phrase τέλεον μέντοι ... ἐξερράγη ("finally, however, ... exploded"; for ἐκρήγνυμι ["break out, burst"], see Rengstorf *s.v.*) draws the readers' attention and prepares for a climax. It may echo a phrase in Herodotus (8.74): "(For a time each man talked quietly to his neighbor, wondering at Eurybiades' folly,) but finally it came out into the open (τέλος δὲ ἐξερράγη)" (trans. Godley; cf. Aelius Aristides, *Sacri serm.* [ed. Dindorf 1.468]).

[1420] The verb ἐγγίγνομαι ("be born in, occur, emerge, pass," Rengstorf *s.v.*) occurs 13 times in Josephus. Six of these occurrences are part of the Herod narrative of *Antiquities* (15.221, 295; 16.75, 176; 17.104, 109). The phrase ἀφορμῆς ἐγγενομένης (literally "starting-point occurring ...") finds a close parallel in Gregory of Nyssa, *Cant. cant.* (ed. Langerbeck 6.55).

[1421] The verb κατακλίνω ("lie down, recline at table," Rengstorf *s.v.*) often occurs in the context of a meal (cf. *Ant.* 6.48), but here the verb refers to resting (cf. aorist infinitive ἀναπαύσασθαι a few words further), probably for a nap at noon (the hottest period of the day). Cf. the story about the death of Mariamme's brother Aristobulus III, in which Josephus relates that the young man and other guests of Alexandra "cooled themselves off from the extreme heat of midday" near the swimming pools of Jericho (15.54). The noun μεσημβρία ("noon") also occurs in 15.54.

[1422] This detail suggests that it was Herod's habit to call for Mariamme when he was resting (see also *Ant.* 15.242 about Herod calling for Mariamme although she was dead).

With Mariamme's refusal to lay down with Herod Josephus moves over to the climax of the dramatic story about the queen's end, which focuses on Salome's framing of Mariamme, alleging that she was planning to have her husband poisoned (15.222-231).

[1423] Herod's great affection (φιλοστοργία) for Mariamme is a recurring motif in the Herod narrative of *Antiquities* (see 15.66, 68, 70, 83; cf. 16.11 concerning Mariamme's sons). *Ant.* 15.83 states that Herod was "overcome by affection for his wife." Here, a small but

he urged her to.¹⁴²⁵ She poured contempt on him¹⁴²⁶ and railed¹⁴²⁷ that he had killed her father¹⁴²⁸ and her brother.¹⁴²⁹ **223** While he took her outrageous [accusation] badly¹⁴³⁰ and was ready to act rashly,¹⁴³¹ his sister Salome,¹⁴³² noticing that his disturbance was rather serious,¹⁴³³ sent his cup-bearer¹⁴³⁴ in, who had been prepared for this long before.¹⁴³⁵ She

Set-up by Salome leads to Mariamme's execution.
War *1.438-439; 443*

---

telling detail is added: Herod *always* felt affection for Mariamme. This may be somewhat overstated, but it would explain why Mariamme could stand her ground at Herod's court despite the sabotage by Salome and Cyprus (see 15.213 with the note to "his sister and mother noticed" and cf. Dositheus' calculation).

¹⁴²⁴ The aorist κατεκλίθη ("did [not] lie down") contrasts with κατακλινόμενος ("lying down") concerning Herod.

¹⁴²⁵ The participle σπουδάζοντος ("although he urged her to," Rengstorf *s.v.* σπουδάζω) is absent in MSS FVE (Niese 372).

¹⁴²⁶ Mariamme treats Herod here the way she used to behave towards Salome and Cyprus (see *Ant.* 15.81, 220). Ilan (1998: 211) argues that the *Antiquities* report about Mariamme's death is modelled on King David's removal of his wife Michal from the court (1 Sam 6:12-23), which likewise mentions Michal's contempt for David. The verb ἐκφαυλίζω ("depreciate, pour contempt on," LSJ *s.v.*) occurs 8 times in Josephus and only in *Antiquities*.

¹⁴²⁷ The verb προσλοιδορέω in the middle and passive voices (here passive) means "insult besides." The verb occurs once elsewhere in Josephus (*Ant.* 7.170; cf. the variant reading of MS M in 13.372 and the noun λοιδορίαις in *War* 1.438).

¹⁴²⁸ Most Greek MSS transmit τὸν πατέρα ("her father"), which is probably the original reading (Niese 372). MS L and E read τὸν πάππον ("her grandfather"), which is historically correct but likely a correction by a copyist (Marcus-Wikgren 106 n. *b*; Schalit 2001: 587 n. 43) on the basis of the parallel passage of *War* (1.437; see *Ant.* 15.238 with the note to "for her not living acceptably with the king"), which reads τὸν πάππον. Since Mariamme's father Alexander had been executed in 49 BCE by Q. Metellus Scipio, the governor of Syria (*Ant.* 14.125), the correct reference should be to Mariamme's grandfather Hyrcanus II. Josephus offers 2 versions of his death in *Antiquities* (15.165-178) and sides with the second version, strongly suggesting that Hyrcanus' execution was orchestrated by Herod (15.174, 178 and see 15.176 with the note to "ordered for the man to be strangled").

¹⁴²⁹ Mariamme thinks aloud what Josephus has already suggested to his readers: Herod was responsible for the death of Mariamme's (grand-)father and brother (*Ant.* 15.53, 55, 58, 174, 178). Small hints in the narrative concerning Jonathan-Aristobulus' death (15.50-56) suggest that Herod was responsible (15.53, 55) and these are taken up in the aftermath of the event, leading to Herod's journey to Antony (15.58, 62-65). The parallel passage of *War* (1.437) reports a similar accusation but does not indicate the context of this reproach: "She publicly reproached him (φανερῶς ὠνείδιζεν αὐτῷ) about what had happened to her grandfather (τὸν πάππον), Hyrcanus, and to her brother, Jonathan" (trans. Sievers/Forte in BJP 1a).

¹⁴³⁰ The phrase χαλεπῶς φέρω ("take badly") also occurs in *Ant.* 15.203, referring to Alexandra and Mariamme's response to their stay and treatment at Alexandrium. For other occurrences, see 15.24 with the note to "took the disgrace of her son badly," and for parallel phrases of χαλεπῶς φέρω plus ὕβρις ("insolence, disgraceful treatment," Rengstorf *s.v.*, or "outrage," LSJ *s.v.* II) as object, Hesiod, *Fragm. astr.* 7.5; Appian, *Bell. civ.* 4.5.32.

¹⁴³¹ For the motif of Herod's rashness in acting, see *Ant.* 15.100 with the note to "out of rashness" and 15.230 with the note to "not to kill her hastily in this way."

¹⁴³² Herod's sister Salome acts at the right moment, as she does during the aftermath of Herod's journey to Mark Antony, when she accuses her husband Joseph of adultery with Mariamme (*Ant.* 15.80-81). Josephus presents Salome as a shrewd and unscrupulous schemer against Mariamme and her sons (see 15.80 with the note to "his sister Salome").

¹⁴³³ Herod's disturbance is emphasized in the earlier episode about Joseph and Mariamme during the aftermath of his journey to Antony, but there Herod "was greatly disturbed" (ἐξετετάρακτο) after Salome's accusation that Joseph had committed adultery with Mariamme (see *Ant.* 15.82 with the note to "he was greatly disturbed"). The noun ταραχή ("disturbance") also occurs with μείζων ("greater, more serious") in *War* 1.245 and *Ant.* 16.229 (concerning the disturbances and dissension within Herod's family; see also 15.22 with the note to "disagreements also arose among persons within his household").

¹⁴³⁴ Cup-bearers were part of the royal court in the eastern Mediterranean world (cf. the Joseph story about the cup-bearer in Pharaoh's dream: Gen 40:1-41:13; Josephus, *Ant.* 2.63-79). Josephus' other references to

had ordered him to say that Mariamme had persuaded him to assist her with preparing a love-potion[1436] for the king. **224** And if[1437] he should be confused[1438] and ask what of all things this was, [the cup-bearer][1439] should say that[1440] Mariamme had this potion[1441] but that he was requested to serve [it].[1442] If [Herod's interest] would not be aroused[1443] because of this love-potion, he [the cup-bearer] should drop the subject.[1444] For it would not cause any danger for him.[1445] Having previously given these instructions[1446] [to the cup-bearer],

---

cup-bearers mostly concern the setting of a royal court (*War* 1.249, 261; *Ant.* 14.333 on the Parthian royal cup-bearer Pacorus [see 15.12 with the note to "the commanders of the Parthians"] and *Ant.* 11.159 concerning Nehemiah, the cup-bearer of the Persian king Xerxes). Cup-bearers were to pour wine for the king (*Ant.* 2.64) and so they had to be absolutely reliable (cf. 2.66) in order to prevent poisoned wine. Herod's father Antipater's being poisoned by Malichus with the aid of a cup-bearer illustrates the need for reliability (*War* 1.226; *Ant.* 14.281). Vössing (2004: 168 n. 2 with references) wonders whether Herod's cup-bearer was a eunuch since it was a practice at the Hasmonean court that cup-bearers were eunuchs (similarly at the royal house of Nicomedia). A later passage about Herod's cup-bearer explicitly states that he was an eunuch (*Ant.* 16.230).

[1435] Salome's act perfectly matches her image in Josephus (see the note to "his sister Salome" above).

The adverbial phrase ἐκ πλείστου ("long before") can also be translated with "in great detail" (LSJ *s.v.* πλεῖστος IV.3). Both possibilities emphasize that Salome had carefully prepared this set up.

[1436] The accusation is plausible because the cup-bearer's nearness to the king could lead to confidential tasks, ordered either by the king or by somebody who needed to approach the king. The offer of a love-potion (φίλτρον, Rengstorf *s.v.*) coming from Mariamme would have appealed to Herod since it would be a signal that Mariamme had overcome her anger and wanted to respond to Herod's love again. The noun φίλτρον is a key-word in this section (see *Ant.* 15.224, 225 [twice], 229). The dangerous potential of a love-potion is also apparent from the stories about the death of Herod's brother Pheroras (*War* 1.583; *Ant.* 17.62).

The verb συγκατασκευάζω means "help to prepare" here (Rengstorf *s.v.*) and implies that Mariamme was involved in the preparation of the love-potion.

[1437] I.e., Herod.

[1438] The aorist ταραχθῇ ("if he should be confused") connects with ταραχῆς in the previous paragraph and puts emphasis on Herod's confusion and disturbance (see *Ant.* 15.223 with the note to "his disturbance was rather serious").

[1439] It is clear that the subject is the cup-bearer since the infinitive λέγειν ("say") follows κελεύουσα ("she [i.e., Salome] had ordered him [i.e., the cup-bearer] to say") of *Ant.* 15.223.

[1440] Dindorf (1845: 594, followed by Marcus-Wikgren 106 but not by Niese 372) notes that there is a lacuna after ὅτι ("[say] that").

[1441] The noun φάρμακον is ambiguous: it can mean "medicine, potion" but also "drug" and especially "(deadly) poison" (Rengstorf *s.v.*; see *War* 1.272, 581-583, 592; *Ant.* 17.69). The word could, therefore, easily have aroused Herod's suspicion (cf. *Ant.* 15.42 with the note to "suspicion"), and this seems to have been exactly what Salome was aiming for.

Marcus-Wikgren (106) conjecture χεούσης ("pouring") instead of ἐχούσης ("having"; assuming that a transposition of χ and ε corrupted the more original reading), which is unnecessary since the transmitted text is perfectly understandable: Mariamme kept the potion until the cup-bearer poured it (cf. *War* 1.593 on Pheroras' wife, who was keeping poison intended to murder Herod).

[1442] The passive participle of παρακαλέω probably means "be requested" here (Rengstorf *s.v.*): the context implies that Mariamme requested the cup-bearer to pour the potion. The cup-bearer's words to Herod confirm this (see *Ant.* 15.225 with the note to "said that it was a potion given by Mariamme").

[1443] Herod is not mentioned explicitly.

These phrases form the beginning of what the cup-bearer should do in case Herod did not respond to the statement about the love-potion. The verb κινέω ("move, arouse") is ambiguous: it can indicate the effect of certain feelings or emotions upon a person, positively or negatively (cf. *Ant.* 15.50 concerning Herod being provoked by jealousy and 15.351 about the Jews' feelings of hatred of Herod). The passive voice can in such contexts mean "be agitated/disquieted/angry" (Rengstorf *s.v.* κινέω).

[1444] With Rengstorf (*s.v.* ἀργός "idle"), who suggests "not to dwell on the matter, drop it" as meanings for τὸν λόγον ἀργὸν ἐᾶν. For other expressions with λόγος and ἀργός, cf. Aesop 287; Clement of Alexandria, *Paed.* 2.6.50; *Strom.* 7.9.54.

[1445] This is the conclusion of Salome's words to the cup-bearer, which explains her previous statement. The cup-bearer's participation in her scheme had to be without danger for him. MSS PFV read οὐδέν instead of οὐδένα, which implies a slightly different translation: "nothing would cause a danger for him."

she [Salome] sent him in[1447] at that particular moment to speak to the king. **225** So he went in, persuasively[1448] as well as rapidly, saying that Mariamme had given him presents[1449] and had persuaded him to give[1450] him [Herod] a love-potion. When he [Herod] got excited about this[1451] and asked him what sort of thing the love-potion was,[1452] he [the cup-bearer] said that it was a potion given by Mariamme,[1453] of which he did not know the power,[1454] and for that reason he was informing him about it.[1455] He believed that this was safer for both himself[1456] and the king. **226** Hearing these words Herod,[1457] who was already in a bad state,[1458] became even more enraged.[1459] The eunuch[1460] who was most faithful to

---

[1446] The verb προδιδάσκω ("instruct previously," Rengstorf *s.v.*) is a *hapax legomenon* in Josephus.

[1447] The verb εἰσπέμπει ("she sent [him] in") repeats the same phrase of *Ant.* 15.223 and rounds off Salome's instructions for the cup-bearer.

[1448] The common meaning of πιθανῶς is "credibly, persuasively" (Rengstorf *s.v.* πιθανός); an alternative translation would be "obediently, docilely" (LSJ *s.v.* πιθανός). Josephus neither tells how Salome succeeded in persuading Herod's cup-bearer to co-operate with her, nor mentions any reward by Salome (see the next note). The cup-bearer may have thought that he would not put his position at risk by participating in the intrigue, as Salome's last remark suggests (see *Ant.* 15.224 with the note to "not cause any danger for him").

[1449] This is the obvious thing to do in order to bribe an official (cf. *War* 1.489; *Ant.* 15.205). It is plausible that Salome had to do something similar in order to assure herself of the cup-bearer's co-operation, but Josephus does not mention this.

[1450] The infinitive ἀναπείθειν echoes πείθοι ("persuaded") of *Ant.* 15.223. In both cases Mariamme is the subject. The combination of ἀναπείθω ("persuade," Rengstorf *s.v.*) and διδόναι ("give") also occurs in 15.168, in which passage Alexandra persuades Hyrcanus II to give a letter to Dositheus in order to arrange an escape to King Malichus.

[1451] Salome's strategy, explained in her instructions to the cup-bearer ("If [Herod's interest] would not be aroused because of this love-potion ...," *Ant.* 15.224), aimed for this response by Herod: διακινηθέντος ("got excited") partly repeats κινηθέντος ("[if Herod's interest] would not be aroused") of 15.224 and adds suspense because of the prefix δια-. The verb is ambiguous (cf. 15.224 with the note to "would not be aroused"): the passive voice can mean "get excited" and "be disturbed/ agitated" (LSJ *s.v.*; Rengstorf *s.v.*).

[1452] Herod's question also connects with Salome's instructions ("... if he would ... ask what of all things this was ...," *Ant.* 15.224), but the vocabulary is different.

[1453] This statement also connects with Salome's instructions ("... [the cup-bearer] should say that Mariamme had this potion but that he was requested to serve [it]," *Ant.* 15.224), which were apparently meticulously obeyed by the cup-bearer. The noun φάρμακον ("potion, drug") also occurs in that passage (see the note to "this potion" about the ambiguity of this phrase).

[1454] The noun δύναμις ("power") indicates the potential power of the potion (cf. Rengstorf *s.v.*: "potentiality, effect"), which is again ambiguous: it could imply a powerful love-potion but also a powerful drug. The cup-bearer's statement adds to the ambiguity implied by the noun φάρμακον (see the previous note) and could easily arouse Herod's suspicion since knowing about the drinks poured to the king was the crucial part of the cup-bearer's job (see *Ant.* 15.223 with the note to "his cup-bearer").

The narrative about the poisoning of Pheroras (17.59-77) results in Varus testing the power of the drug: "... he [i.e., Varus] ... ordered for the poison (τὸ φάρμακον) to be brought before them, so that he would know the force that remained in it (ἵν' εἰδῆ τὴν περιοῦσαν αὐτῷ δύναμιν)" (17.131, my trans.); a prisoner who had been sentenced to death had to drink from the potion and died on the spot (17.132).

[1455] This is the cleverest part of Salome's instructions: informing Herod that he did not know the potential of the potion enabled him to fulfill his duty as cup-bearer (see the previous note and the continuation of the narrative) and execute Salome's instructions. In this way it was safe for him to participate in the scheme, as Salome indicated at the end of her words ("For it would not cause any danger for him ...," *Ant.* 15.224).

[1456] See the previous note.

[1457] For a similar introduction of a response by Herod to disturbing news, cf. *Ant.* 16.235 "Having heard these statements, Herod (became extremely bitter ...) (Τούτων τῶν λόγων ἀκούσας Ἡρώδης)" (my trans.).

[1458] Herod's bad state is explained by Mariamme's refusal to lie with Herod (*Ant.* 15.222-223). The verb διάκειμαι means "be in a certain mental or emotional condition" (Rengstorf *s.v.*). In combination with κακῶς it can indicate being in a bad state in general (this is the most probable meaning here), having an illness or handicap (*Apion* 1.257), or showing a negative attitude

Mariamme he subjected to torture[1461] concerning the drug, knowing that without him nothing big or small could have been done.[1462] **227** Even when put under duress, the fellow[1463] had nothing to say about the things concerning which he was being tortured.[1464] But he did say that the woman's hostility to him [Herod][1465] had arisen because of the stories that Soemus had told her.[1466] **228** While he was still saying these things,[1467] the king

---

towards certain persons (possibly here and in *Ant.* 16.386 with Ernesti's conjecture; see Niese 63). Cf. the related phrase χαλεπῶς διάκειμαι ("be shocked/annoyed/displeased/sulk") in 15.208 (with the note to "Being upset").

[1459] These phrases connect with Herod's reaction to Mariamme's refusal to lie with him (see the previous note): "While he took her outrageous [accusation] badly ..." (*Ant.* 15.223). Niese (373) reads ἠρεθίσθη with MSS PFV and E, which can mean that Herod "was enraged" or "felt disturbed" (Rengstorf *s.v.* ἐρεθίζω). MSS LAMW transmit a passive voice of the related compound verb ἀνερεθίζω, with a slightly different meaning: "was provoked/irritated" (Rengstorf *s.v.*).

[1460] Eunuchs traditionally served at royal courts in the eastern Mediterranean world (see *Ant.* 10.190 paraphrasing Dan 1:8, and *Ant.* 11.191, 260 concerning Queen Esther's eunuchs), as is also apparent from Josephus' brief description of Herod's 3 eunuchs in *War* 1.488 (cf. *Ant.* 16.230-231): "There were three eunuchs who were particularly respected by the king (τρεῖς εὐνοῦχοι τιμιώτατοι τῷ βασιλεῖ), and this was evident by the services they performed: one was in charge of pouring wine, another served dinner, and the third one put him to bed and slept at his side" (trans. Sievers/Forte in BJP 1a; cf. 17.44). Mariamme, being the queen, had probably her own eunuchs (cf. 11.260; further references in Schalit 2001: 411).

E reads οἰνοχόον ("cup-bearer") instead of εὐνοῦχον ("eunuch," Niese 373). The 2 words are closely related, and the epitomist may have stuck to the noun οἰνοχόος given in 15.223. The cup-bearer may, in fact, have been an eunuch, as the passage of *War* 1.488 suggests.

[1461] Herod frequently applied torture as a means to find out the truth (*War* 1.443, 485, 489, 496, 527-529, 577, 584-586, 590-594, 598-599, 606, 635; 2.85; *Ant.* 15.231; 16.246-253, 256, 315, 317-318, 320, 388-391; 17.56-57, 64-65, 69, 77, 79, 93, 105-106, 118-121; cf. 15.358; 17.105-106, 118-119). *Ant.* 17.69, 79 mention the torture of a Samaritan named Antipater and a freedman Bathyllus concerning a drug that had been prepared for poisoning Herod.

Torture was often applied in Graeco-Roman trials and private households. Herod did not distinguish between slaves and free persons. Roman law implied that Roman citizens could not be tortured, but Roman officials and governors had no qualms about torturing anyone else—including foreigners and freedmen without citizen status. Herod was presumably acting not differently from any other monarch, none of whom had anything like the Roman citizenship in his kingdom. Roman monarchs too, even during the early empire, did not bother much about rules when push came to shove. From the 2nd cent. CE onward, free persons were tortured on a more regular basis (Peters 1985: 11-36).

[1462] Obviously Mariamme's most faithful eunuch could have been expected to be familiar with her confidential acts. The formulation of this passage is redundant. The last part of it (οὔτε μεῖζον οὔτε ἔλαττον τι πεπρᾶχθαι "that nothing big or small could have been done") is paralleled by Pseudo-Socrates, *Ep.* 1.6; cf. Aelius Aristides, *Conc.* (ed. Dindorf 1.789); *Sacri serm.* (ed. Dindorf 1.531).

[1463] The expression ὁ ἄνθρωπος ("the man, the fellow") can refer to a specific man (e.g., *War* 2.106; 6.302; *Ant.* 8.49, 234; 13.295; 17.180; 19.223; *Life* 102; *Apion* 1.180, 189, 202), sometimes implying pity in particular contexts ("the poor man/fellow," Rengstorf *s.v.* ἄνθρωπος), which is probably the case here (cf. *Ant.* 17.34 about Pheroras being controlled by women).

[1464] This matches the information about Salome's intrigue: there was no potion, and so the eunuch could not know about it. On Herod's application of torture, see *Ant.* 15.226 with the note to "torture."

[1465] The phrase τῆς γυναικὸς ἔχθος εἰς αὐτόν ("the woman's hostility to him") connects with several other passages about hostility towards Herod. Six out of the 9 occurrences of ἔχθος in Josephus concern Herod: τὸ πρὸς Ἡρώδην ἔχθος ("[his] hatred for Herod") in *War* 1.239; 2.68, 76; *Ant.* 15.71, 227; 17.287. On Mariamme's hatred of Herod and his mother and sister, see *Ant.* 15.211 and 15.213 with the note to "their feelings of hatred towards Mariamme."

[1466] This refers to Soemus' revelation of Herod's secret instructions to kill Mariamme if Herod was not accepted by Octavian as ruler of Judea (*Ant.* 15.185, 205-208).

[1467] The phrase ταῦτα δ' ἔτι λέγοντος draws the readers' attention to what is subsequently narrated (cf. *Life* 259: "While I [i.e., Josephus] was still saying these things [ταῦτ' ἔτι λέγοντος], there were numerous voices from all sides calling me patron and rescuer ...," trans. Mason in BJP 9). For a similar formula, see *Ant.* 1.286.

cried out aloud[1468] and said that Soemus, who was at least at all other times most faithful to him and the monarchy,[1469] would never have utterly betrayed his orders[1470] had he not advanced too far[1471] in his contact with Mariamme.[1472] **229** And he ordered to arrest and kill Soemus immediately.[1473] But to his wife he gave a trial,[1474] having gathered[1475] the

---

[1468] Herod's dismay is apparent from his outcry; his emotional state is going from bad (*Ant.* 15.226) to worse. He responds in a similar way to Mariamme's statement about his secret instruction: "He cried out (ἐβόα) and tore his hair with his hands" (15.86). For phrases similar to μέγα βοήσας ("cried out aloud"), see 7.278; 17.206; cf. 8.219 and adverbial phrases with μεγάλη βολή ("in a loud voice") in the dative or accusative (6.172; 7.380; 8.339; 9.248).

[1469] This is the third and final reference to Soemus' faithfulness to Herod. The 2 previous references are found in *Ant.* 15.185, 205: *Ant.* 15.185 concerns Herod's instructions for Joseph and Soemus to guard Mariamme and Alexandra (see the note to "most faithful to him from the beginning"); *Ant.* 15.205 invokes the reader's suspicion (see the note to "trustworthy at the beginning"). Here Josephus writes in retrospective that Soemus had been "at all other times most faithful (πιστότατος, repeating πιστοτάτους of 15.185) to him ...," which implies that Herod believed that something very exceptional had taken place; otherwise Soemus would have remained faithful to him. This belief is elaborated in the continuation of the narrative (15.228).

The additional phrase "to the monarchy" may be redundant, unless it intends the absence of rebellious acts against Herod as ruler, acts with which particularly Alexandra is associated (see 15.166 with the note to "hoping for a political change").

[1470] The verb καταπροδίδωμι ("betray") occurs once elsewhere in Josephus (*War* 3.137, about betraying the fatherland).

[1471] There may be a *double entendre* here because the verb προσέρχομαι ("go/come to," Rengstorf *s.v.* προσέρχομαι) sometimes refers to sexual intercourse (see *Apion* 2.234: συνουσίᾳ προσελθεῖν "in connection with sexual relations," Barclay in BJP 10 on *Ap.* 2.234, and the next note). Herod's consternation and anger should, therefore, be explained by his conclusion that his wife had committed adultery with Soemus and by his enormous jealousy of possible rivals as sexual partners of Mariamme (see *Ant.* 15.65-67 and 15.82 with the note to "could not bear having a rival").

[1472] The noun κοινωνία can mean "association, contact, fellowship, etc." (Rengstorf *s.v.*), sometimes in connection with a sexual relationship. The word also occurs in the episode about Joseph and Mariamme (see *Ant.* 15.86 with the note to "sexual relationship with her"), in which the sexual connotation is obvious because of the accusation of adultery (15.81). Here the context likewise suggests a sexual connotation (see the previous note).

[1473] Soemus' fate is very similar to that of Joseph, who was immediately executed when Herod concluded that he had committed adultery with Mariamme (*Ant.* 15.87). Since Soemus had been appointed governor of a district (15.217) and had been one of Herod's most loyal officials (see 15.228 with the note to "most faithful to him and the monarchy"), one would expect that Herod would have convened a council meeting to pronounce the death sentence for Soemus (see also the next note). Günther (2005: 112, 116) argues that Soemus was actually executed because of treason and rebellion and not because of adultery. She supports this interpretation by stating that Herod had married another wife in 35/34 BCE (cf. Kokkinos 1998: 202; differently Stern 1974b: 262), the daughter of his brother-in-law Joseph and the sister of Dositheus. Günther argues that Josephus obscures the political dimension of the conflict.

[1474] Kasher (2007: 167) qualifies Mariamme's trial as a show trial like Hyrcanus' in *Ant.* 15.173 (see the note to "after showing the letters to the council"). Nevertheless, Herod must have been aware that executing persons without a trial could trigger serious opposition. When Herod, after his appointment as governor of Galilee, had killed Ezekias and his fellow brigands without a trial (14.159; cf. *War* 1.204), the most prominent Jews complained before Hyrcanus II that the unlawful execution had been neither authorized by Hyrcanus nor by the council (*Ant.* 14.167). Herod was put on trial as a result (14.168-178; van Henten 2008a). This experience as well as his relationship with his Roman patrons may have led Herod to organize trials when he wanted to execute important opponents or close relatives (see *War* 1.654; *Ant.* 17.160-164 on the persons responsible for the demolition of the golden eagle; *Ant.* 15.173 on the execution of Hyrcanus II; and *War* 1.538 [cf. *Ant.* 16.356, 361] on the trial of Herod's sons Alexander and Aristobulus, and cf. *Ant.* 15.98-101 on Herod's consultation of his council in order to decide whether Cleopatra was to be murdered or not). Concerning the rare phrase ἀποδίδωμι κρίσιν ("give/grant a trial"), cf. Polybius 5.16.5.

[1475] The verb συνάγω ("bring together, convene") refers to the council meeting for Mariamme's trial (cf.

persons who were closest to him[1476] and formulating a zealously pursued accusation[1477] about the love-potions and the drugs,[1478] in line with the slanders.[1479] And he was unable to control himself in his speaking[1480] and too angry for a judgment.[1481] And the end was such that those present, knowing in what state he was, voted for her death penalty.[1482] **230** After the verdict was pronounced,[1483] however, an idea occurred to[1484] him as well as to some of those present, namely not to kill her hastily in this way[1485] but to put her in one

---

War 1.538 concerning the trial of Herod's sons by Mariamme: συνῆγε τὸ δικαστήριον "he assembled the court," and *Ant.* 15.173 about the council meeting preceding Hyrcanus II's execution).

[1476] The superlative adjective οἰκειοτάτους is open to several interpretations: it can indicate persons belonging to the same family (cf. *Ant.* 15.40, 218, 239) or close friends (LSJ *s.v.* II; cf. Rengstorf *s.v.* οἰκεῖος), which meanings would imply that the council either existed of close relatives (including Salome and Cyprus, i.e., Mariamme's opponents) or political friends (whether Jews or not; see 15.5 with the note to "the friends around him" and cf. 17.46 concerning the council discussing the accusations against Pheroras' wife), or both (Schalit 2001: 405-06). The last option finds support in the continuation of the narrative—which focuses on Alexandra (see 15.233)—and in a parallel passage of *War* (1.556) about a meeting concerning the children of the executed Alexander and Aristobulus: "Now one day Herod assembled his relatives and friends (συναγαγὼν ... συγγενεῖς τε καὶ φίλους), set the children before them, and, his eyes filled with tears, said ..." (trans. Sievers/Forte in BJP 1a). The selectness of the gathering must have made the chances very slim that Mariamme would not be convicted.

[1477] An alternative translation is "a very carefully prepared accusation": the verb σπουδάζω can mean "pursue zealously" as well as "prepare with great care" (Rengstorf *s.v.*, who prefers the second meaning for this passage).

The phrase κατηγορίαν ποιεῖσθαι ("formulate an accusation") is common in Josephus (*Ant.* 1.319; 16.393; 18.179; 19.12-13, 160; 20.200; *Life* 194, 284) and occurs already in Thucydides (3.61.1). The combination with σπουδάζω, however, is unique and emphasizes that Herod absolutely wanted Mariamme to be executed, which is confirmed by the continuation of the narrative (but see *Ant.* 15.230).

[1478] The positive term φίλτρον ("love-potion"; see *Ant.* 15.223 with the note to "love-potion") and the highly ambiguous noun φάρμακον ("potion, drug, poison"; see 15.224 with the note to "potion") are combined here.

[1479] The phrase κατὰ τὰς διαβολάς ("in line with the slanders") is ambiguous since διαβολή can mean "slander" as well as "accusation" (see *Ant.* 15.81 with the note to "accusing" concerning Salome's accusation that Joseph had committed adultery with Mariamme). It probably concerns a marginal comment by Josephus since it connects with Salome and Cyprus' continuous slanders against Mariamme before Herod (15.213 οὐ μικραῖς ... διαβολαῖς; 15.221 διαβολὰς μείζονας), which would imply that Josephus is hinting at Mariamme's innocence. Schalit (2001: 138) concludes that there can hardly be any doubt that Mariamme was innocent, but Grant (1971: 99) considers Mariamme's guilt a serious possibility. *Ant.* 16.185 refers to false charges of licentiousness fabricated by Nicolaus of Damascus in connection with Mariamme's death.

[1480] Ironically this phrase about Herod (ἀκρατὴς ἐν τῷ λόγῳ) is paralleled in *Ant.* 16.399 by a remark about Herod's sons Alexander and Aristobulus: "(they were) intemperate in their speaking (ἀκρατεῖς δὲ λέγειν)."

[1481] Herod's anger connects with his response to the confession of Mariamme's eunuch (see *Ant.* 15.228-229). The comparative of ὀργίλος ("enraged, furious," Rengstorf *s.v.*) also occurs in *War* 3.23. The only other occurrence of ὀργίλος in Josephus is *Ant.* 19.19.

[1482] Herod's state of mind was apparently such that the persons present at the trial did not dare to oppose him. For a similar situation during the council at which the destroyers of Herod's golden eagle were sentenced, see *Ant.* 17.164. The combination of καταψηφίζομαι and θάνατον ("vote for the death penalty," Rengstorf *s.v.* καταψηφίζομαι) is common (Demosthenes, *Or.* 24.171; 50.48; Philo, *Ebr.* 71; *Mos.* 1.134; Josephus, *Life* 225; Plutarch, *Cic.* 21.3; *Mar.* 8.2; Cassius Dio 74.17.4; 76.8.4).

[1483] The noun γνώμη means "verdict, judgment" here (LSJ *s.v.* III), and the verb διαφέρω "pass (on), pronounce" (Rengstorf *s.v.*). The combination of these meanings is rare.

[1484] The verb ὑπογίνομαι ("grow up after, increase," Rengstorf *s.v.*) occurs once elsewhere in Josephus, also in the Herod narrative (*Ant.* 17.86).

[1485] This note confirms the rapid and extreme changes of Herod's mood (see *Ant.* 15.211-212 with notes) and the servile behavior of the council members (see 15.229 with the note to "voted for her death penalty"), who simply follow Herod's change of mind. Ten of the 17

of the fortresses of the kingdom.[1486] **231** But Salome and her female associates[1487] zealously endeavored[1488] to get the woman[1489] out of the way[1490] and more and more prevailed upon the king, advising him to be on his guard against disturbances of the masses[1491] if she happened to remain alive. So Mariamme was led to her execution[1492] in this way.[1493]

[1485] occurrences of the adjective προπετής ("rash, passionate, thoughtless," Rengstorf s.v.) in Josephus appear in the Herod narrative of *Antiquities*. Five of them concern Herod himself, sometimes emphasizing his rashness (16.262; cf. 16.69, 125 on Herod's sons Alexander and Aristobulus), but more often his self-control (15.82; 16.262, 359, and here). *Ant.* 15.82 offers a close parallel, concerning Salome's accusation of Joseph and Mariamme: "... he continued to control himself not to do anything rash (τοῦ μὴ προπετές τι ποιῆσαι) because of his love [for Mariamme]" (cf. 16.359 about Herod's attitude towards his sons Alexander and Aristobulus). See also the related noun προπέτεια ("rashness"), which occurs frequently in the Herod narrative of *Antiquities* (see 15.100 with the note to "anything out of rashness" and cf. *War* 1.379, 430).

[1486] The noun φρούριον means "fortified place, fortress," sometimes "dungeon" (Rengstorf s.v.). The usual meaning is plausible here since it would make Mariamme's situation similar to her previous stay at Alexandrium, where she had been guarded (*Ant.* 15.185).

[1487] Several passages in the Herod narrative suggest that there were at least 2 factions among the women at Herod's court: one around Alexandra and Mariamme, the other around Salome and Cyprus (see 15.213 with the note to "his sister and mother noticed"). It is plausible that several of Herod's (non-female) friends sided with one of these factions (see 15.35 with the note to "the friends called to their help").

MSS LAMW read τοῖς instead of ταῖς, which implies that Salome's associates were males. Niese (373) considers this reading to be probably right. Nevertheless, the reading ταῖς should be preferred as the *lectio difficilior*: a correction from ταῖς into τοῖς is logical, while the alternative option is not. Moreover, Josephus' hints at female factions elsewhere also favor the feminine article.

[1488] The meaning of σπουδάζω ("endeavor zealously") is very similar to that of the passive participle ἐσπουδασμένην ("a zealously pursued accusation" [i.e., pursued by Herod]) of the same verb in *Ant.* 15.229 and associates Salome's attitude towards Mariamme with Herod's.

[1489] The expression ἡ ἄνθρωπος ("the woman") is here not a simple reference to a specific woman, neither has it a depreciating connotation. The phrase probably expresses pity in certain contexts (i.e., "the poor woman"), as the male equivalent ὁ ἄνθρωπος sometimes does ("the poor fellow"; see *Ant.* 15.227 with the note to "the fellow" and cf. 18.112; 19.34).

[1490] The phrase ἐκποδὼν ποιεῖσθαι plus a personal object ("get [someone] out of the way") is a fixed expression in *Antiquities* (see 15.20 with the note to "get him out of the way"). In 15.77 it is also combined with σπουδάζω ("pursue zealously"), referring to Cleopatra's murderous intentions to get Herod out of the way.

[1491] Salome's hint at disturbances among the population may be explained by the assumption that she expected that Mariamme's fate would arouse protest because she was a member of the Hasmonean house. Cf. Herod's excuse for not sending Aristobulus III to Antony: "So [Herod] wrote in reply that in the event the young man would merely leave the country, everything would become filled with war and disorder (ἅπαντα πολέμου καὶ ταραχῆς ἀναπλησθήσεται) because the Jews had hoped for a change of government and a new regime with a different king" (*Ant.* 15.30). Günther (2005: 115) argues that Josephus' emphasis on the tragic end of Herod's relationship with Mariamme causes readers to overlook the political aspect of Mariamme's downfall.

Josephus refers to "disturbances of the people" (τὰς ταραχὰς τοῦ πλήθους) or rebellions of the crowd in various contexts: *War* 1.347 concerning the siege of Jerusalem by Herod and Sosius; *War* 2.29 concerning the disturbances following Herod's death; *Ant.* 4.35 concerning the revolt of Korah, Dathan, and Abiram described in Num 16; *Ant.* 15.358 concerning the complaints of the Gadarenes against Herod (see also 15.286 concerning the conspiracy to murder Herod during a festival in Jerusalem and 4.151; 10.8).

[1492] The phrase ἤγετο τὴν ἐπὶ θανάτῳ ("was led to her execution," Rengstorf s.v. θάνατος) is elliptical: the verb ἄγω is synonymous with ἀπάγω ("lead off [to execution]," Rengstorf s.v.) and the article τὴν should have been followed by a noun (e.g., ἔξοδον "departure" or ζημίαν "penalty"). Similar elliptical phrases with θάνατος occur elsewhere (LSJ s.v. θάνατος I.2). The phrase is closely paralleled by *Ant.* 19.269 about the execution of Chaereas (ἀπήγετο τὴν ἐπὶ θανάτῳ; see also 15.289 about the conspirators executed by Herod; 2 Macc 7:18; Socrates of Constantinople 7.22.11).

[1493] This remark suggests that the narrative about Mariamme's death comes to a conclusion. The continuation of the narrative switches to Alexandra (*Ant.*

(7.5) 232 Alexandra contemplated about the situation.[1494] Because she herself had little hope of not receiving a similar [treatment] from Herod,[1495] she changed her strategy, contrary to her former boldness,[1496] and in a highly disgraceful way. **233** For wanting to display[1497] her ignorance of the things Mariamme was being accused of,[1498] she leaped up[1499] and cried out, railing at[1500] her daughter, while all were listening,[1501] that she had become bad and ungrateful to her husband[1502] and was suffering a just punishment[1503] for

---

15.232), however, such that there is still another scene before Mariamme's death is finally reported (15.237).

[1494] Instead of reporting on how Alexandra felt about her daughter's execution, Josephus emphasizes that she was considering what was going on. He does so for 2 reasons:

(1) Presenting Alexandra as a tough and egocentric woman, which theme Josephus will elaborate in the subsequent paragraphes (*Ant.* 15.232-236). Unlike Mariamme, Alexandra was very well capable of hiding her emotions and thoughts, as the aftermath of her son Aristobulus III's death shows (15.57-65).

(2) Preparing readers for the final information about Mariamme's death (15.232-236), which starts with Alexandra as focalizer and then switches again to Mariamme, how she went to her death, contrasting the 2 Hasmonean women.

The verb συνθεωρέω ("contemplate," LSJ *s.v.*, or "consider, think over, recognize clearly [?]," Rengstorf *s.v.*) is a *hapax legomenon* in Josephus. For another combination of this verb with τὸν καιρὸν ("the situation"), cf. Polybius 3.102.1.

[1495] Alexandra had not only sided with Mariamme during their stay at Alexandrium (*Ant.* 15.202-205) but also attempted several actions against Herod. E.g., she had masterminded the attempt to escape to the Nabatean king Malichus, which led to the execution of Hyrcanus II (15.166-182), and had been lucky not to have been executed together with him (for her involvement in other actions against Herod, see 15.23 with the note to "Alexandra" and 15.166 with the note to "hoping for a political change"). Herod had become suspicious about her already during the episode that led to Aristobulus III's appointment as High Priest (15.42).

For similar expressions with μικρός ("small"), ἐλπίς ("hope," in the singular or plural), and the verb ἔχω ("have"), see Lysias 25.21; Strabo 2.3.5; Lucian, *Dom.* 13; *Hermot.* 69; *Ind.* 22. The phrase τῶν ὁμοίων τυγχάνω ("obtain/receive similar [things]") also occurs in Josephus, *Ant.* 1.274; 7.43; 16.157.

[1496] Josephus has not used the noun θράσος ("boldness") before in references to Alexandra (cf. *Ant.* 15.177 about Hyrcanus II), but this adjective can easily be connected with previous descriptions of Alexandra taking great liberties in speaking (παρρησία; see 15.37 with the note to "frankness") and her contentious character (φιλόνεικος, 15.62, 166, 168). For references about her rebellious acts, see 15.23, 34 and the previous note, and concerning Salome, 16.66 (cf. 17.147; Mayer-Schärtel 1995: 186).

[1497] The verb ἐμφαίνω ("display, show") is sometimes used for highlighting traits (e.g., Herod's generosity in *Ant.* 15.48, 196; his pride in 15.187; and his independence of spirit in 15.194) or feelings (e.g., Antony's desire for Cleopatra in 15.67 and Herod's grief about Aristobulus III's death in 15.60) of one of the characters in the narrative. In 15.379 it concerns the revelation of certain events. The verb is repeated in 15.234-236.

[1498] This note is ironic: Alexandra could not have been acquainted with Mariamme's attempt to poison Herod since it was set up by Salome. In light of what Josephus writes elsewhere about Alexandra it is plausible to assume that she knew everything about the tensions at the court and therefore realized that her daughter was framed. The combination of ἐμφαίνω with ἄγνοια ("ignorance") occurs also in Christian documents (e.g., Origen, *Exp. Prov.* [PG 17.209]; John Chrysostom, *Hom. Rom.* [PG 60.508-09]). For the phrase αἰτίαν ἔχω ("be accused"), see Thackeray and Marcus 1930-55: 15.

[1499] Alexandra apparently had made up her mind very quickly, and the continuation of the narrative presupposes that she had come to the cold and rational conclusion of gaining nothing from siding any longer with her daughter. Her highly emotional behavior in *Ant.* 15.233-234 strongly contrasts with Mariamme's calm and dignified attitude in 15.235-236. The verb ἐκπηδάω probably means "leap up" here (LSJ *s.v.* I.3).

[1500] The combination of the verbs ἐκπηδάω and λοιδορέω ("revile, rail [at]," Rengstorf *s.v.*) is rare (cf. John Chrysostom, *Hom. Eph.* [PG 62.97]).

[1501] The imperfect ἐβόα ("she cried out") suggest in combination with the verbs ἐκπηδάω and λοιδορέω (see the preceding notes) that Alexandra was putting up a dramatic show. The fact that everybody present heard her implies that she was the focal point. Josephus does not specify the setting of Alexandra's act, but the continuation of the narrative renders it plausible that it concerns the pronouncement of the death sentence for Mariamme, at which time Herod's closest associates and relatives were present (see *Ant.* 15.229 with the note to "the persons who were closest to him").

[1502] This highlights Alexandra's unscrupulous

daring to attempt such acts.[1504] For she had not reciprocated the benefactor of all of them as she ought.[1505] **234** When she even dared[1506] to tear her hair[1507] between such shameful histrionics,[1508] the disapproval of this disgraceful pretense[1509] by the others was, as one

---

behavior: she not only betrays her own daughter but also acts as if she herself had been grateful to Herod, while she had been involved in many more actions against Herod than Mariamme had been (see *Ant.* 15.23 with the note to "Alexandra" and 15.166 with the note to "Alexandra was quarrelsome"). Kasher (2007: 169) notes that this section turns Alexandra into a collaborator in Herod's criminal execution of his wife.

The combination of the adjectives κακός ("bad") and ἀχάριστος ("ungrateful") is unique in Josephus but does occur elsewhere (e.g., Demosthenes, *Or.* 20.55; Plutarch, *Aem.* 31.6; *Alex.* 71.4; Cassius Dio 52.26.7).

The noun ἀνήρ also means "husband" in *Ant.* 15.81, referring to Salome's husband Joseph. Submission to one's husband was standard in Jewish marriages (Mayer-Schärtel 1995: 189).

[1503] Alexandra seems to overdo her betrayal of her daughter. In the light of what Josephus writes about Herod's court and the factions involved, with Alexandra as one of the protagonists, it is likely that she had realized that Mariamme was the victim of a plot. This would imply that Alexandra joined the plotters against Mariamme here, which is sheer opportunism and seems incredible since she often sided with Mariamme (e.g., *Ant.* 15.72-73, 202).

The phrase δίκαια πάσχειν ("suffer justly/just punishment") also occurs in *War* 5.325; *Ant.* 5.166; 16.70; cf. *Ant.* 16.238; *Apion* 2.278 and Theognis 1.746; Aristophanes, *Thesm.* 86; Xenophon, *Anab.* 5.1.15; *Hell.* 4.6.1; 5.3.11; Theophrastus, *Char.* 26.6; Plutarch, *Mor.* (*Suav. viv.*) 1090d.

[1504] The vagueness of the formulation may indicate that Alexandra was unaware of Mariamme's supposed attempt to poison Herod, apart from what had become known by the words of the cup-bearer and the eunuch (*Ant.* 15.225, 227). It may also hint once again at Alexandra's unscrupulous behavior towards her daughter. The noun τόλμημα can mean "bold undertaking, outrage, shameless act" (LSJ *s.v.*; Rengstorf *s.v.*).

[1505] This connects with Mariamme's ungratefulness in the previous sentence and puts massive blame on Mariamme: she not only was ungrateful to Herod as her husband but also neglected her duty as a subject who had benefitted from Herod's benefactions as ruler. Gratitude towards a benefactor (εὐεργέτης; see also *Ant.* 15.19, 190, 193) was a basic expectation (12.206 and see 15.19 with the note to "a considerable number of gifts"). The notion that a ruler is the benefactor of all inhabitants of a state (τὸν πάντων αὐτῶν εὐεργέτην; cf. Polybius 4.38.10; Diodorus 2.36.7; Philo, *Spec.* 1.152; Aelius Aristides, *Iov.* [ed. Dindorf 1.10-11]) is connected with the Hellenistic idea that a ruler is the personification of a state and responsible for the care and protection of all inhabitants. This notion is also expressed in 1 Macc 14:47, in which verse the Hasmonean ruler Simon is called "the protector of them all" (τοῦ προστατῆσαι πάντων, Hölbl 1994: 83, 88; van Henten 2007b: 268; cf. *Ant.* 14.253 concerning Hyrcanus II as the benefactor of everybody and 16.98 about Augustus as "their common benefactor").

The verb ἀμείβω ("give in exchange," in the middle voice, "do in return, reciprocate, reward," Rengstorf *s.v.*), with εὐεργέτης ("benefactor") as object, also occurs in 17.327; 19.184; cf. Aesop 65; 176.2; Dio Chrysostom 41.5; Aelian, *Nat. an.* 6.44.

[1506] The depreciating vocabulary (τολμώσης "she dared") in this paragraph prepares for the rejection of Alexandra, which is narrated in the next lines. Alexandra is here depicted as Mariamme's opposite (Schalit 2001: 569-70).

[1507] This gesture could have been convincing had it been honest, but the reader—like those present—knows from the larger context that it is not. The phrase ἐφάπτεσθαι καὶ τῶν τριχῶν ("tear her hair," perhaps elliptical "seize [Mariamme by] her hair," Rengstorf *s.v.* ἐφάπτω). The Greek lacks a reference to another person and Salome tears her hair (ἐπιδραττομένης τῶν τριχῶν) in vociferous self-defence when she is accused of conspiracy (16.216), so Alexandra's tearing her hair may be intended—according to Josephus' presentation—to express her indignation. The middle voice of the verb ἐφάπτω plus a genitive usually means "touch," but it sometimes has a stronger meaning ("lay violent hands upon," LSJ *s.v.* II d).

[1508] The vocabulary shows that Josephus as narrator clearly repudiates Alexandra's behavior: the phrase μεταξὺ καθυποκρινομένης ἀσχημόνως ("between such shameful histrionics") is unique, and the verb καθυποκρίνομαι ("pretend/subdue by histrionic acts," LSJ *s.v.* I; Rengstorf *s.v.*, who also suggests "play the hypocrite" as meaning) is a *hapax legomenon* in Josephus.

[1509] These words partly repeat the phrase that introduces Alexandra's behavior towards her daughter (cf. λίαν ἀπρεπῶς in *Ant.* 15.232 with ἀπρεποῦς here). The noun προσποίησις ("acquisition," *Ant.* 17.149) can also mean "pretence, hypocrisy" (Rengstorf *s.v.*).

would imagine,[1510] great;[1511] it was especially displayed by her who was sent to death.[1512] **235** For she [Mariamme] did not say one word [to her],[1513] nor was she disturbed[1514] when she looked at[1515] Alexandra's annoying behavior.[1516] Through her attitude[1517] she indicated,[1518] as it were, that her mother had behaved offensively[1519] and [also] that she was more than angry about her evidently shameless behavior.[1520] **236** She, at last, truly went to her death calmly[1521] and without any change of complexion,[1522] clearly[1523] displaying[1524] her nobility[1525]

[1510] This brief note (ὡς εἰκός) conveys Josephus' own opinion once again, see *Ant.* 15.70 with the note to "as was to be expected."

[1511] For the phrase πολλὴ ... ἡ κατάγνωσις ἦν ("the disapproval was ... great"), cf. Petrus Patricius' excerpts of Cassius Dio 160 (ed. Boissevain 3.742).

[1512] With this remark Josephus switches from Alexandra to Mariamme as focalizer and builds up to a climax that highlights Mariamme's impressive behavior during her last moments. The contrast between Mariamme and Alexandra is emphasized by the repetition of the verb ἐμφαίνω ("display"; see *Ant.* 15.233 with the note to "wanting to display" and 15.234-236), which refers to Alexandra in 15.233 and to Mariamme here.

[1513] The literal translation is "did not say one word" (without the person[s] addressed). Yet the expression λόγον διδόναι can mean either "give permission to speak, grant a hearing" (cf. *Ant.* 15.351; 17.304) or "say a word (to)," with the person(s) spoken to indicated in the dative (*War* 2.443; 5.72). The phrase here may be elliptical and connected with the second meaning, implying that Mariamme did not say a word to her mother. If the phrase is to be understood in a general sense, it probably emphasizes that Mariamme did not defend herself. Schalit (2001: 138) concludes that Mariamme was determined to end her tragic life with Herod.

[1514] The participle ταραχθεῖσα ("she was [not] disturbed") echoes ταραχθῇ of *Ant.* 15.224 referring to the possibility that Herod would be disturbed by the love-potion, possibly contrasting Mariamme with Herod. For this motif, see 15.82 with the note to "he was greatly disturbed" and 15.223 with the note to "his disturbance was rather serious."

[1515] MSS LAMW read ἐπέτρεπεν ("handed over, submitted") instead of ἐπέβλεπεν ("looked at, watched," attested by MSS PFV and E; cf. the Latin version). The first reading does not make sense in the context and resulted most probably from a scribal error that changed β to τρ. Ernesti's conjecture ἀπέβλεπεν ("looked at," Niese 374) is unnecessary.

[1516] Rengstorf (*s.v.*) offers, with question marks added, "offensive behaviour" and "insults" as meanings for δυσχέρεια here, but a more general meaning like "annoying behavior" may be more appropriate (cf. Josephus' phrases with the adjective δυσχερής ["difficult,

unpleasant, bad"] in *Ant.* 15.238-239).

[1517] The phrase ὑπὸ φρονήματος is open to several interpretations since φρόνημα can indicate various mental qualities of persons, positive or negative: e.g., a female way of thinking (*Ant.* 15.44 concerning Alexandra), arrogance (15.81 concerning Mariamme), (high) spirit (15.115, 139, 159 concerning the Jews and their Nabatean opponents), and pride or high-mindedness (15.187 concerning Herod). Josephus emphasizes here that Mariamme's mental attitude was admirable because of the way she dealt with the annoying behavior of her mother. Rengstorf (*s.v.* φρόνημα) gives "attitude" as one of the meanings of φρόνημα, but "pride" would also fit.

[1518] The aorist ἐνέφηνεν ("she indicated") with Mariamme as subject repeats the passive aorist ἐνεφάνη of the same verb ἐμφαίνω in *Ant.* 15.234 (for this verb, see also 15.233 with the note to "wanting to display"), also pointing to Mariamme, which adds emphasis to her admirable response to Alexandra's behavior.

[1519] The noun ἁμαρτία probably means "offense" here (Rengstorf *s.v.*).

[1520] The participle ἀσχημονούσης ("behaving shamelessly, conducting oneself disgracefully") connects with the adjective ἀσχήμων ("shameless") in *Ant.* 15.234, also highlighting Alexandra's despicable behavior. The verb ἀσχημονέω is a *hapax legomenon* in Josephus; the related noun ἀσχημοσύνη ("disgraceful behavior, improper conduct," Rengstorf *s.v.*) occurs in 16.223 referring to Salome and is also a *hapax legomenon* in Josephus.

[1521] Literally "in a calm condition" (ἀτρεμαίῳ τῷ καταστήματι). As in the previous paragraph Josephus describes Mariamme's death with rare vocabulary. The adjective ἀτρεμαῖος ("unmoved, calm") is a *hapax legomenon* in Josephus. The noun κατάστημα usually means "condition, position" (cf. *War* 1.40; 2.650; 4.287). Rengstorf (*s.v.*) suggests "bearing, demeanor" as meaning in this passage.

[1522] This note and the preceding one about Mariamme's calm attitude during her last moments (cf. *Ant.* 15.237) associate her with Greek and Roman traditions about noble deaths of famous persons, especially philosophers like Socrates and Seneca (Ronconi 1966; Döring 1979; Baumeister 1983; van Henten and Avemarie 2002: 11-14, 25-30).

The adjective ἀμετάβλητος ("unchanged, unchange-

BOOK FIFTEEN

to those who were looking at[1526] her, even in her last moments.[1527]

(7.6) 237 So Mariamme died this way,[1528] a woman who excelled[1529] in self-control[1530]

---

able," Rengstorf *s.v.*) occurs once elsewhere in Josephus (*Life* 264).

[1523] The expression οὐδ' ... ἄδηλον (literally "not ... invisible") is a case of *litotes*, which adds emphasis to Mariamme's attitude during her last moments.

[1524] This participle, which concludes the Greek sentence, is the fourth occurrence of the verb ἐμφαίνω ("display") in this section and again emphasizes Mariamme's behavior (see also *Ant.* 15.233-235).

[1525] Mariamme's εὐγένεια ("noble ancestry, nobility of birth"), referring to her Hasmonean descent, is a recurring motif in the Herod narrative of *Antiquities*. Several passages refer to the noble ancestry of the Hasmoneans (see 15.14 with the note to "the eminence of his noble ancestry"), and this nobility is particularly emphasized in references to Alexandra and Mariamme (15.73 and see 15.210 with the note to "her superior nobility" concerning Mariamme). In this concluding note about Mariamme's death Josephus suggests that her admirable way of dying matched her nobility of birth, which is a *topos* in noble death traditions (2 Macc 14:42; 4 Macc 8:4, as well as Athenian funeral orations; Loraux 1981; van Henten 1997: 225-27).

[1526] The verb ἐπιθεωρέω ("look at," Rengstorf *s.v.*) is another *hapax legomenon* in Josephus.

[1527] For the date of Mariamme's death, see the next note.

[1528] Mariamme probably died in 29 BCE. Josephus' note that Herod's suspicion extended over a period of 1 year starting from Herod's return from his second visit to Octavian (see *Ant.* 15.221 with the note to "a period of a year") suggests a time after the spring/summer or the autumn of 29 BCE. Schürer-Vermes (1.289, 302), Hoehner (1972: 9), and Smallwood (1976: 71) opt for 29 BCE; Schalit (2001: 114-19) for 30/29 BCE; and Kokkinos (1998: 213, supported by Kasher 2007: 165 n. 23) for 29/28 BCE.

Otto (1913: 51-52) and Schalit (2001: 139-41) wonder why Alexandra was not executed together with Mariamme, particularly since Alexandra was the mastermind of many actions against Herod in *Ant.* 15. Otto assumes that Josephus exaggerated Alexandra's rebellious role greatly and that Herod hardly knew about her intrigues until immediately before her death (which differs from what Josephus writes in 15.42-44). Schalit offers another explanation: Herod's intent to kill all members of the Hasmonean family would have become obvious had he executed both Hasmonean ladies at the same time. He therefore postponed Alexandra's execution and gave the impression that Mariamme was executed because of her adultery and her attempt to poison him (p. 140).

The phrase οὕτως ἀπέθανε and similar formulas are common (e.g., Antiphon, *Caed. Her.* 44; Xenophon, *Hell.* 2.4.1; Plutarch, *Art.* 19.6; Cassius Dio 42.26.1; 46.54.1; 58.25.4). In Josephus they usually form the conclusion of a death report (*War* 7.369, 453; *Ant.* 3.210; 9.123; differently *Ant.* 1.346; 16.319).

[1529] The phrase ἄριστα γεγενημένη (literally "being the best") can in principle refer to either birth or rank. The latter is much more probable here. Two parallel passages in Josephus indicate an exceptional status on the basis of deeds or experience (*Ant.* 5.274; 7.390; cf. Lysias 25.31).

[1530] This is the first out of 6 characteristics that Josephus gives in this brief "obituary" of Mariamme (see Landau 2006: 130-31, 180, who suggests that Josephus uses Mariamme's personal traits to interpret her relationship with Herod). The first remarks concern extremely positive points (cf. ἐν φύσει ["in her character"] further in the sentence, see the note to that phrase): self-control and greatness of mind. They are followed by 2 negative points: lack of reason and contentiousness. The final 2 characteristics are her exceptional beauty and aristocratic behavior.

The philosophical term ἐγκράτεια ("self-control") is connected with the earlier description of Mariamme's attitude during her last moments (*Ant.* 15.236). It is a prominent ethical concept in Stoic philosophy and in other Classical and Hellenistic philosophical schools. Socrates considers it to be a cardinal virtue (Xenophon, *Mem.* 1.5.4), and Aristotle offers elaborate discussions of it (see below). In Stoic philosophy it is a virtue subordinate to σωφροσύνη ("prudence," Diogenes Laertius 7.92; Stobaeus 2.60.20-21). Cleanthes describes it as a force and tension of the soul (Plutarch, *Mor.* [*Stoic. rep.*] 1034d), which explains why ἐγκράτεια is often associated with the moral and rational struggle against passions and certain other feelings (e.g., Galen, *Plac. Hipp. Plat.* 5.7.21-25 [ed. Kühn 5.484-86]). This interpretation of ἐγκράτεια is also important in Jewish philosophical writings such as 4 Maccabees (e.g., 5:34) and the works of Philo, who argues that philosophy teaches ἐγκράτεια, which is interpreted as abstinence from food, sexuality, and the prudent use of the tongue (*Congr.* 79-80; cf. *Spec.* 2.195; further references in Grundmann 1964). Josephus gives a definition of ἐγκράτεια in his presentation of the Essenes, contrasting it with pleasures and emotions: "Whereas these men shun the pleasures as vice they consider self-control and greatness of mind[1531] but lacked[1532] reason;[1533] contentiousness[1534] had the upper hand in her character.[1535] Yet in physical beauty[1536] and dignity[1537] of manners[1538] she surpassed the women of her time[1539] more than one could say.[1540] **238** But the greatest cause of her

---

(ἐγκράτεια) and not succumbing to the passions virtue" (*War* 2.120, trans. Mason in BJP 1b). In *Ant.* 6.63 he mentions ἐγκράτεια together with σωφροσύνη ("prudence, self-control"), which is apparently almost synonymous.

Schalit (2001: 567-71) argues that Nicolaus of Damascus is responsible for all or most of the section of *Ant.* 15.202-239 (see 15.202 with the note to "when he came to the kingdom that time"), such that Mariamme's characteristics may be described in line with Nicolaus' own philosophical preference for the Peripatetic School. Schalit notes that most of the key words in the relevant section are prominent in Aristotle's writings, especially in his *Nicomachean Ethics* (concerning ἐγκράτεια, *Eth. Nic.* 7.1-9 1145a-1152a; see also *Eth. Eud.* 2.3-6 1220b-1223a; *Virt. vit.* 2 1250a; further references in Schalit), but he rightly observes that the descriptions of Mariamme's virtues and vices are more general and popular than Aristotle's descriptions. Schalit further suggests that Mariamme's virtue of self-control is ultimately based upon a feeling of pride and contempt of others (p. 569).

[1531] The noun μεγαλοψυχία ("magnanimity, greatness of mind," Rengstorf *s.v.*; cf. Aristotle's description in *Eth. Nic.* 4.3 1123a-b) sometimes has a negative meaning ("arrogance," LSJ *s.v.* 2). It usually refers to males which may add emphasis to Mariamme's exceptional character: to a certain extent her virtues correspond to those of men. The other occurrences of this word in the Herod narrative of *Antiquities* mostly refer to Herod (see 15.48 with the note to "he showed enough magnanimity").

[1532] The reading ἔλειπεν of MSS FVE (Niese 374) implies a translation such as "continually lacked" if the imperfect has a durative aspect.

[1533] Mariamme lacked ἐπιείκεια ("reasonableness, kindness"), the trait that characterized her grandfather Hyrcanus II (see *Ant.* 14.13; 15.165 with the note to "his reasonable character" and cf. 15.177, 182 about Hyrcanus II and 15.48 about Herod). Cf. Aristotle's description of ἐπιείκεια in *Eth. Nic.* 5.10 1137a-b.

[1534] The adjective φιλόνεικος ("being contentious/ quarrelsome," Rengstorf *s.v.*) expresses a trait that Mariamme shared with her mother Alexandra (see *Ant.* 15.62 with the note to "contentious" and 15.166, 168).

[1535] The phrase ἐν φύσει ("in her character") confirms that Josephus gives a description of Mariamme's character (see also the note to "self-control" above). The noun φύσις and related words sometimes mark characterizations of important persons in Josephus (see *Ant.* 15.89 with the note to "her greedy character" concerning Cleopatra). For phrases similar to (ἐν τῇ) φύσει φιλόνεικον, cf. Galen, *Propr. an.* 4 (ed. Kühn 5.10-11); *Meth. med.* (ed. Kühn 10.20).

[1536] Mariamme's exceptional beauty has been highlighted several times (see *Ant.* 15.23 with the note to "strikingly beautiful"). *Ant.* 15.25 also contains the noun κάλλος ("beauty"; cf. 15.51). For expressions similar to κάλλει δὲ σώματος ("in physical beauty"), cf. *War* 7.118 and *Ant.* 16.122 (referring to Herod and Mariamme's sons).

[1537] The noun ἀξίωμα means "dignity" here and is related to Mariamme's royal status and rank (cf. *Ant.* 15.164, 187; see also 15.51 about Mariamme's brother Aristobulus III and 15.206 about Mariamme and Alexandra).

[1538] The plural of ἔντευξις ("meeting, communication," Rengstorf *s.v.*) can also mean "manners, behavior, speeches" (LSJ *s.v.* 2b, 3).

[1539] Josephus emphasizes that not only Mariamme's beauty but also her dignity of behavior were unique. Mariamme apparently stood out among all women of her time in these respects (as Cleopatra did in other respects: *Ant.* 15.101 "... a woman who held the greatest honor [μέγιστον ἀξίωμα] of all women at that time [τῶν κατ' ἐκεῖνον ἐσχηκυῖαν τὸν χρόνον] ...)."

Ant. 15.238 echoes several words of 15.51 that concern Mariamme's brother Aristobulus: "... he looked extraordinary handsome (κάλλει τε κάλλιστος) and taller than (ὑπεράγων) most youths of his age. Yet it was his dignity (ἀξιώματος) connected with his descent that particularly showed itself in his appearance." Haverkamp's conjecture ὑπερῆρεν ("surpassed," Niese 374, taken over by Marcus-Wikgren 112; see also Naber 1888-1896: 3.xliv, 351) is unnecessary: not only does the reading ὑπερῆγεν attested by the Greek MSS make sense, but the verb ὑπεράγω ("surpass, exceed," Rengstorf *s.v.*) also occurs in *Ant.* 15.51 concerning Aristobulus.

[1540] The expression μειζόνως ἢ φράσαι echoes a phrase in a fragment of Euripides' tragedy *Temenidae* or *Temenus* (*Fragm.* 1083 in ed. Nauck = 727e in ed. Kannicht ll. 9-10) transmitted by Strabo (8.5.6): τὸν δὲ δεύτερον τῆς Μεσσήνης ἀρετὴν ἐχούσης μεῖζον' ἢ λόγῳ φράσαι ("... and the second over Messenia, 'whose fertility is greater than words can express' ..."; trans. Jones).

not living acceptably with the king[1541] or in a pleasant way[1542] arose from just this: while being paid court[1543] because of his love[1544] and not expecting anything unpleasant from him[1545] she kept up a disproportionate[1546] [level] of frankness.[1547] **239** And what happened

---

[1541] Apart from the 2 affairs following Herod's journeys to his patrons (*Ant.* 15.65, 70, 185-186), Josephus leaves us very much in the dark about Mariamme's relationship with the king. His indication that Herod loved her very much (see 15.82 with the note to "loved her terribly") is plausible, which may imply that the relationship was intimate for several years, such that Mariamme would initially have responded to Herod's affection (with Kasher 2007: 165 n. 23; differently Schalit 2001: 131, 586-87, who assumes that Mariamme despised Herod because of his Idumean origin and hated him from the beginning). This is matched by the emotional description of Herod and Mariamme's reconciliation in 15.84 and by 2 hints in 15.209: at Herod's happy return from his visit of Octavian "he told the good news—*as he usually did*—first to his wife" and "he embraced her, *honoring her alone specially, because of his love and the intimacy he felt for her*" (cf. 15.222). It is very hard to go beyond Josephus and make sure about this relationship, but the fact that Herod and Mariamme had 5 children together (*War* 1.435) implies that it cannot have been that bad for several years. This also supports the later date of Mariamme's death as implied by *Antiquities* (29 BCE; Kokkinos 1998: 213 and see 15.237 with the note to "died this way").

Josephus' point that Herod's secret instructions and Mariamme's reactions to them greatly deteriorated the relationship (*Ant.* 15.70, 85-87, 204, 208, 210-211, 222) is plausible. The death of Mariamme's brother Aristobulus III probably also determined Mariamme's attitude towards Herod. Josephus writes that she took it for granted that Herod had caused his death (*War* 1.437; *Ant.* 15.222), which may be an overstatement, but it is plausible that his death made her suspicious and dampened her affection for Herod (Schalit 2001: 132).

The expression κεχαρισμένως ("to please, [live] acceptably," Rengstorf *s.v.*) with a personal object in the dative also occurs in *Ant.* 15.53 (concerning Herod pleasing Aristobulus III) and 16.184 (concerning Nicolaus of Damascus writing to please Herod).

[1542] Josephus' report implies that Mariamme's marriage became increasingly unhappy after Herod's journeys to Mark Antony and Octavian (see the preceding note). The phrase μηδὲ πρὸς ἡδονὴν ζῆν ("not enjoying to live") finds a close parallel in Plutarch, *Pyrrh.* 16.2 about the inhabitants of Tarentum who disliked their treatment by Pyrrhus: "Many therefore left the city, since they were not accustomed to being under orders, and called it servitude not to live as they pleased (δουλείαν τὸ μὴ πρὸς ἡδονὴν ζῆν καλοῦντας, trans. Perrin)."

[1543] MSS LAMW add ἀεί ("all the time," Niese 374).

[1544] Herod's great love (ἔρως) and affection (φιλοστοργία) for Mariamme have been emphasized many times before (*Ant.* 15.66, 68-70, 82-83, 87, 209).

[1545] Within the present context this seems a really cynical remark, but it may refer to an earlier period in which Mariamme still had full confidence in Herod (see the last note of *Ant.* 15.239). Later on Herod's double secret instructions to kill her if he did not return from his trips to Antony and Octavian (15.55, 70, 185-186) greatly disturbed her (see the note to "reason for [her] not living acceptably with the king" above). Earlier references to Mariamme's frankness in her speaking to Herod (see the next note) are also connected with these secret instructions. A further explanation of Josephus' remark could be that it is part of an attempt to put the blame for Mariamme's death on herself instead of Herod (see 15.239), although this would not match the main trend of the preceding narrative (see 15.236 with the note to "even in her last moments").

For a similar combination of προσδοκάω ("expect") and οὐδὲν/μηδὲν δυσχερές ("nothing bad/unpleasant"), see 15.78 referring to Cleopatra's scheming against Herod ("… he did not expect any further unpleasantness …"). Ironically the same word δυσχερές appears in passages which indicate that Octavian might decide to punish Herod during his visit (15.184, 186; see also 15.239 with the note to "suffer something bad").

[1546] The adjective ἀσύμμετρος ("incommensurable, excessive," Rengstorf *s.v.*) is a *hapax legomenon* in Josephus.

[1547] Josephus adds a third negative characteristic of Mariamme (for the other 2, see *Ant.* 15.237), which he singles out as the main reason of all the problems: her frankness (παρρησία, Rengstorf *s.v.*), mainly the great freedom she allowed herself in expressing what she thought and felt (see her statement about the secret instruction in 15.85; cf. 15.210, 222, 239) and her arrogant behavior towards Herod's sister, mother, and Herod himself (see *War* 1.438; *Ant.* 15.219-220, 222 with notes). This trait contrasts with Mariamme's alleged ἐγκράτεια ("self-control") and associates her with her mother Alexandra (see 15.37 with the note to "because of his kin and frankness" and 15.44; nevertheless, *Antiquities* emphasizes Mariamme's frankness only after Herod's secret instructions for Joseph had become known to her: 15.65, 69-70, 85, 222; see the references

to her relatives grieved her also,[1548] and she considered it fit to tell Herod all she felt about these things.[1549] In the end she succeeded[1550] in making the mother as well as the sister of the king hostile towards her,[1551] and even the king himself,[1552] who was the only person in whom she had mistakenly put her trust[1553] not to suffer something bad.[1554]

Excursus: Mariamme's death and Otto's hypothesis about the doublet in Ant. 15.62-87 and 15.161-236

Several scholars discuss the reasons that actually may have caused Mariamme's death. Otto (1913: 51-52) argues that Mariamme was a victim of the severe tensions between Herod and the remaining members of the Hasmonean royal family, which view is supported by a tradition about Mariamme's suicide in the Babylonian Talmud (*b. B. Bat.* 3b-4a; Cohen 1986: 10). Schalit (2001: 131, 566-67, 586-87) rejects most of the details of the— in his opinion—highly embellished narrative about Mariamme's end (see *Ant.* 15.202 with the note to "when he came to the kingdom that time"), but he takes for granted that Mariamme hated Herod from the beginning, that Salome played a major perfidious role, and that Herod ordered his wife's execution. Richardson (1996: 218-20) offers a tentative reconstruction and concludes that an incident in 30/29 BCE led to the execution of both

---

above). *War* 1.437 (cf. *Ant.* 15.222) connects Mariamme's παρρησία with her response to the deaths of her grandfather Hyrcanus II and her brother Aristobulus III: "Her hostility was justified by what had taken place, and she was at liberty to express herself (τὴν... παρρησίαν) because of her husband's passion for her. She publicly reproached him about what had happened to her grandfather, Hyrcanus, and to her brother, Jonathan" (trans. Sievers/Forte in BJP 1a).

[1548] *War* 1.437 and *Ant.* 15.222 are much more explicit and report that Mariamme reproached Herod for killing her (grand-)father and her brother. The expression τὰ περὶ τοὺς οἰκείους refers here to the tragic events in Mariamme's Hasmonean family (for οἰκεῖος meaning "related, relative," see 15.229 with the note to "the persons who were closest to him").

[1549] This phrase repeats the point in the previous paragraph about Mariamme's frankness (see the note to "[level] of frankness").

[1550] With Niese (375), who follows the reading ἐξενίκησεν of E. The verb ἐκνικάω ("achieve by force," metaphorically also "prevail, succeed [in]," Rengstorf *s.v.*; cf. *Ant.* 5.286) also occurs elsewhere in Josephus (*War* 3.536; 7.419; *Ant.* 5.286; 13.132). The reading ἐξεκίνησεν (from ἐκκινέω "move out, put up," LSJ *s.v.*) of the Greek MSS does not make sense. It may easily have resulted from the reading attested by E because of a transposition of ν and κ (for a similar case, see *Ant.* 15.286).

[1551] Herod's mother Cyprus and his sister Salome clearly opposed Mariamme following Herod's journey to Mark Antony (see *Ant.* 15.80 and 15.213 with the note to "his sister and mother noticed"), but it is plausible that they had been hostile towards Mariamme already for a longer period (with Otto 1913: 50; Schürer-Vermes 1.302) in their status of prominent members or even leaders of the rival women factions at Herod's court (see 15.35 with the note to "the friends called to their help").

[1552] On the deterioration of the relationship between Herod and Mariamme, see *Ant.* 15.238 with the note to "reason for [her] not pleasing the king." Herod's hostile attitude largely arose during the aftermath of his journey to Octavian (15.210-215, 229, i.e., in 30/29 BCE; see 15.221 with the note to "returned from Caesar").

[1553] The verb ἀποπιστεύω ("trust mistakenly," Rengstorf *s.v.*) is a *hapax legomenon* in Josephus.

[1554] Mariamme's confidence that Herod would never undertake anything against her because of his extraordinary love for her is also suggested by Soemus' reasoning described in *Ant.* 15.207: "... Herod ... would not be able to deny his wife anything she wanted. For [Soemus] knew that the king's love for Mariamme was beyond description." It is also indicated twice in *War*: "... she was at liberty to express herself *because of her husband's passion for her*" (1.437, trans. Sievers/Forte in BJP 1a; my emphasis) and "... Whereas he was reduced to silence by his passionate love for her ..." (1.438, trans. Sievers/Forte in BJP 1a).

The expression τὸ μὴ παθεῖν τι δυσχερές partly repeats the phrase with δυσχερές ("bad, unpleasant") of *Ant.* 15.238 (see the note to "having nothing bad to expect from Herod") and ironically also echoes the references to Herod's possible sufferings during his journeys to Mark Antony and Octavian (15.65 εἰ πάθοι τι παρ' Ἀντωνίῳ; 15.69 εἰ πάσχοι δεινόν τι; 15.85 εἰ πάσχοι τι χαλεπόν; 15.164 εἰ δὲ καὶ πάσχοι τι; 15.197 μηδὲν ἀνήκεστον παθεῖν; 15.204 εἰ πάσχοι τι δεινόν).

Soemus and Mariamme. Vogel (2002: 113-14) argues that it is impossible to separate fact from fiction.

Looking back to the factors that led to Mariamme's execution according to Josephus' narrative, three issues stand out: (1) the impact of Herod's secret instructions to kill Mariamme if he did not return from his journeys to Mark Antony and Octavian (see *Ant.* 15.221-222), (2) Salome's scheming against Mariamme with her accusation of adultery (15.81) and shrewd intrigue concerning the love-potion (15.223), and (3) Mariamme's difficult character was a major factor (15.237-238).

Mariamme's death was the ultimate outcome of Herod's journey to Octavian with his secret instructions for Joseph and Soemus to kill her (and her mother) if something bad happened to him. A comparison of the present section with the earlier one about Herod's journey to Mark Antony is called for, also because scholars have argued that the earlier episode is a duplicate of the later one (especially Otto, see *Ant.* 15.87 with the note to "he ordered Joseph to be killed"). I will first list the correspondences of both sections (15.62-87 and 15.161-236) and then briefly discuss some of the differences. Finally I will give a brief assessment of the plausibility of the hypothesis that the first story is a duplicate of the second.

The correspondences between the two episodes are:
(1) The point of departure: Herod visits his Roman patron because he has to render account for his deeds (15.64-65 and 15.188, 194), which implies that his position as ruler of Judea is jeopardized (15.65, 67 and 15.161-163, 183).
(2) Herod appoints a substitute ruler (15.65: Joseph, and 15.184, 186: Pheroras) and gives secret instructions to kill Mariamme if something happens to him during his journey (15.65-67 and 15.186; cf. *War* 1.441).
(3) Joseph and Soemus, respectively, reveal Herod's secret instructions to Mariamme and Alexandra (15.68-69 and 15.205-207).
(4) Mariamme/the women is/are shocked because of the cruelty of Herod's secret instructions (15.70 and 15.208, 227; cf. 15.204).
(5) Herod's meeting with his patron turns out very well: his rule is reconfirmed (15.74-79 and 15.187-196), and his patron treats him as a close friend (15.77 and 15.195-196, 199, 217).
(6) Herod returns to Judea after escorting his patron (15.80 and 15.196, 198-201, 209; cf. 15.218 and *War* 1.442).
(7) Salome plays a major role in the downfall of Mariamme by accusing her indirectly of adultery or by framing her (15.80-81 and 15.213, 223-225, 231; cf. *War* 1.441, 443).
(8) Herod is greatly disturbed because of the alleged crimes of his wife. He is torn by emotions of love and hatred (15.82-84 and 15.210-212, 214, 229-230).
(9) During an intimate moment Mariamme reveals to Herod her knowledge about the secret instructions, with a devastating result (15.85-87 and 15.209-210, 222; cf. *War* 1.442).
(10) The caretaker (Joseph/Soemus) is immediately executed (15.87 and 15.227-229; cf. *War* 1.443).

The main differences between the two stories are:
(1) Both accounts contain additional information which is related to the main narrative thread but different in content: the rumor about Herod's death together with Mariamme and Alexandra's plan to flee to the Roman legion (15.71-74, 80), Hyrcanus' death (15.164-182), and Alexandra's disgraceful turn against her daughter (15.232-235).
(2) The immediate causes of Herod's visits of his Roman patrons and the descriptions of the meetings differ: at Alexandra's demand (15.62) Cleopatra forces Antony to order

Herod to clear himself of the accusation concerning the murder of Aristobulus III (15.63-64), while the second journey results from Octavian's defeat of Antony (15.162-163). For the meetings, see 15.74-79 and 15.187-197.

(3) During the second journey Herod moves his family to Masada, but he puts Mariamme and Alexandra under at Alexandrium (15.184-185). The tasks of substitute ruling and caretaking of Mariamme (and Alexandra) are divided among several persons (15.184-185).

(4) The accounts clearly vary most in their final sections (notwithstanding important correspondences). The caretakers are immediately executed in both accounts, but Mariamme is killed only in the later account (of course, she can only be killed once). In 15.82-84 Herod questions Mariamme in private following Salome's accusation, which leads to a temporary reconciliation and then to a severe conflict when Mariamme reveals that she knows about the instructions to kill her (15.85-87). Although this convinces Herod that she has committed adultery with Joseph, he does not execute her (although he does that in *War* 1.443; see below). In 15.229 he arranges a council meeting and has Mariamme convicted.

(5) There are additional minor differences concerning the roles of Mariamme and Alexandra. Herod's first instructions deal only with Mariamme (15.65), whereas his second also concern Alexandra (15.186). In the first section Mariamme and her mother act as a tandem (e.g., 15.69), with Salome and Cyprus as their opponents (15.80; see the next point). In the second Mariamme and Alexandra are guarded together at Alexandrium (15.184, 202-207), but several times Josephus focalizes only Mariamme (e.g., 15.204, 208). Alexandra finally turns against her daughter in 15.232-235.

(6) There are likewise minor differences concerning Salome's role. Sometimes Salome cooperates with her mother Cyprus, and sometimes she acts on her own. E.g., in 15.80 Salome and Cyprus inform Herod about Mariamme and Alexandra's attempt to flee to the Roman legion (Salome and Cyprus also act together in 15.213). In 15.81 Salome accuses Joseph and Mariamme of adultery and in 15.223-225 she implements a carefully prepared trap for Mariamme, which makes Herod conclude that his wife has had a sexual relationship with Soemus (15.227-228).

Notwithstanding the differences between both reports, the correspondences between both stories are so close that one account is plausibly dependent on the other. The fact that *War* has only one (much briefer) account (1.441-443), which parallels both *Antiquities* accounts to a certain extent, further supports this plausibility. Moreover, the sequence of the events (apart from the end) is also very similar in both sections of *Antiquities*; the differences hardly affect the basic chain shared by both. All this renders Otto's argument (see 15.87 with the note to "he ordered Joseph to be killed") about a duplicate account plausible. His hypothesis helps to explain the discrepancy between *War* and *Antiquities* concerning the date and setting of Mariamme's death (see the next note). Josephus' double tradition in *Antiquities* about secret instructions connected with a trip to a Roman patron may be a correction of the account in *War*—which sets Mariamme's death too early—and an attempt to harmonize *Antiquities* with *War* to a certain extent. The hypothesis would also help to explain certain difficult details in *Antiquities*. The fact that Mariamme is not executed in the first account (i.e., the one reporting Herod's visit of Antony) after Herod had become convinced that his wife had committed adultery (*Ant.* 15.85-87) comes as a surprise for the reader. Josephus heightens and then deflates and then heightens again the dramatic tension—will he kill her or won't he? (15.81-87)— so that the reader is almost disappointed that Mariamme is not executed at this stage. The punishment of Joseph in 15.87 may function as a substitution for Mariamme's punishment, which Josephus could not narrate here. The brief narrative of *War* 1.443 is much more coherent and convincing in this connection since it reports the execution of both Joseph and Mariamme.

Another puzzle concerns the figure/s of Joseph the administrator. In the second account a Joseph is mentioned only once, as one of the two caretakers of Mariamme and Alexandra (15.185), and he then disappears from the story, while the Joseph of the first account is again referred to in 15.204 (von Destinon 1882: 113 n. 1). The second Joseph may originally have been identical with the first Joseph of *War* 1.441-443 and the first account of *Antiquities* (Richardson 1996: 219; differently Kokkinos 1998: 153 n. 15). Sandmel (1967: 165 n. 8) considers this possible though beyond verification. A final argument in favor of a duplicate may be the many repetitions and verbal echoes in both accounts (see the notes concerning *Ant.* 15.161-236), although these data can be explained in other ways as well. In short: Otto's hypothesis seems plausible and helps to explain certain details and oddities in the stories, but we lack hard evidence to prove it.

(7.7) 240 The moment she had been done away with,[1555] the king's desire was inflamed even more[1556] because he felt the same as we indicated earlier.[1557] For [his] love for her[1558] was very passionate[1559] and not of the usual kind:[1560] it began fervently.[1561] Despite the

Breakdown and illness of Herod. War 1.444

[1555] Josephus describes Herod's reaction to Mariamme's death in dramatic terms in *Ant.* 15.240-246: he first focuses on Herod's emotions (15.240-242, 244) and then on Herod's illness (15.245-246) after a break out of a pestilential disease (15.243). The verb ἀναιρέω can mean "kill, murder" as well as "remove, do away with" (Rengstorf *s.v.*). The second meaning can be a disparaging way to indicate someone's death aimed for by somebody else. Josephus prepares his readers for the subsequent report of the quick change of Herod's state of mind.

[1556] Herod suddenly desired Mariamme again, which reminds one of Josephus' portrayal of Herod as a person switching from one extreme emotion to another (see *Ant.* 15.211-112 with notes). Nevertheless, Herod's desire for Mariamme is quite understandable since she was no longer available; it is a cross-cultural experience that the longing for a lost person or for something that one cannot get steadily increases. The parallel passage of *War* (1.444) also describes Herod's prompt change of temper after Mariamme's death and his desire for her: "A feeling of regret immediately followed upon his fateful outburst and when his rage subsided, his passionate love was newly reawakened (ὁ ἔρως πάλιν ἀνεζωπυρεῖτο). So intense was the ardor of his desire (τοσαύτη δ' ἦν φλεγμονὴ τῆς ἐπιθυμίας) that he believed she was not dead" (trans. Sievers/Forte in BJP 1a).

There is only one further occurrence of ἐπιθυμία ("desire") referring to Herod's longing for Mariamme (*Ant.* 15.219), but it is telling: "... he [i.e., Herod] was enslaved by his desire [for Mariamme]." The noun ἐπιθυμία may mean "lust" here as well as "longing" in a more general sense (cf. 15.88, 91, 97). For other expressions of ἐξάπτω ("tie, kindle") with μᾶλλον ("more") in Josephus, see *War* 2.490 and *Ant.* 18.67 (concerning Decius Mundus' love for Paulina).

[1557] The translation follows the Greek MSS and E, with Niese (374). Bekker (1855-56: 3.320, followed by Marcus-Wikgren 112-13) proposes to move ὡς to after καὶ πρότερον, which seems more logical: "... for such had been his feeling even earlier, as we have related." Nevertheless, the conjecture is unnecessary: the transmitted text may be elliptical but it makes sense and seems to imply "because he felt the same as [he had felt as] we indicated earlier [i.e., before Mariamme's death]." The text matches the earlier descriptions of Herod's love for Mariamme (see the preceding note). For the formula ὡς ἐδηλώσαμεν ("as we have indicated"), see *Ant.* 15.254 with the note to "as we have indicated."

[1558] The preceding narrative of *Antiquities* emphasizes Herod's love for Mariamme many times, with ἔρως ("love") and φιλοστοργία ("affection") as key terms (see 15.68 with the note to "affection" and 15.82 with the note to "loved her terribly").

[1559] The expression οὐ ἀπαθής (literally "not without passion") is a case of *litotes*, emphasizing that Herod's love for Mariamme was passionate, which matches the continuation of the narrative. Cf. *Ant.* 16.222 concerning Salome being eager to marry the young Nabatean Syllaeus: "Salome did not look at the youngster without passion (οὐκ ἀπαθῶς ὁρῶσα) ..." (my trans.). The opposite of οὐ ἀπαθής involves πάθος ("passion, erotic desire," Rengstorf *s.v.*), which noun is used for Herod's relationship with Mariamme in 15.242 (for different meanings of this word referring to Herod or Mariamme, cf. 15.82, 208, 214).

[1560] The prepositional expression ἐκ συνηθείας functions as a synonym of the preceding οὐ ἀπαθής. The noun συνήθεια means "the usual/habitual" here (Rengstorf *s.v.*), which excludes passion. In *Ant.* 15.209 (see the note to "intimacy") συνήθεια has a different

freedom of their marriage[1562] it was not defeated and even became greater and greater. **241** Moreover, at that time he seemed especially to draw upon himself a certain divine retribution[1563] for doing away with Mariamme. There were frequent callings for her, and also frequent indecorous laments.[1564] He would think up everything possible for diversion,[1565] keeping himself busy with drinking bouts and liaisons,[1566] but none of these things could satisfy him. **242** So he refrained from doing the kingdom's administration[1567] and was so much overcome by his passion[1568] that once he even ordered his servants to call

---

meaning and refers to Herod's intimate relationship with Mariamme.

[1561] Herod loved Mariamme passionately (see the note to "not without passion" above) and she may have loved him too at the beginning of their marriage (see *Ant.* 15.238 with the note to "reason for [her] not pleasing the king"). The adverb ἐνθουσιαστικῶς ("passionately, enthusiastically," Rengstorf *s.v.*) is a *hapax legomenon* in Josephus.

[1562] This phrase (τῇ παρρησίᾳ τῆς συμβιώσεως) is ambiguous because the noun παρρησία can mean "freedom of speech, frankness" as well as "freedom of action" (LSJ *s.v.* 3), and even "licence of tongue" (see *Ant.* 15.238 with the note to "[level] of frankness"). The phrase can, therefore, point either to the open character of the marriage (implying that Herod and Mariamme could say everything to each other) or to the freedom involved in their married life. Rengstorf (*s.v.*) interprets the noun συμβίωσις ("marriage") in a sexual sense: "(freedom) of cohabitation."

[1563] Josephus indicates that Herod suffered terribly after Mariamme's death. Landau (2006: 131) argues that the noun νέμεσις ("punishment, revenge," Rengstorf *s.v.*, or "retribution," LSJ *s.v.*) indicates divine punishment here (see also Marcus-Wikgren 115), although an explicit reference to punishment by God is missing (but note that God is referred to in *Ant.* 15.243). The context of the only other occurrence of this noun in Josephus (*War* 6.176) supports such an interpretation, which also matches Josephus' message in other passages about Herod (e.g., *War* 1.431: "Fortune, however, made [Herod] pay for his public success with troubles at home," trans. Sievers/Forte in BJP 1a). Landau (2006: 180-81) also argues that the word νέμεσις echoes the vocabulary of Greek historians such as Herodotus (e.g., 1.34 on Croesus' downfall caused by divine vengeance).

Kasher (2007: 171-72) argues that Josephus' description of Herod's mental state after Mariamme's death is accurate, and he explains that the king's deep depression was caused by acute feelings of grief and guilt and the incapability to cope with Mariamme's death at the cognitive level.

[1564] Note the parallelism in these 2 subclauses through the repetition of πολλάκις ("frequently") and the related nouns ἀνακλήσεις ("invocations") and θρῆνος ("laments"). The adjective ἀσχήμων ("unseemly, shameless, extravagant"), preceding θρῆνος (cf. John Chrysostom, *Ecl.* [PG 63.807]), echoes the adverb ἀσχημόνως referring to Alexandra's disgraceful behavior (*Ant.* 15.234) and indicates, together with other reactions to Mariamme's death, that Herod's suffering is not likely to evoke sympathy (Landau 2006: 131). One might conclude that laments for Mariamme ordered by Herod were inappropriate since Herod had asked for Mariamme's death, but it should be noted that Josephus' presentation implies that Herod's character was complex (see the excurse about Herod's portrait in *Antiquities* at 17.199). Josephus' description of Herod's response to Mariamme's death (15.240-246) strongly suggests that the king's grief was real, and this matches his earlier report about Herod's grief and mourning following Jonathan-Aristobulus III's death found in 15.60. The implication is that Herod could cause the death of a family member and still experience deep and genuine feelings of grief because of this death.

[1565] An alternative translation is "to amuse [himself]": the noun ψυχαγωγία can mean "entertainment, amusement" (see *Ant.* 15.274; 16.140 in the context of festivals; cf. Dionysius, *Ars rhet.* 1.1) as well as "distraction" (Rengstorf *s.v.*). Even the original meaning ("evocation of souls from the netherworld," LSJ *s.v.* 1) may be relevant here since the phrase connects with Herod's previously mentioned invocations of Mariamme and his order to call for her (*Ant.* 15.242).

[1566] The drinking-bouts and parties (πότους καὶ συνουσίας; similar phrases in Theopompus, *FGH* 115 F 233.5; Isocrates, *Antid.* 286; Plutarch, *Dion* 41.2; Athenaeus 4.61) show what Herod apparently did to distract himself (see the preceding note). Concerning πότος, cf. *Ant.* 15.53, and concerning συνουσία, 15.97 with the note to "have sex with the king."

[1567] The noun διοίκησις concerns the administration of the kingdom here (cf. *Ant.* 15.68, 177; 16.1, 22).

[1568] This phrase connects with the expression οὐ ἀπαθής ("not without passion") of *Ant.* 15.240 (see the note to "very passionate"), although a milder translation of πάθος ("feelings," Rengstorf *s.v.*) may be preferable here. The noun also occurs in the parallel account of *War* (1.444). *Ant.* 16.153 attests a similar combination of πάθος with ἡττάομαι ("be overpowered"), concerning

Mariamme[1569] as if she were still alive and able to answer them.[1570]

243 While he was in this state[1571] a contagious illness broke out,[1572] which destroyed the majority of the masses[1573] and the most high-ranking[1574] of his friends. And it made everyone suspect[1575] that this occurred in connection with God's wrath,[1576] because of[1577] the wicked deed done to Mariamme.[1578] **244** So this kept the king[1579] feeling even worse,

---

Herod's love of honor: "... (he) was strongly dominated by this emotion [or 'passion'] (τούτου τοῦ πάθους ἡττημένος ἰσχυρῶς)" (my trans.); for similar vocabulary, cf. Plutarch, *Per.* 36.5; Cassius Dio 758; Heliodorus 4.10.3; Gregory of Nyssa, *Orat. cons. Pulch.* [ed. Spira 9.464]). A related combination of ἡττάομαι with φιλοστοργία in *Ant.* 15.83 indicates that Herod was overcome with affection for Mariamme (cf. 15.97 about Cleopatra being overcome with [sexual] desire [ἐπιθυμία] and 16.206 about Herod being overcome with love [ἔρως] for Glaphyra).

[1569] The verb καλέω ("call") with Mariamme as object recalls the dramatic conversation between Herod and Mariamme reported in *Ant.* 15.222-223, which is introduced by "When the king was lying down to rest at noon, he called for Mariamme (ἐκάλει τὴν Μαριάμμην) out of the affection he always felt for her."

[1570] This final note is redundant but adds to the drama and also ridicules Herod somewhat. *War* 1.444 suggests that owing to his burning desire Herod could not believe that Mariamme was dead and that he addressed her as if she were still alive (ὡς ζώσῃ προσλαλεῖν).

[1571] In *Ant.* 15.87 a similar phrase (οὕτως δ' ἔχων) makes the transition to the report about Herod's actions in response to his crisis concerning Mariamme (caused by her revelation that she knew about his secret instructions for Joseph). Here it concerns the transition to the report about the epidemic that broke out during Herod's grief.

[1572] This illness is not mentioned in the parallel account of *War* (1.441-444). The adjective λοιμώδης ("pestilential," Rengstorf *s.v.*) also occurs in *War* 6.2, 421 and *Ant.* 15.301 (also in combination with νόσος ["illness"]; cf. already Thucydides 1.23 and subsequent authors, e.g., Aeschines, *Ep.* 1.2; Philo, *Abr.* 136; *Conf.* 22; *Mos.* 1.236; Plutarch, *Cam.* 43.1; *Cor.* 12.4; *Num.* 13.1; Cassius Dio 75.13.2; Herodian 1.12.1). Ancient historians sometimes connect natural disasters and other catastrophes with human conduct (e.g., Thucydides 2.47-55 about the Athenian plague of 430 BCE; further references in Landau 2006: 157 with n. 127). It is also an important motif in the Bible and its paraphrases in Josephus (e.g., *Ant.* 2.313-314 on the final plague in Egypt: the deaths of the firstborn, Exod 12:29-33).

[1573] This implies that the majority of the population was killed, which emphasizes the severity of the epidemic (see also the next note).

[1574] Alternative translations are "most respectable, most esteemed, most valued, dearest" (Rengstorf *s.v.* ἔντιμος; the word ἔντιμος is a *hapax legomenon* in Josephus). The fact that, in addition to the majority of the population, the most high-ranking persons among Herod's friends were killed once again emphasizes the impact of the disaster and puts the focus on the king because losing more than half of his subjects as well as his most important friends could hardly be considered to be a coincidence, as the next sub-clause elaborates.

[1575] The verb ἐξυπονοέω ("suspect," Rengstorf *s.v.*) is a *hapax legomenon* in Josephus.

[1576] The translation is based on the reading τοῦ θεοῦ τοῦτο of MSS LE (followed by Marcus-Wikgren 114). Niese (375) reads τοῦτο with MS P, which is the only Greek MS that lacks an explicit reference to God (the Latin version also refers to God). Although Niese's reading may be preferred as the shorter and the more probable reading, further occurrences of μῆνις ("wrath") in Josephus show that κατὰ μῆνιν τοῦ θεοῦ is a fixed expression (6 occurrences out of a total of 9: *Ant.* 1.164; 2.344; 4.8; 9.104, 246; 15.243, and a related phrase in *War* 6.40; see also *Ant.* 8.112; 15.299). There is no occurrence of κατὰ μῆνιν without a reference to God in Josephus (cf. κατὰ μῆνιν τῆς θεοῦ in Strabo 12.8.9 and κατὰ μῆνιν θεοῦ in Origen, *Comm. Matt.* 10.17). These data render it probable that τοῦ θεοῦ was left out in MS P because of *homoioarcton* (-του ... του-). Since *Ant.* 1.164 indicates that God punished Pharaoh for his desire for Sarah by causing the outbreak of a disease and a rebellion (cf. Gen 12:10-20) and *Ant.* 2.344 concerns God's destruction of the Egyptian army in the Red Sea (cf. Exod 14:23), Vogel (2002: 115) and Landau (2006: 157) conclude that Josephus presents the plague as a divine punishment for Herod here. In line with biblical traditions, not only the king but also his people are punished (see *Ant.* 15.244). Josephus attributes this view to all of Herod's subjects ("it made everyone suspect"), as Landau (2006: 157 n. 131) rightly notes. She argues that this distinction between the people and Josephus as narrator gives credence to the account and presents Josephus as a serious and reliable historian.

[1577] Reading διά with MSS FLAMWE and Marcus-Wikgren (114). Niese's reading τῶν κατά (375, only supported by MS P) does not make sense.

[1578] Josephus uses for the first time strongly negative language in connection with Mariamme's death, which

and finally he made his way to the wilderness.[1580] And being there, under the pretext of a hunt,[1581] he was greatly afflicted[1582] in this wilderness. He endured only for a few days before[1583] he fell into a most terrible illness.[1584] **245** For there was an inflammation[1585] and a soreness[1586] of his occipital bone,[1587] as well as a distortion of his capacity to think.[1588]

---

no doubt targets Herod. Herod's παρανομία ("lawless behavior") is mentioned a few times in *War* (in flashbacks) and more frequently in *Antiquities* (see 15.166 with the note to "lawless behavior").

[1579] Josephus focuses on the impact of the pestilential disease for the king not only because Herod is the main character of this section but also because he is held responsible for the misery (see *Ant.* 15.243 with notes).

[1580] Josephus' remark that Herod retreated to the wilderness points to the emotional collapse of the king at the moment when he had to coordinate the aid for his subjects' sufferings. It implies a double disqualification: Herod was unable to control himself, and he took the wrong priorities by focusing on his own grief. The retreat seems to be a motif added by Josephus in order to show that the king was unfit to rule. The last Babylonian king, Nabonidus (555-539 BCE), suffered from a mental illness and retreated from the civilized world according to the *Nabonidus Chronicle*, Haran inscriptions, and the Qumran *Prayer of Nabonidus* (4Q242; further discussion in Henze 1999). These traditions may originate in Nabonidus' absence from Babylon in 552-543 BCE: he stayed for 10 years at Tayma, an oasis in the Arabian Desert. They partly underlie the story about the dream and madness of the Babylonian king Nebuchadnezzar in Dan 4: the king's dream, explained by Daniel, comes true and he spends 7 times in the wilderness with the animals (Dan 4:15-16, 23, 25, 32-33) before he returns to his senses and acknowledges God's sovereignty (Dan 4:34-37). Like Herod's collapse Nebuchadnezzar's madness is clearly caused by God (Dan 4:25-26, 31). Both traditions about a journey to the wilderness are probably fictitious, although Kasher (2007: 173) argues that Herod actually decided to retreat into the wilderness and that it is plausible that he did this in order to prevent himself from becoming infected by the epidemic disease. The vague information about the wilderness and the reference to the doctors at the beginning of *Ant.* 15.246 do not enhance the plausibility of this detail.

The location of this wilderness is not mentioned. One might think of a Judean wilderness but also of a wilderness near Samaria-Sebaste (the north-east Samarian wilderness, north of Wadi al-Far'a; see Kallner and Rosenau 1939: 63) since *Ant.* 15.246 refers to Samaria.

[1581] Although the hunt merely seems to have been a pretext for Herod's retreat, it indicates at the same time that hunting was a usual kind of entertainment for the king (see also *Ant.* 16.248).

[1582] The rare verb ἐναδημονέω ("be greatly afflicted," LSJ *s.v.*, referring to this passage, or "worry, grieve [in a place]," Rengstorf *s.v.*) is a *hapax legomenon* in Josephus.

[1583] The verb φθάνω plus a negation and followed by a participle (here an infinitive) and καί or εὐθύς indicates that the 2 actions referred to are closely related (LSJ *s.v.* IV.1; cf. the rendering by Rengstorf *s.v.*: "scarcely ... when"). The text suggests therefore that Herod soon fell ill in the wilderness, such that he must have been infected before his retreat.

[1584] This general but at the same time very negative formulation leads up to a more detailed description of Herod's physical illness in the next paragraph. Herod suffered from this illness in addition to his emotional breakdown (*Ant.* 15.240-242).

[1585] The noun φλόγωσις also occurs in the report of Herod's final illness (*Ant.* 17.168). The only further occurrence in Josephus concerns the combustion of a fire (3.63; cf. Thucydides 2.49, who mentions that the first symptoms of the plague described by him were having burned feelings in the head as well as red and inflamed eyes [τῶν ὀφθαλμῶν ἐρυθήματα καὶ φλόγωσις]).

[1586] The noun πεῖσις ("affection, pain," Rengstorf *s.v.*) is a *hapax legomenon* in Josephus. Cobet (followed by Herwaarden and Naber 1888-96: 3.xliv, 352) conjectures πύσις ("suppuration").

[1587] The noun ἰνίον ("back of the head, nape of the neck," Rengstorf *s.v.*) occurs once elsewhere in Josephus, in connection with the High Priest's turban (*Ant.* 3.178). The vocabulary concerning Herod's illness is largely unique (but see the next note), such that it is hard to determine the illness. Kasher (2007: 172-74) discusses several options, including bacterial or viral forms of meningitis, which disease causes a stiffness of the neck and headaches and also matches the epidemic character (see 15.243).

[1588] The noun παραλλαγή is a further *hapax legomenon* in Josephus and can mean "alteration, disturbance" but also "distortion" (e.g., of the vertebrae; Hippocrates, *Art. rep.* 48; LSJ *s.v.*). Rengstorf (*s.v.*) believes that the noun indicates a temporary loss of consciousness here. Another possibility is madness (LSJ *s.v.* IV), which may be supported by the definition of madness (μανία) in Pseudo-Galen, *Def. med.* (ed. Kühn 19.416): "Madness is an ecstatic state of the mind and a change of the usual habits (μανία ἐστὶν ἔκστασις τῆς διανοίας καὶ παραλλαγὴ τῶν νομίμων ... ἐθῶν) when one is healthy

None of the medical treatments[1589] accomplished[1590] improvement. They worked in the opposite direction and led for a while[1591] to desperation.[1592] **246** As many doctors as there were around him[1593]—because on the one hand the illness did not withdraw in any way by the remedies they kept applying,[1594] and on the other hand the king was in no other condition than to live on the dietary food that his illness forced upon him,[1595]—they thought it best to give the king everything he might eat,[1596] leaving the minimal hope[1597] of recovery with the control[1598] over his diet to fortune.[1599] And he was suffering from illness[1600] in this

---

and without fever" (my trans.). Josephus reports a temporary madness for Herod later (*Ant.* 16.259-260; cf. 17.247). Richardson (1996: 218) wonders whether the plague accounts for some of Herod's symptoms.

[1589] Herod was accompanied by doctors, as the next paragraph indicates. The noun θεράπευμα ("medical treatment," Rengstorf *s.v.*) is a *hapax legomenon* in Josephus.

[1590] The verb ἐξανύω ("accomplish, be effective," Rengstorf *s.v.*) is a further *hapax legomenon* in Josephus.

[1591] Reading τέως ("for a while") with MS P and Niese (376). The other Greek MSS read τέλος ("finally"), which is followed by Marcus-Wikgren (114-15). The change from τέως to the more usual word τέλος may derive from an accidental exchange of -ω- and -λο-. Josephus uses τέως also elsewhere (references in Rengstorf *s.v.*).

[1592] For the noun ἀπόγνωσις ("desperation, abandonment [of hope])," see *Ant.* 15.125 and 15.163 with the note to "lost their hope."

[1593] This detail is remarkable because Herod is located in the wilderness according to the context (*Ant.* 15.244). The presence of doctors implies that he stayed at a less deserted place. If Josephus' information is trustworthy here, as some scholars think, this detail requires that one assumes there is an ellipsis in the Greek text: Josephus has left out a journey by Herod, e.g., a transfer to Samaria-Sebaste (where Herod is staying according to the end of the paragraph). Another option is that the wilderness motif was added by Josephus in order to disqualify the king as ruler of the Jews (see 15.244 with the note to "he made his way to the wilderness").

[1594] This statement connects with "They [i.e., the treatments] worked in the opposite direction" of the previous paragraph, highlighting Herod's serious health condition. Despite the deficiency of the treatments, the doctors did not know anything better than to desperately continue them. The noun βοήθημα ("remedy," Rengstorf *s.v.*) occurs once elsewhere in Josephus, in connection with King David, for whom his doctors arranged that he could sleep with the young woman Abishag to be kept warm (*Ant.* 7.343-344). The expression προσφέρω βοηθήματα ("apply remedies") is a medical term (Galen, *Plac. Hipp. Plat.* 9.6.20; 9.7.7 [ed. Kühn 5.766, 779]; Pseudo-Galen, *Intr.* [ed. Kühn 14.677]).

[1595] This remark implies that Herod's situation was not completely hopeless, since he was able to eat. The noun ἀρρωστία has a general meaning ("illness," Rengstorf *s.v.*). In *Apion* 1.146 the word occurs in a quotation from Berossus concerning Nabuchodonosor's death. The only further occurrence in Josephus is *Ant.* 6.361.

[1596] The subject of the passive verb ἐπενεχθείη, attested by the Greek MSS (Niese 376), is the pronoun ἐκεῖνος ("he," referring to the king). The basic meaning of ἐπιφέρω is "bring upon" (LSJ *s.v.*); the middle and passive voices can mean "consume/eat in addition" (LSJ *s.v.* II.2). Naber's conjecture ἐπειχθείη (from ἐπείγω ["press, force"], Naber 1888-96: 3.xliv, 352, supported by Schreckenberg 1977: 137) finds a close parallel in *War* 7.372: "Who would not rush [or 'be eager'] to his death ere he shared their fate [i.e., of the persons captured by the Romans] (τίς οὐκ ἂν ἐπειχθείη πρὸ τοῦ ταὐτὰ παθεῖν ἐκείνοις ἀποθανεῖν)?" (trans. Thackeray). The verb ἐπείγω can also mean "be eager (for)" in the passive voice (Rengstorf *s.v.*)—in which case the translation would be "(everything) he might be eager for"—but such instances are usually followed by an objective genitive (LSJ *s.v.* III.b) or an infinitive (e.g., *War* 7.372) and not by a dative (which is the case here: οἷς).

[1597] The noun δύσελπις ("hopeless, almost desperate," Rengstorf *s.v.*) occurs twice elsewhere in Josephus, both times in *Antiquities* (3.11; 5.41).

[1598] Schreckenberg (1977: 137) erases the ἐν of ἐν ἐξουσίᾳ because common Greek requires a simple instrumental dative here.

[1599] This phrase is ambiguous since τύχη can mean, among other things, "fate, fortune, deity" (see *Ant.* 15.17 with the note to "fortune"). Jewish and Christian readers would conclude that Herod's recovery was in God's hands, but Greeks and Romans would think of fate or fortune. The connection between Rome's rise and fortune (interpreted as chance or personified as a sometimes malevolent force, or in the case of Plutarch as either fortune or a divine force) is a longstanding theme since Polybius, elaborated especially by Plutarch (Eckstein 1995: 254-71; Swain 1996: 151-61).

For a phrase similar to ἀνατιθέντες τῇ τύχῃ ("leaving ... to fate"), see Clement of Alexandria, *Exh.* 4.51: "The Romans, who ascribed their greatest successes to Fortune

Alexandra's attempt to take over the citadels leads to her execution.

way in Samaria, which is called Sebaste.[1601]

(7.8) 247 When[1602] Alexandra, who was staying in Jerusalem,[1603] learned about his situation,[1604] she hurried to get control over the citadels in the city.[1605] **248** There are two: one for the city itself,[1606] the other for the Temple.[1607] Those who hold these [citadels] have the entire people[1608] in their power.[1609] For it is not possible for the sacrifices to take place without these,[1610] and it is impossible for any of the Jews not to present these [sacrifices].[1611]

(Τύχῃ ἀνατιθέντες), and regarded her as a very great deity … (trans. Wilson).

[1600] There is one further occurrence of νοσηλεύω ("be ill," Rengstorf s.v.) in Josephus (*War* 3.156).

[1601] Samaria-Sebaste was part of Herod's territory at least since Octavian's grant (see *Ant*. 15.217 with the note to "Samaria," and for the new name Sebaste, 15.292 with the note to "Sebaste").

[1602] *Ant*. 15.247 introduces a section that focuses on the theme of rebellion against and betrayal of Herod. It starts with Alexandra (15.247-251) and continues with Costobar and other friends (15.252-266), which passage includes a subsection about the Sons of Baba (15.260-266). The section reports that all these opponents were executed.

[1603] Alexandra had been mentioned for the last time in *Ant*. 15.232-235, in connection with Mariamme's trial, which took place in Jerusalem. She apparently did not follow Herod into the wilderness and did not join him in Samaria either. She was staying in the center of power, while Herod, being ill, was away in Samaria. On the basis of the previous descriptions of Alexandra, one would assume that she once elsewhere would attempt to take over the throne (see 15.31-34, 42-43, 47, 59, 62, 87, 166, 183, 185; further references in 15.166 with the notes to "hoping for a political change" and "get a start with bringing their hopes for the future into safer ground again").

[1604] The reading πυθομένη of MSS MVE (Niese 376; the other MSS have the present participle πυνθανομένη) implies the meaning "had learned" and matches the preceding aorist participle διατρίβουσα. Nevertheless, Josephus does combine aorist and present participles in several instances (e.g., *Ant*. 15.233 ἐκπηδήσασα καὶ λοιδορουμένη). The reading πυθομένη is probably a correction of πυνθανομένη; the latter reading would then be original.

[1605] Taking control over the fortresses gave Alexandra a power base (as the next paragraph explains), which confirms that she was planning a coup (see the note to "Alexandra, who was staying in Jerusalem" above). Josephus does not specify the fortified places (for their identifications, see the next notes and Shatzman 1991: 225; Richardson 1996: 220). *War* 5.245, which shares the noun φρούριον ("fortified place, fortress") with *Ant*. 15.247, refers to 2 fortresses (the Antonia and Herod's palace; for a description of this palace, see *War* 5.176-181) and states that the Temple was situated adjacent to the city as its fortified place and the Antonia adjacent to the Temple as its fortification.

[1606] The identification of the fortress protecting the city of Jerusalem is less easy than that of the fortress near the Temple because in the period shortly after Mariamme's death (29 or perhaps 28 BCE; see *Ant*. 15.237 with the note to "Mariamme died this way") Herod's fortified palace (mentioned in *War* 5.245; see the previous note) was still to be built. It probably concerns the cluster of the 3 multi-story towers named Phasael, Hippicus, and Mariamme after the 3 persons whom Herod loved most (2.439; 5.162). They were located west of the Temple Mount in the upper city (close to the Jaffa Gate of the current Old City) and are described in detail in *War* 5.163-171 (further discussion in Netzer 2006: 127-29). Herod's later palace was built to the south of these towers.

[1607] The fortified place that protected the Temple area was the Fortress Antonia, which was located northwest of the Temple precinct and directly connected with its wall. Netzer (2006: 160-61) argues that the fortress was partly integrated into the Temple complex. Herod built it and named it after his first Roman patron, Mark Antony (see *Ant*. 15.292 with the note to "Antonia").

[1608] The noun ἔθνος sometimes refers to the Jewish people as an ethnic entity recognized by outsiders rather than to a population living within a specific territory (cf. *Ant*. 11.184, 303; 15.15; 18.378 referring to the Jews staying in former Babylonia; see 15.15 with the note to "nation of the Jews"). Here, however, the Jewish nation living in its heartland Judea is meant.

[1609] The phrase ὑποχείριον ἔχω ("have in one's power") also occurs in *Ant*. 15.20 concerning Herod and Hyrcanus II and in 15.99 concerning Herod and Cleopatra.

[1610] This way of expressing the prominence of the fortresses may reflect Josephus' interests as a priest. He may have in view events from the time of Antiochus IV through to the recent war against Rome and its antecedents, when control over the population interfered with the sacrificial regimen. The priests were in charge of the sacrifices in the Temple and control over both fortresses implied control over both the city and the Temple complex, such that the supply of sacrificial

They are more ready to sacrifice their lives[1612] than to give up the cult they are accustomed to perform for God.[1613] **249** So Alexandra addressed[1614] those[1615] in charge of these forts,[1616] saying that they ought to hand them over to her[1617] and Herod's sons,[1618] so that somebody else would not push ahead to take over the government[1619] in case he [Herod] exited [life].

---

animals could be stopped. The Temple cult was, therefore, dependent on the support of the political authorities.

[1611] This note is surprising for 2 reasons. First, the Temple did not exist anymore at the time of *Antiquities*' composition. Nevertheless, Josephus sometimes writes about the Jerusalem Temple as if it is still functioning (see *Apion* 2.102-109, discussed by Bauckham 1996, who argues that Josephus could not imagine Judaism without the Temple, p. 347; I thank Michael Tuval, Jerusalem, for this reference). In *War* 6.94 Josephus indicates that the Jewish population was deeply depressed because of the interruption of the daily sacrifices in the Temple. The importance of the Temple cult is also acknowledged by a famous statement of Simon the Righteous: "By three things is the world sustained: by the Law, by the [Temple-]service, and by deeds of loving-kindness" (*m. 'Abot* 1.2, trans. Danby). Second, Josephus' reference to the sacrifice obligation is vague and abstract, especially if compared with the biblical instructions, which not only differentiate between the tasks of the priests and those of the lay persons but also state that the male Jews have to bring sacrifices to the Temple only 3 times a year, during the 3 "pilgrim festivals" (Passover, Pentecost, and Tabernacles, Lev 23; Deut 16:16-17); women were free to bring sacrifices (*m. Ḥag.* 1.1). This vagueness is, however, understandable in the present context, which focuses on the importance of the fortresses in the city and not on the prescriptions for the temple service. Josephus may hint at other reasons why the Temple cult was important: a cosmic function (the Jewish cult in *Ant.* 3.179-187 is a divinely established worship at a place chosen by God, carried out by chosen priests on behalf of the Jews and all humankind) and a symbolic meaning (cf. the annual payment of the Temple tax [a half-shekel equaling two drachmae or denarii in Josephus' time] by all male Jews, also those living in the Diaspora: *War* 7.218; *Ant.* 18.312-313; Trebilco 1991: 13-16, 196-97; Sanders 1994: 52, 156, 163-68).

The verb συντελέω with the meaning "present (a sacrifice)" (Rengstorf *s.v.*) also occurs in *Ant.* 15.51, concerning the young High Priest Jonathan-Aristobulus III.

[1612] Josephus swiftly connects the Temple cult with the Jews' readiness to sacrifice themselves for their culture and identity. A similar readiness is apparent from passages in which Josephus briefly points to the Jews'

fame of dying nobly for a Jewish cause (*War* 2.169-177 [cf. *Ant.* 18.55-62]; 3.475; 5.88, 315, 458; 7.406; *Ant.* 17.256; *Apion* 1.42-43, 190-193; 2.146, 218-220, 225-235; cf. the Jews' response to Gaius' decision to erect a statue of himself in the Temple in *War* 2.184-203; *Ant.* 18.261-288; further discussion in van Henten 2007a).

[1613] The vocabulary partly repeats that of the previous sub-clause (e.g., συντελέω) and also echoes that of *Ant.* 15.51 (e.g., θρησκεία "cult, rites," Rengstorf *s.v.*).

[1614] For the verb προσφέρω with λόγους as object ("address"), see *Ant.* 15.16 with the note to "he addressed."

[1615] The officers in charge are called friends (φίλοι) of the king further on in the paragraph.

[1616] The fortified places of *Ant.* 15.247-248 are clearly meant here, although Josephus uses another noun (φυλακτήριον) this time.

[1617] Alexandra boldly tries to have her own way, apparently on the basis of her royal status and authority, which matches her frank and arrogant attitude in other passages (see *Ant.* 15.37 with the note to "because of her kin and frankness"). She apparently sets herself up as Herod's substitute—which is logical in a way since Herod had not appointed one, while he had done so during his journeys to Antony and Octavian (15.65, 184).

[1618] The sons are not specified. The Greek text suggests that all of Herod's sons who were born before this event are referred to: Antipater, Alexander, Aristobulus IV, and possibly Herod III, Herod IV, and Archelaus (these last 3 sons were born in 28 or 27 BCE; Kokkinos 1998: 208). However, it is plausible to assume that Alexandra appointed herself as the patron of Herod's sons who had "blue" (i.e., Hasmonean) blood through Mariamme I rather than of all of his sons. Herod and Mariamme had 5 children (*War* 1.435; *Ant.* 14.300): 3 boys and 2 girls. One son died early (*War* 1.435), Alexander was born in 36 BCE, and Aristobulus probably in 35 BCE (Kokkinos 1998: 213-14).

[1619] This phrase is ironical because it echoes Herod's accusation of Alexandra in *Ant.* 15.32: "He said that she [i.e., Alexandra] secretly plotted against the throne and was arranging, through Cleopatra, that he would be deprived of his rule and that the young man [i.e., Jonathan-Aristobulus III] would receive the government (παραλάβῃ τὰ πράγματα; cf. ἀντιλαμβάνεσθαι τῶν πραγμάτων in 15.249) instead of him through Antony." For τὰ πράγματα meaning "the matters of the kingdom"

And in case he became healthy[1620] again, none of his nearest relatives[1621] could protect it for him more safely.[1622] **250** They did not agree with these words of hers;[1623] furthermore, having been loyal[1624] in the earlier period, they would remain so[1625] all the more at this time, out of hatred against Alexandra[1626] and because they thought it was impious[1627] to give up on Herod while he was still alive.[1628] For they were old friends;[1629] one of them, Achiab, was even a cousin of the king.[1630] **251** So they immediately reported [it] by sending

---

or "the government," see 15.32 with the note to "the government."

[1620] Alexandra's claim is brilliant: it implies that she was the best substitute for Herod, no matter whether he died or remained alive.

[1621] Alternative translation: "closest friends."

[1622] This statement is clearly ironical in the light of Alexandra's repeated actions against Herod (see *Ant.* 15.247 with the note to "she hurried to get control over the citadels in the city").

The verb διατηρέω ("maintain, keep") also occurs in the description of Herod's secret instructions for Joseph and Soemus (15.184-186), which include the phrase "to do everything possible to secure the kingdom (τὴν βασιλείαν ... διατηρεῖν) for his sons together with his brother Pheroras" (15.186).

[1623] The expression ἐπιεικῶς φέρω means "accept, assent" here (Rengstorf *s.v.* ἐπιεικής; cf. Lucian, *Laps.* 1; John Chrysostom, *Hom. Matt.* [PG 58.772]; *De meretrice* [ed. Abicht 151]).

[1624] Niese (376) reads ἀλλὰ πιστοί ("furthermore, [having been] faithful") with MSS FV and E. Most MSS read the opposite: ἀλλ' ἄπιστοι ("furthermore, [having been] unfaithful"). It is likely that the latter reading is a misinterpretation of the first; in the stage of the uncial MSS both readings were identical, except for the separation of both words. The particle ἀλλὰ has a progressive function here (Denniston 1954: 21-22).

[1625] The aorist διέμειναν links up with the word πιστοί at the beginning of this subclause. For phrases of διαμένω ("maintain, continue to be") with πιστός ("faithful"), cf. Xenophon, *Cyr.* 7.1.45; *Hell.* 6.5.44; 7.2.2; Cassius Dio 6.28.4.

[1626] Josephus does not explain this hatred. On the basis of the preceding narrative one can think of at least 3 possibilities: (1) Alexandra was apparently an arrogant woman who allowed herself great liberties and had plotted against Herod before, and the officers may have known her personally or have, at least, been familiar with her bad reputation; (2) Josephus refers to the mutual hatred of Alexandra and Mariamme on the one hand, and Salome and Cyprus on the other hand (*Ant.* 15.213, 220), and the officers may have supported the faction of Salome and Cyprus; (3) some of the officers were close to Herod. The third option is in line with the last part of this section, and the first two could be additional explanations, although this remains entirely speculative.

[1627] The phrase (μηδ') ὅσιον ὑπολαμβάνειν ("think [something] is against the divine laws"; cf. Philo, *Spec.* 3.27; Theodoretus, *Hist. eccl.* 3.72.3 [ed. Parmentier and Hansen 206.16]; *Quaest. Regn. Paral.* [PG 80.649]) indicates that the attendants considered it to be their religious duty to respect Herod's life (see the next note). Josephus' description of the response of those in charge of the forts to Alexandra's proposal (see *Ant.* 15.249) implies that they interpreted it very negatively: the immediate context indicates that they assumed that Alexandra took Herod's death for granted (see the next note), and their response also presupposes that they took Alexandra's initiative as an attempt to overthrow Herod's rule. The adjective ὅσιος ("holy, appointed by divine decree, pious," Rengstorf *s.v.*) may evoke the divine laws here (cf. ὅσιον οἴεσθαι in 15.281 ["think it is a religious duty"], which concerns faithfulness to the divine laws).

[1628] The obligation to protect and respect the lives of human beings is an important point in Jewish tradition and already emphasized in the Ten Commandments: "You shall not murder" (Exod 20:13; cf. Deut 5:17) and other passages in the Pentateuch (Gen 9:5-6; Exod 21:12-14, 19; Lev 24:17; Num 35:16-34; Deut 19:11-13; see also Josephus' reference to this commandment in his summary of the Decalogue in *Ant.* 3.91-92).

[1629] Josephus' vocabulary implies that these men were not only political friends of Herod, which meant that they had a high status (on the "friends of the king," see *Ant.* 15.5 with the note to "the friends around him"), but also that they had a close connection with the king. This is confirmed by the next detail, which indicates that Achiab was a relative of Herod (see the next note). Their close relationship with Herod explains their refusal to Alexandra's proposal.

[1630] Achiab prevented Herod's suicide near the end of the king's life and was apparently still close to the king at that time (*War* 1.662; *Ant.* 17.184; see also *War* 2.55, 77; *Ant.* 17.270, 292). *War* 2.55 also refers to Achiab as a cousin of the king (ἀνεψιὸς [τοῦ] βασιλέως).

There are 2 explanations for Achiab's relation to Herod (Vogel 2002: 115 n. 23): Achiab may have been (1) a son of Phallion, who was a brother of Antipater (i.e., Herod's father) and died in 40 BCE (Richardson 1996: 221 n. 13), or (2) he was a son of Dositheus' sister (see *Ant.* 15.168-169 with the notes to "Dositheus, one

BOOK FIFTEEN

a message[1631] about Alexandra's plan to the king.[1632] And he ordered, without any delay,[1633] for her to be killed.[1634] He was in a bad state, having hardly and under great pains[1635] escaped from his illness. He was still suffering mentally and bodily[1636] at the same time, with the result that he was hard to please.[1637] He was more than ready to use every kind

---

of his friends" and "Dositheus was a relative of Joseph") and Joseph, Herod's youngest brother (Kokkinos 1998: 153-55; Günther 2005: 112).

Kokkinos (1998: 153) argues that Achiab hated Alexandra because he held her responsible for the death of his father Joseph (15.87). However, in 15.87 Josephus merely notes that Herod held Alexandra partly responsible for the troubles in his family and kept her under guard. The passage also indicates that Herod was primarily responsible for Joseph's death; it was the king who ordered Joseph's execution. Had Joseph been Achiab's father, Achiab would probably have hated Herod for killing his father. Achiab's loyalty to Herod implies that Phallion was more likely his father.

[1631] A message had to be sent because the king was still staying in Samaria-Sebaste (*Ant.* 15.246).

[1632] The officers' swift report to Herod is only logical in the light of their close connection with the king (*Ant.* 15.250). It is puzzling why Alexandra approached them since one would assume that she was aware of their relationship with the king, given that she was a prominent member of the court. Günther (2005: 121) concludes that Alexandra miscalculated the situation.

[1633] The translation follows the reading οὐδὲν ἀναβαλλόμενος of MSS FLAMW. Niese (377) conjectures οὐδὲν ἀναβαλομένους ("[he ordered] them [to kill her] without any delay"). Herod was apparently sound enough to respond immediately to Alexandra's attempt to take over the throne.

[1634] Alexandra is executed immediately, although Herod used to kill prominent family members only after having convened a council (cf. the executions of Hyrcanus II and Mariamme I in *Ant.* 15.165-176, 229-236; see 15.229 with the note to "having gathered"). However, the circumstances are different here, as the continuation of the paragraph indicates: Herod was apparently still in Samaria-Sebaste (15.247) and had barely survived a critical medical condition, which deeply affected his mental and emotional states.

Kokkinos (1998: 182) dates Alexandra's execution to 28/27 BCE. Otto (1913: 52) wonders why Alexandra is executed so late in the Herod narrative while she had been involved in many previous rebellious acts (see 15.166 with the notes to "quarrelsome" and "strongly hoping for a political change"). He therefore suggests that Alexandra became Herod's enemy at a very late stage and that the earlier references to her rebellious acts are fictitious. Kokkinos (1998: 181-82) argues that Herod only dared to take action against Alexandra (and Costobar; see 15.252) after Cleopatra had died, since the queen would have tried to have Herod punished if he executed Alexandra.

Josephus does not offer an obituary of Alexandra after the notification of her death, although one would expect this here because he offers such assessments of Alexandra's father Hyrcanus II (15.179-182) and her daughter Mariamme I (15.237-239) after reporting their deaths. Yet Josephus already commented on Alexandra as a person in 15.233-234, shortly before Mariamme's execution. Josephus' very negative view of Alexandra is not a likely explanation of the absence of a concluding assessment of Alexandra. He does comment on Herod as a person and a ruler after the king's death (17.191-192), while there are several negative remarks about Herod within *Antiquities*' Herod narrative. Moreover, an assessment of Jonathan-Aristobulus III after his death is missing as well (cf. 15.56-57), and Josephus' portrait of him is very positive (see 15.23, 25, 29, 51-52).

Landau (2006: 132) argues that the brief description of Alexandra's execution is a means to anticipate the report of Herod's subsequent "preposterous deed," i.e., the execution of his sons Alexander and Aristobulus IV, but that episode is narrated only much later (16.356-394).

[1635] The noun κακοπάθεια ("distress") is rare in Josephus. Here it means "great pains, arduous effort" (Rengstorf *s.v.*). The 2 other occurrences in Josephus are part of the Herod narrative in *Antiquities* (15.312, referring to distress because of a famine, and 17.347).

[1636] Concerning the phrase ψυχῇ καὶ σώματι κεκακωμένος ("afflicted in mind and body"), see *Ant.* 15.158 with the note to "afflicted in body and soul." For a very different statement about Herod, which also closely connects body and mind, see the praise of Herod in *War* 1.429-430: Josephus emphasizes that Herod's body and soul fully corresponded to each other ("Endowed also with a physique that equalled his genius [σώματι πρὸς τὴν ψυχὴν ἀναλόγῳ] ... in addition to the advantages he had in mind and body [πρὸς δὲ τοῖς ψυχικοῖς καὶ τοῖς σωματικοῖς προτερήμασιν]," trans. Sievers/Forte in BJP 1a), which explains why he was an extremely successful hunter as well as an irresistible fighter (Sievers 2009: 91-4).

[1637] The adjective δυσάρεστος ("discontent, grumbling" and here "in an irritable mood," Rengstorf *s.v.*) occurs once elsewhere in Josephus (*Ant.* 3.23), in which

Execution of Costobar and the Sons of Baba.
War *1.486*

of reason to punish those who fell into his hands.[1638] **252** He even murdered his most indispensable friends[1639]—Costobar,[1640] Lysimachus,[1641] Antipater surnamed Gadia,[1642] and also Dositheus[1643]—for the following reason.[1644]

(7.9) 253 Costobar was Idumean by origin.[1645] Among them he was a member of those of the highest rank[1646] and he had priests of Koze[1647] as ancestors. The Idumeans think that

---

case it characterizes the human race as being discontent and fond of uttering reproaches in cases of misfortune.

[1638] This trait of Herod's character becomes very explicit at the end of his life, when the king is planning a huge mourning session for him by having prominent Jews killed in the hippodrome of Jericho (*Ant.* 17.173-179). Josephus indicates that Herod tended to take his misery out on others in an extreme way, killing them at random, which is part of the tyrannical stereotype (van Henten 2011b). This point is, however, sometimes mollified. Thus the next paragraph shows that Herod actually had a good reason for executing these friends (see 15.252 with the note to "for the following reason"). The verb ὑποπίπτω ("fall under") means "fall into someone's hands" here (Rengstorf *s.v.*).

[1639] Josephus is combining 2 execution reports (Alexandra's and that of part of the administrative elite at Herod's court), although they likely occurred at different moments: Alexandra was executed in 28 (or 28/27) BCE (see *Ant.* 15.251 with the note to "for her to be killed"), and the friends of Herod mentioned here may have been executed in 26/25 BCE (see 15.254 with the note to "governor of Idumea and Gaza"). *Ant.* 15.251-252 therefore is an example of Josephus' technique of synchronizing events that are thematically related (van Henten and Huitink 2007: 225).

Josephus may indicate that the very close friends mentioned here belonged to the Idumean elite at Herod's court since in 15.253 Josephus explicitly states that Costobar, the friend who is mentioned first, was an Idumean, like Herod himself.

The combination of ἀναγκαῖος and φίλος, indicating close friends, is a fixed expression in Josephus (*Ant.* 7.350; 11.254-255; *Life* 223) and also occurs with the superlative ἀναγκαιότατος (*Ant.* 10.5, 59, 229; 13.224). For a political meaning of φίλος, see 15.5 with the note to "the friends around him."

[1640] This theophoric name is of Semitic origin (*qwsgbr*) and means "Qôs is mighty" (Knauf 1999: 675; Ilan 2002: 436-37; see *Ant.* 15.253 with the note to "Koze"). Costobar must have been a very important administrator in Herod's kingdom: Herod appointed him as governor of Idumea and Gaza (15.254) and arranged a marriage for him with his sister Salome (15.254; cf. *War* 1.486).

The subsequent section of *Ant.* 15.253-266 focuses on Costobar. The parallel narrative of *War* (1.486) mentions Costobar in passing, also in a context of betrayal of Herod: he would have supported Herod's brother Pheroras in his attempt to flee to the Parthians. Costobar's fall sets in with Salome's decision to separate from him (*Ant.* 15.259). For further references to Costobar, see Kasher 1988: 55, 64, 74, 143, 150, 214-18, 222-23; Kokkinos 1998: 179-82; Marshak 2011.

[1641] Lysimachus is a familiar Greek name and therefore does not confirm an Idumean provenance (cf. the 2 previous notes). Although this name was also used for Jews, it is uncertain whether Lysimachus considered himself to be Jewish (Ilan 2002: 49-50, 294; cf. the following report about Costobar in *Ant.* 15.253-258). Lysimachus is mentioned again in 15.260.

[1642] Antipater is another familiar Greek name. Both Idumeans and Jews used it (Ilan 2002: 264-65). Herod's father was called thus (or Antipas, *War* 1.19; *Ant.* 14.8, 10) in addition to his Semitic name Gadia (*gdy'*; Schlatter 1913: 35; Schalit 2001: 144), which means "kid" (Marcus-Wikgren 118 n. *d*; Ilan 2002: 366)—although it may be a theophoric name deriving from Gad, a Semitic god of fortune (cf. Tyche in Greek and Fortuna in Latin literature; Ribichini 1999; Ilan 2002: 366-67).

[1643] This Dositheus has already been mentioned in *Ant.* 15.168 (further references there in the note to "Dositheus, one of his friends").

[1644] Important points in the following section about Costobar (*Ant.* 15.253-266) are that he had approached Herod's arch-enemy Cleopatra (15.256) and had hidden the Sons of Baba, who were possible pretenders to the throne (15.260). Both acts were cases of severe betrayal. The other friends mentioned may have been involved in Costobar's acts or in other cases of treason.

[1645] Josephus starts with a flashback concerning Costobar and the Idumeans before coming to the main issue, the Sons of Baba (*Ant.* 15.260). Costobar's family came from Idumea, a region south of Judea, west of the Dead Sea, and east of Gaza, which roughly coincides with the area attributed to the Edomites in the early Second Temple period (Möller and Schmitt 1976: 100; Kokkinos 1998: 36-139). Idumea was from the beginning a part of Herod's kingdom (see 15.2 with the note to "all Judea" and 15.254).

[1646] This suggests, together with Josephus' next remark, that Costobar's family belonged to the priestly elite of the Idumeans (see also the next note). The noun ἀξίωμα can mean, among other things, "dignity, status,

this figure is a god.[1648] **254** Hyrcanus[1649] had changed their way of life[1650] to the habits and customs of the Jews.[1651] When Herod took over the kingdom,[1652] he appointed Costobar as governor of Idumea and Gaza.[1653] He gave him his sister Salome [in marriage][1654] after he

---

rank" (Rengstorf s.v.), sometimes in combination with a statement about someone's descent (see *Ant.* 15.51 with the note to "his dignity connected with his descent" concerning Jonathan-Aristobulus III, who descended from the Hasmonean dynasty).

[1647] Niese (377) reads Κοζαί with MS P, while the other Greek MSS read Κωζέ; they are different spellings of the same divine name. Qôs was the national deity of the Edomites (see *Ant.* 15.252 with the note to "Costobar"). Theophoric names with Qôs (*qws*, "bow") are attested for Edomite royal and non-royal persons. Qôs was originally a Syrian weathergod, and Qôs, Yahweh, Haddu/Hadad, and Baal may be different names for the same deity (Knauf 1999: 677). A small altar with the name "Qôs" on its base was found at Ramat el-Khalil (the location of the oaks [or terebinths] of Mamre, where Abram was living according to Gen 13:18; Josephus refers to this place as "the oak called Ogyges," Feldman in BJP 3 on *Ant.* 1.186), 3 km north of the old city of Hebron, which altar was enclosed by a massive wall erected in Herod's time (Magen 1993). Evidence shows that Qôs was still worshipped in Nabatean territories in the 2nd and 3rd cent. CE (further discussion and references in Dearman 1995: 123-31; Knauf 1999).

The verb ἱερατεύω ("assume the duties of/be a priest") occurs twice elsewhere in Josephus (*Ant.* 3.189; 20.242).

[1648] This is Josephus' diplomatic way of saying that Qôs was one of the Idumean gods. Stating unconditionally that Qôs is an Idumean deity would be at odds with the first commandment to venerate no god other than the God of Israel (Exod 20:2-3; cf. 23:24; 34:14; Deut 6:13). The veneration of Qôs by the Idumeans was a sensitive issue, also because they had converted to Judaism (see *Ant.* 15.254).

[1649] I.e., the Jewish ruler John Hyrcanus, Hyrcanus I (135/134-104 BCE).

[1650] The noun πολιτεία not only means "citizenship" or "constitution" but also a "way of life" (Rengstorf s.v.) associated with a specific ethnic group (2 Macc 6:23A; 8:17; 4 Macc 8:7; 17:9-10; van Henten 1997: 189-90, 197-99, 254-55, 263). This meaning is also apparent from the first lines of a famous inscription from Stobi (Macedonia, probably 3rd cent. CE): "[Claudius] Tiberius Polycharmus, also (called) Achyrius, the father of the synagogue at Stobi, having lived my whole life according to the (prescriptions of) Judaism (ὅς πολιτευσάμενος πᾶσαν πολιτείαν κατὰ τον Ἰουδαϊσμόν), in fulfilment of a vow (have donated) the rooms(?) to the holy place, and the *triclinium* with the *tetrastoa* out of my personal accounts without touching the sacred (funds) at all …" (*CIJ* no. 694). Chester (2012: 120-22) concludes that these lines imply that Polycharmus had lived his life throughout faithful to the Jewish tradition. Claudius Tiberius Polycharmus clearly was an official figure, belonging to the elite, and "life" probably implies "public life," which means that the inscription does not make a stament about this man's personal life but rather indicates that he has enacted his every policy in keeping with the Jewish tradition. The continuation of the *Antiquities* narrative confirms this meaning of πολιτεία: John Hyrcanus forced the Idumeans to adopt the practices of the Jewish people (see the next note), implying that they participated in the Jewish public form of life (calendar, holidays, cult and public devotion). The verb μεθίστημι plus τὴν πολιτείαν as object ("change the way of life, change the form of government") is a common expression in Plutarch (*Caes.* 13.2; *Lyc.* 5.2; *Lys.* 15.1; *Pel.* 25.7; *Pomp.* 20.4; *Sol.* 13.3; cf. Xenophon, *Hell.* 7.1.42; Diodorus 13.34.6; 15.40.4; 15.79.3; Eunapius, *Fragm.* [ed. Dindorf 1.251]).

[1651] John Hyrcanus expanded the Judean territory in several directions and conquered the Idumean cities of Adora and Marissa. He forced the Idumeans to convert to Judaism, which required male circumcision and observance of the other Jewish laws and practices (*War* 1.63; *Ant.* 13.255-258). Accepting the Jewish religion implied, of course, that the worship of deities like Qôs was forbidden. *War* 4.281 indicates that many Idumeans implemented this transition: they protected the Jerusalem Temple and were ready to fight, together with the Jews, for their fatherland (Schürer-Vermes 1.207, 538; 2.3-6). The combination ἔθη καὶ νόμιμα ("habits and customs") also occurs in *Ant.* 14.216 and in *War* 2.160 concerning the Essenes (see also 15.267 with the note to "the ancestral customs").

[1652] This note refers to Herod's final triumph over Antigonus at his capture of Jerusalem in 37 or 36 BCE (see *Ant.* 15.2). The verb παραλαμβάνω with τὴν βασιλείαν as object is a fixed expression for taking over the throne, which occurs ca. 32 times in Josephus (Rengstorf s.v. παραλαμβάνω; see, e.g., 15.16, 40 referring to Herod; 15.180 referring to Hyrcanus II; and 16.92; 17.95 referring to Herod's sons who were apparently planning to take over the throne).

[1653] Richardson (1996: 221) connects Costobar's appointment with his marriage to Salome and situates both events in 34 BCE. Smallwood (1976: 63 n. 10) also

had put Joseph to death,[1655] who had earlier received her in marriage, as we have indicated.[1656] **255** Being glad about receiving these benefactions and very excited about his good luck,[1657] which was more than he had expected,[1658] he gradually went beyond due bounds.[1659] For he did not think it right for him to do what was ordered[1660] by Herod[1661]—although he was the ruler—nor for the Idumeans, who had adopted the customs of the

---

states that both events occurred at approximately the same time but she argues for 37 BCE. Kokkinos (1998: 179 n. 9) argues that the date of Costobar's appointment is ambiguous: in *Ant.* 15.254 Josephus connects it with Salome's marriage, but in 15.260 he mentions 12 years during which Costobar protected the Sons of Baba. If the latter period is in view, it could imply that Costobar became governor shortly after Herod had captured Jerusalem (in 37 or 36 BCE), with the 12 years corresponding to 37-26/25 BCE (Kokkinos 1998: 180). Smallwood (1976: 72 n. 37) and Kasher (2007: 190 n. 28) reconstruct the 12 years as 40/39-29/28 BCE, starting at Herod's appointment as king by the Romans. If Gaza was included in Antony's grant of the coastal area to Cleopatra in 37 (or 36) BCE or given to her as a separate gift (see 15.217 with the note to Gaza), Costobar must have been appointed before this gift, which implies an appointment in 37 BCE at the latest. Furthermore, since Costobar's marriage with Salome took place after the death of Salome's first husband Joseph in 35/34 BCE (see 15.87 with the note to "he ordered Joseph to be killed" and the note to "gave him his sister Salome [in marriage]" below), the appointment and the marriage were 2 separate events. *Ant.* 15.254 does not imply that both events occurred simultaneously; Josephus merely mentions them together (cf. *War* 1.486, which only mentions Costobar's marriage to Salome). For the function of governor (στρατηγός) in Herod's kingdom, see Levine 1975: 17, 155 n. 29 with references; Shatzman 1991: 287 n. 38 (for other practices concerning this office, see Mason 1974: 155-62).

[1654] Costobar and Salome were probably married in 34 BCE (Marcus-Wikgren 121; Richardson 1996: 221; Vogel 2002: 116; Günther 2005: 120). Josephus indicates that Herod orchestrated the marriage (likewise *War* 1.486; cf. 1.566; *Ant.* 16.244; 17.10), but he does not mention Herod's motive, nor does he inform us about Salome's position in this or about the role of their mother Cyprus. A plausible motive would be that the marriage was a way to hold on to Costobar and secure his loyalty (Smallwood 1976: 63). Herod also decided about the marriages of his children, grandchildren, and brother (*Ant.* 16.11, 97; 17.22; Mayer-Schärtel 1995: 202-03).

The formulation δίδωσιν αὐτῷ τὴν ἀδελφὴν Σαλώμην ("He gave him his sister Salome") is elliptical and may be a short-hand formula for γυναῖκα διδόναι ("give as wife") or διδόναι πρὸς γάμον ("give in marriage," Rengstorf *s.v.* δίδωμι; see, e.g., 12.154). For a similar elliptical phrase with διδόναι, cf. 6.204 concerning the marriage of David and Michal.

[1655] The execution of Joseph is reported in *Ant.* 15.87.

[1656] The "we" refers to Josephus as author. He mentions the marriage of Joseph and Salome in passing in his report about Salome accusing her husband of adultery (see *Ant.* 15.81).

The formula ὡς ἐδηλώσαμεν ("as we have indicated") marks cross-references to other passages, sometimes with additional words: 7.330 (plus μικρὸν ἔμπροσθεν ["a little while ago"]); 9.28; 15.240 (plus καὶ πρότερον ["earlier"]); 16.206; *Life* 61 (plus ἐν ἄλλοις ["elsewhere"]).

[1657] The phrase ἤρθη ὑπὸ τῆς εὐτυχίας ("he was excited about his good luck"; about the motif of Herod's fortune as a ruler, see *Ant.* 15.361 with the note to "this state of fortune") is paralleled by Plutarch, *Mor.* (*Fort. Rom.*) 319b concerning the emperor Gaius Caligula.

[1658] This formulation may imply that it was not self-evident that Costobar was appointed as governor of Idumea and Gaza by Herod and that other prominent Idumeans were more likely candidates, or that Costobar did not belong to Herod's closest friends, despite the reference to "his closest friends" in *Ant.* 15.252. It is imaginable that Herod chose Costobar in order to win over a potential enemy (cf. Ronen 1988: 217). The expression παρὰ δόξαν ("contrary to expectation," Rengstorf *s.v.* δόξα) occurs frequently in Josephus (*War* 1.95, 614; 3.289, 518; 4.529; *Ant.* 2.280; 3.210; 5.40; 15.316, 388; 16.269; 18.129, 219; 19.243; *Life* 46, 96).

[1659] Here Josephus offers a psychological explanation for Costobar's behavior: his unexpected great success made him lose sight of reality. The verb ἐκβαίνω ("deviate from") means "exceed all bounds" here (Rengstorf *s.v.*).

[1660] The phrase ποιέω τὸ προσταττόμενον ("do what is ordered") is common in ancient Greek literature (e.g., Isocrates, *Archid.* 7.5; Aristotle, *Rhet.* 1399b 13; Polybius 6.21.2; 6.49.4; Diodorus 2.1.8; 9.31.3; Plutarch, *Lyc.* 11.3; *Sert.* 25.2; Diogenes Laertius 6.36).

[1661] Disobedience to the king is a most serious matter for a governor. Such behavior implies that Costobar did not accept Herod's authority. The subsequent note that Costobar turned to Cleopatra also indicates that he committed treason. It is remarkable that Costobar got

Jews,[1662] to be subject to them.[1663] **256** So he sent out a message to Cleopatra,[1664] saying that Idumea had always belonged to her ancestors[1665] and that therefore it was right to request the territory from Antony.[1666] For he himself was prepared to shift his loyalty to her. **257** And he did this not for the reason that he was more pleased[1667] to be under Cleopatra's rule [than under Herod's], but because he thought that, if Herod was deprived of most of his kingdom,[1668] he would then be easy to attack[1669] and he himself could rule over the Idumean people[1670] and achieve more.[1671] For he kept passing all bounds in his

---

away with this according to Josephus' report (see *Ant.* 15.258).

[1662] The phrase μεταλαμβάνω τὰ Ἰουδαίων ἔθη ("adopt the customs of the Jews") also occurs in *Ant.* 20.139, concerning Epiphanes, the son of King Antiochus of Commagene, who rejected a marriage with Agrippa's sister Drusilla because he did not want to adopt the Jewish customs.

[1663] Several scholars translate this passage as if Costobar was against the Idumeans' conversion to Judaism (e.g., "For he did not think that it was proper … for the Idumeans to adopt the customs of the Jews and be subject to them," trans. Marcus-Wikgren; Kasher 2007: 137). Richardson (1996: 221) concludes that Costobar himself "refused to accept Judaism," although he must have been circumcised in his opinion in order to be able to marry Salome (cf. *Ant.* 16.225). If Costobar was circumcised, this plausibly has happened at 8 days of age, as part of the Jewish custom now adopted in Idumea. In that case his circumcision would not tell us much about his intentions or outlook to Judaism. Josephus' point, therefore, may be different, hinting at Costobar's being dissatisfied with the Idumean subjection to the Jews or the adoption to the Jewish way of life (Josephus writes: "… the Idumeans, who *had adopted* the customs of the Jews …"). This could imply that he could not accept the Idumeans' subjection to the Jews for the very reason that they had adopted the Jewish practices and therefore should be considered to be equal to the Jews (cf. the Idumean loyalty mentioned in *War* 4.281; see *Ant.* 15.254 with the note to "the habits and customs of the Jews"). Another explanation is that he wanted to remain faithful to Idumean practices, which interpretation may be supported by Josephus' introduction of Costobar (15.253), which emphasizes his high status and his ancestry; he descended from a long line of priests of Koze, whom the Idumeans "think … is a god" (note the present tense of νομίζουσιν "think" in 15.253).

[1664] Costobar turned to Cleopatra for help, as Alexandra had done several times before (*Ant.* 15.24, 45, 62; Kokkinos [1998: 181] connects Costobar's letter with Alexandra's appeals to the queen). This makes Costobar's betrayal of Herod even worse since Cleopatra was Herod's biggest enemy (see, e.g., 15.28, 75, 77). Josephus does not indicate why Costobar applied to Cleopatra for help but, if his report is trustworthy, it is highly plausible that he hoped to benefit from his drastic move (Richardson 1996: 221).

[1665] Costobar obviously had to make it attractive for Cleopatra to help him. Supporting a claim that Idumea originally had belonged to the Ptolemaic kingdom and had to be returned to her was one way of doing that. After the Battle of Paneas in 198 BCE Idumea, together with Judea, had been taken over from the Ptolemies by the Seleucids (Schürer-Vermes 1.138). Cleopatra actually attempted to restore the size of the Ptolemaic kingdom to what it had been in the 2nd half of the 3rd century BCE. Josephus emphasizes several times that Cleopatra attempted to expand the territory of her kingdom (see *Ant.* 15.24 with the note to "Cleopatra" and van Henten 2005a).

[1666] Cleopatra received several territorial grants from Antony (*Ant.* 15.77-79, 95-96, 106) and thus became a dangerous competitor of Herod. He even became dependent on Cleopatra because he leased Jericho from her and was guarantor for a Nabatean lease from her (15.106-107).

[1667] The phrase οὐδέν … ἀρεσκόμενος ("he was in no way … pleased") may echo Thucydides 8.48 (cf. also LXX Prov 12:21; Theocritus, *Idyl.* 27.14; Lucian, *Hermot.* 21.6).

[1668] Costobar's reasoning seems to presuppose a context in which parts of Herod's territory would be transferred to Cleopatra, which matches the situation at the time when Antony was giving grants of land to her (see *Ant.* 15.256 with the note to "it was right to request the territory from Antony"). The continuation of the sentence indicates how he would benefit from such a transfer.

[1669] The rare adjective εὐεπιχείρητος ("easy to be attacked," LSJ *s.v.*) occurs once elsewhere in Josephus, with a similar meaning (*Ant.* 1.112; cf. Dionysius, *Ant. rom.* 4.29.4; Strabo 5.3.7; Philo, *Mos.* 1.168; Appian, *Bell. civ.* 2.8.54; 2.18.127; Cassius Dio 86.13).

[1670] Costobar apparently did not intend to take over Herod's entire kingdom but only to separate Idumea from Judea.

[1671] If Costobar's plan was successful, he would replace Herod as ruler of Idumea and thus increase in status and power, although he would remain dependent

hopes,[1672] having significant means[1673] through his family and his wealth,[1674] which he had obtained by a continuous and sordid love of profit.[1675] What he had in mind was no minor thing.[1676] **258** So Cleopatra did ask Antony for this territory,[1677] but she failed to get it. When the matter was told to Herod,[1678] he was prepared to kill Costobar.[1679] Yet because his sister and mother requested it,[1680] he let him go and deemed him worthy of a pardon,[1681] holding him under suspicion[1682] for the rest of his life because of what he had attempted to do at that time.

(7.10) 259 After some time had passed,[1683] it also happened that Salome had a clash

---

on Cleopatra and obliged to demonstrate his loyalty with gifts and services as a friendly king (see *Ant.* 15.5 with the note to "the friends around him"). For phrases similar to μεῖζον πράξειν ("achieve more, do on a grander scale"), see Thucydides 1.130; Libanius, *Ep.* 1178.1.

[1672] The verb ἐπιδιαβαίνω usually means "cross likewise" (see *Ant.* 13.14) and is used metaphorically here (Rengstorf *s.v.*). LSJ (*s.v.* II.1) give "pass all bounds" as the meaning for this passage, which would emphasize Costobar's unbridled ambition.

[1673] The phrase οὐκ ὀλίγας ἀφορμάς (literally "no small means") is a case of *litotes* (cf. Diodorus 19.33.2; Galen, *Alim. facult.* [ed. Kühn 6.479]).

[1674] Costobar's appartenance to the very wealthy aristocracy of Idumea matches the introductory information about him in *Ant.* 15.253, which also mentions his priestly descent.

[1675] This note in passing characterizes Costobar rather negatively as a selfish and greedy person. In *Life* 75 Josephus uses the noun αἰσχροκέρδεια ("greed, vile avarice," Rengstorf *s.v.*) in connection with John of Giscala in a highly critical passage about an issue of pure olive oil: "Yet Ioannes did not say these things in the service of piety, but on account of the most blatant, disgusting greed (δι᾽ αἰσχροκέρδειαν φανερωτάτην)" (trans. Mason in BJP 9; cf. *Life* 224 and the statement of the famous blind seer Teiresias to King Creon of Thebes in Sophocles' *Antigone*: "Rulers, also, are prone to be corrupt (αἰσχροκερδείαν φιλεῖ)" [1056, trans. Lloyd-Jones]).

[1676] The vague phrase οὐδὲν μικρὸν ἐπενόει is a further negative remark about Costobar that points to his unbridled ambition and boldness. The phrase connects with the words "he kept passing all bounds in his hopes" at the beginning of the sentence. Lucian's satire of a contemporaneous prophet named Alexander offers a close parallel: "So he [i.e., Alexander] abandoned petty projects for ever (οὐκέτι μικρὸν οὐδὲν ἐπενόει). He formed a partnership with a Byzantine writer of choral songs, one of those who enter the public competitions, far more abominable than himself by nature" (*Alex.* 6, trans. Harmon). For a similar phrase concerning Domitian before he became emperor, see Cassius Dio 66.3.4: "Domitian became afraid of his father because of what he himself had done and far more because of what he had intended to do; for he was quite ambitious in his projects (οὐδὲν γὰρ μικρὸν ἐπενόει)" (trans. Cary).

[1677] I.e., Idumea (see the previous paragraph).

[1678] The unspecified informant may have been a fellow friend of Costobar who disagreed with his policy, or a spy of Herod (cf. *War* 1.492). Alternative translations for οἱ λόγοι ("the matter") are "the story" and "the negotiations" here (Rengstorf *s.v.* λόγος).

[1679] Herod's intent to have Costobar executed is understandable: Costobar's proposal to Cleopatra as well as his hiding of the Sons of Baba (*Ant.* 15.260-266) were severe cases of treason (see also 15.255 with the note to "by Herod").

[1680] I.e., Salome and Cyprus. Elsewhere Josephus suggests that Salome and Cyprus presided a faction of their own (see *Ant.* 15.35, 185, 213 with notes). Costobar may have belonged to that faction, or his own faction may have occasionally co-operated with it. The immediate context shows that the reason why the 2 women pled for mercy towards Costobar was his marriage with Salome (15.254). This can only be correct if the intervention took place after the execution of Salome's first husband Joseph in 35/34 BCE (see 15.87 with the note to "he ordered Joseph to be killed" and 15.254 with the note to "He gave him his sister Salome [in marriage]").

[1681] Kokkinos (1998: 179-180 n. 9) considers Josephus' information about Costobar's betrayal, Herod's lenient policy towards him, and the date of the event (see *Ant.* 15.254 with the note to "he appointed Costobar as governor of Idumea and Gaza") to be highly ambiguous. Yet if Costobar was married with Salome at this stage, Herod's pardon for Costobar is understandable, and even if he was not yet married, it is plausible that Salome and Cyprus were eager to change Herod's mind, especially if Costobar was close to the women's faction (see the previous note).

[1682] On the motif of suspicion by Herod in the immediate context, see *Ant.* 15.264-265, and for further references in the Herod narrative of *Antiquities*, 15.42 with the note to "he truly did not remain without suspicion."

[1683] This vague chronological marker (χρόνου

with Costobar.[1684] And she immediately sent him a document,[1685] disbanding their marriage,[1686] which [act] was not according to the laws of the Jews.[1687] For with us[1688] it is permitted for a man to do that,[1689] but a divorced woman is not permitted to marry of her

---

διελθόντος) also appears in *Ant.* 10.196. Elsewhere the time lapses are specified, either by the context (1.300) or by an addition, especially ὀλίγου ("a little," 8.328; 9.27; 10.17; 19.300; cf. 13.168). For similar vague expressions, see Demosthenes, *Or.* 23.153; Cassius Dio 52.20.4.

[1684] The verb στασιάζω (πρός) ("rebel, clash, quarrel, etc.," Rengstorf *s.v.*) can be used in descriptions of conflicts between individuals (*Ant.* 12.239; 13.285; 14.77; 18.109). The verb ἐπισυμβαίνω ("happen [further]") occurs once elsewhere in Josephus (15.409).

[1685] The noun γραμματεῖον ("written message/letter," Rengstorf *s.v.*) also occurs in *Ant.* 16.319 (with the meaning "message" or "document"). Marcus-Wikgren (122 n. b) note that Josephus uses the noun γράμματα ("letter") in a similar context in 4.253, in which corresponding passage the LXX (Deut 24:1, 3) has the technical phrase βιβλίον ἀποστασίου ("certificate of divorce"), which renders the expression *sēfer kᵉtîrut* of the biblical Hebrew (Deut 24:1, 3; Isa 50:1; Jer 3:8; cf. Matt 5:31; GELS 1.56). The Rabbinic word for a divorce certificate is *geṭ*. For the phrase γραμματεῖον πέμπω ("send a message"), see Herodian 1.17.6; Libanius, *Or.* 54.35.

[1686] According to Josephus' report Salome takes the initiative (see also the next paragraph), but Mayer-Schärtel (1995: 195-96) notes that this divorce served Herod's political interests as much as Salome's former accusation of her first husband Joseph had done (*Ant.* 15.81).

The verb ἀπολύω ("sever, separate, dissolve [one's marriage]," Rengstorf *s.v.*) is used in contexts of divorce, mostly in situations in which a husband sends away his wife (e.g., 1 Esdr 9:36; Matt 5:31; Luke 16:18). Biblical law prescribes the procedure as follows: "Suppose a man enters into marriage with a woman, but she does not please him because he finds something objectionable about her, and so he writes her a certificate of divorce, puts it in her hand, and sends her out of his house ..." (Deut 24:1). A subsequent husband can act likewise, and the wife is not allowed to remarry a former husband (Deut 24:3-4; Instone-Brewer 1998). The reason for divorce, "something objectionable" (*'erwat dābār*), has been interpreted as adultery, failure to please her partner sexually, or any possible objection. Deut 24 does not indicate that women could divorce from their husband, but several scholars argue that in exceptional cases Jewish women did take the initiative (Hanson 1989-90: 142-51; Richardson 1996: 221 n. 15; Ilan 1996; Satlow 2001: 352 n. 104; see also the next note). The phrase "she left me" in *Life* 415 is sometimes interpreted as if Josephus' first wife divorced him (Thackeray 1926: 153), which allowed him to remarry. Two caveats should be noted, however: (1) the Greek MSS read ἀπαλλάγην instead of ἀπαλλάγη (found in the *editio princeps*), implying that Josephus (i.e., "I") left his wife, and (2) the Greek text does not necessarily imply a divorce (Mason in BJP 9 on *Life* 415 translates "she was released"). Further discussion in Rabello 1981; 1982; Jackson 2005: 346-56; Schwartz 2013: 14-16.

[1687] Biblical law concerning divorce (Deut 24:1-4; see the previous note) focuses on the male partner, as Josephus' paraphrase of it in *Ant.* 4.253 likewise does. It does not explicitly provide a procedure for women, but it does not forbid women to divorce from their husbands either. Second Temple writings offer more specific information about marriage regulations for women. The Qumran community seems to have allowed women to remarry if a spouse had deceased (Shemesh 2009: 117-18). Ilan (1996) as well as Cotton and Qimron (1998) argue that the *Papyrus Ṣe'elim* (XḤev/Se) 13, a document from the Judean Desert (edited by Yardeni 1997: 65-70), confirms that women could divorce their husbands, while Schremer (1998) and Brody (1999), among others, argue that it does not (cf. Instone-Brewer 1999). Cf. Jesus' statement in Mark 10:12: "... and if she divorces her husband and marries another, she commits adultery." In Graeco-Roman contexts it was more common for women to divorce their husbands (e.g., Diodorus 12.18.1). Ilan (1995: 146) suggests that Roman law inspired Salome's deed.

Josephus clearly states here that Salome's decision went against the Jewish law, which implies that he interpreted Deut 24 as a ban on divorce initiated by women. Whether or not the Jewish law allowed Salome to divorce Costobar, she certainly had the support of her brother, as the next paragraph implies (Mayer-Schärtel 1995: 196; Satlow 2001: 352 n. 104).

For phrases similar to κατὰ τοὺς 'Ιουδαίων νόμους ("according to the laws of the Jews"), see *Ant.* 13.318; 14.258; cf. 13.74.

[1688] I.e., among the Jews. Ilan (1995: 143-44) argues that the report about Salome's divorce basically derives from Nicolaus of Damascus and that the comment about the unlawfulness of Salome's behavior would be Josephus' own statement. She refers to the phrase "for with us" in support of this argument.

[1689] See the note to "which [act] was not according to the laws of the Jews" above.

own accord[1690] if her previous husband does not let her go.[1691] **260** Salome truly did not follow the law of the country[1692] but chose to act on her own authority.[1693] She repudiated her married life beforehand[1694] and said to her brother Herod that she had separated from her husband out of her loyalty to him.[1695] For it had come to her knowledge that he [Costobar] was aiming at a rebellion[1696] with Antipater, Lysimachus, and Dositheus.[1697] She confirmed her statement[1698] with the Sons of Baba,[1699] saying that they had been kept safe

---

[1690] Josephus' comment that Salome transgressed the Jewish law is based upon his interpretation of Deut 24:1-4 (see "which was not according to the laws of the Jews" above).

The verb διαχωρίζω ("separate," Rengstorf s.v.) occurs twice elsewhere in Josephus but in contexts different from the breaking off of a marriage (*War* 1.535; *Ant.* 1.28).

[1691] This passage explains Josephus' previous words and connects with Deut 24:4 ("... her first husband, who sent her away ..."). The words τοῦ πρότερον ἀνδρός echo LXX Deut 24:4: ὁ ἀνὴρ ὁ πρότερος ("the former husband"). Niese (378) reads ἐφιέντος with MS P and E, which can be translated "[him] letting her go" or "[him] consenting" (Rengstorf s.v. ἐφίημι). Most Greek MSS read ἀφιέντος ("sending away, divorcing," LSJ s.v. ἀφίημι II.1d), which is the easier and therefore probably secondary reading.

[1692] The phrase τὸν ἐγγενῆ νόμον ("the law of the country") is rare if not unique in ancient Greek literature. The adjective ἐγγενής ("native, indigenous," Rengstorf s.v.) occurs once elsewhere in Josephus, in another context (*Ant.* 16.59).

[1693] The prepositional expression ἀπ' ἐξουσίας (read by MS P and Niese 378) means that Salome acted on her own authority; cf. the same phrase in *Ant.* 15.43 (according to MSS PF) about Alexandra: "... [do nothing] on her own authority ...," and 15.321 about Herod himself.

[1694] The verb προαπαγορεύω ("renounce beforehand," LSJ s.v.) is a *hapax legomenon* in Josephus. Rengstorf (s.v.) suggests "repudiate first" as meaning. The verb may imply a public setting: LSJ (s.v. III) give "make an announcement" as one of the meanings of the simplex verb ἀπαγορεύω. In that case Salome not only gave her husband a divorce certificate but also declared officially her marriage with Costobar to be over. The noun συμβίωσις ("common/married life") means "(freedom of) cohabitation" here (Rengstorf s.v.).

[1695] The Herod narrative of *Antiquities* emphasizes that Salome was keen to suggest to Herod that her deeds were given in by loyalty (εὔνοια) to her brother (e.g., *Ant.* 16.214: "And [she said] that all were eager for her to incur the king's hatred and to get rid of her in every possible way because of the loyalty she had to Herod, always prognosticating his dangers," my trans.). For other cases of Salome's loyalty to Herod, see 15.170-171, 16.83 as well as 17.36 concerning Salome observing the interactions of Pheroras and Antipater.

On the basis of the context one can also think of another motive for Salome revealing Costobar's treason to Herod: she may have wanted Herod's consent for her divorce; revealing her husband's treason at the moment of her request would greatly strengthen her position. Kasher (2007: 133-34) argues along these lines and concludes that Salome had known for a long time about Costobar hiding the Sons of Baba. She would have maintained her marriage as an insurance policy in case Costobar would succeed in a rebellion. She resolved the marriage after she had come to the conclusion that Costobar was no longer useful to realize her political ambitions.

The verb ἀφίστημι ("alienate, etc.") can also mean "separate from" (Rengstorf s.v.; see 1.266 concerning Esau and his Canaanite wives Ada and Alibame and Plutarch, *Galb.* 19.4).

[1696] The phrase νεωτέρων ἐφίεμαι ("aiming at a rebellion") also occurs in *Ant.* 16.135 (cf. *Life* 391 about Justus of Tiberias).

[1697] For Antipater, Lysimachus, and Dositheus, see *Ant.* 15.252.

[1698] The combination of παρέχω ("provide") and πίστις ("pledge, assurance") occurs elsewhere in Josephus and means "make (appear) credible" (Rengstorf s.v. πίστις; *Apion* 2.218; cf. *Ant.* 16.188).

[1699] Josephus explains who the Sons of Baba are in the next paragraphs (*Ant.* 15.261-265). Baba is the Aramaic form (*bb'*) of the Hebrew name Babi (*bby*). The name is attested in Rabbinic literature, papyri from Naḥal Ḥever (XḤev/Se 64; 5/6Ḥev 7; Ilan 2002: 80), and inscriptions (from the late 3rd and 2nd century BCE) from a necropolis at Marissa, a major city in Idumea. These funerary inscriptions are dedicated to Babatha (βαβάτας) and Baba (Βάβα), a sister and brother, the children of Cosnathan, son of Amareus (Oren and Rappaport 1984; Ronen 1988: 214-20). That the Semitic name Baba was used by the Idumeans does not necessarily mean that the Sons of Baba like Costobar were Idumeans, as some scholars argue (Oren and Rappaport 1984: 144 with n. 68; cf. Schalit 2001: 142-43, who argues that there was a close friendship between the families of Costobarus and the Sons of Baba). The conclusion of this section

by him for a period of twelve years now.[1700] **261** And this was really the case, which caused great consternation[1701] for the king when he heard it because it was beyond what he expected.[1702] He was even more disquieted because the matter was unbelievable.[1703]

For the case of Baba's Sons, who had become hostile in their disposition [towards him],[1704] had been dealt with by him before, with effort, but by now they had escaped his memory[1705] because it was a long time ago. **262** His enmity and his hatred towards them[1706] was caused by the following reasons. When Antigonus was holding the throne[1707] and Herod was besieging the city of Jerusalem[1708] with a military force,[1709] out of all the need

---

rather implies that they were related to the Hasmonean dynasty (see 15.266 with the note to "that there was no one left from Hyrcanus' family"). Ronen (1988: 219-20) and Kokkinos (1998: 180) also mention the possibility that the Sons of Baba were connected with a sage called Baba ben Butha, whose eyes Herod had cut out and on whose head he had placed a garland of hedgehog bristles (*b. B. Bat.* 3b-4a; further references in Ben-Shalom 1980: 235-36).

[1700] If this long duration is correct, the period implied may be 37-26/25 BCE (Kokkinos 1998: 180; see *Ant.* 15.254 with the note to "governor of Idumea and Gaza"). Otto (1913: 53-54, followed by Schalit 2001: 144) proposes to read δέκα ("ten") instead of δεκαδύο ("twelve") and therefore reconstructs the period as 37-28/27 BCE. He argues that the context implies that the execution of Costobar and his fellow friends took place not long after Herod's illness and Alexandra's execution (described in 15.244-251). Mahieu (2012: 160-61) argues that the capture of Jerusalem took place in 36 BCE, with the 12 years period referring to 36-25/24 BCE.

[1701] The verb ἐμποιέω ("cause") with ἔκπληξις ("consternation, astonishment, admiration," Rengstorf *s.v.*) as object also occurs in *Ant.* 15.414, in a very different context: concerning the magnificent columns of the Temple. The phrase is rare in ancient Greek literature (see Gorgias, *Fragm.* 11a.4 [ed. Diels and Kranz 2.295]; Pausanias 7.24.8). The combination of the simplex ποιέω and ἔκπληξιν is more common. Cf. the consternation (ἔκπληξις) among Herod's opponents when the king returned unexpectedly successfully from his trip to Octavian (*Ant.* 15.198).

[1702] It is easy to imagine that the duration of Costobar's betrayal (12 years, *Ant.* 15.260), when the Sons of Baba were hidden, was shocking to Herod. A second reason for Herod's consternation apparently was his assumption that the case of Baba's Sons had been settled, as the continuation of the paragraph indicates.

[1703] Josephus' phrase ἐπὶ τῷ παραδόξῳ τοῦ λόγου ("the matter was unbelievable") echoes the words τοῦ λόγου in *Ant.* 15.260 about the statement made by Salome. The words τοῦ λόγου can refer either to that statement or to the matter pointed out by Salome (Rengstorf *s.v.* λόγος; cf. 15.224).

[1704] The hostility that the Sons of Baba felt for Herod is explained by their support of Herod's opponent Antigonus, as the next paragraphs indicate (*Ant.* 15.262-263).

The noun διάθεσις means "disposition" towards a person here (LSJ *s.v.* II.1b), which attitude can be friendly, affectionate, etc., or hostile, as here (cf. 4.250; 6.225; 8.405; 15.70, 85, 131; 16.54, 119, 193).

[1705] Apart from their support of Antigonus, Josephus reports in *Ant.* 15.263 that the Sons of Baba continuously slandered Herod. The phrase τῆς μνήμης ἐξέρχομαι means "fade from memory, be forgotten" (Rengstorf *s.v.* ἐξέρχομαι; cf. *Ant.* 2.202: the Egyptians had forgotten Joseph's benefactions of long time ago).

[1706] For a similar combination of ἔχθρα and μῖσος, cf. *Ant.* 13.130: "Accordingly, he [i.e., Demetrius II] incurred the enmity and hatred of the soldiers (ἔχθρα τοιγαροῦν αὐτῷ καὶ μῖσος ἐκ τούτου γίνεται) ..." (trans. Marcus).

[1707] The Romans had appointed Herod king in 40 BCE, but he had to defeat the Hasmonean ruler Antigonus, the son of Aristobulus II, before he could actually execute his authority as king. With the capture of Jerusalem Herod finally took hold of the throne, in 37 (or 36) BCE (see *Ant.* 15.1-2 with notes). Antigonus' kingship is referred to in 14.469, 478.

[1708] Niese (379) reads τὴν τῶν Ἱεροσολυμιτῶν πόλιν (literally "the city of the Jerusalemites") with MSS FV and E, which reading is common in Josephus (e.g., *Ant.* 5.82; 10.109; 15.71; *Life* 130). Most Greek MSS (supported by the Latin version) read slightly differently: τὴν τῶν Ἱεροσολύμων πόλιν ("the city of Jerusalem"), which is unusual in Josephus but found in Christian passages (e.g., Origen, *Comm. Matt.* 16.26; Gregory of Nyssa, *Hom. opif.* [PG 44.216]; John Chrysostom, *Comm. Isa.* 1.9 [ed. Dumortier 90]; *Hom. 2 Cor.* [PG 61.416]) and may have resulted from the accidental omission of -ιτ- in the noun Ἱεροσολυμιτῶν.

[1709] Herod's siege of Jerusalem with the help of C. Sosius, Antony's lieutenant, is described in *Ant.* 14.468-488 and briefly referred to in 14.176; 15.1; 20.246.

and suffering[1710] that occurred to those besieged there were many who called on Herod as helper[1711] and were already turning towards him with their hopes. **263** But Baba's Sons,[1712] who were of high standing[1713] and had a strong hold on the people,[1714] remained faithful to Antigonus[1715] and continuously spoke slander[1716] about Herod. They kept urging[1717] people to protect together[1718] the kings' rule that was based on birth.[1719] So these men were acting according to such a policy, thinking at the same time that this would be to [their own] advantage.[1720] **264** When the city was seized[1721] and Herod was controlling the

---

[1710] Josephus' report of the siege of Jerusalem in *Antiquities* refers to a lack of provisions and hunger (14.471, 475; cf. *War* 1.449), damage to the Temple (14.476), and widespread killings by the Romans and Herod's soldiers (14.479-480; cf. *War* 1.351-352). Niese (379) reads ὑπὸ δὲ χρείας κακῶν ("out of the need because of the suffering") with MSS PF, but most MSS read ὑπὸ δὲ χρείας καὶ κακῶν ("out of [all] the need and suffering"). The first reading may have resulted from an omission of καί since both καί and κακῶν begin with κα- (i.e., a case of *homoioarcton*).

[1711] This detail is absent in the *Antiquities* report of the siege, but 14.484-486 (cf. *War* 1.356) does note that Herod made an end to the plundering and killing by the Romans by rewarding them out of his own pocket and by purchasing security for the city. *War* 1.358 and *Ant.* 15.2 show that Herod had supporters among the population of Jerusalem, but only here they are told to have been numerous.

[1712] The beginning of this new clause creates an opposition between those calling upon Herod and the Sons of Baba.

[1713] The noun ἀξίωμα can, among other things, point to dignity connected with an aristocratic or even royal descent (*Ant.* 15.51, 164) and to high reputation (15.101). The prepositional expression ἐπ' ἀξιώματος ("of high standing, being influential/respected") is common in Josephus (5.115; 12.187; 15.164, 266; 16.368; 18.142). In 15.164 (see the note to "the only person left of a royal rank") it refers to Hyrcanus II's royal descent. The remark further on "that there was no one left from Hyrcanus' family" (15.266) strongly suggests that the Sons of Baba were related to the Hasmonean family. They may have married into the Hasmonean family, as Herod himself had done in 37 BCE by marrying Mariamme I (see 15.23 with the note to "who was living in wedlock with Herod").

[1714] The adjective δυνατός means "influential" here (Rengstorf *s.v.*). The Sons of Baba were apparently very dangerous opponents for Herod because of their support of Antigonus (see the next clause) and their great influence on the population.

[1715] This point and the slander mentioned in the next phrase explain the enmity between the Sons of Baba and Herod mentioned in *Ant.* 15.262.

The expression πιστός διατελέω means "remain faithful to" here (cf. Isocrates, *Plat.* 26).

[1716] The 2 imperfect tenses διετέλουν (see the preceding note) and διέβαλλον together with the adverb ἀεί ("always") emphasize the firm support of the Sons of Baba for Antigonus and their continuous slander of Herod. The expression διαβάλλω ἀεί ("slander continuously") also occurs in Isaeus 8.36; Cassius Dio 75.15.6; Damascius, *Vit. Isid.* (fragm. 191, ed. Zintzen 167). Josephus does not give the content of the slander. One could think of Herod's bold and violent way of ruling (cf. *Ant.* 14.165; 15.321; van Henten 2011b) but more likely of his being a commoner (see 15.263 with the note to "the kings' rule that was based on birth").

[1717] The form προὔτρεπον ("they kept urging," from προτρέπω "urge, incite, encourage, cause," Rengstorf *s.v.*) is a further imperfect verb with a durative aspect.

[1718] The verb συμφυλάττω ("hold, maintain together," Rengstorf *s.v.*) occurs once elsewhere in Josephus, in a very different context (*War* 4.123).

[1719] The plural "kings" refers to the Hasmonean dynasty. Josephus' remark implies that the Sons of Baba were not only supporting Antigonus as a ruler because he was a member of the Hasmonean royal family but also that they undermined the legitimacy of Herod's kingship. It was common knowledge that Herod was born a commoner (see *Ant.* 14.489-491 as well as 15.2 with the note to "while he was still a commoner"). Herod only became a member of this family through his marriage with Mariamme in 37 BCE. The Sons of Baba apparently ignored Rome's appointment of Herod, as Antigonus himself had done.

[1720] The Sons of Baba would no doubt have benefited from their support of Antigonus had Herod been defeated: Antigonus might have given them an important office or other significant rewards (cf. Dositheus' betrayal of Hyrcanus II because he calculated that Herod would reward him better, *Ant.* 15.169-170). A similar combination of νομίζω ("think") and the infinitive συμφέρειν ("be advantageous") occurs in *War* 2.346.

[1721] This refers to Herod's capture of Jerusalem in 37 (or 36) BCE (see *Ant.* 15.262 with the note to "When Antigonus was holding the throne"). For further phrases combining ἁλίσκομαι ("capture") with ἡ πόλις ("the city") in Josephus, see *War* 7.147; *Ant.* 5.13, 26.

state,[1722] Costobar was appointed to block the ways out of the city[1723] and to guard it,[1724] so that those citizens who were indebted [to Herod][1725] or meddling with politics that were the opposite of the king's policy[1726] would not escape.[1727] But knowing that the Sons of Baba had a good reputation and the respect of the entire people,[1728] and assuming that their deliverance would give him a major role[1729] in the changes in the political situation,[1730] he brought them secretly in safety[1731] and hid them on his family estate.[1732] **265** At that time he assured Herod—for suspicion[1733] about the truth had crossed [Herod's mind]—with oaths[1734] that he truly did not know anything about them,[1735] and he dispelled [Herod's]

[1722] The expression τὰ πράγματα literally means "the matters." It frequently has a political meaning in Josephus, in which cases it can refer to the government or the administration of Judea (see *Ant.* 15.32 with the note to "the government").

[1723] With Niese (379), who reads τὰς διεκβολὰς ἀναφράττειν with MSS AMW and E (MS L reads slightly differently). The noun διεκβολή ("exit, gate," Rengstorf *s.v.*) and the verb ἀναφράττω ("bar," Rengstorf *s.v.*) are both *hapax legomena* in Josephus. MSS PFV and marginal readings in MSS AM read ἐπιβουλὰς ἀνατρέπειν ("to counter plots"; a similar phrase occurs in Athanasius, *Vit. Anton.* [PG 26.965]), which is the easier and therefore probably the secondary reading.

[1724] Cf. *Ant.* 15.6: "... after stationing guards at the gates of the walls, so that nothing would be taken outside together with the corpses," which concerns a similar purpose of preventing citizens from moving valuable things out of the city but does not mention Costobar.

[1725] The context implies that the citizens were indebted to Herod. Costobar had to prevent them from fleeing, which detail is missing from the reports about the aftermath of the capture of Jerusalem (*War* 1.354-359; *Ant.* 14.482-491; 15.1-11). The repayment by Herod's debtors was indispensable, likely because the king was badly in need of money following his generous reward of Sosius and the Roman soldiers and his purchase of Jerusalem's security (*War* 1.356-357; *Ant.* 14.485-486; cf. *War* 1.358; *Ant.* 15.5-7). The phrase τοὺς ὑπόχρεως ("those who were indebted") is a *hapax legomenon* in Josephus.

[1726] The phrase τἀναντία πολιτεύομαι plus a reference to a person in the dative (literally "act in the opposite way to") is closely paralleled by Aelius Aristides, *Plat.* (ed. Dindorf 2.168); Lucian, *Phal.* 1.2; cf. Dionysius, *Ant. rom.* 11.59.2.

[1727] *War* 1.358 reports that Antigonus' supporters were executed: "... he [i.e., Herod] slew those who were of Antigonus' party" (trans. Sievers/Forte in BJP 1a; cf. *Ant.* 15.2). This would no doubt also have befallen the Sons of Baba had Herod had his way.

[1728] This phrase links up with *Ant.* 15.263: "Baba's Sons, who were of high standing and had a strong hold on the people." Note the climax τῷ πλήθει ("the people," 15.263)—τῷ παντὶ πλήθει ("the entire people," 15.264).

[1729] Costobar's self-interest apparently also underlay his decision to approach Cleopatra (*Ant.* 15.257). In both cases he betrayed Herod (see also the next note).

The expression μέγα μέρος ("a great part") also occurs in *War* 1.225; *Ant.* 14.117; 15.307; 19.233.

[1730] The text leaves no doubt about Costobar's strategy: his aim was to rescue the Sons of Baba in order to benefit from a future rebellion in which the Sons would be involved. It is significant that Josephus does not report such a rebellion, whereas there had been several occasions for starting a rebellion during the 12 years of the Sons' concealment (e.g., during Herod's visits to Antony and Octavian, *Ant.* 15.71-73, 183-187). The noun μεταβολή means "political change" in several other Josephan passages (see 15.30 with the note to "had hoped for a change of government"), and the words τὰ πράγματα refer to the matters of the state or to the government (see the note to "the state" above; for other combinations of μεταβολή and πράγματα with a similar meaning, see *War* 2.113; *Ant.* 17.346-347; *Life* 36).

[1731] The verb ὑπεκτίθεμαι ("bring secretly in safety," Rengstorf *s.v.*) is a *hapax legomenon* in Josephus. As important supporters of Antigonus the Sons of Baba would surely have been executed by Herod (see *Ant.* 15.2).

[1732] Josephus does not specify where Costobar's family estate was situated; it was most probably in Idumea (cf. *Ant.* 15.253 with notes).

[1733] Josephus first focuses on Herod (instead of Costobar, the subject of this passage) and then starts a brief parenthesis that reveals Herod's thoughts, introduced by γάρ. For a similar parenthesis, about Mariamme, see *Ant.* 15.185.

The noun ὑποψία ("suspicion") echoes 15.258 (see the note to "holding him under suspicion"): "... holding him [i.e., Costobar] under suspicion (οὐκ ἀνύποπτον ... ἔχων) for the rest of his life ...."

[1734] For other occurrences of πιστόω plus ὅρκοις ("assure with oaths") in Josephus, see *War* 1.532; 4.213; *Ant.* 14.7.

[1735] This phrase is ironical because Costobar apparently knew exactly where the Sons of Baba were hiding (see *Ant.* 15.264 and the continuation of this paragraph).

suspicion.[1736] And again, when the king posted proclamations and rewards[1737] and contrived every kind of inquiry,[1738] he did not come to confess. He believed that the discovery of the men implied that he would be suitably punished[1739] because he had denied[1740] [keeping them] the first time. So he clung to hiding them, not only out of loyalty[1741] but this time also out of necessity.[1742]

266 When these matters were reported to him [Herod] through his sister,[1743] the king sent men to the place where [Baba's Sons] were said to be staying.[1744] He had them killed, along with those jointly accused with them,[1745] such that there was no one left from Hyrcanus' family.[1746] He [Herod] had the throne all to himself[1747] because there was no one

---

[1736] The phrase ἀφεῖτο τῆς ὑπονοίας is slightly ambiguous since it can also mean that Herod let go his suspicion (LSJ s.v. ἀφίημι II.1b), but this requires a change of subject.

[1737] The noun μήνυτρον ("reward for information," Rengstorf s.v.) occurs once elsewhere in Josephus (Ant. 4.220).

[1738] Herod apparently tried every possible means to find out where the Sons of Baba were staying, obviously with the intent to have them killed, which reminds one of his role in the story about the birth of Jesus and the visit of the Three Sages (Matt 2:1-18; van Henten 2008a: 103-08). The climax indicated by πάντα τρόπον ἐρεύνης ἐπινοοῦντος ("tried every possible means to find out") is emphasized by the alliteration (note the *p* and *t* sounds).

[1739] The extremely rare adjective ἀνυποτίμητος (cf. a late parallel in Constantine Porphyrogenitus, Legat. [ed. de Boor 1.2.367]) may mean "that cannot adequately be punished" here (LSJ s.v.). The word also occurs in Ant. 16.402 (cf. ἀνυποτιμήτως in 15.188; 16.277). Rengstorf (s.v.) lists several possible meanings, with question marks added, including "exempt from punishment." The unclear meaning may explain the omission of the preceding οὐκ ("not") in MSS PFVW.

[1740] The phrase ἔξαρνος γίνεσθαι ("deny") is found only here in Josephus, but ἔξαρνος εἶναι (with the same meaning) occurs in Ant. 5.44; 14.282; 16.280. Both phrases are common in ancient Greek literature (see, e.g., for the first phrase Isocrates, Euth. 3; Demosthenes, Or. 23.171; 29.10, and for the second Herodotus 3.66; Plutarch, Pyrrh. 26.9; Sull. 23.3).

[1741] I.e., loyalty to the Sons of Baba (cf. Costobar's offer to be loyal to Cleopatra, Ant. 15.256).

[1742] There was no other option left for Costobar, since his confession would reveal immediately that he had been betraying Herod during the period he had hidden Baba's Sons.

[1743] This passage links up with Salome's disclosure mentioned in Ant. 15.260 and concludes the flashback about Baba's Sons and Costobar's involvement in hiding them.

The transmitted Greek text (περὶ τούτων ἐξαγγελθέντων) requires an adaptation: either περί has to be left out, as suggested by E and Dindorf (1845: 379, τούτων ἐξαγγελθέντων, with περί possibly added because of περιείχετο in the previous paragraph), or ἐξαγγελθέντων should be changed into ἐξαγγελθέντος, as Niese (380) conjectures (περὶ τούτων ἐξαγγελθέντος "When he was informed about these matters"; an absolute genitive without a subject, as is common in Thucydides; examples in Kühner and Gerth 1898-1904: 2.2.81-82). The first reading is preferable since Niese's conjecture does not go well with the next word in the MSS (αὐτῷ "to him").

[1744] Ant. 15.264 identifies this location as Costobar's estate.

[1745] The execution of Baba's Sons is expected in the light of the information given about them in Ant. 15.261-264, but the reference to "those jointly accused with them" is vague. The most likely way to fill this gap is to assume that it concerns the persons involved in hiding Baba's Sons, in addition to Costobar (15.264). These persons are, perhaps, identical with Antipater, Lysimachus, and Dositheus (i.e., the other friends of Herod mentioned in 15.252, 260). Josephus reports the execution of Costobar and the other 3 friends in 15.252, but he only gives a reason for the execution of Costobar. There is a possibility that the other friends were also involved in hiding the Sons of Baba, but Josephus does not say this.

The verb συγκαταιτιάομαι ("be accused together," Rengstorf s.v.) is a *hapax legomenon* in Josephus.

[1746] This remark concerns the Hasmonean royal family; the Hyrcanus referred to is Hyrcanus II, the former High Priest (see Ant. 15.11 with the note to "Hyrcanus the High Priest"). Hyrcanus, his daughter Alexandra, and his grandchildren Mariamme I and Aristobulus III are important characters in book 15 of Antiquities (further references in 15.23-24 with notes). Josephus emphasizes several times that Herod attempted to remove any possible Hasmonean competitor (see 15.164 with the note to "considered it the safest option"). Not all Hasmoneans, however, were a threat to the throne: e.g., Herod's son Antipater married Antigonus' daughter (Ant. 17.92; Marcus-Wikgren 127 n. *c*; Kokkinos 1998: 210-11).

of high rank[1748] to stand in the way of his unlawful acts.[1749]

(8.1) 267 For this reason[1750] he departed even more from the ancestral customs[1751] and

Herod's quadrennial festival in Jerusalem. Attempt to murder him.

The implication of Josephus' statement that there were no competitors left from the Hasmonean family after the execution of the Sons of Baba is, of course, that the Sons were part of this family, although Josephus does not say this explicitly.

[1747] Although Herod had been the sole ruler of the kingdom starting from Antigonus' defeat (*Ant.* 15.262-264), this passage implies that he had no serious rivals for government only from now on. This means that Josephus suggests that the Sons of Baba had been an ongoing threat for Herod.

Josephus' phrase (τὴν βασιλείαν αὐτεξούσιον αὐτῷ) may hint at autocratic government: the combination of βασιλεία ("kingdom, throne, power") and αὐτεξούσιος ("at one's sole disposal," Rengstorf *s.v.*, or "free, absolute," LSJ *s.v.*) also occurs in Philo, *Her.* 301 (cf. Philo, *Ios.* 148) and refers there to God's absolute and sovereign rule of the world (*Her.* 228).

[1748] The phrase μηδενὸς ὄντος ἐπ' ἀξιώματος links up with the words ὄντες ἐπ' ἀξιώματος of *Ant.* 15.263 referring to the Sons of Baba. It emphasizes that there were no longer influential persons who could stand up against Herod (see also the next note). Richardson (1996: 222) concludes differently—also referring to the earlier executions of Joseph and Soemus: "Herod had lost support among the elite upon whom he counted."

The phrase ἐμποδὼν ἵσταμαι ("hinder") occurs in *Ant.* 2.283 and is common in ancient Greek literature (e.g., Herodotus 8.68; Thucydides 1.53; Philo, *Legat.* 313; Plutarch, *Pyrrh.* 12.6).

[1749] With this passage Josephus concludes the section about Costobar and other opponents of Herod (*Ant.* 15.247-266) and prepares his readers for the next section, about Herod's festival in Jerusalem (15.267-291). Josephus emphasizes that since there were no leading figures left who could oppose him, the king had the opportunity to do whatever he liked. The report about the festival shows immediately what the result of this freedom was in Josephus' opinion: the founding of quadrennial games and the issue of trophies are presented as shocking examples of Herod's transgressions of the Jewish laws. Herod was developing into an absolute monarch. The later golden eagle episode (17.148-164) is also presented in this light and explicitly portrays Herod as a tyrant. Eliminating possible competitors and committing lawless deeds both belong to the stereotype of tyrants (van Henten 2011b).

[1750] *Ant.* 15.267 introduces a new episode of the Herod narrative, which focuses on Herod's foundation of quadrennial games in Jerusalem and the response of the Jerusalemites to this initiative (15.267-291; van Henten 2008b). The narrative, which finds no parallel in *War*, can be divided into 3 sections: (1) Josephus first deals with the arrangements for Herod's festival and the newly erected buildings (15.267-276); (2) then he briefly describes the protest of Jerusalem's indigenous population against the newly erected theater (15.277-279)—with its trophies in honor of Octavian (15.272; cf. the later collective protests against Gaius Caligula's statue in the Temple of Jerusalem: Philo, *Legat.* 203-337; Josephus, *War* 2.184-203; *Ant.* 18.261-309, and against the Roman golden shields brought into Jerusalem by Pilate: Philo, *Legat.* 299-305; Josephus, *War* 2.169-174; *Ant.* 18.55-59); (3) and finally he describes the attempt by 10 anonymous male Jewish citizens and a blind man to murder Herod (15.280-290).

The first part of 15.267 ("For this reason ...") connects with the statement in 15.266 that there was nobody of high rank left to withhold Herod from unlawful acts because he had killed them all; not even Costobar or the Sons of Baba could hinder him any longer. Josephus suggests that Herod immediately used this situation to perform something unlawful in Jerusalem (see also the next note).

[1751] This introduction of Herod's innovations, which are described in the next paragraphs, immediately sets the tone. Josephus repeats the accusation in *Ant.* 15.275, 277. The combination of ἐκβαίνω ("abandon") plus τῶν ἐθῶν ("the customs") is also found in 15.328, which connects Herod's deviation from the ancestral customs with his ambition to flatter important Roman persons (for more criticism of Herod because of his transgressions of the ancestral customs, see 16.1-5, 183-187, 395-404; 17.148-164, 180-181).

The expression "the ancestral customs" of the Jews is one of Josephus' container terms that vaguely refer to the Jews' traditional way of life. For similar expressions with τὰ πάτρια ἔθη ("the ancestral customs") in Josephus, see *War* 2.220 (in a variant reading), 279; 4.102; 7.424; *Ant.* 5.90, 101; 9.95 (with τὴν τοῦ θεοῦ θρησκεία), 137; 11.339; 12.255, 271, 280; 13.397; 14.194, 213, 223, 258; 16.1, 35; 19.290; 20.100; *Life* 198; *Apion* 1.317; 2.10. Almost synonymous are "the holy customs" (τὰ ἱερὰ ἔθη, *War* 4.182), "the (ancestral) customs of the Jews" (τὰ [πάτρια] τῶν Ἰουδαίων ἔθη, *War* 7.50; *Ant.* 13.397; 15.254-255; 16.225; 20.17, 38, 139, 146; see also 15.268 with the note to "not according to the tradition"), and "our customs" (τὰ ἡμετέρων ἔθη,

gradually perverted the ancient code[1752] with foreign habits,[1753] although it had previously remained undisturbed.[1754] Because of this we[1755] suffered considerable[1756] harm,[1757] also in

---

Ant. 16.43). The ancestral customs should be guarded (*Ant.* 5.90) and not altered (*Ant.* 5.101) or transgressed (*War* 4.102; *Ant.* 9.95). According to Josephus, these customs are closely related to "the ancestral laws" or "the ancestral constitution" (see Mason 1991: 96–106; Schröder 1996: 49-50).

[1752] An alternative translation is "corrupted the way of life." The noun κατάστασις can mean "existence, situation" or "constitution" (Rengstorf *s.v.*). *Ant.* 6.35 mentions it together with πολιτεία ("constitution, citizenship, way of life") in a reference to the Israelite type of government (Begg in BJP 4 on *Ant.* 6.35; see also ἡ κατάστασις τοῦ πολιτεύματος in *Apion* 2.145, 184 referring to the constitution of the Jews; Barclay in BJP 10 on *Ap.* 2.145, 184). The meanings "way of life," "existence" and "code, constitution" all match the context, because Herod apparently introduced foreign practices in Jerusalem and perverted the Jewish constitution or corrupted the Jewish way of life in this way. The verb ὑποδιαφθείρω ("corrupt gradually," Rengstorf *s.v.*) is a *hapax legomenon* in Josephus.

[1753] Josephus severely criticizes Herod for introducing foreign and unconventional practices. The following report about the quadrennial games (*Ant.* 15.267-276) illustrates his criticism (differently Otto 1913: 76-77 n. *, who argues that *Ant.* 15.267-298 derives from an anonymous source hostile to Herod; see also Schürer 1901-09: 1.366 n. 8 and Levine 1975: 61 concerning 15.280-291). One might ask whether Herod really transgressed the ancestral laws. The narrative about the games and their follow-up does not offer much evidence for Josephus' criticism (as rightly observed by Smith 1999: 229), which is repeated in 15.268, 271, 274-275 (*Ant.* 15.274-275 suggests that combats between wild animals and between humans and wild animals go against the Jewish customs). Lämmer (1973: 222 n. 120) connects Herod's innovations with a rabbinic passage in *Sifra Lev.* (on 18:3) that interprets the foreign practices hinted at in Lev 18:3 ("You shall not do as they do in the land of Egypt, where you lived, and you shall not do as they do in the land of Canaan, to which I am bringing you. You shall not follow their statutes") as visits to the theater, stadium, and circus. In the Second Temple period there was usually only a clash between the foreign and and the Jewish authorities if the foreign customs forced the Jews to transgress the Mosaic Law (see, e.g., the court tales in Dan 3 and 6), or if the Jews felt the Law was violated (e.g. in the case of Pilate's decision to move the Roman standards from Caesarea to Jerusalem, *War* 2.169-174; *Ant.* 18.55-59). Therefore one should not exclude the possibility that the majority of the Jerusalemites tolerated Herod's innovations. The continuation of the narrative implies that only a small group took action against Herod's trophies (*Ant.* 15.280-290; differently Feldman 1993: 41; Richardson [1996: 224] concludes that it remains unclear how widespread the opposition to the trophies was). Similarly, only a limited group of young men decided to destroy Herod's eagle erected in the Temple (17.148-164).

The noun ἐπιτήδευμα in the plural can mean, among other things, "habits, ways of life" (LSJ *s.v.*). *Ant.* 1.61 characterizes Cain as a "teacher of evil practices" (διδάσκαλος πονηρῶν ἐπιτηδευμάτων). The phrase ξενικὰ ἐπιτηδεύματα ("foreign practices") also occurs in Dionysius, *Ant. rom.* 2.19.3; Josephus, *Ant.* 15.275; Eusebius, *Praep. ev.* 2.8.7.

[1754] The adjective ἀπαρεγχείρητος is a *hapax legomenon* in Josephus. LSJ (*s.v.*) offer "not to be tampered with" as meaning here, which fits well if the preceding noun κατάστασις refers to the sacrosanct Jewish constitution (see *Ant.* 3.84, 213, 322, and for a discussion with further references, Rajak 1998). Rengstorf (*s.v.*) gives "undisturbed, inviolate" as meanings. Regardless whether this passage concerns the Jewish constitution or the Jewish way of life, the statement is in any case opportunistic since foreign rulers who previously had captured Jerusalem did interfere with the city's affairs. Josephus himself reports about Antiochus IV's desecration of the Temple, his introduction of idolatrous sacrifices, and his ban on the veneration of the God of the Jews (14.248-256).

[1755] The "we" is not specified, but the preceding passage makes clear that the Jewish people is intended.

[1756] The expression οὐ μικρά (literally "not little") is a case of *litotes* (see *Ant.* 15.150 with the note to "significantly").

[1757] The context implies that the harm mentioned concerns the impact of Herod's foundation of the quadrennial games (see the next paragraph) and his trophies in Octavian's honor (*Ant.* 15.272). Josephus does not specify the harm done and only indicates in general terms that Herod violated the Jewish customs. If one reads between the lines, the narrative even seems to imply that Herod successfully countered the protest triggered by the trophies (see 15.277-279 and van Henten 2008b).

later times, since all the matters that had previously led the masses to proper worship[1758] were neglected.[1759]

268 For first he established an athletic contest[1760] every fifth year[1761] in honor of

---

[1758] The noun εὐσέβεια (among other things, "awe, piety, manner of worship," Rengstorf *s.v.*) often has God as object (e.g., *War* 7.264, 267; *Ant.* 2.196; 4.181; 15.288, 365, 375-376, 386; 17.150). The worship of God is closely connected with faithfulness to the Mosaic commandments (*Ant.* 3.49; 8.290; 14.65; *Apion* 1.60, 212; and passages with εὐσέβεια in 4 Macc; see van Henten 1997: 131-32, 281-84). It sometimes indicates the proper attitude owed to God and humans (see *Ant.* 7.269 referring to David and 16.92, 169). This links up with an aspect of the related Latin word *pietas*, which indicates the appropriate behavior towards deities *and* human persons, especially family members (Hellegouarc'h 1963: 276-79; Latte 1960: 39-40).

[1759] Cf. *Ant.* 11.300; 16.37.

[1760] Athletics were a prominent part of Herod's games in Jerusalem (see the references to athletes and gymnastics in *Ant.* 15.269-270), but other festivities were also part of them. The games thus belonged to the category of *paneguris* festivals, which matched contemporary Roman customs (Bieber 1939: 167-89). In contrast to the horse races (see 15.271), Josephus does not provide details about the athletic contests, which may imply that they included the usual Olympic disciplines: apart from the horse races the single stadium running race (200 m), the double stadium race (400 m), the long distance race (4800 m), the race in armor, the *pentathlon*, wrestling, boxing, and the *pankration* (i.e., a combination of boxing and wrestling; Lämmer 1973: 187; Finley and Pleket 1976: 26-46). Herod also helped to re-organize the Olympic Games and sponsored them (*War* 1.426-427; *Ant.* 16.149).

Josephus does not mention the date of the games' foundation, but the larger context of the narrative (see, e.g., *Ant.* 15.237, 252 with notes) implies that they were organized in the spring or summer of 28 BCE (Otto 1913: 64, 80; Lämmer 1973: 196, 206; Bernett 2007a: 52-53). The location of the games must have been Jerusalem because the new theater and amphitheater mentioned in the next lines were located in or near that city. Schalit (2001: 371) argues that these 2 constructions were built before or in 28 BCE. Mahieu (2012: 160-61) dates the 2 buildings to 25 BCE and the first Jerusalem Games to 5 March 24 BCE.

Several states organized games in honor of Caesar, inspired by the huge triple triumphal festivities held in Rome in August 29 BCE, which celebrated Octavian's victory at Actium as well as his triumph at Illyricum and the annexation of Egypt. (Lämmer 1973: 189 with n. 27; Bernett 2007a: 56-57). Rome organized quadrennial games for Octavian's welfare (*ludi quinquennales pro salute Caesaris*) from 28 BCE onward (Kienast 1999: 79). Lämmer (1973: 189), Schalit (2001: 422), and Bernett (2007a: 56-57) suggest that Herod's games were named *Kaisareia*, although there is no conclusive evidence for this. If so, Herod would have been one of the first rulers to organize such games outside Rome. Other scholars argue that Herod's festival was connected with the *Aktia* (the Latin *Actia* or *ludi Actiaci*), i.e., the games that commemorated Octavian's victory at Actium (differently Bernett 2007a: 56). Since Octavian's *Aktia* were celebrated for the first time only in September 27 BCE (see *Ant.* 15.109 with the note to "the Battle of Actium" and 15.343 with the note to "for the following reason"), they can only have functioned as a model for Herod's games if these latter games were celebrated in a later period (as argued by Mahieu 2012: 160-61).

A few scholars argue that Josephus' report of Herod's festival in Jerusalem is fictitious. If so, it may have been invented by Josephus in order to disqualify Herod as king of the Jews (see 15.282). Geva (2001) argues that Josephus modeled the report on conventional images of Roman city celebrations. Drüner (1896: 66-68) argues that (1) specific information about the festival in Jerusalem is missing; (2) there are striking correspondences between the descriptions of the festivals in Jerusalem and Caesarea (*War* 1.415; *Ant.* 16.137-141), which renders it plausible that the report about Jerusalem is based on the information about the Caesarean Games; and (3) there is no parallel report in *War*, whereas such a report would have fit in with the list of tributes to Augustus (*War* 1.401-428). One could add that the descriptions of Herod's theater and amphitheater are not convincingly supported by archaeological evidence, although this objection vanishes if one assumes that both buildings were of wood (see *Ant.* 15.268 with notes). The parallels in the vocabulary used for the festivals in Jerusalem and Caesarea cannot be denied, but there are significant differences between the 2 festivals as well (see 16.137-141 with notes)—which may result from the fact that Herod took the Jews' religious views into account when organizing his festival in Jerusalem (van Henten 2008b). Mahieu (2012: 177) argues that Herod initiated the Caesarean Games in 8 BCE in order to replace the Jerusalem Games, which might further explain the correspondences between the 2 games mentioned. An additional argument against the hypothesis that the report is fictitious are the tensions between the

Caesar,[1762] and he built a theater in Jerusalem[1763] and subsequently a huge amphitheater[1764]

---

actual information provided by the report and Josephus' own comments: Josephus consistently tries to disqualify Herod because of a supposedly all-embracing attempt to change the Jewish customs.

For a similar formula of καθίστημι ("erect, establish") with ἀγῶνα πενταετηρικόν ("a quinquennial contest") as object, cf. *War* 1.415 (referring to the games founded by Herod in Caesarea, with athletic and musical contests [*Ant.* 16.136-141]) and Cassius Dio 61.21.1.

[1761] The Greek text literally says that the games were quinquennial (like those at Caesarea, *War* 1.415), but the Greeks and Romans counted inclusively: the games took place every 4th year by our exclusive method of counting. Thus, if games were held in 28 and 24 BCE, we would count 4 years from one to the next. The ancients counted 28 as Year 1 and 24 as Year 5 in that cycle, which became Year 1 of the next cycle. "Big games" like the Olympic Games were also labeled quinquennial (e.g., *War* 1.426-427; *Ant.* 16.149), whereas they took place every 4th year (Lämmer 1973: 189; Mahieu 2012: 76 n. 129).

The phrase ἀγὼν πενταετηρικός ("quinqennial contest") also occurs in 2 Macc 4:18; Plutarch, *Arist.* 21.1; *Mor.* (*Amat.*) 748f; *Prov. Alex.* 24.2; Cassius Dio 61.21.1.

[1762] Herod also organized quadrennial athletic and musical contests in Caesarea when the building of this city was completed (*War* 1.414-415; *Ant.* 16.137-138). Herod "dedicated this festival *also* to Caesar" (ἀνετίθει δὲ καὶ τοῦτον τὸν ἀγῶνα Καίσαρι, *Ant.* 16.138, italics added), which associates the Caesarean Games with the festival in Jerusalem. The *War* passage mentions that both the city of Caesarea and its festival were named after "Caesar" (see also *Ant.* 15.364 about the Temple in Jerusalem).

[1763] Josephus explicitly situates the theater within the city of Jerusalem (ἐν Ἱεροσολύμοις). Schalit (2001: 370-71) thinks this is correct (differently Richardson 1996: 187, 224 n. 28). The statement that images of human beings should not be brought into the city (*Ant.* 15.277) confirms a location in Jerusalem. Josephus does not refer to the theater in other episodes (the other references [*Ant.* 15.272, 284-285] all belong to the same section), not even in passages in which a reference to such a landmark (if it were one) would seem natural, as in the detailed descriptions of Jerusalem (*War* 1.401; 5.184-214, 238-247). Nor does he say whether the Jews visited the theater, although a remark in *Ant.* 15.284 suggests that at least some Jews did (see the note to "to the theater").

Several proposals have been made for the location of the theater, mostly on the basis of archaeological remains (differently Aharoni and Avi-Yonah 1977: 139; cf. Patrich 2002b: 231). In the 19th cent. already Schick (1887) associated Herod's amphitheater with traces of a semicircular auditorium cut in the rock on the northern side of a hill ca. 900 m south of Jerusalem, south-south west of Bir Eyub and north of Wadi Yasul (further references in Schürer-Vermes 1.305-06 n. 56). He could not relate it to the theater because of the latter's location within the city. However, the amphitheater does not fit either, since it was located in the plain according to Josephus (see the next note). Reich and Billig (2000a; 2000b) connect recent findings of theater seats near Robinson's Arch, at the southwestern corner of the Temple platform, with Herod's theater. They could belong to Herod's theater or to Hadrian's (the *Chronicon paschale*, a 7th-cent. Christian document, mentions a theater erected by Hadrian in Jerusalem [ed. Dindorf 1.474]; see also the *Chronicon Alexandrinum seu paschale* [PG 92.613]), as other scholars suggest. The outline of these seats, however, is straight rather than curvilinear, which makes it more likely that the seats belonged to a different type of entertainment building, such as Herod's hippodrome/stadium or Hadrian's circus in Jerusalem (Patrich 2002b: 231). Neither Schick's nor Reich and Billig's identifications thus explain Josephus' theater description. Avi-Yonah (1966: 5, 8-9, 16) and Aharoni and Avi-Yonah (1977: 139) suggest that the theater was located ca. 200 m to the west of the southwestern corner of the Temple platform, to the southeast of the upper city, because it was the area where the wealthy "hellenizers" were living. There are, however, neither archaeological remains nor texts to support this location. Richardson (1996: 186-87 with n. 40) locates the theater on the northern slope of er-Ras, the southern side of Wadi es-Shamm, 100 m south of the Hinnom Valley. Patrich (2002b: 231) argues that it is plausible that the theater was located at the head of one of the valleys, with the seats resting against a hillside.

Both Patrich (2002b) and Lichtenberger (2006; cf. Netzer 1999: 56-59) convincingly argue that Herod's theater was of wood. Wooden theaters and amphitheaters were standard during the Late Republic and the Early Empire (Bieber 1939: 326-55; Beacham 1999: 25-35). Herod may have followed Roman rather than Hellenistic conventions for the erection of his theater in Jerusalem, although the shape of the stone theater and the stone hippodrome/stadium at Caesarea as well as the characters of the festivals in Jerusalem and Caesarea (see the notes to *Ant.* 15.269-271) clearly show that the king combined Greek and Roman conventions. A wooden temporary

in the plain,[1765] both conspicuous by their rich decoration,[1766] yet foreign to the customs of

---

building fits in with the description of the trophies (15.272), which seem to have been portable. A wooden construction would also explain the silence about the theater in his descriptions of the Herodian buildings in Jerusalem and give meaning to Josephus' note that Herod's theater at Caesarea was of stone (15.341), suggesting a contrast with the earlier facility in Jerusalem.

Herod also founded theaters in Caesarea, Sidon, and Damascus (*War* 1.415, 422-423; *Ant.* 15.341; cf. *Ant.* 19.329 and 19.335-336; 20.211 on Agrippa I's constructions), and probably at Samaria-Sebaste (as argued by Fulco and Zayadine 1981: 197). Jericho had a theater according to the reading of *Ant.* 17.161 in some MSS.

[1764] It is unclear whether the amphitheater in Jerusalem was of wood or (partially) of stone. Bieberstein and Bloedhorn (1994: 3.400-01) argue for a wooden construction on a stone foundation (see also Patrich 2002b: 235). Wooden amphitheaters were common before the Empire, and both Caligula and Nero still erected such amphitheaters in 38 and 57 CE, respectively (Calpurnius Siculus 7.23-56; Tacitus, *Ann.* 13.31; Suetonius, *Nero* 12; Patrich 2002b: 235). The procurator L. Calpurnius erected one in Antiochia Pisidia in the 2nd cent. CE (Lämmer 1974: 158 n. 229 with references).

It is also unclear which type of building it was, since Josephus uses the words ἀμφιθέατρος/-ov rather loosely (see *War* 1.415 and *Ant.* 15.341 [in Caesarea]; *War* 1.666 and *Ant.* 17.161 [according to Naber's conjecture, Naber 1888-96: 4.xiii, 98], 194 [in Jericho]; *War* 2.490, 492 [in Alexandria]; *Ant.* 19.335-336 [in Beirut]). Herod perhaps erected an amphitheater in the strict sense of the word (Kähler and Forni 1958; Golvin 1988; Golvin and Landes 1990), although it concerns more probably an elongated multi-functional construction with 1 or 2 semicircles with seats at the end(s). A stadium could have such a form, as suggested by an inscription about a stadium at Laodicea on the Lycus (*IGR* IV no. 861; see also Dionysus of Halicarnassus, *Ant. rom.* 4.44.1-2 concerning a hippodrome). The word ἀμφιθέατρον denotes in this period usually a *stadium* or *hippodromos* rather than the Roman oval *amphitheatrum* (which was known in the 1st cent. BCE as a *spectaculum*, Étienne 1965; see also Lämmer 1973: 191, 208-09, 216 with notes; 1974: 152 n. 142; Patrich 2002b: 234-35). Josephus describes the building as exceptionally big (*Ant.* 15.268) and refers to 3 types of horse races within the direct context (15.271), which could not have taken place in an actual amphitheater. Moreover, he does not mention the amphitheater anywhere else, whereas he does refer twice to a hippodrome in Jerusalem, located to the south of the Temple (*War* 2.44; *Ant.* 17.255). Several scholars have, therefore, identified the amphitheater with that hippodrome, sometimes suggesting that the differing vocabulary results from the use of different sources (Lämmer 1973: 191, 208-09 with nn. 49, 174-75; Bernett 2007a: 56). Otto (1913: 80) argues that Herod built not only a theater and amphitheater but also a hippodrome in Jerusalem, which is refuted by Humphrey (1986: 528). Bieberstein and Bloedhorn (1994: 401) suggest that the hippodrome south of the Temple was merely a park (see also Lichtenberger 2006: 296 and *Ant.* 15.271 about the horse races).

Herod implemented a similar cluster of innovations in Caesarea (*War* 1.415 [cf. *Ant.* 15.341; 16.137-141]: contests, a theater, amphitheater, and *agora*; *War* 2.172: a stadium).

[1765] The location of the amphitheater is debated (Lämmer 1973: 191-92 with nn. 45-57; Lichtenberger 2006: 291). Richardson (1996: 187 n. 41) locates it in the Rephaim Plain, southwest of Jerusalem. Other scholars identify it with the hippodrome, which was within the city according to *War* 2.44 (Mason in BJP 1b on *War* 2.44; see also the previous note), but this does not match the location specified here as "in the plain." Avi-Yonah (1966: 8-9) locates it near the southwestern corner of the Temple platform, in the direction to the south, in the western section of the Ophel (cf. Aharoni and Avi-Yonah 1977: 139: in the Tyropoeon Valley). Perowne (1956: 136) suggests the present Baq'a Quarter (further references in Lämmer 1973: 191-92 with nn. 45-57). If Josephus' description is accurate in all the references to the amphitheater and hippodrome (i.e., *War* 2.44; *Ant.* 15.268; 17.255), they were distinguished buildings; the hippodrome may have been built later.

[1766] Since both Herod's new games (*Ant.* 15.269) and his 2 newly constructed buildings are described by means of superlatives, Lämmer (1973: 190) concludes that the theater was probably built of stone, but Patrich (2002b: 233-34) argues that wooden buildings could be monumental and expensively decorated and refers to the stage houses (*scaenae*) of the theaters erected by Lucius Mummius in 144 BCE (Tacitus, *Ann.* 14.21) and the theater built by Lucius Pulcher in 99 BCE, which was decorated with realistic paintings (Pliny the Elder 35.23; see also Vitruvius 5.5.7). The facades of later wooden stage houses, like the one erected by Marcus Aemilius Scaurus in 58 BCE in Rome, were plated in gold, silver, ivory, or marble, and contained columns (see also *Ant.* 19.335 concerning Agrippa's theater in Beirut, which surpassed many others in beauty and expensive decorations).

the Jews.[1767] For the use of them and the competitive showing[1768] of such spectacles are not according to the tradition.[1769] **269** But he truly celebrated the quinquennial feast[1770] in a most splendid way, making announcements to all living close [to Judea][1771] and inviting persons from every people.[1772] And the athletes and everyone else connected with contests[1773] from every country were informed and invited by the hope of the prizes that were offered[1774] as well as the honor of winning.[1775] The most leading professionals in their

---

[1767] Rich decoration as such did not run counter the Jewish laws, but it may have irritated (Jewish) readers (and still do so) who cared for a sober and responsible lifestyle. This criticism links up with the remarks in the introduction of this episode (cf. ἐξέβαινε τῶν πατρίων ἐθῶν in *Ant.* 15.268 with κατὰ τοὺς Ἰουδαίους ἔθους ἀλλότρια in 15.269; see also 15.274 with the note to "the customs long honored by them"). Kienast (1999: 464) notes that festivals like Herod's games generally had positive effects on the population and brought economic advantages with them.

[1768] The noun ἐπίδειξις can mean, among other things, "the act of presenting" (*Ant.* 6.203) and "show, performance" (*War* 1.77 "parade"), sometimes metaphorically (Rengstorf *s.v.*, e.g., *War* 4.368: a "display" of physical power and weapons as if it were a theater performance; Lämmer 1973: 224; see also *Ant.* 15.271 with the note to "eminent show").

[1769] This remark links up with Josephus' criticism that Herod's festival implied a transgression of the Jewish practices, which is also highlighted in *Ant.* 15.267. Herod's games must have been organized in co-operation with non-Jewish guilds of athletes and performers in the arts (Forbes 1955; Pleket 1973; 1975: 81-82). The Judean Jews most probably lacked the necessary know how (cf. 15.269, 275), and Herod needed professional organizations in order to get the best athletes and performers (Lämmer 1973: 188-89). About ancient professional organizations of dancers, musicians, and actors, see Poland 1934; Pickard-Cambridge 1968: 279-321.

The verb παραδίδωμι means "hand down by tradition" here (LSJ *s.v.* I.4).

[1770] The noun *paneguris* (πανήγυρις "festal assembly, feast," LSJ *s.v.* 1; Rengstorf *s.v.*) indicates the festival organized by Herod. Josephus uses the same word for the quadrennial games at Caesarea (*Ant.* 16.140, 142; see 15.268 with the note to "an athletic contest") and the Olympic Games (16.149). The word has a more general meaning in *War* 5.230; *Ant.* 2.45, 47; 5.170, 286. The phrase πανήγυριν ... συντελέω ("organize a feast") is common (e.g., Diodorus 6.7.1; 17.16.4; Strabo 8.4.9; 9.5.15; and especially Diodorus 5.4.2: οἱ Συρακόσιοι πανήγυριν ἐπιφανῆ συντελοῦσι). Many of these celebrations were organized on a local scale and founded in honor of a local deity or a deceased aristocrat. They usually consisted of athletic and other contests, entertainments like drinking bouts and dancing, and cultic procedures (Pleket 1975: 55). Josephus mentions none of these in connection with Herod's festival.

[1771] Josephus does not indicate here whether the persons invited concern the guests or the participants, but the continuation of the sentence indicates that he first focuses on the guests and then on the participants (starting from "And the athletes ..."). Announcing such contests was an official task executed by representatives who were called *theoroi* (Ziehen 1934: 2239-44).

"All living close" (literally "those all around") must denote people near Judea since the festival took place in Jerusalem. Herod may have invited especially the inhabitants of Greek cities in Syria, Transjordan, Egypt, and the coastal plain (Lämmer 1973: 188). Kokkinos (1998: 125) points out that documentary evidence indicates that the Phoenicians took active part in athletic games.

[1772] The translation follows the conjecture of Chamonard (1904: 332), who leaves out the article τοῦ before παντός. The Greek MSS read συγκαλῶν ἀπὸ τοῦ παντὸς ἔθνους (Niese 380), which means "inviting from the entire [i.e., Jewish] people" and is highly improbable (differently Marcus-Wikgren 129 n. *c*) because the sentence suggests a progression from non-Jewish persons in the neighborhood of Judea to an even larger circle of all peoples and states, which is supported by the similar phrase "from every country" (ἀπὸ πάσης γῆς; note that the article is absent) in the next sentence. Herod's ambition must have been to invite as many foreigners as possible in order to add luster to the event. The article τοῦ before παντὸς ἔθνους was perhaps added by a copyist who associated the noun ἔθνους with the Jewish people. Lämmer (1973: 188 with n. 16) also rejects the transmitted text and proposes the reading συγκαλῶν τοὺς ἀπὸ παντὸς ἔθνους ("inviting the inhabitants from every state").

[1773] The noun ἀγώνισμα ("conflict, contest, objective [of a competition]," Rengstorf *s.v.*) can also indicate every kind of person involved in athletic and other contests, including trainers, masseurs, doctors, and theater specialists (Lämmer 1973: 211 n. 7). Several categories of performers are mentioned in *Ant.* 15.270.

[1774] The participle of πρόκειμαι ("be first, lie openly," Rengstorf *s.v.*), which is used as a noun here, indicates things lying ready or on display, or objects being offered.

fields were assembled.[1776] **270** For he set out the biggest prizes[1777] not only for those in connection to the gymnastic contests,[1778] but also for the participants in the musical competitions[1779] and the actors who are called *thumelikoi*.[1780] And a great effort was made[1781] to have all the most famous people come to the contest.[1782] **271** He also displayed[1783]

Five further passages in Josephus include a similar participle and concern prizes (ἆθλα): *Ant.* 8.208, 302; 16.313; 18.173; 19.131. Hence it seems safe to translate τῶν προκειμένων with "the prizes being offered." On prizes given at contests in antiquity, see the next note. Herod probably functioned as ἀγωνοθέτης ("organizer and president of the games"), such that he was responsible for the level of the prizes (cf. *War* 1.415 about Herod's games at Caesarea and *War* 1.426-427; *Ant.* 16.149 about his sponsorship of the Olympic Games).

[1775] MSS FV read εὐεξίαν ("skill") instead of εὐδοξίαν ("honor"). The note builds on the Graeco-Roman agonistic mentality: contestants received prestige only by winning; athletes even qualified their mission as "to win or die" (Weiler 1974; Pleket 1975). There were 2 types of ancient games (details in Pleket 1975: 53-71). (1) The highest category of games consisted originally of the Olympic, Pythian, Nemean, and Isthmian Games. This circuit (*periodos*) of 4 games was later extended with other "great" games like the *Aktia* in Octavian's honor (see *Ant.* 15.109 with the note to "the Battle of Actium"). These games were called the "holy crown contests" and announced in the entire Graeco-Roman world. The winner received, in principle, only an olive wreath or a crown as reward—the main point was the huge glory resulting from winning—although considerable benefits could follow (especially in the athlete's native city: a pension, fixed amounts of money, or entering the city in a solemn procession). (2) The second type of games, sometimes also called "sacred," had a more local character. The winner gained a wreath or crown as well as a valuable object or (later on) a money prize. Herod's games seem to be situated in between both categories: the scale and the expenses made (cf. the superlatives in the next paragraphs) place them at almost the same level as the great games, whereas the prizes being mentioned before the honor match the less important games.

[1776] The superlatives concerning the rewards in *Ant.* 15.270-271 imply that Herod attempted to attract the very best competitors. The vocabulary further suggests that the athletes were professionals specialized in certain disciplines. The word ἐπιτήδευμα ("effort, conduct, etc.," Rengstorf *s.v.*) can also mean "professional performance" in a specific sport (Galen, *Prot.* 9-14 [ed. Kühn 1.20-39]; Lämmer 1973: 188; Pleket 1975: 72-74, 80-89). This professionalism was quite different from other contemporary sport performance: earning income through money prizes did not match the ideology of the wealthy aristocratic circles in which sport was rooted.

[1777] Herod had to offer costly prizes in order to attract good athletes (see the previous note). Whether these rewards included money is left open by Josephus, who refers to great gifts (*Ant.* 15.271), the biggest prizes (15.270), and prizes offered (15.269). At Caesarea even those who were second and third received prizes (*War* 1.415). For a list of prizes during a comparable contest at Aphrodisias (in Asia Minor) with gymnastic, musical, and equestrian disciplines, see Liermann 1889: 168-74 inscription no. 37. *Ant.* 11.35 specifies the victory prize for one of King Darius' guards—competing in giving the most intelligent speech—as purple garments, golden drinking cups, a golden bed, a chariot with a bridle of gold, a head-dress of fine linen, a golden necklace, the chief place after the king, and the honor of being called the king's kinsman.

[1778] The expression γυμνικαὶ ἀσκήσεις ("gymnastic contests") has synonyms in *Ant.* 14.153 (γυμνικοὶ ἀγῶνες) and 16.137 (γυμνικὰ ἀθλήματα).

[1779] *Ant.* 16.137 also mentions a combination of gymnastic and musical contests at the Caesarean Games. About the program of Herod's festival in Jerusalem, see 15.269 with the note to "the quinquennial feast."

[1780] The adjective θυμελικός ("pertaining to the theater," Rengstorf *s.v.*) is a *hapax legomenon* in Josephus. Since the musical performers were usually identical with the θυμελικοί (literally "those who performed on stage"), the καί ("and") before the word θυμελικοῖς is sometimes left out, in line with the Latin version (Niese 381). The translation of such a reading would be "also for the participants in the musical competitions who are called *thumelikoi*." The word θυμελικοί derives from θυμέλη ("hearth"), which originally indicated a central spot in the orchestra of a Greek theater for a hearth or altar (LSJ *s.v.*; Fensterbusch 1936); afterwards it became the name of the podium for the singers and musicians. Josephus' formulation probably reflects the Roman practice, in which the θυμέλη could indicate the λογεῖον ("speaking place, stage," i.e., the location where the actors were performing). If so, the word θυμελικοί means "actors" and not "musicians" here (cf. Plutarch, *Fab.* 4.6; *Sull.* 36; Lämmer 1973: 187 with n. 10).

[1781] The verb διασπουδάζω ("do zealously," in the passive voice "be anxiously done," LSJ *s.v.*) is a *hapax legomenon* in Josephus.

[1782] This note links up with the final words of *Ant.* 15.269, such that the expression "all the most famous

great gifts[1784] to four-horse chariots,[1785] chariots with pairs of horses,[1786] and riding horses.[1787] Everything extravagant and magnificent[1788] that had been pursued[1789] by others independently he imitated faithfully[1790] in his ambition[1791] that the spectacle would work out for him as an eminent show.[1792] **272** All around the theater there were inscriptions in

---

people" probably concerns competitors in the performing arts rather than guests. Herod apparently aimed for the most famous competitors in both the athletic contests (15.269) and performing arts (15.270).

[1783] The aorist προύθηκε ("he displayed") recalls the form προυτίθει of *Ant.* 15.270 (from the verb προτίθημι, with the meaning "hold out [prizes]," Rengstorf *s.v.*; see also the next note).

[1784] The phrase οὐ μικρὰς δωρεάς (literally "no small gifts") is a case of *litotes* (cf. *War* 1.415 about Herod's games in Caesarea: ἆθλα μέγιστα προθείς "supplying excellent prizes").

[1785] About prizes for horse races, see Friedländer 1934: 432-34; Lämmer 1974: 144 n. 31). The noun τέθριππος ("four-horse chariot," Rengstorf *s.v.*) is a *hapax legomenon* in Josephus.

[1786] The noun συνωρίς ("two-horse chariot," Rengstorf *s.v.*) is a further *hapax legomenon* in Josephus.

[1787] The word κέλης ("race horse" or "horse race," Rengstorf *s.v.*) is a *hapax legomenon* in Josephus. Herod's horse and chariot races were Greek-style (Patrich 2007: 119). Races with chariots for 4 horses were very expensive and hard to organize. The information about the 3 kinds of horse races stands out because it is the only reference to specific disciplines, which could imply that Herod himself was especially interested in these races (see Lämmer 1973: 187-88, 202, who argues that Herod may have had 2 motives for organizing these races: [1] they showed that he was capable of organizing races that matched the aristocratic Greek tradition; and [2] he was an excellent and passionate horseman himself [see *War* 1.429] and may even have brought his own horses and chariots to the race). However, Josephus' emphasis on the horse races could also be implicit criticism of the king (cf. Tacitus, *Dial.* 29, who considers passions for actors, gladiators, and horses to be Roman vices).

Horse races usually took place in a hippodrome (Humphrey 1986; Richardson 1996: 224 n. 25), but such a building is not mentioned by Josephus here (cf. *War* 2.44 and *Ant.* 17.255, in which cases he does mention a hippodrome). If the "amphitheater" mentioned in *Ant.* 15.268 was in fact a multi-functional building (see 15.268 with the note to "a huge amphitheater" and Richardson 1996: 187), the races may have taken place there.

[1788] The vocabulary partly repeats that of *Ant.* 15.268 (e.g., πολυτέλεια "great expense, splendor, extravagance"). The noun σεμνοπρέπεια ("splendor, magnificence," Rengstorf *s.v.*) is a *hapax legomenon* in Josephus.

[1789] The verb ἐσπούδαστο echoes διεσπούδαστο ("a great effort was made") of *Ant.* 15.270.

[1790] The overstatement ("*everything ... pursued by others independently he imitated faithfully*") emphasizes Herod's ambition and can be a critical note. The verb ἐκμιμέομαι ("imitate [faithfully]") further occurs in *War* 7.269; *Ant.* 8.316 and in *War* 7.428 (with the meaning "copy exactly," Rengstorf *s.v.*).

[1791] This passage once again indicates that Herod was eager to turn the games into a spectacular show (see also *Ant.* 15.268-269 and cf. 16.140-141) in order to demonstrate his great capabilities as organizer, benefactor, and ruler of Jews and non-Jews alike (Lichtenberger 2006: 287-88). Josephus indicates that his gratitude to Octavian was another important motive (see the next paragraph). Lämmer (1973: 197-99, 208) discusses 2 possible additional motives: (1) a display of control and stability, and (2) a demonstration to the Greeks that Greek practices would be the model in the new Jewish state. Schalit (2001: 417-18) argues that Herod attempted to breach the spiritual wall between Jews and non-Jews and behaved in line with the conventions of the Hellenistic rulers.

The noun φιλοτιμία can mean, among other things, "love of glory" (see *Ant.* 16.138 concerning Caesar's contribution to the games at Caesarea and 16.153, 248), "ambition," and "munificence" (LSJ *s.v.*; Rengstorf *s.v.*). Especially the second and third meanings match Herod's characterization by Josephus, who highlights both the king's ambition to erect new buildings (*War* 1.403, 408, 419; *Ant.* 15.296, 303, 330) and his munificence (*Ant.* 15.312, 315, 328; 16.149-150, 158).

[1792] The final part of *Ant.* 15.271 corresponds closely to a passage in *Ant.* 16.140 about the Caesarean Games: "... so that his (i.e., Herod's) magnanimity became renowned" (my trans.), as has been observed by Drüner 1896: 67-68 (see also 15.268 with the note to "an athletic contest"). The noun ἐπίδειξις ("competitive showing, show") also occurs in 15.268 (see the note to "the competitive showing"). It alludes to the spectacular character of the festival and to the competition between the participants (Ebert 1972: 133-34; Lämmer 1973: 224 n. 144; Pleket 1975; see also 16.140 and 19.335-337

honor of Caesar[1793] and trophies[1794] of the peoples that he[1795] had won during wars,[1796] all

---

about Agrippa I's involvement in the organization of similar entertainments in Beirut).

[1793] The inscriptions in Octavian's honor show Herod's second motive for organizing the festival in Jerusalem: expressing his gratitude and loyalty to Octavian (already indicated in *Ant.* 15.268; see also 15.271 with the note to "in his ambition" and 15.328; 16.137-138). Following the successful meeting in Rhodes (15.187-198), Octavian had become the foundation of Herod's power, such that the king did his best to express his connection with and recognition to Octavian by founding cities, temples, and altars and by organizing games in the emperor's honor (see, e.g., *War* 1.407, 414-415). Such behavior was expected from friendly kings (Suetonius, *Aug.* 59-60). The inscriptions here may have been written on the trophies (see the next note). Previous Jewish rulers already had issued inscriptions honoring Roman leaders: *Ant.* 14.34-36 mentions a golden vine donated by Aristobulus II to Pompey, which Josephus himself had seen in the temple of Jupiter Capitolinus in Rome. This vine bore the inscription "from Alexander, the king of the Jews," which probably refers to Aristobulus' father, King Alexander Janneus (Marcus 467 n. *c*).

[1794] The syntax of the Greek sentence implies that the trophies (τρόπαια; see the next 2 notes, also *Ant.* 15.276-278, 287 and cf. 13.251) were located around the theater, like the inscriptions. Inscriptions on or close to trophies frequently explained the occasions for the trophies' erections (Pliny the Elder 3.136; Pausanias 5.27.11; Tacitus, *Ann.* 2.18). Patrich (2002b: 236) argues that Herod's trophies were located at the front side of the stage. Patrich's references to trophies in the form of shields and bounty stands with body armor include a relief from the Augustan era with very naturalistic body armor (found in Turin, possibly as part of an honorific arch) and a relief on a frieze of a tomb at Petra from the 1st cent. CE. Picard (1957: 283) connects Herod's trophies with Roman trophies found in public city places, like a *forum* or temple (Pausanias 5.27.7; see also Pliny the Elder 3.136; Tacitus, *Ann.* 2.18; Cassius Dio 52.35.6). Several Greek and Roman authors refer to trophies located at the Odeum in Athens—a public building for musical performances erected by Pericles, which had the appearance of a theater—e.g., Pausanias 1.20.4: "Near the sanctuary of Dionysus and the theatre is a structure, which is said to be a copy of Xerxes' tent" (trans. Jones; similar information in Plutarch, *Per.* 13). Vitruvius (5.9.1) is more explicit: "For those who exit on the left side [of the theater of Dionysus] there is the Odeum that Themistocles set up with stone columns and covered over with the masts and yardarms of ships from the Persian war booty" (trans. Rowland; I thank Dr. Peter Eversmann, Amsterdam, for these references).

[1795] I.e., Octavian, who is referred to in the sentence as "Caesar."

[1796] The trophies are the *pièce de résistance* for the Jews in this case (*Ant.* 15.276-279; van Henten 2008b). Trophies were originally memorials of a specific military victory and were situated at the place where the enemy started to flee, which explains their name (the noun τρόπαιον derives from the verb τρέπω ["turn"]; Woelcke 1911; Janssen 1957; Hurschmann 2002). *Ant.* 13.251 reports that Antiochus VII Sidetes erected a trophy at the River Lycus after his triumph over the Parthian general Indates. Herod's trophies commemorated Augustus' victories and were made of refined gold and silver. In 15.276-277 Josephus adds that they appeared to be images of humans surrounded by weapons, and in 15.279 he suggests that they were statues with a wooden frame (see the notes to these passages). These data match the present knowledge about ancient trophies: the basic form of a trophy consisted of a tree stump or a wooden pale with a crossbar (Diodorus 13.24.5), covered by a torso of the defeated enemy and one or more of his weapons (lance, shield, sword, etc.; see also *Ant.* 15.276 with the note to "they" and 15.279 with the note to "the bare wood"). Trophies developed in various ways, including into naval types (e.g., those commemorating the sea battle at Actium [Hölscher 1985; Zachos 2003] and cf. the carvings on the Hasmonean mausoleum at Modein [1 Macc 13:29]). They were represented on reliefs not only at public places but also on vases and coins (Woelcke 1911; Janssen 1957: 60-178). Coins minted in 34 BCE in honor of Caius Sosius, the Syrian governor active at Herod's capture of Jerusalem, bear the image of a Roman trophy flanked by captives representing Antigonus and Judea (Fine 2005: 75 with references). The Romans took over the convention of erecting trophies from the Greeks and adapted it, e.g., by adding images of captured males and females standing or kneeling beside or around the trophies. Such scenes were also depicted on triumphal or honorary arches (Künzl 1988: 76, 123, 128, 132; Hurschmann 2002: 873). Josephus' description stays close to the original Greek type and suggests that the trophies were portable (*Ant.* 15.279). The general character of Herod's trophies, however, fits in with a trend during Augustus' rule, attesting many examples of universal trophies commemorating all of the emperor's victories (Picard 1957: 232-311; Künzl 1988: 132). Whether Herod's trophies had a cultic function is not completely clear from Josephus' vocabulary, which is

of them made for him of refined gold and silver.[1797] **273** And for the equipment[1798] there was nothing, neither costly garment nor dress with precious stones,[1799] that was not on display when the contests were shown.[1800] And wild beasts were also provided;[1801] a great many lions were brought together for him, and all other [wild animals] of extraordinary strength[1802] or of a rather rare kind.[1803] **274** Both engagements of these [animals] against one another and fights against them by humans[1804] who who had been condemned[1805] were

---

ambiguous (see 15.276-279). The main objection for the Jews seems to have been the images of humans on their surfaces (15.277; cf. 2 Macc 5:6 about the wicked High Priest Jason: "... he [i.e., Jason] was setting up trophies of victory over enemies and not over compatriots [πολεμίων καὶ οὐχ ὁμοεθνῶν τρόπαια]").

For the practice of combining trophies with inscriptions, see the note to "trophies" above.

The vocabulary (πολεμήσας ... ἐκτήσατο, with the seemingly superfluous πολεμήσας) may echo a phrase in the *Res gest. divi Aug.* 13 (*esset parta victoriis pax* "... there was peace, secured by victory ...," trans. Shipley), which is typical for the Augustan ideology that war brings peace (see also the Ara Pacis on the Field of Mars in Rome; Galinsky 1996: 107). It is plausible that such a message was expressed by an inscription on or near the trophies.

[1797] The trophies were only covered by gold and silver (see *Ant.* 15.279). The adjective ἄπεφθος ("refined, purified," Rengstorf *s.v.*) is a *hapax legomenon* in Josephus.

[1798] The noun ὑπηρεσία ("service," Rengstorf *s.v.*) refers to the equipment used at the festival (cf. in *Ant.* 15.199, 201 the word indicates extraordinary services provided by Herod to Octavian), as the continuation of the narrative indicates. The utensils and other equipments are described in superlatives in order to add to the glory of the festival.

[1799] The noun σκευή ("equipment, attire") can indicate the dress of a singer, actor, or public officer (LSJ *s.v.* 1). Rengstorf (*s.v.*) proposes, adding a question mark, "utensil" or "ornament."

[1800] The noun ἀγώνισμα ("contest") repeats the vocabulary of *Ant.* 15.269. The verb συνεπιδείκνυμι ("exhibit/present at the same time") is a *hapax legomenon* in Josephus.

[1801] Herod combined the Greek tradition of athletic and other contests with Roman style entertainments. Gladiator combats and shows with wild animals (*venationes*; Futrell 1997: 24-28) were both included in the Caesarean Games (*Ant.* 16.137) and common in Roman festivities to entertain the audience (Friedländer 1934: 487-500; Robert 1940: 309-31). Some Jews of the elite may have been familiar with them, also because Julius Caesar had given, by a decree of 44 BCE, to the Hasmonean High Priest Hyrcanus II and his children as well as to Jewish delegates the privilege to attend gladiatorial combats in Rome in the senatorial box (*Ant.* 14.210; Lämmer 1973: 195). The contests were commonly organized in Greek cities and Roman colonies in the contexts of a ruler's cult, a celebration of an emperor's birthday (or the inauguration of his rule), or a military victory. A visit of Roman officials or military commanders could also induce local authorities to organize such events. Antiochus IV, who had lived for a period in Rome before his accession, may have been the first Greek ruler to organize gladiator and animal fighter combats in the East (in Antioch; Livy 41.20), although this report may be fictitious (Robert 1940: 263-64; Lämmer 1973: 195, 203 with n. 134). It is implausible that Herod organized gladiator combats in Jerusalem (see *Ant.* 15.274 with the notes to "humans" and "who who had been condemned").

The rare phrase παρασκευὴ θηρίων ("supply of wild animals") also occurs in Polyaenus 4.6.7.

[1802] This phrase emphasizes the physical strength of the animals (cf. other passages with ἀλκή ["strength, might"]: *War* 2.580 about Roman soldiers in general; 6.81 about the centurion Julianus; *Ant.* 9.220 about Uzziah's soldiers; 17.278 about the pretender Athronges). The reading τὰς ἄλλας ὑπερβολάς ("the other extreme cases," found in MSS LAMW) instead of τὰς ἀλκὰς ὑπερβαλλούσας ("the other [wild animals] with extraoardinary strength," found in MS P and with slight variations in MSS FE; Niese 381) probably resulted from a wrongful copying of the second reading. It is much more probable that the first reading evolved out of the second by mistake than vice versa.

[1803] The Greek text implies that these animals were rare according to their nature (τὴν φύσιν), which probably denotes their physical appearance. Josephus' very specific formulations again express the spectacularity and extreme costs of the show.

[1804] In addition to animal fights Herod also arranged for combats between animals and humans, usually convicted criminals, which was common practice in the Early Roman period (Friedländer 1934: 498-500; Robert 1940: 320-21; Futrell 1997: 28-29). Out of need of human fighters, administrators sometimes supplied nonprofessional persons even if they had committed relatively light crimes (Cicero, *Pis.* 89). Such entertainment appealed to the Romans and may have had a deterrent

organized. For the foreign visitors[1806] [the experience was one of] shock over the [evident] cost,[1807] combined with riveting entertainment,[1808] given the dangers involved in the spectacle,[1809] whereas for the locals it meant the public dissolution of the customs long honored by them.[1810] **275** For it was very evident [to them][1811] that it was godless to throw humans to the wild beasts[1812] for [other] humans' enjoyment of the spectacle,[1813] and

---

function (Cicero, *Tusc.* 2.41; Lämmer 1973: 196 nn. 84-85). *War* 6.418 reports that, after his victory in 70 CE, Titus transferred most of the Jewish prisoners who were over 17 years old from Jerusalem to the provinces to be executed in the theaters by the sword or by fighting against wild animals (see also *Apion* 1.43).

[1805] Josephus does not specify who these persons are, but forcing convicted persons to fight against wild animals is in line with the usual practice at events like this (see the next note). Josephus does not mention gladiators or professional animal-fighters (*venatores*) during the festival in Jerusalem. Willrich (1929: 82) and Lämmer (1973: 196) argue that Herod deliberately arranged this because he was aware of the Jews' sensitivity in this respect (the Caesarean Games included gladiator combats; see *Ant.* 15.273 with the note to "wild beasts were also provided").

The absolute use of the verb καταγινώσκω stands in for the longer phrase θάνατόν τινος καταγινώσκω ("sentence someone to death"; see *War* 1.545; 7.154; *Ant.* 16.352, 382; *Life* 425; *Apion* 2.265; cf. *Ant.* 18.242; *Apion* 2.263).

[1806] Josephus distinguishes between foreigners and indigenous people (note the opposition τοῖς μὲν ξένοις ... τοῖς δ' ἐπιχωρίοις). The vague reference to "foreigners" probably includes local non-Jews as well (see *Ant.* 15.269 with notes about Herod's invitations).

[1807] The perplexity of the non-Jewish audience concerns the huge expenses here, while the next note highlights the admiration caused by the spectacle itself. Cf. an honorary inscription from Mylasa (in Asia Minor), which refers to the "huge perplexity" (ἔκπληξις μεγίστη) of the audience during a gladiatorial contest (Robert 1940: 174 no. 171 l.12).

[1808] The noun ψυχαγωγία ("pleasure, entertainment," Rengstorf *s.v.*; Lämmer 1974: 106) also occurs in *Ant.* 16.140 about the Caesarean Games (see also *Ant.* 15.241 with the note to "everything possible for diversion").

[1809] Entertainment showing severe dangers and bloody scenes appealed to the Roman taste (Friedländer 1934: 498-500; Futrell 1997: 24; more generally about the penchant for spectacle in Roman society, see Meijer 2007: 1-12, 135-75).

[1810] Josephus returns to his criticism that the festival in Jerusalem abolished the Jewish practices (see *Ant.* 15.267-268 with notes). The vocabulary echoes previous phrases that convey Josephus' criticism (see ἔθος/ἔθη in 15.267-268 and 16.1 about another case of abolishing ancestral customs [κατάλυσις τῶν πατρίων ἐθῶν] by Herod; cf. also similar vocabulary in different contexts: *War* 1.34; 2.393; 4.348; *Ant.* 12.364; 16.36; 19.301; 20.81). Kasher (2007: 188) argues that the entire Jewish community of Jerusalem was furious about the trophies (differently Richardson 2004: 238).

[1811] Instead of ἐκ προδήλου ("clearly, very evidently," Niese 381), MS L reads ἐκ προχείρου ("easy [to see]"), which is a common phrase in Galen (e.g., *Plac. Hipp. Plat.* 2.5.38 [ed. Kühn 5.248]) and Gregory of Nyssa (e.g., *Apol. Hex.* [PG 44.68.48]; see also Didymus, *Gen.* 231.19 [ed. Nautin and Doutreleau 192]).

[1812] Here Josephus expresses the opinion of the indigenous people (see *Ant.* 15.274), which implies severe criticism not only of Herod's festival but also of the non-Jews' festal practices in general given that such combats were common practice (see 15.273-274 with notes).

The verb ὑπορρίπτω ("throw to") occurs once elsewhere in Josephus (*War* 2.90, a passage that is also highly critical about Herod).

[1813] This ethical criticism that human enjoyment at the expense of other humans is godless is not found elsewhere in this episode (Herod's opponents remain silent about it), such that it may well be an objection by Josephus himself (cf. Bergmann 1908: 16-20). Although there are no other explicit passages about fights between animals and between animals and humans in ancient Jewish literature, it is highly plausible that such fights were considered to be problematic by at least some of the Jews. Humans are to take care of animals in the Jewish tradition, and the Torah includes several regulations in order to protect animals (though mostly tame ones). The deaths of wild animals for human entertainment hardly match these ethics (Landmann 1959: 86-88), which is even more true for the deaths of humans. Nevertheless, the sources do not allow us to retrieve whether these considerations were shared by most of the Judean Jews in Herod's day (see also *Apion* 2.213-214, 271; Barclay in BJP 10 on *Ap.* 2.213-214, 271). The combination of τέρψις ("enjoyment") and θέα ("viewing, spectacle") also occurs in *Ant.* 11.188, which is part of Josephus' report of Ahasverus' banquet (see Esth 1). Josephus states that the bowls were "made of

godless too to totally change their practices into foreign customs.[1814] **276** Of all things, however, the trophies caused them the greatest grief.[1815] For thinking[1816] that they[1817] were images [of human persons][1818] surrounded by weapons, they[1819] were greatly[1820] displeased[1821]

---

gold or precious stones for the pleasure of those who beheld them (εἰς τέρψιν ἅμα καὶ θέαν πεποιημένοις)" (trans. Marcus).

[1814] The phrase ξενικὰ ἐπιτηδεύματα ("foreign practices") repeats the vocabulary of *Ant.* 15.267 (see the note to "foreign habits" and 15.281). Josephus criticizes Herod once elsewhere for introducing "foreign practices" with his festival (cf. also 15.268, 271, 274). The repetition of the adjective ἀσεβής ("ungodly, wicked") in this sentence emphasizes that Herod's innovations went against the Mosaic Law, although this criticism is hardly elaborated.

MSS LAMW read ἐξαλλάττειν τοὺς θεσμούς ("change their laws") instead of ἐξαλλάττειν τοὺς ἐθισμούς ("change their customs"), read by MSS PFVE and Niese (381). The first reading probably derives from a change of ἐθισμούς into the rather similar word θεσμούς. The noun θεσμός occurs once elsewhere in Josephus (*War* 4.386; cf. the variant reading θεσμοῖς for ἐθισμοῖς in *Ant.* 16.163). Josephus' point in this section is not that Herod tried to change the Jewish laws, but that he attempted to change the Jewish practices (see 15.267 with notes and 15.281 with the note to "the abandonment of the ancestral customs").

Apart from *War* 7.148 all occurrences of the verb ἐξαλλάττω ("change") are part of the Herod narrative of *Antiquities* (15.17, 275, 281, 300; 16.13, 121).

[1815] This passage indicates a transition in the narrative; Josephus focuses on the trophies in *Ant.* 15.276-279. He first presents the trophies as the main cause of the Jews' resistance against Herod's festival, and then explains why in the next sentences. It should be noted that there is no indication whatsoever in the text that Herod included the usual Graeco-Roman religious rituals in the festival, such as a procession or sacrifices and prayers to the patron deity of the festival (Bernett 2007a: 59-61).

For a similar phrase with λυπέω ("grieve"), cf. *War* 1.208 about Hyrcanus II, who "grieved most especially (μάλιστα δὲ ἐλύπει) over the successes of Herod" (trans. Sievers/Forte in BJP 1a).

[1816] This detail (δοκοῦντες "thinking") is important for 2 reasons: (1) trophies entailed in most—if not all—cases images of human persons, and (2) the vocabulary that describes Herod's trophies is ambiguous (as noted by Bernett 2007a: 64): on the one hand it associates them with images of humans (*Ant.* 15.276-277, 279), on the other hand with idolatry (see 15.279 with the note to "became a cause of laughter"). This raises the question whether Herod's trophies were different from the usual ones.

[1817] The description fits in with the original Greek type of trophies: a dummy of a defeated enemy on a wooden frame and with one or more of his weapons (see *Ant.* 15.272 with the note to "had won during wars").

Several scholars consider the reading τὰς τοῖς ὅπλοις περιειλημμένας ("those being surrounded by weapons") of the Greek MSS (Niese 381) to be corrupt. Niese minor (305), following Ernesti, proposes to strike τὰς. Marcus-Wikgren (130) conjecture αὐτὰ τοῖς ὅπλοις περιειλημμένας ("[that] these were [images] surrounded by weapons"). However, both conjectures are unnecessary; the transmitted text makes sense: "(thinking that) they (i.e., those specimens of the trophies) were (images) surrounded by weapons."

[1818] Josephus specifies the noun εἰκόνας ("images") in *Ant.* 15.277, 279 by adding the word ἀνθρώπων ("of humans"). Images of living creatures—human and non-human alike—go against the second commandment (Exod 20:4-6; Deut 5:8-10; Josephus, *Ant.* 3.91; *Apion* 2.190-191; Richardson 2004: 231-35; Gambetti 2009: 168 n. 4).

Several episodes in Josephus show that the Jews were particularly sensitive to images of living creatures erected in the holy city of Jerusalem (see, e.g., the demolition of Herod's golden eagle in *War* 1.648-655; 2.5-7; *Ant.* 17.148-164). Pontius Pilate's transfer of Roman standards from Caesarea to Jerusalem was met with fierce opposition: the Jews were even willing to sacrifice their lives for stopping this (Philo, *Legat.* 299-305; Josephus, *War* 2.169-174; *Ant.* 18.55-59; Kraeling 1942; Maier 1969). Gaius Caligula's decision to erect a statue of himself in the Temple of Jerusalem triggered a similar response (Philo, *Legat.* 203-337; Josephus, *War* 2.184-203; *Ant.* 18.261-309; see also *Life* 65-67).

Richardson (2004: 238) concludes that Herod respected the second commandment within Judea and permitted images of living creatures outside the area.

[1819] I.e., the indigenous Jews mentioned in *Ant.* 15.274.

[1820] The phrase οὐδὲ μετρίως (literally "not moderately") is case of *litotes* (see *Ant.* 15.119 with the note to "exceedingly").

[1821] About δυσχεραίνω ("be displeased," Rengstorf *s.v.*), see *Ant.* 15.281 with the note to "being annoyed" and 15.369 with the note to "were disgusted about being compelled." Feldman (1993: 41) argues that this reflects the actual response to Herod's initiative and that Josephus' description of the protest indicates fierce Jewish opposition to Herod.

because it is not in keeping with their ancestral practices[1822] to venerate such [images].[1823]

(8.2) 277 It did not escape Herod's notice[1824] that they[1825] were feeling greatly troubled.[1826] But he thought it a bad time to use force against them[1827] and attempted to reconcile and comfort some of them,[1828] trying to do away with their superstition.[1829] Yet he truly did not

---

[1822] This criticism links up with Josephus' introduction of this section in *Ant.* 15.267 (see the note to "he departed even more from the ancestral customs" and the next note). In 15.277 Josephus also emphasizes that the trophies concerned a violation of the Jewish customs (cf. the more general criticisms in 15.267-268).

The phrase (μὴ) πάτριον ἦν (or ἐστι or εἶναι) occurs frequently in connection with practices that do or do not match the Jewish tradition: *Ant.* 1.11; 3.247; 8.193; 14.41, 63 (about keeping the Sabbath); 15.277; 16.169; 18.121; 20.34, 120, 226; *Apion* 1.91; 2.237. See especially *Ant.* 18.121 concerning the Jews' protest against Vitellius, who marched through Judea with his army and its military standards: "For, they said, it was contrary to their tradition (οὐ γὰρ αὐτοῖς εἶναι πάτριον) to allow images (περιορᾶν εἰκόνας), of which there were many attached to the military standards, to be brought upon their soil" (trans. Feldman).

[1823] The statement "it is not according to their ancestral practices to venerate such [images] (τὰ τοιαῦτα σέβειν)" implies a switch in the Jews' objection against Herod's trophies: the previous information denounces a violation of the second commandment (see the note to "images [of human persons]" above), but the present phrase points to the violation of the first commandment (Exod 20:3; Deut 5:7) because of idolatry (i.e., the cultic veneration of the trophies). The expression τὰ ἀγάλματα ("the statues") in *Ant.* 15.279 is important in this connection: it could mean that the trophies were statues in honor of a god (LSJ *s.v.* ἄγαλμα 3 and 5; Rengstorf *s.v.*). The meaning "statue of a god" is implied in 15.339 for the statues of Augustus and Dea Roma standing in the temple near Caesarea's harbor (ἔχων ἀγάλματα, τὸ μὲν Ῥώμης, τὸ δὲ Καίσαρος). Greek games and Roman festivals usually included cultic activities (Futrell 1997: 77-93). Cultic performances in Augustus' honor would have been an obvious and important demonstration of Herod's loyalty towards his patron. Herod organized a cult for Augustus in Samaria-Sebaste, Paneas (i.e., the later Caesarea Philippi), and Caesarea (see 15.339 with the note to "one of Caesar").

Like statues of gods, trophies proper were also usually venerated; they were dedicated to anonymous war gods, the god(s) who had brought victory, Zeus, Nike, or the emperor himself (Herodotus 8.37; Plutarch, *Sull.* 464e; *CIA* II no. 467 l.27 = *SIG* II no. 521 l.27; Woelcke 1911: 138) and sometimes accompanied by sacrifices to these gods (Woelcke 1911: 138, 147-48). The emperor, e.g., dedicated an enemy's military equipment to the gods as a thanksgiving after a victory. The trophies' cultic function is probably the ground for Picard's bold conclusion (1957: 283) that Herod erected the theater and its trophies in order to impose the Roman imperial cult on his subjects, which is highly implausible, however, because it does not match other evidence about the king's religious policy. Smallwood (1976: 84) and Braund (1984: 110) argue that Herod arranged the festival within the limits permitted by the Jewish religion. Apart from perhaps 1 or 2 exceptions, Herod's buildings erected in Jewish environments were not decorated with images of living creatures (note the difference with Caesarea, which had a temple in the emperor's honor containing statues of Augustus and Roma; see above and Richardson 2004: 225-39; van Henten 2008b). Herod probably realized the limitations of showing gratitude and loyalty to Augustus in Jerusalem. The trophies are the only evidence in the report about the festival in Jerusalem pointing to a veneration of deities other than the God of Israel (see also *Ant.* 15.279 with the note to "became a cause of laughter").

[1824] For the verb λανθάνω ("escape [notice]") followed by a negation, see *Ant.* 15.43 with the note to "nothing escaped [their] notice."

[1825] I.e., the indigenous Jews referred to in *Ant.* 15.274, 276.

[1826] This passage introduces Herod's response to the Jews' objection against the trophies. For the verb ἐκταράσσω ("disturb [highly]," Rengstorf *s.v.*), see *Ant.* 15.82 with the note to "he was greatly disturbed."

[1827] This note may hint at Herod's behavior as a tyrant, which would fit the Herod image found in *Antiquities*. His noticeable use of force (βία) is already emphasized in *Ant.* 14.165: "But the chief Jews were in great fear when they saw how powerful and reckless Herod was and how much he desired to be a dictator (ὁρῶντες τὸν Ἡρώδην βίαιον καὶ τολμηρὸν καὶ τυραννίδος γλιχόμενον)" (trans. Marcus; see also 15.321 and the discussion in van Henten 2011b).

[1828] Herod's attempt to appease some of the local Jews seems to have been successful, apart from the radical group mentioned in *Ant.* 15.281. Lämmer (1973: 205) argues that the reconciliation took place on the eve of the new festival, when the trophies were put outside on display, and that the protesters were looking for a pretext

persuade [them],[1830] but they cried out all together, out of annoyance about the things they thought[1831] he was offending them with, that even if they deemed everything [else] bearable,[1832] they would not bear images of humans in the city[1833]—speaking about the trophies. For it was not in keeping with their ancestral customs, they said.[1834] **278** Herod saw that they were troubled[1835] and would not easily change their opinion quickly unless they were appeased.[1836] Having called the most eminent among them[1837] he directed them to the theater, and having shown them the trophies he inquired[1838] what sort of things these

---

to enforce a confrontation that could result in a change of government.

[1829] The word of δεισιδαιμονία ("fear of God, reverence, superstition", Rengstorf *s.v.*) often has a negative connotation, which matches the context here. Koets (1929: 22) and Marcus-Wikgren (132-33) translate "religious scruples," which is perhaps anachronistic. Thackeray and Marcus (1930-55: 126 *s.v.*) give "piety" as meaning, while Kasher (2007: 187-88) argues that Herod took great pleasure in mocking the "superstitious beliefs" of his Jewish subjects (cf. Lämmer 1973: 225 n. 153).

For the combination of δεισιδαιμονία and ἀφαιρέω ("take away"), cf. Plutarch, *Mor.* (*Suav. viv.*) 1100e-f, 1101c; *Nic.* 23.5; Clement of Alexandria, *Ecl.* 28.1.

[1830] In *Ant.* 20.70 the personal object of οὐ μὴν ἔπειθεν ("he failed to persuade") is also to be supplemented on the basis of the context (cf. *War* 3.346).

[1831] The imperfect ἐδόκουν links up with the participle δοκοῦντες ("thinking") of *Ant.* 15.276 (see the note to "thinking") and adds to the ambiguity of this section: in what way were the trophies thought to be irreconcilable with the Jewish religion (see 15.276 with notes) and what was Herod's view about them? The repetition of the verb δοκέω may suggest that the trophies were actually harmless, which may match Herod's own take on them (see 15.279).

[1832] The adjective οἰστός ("bearable," Rengstorf *s.v.*) occurs once elsewhere in Josephus (*Ant.* 17.175), likewise in the Herod narrative of *Antiquities*.

[1833] The problem of the trophies seems to be again that they conveyed images of living creatures (see Josephus' explication at the end of the sentence and *Ant.* 15.276 with the note to "images [of human persons]"). The geographic reference suggests a distinction between Jerusalem (the area within the city walls) and the Judean territory outside the city; the city with the Temple was apparently the most sacred area. Other passages in Josephus that concern objections against images of living creatures sometimes also focus on the city, e.g., the passages about Pilate's decision to move Roman standards bearing images of the emperor from Caesarea to Jerusalem (*War* 2.169-174; *Ant.* 18.55-59, especially *Ant.* 18.55-56 with the phrase τὰς εἰκόνας φέρειν εἰς τὰ Ἱεροσόλυμα; see also 15.276 with the note to "images [of human persons]"). *War* 2.170 states in relation to this transfer that the Jewish laws forbid any kind of sculpted creature (οὐδὲν ... δείκηλον τίθεσθαι) in Jerusalem. See also Josephus' explanation in *War* 1.650 about Herod's violation of the Law by erecting a golden eagle, which passage mentions the Temple as geographical marker: "... for it was unlawful *for the Temple* (κατὰ τὸν ναόν) to contain either images or busts or a work representing some living creature" (trans. Sievers/Forte in BJP 1a, my italics; see also *Ant.* 15.417-419 with notes; further discussion in Schwartz 1996; Tromp 1996).

[1834] The passage οὐ γὰρ εἶναι πάτριον αὐτοῖς repeats the phrase μὴ πάτριον ἦν αὐτοῖς of *Ant.* 15.276, which recurrence emphasizes that the protesters considered the trophies to be a violation of the ancestral customs. There is a different nuance, though: *Ant.* 15.276 concerns the veneration of the trophies, while *Ant.* 15.277 reflects the view that the trophies were images of living creatures.

[1835] The introduction of Herod's response to the protesters (*Ant.* 15.278-279) echoes part of the vocabulary of Josephus' description of the protest in 15.277 (cf. τεταραγμένους ["[they] being troubled"] in 15.278 with ἐκταραττόμενοι ["[they] feeling greatly troubled"] in 15.277; see also the next note).

[1836] The noun παρηγορία ("comfort," here "appeasement," Rengstorf *s.v.*) echoes the imperfect παρηγόρει ("he [i.e., Herod] comforted [some of them]") of *Ant.* 15.277.

[1837] The phrase οἱ ἐπιφανέστατοι ("the most eminent/ prominent/etc.," Rengstorf *s.v.*) is a common expression for a very select group, in various contexts (see *War* 2.243 [the most prominent Samaritans]; 4.335; *Ant.* 11.6; 20.114; *Life* 427; *Apion* 2.239). *Ant.* 11.6 is a close parallel of 15.277: "... summoning the most distinguished (καλέσας τοὺς ἐπιφανεστάτους) of the Jews in Babylon" (trans. Marcus). In *Ant.* 15.269 Josephus uses the superlative ἐπιφανεστάτην to qualify Herod's festival in Jerusalem.

[1838] Herod's response to the protest as described by Josephus is quite clever: it is neither based on the use of force (cf. *Ant.* 15.277), nor on his authority as king. He neither gives in to the protesters by bringing the trophies outside of the city walls (contrary to Pilate, who decided to remove the Roman standards from Jerusalem; see

possibly seemed to be to them.[1839] **279** When they cried out "images of humans,"[1840] [Herod] ordered the decoration that covered[1841] [the trophies] to be removed and showed them the bare wood.[1842] When they were stripped,[1843] the [trophies] immediately became a cause of laughter.[1844] What brought about their[1845] relaxation[1846] most was that previously they too had mocked[1847] the construction of the statues.[1848]

15.277 with the note to "would not bear images of humans in the city"). Herod apparently realized that he could counter the protest only by refuting the protesters' reasoning, which he did by revealing the trophies' true identity. The passage indicates that the king was sensitive to the protesters' religious feelings (Richardson 1996: 188 n. 48; van Henten 2008b: 166; cf. Richardson 2004: 233 concerning the eagle episode).

[1839] Herod's question repeats the verb δοκέω ("seem, think") of *Ant.* 15.276-277 (see 15.276 with the note to "thinking" and 15.277 with the note to "they thought"), which passage turned the trophies into an ambiguous item. The continuation of the narrative in 15.279 builds on this: Herod shows to the protesters that the trophies are not what they seem to be.

[1840] The report of the protesters' response to Herod's question repeats the vocabulary of *Ant.* 15.277 (i.e., the verb ἐκβοάω ["cry out"] and the expressions ἀνθρώπων εἰκόνες/ εἰκόνας ἀνθρώπων ["images of humans"]). The protesters clearly consider the trophies to be a violation of the second commandment (see 15.276 with the note to images [of human persons]").

[1841] The adjective περιθέσιμος ("[intended to] be put around, put around," Rengstorf *s.v.*) is a *hapax legomenon* in Josephus.

[1842] Herod ordered to strip off the decoration from the trophies up to the point that their wooden frames were laid bare (about the construction of trophies, see *Ant.* 15.272 with the note to "had won during wars"), so that any possible association with images and the reason for the protest given in *Ant.* 15.277-278 were eliminated. However, there was more to Herod's demonstration, as the continuation of the narrative indicates.

[1843] The verb ἀποσυλάω ("strip, take away," Rengstorf *s.v.*) occurs once elsewhere in Josephus (*Ant.* 19.323). Its use is humorously ironic here, for a trophy represented military victory and the taking of spoils from the defeated party. Now, to satisfy his critics, Herod is taking the "spoils" from the trophy itself, doing to it what armies did to populations in order to earn trophies.

[1844] The laughter and the mocking (see the note to "had mocked" below) imply a further interpretation of the trophies in addition to the first one (that they were images of humans): they were considered to be idols. Josephus already prepares the readers for this second interpretation in *Ant.* 15.276, when he speaks of the veneration of the trophies (see the note to "venerate such [images]," also the reference to τὰ ἀγάλματα ["the statues"] at the end of that paragraph). The narrative implies that Herod successfully countered the 2 objections that were raised in connection with the trophies (i.e., a violation of the first and second commandments).

That the protesters laughed about the trophies is understandable in the light of the Jewish polemics against idols, which state that the veneration of statues of deities is stupid because they are deceptive; they are fabricated by humans and are exactly what they appear to be: handmade artifacts, pieces of wood with precious metal coverings (Bel 5; Ep Jer 3, 7-15, 39, 45, 50, 54-56, 70-71; *Sib. Or.* 3.27-38, 586-590, 601-607; especially Ep Jer 57-58: "Gods made of wood and overlaid with silver and gold are unable to save themselves from thieves or robbers. Anyone who can will strip them of their gold and silver and of the robes they wear, and go off with this booty, and they will not be able to help themselves").

[1845] I.e., the group of protesters taken to the theater by Herod.

[1846] The MSS transmit several readings here. MSS FAVW, followed by Niese (382), read εἰς διάχυσιν ("to relaxation, to amusement," Rengstorf *s.v.*), MSS PLE εἰς διάλυσιν ("to relief"), and MS M εἰς διάθεσιν ("to goodwill"). The first reading is the more difficult and therefore the more original one; scribes may have replaced the rare noun διάχυσις (one further occurrence in Josephus: *War* 3.507) by more common words.

[1847] The final outcome of the exchange between Herod and the protesters seems to be that both sides agreed upon the trophies' true identity. Herod apparently appeased the protesters (see also *Ant.* 15.280) not by persuading them that the trophies were no idols (they were already convinced of this since the sentence reports that the protesters had mocked the trophies among themselves) but by taking side with the protesters in confirming the trophies' voidness. This was dangerous because Herod ridiculed the trophies made in Octavian's honor; the king could not afford many more of such actions. If this detail is historical, it implies that Herod had miscalculated the sensitivity of the Jews and realized during the festival that the trophies were not acceptable to some of the local Jews. He may have tried to find a way out of this precarious situation by showing that the

(8.3) 280 After he had diverted[1849] the people in this way[1850] and relaxed[1851] the commotion they had suffered because of rage,[1852] most of them[1853] were ready to change their views and no longer be angry,[1854] **281** but some of them[1855] persisted in being annoyed[1856] about the uncommon habits[1857] and considered the abandonment of the ancestral customs[1858] to be the beginning of great disasters.[1859] They thought it was their religious duty to incur any risk[1860] rather than deem it good[1861]—in a situation of great changes in

---

trophies were, in fact, harmless artifacts. The positive image of Herod here does not match the criticism of the king in the previous paragraphs of this episode. Richardson (2004: 238) concludes that Herod was not "a fully Torah-observant Jew"; the king tried to remain "pious" towards the God of the Jews and towards the emperor.

Concerning the phrase ἐν εἰρωνείᾳ τίθεσθαι ("mock"), cf. *War* 4.152; *Life* 367; Mason 2005. Lämmer (1973: 225 n. 150) takes the noun εἰρωνεία here to denote the attitude of somebody who pretends not to know what he or she in fact does know.

[1848] On the association of the trophies with statues, see *Ant.* 15.276 with the note to "venerate such [images]."

[1849] The meaning of παρακρούω is ambiguous: the verb can mean "strike aside, divert" (LSJ *s.v.* 1) or "mislead, deceive" (Rengstorf *s.v.*). The latter meaning would match the criticism in this episode (see *Ant.* 15.267-268 with notes).

[1850] This phrase is the transition to the third section of the episode (*Ant.* 15.280-291), which focuses on an attempt to murder Herod.

[1851] Note the similarity between the verb διαχέω ("disperse, relax") and the noun διάχυσις ("relaxation") in *Ant.* 15.279.

[1852] The complicated formulation includes a word play of ὁρμή ("commotion, turbulence") and ὀργή ("anger, rage").

[1853] Josephus makes a distinction between the majority of the protesters (οἱ μὲν πλείους) and a tiny minority (τινὲς δὲ αὐτῶν, *Ant.* 15.281) that persisted in its resistance against Herod (for the description of this group, see 15.282).

[1854] This implies that Herod's response to the protesters was largely successful (see *Ant.* 15.279 with the note to "they too had mocked"). Smallwood (1976: 84) states that Josephus presents the conspiracy against Herod described in 15.282-290 as a chain reaction set off by Herod's festival.

[1855] See the previous paragraph with the note to "most of them."

[1856] The noun δυσχέρεια ("annoyance") echoes related words in *Ant.* 15.276 (δυσχεραίνω "be displeased") and 15.277 (δυσχέρεια), which links this group with the protest described in 15.276-279 (cf. also the adjective δυσχερής ["bad, unpleasant"] in 15.283). Concerning more repetitions of the preceding vocabulary, see the next notes.

[1857] The opinion of this final group of protesters connects with Josephus' own criticism in the introduction of this episode (see *Ant.* 15.267; note the repetition of ἐπιτηδεύματα ["habits"; cf. 15.269, 275] and ἔθος ["custom"]).

[1858] The phrase καταλύεσθαι τὰ πάτρια echoes the expression "abolition (κατάλυσις) of the customs they held in honor" of *Ant.* 15.274 (see the note there) and the adjective πάτριος ("ancestral") of 15.267, 276, 278. *Ant.* 16.1, which also concerns Herod, offers a close parallel about another case of abolishing ancestral customs (κατάλυσις τῶν πατρίων ἐθῶν).

[1859] Josephus embellishes the criticism of these protesters with a stock phrase (μεγάλων ἀρχή κακῶν) taken from Greek historiography; see Polybius 11.5.9; 18.39.2; 23.5.9; Philo, *Ios.* 12 (concerning Joseph being sold by his brothers, Gen 37:12-36); Michael Psellus, *Chron.* 4.24, which passages may go back to 2 famous episodes: (1) in Thucydides 2.12 the Spartan envoy Menippus concludes at the eve of the Peloponnesian War (431-404 BCE), when the Athenians have sent him back without a hearing: "This day will be the beginning of great evils (μεγάλων κακῶν ἄρξει) for the Hellenes" (trans. Smith), and (2) during the rebellion of the Ionians (499-497 BCE) Herodotus (5.97) remarks concerning the Athenian fleet: "These ships were the beginning of troubles (ἀρχή κακῶν) for Greeks and foreigners" (trans. Godley).

[1860] The verb ἀποκινδυνεύω ("run a/incur any risk," Rengstorf *s.v.*) occurs once elsewhere in Josephus (*Ant.* 14.438).

[1861] These protesters were apparently willing to sacrifice their lives to prevent Herod from changing the Jewish customs (see the next note). In *War* 2.200-201 Josephus uses similar vocabulary when he describes that Petronius was willing to die in preventing the emperor Gaius Caligula from putting a statue of himself in the Temple of Jerusalem (see *Ant.* 15.276 with the note to "images [of human persons]"): "It is rather for me to face the risk (παρακινδυνευτέον ἐμοὶ μᾶλλον ... ἤ). Either, with the God collaborating, I shall persuade Caesar and happily be saved along with you [i.e., the Jews] or, upon his becoming provoked, I shall readily give up my own life for the sake of so many" (trans. Mason in BJP 1b; about Josephus' rhetoric of noble death in general, see van Henten 2007a, also 15.236 with notes concerning Mariamme's death).

their way of life[1862]—to allow Herod to introduce things by force[1863] that ran counter to [their] customs.[1864] He was a king in name[1865] but manifested himself, in fact, as the enemy of the entire people[1866] in his deeds.[1867]

282 For this reason ten male citizens conspired[1868] to plunge themselves into any kind of danger[1869] and put daggers under their clothes.[1870] **283** Among them was a blind person[1871] who, out of indignation over[1872] the things he had heard[1873] about, participated in the conspiracy.[1874] He was incapable of[1875] taking action and contributing something to the

---

[1862] The verb ἐξαλλάττω ("change [utterly]") also occurs in *Ant.* 15.275 (see the note to "totally change their practices into foreign customs"), with τοὺς ἐθισμούς as object (i.e., "change their laws"), also referring to Herod's innovations.

[1863] Once again the vocabulary echoes a previous passage, this time contrasting Herod's own intentions with the radical protesters' opinion: in *Ant.* 15.277 Herod "thought it a bad time to use force (βίαν ἐπάγειν) against them," while here the protesters want to prevent Herod "to introduce things by force (πρὸς βίαν ἐπεισάγοντα)."

[1864] The phrase τὰ μὴ δι' ἔθους ὄντα ("that ran counter to [their] customs") connects with "the uncommon habits (τῶν οὐκ ἐξ ἔθους ἐπιτηδευμάτων)" mentioned previously in this passage (for other occurrences of ἔθος ["custom"] in this episode, see *Ant.* 15.267-268, 274 with the note to "the public dissolution of the customs long honored by them").

[1865] The criticism that Herod was a king in name only occurs once elsewhere in the Herod narrative of *Antiquities* (17.304; cf. 16.4); it is part of the tyrannical image of Herod (van Henten 2011b). It constitutes the upbeat to the radical conclusion that Herod was the enemy of the entire people (see the next note).

[1866] This severe accusation is unique in both *War* and *Antiquities*, but it clearly builds on the previous criticisms in this section (see the previous notes to this paragraph and their references to other passages): Herod's festival was considered to be an unacceptable violation of the Jewish customs and practices, enforcing non-Jewish customs upon the Jews; the statement that the king was the enemy of the entire Jewish people is the logical conclusion of this line of thought. For similar radical criticisms, see the golden eagle episode (*Ant.* 17.148-164) and the Jews' petition to Augustus after Herod's death (17.304-314); both passages depict Herod as a wicked tyrant.

[1867] The opposition "in name" (or "in words")—"in deeds" (λόγῳ μὲν ... τῷ δ' ἔργῳ) is very common in Greek rhetoric. For similar phrases in Josephus, see *War* 1.288; 2.26; *Ant.* 5.289; 18.260; 19.101; *Apion* 2.241. The correspondence between one's words and deeds was considered to be very important (cf. the often mentioned example of Socrates' death, e.g., Cicero, *Tusc.* 1.102-103 and further Döring 1979).

[1868] The continuation of the narrative (*Ant.* 15.284) indicates that it was a conspiracy in order to murder Herod. For the verb συνόμνυμι ("promise by oath, conspire") in a similar context, see *Ant.* 19.38.

[1869] The conspirators were apparently willing to sacrifice their lives (cf. *Ant.* 15.284). The vocabulary is ambiguous: the verb ὑποδύω can mean "go under, plunge into" (LSJ *s.v.* II.1a) or "accept, take on (oneself)" (LSJ *s.v.* II.3b; Rengstorf *s.v.*). The first meaning implies a pejorative connotation, suggesting that the conspirators' plan was doomed to fail; the assistance of the blind man mentioned in the next sentence may support this reading. On the other hand, the expression κίνδυνον ὑποδύεσθαι is elsewhere used with a neutral or even positive import (Herodotus 3.69; Xenophon, *Symp.* 4.35; Plutarch, *Mor.* [*Gen. Socr.*] 576e; see especially Xenophon, *Cyr.* 1.5.12: πάντα δὲ κίνδυνον ἡδέως ὑποδύεσθαι "undergo any danger gladly").

[1870] Several scholars argue that there is a gap in the Greek text here (Niese 382; Marcus-Wikgren 134-35 with n. *a*).

The so-called *Sicarii* were famous for keeping small daggers (*sicae*) under their clothes before murdering someone (see *War* 2.255 [Mason in BJP 1b on *War* 2.255; Brighton 2009] and *Ant.* 20.164; *Life* 293).

[1871] The sequence of the Greek sentence is awkward and can hardly be maintained in the translation. The verb διαφθείρω ("destroy") can mean "be blind" in the perfect passive voice (in combination with τὰ ὄμματα or τοὺς ὀφθαλμούς; LSJ *s.v.* διαφθείρω II).

[1872] The extremely rare noun ἀναξιοπάθεια ("unworthy treatment, indignation") also occurs in *Ant.* 15.37 (see the note to "her unworthy treatment").

[1873] Niese (382) reads ἤκουε ("he had heard about") with MS F and a marginal reading of MS V. Most MSS read ἤκουον ("they had heard about").

[1874] The reading συνωμοσμένος of the Greek MSS is probably a corruption of συνομωμοσμένος ("joining the conspiracy," with Niese 382).

[1875] The phrase οὐχ ... ἱκανός (εἶναι) plus an infinitive ("be unable/incapable to," Rengstorf *s.v.* ἱκανός) also occurs in *Ant.* 16.156, 298.

attack, but he held himself ready to suffer if something bad[1876] happened to them,[1877] such that his incitement of the plotters[1878] of the attack was great.[1879] **(8.4) 284** Having decided this,[1880] they went at a given signal[1881] to the theater,[1882] hoping that[1883] Herod himself would not escape when they fell upon him unexpectedly.[1884] They assumed that they would kill many of the people around him even if they did not get him.[1885] And it would satisfy them, even if they died,[1886] to bring the people and the king himself to reflect upon the outrageous acts he was committing.[1887] So they were very eager to act,[1888] having prepared themselves beforehand.[1889] **285** But one of the men ordered by Herod to closely inquire into such

---

[1876] This phrase may anticipate the failure of the conspiracy described in *Ant.* 15.285-290. The adjective δυσχερές ("bad") echoes the noun δυσχέρεια ("annoyance") and related words in 15.276-277, 281 (see 15.281 with the note to "being annoyed" and 15.316 with the note to "the calamity that befell him"), but here it regards the conspirators' fate instead of Herod's innovations.

[1877] I.e., his fellow conspirators. The blind person apparently decided not to participate in the action—which would hardly have been of any help—but to suffer in solidarity with the other conspirators if they would be caught.

[1878] The expression τοῖς ἐπιχειροῦσι ("the plotters") echoes τὴν ἐπιχείρησιν ("the attack") in one of the preceding subclauses.

[1879] The phrase μὴ μετρίαν (literally "not little") is a case of *litotes*, like οὐδὲ μετρίως (*Ant.* 15.276; see 15.119 with the note to "exceedingly"). Note also the alliteration in μὴ μετρίαν τὴν ὁρμήν, with the repetitions of the *m* and *r* sounds.

[1880] For a similar introduction with ταῦτα γνόντες for an action by the persons involved, see *Ant.* 15.158 with the note to "determined to do this."

[1881] An alternative translation is "(Having decided this) as agreed upon, (they went …)."

The word σύνθημα can mean, among other things, "sign, signal" (LSJ *s.v.*). Rengstorf (*s.v.*) gives "agreement, decision" as meanings here. The phrase ἀπὸ συνθήματος seems to refer to a signal given in a military context (see *War* 3.26; *Ant.* 18.58; Cassius Dio 36.49.1; 62.12.2, and cf. Polybius 3.105.4; Philo, *Ios.* 6; Lucian, *Tox.* 17). The meaning "given signal" fits the context best because the murder attempt's location at the theater required a careful timing taking into consideration the schedule of the performances and the expected moves of Herod (see also *Ant.* 15.285).

[1882] I.e., the theater built in connection with Herod's festival (*Ant.* 15.268). This detail suggests that the Jews of Jerusalem were not used to going to the theater, as Lämmer (1973: 202) observes. This is all the more striking since Josephus so far did not say one word about the Jewish interest in Herod's festival (cf. 15.274).

[1883] The exact plan is not specified. The participle ἐλπίσαντες introduces the description of the strategy of the conspirators given in the remaining part of this paragraph.

[1884] The theater was an obvious place to murder Herod because of the crowd present and the possibility to hide somewhere. This concept is standard in Graeco-Roman literature: wicked tyrants are murdered during a festival and/or at a theater. Famous is the murder of Hipparchus by Harmodius and Aristogeiton during the Panathenean Games (Bengtson 1950: 127). Amphitres murdered the tyrant Leodamas of Milete during the local Didymean Games, in honor of Apollo (Nicolaus of Damascus, *FGH* 90 F 52). Josephus twice refers to the murder of Philip of Macedonia by one of his companions when he was entering the theater (*Ant.* 11.304; 19.95) and describes the murder of Gaius Caligula in great detail (19.14-118); the emperor died during the Palatine Games after he had left the theater (Wiseman 1991; cf. Bathybius' statement in 19.92: "Well then, Cluvius, the programme for to-day will include assassination of a tyrant," trans. Feldman).

[1885] The strategy of the 10 conspirators corresponds to that of contemporary terrorist groups: creating terror among the audience by causing numerous casualties. These men were apparently as evil as Herod himself. A second purpose of the conspiracy is provided by the continuation of the narrative: they intended to provide the king and his people with a clear warning that would make them to reconsider their policies.

[1886] This phrase links up with the statement in *Ant.* 15.282 that the conspirators were willing to accept any danger (see the note to "plunge themselves into any kind of danger" and 15.288 with the note to "which all are obliged to preserve or die for").

[1887] The verb ἐξυβρίζω ("behave insolently, commit an outrage," Rengstorf *s.v.*) connects with the criticism formulated against Herod in *Ant.* 15.281, including that he was considered to be the enemy of the entire people.

[1888] MSS FV read προθεσμίας ("fixed time, previously appointed day") instead of προθυμίας ("eagerness"), which does not make much sense. The second reading probably derives from a scribal lapse, misreading -υ- for -εσ-.

[1889] This note concludes the description of the conspirators' strategy. The participle προκαταστάντες is

matters[1890] and report them [to him][1891] found out about the entire attack and revealed it to the king, who was about to enter the theater.[1892] **286** He[1893] did not consider the report strange,[1894] taking into view the hatred he well knew the masses had for him,[1895] as well as the disturbances that accompanied every single event.[1896] So he retired to the palace[1897] and summoned by name those facing charges.[1898] **287** Being caught in the very act[1899] when

---

missing in MSS LWE. The verb προκαθίστημι ("prepare previously," Rengstorf *s.v.*) occurs twice elsewhere in Josephus, each time within the Herod narrative of *Antiquities* (15.34 [with the meaning "appoint previously"], 381).

[1890] This passage suggests that Herod had spies or a secret service *avant la lettre* at his disposal, which evokes his great distrust (Schalit 2001: 314). Other passages in Josephus support such secret missions, e.g., when Herod was suspicious about his son Alexander plotting against him: "But, secretly sending out spies (κατασκόπους) night and day, he investigated all that was done or said, and immediately put those under suspicion to death" (*War* 1.492, trans. Sievers/Forte in BJP 1a; cf. *Ant.* 16.236 and *War* 1.468). Another secret mission concerns the death of Jonathan-Aristobulus III in one of the royal swimming pools at Jericho (*War* 1.437; *Ant.* 15.50-56). Herod ordered some of Aristobulus' friends to secretly drown him (*Ant.* 15.55) because he considered the young and popular Hasmonean High Priest to be a possible competitor (15.50, 52, 60). Matthew 2 suggests that Herod sent the Three Sages on a secret mission (Matt 2:8) after the religious authorities had revealed him the birthplace of the new king (2:5-6) and the Sages, in private, the precise time of the star's appearance (2:7, 16). This passage implies that Herod implemented a double strategy by combining official assignments with secret missions. This matches the king's behavior in *Antiquities* (France 1979: 116; van Henten 2008a; see also *Ant.* 15.366-367 and Shatzman 1991: 188-89).

[1891] The rare combination of the verbs πολυπραγμονέω (among other things, "inquire closely into," LSJ *s.v.* 3) and διαγγέλλω ("report") also occurs in Plutarch, *Dion* 28.1; Cassius Dio 55.19.1.

[1892] This detail not only confirms that the murder attempt was planned to take place in or near the theater (see *Ant.* 15.284), but also suggests that the plot was revealed to Herod just in time (see also 15.287), which enhances the dramatic character of the report.

[1893] The opening of the sentence (ὁ δ' "He ...") is immediately followed by a parenthesis introduced by οὐ γάρ ("for [he] ... not"). For similar parentheses introduced by οὐ γάρ in Josephus, see *War* 1.138, 318; 2.231; *Ant.* 3.5; 5.16, 305, 351; 6.151; 8.223; 9.31, 131, 192, 224; 13.278; 14.386; 15.325; 16.361; 17.44, 337; 18.69, 108, 154, 287, 317; 19.115; *Life* 83, 153; *Apion* 1.216, 221. As in several other cases, the parenthesis offers an explanation for the act of the key person described in the narrative (see the next note).

[1894] The parenthesis focalizes Herod's feelings concerning the conspiracy. The information that the report did not surprise the king is implausible if one takes the context into account; it goes against the king's great efforts to make a success of his festival in Jerusalem. Even though the festival was apparently mainly organized to impress non-Jewish participants (see *Ant.* 15.269 with notes), it is plausible that Herod was keen on attracting the admiration of his subjects with his initiative as well. However, the Jews' protest against the trophies and the subsequent conspiracy showed that he had been wrong (further discussion in van Henten 2008b).

The adjective ἀνοίκειος ("unsuitable, strange," Rengstorf *s.v.*) occurs once elsewhere in Josephus, likewise in the Herod narrative of *Antiquities* (16.262).

[1895] The dislike, if not hatred, of Herod by the majority of the Jewish population is a theme that reoccurs several times in the Herod narrative of *Antiquities* (see 15.8 [with the note to "out of hatred for Herod"], 10, 304, 315). It is connected with Herod's negative image as a violator of the Jewish customs and his portrayal as a tyrant (van Henten 2011b). About Herod's unpopularity, see also 15.281.

[1896] This note matches the negative relationship between Herod and his Jewish subjects presented in the previous subclause. The danger of disturbances (ταραχαί) among the masses had been the final argument for executing Mariamme (see *Ant.* 15.231 with the note to "on his guard against disturbances of the masses" and 15.30 with the note to "war and disorder").

The verb παρυφίστασθαι ("happen [in consequence]," Rengstorf *s.v.*) is a *hapax legomenon* in Josephus.

[1897] The Greek text interrupts the note about Herod's return to his palace by a parenthesis (see the note to "He" above).

This may be a reference to the Hasmonean palace in Jerusalem that was used by Herod before he built his own palace (see *Ant.* 15.71 with the note to "in the palace" and 15.318 with the note to "he built a palace"), although it is also possible that the Fortress Antonia (mentioned in 15.292) is meant (Kasher 2007: 188 n. 25).

[1898] There is a small ellipsis: Josephus has not reported

Herod's servants fell upon them,[1900] they knew[1901] that they would not escape and made the forced end to their lives[1902] noble[1903] by giving up none of their high spirits.[1904] **288** Feeling no shame,[1905] nor denying the deed, they then showed their drawn swords.[1906] They asserted[1907] that their conspiracy[1908] had been formed nobly and with proper worship,[1909] without any profit or personal interest,[1910] but more importantly for [preserving] the

---

that the 10 conspirators were arrested and moved over to the palace. The first act is related in the next paragraph, while the second act is clearly presupposed because the narrative continues with Herod's interrogation of the conspirators. The verb καλέω together with ὀνομαστί ("call/summon by name") also occurs in *War* 3.294, 385; *Ant.* 1.279; 2.172, 267; 5.348.

[1899] The adjective αὐτόφωρος ("in the very act," Rengstorf *s.v.*) occurs twice elsewhere in Josephus, each time in the Herod narrative of *Antiquities*: *Ant.* 15.48 concerns Alexandra's arrest during her flight to Cleopatra, and *Ant.* 16.213 Pheroras' accusation that Herod was courting his son Alexander's wife Glaphyra.

[1900] This detail partly fills the gap of the narrative in the previous paragraph (see the note to "summoned those under accusation by name"). Shatzman (1991: 189) emphasizes that the conspirators were arrested by Herod's servants and not by his soldiers or bodyguards. This detail perhaps confirms the secrecy of the operation.

[1901] At the moment of the conspirators' arrest Josephus focuses again on their thoughts (cf. in *Ant.* 15.283 the introduction to the conspirators is followed by a description of their motivation).

[1902] Since death was unavoidable, the conspirators apparently decided to make the best out of it. A similar reasoning may underlie the collective suicide at Masada: Eleazar ben Yair persuaded his companions to kill themselves together before the Romans arrived; their situation was hopeless and suicide was the only way to prevent the Romans from harming their wives and children and making them slaves (*War* 7.321). Suicide is presented as a necessity (ἀνάγκη, *War* 7.330, 358, 380, 387; ἀναγκαῖος, 7.352, 382; cf. *Ant.* 15.287: τὴν ἀναγκαίαν καταστροφήν). The noun καταστροφή in combination with βίος or τέλος can indicate the end of a person's life (LSJ *s.v.* II; see *Ant.* 15.376 with the note to "at the end of your life").

[1903] This phrase introduces Josephus' presentation of the conspirators' execution as a noble death (see also *Ant.* 15.281 with the note to "rather than deem it good"), which is elaborated in the next paragraph. This paragraph also offers additional noble death vocabulary (καλῶς καὶ σὺν εὐσεβείᾳ and θνῄσκειν πρό/ὑπέρ).

The verb ἐπικοσμέω ("add ornaments to, decorate, honor," LSJ *s.v.*) is also used in a context of noble death in *War* 6.186, concerning the Roman soldier Longus (for the same verb in different contexts, cf. *Ant.* 8.185; 15.396; 16.138).

[1904] The verb ὑφίημι ("give up," LSJ *s.v.* I.4) combined with φρόνημα ("[high] spirit") occurs frequently in Plutarch (*Caes.* 6.4; *Cat. Min.* 1.2; *Cor.* 9.4; *Demetr.* 18.2; *Pyrrh.* 25.1; see also Dionysius, *Ant. rom.* 7.46.2; 9.54.4; Cassius Dio 68.17.2).

[1905] The particular nuance implied by the absolute use of the verb ἐντρέπω ("turn") remains open, although the verb certainly highlights the conspirators' heroic attitude. Suitable translations are "feeling no remorse/shame" (Rengstorf *s.v.*) as well as "feeling no fear" (LSJ *s.v.* II.4).

[1906] The translation follows Niese's reading κρατούμενα τὰ ξίφη (383), attested by MS L. MSS FAMVWE read κρατούμενοι τὰ ξίφη ("[showed] their swords, holding [them] ..."). The phrase τὰ ξίφη echoes the noun ξιφίδια ("daggers") of *Ant.* 15.282.

[1907] The 3 verbal forms ἐντραπέντες, ἀρνησάμενοι, and ἀνέδειξαν lead to a climax culminating in διωμολογήσαντο ("they asserted"), which highlights the conspirators' confession. The verb διομολογέω ("affirm, assert," Rengstorf *s.v.*) occurs once elsewhere in Josephus (*Ant.* 13.115).

[1908] The noun συνωμοσία ("conspiracy") also occurs once elsewhere in Josephus, in the Herod narrative of *Antiquities*, in connection with Herod's sons Alexander and Aristobulus IV (16.111).

[1909] The noun εὐσέβεια ("piety, proper worship") is also mentioned in the introduction of this episode in connection with Herod's innovations going against the proper worship of God (see *Ant.* 15.267 with the note to "proper worship" and cf. 15.365 about Herod's subjects' belief that the king's measures would put an end to their worship [εὐσέβεια] and change their habits for the worse). There is an obvious contrast between Herod and the conspirators: while Herod corrupts the worship of God, the conspirators defend it and even sacrifice their lives for it. Manaemus' prophecy in 15.375-376 clearly states what Herod should aim for: "For the best policy would be if you would love righteousness and proper worship of God (καὶ πρὸς τὸν θεὸν εὐσέβειαν) as well as reasonableness towards your citizens. ... but you will forget about worship (εὐσεβείας) and what is righteous" (see also 17.150).

[1910] Rengstorf (*s.v.*) gives "personal interest" as meaning for πάθος οἰκεῖον here and in *War* 5.162, but the latter passage seems to concern Herod's personal feelings rather than his personal interest (in naming 3

common customs,[1911] which all are obliged to preserve or die for.[1912] **289** After they had openly declared these things concerning[1913] the plan of their attack, they were led away[1914] with the king's men standing around them. And after enduring every kind of torture[1915] they were killed.[1916] Also not long afterwards,[1917] out of their hatred, some persons[1918] quickly seized the man who had reported these things[1919] and they not only killed him,[1920]

---

towers in Jerusalem after his brother Phasael, his wife Mariamme, and his friend Hippicus). In *Ant.* 15.142 the same expression refers to sufferings (see the note to "sufferings").

[1911] The phrase τῶν κοινῶν ἐθῶν also links up with the introduction of this episode (see ἔθος ["custom"] in *Ant.* 15.267 [with the note to "the ancestral customs"], repeated in 15.268, 274, 281), again contrasting Herod as a violator of the Jewish tradition with the conspirators as its protagonists.

[1912] The phrase θνῄσκειν πρό ("die for") connects with ὑπὲρ τῶν κοινῶν ἐθῶν ("for [preserving] the common customs"; see the previous note) and confirms that the conspirators' interrogation and execution are depicted as a noble death (see *Ant.* 15.287 with the note to "noble").

The conspirators die because of their faithfulness to the Jewish customs, but the Jewish laws are clearly implied (see 15.291). Their motivation links up with brief passages in Josephus about brave ways of dying and about the Jews' contempt of death, sometimes explicitly in connection with faithfulness to the Jewish laws (see, e.g., the motivation given by the persons who demolished Herod's golden eagle in their reply to the king in 17.158-159). In *Against Apion* Josephus emphasizes that, if necessary, every Jew would gladly die for the ancestral laws (1.42-43, 190-193 [quoting Hecataeus]; 2.146, 218-235, 293-294). In 1.42 Josephus notes with respect to the Jews' attitude towards their Sacred Scriptures: "... and it is natural *for all Jews, right from the day of their birth*, to consider them as God's decrees, abide by them, and, if necessary, *gladly die for them* (καὶ ὑπὲρ αὐτῶν, εἰ δέοι, θνῄσκειν ἡδέως)" (trans. Thackeray, my emphasis; cf. Barclay in BJP 10 on *Ap.* 1.42). Smith (1999: 226 n. 116) argues that Josephus praises the conspirators out of self-hatred because he himself failed to commit suicide during the Roman siege of Jotapata.

[1913] The conspirators' frankness is another noble death motif. Socrates figures in Epictetus as a steadfast philosopher who does not shrink away from a tyrant's threats, says what he has to say with full frankness and independence, and accepts torture and even execution (Epictetus 4.1.165; cf. 1.9.25; 4.1.70, 161, 168-169). Jewish and Christian martyrs approved Socrates' attitude, which was an example for many in the early imperial age (van Henten and Avemarie 2002: 14 with references; see also *Ant.* 16.379 about the old soldier Tiro's speech to Herod and 17.160 about the persons who pulled down Herod's eagle).

The rare verb ἐμπαρρησιάζομαι ("speak frankly [about something]," Rengstorf *s.v.*) is a *hapax legomenon* in Josephus. The verb occurs in LXX Job 22:26 (MS A); Polybius 38.12.7; Eusebius, *Vit. Const.* pinax 3.2 (ed. Winkelmann 8); Basil of Caesarea, *Enarr. Isa.* 3.114; 5.174; Gregory of Nyssa, *Ep.* 29.9 (ed. Pasquali 89); *Eun.* 3.2.136 (ed. Jaeger 96).

[1914] The verb ἄγω has probably the meaning of the compound verb ἀπάγω here ("lead off [to execution]," Rengstorf *s.v.*). The simplex ἄγω is also used in *Ant.* 15.231 in connection with Mariamme's execution (see the note to "led to her execution").

[1915] The torture may have been an additional punishment because the conspirators had done more than only attempting to murder the king: they also had disqualified him as king by their statement. The combination of ὑπομένω ("undergo, endure") and πᾶσαν αἰκίαν ("every kind of torture") also occurs in *Ant.* 10.115, about the prophet Jeremiah being tortured by one of the Judean magistrates (cf. also Dionysius, *Ant. rom.* 10.39.1; Justin, *Dial.* 34.8, and see *War* 4.329; 7.273 for similar vocabulary in Josephus).

[1916] Herod's mild and wise reaction to those protesting against the trophies contrasts his harsh punishment of the conspirators, which brutal response is understandable in the light of their attack on his rule and personal life (Lämmer 1973: 206).

[1917] The chronological marker μετ' οὐ πολὺ (δέ) occurs frequently in Josephus (e.g., *War* 1.513; *Ant.* 1.133; 6.176), as does its longer form μετ' οὐ πολὺν δέ χρόνον (e.g., *Ant.* 1.160; 7.298; 10.96).

[1918] This phrase implies that the conspirators had the warm support of other Jerusalemites, which has not been indicated before (but see the next paragraph). Josephus' introduction of the story about the conspiracy even suggests that most inhabitants of Jerusalem had been persuaded by Herod's dealing with the trophies and that only the group of conspirators continued to resist (see *Ant.* 15.280 with the note to "most of them").

[1919] The phrase τὸν ταῦτα μηνύσαντα echoes the aorist κατεμήνυσεν ("he revealed it [to the king]") of *Ant.* 15.285.

[1920] Here Josephus may hint at a correspondence between the deaths of the conspirators, which followed

Herod builds fortified places, including Samaria-Sebaste.
War 1.401; 403

but also divided him up, limb from limb,[1921] and threw him to the dogs.[1922] **290** The event was seen by many of the citizens, but nobody reported it until,[1923] after Herod had arranged a severe[1924] and relentless inquiry,[1925] some women were compelled to testimony under torture[1926] and confessed that they had seen what had been done. And there was punishment for those who had executed it.[1927] He took vengeance for their harsh act upon their entire households.[1928] **291** This persistence of the people[1929] and this imperturbability for the sake

---

upon every kind of torture (see the note above), and the murder of the informant.

[1921] The adverb μέλιστι ("limb from limb," Rengstorf *s.v.*) is a *hapax legomenon* in Josephus.

[1922] The shamefulness of this death is obvious to any reader. The fact that the man was not buried still adds to the shame (1 Kgs 14:11; cf. 2 Kgs 9:10, 37). By being thrown to the dogs the corpse had a status equal to impure prey: "You shall be people consecrated to me; therefore you shall not eat any meat that is mangled by beasts in the field; you shall throw it to the dogs" (Exod 22:31). Josephus' passage may hint at the fate of Queen Jezebel, who was famous for her idolatry and persecution of Israelite prophets and was thrown out of a window by Jehu; her blood spat on the walls, horses trampled upon her, and her flesh was eaten by the dogs (1 Kgs 21:23-24; 2 Kgs 9:30-37; Josephus, *Ant.* 9.122-124). Josephus also refers elsewhere to human bodies that were eaten by the dogs or whose blood was licked by them (*War* 6.367; *Ant.* 6.187; 8.270, 289, 361, 407, 417). Kasher (2007: 189) suggests that this passage derives from a pro-Herodian source.

[1923] The phrase κατεμήνυσεν οὐδείς partly repeats the aorist κατεμήνυσεν ("he revealed it [to the king]") of *Ant.* 15.285 and may be ironical. The contrast between many citizens seeing the informant's shameful death and nobody reporting it to Herod again suggest that the conspirators enjoyed warm support among the population (see also 15.289 with the note to "some persons").

[1924] A few passages in the Herod narrative of *Antiquities* refer to Herod's bitterness or cruelty (πικρός ["bitter, cruel"] in 16.235; πικρία ["bitterness"] in 17.148; cf. *War* 1.494).

[1925] The adjective φιλόνεικος means "pursuing eagerly, relentless" here (Rengstorf *s.v.*). For other passages with the same word referring to Herod, see *Ant.* 15.156 concerning Herod's attitude towards the Nabateans and 16.252 concerning the king's eagerness not to appear as having sentenced his son Alexander hastily to prison (cf. φιλονεικέω ["be intent on"] concerning Herod in *War* 1.411; *Ant.* 16.141).

[1926] The meaning of ἐκβασανίζω, which verb is a *hapax legomenon* in Josephus, is ambiguous. Rengstorf (*s.v.*) offers "compel testimony under torture" but LSJ (*s.v.*) "be put to the question" (not necessarily implying torture) as meanings for this passage. Here torture is likely since starting from Mariamme I's death Herod frequently applies torture in *Antiquities* (see 15.226 with the note to "to torture"). A few passages also connect Herod's (excessive) use of torture with his characterization as a tyrant (*War* 1.586; cf. *War* 2.84-86; *Ant.* 17.66-67; van Henten 2011b: 197-99). Kasher (2007: 189) argues that torture was not unusual in the ancient world, but that Herod applied it in an excessive way.

[1927] The verb ἐνεργέω ("undertake, be active") also occurs in *Ant.* 15.283 concerning the blind supporter of the conspirators.

[1928] Herod's punishment of the perpetrators and their families (πανοικί) apparently functioned as a deterrent. Josephus mentions a few similar severe punishments (*War* 7.365 about the murder of the Jews at Scythopolis by "the Greeks"; *Ant.* 5.11 about Rahab's risk in helping Israel's scouts; 9.168 about God's punishment of Judah's unfaithful inhabitants during the reign of King Joash). The alliteration in this passage (the repetition of the *p* sound) emphasizes the harshness of Herod's punishment.

[1929] This phrase commences the conclusion of the present episode. The paragraph forms the transition to a brief section about some of Herod's building activities (*Ant.* 15.292-298).

Niese has ἡ δ' ἐπιμονὴ τοῦ πάθους with MS P ("The persistence in [the face of] suffering"), presumably in part because of the parallel with the next clause. Niese minor (p. 384) reads ἡ ἐπιμονὴ τοῦ πλήθους ("The persistence of the people") with MSS VFE (and partly P), while MSS LAMW read ἐπιδρομή ("attack") instead of ἐπιμονή. The second reading (probably mistaking -μ- for -δρ-, which automatically led to the change of -ονη into -ομη because of the lexeme -δρομ-) does not match the previous information that only a small minority participated in the coup (15.280-282). Whether the text of MSS LAMW is original or not, it implies that the "attack" of the conspirators had considerable support among the Jerusalemites. The people's persistence may imply a rejection of Herod's festival by the majority of the Jews in Jerusalem. The expression τὸ πλῆθος ("the people, the crowd," sometimes also pejoratively "the rabble"; see *Ant.* 15.2 with the note to "the city's population") also appears in 15.280, 284, 291.

of faithfulness to the laws[1930] would not put Herod at ease—[1931] unless somehow he could take control [of the situation] in complete security.[1932] So he decided to enclose the people from every side,[1933] such that if they would revolt,[1934] the rebellion would not become manifest.[1935]

[1930] Here Josephus uses the noun νόμων ("laws") instead of ἔθων ("customs"), which he repeatedly uses in this episode to highlight Herod's violation of the Jewish customs (see *Ant.* 15.267 with the note to "the ancestral customs"). The perspective in the narrative shifts: the preceding paragraphs suggest that the majority of the Jewish population stopped their protest against the festival, particularly against the trophies (see 15.280: "After he had diverted the people in this way and dissolved the rage …"; note the expression τὸ πλῆθος in that passage, which also occurs here), and that the conspirators were ready to sacrifice their lives for the Jewish customs (see 15.288 with the note to "which all are obliged to preserve or die for"), while the passage here suggests that the people's faithfulness to the Jewish laws was an important factor for Herod.

It is difficult to reconstruct what actually happened during Herod's festival in Jerusalem, but one can make a plausible case that the Jewish response to his initiative was mixed at best. If the scene about taking away the protest against the trophies is reliable (15.276-279), one could argue that Herod tried to make the best out of a hopeless case: the Jews' reaction forced him to be explicit about the trophies' meaning and show that they were harmless in regard to the Jewish religion.

The failed conspiracy seems to have brought an end to the festival in Jerusalem: there are no references to later celebrations, neither in Josephus, nor in any other document (Bernett 2007a: 65). The Jews' reaction to the festival in Jerusalem may have made Herod decide to demonstrate his gratitude and loyalty to his Roman patrons at locations where the sacredness of the ground was not an issue and the Jews did not form the majority of the population. Thus he implemented his plan for a Graeco-Roman style festival at Samaria-Sebaste, which was founded in 27 BCE as a Greek *polis*. Its Herodian buildings include a huge temple for Augustus and a hippodrome, with games and a cult for the emperor (Crowfoot, Kenyon, and Sukenik 1942: 31-129; Avigad 1993; Schalit 2001: 358-65). Later Herod organized a festival at Caesarea, which had obvious connections with a cult for the ruler (see 16.138).

The rare adjective ἀκατάπληκτος ("undaunted," Rengstorf *s.v.*) is a *hapax legomenon* in Josephus. The noun πίστις means "faithfulness" here and refers to the undauntedness of the Jews' loyalty with respect to their laws (Lindsay 1993: 86, 99).

[1931] Josephus uses the phrase (οὐ) ῥᾴδιον ποιεῖν ("put someone in a difficult position," Rengstorf *s.v.* ῥᾴδιος) in a curious way here. Several suggestions have been made to improve the text (Niese 384; Richards and Shutt 1937: 174). However, the transmitted text is understandable.

[1932] This passage transmits Josephus' voice and combines 2 clusters of information about Herod: the episode about the festival in Jerusalem (*Ant.* 15.267-291) and the brief section about Herod's building activities (15.291-298). This connection suggests that the response to the king's festival—with the murder attempt as its aftermath—compelled Herod to improve his security situation. Once again Josephus colors the interpretation of the events in a specific way, by blackening the image of Herod (see van Henten 2008b). It is implausible that Herod's decision to build a series of fortresses was given in by a serious security problem and the need to contain the Jewish population (see already Drüner 1896: 68; Otto 1913: 95, also Bernett 2007a: 69-70; differently Schalit 2001: 340-41, who suggests that the fortresses were to control foreign enemies; see, e.g., *Ant.* 16.277, 284-285, also Vogel 2002: 192; Günther 2005: 215; Udoh 2005: 197 n. 408, and Schalit 2001: 315, who adds that Herod also kept Jewish prisoners in these fortresses). It is improbable that fortresses would protect Herod against murder attempts like the one in the theater. The fortresses served other goals, e.g., demonstrating Herod's loyalty to Rome (see the parallel passages of *War* [1.401, 403, 417-421]) and impressing important guests by providing luxurious accommodation (Günther 2005: 215). For Herod's early period the security motive would make much more sense: the equipment of the fortress at Masada and Herod's flight there were clearly to protect him from internal enemies (*War* 1.264, 286, 294, and especially 7.300, also *Ant.* 14.352-358, 390, 400) as well as from Cleopatra.

For the phrase μετ' πλείονος ἀσφαλείας κρατέω ("rule with greater security"), cf. *Ant.* 15.178 concerning Hyrcanus II, who decided to return to Judea: "He [i.e., Hyrcanus] knew that Herod ruled with full security (κρατοῦντα δὲ μετὰ πάσης ἀσφαλείας) …."

[1933] This is an implausible motivation for Herod's erection of the fortresses (see the previous note and *Ant.* 15.292 with the note to "as a third stronghold").

The verb περιλαμβάνω ("surround") is commonly used in contexts about surrounding cities or fortresses, not peoples. The expression τὸ πλῆθος ("the people") refers to the Jewish population of Jerusalem and probably also of Judea (see 15.280, 284, 289).

[1934] For the verb νεωτερίζω ("revolt"), see *Ant.* 15.8

(8.5) 292 Therefore,[1936] when he had fortified the city by the palace in which he lived[1937] and the Temple with the stronghold near the citadel, which was called Antonia[1938] and built by himself,[1939] he planned[1940] as a third stronghold[1941] against the entire population[1942]

(with the note to "rebelling"), which also concerns the Jewish people rebelling against Herod.

[1935] This is the first passage in the Herod narrative of *Antiquities* in which the noun ἀπόστασις is used with the meaning "rebellion, revolt" (see also 17.176 and cf. 16.337). In 15.183 the verb ἀφίσταμαι means "rebel" in connection with Herod's fear that his mother-in-law Alexandra would start a rebellion. This passage also helps to understand why Herod is eager to contain a possible rebellion: as a friendly king of the Romans he was to maintain peace and order (see 15.5 with the note to "a gift to Antony"); signs of a rebellion would no doubt have made a very bad impression on the emperor.

[1936] *Ant.* 15.292-298 briefly describes a couple of building projects, particularly fortifications. These projects are presented in the light of the security situation of Herod's kingdom and the tendency of the Jewish population to revolt against their king (see especially 15.295). This matches Josephus' comments in 15.291, which forms the transition between the previous section (about the festival in Jerusalem) and the present one. This new section exemplifies Josephus' technique of combining thematically related clusters of information; not all the projects mentioned in it match the period at this stage of the narrative, i.e., ca. 28/27 BCE (with Otto 1913: 76-77; for the date of the festival in Jerusalem, see 15.268 with the note to "an athletic contest," and for the foundation of Samaria-Sebaste in 27 BCE, 15.293): the date for the fortification of the Antonia Fortress (named after Herod's first patron Mark Antony) is most probably situated before Antony's defeat at the Battle of Actium (see also the note to "Antonia" below).

[1937] Herod's first palace (αὐλή) in Jerusalem (also mentioned in *Ant.* 15.43, 71, 286 and in the parallel passage of *War* [1.402]) was a Hasmonean palace (see *Ant.* 15.71 with the note to "the palace"). The noun αὐλή ("court[-yard]") can also mean "palace" in Josephus (Rengstorf *s.v.*; e.g., 15.73). Richardson (1996: 225 n. 31) concludes that Herod restored the Hasmonean palace in the mid or late thirties BCE. Later he built his own splendid palace, adjacent to the 3 royal towers located west of the Temple Mount (see 15.318). Kokkinos (1998: 221-22) assumes that Josephus is referring to Herod's later palace. Since this would imply a chronological inconsistency within the narrative—because the building of that palace is mentioned further on, in 15.318—he argues that Herod started the building preparations already in 29/28 BCE.

[1938] The Antonia Fortress is mentioned for the first time in Josephus in *War* 1.75 (see also *Ant.* 15.247-248, 403, 406, 409, 424; for other references in Josephus, see Schalit 1968: 13). The fortress was named after Herod's first patron, Mark Antony (*War* 1.118, 401; *Ant.* 15.409), which implies that the reconstruction of this fortress took place before the Battle of Actium in September 31 BCE (with Otto 1913: 42) and definitely before the summer of 30 BCE, when Herod switched his allegiance to Octavian (Mahieu 2012: 159), although *War* 1.401 and *Ant.* 15.380-409 connect its building with the renovation of the Temple, set in Herod's 15th or 18th year, respectively (mostly dated to 23/22 and 20/19 BCE; see 15.380, 409 with notes). Josephus offers a detailed description of the fortress in *War* 5.238-246: it was located north of the Temple precinct, at the corner of the western and northern porticoes of the Temple. If the location of the fortress was identical with that of the Baris Fortress (as most scholars argue, see Gibson and Davidson 1996: 230 Fig. 104; Patrich 2011: 564 with Fig. 1, and also 15.403 with the note to "Baris" and the next note) it was damaged during the wars conducted by Pompey (in 63 BCE) and Herod (in 37/36 BCE). It served together with the Hasmonean palace (see the previous note) as Herod's residence in Jerusalem before his own palace was constructed on the western hill (Smallwood 1976: 73-74; Patrich 2009: 66). Herod made it stronger than the Baris Fortress, for his and the Temple's safety (see 15.409). A secret subterranean passage led from the Antonia to the inner Temple (further references in Netzer 2006: 120-26; Ritmeyer 2006: 123-31; Patrich 2009: 55, 64-66 with n. 111 about the archeological remains). Netzer (2006: 160-61) argues that the fortress was even partly integrated into the Temple complex.

[1939] This remark contrasts with *Ant.* 15.403, in which passage Josephus states that the Hasmoneans built the fortress. In *Ant.* 18.91 Josephus specifies that the fortress was originally built by a priest called Hyrcanus, who can be identified with the Hasmonean ruler John Hyrcanus (Simons 1952: 402). These passages imply that Herod only adapted the fortress. The parallel passage of *War* (1.401) adds that Herod restored it at extravagant costs and also notes that it was "no less lavish than a palace" (κατ' οὐδὲν τῶν βασιλείων ἔλαττον, trans. Sievers/Forte in BJP 1a; cf. Josephus description of Samaria-Sebaste in superlative terms in *Ant.* 15.296-298). Ritmeyer (2006: 126-28, 216, 334-37; cf. Bahat 1994: 184-85) argues that Josephus' remark here is correct and connects this with a hypothesis about a location of the

Samaria,[1943] which he called Sebaste.[1944] **293** He intended to make this place no less strong [than the other fortresses][1945] against the countryside; being only a day's journey away from Jerusalem,[1946] it would be most useful with respect to [controlling] both the city and

---

Baris other than that proposed by the majority view (see the previous note). Archaeological data imply in his opinion that the Antonia was a new construction by Herod at the northwest corner of the enlarged Temple Mount, while the Baris Fortress stood at the northwest corner of the previous square Temple Mount. Herod would also have restored this latter fortress between 37 and 31 BCE and called it Antonia (cf. *Ant.* 15.403-409; 18.92), which implies that there were 2 Antonia Fortresses. Ritmyer (2006: 334-37) calls the renovated Baris Fortress the Proto-Antonia.

For Herod as builder, see Levine 1981; Teasdale 1996-97; Roller 1998; Netzer 2006 (also 15.330 with notes), and for a detailed discussion of Herod's fortifications, Shatzman 1991: 217-76.

[1940] Niese (384) reads ἐνόησεν ("he planned") with MSS PFV, while MSS LAM read ἐπενόησεν, which hardly implies a different meaning; both verbs can mean, among other things, "contrive" (Rengstorf *s.v.* ἐπινοέω and νοέω).

The next paragraph explains Herod's strategy.

[1941] The noun ἐπιτείχισμα ("bulwark, rampart," Rengstorf *s.v.*, or "stronghold [placed on the enemy's frontier]," LSJ *s.v.*) preceded by the dative παντὶ τῷ λαῷ (referring to the Jewish people) implies that the entire Jewish population was opposed to Herod (for a similar use of the noun, see Strabo 8.4.2 concerning the Athenian stronghold Pylos in Messenia directed against the Spartans, and Thucydides 1.122; LSJ *s.v.*). Josephus specifies Herod's motivation further in *Ant.* 15.295: the king aimed at arranging maximum control over the Jewish people, who apparently seized every occasion to start a rebellion. The parallel passage of *War* (1.403) about Samaria-Sebaste ("In the region of Samaria he fortified [τειχισάμενος] a city with a magnificent wall of twenty *stadia* ...," trans. Sievers/Forte in BJP 1a) does not mention the issue of security.

[1942] Josephus specifies "the entire population" in *Ant.* 15.293, in which case he refers to "the city [i.e., Jerusalem] and the countryside." The term λαός can refer to the Jewish population or the Jewish people in Josephus (Rengstorf *s.v.*). Such a meaning is plausible here because the Jewish people is consistently depicted as Herod's opponent in this context.

[1943] Josephus returns to Samaria in *Ant.* 15.296 (see also 15.217, 246).

[1944] Samaria was renamed Sebaste after Herod had rebuilt and fortified the city (Strabo 16.2.34; Posidonius, *FGH* 87 F 70; Josephus, *War* 1.64; *Ant.* 15.246, 296).

Sebaste (Σεβαστή) is the Greek equivalent of the Latin *Augusta*, which recalls Octavian's honorary name Augustus (in Greek Σεβαστός; sometimes the Latin title is transcribed as Αὔγουστος). The new name was given to Octavian on 16 January 27 BCE (Kienast 1996: 63), which implies that this date is the earliest possible date for the fortification of Samaria-Sebaste by Herod. Other friendly kings, like Archelaus I of Cappadocia and Pythodoris of Pontus, also renamed cities as Sebaste (Braund 1984: 108; Kienast 1999: 469-70).

Scholars differ on the date of the fortification of Samaria-Sebaste: Otto (1913: 53-54, 76-77), Richardson (1996: 225 n. 32), Bernett (2007a: 67), and Mahieu (2008) argue for 27 BCE because Herod plausibly dedicated Samaria to Augustus shortly after Octavian had accepted his new name of *Augustus-Sebastos* (see *Ant.* 15.109 with the note to "Caesar" and above). Schürer-Vermes (1.290-91 n. 9) and Shatzman (1991: 180 n. 36) suggest ca. 25 BCE because of Herod's 13th regnal year, which is mentioned in 15.299. The earlier date seems more probable (detailed discussion and further references in Mahieu 2008). A parallel passage of *War* (1.401, 403) sets the refoundation in a different chronological framework, in Herod's 15th year (mostly dated in 20/19 BCE). A new era started with Herod's refoundation of the city (Schürer-Vermes 2.163). The city had a mixed population, including former soldiers, local residents, immigrants from surrounding territories, and Jews (Levine 1975: 15-16 with notes). Some coins from Samaria-Sebaste bear the inscription Σεβαστηνῶν ("of the inhabitants of Sebaste") or Σεβαστηνῶν Συρ(ίας) ("of the inhabitants of Sebaste in Syr[ia]"). For a survey of the city's history, see Schürer-Vermes 2.160-64, also Möller and Schmitt 1976: 164-65; Tsafrir, Di Segni, and Green 1994: 220-21 (about Octavian's grant of Samaria to Herod, see *Ant.* 15.217).

[1945] Niese's text (384) is elliptical. Several MSS transmit a different text, but this hardly affects the meaning; the implication of the passage is clear: Samaria-Sebaste was designed as a fortress to control the Jewish people and it was as strong as the 2 fortresses referred to in *Ant.* 15.292 (the royal palace and the Antonia, both situated in Jerusalem). The verb ἰσχυροποιέω ("fortify," Rengstorf *s.v.*) is a *hapax legomenon* in Josephus.

[1946] It was quite common in ancient Greek literature to indicate a distance between 2 locations by the number of days the journey took (see, e.g., Herodotus 1.179; 3.26; 4.122; Xenophon, *Hell.* 3.2.11; Diodorus 17.32.2; Plutarch, *Oth.* 15.4). Josephus applies the same principle

the countryside.[1947] Against the entire people[1948] he built a citadel in what was previously called Straton's Tower;[1949] he named it Caesarea.[1950] **294** As for the Great Plain,[1951] he chose by lot[1952] some of the elite cavalrymen[1953] around him[1954] and founded[1955] a place[1956] called

---

in *Ant.* 5.178; 9.32, 37; 12.192, 335-336; *Apion* 2.21, 23, 116. The straight line distance between Jerusalem and Samaria-Sebaste is ca. 55 km.

[1947] Josephus seems to imply in *Ant.* 15.292-293 that Herod was aiming at controlling the Jewish population in his kingdom from various sides (see 15.292 with the note to "against the entire population"). Here he refers to Jerusalem and its surrounding countryside (χώρα), which is generally considered to denote Judea (for similar references, see *War* 1.154; *Ant.* 11.161, 13.284; 16.1): it is more logical that Samaria-Sebaste was intended as a stronghold against the Judean countryside than against Jerusalem. Yet the geographical markers still do not fit because Samaria-Sebaste was not part of Judea.

[1948] Josephus adds a fourth fortress (Samaria is the third; see *Ant.* 15.292), which clearly shows that he is clustering information that belongs thematically together (see 15.292 with the note to "Therefore"). Caesarea was built considerably later than Samaria-Sebaste (see 15.341 with the note to "a period of twelve years").

The expression τῷ δὲ ἔθνει παντί ("[against] the entire people") connects with παντὶ τῷ λαῷ ("[against] the entire population") of 15.292 and probably also refers to the Jewish people (see 15.292 with the note to "against the entire population").

[1949] About Straton's Tower, see *Ant.* 15.217 with the note to "Straton's Tower." Other friendly kings, like Archelaus I of Cappadocia, Juba II of Mauretania, Polemo I of Pontus and the Bosporus, and possibly Deiotarus Philadelphus of Paphlagonia and Philopator of Cilicia, also refounded earlier cities as Caesarea (Levine 1975: 152 n. 76; Braund 1984: 108 with nn. 22-23; Kienast 1999: 469-71; Bernett 2007a: 69). For many cities with names like Caesarea or Sebaste—referring to the emperor—it remains unclear whether it concerns new cities or the renaming and refounding of already existing cities (Kienast 1999: 469).

[1950] Concerning the renaming of Straton's Tower as Caesarea, cf. *War* 1.80; *Ant.* 13.313; 15.331; 20.173. The present section mentions Caesarea together with Samaria-Sebaste (see already *Ant.* 15.292), although Caesarea was founded considerably later than Sebaste (see 15.293 with the note to "Sebaste" and 15.342 with the note to "when Sebaste was already built as a city"). Herod's founding and construction of Caesarea is described in 15.331-341. The context here strongly suggests that Herod founded Caesarea for security reasons. Such a motive is absent in the introduction to the description of the building of Caesarea (15.331).

[1951] The Great Plain was also called the Valley of Esdraelon (cf. Jdt 3:9), the Valley of Megiddo, or the Valley of Jizreel (Josh 17:16; Judg 6:33; Hos 1:5). It is mentioned in *War* 2.232, 595; 3.39; 4.54; *Ant.* 5.83; 8.36; 12.348; 14.207; 18.122; 20.118; *Life* 115, 126, 318. *Ant.* 12.348 situates it in front of the city of Beth-Shean (i.e., Scythopolis). The valley is situated east of Mount Carmel, in between the regions of Samaria and Galilee. Three other plains are also called "great": the coastal plain of Ptolemais (*War* 2.188; cf. 2.192; Mason in BJP 1b on *War* 2.188), the Jordan Valley (*War* 4.455; *Ant.* 4.100; cf. 5.178), and the modern Beit Netofa Valley, which is also called the Plain of Asochis (*War* 3.59; *Life* 207; Shahar 2004: 228 n. 58).

[1952] Herod apparently selected these men by lot in order to found a colony in the Great Plain (cf. *Ant.* 15.296). The verb ἀποκληρόω ("dispose of by lots, allot," Rengstorf *s.v.*) is a *hapax legomenon* in Josephus.

[1953] Elite cavalrymen could be expected to be very loyal to Herod. They were probably living in Gaba as civilians, like their fellow veterans in Esebonitis and Samaria-Sebaste (about whom Josephus is more explicit in *Ant.* 15.296; Schalit 2001: 181-82). *Ant.* 16.373-375 (about the old soldier Tiro) indicates that there were also veteran soldiers living in Caesarea (Levine 1975: 16). Shatzman (1991: 181) convincingly argues that they could be reconscripted in emergency cases.

Alexander the Great started the practice of establishing military colonies as part of a defense system, and the Romans continued this strategy, e.g., in Asia Minor (Levine 1975: 150-51 n. 59). Herod apparently created colonies for his veterans at several locations (Otto 1913: 80, 90; see 16.285, 292 concerning Trachonitis and 17.23-28 concerning Batanea). Richardson (1996: 225) argues that an important reason for Herod's settling of veterans was an economic one: the veterans no longer received payment but were able to earn a living through the allotment of a piece of fertile land and thus stimulated the economy in this way. Octavian founded several colonies for veterans after his victory at Actium (Kienast 1999: 321-22).

Josephus uses phrases similar to οἱ ἐπίλεκτοι ἱππεῖς ("the elite cavalrymen") in *War* 3.470; 5.52, 258; 6.246; *Ant.* 9.114; cf. *War* 3.120.

[1954] The formulation may imply that Herod commanded these elite riders, which would fit in with the king's interest in horse races (see *Ant.* 15.271 with the note to "riding horses").

[1955] The verb συγκτίζω ("join in founding/colonizing,"

Gaba[1957] for Galilee,[1958] and for Perea[1959] [he colonized] Esebonitis.[1960] **295** So with these [actions] he was, step by step, continuously devising something new[1961] to enhance security.[1962] And he posted garrisons throughout the entire nation[1963] in order to minimize the chance of it falling out of control[1964] into disorder.[1965] The [inhabitants] continually

---

LSJ *s.v.*) occurs once elsewhere in Josephus (*War* 1.422), referring to Herod's building activities.

[1956] The noun χωρίον ("place, area, etc.") can also mean "fortified place" (Rengstorf *s.v.*), which would fit the context (with Kasher 1990: 208). Pastor (2003: 156 n. 19) notes that χωρίον denotes a royal estate here (the word also occurs in *Ant.* 15.297, referring to the specific geographical location of Samaria-Sebaste).

[1957] Gaba (also called Hippeum) is the name of a colony of cavalrymen founded by Herod. It probably existed already as a settlement before Herod's colonization. Jdt 3:10 likely mentions the place, although the Greek spelling in Jdt (Γαιβαί) differs from that in Josephus (Γάβα). Gaba is located at the western end of the Esdraelon Valley, a strategic point. *War* 3.36 situates the city adjacent to Mount Carmel (further references: *War* 2.459; 3.36; *Life* 115, 117-118, and possibly *War* 1.166; *Ant.* 14.88; see Möller and Schmitt 1976: 53-54; Schürer-Vermes 2.164-65; Schalit 2001: 365). Mazar (1952-53) identifies Gaba with el-Harithiyye, on the eastern slope of Mount Carmel; Linn (1988) identifies it with Tell Sush, to the west of Tell Megiddo (see also Marcus-Wikgren 140-41; Schalit 1968: 29; Kasher 1990: 208; Shatzman 1991: 85-86; Netzer 2006: 224).

All settlements mentioned in this paragraph are part of Herod's royal land (Pastor 2003: 155-56).

[1958] The preposition ἐπί ("for") followed by the dative τῇ Γαλιλαίᾳ indicates the purpose of Herod's action (LSJ *s.v.* ἐπί B III.2): Gaba was founded as a military colony in order to control Galilee (Schürer-Vermes 2.164 n. 417; Shatzman 1991: 181). The τε after ἐπί in the Greek MSS should be omitted (Niese 384); otherwise the passage refers to 3 instead of 2 military colonies. The first colony would remain unspecified if τε is included in the text, while Gaba matches the location of the first colony, i.e., in the Great Plain (see the note to "Gaba" above).

Galilee (Γαλιλαία) is mentioned frequently in Josephus. Its location is described in *War* 3.35 (further references in Möller and Schmitt 1976: 64-65).

[1959] In Josephus Perea (Περαία) refers to the Jewish territory east of the Jordan River. *War* 3.46 describes its location: its boundaries are marked by Pella in the north, Machaerus in the south, Philadelphia in the east, and the Jordan in the west (references in Möller and Schmitt 1976: 154-55).

[1960] The formulation is elliptical. It could simply imply that Herod rebuilt the area that was called Esebonitis (i.e., the area around the city of Heshbon-Esbun, north-east of the Dead Sea, *War* 2.458; 3.47; *Ant.* 12.233; Schalit 1968: 46; Möller and Schmitt 1976: 89; Schürer-Vermes 2.165-66; Netzer 2006: 227), but the context implies that Herod established a military colony at Esebonitis (Shatzman 1991: 181-82). Otto (1913: 79-80, 90) argues that Herod founded the settlement at Esebonitis in order to connect the territories east of the Jordan more closely to his kingdom. The city of Heshbon (currently Tell Hesban) existed already in biblical times and was known as a Moabite town in the Hasmonean period; Alexander Janneus conquered it (*Ant.* 13.397).

[1961] The verb ἐπεξευρίσκω ("devise additionally," Rengstorf *s.v.*) is a *hapax legomenon* in Josephus.

[1962] This motivation connects with Josephus' introduction of the current section (see *Ant.* 15.291 with the note to "Therefore") through the repetition of the key word ἀσφάλεια ("security," which also occurs in 15.291, 296, 298).

[1963] Cf. a similar phrase about one of Pompey's commanders in *War* 1.144: διαλαβὼν φρουραῖς τὴν πόλιν ("posting guards throughout the city," trans. Rengstorf *s.v.* διαλαμβάνω).

[1964] The translation follows Niese's text ἀπ' ἐξουσίας ("out of control"; for other meanings, see *Ant.* 15.321 with the note to "using his authority"). The reading ἐπ' ἐξουσίας ("having the license/authority") of MSS LAMW (Niese 385) occurs elsewhere in Josephus (*War* 4.222; *Ant.* 10.103) but does not fit the context here and can easily have derived from a scribal error. For similar cases in which the MSS transmit both the readings ἀπ' ἐξουσίας and ἐπ' ἐξουσίας, see *Ant.* 15.43, 260.

[1965] *Ant.* 15.295 implies not only that Herod's Jewish subjects opposed the king but also that they had an inclination to start a rebellion even if there was only a small reason for discontent (see the next sentence with notes).

For ταραχή ("disorder, unrest") in connection with the possibility of a rebellion by the Jewish people, see 15.30 with the note to "disorder" and the next note.

MSS PFV read προπίπτειν ("fall/plunge into"), while MSS LAMW have προσπίπτειν ("fall upon," Niese 385). The second reading matches the context less and does not fit in with the preposition εἰς ("in[to]"), whereas the first reading does (see *Ant.* 5.292; 6.63, 116). The second reading may derive from a scribal error, adding a -σ- after προ-. Both verbs are common in Josephus and could easily have been exchanged (see *War* 2.37; *Ant.* 6.63; 15.47).

organized disturbances, even after a minor incitement.[1966] [The garrisons] should keep nothing secret if the inhabitants raised trouble.[1967] There were always some [veterans][1968] nearby who could hear about it and prevent it.[1969]

296 At that time, urgently wanting to fortify Samaria,[1970] he arranged many of those who had fought with him against the enemies[1971] and many from the neighboring communities[1972] to take part in the reconstruction work.[1973] He realized his ambitious plan[1974] to erect something new[1975] by himself[1976] because it had not been among the famous cities before,[1977] and he accomplished this ambition[1978] even more in order to enhance

---

[1966] Josephus' suggestion that the Jewish population of Herod's kingdom was very much inclined to rebellion is absurd in the opinion of Morton Smith (1999: 229). The question is whether this stereotypical view reflects the ideas of Herod, Josephus, or both. Rebellion is an important motif in the Herod narrative of *Antiquities* (e.g., 15.8, 30, 165-166, 247-266, 291; cf. also 15.366), which report highlights the rebellious nature of the Jewish people several times (further discussion of this motif in van Henten 2011d).

[1967] The verb παρακινέω ("alter, create disorder") can also mean "act rebelliously" (Rengstorf *s.v.*).

[1968] Josephus does not specify the persons, but the context presupposes former elite cavalrymen (*Ant.* 15.294) and former soldiers (15.296).

[1969] This note connects with Josephus' remark in *Ant.* 15.291 and suggests once again that Herod's measures described in 15.292-298 aimed to control the Jewish population from every side, although there is also a remarkable difference between both passages: *Ant.* 15.291 states that Herod's measures should prevent that a revolt would become manifest outside of the kingdom, while *Ant.* 15.295 suggests that Herod had settled veterans and soldiers at so many places that any initiative to revolt would easily be noticed (cf. 15.285 with the note to "inquire into such matters" concerning Herod's 'secret service') and suppressed. Both passages do not necessarily contradict each other: they may represent different aspects of Herod's rule as a friendly king who had to satisfy his Roman patrons.

[1970] The fortification of Samaria has already been mentioned in *Ant.* 15.292-293. The infinitive τειχίζειν ("fortify") echoes the noun ἐπιτείχισμα ("stronghold") of 15.292.

[1971] Herod's policy in Samaria seems to have been similar to his in Gaba and Esebonitis (*Ant.* 15.294), where the king settled former cavalrymen. His veteran soldiers are not specified and may be infantrymen this time (distinctions between cavalry and infantry were common, e.g., 14.431 about Herod's army), although there is no evidence for this assumption. *War* 1.403 offers the number of the settlers but does not differentiate between soldiers and non-soldiers: "... (he) brought 6,000 colonists (οἰκήτορας) into" the city (trans. Sievers/Forte in BJP 1a).

[1972] Herod apparently settled a new, mixed population at Samaria-Sebaste, existing of veteran soldiers and non-Jewish volunteers from the city's neighborhood. Schalit (2001: 176-80) argues on the basis of an inscription from Magnesia on the Sipylus (*OGIS* no. 229, dated to ca. 244 BCE) that the population of Samaria-Sebaste consisted of 3 categories: veterans, people from the neighborhood, and former inhabitants of Samaria.

[1973] An alternative translation would be "(he arranged ...) to settle." The verb συμπολίζω can mean "settle" or "take part in reconstruction work" (plausibly including the settlement of the builders; Rengstorf *s.v.*; cf. LSJ *s.v.* 3). Levine (1975: 227 n. 4) argues that Herod also maintained close relations with the Samaritans in order to find support against the opposition of many of his Jewish subjects.

[1974] Concerning Herod's φιλοτιμία ("love of glory, ambition, munificence"), see *Ant.* 15.271 with the note to "his ambition" and cf. the introduction in *War* 1.403 to the report about Samaria-Sebaste: "... his generosity (τὸ φιλότιμον) extended to the establishment of entire cities" (trans. Sievers/Forte in BJP 1a).

[1975] The translation follows Niese's reading νέον ("something new"), attested by MSS PFV (Niese 385). Although this may be the best reading according to text-critical criteria, several scholars prefer a different reading on account of the content. Niese minor (308; see also Marcus-Wikgren 140) conjectures νέαν, which results in a slightly different translation: "(to erect the place) as a new city." MSS LAMW (supported by the Latin version) read νεών ("[to erect] a temple"), which reading is preferred by Schalit (2001: 175 n. 97) and might be supported by *Ant.* 15.298 and the parallel passage of *War* (1.403), which both refer to the construction of a temple.

The meaning "erect (a wall or building)" for ἐγείρω is quite common in Josephus (e.g., *War* 1.99; 3.174; 4.56; *Ant.* 8.96; 13.57; 20.191, 228), especially in the Herod narrative of *Antiquities* (15.298, 318, 328, 363, 380, 416; 16.19).

[1976] With Niese minor (308), who reads δι' αὐτοῦ. Niese (385) reads δι' αὑτοῦ ("by him").

[1977] This passage suggests that Herod turned Samaria-Sebaste into a magnificent city, which topic is elaborated in the next paragraphs.

[1978] The vocabulary (τὸ φιλότιμον ἐπετηδεύετο) is

security for himself.[1979] He changed[1980] its name, calling it Sebaste,[1981] and the land nearby, which was the best in the countryside,[1982] he distributed among the colonists[1983]—so that they could live happily[1984]—directly after they had gathered there. **297** And he surrounded the city with a strong wall,[1985] using the steepness of the place as fortification.[1986] And he confined an area that in size was not like that of the first [city],[1987] but was still so big that it did not fall short in any way[1988] of the most highly regarded cities,[1989] for it was twenty *stadia*.[1990] **298** Inside, at the center,[1991] he consecrated a precinct[1992] with a diameter of three

---

very similar to a previous phrase a few lines earlier (ἐπετήδευεν, ὑπό τε φιλοτιμίας; see the note to "He realized his ambitious plan" above, also *War* 1.403).

[1979] This note connects with *Ant.* 15.291, 295, also via the repetition of the noun ἀσφάλεια ("security"; see 15.295 with the note to "enhance security").

[1980] The compound verb ὑπαλλάττω ("change," Rengstorf *s.v.*) occurs 3 times in Josephus and always in the Herod narrative of *Antiquities* (15.47, 193, 296; *Ant.* 15.193 similarly refers to a change of name).

[1981] This phrase (Σεβαστὴν καλῶν) partly repeats "which he called Sebaste" (καλέσας αὐτὴν Σεβαστήν) of *Ant.* 15.292 (see the note there and cf. *War* 1.403: τὸ ἄστυ Σεβαστὴν καλέσας "he named the city Sebaste," trans. Sievers/Forte in BJP 1a).

[1982] *War* 1.403 also refers to the quality of the agricultural land near Samaria-Sebaste: "... (he) allotted them very fertile land (γῆν ... λιπαρωτάτην)" (trans. Sievers/Forte in BJP 1a). The combination of χώρα and ἀρίστη also occurs in *Ant.* 16.142, concerning the city of Antipatris, which was also founded by Herod: "... he erected another city in the plain [i.e., the Plain of Sharon] that is called Kafarsaba. He selected a well-watered place and land excellent for plants (χώραν ἀρίστην)" (my trans.).

[1983] The allotment of pieces of land to colonists matches the practice of founding colonies for veterans (see *Ant.* 15.294 with the note to "elite cavalrymen") and confirms that Herod refounded Samaria-Sebaste as a colony of veterans.

The verb καταμερίζω ("distribute") is a *hapax legomenon* in Josephus. The noun οἰκήτωρ ("inhabitant, settler, colonist") occurs in the parallel passage of *War* (1.403).

[1984] The connection with the previous phrase is obvious: the fertile land around Samaria-Sebaste was a sound basis for a stabile life of the new inhabitants. The phrase ἐν εὐδαιμονίᾳ οἰκεῖν ("live happily") may be inspired by a passage in Plato's *Gorgias* referring to the blissful posthumous life at the Island of the Blessed (*Gorg.* 523b; cf. Plutarch, *Mor.* [*Cons. Apoll.*] 120f). The parallel passage of *War* (1.403) lacks this note but mentions another detail: Herod granted to the inhabitants of Samaria-Sebaste an especially privileged constitution (ἐξαίρετον ... εὐνομίαν), which, like the constitutions of Gaba and Esebonitis, was that of a Greek city with the usual privileges (Otto 1913: 116; Levine 1975: 17).

[1985] Only at this stage, after Samaria-Sebaste has already been mentioned several times, a more detailed description of the rebuilt city commences (cf. the shorter and much more straightforward narrative of *War* 1.403).

In *War* 1.403 Josephus also mentions that Samaria-Sebaste was a walled city: "... he [i.e., Herod] fortified a city with a magnificent wall (καλλίστῳ περιβόλῳ τειχισάμενος, trans. Sievers/Forte in BJP 1a; cf. *Ant.* 15.297 τείχει ... περιέβαλε)." Archaeologists have found sections of this wall and remains of several towers (Schalit 2001: 358-59; Netzer 2006: 84-85). On the west side—not necessarily on all sides—the wall was ca. 3.2 m thick (Netzer 2006: 84).

[1986] Samaria-Sebaste was built on a high hill and had been a fortified place since the period of the Israelite kings. The Hasmonean king John Hyrcanus destroyed the city in 108 BCE, but Gabinius, a Roman governor of Syria, rebuilt it in 55 BCE.

The noun ἐρυμνότης ("fortification, security," Rengstorf *s.v.*) occurs once elsewhere in Josephus, in the next paragraph.

[1987] I.e., Samaria.

[1988] The expression μηδὲν ἀποδεῖν plus a genitive construction ("fall short of ... in any way") also occurs in *War* 7.297; *Ant.* 12.75 (cf. ὀλίγον ἀποδεῖν in *War* 3.95; 4.115 and οὐδὲν ἀποδεῖν in *War* 5.156; *Life* 246; see also Plutarch, *Alex.* 60.12; Galen, *Usu part.* [ed. Kühn 4.70]).

[1989] For the phrase ἐλλογιμώταται πόλεις ("the most renowned cities"), see Isocrates, *Pac.* 68; Strabo 13.1.49 (cf. 13.1.26). The adjective ἐλλόγιμος ("renowned, famous," Rengstorf *s.v.*) occurs once elsewhere in Josephus, in the next paragraph.

[1990] *War* 1.403 mentions the same length for Samaria-Sebaste's city wall. Since a *stadium* (στάδιον) equals ca. 185 m (see *Ant.* 15.168 with the note to *stadia*), 20 *stadia* equal ca. 3.7 km, which length matches the archaeological findings of the wall (Netzer 2006: 84).

[1991] *War* 1.403 likewise indicates that the precinct with the temple building was situated at the center of the city (cf. ἐν μέσῳ with κατὰ μέσην here).

[1992] *War* 1.403 similarly reads "In the middle of this settlement he erected an enormous temple (ναὸν ...

half-*stadia*,[1993] decorated in every possible way, and he erected a sanctuary[1994] in it, which belonged among the most highly regarded in size and beauty.[1995] He adorned the various sections of the city step by step and by all means,[1996] looking after the necessity of his security[1997] by turning it into a splendid fortress[1998] through the fortification of its walls.[1999]

μέγιστον) with an enclosed sacred area around it (περὶ αὐτὸν τέμενος), which measured one and a half *stadia* (τρίων ἡμισταδίων). He dedicated the temple to Caesar (ἀποδειξας τῷ Καίσαρι)" (trans. Sievers/Forte in BJP 1a). The temple's consecration to Augustus is not mentioned explicitly in *Antiquities*, but Josephus seems to hint at it in the elliptical phrase τέμενος ἀνῆκεν ("he consecrated a precinct"). Thucydides (4.116) uses the same phrase for Brasidas' dedication of a former fortification in Lecythus to the deity Athena (cf. Pausanias 2.27.4: ἀνῆκε τῇ Ἀρτέμιδι τέμενος "he ... devoted a precinct to Artemis," trans. Jones). The noun τέμενος ("precinct, temple area") is the usual word for the area of a sanctuary, in contradistinction to the temple proper (here called ναός; see *Ant*. 15.380 with the note to "God's sanctuary").

[1993] The same longitudinal measurement (ἡμιστάδιον) is mentioned in the parallel passage of *War* (1.403; cf. 2.304). A half-*stadium* equals ca. 96 m. The variant readings ἥμισυ σταδίων of MSS FLAMW and *unius et semis stadii* of the Latin version (Niese 385) result in the same measure, 1.5 *stadia* (= ca. 273 m).

[1994] Herod's temple in honor of Augustus (Josephus does not mention that it was a temple for Augustus; Bernett 2007a: 72) at Samaria-Sebaste has been partly excavated. It was an impressive building with a forecourt, standing on a high platform on a hill, which was visible from afar (Hänlein-Schäfer 1985: 34-35; Barag 1993; Schalit 2001: 359-61; Netzer 2006: 82-83, 86-90). It dominated the buildings in the center of the city; it was by far the highest building of the acropolis. The platform was partly raised through substructures and fills. The forecourt was surrounded by double colonnades. The entire complex had a length of ca. 128 m (measured from the supporting wall in the north to the backside of the temple in the south) and a width of ca. 72 m. Both the forecourt and the temple were orientated to the north. The temple was ca. 4.5 m higher than the forecourt and measured ca. 35 x 24 m (for detailed descriptions of the forecourt, temple, and surrounding buildings, see Netzer 2006: 85-91; Bernett 2007a: 68; 72-86). Among the 15 Augustus temples of which the measures are known the temple at Samaria-Sebaste is the fourth largest building (Bernett 2007a: 78).

[1995] The size of the building was impressive (see the previous note). The type of the columns is unclear, and remains of the decorations are missing. The stadium in Samaria-Sebaste probably had Doric columns, and the inner faces of the colonnade's rear walls were likely decorated with frescoes (Netzer 2006: 92).

In *War* 1.414 Josephus uses similar vocabulary for Augustus' temple at Caesarea Maritima: "On a mound right opposite the mouth [of the harbor] was Caesar's temple, remarkable for its beauty and size (κάλλει καὶ μεγέθει διάφορος)" (trans. Sievers/Forte in BJP 1a). Phrases like μεγέθει καὶ κάλλει occur frequently in Josephus (*War* 1.147; 5.161; 7.118, 175; *Ant*. 2.224; 3.166; 4.98; 6.130; 8.176; cf. *Ant*. 5.279; 6.137; 7.238; 8.125, 168; 13.211; 15.25, 51; 16.19; 19.335). The superlative ἐλλογιμώτατος ("most renowned") also occurs in 15.297 referring to the city of Samaria-Sebaste in comparison to other cities.

[1996] Archaeological finds indicate that there was a second temple in Samaria-Sebaste (dedicated to Kore and possibly the Dioscuri), a colonnaded road, a forum, a basilica, a theater, and a stadium. These buildings have been renovated and it is not certain that all of them were created by Herod; most of these buildings probably date from a later period (cf. Schalit 2001: 358-65; Netzer 2006: 83, 92-93; Bernett 2007a: 84-98).

[1997] Once again Josephus emphasizes Herod's concern for security as being the main motive for turning Samaria-Sebaste into a stronghold (note the repetition of the key word ἀσφάλεια ["security"] in *Ant*. 15.291, 295-296, 298).

[1998] The noun φρούριον ("fortress") also occurs in *Ant*. 15.292, referring to the Antonia, and in 15.293, referring to Caesarea Maritima.

[1999] This note echoes previous words concerning Herod's fortification of Samaria-Sebaste: ἐρυμνότης ("fortification") occurs in *Ant*. 15.297 (see the note to "fortification"); περίβολοι ("[surrounding] walls") echoes περιέβαλε ("he surrounded [the city]") of 15.297, and the singular of this noun occurs in the parallel passage of *War* (1.403).

[2000] In his concluding remarks Josephus suddenly adds a second motivation for Herod's rebuilding of Samaria-Sebaste: Herod's love of beauty and his ambition to be remembered on account of his splendid buildings (the structure of the sentence clearly distinguishes 2 motives: τὸ μὲν ἀναγκαῖον τῆς ἀσφαλείας ὁρῶν ... τὸ δ' εὐπρεπὲς "looking after the necessity of his security .... He also made it look good"). In the previous narrative there is just one hint at the

He also made it look good[2000] in order to leave behind for later times memorials[2001] to his benevolence,[2002] which resulted from his love of beauty.[2003]

(9.1) 299 Now in this year,[2004] which was the thirteenth year of Herod's rule,[2005] the greatest calamities befell the country,[2006] either because God cherished wrath[2007] at this

Severe drought in Herod's 13th year.

---

second motive: the noun φιλοτιμία ("love of glory, ambition"; see *Ant.* 15.296 with the note to "his ambitious plan," also 15.330 and the next note).

[2001] For a more elaborate passage with this motive, see *Ant.* 15.328-330, and for a similar phrase concerning Herod seeking posthumous fame, 15.330: "leaving behind ... monuments of his reign (τὰ μνημεῖα τῆς ἀρχῆς τοῖς αὖθις ὑπολιπέσθαι)." Cf. 5.183 concerning Nehemia leaving the city walls of Jerusalem behind as his eternal monument (μνημεῖον αἰώνιον αὐτῷ καταλιπών) and 12.424 concerning Judas the Maccabee leaving behind a non-material monument, the liberation of his nation: "... he left behind him the greatest and most glorious of memorials (μέγιστον αὐτοῦ κλέος καὶ μνημεῖον κατέλιπεν)—to have freed his nation and rescued them from slavery to the Macedonians" (trans. Marcus). Josephus' phrase μνημεῖον ἀπολείπω ("leave behind a memorial") also occurs in Diodorus 1.19.7; 2.13.5; Philo, *Mos.* 1.4; *QG* 4.191a; *Spec.* 4.169; Josephus, *War* 7.376 (about the ruins of Jerusalem as a memorial to those killed).

[2002] Other passages in Josephus highlight Herod's benevolence (φιλανθρωπία) towards cities (especially outside his kingdom) that needed support in building (*War* 1.422-425; *Ant.* 15.328-330; 16.18-19, 146-149).

[2003] There is no further reference in Josephus to Herod's love of beauty (φιλοκαλέω), but the descriptions of several building activities in the present context (e.g. Samaria-Sebaste, *Ant.* 15.296-298; Herodium, 15.323-325; Caesarea Maritima, 15.331-341) support the remark. The archaeological remains testify to Herod's ambition to create beautiful constructions, e.g., at Masada, Herodium, and Caesarea Maritima (Otto 1913: 81-82; Netzer 2006: 300-06).

[2004] The formula "this year" makes Schürer (1901-09: 3.366) and Schürer-Vermes (1.290-91) date the refoundation of Samaria-Sebaste to Herod's 13th regnal year (mentioned in the next phrase), which is converted into 25 BCE (further references in *Ant.* 15.292 with the note to "Sebaste"). However, one should not presuppose a close connection between Josephus previous remarks about Samaria-Sebaste and this dating formula since Josephus is clustering related information (concerning fortresses) that dates from various periods (see 15.292 with the note to "Therefore"). Otto (1913: 76-77) argues that the formula derives from Nicolaus of Damascus, who may have been Josephus' source for 15.299, and that it cannot be used as a clue for the date of the refounding of Samaria-Sebaste.

[2005] The conversion of Herod's 13th regnal year results in the year Nisan 25-Nisan 24 BCE if Nisan (March/April) 37 BCE is taken as the starting point of the calculation (Otto 1913: 67; Schürer-Vermes 1.290-91 with n. 9; Applebaum 1976: 664; Smith 1999: 228). If the regnal years are counted starting from Herod's appointment as king by the Romans in 40 BCE, the year is 28/27 BCE (further discussion in Mahieu 2012: 140-42). Richardson (1996: 222-23 with nn. 17, 19) favors the year 28/27 BCE as the date for the famine described in this section and argues that the preceding year 29/28 BCE had been a Sabbatical year, during which the fields were left fallow. He realizes that the reference to Petronius in *Ant.* 15.307 constitutes a problem for this date since Petronius probably became prefect of Egypt only in 25/24 BCE (see the note to "from Caesar"). Obviously this problem does not exist if one accepts the later date of 25/24 BCE.

[2006] This phrase introduces the disasters described in *Ant.* 15.299-316: a period of severe drought caused illnesses and famine among the population (15.299-304; see also the description of the hunger in Jerusalem during the First Jewish-Roman War [*War* 5.512-518] and Schürer-Vermes 1.457 n. 8; Hamel 1990: 44-52 concerning famines during the 1st cent. CE). Herod's measures to counter this crisis are described in rather positive terms (*Ant.* 15.305-316). Richardson (1996: 223 n. 22) argues that this positive portrayal of Herod derives from Nicolaus of Damascus.

[2007] Josephus implies that there was a close connection between Herod's transgression of the Jewish laws in organizing a festival in Octavian's honor in Jerusalem (*Ant.* 15.267-291) and God's punishment of the Jewish people with a drought (see the continuation of the narrative). About the motif of God's wrath and the formula κατὰ μῆνιν τοῦ θεοῦ in *Antiquities*, see 15.243 with the note to "in connection to God's wrath." *Ant.* 15.243 associates a pestilence among the population with Herod's execution of Mariamme and God's wrath (see also 15.375-376; 16.188; 17.150-151, 155). Droughts as a divine punishment also occur in 7.294-297; 8.319-324; 18.285. The verb μηνίω ("be angry") with God as subject also occurs in 8.112 and *Sib. Or.* 4.51; Diodorus 4.34.2; Dionysius, *Ant. rom.* 3.35.2; Plutarch, *Mor.* (*Amat. narr.*) 775e.

point, or because disaster comes across this way periodically.[2008] **300** For first there were continuous droughts,[2009] and as a consequence of such a condition the land remained barren.[2010] It did not even produce all that it used to bring forth by itself.[2011] Next, since the diet also changed completely because of the lack of cereals,[2012] bodily illnesses[2013] as well as the calamity of the plague[2014] prevailed [during this period], while the people were continuously being attacked by disasters.[2015] **301** Owing to the lack of medical care[2016] and food, the pestilential disease,[2017] which had [already] started severely, was greatly

---

[2008] Josephus presents 2 alternative interpretations for the disasters. The first one matches his own opinion (see the preceding note). Yet the alternative interpretation may ultimately also imply a divine interference since nature was supposed to be orchestrated by a higher cause: Philo (*Her.* 97) refers to the Babylonian astronomers thinking that the world is divine and that good and evil are dependent on the divinely determined orbit of the stars. The philosopher-emperor Marcus Aurelius (5.32) speaks of "the reason that informs all Substance, and governs the Whole from ordered cycle to cycle (κατὰ περιόδους τεταγμένας) through all eternity" (trans. Haines).

[2009] Rain usually falls in Palestine during winter and spring, although sometimes there is little or no rain during the wet season, as the story about Honi the Circle-Drawer implies: people asked Honi to pray for rain since no rain had fallen so far, and Honi drew a circle and said to God that he would not step out of it until it would start raining (*m. Ta'an.* 3:8; *b. Ta'an.* 23a; cf. *Ant.* 14.22; further references in Hamel 1990: 45-46).

The severe drought presupposes that the rainfall was poor during the winter of 25/24 BCE (or 28/27 BCE; see *Ant.* 15.299 with the note to "the thirteenth year of Herod's rule").

[2010] Josephus' rendering of Solomon's prayer at the inauguration of the Temple in Jerusalem (1 Kgs 8; 2 Chr 6) includes a passage (*Ant.* 8.115) that connects the land's barrenness with Israel's sins and divine punishment. The noun γῆ ("land") also occurs together with the adjective ἄκαρπος ("barren") in *War* 5.383, a passage which concerns Egypt in relation to the Ten Plagues (Exod 10:1-20; cf. also Diodorus 3.59.7; Dionysius, *Ant. rom.* 6.17.3; Pseudo-Apollodorus 3.35).

[2011] The MSS and E show many minor differences. The present translation follows the reading καθ' αὐτὴν εἴωθεν ἀναβλαστάνειν φέρουσα of MS W as well as MSS LAM and E with minor variations. Niese (386) conjectures ἀνεβλάστανεν ("[the barren land] ... brought forth ...") instead of ἀναβλαστάνειν and assumes that there is a lacuna before this verb.

[2012] A lack of cereals (σιτία) is the obvious result of a severe drought and causes shortages of bread and porridge, the staple foods for most of the population. Moreover, a drought implies that there are no fresh vegetables and fruits either (Hamel 1990: 46-47), such that vitamins are lacking. Galen (*Reb. suc.* 1.1-3 [ed. Kühn 6.749-51]) describes the consumption of indigestible plants because of famine. Drought often leads to a culmination of calamities, including the deaths of animals and the lack of support for poor people.

The noun δίαιτα ("[way of] life," Rengstorf *s.v.*) also has the meaning "diet" in *Ant.* 15.246 (concerning Herod's illness) and in 16.13. A lack (ἔνδεια) of cereals (σῖτος, σιτία) resulting in hunger is also mentioned in *War* 5.427; 6.419.

[2013] Illnesses are the obvious result of hunger and a limited diet (Hamel 1990: 52-54). Famine studies reveal that the number of infectious diseases increases when a famine is worsening (Pastor 2007: 342 with references).

Josephus distinguishes bodily from mental illnesses. E.g., when he describes Catullus' death as a divine punishment (*War* 7.451-453), he notes that Catullus' mental illness (delusions) was more severe than his bodily illness (ἀλλ' ἦν ἡ τῆς ψυχῆς αὐτῷ νόσος βαρυτέρα, 7.451; see also *Ant.* 15.251 with the note to "suffering mentally and bodily" and 17.238).

[2014] The phrase πάθος λοιμικόν ("calamity/illness of the plague") is a fixed expression (Hippocrates, *Ep.* 2; Erotianus, *Fragm.* 33 [ed. Nachmanson 108]; Strabo 14.1.6; 17.1.7; Plutarch, *Mor.* [*Is. Os.*] 383c; [*Def. orac.*] 419f; [*Quaest. conv.*] 662e).

[2015] This passage introduces Josephus' detailed description of a catastrophic period (starting in the next paragraph, with τό τε γάρ).

The adverb διηνεκῶς ("continuously") echoes the adjective διηνεκεῖς of the first sentence of this paragraph. The verb ἀντεφοδιάζομαι ("be meted out one after another [?]," Rengstorf *s.v.*) is a *hapax legomenon* in Josephus. LSJ (*s.v.*) offer the meaning "be furnished instead of provisions" and indicates that Josephus uses the verb metaphorically here.

[2016] The noun θεραπεία probably means "(medical) care" here, as in several other Josephan passages (e.g., *Ant.* 6.166; 14.368; 19.134, 157).

[2017] The phrase (ἡ) λοιμώδης νόσος ("[the] pestilential disease") also occurs in *Ant.* 15.243 and may allude to Thucydides 1.23 (see *Ant.* 15.243 with the note to "a contagious illness broke out").

intensified. The death of those who were perishing in this way also took away the morale of the survivors[2018] because they were unable to assist with medical treatment during the difficulties.[2019] **302** At any rate, the harvests of that year were really ruined,[2020] and all those that had been stored before[2021] had been consumed; nothing remained to feed their hope for improvement.[2022] The disaster intensified[2023] more than expected, such that not only in that year nothing was left,[2024] but also the sowing seed of the remaining plants was lost,[2025] since the land did not bring forth[2026] in the second year.[2027] **303** The desperate situation forced [them][2028] to improvise in many ways. And it happened that the difficulties were no less for the king himself[2029] because he was deprived of the revenues he received from the land.[2030] He had spent his money,[2031] in connection with his love of honor, on the sums

---

[2018] Josephus clarifies this phrase in the next subclause: the survivors obviously felt down-hearted because they were unable to help the afflicted (cf. by way of contrast *Ant.* 15.246, concerning Herod's illness).

[2019] The translation follows the meaning "medical treatment" of ἐπιμέλεια given by LSJ (*s.v.* 1). The word can also have a more general meaning (e.g., "effort, concern," Rengstorf *s.v.*), in which case the phrase should be translated "by care" or "with treatment."

[2020] Due to the severe drought (*Ant.* 15.300) there were no crops that year (cf. Diodorus 4.61.1).

[2021] Droughts were a familiar phenomenon in Herod's kingdom, and the farmers built up stocks in order to assure survival in a year with a bad harvest (Hamel 1990: 46-47; Pastor 2007: 342).

[2022] The phrase ἐλπὶς χρηστή ("hope for a turn for the better," Rengstorf *s.v.* χρηστός) is a fixed expression (Dionysius, *Ant. rom.* 5.6.3; 5.34.2; Philo, *Cher.* 106; Josephus, *Ant.* 7.234; 8.419; 18.284; Plutarch, *Arist.* 15.4; *Tim.* 12.1; Cassius Dio 12.49.1; 41.15.2; Herodian 1.7.1; 2.14.3).

For other combinations of ὑπολείπω in the passive voice with ἐλπὶς χρηστή, see Philo, *Ebr.* 25; Didymus the Blind, *Fragm. Ps.* Ps. 76:6 794a12 (ed. Mühlenberg 121). Concerning the passive voice of ὑπολείπω combined with ἐλπίς, cf. *War* 1.616; *Ant.* 2.140.

[2023] This phrase echoes previous words: ἐπιτείνω ("increase, grow worse") of *Ant.* 15.301 and κακόν/κακά ("disaster[s]") of 15.299-300.

[2024] The noun ὑπόλοιπον ("remains") echoes the imperfect ὑπελείπετο in a previous subclause within the same paragraph. The statement at the beginning of the paragraph is repeated in order to build up a climax (introduced by "such that not only ... but also ...") highlighting the absence of sowing seed.

[2025] This passage echoes previous expressions (cf. ἀπολωλέναι with ἀπολλυμένων and τῶν περιόντων with τοὺς περιόντας, both in 15.301—although the latter passage refers to persons).

[2026] For the combination of ἀνίημι ("cause to sprout, let grow," Rengstorf *s.v.*) with γῆ ("land"), see *Ant.* 3.183; 12.151.

[2027] With Niese (386), who reads μηδὲ τὸ δεύτερον with MSS LAM. MSS PFVE read μηδέτερον ("neither of the two years"), which is probably a case of haplography.

The drought apparently continued during the second winter, such that the seed was unable to sprout and was lost (or eaten). Richardson (1996: 222 with n. 17) argues that the description matches the extremely difficult situation in a year following a Sabbatical year (i.e., in the post-Sabbatical year 28/27 BCE), when the supplies of seed would be consumed. Pastor (2007: 342) calculates that droughts lasting 2 years occurred on average once every 25 years in Palestine. Successive bad harvests obviously also occurred in non-Jewish areas (Garnsey 1988: 23-24).

[2028] The "them" is added because of the context, though in fact it is Herod who is improvising during this difficult situation, as the continuation of the narrative indicates (Richardson 1996: 222).

[2029] The repetition of the vocabulary underlines that both the king and the population were greatly affected by the drought (cf. τὰς ἀπορίας ["the difficulties"] with ταῖς ἀπορίαις in *Ant.* 15.301; see also the next note).

[2030] Niese (386) reads ἀφῃρημένῳ ("he was deprived of [the revenues]") with MSS PFVE but notes that the reading ἀφῃρημένων ("[the revenues ...] were lost") of MSS LAMW could be correct. The verb ἀφαιρέω ("remove, be deprived of") in the passive voice also occurs in *Ant.* 15.301: "The death of those who kept perishing in this way also took away (ἀφῃρεῖτο) the morale of the survivors ...."

Josephus nowhere provides details concerning Herod's taxation of the agricultural production (the land tax, *tributum soli*; see also 15.365; Udoh 2005: 162-64). A major part of the king's income must have been collected from the revenues of the agricultural sector (Udoh 2005: 163; Pastor 2007: 105-10; 2007: 343), although the amount that the landowners were to pay is unknown. We do know the amount for an earlier period: *Ant.* 14.202-210 concerns a decree issued by Julius Caesar in 47 BCE referring to a tax of one fourth of the crop in the second year (to be paid to the Romans),

with which he was restoring the cities.²⁰³² **304** There was nothing that seemed suitable for help. The disaster had already aroused hatred against him from his subjects.²⁰³³ For [things] not going well is always a welcome reason²⁰³⁴ [for people] to blame those in charge.²⁰³⁵

Herod's measures to counter the famine.

(9.2) 305 Being in such circumstances, he thought about coming to rescue the critical situation.²⁰³⁶ But this was difficult since the neighboring people had no cereals²⁰³⁷ to sell,

---

except in the Sabbatical years, but the interpretation of this passage is much debated (Mahieu 2012: 337-343). Whether Herod levied taxes on properties other than land estates is also unknown, but it is possible that he did (Udoh 2005: 164). Information about censuses conducted by Herod—in connection with the head tax—is likewise missing (Udoh 2005: 164-71). Herod also received income from his royal land: parts of it may have been leased to members of the elite for a fixed amount of money (see *Ant.* 16.250 and cf. 15.106), possibly for part of their harvests. Other income like customs probably also dropped dramatically because of the drought. For further discussions of taxes (including tolls, duties, and sales taxes) during Herod's rule, see Schürer-Vermes 1.372-76; Stern 1974c: 331-32; Applebaum 1976: 661-62, 665; Schalit 2001: 262-98; Udoh 2005: 159-206 (who argues that Herod as a friendly king did not pay tribute to Rome, pp. 118-59; differently Mahieu 2012: 324-49, who argues that 25% of the civil tax revenue of the post-Sabbatical year—i.e., once in 7 years—was paid to Rome).

²⁰³¹ The verb δαπανάω ("spend, consume") also occurs in *Ant.* 15.302, in connection with the supplies that had been consumed.

²⁰³² Apart from the section about the construction of Samaria-Sebaste (*Ant.* 15.292-293, 296-298), *Antiquities* so far did not deal concretely with Herod's contributions to the renovation of (non-Jewish) cities. The note may anticipate 15.328 about such contributions. It is obvious that Herod's many building activities made inroads on the treasury (Schalit 2001: 670). About the various meanings of φιλοτιμία ("love of glory, ambition, munificence"), see 15.271 with the note to "his ambition."

²⁰³³ Rengstorf (*s.v.*) suggests "direct (one's hatred) at someone" as meaning of προκαταλαμβάνω here. That Herod's subjects held the king responsible for the crisis, directly or indirectly, is evident (as the final statement of this paragraph suggests) and also matches Josephus' opinion that the drought was a divine punishment for the king's transgression of the Jewish laws (see *Ant.* 15.299 with the note to "because God cherished wrath").

The expression τοῦ κακοῦ ("the disaster") further occurs in 15.299, 302 (cf. τῶν κακῶν in 15.300). The phrase οἱ ἀρχόμενοι refers to Herod's subjects (likewise in 15.327; 16.4, 115, 151).

²⁰³⁴ Josephus seems to come out with a platitude about politicians and leaders (see also the next note), although there are no close parallels in classical literature. A few passages share the theme of a people's inclination to blame its leaders, including one episode in Josephus: the Israelites complain against Moses several times during their journey through the desert (*Ant.* 3.1-38; cf. Exod 15:22-17:8), which compels Moses to approach God and act as the people's intercessor (3.22-23). He asks God to forgive the people and tries to justify its behavior by referring to the distress and humans' response to misfortune (3.23): "... inasmuch as the race of humanity who experience misfortune is by nature grumbling and fond of having reproaches at hand (φύσει δυσαρέστου καὶ φιλαιτίου τοῦ τῶν ἀνθρώπων ... γένους)" (trans. Feldman in BJP 3). This and the present passage are the only instances in Josephus in which the rare adjective φιλαίτιος ("fond of bringing accusations," LSJ *s.v.*) is found. In Aeschylus' tragedy *The Suppliant Women* King Pelasgus of Argos states: "And let no random word fall against me; for the people is fain to complain against authority (κατ' ἀρχῆς γὰρ φιλαίτιος λεώς)" (*Suppl.* 484-485, trans. Smyth). In his fourth speech against Philip of Macedonia, in a response to an unknown Aristomedes, Demosthenes points to the risk for politicians to be criticized: "Tell me, Aristomedes, why, when you know perfectly well—for no one is ignorant of such matters—that a private station is secure and free from risk, but the life of a politician is precarious (φιλαίτιον), open to attack, and full of trials and misfortunes every day, why do you not choose the quiet, sequestered life instead of the life of peril?" (*Or.* 10.70, trans. Vince; see also Plutarch, *Mor.* [*Praec. ger. rei publ.*] 813a).

²⁰³⁵ The plural οἱ προϊστάμενοι ("the leaders") suggests that Josephus is making a general statement about a people's response to its leaders (see also the preceding note).

²⁰³⁶ This sentence introduces the report about Herod's actions to counter the crisis caused by the drought (*Ant.* 15.305-316), which episode depicts Herod in rather positive terms (see 15.316 with the note to "in their need"). An alternative translation would be "coming to rescue in time" because καιρός can also indicate the right time (Rengstorf *s.v.*).

²⁰³⁷ The noun σιτία ("cereals, food") also occurs in *Ant.* 15.300 (see the note to "cereals").

suffering no less themselves,[2038] and, even if it had been possible to find a little available at high prices, there was no money.[2039] **306** But thinking it right not to neglect[2040] anything[2041] that could bring help, he chopped up[2042] the valuable things of silver and gold[2043] in his own palaces, sparing nothing—neither carefully crafted furniture nor something that was costly because of its artistic quality.[2044] **307** He sent the money to Egypt,[2045] where Petronius had received the prefecture[2046] from Caesar.[2047] This man, to whom no small number of people fled for refuge out of the same need,[2048] was a personal friend of Herod[2049] and wanted to keep his [Herod's] subjects safe. He allowed them first to export grain[2050] and

---

[2038] Neighboring people like the Nabateans and the Syrians were probably suffering from the same drought.

[2039] This note connects with *Ant.* 15.303 (cf. the repetition of χρήματα ["money"]).

[2040] MSS PVF read ἀνελεῖν ("annul [anything]," LSJ *s.v.* ἀναιρέω A II.2) instead of μὴ ἀμελεῖν ("not to neglect [anything]"), attested by MSS LAMW and E (Niese 387). Both infinitives are quite similar. The first reading probably resulted from the second; the inverse direction would require the addition of μή.

[2041] The MSS attest several readings, related to the previous text-critical issue: the reading ἀνελεῖν requires a noun in the accusative, which is attested by MSS PFV (πάντας), while Niese (387) reads μὴ ἀμελεῖν and conjectures πάντος because ἀμελεῖν requires a noun in the genitive (cf. πάντος ἀμελεῖν in Plato, *Pol.* 260e; Gregory of Nyssa, *Sanct. pasch.* [ed. Gebhardt 9.249]). MSS LAMW read πάντως ("[neglect] absolutely [anything]").

[2042] The verb συγκόπτω ("cut up," Rengstorf *s.v.*) occurs once elsewhere in Josephus (*Ant.* 19.138).

[2043] Herod's first step is to provide silver and gold (ultimately money, *Ant.* 15.307) for the purchase of food. The phrase ἀργυρίου καὶ χρυσίου ("silver and gold") probably modifies τὸν κόσμον ("the valuable things"), although it could also denote "silver and gold money" (Rengstorf *s.v.* ἀργύριον; cf. 9.62; 19.71 and see also Marcus-Wikgren 147, who translate "cut up into coinage all the ornaments of gold and silver").

[2044] Josephus' repetitions imply that Herod made a great sacrifice in destroying items of diligent handicraft and beautiful artwork.

[2045] Egypt's agriculture depends on the Nile River. Most of its water comes from Lake Tana in Ethiopia, far away from Palestine. The Egyptian food supplies were, therefore, probably less affected by the drought (Richardson 1996: 223; Pastor 2007: 343).

[2046] The noun ἐπαρχία ("[Roman] province," Rengstorf *s.v.*; Mason 1974: 45, 135-36) refers to the office of prefect of Egypt here. MSS PFVE read τὴν ἀρχήν ("the rule") instead of τὴν ἐπαρχίαν ("the prefecture," with MSS LAMW; Niese 387). The first reading is secondary since it is more probably that the technical term ἐπαρχίαν evolved into ἀρχήν than vice versa.

[2047] The province of Egypt was founded by Octavian after his triumph over Mark Antony and Cleopatra VII in 30 BCE. It had a special status because of its importance as one of Rome's granaries (Kienast 1999: 74). Its prefect belonged to the equestrian class and bore the official title *praefectus Alexandreae et Aegypti* ("prefect of Alexandria and Egypt"; Kienast 1999: 188-89). His most important task was the tax management in Egypt. He was also the highest legal authority and coordinated the grain export to Rome (Stein 1915: 79-119).

Publius Petronius succeeded Aelius Gallus as prefect of Egypt in the second half of 25 BCE (Schürer-Vermes 1.290 n. 8) or in 24 BCE (Mahieu 2012: 142-45) and remained in office until 21 BCE (cf. Strabo 17.1.54; Bagnall 1985: 87, 89).

[2048] Obviously other persons from the region were also seeking refuge in Egypt since this country was probably not, or far less, affected by the drought (see the note to "Egypt"). A similar scenario appears in Gen 42:1-5 (paraphrased in *Ant.* 2.95), when Jacob sends 10 of his sons to Egypt because he had heard that grain was available there; they arrived together with other people from Canaan. The expression διὰ τὰς αὐτὰς χρείας ("out of the same need") recalls διὰ τὰς χρείας of *Ant.* 15.303, referring to Herod's subjects.

[2049] The vocabulary indicates that Petronius was a personal friend (ἰδίᾳ τε φίλος ὢν Ἡρώδῃ; cf. *Ant.* 16.327: οἱ ἴδιοι φίλοι "his [i.e., Antipater's] personal friends") of Herod, and Josephus seems to suggest that Petronius' favoring of Herod resulted from his warm relationship with the king. Obviously, such a friendship did not exclude a business arrangement between these 2 persons (see the note to "its purchase and departure from the harbor" below). Josephus indicates that Herod's "friendships" with Mark Antony and Augustus were also close (see, e.g., 15.77, 189-190, 194-197), but these concern client-patron relationships (see 15.5 with the note to "the friends around him").

[2050] The subject of this clause must be Petronius, whose relationship with Herod apparently made him give priority to Herod's representatives, which was a notorious privilege because Egypt's grain was supposed to be transported to Rome (Garnsey 1988: 255-57).

assisted in anything having to do with its purchase and departure from the harbor,[2051] such that he was a major factor, if not totally responsible, for this help.[2052] **308** After this aid had arrived, Herod[2053] added his own support.[2054] As a consequence he not only completely changed[2055] the opinion of those who had previously thought badly of him,[2056] but also gave a huge demonstration of his goodwill and care.[2057] **309** For first he distributed grain[2058] among all those who were able to accomplish the preparation of the food[2059] by themselves,[2060] taking care that the distribution[2061] was most precise. Since there were many who were not fit enough, out of old age or some other present weakness, to prepare the cereals[2062] for themselves, he next took care of them by putting bakers[2063] to work and

---

[2051] The ships that transported grain from Alexandria to Italy weighed 340 tons, in the Hellenistic period ca. 150 tons. If the number of 80,000 *kor* (*Ant.* 15.314) equals ca. 28,000 tons (see the notes to 15.314), ca. 200 shiploads were brought to Herod's kingdom. Such numbers support the conclusion by Udoh (2005: 204) that Herod's measured up to a "national relief and economic recovery program." The motivation for Petronius' exceptional support may have been his close relationship with Herod, as Josephus indicates at the beginning of this paragraph, but the fact that the prefect supervised the purchase and export of the grain points to an additional reason: Herod's money (see 15.306-307) may have gone partly or even completely into Petronius' pocket.

[2052] MSS LAMW add the words τὸν Ἡρώδη(ν) and imply in this way that Herod was mainly responsible for the aid. The noun βοήθεια ("help") also occurs in *Ant.* 15.306, 313, 315 and echoes the infinitive βοηθεῖν of 15.305. *Ant.* 15.307 refers to Petronius, though, while 15.305, 306 refer to Herod.

[2053] The γάρ at the beginning of the Greek sentence (ὁ γὰρ Ἡρώδης "For Herod") introduces an exemplification (as in *Ant.* 15.309; Denniston 1954: 58-68). This would have worked had Herod been the subject of the previous sentence (as several MSS might suggest; see the previous note), but Petronius functions as its subject, such that the γάρ is problematic and therefore better left untranslated.

[2054] MSS PFV read προστιθείς ("adding"), which reading is followed by Niese (387). The verb προστίθημι has several meanings (LSJ *s.v.*; Rengstorf *s.v.*). The meaning "add" (LSJ *s.v.* III) fits the context well; it does not put Herod in a negative light. The reading προτιθείς ("setting before, presenting," Rengstorf *s.v.* προτίθημι) of MSS LAMW probably results from the omission of the -σ- in προστιθείς.

[2055] The verb ἀντιμεθίστημι ("change completely," Rengstorf *s.v.*) occurs in Josephus only in the Herod narrative of *Antiquities* (see also 15.316; 16.264).

[2056] Several preceding passages of *Antiquities* mention enemies of Herod, or persons thinking badly of him (e.g., 15.2, 5-6, 8, 71, 162-163, 252-266, 280-291).

Concerning the phrase χαλεπῶς ἔχειν ("think badly of, be angry with"), see 15.202 with the note to "were angry."

[2057] Josephus focuses on Herod's care for his subjects during the famine, which topic he elaborates in *Ant.* 15.309-310. The noun εὔνοια can mean, among other things, "(expression of) goodwill" and "love" (Rengstorf *s.v.*). The word is common in the Herod narrative of *Antiquities* but seldom used in connection with Herod's goodwill towards his subjects (see 16.197 concerning Pheroras). An inscription from Athens (*OGIS* no. 414) refers to Herod's εὔνοια: "The people to King Herod friend of Romans because of his good works and goodwill (εὐεργεσίας ἕνεκεν καὶ εὐνοίας) toward the city" (trans. Richardson 1996: 207; cf. *OGIS* no. 417, an inscription from Delos referring to Herod's son Herod Antipas; Richardson 1996: 207, 209-10, 223). The noun προστασία can mean, among other things, "leadership" but also "care, protection" (Rengstorf *s.v.*); cf. the related noun προστάτης ("protector, leader") in *Ant.* 15.159 (see the note to "patron of their people").

[2058] Applebaum (1976: 664) suggests, building on Heichelheim, that Herod provided the grain as a repayable loan, which was a common procedure in ancient society. The noun σῖτος ("grain") also occurs in *Ant.* 15.307.

[2059] For phrases similar to τὰ περὶ τὰς τροφὰς ἐκπονεῖν ("to accomplish the preparation of the food"), cf. Aristotle, *Hist. an.* 588b, 612b.

[2060] Herod apparently divided the population into 2 categories according to their fitness.

[2061] Niese (387) reads ἔκταξιν with MSS PLAMW. The readings ἔκστασιν ("displacement, differentiation," attested by MSS FV) and ἔκτασιν καὶ ἐξέτασιν ("extension and investigation," a marginal reading of MS A) are scribal errors and clearly secondary. The noun ἔκταξις ("distribution," LSJ *s.v.* III; Rengstorf *s.v.*) is a *hapax legomenon* in Josephus.

[2062] The noun σιτία ("cereals") repeats *Ant.* 15.300, 305.

[2063] The noun ἀρτοποιός ("baker," Rengstorf *s.v.*) is a *hapax legomenon* in Josephus.

providing them with the food ready-prepared.²⁰⁶⁴ **310** He also arranged²⁰⁶⁵ that they would pass the winter²⁰⁶⁶ without risks since their need also included²⁰⁶⁷ clothing after their cattle had died and had been totally used up,²⁰⁶⁸ such that they could not use wool or any of the other products to cover their bodies.²⁰⁶⁹ **311** After these items²⁰⁷⁰ had also been provided by him, he threw himself promptly into providing aid to the cities nearby,²⁰⁷¹ giving²⁰⁷² sowing seed to the people in Syria.²⁰⁷³ And this deal brought him no small gain²⁰⁷⁴ since the well-timed favor²⁰⁷⁵ rendered abundant crops, such that there was enough food²⁰⁷⁶ for

---

²⁰⁶⁴ Herod apparently organized a kind of soup kitchen for the weak and needy, which is remarkable for a ruler (Hands 1968: 26-61, who emphasizes that benefactions generally implied that something was to be given in return; Hamel 1990: 219; see also *Ant.* 15.316 with the phrase "beyond expectation" and the note to "in their need"). The combination τροφὴν ἑτοίμην παρέχω ("provide ready-prepared food") also occurs in Hecataeus, *FGH* 264 F 25.1; Diodorus 1.10.1 (cf. Aesop 4.3; Philo, *Spec.* 1.132; Josephus, *Apion* 2.230).

²⁰⁶⁵ The noun ἐπιμέλεια means, among other things, "provision, care" (Rengstorf *s.v.*) and also occurs in *Ant.* 15.308, 315-316 in references to Herod's care (cf. the same word with different meanings in 15.301, 306).

²⁰⁶⁶ The verb διαχειμάζω ("come through the winter," Rengstorf *s.v.*) is a *hapax legomenon* in Josephus.

²⁰⁶⁷ The verb συγκαταλαμβάνω ("comprise also," Rengstorf *s.v.*) is also a *hapax legomenon* in Josephus.

²⁰⁶⁸ The vocabulary seems to imply that part of the cattle had died because of lack of food and diseases (owing to the drought) and that the rest had been slaughtered. In the ancient Mediterranean, farmers usually could hardly afford to feed their cattle well. Animals and humans were competing for food, which was a further reason for killing animals (Pastor 2007: 344). For a survey of domestic animals (sheep, goats, cattle, donkeys, horses, mules, and camels) in Palestine in the rabbinic period and their usual feed, see Krauss 1910-12: 1.111-20, 129-32.

²⁰⁶⁹ Warm clothing is important in Palestine during winter, especially in the hills and mountainous areas like Jerusalem and its neighborhood. Such clothes were prepared from wool and animal skins (cf. Elijah's mantle made from goat skin, 1 Kgs 19:13, and John the Baptist's mantle from camel's hair, Mark 1:6; for a survey of cloths fabricated from wool, leather, and other animal materials, see Krauss 1910-12: 1.136-38 with notes).

²⁰⁷⁰ Josephus does not specify the items, but the close connection with the previous paragraph implies that they concern winter clothes. Herod may have provided wearable clothing and/or raw materials to fabricate such. The lack of precision may indicate that this aspect of Herod's help was added by Josephus (or his source) to embellish Herod's positive portrayal. The need for clothing was likely far less urgent than that for food because clothes last for many years.

²⁰⁷¹ "The cities nearby" (αἱ πλησίον πολεῖς) may be the cities of the Decapolis (the "Ten Cities"; further references in Richardson 1996: 88-91), which are situated east of the Jordan (except for Scythopolis), southeast of the Sea of Galilee, directly bordering Herod's kingdom (see also *Ant.* 15.111-112, 148 with notes). The expression does not denote a fixed group of cities in Josephus since in *War* 2.598 the same phrase refers to other cities. The subsequent reference to Syria favors a reference to the Decapolis.

²⁰⁷² Most MSS read διδούς ("giving"), but Niese (388) reads διαδούς ("distributing, giving," Rengstorf *s.v.*) with MS P, which is presumably the original reading since the -α- in διαδούς was more probably left out than added.

²⁰⁷³ "Syria" likely refers to the region thus called and not to the Roman province of Syria. The region lies roughly north of Herod's kingdom and the Decapolis (see the note to "the cities nearby" above), except for the city of Damascus, which is part of Syria (further references in *Ant.* 15.88 with the note to "Syria").

²⁰⁷⁴ Herod's profit may imply that the distribution of seed was a transaction, such that the Syrians were to pay back Herod, either *in natura* or with money. In combination with the last part of the sentence Josephus' remark could imply that the Syrians had a very generous harvest, which allowed them to feed everybody and pay back Herod.

²⁰⁷⁵ The noun χάρις can mean "good deed, favor" (see *Ant.* 15.16 with the note to "that his favor would be remembered" and Rengstorf *s.v.*). The verb εὐστοχέω further occurs in *War* 1.287; *Ant.* 5.273. LSJ (*s.v.*) give "(blessing) seasonably granted" as meaning here. Instead of εὐστοχηθείσης MSS PFV read εὐθὺς τε χυθείσης ("was shed immediately"), which must be a scribal mistake (it also destroys the word play and alliteration in the phrase εὐστοχηθείσης εἰς εὐφορίαν τῆς χάριτος). The reading ἀστοχηθείσης ("went wrong") of E (Niese 388) does not fit the context and must also be secondary. Herod's purchase was successful because the sowing resulted in a good harvest.

²⁰⁷⁶ The phrase τὰ περὶ τὰς τροφὰς further occurs in *Ant.* 15.309 (which passage also includes the phrase παρέχων ἑτοίμας τὰς τροφὰς ["providing them with the

everybody.²⁰⁷⁷ **312** In short, when the harvest time for the land arrived,²⁰⁷⁸ he sent out over the countryside no fewer than 50,000 men,²⁰⁷⁹ whom he himself had fed²⁰⁸⁰ and kept alive.²⁰⁸¹ In this way he restored his ruined kingdom²⁰⁸² with every kind of effort and care,²⁰⁸³ and not least he also supported the surrounding peoples²⁰⁸⁴ who were in the same distress.²⁰⁸⁵ **313** For no one who had appealed to him out of need²⁰⁸⁶ was left behind without receiving appropriate help:²⁰⁸⁷ peoples, cities, as well as all the private persons²⁰⁸⁸ who got in distress because they were supporting the common people²⁰⁸⁹ received what they asked for when they fled to him for refuge.²⁰⁹⁰ **314** This amounted, when he was

---

food ready-prepared"]) in connection with Herod's arrangements for the Jews.

²⁰⁷⁷ The word context implies that "everybody" refers to the Syrians (see the note to "the people in Syria" above).

²⁰⁷⁸ The translation is based on Niese's reading ὑποφανέντος, attested by most MSS (Niese 388). Niese minor (310) reads "(when the harvest time ...) was starting," with MS W.

²⁰⁷⁹ There is no external evidence in support of this high number, but the analysis of Pastor (2007) leads to the conclusion that Josephus' report of the famine and Herod's aid is all in all plausible in the light of famine studies and common knowledge about the agricultural society of Palestine at the turn of our era.

²⁰⁸⁰ Niese (388) reads ἔθρεψε ("fed") with MSS PF and E. Most MSS read ἐξέθρεψε(ν) ("brought up"), which does not fit the context and is probably a scribal error, possibly under biblical influence (cf. the phrase περιεποιήσατο καὶ ἐξέθρεψεν ["he [i.e., the poor man] brought it [i.e., the ewe lamb] up and it grew up with him"] in Nathan's parable about the little ewe lamb, LXX 2 Sam 12:3).

²⁰⁸¹ The sentence seems to imply that Herod sent out these men to help with the harvest, presumably because the local people had become very weak. This presupposes that Herod also had provided his own subjects with seed (as he had done for the people of Syria; see *Ant.* 15.311). The verb περιποιέω means "save, keep alive" here (Rengstorf *s.v.*).

²⁰⁸² The phrase τὴν βασιλείαν ἀναλαμβάνω ("restore the kingdom") also occurs in Plutarch, *Ant.* 3.4; Cassius Dio 40.9.

²⁰⁸³ For φιλοτιμία ("effort, munificence, etc."), see *Ant.* 15.271 with the note to "ambition" (the noun also occurs in 15.296, 303). For phrases similar to ὑπὸ φιλοτιμίας καὶ σπουδῆς, cf. Polybius 31.12.9; Philo, *Mos.* 2.136; Josephus, *Ant.* 6.292; 7.380; 10.25; 12.83; 14.154; Plutarch, *Aem.* 10.2; *Mor.* (*Stoic. rep.*) 1036b; Cassius Dio 36.24.5.

²⁰⁸⁴ This phrase connects with the reference to the neighboring cities and the inhabitants of Syria (see *Ant.* 15.311 with the note to "the people in Syria"; at least those parts of Syria north and northeast of Herod's kingdom). Other nearby regions were Nabatea (south and southeast of Judea) and Perea (east of the Jordan).

²⁰⁸⁵ The noun κακοπάθεια ("distress, need"; see *Ant.* 15.251 with the note to "under great pains") echoes the participle κακωθεῖσαν ("ruined") in the previous subclause.

²⁰⁸⁶ The phrase ὑπὸ χρείας ("out of need") further occurs in the Herod narrative of *Antiquities* in 15.262 (see the note to "all the need and suffering") and 16.221 (cf. a related phrase in *Ant.* 1.287)

²⁰⁸⁷ Josephus formulates twice that everybody who had appealed to Herod for help was heard: first in a negative clause ("no one was left behind") and subsequently in an enumeration of categories who received help (peoples, cities, and private citizens; see the next note). He does not differentiate between Jews and non-Jews here (cf. *Ant.* 15.311-312) and the next paragraph implies that he intends both.

For the noun βοήθεια ("help"), see *Ant.* 15.307 with the note to "this help." The prepositional phrase κατ' ἀξίαν/κατὰ τὴν ἀξίαν ("properly, deservedly," Rengstorf *s.v.* ἀξία) further occurs in the Herod narrative of *Antiquities* in 15.20; 16.54, 94, 212 (cf. *War* 1.511 concerning Herod and *War* 7.274; *Ant.* 12.210).

²⁰⁸⁸ Josephus mentions 3 categories of groups: peoples (δῆμος, i.e., the collective body of the citizens of a state as well as its assembly; LSJ *s.v.* III), cities (πόλις "[city-] state," LSJ *s.v.* III), and private citizens (ἰδιώτης "private person, ordinary citizen," Rengstorf *s.v.*; see also *Ant.* 15.2 with the note to "a commoner" as well as the next note). For a similar list, cf. Cassius Dio 71.27.3 according to the excerpts of Joannes Antiochenus (ed. Boissevain 3.761).

²⁰⁸⁹ The 3 categories mentioned (see the previous note) differ from the common people (οἱ πλείονες) because they are responsible for the people (the third category probably refers to rich private persons who acted as benefactors of their cities and/or peoples). The verb προΐσταμαι means "support, protect" here (LSJ *s.v.* προΐστημι B II.3; cf. Herod's role as patron or protector [προστάτης] of the Nabateans, *Ant.* 15.159).

²⁰⁹⁰ The phrase ἐπ' αὐτὸν καταφεύγω ("flee to him

making the calculation, to a total of 10,000 *kor*[2091] of cereals—and the *kor* equals ten Attic *medimnoi*[2092]—that were given outside of his realm[2093] and to about 8,000 inside his kingdom.[2094] **315** This care he provided[2095] and the perfect timing[2096] of his support happened to have such a strong impact on the Jews and to be common talk among the other peoples[2097] that the earlier hatred[2098]—aroused by the change of some of the customs[2099]—departed from the kingdom as well as the entire [Jewish] people.[2100] His munificence[2101] in the form

---

for refuge") also occurs in *Ant.* 15.307, in a reference to Petronius.

[2091] The noun κόρος ("*kor*," Rengstorf *s.v.*) is the transcription of the Hebrew dry measure *kōr*, which is used, among other things, for grain (1 Kgs 5:2, 25; Luke 16:7; KBL 2.472, and see the next note).

[2092] The μέδιμνος is a Greek grain measure and exists in an Attic and a Sicilian version (Herodotus 1.192; Polybius 2.15.1; Josephus, *Ant.* 3.321; LSJ *s.v.*). The Attic *medimnos* equals a bushel and a half (i.e., 52.857 liters). Josephus' equation of the *kōr* measure with 10 Attic *medimnoi* is probably incorrect; most scholars assume that the *kōr* equals ca. 7 Attic *medimnoi* (for a different equation, cf. *Ant.* 3.321; Marcus-Wikgren 150 n. *a*; Feldman in BJP 3 on *Ant.* 3.321). GELS (2.264) gives ca. 450 liters for the *kōr* measure, but other scholars propose 370 or 395 liters. LSJ (*s.v.*) state that the *kōr* roughly equals 120 gallons (see also Pastor 2007: 339 n. 17 with references).

[2093] Interestingly, the people outside of Herod's kingdom are mentioned first among those benefiting from Herod's aid, although the amount of grain given to them is far less than that given to Herod's subjects. These foreigners are referred to already in *Ant.* 15.311 ("the cities nearby" and "the people in Syria"), which may indicate that Josephus (or his source) was writing primarily for a non-Jewish audience (Mason 1998; van Henten and Huitink 2009).

[2094] Applebaum (1976: 669) calculates that the 80,000 *kōr* equal 28,155.6 ton of grain.

[2095] The key word ἐπιμέλεια ("care"; see *Ant.* 15.310 with the note to "arranged") introduces and resumes the 2 subsequent paragraphs that describe the impact of Herod's aid on the inhabitants of Herod's kingdom and on the foreigners: Josephus first deals with the king's Jewish subjects (15.315) and then with the non-Jews (15.316).

[2096] For the noun εὐκαιρία ("right moment, suitable time, opportunity") in the Herod narrative of *Antiquities*, see 15.59 with the note to "an opportunity for revenge."

[2097] Various groups of non-Jews have been mentioned in the preceding episode: "the neighboring people" (*Ant.* 15.305), "the cities nearby ... the people in Syria" (15.311), "the surrounding peoples" (15.312), "peoples, cities, as well as all the private persons" (15.313), and "(those) outside of his realm" (15.314).

[2098] In the preceding Herod narrative Josephus has mentioned several times that the king was hated by a considerable part of his subjects (e.g., *Ant.* 15.8, 10, 71, 286; see the next note).

For the phrase τὰ πάλαι μίση, cf. *War* 7.363, in which passage Josephus recalls "the old hatred" (τὸ παλαιὸν μῖσος) of the non-Jewish inhabitants of Caesarea Maritima towards their Jewish fellow citizens in order to explain the murder of Caesarea's Jewish inhabitants by the non-Jewish crowd.

[2099] A combination of a reference to the hatred of Herod by his subjects and an accusation that the king changed the Jewish practices occurs in the report about Herod's festival in Octavian's honor and its aftermath (the change of the Jewish customs [τὰ ἔθη] is described in *Ant.* 15.267-268, 274, 281, 286, 288, the hatred towards Herod in 15.286; see the note to "the hatred he well knew the masses had for him"). Here Josephus may hint at that episode. The hatred towards Herod mentioned in both instances may reflect Josephus' own view rather than that of the majority of the Jewish population (see 15.267 with the note to "foreign habits").

The verb παραχαράττω ("alter") also occurs in *Ant.* 5.306, concerning Samson (who changed, in the company of Delilah, the way of life he grew up with), and in 15.328 about Herod, who "was forced to depart from the Jewish customs and to change many of their practices (πολλὰ τῶν νομίμων παραχαράττειν)" because of his intention to please Octavian (the verb παραχαράττω also occurs in *War* 1.529, with the meaning "falsify," Rengstorf *s.v.*).

[2100] The transmitted Greek text is perhaps corrupt. With Niese (388) the present translation follows the text καὶ τῆς βασιλείας ἐξαιρεθῆναι καὶ τοῦ παντὸς ἔθνους, which is attested by MSS AM, but it should be noted that no further passage in Josephus combines τὰ ἔθη ("the customs", mentioned just before the phrase) with ἡ βασιλεία ("the kingdom/rule") in this way. The reading of MSS PFLVWE leaves out the second καί: "that the earlier hatred—aroused by the change of some of the customs of the kingdom—departed from the entire [Jewish] people." This reading makes more sense, but it is the easier reading and therefore probably not original.

[2101] The noun φιλοτιμία ("munificence") is a further

of aid[2102] in their most terrible distress appeared to be [their] compensation.[2103] **316** He was also famous among the foreign peoples.[2104] It seemed that the calamity that befell him[2105] was beyond description,[2106] but, although it had devastated his kingdom,[2107] it greatly contributed to his good reputation.[2108] For by showing himself[2109] generous beyond expectation[2110] during the disaster,[2111] he completely overturned [the opinion] of the masses,[2112] such that from the beginning onward[2113] he seemed to be unlike the [king] experienced during the earlier events[2114] but like the [king who had] provided care[2115] in their need.[2116]

---

key word in the episode about the drought and the subsequent famine (see *Ant.* 15.303, 312, 315 [with notes], also referring to Herod; cf. 15.296, 298, 328).

[2102] The noun βοήθεια ("help") is also a key word in this episode (see *Ant.* 15.307 with the note to "help").

[2103] Josephus suggests that in the opinion of Herod's subjects the king's aid made up for his changes of the Jewish customs, but this is not very convincing in the light of the previous narrative. Persons like the conspirators against Herod (*Ant.* 15.280-288), who were willing to sacrifice their lives for maintaining the customs, no doubt remained very critical of Herod. The statement may reflect Josephus' own voice and his mainly negative interpretation of Herod's rule.

The rare noun ἀντικατάλλαγμα ("compensation," Rengstorf *s.v.*; in LSJ *s.v.* "satisfaction") is a *hapax legomenon* in Josephus (cf. Onosander 35.4; Pseudo-Socrates, *Ep.* 6.10; Epiphanius, *Haer.* 64.59.1 [ed. Holl 2.494]).

[2104] Obviously Herod's aid to the various groups of non-Jews (*Ant.* 15.311-314) greatly enhanced his reputation among them. The phrase οἱ ἔξωθεν ("the foreigners," also *War* 1.359; 4.179) echoes ἔξω τῆς ἀρχῆς ("[those] outside of his realm") of *Ant.* 15.314 (see the note to "outside of his realm"). For εὔκλεια ("good reputation, renown") concerning Herod, cf. 16.184; 17.163.

[2105] Concerning the phrase τὰ δυσχερῆ συμβαίνω ("the calamity ... befell"), cf. *Ant.* 15.283 (with the note to "something bad" about δυσχερής) concerning the blind man and his fellow conspirators against Herod: "... he [i.e., the blind man] held himself ready to suffer if something bad happened to them (εἴ τι ... συμβαίνοι δυσχερές)," and Euripides, *Fragm.* 963.3 (ed. Kannicht 963); Aristotle, *Cael.* 304a; Demosthenes, *Or.* 39.19; Plutarch, *Mor.* (*Cons. Apoll.*) 102f; (*Def. orac.*) 437b.

[2106] Cf. *Ant.* 5.350 about God's revelation to Samuel concerning the Philistine victory over Israel (1 Sam 3-4): "And God said: 'since you are available, learn of the misfortune—beyond the words and belief of those involved—that will happen to the Israelites (μάνθανε συμφορὰν Ἰσραηλίταις ἐσομένην λόγου μείζονα) ..." (trans. Begg in BJP 4).

[2107] The phrase κακώσαντα τὴν βασιλείαν ("[the calamity had] devastated his kingdom") links up with κακωθεῖσαν αὐτῷ τὴν βασιλείαν ("his ruined kingdom") of *Ant.* 15.312 (cf. 8.303).

[2108] Cf. *Ant.* 16.272, 396 about Herod's reputation or fame (εὐδοξία). The first passage is neutral or even positive, like the current remark; the second is clearly negative and highlights the king's hunger for glory: "(Herod ...) who was insensible and excessive in his desire for the rule and every other fame" (my trans.).

[2109] The participle ἐπιδειξάμενος ("showing himself") echoes ἐπίδειξις ("demonstration") of *Ant.* 15.308.

[2110] The adjective μεγαλόψυχος ("generous, magnanimous") also occurs in *Ant.* 15.201, concerning Herod's extraordinarily generous support of Octavian. About μεγαλοψυχία ("generosity, magnanimity") as an important characteristic of Herod, see 15.48 with the note to "enough magnanimity."

[2111] The noun ἀπορία ("difficulty, need") is repeated several times in this section (*Ant.* 15.301, 303, 310, 313, 316).

[2112] Alternative translation: "redefined his relationship with the masses." Josephus apparently switches again to Herod's Jewish subjects since the masses concerned are changing their opinion of Herod (cf. *Ant.* 15.308, 315). The rare verb ἀντιμεθίστημι ("change completely, transform") also occurs in 15.308 (see the note to "completely changed"). Niese (389) reads (ἀντιμετέστησε) τοὺς πολλούς ("[overturned] the majority/masses") with MS P and E, while the other MSS have τοὺς ὄχλους, which basically means the same.

[2113] This subclause concludes the section of the drought and Herod's aid with a rhetorical statement about Herod's performance as king containing 2 parallel phrases introduced by οἷον ("like"). The prepositional phrase ἐξ ὑπαρχῆς ("in/from the beginning, anew") occurs once elsewhere in Josephus (*Ant.* 15.196).

[2114] Josephus speaks about Herod in an indirect way but clearly intends Herod's previous behavior as king, which had been negatively perceived, as several previous passages suggest (e.g., *Ant.* 15.267-291).

For the phrase ἡ πεῖρα τῶν πάλαι γεγενημένων ("the experience during the earlier events"), cf. the expression πεῖρα τῶν ἤδη γεγενημένων ("through what has already

(9.3) 317 About that time[2117] he also sent an auxiliary force to Caesar[2118] of 500 special men from his bodyguard,[2119] whom Gallus Aelius[2120] led to[2121] the Red Sea.[2122] They were greatly useful to him [Gallus Aelius].

Brief reports about various events, including a new marriage.
War *1.402; 419-421*

---

happened") in 15.193, which refers to Herod's loyalty towards Mark Antony.

[2115] About the key word ἐπιμέλεια ("care"), see *Ant.* 15.315 with the note to "he provided."

[2116] This positive conclusion concerning Herod's intervention matches Josephus' description of Herod's aid to the Jews and non-Jews in *Ant.* 15.305-316. The exceptional scale of the king's support stands out when compared to the responses of other rulers in similar situations of drought. *Apion* 2.60 brackets Cleopatra VII's suicide with her refusal to give corn to the Alexandrian Jews during a famine in 43/42 BCE (cf. Seneca the Younger, *Mal. bell. civ.* = *Anth. Lat.* no. 462; Appian, *Bell. civ.* 4.108; Becher 1966: 65-66, 87, 116; Barclay in BJP 10 on *Ap.* 2.60). The Romans probably did not care much about Josephus' reproach of her refusal, but it must have been sensitive to Jewish readers, who were familiar with the aid granted by the biblical hero Joseph. Joseph took care of his father and the families of his brothers in Egypt during 7 years of famine (Gen 41:53-47:27; Josephus, *Ant.* 2.93-193). He was for Josephus a prime model of a prudent statesman, also because of his self-control (σωφροσύνη), a ruler's most important virtue (Niehoff 1992; Feldman 1992, and see *Ant.* 15.27 with the note to "sexual pleasures"). Another highly praised person on account of providing food to the Jews is Queen Helena of Adiabene. She bought grain in Alexandria—for a large sum—and dried figs in Cyprus to relieve the Jerusalemites' need during a famine in 46/47 CE (*Ant.* 20.51-53, 101). Herod's behavior can clearly be associated with the exceptional supports given by Joseph and Queen Helena, even though helping his needy citizens belonged to his duties as king. The noun χρεία ("need") also occurs in 15.303, 307, 313 in connection with the crisis caused by the drought.

[2117] The section *Ant.* 15.317-325 is a cluster of brief reports about various events set in roughly the same period (15.317 the military support to Aelius Gallus; 15.318 the building of a new palace in Jerusalem; 15.319-322 the marriage with Mariamme II; and 15.323-325 the building of Herodium). The phrase "about that time" is one of Josephus' formulas that indicate synchrony (related phrases in 7.117; 16.136; 20.15; see van Henten and Huitink 2007: 225-27). The formula links up with the introduction of the previous section about the drought: 15.299 "Now in this year, which was the thirteenth year of Herod's rule ...," such that the date for the information given here seems to be the year Nisan 25/Nisan 24 BCE. However, external evidence concerning Aelius Gallus implies that the event likely preceded the drought (see 15.299 with the notes to "this year" and "the thirteenth year of Herod's rule").

[2118] It is plausible that Herod actually sent this force of allied auxiliary troops (συμμαχικόν; cf. *War* 5.47) not to Octavian but to Aelius Gallus, who is mentioned later in this paragraph. Octavian is mentioned because of Herod's being a friendly king of him (see *Ant.* 15.187-201, especially 15.193, 196, 199), which friendship implied military support in times of trouble (see 15.5 with the note to "gift to Antony").

[2119] This information is confirmed by Strabo 16.4.23, who mentions 500 Jews among the Roman allies. Herod's bodyguard included the 400 Gauls who had been Cleopatra's guards and given to Herod by Octavian (see *Ant.* 15.217 with notes; see also 16.314; 17.55). The Nabatean administrator Syllaeus (see 16.220 with the note to "Syllaeus") led another auxiliary force of 1,000 Nabatean soldiers (Strabo 16.4.23). Herod himself probably did not participate in the campaign (Richardson 1996: 230). Concerning σωματοφύλαξ ("bodyguard"), see 16.314 with the note to "bodyguards".

[2120] Josephus inverts the name of this high Roman official. Aelius Gallus was prefect of Egypt in ca. 26-24 BCE and the predecessor of Petronius (attested in *Ant.* 15.307). He is mentioned several times by the famous historian Strabo of Amaseia, who was one of his friends (Strabo 2.5.12; 16.4.22; 17.1.46; 17.1.53-54; Kienast 1999: 311-12).

[2121] MS P and E, supported by the Latin version, read ἐπί ("to"). In the light of what we know about Aelius Gallus' campaign (see the next note), this probably implies a journey from Alexandria (in Egypt) to the western shore of the Red Sea. MSS FLAMVW read περί ("round about"), which implies that Aelius Gallus went all along the shore of the Red Sea to southern parts of the Arabian peninsula (see the next note).

[2122] Josephus does not give the context of the military support given to Aelius Gallus, but we know from other sources that the prefect launched a campaign against the Sabeans in *Arabia Felix* (southern Arabia, roughly equivalent to the area of contemporary Yemen and Oman; about the campaign see *Res gest. divi Aug.* 26; Strabo 16.4.22-24; Pliny the Elder 6.160; Cassius Dio 53.29.3; Kienast 1999: 335-36 with further references). Aelius Gallus crossed the Red Sea with a fleet and went ashore at Leuce Come, a harbor city at the western coast

318 When matters[2123] were increasingly going well[2124] for him again, he built a palace[2125] in the Upper City.[2126] He erected immensely big chambers[2127] and equipped them with the most expensive decorations[2128] with gold,[2129] precious stones,[2130] and paint,[2131] so that[2132]

---

of the Arabian Peninsula, from where he marched south. Augustus' *Res Gestae* and Pliny indicate that the campaign was a success, but Strabo points out that it was a great failure. Pliny's source may have been Juba (Juba II, ca. 50 BCE–23/24 CE, king of Numidia and Mauretania, and author of a natural history of Arabia), who was close to Augustus (Retsö 2003: 402-03 with footnotes). Strabo puts the blame for it on the Nabatean Syllaeus, who would have sabotaged the operation, which seems unlikely since Syllaeus would have been executed in that case (with Richardson 1996: 230; see also Schürer-Vermes 1.290 with n. 8; Kienast 1999: 335; Schalit 2001: 163-64, 407).

[2123] The expression τὰ πράγματα can have a general meaning here ("the matters") or a more specific meaning ("the government/administration"; see *Ant*. 15.32 with the note to "the government").

[2124] This remark implies that Herod's kingdom had recovered from the severe crisis of the drought (*Ant*. 15.299-316) and that his own financial situation had gone back to normal again. The recovery may have taken several years; Josephus does not specify the period. Schürer-Vermes (1.304-05) date the building of the palace to ca. 24 BCE; Otto (1913: 80), Smallwood (1976: 91), and Schalit (2001: 371) to ca. 23 BCE; Richardson (1996: 225 n. 31) to 22 BCE or later. A clue for the date is Marcus Agrippa's authority to act as Augustus' deputy in the East, which was given in 23 BCE (see *Ant*. 15.350 with the note to "Agrippa"). Agrippa had likely been active for some time in that role before Herod decided to name a room in the palace after him (15.318; cf. Kokkinos 1998: 221-2 with n. 53, who argues that the building activities started in 29/28 BCE and that the project was completed in 23 BCE). Mahieu (2012: 158-62) situates the building of the palace in Herod's 15th year (*B.J.* 1.401-402), converted as the year 25 BCE, and makes it coincide with Herod's other building projects in Jerusalem: the theater, amphitheater, and Temple enclosures.

The prepositional phrase πρὸς ἐπίδοσιν ("increasingly") is found a few times in other authors (Aspasius [ed. Heylbut 19.24]; Aelius Aristides, *Dem*. [ed. Dindorf 2.615, 617]; John Chrysostom, *Exp. Ps.* [PG 55.418]). The verb εὐθηνέω ("thrive, flourish, experience an improvement") is also found in *War* 6.300; *Ant*. 7.297; 9.176.

[2125] This is Herod's second palace, which was newly built by him (for his earlier palace, see *Ant*. 15.43, 71, 247 with notes). It was located in the Upper City in the western part of Jerusalem (see the next note and *War* 1.402), adjacent to the three towers Mariamme, Hippicus, and Phasael (*War* 5.175, 183), which meant that the palace was part of Jerusalem's fortifications (see also *Ant*. 15.292 with the note to "the palace in which he lived"). The palace was situated south of these towers, along the western city wall, which was thickened at the palace's place. Archaeological remains confirm this location. *War* 5.176-181 describes the second palace in detail (further discussion in Schalit 2001: 371-72; Netzer 2006: 129-32).

The verb ἐξοικοδομέω ("build, construct, furnish [with]") occurs in Josephus only in the Herod narrative of *Antiquities* (15.318, 324, 425; 16.13; Rengstorf *s.v.*).

[2126] The phrase ἡ ἄνω πόλις ("the Upper City") also occurs in *War* 1.39, 402; 2.424, 426, 530; 5.11, 245, 252, 260, 356, 445; 6.325, 363, 374; 7.26; *Ant*. 7.66; 14.477. The Upper City existed already before the Babylonian captivity, the City of David being too small to host all of Jerusalem's inhabitants. It was located southwest of the Temple and west of the City of David, from which it was separated by the Tyropoeon Valley (the Valley of the Cheesemakers). The first city wall enclosed the Upper City at the west and north sides until Herod's day (*War* 5.142-145; Netzer 2006: 119-21 with a map on p. 121).

[2127] The noun οἶκος, which is also used in the parallel passage of *War* (1.402), usually means "house" or "dwelling-place," but it can also refer to a room, chamber, or dining hall (LSJ *s.v.* I.2). The translation "dining hall" is particularly appropriate here, especially since Josephus seems to hint at huge banquet halls (see the note to "couches that could hold numerous people" and Netzer 2006: 131, who notes that Herod's palace in Jericho also included a gigantic reception and banquet hall, a *triclinium*). The chambers are most probably the two rooms mentioned at the end of this paragraph. *War* 5.177 mentions huge chambers and guestrooms with 100 couches. The adjective ὑπερμεγέθης ("gigantic") further occurs in *Ant*. 15.334 concerning the huge stones that were sank down in Herod's harbor at Caesarea.

[2128] The more elaborate passage about the palace in *War* 5.176-181 notes that the palace was unsurpassed with regard to the costly materials used and the craftsmanship (οὔτε γὰρ πολυτελείας οὔτε κατασκευῆς τινος ἔλειπεν ὑπερβολήν).

[2129] *War* 5.179 refers to silver and gold.

[2130] Precious stones are also mentioned in *War* 5.178.

[2131] The chambers' decorations are clearly extraordinary, but the precise details remain unclear. The meaning

BOOK FIFTEEN   229

each of them had couches that could hold numerous people.[2133] [They varied][2134] in size and name; one was called Caesar's room[2135] and the other Agrippa's[2136] room.

319 He also took a wife for himself.[2137] This was motivated out of sexual desire[2138] because he had no scruples[2139] about living [only] for his own pleasure.[2140] The beginning

---

of the extremely rare last word of the description (περιάλειμμα, which is a *hapax legomenon* in Josephus) is uncertain. LSJ (*s.v.*) gives "pigment" as meaning for this passage, while Rengstorf (*s.v.*) offers "paint, pigment (?)" as meaning. Several conjectures have been proposed for this passage; nevertheless, Hudson's (1726: 771) κατακλιμάτων (meaning unclear, the word is missing in LSJ) as well as Ernesti's (1795: 132) καταποικιλμάτων ("brocades" ?) or περιπετασμάτων ("covering" ?) are hardly an improvement. Niese (389) suspects a lacuna.

[2132] The passage does not connect well with the preceding one about the decorations, which supports Niese's assumption of a lacuna (see the preceding note). According to the current text Josephus switches without any transition from the decorations to the rooms' sizes.

[2133] The noun κλισία means "(banquet) couch, group of guests" (Rengstorf *s.v.*). The word occurs twice elsewhere in Josephus. One of these passages concerns the 72 men who translated the Hebrew Bible into the Greek LXX for Ptolemy Philadelphus (*Ant.* 12.96) and offers an interesting parallel: Ptolemy is so happy with his guests that he organizes a banquet lasting for 12 days (12.98); couches for the guests are ranged in two rows next to or behind Ptolemy's couch, which presupposes a large room functioning as a banquet hall.

[2134] The Greek text is most probably corrupt. Niese (389) supposes a lacuna after ὑποδέχεσθαι: a verb is missing, which is here tentatively added (with Marcus-Wikgren 153).

[2135] Cf. *War* 1.402 (see the next notes). Herod also named two cities after Augustus: Samaria (Sebaste, *Ant.* 15.246, 292, 296, 342) and Straton's Tower (Caesarea Maritima, 15.331-341).

[2136] *War* 1.402 likewise mentions that Herod's palace in Jerusalem contained two very large and extremely beautiful rooms (or buildings; see the note to "chambers" above) named "Caesareum" and "Agrippeum," adding that they were named after Herod's most important "friends" (i.e., Augustus and Marcus Agrippa, Reinhold 1933; Schalit 1968: 3; Roddaz 1984; Taylor 2006: 566). Herod also named new buildings in Jericho after Augustus and Agrippa (*War* 1.407) and Agrippa's name was inscribed on one of the gates of the Temple (1.416).

Marcus Vipsanius Agrippa is here mentioned for the first time in book 15 of *Antiquities* (references in 15.350 with the notes to "Agrippa" and "Caesar's deputy"; see Braund 1984: 82, 122 on ways of honoring one's patrons and the importance of the friendship between Herod and Agrippa).

[2137] *Ant.* 15.319-322 briefly reports Herod's decision to enter into a new marriage, with another Mariamme, the daughter of a priest called Simon (15.320). There is no parallel account in *War*. The phrase προσελάμβανε γάμον αὑτῷ may link up with a biblical convention since in the Bible "taking a wife (for himself)" sometimes indicates the beginning of a marital relationship: "Lamech took two wives; the name of the one was Adah, and the name of the other Zillah" (Gen 4:19); "Abraham took another wife, whose name was Keturah" (Gen 25:1; also Gen 24:4; 34:16; Ruth 1:4; 2 Chr 11:21; 13:21; Ezra 10:44). For related vocabulary in Josephus, see 15.321 with the note to "marry the maiden." The chronological order of the narrative suggests that this new marriage took place in ca. 23 BCE (see 15.318 with the note to "were increasingly going well"). Schürer-Vermes (1.320), Richardson (1996: 235), and Vogel (2002: 121) refer to 24 BCE; Mahieu (2012: 189-90) to 25 BCE. Kokkinos (1998: 221-22) dates it to 29/28 BCE (his date is followed by Günther 2005: 238) and argues that Josephus' association of the marriage with the completion of Herod's new palace (see the previous paragraph and 15.292) is misleading because it actually coincided with the beginning of the building activities in 29/28 BCE. Additional arguments in favor of Kokkinos' hypothesis are the implausibility that Herod remained without a wife for several years after the death of Mariamme I (i.e., during the period 29/28-23 BCE) and that his son by Mariamme II, Herod III, was probably ca. 20 rather than ca. 15 years old (the age implied if the marriage took place in 23 BCE) when he became the designated heir to the throne second after Antipater (*War* 1.573, 588, 600; *Ant.* 17.53, 78). Kokkinos' interpretation implies that *Ant.* 15.319-323 is a flashback.

[2138] Josephus states in plain words that Herod's motivation for this new marriage was sexual desire (κινηθεὶς ἐξ ἐρωτικῆς ἐπιθυμίας). For ἔρως ("[sexual] love"), see Rengstorf (*s.v.*) and *Ant.* 15.29 with the note to "erotic diversion", and for ἐπιθυμία ("desire, [sexual] lust"), 15.88 with the note to "his passion for her."

[2139] The rare noun ὑπολογισμός ("reflection, scruple," Rengstorf *s.v.*) is a *hapax legomenon* in Josephus.

[2140] The passage is ambiguous because the adjective οἰκεῖος can be interpreted in two different ways: it can indicate family matters and family relations, but also one's own interests or issues (Rengstorf *s.v.*). The first meaning implies as translation "because he had no high regard for a happy family life." The second interpretation

of his marriage was as follows. **320** There was a Simon from Jerusalem,[2141] a son of a certain Boethus from Alexandria,[2142] who was one of the distinguished priests. He[2143] had a daughter[2144] who was considered to be the most beautiful of the women of that time.[2145] **321** So when there was common talk among the Jerusalemites[2146] about her, Herod was initially excited[2147] by the report,[2148] but when he saw her,[2149] the beauty of the girl overwhelmed him.[2150] Yet he rejected[2151] the thought of accomplishing everything by using

---

is more plausible, especially since in a similar passage in Josephus the biblical Joseph explains his refusal to sleep with Mrs. Potiphar as follows: "but it was for the sake of virtue and self-control that we were condemned to endure the punishment of evil-doers, since I did not wish, for the sake of my own pleasure (μετ' οἰκείας ἡδονῆς), to insult the one who had done these things for us" (*Ant.* 2.69, trans. Feldman in BJP 3). Non-Jewish passages that combine οἰκεῖος and ἡδονή ("desire, pleasure") also support the second interpretation (see especially Plato, *Resp.* 587b, who associates true and personal pleasures with kingship).

[2141] The priest Simon, son of Boethus, is also mentioned in *Ant.* 15.322; 17.78; 18.109, 136 but not in *War* (Schalit 1968: 113). The explicit reference to Jerusalem may intend to contrast him with Ananel, a former High Priest appointed by Herod, who was of Babylonian origin (see 15.22 with the note to "Ananel").

[2142] Simon's father Boethus came from Alexandria. The family of Boethus developed into one of the families of the High Priesthood (see *Ant.* 15.322 with the note to "the office"). *Ant.* 19.297 mentions another Simon, son of Boethus, who was appointed High Priest by Agrippa I (Schalit 1968: 113).

[2143] I.e., Simon. Schürer-Vermes (1.320-21; 2.229) indicate that other passages mention Boethus as the father of the woman (cf. Richardson 1996: 243) but do not offer specific references. Some scholars deduce from *Ant.* 19.297 (see the previous note) that she was the daughter of Boethus since it refers to Boethus as a father and directly afterwards to a daughter married to Herod (see especially Schwartz 1990: 185-86). Schalit (1968: 28) rejects such a reading because the reference to Boethus as a father is part of a parenthesis and his fatherhood does not concern the woman in question. Stern (1976a: 605) argues that Josephus made a mistake in 19.297 and that he meant to refer to Simon ben Boethus as the father of the woman. Kokkinos (1998: 220) argues that Boethus functions as a family name in 19.297 and that Simon ben Boethus is implied, also because he is mentioned elsewhere as father of the woman (17.78; 18.109, 136). Unfortunately the references in the *War* (1.562, 573, 599, see the next note) do not mention the name of this priest. The name Simon Boethus resembles the inscription "Shimon Bothon" (שמון בוטון, *šimôn bôṭôn*) found on an ossuary from Jerusalem (*CIJ* no. 1246; Kokkinos 1998: 218 n. 40; Ilan 2002: 348).

[2144] *War* (1.562, 573, 599) mentions her name, Mariamme, and also indicates that she was "the daughter of the High Priest." Her son by Herod, also named Herod (Herod III), is mentioned in *War* 1.562, 573 (further references in Kokkinos 1998: 207-08; 222-23; 265-68).

[2145] This statement clarifies Herod's behavior described in the next two paragraphs, which characterize Herod as a powerful macho man who can easily afford to take the most beautiful woman and arrange a marriage with her. The translation follows Niese (389), who reads καλλίστην τῶν τότε νομιζομένην with MS P. The other Greek MSS read καλλίστην τῶν τότε νομιζομένων ("the most beautiful [woman] as people at that time thought").

[2146] For similar vocabulary, see *Ant.* 15.71 about the rumor in Jerusalem that Mark Antony had tortured and killed Herod.

[2147] The subsequent lines and the next paragraph focalize Herod, describing his feelings and his strategy to acquire this remarkable woman. The verb κίνεω ("move, arouse, be excited [in the passive voice]") also occurs in the introductory passage about Herod's new marriage (*Ant.* 15.319).

[2148] By first referring to an anonymous report about the fame of this Mariamme and subsequently describing Herod's response to the beauty of the girl Josephus creates a climax that highlights her exceptional beauty. Josephus builds this climax by two steps (indicated by τὸ μὲν πρῶτον and ὡς δὲ καί) that differentiate between two senses: he first focuses on Herod *hearing* about the priest's daughter and then on the king actually *seeing* her. Josephus does not tell whether Herod was actually searching for a new wife, neither whether he arranged for a meeting or saw the girl by coincidence.

[2149] Although Josephus does not say so explicitly, it is plausible that Herod made arrangements for a meeting with the girl. That implies that Herod wanted to see for himself, and apparently only by seeing the girl Herod realized how exceptionally beautiful she was (see the previous note).

[2150] Josephus uses the noun ὥρα ("beauty") also in *Ant.* 15.25, 29, 60, when he refers to the exceptional beauty of Mariamme I and her brother Aristobulus III.

his authority,[2152] suspecting, which was true, that he would be accused of using force[2153] as well as of tyrannical behavior.[2154] Therefore he considered it better to marry the maiden.[2155] **322** Because Simon was not illustrious enough for his family[2156] but too important to be treated with contempt, he pursued his desire[2157] in a quite reasonable way, by increasing their status and making them more glorious.[2158] Indeed he immediately removed the High Priesthood[2159] from Jesus, the son of Phabes.[2160] He appointed Simon to

---

The combination of ἐκπλήσσω ("astonish, etc.") with ὥρα also occurs in Plutarch, *Alc.* 4.1, concerning Alcibiades.

[2151] The verb ἀποδοκιμάζω ("reject," Rengstorf *s.v.*) is a *hapax legomenon* in Josephus.

[2152] The phrase ἀπ' ἐξουσίας ("by ... his authority") is used with this same meaning in *Ant.* 15.43, 260 (see the note to "on her own authority"), although it could here also refer to Herod's power (cf. 6.61). It may hint at Herod's apparent inclination to tyrannical behavior, which shines through in several passages in the Herod narrative of *Antiquities* (e.g. 15.6-7, 252; 16.4; see the note to "tyrannical behavior" below). *Ant.* 19.65 notes about Calistus, a freedman of Gaius: "His power was no less than a tyrant's. For he was a great taker of bribes, and most contemptuous of rights, with none to match him. His authority had been exercised beyond all reason (ἐξουσίᾳ χρησάμενος παρὰ τὸ εἰκός)" (trans. Feldman). Herod could easily have used his authority or power to bring the girl over to his palace; it is significant that he did not do so.

[2153] Cf. *Ant.* 15.277 concerning the protest against the trophies, in which case too Herod decides not to apply force.

[2154] Josephus hints here at Herod's use of force and at the king's tyrannical behavior (εἰς βίαν καὶ τυραννίδα διαβληθήσεται) but reports that Herod decided to handle this in a prudent way in order to save his reputation. Nevertheless, the suggestion that Herod was a tyrant is made once more. For βία ("force") and τυραννίς ("tyranny") as parts of the semantic field of tyranny in connection with Herod, see *Ant.* 14.165, a passage that expresses the fear of prominent Jews of Antipater (Herod's father) and his sons, with the focus on Herod: "But the chief Jews were in great fear when they saw how violent and bold Herod was, and how much he longed for a rule as a tyrant (ὁρῶντες τὸν Ἡρώδην βίαιον καὶ τολμηρὸν καὶ τυραννίδος γλιχόμενον)." The immediate cause of this fear was Herod's execution of Ezekias and his fellow brigands (14.159, 165-169). About the semantic field of tyranny, cf. *War* 7.261 referring to the so-called *Sicarii* ("dagger people"; see *War* 2.255) and *Ant.* 5.339 referring to the sons of Eli (further discussion in van Henten 2011b).

[2155] The decision to marry the girl implied that Herod needed permission from her father for the marriage. This is already apparent from biblical passages. In *Ant.* 1.337-338 Sychem arranges for his father Emmor to get permission from Jacob to marry Dinah (Gen 34): "And Sychemmes ... being amorously disposed toward her, he implored his father to take the maiden in marriage for him (ἱκετεύει τὸν πατέρα λαβεῖν αὐτῷ πρὸς γάμον τὴν κόρην)" (*Ant.* 1.337, trans. Feldman in BJP 3). Cf. also 1.242-252 (esp. 1.253) concerning Abraham's servant asking Laban, Rebecca's brother, and her mother permission for Isaac to marry Rebecca. In ancient Judaism marriage was a contract which determined the *môhar* (bride price) and dowry as economic protections of the wife and which presupposed the consent of the wife's father (see the conclusion of this paragraph, Tob 7:12-13, and the discussion in Collins 1997: 107-15). In *Ant.* 14.300 Josephus mentions Herod's engagement with Mariamme in a passage in which he also refers to Herod's first wife, Doris, by way of a flashback. Josephus writes about this engagement : "And when he [i.e., Herod] arrived in Jerusalem, Hyrcanus [i.e., Hyrcanus II] and the people wreathed his head with crowns. As Herod had already become connected by an agreement of marriage (ἐγεγάμβρευτο ... καθ' ὁμολογίαν) with the family of Hyrcanus, he [Hyrcanus] was for that reason more protective of him ... (trans. Marcus)."

[2156] I.e., Herod's family. This detail implies that the status of Herod's future wife's family was important for Herod. Mariamme I had descended from the Hasmonean royal and high priestly family (see *Ant.* 15.23 with notes), and the new Mariamme could not compare unfavorably with her.

[2157] This phrase with ἐπιθυμία ("desire") links up with *Ant.* 15.319 (see the note to "sexual desire").

[2158] Herod's policy is fully consistent with his reasoning indicated in the previous lines; the decision to give the High Priesthood to Simon, reported in the next sentence, is the logical outcome. Obviously Herod could not arrange for a royal status of Simon's family, but by making Simon High Priest Mariamme II equaled her predecessor at least partly in rank.

[2159] Similar formulation in *Ant.* 15.39, in which passage Josephus mentions that Herod deposed Ananel as High Priest.

[2160] Jesus, the son of Phabes, is mentioned only once as High Priest in Josephus (Schalit 1968: 60). Josephus does not indicate when Jesus was appointed. Jesus's

the office[2161] and contracted the marriage with him.[2162]

(9.4) 323 After his marriage was performed,[2163] he built another fortress[2164] near the areas in which he had defeated the Jews[2165] when Antigonus[2166] was controlling the political

---

father's Greek name (or his family name) is spelled out in various ways in the MSS (also Phoabes and Phobes, Niese 390). Schürer-Vermes (2.229 n. 6) indicate that the correct name is Phiabi, which form is attested in Rabbinic sources. Kasher (1985: 119-35), Stern (1974b: 274; 1976a: 604-05, 607), Hengel (1989: 14), Richardson (1996: 244-45), and Kokkinos (1998: 217-18) argue that Jesus, son of Phiabi, came from Egypt and descended from Onias III (?), who had founded a Jewish temple at Leontopolis (cf. Vogel 2002: 121, who considers this connection to be possible). Through his appointment Herod perhaps attempted to connect both this Zadokite family and the Egyptian Jews closer with his kingdom. Some support for this hypothesis is found in the fact that a Greek version of the name (Phabeis) is attested in a funerary inscription from Tell el-Yehudiye (Leontopolis, *CIJ* no. 1510 = *JIGRE* no. 33 l. 5 with pp. 69, 72). Josephus mentions two other High Priests from the family of Phabi: Ishmael, son of Phabi (*Ant.* 18.34, High Priest in 15-16 CE), and another Ishmael, son of Phabi (20.179, 194-195, High Priest in 59-61 CE, Schürer-Vermes 2.229-31). He also mentions several persons with the name Jesus (Hebrew or Aramaic equivalents: Jehoshua, Joshua, and Jeshua), which was a common name in the Second Temple period (Ilan 2002: 126-29), and distinguishes between them by adding the name of their father or the surname (Schürer-Vermes 1.431 n. 5 provide a list).

[2161] This may have been the beginning of the close connection of the family of Boethus with the High Priesthood. From Herod's time onward the High Priesthood became the prerogative of a few priestly families: the family of Phiabi (see the previous note), that of Ananus or Annas, and that of Boethus (Schürer-Vermes 2.229-34). It is possible—though not probable—that Ananel was the first High Priest from the family of Boethus (Schürer-Vermes 2.229 with n. 5, but cf. *Ant.* 15.22 with the note to "Ananel"). *Ant.* 17.78 reports that Herod later deposed Simon the son of Boethus as High Priest.

[2162] This final statement indicates that Mariamme's father was a decisive factor in the arrangement of the marriage (see also *Ant.* 15.321 with the note to "marry the maiden"). The High Priesthood greatly enhanced the status of Simon's family, as stated previously in this paragraph.

[2163] This chronological marker forms the transition between the report about the marriage between Herod and Mariamme II (*Ant.* 15.319-322) and that about the building of a new fortress (15.323-325; cf. *War* 1.419-421).

The phrase κῆδος συνάπτω ("form an alliance through marriage, contract a marriage," LSJ *s.v.* συνάπτω II.2) also occurs in Thucydides 2.29; Philo, *Fug.* 49.

[2164] The fortress was called Herodium (*War* 1.419). The time marker in the previous phrase implies that the fortress was built after the wedding (for the date of the wedding see *Ant.* 15.319 with the note to "took a wife for himself"). Several scholars argue for 24 or 23 BCE, or later. Shatzman (1991: 230) gives ca. 23 BCE as date; Roller (1998: 33, 164) gives 25-22 BCE; Mahieu (2012: 190-91) argues for 25 BCE. Kasher (2007: 181 n. 1) argues for an even earlier date (29/28 BCE), which is connected with his early date for the marriage of Herod and Mariamme II.

The site of Herodium has been identified with Jebel Fureidis, southeast of Bethlehem, ca. 12 km from Jerusalem (Schalit 2001: 357; Netzer 2006: 179). Herodium was a large and unique complex, with a royal residence on top of an adapted and fortified hill as well as a lower cluster of buildings containing a palace and a large pool (see 15.324-325 and the detailed discussion in Netzer 2006: 179-201). The entire site extends over an area of ca. 25 ha. *War* 1.419 mentions two fortresses with the name Herodium and notes that the first one was built "on the mountain towards Arabia" as a remembrance of Herod himself, which matches the context: 1.419 follows a passage with brief notes about other constructions named after relatives of Herod (1.417-418). Since the second fortress was also named after Herod, it was also built in memory of Herod (Netzer 2006: 180). Josephus mentions that Herod was buried at Herodium (*War* 1.669, 673; *Ant.* 17.199; Netzer 2006: 180, 198), but he does not provide details. Prof. Ehud Netzer has claimed having found Herod's tomb near the top of the monumental staircase of the Herodium Fortress at Jebel Fureidis, together with remains of a rare sarcophagus (press conference in Jerusalem on 8 May 2007; lecture at the Netherlands Institute for Advanced Study, Wassenaar, on 3 June 2008). Lichtenberger (1999: 113-15) and Netzer (2006: 181 n. 15) argue that the first Herodium never existed.

Through the verb προσκατεσκευάσατο ("he built another [fortress]") Josephus connects this passage with his report about fortified places built by Herod (*Ant.* 15.292-298).

[2165] The association of the location of the fortress and this defeat implies that the fortress served as a

affairs and he[2167] was deprived of the rule.[2168] **324** This fortress is about sixty stades away from Jerusalem;[2169] it is a natural stronghold and most suitable for construction work.[2170] For there is a hill reasonably close-by,[2171] the top of which has been raised by human hands,[2172] so that it has a circular shape in the form of a breast.[2173] It is provided with a

---

commemoration of Herod's victory, which is pointed out in rather general terms in the next subclause (see the next three notes).

[2166] Josephus refers here to the power struggle between Herod and Antigonus in 40-37/36 BCE, which is also mentioned in 15.1-11 (see 15.1 with the note to "they took Antigonus captive"). The reference to location of the fortress in connection with this victory is missing in the parallel report of *War* (1.419-421) and particularly notable because of the long interval between Herod's triumph over Antigonus (in 37 or 36 BCE (see 15.7 with the note to "at that time") and the building of this fortress in the twenties (see the note to "another fortress" above). Moreover, the conflict ended when Antigonus surrendered in Jerusalem (*Ant.* 14.481; 15.1) rather than in Herodium. Elsewhere Josephus connects the fortress' location with the dramatic flight of Herod and his family from Jerusalem to Masada. During the journey Herod's mother got an accident: her chariot overturned and Herod almost committed suicide. Nevertheless, Herod fought against the Parthians and defeated his Jewish opponents during this trip. *War* 1.265 reports: "In his flight, he found the Judeans even more an encumbrance than the Parthians; they harassed him continually and at a distance of sixty stades from the city, they engaged in a battle that lasted a long time. Here Herod was victorious and he slew many of them. It was here, too, that he founded a city as a memorial to his victory. He adorned it with the most sumptuous palaces and constructed an exceptionally well-fortified citadel, calling it Herodion after his own name" (*War* 1.265, trans. Sievers/Forte in BJP 1a; cf. *Ant.* 14.355-360). Netzer (2006: 179-80) argues that Herod was emotionally deeply attached to this location because of the flight, his mother's accident, and the battle; all would have taken place on the same day. Additional motives for building Herodium may have been the suitability of the location and the fact that there was already a summer palace (Netzer 2006: 181-83). Since the fortress was built on the highest hill in the countryside, it must have been visible from Jerusalem, such that it suited the purpose of being a monument for Herod well (see the note to "another fortress" above).

[2167] I.e., Herod.

[2168] An alternative translation would be "had been driven out of the realm"; the noun ἀρχή can mean, among other things, "realm" as well as "rule, throne" (Rengstorf *s.v.*). In the latter case ἡ ἀρχη may be synonymous with τὰ πράγματα ("the matters," i.e., "the power"; see *Ant.* 15.32 with the note to "the government"). The phrase τῆς ἀρχῆς ἐκπίπτω ("lose power") is common (e.g., Dionysius, *Ant. rom.* 4.7.3; 6.1.4; Plutarch, *Mor.* [*Reg. imp. apophth.*] 176d; [*Mulier. virt.*] 250a; Athenaeus 14.6.28).

[2169] *War* 1.419 provides the same information. Sixty stades equal ca. 11 km (about the location of the fortress see *Ant.* 15.323 with the note to "another fortress").

[2170] Josephus points here to a double advantage of the location: the area apparently was a stronghold by itself and it was also a convenient place for the construction (κατασκευή) of a fortress. The next sentence gives a clarification: there stood a hill that could be adapted (Shatzman 1991: 230).

[2171] The description of Herodium starts with the center (the fortress on top of the hill) and then moves on to the periphery: the site, the aqueduct, the lower city, and the palaces at the base of the hill (Shahar 2004: 232-33, who compares this manner to Strabo's way of topographical descriptions). The description in *War* 1.419 includes the same word κολωνός ("hill"), which occurs once elsewhere in Josephus (*Ant.* 15.339 concerning the location of Augustus' temple at Caesarea Maritima). There are small differences between *War* 1.419-420 and *Ant.* 15.324: in *War* the fortress is identical with the hill, whereas in *Antiquities* the fortress is close to the hill; *War* states that the hill was entirely artificial, while *Antiquities* correctly suggests that an existing hill was adapted in its form (Richardson 2004: 257-58; see also the next note).

[2172] The fortress was built on top of the hill. A conical fill was erected around the building (by artificially heightening the hill outside the fortress), which caused several stories in the fortress to be below ground-level. The diameter of the cone was ca. 180 m, its gradient ca. 32°. The fortress was round, having two round walls with an outer diameter of 63 m as casing (details and figures in Netzer 2006: 182-88).

[2173] The archaeological findings prove this plastic description to be adequate. The conic structure of the hill together with the round fortress on top in the center can be associated with a breast, the fortress being its nipple. The same adjectives χειροποίητος ("made by human hands") and μαστοειδής ("in the shape of a female breast," Rengstorf *s.v.*) occur in *War* 1.419 in a somewhat compacter description of the hill (it is repeated in 1.420). The word μαστοειδής does not occur elsewhere in Josephus. See also *War* 7.189 about two hills near Baaras-Baaru (with a cold and a hot water spring), east

series[2174] of round towers[2175] and has a steep way up built with 200 steps out of hewn stone.[2176] Inside the hill there are costly royal residences,[2177] made for security and at the same time for embellishment.[2178] **325** Around the foot of the hill there are places of resort[2179] with a structure[2180] worth seeing,[2181] in particular because of the supply of water[2182]—water is absent in this area—,[2183] which is built over a long distance and at great expense.[2184] The flat areas around it were built over, not inferior to any city,[2185] while the

---

of the Dead Sea, the shapes of which are compared to female breasts (ὡσανεὶ μαστοί).

[2174] The verb διαλαμβάνω ("intersperse, etc.") also occurs in the parallel passage of *War* (1.420) in connection with the construction of the staircase.

[2175] The towers are also mentioned in *War* 1.420 (with the same noun πύργος). The fortress had 4 towers: 1 main multi-story tower to the east (which was round and considerably higher than the rest of the fortress) and 3 semi-circular extensions to the casing (facing north, west, and south, Netzer 2006: 183-86). The adjective κυκλοτερής ("circular, round," Rengstorf *s.v.*) occurs once elsewhere in Josephus (*War* 2.190).

[2176] *War* 1.420 provides a similar description with a slightly different vocabulary: both passages mention the noun ἄνοδος ("way up") but its steepness is not mentioned in *War*; *War* notes instead that the hill was moderately high) and also mentions the 200 steps (*Ant.* 15.324 uses the noun βαθμίς, while *War* 1.420 employs βαθμός and adds that the steps were made of white marble). The monumental entrance to the fortress was on the northeast (Netzer 2006: 187).

[2177] The meaning of καταγωγή (translated with "residence") is uncertain here. Elsewhere in Josephus the word can mean, among other things, "landing place (within a harbor)" (*Ant.* 15.332) or "accommodation" (Rengstorf *s.v.*). It may refer here to rooms where important guests were received (cf. *Ant.* 16.128), but the context and archaeological findings indicate that these spaces were within the hill (built-in, so to say). The construction was ca. 30 m high and may have had 7 stories. The western part included the rooms of a royal mansion, while the eastern part contained a large courtyard surrounded by colonnades (Netzer 2006: 182-89). *War* 1.420 offers vocabulary partly different from that of *Antiquities*: "(Herod) ... filled the enclosure with splendid palaces (βασιλείοις πολυτελεστάτοις; cf. *Ant.* 15.324 καταγωγαὶ βασίλειοι πολυτελεῖς), so that not only the interior of the buildings had a magnificent appearance, but also the outer walls" (*War.* 1.420, trans. Sievers/Forte in BJP 1a; cf. *War* 1.265 and the description in superlative forms of Herod's new palace in Jerusalem in *Ant.* 15.318).

[2178] This detail is absent in *War*. Herod apparently combined the arrangement of security (see *Ant.* 15.327: "building a stronghold for [defending] himself against his [own] subjects ") with the construction of a splendid settlement, which policy matches Aristotle's remark about the preferred way of building cities: security combined with beauty (*Pol.* 1330b). Netzer (2006: 181) considers security for Herod and his family during periods of unrest to have been the primary purpose of the fortress. Shatzman (1991: 231-32) notes that Herod needed a new urban and administrative center because of the decline of the city of Beth-Zur, west of Herodium. This change may be reflected also by the fact that Herodium and not Beth-Zur is mentioned in a list of toparchies or capitals of a toparchy (*War* 3.55, Schürer-Vermes 2.190-96; Netzer 2006: 180, 191).

[2179] *War* 1.421 uses the noun βασίλεια ("palaces") for these buildings. Lower-Herodium was located north of the hill. It included a large garden complex (130 x 110 m) around a big pool, a large palace (130 x 55 m), a bath house, and a monumental building at the western end of a large course (350 x 30 m, Netzer 2006: 189-99).

[2180] The noun κατασκευή ("structure") also occurs in the previous paragraph, with a slightly different meaning (see *Ant.* 15.324 with the note to "construction work").

[2181] The adjective ἀξιοθέατος ("worth seeing," Rengstorf *s.v.*) is a *hapax legomenon* in Josephus.

[2182] This phrase presupposes a water supply system like an aqueduct. *War* 1.422, a passage which immediately follows upon the passage about Herodium (*War* 1.419-421), includes a very similar sentence: "He built an aqueduct (ὑδάτων εἰσαγωγήν) for the Laodiceans who lived on the coast" (*War* 1.422, trans. Sievers/Forte in BJP 1a).

[2183] This is not entirely true; nevertheless, there is certainly no permanent water source near Herodium.

The Greek sentence has a parenthesis introduced by οὐ γάρ. For further examples of such parentheses in the Herod narrative of *Antiquities*, cf. 15.50, 124, 185, 286 (with the note to "He").

[2184] Netzer (2006: 180) states that water was led to Herodium from a spring located ca. 5 km away, in the current village of Urtas, which lies close to Solomon's Pools.

[2185] Niese (390, likewise Niese minor 312) changes πόλεως (attested by most MSS) into πόλις (implying a translation such as "a city not inferior to any other"). However, Josephus creates a distinction between the flat areas (τὰ δ' ἐπίπεδα) and the hill (ὁ λόφος), which both

hill serves[2186] as an *acropolis*[2187] for the other residences.

(9.5) 326 Since all matters he had hoped for were proceeding well for him,[2188] as they should, he did not have any suspicion[2189] whatsoever of disturbances in his kingdom.[2190] He domesticated his subjects in two ways: through fear,[2191] by being merciless in his punishments,[2192] and through care,[2193] by showing himself generous[2194] when circumstances

Summary of Herod's deeds.

---

served as construction grounds for Herod. This implies that the attested word ἐλάσσω goes with τὰ ἐπίπεδα and does not have to be changed into ἐλάσσων, as Niese does. *War* 1.421 shares the word πόλις (in the accusative) with *Ant*. 15.325 but is more modest in its comparisons: "Therefore, because of the fact that the fortress had everything, it seemed to be a city (πόλιν εἶναι δοκεῖν), whereas by its size [it was] only a palace." (trans. Sievers/Forte in BJP 1a). Since Herodium was an administrative center (see 15.324 with the note to "for embellishment"), Lower-Herodium must have included, in addition to living quarters for the staff of the fortress and the palace, buildings for the administration of the area.

[2186] In consequence of the text-critical argument in the previous note, the participle ἔχουσα ("having," with πόλις as its subject) attested by the MSS should be changed into ἔχοντα (as an attributive particle going with τὸν λόφον), which conjecture was suggested already by Hudson (1726: 772 n. c; Marcus-Wikgren 156). The change of ἔχοντα into ἔχουσα could easily have been caused by a scribal error, especially in the minuscule MSS. The transmitted text obviously has to be amended either in the way proposed by Niese (see the previous note), or in the way proposed here.

[2187] The noun ἀκρόπολις can mean "castle, fortress" (Rengstorf *s.v.*) as well as "upper city" (LSJ *s.v.* I.1). The latter meaning is more plausible because Josephus is focusing on the settlement rather than on the fortifications.

[2188] The brief assessment of Herod's situation reflects Josephus' own voice and makes a transition to the section of *Ant*. 15.326-341, which once again highlights Herod's violation of the Jewish practices (15.328-329). For similar transitions in the Herod narrative of *Antiquities*, cf. 15.218, 291. The section 15.326-341 first focuses on Herod's benefactions outside his kingdom (15.326-330) and then describes in detail the construction of the harbor city of Caesarea Maritima (15.331-341).

[2189] About Herod's suspicion as a recurring theme in *Antiquities*, see 15.35, 42 with the notes to "being under suspicion" and "without suspicion." Significantly this note presupposes that Herod's suspicion had been taken away, in contrast to other passages. The divergence is explained in the following subclauses.

[2190] This note is significant in connection with Josephus' previous information about Herod's motivation for constructing new fortresses (*Ant*. 15.291-292, 295). The fortresses were apparently to enhance Herod's security against the inhabitants of his kingdom who "continuously organized disturbances (ταραχαί), even after a minor incitement" (15.295). Since references to the possibility of such disturbances appear in book 15 of *Antiquities* only until the present note (e.g., 15.30, 73, 231, 286, 295), the readers can conclude that Herod's building of new fortresses was efficient. Nevertheless, the continuation of the narrative gives other reasons for Herod's secure position.

[2191] Josephus suggests here that fear (φόβος) was an important means for Herod in securing his position, but there are actually not many passages in the Herod narrative of *Antiquities* that highlight fear felt for Herod by his subjects: 14.427 about brigands being executed in Galilee; 15.44 about Herod's mother-in-law Alexandra; and 15.358 about the Gadarenes (cf. 17.67, 206-207 and see also the next note).

[2192] The Herod narrative of *Antiquities* reports many executions ordered by Herod, including those of his wife Mariamme I and other close relatives (*Ant*. 15.87, 176, 229-236, 251-252, 284-289; 16.379-394; 17.156-164, 187). One could question whether all of these cases were just, but several clearly were in response to betrayal or military opposition (e.g., 14.283, 288-289: the execution of Malichus, the murderer of Herod's father; 14.432-433: rebels in Galilee; 14.336, 15.2, 5-6: other opponents; 15.251: Alexandra; 15.252-266: Costobar and other friends as well as the Sons of Baba). Josephus suggests time and again that Herod was extremely severe in his punishments (e.g., 15.356: "For more than anyone else he had the reputation of being inexorably harsh [δυσπαραίτητος] towards his own people, but of being generous to foreigners by letting them go after they had done wrong"; see also 15.251, 290, 356, 366; 16.1-4, 151). This particularly pertains to the sections about Herod's last period: the golden eagle episode and the king's brutal plan to kill a great number of prominent Jews in the hippodrome of Jericho after his death in order to guarantee that many would be mourning (17.148-164, 174-181 with Josephus' comments in 17.180-181).

For the combination of ἀπαραίτητος ("implacable, unrelenting," Rengstorf *s.v.*) and τιμωρία ("punishment"), cf. *Apion* 2.292 concerning the Jewish laws (Barclay in

suddenly changed.[2195] **327** He enclosed himself with security on [Judea's] outside,[2196] as if he were building a stronghold[2197] for [defending] himself against his [own] subjects,[2198] for he treated [foreign] cities kindly and generously.[2199] He paid court to their leaders[2200] and gave each of them opportune supplies,[2201] which enhanced their gratitude to him.[2202] And

---

BJP 10 on *Ap.* 2.292) and Diodorus 10.21; Dionysius, *Ant. rom.* 4.58.2; Philo, *Spec.* 3.42; 3.76; Cassius Dio 36.16.2.

[2193] Herod's care (ἐπιμέλεια, see also 15.308) for his subjects is highlighted in the episode about the king's response to the drought (*Ant.* 15.299-316, especially 15.308-310, 315-316).

[2194] The adjective μεγαλόψυχος ("generous, magnanimous") also characterizes Herod in the conclusion of the episode about the drought (see also *Ant.* 15.48 with the note to "magnanimity" and 15.201 concerning Herod's extraordinarily generous support to Octavian).

[2195] The noun περιπέτεια ("[sudden] change, crisis") occurs once elsewhere in Josephus, in a different context, in the prologue to *Antiquities* (1.13). The plural here suggests that there were several crises during which Herod arranged aid, although the narrative reports only one: Herod's response to the severe drought (*Ant.* 15.299-316).

[2196] This passage links up with *Ant.* 15.291-298, which indicates that Herod built several strongholds to protect himself against his own subjects (see 15.291-292, 295 with notes as well as the next note). Some of these fortified places were located at the border of his kingdom, like Caesarea Maritima and Esebonitis. The noun ἀσφάλεια is a key word in the section 15.291-298. Herod apparently focused on security for his rule from an internal perspective (15.291-298) and on strengthening the external support for his rule through benefactions and assistance from his Roman patrons (15.327-328).

The phrase ἡ ἔξωθεν ἀσφάλεια (" security on the outside") also occurs in *War* 2.572 concerning Josephus' measures in Galilee during the war against Rome: he first ensured himself of the support of the Galileans (2.569-571) and subsequently fortified many places there because he assumed that the Romans would attack Galilee first (2.572-574). Thus these fortifications enhanced the security against attackers from the outside.

[2197] The noun ἐπιτείχισμα ("stronghold") occurs twice elsewhere in Josephus. In *Ant.* 15.292 it concerns a literal meaning: "… he planned against the entire population Samaria as a third stronghold." A metaphorical meaning which is similar to the passage here occurs in *War* 1.448 about Herod's decision to use Antipater as "a bulwark" against his other sons Aristobulus and Alexander: "Fed up as a result of these false accusations, Herod called back Antipater, Doris' son, to function as a bulwark (ὥσπερ ἐπιτείχισμα) against his (other) sons, and began to honor him above the others in every way" (trans. Sievers/Forte in BJP 1a; cf. Athanasius, *Syn.* 45.8 [ed. Opitz 271]).

[2198] The same motive is mentioned in *Ant.* 15.291: "So he decided to enclose the people from every side …" (see also 15.292 about Samaria as a stronghold "against the entire population").

[2199] Josephus switches here from Herod's own kingdom to other territories. Benefactions to other states contributed to a secure position for the king (Braund 1984: 79) and demonstrated his aspiration to be a respected ruler in the eastern Mediterranean world (Levine 1975: 11-13).

The adverb φιλανθρώπως ("generously") suggests in combination with the next subclause that Herod supported cities outside his kingdom, although the word can also be used together with the preceding verb ὁμιλέω ("associate with, etc.") in a more general way (e.g., Polybius 11.24a; Diodorus 27.6.1-2). Josephus does not provide details here, while he does in *War* 1.422-425 (see also *Ant.* 15.298; 16.18-19, 24-26, 146-149). Herod's impressive building activities within and outside his kingdom match Augustus' policy in this respect. Augustus was extremely active as builder in Rome, the cities in Italy, and Rome's provinces (Kienast 1999: 408-49). This building activity outside the city of Rome was an important innovation (Kienast 1999: 417-18). About benefactions to cities in the Hellenistic period in general, see Bringmann and von Steuben 1995.

[2200] There are several cases in the Herod narrative of *Antiquities* in which Josephus reports about Herod paying court to (θεραπεύω) leaders (see 15.328 with the note to "the court he paid to Caesar and the most powerful Romans"), though not specifically to leaders of cities, such that this is a unique statement. However, such behavior is what one would expect from a prominent leader who aimed at enhancing his power base (cf. 17.81 about Herod's son Antipater: "He had been paying court [περὶ θεραπείαν … ἐγεγόνει] to the most important men …"). Levine (1975: 151 n. 67) notes that the kings of Pergamum maintained warm relations with the cities along the Ionian coast through gifts.

[2201] Richardson (1996: 223 n. 20) takes this to be an allusion to the allocation of food supplies to neighboring Syrian cities during the famine (*Ant.* 15.311-314).

[2202] This point links up with the remark at the beginning of this paragraph about Herod arranging

he naturally behaved generously,[2203] as is appropriate for a king,[2204] such that his [power] increased in every way[2205] since all things went better and better.[2206]

328 Because of his ambition[2207] to establish such [security][2208] and because of the court he paid to Caesar and the most powerful Romans,[2209] he was forced to depart from the Jewish customs[2210] and to change many of their practices.[2211] He founded cities[2212] out of

---

security from the outside. The Roman leaders' gratitude would, from Herod's perspective, no doubt pay off in the future (as the last subclause of this paragraph indicates; cf. *War* 1.400; *Ant.* 15.360-361). Herod's rule depended very much on Augustus' support (cf. Augustus' deposition of Herod's successor Archelaus after a rule of ca. 10 years in Judea, *Ant.* 17.342-344, 355). About Herod as a friendly king of the Romans, see 15.5 with the note to "gift to Antony" and 15.127-129, 330.

[2203] Josephus notes here that generosity (μεγαλοψυχία) was an important trait of Herod (μεγαλόψυχον φύσει; a similar expression occurs in *War* 5.162, also about Herod; cf. Diodorus 17.74.4 concerning Alexander the Great and the next note). *Ant.* 16.153 makes a similar statement. Herod's generosity is a recurring motif in the *Antiquities* narrative about him (see 15.48 with the note to "magnanimity").

[2204] The emperor Julian the Apostate states in his speech *The Heroic Deeds of the Emperor Constantius* (also called *On Kingship*) that love of labor and generosity are appropriate characteristics for a king (φιλόπονος δὲ ὢν φύσει καὶ μεγαλόψυχος, *Regn.* 28 [ed. Bidez 1.1.162; cf. *Cyn. ind.* 20 [ed. Rochefort 2.1.172] and Dio Chrysostom 32.95 concerning Trajan's generosity).

[2205] Philo, *Det.* 14, about Jacob's household that was growing in every respect as time progressed, offers a close parallel (πάντα διὰ πάντων ἔλαβεν αὔξησις).

[2206] The translation follows the reading προχωρούντων attested by MS P (Niese 391). The other MSS read προσχωρούντων, which results in a translation like "because more and more people were choosing his side." This reading does not fit the context and may have been caused by the addition of a σ to προχωρούντων, possibly because the verb προσχωρέω ("come to, go over to someone's side") is more common in Josephus than προχωρέω ("proceed"). An additional argument in favor of the reading of MS P is that the same verb occurs in *Ant.* 15.326.

[2207] The noun φιλοτιμία can mean several things, including "love of glory" (*Ant.* 16.138, 153, 248), "munificence," and "ambition" (see 15.194 with the note to "magnanimous and generous" and 15.271 with the note to "ambition"; Landau 2006: 123, 168, 171 n. 173). The last meaning matches the context best.

[2208] The phrase εἰς τοῦτο can be interpreted in several ways, but the next word (θεραπεία; see the next note)

renders it plausible that it refers to Herod's strife for more security by cultivating relations with other states and with his patrons.

[2209] Josephus notes several times that Herod courted his Roman patrons (as his father Antipater already had done [*War* 1.187] and his son Antipater would do later on [1.554]). *Ant.* 15.75 reports about Herod's favors (θεραπεία) to Mark Antony and associates them with gifts (δῶρα; see also 15.5 with the note to "gift to Antony"; 15.200). Josephus states in 15.199 that Herod received his new patron Octavian "with every royal service" (πάσῃ τῇ βασιλικῇ θεραπείᾳ) in Ptolemais. In 15.103 he notes that Herod conciliated (θεραπεύσας) Cleopatra with gifts. Herod's favors to his Roman patrons also included honors (the naming of cities, buildings, or rooms after one of them [*War* 1.118; *Ant.* 15.318, 363-364] and the organization of festivals in Augustus' honor [15.268; 16.138]); also services (15.200-201, 318, 363; 16.21-22), and festive receptions (e.g., 15.199; 16.12-15). Two specific favors, founding cities and erecting temples, are mentioned at the end of this paragraph. Herod also offered favors to Marcus Agrippa (*War* 1.118; *Ant.* 15.350-351; 16.12-15, 21-22, 60, 157).

[2210] The combination of ἐκβαίνω ("abandon") plus τῶν ἐθῶν ("the customs") also occurs in *Ant.* 15.267, the introduction to the episode about Herod's festival in Augustus' honor in Jerusalem. It is doubtful whether Herod's strategy to court his Roman patrons required that the Jewish customs were violated. Nevertheless, some of the obvious conventions in this connection, like the erection of a temple in the emperor's honor (see *Ant.* 15.339), clearly opposed the Jewish customs. The crucial question is whether Herod's Jewish subjects were affected by such measures, as *Ant.* 15.267 suggests (see the note to "the ancestral customs" and the next paragraph).

[2211] This phrase (καὶ πολλὰ τῶν νομίμων παραχαράττειν) is almost synonymous with the previous remark (cf. *Ant.* 15.254, which refers to the customs and habits of the Jews in connection with the Idumeans, who had to switch to a Jewish way of life: "Hyrcanus [i.e., John Hyrcanus] had changed their way of life to the habits and the customs of the Jews [τὰ Ἰουδαίων ἔθη καὶ νόμιμα]"). Concerning παραχαράττω ("alter"), see 15.315 with the note to "the change of some of the customs," and for the rare combination of this verb with

his ambition[2213] and erected temples,[2214] **329** although not in the [territory] of the Jews[2215] for they would not have tolerated this[2216] because such matters as statues[2217] and figures molded in relief[2218] according to the manners of the Greeks[2219] are forbidden for us[2220] to venerate,[2221] but outside of the territory[2222] and in the neighboring areas[2223] he built such

---

τὰ νόμιμα, John Chrystom, *Fragm. Jer.* (PG 64.768); Theophylact Simocatta 5.13.7.

[2212] Herod refounded Samaria and named it Sebaste after Augustus (*War* 1.119, 403; *Ant.* 15.246, 292-298; see 15.292 with the note to "Sebaste"). He created a harbor city at the location of Straton's Tower and called its harbor Sebastus (*War* 1.613; *Ant.* 17.87) and its city Caesarea after Augustus (*War* 1.408-416; *Ant.* 15.331-341). *War* 1.407 makes an overstatement concerning Herod's founding of settlements in Augustus' honor: "In short, it is impossible to mention any significant place in his realm that he left without [attributing] some sign of honor to Caesar. After he filled his homeland with temples, he outdid himself by bestowing honors on his [i.e., Caesar's] province, and in many cities he erected monuments to Caesar" (trans. Sievers/Forte in BJP 1a). Herod also rebuilt the harbor city of Anthedon, north of Gaza, and renamed it Agrippeion or Agrippias after Marcus Agrippa (*War* 1.87, 119, 416; *Ant.* 13.357).

[2213] This second occurrence of φιλοτιμία in this paragraph may again refer to Herod's ambition or to his love of honor (see the note to "ambition" above). Concerning φιλοτιμία in connection with the founding of cities, cf. Philo, *Opif.* 17.

[2214] Herod erected temples in Augustus' honor at Paneion-Baneas (*War* 1.404-406; *Ant.* 15.363-364) and at Caesarea Maritima (*War* 1.414; *Ant.* 15.339).

[2215] Josephus explains the distinction between the Jewish and non-Jewish territories in the next subclause. The Jewish territory could be identical with Judea (see *Ant.* 15.2 with the note to "all Judea") and probably does not concern Herod's entire kingdom because in that case the temples in Caesarea Maritima and Banias would be included, which would contradict Josephus' statement here. Levine (1975: 152 n. 71) argues that Josephus presents Caesarea as a non-Jewish city in *Antiquities*.

A noun has to be added in the Greek text, most probably the word χώρα ("territory"), which occurs in the opposite phrase later in the paragraph (τὴν δ' ἔξω χώραν; cf. ἡ Ἰουδαίων χώρα in *War* 1.21; *Ant.* 13.57, 145; 14.250, and ἡ γῆ τῶν Ἰουδαίων in *War* 7.216; *Ant.* 15.121).

[2216] Cf. *Ant.* 15.277 about the Jerusalemites' response to the trophies in Augustus' honor: "… they would not bear images of humans in the city …."

[2217] The noun ἄγαλμα can mean "image" or "statue" (Rengstorf *s.v.*). In Josephus the majority of the occurrences refers to images of deities: *War* 7.136 Roman deities in general; 7.151 Nike (the goddess of victory); *Ant.* 18.79 Isis (cf. 15.279; 19.11; *Apion* 1.199). It is probable, therefore, that the word here also refers to statues of deities.

[2218] The noun τύπος can mean, among other things, "impression, picture, sculpture" (Rengstorf *s.v.*; see also *Ant.* 16.319). Because of the context the word probably refers to images of living creatures cast in a mold, like sculptures or reliefs (see also the next note).

[2219] Expressions like πρὸς τὸν Ἑλληνικὸν τρόπον point to various Greek conventions (e.g., Herodotus 7.89; Xenophon, *Cyr.* 2.2.28; Diodorus 1.11.2; 20.58.3; Dionysius, *Ant. rom.* 1.38.4; Strabo 17.1.42; Cassius Dio 72.17.3); here it concerns the Greek practice to put sculptures and reliefs on the outside of temples, which represented deities, humans, and mythological creatures like giants and centaurs (on metopes, friezes, pediments, roofs etc.).

[2220] *Ant.* 18.55 is even more explicit about Pontius Pilate's transfer of Roman standards (which included busts of the emperor) to Jerusalem: "… for our law forbids the making of images" (trans. Feldman; see also *Life* 65).

The verb ἀπαγορεύω ("prohibit, forbid, etc.," Rengstorf *s.v.*) frequently refers to a specific ban by the Jewish laws, usually the written laws of the Pentateuch (*Ant.* 3.260, 318; 8.191; 12.145-146; 18.264; *Life* 65, 128).

[2221] Jewish readers will easily connect Josephus' remark with the Second Commandment, which forbids the making of idols or images of any living creature (Exod 20:4-6; Deut 5:8-10; cf. *Ant.* 3.91; 17.151; *Apion* 2.190-191 and see *Ant.* 15.276 with the note to "venerate such [images]"). For non-Jewish readers the remark remains an unspecified reference to the Jewish laws. Josephus' note that Herod did not transgress the Second Commandment in the Jewish territory is fairly adequate, as is apparent from the archaeological remains of Herod's buildings in Jewish locations. Herod probably tried to avoid such images in public spaces of Judea, but privately he did not (Fine 2005: 74-79; differently Jacobson 2001a: 103; Richardson 2004: 230; see also *Ant.* 15.279 with the note to "they too had mocked"). A recent find by Ehud Netzer and his team in Herodium (a non-Jewish place) of a room near the monumental tomb of the fortress displays magnificent fresco's, and the walls of the caldarium of the upper-bath-house show pictures of

BOOK FIFTEEN

things. **330** Towards the Jews he defended himself[2224] [by saying] that he did these things not out of his own decision but on the basis of a command and [other] orders.[2225] He pleased Caesar and the Romans by aiming more for their honors[2226] than for his own customs.[2227] In short, he was aiming for his own [glory][2228] or even seeking the honor of[2229] leaving behind for posterity[2230] monuments[2231] of his reign that were [even] bigger.[2232]

---

birds (email from Prof. Joseph Patrich, Jerusalem to me on 1 May 2009). The same geographic division between Jewish and non-Jewish territories and images of living creatures applies to the Herodian coinage: Hellenistic-Roman influences are found only on coins minted outside of the Jewish territory (Mahieu 2012: 391-93, 556-57). The golden eagle on a Jerusalem Temple gate may be the exception to the rule (*War* 1.648-655; 2.5-7; *Ant*. 17.148-164). Fine (2005: 69-81) argues that images by themselves were not problematic; they were considered to be offensive only if they were associated with idolatry.

[2222] This phrase (τὴν δ' ἔξω χώραν) contrasts the previous expression "in the [territory] of the Jews" (see 15.329 with the note to "the [territory] of the Jews"). Assuming that the first phrase refers to Judea, the second one would refer to other territories within Herod's kingdom.

[2223] This expression may be synonymous with the previous one or denote a wider extension, i.e., areas outside Herod's kingdom where Herod likewise erected buildings or contributed to them (see *Ant*. 15.327 with the note to "[Judea's] outside").

[2224] An alternative translation would be "he apologized to the Jews" (cf. *War* 1.457 after Herod's return from a trip abroad: "Upon his arrival in Jerusalem, Herod assembled the people, introduced his three sons, and apologized for [ἀπελογεῖτο] his absence"). Both meanings of ἀπολογέομαι ("defend" or "apologize," Rengstorf *s.v.*) are possible here.

[2225] This remark is highly implausible in the light of indications in Josephus, which suggest that Herod was very eager to show his loyalty and gratitude to his most important Roman patron, Octavian-Augustus (e.g., *War* 1.404-406, 414; *Ant*. 15.268, 339, 363-364).

The combination ἐξ ἐντολῆς καὶ προσταγμάτων ("on the basis of a command and orders") is a bit bizarre because προστάγματά is almost synonymous with ἐντολή. The expression may echo a frequent phrase in the LXX referring to God's commands and orders (τὰ προστάγματά καὶ αἱ ἐντολαί, LXX Gen 26:5; 3 Kgs 3:14; 8:58; 9:6; 11:11, 38; 2 Chr 7:19; 2 Esd 7:11; 11:7; 19:13-14).

[2226] This note may anticipate the report about Herod's foundation of Caesarea in Augustus' honor (*Ant*. 15.331-341). Paying homage to one's patrons was an obvious activity for a friendly king, and Josephus reports several times about Herod giving several kinds of honors to Mark Antony (*War* 1.401), Octavian-Augustus (*War* 1.407, 414; *Ant*. 16.129; 17.87), and Marcus Agrippa (*Ant*. 16.22, 51; see also 15.328 with notes). Herod at the same time benefited from honors and presents from his patrons (*War* 1.396; *Ant*. 14.445; 15.76-77, 195, 198; 16.129). For a further general statement about Herod's relationships with his Roman patrons and his own subjects, see *Ant*. 16.157 "But evidence for me that this was his greatest emotion is also what happened with the honors for Caesar, Agrippa, and his other friends (κατὰ τὰς Καίσαρος καὶ Ἀγρίππα καὶ τῶν ἄλλων φίλων τιμάς). For with the very favors he was paying court to those higher in rank he was expecting to be paid court himself" (my trans.).

For references concerning friendly kingship, see 15.5 with the note to "gift to Antony."

[2227] I.e., the customs of Herod's Jewish subjects. Concerning Josephus' repeated accusation that Herod abandoned the Jewish customs, see *Ant*. 15.267, 328 (with the note to "depart from the Jewish customs"). The phrase τὰ οἰκεῖα ἔθη ("[their] own customs") also occurs in 16.61, in connection with the Ionian Jews.

[2228] Josephus emphasizes this aspect through the repetition of the verb στοχάζομαι ("aim at, be intent on," Rengstorf *s.v.*), which is followed by a reflexive pronoun (literally "aiming for himself"). Enhancing one's own glory by courting one's patrons is an obvious thing to do, as *Ant*. 15.327 implies (see the note to "paid court to their leaders"), but Josephus presents it as a criticism here. Kasher (2007: 183-84) argues that the constructions of Herodium and other buildings indicate that Herod suffered from megalomania.

[2229] An alternative translation of φιλοτιμούμενος would be "showing the ambition of." For φιλοτιμία ("ambition" or "love of honor") in connection with Herod, see *Ant*. 15.194, 271, 303, 328 with the note to "his ambition."

[2230] For the motive of leaving behind a monument for posterity, see *Ant*. 15.298 with the note to "leave behind for later times memorials."

[2231] *Ant*. 15.298, the concluding paragraph about the rebuilding of Samaria-Sebaste, offers a similar passage ("leave behind for later times memorials to his benevolence") without a critical undertone. Josephus' remark is ironic in the opinion of Landau (2006: 168), but one can hardly deny that the remains of Herod's buildings at, e.g., Caesarea and Jerusalem still indicate

Because of this he let himself be drawn into the restoration of cities,[2233] and he went to the greatest expense for this [goal].[2234]

Building of Caesarea Maritima. War 1.408-415

(9.6) 331 Observing that there was also an area near the sea[2235] that was most suitable for holding a city,[2236] which was previously called Straton's Tower,[2237] he devoted himself

---

that they must have been very impressive while they were still intact.

[2232] Josephus does not indicate in comparison to what these monuments of Herod were bigger, but one can think of the building activities reported in the previous sections (e.g., Samaria and Herodium, *Ant.* 15.292-298, 323-325). Josephus' remark, together with the concluding subclause of this paragraph, anticipates the report about the building of Caesarea in the next section (15.331-341), which concerns a huge construction project.

[2233] This note makes the transition to the report about the set-up and building of Caesarea (*Ant.* 15.331-341). Caesarea, like Samaria-Sebaste (15.292-298), concerns a refoundation and renovation of an existing city (see 15.331).

[2234] *Ant.* 15.332 and 15.341 refer to Herod's expenses involved in the building of Caesarea. *Ant.* 15.396 contains a further superlative formula concerning Herod's spending: Herod surpassed previous rulers with the money spent for the renovation of the Jerusalem Temple. *Ant.* 16.13 notes that Herod's fortresses Alexandrium, Herodium, and Hyrcania were built at great expense (cf. 15.274 about the festival in Jerusalem). See also *Ant.* 16.24 concerning Herod's generosity to foreign cities.

[2235] *Ant.* 15.331-341 reports about Herod's foundation of the city of Caesarea (Maritima) at the location of the former city of Straton's Tower (see the note below). The passage finds a close parallel in *War* (1.408-415). The introduction (1.408) of that passage is similar to that of *Antiquities* and also shares the participle κατιδών ("observing, attracting attention") as its first word: "A city on the coast, called Strato's Tower, attracted his attention ...." (trans. Sievers/Forte in BJP 1a).

The notes concerning Caesarea's location near the sea are comparable to the description of Samaria-Sebaste (*Ant.* 15.292-298), the suitable location of which is also noted: it was only a day trip from Jerusalem (15.293) and surrounded by fertile soil (15.296). *Antiquities* mentions the account about Samaria-Sebaste directly after that about Caesarea (15.342); both cities are mentioned together in 15.292-293. Herodium was also built at a location that was most suitable (see 15.324 with the note to "most suitable for construction work").

Caesarea soon had a mixed population, consisting of Jews and non-Jews (including Romans, merchants, and tax farmers). Jewish inhabitants lived scattered all over the city (Patrich 2007: 93, 109). Herod most probably did not design it as a Jewish city, otherwise he would not have erected a temple with statues of Augustus and Roma in it (see 15.328-329, 339; Levine 1975: 16-17). This argument was also brought forward by the non-Jewish inhabitants of Caesarea against their Jewish fellow citizens who claimed that the city was Jewish because it was founded by a Jew (i.e., Herod; *War* 2.266).

Herod probably had several motives for founding Caesarea: he clearly intended to show his loyalty and gratitude to Augustus by naming the new city Caesarea (see 15.293 with the note to "Caesarea," also 15.339) and to create an image of himself as a successful builder and ruler–Caesarea was his most extensive and prestigious building project (cf. Schalit 2001: 341, who emphasizes that Herod was a Hellenistic ruler who loved splendor and glory). Herod probably also built the city for economic reasons (see the next note) and to improve his relationship with prominent non-Jews (Levine 1975: 12-14). And last but not least, Caesarea also became the administrative capital of the kingdom (Patrich 2007: 93).

[2236] The suitability of the area can be taken in a strict as well as in a broad sense. Its location on the coastal Plain of Sharon provided ample space to build a new city, and Mount Carmel was relatively close, such that the city's water supply was fairly easy to arrange. Moreover, the city had wells (Netzer 2006: 101-03; Patrich 2007: 120-21, who notes that it is uncertain whether there was an aqueduct already in Herod's time). In a broader perspective the location could give an important stimulus to commerce and other economic activities in Herod's kingdom given the good road connections with Egypt, the Phoenician coast, Antioch, Asia Minor, Scythopolis, Damascus, Palmyra, the Red Sea area (via Gaza), and the Euphrates area (Charlesworth 1926: 36-56; Schalit 2001: 340). The Plain of Sharon as the city's hinterland provided access to the Valley of Esdraelon, Galilee, and the fertile hills of Samaria (Stern 1974b: 257; Levine 1975: 12 with n. 63). The tolls in Caesarea must have been an important source of income for Herod (Udoh 2005: 172).

Dionysius (*Ant. rom.* 1.85) offers a close parallel to Josephus' phrase (χωρίον ἐπιτηδειότατον δέξασθαι πόλιν "an area ... most suitable for holding a city") concerning the location of the city of Remoria near the Tiber (ἔστι δὲ τὸ χωρίον ἐπιτήδειον ὑποδέξασθαι πόλιν). The parallel report of *War* (1.408) also shares several words with *Ant.* 15.331, but it has a different

to making a magnificent layout.²²³⁸ And he set it all up, very carefully,²²³⁹ with buildings of white stone,²²⁴⁰ adorning it with a most costly palace²²⁴¹ and public buildings,²²⁴² **332** also with a harbor, which was the biggest project and created the most work.²²⁴³ [This harbor] was free from inundation²²⁴⁴ [and] similar in size to Pireus.²²⁴⁵ It has internal landing places²²⁴⁶ and second anchorages.²²⁴⁷ Its construction²²⁴⁸ is admired by all because

---

tenor: "… it was suited for welcoming his generosity because of its favorable position (διὰ δὲ εὐφυίαν τοῦ χωρίου δέξασθαι δυναμένην τὸ φιλότιμον αὐτοῦ)." Cf. *Ant.* 5.68 about Silo as location for the Tabernacle.

²²³⁷ Similar phrases in *War* 1.156, 408; *Ant.* 15.293. Straton's Tower was founded by the Sidonians and located on the coast, ca. 35 km south of the current city of Haifa (further references in 15.217 with the note to "Straton's Tower"). *War* 1.408 notes that Straton's Tower was dilapidated.

²²³⁸ This passage suggests that Herod was actively involved in the building activities as a city planner and architect (about Herod as builder, see Roller 1998; Lichtenberger 1999; Japp 2000; Netzer 2006).

The noun διαγραφή ("outline, plan," Rengstorf *s.v.*) occurs once elsewhere in Josephus, concerning David giving to Solomon a plan for the building of the Temple (*Ant.* 5.375).

²²³⁹ The phrase οὐ παρέργως (literally "not incidentally") is a case of *litotes*, which phrase also occurs in *War* 7.136; *Ant.* 1.9; 20.157; *Apion* 1.183, 216.

²²⁴⁰ The parallel report of *War* (1.408) includes a similar note: "He entirely rebuilt it with white stone (πᾶσαν ἀνέκτισεν λευκῷ λίθῳ)" (trans. Sievers/Forte in BJP 1a), although *Antiquities* uses πέτρος instead of λίθος for "stone." Marcus-Wikgren (159 n. *d*) and Oleson and Raban (1989-94: 1.52) state that marble is intended. Archaeological finds, however, imply that most buildings at Caesarea were made out of local *kurkar*, which was plastered and sometimes also provided with *stucco* (Patrich 2007: 100-01).

²²⁴¹ The plural βασίλεια, which also occurs in the parallel passage of *War* (1.408 καὶ λαμπροτάτοις ἐκόσμησεν βασιλείοις), can either mean "palace" or "palaces" (Rengstorf *s.v.*), such that an alternative translation would be "most costly palaces." Nevertheless, the excavations reveal that Herod built only one palace, at a special spot: a *kurkar* salient that jumps into the sea ca. 450 m south of the harbor. Herod expanded this beautiful promontory palace over 2 terraces with a view to the festival, which would be held at the completion of Caesarea, in order that he could host important guests in it. This palace (the "lower terrace") was a two-story building (110 x 55 m) with a rock-cut rectangular pool at its center. The pool was ca. 35 x 18 m wide (and 2 m deep) and positioned within a peristyle court, which provided access to a *triclinium* and other rooms. The added "upper terrace" was built adjacent to the "lower terrace" and bonded with the hippodrome stadium at its northeastern corner. It had a large peristyle courtyard (64 x 32 m) and a large wing of rooms along the north side. Its western section included a large basilical hall (ca. 15 x 17 m), which may have functioned as an audience hall. The southern side of the palace was almost entirely eroded (Netzer 1986; 2006: 106-12; Patrich 2007: 110-13).

²²⁴² This detail is missing in *War*, which also has no parallel for δίαιται πολιτικαί ("public buildings," LSJ *s.v.* δίαιτα). In his *De architectura* (5 preface 5), a work written for Augustus, Vitruvius mentions the public buildings (*loci publici*) that each city should have: a *forum* (marketplace), a *basilica* (assembly hall), a treasury, a prison, a *curia* (council house), a theater with adjoining porticoes, baths, a *palaestra* (wrestling school), a harbor, and ship yards. Archaeological remains confirm that Caesarea contained several of these buildings, of which the harbor, mentioned in the next paragraph, was the most important (see also *Ant.* 15.339-341). The parallel passage of *War* (1.408) highlights Herod's magnanimous character: "Above all he demonstrated in this way his innate magnanimity (τὸ φύσει μεγαλόνουν; cf. 1.400, 428) …."

²²⁴³ The complicated and long Greek sentence of *Ant.* 15.331-332 has to be broken up in English. The beginning of 15.332 puts emphasis on the harbor as the last and biggest project mentioned in the sentence. The construction of the harbor is described in detail in 15.334-338.

²²⁴⁴ The adjective ἄκλυστος ("free from inundation," LSJ, or "sheltered from the sea," Rengstorf *s.v.*) is a *hapax legomenon* in Josephus (cf. Diodorus 3.44.7; 17.104.8; Strabo 6.3.6; Arrian, *Ind.* 26.10; Oppian of Corycus 1.226; 4.450).

²²⁴⁵ *War* 1.410 says that Caesarea's harbor was even bigger than Pireus' (μείζονα τοῦ Πειραιῶς λιμένα κατεσκεύασεν). Archaeological research shows that the statements of both *War* and *Antiquities* are exaggerated: Caesarea Maritima had a middle sized harbor (Lehmann-Hartleben 1923: 180; Lämmer 1974: 140 n. 7; Schalit 2001: 339, referring to Foerster).

²²⁴⁶ The noun καταγωγή ("landing, entrance, etc.," Rengstorf *s.v.*) refers here to the space of the enclosed harbor (see *Ant.* 15.334-336), which offered a safe berth for ships. The word also occurs in *War* 1.413; *Ant.*

there were no local materials that were necessary[2249] for such a magnificent work.[2250] It was accomplished[2251] with imported materials[2252] and at great expense.[2253] **333** The city lies in Phoenicia,[2254] along the passage to Egypt,[2255] between Joppa and Dora.[2256] These are

---

15.337, in which cases it refers to the accommodation for the sailors arriving at Caesarea. Oleson and Raban (1989-94: 1.52) translates with "quays" here.

[2247] The expression δευτέρους ὑφόρμους (translated as "second anchorages") has no parallels, and we can only guess what it refers to exactly. It might indicate that the harbor offered to ships a 2nd place to anchor in addition to the anchorages at the shore (cf. *Ant.* 15.333) or refer to a 2nd row of ships lying at anchor behind those directly connected with the quay. The noun ὕφορμος ("anchorage," Rengstorf *s.v.*) is a *hapax legomenon* in Josephus.

[2248] The noun δόμησις ("building, construction") also occurs in *War* 1.411 but with a different tenor: *Antiquities* focuses on the materials used for the construction, while *War* highlights the technicality of the construction in the sea ("Despite the entirely adverse nature of the terrain, he struggled with the difficulties so that the solidity of the construction was not damaged by the sea." Trans. Sievers/Forte in BJP 1a).

[2249] The materials for the mole (concrete with volcanic ash—*pozzolana*—as active ingredient) and for the double-walled frameworks (wood into which concrete was poured; see *Ant.* 15.334 with the note to "enormous stones") came from Italy or Greece and Eastern Europe, respectively (Richardson 2004: 261; Netzer 2006: 100).

The noun ἐπιτηδειότης ("necessary material," Rengstorf *s.v.*) is a *hapax legomenon* in Josephus.

[2250] The noun μεγαλουργία ("magnificence") also occurs in *Ant.* 15.414, concerning the columns of the portico of Herod's Temple in Jerusalem.

[2251] The verb ἐκτελειόω ("accomplish, complete," Rengstorf *s.v.*) is a *hapax legomenon* in Josephus.

[2252] See the note to "no local materials that were necessary" above.

[2253] This note links up with the phrase "he went to the greatest expense for this" (*Ant.* 15.330), concerning Herod's aid to foreign cities. *Ant.* 16.13 mentions Samaria-Sebaste and Caesarea as well as fortresses that Herod had built at great expense (πολλαῖ δαπάναις; cf. 15.274; 16.154, 182).

[2254] In this paragraph Josephus first points out the location of Caesarea. His information is rather similar to that given in the parallel passage of *War* (1.409): "For from Dora to Joppa (μεταξὺ γὰρ Δώρων καὶ Ἰόππης; cf. *Ant.* 15.333 Ἰόππης μεταξὺ καὶ Δώρων), midway between which the city is situated, the coast was without a port, so that sailing along the coast of Phoenicia (τὸν τὴν Φοινίκην) on the way to Egypt entails dropping anchor in the open sea because of the threat of the south-west wind (διὰ τὴν ἐκ λιβὸς ἀπειλήν) ..." (*War* 1.409, trans. Sievers/Forte in BJP 1a). Both passages mention Phoenicia, but there is a significant difference: *War* points to a sea trip along the coast from Egypt to Phoenicia to the north, without connecting Caesarea directly with Phoenicia, while *Antiquities* locates Caesarea within Phoenicia. In the 1st cent. BCE "Phoenicia" usually refers to the coastal area between Mount Carmel to the south and the territory around the city of Gabala to the north, including the Bekaa Valley (Grainger 1991: 5-19, 113-14); sometimes the Palestinian coast was included as well. Thus concerning Antony's grant of coastal cities and other areas to Cleopatra in 37 BCE, Plutarch (*Ant.* 36) refers to Phoenicia, while Cassius Dio (49.32.4-5) to Phoenicia and Palestine (see *Ant.* 15.95 with the note to "and Egypt"). Dionysius Periegetes (904-912) associates Gaza and Joppa with Phoenicia by pointing to Phoenician inhabitants (Kokkinos 1998: 117 n. 105). Möller and Schmitt (1976: 190) note that the coastal city of Dor-Dora, north of Caesarea (see the note to "Dora" below), was considered to be part of Phoenicia. Josephus apparently takes Phoenicia in a broad sense here, referring to the entire coastal line running from Egypt to Asia Minor. The implication of his presentation seems to be that Caesarea was not part of the Jewish territory (see also *Ant.* 15.331 with the note to "an area near the sea").

The phrase ἡ πόλις κεῖται ("the city lies"; see already Herodotus 1.142; Thucydides 1.46) occurs in *War* 1.409 (also referring to Caesarea); 3.52 (Jerusalem); 4.2 (Gamala); 7.224 (Samosata); *Ant.* 12.348 (Scythopolis); 15.410 (Jerusalem); *Apion* 2.10 (Heliopolis).

[2255] Cf. the parallel passage of *War* (1.409), which refers to a journey by sea along the Phoenician coast to Egypt (see the previous note).

[2256] Caesarea was considerably closer to Dora than to Joppa: it was located ca. 12 km south of Dora and ca. 52 km north of Joppa-Jafo. Herod captured Joppa at the beginning of his rule (see *Ant.* 14.396-397 and 15.2 with the note to "all Judea"). Dora was founded by the Phoenicians. It became part of Alexander Janneus' territory (13.324) but was separated again from the Judean territory by Pompey. It remained an independent city and never became part of Herod's territory (13.324, 326, 334-335; 14.76; Möller and Schmitt 1976: 84-85; Schürer-Vermes 2.118-20).

small cities along the coast,[2257] where it is difficult to anchor[2258] because of the fierce blowing of the south-west winds,[2259] which are continuously[2260] dragging the sand[2261] from the sea[2262] to the beach[2263] and do not offer a gentle landing place.[2264] Most of the time it is necessary that the merchants ride at anchor.[2265] **334** Setting right this difficult[2266] condition of the area and having drawn the circular outline[2267] for the harbor sufficiently big enough for anchoring[2268] close to the shore[2269] with big fleets, he sank down enormous stones[2270]

[2257] Josephus starts here his explanation why Herod decided to build an artificial harbor at Straton's Tower (*Ant.* 15.333-334). The parallel passage of *War* (1.409), which shares the adjective παράλιος ("coastal") with *Ant.* 15.333, similarly notes that there were no harbors along the coast between Dora and Joppa.

The word πολισμάτιον is the diminutive of πόλισμα ("[buildings of] a city," LSJ *s.v.*) and a *hapax legomenon* in Josephus.

[2258] There is no natural harbor at this part of the coast. The adjective δύσορμος ("with bad anchorage," LSJ *s.v.*) is a *hapax legomenon* in Josephus.

[2259] *War* 1.409 and *Ant.* 15.333 share the noun λίψ ("south-west, south-wester," Rengstorf *s.v.*). There is one further occurrence of this word in Josephus (*Ant.* 3.294; 3.34).

[2260] With Niese 392. MSS FLAMVW lack the adverb ἀεί ("continuously"). The word may have been left out because it conflicts with the expression "most of the time" found in the final subclause of this paragraph.

[2261] The noun θίς ("sand," Rengstorf *s.v.*) is a *hapax legomenon* in Josephus.

[2262] The noun πόντος ("[open] sea," LSJ *s.v.*) occurs once elsewhere in Josephus, referring to the Euxine Sea in the story of Jonah (*Ant.* 9.213).

[2263] In addition to the winds that were blowing the ships to the shore, shifting sandbanks may also have made anchorage along this coast difficult.

[2264] Niese (392) leaves out the word μειλίχιος ("smooth") with MS P, but all the other Greek MSS include this adjective. Niese's reading implies "do not offer a landing place" as translation. The word μειλίχιος occurs once elsewhere in Josephus, as a noun (τὸ μειλίχιον "friendliness," *War* 7.71; Rengstorf *s.v.* μειλίχιος). The noun καταγωγή ("landing, landing place") also occurs in *Ant.* 15.332.

[2265] The implication of Josephus' explanation seems to be that the ships had to keep a safe distance from the shore most of the time, such that the merchandise had to be transferred to small boats in order to bring it ashore. *War* 1.409 also notes that the ships had to stay away from the shore but focuses on the effect of the winds on the water: "For even when the wind blows moderately, it sends the waves up to such a height against the cliffs, that the waves' backward flow stirs up the sea to the greatest distance." (trans. Sievers/Forte in BJP 1a).

The verb ἀποσαλεύω ("ride at anchor," LSJ *s.v.*; cf. Rengstorf *s.v.* "be exposed to the sea, lie [at anchor]" and *War* 1.409 σαλεύειν ἐν πελάγει "dropping anchor in the open sea") occurs once elsewhere in Josephus, with a different meaning (*War* 7.62 "be alarmed," Rengstorf *s.v.*).

[2266] Niese (392) reads δυσδιάθετον ("difficult to regulate," Rengstorf *s.v.*), following MS P (δυσδυάθετον) with a slight change. MSS FLAMMVW and E read δύσθετον ("unfavorable"), which would be a *hapax legomenon* in Josephus. This reading probably results from a contraction of the reading δυσδιάθετον and should, therefore, be considered to be secondary. Schreckenberg (1967-69: 70-71) proposes δυσίατος ("incurable"), which adjective occurs once elsewhere in Josephus (*War* 7.451), but there is no need to change the transmitted text.

[2267] The harbor had 3 basins, the major part of which was built into the open sea. It had 2 piers (or breakwaters), one at the north side and one at the south-west, with the entrance to the north (see *Ant.* 15.337 with notes). For the report of the maritime excavations of the harbor, see Oleson and Raban 1989-94; Raban and Holum 1996.

The noun κύκλος ("ring, circle") also occurs in the parallel report of *War* (1.413), but there it is used adverbially in connection with the quay: "... the entire circular quay (τὸ πᾶν κύκλῳ νάγμα) in front of them [i.e., the vaulted chambers] formed an extensive promenade for those disembarking." For the combination of the verb περιγράφω ("draw') with κύκλος ("circle") and λιμήν ("harbor"), cf. Heron, *Diop.* 17.1.

[2268] The verb ἐνορμέω ("to lie at anchor in the harbor," Rengstorf *s.v.*) is a *hapax legomenon* in Josephus.

[2269] The noun χέρσος (literally "dry land," Rengstorf *s.v.*) is a *hapax legomenon* in Josephus.

[2270] Josephus' description does not completely match the archaeological findings: the base of the mole was constructed from poured concrete, put underwater into place with a wooden construction that could sink at the appropriate location. This technique was quite recent; Vitruvius describes it in his *De architectura* (5.12.2-6). Underwater the concrete blocks looked like huge stones (Richardson 2004: 260-61). Many of the blocks were ca. 30 m³ (ca. 90 tons) or more in volume (Netzer 2006: 100).

to a depth of about twenty fathoms.[2271] Most of them had a length of fifty feet,[2272] a breadth of no less than eighteen feet, and a depth of nine feet,[2273] but some were bigger or smaller than these.[2274] **335** The construction that he threw in the sea as a barrier[2275] was as big as[2276] 200 feet [wide].[2277] Half of this he set up against the surf[2278] in order to keep off the high breaking waves there.[2279] For this reason this is called a breakwater.[2280] **336** The other half

---

The adjective ὑπερμεγέθης ("gigantic, immense," Rengstorf s.v.) also occurs in the description of the 2 huge rooms in Herod's palace in Jerusalem, which were named after Caesar and Agrippa (*Ant.* 15.318).

[2271] I.e., ca. 37 m. Cf. *War* 1.411 "... he submerged into twenty fathoms of water stone blocks (καθίει λίθους ἐπ' ὀργυιὰς εἴκοσιν εἰς τὸ πέλαγος) ...." (trans. Sievers/Forte in BJP 1a). The noun ὀργυιά ("the length of the outstretched arms," LSJ s.v.; see *Ant.* 15.413) indicates a unit of length equal to 6 feet and 1 fathom (ca. 1.85 m). The word also occurs in the parallel passage of *War* (1.411) and still once elsewhere in Josephus (*Ant.* 15.413 concerning the thickness of the columns of the Temple's portico).

[2272] The foot (πούς) is a common unit of length in antiquity (LSJ s.v. 3), equaling roughly 30 cm: the Attic and Roman feet are ca. 29.5 cm; the Olympic foot is 32.1 cm. The same measurement occurs in the passage of *War* (1.411) and the same unit in *War* 1.412; *Ant.* 15.335, 413, 415.

[2273] *War* 1.411 offers similar measurements: "... most of which measured fifty feet in length, nine in depth, and ten in breadth (ὧν ἦσαν οἱ πλεῖστοι μῆκος ποδῶν πεντήκοντα, βάθος ἐννέα, εὖρος δέκα) ...." (trans. Sievers/Forte in BJP 1a).

[2274] The parallel passage of *War* (1.411) is slightly briefer and different: "... some were even larger (τινὲς δὲ καί μείζους)." (trans. Sievers/Forte in BJP 1a).

[2275] The rare noun ἐνδόμησις ("thing built in, mole, breakwater," LSJ s.v.; Rengstorf s.v.) is a *hapax legomenon* in Josephus. It occurs a few times elsewhere, although only in Christian literature (e.g., John of Damascus, *Vit. Barl. Joas.* 94 [ed. Woodward and Mattingly 158.23]). A variant reads ἐνδώμησις ("enclosing with a wall," Niese 392), which noun is also attested in Rev 21:18 and in an inscription from Smyrna (*SIG* no. 996 l. 30; LSJ s.v.). *War* 1.412 uses the noun τεῖχος ("wall") for "mole" (Marcus-Wikgren 161 n. *d*; Rengstorf s.v.): "When the underwater foundation was completed, he then extended a mole (τεῖχος) two hundred feet in breadth above the water." (trans. Sievers/Forte in BJP 1a). For a detailed report of the archaeological findings concerning the breakwaters, see Oleson and Raban 1989-94: 1.101-203.

[2276] Niese (392), who reads ὅσον ἦν ἐβάλλετο ("[the construction] ..., which was as big as ? he threw ...") with MS P, indicates that the transmitted Greek text is corrupt. The description in *War* is clear (see the next note).

[2277] *War* 1.412 says more specifically that the mole was 200 feet wide. In fact, there were 2 breakwaters: a northern and a southern one. The debris of the northern breakwater implies that it had a rectangular outline, which was ca. 60-65 m wide and ca. 250 m long in the east-west direction. The southern breakwater formed a great arc (running first [roughly] east-west), then making a curve (running north-south), and finally making another curve towards the end of the northern breakwater. Its width varied, and its length was ca. 750 m (about the southern and northern breakwaters, see Raban and Oleson and Raban 1989-94: 1.104-31, 157-60, 279-86). Josephus' number of 200 feet, therefore, can hardly apply to the main construction of the southern and northern breakwaters and may rather pertain to a section of the outer construction of the southern breakwater.

[2278] The transmitted Greek text is probably corrupt again. Niese (393) and others follow the conjecture proposed by Coccejus: προβέβλητο κυματωγαῖς. The noun κυματωγή ("place where the waves break," LSJ s.v.) would be a *hapax legomenon* in Josephus (Rengstorf s.v.). The readings κυμαγωγίαις and κυμαγωγαῖς of MSS FLMVE and MSS AW, respectively, are nouns that are not attested in ancient Greek literature. The reading κυματώσαις of MS P is an existing noun (κυμάτωσις) meaning "flow (of the tide)" (LSJ s.v.), but this does not fit the context well. It is, however, associated with storms and high seas in Philo, *Mos.* 2.255; *Opif.* 63.

[2279] The description of the breakwater is again more specific in the parallel report of *War* (1.412): "... one hundred feet of which were built out to break (the assault of) the waves (πρὸς τὴν ἀνακοπὴν τοῦ κύματος)." (trans. Sievers/Forte in BJP 1a).

The verb περικλάω ("break") occurs once elsewhere in Josephus (*Ant.* 19.226; Rengstorf s.v.).

[2280] Instead of the noun προκυμάτια attested by MSS FLAMW, Niese (393) reads προκυμία ("breakwater," LSJ s.v.), following *War* 1.412: προκυμία γοῦν ἐκλήθη ("whence the name 'breakwater'"). The noun προκυμία does not occur elsewhere in Josephus. The archaeological remains imply that a segmented construction outside the main body of the southern breakwater functioned as the actual breakwater and that a wall with sloping faces on both sides served as the subsidiary breakwater. The width of the main breakwater from the outside to its

contained a stone wall,[2281] equipped at intervals with towers.[2282] The biggest of these is called Drusus,[2283] a most beautiful construction,[2284] taking its name from Drusus, Caesar's stepson, who has died young.[2285] **337** Vaults[2286] were built inside it,[2287] containing a row of shelters[2288] for the sailors.[2289] Before them a wide quay[2290] enwreathed the entire harbor around,[2291] [enabling] a most pleasant walk[2292] for all who wish to. And the entrance,[2293] or mouth,[2294] has been made to the north[2295] [because] this wind brings the clearest weather.[2296]

---

inner edge was ca. 65 m, which roughly matches Josephus' reference to 200 feet (Oleson and Raban 1989-94: 2.284-85, 288).

[2281] Similarly *War* 1.412, with partly the same vocabulary: "... the rest supported a stone wall (λιθίνῳ τείχει) ..." (trans. Sievers/Forte in BJP 1a).

[2282] The verb διαλαμβάνω ("intersperse," Rengstorf *s.v.*) occurs in *Ant.* 15.324 in connection with the building of a series of towers at Herodium. The parallel report of *War* (1.412) also combines διαλαμβάνω with πύργοις ("towers").

[2283] *War* 1.412 indicates that all the towers of the mole were huge (μέγιστος; see also *War* 5.177, 242 and Aristotle, *Pol.* 1331a; Diodorus Siculus 2.7.3; 14.18.8), while *Antiquities* uses this adjective to note that the tower called after Drusus was the biggest.

[2284] *War* 1.412 uses different vocabulary to point out that the Drusus Tower was the most important and most beautiful tower of the breakwater.

[2285] Likewise *War* 1.412, which also shares the word πρόγονος (meaning "ancestor, stepson" here, Rengstorf *s.v.*) with *Ant.* 15.336. Drusus the Elder (i.e., Nero Claudius Drusus) was the brother of the later emperor Tiberius and Augustus' adoptive son. He is also mentioned in *Ant.* 18.143, 180 (Schalit 1968: 40; further references in Kienast 1996: 68-69; Kienast 1999: 125). Josephus does not offer a specific reason for this honor to Drusus the Elder. There is no evidence of a special relationship between Herod and Drusus. Caesarea may have been completed shortly after Drusus' death in 9 BCE, such that the tower would have been thus called in his commemoration (Braund 1984: 109). This would imply that Herod would have honored Augustus by naming the tower after Drusus.

[2286] The noun ψαλίς ("vault") occurs in Josephus only here and in the parallel passage of *War* (1.413).

[2287] Rengstorf (*s.v.*) gives the meaning "build in to" for the verb ἐμποιέω.

[2288] The noun καταγωγή ("landing place, accommodation, etc.") also occurs in *Ant.* 15.332-333, in which case it refers to landing places for ships in the harbor (see 15.332 with the note to "internal landing places"). Here as well as in the parallel passage of *War* (1.413) it indicates an accommodation for sailors (Rengstorf *s.v.*).

[2289] The noun ναυτίλος ("seamen," Rengstorf *s.v.*) used in the plural is a *hapax legomenon* in Josephus. About Herod's navy, see Shatzman 1991: 186-87.

[2290] The noun ἀπόβασις ("quay," Rengstorf *s.v.*) is a further *hapax legomenon* in Josephus. The vocabulary for the description of the quay in *War* 1.413 is closely similar to that in *Ant.* 15.337, although it also varies, using identical or related words in differing ways: "... the entire circular quay (τὸ πᾶν ... κύκλῳ νάγμα; cf. *Ant.* τὸν πάντα λιμένα) in front of them (πρὸ αὐτῶν, i.e., the vaulted chambers; *idem* in *Ant.*) formed an extensive promenade (πλατὺς περίπατος; cf. *Ant.* ἀπόβασις πλατεῖα) for those disembarking (τοῖς ἀποβαίνουσιν) ..." (trans. Sievers/Forte in BJP 1a).

[2291] The verb περιστεφανόω ("enwreathe, surround," Rengstorf *s.v.*) occurs twice elsewhere in Josephus (*Ant.* 6.108 concerning the location of a military camp and 12.80 concerning the decoration of the rim of a mixing vessel). The dative κύκλῳ ("around") also occurs in *War* 1.413 (see the previous note). The combination of both words also occurs in *Ant.* 6.108 about a camp's location on a cliff "surrounded by a ring of rocks (ἐν κύκλῳ περιστεφανούσης)."

[2292] Cf. Plutarch's reference in his *Symposiacs* to the common saying "the pleasantest sailing is along the coast, while the pleasantest walk is by the sea (περίπατος δ' ὁ παρὰ θάλατταν ἥδιστος)" (Plutarch, *Mor.* [*Quaest. conv.*] 621d, trans. Clement and Hoffleit). The noun περίπατος ("walk, promenade," Rengstorf *s.v.*) also occurs in the parallel passage of *War* (1.413), but there it means "promenade" (see above and *Ant.* 15.366).

[2293] Likewise *War* 1.413, which shares the noun εἴσπλους ("entrance [of a harbor]," Rengstorf *s.v.*) with *Ant.* 15.337. The word occurs once elsewhere in Josephus, referring to the narrow entrance of Alexandria's harbor (*War* 4.612). The entrance to Caesarea's harbor was between 20 and 30 m wide.

[2294] The noun στόμα ("mouth") is redundant and also occurs in the parallel passage of *War* (1.413).

[2295] Instead of the noun βορρᾶς ("north, north wind"), *War* 1.413 has the closely related word βορέας (cf. also the adjective βόρειος ["northern"] concerning the entrance of the harbor, 1.413).

[2296] Likewise *War* 1.413, which shares the words ἀνέμων ("wind") and αἰθριώτατος ("clearest") with *Ant.* 15.337.

338 The foundation[2297] of the entire wall[2298] on the left of those who sail into[2299] the harbor is a piled-up tower[2300] to hold off [the water] most robustly; on the right two big stones,[2301] bigger than the stronghold opposite them,[2302] are standing upright as a pair.[2303] **339** And a series of buildings[2304] stand in a circle around the harbor,[2305] constructed with the smoothest

---

[2297] The noun βάσις ("foot, base") also occurs in the description of the hill upon which Herodium was built (*Ant.* 15.325). Rengstorf (*s.v.*) gives "(outermost) end" as meaning here.

[2298] The adjective περίβολος also functioned as a noun, meaning, among other things, "(surrounding) wall, temple area," but Rengstorf (*s.v.*) gives "ring shaped mole, quay" as meanings here.

[2299] Part of Josephus' description of Caesarea takes a panoramic viewpoint by inviting the readers to look at Caesarea's harbor as if they were sailing in to it (*Ant.* 15.338-339). Other classical authors likewise provide topographical information from the perspective of an anonymous traveler on a boat that sails into or around a specific place. E.g., Thucydides 1.24.1: "There is a city called Epidamnus on the right hand as one sails into the Ionian gulf ..." (trans. Smith). This description presents the viewpoint of somebody who is sailing away from the Mediterranean basin. See also Appian's preface to his *Foreign Wars* (about the territories ruled by the Romans), which includes the following passage: "In the Ocean they [i.e., the Romans] rule most of the Britons; to one that enters through the Pillars of Heracles [i.e., the promontories that flank the entrance to the Strait of Gibraltar] into this sea [i.e., the Mediterranean Sea] and that sails around again to the same Pillars they rule all islands, and all the main-lands that run down to the sea" (translation and discussion in Pitcher 2012: 222-24; similar vocabulary in Strabo 7.3.15; 7.4.5; 11.2.10; 11.7.11; Procopius, *Aed.* 1.8.2). The participle εἰσπλεόντων ("sailing into," also *Ant.* 15.339) echoes εἴσπλους ("entrance") in 15.337. Apart from here and the parallel passage of *War* (1.413), the verb occurs only in the next paragraph.

[2300] An alternative translation would be "a compressed stronghold," but that does not fit the context well. MSS AMVW read πύργος περιηγμένος or πύργος ... ιηγμένος ("a [rotated] tower") instead of πύργος νενασμένος attested by MS P, which reading is followed by Niese. The Homeric verb νάσσω ("squeeze close, press, stamp down," LSJ *s.v.*) occurs once elsewhere in Josephus (*War* 1.337), referring to houses packed with heavily armed troops (πᾶσα ὁπλιτῶν οἰκία νένακτο)." Rengstorf (*s.v.*) offers "be filled in, be solid" as meanings for νάσσω in the passive voice.

[2301] Similarly *War* 1.413, although the size of the stones is not indicated in *War*. The "stones" were in fact towers (see the next note).

[2302] Cf. *War* 1.413. Concerning the remains of the tower located northwest of the northern breakwater and the twin towers situated west of the harbor's entrance channel, see Oleson and Raban 1989-94: 1.127-30 and 1.149-51 (written by Vann).

[2303] Similarly *War* 1.413 (ὀρθοὶ λίθοι ... συνεζευγμένοι), which passage offers a roughly similar description of the harbor's entrance but adds information about colossal statues supported by columns: "At the mouth (ἐπὶ τοῦ στόματος) [of the harbor] colossal statues (κολοσσοὶ) were supported by columns, three on each side (ἑκατέρωθεν). A massive tower (πύργος ναστός) held up [the columns] on the left of vessels entering (εἰσπλεόντων) [the harbor], while two stone blocks standing upright (δύο ὀρθοὶ λίθοι) and clamped together (συνεζευγμένοι) [held up] those [columns] on the right, whose height surpassed that of the rim of the tower on the opposite side (τοῦ κατὰ θάτερον χεῖλος πύργου μείζονες)" (*War* 1.413, trans. Sievers/Forte in BJP 1a, slightly adapted)."

[2304] An alternative translation would be "a series of houses" since οἴκησις can mean "house, building, dwelling" as well as "place of residence" (Rengstorf *s.v.*). *War* 1.414 refers explicitly to houses (see the next note). A translation like "houses," however, does not fit the grid system of Caesarea's city plan: the houses of the city were located within the grid, in the *insulae* between the streets (see the next note), such that Josephus may here vaguely refer to public buildings that were situated outside of the grid plan, like the temple, theater, amphitheater, and royal palace (see *Ant.* 15.331 with the note to "a most costly palace").

[2305] The description in *War* 1.414 is different: "The houses (οἰκίαι) adjacent to the harbor were also of white stone, and the streets of the city, marked out at equal distances from each other, led down to it." (trans. Sievers/Forte in BJP 1a). Contrary to other Herodian cities, Caesarea was built according to an orthogonal grid, possibly inspired by Alexandria's city plan. This is confirmed by the descriptions of its streets in *War* 1.414 and of its drainage and sewage system in *Ant.* 15.340. The city had 4 north-south streets (*cardines*) and at least 7 east-west streets (*decumani*), with rectangular blocks for housing in between (*insulae*, Patrich 2007: 95-96, 104-05). Patrich (2007: 104, 122-24) argues that there was also a diagonal street leading up to Augustus' temple from the east. Caesarea most probably included all the public buildings that were usually part of a Hellenistic

stone.[2306] In the middle is a mound,[2307] on which a temple for Caesar is built,[2308] visible to all who sail in.[2309] It has statues,[2310] one of Rome[2311] and one of Caesar.[2312]

---

city (see also 15.331 with the note to "public buildings") and was surrounded by a semi-circular city wall at its south, east, and north sides (Netzer 2006: 96-99; Patrich 2007: 101-04).

[2306] The adjective λειότατος ("most smoothly") probably refers to carefully polished stones (see also *War* 5.239 and *Ant.* 15.331 with the note to "buildings of white stone").

[2307] The platform on which the temple stood was ca. 13 m above sea level and partly based on a natural ridge of *kurkar*, which was filled in on the sides. It was rectangular in shape (ca. 100 x 90 m), but the eastern side was curvilinear. At the ends of the western side westward-projecting wings were built (21 x 9.5 m). A massive pier (20 x 10 m) housed a staircase leading up to the temple from the west side, which shows that the west, visible from the sea, was the temple's front side. The temple itself was 46.4 m long, 28.6 m wide, and ca. 21 m high. It had colonnades on all sides, in Corinthian style and with Attic bases (Holum 1999; Netzer 2006: 103-06; Patrich 2007: 105-08). The noun κολωνός ("hill, mound," LSJ *s.v.*; Rengstorf *s.v.*) occurs twice elsewhere in Josephus, both times referring to the hill on which Herodium was built (*War* 1.419; *Ant.* 15.324).

[2308] In the parallel version of *War* (1.414) the description and most of the vocabulary are again different: "On a mound (ἐπὶ γηλόφου; cf. *Ant.* 15.339 κολωνός τις) right opposite the mouth [of the harbor] was Caesar's temple (ναὸς Καίσαρος; cf. *Ant.* νεὼς Καίσαρος), remarkable for its beauty and size" (trans. Sievers/Forte in BJP 1a). Patrich (2007: 108-09) argues on the basis of city coins and a marble statue of Tyche dating from the 2nd cent. CE that Caesarea also had a temple of Tyche.

[2309] This detail is missing in *War*. Archaeological research confirms that this temple of Augustus was located on a terrace and visible from afar at sea (Schalit 2001: 336-37). Concerning τοῖς εἰσπλέουσιν ("those who sailed in"), see *Ant.* 15.338 with the note to "those who sail into." Vogel (2002: 196) states that the harbor with its view on Augustus' temple was Herod's "visiting card," presenting his kingdom as a stabile part of the Roman Empire.

[2310] See the next two notes. For ἀγάλματα meaning "statues (of gods)," see *Ant.* 15.276 with the note to "venerate such [images]."

[2311] Roma (Ῥώμη) is the toponym for the capital of the Roman Empire. According to legends, the name goes back to Romulus, the founder and first ruler of Rome (Livy 1.7.3), or to the name of a Trojan woman called Rhome (Ῥώμη; this tradition is part of the legend that Odysseus and Aeneas founded Rome, see Dionysius, *Ant. rom.* 1.72.2). In the Greek world Roma was the personification of the Roman people and the Roman state, analogous to Demos as the personification of Athens. Such personifications were deified and honored with cults and festivals. In line with Rome's presence in the eastern part of the Mediterranean world from the beginning of the 2nd cent. BCE onward, cults of Roma were founded at several places, with temples, altars, priests, and Romaia festivals (at Smyrna in 195 BCE, Chalcis in 194 BCE, Delfi and Lycia in 189 BCE, Alabanda in 170 BCE). The supreme deity, Zeus or Jupiter, usually joined Roma, although not so much as the patron deity of Rome but rather as the protector of oaths and treaties. In the Imperial period the emperor was frequently venerated together with Roma and associated with Zeus/Jupiter, whose characteristics were transferred to the emperor. Roma changed from a symbol of military hegemony into a representation of the empire. Shortly after the Battle of Actium (in 31 BCE), temples for Roma and Augustus were founded in several cities in various provinces of Asia Minor (Pergamum in Asia, Nicomedia in Bithynia, and Ancyra in Galatia; see the next note). Tacitus (*Ann.* 4.37.3) presents the relevant cult in Asia as venerating Augustus and the city of Rome, but Greek inscriptions show that the goddess Roma was worshipped. Local cults for Roma and the emperor came also into being, e.g., in Caesarea Maritima. She was depicted with a mural crown, a crested helmet, a *modius*, and sometimes bareheaded (van Henten 1999; for the association of Roma with Hera, see the next note).

[2312] By way of exception the *Antiquities* report concerning the statues of Augustus and Roma is shorter than the parallel version of *War* (1.413). It also mentions the statues in a reversed order. The extra information in *War* 1.414 describes the statues: "In it was a colossal statue (κολοσσός; cf. *Ant.* 15.339 ἀγάλματα) of Caesar, not inferior to the Olympian Zeus, after which it was modelled, and [a statue] of Rome, matching that of Hera at Argos." (trans. Sievers/Forte in BJP 1a). Pheidias' massive (12–14 m high) statue of Olympian Zeus, made in the 5th century BCE was considered one of the wonders of the ancient world. Its appearance is known from a downsized Roman copy (currently in the Hermitage Museum, St. Petersburg). Zeus is clad in a heroic *himation*. In his right hand he holds a small winged Victory (Nike) standing on a globe, indicating his rule of the world, and in his left a sceptre. He is accompanied by his symbol, the eagle. The same

The city itself is called Caesarea,[2313] and it is most beautiful both in building materials and construction.[2314] **340** The water channels under it and the sewers[2315] are no less carefully constructed than what is built on top of them.[2316] Some of these lead at equal intervals[2317] to the harbor and the sea, but one crosswise channel[2318] connects them all from below, so that the rainwater and the refuse[2319] of the inhabitants can be led out conveniently.[2320]

---

museum has a statue of Augustus as Olympian Zeus, which was probably similar to the statue that Herod placed in Augustus' temple in Caesarea. The bearded and long-haired head of Zeus is replaced by the head of the young Augustus head. Josephus states that Roma was depicted as Hera of Argos, which may be modeled on a huge sculpture made by Polycleitos (5th century BCE, Taylor 2006: 571-72).

The veneration of (deceased) rulers was a Greek custom that was adapted by Octavian-Augustus to the new political situation in the Mediterranean world after Actium (31 BCE). There were 2 types of cults: (1) dynastic cults set up by the rulers themselves, which legitimized their power as rulers, and (2) cults organized by others (like individual rulers, cities, or provinces), which reciprocated the benefactions of the ruler venerated. In both cases the cults were part of a mutually advantageous relationship. Price (1984: 248) argues that "the (imperial) cult was a major part of the web of power that formed the fabric of society." The first provincial cults for Octavian were established at Pergamum in Asia (in 29 BCE) and at Nicomedia in Bithynia shortly after his triumph at Actium, which initiatives were taken by the provinces (Tacitus, *Ann.* 4.37; Suetonius, *Aug.* 52; Cassius Dio 51.20.7). The cults were dedicated to the ruler (i.e., Augustus) and to Roma (see the previous note). In that same period Octavian himself decreed that a cult of Roma and Divus Julius ("the divine Julius [Caesar]") had to be set up in the Roman provinces of Asia (at Ephesus) and Bithynia (at Nicea). The cults initiated by the provinces themselves were celebrated by the indigenous worshippers; the ones for Rome and Divus Julius by the Romans present in the provinces. Shortly after the incorporation of Galatia into the Roman Empire a temple for Roma and Augustus was built at Ancyra (probably around 25-20 BCE). In the western part of the empire a cult of the emperor was established in 12 BCE when the Gallic provinces dedicated an altar to Roma and Augustus at Lugdunum (Fishwick 1987-2005). Herod's cult of Augustus in Caesarea matches the 2nd type of ruler cult, and Caesarea became the center of the cult of the emperor in Palestine (Bernett 2007a: 110-26). The temple included statues of Augustus and Dea Roma (see *Ant.* 15.339). Lämmer (1974: 102-03) argues on the basis of analogue cases in Pergamum and elsewhere that both Augustus and his wife Livia were venerated as protector gods during the quadrennial games at Caesarea (see 16.136-141): Augustus as Zeus Olympius and Livia as Hera-Roma. Herod also built temples for Augustus in Samaria-Sebaste, Paneas-Caesarea Philippi, and probably also at Sidon, Damascus, and Nicopolis (Braund 1984: 113; Schalit 2001: 358-65; Kienast 1999: 252; Bernett 2007a; 2007b). A dedicatory inscription on the base of a statue from Herod (*OGIS* no. 415) renders it plausible that the king also contributed to the building of a temple of Baʿal Shamim at Siʿa, near Canatha-Qanawat (Richardson 1996: 184-85, 206-07; about the location, see *Ant.* 15.112 with the note to "Canata"). *War* 1.422 mentions briefly that Herod also built temples (ναούς) in Tyre and Berytus.

[2313] The city was officially called Καισάρεια Σεβαστή (Caesarea Augusta; see also *Ant.* 15.292 with the note to "Sebaste"). The parallel version of *War* (1.414) mentions the homage to Augustus explicitly: "He [i.e., Herod] dedicated the city to the province, the harbor to those who sail in nearby waters, and the glory of this foundation, which he called Caesarea, to Caesar" (trans. Sievers/Forte in BJP 1a).

[2314] The alliteration of the k sound (καλλίστης καὶ τῆς ὕλης καὶ τῆς κατασκευῆς) adds emphasis to Josephus' point that Caesarea was a most remarkable city in regard with both its building materials and architecture (cf. the polished stones of the construction [κατασκευή] earlier in this paragraph; see the note to "the smoothest stone").

[2315] The noun λαύρα ("passage, sewer," LSJ *s.v.*; Rengstorf *s.v.*) is a *hapax legomenon* in Josephus.

[2316] The sewage system was covered (Patrich 2007: 95, 123). The verb ὑπεροικοδομέω ("be built over something" in the passive voice, Rengstorf *s.v.*) occurs once elsewhere in Josephus (*War* 5.186).

[2317] The noun διάστημα ("distance, interval," Rengstorf *s.v.*) also occurs in the parallel passage of *War* (1.414), but there it points to the grid system of the streets rather than the sewerage. For a close parallel of κατὰ σύμμετρα διαστήματα, cf. Polyaenus 2.31.4 (concerning a series of epiphanies of the Dioscuri during a nightly sacrificial assembly of Lacedaemonians) and Pseudo-Plutarch, *Hom.* 2.38 (ed. Kindstrand 24).

[2318] The description suggests that there was one main sewer channel draining the wastewater off to the sea. The adjective ἐγκάρσιος ("transverse," Rengstorf *s.v.*) is a *hapax legomenon* in Josephus.

[2319] The sewerage system transported excess rainwater

Furthermore, when the sea intrudes[2321] from the outside, it can flow through and flush the entire city from below.[2322] **341** He also built a theater in it,[2323] out of stone,[2324] and further back[2325] on the south side of the harbor an amphitheater,[2326] which can hold a great crowd of people[2327] and is suitably situated for having a view over the sea.[2328] In fact, the city was completed this way in a period of twelve years[2329] because the king did not grow weary

---

and the inhabitants' refuse. The noun λῦμα can mean "washing water, dirt" as well as "refuse" (LSJ *s.v.*; Rengstorf *s.v.*).

[2320] The construction of this athwart channel apparently prevented the flooding of one or more of the other channels. The verb συνεκδίδωμι ("join in giving out, yield up together," LSJ *s.v.*; Rengstorf *s.v.*, who suggests "be washed away [together]" as meaning for this passage) is a *hapax legomenon* in Josephus.

[2321] Niese (394) reads ἐπείγηται ("intruded," Rengstorf *s.v.* ἐπείγω), following MS P. The other Greek MSS read ἐπιγένηται ("was coming in"), which may have evolved out of the reading of MS P or vice versa.

[2322] The description suggests that the sewerage system enabled a flow in 2 directions: the waste water went into the sea, while the sea itself could stream in (most probably during high water), so that the system was flushed. The parallel report about Caesarea in *War* 1 does not mention the sewerage system. The verb ὑποκλύζω ("wash from below," Rengstorf *s.v.*) is a *hapax legomenon* in Josephus.

[2323] Herod's theater has been excavated and is still well visible. It is located ca. 150 m from the sea, southeast of the harbor. It is relatively small and could receive between 3,500 and 5,000 spectators (Lämmer 1974: 120; Netzer 2006: 113; Patrich 2007: 115, with various calculations). It had a horseshoe-shaped *cavea*, an *orchestra*, and a stage with a *scaenae frons*. The diameter of the *cavea* was ca. 85 m and that of the *orchestra* ca. 35 m. The stage was ca. 9.5 m wide and ca. 50 m long (further references in Frova and Dell'Amore 1965: 157-234; Lämmer 1974: 128-30; Patrich 2002a; Netzer 2006: 112-15; Patrich 2007: 113-16).

[2324] Niese (394) leaves out the phrase ἐκ πέτρας, following MS P and the Latin version, but most Greek MSS include both words. Copyists may have considered these words to be redundant since for them it was obvious that a theater was built of stone. Nevertheless, theaters could also be built of wood in Herod's period (see *Ant.* 15.268 with the note to "a theater in Jerusalem"). The words make sense, therefore, and may emphasize Herod's innovative switch from a wooden to a stone theater (Lichtenberger 2006: 290). A stone theater required a much greater effort and the import of building materials to the sandy coastal area of Caesarea.

[2325] Lämmer (1974: 120-21), building on a suggestion by Ebert, proposes to transfer the καί attested after πέτρας to a position before ὄπισθεν, such that the theater would have been located south of the harbor and the amphitheater further back. This does not match the archaeological excavations, which show that the theater was furthest to the south.

[2326] The parallel report of *War* (1.415) mentions, in addition to a theater and an amphitheater, also marketplaces. The amphitheater was most probably a hippodrome stadium building that was named ἀμφιθέατρον by Josephus because of its elongated form and U-turn (see also *Ant.* 15.268 with the note to "a huge amphitheater"; cf. *War* 2.172, which mentions a stadium). The hippodrome stadium (briefly "hippo-stadium," a term coined by Humphrey 1996) has been excavated in the 90's of the previous century. It was located northwest of the theater and had a maximum length (including the U-turn) of ca. 310 m; its width was ca. 68 m. The *arena* was 300 m long and 50.35 m wide. There were 12 rows with seats along the eastern, southern, and western sides. The starting gates were at the north side and contained 12 cells in Herod's time, for races of 12 horses or chariots (Lämmer 1973: 216 n. 47; 1974: 115-27; Humphrey 1996; Patrich 2001; 2002a; 2007: 116-20). The stadium was built for the games held at the completion of Caesarea (Netzer 2006: 117; for the games, see *Ant.* 16.136-141).

[2327] *Life* 277 offers a rather similar phrase concerning the synagogue of Capernaum: "... able to accommodate a large crowd (πολὺν ὄχλον ἐπιδέξασθαι δυνάμενον)" (trans. Mason in BJP 9 on *Life* 277). *War* 1.415 mentions that Herod built the theater, amphitheater, and marketplaces in a manner worthy of the name of the city (i.e., the emperor's name).

[2328] The parallel report of *War* (1.415) mentions in addition Caesarea's marketplaces (ἀγοράς; or the singular "marketplace" according to some MSS). The verb ἀποπτεύω echoes the adjective ἄποπτος ("visible," Rengstorf *s.v.*) in *Ant.* 15.339 and is a *hapax legomenon* in Josephus.

[2329] Josephus also refers to the completion of the building activities in *Ant.* 16.136 and mentions 10 years in that connection: "The entire building project was finished in its tenth year (δεκάτῳ ἔτει πρὸς τέλος ἐλθούσης; my trans.)." This implies that there is a discrepancy between the period that the building activities lasted given here (i.e., 12 years) and that given in *Ant.* 16.136 (i.e., the 10th year).

Herod sends his sons Alexander and Aristobulus to Rome.
War 1.435; 445

of the work[2330] and was able to pay its expenses.[2331]

(10.1) 342 Being busy with these [activities][2332] and when Sebaste was already built as a city,[2333] he decided to send his sons Alexander and Aristobulus[2334] to Rome[2335] in order

---

Josephus mentions in 16.136 that the completion of Caesarea coincided with Herod's 28th regnal year and the 192nd Olympiad (i.e., summer 12-summer 8 BCE). He also reports in book 16 that the completion was followed by the foundation of quadrennial games (16.137). *War* 1.415 dates the foundation of these games to the 192nd Olympiad. Otto (1913: 78), Schürer-Vermes (1.291, 293), Stern (1974b: 257), Levine (1975: 11 with n. 53), Foerster (1976: 986), Richardson (1996: 231 n. 48; 2004: 267), and Netzer (2006: 94) take the capture of Jerusalem (mostly dated to 37 BCE) as the starting point for the conversion of the 28th year and conclude that the 12 years concern the period 23/22-10/9 BCE. Kokkinos (1998: 370) proposes 23-13 BCE (according to the 10 years mentioned in *Ant.* 16.136) or less likely 24-12 BCE (further references in Mahieu 2012: 166). Mahieu herself (pp. 166-78) argues that Herod chose the date of his capture of Jerusalem (5 March [36 BCE] in her opinion) as Caesarea's dedication day, and that only 5 March 8 BCE matches Josephus' references to the 28th regnal year (counted from 36 BCE) and the 192nd Olympiad. In Mahieu's opinion there would be no discrepancy between the 12 years and the 10th year: the 10th year would mark the start of the work in 20 BCE (reckoned from Augustus and Herod's meeting in Syria at the end of 30 BCE)—instead of marking its duration— with the work ending 12 years later, in 8 BCE (pp. 178-80).

[2330] The word ἐργασία ("work, construction") also occurs in *Ant.* 15.332, in connection with the building of Caesarea's harbor.

[2331] The expenses (δαπάναι) are also emphasized in *Ant.* 15.332. The parallel report of *War* (1.415) continues with a brief description of the foundation of the quadrennial games at Caesarea. Such a description is absent here but is given in *Ant.* 16.136-141.

[2332] Josephus switches here to a new cluster of events via a transition that indicates the time frame of the events. The expression "these [activities]" refers in the present context to the building of Caesarea (see *Ant.* 15.331-341). The subsequent time reference mentions the building of Samaria-Sebaste (see the next note). The combination of both time markers is somewhat misleading since there was a considerable gap between the building of Caesarea and that of Samaria-Sebaste. The time setting of the section *Ant.* 15.342-364, which starts with the report of Herod sending his sons Alexander and Aristobulus IV to Rome (15.342-343), matches the period in which Samaria-Sebaste was built (see the next note) better than the time in which Caesarea was constructed.

The main figure in the section 15.342-364 is a local ruler named Zenodorus (15.344). *Ant.* 15.343-349 relates Zenodorus' attack on the inhabitants of Damascus and the transfer of his territory of Trachonitis, Batanea, and Auranitis to Herod; *Ant.* 15.350-353 reports about Herod's conflict with the Gadarenes, in which Zenodorus played a prominent role; and *Ant.* 15.354-364 concerns Augustus' grant of Zenodorus' dominion to Herod, Zenodorus' death, and the building of a temple near Paneion, in Zenodorus' territory.

[2333] Caesarea and Samaria-Sebaste have been mentioned together several times in the preceding paragraphs (*Ant.* 15.292-293), although Samaria-Sebaste was built much earlier, starting from 27 BCE or a few years later (see 15.292 with the note to "Sebaste").

The verb πολίζω ("build a city," Rengstorf *s.v.*) is a *hapax legomenon* in Josephus. Mahieu (2012: 133 n. 41) suggests "found" as translation; she notes that the fact that Samaria was called Sebaste in 27 BCE does not necessarily imply that the building activities were finished in that year. Josephus does not refer to a specific year here, and his phrase "built as a city" can perhaps be interpreted as a reference to the refoundation of Samaria and the start of Herod's building activities as a consequence.

[2334] This is the first time that these two sons of Herod by Mariamme I are mentioned in *Antiquities*. They will figure prominently in book 16, from 16.11 onward. The precise dates of their births are unknown. The eldest, Alexander, was plausibly born in 36 BCE and Aristobulus IV in 35 BCE at the earliest given that Herod married Mariamme in 37 BCE (see 15.23 with the note to "living in wedlock with Herod"; Hoehner 1972: 13 n. 4; Kokkinos 1998: 213-14; Mahieu 2012: 187-88).

[2335] The purpose of the visit was meeting Augustus according to the next phrase, but parallel passages of *War* indicate that the boys stayed in Rome for a long period and mention their education explicitly in passing (1.435, 445). Herod, therefore, sent his sons to Rome to provide them with a proper elite education. The full cycle of this education included the *ludus litterarius* (reading, writing, and arithmetic) from the age of 7 until the age of 11 or 12, the *ludus grammaticus* (Latin and Greek grammar) from the age of 11 or 12 until usually 15, and the *schola rhetoris* (rhetoric) until the age of 18 to 20 (Bonner 1977: 34-75; Eyben 1993: 128-31).

War 1.435 refers to an anonymous 3rd son, the

to meet[2336] with Caesar.[2337] **343** When they arrived, there was accommodation[2338] for them in the house of Pollio,[2339] one of the persons who did his utmost[2340] to be friends with

---

youngest of the three, who died during his education in Rome. Archelaus, Philip, Antipas, and Herod junior were educated in Rome as well (*War* 1.602-603; *Ant.* 17.20-21, 80). Agrippa I was brought up in Rome together with Drusus the Younger, Tiberius' son (*Ant.* 18.143).

[2336] The variant reading ἐντευξομένους of E (Niese 394) can mean "meet with" but also "get an interview with" (LSJ *s.v.* ἐντυγχάνω 4).

[2337] The education of the sons of friendly kings in Rome became standard practice under Augustus (Braund 1984: 9-17), as a passage in Suetonius (*Aug.* 48) that describes Augustus' policy concerning friendly kings indicates: "He [i.e., Augustus] also united the kings with whom he was in alliance by mutual ties, and was very ready to propose or favour intermarriages or friendship among them. He never failed to treat them with all consideration as integral parts of his empire, regularly appointing a guardian for such as were too young to rule or whose minds were affected until they grew up or recovered; and he brought up the children of many of them and educated them with his own (*plurimorum* [i.e., *regum*] *liberos et educavit simul cum suis et instituit*; trans. Rolfe). Cassius Dio (51.15.5-6) notes that Juba II stayed with Augustus, and Plutarch (*Ant.* 87.1) and Suetonius (*Aug.* 17.5) report that, apart from Caesarion, Cleopatra's children also stayed with him. Some kings even sent their sons to Rome already in the 2nd cent. BCE. Ariarathes IV of Cappadocia sent his son, the future Ariarathes V, immediately before Rome's victory at Pydna in 168 BCE (Livy 42.19). According to Livy the purpose was education, although this may be a projection of the Augustan practice into earlier times (Braund 1984: 17 n. 9). In 167 BCE Prusias II of Bithynia brought his son, the future Nicomedes II, to Rome, accompanied by a large retinue (Livy 45.44).

Education seems to have been the main purpose of these stays in Rome, but the kings often had other motives as well, e.g., carrying over the relationship with Rome to the next generation and preparing a son's future rule; there was a close connection between being educated in Rome and taking over the throne at home (Braund 1984: 11; Smallwood 1976: 102). Moreover, these "royal students" were potential hostages from a Roman perspective (Braund 1984: 12): the Parthian king Phraates IV sent 4 sons (2 with their wives) and 4 grandsons to Rome as hostages in 10 BCE; the young among them were educated in Rome at the same time (*Res gest. divi Aug.* 32; Strabo 16.1.28; further references in Braund 1984: 9-21; Kienast 1999: 316 n. 356 and 501-02; Kasher 2007: 207-08).

According to the context of the narrative the trip of Herod's sons to Rome fell between the refoundation of Samaria-Sebaste (probably in 27 BCE, with 16 January 27 BCE as *terminus post quem*; see *Ant.* 15.292 with the note to "Sebaste") and Augustus' grant of Trachonitis, Batanea, and Auranitis to Herod (which has been dated between 27 and 22 BCE). Schürer-Vermes (1.291, 321) and several other scholars date the trip to 23 BCE (Braund 1984: 10; Schalit 2001: 423, 588; Günther 2005: 129, 154, 258). Kokkinos (1998: 369) argues for 24 BCE; Otto (1913: 68-71), Hoehner (1972: 9 with n. 4), and Richardson (1996: 231) for 22 BCE, in line with Caesarea's refoundation in (supposedly) 22 BCE. Mahieu (2012: 186-89) argues for 27 BCE, immediately after the refoundation of Samaria-Sebaste: Augustus was in Rome from August 29 BCE until the early summer of 27 BCE, and the year 27 BCE would match the ages of Alexander and Aristobulus in relation to their primary education (see the note to "Rome" above). Such an early date is possible, although the boys could also have met with Augustus after his return to Rome from his trip to Gaul and Spain (in 24 BCE). Moreover, *War* 1.435 refers to a 3rd son, who was younger than Alexander and Aristobulus IV. This implies that, if the trip occurred a few years later than 27 BCE, the ages of the 3 boys would still roughly fit the customary age for the *ludus litterarius*. On the other hand, Josephus doesn't specify in *War* 1.435 that the 3 sons were sent simultaneously to Rome and the fact that *Antiquities* mentions only 2 sons here may imply that the 3rd son was sent to Rome at a later time.

Alexander and Aristobulus lived in Rome until 18 or 17 BCE (see *War* 1.445 and *Ant.* 16.6 with notes; Schürer-Vermes 1.321).

[2338] The noun καταγωγή ("landing, accommodation") occurs twice in the report about the building of Caesarea (*Ant.* 15.332, 337, see 15.332 with the note to "internal landing places").

[2339] Alexander and Aristobulus could have stayed in Augustus' palace (see the note to "Caesar's residence" below), but Herod apparently decided lodge them with Pollio (for different spellings of his name in the MSS, see Niese 394). Pollio is a Latin family name (a *cognomen*), which was common in several Roman clans (e.g., the Asinii). Josephus does not specify which Pollio is concerned here. Several scholars opt for C. Asinius Pollio (mentioned in *Ant.* 14.138), who had been consul in 40 BCE and may have had a great interest in Judaism (Otto 1913: 69; Feldman 1953; 1958-59; 1985; Marcus-Wikgren 165 n. *g*; Kienast 1999: 312). Bowersock (1965:

Herod.[2341] And it was even permitted [for them] to stay at Caesar's residence.[2342] For he received the boys with the greatest benevolence.[2343] He also granted Herod the right to secure the throne for whomever [of his children] he wanted[2344] and also gave him the territory of Trachon, Batanea, and Auranitis,[2345] which he[2346] had received[2347] for the following reason.[2348]

---

55 n. 3), Grant (1971: 145), and Smallwood (1976: 89 with n. 103) argue that P. Vedius Pollio may have been the boys' host; he was a rich friend of Augustus (further references concerning both proposals in Richardson 1996: 231 n. 49). Willrich (1929: 184-85) and Braund (1983; 1984: 10) argue that Pollio was merely a Jew residing in Rome (cf. Pollio as the name of a Jew in *Ant.* 15.3-4, 370). In that case Pollio may have been both the host and the tutor of the boys.

[2340] The phrase μάλιστα σπουδάζω περί ("do his utmost for, favor [someone] most eagerly") also occurs in *War* 1.432; *Ant.* 1.265, 277.

[2341] This friendship with Herod is open to several interpretations. It may concern a personal friendship—especially if a high Roman official like C. Asinius Pollio or P. Vedius Pollio is meant—or a *clientela* relationship with Herod, in which case Pollio was plausibly a prominent Roman Jew (for proposed identifications of Pollio, see the note to "in the house of Pollio" above).

For a close parallel of σπουδασάντων περὶ τὴν φιλίαν, see Strabo 16.1.28 about the Parthian king Phraates IV: "Phraates, his successor, was so eager for friendship with Caesar Augustus (τοσοῦτον ἐσπούδασε περὶ τὴν φιλίαν τὴν πρὸς Καίσαρα τὸν Σεβαστόν) that he even sent him the trophies ..." (trans. Jones). For the context of Josephus' remark, see *Ant.* 15.11 with the note to "the Parthians," and for another parallel, Appian, *Hist. rom.* 11.23.

[2342] Assuming that Pollio was the boys' host, as the beginning of this paragraph implies (see the note to "in the house of Pollio" above), this remark either means that Herod's sons received permission to stay at Augustus' place but did not do so (except for some visits) or that they stayed part of the time with Augustus. Kienast (1999: 312 n. 338) concludes that the boys frequently stayed at the emperor's palace and met there the freedman Celadus, who was highly esteemed by the emperor (cf. *War* 2.106-107; *Ant.* 17.332; Suetonius, *Aug.* 67.1; *PIR*² 2.142 no. 616). Richardson (1996: 231) argues that the boys stayed first with Pollio and then with Augustus.

[2343] Augustus' benevolence towards Herod's sons demonstrates the good relationship that existed between Herod and the emperor in this period. The refoundation of Samaria as Sebaste shortly before (see *Ant.* 15.292 with the note to "Sebaste") demonstrates how import this relationship was for Herod.

[2344] The right to choose one's own successor may have been exceptional in the context of Augustus' friendly kings (Otto 1913: 62-64). Josephus refers to this right again in *War* 1.454, 458; *Ant.* 16.92, 129. Schalit (2001: 159-60) relativizes the scope of this right by arguing that Herod could only put forward a successor. Archelaus' journey to Rome to receive Augustus' approval for being Herod's successor (*Ant.* 17.202, 219-223) supports his view.

[2345] Batanea is a section of the territory that is called Bashan in the Bible, with Ashtaroth and Edrei being its main cities. It is located east of the Sea of Galilee and the Golan area, and west of Trachonitis and Auranitis (Schürer-Vermes 1.336-37; Möller and Schmitt 1976: 38; Richardson 1996: 141). Its broad and fertile plains were suitable for cattle, agriculture, and the production of timber.

Auranitis is the Greek name for the Hauran region (mentioned already in Ezek 47:16, 18), i.e., the mountainous area around the peak of Jebel Hauran, east of Batanea and south of Trachonitis. Nabateans were living in the southern part of this region (see *Ant.* 15.111 with the note to "Arabia"; Schürer-Vermes 1.337; Richardson 1996: 141). Part of Auranitis was apt for agriculture because of its fertile volcanic soil.

For Trachonitis, see *Ant.* 15.344 with the note to "Trachonitis." After Herod's death the territory of Trachonitis, Batanea, and Auranitis was given to Herod's son Philip (*War* 2.95; *Ant.* 17.319).

[2346] I.e., Herod (see the next note).

[2347] MSS WE and an excerpt by Constantine Porphyrogenitus (*Legat.* 369) do not have the participle παραλαβών ("having taken over"). The omission of παραλαβών is understandable because this participle requires a switch of subject (Herod in stead of Augustus), which is awkward. The participle is missing in the parallel passage of *War* (1.398). MSS WE and Constantine's excerpt imply a smoother reading: "... he [i.e., Augustus] also gave him the territory of Trachon, Batanea, and Auranitis for the following reason."

[2348] The parallel passage of *War* (1.398) introduces the reason for the grant with a similar phrase (ἐξ αἰτίας τοιᾶσδε "the reason for this was as follows") and dates this grant "after the first Actiad," i.e., after the first period of the Actian era and the first Actian Games, which implies a date after September 27 BCE: the first Actian cycle (lasting 4 years) was September 31-September 27

344 A certain Zenodorus[2349] had leased the estate of Lysanias.[2350] The revenues did not satisfy him,[2351] so he increased his income[2352] by having bands of robbers in Trachonitis.[2353]

Transfer of Zenodorus' territory to Herod.
War *1.398-400*

BCE, and the first Actian Games were probably celebrated in September 27 BCE (Lämmer 1974: 109 with n. 110; Kasher 2007: 206; Mahieu 2012: 134-35; see also *Ant.* 15.109 with the note to "the Battle of Actium" and 15.268 with the note to "an athletic contest"). Mahieu (2012: 133-37) argues for 27 BCE as the date of the grant. Other scholars date the grant a few years later: Schürer-Vermes (1.256, 291, 319) dates it from the end of 24 or the beginning of 23 BCE (cf. Richardson 1996: 232, 24/23 BCE) to ca. 23 BCE or 23/22 BCE; Avi-Yonah (1974: 92), Stern (1974b: 236), Kasher (1988: 157), and Schalit (2001: 423) opt for 23 BCE; Shatzman (1991: 170-71) and Günther (2005: 258) for 23/22 BCE; Otto (1913: 68-69 with n. *) and Hoehner (1972: 9 with n. 4) for 22 BCE.

[2349] About Zenodorus, see the next note. Josephus explains in a flashback (*Ant.* 15.344-348) why Augustus granted Zenodorus' territory of Trachonitis, Batanea, and Auranitis to Herod: Trachonitis was a robbers' den and Zenodorus had struck a deal with the robbers rather than controlling them (see also the next note). The much briefer parallel passage of *War* (1.398-400) begins in a similar way: first Josephus mentions the grant of Trachonitis, Batanea, and Auranitis and then he explains this gift by referring to Zenodorus.

[2350] The parallel passage of *War* (1.398) similarly reads: "Zenodorus, who had contracted for Lysanias' estate (Ζηνόδωρος ὁ τὸν Λυσανίου μεμισθωμένος οἶκον) ..." (trans. Sievers/Forte in BJP 1a). Lysanias of Chalcis, who was also king of the Itureans, is meant (further references in *Ant.* 15.92 with the note to "Lysanias, the son of Ptolemy"). Josephus specifies Lysanias' territory in 15.360: "Ulatha, Paneas and the country surrounding it" (see 15.360 with notes). Trachonitis, mentioned in the next subclause, was located east of this region. The context of Augustus' grant of Trachonitis, Batanea, and Auranitis to Herod (15.344, 348) and the deposition of Zenodorus (15.349) imply that these regions were part of Zenodorus' dominion (see also 15.349 with the note to "because his territory was taken away from him"). They may have partly overlapped with "Ulatha, Paneas and the country surrounding it" (see above). After Lysanias' death (15.92), in 36 or 34 BCE, Zenodorus (who was probably a member of the Iturean elite) had leased Lysanias' territory from Cleopatra. Cassius Dio (54.9.3) refers to a tetrarchy of Zenodorus (possibly Trachonitis, Batanea, and Auranitis), and an inscription from Heliopolis-Baalbek (*CIG* no. 4523) mentions a "Zenodorus, son of the tetrarch Lysanias." Several coins refer to a tetrarch and high priest named Zenodorus (*BMC* 20.281). In all these cases it may concern the Zenodorus mentioned in Josephus, although not all scholars agree with this identification (discussion in Schürer-Vermes 1.565-67; Mahieu 2012: 136). The references to Zenodorus' ἐπαρχία ("territory") in *Ant.* 15.349, 352 and the coins referring to Zenodorus as tetrarch may imply that Zenodorus had been appointed tetrarch by Octavian after Actium (Smallwood 1976: 86), but this is not stated explicitly by Josephus or other sources. Zenodorus died in 20 BCE (*Ant.* 15.359; further discussion in Kasher 1988: 143-44, 157-60; 2007: 206; Shatzman 1991: 170-71, 293-98; Overman, Olive, and Nelson 2007: 180-82). Like Lysanias, Zenodorus had the task of controlling the gangs of robbers in this area (Buchheim 1960: 19; Schürer-Vermes 1.565-66; Kasher 1988: 151; Shatzman 1991: 292-94).

[2351] Zenodorus had to earn at least enough money to pay the sum of the lease (see the note to "leased the estate of Lysanias" above). This detail is missing in the parallel passage of *War* (1.398), and Josephus does not provide further specifics, apart from the information that Zenodorus cooperated with the robbers in order to enhance his income.

[2352] The noun πρόσοδος ("income") links up with the plural προσόδους ("revenues") in the previous subclause and emphasizes that Zenodorus struck a deal with the robbers for financial reasons. Vogel (2002: 140) suggests that Zenodorus' motive was greediness.

[2353] The name (of the area) Trachon (ὁ Τράχων "the Rough Area," see below; cf. *War* 1.398; *Ant.* 13.427; the standard Graecized form is ἡ Τραχωνῖτις, e.g., *War* 2.215; *Ant.* 1.145; 17.25; Schalit 1968: 119) refers to a region in the neighborhood of Damascus (Strabo 16.2.20, who refers to 2 hills called Τραχῶνες ["the Roughed Ones"]). It is located northeast of Batanea and north of Auranitis (see *Ant.* 15.343 with the note to "the territory of Trachon, Batanea, and Auranitis"). Eusebius (*Onom. s.v.* Ἰτουραία) and several rabbinic passages note that Trachonitis bordered the city of Bostra (Schürer-Vermes 1.337). As the Greek name implies (τράχων means "rugged, stony," LSJ *s.v.*), it was a rough region, with many small volcanic cones (see also the description in *Ant.* 15.346-348), and hardly suitable for settlement (Schürer-Vermes 1.337; Möller and Schmitt 1976: 184-85; Richardson 1996: 141). The rugged area together with its lack of inhabitants was a perfect base of operation for robbers. The parallel passage of *War* (1.398) and *Ant.* 16.285, 347; 17.26 (also Strabo 16.2.20) also note that robbers were living in Trachonitis.

For there were inhabitants who lived in these areas out of desperation,[2354] who kept plundering the area of the Damascenes,[2355] but Zenodorus did not stop them and shared in the profits himself.[2356] **345** The people living in the adjacent areas[2357] suffered badly[2358] and complained to Varro,[2359] who was the governor at that time.[2360] They asked him to write to Caesar about Zenodorus' criminal behavior.[2361]

When these things were reported to him, Caesar wrote in answer to remove the bands of robbers.[2362] He allotted the land[2363] to Herod[2364] in the expectation that[2365] through his

---

[2354] These people apparently had no other option but to live as freebooters and join gangs of robbers. One can think of criminals, runaway slaves, impoverished mercenaries, veterans, and Nabateans (cf. *Ant.* 15.352 referring to raids by them). Josephus describes them in greater detail in 15.346.

[2355] The noun δαμασκηνός ("inhabitant of Damascus") also occurs in the parallel passage of *War* (1.398). The rather vague passage may imply that the robbers operated in the city of Damascus and/or plundered the caravan trade on the roads to and from Damascus.

[2356] The parallel passage of *War* (1.398) is much briefer and only notes that Zenodorus was "continually sending (οὐ διέλειπεν) out the brigands of Trachonitis (τοὺς ἐκ τοῦ Τράχωνος λῃστάς) against the inhabitants of Damascus." (trans. Sievers/Forte in BJP 1a).

[2357] This phrase (οἱ πλησιόχωροι) can be synonymous with "the Damascenes" in the previous paragraph (as *War* 1.398 implies), but it can also have a more general meaning, in which case it may refer to the inhabitants of the city of Bostra (south of Trachonitis), Batanea, and Auranitis (see *Ant.* 15.343 with the note to "the territory of Trachon, Batanea, and Auranitis").

[2358] The phrase κακῶς πάσχω ("suffer badly") occurs several times in Josephus and only in *Antiquities* (see 15.118 with the note to "were faring badly").

[2359] An alternative translation would be "called upon Varro ... for help" (LSJ *s.v.* καταβοάω IV). A governor with the name Varro is also mentioned in the parallel passage of *War* (1.398-399). The identification of this Varro depends on the date when his office started. Dabrowa (1998: 17-18) and Eck (2002a: 1130) assume that it began in 25 or 24 BCE, in which case he may be identified with Marcus Terentius Varro, who subdued the Salassi in the Alps in 25 BCE (Strabo 4.6.7; Cassius Dio 53.25.3-5; Schürer-Vermes 1.256). If the grant of Trachonitis, Batanea, and Auranitis took place in 27 BCE (as argued by Mahieu 2012: 133-37; see *Ant.* 15.343 with the note to "for the following reason"), Varro would have become governor in 27 BCE. Mahieu (2008: 189; 2012: 137-38) considers it likely that Varro started his governorship right after the change of the Roman administration of the provinces in 27 BCE, when Augustus divided the provinces between the Senate and himself. Augustus had to appoint legates in his name after this change and Varro may have been one of them. This earlier date would render the identification with Marcus Terentius Varro impossible. Varro remained in office until 23 BCE, when Marcus Agrippa succeeded him (Schürer-Vermes 1.256).

War 1.398 notes that the inhabitants of Damascus turned to Varro for help (καταφυγόντες; cf. κατεβόων here in *Ant.*).

[2360] The verb ἡγεμονεύω means to "be the (Roman) governor (of Syria)" in this passage (see the previous note and cf. explicitly *War* 7.59). *War* 1.398 refers to Varro as ὁ ἡγεμὼν τῆς Συρίας ("the governor of Syria").

[2361] This implies that Zenodorus' deal with the robbers from Trachonitis was common knowledge. The inhabitants of Damascus and/or the people living in the neighborhood of Trachonitis apparently asked Varro to file a complaint with the emperor, which assumption is confirmed by the reference to Augustus' response in the next sentence. *War* 1.398 is slightly less specific: the Damascenes asked Varro "to report their unfortunate situation to Caesar" (trans. Sievers/Forte in BJP 1a).

[2362] The first part of Augustus' response to the complaint (see the previous note) concerns his order to Varro to eliminate the robbers (likewise in *War* 1.398, which shares the verb ἐξαιρέω ["remove, take out"] with *Ant.*).

The expression τὰ λῃστήρια ("the bands of robbers") repeats the vocabulary of *Ant.* 15.344. *War* 1.398 uses the singular of this same noun.

[2363] I.e., Trachonitis, Batanea, and Auranitis (see *Ant.* 15.343-344).

[2364] The second element of Augustus' response reports Zenodorus' punishment: his land was taken away and allotted to Herod. The continuation of the narrative indicates that Augustus expected Herod to stop the brigandage in the area (cf. *Ant.* 16.285, 347; 17.26). The *War* report (1.399) is slightly different: it indicates that Varro undertook a campaign against the robbers (likewise Strabo 16.2.20), purged Trachonitis of them, and took away this territory from Zenodorus, and that Augustus only later (ὕστερον) gave it to Herod.

[2365] The ὡς in this clause may introduce indirect speech referring to Augustus' letter of response (LSJ *s.v.* ὡς III I.2).

care the region of Trachonitis would cause no more trouble to the people of the neighborhood.[2366] **346** For it was not easy at all to stop[2367] those who had made their habit of robbing and had no other means of making a living,[2368] since they had no cities nor possessed fields,[2369] but only underground refuges and caves,[2370] and they were living together with their cattle.[2371] Nevertheless, they had arranged water supplies[2372] and stores of grain,[2373] which enabled them[2374] to hold out for a long time in their hiding places.[2375] **347** And the entrances were really narrow—people [could only] enter one by one[2376]—but the places inside were unbelievably big[2377] and constructed to provide a lot of space.[2378] The ground above their dwellings was not high but on the same level as the ground that surrounded it.[2379] The area existed entirely of rough rocks, which were scarcely passable,[2380] unless one used the paths[2381] with a guide.[2382] For even these unfold themselves[2383] not straight but have many bends.[2384] **348** Now when they were prevented from harming[2385]

[2366] See also *Ant.* 15.348. *War* 1.399 reports that Varro took action against the robbers (see the note to "Herod" above).

The phrase οἱ πλησίον (literally "those who are nearby") links up with the expression οἱ πλησιόχωροι at the beginning of this paragraph (see the note to "people living in the adjacent areas"). The phrase also occurs in *Ant.* 15.305, 348. In *War* 7.260 it means "one's fellow men" (Rengstorf *s.v.*).

[2367] *Ant.* 15.346-348 explains why it was complicated to combat the robbery.

For a similar combination of ῥᾴδιον ἐστιν ("it is easy") and ἐπέχω ("stop") in a different context, see Plutarch, *Mor.* (*Cohib. ira*) 454e.

[2368] The geographical conditions made it hard to survive as farmers in this region (Shatzman 1991: 173 with n. 10). The noun βίος means "livelihood" here (Rengstorf *s.v.*).

[2369] *Ant.* 15.346-347 offers a detailed description of the home base of the robbers in Trachonitis, which is absent in *War*. Josephus may have taken his information from a source (cf. several words in 15.347 are unique). The passage matches other statements about the region of Trachonitis in Josephus (see 15.344 with the note to "Trachonitis") and explains why there were hardly any other inhabitants than the robbers This particular situation gave the robbers free play in preparing their hiding places and raids.

[2370] Strabo (16.2.20) confirms that there were deep caves in Trachonitis, owing to volcanic activity in the past (Huguet 1985: 9).

[2371] This detail emphasizes the robbers' very basic lifestyle (cf. *Ant.* 10.216, 242 [paraphrasing Dan 4] about Nebuchadnezzar living temporarily with the wild beasts and Mark 1:13 about Jesus living with the wild beasts in the wilderness for 40 days).

[2372] The plural of συναγωγή refers to devices for the collecting of water here (Rengstorf *s.v.*).

[2373] The noun προπαρασκευή means "preparation" in *War* 2.604, but here, in combination with σιτίων, "stores (of grain)" (Rengstorf *s.v.*; less likely, though also possible, "pre-prepared [food]"). There are no further occurrences of this word in Josephus.

[2374] The translation follows Niese (395), who reads αἵ with MS P. Most Greek MSS have καί instead of αἵ, which results in a slightly different translation: "... so that they were able (to) ...."

[2375] The caves in Trachonitis were apparently the permanent places to which the robbers could fall back. They needed such shelter since they had no option but to rob for making a living, as the beginning of this paragraph reports. Their "job" implied that they had to secure supplies of water and food in order to survive during periods in which they were unable to make raids or had to hide for armed groups searching for them.

[2376] Similar vocabulary in Eusebius, *Comm. Ps.* (PG 23.129).

[2377] Strabo (16.2.20) notes that a famous cave in the area could host 4,000 persons.

[2378] This suggests that the robbers constructed large spaces inside the caves, which seems implausible, although they may have adapted the caves here and there to enhance their comfort. The apparent exaggeration highlights the robbers' determination and toughness, in accordance with the beginning of *Ant.* 15.346, which emphasizes that it was difficult to stop the robberies.

[2379] Josephus states twice, in different words, that there was no elevation of the ground above the robbers' dwellings, which may highlight that the dwellings in the caves were invisible to somebody standing above them.

[2380] The adjective δύσοδος ("difficult of access, impassable," Rengstorf *s.v.*) is a *hapax legomenon* in Josephus

[2381] The noun τρίβος ("path," Rengstorf *s.v.*) is also a *hapax legomenon* in Josephus.

[2382] The noun ὁδηγία ("showing the way," Rengstorf *s.v.*) is a further *hapax legomenon* in Josephus (Rengstorf *s.v.*).

[2383] The verb ἐξελίττω ("unroll, unfold," LSJ *s.v.*) is again a *hapax legomenon* in Josephus.

[2384] The alliteration of the l sound in the concluding phrase ἀλλὰ πολλὰς ἕλικας ἐξελίττονται draws

the people in the neighborhood,[2386] it was their habit to rob even each other, such that every kind of lawlessness was committed[2387] in the meantime.[2388]

After Herod had received the grant from Caesar,[2389] he entered the country,[2390] using the experience of guides.[2391] He put an end to the villains[2392] and provided a secure peace to the surrounding people.[2393] **(10.2) 349** But Zenodorus,[2394] who was at first angry because his territory was taken away from him,[2395] then became even more angry out of jealousy[2396] because Herod had taken the rule over from him.[2397] He went up to Rome to accuse him,[2398] but he returned without success.[2399]

---

attention to the uniqueness of the landscape and emphasizes that it was absolutely inhospitable.

[2385] Cf. *Ant.* 17.26 about the robbers from Trachonitis, which passage shares the noun λῃστεία ("robbery") with *Ant.* 15.348 and has the verb κακουργέω ("cause harm") instead of the noun κακούργημα ("offence, crime").

[2386] The phrase οἱ πλησίον ("their neighbors") repeats the vocabulary of *Ant.* 15.345 (see the note to "the people of the neighborhood").

[2387] This concluding statement forms the climax of the description of the robbers and their home base in Trachonitis and characterizes Trachonitis as a hotbed of crime and anarchy.

[2388] The adverbial phrase ἐν τούτῳ ("in the meantime," LSJ *s.v.* οὗτος C.VIII.6b) is idiomatic and anticipates Herod's action against the robbers narrated in the subsequent part of this paragraph. The phrase constitutes the very end of the flashback about Zenodorus and the robbers that starts in *Ant.* 15.344 (see the note to "A certain Zenodorus").

[2389] *Ant.* 15.348 continues the narrative of 15.343, with 15.344-348 being a flashback in between.

The noun χάρις means "grant" here (LSJ *s.v.* III.1b). It concerns Augustus' grant of Trachonitis, Batanea, and Auranitis (*Ant.* 15.343).

[2390] Herod himself dealt with the robbers, as he had done much earlier with Ezekias and his fellow brigands, who were active in parts of Syria (*War* 1.204; cf. *Ant.* 14.159). The verb παρέρχομαι ("pass, enter") also occurs in the description of the entrances of the caves in which the robbers were living.

[2391] The word ὁδηγός ("guide") echoes the noun ὁδηγία ("showing the way") in *Ant.* 15.347.

[2392] The verb πονηρεύομαι ("do evil," Rengstorf *s.v.*) is a *hapax legomenon* in Josephus.

[2393] The phrase οἱ πέριξ ("the surrounding people") links up with οἱ πλησίον referring to the robbers' neighbors in *Ant.* 15.345 and at the beginning of this paragraph. Herod apparently fulfilled the former task of Zenodorus, i.e., controlling the gangs of robbers (see 15.344 with the note to "A certain Zenodorus"), with great success.

The *Antiquities* report differs in certain details from the much briefer description in *War* (1.398-399), in which Varro takes action against the robbers (see 15.345 with the note to "Varro"). *Antiquities*, therefore, presents Herod in a more positive light than *War* does in this respect.

[2394] Concerning Zenodorus, see *Ant.* 15.344 with the note to "A certain Zenodorus."

[2395] The noun ἐπαρχία can mean "province" but also more generally "territory" in the Imperial period. Marcus-Wikgren (168 n. *a*) argue that it refers to Zenodorus' tetrarchy. Zenodorus' dominion most probably included Trachonitis, Batanea, and Auranitis (see *Ant.* 15.344 with the note to "the estate of Lysanias") and "Ulatha, Paneas and the country surrounding it" (15.360, laying [partly] west of the former territories). Since the latter territories were given to Herod after Zenodorus' death, the noun ἐπαρχία refers here to Trachonitis, Batanea, and Auranitis.

[2396] Zenodorus and Herod were competitors, being both friendly kings of the Romans in roughly the same region (Braund 1984). The context explains Zenodorus' jealousy: Augustus clearly had much more goodwill for Herod than for Zenodorus and appointed Herod as ruler over Zenodorus' territory (see also the next note).

[2397] This remark confirms that Trachonitis, Batanea, and Auranitis were parts of Zenodorus' territory that had been granted by Augustus to Herod (see the note to "because his territory was taken away from him" above and *Ant.* 15.344). The much shorter parallel narrative of *War* (1.399) reports that Zenodorus' territory was later given to Herod.

[2398] I.e., Herod. Zenodorus attempted to change Augustus' decision and apparently had no other means of doing so but to bring an accusation against Herod, plausibly after the robbers had been subdued. Josephus does not inform us about the kind of accusation, but it goes without saying that he complained of extremely severe actions by Herod. Since Augustus must have known that Herod was successful in dealing with the robbers, as *Ant.* 15.348 implies, he probably turned a blind eye to Herod's measures in Trachonitis. The precise date of Zenodorus' visit to Rome is unknown.

[2399] See the previous note. The *praesens historicum* ἀναστρέφει ("he returned") helps to enliven the narrative

350 Agrippa[2400] was sent as Caesar's deputy[2401] to the region across the Ionian Sea.[2402] Herod met him when he was wintering in Mytilene,[2403] for he was a very close friend and companion.[2404] He then returned[2405] to Judea. **351** And some of the Gadarenes[2406] went to Agrippa[2407] trying to accuse him,[2408] but [Agrippa] did not even give them the opportunity

Agrippa and Caesar support Herod in his conflict with the Gadarenes.
War *1.399*

(Blass, Debrunner, and Rehkopf 1976: 265-66; cf. the verbal form πέμπεται in the next paragraph), while the succinct final clause with the alliteration of the a sound (ἄπρακτος ἀναστρέφει) adds emphasis to the unsuccessfulness of Zenodorus' trip.

[2400] The section *Ant.* 15.350-359, starting with a reference to Agrippa, concerns complains of the Gadarenes against Herod. This Agrippa is Marcus Agrippa, who has been previously mentioned in *Ant.* 15.318 (for further references in Josephus, see Schalit 1968: 3). Marcus Vipsanius Agrippa was born in Dalmatia in 64/63 BCE. He became acquainted with Octavian-Augustus in Rome at the school of rhetoric, accompanied him on his trips to Spain and Apollonia (in Illyria) in 46-44 BCE, and fulfilled many important tasks afterwards. In 23 BCE Augustus, who was very ill at that time, handed his signet ring over to Agrippa. Somewhat later Agrippa married Augustus' daughter, Julia. Telling is a statement of Mecaenas to Augustus about Agrippa: "You have made him so great that he must either become your son-in-law or be slain" (Cassius Dio 54.6.5, trans. Cary; further references in Reinhold 1933; Roddaz 1984 and the next note).

[2401] Agrippa received, probably in 23 BCE, the privilege to act as Augustus' deputy in the provinces attributed to him, such that his authority (*imperium*) went beyond that of all others except Augustus'. The details of his *imperium* are unknown (discussion in Kienast 1999: 108-09).

[2402] I.e., to the East. The Ionian Sea is a part of the Mediterranean Sea, south of the Adriatic Sea, between Epirus and Italy. The name Ἰόνιος derives from Io, the daughter of Inachus, who swam across this sea (Aeschylus, *Prom.* 840; see LSJ *s.v.*). The Ionian Sea is also mentioned in *War* 1.183; *Ant.* 14.123.

[2403] Mytilene (also mentioned in *Ant.* 16.20; Josephus writes Μιτυλήνη instead of the usual spelling Μυτιλήνη) is the name of the main city on the island of Lesbos, near the Hellespont. Marcus Agrippa probably stayed in Mytilene from 23 until 21 BCE (Tacitus, *Ann.* 14.53; Suetonius, *Aug.* 66.3; Suetonius, *Tib.* 10.1; Cassius Dio 53.32.1; 54.6; Schürer-Vermes 1.256; Kienast 1999: 72). Herod's visit may, therefore, be dated to the winter of 23/22 or of 22/21 BCE (Shatzman 1991: 293; Günther 2005: 132). Several scholars prefer the winter of 23/22 BCE, assuming that Herod was keen to show his loyalty to Agrippa as soon as it was feasible (Schürer-Vermes 1.291 n. 11; Kasher 1988: 159 n. 76; Richardson 1996:

232; differently Otto 1913: 70; Schalit 2001: 424; Günther 2005: 132; Mahieu 2012: 135).

Kokkinos (1998: 221-22) and Kasher (2007: 207) argue that there is a close connection between the grant (mentioned in *Ant.* 15.343) and Herod's visit to Agrippa (15.350), but this is not necessarily the case: the grant could have been assigned already at the end of 27 BCE and the visit taken place in the winter of 23/22 or 22/21 BCE (Mahieu 2008: 188; 2012: 135-36).

[2404] The Greek subclause indicating the close relationship between Herod and Marcus Agrippa is a parenthesis introduced by ἦν γάρ (for similar parentheses, see *Ant.* 15.325 with the note to "—water is absent in this area—").

Agrippa was the most important person after Augustus in the Roman Empire at that time (see the note to "Agrippa" above and 15.361 with the note to "Agrippa"). Josephus' remark about Herod being Agrippa's friend and companion (φίλος καὶ συνήθης; for the same pair of words, see *War* 1.544; *Life* 180, 192, 204; Mason in BJP 9 on *Life* 180), which is further qualified with the phrase εἰς τὰ μάλιστα (literally "to the most"), suggests that this relationship went beyond "business" and that they really were close. Such a friendship is confirmed by other passages (e.g., *Ant.* 15.318, 361 and 16.12-15 about Agrippa's visit to Jerusalem; Richardson 1996: 232-33; and also the note to "did not even give them the opportunity to speak" below). Herod's intervention on behalf of the citizens of Ilios-Troy in 16 or 15 BCE, when Agrippa wanted to punish them because his wife, Julia, had almost been drowned in their city (Nicolaus of Damascus, *FGH* 90 F 134; cf. *Ant.* 16.26), also points to a close relationship between Herod and Agrippa (Richardson 1996: 233).

[2405] Most Greek MSS read the *praesens historicum* ἀναστρέφει ("he returned"), which is also found at the end of *Ant.* 15.349, but Niese (396) reads the imperfect ἀνέστρεφεν with MS P and E.

[2406] I.e., the citizens of the Decapolis city of Gadara, which was located south-east of Lake Gennesaret. Since Gadara was added to Herod's territory by Octavian in 30 BCE (*War* 1.396; *Ant.* 15.217; see also 15.354), Herod had been ruling over the city for ca. 7 years thus far.

[2407] Given that Josephus does not indicate a change of place for Agrippa, the Gadarenes probably visited Agrippa in Mytilene, like Herod had done (*Ant.* 15.350).

[2408] I.e., Herod. Niese (396) reads αὐτοῦ ("him") with MS P and E, but the other MSS read Ἡρώδου ("Herod"),

to speak[2409] and sent them to the king in chains.[2410] And the Arabs,[2411] who had been hostile to Herod's rule[2412] for a long time,[2413] caused trouble and attempted at that time to revolt against his administration[2414] with a fair reason,[2415] so they thought. **352** For Zenodorus, who was at this stage despairing of[2416] his own situation,[2417] had previously managed to lease to[2418] them[2419] a part of his territory,[2420] Auranitis,[2421] for fifty talents.[2422] Since this

---

which is the easier and therefore probably the secondary reading.

Josephus does not give the content of the accusation. Günther (2005: 132) argues that it was similar to a later accusation before Augustus (*Ant.* 15.354), which refers explicitly to severe commands and a tyrannical rule. There is a certain analogy between Zenodorus accusing Herod before Augustus (15.349) and the Gadarenes accusing the king before Agrippa (cf. the repetition of the verb κατηγορέω in 15.349, 351; see also 15.357).

[2409] Agrippa apparently reasoned that the Gadarenes were under Herod's authority and that their complaint meant that they did not recognize the king's position. He therefore sent them to Herod in chains, which implies once again that Agrippa and Herod had a close relationship (Richardson 1996: 233; Vogel 2002: 141; see *Ant.* 15.350 with the note to "a very close friend and companion" and 15.361 with the note to "Agrippa").

[2410] The later flashback (*Ant.* 15.356) to this episode adds that Herod did not do any harm to these Gadarenes and released them.

[2411] "The Arabs" probably refers to the Nabateans in general (see *Ant.* 15.107 with the note to "The Arab") or a specific group among them, in particular those Nabateans who were living in Auranitis and/or its neighborhood (Shatzman 1991: 294).

[2412] In previous sections Josephus describes several hostilities between Herod and the Nabateans (see *Ant.* 15.106-108 concerning Malichus I's slowness in paying back Herod; 15.111-160 concerning several battles between Herod and the Nabateans; and 15.165-178 concerning Malichus I's possible involvement in treason by Hyrcanus II).

The phrase δυσμενῶς ἔχω ("be hostile [to]") also occurs in *Ant.* 1.166; 2.322; 13.432; 15.365; 16.90.

[2413] Shatzman (1991: 294) argues that the narrative refers here to the battles described in *Ant.* 15.111-160 and that it at the same time implies that part of the Nabateans had become subjects of Herod, as the continuation of the narrative shows (see the note to "revolt against his administration" below). If so, the passage may link up with *Ant.* 15.159, which states that the Nabateans acclaimed Herod patron (or ruler) after their defeat by him. The exact meaning of 15.159, however, remains unclear (see the note to "acclaimed him patron of their people"). Another possibility is that Josephus refers here to the Nabateans who were living within Herod's kingdom, e.g., in Auranitis, which had previously been part of Zenodorus' territory (15.343-344, 349, 352). Shatzman (1991: 294) also points to the selling off of the private property of Herod's son Archelaus (*Ant.* 17.344, 355; 18.26) and argues that Auranitis was the private property of Zenodorus.

[2414] The expression τὰ πράγματα can mean, among other things, "power, government, administration" (see *Ant.* 15.32 and 15.189 with the note to "the Commonwealth would fall to him").

[2415] The combination of εὔλογος ("justified, plausible") and αἰτία ("reason") also occurs in *Ant.* 7.388, concerning David's instructions to find a good reason to kill his enemy Sumuis (biblical name: Shimei), the son of Gera.

[2416] For similar cases of a participle of ἀπογινώσκω plus ἤδη ("despairing already of"), cf. Diodorus 15.71.6; 16.13.1; 18.21.3; Appian, *Bell. civ.* 1.10.90.

[2417] This remark is obvious in the light of the previous information about Zenodorus: he had been deprived of Trachonitis, Batanea, and Auranitis (*Ant.* 15.343-344, 349) and unsuccessful in his accusation against Herod before Augustus (15.349).

[2418] Zenodorus apparently had been in desperate need of money (cf. *Ant.* 15.344) and he most probably had struck his deal with the Nabateans without permission from Augustus (with Shatzman 1991: 294); otherwise Augustus would have taken arrangements for the Nabateans when he made his grant to Herod.

The verb ἀποδίδωμι can mean, among other things, "lease (to)" as well as "sell" (Rengstorf *s.v.*). Most scholars assume that the Nabateans bought Auranitis from Zenodorus (e.g., Kasher 1988: 159; Schalit 2001: 327), although the meaning "leased" seems more plausible in the light of the 50 talents mentioned further on (see the note to "fifty talents"; cf. Günther 2005: 130-31, who argues that the deal was different from a sale).

[2419] I.e., the "Arabs" mentioned in *Ant.* 15.351 (referring to Nabateans; see the note to "the Arabs").

[2420] The noun ἐπαρχία ("territory") also occurs in *Ant.* 15.349 referring to Zenodorus' territory (l.c. with the note to "because his territory was taken away from him").

[2421] That Auranitis was part of Zenodorus' territory is confirmed by *Ant.* 15.343-344 (see 15.351 with the note to "for a long time").

[2422] The amount of 50 talents is a reasonable sum for

region was included in Caesar's gift,[2423] they kept disputing[2424] [this gift], claiming they were unjustly deprived of it.[2425] They frequently made raids[2426] and intended to use force,[2427] but they went to court to assert their claim on other occasions.[2428] **353** They also induced the poor among his [Herod's] soldiers [to defect].[2429] They were hostile to him[2430] and always putting their hope on[2431] becoming involved in a rebellion,[2432] in which those who do badly in life rejoice most.[2433] Although Herod knew that these things had been happening for a long time,[2434] he still did not use force[2435] against them but tried to assuage them[2436]

---

an annual lease of this territory (cf. the 200 [or 400] talents for the territories that Herod leased from Cleopatra; see *Ant.* 15.96, 106-107).

[2423] I.e., Augustus' grant of Trachonitis, Batanea, and Auranitis to Herod (*Ant.* 15.343).

[2424] Günther (2005: 131) argues that the Nabateans had become self-confident following Aelius Gallus' defeat in South Arabia (see *Ant.* 15.317 with the note to "the Red Sea") and the severe drought in the Syrian region (15.299-316).

The verb διαμφισβητέω ("dispute," Rengstorf *s.v.*) occurs once elsewhere in Josephus (*Ant.* 14.38).

[2425] From the perspective of the Nabateans, Augustus' grant of Auranitis to Herod could easily have been perceived as unfair since they were obliged to pay Zenodorus 50 talents for the lease (see above with the note to "fifty talents"). Even if this lease contract was annulled, Herod may have forced them to pay (as a tribute) considerably more than 50 talents. The unfairness would have been even greater if Zenodorus had sold the territory to them.

[2426] Shatzman (1991: 294) argues that these raids were undertaken in Auranitis.

[2427] This description is quite vague. The Nabateans apparently used various means to acquire what they thought was their rightful position in Auranitis (see also the previous and the next note). Since the Nabateans clearly rejected Augustus' grant of Auranitis to Herod, they were not recognizing the emperor's authority. They clearly did not accept Herod as their ruler either. This seems to have been a reckless strategy, but Herod did not punish them for that and tried to appease them (see *Ant.* 15.353).

[2428] Again the description is tantalizing vague. Which court could this have been? Not one of the courts in Herod's kingdom since the Nabateans did not accept Herod's authority (see the previous note). They could have appealed to Marcus Agrippa, like the Gadarenes did (see *Ant.* 15.351; Kasher 1988: 159 assumes that they actually did so), but that does not seem smart at all because they apparently did not accept the emperor's authority either (see the previous note). Josephus' information is too limited for developing a plausible interpretation of what actually happened. He may even have invented the story in order to present a further case (in addition to the Gadarenes', 15.351) of non-Jewish subjects who were most unhappy with Herod as their ruler.

[2429] Obviously poor soldiers were dissatisfied and thus an easy prey for opponents who wanted to start a rebellion. Shatzman (1991: 190) rightly concludes that this passage does not necessarily mean that Herod's soldiers were badly paid; the soldiers may have been poor before joining the king's army. Herod's rule depended heavily on a loyal army, which renders it plausible that Herod's soldiers were paid reasonably well. For similar vocabulary, cf. Diodorus 33.21a.1.

[2430] Kasher (1988: 159) argues that part of these soldiers were Nabateans who had enrolled in Herod's army after having been defeated by him during the rule of Malichus I (see *War* 1.384; *Ant.* 15.156), which would explain their hostility: they may have had no other option but to enroll in Herod's army and remained hostile to him because of their defeat.

[2431] With Niese (396), who reads ἐπελπίζοντες ἀεί (cf. Polybius 4.35.6). MSS FLAM read ἐπελπίζοντες ἀεί ("[who were] always hoping").

[2432] For νεωτερισμός ("uprising"), see *Ant.* 15.30 with the note to "a new regime."

[2433] This is one of Josephus' truisms, which reflect his own voice (see especially "success breeds envy," which expression is repeated in various forms: *War* 1.208; *Ant.* 10.250; *Life* 122; cf. *War* 1.77; *Ant.* 13.288; Mason in BJP 9 on *Life* 122). Other truisms in Josephus are "Good people are made better by hope of a reward after death; wicked persons are restrained by fear of punishment" (*War* 2.157), "No one should be called happy before his death" (*War* 5.461, echoing a statement by Solon in Herodotus 1.32.7), and "Some children are not like their parents: kind and moderate ones can come from vile parents, just as those born from good parents sometimes show themselves depraved" (*Ant.* 6.33; I owe these references to Steve Mason, Aberdeen; cf. *Ant.* 15.42 with the note to "as is likely in a case of reconciliation").

[2434] The vague time indication implies that the Nabateans were undertaking activities against Herod's rule for a considerable period, which echoes Josephus' remark in *Ant.* 15.351: "And the Arabs who had been

with a calculated approach.[2437] He did not think it was suitable to provide a pretext[2438] for them to cause disturbances.[2439]

(10.3) 354 When the seventeenth year of his [Herod's] reign[2440] had already started,[2441] Caesar came to Syria.[2442] And at that time[2443] most[2444] of the inhabitants of Gadara[2445]

---

hostile (δυσμενῶς ἔχοντες; cf. 15.353: δυσμενεῖς ἦσαν) to Herod's rule for a long time"; the reason for their hostility given by Josephus is Augustus' grant of Auranitis to Herod (*Ant*. 15.343, 351-352). The next time marker in the narrative concerns Augustus' visit of Judea in Herod's 17th year (probably in 20 BCE; see 15.354 with the note to "reign"), such that "for a long time" would mean at least a few years.

[2435] Josephus uses the adjective δυσμενής with variant meanings in this paragraph: in connection with the soldiers mentioned previously the word means "hostile" (cf. δυσμενῶς ἔχειν in *Ant*. 15.351 concerning "the Arabs"), while here it is used as a substantive meaning "forcible measures" (Rengstorf *s.v.* δυσμενής).

[2436] For a similar prudent response, cf. Herod's reaction to the protest against the trophies in Jerusalem (*Ant*. 15.277), which shares the verb παρηγορέω ("comfort, appease") with this passage.

[2437] Günther (2005: 133) supposes a connection between the actions of the Nabateans against Herod (*Ant*. 15.351-353) and the complaints of the Gadarenes (15.351, 354); *Ant*. 15.354 would suggest that Herod did retaliate the Nabateans' actions.

The noun ἐπιλογισμός ("calculation, prudence," Rengstorf *s.v.*) is a *hapax legomenon* in Josephus (for the phrase ἐξ ἐπιλογισμοῦ, cf. Philo, *Leg*. 3.102; *Plant*. 123; *Sacr*. 35; *Somn*. 1.75; Plutarch, *Mor*. [*Fat.*] 571d).

[2438] The phrase ἀφορμὰς ἐνδίδωμι ("provide a pretext, give reason") also occurs in *Ant*. 18.333 (cf. Philo, *Spec*. 2.93; Plutarch, *Per*. 33).

[2439] This statement is surprising: it is inconsistent with the preceding narrative, which suggests that the Nabateans caused disturbances (*Ant*. 15.351), made raids, and approached Herod's soldiers (15.352-353).

For the motif of ταραχή ("disorder, disturbance, [internal] rebellion") in the Herod narrative of *Antiquities*, see 15.30 with the note to "war and disorder"; 15.72-73, 239, 326 (with the note to "disturbances in his kingdom"; also van Henten 2011b).

[2440] Herod's 17th year can be 24/23 BCE or 21/20 BCE, depending on whether one takes Herod's appointment in 40 BCE or his capture of Jerusalem in 37 BCE as point of departure. Most scholars assume that the year concerns Nisan (March/April) 21/Nisan 20 BCE (e.g., Schwartz 1907: 265-66; Schürer-Vermes 1.291-92; Smallwood 1976: 88 n. 97). Mahieu (2012: 146-47) argues for March 20/March 19 BCE, in consequence of her argument that Herod captured Jerusalem in 36 rather than 37 BCE (pp. 60-64).

[2441] With Niese (396), who reads προελθόντος with MSS PFLAM. MS V and E have παρελθόντος ("had passed"), and MS W προσελθόντος ("had come"). Marcus-Wikgren (170), Schürer-Vermes (1.292), and Kokkinos (1998: 167 n. 60), among others, prefer the reading of MS V and E, which has the advantage that Augustus' visit can be easily combined with the reference to Herod's 17th year. The visit took place after the spring of 20 BCE (see the next note), i.e., after the 17th year had already passed. However, the reading of MS V and E seems to be the *lectio facilior*. Niese's reading can imply a contradiction between the date of Augustus' visit and Herod's 17th year, but this is not the case if Mahieu's year conversion is followed (see the previous note).

[2442] Cassius Dio (54.7.4-6) situates Augustus' visit to Syria in the spring of 20 BCE (Kasher 1988: 159; Richardson 1996: 233; Schalit 2001: 274 n. 435; Mahieu 2012: 146). In *War* 1.399 Josephus notes that the visit occurred in the 10th year after Augustus' first visit to Syria (which took place in 30 BCE, *Ant*. 15.199-201). Unfortunately Josephus does not specify Augustus' itinerary. Richardson (1996: 234) makes a calculated guess and thinks that Herod entertained Augustus at Paneas (15.363-364) and organized a royal procession to Samaria-Sebaste, with its temple of Augustus and Roma. Afterwards he would have arranged a visit to Caesarea, where another temple of Augustus and Roma was located. It is plausible that Augustus visited Gadara during this trip (see 15.357-358 with the note to "prepared to defend himself").

[2443] With this phrase Josephus connects the Gadarenes' complaint against Herod (*Ant*. 15.353-359) with Augustus' visit to Syria of 20 BCE. Thematically the complaint is connected with 2 previous sections (15.343-349 about Augustus' grant of Trachonitis, Batanea, and Auranitis to Herod, and 15.350-353 about Herod's visit to Marcus Agrippa). Both sections are related to Josephus' description of Herod's final problems with Zenodorus (15.354-360), which are connected with the complaint. The thematic connections do not necessarily imply, however, that the events described occur in the same period (Mahieu 2008: 188 and see 15.350 with the note to "Mytilene").

[2444] Compare Josephus' description of the Gadarenes' earlier complaint against Herod, before Agrippa, which refers to "some of the Gadarenes." The change from

complained about Herod,[2446] claiming that he was severe in his commands and tyrannical.[2447] **355** They dared to make these charges especially because Zenodorus[2448] insisted on accusing him.[2449] He assured them under oath that he would not leave any way untried to remove them from Herod's kingdom[2450] and add[2451] them to Caesar's administration.[2452] **356** Persuaded by these [assurances][2453] the Gadarenes made a loud outcry.[2454] They found

---

"some" to "most" suggests that Herod's rule had become more severe during the few years between the visits of Agrippa and Augustus.

[2445] Gadara is one of the Decapolis cities. It is located on a hill south of the Yarmuk River, ca. 10 km southeast of Lake Gennesaret. The city was included in Octavian's grant of several territories and cities to Herod after the defeat of Mark Antony and Cleopatra (*War* 1.396; *Ant.* 15.217).

[2446] This is the second complaint against Herod before a high Roman official by a group of Gadarenes narrated by Josephus (see *Ant.* 15.351 about the complaint before Marcus Agrippa).

The verb καταβοάω ("complain") also occurs in 15.345, concerning the people living in the neighborhood of Trachonitis who suffered from the robbers and complained before Varro.

[2447] See also *Ant.* 15.357, which passage indicates that the Gadarenes accused Herod of outrageous acts, robberies, and destructions of temples. Both this very serious accusation and the present strong complaint about Herod's tyrannical rule are contradicted by a detail in the continuation of the narrative: in 15.356 Josephus notes that Herod had not punished the Gadarenes whom Agrippa had sent to him as prisoners. The complaint does match, however, a trend in Josephus' presentation of Herod as ruler; it is in line with brief references in *Antiquities* that point to Herod's supposed tyrannical rule and behavior. E.g., *Ant.* 14.165: "But the chief Jews were in great fear when they saw how violent and bold Herod was, and how much he longed for a rule as a tyrant (τυραννίδος γλιχόμενον)" (trans. Marcus); 15.70 about the thoughts of Mariamme I and Alexandra: "Yet the women, as is likely, did not grasp the affection of Herod's disposition to them but the cruelty of it: if he would die, they would not escape destruction and a tyrannical death (θανάτου τυραννικοῦ). So they considered the deeper sense of what was said to be cruel"; 15.321 concerning Herod marrying Mariamme II: "Yet he rejected the thought of accomplishing everything by using his authority, suspecting, which was true, that he would be accused of using force as well as of tyrannical behavior (εἰς βίαν καὶ τυραννίδα διαβληθήσεσθαι). Therefore he considered it better to marry the maiden"; 16.4 in connection with Herod's new law concerning burglary: "That the punishment, as it was laid down then, became hard and unlawful, demonstrated his arrogance; whereby he was keen on imposing the punishment not in a king-like but in a tyrannical way (τυραννικῶς), neglectful of the public interest of his subjects" (my trans.). Josephus becomes much more explicit about this when he describes the last period of Herod's life (further discussion in van Henten 2011b; cf. Schalit 2001: 305, who argues that 15.354-359 implies that Herod treated the Greek cities in his kingdom as harsh as the Jewish ones).

[2448] Concerning Zenodorus, see *Ant.* 15.344 with the notes to "A certain Zenodorus" and "had leased the estate of Lysanias."

[2449] Zenodorus' behavior is understandable in the light of the previous paragraphs in which Josephus reports that Zenodorus was angry with Herod and jealous as well because Augustus had given his territory to the king (*Ant.* 15.343-349). In 15.349 Josephus notes that Zenodorus even went to Rome in order to accuse Herod. Zenodorus and the Gadarenes apparently had a common enemy in the person of Herod. That they were in touch with each other is obvious; Zenodorus' former territory (Trachonitis, Batanea, and Auranitis, 15.344) was close to Gadara.

Cf. *Ant.* 15.193-194, 201.

[2450] The aim of the Gadarenes to be disconnected again from Herod's kingdom becomes obvious here and should be considered in the light of their accusation and of the fact that they had become part of the kingdom only ca. 10 years earlier (see *Ant.* 15.351 with the note to "some of the Gadarenes"). Zenodorus no doubt acted out of self-interest by setting himself up as the supporter of the Gadarenes' cause: it helped him to weaken Herod's position and he could have benefited had the charges against Herod been declared valid by the Romans.

[2451] Niese (397) considers the Greek text with the infinitive προσθήσειν ("add") to be corrupt (see also the next note).

[2452] This seems to imply that Gadara wanted to become part of the Roman province of Syria (Stern 1974b: 251), which actually happened after Herod's death (see *Ant.* 17.320).

[2453] For a similar phrase with a passive participle aorist of ἀναπείθω and the demonstrative pronoun τούτοις, cf. *War* 2.183 about Herod Antipas, who let himself be persuaded by his wife Herodias to travel to

encouragement in the fact that Herod had released²⁴⁵⁵ those who had been handed over by Agrippa for punishment²⁴⁵⁶ and that he had not done them any harm.²⁴⁵⁷ For more than anyone else²⁴⁵⁸ he had the reputation of being inexorably harsh²⁴⁵⁹ towards his own people,²⁴⁶⁰ but of being generous²⁴⁶¹ to foreigners²⁴⁶² by letting them go²⁴⁶³ after they had done wrong.²⁴⁶⁴ **357** So they accused him of outrageous acts,²⁴⁶⁵ robberies,²⁴⁶⁶ and

---

the emperor Gaius Caligula in order to be elevated to the status of a king. Antipas' trip had the opposite result: he was exiled to Spain (cf. *Ant.* 18.247-252; Mason in BJP 1b on *War* 2.183). Here the phrase anticipates perhaps already the remark that the Gadarenes were ill-advised (15.358). *Ant.* 15.64 offers a similar phrase (τούτοις ἀναπειθόμενος "having been persuaded by these [words]") about Cleopatra's advice to Mark Antony to punish Herod for having Aristobulus III killed.

²⁴⁵⁴ The phrase οὐ μικρὰν καταβοὴν ἐποιήσαντο (literally "made not a small outcry") is a case of *litotes*.

²⁴⁵⁵ Niese (397) reads διιέντος (from διίημι "release," LSJ *s.v.* II.3; Rengstorf *s.v.*) following MS P. MSS FAMV read διαφέντος ("dismissed"), and MSS LW διαφέροντος ("carried over").

²⁴⁵⁶ This passage links up with Josephus' reference to the previous complaint by the Gadarenes (*Ant.* 15.351), in which he briefly notes that Agrippa did not even offer them the opportunity to speak and sent them in chains to Herod (see also 15.354 with the note to "most").

²⁴⁵⁷ This remark contradicts the Gadarenes' complaint about Herod being a tyrannical ruler (*Ant.* 15.354, 357) and suggests a particularly merciful attitude of the king towards the Gadarenes. For other occurrences of the phrase (μηδὲν) κακὸν ἐργάζομαι ("do [no] harm") in Josephus, see *Ant.* 7.51; 9.58, also 6.353; 7.235; 10.124; 11.114.

²⁴⁵⁸ For phrases similar to εἴ τις καὶ ἄλλος ("more than anyone [or 'anything'] else"), see Xenophon, *Anab.* 1.4.15; Philo, *Ios.* 69; *Prob.* 53; *Spec.* 1.327; 4.101; Plutarch, *Ages.* 25.3; Diogenes Laertius 4.62; Athenaeus 14.23.

²⁴⁵⁹ The adjective δυσπαραίτητος ("inexorable, relentless," Rengstorf *s.v.*) occurs once elsewhere in Josephus (*Ant.* 16.151, which is a further passage in which Josephus characterizes Herod as a ruler and as a person).

²⁴⁶⁰ The phrase οἱ οἰκεῖοι frequently refers to Herod's relatives or household in Josephus' Herod narratives (e.g., *War* 1.263, 281, 292-294 in connection with Herod's flight from Jerusalem, also *Ant.* 16.156, 159). Sometimes the phrase has a broader meaning, indicating fellow Jews (Rengstorf *s.v.*), which meaning is probable here because of the opposition "his own people"—"foreigners" (οἱ ἀλλότριοι).

²⁴⁶¹ Concerning the adjective μεγαλόψυχος ("high-minded, magnanimous, liberal," Rengstorf *s.v.*), cf. the related noun μεγαλοψυχία ("greatness of mind, generosity," Rengstorf *s.v.*) in *Ant.* 16.153. For further references to this trait of Herod in Josephus, see 15.48 with the note to "magnanimity."

²⁴⁶² Josephus' general statement about Herod's different attitudes towards Jews and non-Jews here is remarkable in the context of the Gadarenes' complaint. It most probably stems from Josephus himself since it matches another long statement about Herod's differing attitudes towards fellow Jews and non-Jews (*Ant.* 16.150-159; see below). If the statement here is accurate, the complaint by the Gadarenes becomes hard to understand because there would be not much to complain about. The discrepancies in this section (see also 15.354, 357 with notes) may be explained by the assumption that Josephus adapted his source's text (probably from Nicolaus of Damascus) about this episode by changing Herod's depiction as a ruler in such a way that it better fitted his overall presentation of Herod.

There is a significant parallel to this statement in 16.150-159, which passage follows a description of Herod's benefactions to people outside his kingdom (16.146-149) and points to the alleged ambiguity of Herod's behavior (16.150-151) towards subjects and non-subjects: the king was very generous towards non-subjects, while harsh towards the Jewish people in his kingdom. Josephus' own view largely supports this ambiguity and he gives his own explanation for it (16.152-159; see further the commentary on that passage). The connection between 15.356 and 16.150-159 is supported by the correspondences of the vocabulary in both passages (δυσπαραίτητος in 15.356 and 16.151, οἱ οἰκεῖοι in 15.356 and 16.156, and μεγαλόψυχος/μεγαλοψυχία in 15.356 and 16.153; see also the previous notes).

²⁴⁶³ The verb ἀφίημι means "leave unpunished, pardon" here (Rengstorf *s.v.*; cf. *Ant.* 15.371).

²⁴⁶⁴ With these last words Josephus returns again to the situation of the Gadarenes.

²⁴⁶⁵ There is no other passage in Josephus mentioning explicitly outrageous acts (ὕβρεις) by Herod (similar vocabulary in Strabo 15.1.64).

²⁴⁶⁶ There are no other passages in Josephus referring to robberies (ἅρπαγες) by Herod; *War* 1.355 and *Ant.* 14.484 even report that Herod attempted to prevent the plundering of Jerusalem (τὰς κατὰ τὴν πόλιν ἅρπαγας, *Ant.* 14.484) by Sosius' soldiers.

destructions of temples.[2467] But Herod, remaining calm,[2468] was prepared to defend himself.[2469]

Caesar welcomed him cordially without having changed his benevolence[2470] in any way because of the crowd's tumult.[2471] **358** And the speeches about these things were given during the first day,[2472] but the inquiry[2473] did not proceed further on the following days. For the Gadarenes saw what the outcome of the decision[2474] of Caesar himself and the council[2475] would be. They supposed, as was to be expected, that they would be surrendered to the king.[2476] Out of fear of torture[2477] some of them cut their own throats during the

---

[2467] The combination of outrageous acts, robberies, and destructions of temples must at least be a gross overstatement (see also the 2 previous notes) since it is improbable that Herod committed all these wicked acts at Gadara (cf. Richardson 1996: 233 n. 61, who considers the destructions of temples at Gadara to be "particularly odd"). The accusation doesn't fit Josephus' previous statement about Herod's lenient attitude towards the Gadarenes (see *Ant.* 15.356 with the note to "he had not done them any harm"), but it does match elements of the tyrannical stereotype, which often includes accusations of outrageous acts (also towards the gods or God), plundering, and destructions of temples, as passages about Cambyses, Antiochus IV, Nero, and Domitian show (e.g., *Sib. Or.* 5.107-110, 150-151, 226 about Nero; more references and further discussion in van Henten 2000; 2011b). Josephus' portrayal of Cleopatra incorporates elements of this stereotype, referring, among other things, to her violations of temples and tombs (*Ant.* 15.90; *Apion* 2.58; van Henten 2005a).

[2468] Herod's calmness presupposes a prudent and self-assured attitude, which is at odds with the accusation of the Gadarenes and the presentation of Herod as a tyrannical ruler. The verb ἀταρακτέω ("remain calm," Rengstorf *s.v.*) is a *hapax legomenon* in Josephus.

[2469] Herod apparently had anticipated the accusation of the Gadarenes and prepared his defense before Augustus, which again suggests that he was a clever ruler. Being well-prepared for one's defense is a virtue according to 1 Pet 3:15: "Always be ready to make your defense (ἕτοιμοι ἀεὶ πρὸς ἀπολογίαν) to anyone who demands from you an accounting for the hope that is in you ...."

[2470] Augustus' benevolence (εὔνοια) towards Herod is mentioned for the first time in *Ant.* 15.193-194, concerning Herod's journey to Octavian after the Battle of Actium.

[2471] The tumult (ταραχή) of the crowd of Gadarenes could easily have irritated Augustus, not only because unrest was always something bad, but also because it might have indicated that Herod did not succeed in his task of guaranteeing peace and order in the territories that had been added to his kingdom (see *Ant.* 15.5 with the note to "a gift to Antony"). The combination of ταραχή ("tumult, disturbance") and πλῆθος ("crowd, masses") occurs several times in Josephus (see 15.231 with the note to "disturbances of the masses").

[2472] The vocabulary in *Ant.* 15.358 (οἱ λόγοι "the speeches" and ἡ διάγνωσις "the inquiry") suggests that there was a court meeting, apparently at Gadara (see the continuation of the narrative and 15.354). "The speeches" probably refer to speeches elaborating the accusation against Herod by legal representatives of the Gadarenes as well as the defense by the king. In contradistinction to the earlier complaint, when Marcus Agrippa did not even give the Gadarenes a hearing (15.351), the Gadarenes were now allowed to speak during the meeting.

[2473] The noun διάγνωσις can mean "(judicial) inquiry" (LSJ *s.v.* II; Rengstorf *s.v.*) and is sometimes the equivalent of the Latin *cognitio* ("judicial inquiry"), as the governor Festus' explanation to King Agrippa (concerning Paul's appeal to the emperor) in Acts 25:21 shows: "But when Paul had appealed to be kept in custody for the decision (εἰς τὴν τοῦ Σεβαστοῦ διάγνωσιν) of his Imperial Majesty, I ordered him to be held until I could send him to the emperor" (see also *Ant.* 15.77).

[2474] The noun ῥοπή ("turn of the scale, change") can also mean "decision" (LSJ *s.v.* I). Rengstorf (*s.v.*) suggests the meaning "inclination" here.

[2475] The council (συνέδριον, Latin *consilium*) of the emperor was a flexible institution with varying staffing, dependent on the occasion. The emperor's friends as well as senators and members of the equestrian rank served as its members (cf. *War* 2.81 and *Ant.* 17.301; further references in *War* 2.25, 93; *Ant.* 17.317). It had a political as well as a juridical function. Augustus founded this *consilium principis* (Cassius Dio 52.15), and his successors maintained it (Suetonius, *Tib.* 55; Crook 1955: 31-55; Kienast 1999: 181; Mason in BJP 1b on *War* 2.25).

[2476] This expectation seems plausible in the light of the result of the Gadarenes' previous complaint against Herod before Marcus Agrippa, who decided to send the complainants as prisoners to Herod.

[2477] The extreme reaction of the Gadarenes to their failure in persuading Augustus is hardly explained in the

night,²⁴⁷⁸ some threw themselves from high places,²⁴⁷⁹ while others died by falling into the river out of free will.²⁴⁸⁰ **359** These deaths were considered to be a condemnation²⁴⁸¹ of their rashness²⁴⁸² and wrongdoing.²⁴⁸³ For that reason²⁴⁸⁴ Caesar acquitted Herod of the charges²⁴⁸⁵ without delay.²⁴⁸⁶

---

narrative. Their fear that Herod would torture them is curious in the light of Herod's reaction to their earlier complaint: Herod decided not to punish them (*Ant.* 15.356). Although it is implausible that Herod would have had the Gadarenes getting off scot-free for a second time, their fear and various ways of committing suicide seem out of proportion in connection with Herod's attitude towards them sofar. The reaction of the Gadarenes would be understandable in an utterly hopeless situation, in which they would rather commit suicide than be at the mercy of a cruel enemy. The inconsistencies in the narrative may be explained by the assumption that Josephus himself invented the self-killings of the Gadarenes in order to enhance the drama in his description of Herod's dealings with them; they match Josephus' depiction of Herod as a tyrannical ruler perfectly (see 15.354 with the note to "tyrannical").

²⁴⁷⁸ The suicides of the Gadarenes are only understandable in a context in which the Gadarenes were doomed to die anyway (see also the previous note), such that they decided to commit suicide rather than be executed by the enemy or be sold as slaves (cf. Phasael's suicide reported in *Ant.* 14.367, and the Masada suicide in *War* 7.389-401; further discussion in van Henten 2007a).

²⁴⁷⁹ Hurling oneself down from a wall, building, or mountain ridge was a well-known type of suicide in antiquity. Cecrops' daughter Agraulos (also named Aglaulus) plunged herself from a wall and sacrificed herself for her fatherland Attica in this way (Philochorus, *FGH* 328 F 105). Menoeceus thrust his sword through his throat and jumped from the walls of Thebes in order to save his city from the people of Argos (Euripides, *Phoen.* 1090-1092; Statius, *Theb.* 10.756-779). The elder Razis committed suicide in a similar way in 2 Macc 14:37-46 (van Henten 1997: 144-50). The suicide of the inhabitants of Gamla during the first war against Rome (*War* 4.79-80) deserves special attention: since there was no hope of salvation, the males first threw their wives and children and then themselves down from a ridge (see also the next note).

²⁴⁸⁰ Drowning oneself was another well-known way of committing suicide in antiquity. A famous case is the death of Hadrian's friend Antinous, who drowned himself voluntarily in the Nile in order to save Hadrian's life (Cassius Dio 69.11; Historia Augusta, *Hadr.* 14.5-7; further discussion and references about hurling oneself down and drowning as self-killings in Schwenn 1915:

29-31, 42-43, 127, 131-32, 152, 154, 182-84; Schmitt 1921: 96-97; Versnel 1981: 152-56). As the example of Gamla suggests (see the previous note), the inhabitants of a city besieged by the Romans in their hopeless situation sometimes opted for collective suicide rather than undergoing a brutal punishment by the Romans (discussion and references in Cohen 1982).

²⁴⁸¹ The suicides of the Gadarenes were apparently interpreted as proof that their accusation against Herod was unjustified. The noun κατάγνωσις ("[moral] condemnation, disapproval," LSJ *s.v.* I-II; Rengstorf *s.v.*) occurs twice elsewhere in the Herod narrative of *Antiquities*: once in connection with Herod's plan to murder Cleopatra, which act would have showed Herod's stubbornness and condemnation (κατάγνωσις) of Antony's behavior (15.101), and once concerning the disapproval of Alexandra's disgraceful behavior at the time of Mariamme's execution (15.234).

²⁴⁸² The noun προπέτεια ("rashness") occurs in *Antiquities* only in the Herod narrative, several times concerning Herod himself (e.g., 16.255; see 15.100 with the note to "out of rashness"). Rengstorf (*s.v.*) proposes the translation "impudence" for this passage.

²⁴⁸³ The conjecture καὶ οὐχ ἁμαρτίας ("and not of wrongdoing") by Richards and Shutt (1939: 174), instead of the reading καὶ ἁμαρτίας (attested by the MSS; Niese 397), is unnecessary because the phrase refers to the Gadarenes and not to Herod (in contrast to Richards and Shutt's assumption).

²⁴⁸⁴ The translation follows the reading ὅθεν ("whence"), attested by E and favored by Niese minor (317). The reading ἔνθεν ("thence") of the other MSS is probably a scribal error for ὅθεν.

²⁴⁸⁵ Josephus does not inform us about Herod's speech of defense, apart from his remark in *Ant.* 15.357 that the king was well-prepared to defend himself. The sequence of events may imply that Herod or his lawyer had produced a successful speech of defense (cf. 15.358 and Günther 2005: 133), but a plausible motive for Augustus' decision is his faith in Herod as a successful guarantor of order in this unstable region.

For ἀπολύω with the meaning "acquit (of a charge)," see LSJ *s.v.* I.2b and *Ant.* 12.263.

²⁴⁸⁶ Otto (1913: 71) and Schürer-Vermes (2.134 n. 249) refer to city coins from Gadara from the year 44 of the city's era (= 21/20 BCE) displaying the head of Augustus, which coins F. de Saulcy interpreted in 1875 as being minted by Herod in gratitude for Augustus'

Now another instance of extraordinary[2487] good luck came along as well,[2488] in addition to what had already happened. For Zenodorus got a ruptured intestine[2489] and, while blood was draining away[2490] because of his illness, he departed life[2491] in Antioch in Syria.[2492] **360** Caesar also gave his portion of land,[2493] which was not small, to Herod.[2494] It lay between Trachonitis[2495] and Galilee:[2496] Ulatha,[2497] Paneas,[2498] and the country surrounding

Grant of Zenodorus' dominion to Herod. Building of temple near Paneion.
War 1.400;404-406; 483

---

support. For the verb μέλλω having the meaning "delay" (frequently with a negation), see LSJ *s.v.* III.

[2487] This phrase (literally "not moderate") is a case of *litotes*.

[2488] Zenodorus' illness described in the next subclauses is taken as a fortunate coincidence for Herod. The rare verb ἐπισυμπίπτω ("happen further," Rengstorf *s.v.*; cf. Philo, *Spec.* 1.62, though with a different meaning) is a *hapax legomenon* in Josephus.

[2489] A ruptured intestine is a lethal illness if no surgery is undertaken; it causes infection of the abdominal cavity. Josephus does not mention medical treatment of Zenodorus, who was doomed to die with such an illness. He does not explicitly say that Zenodorus' illness was considered to be a punishment for his misdeeds, although this type of illness could easily have been associated with a divine punishment of a wicked person (cf. 2 Macc 9:5 concerning Antiochus IV: "But the all-seeing Lord, the God of Israel, struck him with an incurable and invisible blow. As soon as he stopped speaking, he was seized with a pain in his bowels [τῶν σπλάγχνων ἀλγηδών], for which there was no relief, and with sharp internal tortures …").

[2490] Rengstorf (*s.v.*) suggests the translation "be lost" for ὑποχωρέω ("go back") here.

[2491] The parallel passage of *War* (1.400) is much briefer and does not specify in which way Zenodorus died. The phrase ἐκλείπω τὸν βίον ("depart life, pass away") also occurs in *Ant.* 19.356; 20.26 (cf. Polybius 38.1.7; Diodorus 1.72.2; Philo, *QG* 4.169; Plutarch, *Mor.* [*Cons. Apoll.*] 107e, [*Apoph. lac.*] 234e).

[2492] I.e., Antioch on the Orontes (see also *Ant.* 17.24). Josephus does not inform us why Zenodorus was in Antioch when he died. It is possible that Augustus' council mentioned in 15.358 assembled in Antioch and that Zenodorus wanted to be at that same place in order to act quickly if the accusation of the Gadarenes was found justified.

[2493] The noun μοῖρα can mean "portion of land, part of a region" in Josephus (Rengstorf *s.v.*; see also *War* 2.382; 3.56, 445; *Ant.* 1.136; 2.190; 20.159).

[2494] Kasher (1988: 160) argues that Augustus' grant of the remaining territory of Zenodorus (for Augustus' previous grant of a part of Zenodorus' territory—Trachonitis, Batanea, and Auranitis—to Herod, see *Ant.* 15.343) was given in by political pragmatism and demographic developments: Herod had proved to be successful in controlling rough territories where robbers were hiding, and Jews as well as converted Itureans were living in Zenodorus' territory. Later Herod strengthened the Jewish connection by founding a military colony of Babylonian Jews in Batanea (17.23-29) and settling 3,000 Idumeans in Trachonitis (16.285; see also Shatzman 1991: 171; Günther 2005: 132). For a similar grant of a portion of land by an emperor to a Jewish king, cf. Nero's grant of a part of Galilee to Agrippa II (καὶ τὸν Ἀγρίππαν δὲ δωρεῖται μοίρᾳ τινὶ τῆς Γαλιλαίας, 20.159).

[2495] Concerning the name and the location of Trachonitis, see *Ant.* 15.344 with the note to "Trachonitis."

[2496] The parallel passage of *War* (1.400) has a similar Greek formulation.

[2497] Ulatha (Οὐλάθα) is only mentioned here in Josephus (Schalit 1968: 94; in *Ant.* 17.25 the same name indicates a place near Antioch on the Orontes). It is unclear whether Ulatha refers to a town or region. The context implies that the name refers either to the Hula Valley (including Lake Hula), north of the Sea of Galilee, or to a town or village in its neighborhood (Möller and Schmitt 1976: 192).

[2498] Paneas (Πανεάς; the Greek MSS read τὴν Πανιάδε [from Πανιάς]; Niese 397) is the name of a territory near the source of the Jordan River (currently named Banyas; for the name, see *War* 2.168; *Ant.* 17.189; 18.28; Schalit 1968: 96; Möller and Schmitt 1976: 115; Berlin 1999: 27-28; Overman, Olive, and Nelson 2007: 189-92; see also *Ant.* 15.363 with the note to "the place called Paneion"). Herod's son Philip (re)founded the city Paneas of this area as Caesarea Philippi, probably in 3 or 2 BCE (*War* 2.168; *Ant.* 18.28; Schürer-Vermes 2.169-71; differently Mahieu 2012: 258-59, 398). King Agrippa II refounded the city as Neronias in 60/61 CE.

[2499] The grant probably consisted of the territory of Paneas, the Hula Valley (Ulatha), and the Golan area (i.e., Gaulanitis; Avi-Yonah 1974: 92). In *War* 1.400 Josephus does not mention Ulatha and Paneas but simply states that Augustus gave Herod all the land between Trachonitis and Galilee, i.e., the area around Paneas, Gaulanitis, and Batanea, which had already previously been given to Herod according to *Ant.* 15.343. Schürer-Vermes (1.566) argue that the territory referred to here is identical with the "estate" of Lysanias mentioned in 15.344. Kokkinos (1998: 281 with n. 64) argues that "the country surrounding it" refers to Mount Hermon and possibly also Abilene.

it.²⁴⁹⁹ He also made him²⁵⁰⁰ associate with²⁵⁰¹ the procurators of Syria,²⁵⁰² ordering them to do everything with his [Herod's] consent.²⁵⁰³

361 On the whole he advanced to this state of fortune,²⁵⁰⁴ while two men managed the rule over Rome—which is so big:²⁵⁰⁵ Caesar²⁵⁰⁶ and next to him²⁵⁰⁷ Agrippa,²⁵⁰⁸ in keeping

---

²⁵⁰⁰ Niese (397) reads αὐτήν ("her, it," probably referring to μοῖρα ["portion of land"] at the beginning of the sentence) with MS P. He assumes that the reading αὐτόν ("him," i.e., Herod) attested by the other Greek MSS (supported by the Latin version) can hardly be correct and that there is a lacuna in the Greek text. Nevertheless, the reading αὐτόν makes sense, although it causes a historical problem concerning Herod's financial authority in Syria (see the note to "the procurators of Syria" below).

²⁵⁰¹ The verb ἐγκαταμίγνυμι ("intermingle/associate with," Rengstorf *s.v.*) occurs once elsewhere in Josephus (*War* 2.176: Pilate orders his soldiers to mix, in common clothing, with the Jewish crowd).

²⁵⁰² The verb ἐπιτροπεύω ("administer, be governor") can refer to the Roman office of procurator (LSJ *s.v.* 4; similarly ἐπίτροπος can be the equivalent of the Latin term *procurator*; Mason 1974: 49; 142-43; Eck 2008). The title *procurator* can refer to several Roman offices (survey in Eck 2001); here it refers to officials in the imperial Roman provinces who were responsible for the imperial possessions and funds in the provinces as well as the payments of the soldiers. They were appointed by the emperor and reported back to him as his private agents (Goodman 1997: 108-09; Udoh 2005: 134).

²⁵⁰³ Augustus' decision implies that the procurators of the province of Syria were to cooperate closely with Herod, such that Herod had an important say in the financial matters of the province. Several scholars doubt whether this decision is historical and whether it had to be taken literally by the Syrian procurators (e.g., Schürer-Vermes 1.319). It was perhaps only an honorary matter that reflected Herod's status as the most important local ruler in the region in consequence of the expansion of his kingdom with Zenodorus' territories (*War* 1.398-399; *Ant.* 15.343-348, 360; see Braund 1984: 84-85, 90 n. 97, who notes that Herod's new status in Syria is sandwiched by references to Augustus' donations of Zenodorus' territories to Herod, likewise Udoh 2005: 149-50, 192 with nn. 188 and 386). Schürer-Vermes (1.319 n. 122) argue that this passage derives from Nicolaus of Damascus and reflects his overstatement of Herod's power and status. Gabba (1990) argues that Herod was involved in tax-collecting activities. Cimma (1976: 311) argues that the decision implied that the procurators of Syria had to ask for Herod's permission to act against bandits (cf. Richardson 1996: 234). Braund (1984: 84-85) points to conventions concerning friendly kings and to the analogies between the positions of friendly kings and Roman officials, such that they sometimes could switch position. Lucceius Albinus was governor of Mauretania in 69 CE and assumed the royal *insignia*, taking the name Juba (Tacitus, *Hist.* 2.58); Juba had been the name of 2 kings (Juba I of Numidia and Juba II of Mauretania). There is also an example of the opposite move: following the Roman conquest of the Cottian Alps in 14 BCE, King Donnus no longer ruled this territory, but Donnus' son Cottius I was appointed prefect there (in 44 CE Claudius bestowed the royal title again, on Donnus' grandson Cottius II; *ILS* nos. 94 and 848; Cassius Dio 60.24.4). The parallel passage of *War* (1.399) mentions the appointment of Herod as being even more important; the king would have become procurator of all Syria: "Then, when he [i.e., Caesar] came back to this province ten years later, he also made him [i.e., Herod] procurator of all Syria (Συρίας ὅλης ἐπίτροπον), so that the [other] procurators (τοις ἐπιτρόποις) were permitted to take no action without obtaining the latter's [i.e., Herod's] consent" (trans. Sievers/Forte in BJP 1a). Kasher (1988: 160) considers this appointment to be improbable. Several scholars emend Συρίας ὅλης in *War* 1.399 into Συρίας κοιλῆς, such that Herod would have been the procurator not of Syria but of Coele-Syria (Otto 1913: 71-72 with n. *; Marcus-Wikgren 175 n. *c*; Schürer-Vermes 1.319; Braund 1984: 89 n. 92).

²⁵⁰⁴ Herod's fortune (εὐτυχία) as a ruler is a recurring motif in the Herod narrative of *Antiquities* (see 15.255, 376; 16.64, 76-77, and cf. a similar statement in different words in the parallel passage of *War* [1.400]; see also *Ant.* 6.129 about Saul), but several passages emphasize that his success as a ruler was in strong contrast with the disastrous events within his family (see especially 16.76-77; cf. 17.94-95).

²⁵⁰⁵ Here Josephus refers in passing to the greatness of the Roman empire. For a similar statement, see *War* 7.132-133 (τῆς Ῥωμαίων ἡγεμονίας ... τὸ μέγεθος, 7.133), which emphasizes the greatness of the Roman *imperium* as the main point of the Flavian triumphal procession celebrating the victory over the Jewish people (Beard 2003; Eberhardt 2005). About the motif of the greatness of Rome, cf. Polybius 2.22.2; Appian, *Hist. rom.* preface 43; Cassius Dio 62.7.

Mason (2003: 573-89) discusses other Josephan passages about the Roman political system in which Josephus compares that system with the Jewish constitution.

with his affection for him.[2509] Caesar honored no one more after Agrippa than Herod,[2510] while Agrippa assigned the first place of friendship,[2511] after Caesar, to Herod.[2512]

362 Having such opportunity to speak,[2513] [Herod] asked from Caesar a tetrarchy[2514] for

---

[2506] I.e., Augustus (references in *Ant.* 15.109 with the note to "Caesar").

[2507] Instead of μετ' αὐτόν ("next to him"), attested by MSS FLVE (Niese 398), Richards and Shutt (1939: 174) read μετ' αὐτοῦ ("with him") on the basis of the Latin version.

[2508] I.e., Marcus Vipsanius Agrippa, who became Augustus' deputy probably in 23 BCE (with *imperium proconsulare* in the East; see *Ant.* 15.350 with the notes to "Agrippa" and "Caesar's deputy"). Agrippa was designated successor to Augustus (Cassius Dio 53-54) and in 21 BCE he married Augustus' daughter Julia, who later gave birth to 3 possible successors for Augustus: Gaius, Lucius, and Agrippa Postumus (Richardson 1996: 232-33).

[2509] I.e., Augustus' affection for Agrippa. The phrase κατὰ τὴν πρὸς αὐτὸν εὔνοιαν echoes *Ant.* 15.193-194 concerning the relationship between Octavian and Herod (cf. 15.194 τῆς πρὸς ἐκεῖνον εὐνοίας referring to Octavian's benevolence towards Herod and 15.387). The context implies that εὔνοια has a different nuance than goodwill or loyalty here because it presupposes an intimate relationship between Augustus and Agrippa. The word may, therefore, be translated by "affection, love" or "attachment" (Rengstorf *s.v.*).

[2510] This passage suggests that for Augustus Herod was the third person in importance within the Roman empire, i.e., after Augustus himself and Marcus Agrippa, which implies that Augustus had great confidence in Herod's capabilities as a friendly king (about friendly kings, see *Ant.* 15.5 with the note to "a gift to Antony"). Other details in the Herod narrative can be interpreted in support of such a close relationship between Herod and Augustus, e.g., the education of Herod's sons in Rome (15.342-343) and Herod's legacies of 1,000 talents to Augustus and of 500 talents to Augustus' wife (Julia), children, friends, and freed persons (17.146; cf. 17.190). However, this is not ample evidence; one could even argue that both the education of Herod's son and the legacies only confirm the mutual beneficial relationship between Augustus and Herod. Richardson (1996: 234) doubts whether Augustus and Herod were close friends and states that there is not enough evidence to prove this. Two undated honorary inscriptions call Herod Friend of Caesar (φιλοκαίσαρ) and Friend of Rome (φιλορώμαιος): *IG* II² no. 3440 (= *OGIS* no. 414) and *IG* II² no. 3441 (= *OGIS* no. 427; Smallwood 1976: 71; Kienast 1999: 309, although the identification with Herod the Great is not entirely certain.

The verb προτιμάω means "honor above others" here (Rengstorf *s.v.*; see also 15.209 with the note to "specially").

[2511] This links up with *Ant.* 15.350, which passage calls Herod a very close friend and companion (εἰς τὰ μάλιστα φίλος καὶ συνήθης) of Agrippa (see the note to "he was a very close friend and companion"). The parallel passage of *War* (1.400) likewise tells us that Herod enjoyed Augustus' and Agrippa's special favors (ἐφιλεῖτο). Richardson (1996: 233) argues that Agrippa and Herod were indeed close friends, not only because they had to cooperate with each other (since Agrippa was Augustus' deputy in the East), but also because they had a lot in common: both were coming from the countryside, very wealthy, ambitious patrons of public works, successful military commanders, and keen supporters of Augustus.

For the phrase "assigned the first place of friendship" (πρῶτον ἀπεδίδου φιλίας τόπον), cf. *Ant.* 15.21 concerning Herod's treatment of Hyrcanus II, who received special honors from Herod and was given "the first place (τὸν πρῶτον ἔνεμε τόπον) in the assemblies."

[2512] The repetitive vocabulary with various phrases of μετά plus an accusative ("after, next to") and the pairs Caesar—Agrippa, Caesar—Agrippa, and Agrippa—Caesar together emphasize not only that Augustus and Agrippa were numbers one and two in the empire, but also that they shared the same attitude towards Herod since they considered him to be the third most important person after themselves. Cf. the similar but simpler statement in the parallel passage of *War* (1.400): "But what was greater than all this in Herod's eyes was that next after Agrippa, he enjoyed Caesar's special favor (ἐφιλεῖτο), and next after Caesar, he enjoyed Agrippa's [special favor]" (trans. Sievers/Forte in BJP 1a).

[2513] Herod's apparent close relationship with both Augustus and Marcus Agrippa allowed him to discuss important matters of administration with them. E.g., the arrangement of a tetrarchy for Pheroras (see the next notes) required a change in the arrangement of Herod's territory.

[2514] For the territory of Pheroras' tetrarchy, see the note to "from the kingdom" below. A tetrarchy (τετραρχία) usually concerns a relatively small territory, and a tetrarch (ruling in theory over one fourth of the territory; see *SIG* 3 no. 274; Euripides, *Alc.* 1154; Demosthenes, *Or.* 9.26) basically had a lesser status than a king (Schürer-Vermes 1.334). Many rulers in the East were called tetrarchs in the periods of the Late Republic

his brother Pheroras.[2515] He himself had assigned [him] a revenue of one hundred talents[2516] from the kingdom,[2517] so that, if [Herod] suffered from something,[2518] Pheroras' affairs would be secure and his sons would not get hold of it.[2519]

363 When [Herod] returned home,[2520] after he had escorted Caesar to the sea,[2521] he erected a most beautiful temple[2522] of white stone[2523] for him[2524] in Zenodorus' territory,[2525]

---

and the Early Empire. For a list of tetrarchies in the regions of the Decapolis and Inner Syria, see Pliny the Elder 5.74, 81-82. Mark Antony had appointed both Phasael and Herod tetrarchs of Judea (*War* 1.244; *Ant.* 14.326).

[2515] Pheroras was Herod's youngest brother (see *Ant.* 15.184 with the note to "Pheroras").

[2516] Herod apparently arranged for a fixed revenue for Pheroras' tetrarchy in order to secure his brother's income, as the continuation of the narrative also implies. Concerning Herod's procedure of assigning revenue to Pheroras, cf. *Ant.* 16.250 about a comparable assignment by Herod to his son Antipater: "And a letter ... was also found, in which he [i.e., Antipater's stepbrother Alexander] blamed their father [i.e., Herod] for acting unjustly by assigning a territory (χώραν ἀπονέμοντα) to Antipater that yielded a revenue of two hundred talents (πρόσοδον διακοσίων ταλάντων φέρουσαν; cf. 15.362 πρόσοδον ἑκατὸν ταλάντων)" (my trans.).

[2517] This addition seems unclear at a first glance, but the parallel passage of *War* (1.483) indicates that Herod arranged for a fixed income of 100 talents per year, which was paid (or guaranteed; see below) out of the royal treasury. *War* 1.483 implies that Pheroras received not only the 100 talents, but also the revenues of the territory across the Jordan given to him by Herod (as Udoh 2005: 144 n. 158, 183-84 rightly notes). This territory was most probably identical with Perea (*War* 1.586), which was part of Herod's kingdom (as presupposed in *Ant.* 15.294). *Ant.* 15.362 could therefore, contrary to *War* 1.483, indicate that Herod assigned Perea to his brother Pheroras with a guaranteed income of 100 talents (i.e., the revenues from Perea no longer went to Herod but to Pheroras). Such a move may have preceded Herod's request to Augustus to have his brother appointed as tetrarch. Momigliano (1934: 46-48) prefers Josephus' information in *Antiquities* to the, in his view, clumsy passage of *War* 1.483 and concludes that Pheroras only received the 100 talents.

[2518] Josephus hints with this phrase (εἰ καί τι πάσχοι) at an unforeseen development that could lead to Herod's death. For passages with the same implication and with similar vocabulary, see *Ant.* 15.65, 69, 85 (in the context of a possible punishment of Herod by Mark Antony) and 15.164, 204 (hinting at a punishment by Octavian; see also 17.67, 83).

[2519] I.e., the territory of Pheroras' tetrarchy, Perea (see the note to "from the kingdom" above). The translation follows Niese (398), who reads αὐτῆς with MS P. The other MSS read αὐτοῦ ("his"), referring to Herod's sons. This reading could imply a translation like "that his sons would not get hold [of it]" or "that his sons would not be ruler" (for this meaning of κρατέω, see Rengstorf *s.v.*). The latter meaning matches a later passage in the Herod narrative of *Antiquities* (17.67), referring to Pheroras and Herod's son Antipater: "For even now, he [i.e., Antipater] lamented, Herod would rather order for the power to be given to his brother [i.e., Pheroras] than to his son [i.e., Antipater] if he [i.e., Herod] would suffer something (εἴ τι πάσχειν αὐτόν)" (my trans.).

[2520] The verb ἐπανήκω ("return, come back," Rengstorf *s.v.*) implies that Herod returned home (probably to Jerusalem), likely from a place outside of his kingdom (cf. *War* 1.442 about Herod's return from his journey to Mark Antony and *Ant.* 16.271 about the king's return from a trip to Rome). The last geographic information mentioned concerns Gadara (15.354), such that the meeting of Augustus' council (15.357-358) may have taken place there (Antioch is another option, see 15.359 with the note to "Antioch in Syria"). Gadara had been part of Herod's kingdom since 30 BCE (see 15.217 with the note to "Gadara").

[2521] Josephus does not specify the places from where (possibly Gadara; see the previous note) and whereto (on the coast) Herod escorted Augustus (concerning προπέμπω ["escort"], cf. *Ant.* 15.103 with the note to "escorted her to Egypt"). We do know that Augustus traveled to Samos and Athens afterwards, before arriving back in Rome on 12 October 19 BCE (*Res gest. divi Aug.* 11; Cassius Dio 54.10; Kokkinos 1998: 167 n. 60). The place on the coast could have been Caesarea (cf. Richardson 1996: 234) or Ptolemais (cf. *Ant.* 15.199).

[2522] Herod's temple built in honor of Augustus (see the note to "for him" below) is also mentioned in the parallel passage of *War* (1.404). Contrary to Herod's (re)building of Samaria-Sebaste (see *Ant.* 15.296-298) and Caesarea Maritima (15.331-341), which both concerned a cluster of buildings, Josephus only mentions Herod's building of a temple in the Paneion area (see the note to "the place called Paneion" below).

The precise location of the temple in honor of Augustus is debated. Ma'oz (1993; 1996) argues, partly on the basis of the finding of pottery from the Augustean period, that it was situated directly in front of the grotto close to the place called Paneion.[2526] **364** There is a most beautiful[2527] cave in the mountain[2528] with beneath it[2529] a place where a landslide has occurred,[2530] of an abrupt[2531]

---

described by Josephus (see 15.364 with the note to "cave in the mountain"). Lichtenberger (1999: 150-53), Netzer (2006: 221-22), and Bernett (2007b: 226) argue for a location on a terrace west of the grotto, referring to remains of the so-called *opus reticulatum* technique (elsewhere also used by Herod) and the reconstructed set up of the building. Overman, Olive, and Nelson (2007) argue that the remains of a possibly Herodean building at the 2 locations close to the grotto are scant and that it is much more probable that the temple was located 3.5 km southwest of Paneas-Caesarea Philippi, at Horvat Omrit. At this location a temple complex has been excavated, of which one phase closely reflects the style of temples built in honor of Augustus elsewhere (e.g., the Augusteum at Pula). This temple (called by the excavators "temple I") was ca. 20 m high and stood upon a high podium in Corinthian order with a plaza around it; it had a prostyle and a tetrastyle. This form closely resembles the representation of the front of the temple on the famous coin from Banyas of Philip the tetrarch (further discussion and references in Berlin 1999; Netzer 2006: 218-22; Taylor 2006: 573; Bernett 2007a: 239-48; 2007b: 225-26; Overman and Schowalter 2011).

The adjective περικαλλής ("especially beautiful," Rengstorf *s.v.*, here in the superlative) occurs twice elsewhere in Josephus in connection with building activities of Herod: in *War* 1.402 concerning the 2 large buildings in Jerusalem named after Augustus and Marcus Agrippa (cf. *Ant.* 15.318 with notes) and in *War* 1.412 concerning the Drusus Tower at the harbor of Caesarea (see *Ant.* 15.336, also 15.364).

[2523] The parallel passage of *War* (1.404) states that the temple was built of white marble (see the next note). This could, though not necessarily, be implied by *Ant.* 15.363 as well (see 15.331 with the note to "buildings of white stone" concerning buildings in Caesarea, and Fischer and Kushnir-Stein 1994).

[2524] See also *Ant.* 15.364. The founding of a temple in honor of Augustus (usually called an *Augusteum*) must mainly have been Herod's response to the grant of additional territories from Zenodorus (15.360), as the parallel passage of *War* (1.404) states in rather general terms: "Furthermore, when Caesar gave him additional land, he [i.e., Herod] dedicated a temple of white marble to him (ναὸν αὐτῷ λευκῆς μαρμάρου καθιδρύσατο) there also, near the sources of the Jordan, at a place called Paneion" (trans. Sievers/Forte in BJP 1a). Augustus' continued support of Herod, as shown during the issue of the Gadarenes' complaint (*Ant.* 15.354-359), may have been an additional reason (Overman, Olive,

and Nelson 2007: 183). If the temple was Herod's response to Augustus' grant of Zenodorus' territories, then the building activities probably started in 20 BCE (cf. Otto 1913: 65; Roller 1998: 190; Günther 2005: 258; Mahieu 2012: 167).

[2525] I.e., Ulatha, Paneas, and the country surrounding it (*Ant.* 15.360).

[2526] The expression τὸ Πάνειον/τὸ Πάνιον is the name of the cave where the Jordan River wells up (as implied by the parallel passage of *War* [1.404] and by *War* 3.509; *Ant.* 15.364; for the same name, see also *War* 3.513-514; Möller and Schmitt 1976: 115). Obviously the cave is part of the Paneas-Banyas area (see *Ant.* 15.360 with the note to "Paneas"). Paneion is mentioned for the first time in connection with Antiochus III's defeat of Ptolemy V's army at this location in 198 BCE (Polybius 16.18.2; see also Pliny the Elder 36.49). The name derives from the deity Pan, to whom the grotto was dedicated (Schürer-Vermes 2.169; Berlin 1999: 31-34). To the east of the cave niches in honor of Pan were hewn in the rock and below them traces of shrines have been found (Netzer 2006: 219).

Herod may have chosen the location near the grotto because there was already a cult for Pan and perhaps also one for the Ptolemies or Seleucids at this place. In case Horvat Omrit was the actual location of the temple (see the note to "a most beautiful temple" above), there may have been similar reasons for Herod's choice: it functioned already as a cult centre and it was situated—like Paneas—in the middle of the important commercial road between Tyre and Damascus as well as close to the main north-south road in this area (Günther 2005: 218-19).

About Josephus' description of Paneion, see Kushnir-Stein 2007. The name Πάνειον together with a passive form of καλέω ("call") also occurs in the parallel passage of *War* (1.405).

[2527] Note the repetition of περικαλλής ("especially beautiful") in *Ant.* 15.363-364 (see 15.363 with the note to "a most beautiful temple").

[2528] Josephus' description of the location of the cave (σπήλαιον; the parallel passage of *War* [1.404-406] has ἄντρον) is adequate: the grotto lies on a narrow terrace measuring 250 ft, beneath one of the cliffs of Mount Hermon and above a ravine from which one of the sources of the Jordan River issues forth (Berlin 1999: 28-29). The location is currently a major tourist site.

[2529] I.e., the mountain. Josephus describes the location of the cave from 2 perspectives: from the top of the mountain looking downward (ὑπ' αὐτό) and from the

and impassable[2532] depth,[2533] full with still water, and above it a huge mountain.[2534] Beneath the cave the sources of the River Jordan spring up.[2535] Herod further adorned[2536] this place,[2537] although it was already most remarkable,[2538] with the temple[2539] that he consecrated to Caesar.[2540]

Herod's tax cut and severe measures regarding his Jewish subjects.

(10.4) 365 At that time[2541] Herod also remitted the third part of the taxes[2542] to the

---

cave looking up to the mountain (καθύπερθε δ' ὄρος).

[2530] The translation of the rare noun ὀλίσθημα ("slip, [land]slide," LSJ *s.v.*; Rengstorf *s.v.*) follows the meaning given by LSJ (*s.v.*, referring to an inscription from Priene from the 2nd cent. BCE containing the same word; Hiller von Gaertringen 1906: no. 42 ll. 10 and 42). The cave is situated at the beginning of the bed of the Jordan River (see *Ant.* 15.363 with the note to "to the place called Paneion"), which is part of a gorge for its first few kilometers, and at the bottom of an extremely steep mountain. The particularity of the landscape there could indeed be interpreted as a landslide. The noun ὀλίσθημα is a *hapax legomenon* in Josephus.

[2531] The passive perfect participle of ἀπορρήγνυμι ("break off") means "falling off steeply" here (Rengstorf *s.v.*).

[2532] Niese (398) reads ἄβατον ("difficult to traverse, inaccessible," Rengstorf *s.v.*) with MSS PW. MSS FLAMV and E read ἄφατον ("unspeakable"); the Latin version has *inaccessibilis* ("inaccessible"). The reading ἄφατον probably derived from a scribal error (confusing the consonants -β- and -φ-). The adjective ἄφατος occurs once elsewhere in Josephus (*Apion* 2.190), while ἄβατος is more common (references in Rengstorf *s.v.*).

[2533] The alliteration of the *a* and *p/b* sounds in the phrase βάθος ἀπερρωγὸς ἄβατον ("of an abrupt and impassable depth") emphasizes the extraordinary character of this location where the Jordan River appears above the ground. The parallel passage of *War* (1.405) offers a similar description in mostly different words: "There, a mountain peak (κορυφή τις ὄρους) rises to an overwhelming height, and, near the foot of the side of the mountain, a dark cave opens from below, through which a precipitous chasm plunges down into an immense depth (εἰς ἀμέτρητον ἀπορρῶγα βαθύνεται). No length of rope is sufficient to reach the great quantity of still water (ὕδατος ἀσαλεύτου) and measure the bottom" (trans. Sievers/Forte in BJP 1a).

[2534] The mountain is not particularly high but seems huge to somebody who is standing close to the entrance of the cave, from which position it is impossible to see the top because of the extremely steep incline.

[2535] The parallel passage of *War* (1.406) also combines the verb ἀνατέλλω ("spring [up]," Rengstorf *s.v.*) with αἱ πηγαί ("the sources"): "From outside and below the cave the sources spring up (ἀνατέλλουσιν αἱ πηγαί)" (trans. Sievers/Forte in BJP 1a; cf. *War* 2.168). Josephus adds in 1.406 a note that some people think that the location of the cave contains also the source of the River Jordan (which Josephus himself suggests here and in *War* 1.404-405; 2.168; *Ant.* 18.28; cf. *War* 3.57). He also announces in 1.406 that he will give a detailed description later on in *War*, which he does in 3.509-514, when he points out that the water of the Jordan River derives from Lake Phiala (Birket er-Ram, ca. 6 km east of the cave), from which it streams to the location of the cave through an underground channel. In *Ant.* 1.177 he explains that the neighborhood of Dan (which is close to the area of Paneas) contains one of the sources of the Jordan (associating the name Dan with the second part of the name Jor-dan; Feldman in BJP 3 on *Ant.* 1.177; see also *Ant.* 8.226).

[2536] The verb προσκοσμέω ("adorn even more, enrich," Rengstorf *s.v.*) occurs once elsewhere in Josephus (*War* 5.563, concerning donations of the Roman emperor to the Jerusalem Temple).

[2537] The noun τόπος ("place") also occurs in the parallel passage of *War* (1.404) but in a different way by specifying the location of the temple for Augustus ("... near the sources of the Jordan, at a place called Paneion [καλεῖται δὲ Πάνειον ὁ τόπος]," trans. Sievers/Forte in BJP 1a).

[2538] For similar vocabulary, though with a different meaning, cf. *Ant.* 16.165.

[2539] Cf. the repetition of ναός ("temple") in *Ant.* 15.363-364. The noun also occurs in the parallel passage of *War* (1.404).

[2540] As in Caesarea (*Ant.* 15.339) and in Samaria-Sebaste (15.298), Herod founded the temple in Paneas in honor of Augustus, with a cult for Augustus and Roma (for Herod's contribution to the imperial cult, see 15.339 with the note to "one of Caesar").

There are 3 further occurrences of the verb ἀφιερόω ("consecrate," Rengstorf *s.v.*) in Josephus, one of which concerns the consecration of the Tabernacle (*Ant.* 3.201).

[2541] With a brief formula (τότε καί) Josephus synchronizes his note about Herod's tax cut with the previous events (van Henten and Huitink 2007: 225-27), which are all associated with the date provided in *Ant.* 15.354 (Herod's 17th regnal year; see 15.354 with the note to "reign"). Schürer-Vermes (1.315) and Mahieu (2012: 158) date the remission of the taxes to 20/19 BCE.

[2542] Josephus means the taxes on agricultural pro-subjects of the kingdom[2543] under the pretext that they could recover from their lack of produce,[2544] but mainly because he wanted to win over those[2545] who were hostile.[2546] For they continued to be ill disposed[2547] on account of the introduction[2548] of such practices[2549] in the belief that their worship would be put to an end[2550] and their customs changed for the worse.[2551] So there were discussions among[2552] all of those[2553] who felt continually provoked[2554] and troubled.[2555] **366** But he also paid great attention[2556] to such matters by

---

duction (Pastor 1997: 105-10; Udoh 2005: 205; other types of taxation under Herod include a sales levy and custom duties; further references in *Ant.* 15.303 with the note to "the revenues he received from the land"). It is impossible to calculate with certainty how much a tax reduction of one third implied since Josephus nowhere specifies the tax rate on farm produce. If Herod used the Roman rate of 12.5%, the reduction would be 4.2%, but there may have been different rates for various kinds of products (Pastor 1997: 106).

[2543] For other tax cuts by Herod, see *Ant.* 16.64 and cf. *War* 1.427-428, in which passage Josephus states that going through Herod's taking over of debts and taxes from others in detail would be never-ending, which he illustrates with a reference to Herod lightening the annual tax for several cities in Asia Minor and Syria. This implies, perhaps, that *War* 1.427-428 refers to a reduction of Herod's tax income from overseas (Gabba 1990: 163; Pastor 1997: 107), but it is more plausible that the passage means that Herod paid off the debts of these cities in Asia Minor and Syria, as argued by Udoh (2005: 192-93).

[2544] Herod apparently presented the tax cut (on agricultural produce; see the note to "remitted the third part of the taxes" above) as a relief after one or more bad harvests. Josephus adds, however, that the king had another motive for the cut (see the next note).

Josephus uses the noun ἀφορία ("barrenness, dearth, unproductiveness," Rengstorf *s.v.*) also in connection with Joseph's explanation of Pharaoh's dreams (Gen 41), which predicted 7 years of plenty followed by 7 years of famine (*Ant.* 2.85, 97; see also 7.93).

[2545] For the verb ἀνακτάομαι with the meaning "win over (someone)," cf. *Ant.* 15.75 about Herod winning over Antony with the help of gifts.

[2546] Josephus also implies elsewhere in the Herod narrative of *Antiquities* that the king's subjects were hostile to him (e.g., 15.280, 291). Pastor (1997: 106) rightly notes that Josephus' comment here shows his anti-Herodian bias. It is improbable that a tax cut would have ended the hostility of Herod's subjects if their criticism of him was based on religious and cultural objections.

[2547] For the phrase χαλεπῶς φέρω ("take badly"), see *Ant.* 15.24 with the note to "took the disgrace of her son badly."

[2548] The noun ἐξεργασία ("realization, carrying out," Rengstorf *s.v.*) occurs once elsewhere in Josephus (*War* 1.18), in which passage it means "elaboration" (referring to Josephus' report of the first war against Rome).

[2549] This remark seems out of place here because it is highly implausible that Herod's tax cut was associated with practices that went against the Jewish traditions (see also the note to "who were hostile" above).

The term ἐπιτηδεύματα ("habits, practices"; see *Ant.* 15.267 with the note to "foreign habits") occurs several times in the episode about the trophies in Jerusalem (15.267, 269, 275, 281), in which the reproach against Herod fits the context much better (see also 15.368 and the note to "that their worship would be put to an end" below).

[2550] This motivation for the hostility of Herod's subjects reminds one once again of the episode about the trophies (*Ant.* 15.267-291), especially of its introduction (15.267): "... he departed even more from the ancestral customs and gradually corrupted the [Jewish] way of life with foreign habits (ξενικοῖς ἐπιτηδεύμασιν), although it had previously remained undisturbed. Because of this we [i.e., the Jews] suffered considerable harm, also in later times, since all the matters that had previously led the masses to proper worship (ἐπὶ τὴν εὐσέβειαν) were neglected." The noun εὐσέβεια ("worship") occurs twice in the passage about the trophies (see 15.267 and 15.288 with the notes to "proper worship").

[2551] The verb μεταπίπτω ("change," Rengstorf *s.v.*) also occurs in the report about the trophies: the protesters could not accept Herod's change of the Jewish practices (*Ant.* 15.267-268, 274, 281, 288; see 15.267 with notes).

[2552] Niese (398) conjectures διά ("by, through, between") instead of δέ ("but"; see also the next note).

[2553] The phrase λόγοι διὰ πάντων ἐγίνοντο is perhaps pejorative, which would imply a translation like "(So) there were mutterings by all of them" (cf. *Ant.* 16.373: "When he [i.e., Herod] came to Caesarea, everybody was immediately talking [γίνεται λόγος εὐθὺς ἅπασι] about his sons, and the kingdom was in suspense because the people were waiting [to see] how the case against them would turn out some day," my trans.).

[2554] The context implies that the subjects of Herod's kingdom were provoked by the king's actions, which is remarkable in the light of the tax cut arranged by Herod (see the note to "remitted the third part of the taxes" above).

Concerning the verb παροξύνω ("incite, provoke,"

taking away their opportunities[2557] and ordering them [the subjects] to always be at work.[2558] No gatherings were permitted to the people in the city,[2559] nor meetings during a walk[2560] or at a meal,[2561] for everything was watched.[2562] And the punishments for those detected[2563]

Rengstorf *s.v.*), cf. *Ant.* 15.50 about Aristobulus III's popularity among the Jewish population and Herod's jealousy inciting the king to murder Aristobulus. For the phrase παροξύνω ἀεί ("provoke continuously"), cf. Cassius Dio 46.8.4.

[2555] For the verb ταράσσω ("trouble, disturb," Rengstorf *s.v.*) and its further occurrences in Josephus' Herod narratives, see *Ant.* 15.82 with the note to "he was greatly disturbed" and cf. Matt 2:3 (van Henten 2008a: 104, 114-15). For the combination of παροξύνω and ταράσσω, cf. Plutarch, *Mor.* (*Coni. praec.*) 144e, (*Quaest. conv.*) 656e, 657a.

[2556] The noun ἐπιμέλεια ("care, attention," Rengstorf *s.v.*) is ambiguous. It can have a neutral meaning ("care"; cf. *Ant.* 15.216), but also a negative connotation (as in 15.44 concerning Herod's treatment of his mother-in-law Alexandra). In the general statement about Herod's behavior towards his subjects found in 15.326, ἐπιμέλεια has a positive meaning (see the note to "through care"): "He domesticated his subjects in two ways: through fear (φόβος), by being merciless in his punishments, and through care (ἐπιμέλεια), by showing himself generous when circumstances suddenly changed."

[2557] The context implies that εὐκαιρία ("right moment, suitable time, opportunity") concerns activities against Herod, such as Alexandra's plans (see *Ant.* 15.59 with the note to "an opportunity for revenge"). It is plausible to think of attempts to revolt. *Ant.* 17.148 connects the destruction of the golden eagle that Herod had erected on a Temple gate with the king's fatal illness, which apparently offered a good opportunity to stand up against Herod (van Henten 2011d; see also 15.295 about Herod's subjects, who "continuously organized disturbances, even after a minor incitement").

[2558] Herod's order as described here suggests that the king attempted to fully control his subjects (see the continuation of the narrative and *Ant.* 15.326-327) and achieve maximum security for his rule. Various Josephan passages emphasize Herod's actions to enhance his security (e.g., 15.291-292, 295). The focus on labor here reminds one of the oppression of the Israelites by the Egyptians before the Exodus (*Ant.* 2.201-204; Exod 1:8-14). The noun πόνος in the plural means "work, labor" here (as in *Ant.* 1.33 concerning the Sabbath commandment).

[2559] This is another obvious strategy to control the population. The phrase τοῖς περὶ τὴν πόλιν can refer to the inhabitants of Jerusalem (being the most important city of the kingdom), but πόλις ("city") can also have the meaning "community of citizens" (LSJ *s.v.* III), which would imply that the ban concerned political meetings (either in Jerusalem or in the entire kingdom). The first meaning, however, is more probable because of the opposition "in the city"—"along the road" at the end of this paragraph.

[2560] For περίπατος ("walk, promenade"), see *Ant.* 15.337 with the note to "a most pleasant walk."

[2561] Herod apparently decided for a general ban on gatherings, whether for political or for practical reasons. It is important to note that this harsh ban is not supported by other passages in Josephus' Herod narratives (see also the next note).

The noun δίαιτα ("daily life, [usual] food, etc.," Rengstorf *s.v.*) denotes what belongs to the necessities of life. It refers to daily life in *Ant.* 15.43, 185, and to food or diet in 15.246, 300.

[2562] There is no close parallel to this passage, but the statement matches the tenor of other Josephan passages about Herod. According to *Antiquities* the king was highly suspicious of opposition, also within his own family (e.g., 15.42 [see the note to "he truly did not remain without suspicion"], 183, 210, 258; 16.90, 108, 119, 223, 324, 334). This trait may be part of the tyrannical stereotype, which Josephus applies to Herod in some of his passages in *Antiquities* (detailed discussion in van Henten 2011b). In *War* 1.492-497 (cf. *Ant.* 15.235-254) Josephus describes Herod's reaction to his fear that his son Alexander is plotting against him. Alexander was later executed at Herod's command, together with his brother Aristobulus IV (*War* 1.551; *Ant.* 16.394). Herod's suspicion frightened him terribly and made him send out spies day and night (*War* 1.492). In 1.586 female slaves are put to torture and testify against Antipater, another son of Herod: Antipater (who was scheming wickedly against his father) and Herod's brother Pheroras would have said to each other that "after Alexander and Aristobulus, Herod would go after them and their wives. For after [what he did to] Mariamme and her offspring, he would spare no one. It would be better, then, to flee as far away as possible from the beast (φεύγειν ὡς πορρωτάτω τοῦ θηρίου)" (trans. Sievers/Forte in BJP 1a; cf. *Ant.* 17.66-67). According to the women Antipater would also have said to Pheroras: "It is impossible, however, to escape from such a bloodthirsty beast (ἐκφυγεῖν οὕτω φονικὸν θηρίον), in whose eyes we do not even have the right to show our affection for anyone …" (*War* 1.589, trans. Sievers/Forte in BJP 1a).

[2563] Concerning the verb φωράω ("detect, discover,"

were severe,[2564] and many were taken openly as well as secretly[2565] to the fortress Hyrcania[2566] and done away with.[2567] In the city[2568] as well as along the road[2569] there were people watching those who were meeting together.[2570] **367** They even say[2571] that he himself was concerned to[2572] take part in this.[2573] He frequently disguised himself as a private citizen[2574] and mingled[2575] by night[2576] with the crowds to try and find out the opinions they had about his rule.[2577] **368** Now as to those[2578] who remained obstinate[2579] in every possible

---

Rengstorf s.v.) in connection with criminal behavior, cf. Ant. 15.265; 17.110, 127, 129, 143.

[2564] Josephus emphasizes several times that Herod was severe in the punishments of both his subjects and his relatives (e.g., Ant. 15.326 with the note to "being merciless in his punishments").

[2565] The combination of secret and for everybody visible transports of prisoners suggests maximum deterrence: the openness sets the example, while the discovery afterwards of people having been taken away is an ominous experience.

[2566] Hyrcania was a Hasmonean fortress that was destroyed by Gabinius and rebuilt by Herod. Herod used the fortress as a prison for special enemies (Ant. 14.89 and here). It is usually identified with the site of Khirbet Mird in the Judean Desert, 6 km northeast of Marsaba (Schürer-Vermes 1.268, 307, 315).

[2567] Execution is an extremely hard punishment for people accused of gathering, which is the crime presupposed by the context (above). Herod's victims at Hyrcania were perhaps guilty of other crimes, but Josephus does not inform us about that. Another explanation of this detail might be that Josephus overstates Herod's harshness in order to depict him as a tyrant (see Ant. 15.354 with the note to "tyrannical").

[2568] I.e., Jerusalem (see the note to "the people in the city" above).

[2569] The term ὁδοιπορία ("journey") occurs 12 times in Josephus, but only in Antiquities. Here it means "open road" (Rengstorf s.v.).

[2570] This information implies that some of Herod's subjects openly defied Herod's ban despite the obvious danger of being arrested and executed. This reminds one of the attitude of the conspirators who tried to murder Herod after the king had put up trophies in Jerusalem (Ant. 15.280-289). For the phrase σύνειμι εἰς/ἐπὶ ταὐτόν ("associate/collide with," Rengstorf s.v.), cf. 16.9.

[2571] Josephus' reference to the anonymous source introduces a climax, intensified by the particle ἤδη ("even," Kühner and Gerth 1898-1904: 2.2.122).

[2572] The verb ἀμελέω plus a negation literally means "not neglect to" (Rengstorf s.v.).

[2573] Herod's decision to participate in the illegal gatherings, as described in the continuation of the narrative, is remarkable. It must have been very dangerous since his opponents probably would have killed him if recognizing him (as the episode about the trophies implies; see Ant. 15.282-284). Moreover, participating in the meetings that he himself had banned would also have undermined his authority if he was discovered. The decision implies that Herod was a pathetic and lonely ruler, which matches again the tyrannical stereotype. Schalit (2001: 314) considers this story to be part of a legend that shows how unpopular Herod was. Kasher (2007: 208-09) argues that the description is reliable and that the king's policy towards his subjects as described by Josephus reflects Herod's actual suspicious and paranoid character.

[2574] This detail is implausible since it was dangerous for Herod to mix with the crowd (see the previous and the next note). It is ironic in the light of Josephus' repeated remark that the king was born as a commoner (see Ant. 14.489-491 and 15.2 with the note to "commoner"; 15.263 with the note to "the kings' rule that was based on birth").

For similar phrases with (ἐν) σχήματί τινος ("in the guise of," Rengstorf s.v.) and ἰδιώτης ("commoner"), cf. War 1.387 (concerning Herod visiting Octavian); Ant. 8.266; Diodorus 31.18.2; 38-39.1.1; Philo, QG 4.206 ("... let the king also put on the guise of a commoner [ἰδιώτου σχῆμα] if he is not able in another way to obtain benefit for his realm and his subjects," trans. Marcus); Spec. 2.208; Dio Chrysostom 4.97; Plutarch, Mor. (Par. min.) 305f; Herodian 2.12.1.

[2575] The expression καταμίγνυμι εἰς ("mingle with," Rengstorf s.v.) is a hapax legomenon in Josephus.

[2576] That Herod did this at night (νύκτωρ) is obvious in the light of the danger involved in meeting with crowds consisting of his subjects (see the note to "take part in this" above).

[2577] This detail is also not very plausible: Ant. 15.366 indicates that some of Herod's subjects openly ignored his ban on gathering, which makes their criticism of the king obvious, and Ant. 15.365 states that the subjects felt continuously provoked and troubled by Herod. Moreover, Josephus' repeated remarks that Herod built or restored several fortresses in order to enhance his security with a view to possible rebellions imply that Herod knew that his subjects were very critical of his rule (e.g., 15.291-292, 295).

Several conjectures have been made in order to improve the transmitted text (Niese 399), entailing

way, such that they would not accommodate themselves to[2580] his practices,[2581] he took vengeance upon[2582] them all in various ways. As to the rest of the people[2583] he demanded they submit themselves by oath[2584] and be faithful.[2585] He forced them at one occasion[2586] to confirm their loyalty[2587] to him by oath[2588] and to truly observe his rule. **369** So most of them yielded to the things he demanded,[2589] out of submissiveness or fear,[2590] but those who were staying true to a brave attitude[2591] and were disgusted about being compelled,[2592]

---

different interpretations. For the phrase πεῖραν λαμβάνω with the meaning "get to know, obtain evidence" (Rengstorf s.v.), cf. Ant. 2.60.

[2578] Josephus reports that Herod divided the population into 2 categories (cf. τοὺς μὲν ... τὸ δ' ἄλλο πλῆθος), with the obvious aim of eradicating any remaining opposition.

[2579] The rare verb ἐξαυθαδίζομαι ("be rebellious/stubborn," Rengstorf s.v.) is a *hapax legomenon* in Josephus. Cf. the noun αὐθάδεια ("stubbornness") in Ant. 15.101; 16.399 and the adjective αὐθάδης ("stubborn, rebellious") in 16.79.

[2580] The verb συμπεριφέρω in the passive voice means "accommodate/adapt to" (LSJ s.v. II.3). The verb also occurs in Ant. 12.65 meaning "present (itself)" and in 19.147 meaning "be" (Rengstorf s.v.). The variant reading συμπαραφέσθαι of MS V is corrupt and the reading συμπαραφύεσθαι ("grow together") of the *editio princeps* (Niese 399) does not fit the context.

[2581] This detail links up with the episode about the trophies (e.g., the reproach in Ant. 15.267, 275 that Herod introduced ξενικὰ ἐπιτηδεύματα ["foreign practices"]) and with 15.365 (see the note to "such practices").

[2582] The verb ἐπέξειμι can mean, among other things, "punish, persecute, take vengeance on" (Rengstorf s.v.). It sometimes implies in the Herod narrative of *Antiquities* that Herod's enemies were or would be executed (see 15.290 and 16.106, 356 concerning Herod's sons).

[2583] For τὸ πλῆθος referring to the Jewish population of Herod's kingdom or the Jewish people, see Ant. 15.2 with the note to "the city's population."

[2584] Herod demanded his subjects to make an oath of loyalty to him (see the continuation of the paragraph), which oath is commonly dated to the year of Augustus' visit, i.e., 20 BCE (Mahieu 2012: 158). Kokkinos (1998: 171 with n. 77) dates the oath to 19 BCE. The former date, among other reasons, renders it plausible that the oath was also an oath of loyalty to the emperor (as Herrmann [1968: 98-99] and Kienast [1999: 252] argue), although Josephus does not mention this (differently Braund 1984: 115, who states that an oath of allegiance to the emperor and Herod is without parallels and that it is unlikely that Augustus instructed Herod to arrange such an oath). If the oath was a confirmation of loyalty to Augustus, it was, perhaps, connected with the emperor cult (see Ant. 15.364 with the note to "that he consecrated to Caesar").

Concerning the combination of ἀξιόω ("ask, demand"), ὅρκος ("oath"), and πίστις ("pledge"; see the next note), cf. Ant. 7.24 concerning Saul's commander Abner, who moved over to David (2 Sam 3) and asked David for a sworn pledge (παρὰ Δαυίδην λαβεῖν ὅρκους τε καὶ πίστεις ἠξίου).

[2585] The noun πίστις ("trust," Rengstorf s.v.) can have several nuances in Josephus (Lindsay 1993: 77-82), including "pledge" (see Ant. 15.69 with the note to "making assurances"), "faithfulness" (see 15.291 with the note to "this imperturbability for the sake of faithfulness to the laws"), and "trust (in someone's loyalty)." Here it refers to the loyalty of the Jewish people to Herod (Rengstorf s.v.; Lindsay 1993: 79). Cf. 16.48, 51 concerning the loyalty of Herod's sons to their father, as well as 17.32 concerning Antipater's supposed loyalty to Herod.

[2586] The use of the verb συναναγκάζω ("join in compelling, compel in the same time," Rengstorf s.v.) shows Josephus' own disapproval of this oath (cf. καταναγκάζω ["compel," Rengstorf s.v.] in Ant. 15.369).

[2587] For εὔνοια meaning "loyalty" (Rengstorf s.v.) in various contexts in the Herod narrative of *Antiquities*, see 15.68, 193-194, 201; 16.60, 82; 17.32, 179.

[2588] The adjective ἐνώμοτος ("confirmed by oath," Rengstorf s.v.) is a *hapax legomenon* in Josephus.

[2589] I.e., the oath. Cf. the repetition of ἠξίου ("he demanded") in Ant. 15.368-369.

[2590] The phrase κατὰ θεραπείαν καὶ δέος ("out of submissiveness or fear") is unique in Josephus. It may be associated with the tyrannical stereotype (van Henten 2011b) because submissiveness and fear are obvious responses to the regime of a tyrant. The noun θεραπεία can mean, among other things, "servility, flattery" (Rengstorf s.v.).

[2591] An alternative translation of φρόνημα that fits the context well would be "resoluteness" (Rengstorf s.v.). The noun can express several nuances of "pride" (cf. Ant. 15.128 "proud designs"; 15.187 with the note to "his enormous pride"; 15.287 "high spirits").

[2592] As in the report about the trophies Josephus points out that the majority of the population went along with Herod (at least in the end) and that a minority persisted in opposing the king. In the episode about the trophies

he got rid of[2593] using every possible way.[2594] **370** He also tried to persuade[2595] Pollio the Pharisee and Samaias,[2596] and their group,[2597] as well as most of those who were connected with them[2598] to take the oath.[2599] Although they did not consent, they were not punished in the same way as the [others] who had refused,[2600] since they were held in respect because of Pollio.[2601]

371 Those who are called by us Essaioi[2602] were also exempted from this obligation.[2603]

Manaemus' prophecy that Herod would become king.

---

they are the conspirators who tried to murder the king and were executed afterwards (*Ant.* 15.280-289). Josephus as narrator seems to sympathize with the minority group here; the noun θεραπεία ("submissiveness"; see the note to "submissiveness or fear" above) can easily be interpreted in a depreciating way. The vocabulary also echoes the episode about the trophies: the verb δυσχεραίνω ("be displeased," Rengstorf *s.v.*) occurs in 15.276 to express that the Jews in Jerusalem were greatly displeased (οὐ μετρίως ἐδυσχέραινον) because the trophies went against the ancestral practices (see also 15.281 with the note to "being annoyed").

[2593] The phrase ἐκποδών ποιέομαι ("do away with") is a euphemism for "murder" or "execute" someone (see *Ant.* 15.20 with the note to "get him out of the way").

[2594] This detail suggests again that Herod was an evil king. That Herod eliminated everybody among his Jewish subjects who stood up against him already shows that he was an extremely harsh ruler, but that he used all kinds of ways to achieve this purpose implies that he was wicked and evil. The alliteration of the *p* sound in the phrase παντὶ τρόπῳ ἐκποδὼν ἐποιεῖτο further emphasizes this.

[2595] The imperfect συνέπειθε from συμπείθω ("[seek to] persuade," Rengstorf *s.v.*; see also *Ant.* 15.21 with the note to "to be persuaded") is an *imperfectum de conatu* (Blass, Debrunner, and Rehkopf 1976: 268) since Herod obviously did not succeed in persuading this group.

[2596] With this reference to Pollio and Samaias the passage links up with *Ant.* 15.2-3, which concerns Herod's supporters and enemies as well as the king's treatment of both. Pollio and Samaias are mentioned in 15.3 as persons who were greatly honored by Herod (about hypotheses to identify these 2 scholars and about their connection with the Pharisees, see 15.2-4 with notes).

[2597] I.e., the Pharisees (Mason 1991: 263). The continuation of the narrative indicates that the Pharisees were opponents of Herod.

[2598] This vague reference could point to the supporters or pupils of the Pharisees. The verb συνδιατρίβω means "spend time with, live constantly together" (LSJ *s.v.*). Rengstorf (*s.v.*) gives "be a disciple (/follower)" as meaning for this passage.

[2599] I.e., the oath of loyalty mentioned in *Ant.* 15.368. There is a similar report in 17.41-45, in which Josephus also mentions that the Pharisees refused to swear loyalty to Herod.

[2600] The Pharisees apparently formed an exception: although they disobeyed Herod's command to take the oath of loyalty, they were not punished (see *Ant.* 15.369). The next sub-clause gives the reason for this exception. For the phrase οὔθε τοῖς ἀρνησαμένοις κολάσθηναι (or ἐκολάσθηναι) ("they were not punished ... as the [others] who had refused"), cf. Clement of Alexandria, *Strom.* 4.12.84.

[2601] This detail also links up with *Ant.* 15.2-4, in which episode Josephus indicates, with different vocabulary, that Herod had particularly high regard (ἐτιμῶντο μάλιστα, 15.3) for Pollio and his pupil Samaias. The passage here implies that the Pharisees opposed Herod, but that the king accepted their behavior and still favored them (Mason 1991: 263).

For the noun ἐντροπή ("respect, regard"), cf. 16.187, 241, 400.

[2602] *Ant.* 15.371-372 is a brief transitory passage that allows Josephus to continue smoothly with his report about Manaemus the Essene (15.373-379).

This is the first reference to the Essaioi (Ἐσσαῖοι) in the Herod narrative of *Antiquities*. In 15.372 Josephus uses the variant name Ἐσσηνοί "Essenes" (discussion of the variants by Mason in BJP 1b on *War* 2.113; see also *Ant.* 15.372-373, 378; further references in Schalit 1968: 46). Josephus presents the Essenes as a Jewish group here ("by us" implies "by us Jews"). The name "Essene" derives perhaps from the Syriac word *hase'* ("pious"; discussion in Schürer-Vermes 2.558-60). Philo notes that there were more than 4,000 of them (*Prob.* 75; cf. Josephus, *Ant.* 18.21), living in many towns of Judea (*Hyp.* 1), such that they cannot be fully identical with the Qumran community. There are 2 more elaborate passages about the Essenes in Josephus (*War* 2.119-161 and *Ant.* 18.11, 19-22), in which Josephus describes the Essenes as one of the 3 philosophical schools of contemporary Judaism (*War* 2.119-166; *Ant.* 13.171-173; *Life* 10-12; *Ant.* 18.9-25 mentions a 4th philosophy, which is very different from the others and an innovation that led to disaster according to Josephus; further discussion and references in Schürer-Vermes 2.555-97; Vermes and Goodman 1989; Nodet 2005: 368, 371-79; Mason in BJP 1b on *War* 2.119-166).

For the phrase οἱ Ἐσσαῖοι καλούμενοι ("those who

This movement[2604] has a way of life[2605] that was introduced[2606] by Pythagoras[2607] among the Greeks.[2608] I will describe[2609] these people elsewhere most carefully[2610] in great detail.[2611]

---

are called Essaioi"), cf. Philo, *Hyp.* 198; Eusebius, *Praep. ev.* 8.11.1; George Hamartolus, *Chron.* 8.5 (ed. de Boor 344); idem, *Chron. brev.* (PG 110.408).

[2603] With these words Josephus explicitly states that the Essenes formed the second group that was exempted from the obligation of the oath of loyalty (the Pharisees being the first group; see *Ant.* 15.370 with the note to "their group"). The story of Manaemus reported in 15.373-379 clarifies Herod's decision to exempt the Essenes from the obligation of the vow, as 15.372 ("the reason why") indicates, but it is hardly a satisfactory explanation. There must have been further reasons for exempting the Essenes from the oath, but we can only guess which ones. Perhaps Herod took into account that the Essenes avoided swearing oaths in general (apart from the oath when entering the community, *War* 2.139-142; 1QS 5.8). An additional reason may have been that the Essenes were important for their support against Hasmonean enemies (Gray 1993: 97-98).

The phrase ταύτης τῆς ἀνάγκης ("this obligation") echoes both συνηνάγκαζεν ("he forced them at one occasion") in *Ant.* 15.368 and καταναγκάζεσθαι ("being compelled") in 15.369. For ἀφίημι (here used in the passive voice: "be remitted"), cf. 15.356 with the note to "letting them go," and for the passive of ἀφίημι with τῆς ἀνάγκης in a different context, Cassius Dio 53 (table of contents).

[2604] The noun γένος ("race, offspring, descent") can also mean "class" or "kind" (LSJ *s.v.* V), which could apply to a group. Rengstorf (*s.v.*) offers "sect, fellowship, association, movement" as meanings for this passage. An alternative interpretation would be that γένος here indicates a group with a common origin, which may be implied by the references to individuals who are called Essenes by birth or origin: *War* 1.78 (Ἐσσαῖος ἦν γένος) and *Ant.* 13.311 (Ἐσσηνὸν μὲν τὸ γένος) about Judas; *War* 2.113 (Σίμων τις Ἐσσαῖος τὸ γένος) and *Ant.* 17.346 (Σίμων ἀνὴρ γένος Ἐσσαῖος) about Simon the Essene. Pliny the Elder (5.73) considers the *Esseni* to be a distinct tribe or even a race (*gens*), but he also mentions their practice of adopting children of others (similarly Josephus, *War* 2.120), such that γένος cannot refer to an ancestral group. The contexts of similar references in *War* 2.119 and *Ant.* 13.172 indicate that the noun refers to a Jewish movement (or school; cf. the related noun αἵρεσις in *War* 2.118, 122) of philosophers (Mason in BJP 1b on *War* 2.118). The reference to Pythagoras' way of life in the continuation of the narrative supports this interpretation.

[2605] The noun δίαιτα ("diet, way of life"; see *Ant.*

15.366 with the note to "a meal") sometimes refers to a specific way of life of a particular Jewish group (e.g., *War* 2.137-138, 151, 155, 160 concerning the Essenes and *Ant.* 18.12, 15 concerning the Pharisees). Mason (in BJP 1b on *War* 2.137) translates the noun in *War* 2.137-138, 151, 155, 160 with "regimen" and points out that it sometimes indicates a philosophical lifestyle (referring to Plutarch, *Mor.* [*Virt. vit.*] 100d; Epictetus, *Diatr.* 3.22.87; Philostratus, *Vit. Apoll.* 5.22).

[2606] An alternative translation is "taught" (Rengstorf *s.v.*). The verb καταδείκνυμι occurs twice elsewhere in Josephus (*Ant.* 10.151; 11.80).

[2607] This is the only reference to Pythagoras in *War* and *Antiquities*; he is not mentioned in Josephus' other passages about the Essenes (but cf. *Apion* 1.14, 162, 164; 2.14, 168). Pythagoras was born in ca. 580 BCE on the island of Samos and founded a philosophical school at Croton in Southern Italy. He is world-famous because of the mathematical proposition named after him (although it is uncertain whether he formulated it; it is very difficult to differentiate Pythagoras' own ideas from those of the later Pythagoreans). Pythagoras paid great attention to cosmology, the symbolic meanings of numbers, and the notion of the migration and eternal existence of the soul. He assumed a close connection between one's deeds and the posthumous fate of one's soul. As a consequence his followers were famous for their ascetic lifestyles (further information in Riedweg 2007; for the reception of Pythagoras in Hellenistic passages, see Thesleff 1965). Pythagoras' emphasis on one's deeds and the particular Pythagorean lifestyle make Josephus' association of the Essenes with Pythagoras quite understandable (see further Taylor 2004, who considers the Pythagoreans' permanent state of high purity, with its accompanying prescriptions and prohibitions, to be the most singular feature of their lives, p. 100).

[2608] Sometimes the noun "Greeks" (Ἕλληνες) refers to non-Jews, but here, as in *Ant.* 15.136 (with its binary opposition Greeks—barbarians) and in *War* 2.156, it refers to ethnic Greeks, as the additional reference to Pythagoras also implies.

[2609] The verb διέξειμι ("go through") can also mean "describe (in detail)" in Josephus (Rengstorf *s.v.*; cf. *War* 1.9, 27; 4.496). It indicates that this passage is a cross-reference to a more elaborate passage about the Essenes, *Ant.* 18.11, 19-22 or *War* 2.119-166 (although the latter passage had already been published when Josephus was writing this; for a similar function of διέξειμι, see *Ant.* 1.160).

[2610] Niese (399) reads σαφέστερον ("more clearly")

372 It is worthwhile telling[2612] the reason why he [Herod] held the Essenes in honor.[2613] He thought more highly[2614] of them than the limits of human nature imply.[2615] For the story[2616] does not appear to be unseemly in the genre of history,[2617] intimating[2618] also the public opinion[2619] about them.

(10.5) 373 A certain[2620] Essene[2621] was named Manaemus.[2622] His conduct of life[2623]

---

with MSS FLV, but MSS PAMW have ἀσφαλέστερον ("more carefully/securely"), which is supported by the Latin version (certius). It seems that ἀσφαλέστερον is the more original version, not only because of the Latin version, but also because Josephus uses the verb διέξειμι twice elsewhere in connection with his work as a historian (War 1.9; 4.496) and in both of these passages he clearly refers to accuracy (ἀκρίβεια).

[2611] In Ant. 18.11, 19-22 Josephus returns to the topic of the Essenes and informs his readers (18.11) that he has dealt with the Essenes in book 2 of War (i.e., in 2.119-166, which is obviously the most detailed passage about the Essenes).

[2612] The phrase εἰπεῖν ἄξιον, which is found at the end of the Greek clause, indicates that this passage is a comment by the narrator (cf. Thucydides 2.54; Strabo 1.2.7; Cassius Dio 47.17.4).

[2613] The phrase τοὺς δὲ Ἐσσηνοὺς ... ἐτίμα ("he held the Essenes in honor") is repeated with slight variations in Ant. 15.378 and creates an inclusio containing the story about Manaemus the Essene (15.373-378).

Being esteemed or treated with great respect (τιμάω, Rengstorf s.v.) by Herod was exceptional. Philo emphasizes several times that the Essenes were held in honor even by tyrannical rulers (Prob. 88-91; cf. Eusebius, Praep. ev. 8.11.18). In Ant. 15.40 Josephus reports that Ananel, who was appointed High Priest by Herod, was treated with respect and honored by him (τοῦτον ... ἐτίμησεν; cf. War 1.576, 646; 2.7; Ant. 16.78, 303; 17.207, although τιμάω has different nuances in these passages).

[2614] The phrase μεῖζον φρόνεω (literally "have over-high thoughts," LSJ s.v. φρόνεω II.2b) also occurs in Ant. 15.123, 143, in connection with Herod's battle against the Nabateans (cf. 1.155; 5.301).

[2615] This comment emphasizes that Herod thought highly of the Essenes and also anticipates, through the hint at a supernatural dimension, the motif that the Essenes had knowledge about the future by divine revelations (see Ant. 15.373).

Josephus' vocabulary here is closely paralleled by a passage in Libanius (Prog. 11.9.3): "... I have thought too highly of human nature (μεῖζον ἐφρόνησα τῆς θνητῆς φύσεως) ..." (my trans.). It also recalls a passage from Sophocles (Fragm. 590, transmitted in Stobaeus 3.22.22): "Human nature must think human thoughts (θνητὴν δὲ φύσιν χρὴ θνητὰ φρονεῖν), knowing that there is no master of the future, of what is destined to be accomplished, except Zeus" (trans. Lloyd-Jones).

[2616] For λόγος meaning "story" (LSJ s.v. V.3), cf. Ant. 15.71, 258.

[2617] Here Josephus claims that stories (see the previous note) do belong to the genre (γένος has the specific meaning "genre" here; Rengstorf s.v.) of historiography. The common meaning of the noun ἱστορία is "inquiry, investigation," but the word sometimes has the specific meaning "history" (i.e., the craft of writing history) in Josephus (Rengstorf s.v., also in 2 Macc 2:24, 30, 32; see van Henten 1997: 20). The story about Manaemus is useful in the context of Josephus' report: it exemplifies the opinion of the Jews about the Essenes, as Josephus states in the next line. The phrase τὸ τῆς ἱστορίας γένος is unique in Josephus, but a few related phrases do refer to historiographical conventions (e.g., War 1.11 ὁ τῆς ἱστορίας νόμος "the rule of historiography"; cf. 1.16; 5.10). The "rule/law of history" is a conventional phrase, which Lucian (Hist. conscr. 41) connects with Thucydides' principle of impartiality. Cicero (De or. 2.62; Leg. 1.5) also mentions this law and connects it with telling the truth, as Josephus does in War 1.11, 16 (Mason in BJP 1a on War 1.11). Sometimes Josephus explicitly goes beyond the convention of giving accurate and truthful reports. In 1.11-12, e.g., he includes partisan lamentations in writing history (Mader 2000: 2-3; see also Ant. 15.379: "Now we have deemed it fit to make these matters clear to the readers—even though they may seem incredible—..."). Landau (2006: 123-24) argues that the story about Manaemus is a Herodotean-style anecdote, combining prophecy, the divine favor bestowed upon a young person, and "the Herodotean notion of an ever-changing fortune."

[2618] For the verb παραδηλόω ("intimate, mention in passing"), see Ant. 15.103 with the note to "by intimating."

[2619] LSJ (s.v. II.3) offer "public opinion" as meaning for ὑπόληψις. An alternative translation would be "good reputation" (Rengstorf s.v.), as in Ant. 15.264 about the Sons of Baba. The first translation seems preferable because Josephus is making a distinction in this paragraph between Herod's high regard for the Essenes and the opinion of other Jews about them (see also 15.378-379).

[2620] The formula ἦν τις or ἦν δέ τις ("[there] was a

attested in every way to his excellence,[2624] but he also had foreknowledge from God of what was to come.[2625] When this man observed Herod, who was still a boy and going to

---

certain [person]") introduces the story about Manaemus. For similar formulae introducing a key person in the narrative, see *Ant.* 5.257 (concerning Jephtha); 6.45 (Saul); 6.295 (Nabal); 8.236 (the false prophet of Bethel); 9.239 (Nahum); 12.265 (Mattathias, the father of the 5 Maccabean brothers) and cf. *War* 4.503 (Simon bar Giora).

[2621] See *Ant.* 15.371 with the note to "Essaioi."

[2622] The Essene Manaemus (Μανάημος; MSS FM and E read Μανάιμος; Niese 400) is mentioned in Josephus only in this story (*Ant.* 15.373-374, 377-378). The name Μανάημος does occur elsewhere in Josephus: referring to Menahem, a king of Israel (*Ant.* 9.229, 232-233; cf. 2 Kgs 15:17-22), and to Menahem, a son of Judas the Galilean (*War* 2.433, 437, 440, 442, 446-449; *Life* 21, 46; Schalit 1968: 81). The form Μανάημος (in the LXX: Μαναήμ or Μαναήν) is the Greek equivalent of the Hebrew name *Mĕnaḥēm* (Ilan 2002: 185-88, also for other occurrences of this name).

The context of the story implies that Manaemus was not a resident of Qumran (Gray 1993: 98, who calculates that the first meeting between Manaemus and Herod took place in the 60's of the 1st cent. BCE). Ilan (1998: 225-28) argues that Josephus' story about Manaemus is based on Nicolaus of Damascus.

[2623] The phrase ἡ προαίρεσις τοῦ βίου ("conduct of life, lifestyle") also occurs in *Apion* 2.210, referring to a lifestyle in accordance with the Jewish laws. For the same phrase in various other contexts, cf. Plato, *Def.* 413a; Demosthenes, *Or.* 23.141; 48.56; Diodorus 12.19.3; Philo, *Agr.* 60; *Cher.* 32; Dionysius, *Ant. rom.* 5.71.2; *Acts Apoll.* 27.

[2624] Manaemus' deeds exemplified his moral excellence (καλοκαγαθία "excellence, uprightness, moral perfection," Rengstorf *s.v.*). This term became important in self-definitions from the Sophists in Athens in the 2nd half of the 5th cent. BCE. In the 4th cent. BCE it became a status symbol for rich citizens from Athens who supported their city generously. In later passages the term expresses a common moral virtue (Bourriot 1995). Philo uses it frequently (e.g., *Prob.* 75, 91 in connection with the Essenes), and it also occurs in 4 Macc (1:8 [Codex Sinaiticus], 10; 3:18; 11:22; 13:25; 15:9). The notion that one's conduct has to reflect one's ethical views is a commonplace in popular ancient philosophy, which is re-interpreted from a Jewish perspective in 4 Maccabees. The Maccabean martyrs exemplify the philosophical proposition made in 4 Macc 1:1 ("Since I am about to discuss an eminently philosophical subject—whether pious reason is absolute master of the passions ...," trans. *NETS*) and are striving for excellence in line with the Jewish religion and laws (van Henten 1997: 286).

The noun καλοκαγαθία occurs in Josephus only in the Herod narrative of *Antiquities*, with 2 of the 3 occurrences belonging to the story about Manaemus (15.373, 379; 16.178). For the combination of καλοκαγαθία and μαρτυρέω ("attest"), cf. Philo, *Mos.* 1.59 about Jethro giving Moses his most beautiful daughter (Zipporah) in marriage: "Accordingly, he [i.e., Jethro] gave him [i.e., Moses] the fairest of his daughters in marriage, and, by that one action, attested all his noble qualities (δι' ἑνὸς ἔργου πάνθ' ὅσα τῶν εἰς καλοκἀγαθίαν μαρτυρήσας), and showed that excellence standing alone deserves our love ..." (trans. Colson).

[2625] Manaemus' knowledge of the future is highlighted in the Greek text (καὶ τἄλλα ... καί). Elsewhere Josephus also accredits the Essenes with foreknowledge of the future (*War* 1.78-80; 2.159; *Ant.* 13.311-313; Smith 1987: 248-50; Beall 1988: 109; Gray 1993: 80-111) as well as with the explanation of dreams, which of course requires divine foreknowledge (Gnuse 1996: 132-33, 245-46, 248, 250-54). Josephus offers 2 further reports about individual Essenes predicting the future. According to *War* 1.78-80; *Ant.* 13.311-313 the Essene Judas predicted that Antigonus, the brother of Aristobulus I (104-103 BCE), would be murdered at a place called Straton's Tower. And the Essene Simon explains the dream of Herod's son Archelaus in *War* 2.112-113; *Ant.* 17.246.

For other passages with vocabulary related to πρόγνωσιν ἐκ θεοῦ τῶν μελλόντων ("having foreknowledge from God of what was to come"), see *Ant.* 8.234; 13.300; 17.43, and Philo, *Mos.* 2.190 (cf. *Somn.* 2.2). *Ant.* 8.225-235 (cf. 1 Kgs 12:25-13:10; 2 Chr 9:29; 13:8) offers an interesting parallel. King Jeroboam had built a sanctuary at Bethel with a golden statue of a heifer and planned to offer sacrifices there. A man of God, identified as Jadon (Iddo in the Bible), stood up against Jeroboam and addressed his altar. He said that God had foretold him that someone from the line of David named Josias (Josiah in the Bible) would sacrifice upon the altar the bones of those who misled the people. As a sign the altar was broken, and when Jeroboam stretched out his hand against the prophet it became paralyzed. *Ant.* 8.234 says about the prophet that he possessed divine foreknowledge (θείαν ἔχοντα πρόγνωσιν). Jeroboam admired the prophet because of his self-control (ἐγκράτεια, 8.235), but he feared that the prophecy would change his fortunes. *Ant.* 13.300 states

his teacher[2626] as usual, he addressed him as King of the Jews.[2627] **374** Herod thought that he [Manaemus][2628] did not know him or was making fun of him[2629] and reminded him that he was a private citizen.[2630] But Manaemus laughed gently,[2631] patted him with his hand on his buttocks,[2632] and said: "But truly, you will be king.[2633] You will rule happily.[2634] For

---

in a concluding note about John Hyrcanus (135/134-104 BCE) that God had given him 3 great privileges: the leadership of the Jewish nation, the High Priesthood, and the gift of prophecy (προφητεία). Josephus explains the last point: "for the Deity (τὸ θεῖον) was with him and enabled him to foresee and foretell the future (τὴν τῶν μελλόντων πρόγνωσιν παρεῖχεν αὐτῷ τε εἰδέναι καὶ προλέγειν) ... (trans. Marcus)."

[2626] Herod most probably received an elite education, but apparently not abroad, in contradistinction to his own sons. The reference to Herod being still a boy (παῖς; cf. Manaemus patting Herod on his buttocks in *Ant.* 15.374 and the considerable interval between the prophecy and Herod's response to it in 15.377) may imply that the level of education here concerns the first cycle of education (the *ludus litterarius*, i.e., reading, writing, and arithmetic from the age of 7 until 11 or 12), or the second (the *ludus grammaticus*, i.e., Latin and Greek grammar from the age of 11 or 12 until 15; see 15.342 with the note to "with Caesar").

For φοιτάω εἰς τίνος διδάσκαλου (sc. οἶκον, "resort to a person as a teacher," LSJ *s.v.* 5), cf. Aristophanes, *Eq.* 1235; Xenophon, *Cyr.* 1.2.6; 2.3.9; Plato, *Alc. mai.* 109d; Philo, *Congr.* 122.

[2627] Manaemus' addressing of Herod as King of the Jews foretold Herod's appointment as king by the Romans (*War* 1.281-285; *Ant.* 14.379-389). The title "King of the Jews" (βασιλεύς Ἰουδαίων or βασιλεύς τῶν Ἰουδαίων) is mentioned in connection with Herod in *Antiquities* for the first time in 14.9, which passage already says that Herod would become king because of "some change of fortune" (other references to this title in *War* 1.282; *Ant.* 15.409; 16.291, 311; cf. *War* 6.103-104 concerning Jehoiachin; 6.439 concerning David; 7.171 concerning Alexander Janneus; *Ant.* 6.98 concerning Saul; 7.72 concerning David; and 14.36 concerning Aristobulus II). The same title is mentioned several times in the Passion narratives of the New Testament (e.g., Mark 15:2, 9, 12, 18, 26 and parallels; Brown 1994: 476-78, 731, 763, 823-30, 1151).

[2628] See *Ant.* 15.373.

[2629] The verb κατειρωνεύομαι ("mock, ridicule," Rengstorf *s.v.*) also occurs in *War* 2.26 concerning Antipater's accusation that Archelaus was secretly making fun of Augustus, and in 2.153 about the Essenes mocking their torturers or regarding them ironically (Mason in BJP 1b on *War* 2.153 with Excursus 1; see especially *War* 2.151-158, also 4.127; 7.270 and 2.29 with a different meaning).

[2630] About the motif of Herod being a commoner (ἰδιώτης), see *Ant.* 15.2 with the note to "commoner." The noun also occurs in *War* 1.432, 665 concerning Herod (cf. also *Ant.* 11.31 concerning Darius, son of Hystaspes, and 13.220 concerning Tryphon; both Darius and Tryphon were not born into kingship). The noun is also used in *War* 1.44; *Ant.* 19.213, with different meanings.

[2631] Manaemus' gentle laughter fits a situation in which an adult man is trying to put a boy at ease, but the motif of his laughter may also hint at a superior status in relation to Herod. The passage that mentions that the Essenes ridiculed their tortures (*War* 2.153) refers to laughing at their bodily sufferings (μειδιῶντες ἐν ταῖς ἀλγηδόσιν). The famous Rabbi Aqiva was brought to trial before Turnus Rufus when it was time for the recital of the Shema; his reciting of the Shema and laughing triggered the ruler's response that he was either a sorcerer or despised the tortures (*y. Ber.* 9.7; van Henten and Avemarie 2002: 151-53).

[2632] This detail suggests friendly conduct from Manaemus towards Herod and also indicates that the future king was still a boy at the time, in accordance with the reference to his education in *Ant.* 15.373 (see the note to "going to his teacher"). The gesture functions as a prophetic sign, as Manaemus himself further on suggests: "Remember Manaemus' pats ...." Israelite prophets sometimes combined their prophecies with prophetic signs. A classic case is Jer 19, in which chapter the prophet Jeremiah endorses his prophecy of doom by breaking a potter's jug in front of those who accompanied him (Jer 19:10). The reference to Herod's buttocks may, therefore, also have a symbolic meaning, hinting at Herod sitting on a throne as a king (Meyer 1940: 143 n. 16; 1968: 823).

The noun γλουτός is a *hapax legomenon* in Josephus and means "backside" and in the plural "seat" (Rengstorf *s.v.*). For a parallel to τύπτων ... κατὰ τῶν γλουτῶν ("patting him on his buttocks"), cf. Pseudo-Justin, *Orat. gent.* 3.11 (ed. von Otto 12).

[2633] The Greek sequence is different: "[he] said" follows upon "But truly, you will be king," which highlights these first words of Manaemus' prophecy. They express the most important point; the following lines of the prophecy (*Ant.* 15.375-376) mention what Herod's kingship will entail. Aune (1983: 146) classifies

you were deemed worthy by God.[2635] Remember Manaemus' pats,[2636] so that this too will be a token[2637] of the changes that take place in accordance with fortune.[2638] **375** For the best policy[2639] would be if you would love[2640] righteousness[2641] and proper worship of God[2642] as well as reasonableness towards your citizens.[2643] But beware, for I know,[2644]

Manaemus' prediction as a recognition oracle, comparing it with Josephus' predictions to Vespasian (*War* 3.399-405), Samuel's prediction of David's kingship (1 Sam 16:11-13; *Ant.* 6.162-165), and Rabbi Aqiva's proclamation of Bar Kokhba as Messiah (*y. Ta'an.* 4.8; *Lam. Rab.* 2.4).

[2634] The reading ἀπάξεις ("diverting" or "leading away") of almost all Greek MSS does not go well with the adverb εὐδαιμόνως ("fortunately, happily"). Richards and Shutt (1937: 174) conjecture ἐπάρξεις, offering "you will have a happy reign" as translation of καὶ τὴν ἀρχὴν εὐδαιμόνως ἐπάρξεις. In support of their conjecture they note that Josephus uses the verb ἐπάρχω ("rule over") twice in references to administrators (*Ant.* 9.2; 19.14). Niese (400) conjectures κατάξεις ("bringing down") or διάξεις ("drawing apart"). The reading ἀπάρξεις (perhaps "you will begin") of MS W is a further support of Richards and Shutt's conjecture. The majority reading ἀπάξεις can easily have evolved out of ἀπάρξεις by dropping the -ρ-, and this form ἀπάρξεις may further derive from the accidental change of ε- into α- at the beginning of the word ἐπάρξεις. The interpretation that follows from this reading fits in with other Josephan passages about Herod, which imply that he was a successful ruler but very unfortunate in his personal life (see especially 16.75-77).

[2635] Manaemus' prophetic status (see *Ant.* 15.373 with the note to "had foreknowledge from God of what was to come") allows for this claim that Herod's kingship was decided for by God (see also the hint at the change of Herod's fortune in 14.9 [see 15.373 with the note to "addressed him as King of the Jews"] as well as 15.198, in which passage Josephus notes that Herod's visit to Octavian was successful because of God's consent).

For similar vocabulary, see 6.284 about Saul being counted worthy of the kingship by God (τὸν ὑπὸ τοῦ θεοῦ βασιλείας ἀξιωθέντα) and 13.299 about John Hyrcanus.

[2636] This point refers to Manaemus' gesture of patting Herod on his buttocks mentioned shortly before.

[2637] Manaemus' explanation confirms that his gesture is symbolic (a σύμβολον "sign"; cf. *Ant.* 6.28 and see the note to "patted him with his hand on his buttocks" above).

[2638] The noun τύχη ("fortune, chance, fate") refers indirectly to God here, as the references to God (θεός) in the immediate context imply (*Ant.* 15.373-374; see also 14.9 and 15.17 with the note to "fortune"). The noun μετάπτωσις ("change") occurs once elsewhere in Josephus, also in *Antiquities* (17.303, referring to a change of government).

[2639] The noun λογισμός means "reasoning" leading to virtuous behavior here (cf. the virtues mentioned by Manaemus), which is similar to the use of this noun in 4 Macc (e.g., 6:7; van Henten 1997: 270-88), although Josephus' passage misses the philosophical setting present in 4 Macc.

[2640] The construction of εἰ followed by the optative ἀγαπήσειας ("if you would love") indicates that Manaemus first formulated a possibility that would not become true (Kühner and Gerth 1898-1904: 2.2.477-78).

[2641] This part of Manaemus' statement hints at a motif ("loving righteousness") that is important in the LXX. Manaemus applies it to rulers, as the opening verse of the Wisdom of Solomon (1:1, 1st cent. BCE or CE) likewise does: "Love justice (ἀγαπήσατε δικαιοσύνην), you who rule the earth; be mindful of the Lord in goodness, and seek him in singleness of heart" (trans. Winston 1979: 99). The phrase καὶ εἰ δικαιοσύνην ἀγαπήσειας echoes Wis 8:7: "If one loves justice (εἰ καὶ δικαιοσύνην ἀγαπᾷ τις), the fruits of wisdom's labor are virtues; self-control (σωφροσύνην) and understanding (φρόνησιν) are her teaching, justice (δικαιοσύνην) and courage (ἀνδρείαν), and in the life of humankind nothing is more useful than these" (trans. Winston 1979: 191). The condition "If one loves justice ..." is followed by a reference to the 4 cardinal virtues (including "justice") obtained as a consequence. Manaemus mentions only the cardinal virtue of justice and not those of self-control, understanding, and courage, but he does mention "piety" (εὐσέβεια; see the next note), which replaces "understanding" (φρόνησις) in some Jewish references to the cardinal virtues (4 Macc 1:18; 5:23; Philo, *Decal.* 119; *Spec.* 4.147; Winston 1979: 194; van Henten 1997: 277, 281-82). For other LXX passages with this motif (concerning God loving justice), see LXX 1 Chr 29:17; LXX Ps 44:8; LXX Prov 15:9; LXX Isa 61:8. LXX Ps 44:7-8 refers to the kingship of God in connection with an anointed ruler: "Your throne, O God, is for ever and ever. A rod of equity is the rod of your rule; you loved righteousness (ἠγάπησας δικαιοσύνην) and hated lawlessness. Therefore God, your God, anointed you ..." (trans. *NETS*). For similar vocabulary, cf. Aesop 34 (title); Plato, *Resp.* 472b; Clement of Alexandria, *Strom.* 6.11.95.

[2642] Manaemus mentions justice and piety (or respect,

because I have knowledge of everything,[2645] that you will not be such [a ruler].[2646] **376** For you will surpass any other person in the amount of fortune you have[2647] and you will

---

proper worship [when referring to a deity], εὐσέβεια) together because he focuses on Herod's future kingship with respect to his citizens as well as to God. The noun εὐσέβεια (*pietas* in Latin) sometimes refers to worship of God in specific contexts in Josephus (see *Ant.* 15.267 with the note to "proper worship"), and some of the relevant passages have vocabulary similar to that in Manaemus' statement: e.g., *Ant.* 9.16 refers to King Jehoshaphat's worship as τῇ πρὸς τὸ θεῖον εὐσεβείᾳ. The distinction between one's attitudes to humans and to God in connection with both virtues is explicit in 18.117 (about John the Baptist): "... he was a good man and had exhorted the Jews to lead righteous lives, to practice justice towards their fellows and piety towards God (τὰ πρὸς ἀλλήλους δικαιοσύνῃ καὶ πρὸς τὸν θεὸν εὐσεβείᾳ χρωμένοις)" (trans. Feldman; see also *War* 2.139 on the Essenes; Mason in BJP 1b on *War* 2.139 with Excursus 1). This distinction is made already in Classical Greek passages (with a polytheistic focus), e.g., Isocrates, *Panath.* 124: "For they [i.e., Athen's ancestors] administered both the affairs of the state and their own affairs as righteously and honorably as was to be expected of men who were descended from the gods, who were the first to found a city and to make use of laws, who at all times had practiced reverence in relation to the gods and justice in relation to humankind (εὐσέβειαν περὶ τοὺς θεούς, δικαιοσύνῃ δὲ περὶ τοὺς ἀνθρώπους)" (trans. Norlin, slightly adapted). Plato (*Def.* 412e) defines εὐσέβεια as "justice towards the gods" (δικαιοσύνῃ περὶ θεούς). The combination of righteousness (δικαιοσύνῃ) and proper worship (εὐσέβεια) occurs often in Josephus (*Ant.* 6.265 concerning King Saul; 8.121 concerning King Solomon; 8.314 concerning King Asa; 8.299-300 concerning Jehu's prophecy of warning to King Baasha; 9.16 concerning King Jehoshaphat; 9.236 concerning King Jotham of Judah; 10.49-51 concerning King Josiah; 12.56 concerning King Ptolemy II Philadelphus; 14.283 concerning Herod's father Antipater; 18.117 concerning John the Baptist; see Gray 1993: 99-100, who argues that practicing justice and piety implies that one keeps the commandments of the Law). See also *Apion* 2.146, 170, 291 and cf. Isocrates, *Pac.* 33-34; *Panath.* 183; Diodorus 1.2.2; 5.8.3; Dionysius, *Pomp.* 6.6 (Mason 1991: 85–89; Kienast 1999: 97).

[2643] "Reasonableness, generosity, magnanimity" are possible nuances of the noun ἐπιείκεια (Rengstorf *s.v.*), which is another virtue of good rulers. Josephus uses the noun 3 times in remarks about Hyrcanus II (*Ant.* 15.165 [see the note to "his reasonable character"], 177, 182; cf.

12.122 concerning the Romans; 16.367 concerning the trial of Herod's sons; 3 Macc 3:15 concerning Ptolemy IV Philopator; and Wis 2:19; 12:18; Bar 2:27 concerning God). The phrase ἐπιείκεια πρὸς τοὺς πολίτας is paralleled by Diodorus 37.10.2.

[2644] Cobet's conjecture οἶμαι ("I think," Naber 1888-96: 3.xlvii, 375) instead of οἶδα ("I know," Niese 400) is unnecessary and weakens Manaemus' statement. Manaemus knows because of divine revelation (*Ant.* 15.373).

[2645] These words should not be taken in the absolute sense, which would imply that Manaemus compares himself to God. The context implies that the phrase means that Manaemus had knowledge about Herod's entire future. The motif itself is a *topos* in various passages about persons who have special relationships with the gods or God and therefore "have knowledge of everything" (e.g., Pseudo-Clement, *Hom.* 2.6.1; Dio Chrysostom 33.4; van Unnik 1979; Gray 1993: 100-01).

For a similar but more explicit formulation, cf. *War* 2.102 about the teacher of someone who pretended to be Herod's son Alexander: "... who knew everything that happened throughout the kingdom (πάντα τὰ κατὰ τὴν βασιλείαν ἐπιστάμενος) ..." (trans. Mason in BJP 1b).

[2646] The continuation of the prophecy mentions why Herod would not be a good ruler, emphasizing, among other things, that he would forget about justice and proper worship (*Ant.* 15.376).

[2647] Herod's being fortunate (εὐτυχία "fortune") as a ruler is a recurring motif in *Antiquities* (see 15.361 with the note to "this state of fortune"). Here Manaemus at least intends that Herod would become fortunate as a king because of God's interference since he indicates at the end of this paragraph that God would punish Herod at the end of his rule. God's support for Herod is mentioned much more explicitly in 14.462-464, reporting Herod's rescue from a murder attempt following his victory over Pappus, Antigonus' commander. Josephus notes there that Herod escaped "by the providence of God" (κατὰ θεοῦ πρόνοιαν, 14.462). In another brief report Josephus emphasizes twice that Herod was rescued by God's interference (15.455). Schalit (2001: 459-60) considers these references to be propaganda for Herod suggesting that he was chosen king by God. Cf. Plutarch, *Mor.* (*Alex. fort.*) 344a about Alexander the Great as a fortunate king (εὐτυχὴς βασιλεύς) because he was protected by Fortune (Τύχη). For similar vocabulary, cf. Dio Chrysostom 39.2: "for it is fitting that those whose city was founded by the gods ... prove to be ... to some extent superior to the others in good

receive eternal glory,[2648] but you will forget about[2649] worship and what is righteous.[2650] But these acts will surely not escape God's notice[2651] when at the end of your life[2652] his wrath over them will be remembered."[2653]

377 For the moment[2654] Herod did not even slightly note[2655] these predictions[2656] because he lacked hope in them. But at the height of his power,[2657] after he had been gradually elevated until he ruled as king[2658] and also enjoyed good fortune,[2659] he sent for Manaemus[2660]

---

fortune (διοίσουσί τι τῶν ἄλλων εὐτυχία)" (trans. Crosby). The term εὐτυχία is absent in *War*.

[2648] Various passages in the Herod narrative of *Antiquities* imply that Herod was keen on having a good reputation, also for posterity (see 15.330 with notes); he "loved honor" (for passages with φιλοτιμία ["ambition" or "love of honor"], see 15.271 with the note to "ambition").

[2649] The phrase λήθην ἔχειν ("forget," Rengstorf *s.v.*) also occurs in *Ant.* 3.14; 11.52.

[2650] This takes up Manaemus' earlier point about loving justice and proper worship as being proof of a good ruler (*Ant.* 15.375). Manaemus' statement implies that Herod would not be a good ruler. *War* 1.400 depicts Herod in a different way: "Then he advanced to the greatest prosperity; his high-mindedness rose even more, and the better part of his noble character was directed towards piety (τὸ πλέον τῆς μεγαλονοίας ἐπέτεινεν εἰς εὐσέβειαν)" (trans. Sievers/Forte in BJP 1a).

[2651] There is a Greek word play in Manaemus' statement, contrasting Herod's forgetting (λήθην ἕξεις) about justice and proper worship with this behavior not escaping God's notice (οὐκ ἂν λάθοι τὸν θεόν). For other occurrences of λανθάνω ("escape notice, etc.") referring to God in Josephus, see *Ant.* 2.129; 8.269; *Life* 83.

[2652] The combination ἡ καταστροφή τοῦ βίου ("the end of life," of a certain person) is a fixed expression in Josephus (*Ant.* 2.154; 10.241; cf. 16.72) and also frequently appears in other Greek authors (e.g., Polybius 5.54.4-5; Diodorus 1.58.3; 4.34.5; Strabo 6.3.9).

[2653] Manaemus announces that God will punish Herod for his behaving as a bad ruler. This prediction is taken up again in the Herod narratives about Herod's final period, particularly in *Antiquities*, which work hints at God's interference during Herod's final days of tremendous physical sufferings (17.168-173; see especially 17.168 and cf. *War* 1.656-659). Schalit (2001: 459 n. 1069) surmises that the original version of Manaemus' prophecy only contained the prediction of Herod's kingdom.

[2654] Here Josephus switches from Manaemus' prophecy to Herod's reaction upon it. He points to a double response by Herod: an immediate reaction (introduced by αὐτίκα; see also the next note) and a second one after Herod had become king ("after he had been ... exalted").

[2655] The phrase προσέχω τὸν νοῦν (here "note," Rengstorf *s.v.*) also occurs in *Ant.* 16.233, with a different meaning.

[2656] That Herod did not pay much attention to Manaemus' prophecy is what one would expect of a boy (cf. *Ant.* 15.373-374), being focused on mundane matters. It is plausible that at that time Herod did not know who Manaemus was.

[2657] It is an obvious thing after having tasted the power of kingship to ask how long it will last. That Herod apparently did this at the height of his power (ἐν τῷ μεγέθει τῆς ἀρχῆς) implies perhaps that it was at a crucial moment. Cf. Philo, *Plant.* 92: "It is a strong bulwark of cheerfulness of spirit and freedom from danger to have reposed our confidence in a King [i.e., God] who is not urged by the greatness of his dominion (βασιλεῖ δὲ πεπιστευκέναι μὴ τῷ μεγέθει τῆς ἀρχῆς) to inflict injuries on his subjects, but whose love for humankind makes it his delight to supply what is lacking to each one" (trans. Colson and Whitaker, slightly adapted; cf. Appian, *Hist. rom.* 11.7.3 about Antiochus III; Cassius Dio 66.1 [ed. Boissevain 1.295] about Alexander the Great).

Mahieu (2012: 303) argues that "the height of his power" points to Augustus' confirmation of Herod's rule in 30 BCE. Herod's question "whether there would be ten more years of rule" (*Ant.* 15.378) would match the fact that Herod had been ruling for 10 years thus far (40-30 BCE; see also *Ant.* 15.378 with the note to "even twenty").

[2658] The infinitive βασιλεύειν ("be king") echoes Manaemus' term of address "King (βασιλέα) of the Jews" in *Ant.* 15.373 and his prophecy in 15.374 that Herod would become king (βασιλεύσεις).

[2659] Herod's fortune as a ruler makes him realize in Josephus' presentation that Manaemus' prophecy had become true, which is indicated by εὐτυχεῖν ("enjoy good fortune") linking up with εὐτυχία ("fortune") in *Ant.* 15.376 (see the note to "the amount of fortune you have" and the previous note).

[2660] That Herod summoned Manaemus implies that the sage was still alive and that Herod remembered his prophecy. As an adult Herod apparently knew Manaemus, which is plausible in the light of Manaemus being introduced in *Ant.* 15.373 as an Essene with an exemplary way of life and receiving divine revelations. The meeting

and by asking him[2661] tried to find out for how long he would rule. **378** But Manaemus did not say anything at all.[2662] When he remained silent,[2663] he [Herod] inquired further,[2664] [asking] only whether there would be ten more years of rule. When he [Manaemus] said "even twenty[2665] or thirty," he did not put a limit[2666] to the complete period.[2667] Even with this [answer] Herod was satisfied[2668] and he let Manaemus go after entertaining him hospitably.[2669] And from that time on[2670] he continued to honor all the Essenes.[2671] **379** Now

---

may have taken place at the court in Jerusalem or in one of Herod's palaces elsewhere. There is no indication that Manaemus served at the court (Gray 1993: 98).

[2661] The verb διαπυνθάνομαι ("question, find out," Rengstorf s.v.) occurs twice elsewhere in Josephus (*War* 1.244; 4.415).

[2662] Josephus does not specify why Manaemus remained silent. The silence could either express disinterest, or be a signal that the prophecy was clear enough, or show contempt for Herod. The second option is perhaps confirmed by the answer that Manaemus ultimately gives: he does not give an indication of the duration of Herod's rule, which matches his prophecy further on not mentioning the length of the rule either (Mahieu [2012: 302-03], however, interprets the reference to 20 and 30 years in *Ant.* 15.378 as an indication of a duration; see the note to "even twenty" below). The third interpretation can be associated with a characteristic of certain martyrdom accounts in which the martyrs remain silent during interrogations by foreign rulers, which behavior causes a reversal of the power relations between the 2 antagonists (e.g., 2 Macc 7:25; 4 Macc 6:5, 9-11; *b. Ber.* 61b about Rabbi Aqiva; cf. Jesus' silence in front of Herod Antipas in Luke 23:8-9; van Henten 2009).

[2663] Manaemus' silence is emphasized by the alliteration of the *s* and *p* sounds in τὸ μὲν σύμπαν οὐκ εἶπεν· ὡς δὲ σιωπῶντος αὐτοῦ.

[2664] The verb προσπυνθάνομαι ("put an additional question") links up with διαπυνθάνομαι ("question") in *Ant.* 15.377. This verb occurs once elsewhere in Josephus, also in the Herod narrative of *Antiquities* (16.223), in which case it means "ask (someone else) besides" (Rengstorf s.v.).

[2665] Richardson (1996: 257 n. 69) concludes that if this reference is reliable, the meeting of Manaemus and Herod should have taken place before 21 (or perhaps 18) BCE, i.e., before Herod's 20th year as king (reckoned from Herod's appointment in 40 BCE or his capture of Jerusalem in 37 [or 36] BCE). This would be supported by the reference to Herod's 18th year in *Ant.* 15.380, which passage follows shortly after the present one. Gray (1993: 95, 98) points out that the context of the story suggests a setting in ca. 20 BCE (see 15.354 with the notes to "reign" and "Syria") and dates this second meeting between 23 and 20 BCE. Mahieu (2012: 302-03) situates the meeting in 30 BCE (see 15.377 with the note to "at the height of his power") and argues that the 20 and 30 years were still to come: Herod would still rule for 20 years (30-10 BCE) until his falling into Augustus' disgrace in 10 BCE, and for 30 years (30 BCE-1 CE) until his death (which she situates in 1 CE).

[2666] The phrase ὅρον ἐπιτίθημι ("put a limit to") also occurs in *War* 4.348, referring to a limit to transgressions.

[2667] The leaping point of this passage seems to be that Manaemus does not indicate the end of Herod's rule. In the light of the preceding narrative, one can surmise that Manaemus must have known for how long Herod would rule, but apparently he was not willing to disclose this to the king. This puts the king in his place and suggests that Herod had to resign himself to God's will. Mahieu (2012: 303), however, argues that Josephus himself added the phrase that Manaemus "did not put a limit to the complete period" in order to justify the discrepancy with his own chronology, which did not have 20 or 30 years between the meeting and Herod's death (which Josephus would situate in 3 BCE).

[2668] The phrase καὶ τούτοις implies that Manaemus' answer can hardly have been optimal from Herod's perspective since the sage did not indicate the precise period, but the reference to 20 or even 30 years of kingship seems to have been reassuring enough for Herod. Josephus leaves it open whether Herod picked up Manaemus' putting the king's power into perspective or not. If not, Herod appears to be a simple-minded person who was happy with Manaemus' prediction that he would rule for a long period of at least 20 or 30 years. The king seems in any case to have forgotten the negative points of the previous prophecy referred to in 15.376.

For the phrase καὶ τούτοις ἀρκεσθείς ("even with this [answer] (Herod) was satisfied"), cf. *War* 2.116 about Glaphyra's various marriages: "Although the marriage in Libya was enough for you, not being satisfied with this (οὐκ ἀρκεσθεῖσα τούτῳ) you double back to my hearth—a third husband ..." (trans. Mason in BJP 1b).

[2669] Given the context the verb δεξιόομαι cannot mean "greet" or "welcome (friendly)" here. It probably indicates that Herod entertained Manaemus hospitably (Rengstorf s.v.; cf. *Ant.* 2.123 about Joseph receiving his brothers) or perhaps that Herod paid respect to Manaemus (LSJ [s.v.] also give the meaning "honor" with respect to the gods).

we have deemed it fit to make these matters clear to the readers[2672]—even though they may seem incredible[2673]—and inform them about what happened among us.[2674] Because

---

[2670] The phrase ἀπ' ἐκείνου ("from that ... on") is elliptical for ἀπ' ἐκείνου τοῦ χρόνου ("from that date"; cf. *Apion* 1.11).

[2671] This point links up with the introduction of the story about Manaemus (*Ant.* 15.372): "It is worthwhile telling the reason why Herod held the Essenes in honor (τοὺς δὲ Ἐσσηνοὺς ἀφ' οἵας αἰτίας ἐτίμα)." Note the repetition of the verb τιμάω ("[hold in] honor") in 15.372, 378 with the Essenes (τοὺς Ἐσσηνούς) as object. The combination of διατελέω ("continue to") and the participle τιμῶν also occurs in 8.194; 17.200 (concerning Archelaus paying respect to his father); *Life* 423.

[2672] The conclusion of the story about Manaemus implies more clearly that the readers may benefit from this story (see also the next note). This would be in line with Josephus' pragmatic approach to history (Attridge 1976: 41-70; Villalba i Varneda 1986), paying attention to the moral implications of the history told. The preface of *Antiquities*, e.g., highlights that God "grants a happy life to those who follow Him and surrounds with great misfortunes those who transgress virtue" (trans. Feldman in BJP 3 on *Ant.* 1.20). Another example is the conclusion of the section about the dreams of Archelaus and Glaphyra at the end of book 17: "Therefore, I thought it was good to speak about such things. Let anyone for whom these things are unbelievable benefit from his own view, but let there be no hindrance to anybody who takes them into account for the sake of virtue" (my trans.).

For other references to the readers (οἱ ἐντυγχάνοντες, literally "those who encounter") of (one of) Josephus' works, see *Ant.* 1.15, 129; 4.196-197; 8.26; 20.258; *Life* 345; *Apion* 1.1, 220; 2.136, 147. The verb ἐντυγχάνω ("encounter, come across") can mean "read" in the context of writing and books (almost synonymous with ἀναγινώσκω, "read"), but it should be noted that reading practices in antiquity often differed from our practice of silent reading.

[2673] An alternative translation of παράδοξος is "unusual," but "unbelievable" or "incredible" are the preferable meanings here since they match the references to the supernatural factor in the story about Manaemus, the role of God (*Ant.* 15.372, 374-376). This unusual nature of the account also links up with its introduction, which raises the issue whether Manaemus' story would fit the genre of historiography (see 15.372 with the note to "unseemly in the genre of history"). Cf. similar statements in the introductions to the stories about the Essene Judas (*War* 1.78-80; *Ant.* 13.311-313), which passages note that the reader may be astonished by the story he is going to tell (*Ant.* 13.311 μάλιστα δ' ἄν τις θαυμάσειε; Gray 1993: 94).

The remarkable aspect of the story here most probably concerns the key person Manaemus, who is a model because of his moral excellence (see 15.373 with the note to "attested in every way to his excellence"). Gray (1993: 100) concludes that Manaemus, unlike Herod, did live according to the key virtues of justice and proper worship highlighted in 15.376. In *War* 2.139 Josephus mentions that the entrance vow of the Essenes focused on justice and proper worship: "... first, that he will observe piety toward the deity (εὐσεβήσειν τὸ θεῖον); then, that he will maintain just actions toward humanity (τὰ πρὸς ἀνθρώπους δίκαια φυλάξειν) ..." (trans. Mason in BJP 1b). Jewish readers could associate Manaemus with the prophets of Israel; Graeco-Roman readers with sages like the Sibyls, who predicted the future by their oracles (further references about these as well as other oracles in Burkert 1985: 114-18).

For phrases similar to εἰ καὶ παράδοξα ("even if they may seem unusual"), cf. Aelius Aristides, *Pan.* 108, 176; Lucian, *Dial. mort.* 19.1; Galen, *Diff. resp.* (ed. Kühn 7.851.17).

[2674] An alternative but less likely translation of τῶν παρ' ἡμῖν (literally "the matters among us") would be "the persons among us." The phrase can theoretically indicate persons, although persons are usually specified in such phrases in Josephus (e.g., τῶν παρ' ἡμῖν ἀρχιερέων ["our High Priests"] in *Ant.* 1.11 or τῶν πρώτων ἀνδρῶν παρ' ἡμῖν ["the most prominent men among us"] in 18.64). There is a close parallel in *Ant.* 1.9: "Moreover, besides these considerations that I have stated, I took into account, not incidentally, both whether our ancestors were willing to transmit and whether some of the Greeks themselves were eager to know about our affairs (γνῶναι τὰ παρ' ἡμῖν)" (trans. Feldman in BJP 3). This passage concerns considerations whether Jews and non-Jews were willing to communicate about the history of the Jews (see also the next note). The reference here focuses, of course, on the acts of Manaemus, as the final lines of the paragraph also indicate.

Since Herod behaved like a foreign king (as several Josephan passages suggest; e.g., 15.267-268, 275, 281 with notes) and thus did not belong to those "among us," the Herod narrative of *Antiquities* should perhaps not be considered to be Jewish history. However, this point is not made explicit here.

many persons[2675] by their excellence[2676] are through such events awarded knowledge about the divine things.[2677]

(11.1) 380 Now[2678] at that time,[2679] in the eighteenth year of Herod's rule,[2680] after the

Renovation and expansion of the Temple complex.
War *1.401*

[2675] The crux of this concluding passage is the question to what or whom the phrase πολλοί διὰ τοιούτων ("many persons are through [or 'during'] such events" or "many persons are through such persons"), which phrase is attested by all MSS except MS P (Niese 401), refers. In the immediate context there is only one phrase that connects with the plural διὰ τοιούτων: the phrase τῶν παρ' ἡμῖν, which probably denotes events (see the previous note). In line with this, the passage may be translated as "This is because many persons by their excellence are through [or 'during'] such events awarded knowledge about the divine things." The "many persons" must refer to special persons since they are awarded knowledge of the divine. Taking the context (*Ant.* 15.372) into account, this probably refers to the Essenes, who like Manaemus (15.373) had access to divine knowledge. This interpretation is supported by other references to Essenes having predictive powers in Josephus (see 15.373 with the note to "foreknowledge from God of what was to come"). Although understandable, the attested reading πολλοί διὰ τοιούτων remains far from smooth. This explains why many commentators and translators (e.g., Niese 401; Marcus-Wikgren 182) follow Coccejus' conjecture erasing διά. This simplifies the text and implies a translation like the one given by Marcus-Wikgren (183): "... because many of these men ..." (codex P reads τούτων ["these"] instead of τοιούτων ["such"]). "Many of such [persons]" would then most probably refer to the Essenes.

[2676] The noun καλοκαγαθία ("excellence") also occurs in the introduction of Manaemus in *Ant.* 15.373 (see the note to "attested in every way to his excellence").

[2677] Whether Coccejus' conjecture is followed or not (see the note to "Because many persons" above), Josephus' point seems to be that many more Jewish persons (i.e., other Essenes) due to their excellence were deemed worthy of knowledge of divine things, which implies that the Jewish nation was special because of its many prophetic figures.

The rare phrase ἡ τῶν θείων ἐμπειρία ("the knowledge about the divine things") also occurs in Marcus Aurelius 3.1.1 and cf. ἐμπειρία θείων καὶ ἀνθρωπίνων ("knowledge about divine and human things") in the Scholia on Sophocles' *Oed. tyr.* 300 (ed. Papageorgius 179). Gray (1993: 101) interprets it as "esoteric knowledge of an all-encompassing sort."

[2678] The final section of book 15 of *Antiquities* (15.380-425) focuses on Herod's renovation of the Jerusalem Temple, highlighting not only the former glory of the city of Jerusalem but also Herod's fame as an ambitious builder (as the introduction in 15.380 states; cf. 15.382, 384 and the much briefer report about Herod's renovation of the Temple in *War* 1.401). The focus on the Herodian Temple in the concluding section of book 15 corresponds with the importance of the Temple elsewhere in *Antiquities*, which is also shown by the Temple-orientated ring composition of this work (Mason in BJP 3 xx-xxii; BJP 9 xxiii-xxiv; Mason 2003; Landau 2006: 124; differently Bilde 1988: 89-92, who interprets *Ant.* 1-10 and 11-20 as constituting 2 parallel halves, each ending with a destruction of the Temple).

The section 15.380-425 includes a speech by Herod that prepares the citizens for the Temple project and also expresses the king's motivation for it (15.381-387). *Ant.* 15.388 describes the response of the Jerusalemites to Herod's plan, focusing on their concern that the existing Temple has to be destroyed for the realization of Herod's project. *Ant.* 15.389-390 describes Herod's reaction to the Jerusalemites' response as well as his preparations, and forms the transition to the subsequent description of the Temple project. The next paragraphs (15.391-425) are remarkable from a narratological point of view because Josephus combines the report of the building activities with descriptions of various parts of the Temple complex (van Henten and Huitink 2012). Josephus' account displays a complex technique here, moving from the center to the periphery and vice versa (Shahar 2004: 232-35). He starts with the renewal of the foundations of the sanctuary, located in the center of the complex, and with the description of this building (15.391-395). In 15.396 he moves on to the outside of the complex with the porticoes along the exterior walls. In 15.397 he once again changes the perspective and describes Herod adapting the Temple Mount in order to create several flat platforms, moving from the outside to the area around the sanctuary (15.397-401). From 15.402 (note the vocabulary switching from νεώς/ναός ["sanctuary"] to ἱερόν ["Temple"]) until 15.417 the focus is on the entire Temple complex, describing its exterior from various angles. Josephus starts with the Antonia Fortress at the Temple's northwest corner (15.403, 409) and adds an excursus about the location where the robe of the High Priest was kept (15.403-408). In 15.410 he moves on to events related before,[2681] he undertook an extraordinary[2682] work: his own[2683] construction

a description of the west side with its 4 gates. *Ant.* 15.411-416 concerns the south side with the 2 main gates and the Royal Portico, which is described in detail. From 15.417 onwards Josephus zooms in, moving from the outer precinct to the precinct only accessible to Jews, and then on to the women's court and the inner enclosure in which the sanctuary was located (15.417-419). In 15.420 he notes that the exterior sections of the Temple were rebuilt in 8 years, and in 15.421 he switches for the last time to the sanctuary and informs that it was rebuilt in 1 year and 5 months. He continues with a description of the celebrations held after the completion of the renovation, which festival coincided with the celebration of the king's accession to the throne (15.421-423). *Ant.* 15.424 focuses on the secret tunnel that gave Herod access to the sanctuary area from the Antonia Fortress. *Ant.* 15.425 forms the conclusion of book 15 and highlights God's interference in the renovation activities.

[2679] The word τότε ("at that time") sometimes functions as a brief formula in Josephus to introduce a report about something happening in roughly the same period as the other events narrated, implying that Josephus synchronizes all these events (van Henten and Huitink 2007: 225-27). The same word occurs in *Ant.* 15.365 in the introduction to the report about Herod's tax remittance. The previous date indication given by Josephus is the 17th year of Herod's reign in 15.354 (see the note to that year), which together with the τότε formula of 15.365 implies that the events described in 15.354-379 are to be situated in Herod's 17th regnal year.

[2680] The 18th year of Herod's reign could be 23/22 BCE or 20/19 BCE, depending on whether Herod's appointment as king in 40 BCE or his capture of Jerusalem in 37 BCE (or 36 BCE, with Mahieu 2012) is the point of departure for the calculation of Herod's regnal years. Most scholars believe that the 18th year corresponds to 20/19 BCE (e.g., Otto 1913: 83-84; Simons 1952: 399; Schürer-Vermes 1.292; Smallwood 1976: 92 n. 112; Schalit 2001: 372). Mahieu (2012: 147-49) proposes 19/18 BCE, arguing that Herod captured Jerusalem in 36 rather than 37 BCE (2012: 60-64; cf. Roller 1998: 260, who concludes that the rebuilding started in 18 BCE).

War 1.401 dates the renovation of the Temple to Herod's 15th instead of his 18th regnal year. The difference is sometimes attributed to differing points of departure from which the years were counted: the 18th year mentioned in *Ant.* 15.380 would be reckoned from Herod's appointment in 40 BCE, while the 15th year in *War* 1.401 from his capture of Jerusalem in 37(36) BCE (Corbishley 1935: 26-27; see above). However, this explanation is implausible because the context in *Antiquities* mentions Herod's 17th year in connection with Augustus' visit of 20 BCE (15.354 with notes), such that *Antiquities* seems to reckoned Herod's years from 37(36) BCE; reckoning the 18th year from 40 BCE would also situate the work at the Temple before that visit (Mahieu 2012: 147-48). The date of *Ant.* 15.380 should apparently be preferred and the reference to Herod's 15th regnal year in *War* 1.401 may be a mistake, as several scholars argue (Otto 1913: 81-82; Schürer-Vermes 1.292 n. 12; Schalit 2001: 372-73 with n. 776; differently Vogel 2002: 161, who follows *War* 1.401 and dates the beginning of the building activities to 23/22 BCE). Mahieu (2012: 148-49), however, claims that the 15th year dates the building activities at the outer sections, while the 18th year those at the Temple building. The first works would have started in 26/25 BCE (Herod's 15th year reckoned from 40 BCE), while the latter in 19/18 BCE (the 18th year reckoned from 36 BCE; see above). Both initiatives would have been completed in 18/17 BCE: the outer sections in 8 years (26/25-18/17 BCE; cf. the 8 years mentioned in *Ant.* 15.420) and the Temple building in 1½ year (19/18-18/17 BCE; cf. the 1½ years mentioned in *Ant.* 15.421).

[2681] This phrase points to the chronological order of the narrative, which is confirmed by the preceding reference to Herod's 18th regnal year. About the basic chronological set up of *War* and *Antiquities*, see van Henten and Huitink 2007: 215-16.

For phrases similar to τὰς προειρημένας πράξεις (literally "the deeds mentioned before"), see *Ant.* 5.197; 7.316.

[2682] For Josephus' use of an aorist participle of τυγχάνω ("happen to be at") with the negation οὐ and an article, see *Ant.* 15.33 with the note to "extraordinary dangers."

[2683] Niese (401) reads δι' αὐτοῦ ("by him[self]") with most of the MSS, which reading is paralleled by *Ant.* 15.292 concerning the construction of the Antonia Fortress: "... the stronghold near the citadel, which was called Antonia and built by himself (κατασκευασθὲν δι' αὐτοῦ according to MS P; cf. 15.380: δι' αὐτοῦ κατασκευάσασθαι)." Marcus-Wikgren (184) read δι' αὐτοῦ ("by himself alone," LSJ *s.v.* III.1a) with MS A, i.e., "at his own expense." This implication is perhaps also intended by the reading δι' αὐτοῦ. In that case Josephus emphasizes that Herod himself financed the renovation of the Temple and did not put the burden upon his subjects (e.g., by raising taxes), nor used money from the Temple treasury (Richardson [1996: 247] argues that Herod used his own as well as state money but not resources from the Temple; cf. Applebaum 1976: 666;

of God's sanctuary,[2684] enlarging its precinct[2685] and raising it to a more fitting[2686] height. He thought that to accomplish this[2687] would be the most magnificent of all his deeds[2688]—which it was[2689]—and be enough for his everlasting remembrance.[2690] **381** Understanding that the mob[2691] was not prepared and would not easily accept it,[2692] in view of the immense

Herod's speech about the rebuilding of the Temple.

---

for discussions of Herod's personal resources, see Schalit 2001: 257-98; Udoh 2005: 190-206).

[2684] Although the section *Ant.* 15.380-425 deals with the renovation of the entire Temple complex, the phrase ὁ νεώς/ναός τοῦ θεοῦ ("God's sanctuary," *War* 4.151; *Ant.* 8.119, 139; 9.5, 161, 254; 11.6, 14, 58; 18.261; cf. *Ant.* 12.257; *Apion* 2.193) actually refers to the inner sanctuary of the Temple (Jouön 1935: 331-36; Simons 1952: 392; Rengstorf *s.v.*; see also *Ant.* 15.380, 385-386, 389, 391-392, 394, 396, 401, 419, 421, 423, 425). For discussions of Herod's renovation of the Temple, see Simons 1952: 393-403; Schalit 2001: 372-97; Netzer 2006: 137-78; Patrich 2009.

[2685] The adjective περίβολος used as a substantive means "surrounding wall" or an area protected by such a wall, including a "temple area" (cf. *Ant.* 15.338, 410, 417; Rengstorf *s.v.*). A problem in this section about the Temple (15.380-425) is which area exactly is intended in each of the occurrences of the word περίβολος. Sometimes, as is the case here, it denotes the entire Temple precinct (see also 15.410, 417; cf. 15.420), other times rather an inner enclosure (e.g., in 15.417-418 it refers to 2 inner enclosures within the Temple complex; for still other passages attesting this word in this section, see 15.400, 416-418, 420; cf. 17.259).

[2686] Niese (401) reads ἀξιοπρεπέστερον ("more fitting") with MS P and Zonaras, while the other MSS read ἀξιοπρεπέστατον ("most fitting"). The adjective ἀξιοπρεπής ("in keeping with dignity, fitting") occurs twice elsewhere in Josephus (*Ant.* 11.356; 17.81).

[2687] The verb ἐκτελέω ("complete, perform," Rengstorf *s.v.*) also occurs in *Ant.* 15.341, in connection with the completion of Caesarea.

[2688] The adjective περίσημος ("remarkable, magnificent," here in the comparative περισημότερον) is repeated in *Ant.* 15.423 and does not occur elsewhere in Josephus. MSS FLV read the comparative ἐπισημότερον ("most glorious/famous"), which may derive from the rather similar word περισημότερον since the adjective ἐπίσημος is much more common than περίσημος in Josephus (Rengstorf *s.v.*). In *War* 1.401 Josephus also highlights the splendor of the Temple.

[2689] This short comment by Josephus already anticipates the successful achievement of Herod's plan to renovate the Temple and implies at the same time that the renovation of the Temple was Herod's greatest project as a builder.

[2690] Other passages also emphasize Herod's eagerness to be remembered for eternity, which ambition he pursued, among other things, by leaving behind magnificent buildings (e.g., *War* 1.403, 419, 427; *Ant.* 15.298, 328-330; 16.153; 17.163; Schalit 2001: 341). In 15.298 Josephus notes in connection with Herod's building activities at Samaria-Sebaste that he "also made it look good in order to leave behind for later times memorials to his benevolence (μνημεῖα φιλανθρωπίας) that resulted from his love of beauty" (see also the summary in 15.330: "In short, he was aiming for his own [glory] or even seeking the honor of leaving behind for posterity monuments of his reign [μνημεῖα τῆς ἀρχῆς] that were [even] bigger. Because of this he let himself be induced to the restoration of cities, and he went to the greatest expense for this [goal]"). Richardson (1996: 247) argues that Josephus' description of Herod's motive for rebuilding the Temple is plausible (cf. Roller 1998: 260, who assumes that the subsequent speech derives from Herod's memoirs or from Nicolaus of Damascus and that it reflects Herod's actual motivation).

The phrase μνήμη αἰώνιος ("everlasting remembrance") occurs several times in Josephus, but only in *Antiquities* (1.235; 6.343; 10.266; 13.63; cf. 11.83; see especially 6.343-344 and 10.266 concerning King Saul and the Prophet Daniel as model figures, as well as 13.63 about the High Priest Onias building a temple at Leontopolis in order to acquire everlasting fame and glory for himself [μνήμην καὶ δόξαν αἰώνιον]).

[2691] Like Polybius and several other historians Josephus uses the phrase τὸ πλῆθος ("the multitude") in a mildly pejorative or at least pitying way, which implies a translation such as "the mass/mob" or "the rabble" (Mason in BJP 9 on *Life* 31).

[2692] On the basis of Josephus' previous information about the Jews' responses to Herod's measures (e.g., *Ant.* 15.267, 274-275, 277, 368), it is fully understandable that they would be suspicious about any action by Herod that concerned the Temple. Concerning the phrase οὐχ ἕτοιμον τὸ πλῆθος ("the people were not prepared"), cf. the (inverse) attitude of the Israelites towards Moses described in 3.212: "... he [i.e., Moses] saw that the people were ready (τὸ πλῆθος ... ἕτοιμον) to confer on him" (trans. Feldman in BJP 3).

size of the enterprise,[2693] he thought it wise to undertake the entire project after preparing[2694] them with a speech.[2695]

So he convened them[2696] and said the following:[2697]

382 "To speak about my other deeds in connection with the kingship,[2698] my fellow countrymen,[2699] is, I assume, superfluous,[2700] and yet they came about in such a way that

---

[2693] The Temple complex covered an area of more than 14 ha (= 35 acres). The western wall was ca. 485 m long and the eastern wall ca. 470 m. The northern and southern walls were shorter, measuring ca. 315 and 280 m respectively (Netzer 2006: 160; cf. Sanders 1994: 57-58, who gives 488, 466, 315, and 281 m as the lengths of these walls). Sanders (1994: 58) compares the size of Herod's Temple complex with those of famous ancient temples and notes that the Acropolis at Athens was considerably smaller: 240 m long and 120 m wide in the middle. The temple complex at Olympia was 210 m long and 170 m wide (for similar comparisons, see Patrich 2009: 54). The vocabulary indicating the huge scale of Herod's enterprise here is taken up again later in this section: the noun μέγεθος ("greatness, size") reappears in *Ant.* 15.385-388, 392, 395, 399 (see also 15.386 with the note to "on the same scale" and the noun ἐπιχείρησις ["enterprise, undertaking"] in 15.384).

[2694] The verb προκαθίστημι ("appoint/prepare previously," Rengstorf *s.v.*) occurs 3 times in Josephus (*Ant.* 15.34, 284, 381).

[2695] That Herod decided to give a speech to the mob shows, according to Josephus' presentation, the king's self-confidence that he would persuade his subjects of his project being worthwhile to undertake. The passage may also reflect Josephus' ambivalent attitude toward speechifying; the mob needs speeches to be moved in one direction or another (Mason 2011).

Speeches imply a change of rhythm in the narratives, which almost come to a stand-still. Josephus applies this device many times (Runnalls 1971; 1999; Mason 2011). Ancient speeches also often mark important events and highlight persons or forces that determine these events (Michel 1984: 945; a good example of this function is Herod's commander speech in *Ant.* 15.127-146; see van Henten and Huitink 2007: 227-28). Herod's speech in 15.382-387 highlights the main event of the final section of book 15, the renovation of the Temple (Richardson 1996: 247).

[2696] In *Ant.* 16.132 Herod also assembles the population in order to deliver a speech on a special occasion (cf. *War* 2.1-3; *Ant.* 17.200-205; Schalit 2001: 304).

[2697] The verb συγκαλέω ("call together, convoke, summon," Rengstorf *s.v.*) frequently occurs in phrases that introduce a direct or indirect speech, sometimes combined with a verb meaning "say" (here ἔλεγε). See *Ant.* 3.75 concerning Moses addressing the multitude of the Israelites before ascending Mount Sinai (συγκαλέσας τὴν πληθὺν ... ἔλεγεν), also 3.84; 6.40, 60, 251; 7.26-27, 228, 370; 8.226; 9.260 (concerning Hezekiah addressing the people, the priests, and the Levites when he came to power [συγκαλέσας τὸν λαὸν ... ἐδημηγόρησεν ... λέγων]); 11.168; 12.357; 13.197; 18.279; 19.78 (concerning Cherea and his accomplices [συγκαλέσας τοὺς συνωμότας ... εἶπεν]).

[2698] Herod's reference to his other deeds during his reign puts the project to renovate the Temple explicitly in the light of his achievements as a king, which is elaborated in the continuation of the speech. The body of the speech (*Ant.* 15.383-387) briefly mentions the benefits of Herod's rule and his building activities and then focuses on the new project of restoring the Temple to its original splendor.

[2699] Herod's term of address ἄνδρες ὁμόφυλοι ("fellow countrymen," literally "compatriot men") refers to his fellow Jews. According to ancient gender conventions women were frequently not referred to in such titles (cf. Peter addressing the crowd in Acts: 2:14 ἄνδρες Ἰουδαῖοι καὶ οἱ κατοικοῦντες Ἰερουσαλημ ["Men of Judea and all who live in Jerusalem"; 2:22 ἄνδρες Ἰσραηλῖται ["Men, Israelites"]). The word ὁμόφυλος ("of the same descent, belonging to the same tribe") occurs in Josephus mostly in Israelite or Jewish contexts (although in *Ant.* 6.187 it refers to the Philistines and in *War* 2.210 to the Romans). A number of times the meaning of the word is generic: people of the same nation should know each other (*Ant.* 4.204) and preserve each other's lives rather than harm each other (7.17; 8.223); compatriot bloodshed is the most horrific kind of bloodshed (*War* 1.27; 2.210, 466, 483; cf. *Ant.* 9.231; 19.330). The combination ἄνδρες ὁμόφυλοι also occurs elsewhere in Josephus as a term of address (*Ant.* 6.251; 8.227; *Life* 141).

[2700] The beginning of Herod's speech is a nice example of *apophasis*, i.e., attracting attention to something by saying that it is unnecessary to mention it (Lausberg 1998: 186). In fact the speech continues with a comment concerning the consequences of his deeds for himself as well as his subjects, which means that the phrase highlights his achievements rather than passing over them.

there was less honor for me from them,[2701] while they brought more security for you.[2702] **383** For I have neither neglected to give you support for your needs in your worst times,[2703] nor cared more about my own protection than about all of you[2704] during my building projects.[2705] I think I have brought the nation of the Jews,[2706] with God's will,[2707] to a situation of such happiness[2708] as it did not have before.[2709] **384** The buildings that were

---

[2701] Herod complains that the Jewish people did not honor him enough for his achievements. For metaphorical meanings of κόσμος ("honor, credit"), see LSJ (*s.v.* II.2) and the next note. Elsewhere the Herod narrative of *Antiquities* implies that many subjects were very critical about their king (e.g., 15.280, 291, 365 with notes).

[2702] The main point of Herod's argument, in Josephus' presentation, is that he acted for the benefit of his subjects rather than out of self-interest (Schalit 2001: 470-71, who assumes that this reflects Herod's own view and his attempt to imitate Augustus in this respect). Herod's focusing on the achieved security (ἀσφάλεια) ties in with security being the motive alleged for several of his building activities in the Herod narrative of *Antiquities* (see 15.291-292, 295-296, 298 about the building of the royal palace in Jerusalem, the Antonia Fortress, and the city of Samaria-Sebaste; 15.324 about the Herodium Fortress; 15.409 about the Antonia; 16.143-144 about the Cyprus Fortress near Jericho and the Phasael Tower in Jerusalem; and 17.23 about the Jewish military settlement in Batanea). Some of these passages, however, suggest that these fortified places served Herod's own security rather than the people's (e.g., 15.291, 295-296). Providing security for subjects is highlighted as an important task of rulers in 1 Macc 14:29, 33-34, 36 (about Simon the Maccabee's protection of the Temple as well as his fortification of the towns of Judah, Joppa, and Gazara; discussion and further references in van Henten 2007b: 266-69).

[2703] This statement about Herod's previous support in times of crisis links up with the disasters narrated in *Ant.* 15.299-316: a period of severe drought resulted in illnesses and famine among the population (15.299-304), and Herod provided efficient support to his subjects (15.305-316). Several words in 15.383 echo passages of the section 15.299-316 (15.306: ἀμελέω "neglect"; 15.316: δυσχερής "difficult"; 15.303, 307, 313, 316: χρεία "need").

[2704] Concerning the security motif, see the note to the last phrase in *Ant.* 15.382. This passage is ironic if one connects it with statements that emphasize Herod's ambition and eagerness for fame in relation to his building projects (see 15.380 with the note to "everlasting remembrance").

The extremely rare adjective ἀνεπηρέαστος ("unmolested, unimpaired, unattacked," Rengstorf *s.v.*), which is attested only once before Josephus' work (Diodorus 31.8.7), occurs in *Antiquities* only in the context of official statements (see 13.53 concerning Demetrius I's decree setting the Jewish inhabitants of his realm free and guaranteeing they will be not molested; 14.204 concerning Julius Caesar's decree that the Jews will be free from any kind of molestation; and 16.60 concerning Marcus Agrippa's confirmation that the Jews in Ionia can observe their own practices without being molested, also 16.63).

[2705] This motif is connected with the end of the previous paragraph stating that the building projects (κατασκευάσματα) were to provide security for Herod's subjects (see the last note to *Ant.* 15.382). The noun κατασκεύασμα ("[artistically produced] object/building," Rengstorf *s.v.*) also occurs in 16.19, concerning Herod supporting the restoration of the portico of Chios (cf. 16.183, with the same word referring to David's tomb in Jerusalem).

[2706] For the phrase τὸ Ἰουδαίων ἔθνος ("the nation of the Jews"), see *Ant.* 15.15 with the note to "nation of the Jews."

[2707] Herod's claim of divine support links up with Manaemus' predictions narrated in *Ant.* 15.373-379 (especially 15.374) and is taken up again in 15.387. Herod also refers to God's support in his commander speech before the decisive battle with the Nabateans in 31(30) BCE (15.127-146, especially 15.130, 135-136, 138, 144); in 15.135 Josephus has Herod say: "So, is there still any question for you [i.e., Herod's soldiers] as to whether these wrongdoers [i.e., the Nabateans] ought to be punished, when God, too, wants this (τοῦτο καὶ τοῦ θεοῦ βουλομένου) and always commands us to hate insolence and wrongdoing?" The combination of βούλησις ("will") and (τοῦ) θεοῦ ("of God") occurs frequently in *Antiquities* (*Ant.* 1.157, 170, 223, 254; 2.161, 171, 232, 347; 3.208; 4.67, 109, 127, 235; 5.120, 278; 6.137; 7.90; 8.2, 218, 241, 295, 328, 389; 9.132; 10.7; 11.55, 237; 12.26; once in *Apion*: 2.184) and never in *War* or *Life*.

[2708] The noun εὐδαιμονία can mean, among other things, "good fortune" and "prosperity" (Rengstorf *s.v.*). Schalit (2001: 326 n. 634, 457 n. 1062) assumes that Josephus renders Herod's intention truthfully here and concludes that Herod aimed at his citizens' happiness as well as their prosperity.

accomplished by us one after the other[2710] and were erected within the country[2711] and in the cities[2712] as well as in the newly acquired territories[2713] really increased the splendor of our[2714] people most wonderfully.[2715] It seems superfluous to me to tell[2716] this to people who know it.[2717] But I shall now reveal that the enterprise that I now desire to undertake[2718] will become absolutely[2719] the most pious and wonderful[2720] enterprise of our time.[2721] **385** For

---

[2709] This self-confident claim about the people's unprecedented prosperity in a context referring to Herod's building projects (see also the next paragraph) implies that these projects contributed significantly to the nation's welfare. This claim makes sense since the projects must have attracted all kinds of economic activity and created many jobs. The construction of the Temple as well as the other activities may have boosted the economy of the kingdom and provided work to thousands of laborers (Richardson 1996: 193-94, 223, 236-37; Pastor 1997: 110-27). In *Ant.* 20.219 Josephus mentions that more than 18,000 workers became unemployed when the Temple was finally completed (in the emperor Nero's day). Nevertheless, the claim contrasts sharply with the opinion of many scholars that Herod's rule was particularly harsh for his subjects, which is also suggested by passages in Josephus (e.g., 17.304-310 about the complaints expressed before Augustus after Herod's death; in 17.307 the Jewish delegation states that Herod had reduced the nation to poverty). Udoh (2005: 113-206 with references), however, argues that Josephus' very negative view of Herod's rule and the supposed harsh taxations by him are not supported by serious evidence and therefore implausible.

The phrase ἄγω πρὸς εὐδαιμονίαν ("bring to [a situation of] happiness") also occurs in Xenophon, *Mem.* 2.1.11; Philo, *Contempl.* 12; *Mos.* 2.189; *Plant.* 38.

[2710] Herod connects the prosperity of his subjects with his building projects (the κατασκευάσματα mentioned in *Ant.* 15.383; see the note to "building projects"). He does not mention them specifically, which would not fit in with a speech, but previous narrative sections report several building projects, including in Jerusalem, Samaria-Sebaste, Herodium, and Caesarea (15.296-298, 318, 323-325, 331-341; surveys in Roller 1998; Netzer 2006).

The phrase κατὰ μέρος ἐξεργάζομαι ("accomplish one after the other") also occurs in Polybius 3.26.5; Galen, *Hipp. aphor.* (ed. Kühn 17b.608.16).

[2711] I.e., military settlements like Gaba in Galilee (*Ant.* 15.294) as well as fortified places like Herodium (15.323-325), Alexandrium (15.185), and Masada (15.184).

[2712] I.e., cities like Samaria-Sebaste and Caesarea Maritima, and probably also those of Agrippias, Antipatris, and Phasaelis (Bernett 2007a: 162 n. 468).

[2713] The Herod narrative of *Antiquities* reports building activities in the territories that were added to Herod's kingdom (e.g., 15.363-364 about the temple in Augustus' honor near Paneion).

The adjective ἐπίκτητος ("newly acquired," Rengstorf *s.v.*) is a *hapax legomenon* in Josephus.

[2714] The reading ὑμῶν ("your") of MS V implies that Herod was not regarded as belonging to the Jewish people.

[2715] The alliteration in the phrase κόσμῳ τῷ καλλίστῳ emphasizes the splendor of the people. Note also the repetition of κόσμος in *Ant.* 15.382, 384, with different nuances ("credit" and "splendor").

[2716] For a close parallel to περίεργά μοι δοκεῖ λέγειν ("It seems superfluous to me to tell"), see Demosthenes, *Or.* 43.21 (περίεργον δή μοι δοκεῖ λέγειν) and cf. Isaeus 1.17, 32; Aristotle, *Pol.* 1315a; Anaximenes of Lampsacus 29.7; Hermogenes, *Stat.* 1 (ed. Rabe 34.18).

[2717] Herod's argument that it is unnecessary to elaborate on his building projects is obvious; he could assume that his subjects were familiar with them. The Herod narrative of *Antiquities* confirms that he undertook prestigious building projects (see several of the previous notes). The adjective περίεργος ("unnecessary," Rengstorf *s.v.*) occurs once elsewhere in Josephus (*Apion* 1.16, in a different context).

[2718] The alliteration and repetition in the phrase τὸ δὲ τῆς ἐπιχειρήσεως, ᾗ νῦν ἐπιχειρεῖν ἐπιβάλλομαι (cf. ἐπιχείρησις in *Ant.* 15.381) can hardly be rendered literally in English. The phrase creates a climax and focuses the attention of the audience (and the readers) on the grand new project, the renovation of the Temple.

[2719] The MSS read παντός ("of all"), which is erroneous. Bekker proposes πάντως ("at any rate, absolutely") or πάντων ("of all [enterprises]"; see Niese 402).

[2720] Via a unique combination of the superlatives εὐσεβέστατον καὶ κάλλιστατον Herod characterizes the renovation as a splendid and most pious enterprise. The combination of these superlatives is found only here (but see *Ant.* 7.374 and *Apion* 2.293 for a combination of their root terms). The superlative κάλλιστατον echoes the adjective καλλίστῳ in the preceding sentence. The term εὐσεβέστατον ("most pious") is appropriate since the Temple housed the sacrificial cult for the God of Israel, and its magnificence demonstrated the Jews' high regard for God (for εὐσέβεια and related terms, see *Ant.* 15.267 with the note to "proper worship"; the noun

this is the sanctuary[2722] that our ancestors[2723] built for the greatest God[2724] after their return from Babylon.[2725] With regard to its size it lacks sixty cubits[2726] in height.[2727] For the first

---

occurs 3 times in 15.386-387 in references to the Temple; for the importance of this word in Josephus, see Mason 1991: 85-90).

Landau (2006: 139) considers Herod's statement to be highly ironic. It may be indeed an exaggeration to a certain extent, but Herod's Temple was, as a matter of fact, an extraordinary building given its size and adornments (Sanders 1994: 51-69; see also 15.381 with the note to "the immense size of the enterprise").

[2721] The phrase ἐφ' ἡμῶν can mean "among us" (i.e., indicating the location) as well as "in our time" (perhaps even "of our rule," LSJ s.v. ἐπί A.I-II).

[2722] After 3 paragraphs of introduction (with a climax at the end of the last paragraph) Herod now discloses that his grandest project concerns the Jerusalem Temple. The noun τὸν ναόν, referring to the (inner) sanctuary of the Temple, links up with the phrase τὸν ναὸν τοῦ θεοῦ in Ant. 15.380 (see the note to "sanctuary"). Herod refers here to the Second Temple (see the next note).

[2723] The continuation of the speech indicates that Herod does not refer to the First Temple, built by Solomon (1 Kgs 5-8; 2 Chr 2-7), but to the Second Temple, built after the return from the Babylonian captivity. The Book of Ezra attributes the construction of this Temple to Zerubbabel and situates it in the reign of an unspecified king Darius (Ezra 4:1-5, 24; 5:1-2; 6:1-15; cf. Hag 1:1, 15; 2:1, 10; Zech 1:1, 7; see also Ezra 1 concerning Cyrus' involvement). Ezra 6:15 reports that the building was finished on the 3rd day of Adar in the 6th year of King Darius. Scholars usually date the reconstruction to 520-515 BCE, during the reign of the Persian king Darius I (522-486 BCE; cf. infra), but there are chronological difficulties concerning this date (I thank Bieke Mahieu, Leuven, for pointing this out to me). For instance, the king Darius mentioned in Ezra is supposed to have reigned after King Ahasuerus-Xerxes (Ezra 4:6, 24), but Darius I (522-486 BCE) ruled before Xerxes I (486-465 BCE). Josephus presents the Jewish history during the Persian period in a clear chronological order (Ant. 11.1-320; van Henten and Huitink 2007: 215-16) and indicates that King Cyrus (II) gave permission to rebuild the Temple (11.12-18), but that neighboring peoples, especially the Cutheans (who had settled in Samaria), hindered the building activities (11.19-20). The reconstruction of the Temple was completed by Zerubbabel and Jeshua during the reign of King Darius, the son of Hystaspes (Ant. 11.31-32, 59, 62-63, 79-119), i.e., Darius I (Herodotus 3.71; further discussion and references in Grabbe 2004-08: 1.216-18, 276-85; on the chronological problems and alternative dates, see also Dequeker 1993; 1997).

[2724] The greatest God (ὁ μέγιστος θεός) as name for the God of Israel occurs frequently in Antiquities (6.86; 7.353; 9.133, 211, 288, 289; 10.68; 11.90 [referring to the Jerusalem Temple]; 12.257 [the Samaritan temple on Mount Gerizim]; 13.64, 67 [the Jewish temple at Leontopolis]; cf. also 11.3) but not in the other Josephan works.

[2725] The phrase μετὰ τὴν ἐκ Βαβυλῶνος ἐπάνοδον (MSS FVE read ... ἀνάστασιν ["rising"]; Niese 402) is a fixed expression for the Judeans' return from the Babylonian captivity, which departure was permitted by the Persian king Cyrus II in his first year (539-538 BCE, 2 Chr 36:22-23; Ezra 1; 3:7; 4:3; 5:13-17; 6:3-5; Josephus, Ant. 11.1). Josephus uses the same vocabulary in Ant. 13.5 in another short-hand reference to that return. Similar phrases occur in early Christian passages (Pseudo-Justin, Quaest. resp. 484a [ed. von Otto 222]; Epiphanius, Haer. 8.6.1; 10.5; 42.11.15.26 [ed. Holl 1.191, 204; 2.136]; frequently in Eusebius, e.g., Hist. eccl. 1.6.6; Praep. ev. 10.9.2). An interesting reference concerns the end of the Life of Zechariah in Codex Coislianus (205), which notes that David composed, through prophetic inspiration, the Hallel Psalms (i.e., Ps 113-118) for the prophets Haggai and Zechariah, so that with these psalms they could start praising God for the return from Babylon (περὶ τῆς ἐπανόδου ἀπὸ Βαβυλῶνος; Schwemer 1995-96: 2.174).

[2726] The cubit (πῆχυς) is traditionally the distance between a man's elbow and the end of his middle finger. The Greeks had a wide range of standards for the foot (πούς) and for the cubit. The Roman foot (pes) was fixed as 11.65 modern inches (= 29.6 cm). "The Roman cubit (cubitus) was 1.5 ft (= 44.5 cm), such that 60 cubits were 90 ft. The "royal" or Egyptian cubit was ca. 20.6 inches (= 52.3 cm). Ritmeyer (2006: 170-73) argues that several cubit measurements were at use in Judea."

[2727] This number of 60 cubits is huge (cf. MS V and E read "seven" instead of "sixty," Niese 402). Since in Ant. 8.64-65 Josephus gives the height of Solomon's Temple as 120 cubits (Simons [1952: 397] concludes that Josephus' description of Solomon's Temple reflects Herod's Temple), the height of Zerubbabel's Temple would have been only half of that of Solomon's Temple (see the next note). 1 Kgs 6:2 indicates that Solomon's Temple was 60 cubits long, 20 cubits wide, and 30 cubits high. Other references concerning the Second Temple mention a breadth and height of 60 cubits (Ezra 6:3; likewise 1 Esd 6:25; Josephus, Ant. 11.13, 99). In contrast to Herod's claim here, the biblical data suggest

sanctuary, which Solomon built up,[2728] exceeded it in height by this much.[2729] **386** And no one should accuse our ancestors[2730] of neglect of proper worship.[2731] For the sanctuary[2732] was not made smaller because of them, but Cyrus[2733] as well as Darius,[2734] the son of Hystaspes,[2735] gave those measurements for the building.[2736] Our ancestors were subject to them and their descendants,[2737] and after them to the Macedonians.[2738] Therefore they did not have the opportunity[2739] to rebuild the first archetype of proper worship[2740] on the same

---

that the Second Temple was double as high as the First Temple.

[2728] Here Herod refers to the First Temple, built by Solomon (1 Kgs 5-8; 2 Chr 2-7; Josephus, *Ant.* 8.57-123; see also the first 2 notes to this paragraph).

[2729] The difference in height between the First and Second Temples is 60 cubits according to this passage, which fits in with Solomon's Temple being 120 cubits high (*Ant.* 8.64-65) and the Second Temple 60 cubits (Ezra 6:3). *Ant.* 8.64 gives the total height of Solomon's Temple as 120 cubits, and *Ant.* 8.65 that of the vestibule in front of the sanctuary likewise as 120 cubits: "Thus the height [of the structure; i.e., of the sanctuary] was sixty cubits (ὕψος ἦν ἑξήκοντα πηχῶν) .... On top of this was raised up another [building] of equal dimensions, so that the total height of the sanctuary was 120 cubits (τὸ πᾶν ὕψος τῷ ναῷ πηχῶν ἑκατὸν καὶ εἴκοσι) .... They set up its [i.e., the sanctuary's] vestibule in front, [this being] twenty cubits in length; it extended the width of the building. Its breadth was ten cubits and it was erected to a height of 120 cubits" (8.64; trans. Begg in BJP 5). Marcus-Wikgren (186 n. *a*) suggest that the information in 8.64 is based on the height of the porch in front of the sanctuary given by 2 Chr 3:4 (see also Begg in BJP 5 on *Ant.* 8.64-65). Herod's point that the Second Temple was half the height of Solomon's underpins the contrast between the Second Temple and Herod's (see *Ant.* 15.387).

[2730] I.e., those who built the Second Temple (see the beginning of *Ant.* 15.385). The phrase τῶν πατέρων ("the ancestors") links up with the words πατέρες ἡμέτεροι ("our ancestors") in 15.385.

[2731] This statement links up with the content of the previous paragraph, in which the Second Temple is presented as being lower than the First Temple. The continuation of Herod's speech indicates that the ancestors were not to be blamed for the smaller size of the Second Temple. The noun εὐσέβεια ("proper veneration") echoes the adjective εὐσεβέστατον ("most pious") of *Ant.* 15.384, which is also used in connection with the Temple. For the phrase ἀμέλεια εὐσεβείας ("neglect of proper veneration"), cf. the accusation against Herod in 15.267 (ἀμεληθέντων ὅσα πρότερον ἐπὶ τὴν εὐσέβειαν "all the matters that had previously [led the masses] to proper worship were neglected"); also 15.375-376.

[2732] For the expression ὁ ναός ("the sanctuary"), see *Ant.* 15.380 with the note to "sanctuary."

[2733] I.e., Cyrus II (see *Ant.* 15.385 with the note to "Babylon" and the next notes).

[2734] I.e., Darius I (see *Ant.* 15.385 with the note to "ancestors" and the next note).

[2735] "Darius, the son of Hystaspes" is also mentioned in *Ant.* 11.31 and *War* 1.476 (in connection with Glaphyra's descent, although this passage refers perhaps to another Darius, who also had a Hystaspes as father). The additional information in Josephus' report on the Persian period (11.31) that Darius is called "the son of Hystaspes" implies that he is referring to Darius I. As a consequence the Cyrus mentioned here must concern Cyrus II.

[2736] The Book of Ezra mentions a king Cyrus as well as a king Darius in connection with the rebuilding of the Second Temple (see *Ant.* 15.385 with the note to "ancestors"). Ezra 6:3-4 and Josephus (*Ant.* 11.13, 99) state that King Cyrus determined the measures of the new Temple, with a height and breadth of 60 cubits each (see also 1 Esd 6:24-25). King Darius may have been added here by Josephus because the Temple was completed during his reign (Ezra 6).

[2737] That the Judean Jews were subjected to the Persian rule after the Babylonian captivity must have been well known among the Jews, also through the Books of Ezra-Nehemiah and Daniel (Grabbe 2004-08: 1.1-360). Josephus may have added this detail for non-Jewish readers, who were hardly or not at all familiar with Jewish history.

[2738] I.e., Alexander the Great and his successors. Alexander created a new empire after his victory over the Persians; Palestine first became part of the Ptolemaic kingdom and subsequently of the Seleucid kingdom (details in Schürer-Vermes 1.125-36; Grabbe 2004-08: 2.1-224). Alexander's takeover also appears in other Josephan passages (see especially *Ant.* 11.304-347, which passage reports a sacrifice made by Alexander in the Jerusalem Temple [11.326-339]). The name Μακεδόνες ("Macedonians") occurs, among other passages, in 11.304 (referring to Alexander's father Philip as King of the Macedonians), 313, 315-316, 326.

[2739] The builders of the Second Temple being subject to the Persian rule and the size of their Temple being determined by the Persian kings (see the previous notes

scale.²⁷⁴¹ **387** But after that, I now²⁷⁴² rule, by the will of God,²⁷⁴³ and there is a long period of peace²⁷⁴⁴ as well as the possession of wealth²⁷⁴⁵ and an abundance of revenues.²⁷⁴⁶ Most

---

to this paragraph) account for the Second Temple being smaller and therefore less glorious than the First Temple.

The noun εὐκαιρία ("right moment, opportunity," Rengstorf s.v.) occurs 7 times in Josephus and only in *Antiquities*; 6 occurrences of which belong to the Herod narrative (15.59, 315, 327, 366, 386; 16.301; cf. 18.54).

²⁷⁴⁰ The rare phrase τὸ τῆς εὐσεβείας ἀρχέτυπον refers to the First Temple as the place of worship of the God of Israel (for εὐσέβεια, see *Ant.* 15.384 with the note to "pious and wonderful" as well as 15.267 with the note to "proper worship"). So far Herod has only indicated the measures of the Second Temple (see 15.385-386). The noun ἀρχέτυπον ("archetype, model," LSJ s.v.; Rengstorf s.v.) is a *hapax legomenon* in Josephus, while a favorite word in Philo. Phrases similar to ἀρχέτυπον τῆς εὐσεβείας, however, only occur in patristic literature, although never in connection with the Temple (John Chrysostom, *Hom. 2 Tim.* [PG 62.643]; Theodoretus, *Int. Dan.* [PG 81.1313, 1345]; *Int. ep. Paul.* [PG 82.632, 769]).

²⁷⁴¹ The smaller size of the Second Temple is the main point in Herod's argument and subsequently makes him contrast the fortunate circumstances for his initiative with the limited possibilities for the builders of the Second Temple. The noun μέγεθος ("size, greatness") applies here to the size of the Second Temple and occurs already in the introduction of the speech (*Ant.* 15.381), referring to the size of Herod's enterprise. The word reoccurs in 15.388, 395, 399 in connection with Herod's own project (cf. 15.392 about the sizes of the stones).

²⁷⁴² A combination of particles (ἐπειδὴ δὲ νῦν) introduces Herod's motivation for his project and creates a contrast between his rule and that of those responsible for the Second Temple. By focusing upon himself Herod also expresses that there are no foreign overlords at this moment and that he is the ideal leader to carry out the ambitious plan of renovating the Temple because he has the financial resources to do it and is supported by God as well as the Romans, as he explains in the next lines.

²⁷⁴³ The phrase ἄρχω θεοῦ βουλήσει links up with σὺν τῇ τοῦ θεοῦ βουλήσει in *Ant.* 15.383 (see the note to "with God's will"). Herod's claim that he is ruling with God's assent seems bold in the light of the criticism by his subjects (see, e.g., 15.368), but it is supported by the episode about Manaemus (15.373-379). Herod does not refer to that episode in his speech; he simply claims in a self-confident way to enjoy God's support, which statement is elaborated in the continuation of the speech by pointing out that the king is a most successful ruler.

This claim would have appealed to Herod's Roman patrons.

²⁷⁴⁴ A stable period of peace is an ideal situation according to both Jewish and non-Jewish writings. 2 Macc 3:1 describes the situation in Judea during the leadership of the High Priest Onias III as follows: "While the holy city was inhabited in unbroken peace (μετὰ πάσης εἰρήνης) and the laws were strictly observed because of the piety (εὐσέβεια) of the high priest Onias and his hatred of wickedness." 1 Macc 14:8-12 describes another peaceful situation, during the rule of Simon the Hasmonean (143/142-135/134 BCE), which section includes allusions to biblical passages: "(8) They tilled their land in peace; the ground gave its increase, and the trees of the plains their fruit. (9) Old men sat in the streets, they all talked together of good things .... (11) He established peace in the land, and Israel rejoiced with great joy. (12) All the people sat under their own vines and fig trees, and there was no one to make them afraid" (cf. 1 Macc 14:4; Mic 4:4; Zech 8:4-5). According to the Roman ideology the emperor was the guarantor of peace and order (e.g., Dio Chrysostom 1.73-75; Aelius Aristides, *Rom.* [ed. Dindorf 335-36]).

²⁷⁴⁵ Wealth was important for ancient rulers since many projects depended on their benefactions (Danker 1982). Other Josephan passages depict Herod as a generous benefactor, especially towards non-Jews (see *Ant.* 15.19 with the note to "gifts," also 15.37, 233, 326-330, 356; 16.24, 146-149). *War* 1.205 expresses the gratefulness of the Syrians towards Herod for restoring peace and saving their possessions (ὡς εἰρήνην αὐτοῖς καὶ τὰς κτήσεις ἀνασεσωκώς). The eulogy for the Hasmonean leader Simon in 1 Macc 14:4-15 (see the previous note) also focuses on Simon's personal wealth, which enabled him to support his subjects and enhance the glory of the Temple: "(10) He supplied the towns with food, and furnished them with the means of defense .... (14) He gave help to all the humble among his people .... (15) He made the sanctuary glorious, and added to the vessels of the sanctuary" (cf. the decree in recognition of Simon in 1 Macc 14:25-49, especially 14:32-34).

²⁷⁴⁶ Herod's income resulted from taxes (taxes on agricultural production, sales levies, and custom duties; see *Ant.* 15.365 with the note to "taxes") and from revenues from the production of rare products like dates and balsam in the area of Jericho (15.96).

The phrase κτῆσις χρημάτων ("possession of wealth") is common from Thucydides onward (e.g., 1.8.3; 1.13.1, also Dio Chrysostom 4.100; 55.9; Plutarch,

importantly, the Romans,[2747] who control practically[2748] the entire world,[2749] are my friends[2750] out of loyalty.[2751] So I will try to set right what has been neglected[2752]—albeit out of necessity and because of our servitude[2753] in the earlier period—and to repay God with perfect worship[2754] in return for having received this kingdom."[2755]

Mor. [*Lib. ed.*] 4e, [*Frat. amor.*] 484c).

[2747] Highlighting the importance of the Romans in a speech to the Jewish people also puts the focus upon Herod as the leader of the Jews (see also the continuation of the narrative: "the Romans ... are my friends"), because the current friendship with the Romans was based upon the relationship between Herod and Augustus, who was the king's Roman patron at this stage of his career (see *Ant.* 15.193, 195, 199, 217, 361 with notes; cf. 15.409). The friendship between the Romans and the entire Jewish people was, in fact, much older: the first treaty of friendship between the 2 nations dates from the period of Judas Maccabeus (1 Macc 8:17-32; Josephus, *War* 1.38; *Ant.* 12.419; see also *War* 1.48; *Ant.* 13.259-266; 14.143-148, 265-267, 320). The reference to the Romans' friendship with the Jews as being the most important factor for the prosperity of the Jews may also be connected with Josephus' broader purposes and his audience in Rome, in which case it would emphasize that the well-being of the Jewish people is highly dependent on a good relationship between Jews and Romans (for Josephus' aim and purposes in *Antiquities*, see Mason 1998; 2003).

[2748] The formula ὡς ἔπος εἰπεῖν ("so to speak, almost," LSJ *s.v.* ἔπος II.4; Rengstorf *s.v.*) is unique in Josephus but common in Greek literature starting from Plato (*Apol.* 22d; *Phaed.* 66a; Heb 7:9; cf. Polybius 1.1.2; 1.64.3 etc.; Dionysius, *Pomp.* 6.4; Plutarch, *Arist.* 26.5; *Rom.* 9.7, and frequently in Philo, e.g., *Det.* 73; *Opif.* 13, 88). The noun ἔπος ("word") is a *hapax legomenon* in Josephus.

[2749] This statement links up with *Ant.* 15.361 (see the note to "big") about the greatness of Rome.

[2750] Many passages in the Herod narratives of *War* and *Antiquities* support this point: Herod was a friend of his first patron, Mark Antony (*War* 1.386, 390; *Ant.* 15.131, 162, 183, 189, 195, 409), and afterwards a friend of Augustus (*Ant.* 15.193, 195, 199, 217, 361). The word "friend" has first and foremost a political meaning in this connection (see 15.5 with the note to "the friends around him"), although *War* 1.400 and *Ant.* 15.361, among other passages, also suggest that Herod had special relationships with Augustus and Marcus Agrippa.

[2751] This detail may hint at Herod's good relationship with Augustus. The Herod narrative of *Antiquities* mentions several times Augustus' loyalty (εὔνοια) towards Herod. The report about Herod's journey during which he successfully moved over to Octavian-Augustus as his patron (15.187-198) already mentions Octavian's loyalty towards Herod (15.193-194). The report about Herod's conflicts with the Gadarenes (15.351-359) likewise refers to this loyalty of the emperor (15.357). Another passage about the relationship between Herod and Augustus (15.361) also includes the term εὔνοια, but there the word means "affection" rather than "loyalty," which presupposes a close relationship between both men. Concerning the loyalty of other Romans towards Herod, cf. 14.274 about Herod becoming friendly with Cassius. A few further passages emphasize the loyalty of Jewish leaders towards the Romans (*War* 1.284; *Ant.* 14.212, 384). For the phrase δι' εὐνοίας ("out of loyalty") in the context of friendship, see Thucydides 2.40.4.

[2752] The verb παραμελέω ("disregard, overlook," Rengstorf *s.v.*) occurs once elsewhere in Josephus (*Ant.* 10.90).

[2753] I.e., subjection (δουλεία) to foreign rulers. Herod refers briefly again to the period following the return from Babylon, when the Judeans were subjected to the Persian rule. Herod presses home the point prepared for in *Ant.* 15.386 that the Temple renovated by him will outdo the Second Temple, which was smaller than Solomon's because the Persian kings had determined its size. The connection is strengthened by means of the noun δουλεία echoing the participle δουλεύσαντες ("being subject") found in 15.386. However, Josephus may hint at the same time at "slavery," the more literal and common sense of δουλεία. Greek and Roman political discourses are full of the freedom—slavery dialectic. It also pervades Josephus' *War*, in which δουλεία clearly means political enslavement in contrast to "freedom" (ἐλευθερία; see, e.g., the speech of Agrippa II in *War* 2.346-401 [Mason in BJP 1b on *War* 2.346, 349, 355-356] and 2.87, 259).

[2754] The verb ἀποδίδωμι plus an object and an adjective means "make something (so and so)" (LSJ *s.v.* I.5). The noun εὐσέβεια ("[proper] worship") is a key word in this speech and refers to the worship in the Temple (see *Ant.* 15.384, 386 with the notes to "pious and wonderful" and "proper worship").

[2755] Interestingly, Herod himself confirms here that he received his kingdom because of God's interference, which is an important theme in the Manaemus episode (*Ant.* 15.373-379, especially 15.374-376; see 15.383 with the note to "with God's will").

Building or enlarging a temple was a conventional way among rulers to express gratitude towards a patron deity. Thus Augustus expanded the temple of Apollo at

(11.2) 388 Herod said these things,[2756] and the speech perplexed most of them[2757] because it had fallen upon them unexpectedly.[2758] The fact that his hoped-for project was incredible[2759] did not upset[2760] them, but they were greatly troubled [by the prospect] that he, after first tearing down the entire work,[2761] would not manage to bring his plan to completion.[2762] The risk appeared rather large to them, and the size of the enterprise[2763] seemed hard to handle.[2764] **389** While they were in such a state,[2765] the king tried to encourage them,[2766] saying that he would not take down the sanctuary[2767] before all the preparation for its completion had been taken.[2768] And he did not lie with this promise.[2769] **390** For he prepared a thousand wagons[2770] that would carry the stones, selected ten

---

Nicopolis (near Actium) following his triumph of 31 BCE; he also built a new temple for his patron deity on the Palatine Hill (Suetonius, *Aug.* 18.2; Cassius Dio 51.1.1-3).

[2756] Similar formula including ταῦτα and the aorist εἶπεν (or similar forms, "he/she said these things") frequently conclude a passage of direct speech in Josephus (*War* 1.80, 84, 466, 598; 2.212, 474; 3.355, 403; 6.58; *Ant.* 1.317; 2.166, 287; 3.89; 4.35, 51, 194; 5.99; 6.22, 92, 174; 7.52, 221, 257, 271; 8.30, 229, 233, 245, 323; 9.37, 263; 10.178; 11.58, 95, 172, 336; 12.24, 271; 13.318; 18.186, 233, 338; 20.28, 60; *Life* 136, 388).

[2757] The response to Herod's speech matches the king's awareness in *Ant.* 15.380-381 that the people had to be prepared for the huge enterprise of renovating and expanding the Temple.

The phrase τοὺς πολλούς can also be translated with "the multitude" and links up with Josephus' introduction of Herod's speech in *Ant.* 15.382 (cf. τὸ πλῆθος in 15.381 and its note to "the mob").

[2758] Rengstorf (*s.v.*) gives "to come up (suddenly) for discussion" as meaning for ἐμπίπτω here (cf. *Ant.* 16.400).

[2759] The rare phrase τὸ τῆς ἐλπίδος ἄπιστον ("the incredibility of his hoped for project") echoes a passage in Euripides (*Suppl.* 479: ἐλπὶς γάρ ἐστ' ἄπιστον "hope is delusive," trans. Way; cf. Heliodorus 10.13.1). The adjective ἄπιστος ("incredible") is repeated in *Ant.* 15.416, 425.

[2760] The alliteration of the *p* sound in the phrase τὸ ... τῆς ἐλπίδος ἄπιστον οὐκ ἐπήγειρεν adds emphasis to Herod's daring project of renovating the Temple.

[2761] I.e., the Temple, as specified in *Ant.* 15.389.

[2762] The multitude apparently assumed that Herod would not succeed in rebuilding the Temple, such that a destroyed Second Temple would be the only outcome, which was totally unacceptable for most of Herod's subjects.

For a phrase related to πρὸς τέλος ἀγαγεῖν τὴν προαίρεσιν ("bring his plan to completion"), see *Ant.* 16.392 concerning Herod's plan to execute his sons (τέλος ἐπιθεῖναι τῇ προαιρέσει "[he finally hastened now] to bring his plan to fulfillment"; cf. 12.110 and Hecataeus of Abdera, *FGH* 264 F 25.54 [ed. Jacoby 3A.37]; Diodorus 1.64.13; 14.17.2).

[2763] The phrase τὸ μέγεθος τῆς ἐπιβολῆς ("the size of the enterprise") is a variant of τὸ μέγεθος τῆς ἐπιχειρήσεως of *Ant.* 15.381 (note the repetition of μέγεθος). Once more the size of Herod's Temple is emphasized.

[2764] The adjective δυσεγχείρητος ("difficult to carry out/realize," Rengstorf *s.v.*) is a *hapax legomenon* in Josephus. The word is extremely rare; this is the only occurrence in literature before the 3rd cent. CE.

[2765] Phrases with a participle of διάκειμαι plus a personal pronoun and οὕτως ("person X being in a certain state/mood") also occur elsewhere in Josephus (*Ant.* 3.83; 8.257; cf. *War* 3.184-185; *Ant.* 14.172). *Ant.* 3.83 summarizes the gloomy mood of the Israelites following God's theophany at Mount Sinai (3.79-82), leading up to the climax of Moses' comforting return (3.83). Here the phrase similarly marks a contrast between the mood of the people and that of their leader.

[2766] The verb παραθαρσύνω/παραθαρρύνω ("encourage") occurs in Josephus only in *Antiquities* (15 times). The introduction of Herod's commander speech in 15.126 includes this verb, with Herod as subject.

[2767] This phrase connects with the words καταλῦσαι τὸ πᾶν ἔργον ("tearing down the entire work") of *Ant.* 15.388. Concerning the noun ναός denoting the inner sanctuary of the Temple, see 15.380 with the note to "sanctuary."

[2768] Herod responds self-confidently to the multitude's fear that the Second Temple would be torn down and not rebuilt (as formulated in *Ant.* 15.388).

[2769] Josephus' clear-cut statement not only implies that Herod would be successful with his project but also anticipates the report about Herod's renovation of the Temple (*Ant.* 15.391-421).

Concerning the phrase οὐκ ἐψεύσατο ("he did not lie") combined with the verb προλέγω ("promise"), cf. Xenophon, *Ages.* 1.29; *Hell.* 3.4.21; Libanius, *Ep.* 278.1.

[2770] This huge number of wagons may be exaggerated; it points, though, to the gigantic scale of Herod's enterprise (cf. *Ant.* 15.380-381, 388). The claim becomes still more impressive if one takes into consideration the

Description of the Temple and the building activities ending with celebration.
War 1.401

thousand[2771] of the most experienced workers,[2772] and purchased priestly robes[2773] for a thousand priests. He taught[2774] some to be builders and others as craftsmen,[2775] and started with the construction when everything had eagerly been prepared by him.[2776]

(11.3) 391 After removing the old foundations and laying other ones,[2777] he erected the sanctuary upon them[2778] with a length of one hundred cubits ...[2779] and a height of twenty[2780]

---

sizes of the stones (see 15.396). The round numbers 1,000, 10,000, and again 1,000 in this paragraph render it plausible that Josephus adapted or even invented them (but see the next note). The noun ἅμαξα ("carriage, wagon") occurs in Josephus only in *Antiquities* (10 times).

[2771] See the previous note. Warszawski and Peretz (1992) make a detailed estimation of the labor force needed for Herod's Temple renovation, arguing that it involved 50,000 man-years of labor, such that a permanent crew of 7,000-8,000 laborers was employed, to which 2,000-3,000 extra workers have to be added for support and transportation. Hence the number of 10,000 laborers may be fairly adequate. In *Ant.* 20.219 Josephus mentions that when the renovation of the Temple was completed, during Albinus' governorship (62-64 CE), 18,000 laborers became unemployed. Pastor (2003: 163) uses these numbers as the basis for his calculation that Jerusalem had a population of ca. 40,000 persons or more (see also 15.383 with the note to "as it did not have before").

[2772] The alliteration of the *r*, *p*, and *m* sounds in the phrase ἐργάτας δὲ μυρίους τοὺς ἐμπειροτάτους ἐπιλεξάμενος adds emphasis to Josephus' note about the workers.

[2773] Concerning the number of 1,000 priestly vestments (see the note to "a thousand wagons" above), cf. 1 Esd 5:44-45, which passage mentions that some heads of the families that returned from the Babylonian captivity vowed, when they came to the area of the Temple, that "they would erect the house on its site, and that they would give to the sacred treasury for the work a thousand minas of gold, five thousand minas of silver, and one hundred priests vestments." The combination of ἱερατικός ("priestly") and στολή ("robe") occurs, apart from the *History of Alexander the Great* (Pseudo-Callisthenes), only in Jewish and Christian writings, including Josephus (*Ant.* 3.107, 279; 6.359; 8.93; 9.223; 15.403, also 6.359) and 1 Esd 4:54; 5:44; 2 Macc 3:15.

[2774] This detail seems to indicate that Herod himself instructed the craftsmen, which contradicts the previous statement that Herod selected "the most experienced workers." It may therefore mean that Herod took the initiative for these activities. However, although Herod is clearly the central figure in this section and presented as the main organizer, it is implausible that he executed some of the tasks himself (in contrast to what this passage and *Ant.* 15.391 seem to imply). Montacutius and Cotelerius read ἐπιτάξας ("commanding") or διατάξας ("ordering") instead of διδάξας ("instructing"), but there is no need to change the transmitted text (Niese 403; Marcus-Wikgren 188).

[2775] The noun τέκτων does not necessarily mean "carpenter," although most scholars assume this meaning in reference to the trade of Jesus' father Joseph (Matt 13:55; Mark 6:3). The word can have a more general meaning like "craftsman" or "builder" (Rengstorf *s.v.*). Like 15.390, *Ant.* 7.66 mentions "builders" or "masons" (οἰκοδόμους) and "craftsmen" or "carpenters" (τέκτονας) together, in a reference to the building of King David's palace in Jerusalem. Ilan (1998) argues that such analogies between Herod and David were created by Nicolaus of Damascus, whose work Josephus used as a source.

[2776] The verb προευτρεπίζω ("make ready before, prepare [someone] for," Rengstorf *s.v.*) occurs twice elsewhere in Josephus (*Ant.* 20.85, 136). It links up with the verb εὐτρεπίζω ("prepare") at the beginning of this paragraph. The final sub-clause again adds emphasis through alliteration (of the *p* sound).

[2777] Although Josephus continues with a description of the renovation of the sanctuary, he first focuses on the new foundations since these were necessary for the entire Temple complex, Herod's Temple being much larger than its predecessor and covering an area of more than 14 ha (Netzer 2006: 160; see also *Ant.* 15.381 with the note to "size of the enterprise"). This passage implies that the foundations of the sanctuary were replaced. The paragraph later connects this replacement with the danger of subsidence. The phrase ... θεμελίους καὶ καταβαλόμενος ἑτέρους ("... foundations and laying other ones") echoes *Ant.* 11.93, concerning Sanabasarus-Sheshbazzar, who laid the foundations of the Second Temple.

[2778] The phrase τὸν ναὸν ἤγειρε ("he erected the sanctuary") also occurs in *Ant.* 20.228, concerning Solomon erecting the First Temple.

[2779] Niese (403), Marcus-Wikgren (188-89), and other scholars assume that several words are missing here.

[2780] Dindorf indicates that the lacuna in the Greek text (see the previous note) begins after the word εἴκοσι ("twenty," Niese [403]).

extra,[2781] which went down in the course of time, after the foundations had settled.[2782] We decided to raise the height[2783] again in the time of Nero.[2784] **392** The sanctuary was built of white and mighty stones;[2785] the size of each was about twenty five cubits in length, eight in height, and twelve in width.[2786] **393** The sides of the entire [sanctuary][2787] were lowest,[2788] as was also the case with the Royal Portico.[2789] The most central part was the

---

[2781] This passage implies that the sanctuary's height was 120 cubits. The Latin version (*altitudine centum viginti* [*cubitorum*]) confirms this height of 120 cubits (Niese 403). In *War* 5.207 (belonging to an elaborate passage about the Temple) Josephus indicates that the height and breadth of Herod's sanctuary were 100 cubits, which matches *m. Mid.* 4.6 referring to a length, breadth, and height of 100 cubits (Netzer 2006: 143, 150, who concludes that these numbers are accurate). In *War* 5.36-37 Josephus mentions that King Agrippa II (50-92/93 CE) took preparations to expand the height to 120 cubits at the demand of the Jewish people and the leading priests. This height of 120 cubits matches the height of Solomon's Temple according to Josephus' calculation (see *Ant.* 15.385 with notes). *War* 5.215 mentions that the height of the inside of the sanctuary (from the ground floor to the top) was 60 cubits.

[2782] Josephus seems to suggest that Agrippa II's additional 20 cubits were meant to restore the original height of Herod's sanctuary; the foundations had gone down in the course of time.

The verb συνίζω ("sink, settle" [in relation to foundations], Rengstorf *s.v.*) occurs once elsewhere in Josephus (*Ant.* 4.51, with the meaning "sink," referring to the earth opening up and swallowing those rebelling against God; cf. Num 16:31-32).

[2783] Literally "this."

[2784] The "we" is surprising and may proleptically refer to the Jewish people and priests who decided to expand the height of the sanctuary by 20 cubits in Josephus' day (*War* 5.36; see *Ant.* 15.391 with the note to "extra"; Marcus-Wikgren 190 n. *a*). This interpretation fits the reference to Nero's reign (54-68 CE).

[2785] "White stone" (λευκός λιθός) is sometimes interpreted as denoting (white) marble (cf. Rengstorf *s.v.*), but the phrase need not refer to marble: Josephus mentions twice that various buildings in Herod's harbor city of Caesarea were made of white stone (*War* 1.408, 414); the archaeological findings show that most of them were made out of local *kurkar*, which was plastered and sometimes also provided with *stucco* (Patrich 2007: 100-01). Josephus states that Solomon's Temple and palace were built of white stone (*Ant.* 8.64, 139; see also *War* 7.286 concerning Masada; *Ant.* 12.230 concerning the Trans-Jordanian palace of the Tobiad Hyrcanus; 13.211 concerning the mausoleum of the Maccabees; and 20.221-222 concerning Solomon's Temple and the paving of Jerusalem). In *War* 5.190 Josephus explicitly refers to white marble in connection with the pillars of the Temple porticoes (μονόλιθοι λευκοτάτης μαρμάρου). The masonry for the Temple was quarried in the area of Jerusalem and mostly consisted of hard limestone known as *meleke* ("royal"; Netzer 2006: 160-02).

[2786] These sizes are huge; 25 cubits are more than 12 m (ca. 37.5 ft). In *War* 5.163 Josephus gives this same number of 25 cubits for the length and breadth of the Hippicus Tower and in 5.190 for the height of the pillars of the Temple porticoes. He refers to even higher numbers in connection with the stones of the sanctuary: some of them were 45 cubits long, 5 cubits high, and 6 cubits wide (5.224), while the stones of the foundation measured 40 cubits (5.189). The largest stone found so far, at the western side north of Wilson's Arch, is 12 m long, 3 m high, and ca. 4 m thick (the weight of this stone is estimated at 400 metric tons, Patrich 2009: 50).

[2787] Josephus switches to a description of the entire Temple complex by taking a panoramic viewpoint. He first focuses on the sanctuary (cf. the sentence beginning with καὶ παντὸς αὐτοῦ [literally "of the entire of it [i.e., the sanctuary]"]) in the way it would appear to somebody looking down on it from one of the neighboring hills, e.g., from the Mount of Olives (cf. the continuation of this paragraph; for Josephus' use of space as a narrative tool, see van Henten and Huitink 2012). After offering a picture of the sanctuary Josephus zooms in on other specific parts of the complex.

[2788] The shape of the sanctuary is compared to a lion in *m. Mid.* 4.7. In *War* 5.208 Josephus mentions 100 cubits as the height and width of the sanctuary's front and notes that the building was 40 cubits less wide behind the front.

[2789] Josephus uses the phrase ἡ βασίλειος στοά ("the Royal Portico") only here and in *Ant.* 15.411, when he is giving a detailed description of this portico (15.411-416; see also *War* 5.220-221). The name derives perhaps from the fact that Herod ordered this portico to be built, possibly as a compensation for the fact that he, as a non-priest, could not enter the inner enclosure of the sanctuary (Netzer 2006: 170). Since this explanation faces the problem that Herod ordered the construction of the other porticoes as well, we may think of another reason: the name of the portico may be connected with its function, Herod may have been meeting with people as king in the

highest,[2790] such that it was visible all around[2791] from a distance of many *stadia*[2792] for the people who inhabit the countryside,[2793] and even better for the people who would happen to live opposite to it[2794] or approach it.[2795] **394** The doors at the entrance,[2796] which with their lintels[2797] were of the same height as the sanctuary,[2798] he adorned with multicolored curtains,[2799] with floral designs[2800] in purple dye,[2801] and with columns woven in.[2802]

---

portico (cf. Pausanias 1.3.1 concerning the district of Cerameicus in Athens: "First on the right is what is called the Royal Portico, where sits the king when holding the yearly office called the kingship ...," trans. Jones; Simons 1952: 401 with n. 1; Schalit 2001: 382 with n. 810).

The name "Royal Portico" is common in Greek literature (e.g., Aristotle, *Ath. pol.* 7.1; Demosthenes, *Or.* 25.23; Philostratus, *Vit. Apoll.* 4.20), but the form of Herod's colonnaded hall (see the description in *Ant.* 15.411-416) is that of a Roman civil *basilica* (i.e., an oblong colonnaded hall; Netzer 2006: 165-71). The oldest specimens of such halls date from the 2nd cent. BCE (e.g., the Basilica Porcia in Rome, built in 184 BCE). Herod's Royal Portico may, therefore, have had a similar function as a Roman *basilica*, i.e., assembling people for the sale of sacrificial items, money changing, and court meetings (Patrich 2009: 61-62, 68-69 with references).

[2790] I.e., the sanctuary itself, which stood within the priestly court. It is described in greater detail in *Ant.* 15.421-423.

[2791] For another occurrence of περίοπτος ("highly visible") with persons in the dative as the indirect object, see *War* 3.232 concerning the brave self-sacrifice of Eleazar during the capture of Jotapata-Yodfat ("his bravery was visible for all," trans. Thackeray).

[2792] The ancient length measure of the *stadion* (στάδιον) equals ca. 185 m (see *Ant.* 15.168 with the note to "*stadia*"). Josephus thus clearly indicates that the sanctuary was visible from a long distance.

[2793] Josephus refers here to the countryside (χώρα) of Jerusalem (see *Ant.* 15.293 with the note to "countryside").

[2794] Josephus is evidently speaking about the dominant presence of the Temple from his own experience. "To live opposite" the Temple would visually apply best to people living in the Upper City, to the west of the Temple. One can also think of people living on nearby hills (see also the first note to this paragraph), especially at the City of David, the Mount of Olives, or Mount Scopus. From all these locations, which are higher than the Temple Mount, the sanctuary was a clear focal point.

[2795] This note continues the evocation of a visual experience, this time that by travelers approaching Jerusalem by one of the ancient roads, e.g., the roads coming from Joppe-Jafo, Samaria, Jericho, Antipatris, or Beersheva (Beauvery 1957; Wilkinson 1975; Har-El 1981; Roll 1983; Fischer, Isaac, and Roll 1996).

[2796] Josephus resumes his tour along the marvels of the Temple. The reference to "the doors at the entrance" takes the perspective of someone standing in front of the sanctuary, viewing through the vestibule unto the doors of the sanctuary. There was a portal without doors in the front side of the vestibule and 2 sets of folding doors at its end side, giving access to the sanctuary. These doors measured 55 x 16 cubits according to Josephus (*War* 5.211) and 20 x 10 cubits according to the Mishnah (*m. Mid.* 4.1; Netzer 2006: 148). Josephus must be referring to these doors (see also the next notes). The vestibule is described in greater detail in *War* 5.208-209.

Josephus' description of the sanctuary's entrance foregoes the entrance to the vestibule (i.e., the portal without doors), perhaps because a position right in front of the sanctuary seems to be the point of departure for the description. This portal measured 70 x 25 cubits according to *War* 5.208 and 40 x 20 cubits according to *m. Mid.* 3.7. It was the sanctuary's main source of light.

[2797] The word ὑπερθύριον ("lintel," Rengstorf *s.v.*) is a *hapax legomenon* in Josephus.

[2798] According to the height of the sanctuary given in *Ant.* 15.391, the doors (together with their lintels) that gave access to the sanctuary would thus have been 120 cubits high. However, other sources give the height of the sanctuary as 100 cubits (see 15.391 with the note to "extra").

[2799] The noun ἐμπέτασμα ("curtain") occurs once elsewhere in Josephus (*Ant.* 12.318). Several MSS read ἐκπέτασμα (literally "that which is spread out," Rengstorf *s.v.*), which is a *hapax legomenon* in Josephus. The related and more elaborated passage of *War* (5.212) mentions 1 curtain (καταπέτασμα) hanging in front of the doors, being as long as the doors and woven in various colors (cf. ποικίλοις ["multicolored"] in *Ant.* 15.394 with ποικιλτός ["woven in various colors"] in *War* 5.212), including purple. Josephus interprets the 4 colors (white, violet, scarlet red, and purple) mentioned in *War* symbolically (5.213-214). The curtains were placed every morning in front of the doors of the sanctuary (Netzer 2006: 151).

[2800] The noun ἄνθος is poly-interpretable here: it can mean "flower" or "floral design" as well as "(brilliant) color" (Rengstorf *s.v.*; cf. Marcus-Wikgren 193, who translate "[with purple] colours"). Cf. Josephus' description of the priestly robes, which have flowers

395 Above them, below the cornice,[2803] a golden vine[2804] was spread out, with bunches of

---

woven in to them (ἄνθη ... ἐνύφανται), embroidered with scarlet and purple together with hyacinth and fine linen (*Ant.* 3.154). The curtain of the Tabernacle also has all kinds of flowers on it (3.126: ἄνθεσι παντοίοις).

[2801] The word ἁλουργής ("purple, purple-colored") occurs twice elsewhere in Josephus (*Ant.* 8.183 referring to purple-colored garments sent as a gift to Solomon and 17.197 referring to the purple cover of Herod's bier).

[2802] Niese minor (322) notes that the reading ἐνυφασμένους (entailing a rather loose connection between the curtains and the columns) transmitted by the MSS is corrupt. The *editio princeps* offers the reading ἐνυφασμένοις and implies that the curtains had (a design of) columns woven into them, which is the most plausible case and which may be inspired by Josephus' description of the Tabernacle: in *Ant.* 3.124 he states that 5 golden pillars (κίονες; cf. κίονας in 15.394) stood at the entrance of the Tabernacle: "In front, through which they had made the entrance, stood golden pillars, resting on bronze bases, five in number. They covered the Tent with curtains (ὕφεσι) of fine linen in which purple, hyacinth, and scarlet hues were blended" (trans. Feldman in BJP 3; cf. Exod 26:32). The Latin version refers to golden flowers surrounding the relevant columns (*aureos flores ambientes columnas*, Niese 403).

[2803] The translation follows Selden's conjecture (below). The MSS, with one minor exception, read τριχώμασιν (from τρίχωμα "[heavy] hairiness," Rengstorf *s.v.*; one further occurrence in Josephus: *Ant.* 1.258; see also Euripides, *Iph. taur.* 73). Since this word does not make sense, it is most probably corrupt. Selden (Niese 403) conjectures θριγχώμασιν ("cornice," LSJ *s.v.* θρίγχωμα; LSJ [Suppl. 72] give the spelling θρίγκωμα; cf. Plutarch, *Mor.* [*Quaest. conv.*] 685b), which is taken over by Niese minor 322 (with a variant spelling); LSJ *s.v.* θρίγχωμα; Marcus-Wikgren 190 and others.

[2804] Here Josephus refers to 1 golden vine, while in the parallel passage of *War* (5.210) he mentions that golden vines covered the sanctuary's vestibule (εἶχε δὲ καὶ τὰς χρυσᾶς ὑπὲρ αὐτῆς ἀμπέλους). Tacitus (*Hist.* 5.5) confirms the singular form and rejects the interpretation made by some that the vine implies that the Jews venerated Bacchus. The Mishnah also mentions 1 golden vine (*m. Mid.* 3.8), from which leafs and berries donated by visitors were hanging.

The vine at the entrance of the sanctuary may imply that Herod's architects were familiar with the Neo-Attic vine-scroll motif, which was introduced during Augustus' rule and became an integral part of the ornamental repertoire of the Corinthian style in the Imperial period. It was used in entablature friezes and soffit panels and sometimes also in capitals and great panels (e.g., in the Ara Pacis). Vine scrolls are displayed in the friezes of several Augustan temples, including the temple of Mars Ultor on the Augustan forum in Rome (Emerick 1998: 242-44).

The application of a Roman architectural convention does not exclude the possibility that the vine had at the same time a symbolic meaning, although we can only speculate about this by comparing it with Jewish and non-Jewish parallels. Designs of vines and grapes were used in several Jewish contexts: they are found on tombs, ossuaries, coins, and later also in synagogues (Michel-Bauernfeind 2.253-54; Hachlili 2005: 46-47, 133-46, 154-55, 289; Patrich 1993-94). Symbolic interpretations often focus on the association of Israel with a vine, attested in several biblical passages (e.g., in Ps 80:8-19 Israel is the vine brought from Egypt by God, also Jer 2:21; Hayward 1996: 161). Ezek 17:5-10 probably links a vine with the Judean king Zedekiah. Goodenough interprets a vine found at Palmyra as symbolizing the anticipation of future life (1953-68: 6.67-68) and he associates the vine at Herod's Temple with the ritual of drinking wine (1953-68: 5.103). In Matthew's version of the New Testament parable of the wicked tenants the vine imagery symbolizes the Kingdom of God, focusing on the fruits produced by the vineyard: "Therefore I [i.e., Jesus] tell you, the kingdom of God will be taken from you and given to a people that produces the fruits of the kingdom" (Matt 21:43).

Associations of golden vines with the power of rulers are found in various non-Jewish contexts. In *Ant.* 14.34-36 Josephus reports that Aristobulus II sent a golden vine worth 500 talents to Pompey, who was on his way to Coele-Syria. Josephus states that Strabo confirms this gift (although Strabo refers to either a vine or a garden) and that he himself has seen this gift in the temple of Jupiter Capitolinus (14.36). As precious decorations golden vines were also part of the royal paraphernalia of the Persian kings, the precise symbolic meaning of which is unknown according to Kuhrt (2007: 473). Briant (2002: 236-37), however, argues that the vines functioned as symbols of fecundity and refers in this connection to a dream of the Median king Astyages shortly after his daughter Mandane had married the Persian Cambyses I (Herodotus 1.108). In the dream a vine grew from Mandane's private parts and spread over Asia. The Magi interpreted this as predicting that Mandane's son would usurp the Median throne. Herodotus (7.27) also records that an extremely rich Lydian, called Pythius, offered to the Persian king Darius

grapes[2805] hanging down from it.[2806] It was a marvel of size and artistry[2807] to those who saw[2808] how much of the construction was made out of expensive material.[2809] **396** He surrounded the sanctuary[2810] with very large porticoes,[2811] building everything in proportion.[2812] He surpassed his predecessors in expenses,[2813] such that no other person was reputed to have adorned the sanctuary more. Both[2814] were[2815] combined with the wall,[2816]

---

a golden plane tree and a golden vine. Diodorus (19.48.7) relates that Antigonus Monophthalmus found a golden climbing vine in the citadel of Susa after he had captured this stronghold in 316 BCE. Pseudo-Callisthenes (3.28.10-14) relates that one of the buildings belonging to the palace of the Persian king in Egypt contained a golden eagle and a golden vine.

[2805] The bunches of grapes (βότρυες) are also mentioned in *War* 5.210 (for *m. Mid.* 3.8, see the previous note).

[2806] The verb ἀπαιωρέω ("hold up, let hang down"; "hang down" in the passive voice) occurs once elsewhere in Josephus (*Ant.* 11.234, in another context). The verb is first and foremost attested in the middle/passive voice; its active voice is found in Josephus (11.234) and Alciphron (LSJ *s.v.*). A passive form in combination with βότρυς also occurs in Gregory of Nyssa, *Vit. Mos.* 2.267 (ed. Daniélou 288).

[2807] Josephus uses a similar combination of both magnitude (μέγεθος) and artistry (τέχνη) when describing the remarkable sight of the statues of the gods in Vespasian's triumphal march in Rome (*War* 7.136).

[2808] The detail τοῖς ἰδοῦσιν ("those who saw") once again suggests that Josephus is attempting to visualize the Temple for his readers (see the first note to *Ant.* 15.393).

[2809] In both *War* and *Antiquities* Josephus emphasizes several times that Herod's building projects used expensive materials (cf. πολυτέλεια ["costliness"] in *War* 1.401 concerning Herod's restoration of the Antonia fortress; 1.418 concerning the Phasael Tower; 2.49 concerning the colonnades of the Temple; *Ant.* 15.199 concerning the 150 residences in Jerusalem; and 15.268 concerning the amphitheater in Jerusalem). The phrase πολυτέλεια τῆς ὕλης ("costliness of material") also occurs in *Ant.* 12.77, concerning the table of shewbread donated to the Temple by Ptolemy II Philadelphus (cf. also Philo, *Spec.* 1.276).

[2810] The noun νεώς/ναός usually refers to the sanctuary. Since this paragraph focuses on the entire Temple complex, Simons (1952: 392) argues that ναός has a wider meaning here (and perhaps also in *Ant.* 15.401). Nevertheless, Josephus' statement still makes sense if the word refers to the sanctuary, which was located more or less in the middle of the porticoes along the outer walls.

[2811] Josephus switches the view from the sanctuary to another part of the Temple complex, the colonnades along the walls. On the south side stood the more elaborate Royal Portico (mentioned in *Ant.* 15.393), while the other 3 sides had double colonnades (see also *War* 1.401; 5.190 and cf. *Ant.* 8.98; Netzer 2006: 164-71).

[2812] It is not exactly clear what the phrase ἅπαντα πρὸς τὴν ἀναλογίαν ἐπιτηδεύων means. The noun ἀναλογία ("[mathematical] proportion," Rengstorf *s.v.*) is a *hapax legomenon* in Josephus and has a range of further meanings ("[grammatical] analogy, relation, resemblance," LSJ *s.v.*). The Royal Portico on the south side was larger and more elaborate than the 3 porticoes on the west, north, and east sides (see *Ant.* 15.411-416). These latter 3 porticoes all looked identical and consisted of double colonnades with a width of ca. 15 m and a height of ca. 12.5 m; their lengths varied in accordance with the differing lengths of the outer walls of the Temple complex, on which they were standing (calculations by Netzer 2006: 164, based on Josephus' measures given in *War* 5.190-192; see also the previous note and 15.381 with the note to "the immense size of the enterprise"). On the basis of *War* 6.166 and the lack of evidence that Herod used roof tiles, Netzer (2006: 164 with n. 97) argues that the roofs of the 3 porticoes were flat, but this is far from conclusive. At the northwestern corner the Antonia Fortress was attached to the wall, while at the other 3 corners the walls had higher and wider sections (Netzer 2006: 163-64).

[2813] This comment clarifies the introductory remark in *Ant.* 15.380 that Herod's construction of God's sanctuary was "his own" (or built "by himself") since it shows that he financed the project. In taking care of the expenses for the Temple construction Herod apparently surpassed the investments of the builders of the First and Second Temples. If the notice specifically concerns the payment of the porticoes, as the context suggests, it may also mean that the Temple had (partial) colonnades in its earlier stages (Netzer 2006: 165 n. 100). Other Josephan passages likewise emphasize that Herod spent great sums of money on his projects (15.330, 332, 341; 16.13, 24, 154, 182; cf. also 15.274).

[2814] The problem here is to what the word ἄμφω ("both") refers. The immediate context speaks about 2 items: the sanctuary and its surrounding porticoes. The simplest reading is therefore that "both" refers to the sanctuary and the porticoes, implying that both were

and the wall[2817] itself was the greatest work heard about by humans.[2818] **397** The hill[2819] was a rocky ascent;[2820] it sloped gently upwards[2821] towards the eastern part of the city,[2822] to the highest summit. **398** This hill was surrounded by our[2823] first king Solomon[2824] in

---

"with a wall" or "with the wall" (according to MS P; see the next notes). The word "both" is sometimes interpreted as referring to 2 colonnades (e.g., Marcus-Wikgren 193; Meijer-Wes 3.207), but that would be at odds with the information that all 4 sides of the Temple complex had colonnades along the wall. If the linking of "both" with colonnades is nevertheless correct, it perhaps refers to the double rows of columns in the porticoes on the west, north, and east sides (the Royal Portico had 4 rows of columns); *War* 5.190 indicates that all the porticoes had double rows of columns: "All porticoes (αἱ στοαὶ πᾶσαι) had double rows (διπλαῖ) ..." (trans. Thackeray). There is still another explanation: in *Ant.* 20.221 Josephus attributes the construction of the eastern portico to Solomon (see also *War* 5.184-185; the passages John 10:23; Acts 3:11; 5:12 also refer to "Solomon's Portico"; see also *Ant.* 15.401 with the note to "double portico"). This would imply that Herod built only 2 double porticoes (the porticoes on the north and west sides; communication by Prof. Joseph Patrich [Jerusalem], see also Simons 1952: 401). According to the Latin version 2 porticoes were supported by large walls (*porticus autem duae maximis parietibus fulciebantur*, Niese 404)

[2815] Niese minor (322) notes that the transmitted Greek text is corrupt. Marcus-Wikgren (192 n. 2) state that a verb is missing after ἦσαν.

[2816] The translation follows Niese (404), who reads μετὰ τοῦ τείχος with MS P. The other MSS read μεγάλου τείχος ("of a big wall"), which probably derives from the reading of MS P, changing the first τ into γ and the second τ into λ. Marcus-Wikgren (192) conjecture μετὰ μεγάλου τείχος ("combined with a big wall"), supposing a case of haplography, which is unlikely.

[2817] In *Ant.* 15.396-400 Josephus focuses on this surrounding wall, another conspicuous item of the Temple complex (Netzer 2006: 162-64). The sanctuary was standing on a platform surrounded by an outer wall; the porticoes were standing on that wall (Busink 1970: 68).

[2818] Constructing the wall of the Temple complex must have been an enormous project because Herod had to expand the plateau on which the Temple was standing; the shape of the Temple Mount had to be adapted before the wall could be built, as Josephus indicates in the next paragraphs.

Concerning the phrase ἔργον μέγιστον ἀνθρώποις ἀκουσθῆναι ("[the wall itself] was the greatest work heard about by humans"), cf. Aelius Aristides, *Pan. Cyz.* (τὸ ἔργον μέγιστον τῶν εἰς ὄψιν ἐλθόντων ἀνθρώποις, ed. Dindorf 1.382).

[2819] I.e., the Temple Mount. Josephus switches his focus once again, concentrating now on Herod's adaptation of the hill.

[2820] The adjective ἀνάντης ("uphill, steep," LSJ *s.v.*; "sloping upwards," Rengstorf *s.v.*) is a *hapax legomenon* in Josephus. *War* 5.184 indicates that the hill was precipitous and steep (κατάντης) from all sides.

[2821] The verb ὑπτιόομαι ("slope upwards," a verb always used in the passive, Rengstorf *s.v.*) is a *hapax legomenon* in Josephus. It is extremely rare and attested before Josephus only in Aeschylus, *Pers.* 418-419 ("the hulls of our vessels rolled over [ὑπτιοῦτο] ...," trans. Smyth). The attribute ἠρέμα ("gentle") hardly matches the rockiness and difficult access of the Temple Mount that Josephus emphasizes elsewhere, but the word is adequate if it refers to the situation after Herod's adaptation of the hill, when the Temple became easily accessible from the east side (see *Ant.* 15.410).

[2822] The Temple was located in the eastern part of the city. The adjective ἑῷος ("eastern") occurs 5 times in Josephus, 4 of which belong to *Ant.* 15-17 (*War* 7.293; *Ant.* 15.397, 401, 411; 17.255; note that 15.401 and 15.411 also concern the description of the Temple).

[2823] The reference to Solomon as "our king" implies that Josephus associates himself with the Jewish people and at the same time that his audience included non-Jews. In *Ant.* 1.5-12 Josephus identifies himself as a Jewish (or Judean) spokesman to the non-Jewish (or non-Judean) world (further discussion by Mason in BJP 3 xvii-xx).

[2824] Josephus here interrupts his visual tour of the Temple and inserts a short excursus about the construction of the outer wall (*Ant.* 15.398-400) in order to give his readers further reasons to admire Herod's extraordinary project, although he starts with Solomon, the builder of the First Temple. Solomon's and Herod's building activities were partly identical: both kings had to create a platform on which the Temple complex could stand, but Herod's platform was considerably bigger; he expanded the platform (having already been expanded by the Hasmoneans) to the north and south and more modestly to the west, but not to the east (Sanders 1994: 56; Netzer 2006: 160). Simons (1952: 394, 397) argues that Josephus presents Solomon's Temple as the model for Herod's (see also 15.385 with the note to "in height").

The MSS read ὁ πρῶτος ἡμῶν βασιλεὺς Σολομών ("our first king Solomon"), which is incorrect since Saul

his wisdom[2825]—received from God[2826]—with large works[2827] above at the top.[2828] He[2829] surrounded it from below with huge stones[2830] bound together with lead,[2831] starting at the foot, around which a deep ravine runs.[2832] He continuously took [soil][2833] from the area inside while he was advancing the height [of the wall], **399** such that the size and height of the building, which had become square,[2834] were immense.[2835] The great sizes of the stones[2836] could be seen at the surface[2837] from the front.[2838] But inside[2839] the [stones] were

---

was the first king of the Israelites (1 Sam 9-10). Holwerda therefore suggests to erase the article ὁ (Niese 404), so that πρῶτος can be interpreted as "[our King Solomon] first" (see also Marcus-Wikgren 192 n. *b*).

[2825] The noun ἐπιφροσύνη ("wisdom, inspiration," Rengstorf *s.v.*) is a *hapax legomenon* in Josephus.

[2826] Niese (404) leaves out the words τοῦ θεοῦ ("from God, God's") after κατ' ἐπιφροσύνην because they are absent in MS P. However, they are attested by the other Greek MSS and the Latin version. The words make explicit what is probably intended by MS P as well, namely that Solomon adjusted the Temple Mount according to God's wise plan. The expression κατ' ἐπιφροσύνην θεοῦ ("according to God's wisdom") occurs twice in Philo (*Agr.* 169; *Mos.* 1.85; cf. *Migr.* 123; *QG* 3.18; *Sobr.* 18).

[2827] Perhaps "fortification works" (with LSJ *s.v.* ἐργασία II.5).

[2828] In order to get a rectangular platform Solomon had to flatten the top of the hill and to add enormous amounts of soil and stones at the foot.

[2829] Since there is no change of subject in the Greek text, the subject must be Solomon (if the transmitted text is reliable). However, given that the gigantic stones are obviously more typical of Herod's platform (cf. *Ant.* 15.392), Herod would make a better subject for this clause. Such a change of subject is possible if one follows Holwerda's conjecture (see the note to "first king Solomon"). Simons (1952: 394) argues that the Greek text originally mentioned Herod as subject.

[2830] The walls were built of ashlars laid in courses of 0.75-1.40 m high (on the average 1-1.2 m). There were courses of headers, courses of stretchers, and mixed courses (a "header" is a brick laid in such a way that only its end is visible; a "stretcher" is a brick laid so that its side is visible). The lengths of the headers were usually 0.80-1.10 m, while those of the stretchers 2-4 m. The largest stone, found in a course ca. 10 m below the platform level, was more than 12 m long and 3 m high (Netzer 2006: 162). Instead of the reading ἠλιβάτοις ("huge, steep," Rengstorf *s.v.*) attested by MS M, MSS PLW read κατὰ λίβα ταῖς ("in/to the southwest the ..."; similarly the Latin version), which makes no sense (Simons 1952: 394 with n. 1) and may derive from the reading ἠλιβάτοις. The adjective ἠλίβατος is a *hapax legomenon* in Josephus.

[2831] This detail is not supported by the archaeological findings: the outer wall surrounding the Temple was most probably built dry, without any bonding materials, neither lead nor iron; there is no bonding material whatsoever seen on the extant remains of the entire outer wall (Netzer 2006: 162; communication by Prof. Joseph Patrich, Jerusalem). The detail may have been added by Josephus to emphasize the strength of the walls.

The word μόλιβδος ("lead," LSJ *s.v.*: μόλυβδος) is a *hapax legomenon* in Josephus, but there are several close cognates (*War* 5.275; 6.278; 7.299; *Apion* 1.307).

[2832] To the east of the Temple complex lies the Kidron Valley, which is called a "deep ravine" (βαθεῖα φάραγξ) in *War* 5.70 (cf. 5.141; *Ant.* 14.57, 61) and "the eastern ravine" in *Ant.* 15.411. It is a steep valley running from north to southeast and south of the Temple complex (see also the description in 20.221 referring to the Temple's eastern portico: "This portico was part of the outer temple, and was situated in a deep ravine [κειμένη ἐν φάραγγι βαθείᾳ]," trans. Feldman).

[2833] Niese (404) and Marcus-Wikgren (192) read ἀπολαμβάνων αἰεί τι ("taking something continuously from") with Hudson's conjecture. The present translation is based on the reading ἀπολαμβάνων αἰεί τε ("and taking continuously from") of MSS PFLAMW, which is elliptical (the object—soil or stones—is implied). The archaeological analysis shows that the builders moved blocks of stone (communication by Prof. Joseph Patrich, Jerusalem).

[2834] The reference to the square dimension of the Temple complex implies that Josephus returns here to his visual description, as the next clause explicitly says. Standing in front of one section of the wall, one indeed perceived the complex as a square structure owing to the high and vertical wall and to the flat surface of the wall on which the porticoes were standing. A view from one of the hills nearby would also imply a square appearance because the platform was more or less rectangular with corners of ca. 90 ° (cf. in *War* 6.311 Josephus states that when the Antonia was demolished the Jews turned the Temple into a square [τετράγωνος] construction).

[2835] This comment is accurate if one takes the actual size of the Temple complex into account (see *Ant.* 15.381 with the note to "the immense size of the enterprise").

[2836] On the sizes of the stones, see *Ant.* 15.398 with the note to "huge stones" (about the material of the

firmly secured[2840] with iron[2841] in order to keep their joints[2842] fixed together forever. **400** When the construction[2843] reached the top of the hill[2844] this way, he fixed[2845] its summit, filled the hollow spaces near the walls,[2846] and made a flat[2847] and smooth surface on the top.[2848] This was the entire enclosed area,[2849] having a circumference of four

---

stones, see 15.392 with the note to "white and mighty stones").

[2837] The phrase κατὰ τὴν ἐπιφάνειαν ("at the surface") occurs twice in Josephus: here and in the next paragraph.

[2838] Once more Josephus invites his readers to take the perspective of somebody standing in front of one of the marvels of the Temple, this time before its outer wall (see the note to "square" above as well as *Ant.* 15.394, 401 with notes).

[2839] Josephus returns here to his excursus on the construction of the Temple wall and the platform.

[2840] The verb διασφαλίζομαι ("secure [firmly]," Rengstorf *s.v.*) occurs once elsewhere in Josephus (*War* 4.442, in a military context).

[2841] In contradistinction to Josephus' remark about the huge stones of the precinct being connected by lead in *Ant.* 15.398 (which may refer to Solomon's Temple), Josephus states here that the stones of the outer Temple wall were joined together by iron (σίδηρος). Archaeology reveals, though, that the ashlars were laid next to each other without any binding material (see 15.398 with the note to "bound together with lead").

[2842] The noun ἁρμογή ("joining, joint," Rengstorf *s.v.*) is a *hapax legomenon* in Josephus.

[2843] I.e., the construction of the wall. The word ἐργασία ("work") also occurs in *Ant.* 15.398. In both cases it means "construction, construction (work)" (Rengstorf *s.v.*).

[2844] Josephus rounds off his excursus on the construction of the Temple wall and moves on to the top of the complex, on which the sanctuary was standing. The noun λόφος ("hill, mountain") also refers to the Temple Mount in *Ant.* 15.397.

[2845] The context implies that the top of the Temple Mount was leveled (see *Ant.* 15.398 with notes), although it is uncertain whether the verb ἀπεργάζομαι has the specific meaning of "level"; it can mean, among other things, "finish, complete" (LSJ *s.v.*; Rengstorf [*s.v.*] offers "level off, plane" as meanings here).

[2846] The empty space between the wall and the top of the hill had to be filled up in order to construct the flat platform on which the sanctuary was standing (see the next sub-clause).

[2847] The adjective ἰσόπεδος ("of the same level, equally high," Rengstorf *s.v.*) occurs twice elsewhere in Josephus, both times in connection with the Temple (*War* 5.197 concerning the inner court of the sanctuary; *Ant.*

8.97 referring to the platform of Solomon's Temple).

[2848] For the description of a similar procedure in connection with the construction of Solomon's Temple, see *Ant.* 8.97, which passage shares the words φάραγξ, βαθύς/βάθος, ἰσόπεδος, and κορυφή with 15.400. Note the alliteration of the *p* sound in this clause.

[2849] According to the context the phrase τὸ πᾶν περίβολος ("the entire enclosed area") would not refer to the entire Herodian Temple precinct (differently Simons 1952: 395, who argues that the clause must refer to the outer wall of the Temple). The indications that the circumference was 4 *stadia* long and that each side was 1 *stadion* long (see the next note) do not fit the measures of the entire complex (see the next note and cf. *War* 5.192 mentioning 6 *stadia*). Josephus probably describes the leveled enclosed area at the summit, which was confined by a barrier, the *sôreg* (*m. Mid.* 2.3; see *Ant.* 15.417 with the note to "stone partition"), and surrounded the sanctuary of the Temple and the *ăzārâ* (the Priests' Court). The adjective πᾶν should therefore be understood in a relative sense, referring to the "entire" area within this barrier (Netzer 2006: 140). Patrich (2011) argues that this space corresponds to the area created by the High Priest Simeon the Just that is mentioned in Sir 50:2 in a reference to the renovations Simeon made to the Temple: "He [i.e., the High Priest Simon] laid the foundations for the high double walls, the high retaining walls for the temple enclosure (ἀνάλημμα ὑψηλὸν περιβόλου ἱεροῦ)." The porticoes that Simon built around this Temple "enclosure" are identical with the *sôreg* surrounding the precinct. Josephus refers to the precinct forbidden to the Gentiles (probably Simeon's precinct) as a περίβολος in *Ant.* 12.145. This area was surrounded by porticoes (12.141). It was fortified by Judas Maccabeus, destroyed by Antiochus V, and refortified by the Hasmonean leader Jonathan (13.181; see also 14.5 and cf. the plural τοὺς τῶν ἁγίων περιβόλους in *War* 4.182).

[2850] The ancient length standard of the Greek *stadion* (στάδιον) has several conversions (see *Ant.* 15.168 with the note to "*stadia*"). If it equals ca. 185 m here, in line with the Roman *stadium*, the complex was square and ca. 185 m long and wide. A similar square form is mentioned in *m. Mid.* 2.1, referring to a length and width of 500 cubits (= ca. 222 m according to the Roman cubit, or ca. 261 m according to the royal or Egyptian cubit), which measure equals the size given in Ezek 45:2 for the square plot around the sanctuary. Busink (1970: 63 with

stadia,[2850] each side taking one *stadion*.[2851] **401** Within it,[2852] above, at the top itself, ran[2853] another stone wall,[2854] which had on the eastern ridge[2855] a double portico[2856] of the same length as[2857] the wall—the sanctuary being in the middle[2858]—facing its doors.[2859] Many former kings decorated this [portico].[2860] **402** Around[2861] the entire Temple,[2862] spoils[2863]

---

n. 400) argues that the size of the square form in *Ant.* 15.400 is taken from Ezek 45:2, despite the fact that Ezekiel mentions 500 cubits, whereas 1 *stadion* equals roughly 400 cubits. Businck (1970: 38-39) and Schalit (2001: 376) argue that the 4 *stadia* concern the size of Solomon's Temple. For a discussion of the area that may be referred to, see the previous note.

[2851] The measure of 1 *stadion* (equaling 185 m) deviates considerably from the length of every side of the Temple complex based upon archeological data (see *Ant.* 15.381 with the note to "enterprise"). The notion of a square surface is valuable, though: looking from one of the hills opposite the eastern wall, e.g., from the Mount of Olives (see 15.393 with the note to "The sides of the entire [sanctuary]") one has the impression that the complex was square. Some sources do suggest such a square construction (e.g., *m. Mid.* 2.1; see the previous note). Nevertheless, since the measure of 1 *stadion* hardly fits the real measures of the Temple complex, the reference apparently concerns a smaller square area, most probably the area forbidden to the Gentiles (see the note to "the entire enclosed area").

[2852] I.e., within the "enclosed area" mentioned in *Ant.* 15.400.

[2853] The same verbal form περιθεῖ (from περιθέω, "run about/around") occurs in *Ant.* 15.398 referring to the deep ravine. Since the verb occurs elsewhere in Josephus only in *War* 1.412; 4.223; *Ant.* 3.140, the present case may be another example of Josephus' practice of re-using a word in a short space and then dropping it (see Mason in BJP 9 lii-liii).

[2854] This was the inner, rectangular enclosure, called *ăzārâ* in Hebrew, which surrounded the sanctuary, the Court of the Priests, and the Court of the Men and was located to the west of the Court of the Women (Netzer 2006: 142-59; cf. Simons 1952: 395). If the *bîrâ* ("fortress") mentioned in Neh (2:8; 7:2) refers to this area, there may have been already such a wall from Nehemiah's time onward (as argued by Patrich 2011: 569). In *War* 5.196 Josephus mentions that this wall was 25 cubits high measured from the inside and 40 cubits high measured from the surface of the outer court.

[2855] I.e., the side of the wall at the eastern ridge of the Temple Mount, which is confirmed by the final subclause of this paragraph. The word ῥάχις ("ridge," Rengstorf *s.v.*) is a *hapax legomenon* in Josephus.

[2856] This description implies that the eastern wall around the inner court (*ăzārâ*) included a double portico, which is confirmed by the Mishnah mentioning 2 roofed strips facing the sanctuary on the east side, which were both 11 cubits broad and 135 cubits long and were called the Court of Israel (*ăzārat yiśrā'ēl*) and the Court of the Priests (*ăzārat hakkōhănîm*; *m. Mid.* 2.5-6; see also *Ant.* 15.419 with the note to "third precinct"). The roofs of both strips must have been supported by a portico each, which matches Josephus' reference to a double portico (I owe this reference to Prof. J. Patrich, Jerusalem). The rather specific phrase στοά διπλή ("double portico," i.e., a portico with a double colonnade, like the porticoes standing on the northern and western walls of the Temple; see 15.396 and *War* 5.190) occurs twice elsewhere in Josephus: in *Ant.* 8.98 it refers to the porticoes of the (outer) precinct of Solomon's Temple; in *War* 5.190 to the porticoes on the walls of Herod's Temple. There is evidence for another portico, probably from the Hasmonean period, which was located on the inside of the eastern outer wall, on a lower level than the Herodian court (the Herodian eastern wall was an extension of the Hasmonean precinct). Josephus attributes this portico to Solomon (*Ant.* 20.220-221). It is mentioned several times in the New Testament as "Solomon's Portico" (Patrich 2011: 570; see also 15.396 with the note to "Both").

[2857] The adjective ἰσομήκης ("equally long," Rengstorf *s.v.*) occurs twice elsewhere in Josephus (see *War* 1.425 concerning the portico of Antioch's main street, which was financed by Herod, and 5.212 concerning the curtain at the entrance of the Temple sanctuary).

[2858] The construction of the inner enclosure with the Court of the Women in front of it must have looked symmetrical. For somebody standing on the east side, in front of the gate of the inner enclosure or the gate of the Women's Court, the sanctuary was in the middle of the enclosure (see Netzer 2006: 142-45, with a reconstruction of the plan of the inner enclosure on pp. 144-45). Concerning the doors of the sanctuary, see *Ant.* 15.394 with the note to "doors at the entrance."

[2859] This detail confirms that it concerns the eastern part of the wall of the inner enclosure, which had a gate that enabled someone to see the entrance of the sanctuary. The center of that eastern wall formed a straight line with the entrance of the sanctuary's vestibule (see also the previous note).

[2860] The verb κατασκευάζω means "decorate" here (Rengstorf *s.v.*; see also *Ant.* 15.318). The fact that

from foreigners[2864] were fixed.[2865] All these King Herod[2866] set up as a votive offering[2867] after he had added all those that he took from the Arabs.[2868]

(11.4) 403 On the north side[2869] was a citadel built, well-fenced[2870] and standing at a corner. It was remarkable in strength. The kings and High Priests[2871] from the family of

---

former kings had contributed something to the decoration of this portico implies that it already existed before Herod's renovation (Simons 1952: 395). Non-Jewish kings honored the Temple with gifts, as several biblical and Hellenistic-Jewish passages indicate: the First Book of Kings mentions gifts by King Hiram of Tyre and the Queen of Sheba (1 Kgs 7:13-46; 9:11-14; 10:1-10). 2 Macc 3:2 reports that foreign kings honored the Temple and glorified it with the finest presents during the High Priesthood of Onias III (see also *War* 2.412-413; *Let. Aris.* 42, 51-82; 2 Macc 2:13; 5:17; Philo, *Legat.* 157, 317-319).

[2861] Cf. the inscriptions and trophies in Augustus' honor, which were located "all around" (κύκλῳ) Herod's theater in Jerusalem (*Ant.* 15.272).

[2862] Josephus switches his perspective once again, which is also apparent from the vocabulary: in the previous paragraph he uses the word ναός/νεώς ("sanctuary," referring to the sanctuary within the inner enclosure of the Temple; see *Ant.* 15.380 with the note to "sanctuary"), while here he uses the word ἱερόν ("temple," referring to the entire Temple complex). Hence the spoils were located at accessible areas along the outer walls.

[2863] Such spoils (σκῦλα) were usually weapons taken from enemy soldiers, or reliefs (i.e., trophies) representing spoils (Diodorus 14.29; Plutarch, *Tim.* 29.6; see also *Ant.* 15.272 with the note to "trophies" and the next note).

[2864] Or "from barbarians." The spoils were apparently taken from non-Jews and put in or near the Temple already before Herod's time (Simons 1952: 395). They commemorated the Jews' military victories over foreign enemies (cf. Herod's defeat of the Nabateans mentioned in the next sentence and described in *Ant.* 15.147-160). The adjective βαρβαρικός ("of speaking a foreign language, pertaining to a foreign people," Rengstorf *s.v.*) sometimes has the pejorative meaning "barbaric." It has this meaning in *War* 4.45, in which passage it includes the Jews. The only other occurrence in Josephus is *Ant.* 1.93, referring to foreign histories written by non-Greeks. Here the word seems to have a neutral meaning ("foreign," i.e., "non-Jewish"). In some instances Josephus re-interprets the common distinction between Greeks and foreigners/barbarians ("Ελληνες—βάρβαροι) as a differentiation between Jews and non-Jews (see the noun βάρβαρος in *Ant.* 15.136 and van Henten 2011a).

For the phrase σκῦλα βαρβαρικά ("spoils from foreigners"), see Plutarch, *Tim.* 29.6 and cf. Euripides, *Elec.* 7; Diodorus 14.29.4.

[2865] Josephus does not specify the exact location of the spoils. Netzer (2006: 165 n. 100) argues that they were affixed to the rear wall of the colonnades (mentioned in *Ant.* 15.396) or to the outer faces of the surrounding walls of the Temple complex.

[2866] Herod is mentioned several times with his label "King" in this section (see also *Ant.* 15.404, 409, 420). About this title referring to Herod, see 15.1 with the note to "captive," 15.5 with the note to "gold," and 15.9 with the note to "king."

[2867] An alternative translation would be "dedicated [to God]" (with Simons 1952: 395 n. 2). The verb ἀνατίθημι can mean, among other things, "set up, set up as (a votive offering)" or "offer (a gift to God)" (Rengstorf *s.v.*). The last meaning occurs frequently in Josephus (e.g., *Ant.* 3.219 and 6.192, 244 referring to Goliath's sword dedicated to God by David; cf. 1 Sam 21:9; see also *War* 1.357; *Ant.* 7.104, 108; 8.259; 14.488 and *Apion* 2.48 referring to votive offerings to God by Ptolemy III Euergetes in order to commemorate a victory over the Seleucids). Since Josephus is describing the location of the spoils, the meaning "set up as (a votive offering)" seems more plausible.

[2868] This probably refers to the spoils that Herod took from the Nabateans during the decisive battle against them (*Ant.* 15.147-160).

[2869] The viewpoint remains on the outside of the Temple, focusing now on the Antonia Fortress (*Ant.* 15.409) located on the north side of the precinct. Josephus also mentions the Antonia in 15.406, 424 (for further information about this fortress, see 15.292 with the notes to "Antonia" and "built by himself").

The phrase ἡ βόρειος πλευρά ("the north side") does not occur elsewhere in Josephus (but see Hecataeus of Abdera, *FGH* 264 F 25.63 [ed. Jacoby 3A.43]; Diodorus 1.64.8; Strabo 2.1.14, 27).

[2870] The word εὐερκής ("strongly fortified," Rengstorf *s.v.*) is a *hapax legomenon* in Josephus.

[2871] Herod's predecessors, i.e., the rulers of the Hasmonean dynasty (see the next note), were exceptional because they were both the political and religious leaders of the Jews. The key document about the Hasmonean ideology of rulership is the honorary decree for Simon

the Hasmoneans[2872] had built it before Herod[2873] and called it Baris.[2874] It functioned as a depository of their priestly robe,[2875] in which the High Priest dresses himself[2876] only when he needs to sacrifice. **404** King Herod[2877] kept this robe safe in this place[2878] and after his death[2879] it remained under the supervision of the Romans[2880] until the time of Tiberius

---

and his sons transmitted in 1 Macc 14:25-49 (set in 140 BCE). Simon the Hasmonean is not called a king in this decree, but the document presents his power in the ideological framework of the Hellenistic kings. It reconfirms that Simon was the Jews' political and military leader as well as their High Priest (14:35, 38, 41-42). 1 Macc 14:41 reports the Jews' decision to appoint Simon to these positions forever, or at least, "until a trustworthy prophet should arise" (further discussion in van Henten 2001; 2007b).

[2872] The noun Hasmonean (Ἀσαμωναῖος, also *War* 1.19, 36; *Ant.* 11.11; 12.265; 14.490-491; 16.187; 17.162; 20.190, 238, 247, 249) refers to a member of the dynasty of the Jewish Hasmonean leaders, who were also called "the Maccabees" (e.g., Eusebius, *Dem. ev.* 8.2.93). The latter name derives from Judah/Judas the Maccabee, one of the members of this family, while the name Hasmonean derives from Hashmon, the great-grandfather of the priest Mattathias who began the rebellion against the Seleucids (*Ant.* 12.265; further references in Schürer-Vermes 1.156-242; Sievers 1990; van Henten and Joubert 1996). 1 Maccabees describes how this family rebelled against Antiochus IV, starting with Mattathias' refusal to participate in a sacrifice ordered by Antiochus (1 Macc 2:15-28, also *Ant.* 12.265-272). Mattathias belonged to the priestly tribe of Yehoyarib (1 Chr 24:7). 1 Maccabees is the most important source for the first 3 generations of the Hasmonean dynasty (i.e., Mattathias, his 5 sons [including Judas], and John Hyrcanus [one of Mattathias' grandsons]). Josephus describes their rules in *Ant.* 12.265-14.491. Goldstein (1976: 17-20) argues that the absence of the name Hasmonean from 1 Maccabees implies that it had a derogatory connotation.

[2873] Differently in *Ant.* 15.292 (see the note to "built by himself").

[2874] The former name (Baris) of the fortress also occurs in *War* 1.75, 118, 353; *Ant.* 13.307; 14.481; 15.409; 18.91-92. It derives from the Greek noun βᾶρις, which means "large house, tower, stronghold" in Hellenistic-Jewish passages (see 2 Chr 36:19; Dan 8:2 in Theodotion's version; Josephus, *Life* 246; LSJ *s.v.* 2; GELS *s.v.*). It sometimes corresponds to the Hebrew/Aramaic noun *bîrâ* ("fortress," e.g., Ezra 6:2; Neh 2:8; Esth 8:14; see *Ant.* 15.401 with the note to "wall"). Contrary to 15.292 Josephus here seems to identify the Baris Fortress with the Antonia (see 15.406), which is incorrect according to Ritmeyer (see 15.292 with the notes to "Antonia" and "built by himself").

[2875] The phrase ἱερατικός στολή ("priestly robe") also occurs in *Ant.* 15.390 (see the note to "priestly robes"; cf. 15.405: ἱερὰ στολή). For similar vocabulary, cf. 18.93: τῆς στολῆς τοῦ ἀρχιερέως ἀποκειμένης.

[2876] The High Priest wore magnificent garments during the performance of his priestly duties. Biblical and non-biblical passages offer descriptions of his vestments (e.g., Exod 28; Sir 45:7-13; 50:5-11; Philo, *Mos.* 2.109-126, 135). Josephus describes them in *War* 5.231-236; *Ant.* 3.159-187 (details in Feldman in BJP 3 on *Ant.* 3.159-187). On the Day of Atonement the High Priest wore a simpler, but still costly, white garment (Lev 16:4; Josephus, *War* 5.136; Schürer-Vermes 2.276 n. 7).

[2877] Exactly the same title (Ἡρώδης ὁ βασιλεύς) occurs in *War* 2.266 in a reference to Herod's construction of Caesarea Maritima (see also *Ant.* 15.409 and in general Goodblatt 1998: 19-23).

[2878] *Ant.* 15.404-409 offers a proleptic excursus about the location where the high priestly garments were kept and about those having the authority over them. The Antonia was the safest place in the Temple area. In *Ant.* 18.91-92 Josephus reports that the Hasmoneans kept the high priestly garments in the Antonia (see also 15.403 and cf. 15.292 with the note to "built by himself") and that they were the custodians of them. Herod retained them in the fortress and apparently acted as their custodian until his death (see also the next note). Otto (1913: 111-13) and Schalit (2001: 312-13) argue that taking custody of the high priestly garments was part of Herod's strategy to control the priesthood and the Temple (with its treasury).

[2879] I.e., in 4 BCE (or 1 BCE or 1 CE). On the one hand Josephus states here that the high priestly robe was under the control of the Romans starting from Herod's death (without specifying whether this was directly after the king's death) until Tiberius' day (see the last note to this paragraph). On the other hand in *Ant.* 18.93 he reports that Archelaus kept the garments in the Antonia as his father had done and that the Romans took over the supervision when they removed Archelaus from his office (in 6 CE), which seems more plausible.

[2880] *Ant.* 15.405 implies that the Romans guarded the high priestly garments starting from Herod's death up to Vitellius' visit (cf. the previous note). *Ant.* 18.93-94 offers additional information: the Romans apparently removed the garments from the Antonia and kept them in a stone building (the vocabulary is clearly different from that referring to the Antonia). *Ant.* 15.406 (see the

Caesar.[2881] **405** During his reign[2882] Vitellius,[2883] the governor of Syria,[2884] visited Jerusalem[2885] and because the people gave him a most magnificent reception[2886] he wanted to return to them their beneficence.[2887] Since they appealed to him to have the priestly robe under their own authority,[2888] he wrote to Tiberius Caesar[2889] about these matters and Tiberius yielded it. So the authority over the robe[2890] remained with the Jews until King Agrippa died.[2891] **406** After him[2892] Cassius Longinus,[2893] the governor[2894] of Syria[2895] at that

---

note to "Antonia") likewise implies that another location is meant. During their stay in this building the seal of the priests and the treasurers protected the garments. *Ant.* 18.93-94 further implies that the Romans restricted the use of the garments to the 3 main holidays (i.e., Passover/Pesach, Pentecost/Shavuot, and Tabernacles/Sukkot) and to the Day of Atonement (Schürer-Vermes 1.379).

[2881] The emperor Tiberius ruled from 19 August 14 CE to 16 March 37 CE (Kienast 1996: 76-79). His full name was Tiberius Claudius Nero (for other references to him in Josephus, see Schalit 1968: 118).

[2882] I.e., the reign of Tiberius (see the previous note).

[2883] Lucius Vitellius was born before 5 BCE and died in or after 51 CE. He was the youngest son of Publius Vitellius, a knight from Luceria (in Southern Italy). He served as a steward under Augustus and became close with Antonia, the daughter of Mark Antony and the widow of Augustus' adoptive son Drusus, which granted him access to the imperial court. He was consul in 34 CE and appointed governor of Syria in 35 CE (*Ant.* 18.88; Tacitus, *Ann.* 6.32, 41). He suspended Pontius Pilate as governor of Judea in the winter of 36/37 CE, or in the subsequent spring, and was recalled to Italy by Caligula, probably in 39 CE (Schürer-Vermes 1.262-63, 386-88; Eck 2002b; Mahieu 2012: 405-07). Vitellius is mentioned frequently in book 18 of *Antiquities* (references in Schalit 1968: 94; see also 15.407 with the note to "Vitellius").

[2884] The word ἡγεμών means "governor of a province" here (Rengstorf *s.v.*). Syria became a province of Augustus in January 27 BCE, from which time on Augustus and his successors appointed its governor, who was called a *legatus* ("envoy [of the emperor]"; Millar 1993b: 31-32; for Vitellius, see the previous note as well as *Ant.* 18.88; for the Roman province of Syria, Millar 1993b: 31-38).

[2885] This visit must have taken place soon after Pontius Pilate's deposition as governor in 36/37 CE. *Ant.* 18.90 and 18.95 offer a slightly more elaborate description of the visit and connect it with the Feast of Passover (probably in 37 CE, with Schwartz 1990: 62, 64; differently Mahieu 2012: 404-05: Passover 36 CE). For a similar combination of the verb ἐπιδημέω ("visit for a while, sojourn") and τοῖς Ἱεροσολύμοις, see *Life* 200.

[2886] Similarly *Ant.* 18.90, with different vocabulary. Josephus does not explain why Vitellius received a splendid reception from the Jerusalemites. It was perhaps due to Vitellius' good reputation as an administrator. If Mahieu's argumentation (2012: 407) is correct that Vitellius came to visit Palestine because the tetrarchy of Herod's son Philip had recently become an annex to the province of Syria, the Jerusalemites may have welcomed him as the new ruler of an adjacent, related district.

[2887] This detail remains implicit in *Ant.* 18.90.

[2888] This request may have been given in by a wish for autonomy in religious matters; its approval would allow the High Priest to use his garments every day and not only during the 3 main festivals and on the Day of Atonement (see *Ant.* 15.404 with the note to "Romans").

The vocabulary here (τὴν ἱερὰν στολὴν ὑπὸ τὴν αὐτῶν ἐξουσίαν ἔχειν "have the priestly robe under their own authority") is almost identical to that of *Ant.* 20.7 concerning a request to Fadus (see 15.406). In 18.90 Josephus formulates the change concerning the high priestly garments in slightly different terms, indicating that the garments and ornaments would be kept in the Temple under the custody of the priests, as had been the case before. He further adds that Vitellius also remitted the taxes on the sale of agricultural products.

[2889] Such a letter is not mentioned in *Ant.* 18.90, which paragraph merely states that Vitellius agreed that the High Priest's garments and ornaments would be kept in the Temple under the custody of the priests. A letter to the emperor may not have been strictly necessary, but it was common practice for governors to request the emperor for advice, and for emperors to send out instructions (*mandata*) to governors, whether or not as responses to requests (Goodman 1997: 109-10).

[2890] The words ἐξουσία ("authority") and στολή ("robe") also occur in the request of the Jerusalemites previously formulated in this paragraph (see also *Ant.* 20.7).

[2891] Other passages imply that King Agrippa I is meant here. This is the first reference to Agrippa I in *Antiquities*. He figures prominently in book 18 (references in Schalit 1968: 3; cf. *War* 2.178-220). Agrippa was the grandson of Herod and Mariamme I, and the son of Aristobulus IV (who was executed together with his brother Alexander by Herod) and Berenice (*War* 1.552). He was born in 11 or 10 BCE and was educated in Rome, where he became close with Tiberius' son Drusus. In 37 CE Caligula gave him the tetrarchy of Philip and

time, and Cuspius Fadus,[2896] the procurator of Judea,[2897] ordered the Jews[2898] to deposit the robe in the Antonia.[2899] **407** For [Longinus and Fadus said][2900] it was necessary for the Romans to be masters of it,[2901] as they had been before.[2902] Then [the][2903] Jews sent[2904]

---

that of Lysanias and allowed him to use the title "king." Gaius Caligula added Herod Antipas' tetrarchy to Agrippa's territory in 39 (or 40) CE (Mahieu [2012: 272-73] argues for 39 CE). Claudius appointed him king of Judea and Samaria in 41 CE, such that his territory became basically the same as that of his grandfather Herod the Great (further information in Schürer-Vermes 1.442-53; Schwartz 1990; Kokkinos 1998: 271-304). Agrippa's death is described in Josephus (*Ant.* 19.343-352) and Acts (12:19-23). These passages show strong similarities: both suggest that a flattering crowd deified Agrippa, that he did not reject this, and that his painful death was a consequential, divine punishment (Acts 12:23 states that his body was eaten by worms). Most scholars argue that Agrippa died in Caesarea Maritima in March 44 CE during or shortly after a festival in honor of the emperor (e.g., Schwartz 1907: 262-67; Schürer-Vermes 1.452-53; Smallwood 1976: 199; Kokkinos 1998: 300-02). Schwartz (1990: 107-11, 145-49) argues for an earlier date, between September/October 43 CE and January/February 44 CE, by preference at the beginning of this period, when the quadrennial festival founded by Herod the Great would have been celebrated in Caesarea (see *Ant.* 16.138). Kokkinos (1998: 302 with nn. 134-35) criticizes Schwartz, noting that Agrippa was still alive when Marcus Julius Alexander, the husband of his daughter Berenice, died (*A.J.* 19.277), while Alexander died after 25 January 44 CE. On the basis of an ostracon from Myos Hormos dated between 26 May and 25 June 44 CE and referring to Marcus Julius Alexander, Mahieu (2012: 172-74) argues against March 44 CE; she proposes early August 44 CE as the probable date of Agrippa's death. For other references to Agrippa's death in Josephus including the verb τελευτάω ("die"), see *Ant.* 18.194; 20.1, 9, 15.

[2892] Literally "after this (one)," i.e., after Agrippa I.

[2893] G. Cassius Longinus was the governor of Syria from 44/45 until 49/50 CE, being the successor of Vibius Marsus. He was a famous jurist and a *consul suffectus* in 30 CE (Schürer-Vermes 1.264). He is also mentioned in *Ant.* 20.1, together with a reference to the death of Agrippa I (see also 20.7).

[2894] The verb διοικέω means "be governor" or "administer" here (see the next note and Rengstorf *s.v.*).

[2895] On the office of the governor of Syria, see *Ant.* 15.405 with the note to "governor of Syria."

[2896] After the death of Agrippa, Cuspius Fadus was sent as a procurator to Judea (*War* 2.220). He was succeeded by Tiberius Julius Alexander, most probably in 46 CE. For the scarce information about the cognomen *Fadus* and the family name *Cuspius*, see Mason in BJP 1b on *War* 2.220 with the note to "Cuspius Fadus." In *Ant.* 19.363-366 Josephus reports that one of the reasons for sending Fadus to Judea was preventing the Syrian governor Marsus, who had had a conflict with Agrippa, to be present in Judea.

[2897] Fadus is also mentioned as the procurator of Judea (ὁ τῆς Ἰουδαίας ἐπίτροπος) in *Ant.* 20.2, 97.

[2898] Josephus mentions the same episode in *Ant.* 20.6, specifying that Fadus sent for the chief priests and the leaders of the Jerusalemites and urged them to deposit the full-length tunic and the sacred robe (τὸν ποδήρη χιτῶνα καὶ τὴν ἱερὰν στολήν) of the High Priest in the Antonia under the authority of the Romans.

[2899] I.e., the Fortress Antonia, where Herod had previously kept the robe (see *Ant.* 15.404 and for further references, 15.292 with the note to "Antonia"). This implies that the Jews kept the high priestly garments at another place during the interval between Vitellius' (see 15.405) and Fadus' governorships, or even during the interval between the rule of Herod the Great or his son Archelaus and that of Fadus. *Ant.* 18.93-94 seems to confirm this: the Romans apparently removed the high priestly garments from the Antonia and kept them in a stone building (the vocabulary concerning this building is clearly different from that referring to the Antonia here). Schwartz (1990: 64-65) argues that Fadus wished to restore the *status quo ante*, i.e., the situation before Vitellius' concession and adds that Fadus probably had a political motive for doing so: the control of the high priestly garments was an important means to supervise potentially dangerous competitors.

[2900] The Greek infinitive construction indicates that it concerns indirect speech by Longinus and Fadus. They are expressing their reason for returning the authority over the priestly garments to the Romans.

[2901] This point of view implies that Longinus and Fadus were of the opinion that the Roman rule over Judea included the control over the garments of the High Priest, who was the most important Jewish leader following Agrippa's death. In retaking this authority they undid the concession made by Vitellius (see *Ant.* 15.405).

[2902] Cf. *Ant.* 20.6, in which case Josephus only mentions Fadus and suggests that Fadus wanted to restore the previous situation (see the note to Vitellius further on in this paragraph about Schwartz' interpretation of the events; cf. καθὼς καὶ πρότερον ἦσαν ["as they were before"] here with καθὰ δὴ καὶ πρότερον ἦν ["as

envoys to Claudius Caesar[2905] to petition him[2906] about these matters.[2907] After they had arrived[2908] the younger King Agrippa,[2909] who happened to be in Rome,[2910] asked for the authority[2911] from the emperor and received it,[2912] while the emperor gave instructions to Vitellius,[2913] who was the governor[2914] of Syria. **408** Previously[2915] it[2916] had been under the

---

they had been in the past"] in 20.6).

[2903] The article is missing in the Greek text, although one would expect it since Josephus is referring to "the Jews" (τοὺς Ἰουδαίους) in the previous paragraph. Implied articles are quite common in Josephus (e.g., *War* 1.1, 151, etc.). Without the article the text literally means "[some of the] Jews," which does not fit the context because it is implausible that envoys were sent by some of the Jews. In the majuscule MSS the article (OI) may easily have been left out by haplography in the reading ΟΥΝΟΠΟΥΔΑΙΟΙ (I owe this explanation to Omert J. Schrier, Amsterdam).

[2904] MS P has a long lacuna, starting from this sentence (which in the Greek text begins with πέμπουσιν) until the end of *Ant.* 15.408, such that it completely lacks the section about the Jews' petition.

[2905] I.e., the emperor Claudius (41-54 CE), whose full name at birth was probably Tiberius Claudius Drusus (Kienast 1996: 90-92) and at his accession Tiberius Claudius Caesar Augustus Germanicus. Claudius is mentioned frequently in *War* 2 and *Ant.* 19-20 (references in Schalit 1968: 75).

[2906] The verb παρακαλέω ("petition, appeal to"; see Rengstorf *s.v.*; Mason in BJP 9 on *Life* 62; and the next note) with the emperor Claudius as object occurs with a slightly different meaning in *Ant.* 20.9 about Agrippa II entreating Caesar (παρακαλεῖ τὸν Καίσαρα).

[2907] The authority over the high priestly garments must have been a sensitive matter, which is confirmed by the more elaborate version of this episode in *Ant.* 20.6-14 (see below).

The phrase "petition ... about these matters (περὶ τούτων παρακαλέσοντας)" links up with the Jews' request to Vitellius (15.405) through the repetition of the verb παρακαλέω ("beseech, appeal to," among other meanings). Since Longinus and Fadus wanted to undo the concession made by Vitellius, the Jews petitioned the emperor. According to 20.7 the chief priests and the leaders of the people petitioned (παρεκάλουν) Fadus and Longinus. The latter had come to Jerusalem with a large force out of fear that the Jews would revolt. Fadus and Longinus allowed the Jewish leaders to send a delegation to Rome and accepted to wait for the emperor's decision on the condition that their children would be hostages of the Romans (20.7-8).

[2908] I.e., the envoys in Rome.

[2909] I.e., Agrippa II. Agrippa II was the son of Agrippa I and Cyprus (*War* 2.220). His full name was Marcus Julius Agrippa. He was born in 27/28 CE and educated in Rome in Claudius' house (*Ant.* 19.363; 20.9, 12), so that he knew the emperor quite well. Most scholars conclude that Agrippa II died in 92/93 CE, but Kokkinos argues on the basis of Photius (*Bibl.* 33), inscriptions, and numismatic evidence that he died in 100 CE. Claudius wanted to give Agrippa II the kingdom of his father at the latter's death in 44 CE, but Agrippa II was considered to be still too young (*Ant.* 19.360-362). In 50 CE (according to Kokkinos [1998: 318] in late 48 CE) Claudius appointed Agrippa II King of Chalcis and also granted him the right to nominate and depose the High Priests. In 53 CE he gave him the tetrarchy of Philip (Batanea, Trachonitis, and Gaulanitis) as a replacement for the kingdom of Chalcis. Nero added the cities of Tiberias, Tarichea, and Julias (with their surrounding areas). Agrippa II is mentioned frequently in *War* 2-3, *Ant.* 20, and *Life* (references in Schalit 1968: 3). During his early years in Rome he used his excellent connections at the imperial court to support the cases of Jews (apart from this passage, see also *Ant.* 20.134-136 concerning the conflict with Cumanus and the Samaritans; further discussion and references about Agrippa II in Schürer-Vermes 1.471-83; Kokkinos 1998: 317-42, 396-99).

[2910] Agrippa II, who was probably ca. 16 years old at the time of this petition, lived in Rome until he received the kingdom of Chalcis (see the previous note).

[2911] I.e., the authority (ἐξουσία) over the high priestly garments (see *Ant.* 15.405-406 with notes). The same request appears in 20.9.

[2912] This implies that Claudius restored the situation as implemented by Vitellius, which is confirmed by *Ant.* 20.12 (about Vitellius' concession, see 15.405). Josephus does not inform us of Claudius' motive; it was probably his good relationship with Agrippa II (see the note to "who happened to be in Rome" above).

[2913] The reference to Vitellius as the governor of Syria, found in all the MSS, is anachronistic: Vitellius was no longer governor of Syria at the death of Agrippa I (in 43 or 44 CE; see *Ant.* 15.405 with the note to "until King Agrippa died"); Caligula (37-41 CE) had replaced him by Publius Petronius (*Ant.* 19.316; 20.1; Schürer-Vermes 1.263), probably in 39 CE (see *Ant.* 15.405 with the note to "Vitellius"). Vitellius became a very prominent administrator in Rome: he was consul in the years 43 and 47 CE and took care of the government

seal[2917] of the High Priest[2918] and the treasurers.[2919] One day before [every] festival the treasurers[2920] would go up to the commander of the Roman garrison.[2921] They would inspect their own seal and take the robe.[2922] Subsequently, when the festival was over, they returned it again[2923] to the same place[2924] and deposited it after showing the commander of the

---

during Claudius' invasion of Britain in 43 CE (Suetonius, *Vit.* 2; Eck 2002b). Schwartz (2013: 34-36) notes that the Greek text is authentic, but wrong. Josephus either is mixing up the governor Vitellius with another governor (the Syrian governor Longinus, mentioned in *Ant.* 15.406, or the Judean procurator Fadus, 20.9, 14), or he is referring to Vitellius' actions in Rome. The first option is confirmed by the more elaborate parallel passage found in 20.6-14, in which Josephus connects Longinus and Fadus with the petition (20.7, as the context of 15.407 likewise implies; see 15.406). *Ant.* 20.6-14 quotes a letter from Claudius (20.11-14), which refers to the emperor's instructions to Fadus about this matter (20.14) and to the precedent set by Vitellius (20.12). The latter passage perhaps caused the confusion of Vitellius with Longinus/Fadus.

[2914] Niese (405) reads ἀντιστρατήγῳ ("propraetor, someone who acts as governor," LSJ *s.v.* ἀντιστράτηγος) with MS W, which reading reflects the official title of the governor of Syria, i.e., *legatus Augusti pro praetore* (in Greek πρεσβευτής Σεβαστοῦ ἀντιστράτηγος; Mason 1974: 106-08). The other MSS read ὄντι στρατηγῷ ("being governor"; στράτηγος means, among other things, "governor of a province," Rengstorf *s.v.*). The one reading can easily have resulted from the other by an exchange of the first letters α and ο (in either direction).

[2915] It is not immediately clear which period is meant by Josephus. If the adverb "previously" links up with *Ant.* 15.404 (concerning Herod storing the high priestly robe in the Antonia), *Ant.* 15.408 would refer to the period before Herod's rule. If the word is connected with the immediate context (15.407), it has to refer to the period before Claudius granting the Jews themselves the custody of the high priestly garments, probably to Vitellius' concession (see 15.405 with the note to "under their own authority" and 15.406 with the note to "in the Antonia").

[2916] I.e., the robe of the High Priest (see *Ant.* 15.406 and 18.93).

[2917] The seal guaranteed that the robe remained in its protected place until it was removed by those entitled to do so, as the continuation of the narrative indicates; the seal assured the priests that nobody had touched the high priestly robe while being stored (cf. the subsequent reference to the treasurers inspecting the seal before picking up the robe). The sealed storage place may also have been important to the Romans by ensuring that the robe was not taken elsewhere (cf. Longinus' fear that the Jews would revolt because of Fadus' request to bring the high priestly robe and tunic under the Romans' control, *Ant.* 20.7). Dan 6:17 describes a similar purpose for King Darius' seal (an imprint of the king's signet ring in clay); it prevented that someone would open the lion's den (and interfere with Daniel's punishment) before the king ordered to open it.

[2918] The parallel passage found in *Ant.* 18.93 has a slightly different formulation and refers to the seal of the priests (ὑπὸ σφραγῖδι τῶν τε ἱερέων).

[2919] Likewise in *Ant.* 18.93. Josephus refers here to the treasurers (γαζοφύλακες) of the Temple, who were of priestly decent (11.136) and in charge of the treasury of the Temple (τὸ γαζοφυλάκιον, Neh 10:38; 1 Macc 14:49; 2 Macc 3:6; John 8:20). In Herod's Temple the treasury, which consisted of a cluster of magnificent storage rooms, was located on the north side of the Court of the Women (*War* 5.200; cf. *Ant.* 19.294; *m. Šeqal.* 6.5-6).

[2920] For the treasurers, see the previous note. *Ant.* 18.94 indicates, with similar vocabulary, that the robe was removed from its storage 7 days before one of the main festivals and on the Day of Atonement (see *Ant.* 15.404 with the note to "under the supervision of the Romans").

[2921] Until the First Jewish-Roman War one auxiliary Roman force was stationed in Judea, recruited from non-Jewish local inhabitants, e.g., from Samaria and Caesarea Maritima (Schürer-Vermes 1.362-67). One cohort was stationed in Jerusalem, with a tribune or commander of 1,000 (χιλίαρχος) as its commander (*War* 2.11, 224; John 18:12; Acts 21:31; see Mason in BJP 1b on *War* 2.224 with the note to "cohort"). This commander is probably identical with the φρούραρχος ("commander of a garrison") mentioned here and in *Ant.* 18.93-95 (Schürer-Vermes 1.366). Since the Antonia Fortress was the quarters of this cohort (*War* 5.244), the present sentence may imply that the robe was stored in the Antonia, as it had been during Herod's rule.

[2922] *Ant.* 18.94 indicates that the commander of the garrison returned the robe to the priests and treasurers before the festivals (see *Ant.* 15.404 with the note to "Romans"). The robe was then purified, before the High Priest put it on.

[2923] *Ant.* 18.94 mentions with partially the same vocabulary (τῆς ἑορτῆς and αὖθις) that the High Priest himself returned the robe.

garrison a seal that matched.[2925] **409** Now these matters were mentioned in passing[2926] because of the painful experiences[2927] that happened later.[2928]

At that time,[2929] when Herod, the King of the Jews,[2930] had made this fortress[2931] stronger for the security and protection of the Temple,[2932] he named it Antonia,[2933] doing a favor for Antony,[2934] who was his friend[2935] and ruler of the Romans.[2936] **(11.5) 410** In the western section[2937] of the precinct[2938] stood four gates.[2939] One led to the palace[2940] and, traversing

---

[2924] Josephus does not specify the location, but the reference to the commander of the Roman garrison stationed in Jerusalem may imply that it concerns the Antonia (see *Ant.* 15.404, 407 with notes), in contradistinction to 18.93-94 referring to a stone building apparently different from the Antonia (see 15.404 with the note to "under the supervision of the Romans" and 15.406 with the note to "Antonia").

[2925] In the light of the previous information this description implies that a new seal, identical to the previous one, was attached to the storage place to guarantee that the robe would remain in its place.

[2926] With this sentence Josephus rounds off the digression found in *Ant.* 15.404-409 about the storage of the high priestly garments.

For the verb παραδηλόω (meaning, among other things, "mention in passing"), see 15.103 with the note to "intimating."

[2927] The excursus of *Ant.* 15.404-409 indicates that the authority over the high priestly garments was very important to the Jews and their leaders (see 15.405, 407 with notes), such that the switch from Jewish to Roman authority—as described in the previous paragraphs—must have been painful for them, which engenders the translation "painful experiences"; the noun πάθος can have many nuances (Rengstorf *s.v.*). Other renditions of πάθος that fit the context well are "disaster, misfortune," meanings which occur several times elsewhere in the Herod narrative of *Antiquities* (e.g., 15.57, 142).

[2928] Landau (2006: 169) characterizes this passage as a short intervention creating anticipation and suspense. Josephus reveals the most important aspects of these events in the summary found in *Ant.* 15.404-409. He deals more elaborately with them in 18.92-95 and 20.6-14, i.e., at the proper places (according to a chronological order).

[2929] With this time marker Josephus returns to the description of Herod's renovation of the Temple, focusing once again on the Antonia, which has been mentioned already in *Ant.* 15.403.

[2930] The royal title ὁ τῶν Ἰουδαίων βασιλεύς Ἡρώδης links up with Herod's title mentioned in *Ant.* 15.404 (Ἡρώδης ὁ βασιλεύς). The 2 titles together form an *inclusio* concerning the digression about the High Priest's garments.

[2931] The expression "this fortress" refers back to the fortress mentioned in *Ant.* 15.403. Josephus uses the common noun βᾶρις ("fortress"), which at the same time also alludes to the "Baris" Fortress (later renamed "Antonia"; see 15.403).

[2932] The protection of the Temple at its north side was Herod's most important security concern because that side lacked a natural protection (like the Kidron Valley on the east side) and a city wall (as a defense line). The plain located north of the Temple turned that side into the obvious place to start an attack on the Temple. The remark that the Antonia was to protect the Temple differs from the motif highlighted elsewhere that Herod constructed fortified places in order to protect himself from the Jewish people (e.g., *Ant.* 15.291, also 15.292, in which case the Antonia is mentioned as well, and 15.296, 298).

The combination of ἀσφάλεια and φυλακή ("security and protection") also occurs, in various contexts, in *War* 3.440; 5.484; *Ant.* 5.57, 90; 11.156; 14.169; 15.295.

[2933] See *Ant.* 15.292 with the note to "Antonia."

[2934] I.e., Mark Antony (see *Ant.* 15.5 with the note to "Antony"). In *War* 1.401; *Ant.* 18.92 Josephus likewise notes that the fortress was named Antonia as a token of Herod's friendship with Antony. The phrase χαριζόμενος ... Ἀντωνίῳ ("as a favor to Antony") also occurs in *Ant.* 14.383, concerning Octavian doing a favor to Antony in agreeing with Herod's appointment as king.

[2935] Mark Antony was actually Herod's "friend" (we would say "patron"; see *Ant.* 15.5 with the note to "Antony"). For Herod being a political "friend" of Antony, see 15.5 with the note to "the friends around him," and for other references to this friendship, *War* 1.386; *Ant.* 15.131, 162, 189; 18.92. At the same time this friendship was also a close personal relationship (15.161-162, 183, 189).

[2936] Mark Antony was one of the triumvirs following Julius Caesar's death and the most powerful Roman official in the East during the years before the Battle of Actium (in 31 BCE; see *Ant.* 15.5 with the note to "Antony"). Braund (1984: 119 n. 65) notes that it is remarkable that Herod did not rename the fortress after Antony's defeat by Octavian. Herod apparently did not want to cover up his previous great loyalty to Antony (cf. also *War* 1.387-389; *Ant.* 15.187-196).

[2937] The viewpoint in the description switches from the north side of the Temple complex to its west side. The combination of ἑσπέριος and μέρος ("western section," here in the plural) also occurs in *Apion* 1.67

the ravine in the middle,[2941] provided a passage.[2942] Two others[2943] led to the suburb,[2944] and the remaining one[2945] to the rest of the city.[2946] It was distinct by the many steps going down[2947] to the ravine[2948] and from there uphill again.[2949] For the city lay opposite to the Temple,[2950] having the form of a theater[2951] and being surrounded by a deep ravine along

---

concerning the Ibyrians occupying a large section of the western world (τοσοῦτο μέρος τῆς ἑσπερίου γῆς).

[2938] The word περίβολος refers to the entire Temple complex here, as in *Ant.* 15.380 (see the note to "precinct") and 15.417 (cf. 15.420).

[2939] This description is confirmed by archaeological evidence (Netzer 2006: 172-73; Patrich 2009: 59-61). The gates can be identified (from north to south) as Warren's Gate, the gate above Wilson's Arch, Barclay's Gate, and the gate above Robinson's Arch (see the next notes).

[2940] This remark perhaps refers to Herod's palace in the western section of the city, at the location of the 3 towers Hippicus, Phasael, and Mariamme. The western and northern walls of that palace were incorporated into the city wall of the west side of Jerusalem. Netzer (2006: 172) argues that the palace meant is the Hasmonean palace, located opposite the Temple Mount, which is plausible since the text implies proximity between the gate (see the next note) and the palace.

[2941] The gate that gave access to the Hasmonean (or perhaps Herod's) palace has not been preserved. It was called the Coponius Gate in antiquity and located at the spot where the Gate of the Chain has been since the time of the Crusaders. The passageway connecting the Temple with the royal palace crossed the Tyropoeon Valley (the Valley of the Cheesemakers [see *Ant.* 15.318 with the note to "the Upper City"], *War* 5.140) to the west and south-west of the Temple complex. Remains of a viaduct are still visible at the place where a bridge ended in Herod's time. This bridge served as a major connection between the Temple and the Upper City (Netzer 2006: 172). The viaduct, dating from after 70 CE, is called Wilson's Arch after its discoverer, Sir Charles Wilson (Marcus-Wikgren 198 n. *a*).

[2942] The verb ἀπολαμβάνω ("take from, receive") in the passive voice probably has the not very common meaning "bridge, traverse" here (Rengstorf *s.v.*).

[2943] These 2 gates are Warren's Gate (the most northern gate, located 230 m north of the Temple Mount's southwest corner and ca. 50 m north of Wilson's Arch) and Barclay's Gate (located south of Wilson's Arch and ca. 80 m north of the Temple Mount's southwest corner, Netzer 2006: 172-73). Both gates were located in the lower parts of the outer wall, accessible to pedestrians walking down the shop-lined avenue (see the next note). Warren's Gate was already damaged in antiquity, but the corridor leading directly up from it to the paved square around the sanctuary is still extant. It was 5.5 m wide and ca. 26 m long and contained a flight of stairs, following the slope eastward up to the Temple platform (Netzer 2006: 172). Barclay's Gate gave access to the square around the sanctuary through a corridor being 5.8 m wide. After ca. 21 m heading east from the gate, it continues southward for more than 13 m. The huge monolithic lintel (7.5 m long and 2.1 m high) above the gate has survived and can still partly be seen near the southeastern corner of the western wall (Patrich 2009: 59-60 with illustration 32).

[2944] Archaeological evidence confirms that both gates, being lower than the ones at Wilson's and Robinson's Arches, opened on to the lower avenue with shops that ran along the western wall of the Temple complex (Patrich 2009: 59-60 with a drawing), which avenue led from the city to the suburb (τὸ προάστειον) of Bezetha, located north of the city wall in Herod's time (Simons 1952: 58).

[2945] I.e., the gate above Robinson's Arch, which was 15.5 m wide (Ritmeyer 2006: 46) and located directly opposite the west end of the Royal Portico (see *Ant.* 15.411). The arch known as Robinson's Arch was a huge monumental stairway that connected the Temple complex with the avenue that ran along the foot of the western wall. It was built on arches and included several shops.

[2946] The continuation of the description implies that Josephus is referring to the City of David on Mount Ophel, located south of the Temple (see also the next notes). The phrase ἡ ἄλλη πόλις ("the rest of the city, the other city") also occurs in *War* 5.335; 6.413; *Ant.* 20.165.

[2947] The stairs on Robinson's Arch first descended in a westerly direction and then made a turn to the south, going down to the Tyropoeon Valley.

[2948] I.e., the Tyropoeon Valley referred to a few lines earlier (as "the ravine in the middle").

[2949] In its southern direction the passage, after crossing the Tyropoeon Valley, went uphill again and provided access to the City of David. Sections of a Herodian street leading from Robinson's Arch to the Pool of Siloam (located in the very south of the City of David) have been excavated (Patrich 2009: 59, 62, 65).

[2950] Viewed from the western wall the main city was indeed situated opposite the Temple.

[2951] This is another example of a *simile* that helps the reader to imagine the specifics of a location described by Josephus (cf. the comparison of Gamla with the back of

the entire southern side.²⁹⁵² **411** Its fourth side²⁹⁵³ had its face to the south and it had gates²⁹⁵⁴ in the middle. On it stood the Royal Portico,²⁹⁵⁵ which had three sections,²⁹⁵⁶ running in length²⁹⁵⁷ from the eastern ravine²⁹⁵⁸ to the western [ravine].²⁹⁵⁹ It was not possible to extend it further.²⁹⁶⁰ **412** This work was the most remarkable²⁹⁶¹ of those under the sun.²⁹⁶² For the difference in height with the ravine was huge,²⁹⁶³ and for someone who

---

a camel in *War* 4.5 and that of Herodium with a woman's breast in *Ant.* 15.324; see the note there to "form of a breast"). The comparison makes sense if the Temple is seen as the stage of the theater. The adjective θεατροειδής ("theatric," Rengstorf *s.v.*) is a *hapax legomenon* in Josephus, but the word does occur in non-Jewish contemporary authors (Posidonius, *FGH* 87 F 70; Diodorus 2.10.2; 16.76.2; 19.45.3; 20.83.2; Strabo 4.1.4; 9.3.3; 14.2.15; 16.2.41).

²⁹⁵² This ravine is the Hinnom Valley, located south of Jerusalem. The phrase βαθεῖα φάραγξ ("deep ravine") also occurs in *Ant.* 15.398, referring to the Kidron Valley.

²⁹⁵³ Josephus does not refer explicitly to the 3 other sides in the previous paragraphs, but he does move from the east part of the sanctuary (*Ant.* 15.401) to the north side (15.403), and from the north side to the west section (15.410). When he now switches to the south side, he comes to the fourth side according to his changes of perspective. The alliteration of the *m* sound in this sentence (μέτωπον ... μεσημβρίαν ... μὲν ... μέσον) perhaps highlights the magnificent construction of the south side, with its extensive layout of stairs, plazas, and gates (see the next note). Its gates constituted the main entrance to the Temple, through which thousands of pilgrims reached the Temple during the 3 main holidays (see 15.404 with the note to "Romans").

²⁹⁵⁴ Josephus does not specify the number of the gates in the southern Temple wall. *M. Mid.* 2.2 and archeological data indicate that there were 2 (the so-called Huldah Gates): the Double Gate (ca. 12 m wide) lies ca. 110 m east of the southwest corner of the Temple complex, and the Triple Gate (measures unknown Ritmeyer 2006: 77 gives 51 ft [ca. 15.5 m] for the present Triple Gate and states [p. 79]: "Its present width is greater than that of the Double Gate and may reflect, as we shall see, that of the original Herodian gate"; he proposes 50 ft [ca. 15.1 m] for Herod's gate [p. 79]) ca. 90 m west of the southeast corner. Netzer (2006: 174) argues that both gates were originally double gates and that the east gate received a third opening in the Middle Ages. Ritmeyer (2006: 79-80) argues that Herod built a double and a triple gate (i.e., the current Triple Gate), because the latter gate is wider than that of the Double Gate and therefore this gate has to have been a triple gate from its origin onward. From both gates underground passages with decorated ceilings gave access to the precinct; the 2 underground corridors of the Double Gate were separated by a colonnade. In front of the gates, plazas were located, which were constructed on top of a large fill. Two broad stairways led up from the plazas to the gates. The one leading to the Double Gate was ca. 65 m wide and the one to the Triple Gate ca. 15 m. Remains of the staircase leading up to the Double Gate can still be seen (Netzer 2006: 173-75; Patrich 2009: 59-66).

²⁹⁵⁵ The Royal Portico has already been mentioned in *Ant.* 15.393 (see the note to "the Royal Portico").

²⁹⁵⁶ Netzer (2006: 166-67) and Patrich (2009: 62) conclude that the portico's structure was similar to that of a Roman civil *basilica* (further references in *Ant.* 15.393 with the note to "the Royal Portico"). The adjective τριπλοῦς ("threefold") occurs once elsewhere in Josephus (*War* 3.262, in a very different context).

²⁹⁵⁷ The portico was constructed along the southern wall from the west to the east corners (as the next phrases also indicate) since the 2 ravines mentioned ran adjacent to the southwest and southeast corners.

²⁹⁵⁸ This ravine (φάραγξ) is the Kidron Valley (see *Ant.* 15.398 with the note to "a deep ravine runs").

²⁹⁵⁹ Josephus mentions this ravine (i.e., the Tyropoeon Valley) also in *Ant.* 15.410 (see the note to "the ravine in the middle" and cf. the repetition of the adjective ἑσπέριος ["western"] in 15.410-411).

²⁹⁶⁰ The 2 ravines, which were quite steep at the portico's location, made an extension of the portico very difficult, if not impossible.

²⁹⁶¹ This superlative links up with similar vocabulary concerning the Temple (see *Ant.* 15.380, 384; for similar superlative references to other buildings of Herod, cf. 15.268, 296-298, 318).

The rare adjective ἀξιαφήγητος ("remarkable," literally "worth speaking of," Rengstorf *s.v.*) is a *hapax legomenon* in Josephus. There are a few occurrences in non-Jewish authors, from a (slightly) later period (e.g., Appian, *Bell. civ.* 4.3.16; Athenaeus 2.1.75; Cassius Dio 48.50.4; 63.3).

²⁹⁶² The Royal Portico, which was accessible to Jews and non-Jews alike, was probably the most magnificent secular building of Herod (Netzer 2006: 170). Josephus uses the same phrase τῶν ὑφ' ἡλίῳ ("of those under the sun") in *War* 2.365 concerning the Greeks being the most noble persons on earth: "They (i.e., the Hellenes), who take first place in nobility of all those under the sun" (trans. Mason in BJP 1b; cf. 2.380). With a slightly different phrase (τῶν ὑπὸ τὸν ἥλιον), Josephus interprets

would hang over the top[2964] it would be unbearable to look down[2965] from above to the bottom. The portico rose up from it[2966] at a huge height, such that if someone would take a look[2967] from the peak of its roof,[2968] combining both depths, he would become dizzy[2969] because his view would not reach the bottom,[2970] which was immeasurably deep.[2971] **413** Four[2972] rows of columns were standing opposite each other;[2973] the fourth row[2974] was connected to a stone-built[2975] wall.[2976] The thickness of each column comprised about the measure of three persons with their outstretched arms joining each other,[2977] but the height

---

Balaam's oracle in *Ant.* 4.115 as a prophecy that the Israelites may become the happiest people on earth (see also 8.49; 18.46; for further references about the sun and being under the sun in Josephus, see Mason in BJP 1b on *War* 2.128).

The phrase "those under the sun" is perhaps an allusion to the Book of Ecclesiastes (Qohelet), which includes ca. 25 expressions containing the words "under the sun" (ὑπὸ τὸν ἥλιον, e.g., Eccl 1:3, 9, 14; 2:3, 11), which vocabulary in the Bible is peculiar to this book. It refers to all kinds of sublunary things and is paralleled by the expressions "under heaven" (1:13; 2:3; 3:1) and "upon the earth" (8:14, 16; 11:2). However, such an allusion to Ecclesiastes is far from certain; non-Jewish authors also use this phrase (already Homer, *Il.* 4.44; 5.267; *Od.* 2.181; 11.498, 619; 15.349; Euripides [*Alc.* 151] characterizes Alcestis, who sacrifices her life for her husband Admetus, as the noblest woman by far under the sun [γυνή τ' ἀρίστη τῶν ὑφ' ἡλίωι μακρῶι]).

[2963] The difference in height between the top of the Royal Portico and the bottom of the southern wall of the precinct bordered by both ravines must have been huge. Netzer (2006: 162) notes that the construction of the 2 southern corners was an enormous job. He calculates that the southwestern corner was founded on bedrock ca. 31.5 m below the level of the platform on which the sanctuary was standing, and the southeastern ca. 41.5 m below it. The height of the portico still has to be added to these measures (i.e., more than 15 m on the side and more than 30 m in the middle; see *Ant.* 15.415 with notes).

[2964] Josephus changes the viewpoint to someone standing on the edge of the portico and looking straight down, highlighting in this way the heights of the portico and the wall below it. The verb εἰσκύπτω ("lean over, bend forward," Rengstorf *s.v.*) is a *hapax legomenon* in Josephus. Instead of εἰσκύπτοι MSS AM read ἐκκύπτοι ("peeped out of," Niese 407), which reading does not change the meaning much and can easily have resulted from εἰσκύπτοι. The verb ἐκκύπτω does not occur elsewhere in Josephus (Rengstorf *s.v.*), but it is found in writings with which Josephus shows affinities (LXX, 1 Maccabees, Diodorus, Strabo, Philo, and Plutarch).

[2965] Being unable to look down because of the height can easily be associated with a dizzying effect or fear of height (see the continuation of this paragraph).

[2966] I.e., from the bottom.

[2967] It is remarkable that Josephus once again invites the reader to look down from the top of the Royal Portico (likewise again via a phrase introduced by εἴ τις ["if someone"] followed by a verb in the optative mood), but this time he describes the consequences more elaborately than in the previous sentence. The verb διοπτεύω ("look down," Rengstorf *s.v.*) is a *hapax legomenon* in Josephus.

[2968] The Greek text given by Niese (407, ἀπ' ἄκρου τοῦ ταύτης τέγους) is understandable but strange and probably corrupt. Richards and Shutt (1937: 174) conjecture ἀπ' ἄκρας τοῦ τρίτου τέγους ("from the top of the third roof") on the basis of the Latin version.

[2969] The verb σκοτοδινιάω ("be overcome by dizziness," Rengstorf *s.v.*) is a *hapax legomenon* in Josephus (cf. Philo, *Ios.* 142; *Opif.* 71; *Spec.* 1.38).

[2970] The word βυθός ("depth, bottom") is repeated from the previous sentence.

[2971] In *Ant.* 15.413-415 Josephus provides details about the measures of the Royal Portico.

[2972] The adjective τέτραρχα ("fourfold," Rengstorf *s.v.*) is a *hapax legomenon* in Josephus.

[2973] The adjective ἀντίστοιχος ("ranged opposite in rows, standing over against," LSJ *s.v.*; Rengstorf *s.v.*) is a *hapax legomenon* in Josephus.

[2974] Niese (407) reads στοῖχος ("row of columns," Rengstorf *s.v.*) with MS L, while all the other Greek MSS read τοῖχος ("wall," which noun also occurs in *Ant.* 15.416 and other passages in Josephus). The noun στοῖχος is a *hapax legomenon* in Josephus, but it fits the context much better than the word τοῖχος (which reading must have resulted from the omission of the σ, either by accident or because τοῖχος is the more common word in Josephus).

[2975] The adjective λιθοδόμητος ("built of stone," Rengstorf *s.v.*) is a *hapax legomenon* in Josephus.

[2976] There were 3 freestanding rows; the fourth row concerned columns built into the south wall of the Temple precinct (Netzer 2006: 166).

[2977] The diameter of the columns was, according to Josephus' information, ca. 5.55 m. The noun ὀργυιά (literally "the length of the outstretched arms," LSJ *s.v.*; see also *War* 1.411; *Ant.* 15.334) indicates a measure that equals 6 ft (ca. 1.85 m; see *Ant.* 15.334 with the note to

BOOK FIFTEEN   315

of them was twenty-seven feet,[2978] having a double rounded molding as base.[2979] **414** The number of all of them together was 162.[2980] Their capitals[2981] were fashioned artfully[2982] in the Corinthian style with carvings,[2983] which caused astonishment[2984] because of the magnificence of the ensemble.[2985] **415** Since there were four rows[2986] they created three separate spaces in between the porticoes.[2987] The two on the side were made in the same way; the width of each of them was thirty feet,[2988] their length a *stadion*,[2989] and their height more than fifty feet.[2990] The width of the one in the middle was one and a half[2991] times as

---

"twenty fathoms"). If the formulation is to be taken literally, it would emphasize the size of the columns clearly; it is very easy to imagine the size if one thinks of 3 persons standing with outstretched arms next to each other. However, this detail cannot be correct; Netzer (2006: 167-69) states that the diameter of the columns was 1.5 m (on the basis of the remains of the gates in the south wall and the proportions of the colonnades in other Herodian and Nabatean buildings) and that the intercolumniation (i.e., the measure at the bottom of the shaft from one heart of a column to another) was ca. 6 m. This number results with 40 columns per row in a total length of 240 m.

[2978] I.e., ca. 9 m if the foot (πούς), which was a common unit of length in antiquity, equals ca. 30 cm in Josephus (see *Ant.* 15.334-335 with the note to "fifty feet"). Netzer (2006: 167) argues that the number should be corrected to 47 ft (ca. 15.7 m) since it does not match the classical proportions (45-50 ft) nor the height of the aisles given by Josephus ("more than fifty feet"). Many of the other measures of the Temple are given in cubits (see, e.g., *Ant.* 15.385, 391-392). Schalit (2001: 381-82) concludes that Josephus exaggerates some of the measures of the Royal Portico.

[2979] The translation is based upon the reading ὑπειλημμένης of MSS FL, a perfect passive participle from ὑπολαμβάνω. The verb can mean "bear up, support" (LSJ *s.v.* I.1b). Josephus uses a similar participle of this verb in *Apion* 1.162 (in a different context). Niese (407) conjectures ὑπειλημένης, a participle from the rare verb ὑπειλέομαι ("creep under," LSJ *s.v.*; "to run underneath," Rengstorf *s.v.*), which verb would be a *hapax legomenon* in Josephus. This conjecture implies a slight change of the reading of MSS FL and seems to be unnecessary.

[2980] Netzer (2006: 167) argues that the actual number of the columns was 160 since the 4 rows suggest that the total number of the columns was divisible by 4.

[2981] The noun κιονόκρανον ("capital [of a column]," Rengstorf *s.v.*) occurs twice elsewhere in Josephus (*Ant.* 3.109-110, referring to the capitals of the bronze shafts of the tabernacle).

[2982] The verb ἐπεξέργαζω ("fashion artfully," Rengstorf *s.v.*) is a *hapax legomenon* in Josephus.

[2983] The Corinthian style was one of the common types of architecture in antiquity, together with the Doric and Ionic orders. Corinthian-style capitals of columns (i.e., the space between the shaft and the abacus) were the most ornate, with their typical vegetal shape consisting of a bell-shaped molding (*echinus*) adorned with spirals and vegetal motifs; acanthus leaves reached up the bell to cover the capital (Biers 1980: 200-02; Wilson Jones 1989; 1991). The noun γλυφή ("sculpture, carving") also occurs in *Ant.* 15.416 as well as in 19.7 (concerning sculptures of Greek temples) and 19.185 (concerning a gem with Caligula's image).

[2984] The phrase ἔκπληξιν ἐμποιέω ("cause perplexity/consternation/admiration") also occurs in *Ant.* 15.261, in a different context. Cf. the 7 pyramids built by the Hasmonean Simon for his parents and brothers, which were "made as to excite wonder by their size and beauty (εἰς ἔκπληξιν μεγέθους τε ἕνεκα καὶ κάλλους πεποιημένας)" (13.211, trans. Marcus; see also 7.176; 8.170).

[2985] This links up with the superlatives in *Ant.* 15.412 (references in 15.411 at the note to "Royal Portico"). The noun μεγαλουργία ("great achievement, magnificence") also occurs in the description of Caesarea Maritima (15.332), a further impressive specimen of Herod's building projects.

[2986] Likewise in *Ant.* 15.413.

[2987] The 4 rows of columns create 3 spaces from the perspective of the longitudinal axis.

[2988] Ca. 10 m (see *Ant.* 15.413 with the note to "feet").

[2989] Ca. 185 m (see *Ant.* 15.168 with the note to "stades"). The actual length of the portico must have been more. Netzer (2006: 167, 169) calculates that it was close to 240 m (see 15.413 with the note to "joining each other"). The Latin version attests 3 stades (Niese 407), but this does not match the length of the southern wall of the Temple precinct, which was ca. 280 m (see 15.381 with the note to "enterprise"). Josephus also refers to the stade (στάδιον) as a measure in 15.393, 400.

[2990] I.e., more than ca. 15 m (1 ft equals ca. 30 cm). Netzer (2006: 169) assigns 17 m to the overall height of the aisles.

[2991] The other 2 spaces being 30 ft wide, the middle one must have measured 45 ft (ca. 13.5 m). The adjective ἡμιόλιος ("one and a half," Rengstorf *s.v.*) is a *hapax legomenon* in Josephus.

much, and its height twice as much,[2992] as it rose much higher than those on each of its sides.[2993] **416** The ceilings[2994] were furnished with deeply cut[2995] woodcarvings[2996] in all kinds of forms,[2997] and the middle [ceiling] was raised to a higher height.[2998] The wall at the front[2999] was cut all around[3000] with architraves.[3001] It had embedded[3002] columns and was polished[3003] in its entirety, such that [the construction] was unbelievable[3004] to those who do not know it[3005] and was looked at with astonishment[3006] by those who happened to

---

[2992] I.e., more than 30 m. Netzer (2006: 169) gives 27 m as the overall height of the portico's central hall.

[2993] Netzer (2006: 169) tentatively suggests that there was a second level in the middle, created by rows of columns (ca. 9 m high) on top of the others. Through the open spaces between these columns plenty of light shone into the portico (Netzer 2006: 166). Resuming all the numbers given by Josephus, the portico was 105 ft (ca. 33 m) wide, 1 stade (ca. 185 m) long, and in the middle section more than 90 ft (ca. 27.7 m) high.

[2994] There are no remains of roof tiles from Herod's buildings. Netzer (2006: 169) assumes the roofs of the portico were flat (cf. Schalit 2001: 381-82 with n. 806 and 15.396 with the note to "building everything in proportion").

[2995] The translation is based upon the reading βαθυξύλοις of most MSS. The adjective βαθύξυλος ("with deep wood, deeply carved" [concerning coffered ceilings], LSJ s.v. [referring to this passage]; Rengstorf s.v.) is a *hapax legomenon* in Josephus. Niese (407) reads ξύλοις ("wood").

[2996] The plural γλυφαί ("carvings") also occurs in *Ant.* 15.414 (see the note to "carvings") concerning the portico's capitals in the Corinthian style.

[2997] There are no remains of the ceilings. Fragments found from other sections of the building were decorated with delicate *stucco* (Ben-Dov 1985: 124-25, and 126-27 for a drawing of the interior of the Portico; Netzer 2006: 170), such that the ceilings might have been as well.

[2998] For the meaning "raise" (i.e., "erect [a wall or a building]") of the verb ἐγείρω, see *Ant.* 15.296 with the note to "erect something new."

[2999] Josephus probably refers to the south side of the Royal Portico, a wall with built-in columns (located at the south wall of the Temple precinct, near the main gates). Netzer (2006: 169), however, concludes that this front wall is the wall on top of the first level of the Royal Portico, which was likewise a wall with built-in columns. The adjective προμετωπίδιος ("front-," Rengstorf s.v.) is a *hapax legomenon* in Josephus.

[3000] MSS FV read περιτετμημένου ("cut all around"), which seems to be the more difficult and therefore the preferable reading (with Marcus-Wikgren 202-03). Niese (407) follows the reading περιδεδομημένου ("built all around") of MSS PLAMW and MS F (a marginal reading). The verb περιδομέω does not occur elsewhere in Josephus (Rengstorf s.v.), while the verb περιτέμνω ("cut around, circumcise") is quite common. The one reading could easily have evolved into the other, especially in minuscule writing. The verb περιτέμνω is likely the original one since the participle ἐνδεδομημένους ("built in") attested a few lines later may have caused a change from περιτετμημένου into περιδεδομημένου.

[3001] The "architrave" (ἐπιστύλιον, Rengstorf s.v.) is the lintel or beam that rests on the capitals of columns. Josephus' formulation implies that there was a continuous architrave all around the portico. The word is a *hapax legomenon* in Josephus.

[3002] The verb ἐνδομέω ("build into," Rengstorf s.v.) is a *hapax legomenon* in Josephus.

[3003] A few other passages concerning Herod's building projects refer to hewn or polished (ξεστός) stone (see *War* 1.425; *Ant.* 16.148 concerning the main street of Antioch, where Herod provided a portico and polished marble for a length of 20 stades, also *Ant.* 15.324 about the stairs at Herodium).

[3004] The formulation is elliptical; it is unclear to what the plural ἄπιστα ("unbelievable") is referring.

[3005] The exceptional beauty of the south side of the Temple complex is further highlighted via rhetorical means making explicit what the effect was for 2 categories of people: those familiar with its magnificence (the persons mentioned later on in the sentence) and those who were not. Niese (407) reads τοῖς οὐκ εἰδόσι ("for those who do not know it") with the Greek MSS. Cocceius (followed by Naber 1888-96: 3.xlviii, 382; Marcus-Wikgren 202) conjectures τοῖς οὐκ ἰδοῦσι ("for those who did not see it"), which makes the entire statement even more coherent (note the correspondence between "those who did not see it" and "those who happened to see it"). Although the conjectured reading ἄπιστα τοῖς οὐκ ἰδοῦσι is paralleled by a few other passages (Agatharchides, *Mar. Erythr.* 35; Photius, *Bibl.* 250), it seems unnecessary here since the transmitted text makes perfect sense (for vocabulary similar to ἄπιστα τοῖς οὐκ εἰδόσι, cf. Hippolytus, *Haer.* 5.16.15).

[3006] The perplexity caused by the sight of the south side of the Temple complex is also highlighted in *Ant.* 15.414, which paragraph focuses on the columns of the Royal Portico (note the repetition of ἔκπληξις ["perplexity"] in 15.414, 416).

see it.³⁰⁰⁷ **417** Such was the first precinct.³⁰⁰⁸ In the middle,³⁰⁰⁹ at close distance, was a second [precinct],³⁰¹⁰ accessible through a few steps.³⁰¹¹ An enclosure³⁰¹² with a stone partition³⁰¹³ surrounded it, preventing foreigners³⁰¹⁴ from entering through an inscription³⁰¹⁵

---

³⁰⁰⁷ The adjective θεατός ("seen, observed," Rengstorf *s.v.*) is a *hapax legomenon* in Josephus.

³⁰⁰⁸ This formula indicates a further switch of perspective. From *Ant.* 15.402 to 15.416 the focus is on the outside of the Temple (as signaled by the word ἱερόν ["Temple"] in 15.402), describing it from the viewpoints going from the north/northwest side to the west and south sides. Hence this "first precinct" must be the entire precinct of the Temple (for the various meanings of περίβολος, see 15.380, 400 with notes). The phrase πρῶτος περίβολος ("first precinct, first surrounding wall") also occurs in *War* 4.204; 6.150 (in both cases referring to the Jerusalem Temple). This precinct was accessible to Jews and non-Jews alike.

³⁰⁰⁹ Schwartz (2013: 163-64 with footnote 120) connects the description of the inside of the Temple complex in *Ant.* 15.417-419 and the phrase "in the middle" (ἐν μέσῳ) with the idea that the Holy of Holies (located in the sanctuary of the Temple) was the holiest center of a series of concentric circles of holiness, as expressed in the Mishnah (*m. Kel.* 1.6-8). Other passages in Josephus also reflect this notion (*War* 5.207, 227; *Apion* 1.198; 2.102-104). In *Apion* 1.198 Josephus notes that the Temple was "roughly in the middle of the city" (κατὰ μέσον), which may quote Pseudo-Hecataeus and perhaps should be taken symbolically (Barclay in BJP 10 on *Ap.* 1.198). Similarly in *War* 5.207 Josephus indicates that the sanctuary was roughly in the middle of the Temple complex (ὁ ναὸς κατὰ μέσον κείμενος).

³⁰¹⁰ As Josephus explains in the next lines of this paragraph, this second precinct was an area accessible to Jews only. This court was surrounded by a balustrade called the *sôreg* in Hebrew (*m. Mid.* 2.3; see also *Ant.* 15.400 with the note to "the entire enclosed area"). It was higher than the level of the outer court (cf. *War* 5.187; Patrich 2011: 571 n. 30). According to the Mishnah it measured 500 x 500 cubits (ca. 222 x 222 m; Netzer 2006: 140). The sanctuary was located within this enclosure, but not exactly in its center. *M. Mid.* 2.1 indicates that the space south of the sanctuary, within this enclosure, was the largest. The east side of the enclosure probably consisted of the eastern wall of the Temple complex. Most scholars argue that the northern boundary aligned with the current northern edge of the platform on which the Dome of the Rock (the al-Haram ash-Sharif) is standing, and the western boundary with the western side of that platform (Netzer 2006: 176 with references). This enclosure was perhaps identical with the platform of 500 x 500 cubits created by the High Priest Simeon the Just (Simeon II), which was maintained by the Hasmoneans (Patrich 2009: 43, 47; 2011; Ritmeyer [2006: 146-64] discusses several other proposals concerning the location and history of the 500 x 500 cubits square).

³⁰¹¹ The vocabulary here echoes that found in *Ant.* 15.410 (cf. προσβατός ["accessible"] here with πρόσβασις ["ascending, access"] in 15.410; the word βαθμίς ["step"] occurs in both passages), and there is a close parallel in 19.216 (προσβατὸν ὀλίγαις βαθμῖσι, in a different context).

³⁰¹² The rare noun ἑρκίον ("enclosure, wall," Rengstorf *s.v.*), referring to the *sôreg* (see the note to "second [precinct]" above), is a *hapax legomenon* in Josephus (cf. Homer, *Il.* 9.476; *Od.* 18.102; Apollonius of Rhodes, *Arg.* 2.1073). The word is a diminutive of ἕρκος ("fence, enclosure"; cf. Philo of Byblos, *Verb. sign.* 61).

³⁰¹³ The noun δρύφακτος ("barrier, fence," Rengstorf *s.v.*) also occurs in *War* 5.193 (likewise together with the adjective λίθινος ["stone"], referring to the same barrier); 6.124 (in Titus' ironic reference to the barrier); *Ant.* 13.373 (about a wooden barrier around the altar and the sanctuary, put there at the order of Alexander Janneus). Cf. the related word τρύφακτος in the extant warning inscriptions of the Temple (see the note to "inscription" below and Llewelyn and van Beek 2011: 18). The barrier was constructed with pillars and stone plates. It was 3 cubits (ca. 1.35 m) high (*War* 5.194; Patrich 2009: 55).

³⁰¹⁴ In *War* 5.194 Josephus uses the word ἀλλόφυλος instead of ἀλλοεθνής when referring to these inscriptions (see the next note). These adjectives are a combination of ἄλλο- ("different") with -φυλος (deriving from φυλή ["tribe, nation"]) or -εθνής (deriving from ἔθνος ["people"]) and mean "foreign, belonging to a different people." The extant inscriptions (see the next note) use a different but closely related word (ἀλλογενής "of alien descent, non-Jew," Llewelyn and van Beek 2011: 17).

³⁰¹⁵ The *sôreg* bore inscriptions warning non-Jews that they were not allowed to enter the area (with the death penalty as the sanction; see the next note); they probably were located near the gates. Josephus refers elsewhere to these inscriptions (*War* 5.194; 6.125-126; cf. 4.182; *Ant.* 12.145; Philo, *Legat.* 212; Acts 21:26-29) and indicates there that the inscriptions were in Greek and Latin script. Epigraphic evidence confirms the existence of such inscriptions: 2 copies of the Greek inscription have been found (*CIIP* no. 2 [see I.1.42-45]; *CIJ* no. 400; *OGIS* no. 598; Llewelyn and van Beek

by threatening them with the death penalty.³⁰¹⁶ **418** The inner precinct³⁰¹⁷ had triple gateways³⁰¹⁸ in the southern and northern areas,³⁰¹⁹ standing at equal distances from each

---

2011), but no copies of the Latin one. The most complete inscription reads: "No foreigner is to enter within the balustrade (τρυφάκτου) and forecourt around (περιβόλου) the sacred precinct. Whoever is caught will himself be responsible for (his) consequent death (ἑαυτῶι αἴτιος ἔσται διὰ τὸ ἐξακολουθεῖν θάνατον)" (trans. Price in *CIIP*). It is unclear when the *sôreg* was constructed. Patrich (2011) argues that it was an innovation by Simeon the Just, which may have been triggered by Ptolemy IV's attempt to enter the Holy of Holies (see also the note to "a second [precinct]" above). Schürer-Vermes (1.175-76 with n. 6) doubt whether it existed before the time of Alexander Janneus (103-76 BCE).

³⁰¹⁶ The preserved text of the warning inscription (see the previous note) as well as *War* 6.126 indicate that the death penalty was the sanction put on the violation of this ban. Titus states in 6.126 that the Romans had given the Jews the authority to execute violators. The adjective θανατικός ("fatal," Rengstorf *s.v.*) occurs once elsewhere in Josephus (3.103 concerning laws that prescribe the death penalty).

³⁰¹⁷ The phrase ὁ ἐντὸς περίβολος ("the inner precinct"; cf. *War* 5.7: ὁ ἐνδότερος τοῦ νεὼ περίβολος "the inner enclosure of the sanctuary") can, by itself, refer to either the area enclosed by the *sôreg* (see the previous paragraph with notes) or to the inner court of the Temple complex (i.e., the area surrounding the sanctuary, containing the Court of the Women, the Court of Israel, and the Court of the Priests; see *Ant.* 15.419 with notes). The context implies that Josephus means the latter (as in *War* 5.7). The wall of this inner enclosure was 25 cubits (ca. 12 m) high, measured from the inside, and 40 cubits (ca. 18 m) high, measured from the outer court (*War* 5.196). This area also included the altar on which the animals were slaughtered (in front of the sanctuary; see *Ant.* 15.420), offices and porticoes on the north and south sides, and a walkway (the *ḥêl* in Hebrew) around the wall on the north, west, south, and (part of the) east sides of this area (Netzer 2006: 139-40 and see below). *War* 5.195-198 indicates that 14 steps were leading up from the second enclosure (i.e., the one surrounded by the *sôreg*) at a distance of 10 cubits (ca. 4.5 m) from the wall of the inner enclosure. There were 5 more steps in front of the 6 gates leading to the sanctuary (see the next note). The platform on which the sanctuary was standing (including the *ḥêl*) was 15 cubits (ca. 6.7 m) higher than the second enclosure (*War* 5.196).

³⁰¹⁸ There are variations among the readings of the MSS, but basically without significant differences in meaning. The translation is based on Niese's text τριστοίχους πυλῶνας (408), which probably implies that both the northern and southern walls around the sanctuary had 3 gates at equal distance from each other. Schalit (2001: 386 with n. 826) offers an alternative interpretation of τρίστοιχος ("triple"), each gateway having 3 entrances, the main one in the middle and 2 smaller ones on the sides. The 6 gates in the northern and southern walls of the inner enclosure were part of gatehouses. The portals expanded behind the entrances, which were huge. In *War* 5.202 Josephus states that each of them had 2 doors (θύραι) being 15 cubits wide and 30 cubits high (i.e., together 30 x 30 cubits, ca. 13.3 x 13.3 m). *M. Mid.* 2.3 gives 10 x 20 cubits as measures (ca. 4.5 x 9 m; Netzer 2006: 154-55). *M. Mid.* 1.4-5 lists these gates and names them (also mentioning the Nicanor Gate (*šaʿar niqqannôr*): House of the Hearth (*bêt hammôqēd*), Gate of Light (*šaʿar hannîṣôṣ*), Water Gate (*šaʿar hammāyim*), Fuel Gate (*šaʿar haddeleq*), Gate of the Sacrifice (*šaʿar haqqorbān*), and Gate of the First Born (*šaʿar habbĕkôrôt*). Netzer (2006: 158-59) wonders whether the last 3 gates ever served as entrances and argues that they were rather added to create a uniform and esthetically satisfying appearance. In *War* 5.200 Josephus indicates that there were no gates in the western wall and in 5.198-200 he provides different numbers for the gates in the northern and southern walls: there were 4 gates on each of the northern and southern sides of the inner precinct (i.e., 8 in total), 2 of which did not give access to the inner enclosure (the area directly around the sanctuary) but to the Court of the Women. This latter court lay in front of the entrance to the sanctuary, at its eastern side, being ca. 7.5 cubits (ca. 3.4 m) lower than the area of the inner enclosure (Netzer 2006: 156). In 5.198 Josephus indicates that the inner enclosure had 10 gates in total; in addition to the 8 gates mentioned above (on the northern and southern sides), there were 2 on the eastern side: the gate that gave access to the Court of the Women (the Beautiful Gate; see the note to "large gateway" below and *Ant.* 15.424 with the note to "its eastern gate") and the so-called Nicanor Gate (giving access to the Court of Israel from the Court of the Women). The 9 outer gates (i.e., not the Nicanor Gate), with their jambs and lintels, were plated in gold and silver donated by Alexander, the brother of Philo of Alexandria (further details in *War* 5.201-206; *Ant.* 18.259; Patrich 2009: 55).

³⁰¹⁹ For a similar phrase, cf. *Ant.* 15.410 (κατὰ ... τὸ νότιον κλίμα "along the southern side").

other.³⁰²⁰ There was one large gateway³⁰²¹ in the eastern area,³⁰²² which we, being clean,³⁰²³ used to enter together with our wives.³⁰²⁴ **419** Further within this precinct³⁰²⁵ was the sacred area,³⁰²⁶ which was inaccessible to women.³⁰²⁷ And deeper inside this precinct was a third

---

³⁰²⁰ The phrase ἀλλήλων διεστῶτας ("standing at equal distances from each other," Rengstorf *s.v.*) is paralleled by *War* 7.189 (ἀλλήλων ὀλίγῳ διεστῶτας, concerning 2 closeby hills near Baaras-Baaru, east of the Dead Sea).

³⁰²¹ It is not immediately clear to which gate this remark refers if it is to be connected with the final words of the paragraph. The "large gateway" may denote the gate that gave access to the Court of the Women (see below) or, more probably, the so-called Nicanor Gate. The Nicanor Gate was much larger than the other 9 gates and crafted from differing material, of Corinthian bronze (*War* 5.201; *m. Mid.* 2.3). It was named after a wealthy Alexandrian Jew, whose family tomb was found on Mount Scopus (Patrich 2009: 55). A semicircular flight of 15 stairs gave access to the Nicanor Gate (*m. Mid.* 2.5; Netzer 2006: 157). It formed the passage from the Court of the Women to the Court of Israel. Since women were usually not allowed to pass through this gate (*War* 5.199), whereas Josephus states at the end of this paragraph that Jewish women were allowed to pass through the relevant gate, scholars have concluded that Josephus is meaning the gate that gave access to the Court of the Women. This latter gate may be identical with the Beautiful Gate mentioned in Acts 3:2, 10. Spiess (1881: 74-75) emends the text so that it refers to both gates (likewise Schalit 2001: 390-91 with n. 842). However, given that the size of the gate is highlighted, Josephus is probably describing the Nicanor Gate and may simply have made a mistake concerning the access of the women (see also *Ant.* 15.419 with the note to "women").

³⁰²² Literally "in the direction of the sun beams" (κατὰ ἡλίου βολάς, Rengstorf *s.v.*), which echoes the vocabulary from tragic poets (especially Euripides, *Orest.* 1259; cf. Euripides, *Bacch.* 458; *Ion* 1134; Sophocles, *Aj.* 877; Lucian, *Anach.* 16).

³⁰²³ I.e., ritually clean (ἁγνοί). In *War* 5.227 and *Apion* 2.103 Josephus specifies that menstruating women were not allowed to enter the Temple. Men who had not completely purified themselves were not allowed to enter the inner precinct (*War* 5.227; *Apion* 2.104). In *War* 5.227 he adds that priests were also not allowed to enter that precinct if they had not recently undertaken a ritual cleaning, and in *Apion* 2.104 that the priests could enter the Priestly Court only if they were wearing their priestly vestments, and that the High Priest could enter the inner sanctuary only in the high priestly garments (see Bauckham 1996 and Barclay in BJP 10 on *Ap.* 2.103-

104). Even more specific is *m. Kel.* 1.6-9, which points to several levels of purity connected with differing areas of the Temple (see also *Ant.* 15.417 with the note to "in the middle"). No man suffering from spermatorrhoea (cf. Lev 15:1-18; Deut 23:10-11) and no woman being impure because of menstruation or childbirth were to enter the Temple. The area directly inside the barrier (see *Ant.* 15.418 with the note to "inner precinct") was inaccessible to the Gentiles and those unclean because of contact with a corpse. The Court of the Women was forbidden to those of "this day's immersed" (i.e., those who only after the last sunset had taken a ritual bath to purify themselves). The Court of the Israelites was forbidden to those who were "un-atoned" (i.e., those who had not made the sacrifice prescribed in the case of an offence; Schürer-Vermes 2.285 n. 58; Bauckham 1996: 330). For a detailed discussion of the differences between *Ant.* 15.418-419, *Apion* 2.102-104, and *m. Kel.* 1.6-9 concerning the restrictions on entering the various areas of the Temple, see Bauckham 1996: 328-34.

³⁰²⁴ If this detail is correct, Josephus is referring to the Court of the Women (see the note to "large gateway" above). This court was a square, enclosed forecourt attached to the inner enclosure's eastern side (see the next note). According to the Mishnah (*m. Kel.* 1.8; *m. Mid.* 2.5) it measured 135 x 135 cubits (ca. 60 x 60 m). It had 4 segregated areas of 40 x 40 cubits at the corners, used for various purposes connected with the sacrificial cult, and was entered through 3 gates: one at the northern, one at the southern, and one at the eastern side. The Nicanor Gate at the western side connected the Court of the Women with the Court of Israel (Netzer 2006: 140, 160; see also the notes to "triple gateways" and "one large gateway" above).

The name "Court of the Women" is somewhat misleading since the Jewish men also came to this court for various sacrificial purposes and had to cross this court on the way to the Court of Israel and the Court of the Priests.

³⁰²⁵ Josephus is referring to the inner precinct mentioned in *Ant.* 15.418, i.e., the area surrounding the sanctuary (including the Court of Israel and the Court of the Priests; see the next notes).

³⁰²⁶ In calling the area of the inner enclosure "the sacred area" (τὸ ἱερόν), Josephus implies that this area was more sacred than the other parts of the Temple complex. In *War* 5.207 he calls the sanctuary "the holy sacred area" (τὸ ἅγιον ἱερόν; for the idea of increasing levels of sacredness, see *Ant.* 15.417 with the note to "in

precinct,[3028] into which only the priests were allowed to enter.[3029] The sanctuary[3030] was within this [precinct][3031] and in front of it was an altar,[3032] on which we used to bring the burnt offerings to God.[3033] **420** King Herod[3034] passed into none of these three [areas]:[3035]

---

the middle" and 15.418 with the note to "clean").

[3027] Since the next description concerns the area deeper inside the precinct, accessible only to the priests, Josephus is probably referring to the Court of Israel here (called ăzārat yiśrā'ēl in Hebrew; see *Ant.* 15.400-401 with notes and the next note). Women were allowed to enter this area for specific reasons. After childbirth they sacrificed burnt and sin offerings there (*t. 'Arak.* 2:1; cf. Luke 2:24; Schürer-Vermes 2.261 with n. 11). Women who wanted to bring a thank-offering (in Hebrew *šelem*, plural *šᵉlāmîm*), a voluntary offering (*nᵉdābâ*), or a burnt offering (*'ōlâ*), or who desired to make a nazirite vow, had to perform this in person in the relevant court. They also entered the court for prayer and penitence. There was a special gate giving them access to it, called the Women's Gate (*m. Mid.* 2.6; *m. Šeqal.* 6.3; I owe these references to Prof. J. Patrich, Jerusalem).

[3028] The number "third," together with the reference to the priests further on in the sentence, confirms that Josephus is referring to the 3 distinct, well-known, enclosed areas near the sanctuary: the Court of the Women, the Court of Israel, and the Court of the Priests. The latter court (called *ăzārat hakkōhănîm* in Hebrew) was part of the open space surrounding the sanctuary, which area on its eastern side included 2 roofed strips with porticoes: one for the priests and the other for the Jewish men (i.e., the Court of Israel). Both strips were 11 cubits (ca. 5 m) wide (see *Ant.* 15.401 with the note to "a double portico"). Most parts of the Court of the Priests were only accessible to priests and Levites. It was located on the highest point of the Temple Mount, on a square platform built partly on the bedrock and partly on the fills. It was ca. 3.5 m higher than its surroundings. According to *m. Mid.* 2.6 the court measured from its western to its eastern sides 187 cubits (ca. 83.5 m) and from its northern to its southern sides 135 cubits (ca. 60 m). The main part of the court was located in front of the sanctuary, at its eastern side (an area of 135 x 76 cubits, ca. 60 x 34 m). The 6 gatehouses at the northern and southern walls (see *Ant.* 15.418 with the note to "triple gateways") occupied considerable space within the court. Offices and porticoes were built between the gatehouses (*War* 5.200; further details in Netzer 2006: 138-42, 153-55; Patrich 2009: 55).

[3029] This confirms that Josephus is referring to the Court of the Priests (see the note to "third precinct" above).

[3030] Josephus briefly returns to the sanctuary (ὁ ναός; for the vocabulary, see *Ant.* 15.380 with the note to "sanctuary"), which he describes in greater detail in 15.392-395.

[3031] I.e., the inner enclosure of the Court of the Priests. The words "the sanctuary was within this [precinct]" (ὁ ναὸς ἐν τούτῳ) are missing in the important MS P as well as in the Latin version. Niese (408) doubts whether the words were part of the original text and puts them in square brackets, although he includes them without any further notice in his minor edition (326). The continuation of the sentence (καὶ πρὸ αὐτοῦ "and in front of it") implies that the words were part of the original text: they make sense if "it" refers to the sanctuary, in front of which the altar was standing; if "it" refers to the inner enclosure, they become problematic because the altar was inside of that enclosure (see also the next notes).

[3032] The altar was a square, stepped construction, 8 cubits (ca. 3.6 m) high. It measured 32 x 32 cubits (ca. 14.2 x 14.2 m) at its bottom and 26 x 26 cubits (ca. 11.6 x 11.6 m) at its top. It had horns at its 4 corners and was approached from the south via a ramp that was 34 cubits (ca. 15.1 m) long. The sacrificial animals were prepared and slaughtered at the north side of this platform (Netzer 2006: 154).

[3033] Burnt offerings are mentioned frequently in the Bible, but Josephus' exact vocabulary here (τὰς θυσίας ὁλοκαυτέω "burn the offerings completely, offer the burnt offerings," Rengstorf *s.v.*) does not occur in the LXX. A burnt offering (in Hebrew *'ōlâ*), sometimes also called a whole offering (*kālîl*), has an atoning function according to Lev 1 (cf. Exod 29:15-18): "You shall lay your hand on the head of the burnt-offering, and it shall be acceptable in your behalf as atonement for you" (Lev 1:4). The group of animals that were sacrificed as burnt offerings consisted of bulls, he-goats, rams, and doves. Their blood was splashed or poured out against the altar, and subsequently the corpses were burned (Miller 2000: 107-09). Exod 29:18 and Lev 1:9, 13, 17 both imply that burnt offerings were considered to be offerings whose fire spread an odor pleasing to God. In *Ant.* 9.155 (in connection with King David; cf. 10.53) Josephus indicates that the priests twice a day brought burnt and incense offerings.

[3034] About this title, see *Ant.* 15.402 with the note to "King Herod."

[3035] The context at first glance suggests that Josephus is referring to 3 courts (cf. the translation in Marcus-Wikgren 205: "Into none of these courts ..."—ignoring the word "three"): the Court of the Women, the Court of Israel, and the Court of the Priests (described in *Ant.*

not being a priest, he was prevented from doing so.³⁰³⁶ But he engaged himself in the construction work of the porticoes³⁰³⁷ and the outer enclosed areas³⁰³⁸ and built those in eight years.³⁰³⁹

(11.6) 421 When the sanctuary³⁰⁴⁰ had been built by the priests,³⁰⁴¹ in a year and five months,³⁰⁴² all of the people were filled with joy.³⁰⁴³ After they first brought thank-

---

15.418-419). However, the next sentence and the fact that Herod had access to the Court of Israel imply that the 3 areas mentioned in 15.419 are intended: the inner enclosure (i.e., the Court of the Priests), the sanctuary itself, and the area of the altar. This observation offers an additional reason to consider the phrase "the sanctuary was within this [precinct]" to be part of the original text (see 15.419 with the note to "this [precinct]").

³⁰³⁶ Unlike his Hasmonean predecessors Herod was neither a priest nor of royal descent (see *Ant.* 15.2 with the note to "commoner").

³⁰³⁷ The description of the Temple precincts switches here to a brief narration concerning the building process of the Temple (on the combination of narrative and descriptive passages in the section *Ant.* 15.380-425, see 15.380 with the note to "Now").

The areas that were accessible to Herod were renovated by the king himself according to this paragraph, which remark once again puts emphasis on Herod's personal involvement in the rebuilding of the Temple. The passage has been interpreted as evidence that Herod himself acted as an architect, but this is not necessarily the case (Roller 1998: 261 with n. 47). The relevant porticoes are the Royal Portico along the south wall of the Temple complex (15.393, 411-416) and the 3 double colonnades along its other exterior walls (15.396).

³⁰³⁸ The plural οἱ ἔξω περίβολοι ("the outer enclosed areas"; cf. *Ant.* 17.259: ὁ ἔξω περίβολος referring to the outer court of the Temple) probably denotes the outer court of the Temple complex as well as the area enclosed by the *sôreg*. Both areas are clearly distinguished in the previous description (for the outer court, see 15.417, and for the area enclosed by the *sôreg*, 15.400, 417). The construction of the outer court with its porticoes was a prominent part of Herod's Temple project.

³⁰³⁹ If Herod's 18th year, in which the building activities began (*Ant.* 15.380), corresponds to the year 20/19 BCE—as most scholars think (see the note to "the eighteenth year of Herod's rule") —the exterior parts of the Temple were completed in the year 12/11 BCE (i.e., Herod's 26th year).

³⁰⁴⁰ Josephus abandons the description of the Temple for a moment and focuses instead on the completion of the building activities and the festivities that accompanied it (*Ant.* 15.421-423).

Most of the area of the sanctuary (ὁ νεώς/ναός; see 15.380 with the note to "sanctuary") was inaccessible to non-priests (see 15.419 with notes), such that the priests themselves had to act as the builders. The order of presentation clearly suggests that the outer sections of the Temple complex were built first and the sanctuary afterwards. Some scholars suggest, however, that the work started with the sanctuary (Perowne 1956: 177, who refers to the worries of the population formulated in 15.388-389 that Herod would not complete the project and their joy here that it was completed so quickly; Günther 2005: 210-11; Schürer-Vermes [1.292 n. 12] mention this possibility). Other scholars conclude that both building projects overlapped (discussion in Mahieu 2012: 149-50; cf. Simons 1952: 399).

³⁰⁴¹ See the previous note.

³⁰⁴² Although Josephus does not say so explicitly, this note seems to imply that the entire renovation of the Temple complex was completed at that moment. The renovation took 9 years and 5 (or perhaps 6) months, if the number given here and the 8 years mentioned in 15.420 are to be added to each other. The combination with the reference to Herod's 18th year as the starting point for the building activities (*Ant.* 15.380) situates the completion of the work in Herod's 27th or 28th year (i.e., in the period 11-9 BCE; see also 15.420 with the note to "eight years"). Otto (1913: 81) dates the completion to 10 BCE, Schalit (2001: 372-73) to 9/8 BCE. Mahieu (2012: 147-52) proposes that the entire building project took 8 years and that it started in Herod's 15th regnal year, which results in 18/17 BCE as the year of the completion; other passages such as Marcus Agrippa's visit to Jerusalem in the autumn of 15 BCE, with his sacrifice of a hecatomb at the Temple (*Ant.* 16.12-15), and Herod's trip to Rome in 12 BCE, with the Temple being presented as having been built already (16.115), would suggest that the renovation of the Temple was already finished before these 2 events. Mahieu also argues that both the outer parts and the sanctuary were completed at the end of the 8 years (mentioned in 15.420) because there was only one festival that commemorated the completion of the Temple. This is not a compelling argument, however: other traditions about festivals commemorating the dedication or re-dedication of the Temple do not differentiate between a festival for the sanctuary and one for the rest of the Temple complex (see 15.422 with the note to "the king sacrificed three hundred oxen to God"); it is very well possible that the building of the sanctuary

offerings³⁰⁴⁴ to God³⁰⁴⁵ for the swiftness [of the renovation]³⁰⁴⁶ and afterwards also for the king's enthusiasm,³⁰⁴⁷ they feted and applauded³⁰⁴⁸ the restoration.³⁰⁴⁹ **422** And the king

---

took place after the rest of the building activities had been finished and that there was only one festival of commemoration, at the final completion. Smallwood (1976: 282 n. 89) argues that John 2:20 may indicate that the building activities were still ongoing 46 years after the work had started; only the main structures would have been completed during Herod's reign. *Ant.* 20.219 also indicates a much later date (see 15.390 with the note to "ten thousand").

Niese (408) reads καὶ μησὶν πέντε ("and five months") with MS P and the Latin version, while the other Greek MSS read καὶ μησὶν ἕξ ("and six months"), as Marcus-Wikgren (204) do. Niese's reading is preferable as the *lectio difficilior*: it is more probable that scribes changed "a year and five months" into "a year and six months" accidentally (assuming that the more round number of 1½ years was meant) than the other way around (see also Schalit 2001: 373 n. 776; Mahieu 2012: 157 n. 146).

³⁰⁴³ The people's joy is obvious; the rebuilding of the Temple was completed (see the previous note). Its reaction is somewhat ironic in view of its skepticism (described in *Ant.* 15.388) about Herod's enterprise.

For similar vocabulary (a passive form of πληρόω with a genitive of χαρά ["be filled with joy"]), cf. 2 Macc 3:30 concerning the Jerusalemites' response to God's punishment of Heliodorus, who tried to plunder the Temple: "And the temple ... was filled with joy and gladness (χαρᾶς καὶ εὐφροσύνης ἐπεπλήρωτο), now that the Almighty Lord had appeared" (cf. *War* 3.28, with an active form of πληρόω).

³⁰⁴⁴ Niese (408) reads τὰς εὐχαριστηρίους (from the adjective εὐχαριστηρίος "expressing gratitude," LSJ *s.v.*) instead of τὰς εὐχαριστίας (attested by MSS FLAMWV and followed by Marcus-Wikgren 204). Niese's reading is found only in MS P and has no parallels in Josephus' corpus. It is the *lectio difficilior*, but it has the disadvantage of being elliptical; it requires an additional noun in the plural, e.g., θυσίας ("sacrifices," resulting in a translation of τὰς εὐχαριστηρίους θυσίας like "the thank-offerings"). Such a noun is present in related phrases (Heliodorus 10.2.1; John Chrysostom, *Hom. Gen.* [PG 53.252]; see also the sacrifices described in *Ant.* 15.422). The reading τὰς εὐχαριστίας attested by the other Greek MSS (supported by the Latin version) is the *lectio facilior* and seems to be secondary; the rare phrase τὰς εὐχαριστηρίους was obviously adapted to a more common one (probably by accident, perhaps by omitting -ηρίους θυσ- in the phrase τὰς εὐχαριστηρίους θυσίας). The expression εὐχαριστίας ποιοῦμαι ("give thanks") is a *hapax legomenon* in Josephus, but it is common in Philo (*Spec.* 1.97, 144, 210, 229). A translation based on MSS FLAMWV may be: "They first brought thanks to God for the swiftness [of the renovation] and afterwards also for the king's enthusiasm, and then they feted and applauded the restoration."

³⁰⁴⁵ God is thanked first by the Jerusalemites, which matches Josephus' own view that God was responsible for Herod's success, as several other passages in the Herod narrative of *Antiquities* indicate (e.g., 15.373-374; cf. 1.20). God's role in the rebuilding is highlighted once again in the concluding paragraph of this section (see 15.425 with the note to "God in view").

³⁰⁴⁶ The matter that was swiftly executed is unspecified in the Greek text, but the context indicates that it concerns the rebuilding of the Temple. This links up with *Ant.* 15.388 expressing the population's fear that Herod would never finish his project.

³⁰⁴⁷ The phrase τῆς προθυμίας τοῦ βασιλέως (literally "[of/for] the eagerness of the king") is problematic; it does not connect well with the subsequent Greek words in this sentence. Several interpreters connect it with the verbal expression εὐχαριστίας ποιοῦμαι of MSS FLAMWV (see the previous notes), such that the people would have thanked God for both his swift action in the Temple renovation and Herod's enthusiasm for it, which means that God was responsible for Herod's acting. The variant reading τῇ προθυμίᾳ attested by MSS FLAMWV (probably an adaptation influenced by the preceding dative τῷ θεῷ) may denote that both God and Herod were thanked, God first. However, the Greek text does not really make sense this way: it is problematic to take προθυμία as the indirect object of τὰς εὐχαριστηρίους ποιοῦμαι or τὰς εὐχαριστίας ποιοῦμαι. It is also implausible to interpret the phrase τῆς προθυμίας τοῦ βασιλέως as the object of the participle ἑορτάζοντες since the verb ἑορτάζω usually goes with the accusative (LSJ *s.v.*).

³⁰⁴⁸ The verb κατευφημέω ("applaud, extol," LSJ *s.v.*; Rengstorf *s.v.*, who offers "to praise [/celebrate] with blessings [/with cries of joy?]" as meaning) is a *hapax legomenon* in Josephus and has only 17 occurrences attested in the TLG. It occurs, however, in several writings roughly contemporaneous with Josephus (*Let. Aris.*, 3 Maccabees, Dionysius, and 4 times in Plutarch). In 3 Macc 7:13 the verb occurs in the Jews' reaction to the Ptolemaic king's permission to destroy everywhere in his kingdom those who had transgressed the Law of God (7:12): "When they had applauded him (κατευφημήσαντες αὐτόν) in fitting manner, their

sacrificed three hundred oxen oxen to God,[3050] and the others[3051] [sacrificed animals] according to their means,[3052] the number of which is impossible to tell.[3053] For the capability of telling it according to the truth eludes us.[3054] **423** For[3055] that appointed day[3056]—in

---

priests and the whole multitude shouted the Hallelujah and joyfully departed" (7:13, trans. *NRSV*).

[3049] The noun ἀνάκτισις ("reconstruction, restoration," Rengstorf *s.v.*) is a *hapax legomenon* in Josephus. This is the oldest attested usage; the other occurrences appear in early and late-antique Christian literature.

[3050] Josephus does not specify what kind of sacrifice Herod offered. One could think of a thank-offering, which seems appropriate and also fits the context. Thank-offerings are described in Lev 7:12-18; 22:18-30 (see also Ps 22:22 with the reference to the midst of the congregation). However, since they were basically individual sacrifices (although performed in a public setting; Miller 2000: 104-05, 118-21, 129), it is preferable to interpret Herod's sacrifice in line with the tradition of the (Israelite or Judean) kings offering a sacrifice during a (re-)dedication of the Temple, usually during a festival (Pesach, Sukkot, or Hanukkah). Solomon set the trend during the dedication of the First Temple. 1 Kgs 8:62-64 describes his sacrifices as follows: "(62) Then the king, and all Israel with him, offered sacrifice before the Lord. (63) Solomon offered as sacrifices of well-being (*šᵉlāmîm*; LXX: τὰς θυσίας τῶν εἰρηνικῶν) to the Lord twenty-two thousand oxen (βοῶν δύο καὶ εἴκοσι χιλιάδας) and one hundred twenty thousand sheep. So the king and all the people of Israel dedicated the house of the Lord. (64) The same day the king consecrated the middle of the court that was in front of the house of the Lord; for there he offered the burnt-offerings and the grain offerings and the fat pieces of the sacrifices of well-being, because the bronze altar that was before the Lord was too small to receive the burnt offerings and the grain offerings and the fat pieces of the sacrifices of well-being." 2 Chr 7:1-5 describes the same sacrifice, adding that fire came down from heaven consuming the burnt offering and that the glory of the Lord filled the Temple (7:1). Ezra 3:2-6 indicates that the High Priest Jeshua together with his fellow priests and Zerubbabel (the grandson of the Judean king Jehoiachin) rebuilt the altar and offered burnt offerings (*'ōlôt*; LXX: ὁλοκαυτώσεις; cf. also 1 Esd 1:1-22; 1 Macc 4:53; 2 Macc 10:3) during the dedication of the Second Temple. Burnt offerings consisted of bulls according to Lev 1:5 but of oxen according to *Ant.* 3.226. The number here of 300 oxen sacrificed by Herod is huge; however, it pales into insignificance when compared with the 22,000 oxen sacrificed by Solomon (1 Kgs 8:63; 2 Chr 7:5). Josephus' reference to Solomon's dedication of the Temple mentions 12,000 calves and 120,000 sheep (cf. also King Hezekiah sacrificing 70 oxen during Passover in *Ant.* 9.270).

[3051] I.e., the other Jews. The priests were obviously the officials to coordinate the sacrifices, but Josephus is contrasting the king, who paid for a lavish sacrifice, with the others (the non-kings, i.e., the people), who furnished only what they could. This passage may build on traditions concerning (re-)dedications of the Temple (see the previous note); the fact that both the king and the Jewish population are mentioned here as the ones who participate in the sacrifices is in line with these traditions: 1 Kgs 8:62-64 indicates that not only Solomon performed sacrifices during the dedication of the First Temple but also the rest of the people ("all Israel," i.e., "a great assembly, people from Lebo-hamath to the Wadi of Egypt …," 1 Kgs 8:65). 2 Chr 7:3-5 refers to "all the people of Israel" and "all the people" in addition to Solomon and "the priests" (7:1-2). 1 Macc 4:42, 52-56 refer to blameless priests sacrificing during the re-dedication of the altar, during which "all the people" worshiped and blessed God (4:55). In 2 Macc 10:1-8 this re-dedication is performed by "Maccabeus [i.e., Judas the Maccabee] and his followers" (10:1).

[3052] The Greek text of the subclause "and the others [sacrificed animals] according to their means" is elliptical: a verb is missing, and the article οἱ is dangling. The narrative does not specify the kind of animals; their categories and numbers plausibly varied at this occasion. Lev 1 describes the procedures concerning burnt offerings and mentions bulls, he-goats, rams, and doves as the animals that could be sacrificed as burnt offerings (see *Ant.* 15.419 with the note to "bring the burnt offerings to God").

[3053] The implication of this cliché is that the sacrifices brought by the other Jews were innumerable. For a similar statement concerning the number of the Israelites who stayed behind in Mesopotamia when Ezra and his fellows returned to Jerusalem, cf. *Ant.* 11.133.

[3054] The note that the sacrifices brought by the Jewish population were so high in number (see the previous note) that it is impossible to give the exact number can be connected with Josephus' aim to present a trustworthy and precise report of the events (*War* 1.3, 6, 9, 25-26; 7.454-455; *Ant.* 3.230; 8.56; 9.208; Mader 2000: 6-7).

The verb ἐκφεύγω means "elude" here (Rengstorf *s.v.*).

[3055] This paragraph explains why there were so many sacrifices (*Ant.* 15.422).

[3056] Josephus does not specify this day (but see the next 2 notes).

connection with the work on the sanctuary[3057]—and the day of the king's accession to the throne,[3058] which they celebrated customarily,[3059] fell on the same date.[3060] So because of both occasions a most notable feast was held.[3061] **(11.7) 424** There was also a secret passage[3062] built for the king, leading from the Antonia[3063] as far as the inner sacred area,[3064]

The noun προθεσμία ("time appointed beforehand, fixed date," Rengstorf *s.v.*) occurs 12 times in Josephus (8 times in the Herod narrative of *Antiquities*: 15.108, 378, 423; 16.136, 279, 282, 343, 348). Sometimes this word indicates the end of a period, as in the discussion between Herod and Manaemus about the duration of Herod's rule (15.377-378; see also 16.279, 282, 343).

[3057] The fact that the sanctuary is mentioned here specifically (ὁ ναός; see *Ant*. 15.380 with the note to "sanctuary") implies, together with the chronological order (see 15.421 with the note to "sanctuary"), that the sanctuary was finished last (for other opinions, see the same note). Josephus mentions in passing in 20.219 that the Temple renovation was only completed during the governorship of Albinus (62-64 CE).

[3058] Like the "appointed day," Josephus does not specify this day either. It is plausible to assume that it refers either to the day on which Herod was appointed king by the Romans or to the day on which he captured Jerusalem (Schürer-Vermes [1.287, 292 n. 12] opts for the latter possibility). The former is mentioned specifically as "the first day" of Herod's rule in *War* 1.285, in connection with a banquet given by Mark Antony: "On the first day of Herod's kingship (τὴν δὲ πρώτην Ἡρώδῃ τῆς βασιλείας ἡμέραν), Antony entertained [him] with a banquet" (trans. Sievers/Forte in BJP 1a). It is referred to in *Ant* 14.389 (τὴν πρώτην ἡμέραν τῆς βασιλείας ἡμέραν) in connection with festivities organized by Mark Antony. Mahieu (2012: 54-60, 67-68, 75-84) argues for 18 November as the day commemorating Herod's appointment (linking it to the New Year's Day of the Tyrian calendar) and for 5 March as the day commemorating his capture of Jerusalem. She considers the first option to be more probable for Herod's Temple dedication because the vocabulary here echoes that of the episodes describing Herod's appointment in Rome (2012: 152-53). It cannot be excluded, however, that the date celebrating Herod's accession was an invented day, simply because a day had to be chosen.

[3059] The day on which a king acceded to the throne was often a public holiday in the Hellenistic period (concerning the Ptolemaic kings, see the Memphis decree of 196 BCE commemorating the coronation of Ptolemy V Epiphanes, inscribed on the famous Rosetta Stone; Greek version in *OGIS* no. 90; *SB* nos. 8232 and 8299; *SEG* 8 nos. 463 and 784; 16 no. 855; 33 no. 1357; also Hölbl 1994: 73, 76; van Henten 2007b: 273-74).

Herod apparently followed this convention. Matt 14:6 and Mark 6:21 mention a holiday (γενέσια) of Herod Antipas, during which he gave a banquet for his courtiers, officers, and the leaders of Galilee. This day was either his actual birthday or, as some scholars think, the anniversary of his accession to the throne (Hoehner 1972: 160-61 with n. 5; Schürer-Vermes 1.346-48 with n. 26; Schwartz 2013: 16-18).

[3060] The festival commemorating the completion of the Temple construction was apparently set on Herod's accession day (i.e., probably on the day he was appointed king by the Romans; see the note to "throne" above).

[3061] Former completions or renovations of (parts of) the Temple had likewise been celebrated with festivals of dedication (e.g., the Festival of Hanukkah, celebrated from 25 Kislev until 2 or 3 Tevet, 1 Macc 4:59; 2 Macc 1:9, 18; 10:1-8). Such a celebration sometimes coincided with another festival. Thus the dedication of the First Temple followed the celebration of the Feast of Tabernacles (held from 15 until 22 Tishri, 2 Chr 7:8-10; cf. LXX 3 Kgs 8:65). Some 2 centuries later King Hezekiah invited all Israel and Judah, and Ephraim and Manasse, to participate in the Passover Festival in order to celebrate a purification and dedication of the Temple (2 Chr 30:1). This Passover Feast did exceptionally not take place in the month of Nisan but during 2 cycles of 7 days starting on 14 Iyar (2 Chr 30:13, 15, 23). The dedication of the altar under the supervision of Jeshua and Zerubbabel, which preceded the building of the Second Temple, was connected with the Festival of Tabernacles (Ezra 3:1-5). The later, new Festival of Dedication (also called Hanukkah) was modeled after the Feast of Tabernacles (2 Macc 1:9, 18; 10:5-6). Mahieu (2012: 147-53; see also the note to "throne" above) argues that the festival was celebrated on 18 November 18 BCE.

[3062] Josephus is returning to his description of the Temple complex. The relevant passage was most probably a tunnel (cf. the phrase "underground passage" further on in this sentence). For phrases similar to κρυπτὴ διώρυξ ("secret passage"), see Herodotus 3.146; Strabo 5.3.11; 5.4.7; Cassius Dio 71.18.

[3063] I.e., the fortress at the northwest corner of the Temple precinct (see *Ant*. 15.403, 406, 409 with the relevant notes).

[3064] I.e., the area containing the sanctuary, described in *Ant*. 15.391-395, 417-419.

to its eastern gate.[3065] On this he built a tower for himself[3066] in order to be able to go up into it[3067] through the underground passage[3068] and protect himself[3069] against a rebellion of the people[3070] against their kings. **425** People say[3071] that in the period in which the sanctuary was built[3072] there were no rains during the daytime,[3073] but the rains fell during the night, so that the operations were not hindered.[3074] Our fathers[3075] passed this story down to us.[3076] It is not incredible if one also has the other manifestations of God in view.[3077] So this was the way in which the building of the sanctuary was finished.[3078]

[3065] The eastern gate of the sanctuary may be identical with the gate that gave access to the Court of the Women (Patrich 2009: 68-69 with n. 81) or with the Nicanor Gate (see *Ant.* 15.418 with the note to "large gateway"). Especially the latter gate, having a tower on top of it (see the next note), provided Herod with a superb view over the sanctuary area. At the same time Herod himself may have been visible to many persons present in the area.

[3066] Once again Herod's personal involvement in the building activities is emphasized, but here it concerns Herod's own interest (see the next notes).

[3067] I.e., the tower on top of the gate (see the previous notes).

[3068] I.e., the secret passage mentioned previously.

[3069] This remark probably refers to the underground passage that enabled Herod to enter the area of the sanctuary without passing through the crowd. This detail is connected with the security motif highlighted by Josephus in several other passages of book 15 of *Antiquities* (e.g., 15.291-298).

[3070] Josephus once again mentions that the Jewish people intended to revolt against Herod, or, at least, that Herod was afraid that the Jews would do so. This motif occurs already in Herod's response to Antony's request to send Aristobulus over (*Ant.* 15.30) and is especially present in *Antiquities* (van Henten 2011d).

[3071] The introductory formula λέγεται (literally "it is said that") occurs 13 times in Josephus (*War* 7.300; *Ant.* 1.93, 239; 8.349; 13.282, 321; 14.36, 138; 15.425; 19.9, 269; *Apion* 1.165, 250). It introduces anonymous traditions, e.g., about an expedition by Abraham's grandson Eophren (*Ant.* 1.239), about Moses receiving the Law at Mount Sinai (8.349), and the explanation of Aristobulus I's hatred of his son Alexander Janneus (13.321; cf. *Apion* 1.165 concerning Pythagoras [see Barclay in BJP 10 on *Ap.* 1.165] and anonymous introductions of traditions found in rabbinic passages, e.g., about John Hyrcanus hearing a divine voice in the Temple saying that his sons had defeated Antiochus Cyzicenus [*t. Soṭ.* 13.5; cf. *Ant.* 13.282]; see Cohen 1986: 7-8; Schwartz 2013: 107-08).

[3072] I.e., in the period of 1 year and 5 (or 6) months (*Ant.* 15.421).

[3073] In Israel rain falls in autumn, winter, and (early) spring, such that the miracle lasted for one or two rain seasons, depending on the starting point of the building activities. The tradition mentioned here is supported by the Babylonian Talmud: "Likewise we find [what] happened in the days of Herod when the people were occupied with the rebuilding of the Temple. [At that time] rain fell during the night but in the morning the wind blew and the clouds dispersed and the sun shone so that the people were able to go out to their work, and then they knew that they were engaged in sacred work" (*b. Ta'an.* 23a, trans. Rabbinowitz, slightly adapted; see Malter 1967: 334-35; Cohen 1986: 8).

[3074] The rare verb κωλυσιεργέω ("impede work," Rengstorf *s.v.*) is a *hapax legomenon* in Josephus. Outside Josephus it is attested only 5 times: once in Polybius (6.15.5) and 4 times in Philo (*Conf.* 163; *Gig.* 31; *Leg.* 1.103; *Post.* 79). It is one of many cases in which Josephus uses conspicuously "Philonic" language, see the Philo index by Mason in BJP 1b p. 476-78].

[3075] When Josephus is not referring to immediate parents, the most common meaning of the plural οἱ πατέρες (literally "the fathers") in Jewish contexts is "the/our ancestors." Obviously the ancestors were generally held in great honor, and Josephus also mentions them in a honorific sense (e.g., *War* 5.382-386; *Ant.* 4.54, 295; 5.171; 6.89). The noun πατήρ sometimes functions as an honorary title in Josephus (Rengstorf *s.v.*), like its equivalent 'āb in the Hebrew Bible (e.g., 2 Kgs 2:12; KBL *s.v.*). The latter meaning is common in 2 rabbinic writings (*m. 'Abot* and *'Abot R. Nat.*; Jastrow 1.1-2), in which "fathers" is synonymous with "sages." It is possible that Josephus is hinting at a similar meaning here.

[3076] The idea that the ancestors transmitted important traditions occurs already in Ps 44:2 (LXX 43:2); 78:3 (LXX 77:3).

[3077] In this concluding paragraph, with its reference to the other manifestations of God (τὰς ἄλλας ἐμφανείας τοῦ θεοῦ), Josephus points out once again that God was responsible for the events during Herod's reign (see also *Ant.* 15.4 and 15.373-374 with notes and van Henten 2011c). Divine providence is also a favorite theme in other passages of *Antiquities*: military defeats are considered to be caused by God (e.g., 8.279-280; 12.307; 15.137-138, 144-146; cf. *War* 7.323-336). The word ἐμφάνεια ("manifestation") occurs once elsewhere in

Josephus (*Ant.* 15.136), in Herod's commander speech (concerning heavenly messengers who make God known [εἰς εμφάνειαν ἄγειν] to humans).

[3078] The concluding sentence focuses on the rebuilding of the sanctuary (for the Temple section being a mixture of narrative and description, see the first note at *Ant.* 15.380). The sanctuary is mentioned at the end of the section, probably because its renovation was the last phase of the building activities (see 15.421 with the note to "sanctuary") and because the miracle of the rain, which manifested God's role (see the previous note), was specifically connected with the sanctuary.

BIBLIOGRAPHY

Works that appear in the abbreviation list (e.g., Schürer-Vermes) have been omitted from the bibliography here since the commentary does not refer to them by the years of their editions and since their bibliographical data already appear in the abbreviation list.

Abel, F.-M. (1949). *Les livres des Maccabées*. Études bibliques. Paris: Gabalda.
Aharoni, Y. and M. Avi-Yonah (1977). *The Macmillan Bible Atlas*, revised edn. New York, N.Y.: Macmillan.
Albert, S. (1980). *Bellum iustum: Die Theorie des "gerechten Krieges" und ihre praktische Bedeutung für die auswärtigen Auseinandersetzungen Roms in republikanischer Zeit*. Frankfurter Althistorische Studien 10. Kallmünz: Lassleben.
Alföldi, A. (1971). *Der Vater des Vaterlandes im römischen Denken*. Darmstadt: Wissenschaftliche Buchgesellschaft.
Aliquot, J. (1999-2003). "Les Ituréens et la présence arabe au Liban du IIe siècle a.C. au IVe siècle p.C." *MUSJ* 56: 161-190.
Applebaum, S. (1976). "Economic Life in Palestine." Pp. 631-700 in *The Jewish People in the First Century: Historical Geography, Political History, Social, Cultural and Religious Life and Institutions*, vol. 2, ed. S. Safrai et al. CRINT 1.2. Assen: Van Gorcum.
Attridge, H. W. (1976). *The Interpretation of Biblical History in the* Antiquitates Judaicae *of Flavius Josephus*. HDR 7. Missoula, Mont.: Scholars Press.
Aune, D. E. (1983). *Prophecy in Early Christianity and the Ancient Mediterranean World*. Grand Rapids, Mich.: Eerdmans.
Avigad, N. (1993). "Samaria (City)." *NEAEHL* 4.1300-10.
Avi-Yonah, M. (1966). *A Short Guide to the Model of Ancient Jerusalem*. Jerusalem: Holyland Hotel.
Avi-Yonah, M. (1974). "Historical Geography." Pp. 78-116 in *The Jewish People in the First Century: Historical Geography, Political History, Social, Cultural and Religious Life and Institutions*, vol. 1, ed. S. Safrai et al. CRINT 1.1. Assen: Van Gorcum.
Badian, E. (1996). "Amicitia." *DNP* 1: 590-91.
Bagnall. R. S. (1985). "Publius Petronius: Augustan Prefect of Egypt." Pp. 85-93 in *Papyrology*, ed. N. Lewis. YCS 28. Cambridge: Cambridge University Press.
Bagnall, R. S. and R. Cribiore (2006). *Women's Letters from Ancient Egypt, 300 BC–AD 800*. Ann Arbor, Mich.: University of Michigan Press.
Bahat, D. (1994). "The Western Wall Tunnels." Pp. 177-90 in *Ancient Jerusalem Revealed*, ed. H. Geva. Jerusalem: Israel Exploration Society.
Barag, D. (1993). "King Herod's Royal Castle at Samaria-Sebaste." *PEQ* 125: 3-18.
Baron, C. A. (2012). *Timaeus of Tauromenium and Hellenistic Historiography*. Cambridge : Cambridge University Press.
Bartels, J. (2001). "Sosius, S.C." *DNP* 11: 745-46.
Basset, L. (1997). " Ἀλλ' ἐξόλοισθ' αὐτῷ κοαξ: Réexamen des emplois de ἀλλά à la lumière de l'énonciation dans *Les grenouilles* d'Aristophane." Pp. 75-99 in *New Approaches to Greek Particles*, ed. A. Rijksbaron. Amsterdam Studies in Classical Philology 7. Amsterdam: Gieben.
Bauckham, R. J. (1996). "Josephus' Account of the Temple in *Contra Apionem* 2.102-109." Pp. 327-47 in *Josephus'* Contra Apionem*: Studies in Its Character and Context with a Latin Concordance to the Portion Missing in Greek*, ed. L. H. Feldman and J. R. Levison. AGJU 34. Leiden: Brill.
Baumann, U. (1983). *Rom und die Juden: Die römisch-jüdischen Beziehungen von Pompeius bis zum Tode des Herodes (63 v. Chr.–4 v. Chr.)*. Studia Philosophica et Historica 4. Frankfurt am Main: Lang.
Baumeister, T. (1983). "'Anytos und Meletos können mich zwar töten, schaden jedoch können sie mir nicht': Platon, Apologie des Sokrates 30c/d bei Plutarch, Epiktet, Justin Martyr und Clemens Alexandrinus." Pp. 58-63 in *Platonismus und Christentum: Festschrift für Heinrich Dörrie*, ed. H.-D. Blume and F. Mann. JAC 10. Münster: Aschendorff.
Beacham, R. C. (1999). *Spectacle Entertainments of Early Imperial Rome*. New Haven, Conn.: Yale University Press.

Beall, T. S. (1988). *Josephus' Description of the Essenes Illustrated by the Dead Sea Scrolls*. SNTSMS 58. Cambridge: Cambrdige University Press.

Beard, M. (2003). "The Triumph of Flavius Josephus." Pp. 543-58 in *Flavian Rome: Culture, Image, Text*, ed. A. J. Boyle and W. J. Dominik. Leiden: Brill.

Beaujeu, J. (1982). "L'enfant sans nom de la IVe Bucolique." *Revue des études latines* 60: 186-215.

Beauvery, R. (1957). "La route romaine de Jérusalem à Jericho." *RB* 64: 72-101.

Becher, I. (1966). *Das Bild der Kleopatra in der griechischen und lateinischen Literatur*. Deutsche Akademie der Wissenschaft zu Berlin: Schriften der Sektion für Altertumswissenschaft 51. Berlin: Akademie Verlag.

Begg, C. T. (2000). *Josephus' Story of the Later Monarchy (AJ 9,1-10,185)*. BETL 145. Louvain: Peeters.

Bekker, I. (1855-56). *Flavii Iosephi opera omnia: Ab Immanuele Bekkero recognita*. 6 vols. Leipzig: Teubner.

Ben-Dov, M. (1985). *In the Shadow of the Temple: The Discovery of Ancient Jerusalem*. New York, N.Y.: Harper & Row.

Bengtson, H. (1950). *Griechische Geschichte von den Anfängen bis in die römische Kaiserzeit*. Handbuch der Alterumswissenschaft 3.4. Munich: Beck.

Bengtson, H. (1974). *Zum Partherfeldzug des Antonius*. SBAW Phil.-hist. Kl. 1974/1. Munich: Bayerische Akademie der Wissenschaften.

Ben-Shalom, I. (1980). *The Shammai School and Its Place in the Political and Social History of Eretz Israel in the First Century A.D.* Ph.D. diss., Tel-Aviv (Hebrew).

Bergmann, J. (1908). *Jüdische Apologetik im neutestamentlichen Zeitalter*. Berlin: Reimer.

Berlin, A. M. (1999). "The Archaeology of Ritual: The Sanctuary of Pan at Banias/Caesarea Philippi." *BASOR* 315: 27-45.

Bernett, M. (2007a). *Der Kaiserkult in Judäa unter den Herodiern und Römern: Untersuchungen zur politischen und religiösen Geschichte Judäas von 30 v. bis 66 n. Chr.* WUNT II.203. Tübingen: Mohr Siebeck.

Bernett, M. (2007b). "Der Kaiserkult in Judäa unter herodischer und römischer Herrschaft: Zu Herausbildung und Herausforderung neuer Konzepte jüdischer Herrschaftslegitimation." Pp. 205-51 in *Jewish Identity in the Greco-Roman World/Jüdische Identität in der griechisch-römischen Welt*, ed. J. Frey, D. R. Schwartz, and S. Gripentrog. AGJU 71. Leiden: Brill.

Berthelot, K. (2003). *Philanthrôpia judaica: Le débat autour de la 'misanthropie' des lois juives dans l'Antiquité*. JSJSup 76. Leiden: Brill.

Bickerman, E. J. (1938). *Institutions des Séleucides*. Bibliothèque archéologique et historique 26. Paris: Geuthner.

Bickerman, E. J. (1947). "La Coele-Syria: Notes de géographie historique." *RB* 54: 256-68.

Bieber, M. (1939). *The History of the Greek and Roman Theatre*. Princeton, N.J.: Princeton University Press.

Bieberstein, K. and H. Bloedhorn (1994). *Jerusalem: Grundzüge der Baugeschichte vom Chalkolithikum bis zur Frühzeit der osmanischen Herrschaft*. 3 vols. Beihefte zum Tübinger Atlas des Vorderen Orients: Series B 100.1-3. Wiesbaden: Reichert.

Biers, W. R. (1980). *The Archaeology of Greece: An Introduction.* Ithaca, N.Y.: Cornell University Press.

Bilde, P. (1988). *Flavius Josephus between Jerusalem and Rome: His Life, His Works and Their Importance*. JSPSup 2. Sheffield: Sheffield Academic Press.

Blass, F., A. Debrunner, and F. Rehkopf (1976). *Grammatik des neutestamentlichen Griechisch*, 14th edn. Göttingen: Vandenhoeck & Ruprecht.

Blundell, W. M. (1989). *Helping Friends and Harming Enemies: A Study in Sophocles and Greek Ethics*. Cambridge: Cambridge University Press.

Bonner, S. F. (1977). *Education in Ancient Rome: From the Elder Cato to the Younger Pliny*. London: Methuen.

Bourriot, F. (1995). *Kalos kagathos–kalokagathia: D'un terme de propagande de sophistes à une notion sociale et philosophique: Étude d'histoire athénienne*. 2 vols. Spudasmata 58. Hildesheim: Olms.

Bowersock, G. W. (1965). *Augustus and the Greek World*. Oxford: Clarendon.

Braund, D. C. (1983). "Four Notes on the Herods." *CQ* 33: 239-42.

Braund, D. C. (1984). *Rome and the Friendly King: The Character of the Client Kingship*. London: Croom Helm.

Braund, D. C. (1988). "Client Kings." Pp. 69-96 in *The Administration of the Roman Empire, 241 BC–AD 193*, ed. D. C. Braund. Exeter Studies in History 18. Exeter: University of Exeter Press.

Brenk, F. E. (1992a). "Plutarch's Life 'Markos Antonios': A Literary and Cultural Study." *ANRW* II.33.6: 4347-469, 4895-915.

Brenk, F. E. (1992b). "Antony-Osiris, Cleopatra-Isis: The End of Plutarch's *Antony*." Pp. 159-82 in *Plutarch and the Historical Tradition*, ed. P. A. Stadter. London: Routledge.

Brenner, A. (2003). "Are we Amused? Small and Big Differences in Josephus' Re-Presentations of Biblical Female

Figures in the *Jewish Antiquities* 1-8." Pp. 90-106 in *Are we Amused? Humour about Women in the Biblical Worlds*, ed. A. Brenner. JSOTSup 383. London: T&T Clark.

Brentjes, B. (1997). "Armenia." *DNP* 2: 10-11.

Briant, P. (2002). *From Cyrus to Alexander: A History of the Persian Empire*. Winona Lake, Ind.: Eisenbrauns.

Brighton, M. A. (2009). *The Sicarii in Josephus's* Judean War*: Rhetorical Analysis and Historical Observations*. SBLEJL 27. Atlanta, Ga.: SBL.

Bringmann, K. and H. von Steuben (1995). Schenkungen hellenistischer Herrscher an griechische Städte und Heiligtümer. 2 vols. in 3. Berlin: Akademie Verlag.

Brody, R. (1999). "Evidence for Divorce by Jewish Women?" *JJS* 50: 230-34.

Broughton, T. R. S. (1951-86). *The Magistrates of the Roman Republic*, with M. L. Patterson. 3 vols. Philological Monographs of the American Philological Association 15.1-3. New York, N.Y.: American Philological Association; Atlanta, Ga.: Scholars Press.

Brown, R. E. (1994). *The Death of the Messiah: From Gethsemane to the Grave: A Commentary on the Passion Narratives in the Four Gospels*. 2 vols. ABRL. New York, N.Y.: Doubleday.

Buchheim, H. (1960). *Die Orientpolitik des Triumvirn M. Antonius: Ihre Voraussetzungen, Entwicklung und Zusammenhang mit den politischen Ereignissen in Italien*. Abhandlungen der Heidelberger Akademie der Wissenschaften: Philosophisch-historische Klasse 1960/3. Heidelberg: Winter.

Burkert, W. (1985). *Greek Religion: Archaic and Classical*. Cambridge, Mass.: Harvard University Press.

Busink, T. A. (1970). *Der Tempel von Jerusalem: Von Salomo bis Herodes: Eine archäologisch-historische Studie unter Berücksichtigung des westsemitischen Tempelbaus*, vol. 1: *Der Tempel Salomos*. Studia Francisci Scholten Memoriae Dicata 3. Leiden: Brill.

Chadwick, H. (1962). "Enkrateia." *RAC* 5: 343-65.

Chamonard, J. (1904). *Oeuvres complètes de Flavius Josèphe traduites en français sous la direction de Théodore Reinach*. Vol. 3. Paris: Leroux.

Charlesworth, M. P. (1926). *Trade-Routes and Commerce of the Roman Empire*, 2nd edn. Cambridge: Cambridge University Press.

Chaumont, M.-L. (1976). "L'Arménie entre Rome et l'Iran, I: De l'avènement d'Auguste à l'avènement de Dioclétien." *ANRW* II.9.1: 71-194.

Chester, A. (2012). "The Relevance of Jewish Inscriptions for New Testament Ethics." Pp. 107-45 in *Early Christian Ethics in Interaction with Jewish and Greco-Roman Contexts*, ed. J. W. van Henten and J. Verheyden. Studies in Theology and Religion 17. Leiden: Brill.

Cimma, M. R. (1976). *Reges socii et amici populi Romani*. Università di Roma: Pubblicazioni dell'Istituto di Diritto Romano e dei Diritti dell'Oriente Mediterraneo 50. Milan: Giuffrè.

Clavadetscher-Thürlemann, S. (1985). *Polemos dikaios und bellum iustum: Versuch einer Ideengeschichte*. Zürich: Juris.

Cohen, S. J. D. (1979). *Josephus in Galilee and Rome: His* Vita *and Development as a Historian*. Columbia Studies in the Classical Tradition 8. Leiden: Brill.

Cohen, S. J. D. (1982). "Masada: Literary Tradition, Archaeological Remains, and the Credibility of Josephus." *JJS* 33: 385-405.

Cohen, S. J. D. (1986). "Parallel Historical Tradition in Josephus and Rabbinic Literature." Pp. 7-14 in *Proceedings of the Ninth World Congress of Jewish Studies, Jerusalem, August 4-12, 1985*, division B: *The History of the Jewish People*, vol. 1: *From the Second Temple Period until the Middle Ages*. Jerusalem: World Union of Jewish Studies.

Colledge, M. A. R. (1967). *The Parthians*. Ancient Peoples and Places 59. London: Thames & Hudson.

Collins, J. J. (1997). "Marriage, Divorce, and Family in Second Temple Judaism." Pp. 104-62 in *Families in Ancient Israel*, ed. L. G. Perdue, J. Blenkinsopp, J. J. Collins, and C. L. Meyers. The Family, Religion, and Culture. Louisville: Westminster John Knox.

Collomb, P. (1947). "La place de Josèphe dans la technique de l'historiographie hellénistique." Pp. 81-92 in *Mélanges 1945: Études historiques*. Publications de la Faculté des Lettres de l'Université de Strasbourg 106. Paris: Les Belles Lettres.

Corbishley, T. (1935). "The Chronology of the Reign of Herod the Great." *JTS* 36 (1935): 22-32.

Cotton, H. M. and E. Qimron (1998). "XḤev/Se ar 13 of 134 or 135 CE: A Wife's Renunciation of Claims." *JJS* 49: 108-18.

Crook, J. (1955). *Consilium principis: Imperial Councils and Counsellors from Augustus to Diocletian*. Cambridge: Cambridge University Press.

Crowfoot, J. W., K. M. Kenyon, and E. L. Sukenik (1942). *Samaria-Sebaste: Reports of the Work of the Joint*

Expedition in 1931-1933 and of the British Expedition in 1935, vol. 1: *The Buildings at Samaria*. London: Palestine Exploration Fund.

Dabrowa, E. (1989). "Les héros de luttes politiques dans l'État parthe dans la première moitié du Ier siècle de notre ère." *Iranica antiqua* 24: 311-22.

Dabrowa, E. (1998). *The Governors of Roman Syria from Augustus to Septimius Severus*. Antiquitas Reihe 1: Abhandlungen zur alten Geschichte 45. Bonn: Habelt.

Danker, F. W. (1982). *Benefactor: Epigraphic Study of a Graeco-Roman and New Testament Semantic Field*. St. Louis, Mo.: Clayton.

Davies, R. W. (1971). "The Roman Military Diet." *Britannia* 2: 122-42.

Davies, William D. (1954). "A Note on Josephus, *Antiquities* 15.136." *HTR* 47: 135-40.

de Jong, I. J. F. (1987). "The Voice of Anonymity: *tis*-Speeches in the Iliad." *Eranos* 85: 69-84.

de Jong, I. J. F. (1997). "Narratological Theory on Time." Pp. 1-14 in *Time in Ancient Greek Literature*, ed. I. J. F. de Jong and R. Nünlist. Mnemosyne Suppl. 291. Leiden: Brill.

De Temmerman, K. (2006). *Personages op papyrus: Een narratologische analyse van de retorische karakteriseringstechnieken in de Oudgriekse roman*. Ph.D. diss., Gent.

Dearman, J. A. (1995). "Edomite Religion: A Survey and an Examination of Some Recent Contributions." Pp. 119-36 in *You Shall not Abhor an Edomite for He is Your Brother: Edom and Seir in History and Tradition*, ed. D. V. Edelman. SBLABS 3. Atlanta, Ga.: Scholars Press.

Degrassi, A. (1954). *Fasti Capitolini: Recensuit, praefatus est, indicibus instruxit*. Corpus Scriptorum Latinorum Paravianum. Turin: Paravia.

Denniston, J. D. (1954). *The Greek Particles*, 2nd edn. Oxford: Clarendon.

Dequeker, L. (1993). "Darius the Persian and the Reconstruction of the Jewish Temple in Jerusalem (Ezra 4,24)." Pp. 67-92 in *Ritual and Sacrifice in the Ancient Near East*, ed. J. Quaegebeur. OLA 55. Louvain: Peeters.

Dequeker, L. (1997). "Nehemia and the Restoration of the Temple after the Exile." Pp. 547-67 in *Deuteronomy and Deuteronomic Literature: Festschrift C. H. W. Brekelmans*, ed. M. Vervenne and J. Lust. BETL 133. Louvain: Peeters.

Diels, H. and W. Kranz (1954). *Die Fragmente der Vorsokratiker: Griechisch und deutsch*, 7th edn. 3 vols. Berlin: Weidmann.

Dindorf, W. (1845). ΦΛΑΒΙΟΥ ΙΩΣΗΠΟΥ ΤΑ ΕΥΡΙΣΚΟΜΕΝΑ = *Flavii Iosephi opera: Graece et Latine recognovit Guilelmus Dindorfius*, vol. 1. Paris: Didot.

Döring, K. (1979). *Exemplum Socratis: Studien zur Sokratesnachwirkung in der kynisch-stoischen Popularphilosophie der frühen Kaiserzeit und im frühen Christentum*. Hermes Einzelschriften 42. Wiesbaden: Steiner.

Dover, K. J. (1978). *Greek Homosexuality*. London: Duckworth.

Downey, G. (1961). *A History of Antioch in Syria from Seleucus to the Arab Conquest*. Princeton, N.J.: Princeton University Press.

Drüner, H. (1896). *Untersuchungen über Josephus*. Marburg: Hamel.

Eberhardt, B. (2005). "Wer dient wem? Die Darstellung des flavischen Triumphzuges auf dem Titusbogen und bei Josephus (*B.J.* 7.123-162)." Pp. 257-77 in *Josephus and Jewish History in Flavian Rome and Beyond*, ed. G. Lembi and J. Sievers. JSJSup 104. Leiden: Brill.

Ebert, J. (1972). *Griechische Epigramme auf Sieger an gymnischen und hippischen Agonen*. ASAW Phil.-hist. Kl. 63.2. Berlin: Akademie Verlag.

Eck, W. (1995). *Die Verwaltung des Römischen Reiches in der Hohen Kaiserzeit: Ausgewahlte und erweiterte Beiträge*, vol. 1. Arbeiten zur Römischen Epigraphik und Altertumskunde. Basel: Reinhardt.

Eck, W. (2001). "Procurator." *DNP* 10: 366-69.

Eck, W. (2002a). "Varro." *DNP* 12.1: 1130.

Eck, W. (2002b). "L. Vitellius." *DNP* 12.2: 261-62.

Eck, W. (2008). "Die Benennung von römischen Amtsträgern und politisch-militärisch-administrativen Funktionen bei Flavius Iosephus: Probleme der korrekten Identifizierung." *ZPE* 166: 218-26.

Eckhardt, B. (2008). "Herodes der Grosse als Antiochus *redivivus* in apokrypher und josephischer Deutung. Mit einem Ausblick auf eine konstruktivistische Herodesforschung." *Klio* 90: 360-73.

Eckstein, A. M. (1990). "Josephus and Polybius: a Reconsideration." *Classical Antiquity* 9: 175-207.

Emerick, J. J. (1998). *The Tempietto del Clitunno near Spoleto*. University Park, Pa.: Pennsylvania State University Press.

Ernesti, J. A. (1795). *Observationes philologico-criticae in Aristophanis* Nubes *et Flavii Iosephi* Antiquitates Iudaicas. Leipzig: Fritsch.

Étienne, R. (1965). "La naissance de l'amphithéâtre: Le mot et la chose." *Revue des études latines* 43: 213-20.

Eyben, E. (1993). *Restless Youth in Ancient Rome*. London: Routledge.
Feldman, L. H. (1953). "Asinius Pollio and His Jewish Interests." *TAPA* 84: 73-80.
Feldman, L. H. (1958-59). "The Identity of Pollio, the Pharisee, in Josephus." *JQR* 49: 53-62.
Feldman, L. H. (1985). "Asinius Pollio and Herod's sons." *CQ* 35: 240-43.
Feldman, L. H. (1992). "Josephus' Portrait of Joseph." *RB* 99: 379-417, 504-28.
Feldman, L. H. (1993). *Jew and Gentile in the Ancient World: Attitudes and Interactions from Alexander to Justinian*. Princeton, N.J.: Princeton University Press.
Fensterbusch, C. (1936). "Θυμέλη." *PW* 6.A.1: 700-04.
Fine, S. (2005). *Art and Judaism in the Greco-Roman World: Toward a New Jewish Archaeology*. Cambridge: Cambridge University Press.
Finkelberg, M. (2002). "Virtue and Circumstances: On the City-State Concept of *arete*." *AJP* 123: 35-49.
Finley, M. I. and H. W. Pleket (1976). *The Olympic Games: The First Thousand Years*. London: Chatto & Windus.
Fischer, M. L., B. H. Isaac, and I. Roll (1996). *Roman Roads in Judaea, II: The Jaffa-Jerusalem Roads*. British Archaeological Reports International Series 628. Oxford: British Archaeological Reports.
Fischer, M. L. and A. Kushnir-Stein (1994). "Josephus on the Use of Marble in Building Projects of Herod the Great." *JJS* 45: 79-85.
Fishwick, D. (1987-2005). *The Imperial Cult in the Latin West: Studies in the Ruler Cult of the Western Provinces of the Roman Empire*. 3 vols. in 8. EPRO 108; Religions in the Graeco-Roman World 145-148. Leiden: Brill.
Foerster, G. (1976). "Art and Architecture in Palestine." Pp. 971-1006 in *The Jewish People in the First Century: Historical Geography, Political History, Social, Cultural and Religious Life and Institutions*, vol. 2, ed. S. Safrai et al. CRINT 1.2. Assen: Van Gorcum.
Forbes, C. A. (1955). "Ancient Athletic Guilds." *CP* 50: 238-52.
France, R. T. (1979). "Herod and the Children of Bethlehem." *NovT* 21: 98-120.
Fraser, P. M. and E. Matthews, eds. (1987-2010). *A Lexicon of Greek Personal Names*. 5 vols. in 6. Oxford: Clarendon.
Freyne, S. (1980). *Galilee from Alexander the Great to Hadrian, 323 BCE to 135 CE: A Study of Second Temple Judaism*. University of Notre Dame Center for the Study of Judaism and Christianity in Antiquity 5. Wilmington, N.C.: Glazier.
Friedländer, L. (1934). *Sittengeschichte Roms*. Wien: Phaidon.
Fromentin, V. (2001). "L'histoire tragique a-t-elle existé?" Pp. 77-92 in *Lectures antiques de la tragédie grecque*, ed. A. Billault and C. Mauduit. Collection du Centre d'Études et des Recherches sur l'Occident Romain N.S. 22.
Frova, A., G. Dell'Amore, et al. (1965). *Scavi di Caesarea Maritima*. Milan: Cassa di Risparmio delle Provincie Lombarde.
Fündling, J. (2003). "Ventidius Bassus, P." *DNP* 12.2: 14-16.
Fulco, W. J. and F. Zayadine (1981). "Coins from Samaria-Sebaste." *ADAJ* 25: 197-225, 412-18.
Funke, H. (1965-66). "Univira: Ein Beispiel heidnischer Geschichtsapologetik." *JAC* 8-9: 183-88.
Futrell, A. (1997). *Blood in the Arena: The Spectacle of Roman Power*. Austin, Tex.: University of Texas Press.
Gabba, E. (1990). "The Finances of King Herod." Pp. 160-68 in *Greece and Rome in Eretz Israel: Collected Essays*, ed. A. Kasher, U. Rappaport, and G. Fuks. Jerusalem: Israel Exploration Society.
Gafni, I. M. (1997). *Land, Center and Diaspora: Jewish Constructs in Late Antiquity*. JSPSup 21. Sheffield: Sheffield Academic Press.
Galinsky, K. (1996). *Augustan Culture: An Interpretative Introduction*. Princeton, N.J.: Princeton University Press.
Gambetti, S. (2009). *The Alexandrian Riots of 38 CE and the Persecution of the Jews: A Historical Reconstruction*. JSJSup 135. Leiden: Brill.
Garnsey, P. (1970). *Social Status and Legal Privilege in the Roman Empire*. Oxford: Clarendon.
Garnsey, P. (1988). *Famine and Food Supply in the Graeco-Roman World: Responses to Risk and Crisis*. Cambridge: Cambridge University Press.
Garnsey, P. (1999). *Food and Society in Classical Antiquity*. Key Themes in Ancient History. Cambridge: Cambridge University Press.
Gehrke, H.-J. and B. von Reibnitz (1998). "Freundschaft." *DNP* 4: 669-74.
Gera, D. (1998). *Judaea and Mediterranean politics, 219 to 161 BCE*. Brill's Series in Jewish studies 8. Leiden: Brill.
Geva, H. (2001). "Review of *The History and Architecture of the Theatres in Roman Palestine* [A. Segal]" (Hebrew). *Qad* 34: 67-68.
Gibson, S. and D. M. Jacobson (1996). *Below the Temple Mount in Jerusalem: A Sourcebook on the Cisterns, Subterranean Chambers and Conduits of the Ḥaram al-Sharīf*. BAR International Series 637. Oxford: Tempus Reparatum.

Gnuse, R. K. (1996). *Dreams and Dream Reports in the Writings of Josphus: A Traditio-Historical Analysis.* AGJU 36. Leiden: Brill.

Goldstein, J. A. (1976). *I Maccabees: A New Translation with Introduction and Commentary.* AB 41. Garden City, N.Y.: Doubleday.

Goldsworthy, A. K. (1996). *The Roman Army at War, 100 BC–AD 200.* Oxford Classical Monographs. Oxford: Clarendon.

Golvin, J.-C. (1988). *L'amphithéâtre romain: Essai sur la théorisation de sa forme et de ses fonctions.* 2 vols. Publications du Centre Pierre Paris 18. Paris: de Boccard.

Golvin, J.-C. and C. Landes (1990). *Amphithéâtres et gladiateurs.* Paris: Presses du CNRS.

Goodblatt, D. M. (1998). "From Judeans to Israel: Names of Jewish States in Antiquity." *JSJ* 29: 1-36.

Goodenough, E. R. (1953-68). *Jewish Symbols in the Greco-Roman Period.* 13 vols. Bollingen Series 37. New York, N.Y.: Pantheon Books.

Goodman, M. D. (1997). *The Roman World, 44 BC–AD 180.* With the assistance of J. Sherwood. Routledge History of the Ancient World. London: Routledge.

Grabbe, L. L. (2004-08). *A History of the Jews and Judaism in the Second Temple Period.* 2 vols. Library of Second Temple Studies 47, 68. London: T&T Clark.

Grainger, J. D. (1991). *Hellenistic Phoenicia.* Oxford: Oxford University Press.

Grant, M. (1970). *The Ancient Historians.* London: Weidenfeld & Nicolson.

Grant, M. (1971). *Herod the Great.* New York, N.Y: American Heritage.

Grant, M. (1972). *Cleopatra.* London: Weidenfeld & Nicolson.

Gray, R. (1993). *Prophetic Figures in Late Second Temple Jewish Palestine: The Evidence from Josephus.* New York, N.Y.: Oxford University Press.

Gruen, E. S. (2001). "Jewish Perspectives on Greek Culture and Ethnicity." Pp. 62-93 in *Hellenism in the Land of Israel,* ed. J. J. Collins and G. E. Sterling. Christianity and Judaism in Antiquity 13. Notre Dame, Ind.: University of Notre Dame Press.

Grundmann, W. (1964). "ἐγκράτεια." *TDNT* 2: 339-42.

Günther, L.-M. (2005). *Herodes der Grosse.* Gestalten der Antike. Darmstadt: Wissenschaftliche Buchgesellschaft.

Gurval, R. (1995). *Actium and Augustus: The Politics and Emotions of Civil War.* Ann Arbor, Mich.: University of Michigan Press.

Hachlili, R. (2005). *Jewish Funerary Customs, Practices and Rites in the Second Temple Period.* JSJSup 94. Leiden: Brill.

Hackl, U., B. Jacobs, and D. Weber (2010). *Quellen zur Geschichte des Partherreiches: Textsammlung mit Übersetzungen und Kommentaren.* 3 vols. NTOA 83-85. Göttingen: Vandenhoeck & Rupprecht.

Hackl, U., H. Jenni, and C. Schneider (2003). *Quellen zur Geschichte der Nabatäer: Textsammlung mit Übersetzung und Kommentar.* NTOA 51. Göttingen: Vandenhoeck & Ruprecht.

Halfmann, H. (2011). *Marcus Antonius.* Gestalten der Antike. Darmstadt: Wissenschaftliche Buchgesellschaft.

Hamel, G. (1990). *Poverty and Charity in Roman Palestine, First Three Centuries CE.* University of California Publications: Near Eastern Studies 23. Berkeley, Calif.: University of California Press.

Hands, A. R. (1968). *Charities and Social Aid in Greece and Rome.* Aspects of Greek and Roman Life. Ithaca, N.Y.: Cornell University Press.

Hänlein-Schäfer, H. (1985). *Veneratio Augusti: Eine Studie zu den Tempeln des ersten römischen Kaisers.* Archaeologica 39. Rome: Bretschneider.

Hanson, K. C. (1989-90). "The Herodians and Mediterranean Kinship. Part 1: Genealogy and Descent; Part 2: Marriage and Divorce; Part 3: Economics." *BTB* 19: 75-84; 19: 142-51; 20: 10-21.

Har-El, M. (1981). "Jerusalem and Judea: Roads and Fortifications." *BA* 44: 8-19.

Harris, W. V. (1979). *War and Imperialism in Republican Rome, 327-70 B.C.* Oxford: Clarendon.

Hawley, J. S. (1994). *Sati, the Blessing and the Curse: The Burning of Wives in India.* New York, N.Y.: Oxford University Press.

Hayward, C. T. R. (1996). *The Jewish Temple: A Non-Biblical Sourcebook.* London: Routledge.

Hellegouarc'h, J. (1963). *Le vocabulaire latin des relations et des partis politiques sous la République.* Publications de la Faculté des Lettres et Sciences Humaines de l'Université de Lille 11. Paris: Les Belles Lettres.

Hengel, M. (1989). *The Hellenization of Judaea in the First Century after Christ.* London: SCM.

Henze, M. (1999). *The Madness of King Nebuchadnezzar: The Ancient Near Eastern Origins and Early History of Interpretation of Daniel 4.* JSJSup 61. Leiden: Brill.

Herman, G. (1980-81). "The 'Friends' of the Early Hellenistic Rulers: Servants or Officials?" *Talanta* 12-13: 103-49.

Herrmann, P. (1968). *Der römische Kaisereid: Untersuchungen zu seiner Herkunft und Entwicklung*. Hypomnemata 20. Göttingen: Vandenhoeck & Ruprecht.

Hiller von Gaertringen, F. (1906). *Inschriften von Priene*. Königliche Museen zu Berlin. Berlin: Reimer.

Hiller von Gaertringen, F. (1931). "Rhodes." *PW* Suppl. 5: 731-840.

Hoehner, H. W. (1972). *Herod Antipas*. SNTSMS 17. Cambridge: Cambridge University Press.

Hölbl, G. (1994). *Geschichte des Ptolemäerreiches: Politik, Ideologie und religiöse Kultur von Alexander dem Grossen bis zur römischen Eroberung*. Darmstadt: Wissenschaftliche Buchgesellschaft.

Holder, P. A. (1980). *Studies in the* Auxilia *of the Roman Army from Augustus to Trajan*. British Archaeological Reports International Series 70. Oxford: British Archaeological Reports.

Hölscher, T. (1985). "Denkmäler der Schlacht von Actium: Propaganda und Resonanz." *Klio* 67: 81-102.

Holum, K. G. (1999). "The Temple Platform: Progress Report on the Excavations." Pp. 13-34 in *Caesarea Papers, II: Herod's Temple, the Provincial Governor's Praetorium and Granaries, the Later Harbor, a Gold Coin Hoard, and Other Studies*, ed. K. G. Holum, A. Raban, and J. Patrich. Journal of Roman Archaeology Suppl. 35. Portsmouth, R.I.: Journal of Roman Archaeology.

Hudson, J. (1720). ΦΛΑΒΙΟΥ ΙΩΣΗΠΟΥ ΤΑ ΕΥΡΙΣΚΟΜΕΝΑ = *Flavii Iosephi opera, quae reperiri potuerunt, omnia*, vol. 1. Oxford: Sheldonian Theatre.

Huguet, F. (1985). "Aperçu géomorphologique sur les paysages volcaniques du Hauran (Syrie méridionale)." Pp. 5-17 in *Hauran, I: Recherches archéologiques sur la Syrie du sud à l'époque hellénistique et romaine*, ed. J.-M. Dentzer. Bibliothèque archéologique et historique de l'Institut Français d'Archéologie du Proche-Orient: Beyrouth-Damas-Amman 124. Paris: Geuthner.

Humphrey, J. H. (1986). *Roman Circuses: Arenas for Chariot Racing*. London: Batsford.

Humphrey, J. H. (1996). "Amphitheatrical Hippo-Stadia." Pp. 121-29 in *Caesarea Maritima: A Retrospective after Two Millennia*, ed. A. Raban and K. G. Holum. Documenta et Monumenta Orientis Antiqui 21. Leiden: Brill.

Hurschmann, R. (2002). "Tropaion." *DNP* 12.1: 872-73.

Huss, W. (2001). *Ägypten in hellenistischer Zeit, 332-30 v. Chr.* Munich: Beck.

Huzar, E. G. (1978). *Mark Antony: A Biography*. Minneapolis, Minn.: University of Minnesota Press.

Ilan, T. (1995). *Jewish Women in Greco-Roman Palestine: An Inquiry into Image and Status*. TSAJ 44. Tübingen: Mohr Siebeck.

Ilan, T. (1996). "Notes and Observations on a Newly Published Divorce Bill from the Judean Desert." *HTR* 89: 195-202.

Ilan, T. (1998). "King David, King Herod and Nicolaus of Damascus." *JSQ* 5: 195-240.

Ilan, T. (1999). *Integrating Women into Second Temple History*. TSAJ 76. Tübingen: Mohr Siebeck.

Ilan, T. (2002). *Lexicon of Jewish Names in Late Antiquity*, part 1: *Palestine 330 BCE–200 CE*. TSAJ 91. Tübingen: Mohr Siebeck.

Instone-Brewer, D. (1998). "Deuteronomy 24:1-4 and the Origin of the Jewish Divorce Certificate." *JJS* 49: 230-43.

Instone-Brewer, D. (1999). "Jewish Women Divorcing Their Husbands in Early Judaism: The Background to Papyrus Şe'elim 13." *HTR* 92: 349-57.

Jackson, B. S. (2005). "The Divorces of the Herodian Princesses: Jewish Law, Roman Law or Palace Law?" Pp. 343-68 in *Josephus and Jewish History in Flavian Rome and Beyond*, ed. G. Lembi and J. Sievers. JSJSup 104. Leiden: Brill.

Jacobson, D. M. (2001a). "Herod the Great Shows his true Colors." *Near Eastern Archaeology* 64: 100-04.

Jacobson, D. M. (2001b). "Three Roman Client Kings: Herod of Judaea, Archelaus of Cappadocia and Juba of Mauretania." *PEQ* 133: 22-38.

Jameson, M. H. (1991). "Sacrifice before Battle." Pp. 197-227 in *Hoplites: The Classical Greek Battle Experience*, ed. V. D. Hanson. London: Routledge.

Janssen, A. J. (1957). *Het antieke tropaion*. Verhandelingen van de Koninklijke Vlaamse Academie voor Wetenschappen, Letteren en Schone Kunsten van België: Klasse der Letteren 27. Brussels: Koninklijke Vlaamse Academie.

Japp, S. (2000). *Die Baupolitik Herodes' des Grossen: Die Bedeutung der Architektur für die Herrschaftslegitimation eines römischen Klientelkönigs*. Internationale Archäologie 64. Rahden: Leidorf.

Jones, A. H. M. (1937). *The Cities of the Eastern Roman Provinces*. Oxford: Clarendon.

Jones, A. H. M. (1938). *The Herods of Judaea*. Oxford: Clarendon.

Joubert, S. (2000). *Paul as Benefactor: Reciprocity, Strategy and Theological Reflection in Paul's Collection*. WUNT II.124. Tübingen: Mohr Siebeck.

Jouön, P. (1935). "Les mots employés pour désigner 'le Temple' dans l'Ancien Testament, le Nouveau Testament et Josèphe." *RSR* 25: 329-43.

Kähler, H. and G. Forni (1958). "Anfiteatro." *Enciclopedia dell'arte antica, classica e orientale* 1: 374-90.
Kallner, D. H. and E. Rosenau (1939). "The Geographical Regions of Palestine." *Geographical Review* 29: 61-80.
Kaplan, J. (1977). "Lod." *EAEHL* 3: 753-54.
Kasher, A. (1985). *The Jews in Hellenistic and Roman Egypt: The Struggle for Equal Rights*, revised English edn. TSAJ 7. Tübingen: Mohr Siebeck.
Kasher, A. (1988). *Jews, Idumaeans, and Ancient Arabs: Relations of the Jews in Eretz-Israel with the Nations of the Frontier and the Desert during the Hellenistic and Roman Era (332 BCE–70 CE)*. TSAJ 18. Tübingen: Mohr Siebeck.
Kasher, A. (1990). *Jews and Hellenistic Cities in Eretz-Israel: Relations of the Jews in Eretz-Israel with the Hellenistic Cities during the Second Temple Period (332 BCE–70 CE)*. TSAJ 21. Tübingen: Mohr Siebeck.
Kasher, A. (2007). *King Herod: A Persecuted Persecutor: A Case Study in Psychohistory and Psychobiography*. SJ 36. Berlin: de Gruyter.
Kennedy, D. L. (1996). "Syria." *CAH* 10: 703-36, 1100-04, 2nd edn.
Kienast, D. (1996). *Römische Kaisertabelle: Grundzüge einer römischen Kaiserchronologie*, 2nd edn. Darmstadt: Wissenschaftliche Buchgesellschaft.
Kienast, D. (1999). *Augustus: Prinzeps und Monarch*, 3rd edn. Darmstadt: Wissenschaftliche Buchgesellschaft.
Klauck, H.-J. (1992). *Gemeinde zwischen Haus und Stadt: Kirche bei Paulus*. Freiburg: Herder.
Klausner, J. (1949-51). *Hisṭoriyah šel ha-bayit ha-šeni* (Hebrew). 5 vols. Jerusalem: 'Aḥi'asaf.
Klengel, H. and E. M. Ruprechtsberger (2001). "Syrien." *DNP* 11: 1170-81.
Knauf, E. A. (1999). "Qôs." *DDD* 674-77, 2nd ed.
Knoche, U. (1934). "Der römische Ruhmesgedanke." *Phil* 89: 102-24.
Koets, P. J. (1929). *Deisidaimonia: A Contribution to the Knowledge of the Religious Terminology in Greek*. Purmerend: Muusses.
Kokkinos, N. (1998). *The Herodian Dynasty: Origins, Role in Society and Eclipse*. JSPSup 30. Sheffield: Sheffield Academic Press.
Konstan, D. (1997). *Friendship in the Classical World*. Key Themes in Ancient History. Cambridge: Cambridge University Press.
Kötting, B. (1973). "'Univira' in Inschriften." Pp. 195-206 in *Romanitas et christianitas: Studia Iano Henrico Waszink, A.D. VI Kal. Nov. A. MCMLXXIII, XIII lustra complenti oblata*, ed. W. den Boer, P. G. van der Nat, and C. M. J. Sicking. Amsterdam: North-Holland.
Kraeling, C. H. (1942). "The Episode of the Roman Standards at Jerusalem." *HTR* 35: 263-89.
Kraemer, D. (2000). *The Meanings of Death in Rabbinic Judaism*. London: Routledge.
Krauss, S. (1910-12). *Grundriss der Gesamtwissenschaft des Judentums: Talmudische Archäologie*. 3 vols. Schriften herausgegeben von der Gesellschaft zur Förderung der Wissenschaft des Judentums. Leipzig: Fock.
Kühner, R. and B. Gerth (1898-1904). *Ausführliche Grammatik der griechischen Sprache, II: Satzlehre*, 3rd edn. Vol 2 in 2. Hanover: Hahnsche Buchhandlung.
Kuhrt, A. (2007). *The Persian Empire: A Corpus of Sources from the Achaemenid Period*. London: Routledge.
Künzl, E. (1988). *Der römische Triumph: Siegesfeiern im antiken Rom*. Beck's Archäologische Bibliothek. Munich: Beck.
Kushnir-Stein, A. (2007). "Josephus' Description of Paneion." *Scripta Classica Israelica* 26: 87-90.
Lämmer, M. (1973). "Griechische Wettkämpfe in Jerusalem und ihre politischen Hintergründe." *Kölner Beiträge zur Sportwissenschaft* 2: 182-227.
Lämmer, M. (1974). "Die Kaiserspiele von Caesarea im Dienste der Politik des Königs Herodes." *Kölner Beiträge zur Sportwissenschaft* 3: 95-164.
Landau, T. (2006). *Out-Heroding Herod: Josephus, Rhetoric, and the Herod Narratives*. AGJU 63. Leiden: Brill.
Landmann, M. (1959). *Das Tier in der jüdischen Weisung*. Heidelberg: Schneider.
Langlands, R. (2006). *Sexual Morality in Ancient Rome*. Cambridge: Cambridge University Press.
Laqueur, R. (1920). *Der jüdische Historiker Flavius Josephus: ein biographischer Versuch auf neuer quellenkritischer Grundlage*. Giessen: von Münchow.
Latte, K. (1960). *Römische Religionsgeschichte*. Handbuch der Altertumswissenschaft 5.4. Munich: Beck.
Lausberg, H. (1998). *Handbook of Literary Rhetoric: A Foundation for Literary Study*, ed. D. E. Orton and R. D. Anderson. Leiden: Brill.
Lebram, J. C. H. (1975). "König Antiochus im Buch Daniel." *VT* 25: 737-72.
Lehmann-Hartleben, K. (1923). *Die antiken Hafenanlagen des Mittelmeeres: Beiträge zur Geschichte des Städtebaus im Altertum*. Klio Suppl. 14. Leipzig: Dieterich.

Leimbach, R. (1985). *Militärische Musterrhetorik: Eine Untersuchung zu den Feldherrnreden des Thukydides.* Stuttgart: Steiner.

Lendle, O. (1992). *Einführung in die griechische Geschichtsschreibung: Von Hekataios bis Zosimos.* Die Altertumswissenschaft. Darmstadt: Wissenschaftliche Buchgesellschaft.

Levine, L. I. (1975). *Caesarea under Roman Rule.* SJLA 7. Leiden: Brill.

Levine, L. I. (1981). "Towards an Appraisal of Herod as a Builder." Pp. 62-66 in *The Jerusalem Cathedra: Studies in the History, Archaeology, Geography and Ethnography of the Land of Israel*, vol. 1, ed. L. I. Levine. Jerusalem: Yad Ben-Zvi.

Levine, L. I. (1998). *Judaism and Hellenism in Antiquity: Conflict or Confluence?* Seattle, Wash.: University of Washington Press.

Lévy, E. (1984). "Naissance du concept de barbare." *Ktema* 9: 5-14.

Lichtenberger, A. (1999). *Die Baupolitik Herodes des Grossen.* Abhandlungen des deutschen Palästina-Vereins 26. Wiesbaden: Harrassowitz.

Lichtenberger, A. (2006). "Jesus and the Theater in Jerusalem." Pp. 283-99 in *Jesus and Archaeology*, ed. J. H. Charlesworth. Grand Rapids, Mich.: Eerdmans.

Liermann, O. (1889). *Analecta epigraphica et agonistica.* Dissertationes Philologicae Halenses 10.1. Halle: Niemeyer.

Lifshitz, B. (1977). "Études sur l'histoire de la province romaine de Syrie." *ANRW* II.8: 3-30.

Lightman, M. and W. Zeisel (1977). "Univira: An Example of Continuity and Change in Roman Society." *CH* 46: 19-32.

Lindner, H. (1972). *Die Geschichtsauffassung des Flavius Josephus im* Bellum Judaicum*: Gleichzeitig ein Beitrag zur Quellenfrage.* AGJU 12. Leiden: Brill.

Lindner, H. (1974). "Eine offene Frage zur Auslegung des *Bellum*-Proömiums." Pp. 254-59 in *Josephus-Studien: Untersuchungen zu Josephus, dem antiken Judentum und dem Neuen Testament: Otto Michel zum 70. Geburtstag gewidmet*, ed. O. Betz, K. Haacker and M. Hengel. Göttingen: Vandenhoeck & Ruprecht.

Lindner, H. (2002). "Der Bau des grösseren Temples (A 15:380-390): Herodianische Propaganda und Josephus' Auffassung der jüdischen Geschichte." Pp. 152-60 in *Internationales Josephus-Kolloquium, Paris 2001: Studies on the Antiquities of Josephus*, ed. F. Siegert and J. U. Kalms. Münsteraner Judaistische Studien 12. Münster: LIT.

Lindsay, D. R. (1993). *Josephus and Faith: Pístis and Pisteúein as Faith Terminology in the Writings of Flavius Josephus and in the New Testament.* AGJU 19. Leiden: Brill.

Linn, M. (1988). "The Location of Geva Parashim" (Hebrew). Pp. 219-23 in *Geva: Archaeological Discoveries at Tell Abu-Shusha, Mishmar Ha-'Emeq*, ed. B. Mazar. Jerusalem: Israel Exploration Society.

Llewelyn, S. R. and D. van Beek (2011). "Reading the Temple Warning as a Greek Visitor." *JSJ* 42: 1-22.

Loraux, N. (1981). *L'invention d'Athènes: Histoire de l'oraison funèbre dans la 'cité classique'.* Civilisations et Sociétés 65. Paris: Mouton.

Lüderitz, G. (1983). *Corpus jüdischer Zeugnisse aus der Cyrenaika.* Beihefte zum Tübinger Atlas des Vorderen Orients: Series B 53. Wiesbaden: Reichert.

Luraghi, S. (2003). *On the Meaning of Prepositions and Cases: The Expression of Semantic Roles in Ancient Greek.* Studies in Language Companion Series 67. Amsterdam: Benjamins.

Luschnat, O. (1942). *Die Feldherrnreden im Geschichtswerk des Thukydides.* Philologus Suppl. 34.2. Leipzig: Dieterich.

Luzzato, M. J. and A. Wittenburg (1996). "Aisopos." *DNP* 1: 360-66.

Mader, G. (2000). *Josephus and the Politics of Historiography: Apologetic and Impression Management in the* Bellum Judaicum. Mnemosyne Suppl. 205. Leiden: Brill.

Magen, Y. (1993). "Mamre." *NEAEHL* 3.939-42.

Magie, D. (1950). *Roman Rule in Asia Minor to the End of the Third Century after Christ.* 2 vols. Princeton, N.J.: Princeton University Press.

Mahieu, B. (2008). "The Foundation Year of Samaria-Sebaste and Its Chronological Implications." *Ancient Society* 38: 183-96.

Mahieu, B. (2012). *Between Rome and Jerusalem: Herod the Great and His Sons in Their Struggle for Recognition: A Chronological Investigation of the Period 40 BC-39 AD, with a Time Setting of New Testament Events.* OLA 208. Louvain: Peeters.

Maier, P. L. (1969). "The Episode of the Golden Roman Shields at Jerusalem." *HTR* 62: 109-21.

Malter, H. (1967). *The Treatise Ta'anit of the Babylonian Talmud*, 2nd edn. Philadelphia, Pa.: Jewish Publication Society.

Mantovani, M. (1990). *Bellum iustum: Die Idee des gerechten Krieges in der römischen Kaiserzeit.* Geist und Werk der Zeiten 77. Bern: Lang.

Ma'oz, Z. U. (1993). "Banias." *NEAEHL* 1.136-43.
Ma'oz, Z. U. (1996). "Banias, Temple of Pan—1993." *Excavations and Surveys in Israel* 15: 1-5.
Marincola, J. (1997). *Authority and Tradition in Ancient Historiography*. Cambridge: Cambridge University Press.
Marincola, J. (2003). "Beyond Pity and Fear: the Emotions of History." *Ancient Society* 33: 285-315.
Marshak, A. K. (2011). "Rise of the Idumeans: Ethnicity and Politics in Herod's Judea." Pp. 117-129 in *Jewish Identity and Politics between the Maccabees and Bar Kokhba: Groups, Normativity, and Rituals*, ed. B. Eckhardt. JSJSup 155. Leiden: Brill.
Mason, H. J. (1974). *Greek Terms for Roman Institutions: A Lexicon and Analysis*. ASP 13. Toronto: Hakkert.
Mason, S. (1991). *Flavius Josephus on the Pharisees: A Compositional-Critical Study*. StPB 39. Leiden: Brill.
Mason, S. (1998). "Should Any Wish to Enquire Further (*Ant.* 1.25): The Aim and Audience of Josephus's *Judean Antiquities/Life*." Pp. 64-103 in *Understanding Josephus: Seven Perspectives*, ed. S. Mason. JSPSup 32. Sheffield: Sheffield Academic Press.
Mason, S. (2003). "Flavius Josephus in Flavian Rome: Reading on and between the Lines." Pp. 559-89 in *Flavian Rome: Culture, Image, Text*, ed. A. J. Boyle and W. J. Dominik. Leiden: Brill.
Mason, S. (2005). "Figured Speech and Irony in T. Flavius Josephus." Pp. 243-88 in *Flavius Josephus and Flavian Rome*, ed. J. Edmondson, S. Mason, and J. B. Rives. Oxford: Oxford University Press.
Mason, S. (2011). "Being Earnest, Being Playful: Speech and Speeches in Josephus and Acts." *Sapientia Logos* 3: 101-82.
Mattern-Parkes, S. P. (2003). "The Defeat of Crassus and the Just War." *The Classical World* 96: 387-396.
Mayer-Schärtel, B. (1995). *Das Frauenbild des Josephus: Eine sozialgeschichtliche und kulturanthropologische Untersuchung*. Stuttgart: Kohlhammer.
Mazar, B. (1952-53). "Beth She'arim, Gaba, and Harosheth of the Peoples." *HUCA* 24: 75-84.
McLaren, J. S. (1991). *Power and Politics in Palestine: The Jews and the Governing of Their Land, 100 BC–AD 70*. JSNTSup 63. Sheffield: JSOT.
Meeks, W. A. (1968). "Moses as God and King." Pp. 354-71 in *Religions in Antiquity: Essays in Memory of Erwin Ramsdell Goodenough*, ed. J. Neusner. SHR 14, Leiden: Brill.
Meijer, F. (2007). *The Gladiators: History's Most Deadly Sport*. New York, N.Y.: Thomas Dunne Books.
Meyer, R. (1940). *Der Prophet aus Galiläa: Studie zum Jesusbild der drei ersten Evangelien*. Leipzig: Lunkenbein.
Meyer, R. (1968). "προφήτης ktl." *TDNT* 6: 812-828.
Michel, O. (1984). "Die Rettung Israels und die Rolle Roms nach den Reden im 'Bellum Iudaicum'." *ANRW* II.21.2: 945-76.
Millar, F. (1993a). "Hagar, Ishmael, Josephus and the Origins of Islam." *JJS* 44: 23-45.
Millar, F. (1993b). *The Roman Near East, 31 BC–AD 337*. Cambridge, Mass.: Harvard University Press.
Miller, P. D. (2000). The Religion of Ancient Israel. Library of Ancient Israel. Louisville, Ky.: Westminster John Knox.
Mitford, T. B. (1980). "Cappadocia and Armenia Minor: Historical Setting of the *Limes*." *ANRW* II.7.2: 1169-228.
Mittmann, S. and G. Schmitt (2001). *Tübinger Bibelatlas: Auf der Grundlage des Tübinger Atlas des Vorderen Orients (TAVO)*. Stuttgart: Deutsche Bibelgesellschaft.
Möller, C. and G. Schmitt (1976). *Siedlungen Palästinas nach Flavius Josephus*. Beihefte zum Tübinger Atlas des Vorderen Orients: Series B 14. Wiesbaden: Reichert.
Momigliano, A. D. (1934). "Herod of Judaea"; "The Roman Government of Palestine"; "The Jewish Rebellion"; "The Campaigns of Vespasian"; "The Siege and Fall of Jerusalem"; "Josephus as a Source for the History of Judaea." *CAH* 10: 316-39, 850-55, 855-58, 859-61, 861-65, 884-87.
Mørkholm, O. (1966). *Antiochus IV of Syria*. Classica et Mediaevalia: Dissertationes 8. Copenhagen: Gyldendal.
Mussies, G. (1999). "Artemis." *DDD* 91-97, 2nd ed.
Myers, E. A. (2010). *The Ituraeans and the Roman Near East: Reassessing the Sources*. Cambridge: Cambridge University Press.
Naber, S. A. (1888-96). *Flavii Iosephi opera omnia: Post Immanuelem Bekkerum; recognovit Samuel Adrianus Naber*. 6 vols. Leipzig: Teubner.
Najman, H. (2000). "Angels at Sinai: Exegesis, Theology and Interpretive Authority." *DSD* 7: 313-333.
Negev, A. (1977). "The Nabateans and the Province Arabia." *ANRW* II.8: 520-686.
Netzer, E. (1986). "The Promontory Palace." Pp. 149-77 in *Excavations at Caesarea Maritima, 1975, 1976, 1979: Final Report*, ed. L. I. Levine and E. Netzer. Qedem 21. Jerusalem: Hebrew University of Jerusalem.
Netzer, E. (1996). "The Palaces Built by Herod: A Research Update." Pp. 27-54 in *Judaea and the Greco-Roman World in the Time of Herod in the Light of Archaeological Evidence*, ed. K. Fittschen and G. Foerster. Abhandlungen der Akademie der Wissenschaften zu Göttingen: Phil.-hist. Kl. 3.215. Göttingen: Vandenhoeck & Ruprecht.

Netzer, E. (1999). *Die Paläste der Hasmonäer und Herodes' des Grossen*. Sonderhefte der antiken Welt. Mainz am Rhein: von Zabern.

Netzer, E. (2001). *Hasmonean and Herodian Palaces at Jericho: Final Reports of the 1973-1987 Excavations*, vol. 1: *Stratigraphy and Architecture*. Jerusalem: Israel Exploration Society.

Netzer, E. (2006). *The Architecture of Herod, the Great Builder*. TSAJ 117. Tübingen: Mohr Siebeck.

Neusner, J. (1962). *A Life of Rabban Yohanan ben Zakkai, ca. 1-80 CE*. StPB 6. Leiden: Brill.

Neusner, J. (1969). *A History of the Jews in Babylonia. I: The Parthian Period*, 2nd edn. StPB 9. Leiden: Brill.

Neusner, J. (1970). *Development of a Legend: Studies on the Traditions concerning Yohanan ben Zakkai*. StPB 16. Leiden: Brill.

Neyrey, J. H. (1998). *Honor and Shame in the Gospel of Matthew*. Louisville, Ky.: Westminster John Knox.

Niehoff, M. (1992). *The Figure of Joseph in Post-Biblical Jewish Literature*. AGJU 16. Leiden: Brill.

Nodet, É. (2005). *La crise maccabéenne: Historiographie juive et traditions bibliques*. Josèphe et son temps 6. Paris: Cerf.

Oehler, J. (1921). "Keryx (2)." *PW* 11.1: 349-57.

Oleson, J. P., A. Raban, et al. (1989-94). *The Harbours of Caesarea Maritima: Results of the Caesarea Ancient Harbour Excavation Project, 1980-1985*. 2 vols. BAR International Series 491, 594. Oxford: British Archaeological Reports.

Olson, R. S. (2010). *Tragedy, Authority, and Trickery: The Poetics of Embedded Letters in Josephus*. Hellenic Studies 42. Washington, D.C.: Center for Hellenic Studies.

Oppenheimer, A. (1983). *Babylonia Judaica in the Talmudic Period*. Beihefte zum Tübinger Atlas des Vorderen Orients: Series B 47. Wiesbaden: Reichert.

Oren, E. D. and U. Rappaport (1984). "The Necropolis of Maresha–Beth Govrin." *IEJ* 34: 114-53.

Osborne, M. J. and S. G. Byrne (1994). *A Lexicon of Greek Personal Names*, vol. 2: *Attica*. Oxford: Clarendon.

Otto, W. (1913). "Herodes." *PW* Suppl. 2: 1-205.

Overman, J. A., J. Olive, and M. C. Nelson (2007). "A Newly Discovered Herodian Temple at Khirbet Omrit in Northern Israel." Pp. 177-95 in *The World of the Herods*, ed. N. Kokkinos. Oriens et Occidens 14. Stuttgart: Steiner.

Overman, J. A. and D. N. Schowalter (2011). *The Roman Temple Complex at Horvat Omrit: An Interim Report*. BAR International Series 2205. Oxford: Archaeopress.

Parker, R. (2000). "Sacrifice and Battle." Pp. 299-314 in *War and Violence in Ancient Greece*, ed. H. van Wees. London: Duckworth & Classical Press of Wales.

Pastor, J. (1997). *Land and Economy in Ancient Palestine*. London: Routledge.

Pastor, J. (2003). "Herod, King of Jews and Gentiles: Economic Policy as a Measure of Evenhandedness." Pp. 152-64 in *Jews and Gentiles in the Holy Land in the Days of the Second Temple, the Mishna and the Talmud*, ed. M. Mor, J. Pastor, A. Oppenheimer, and D. R. Schwartz. Jerusalem: Yad Ben-Zvi.

Pastor, J. (2007). "Josephus as a Source for Economic History: Problems and Approaches." Pp. 334-46 in *Making History: Josephus and Historical Method*, ed. Z. Rodgers. JSJSup 110. Leiden: Brill.

Patrich, J. (1993-94). "The Golden Vine, the Sanctuary Portal, and Its Depiction on the Bar-Kokhba Coins." *JJA* 19-20: 56-61.

Patrich, J. (2001). "The *carceres* of the Herodian Hippodrome/Stadium at Caesarea Maritima and Connections with the Circus Maximus." *Journal of Roman Archaeology* 14: 269-83.

Patrich, J. (2002a). "Herod's Hippodrome/Stadium at Caesarea and the Games Conducted Therein." Pp. 29-68 in *What Athens Has to Do with Jerusalem: Essays on Classical, Jewish, and Early Christian Art and Archaeology in Honor of Gideon Foerster*, ed. L. V. Rutgers. Interdisciplinary Studies in Ancient Culture and Religion 1. Louvain: Peeters.

Patrich, J. (2002b). "Herod's Theatre in Jerusalem: A New Proposal." *IEJ* 52: 231-39.

Patrich, J. (2007). "Herodian Caesarea: The Urban Space." Pp. 93-129 in *The World of the Herods*, ed. N. Kokkinos. Oriens et Occidens 14. Stuttgart: Steiner.

Patrich, J. (2009). "538 BCE-70 CE: The Temple (*Beyt Ha-Miqdash*) and Its Mount." Pp. 36-71 in *Where Heaven and Earth Meet: Jerusalem's Sacred Esplanade*, ed. O. Grabar and B. Z. Kedar. Jerusalem: Yad Ben-Zvi.

Patrich, J. (2011). "The Pre-Herodian Temple II: The Building Project of Simeon the Just on the Temple Mount." *RB* 118: 558-74.

Pédech, P. (1964). *La méthode historique de Polybe*. Collection d'Études Anciennes. Paris: Les Belles Lettres.

Pelling, C. B. R. (1988). *Plutarch: Life of Anthony*. Cambridge Greek and Latin Classics. Cambridge: Cambridge University Press.

Perowne, S. (1956). *The Life and Times of Herod the Great*. London: Hodder.

Peters, E. (1985). *Torture*. New Perspectives on the Past. Oxford: Blackwell.
Petit, F. (1978). *Philon d'Alexandrie: Quaestiones in Genesim et in Exodum: Fragmenta Graeca*. Les œuvres de Philon d'Alexandrie 33. Paris: Cerf.
Pfeijffer, I. L. (1999). *First Person Futures in Pindar*. Hermes Einzelschriften 81. Stuttgart: Steiner.
Pflaum, H.-G. (1940). "Essai sur le *cursus publicus* sous le Haut-Empire romain." Pp. 189-390 in *Mémoires présentés par divers savants à l'Académie des Inscriptions et Belles Lettres* 14. Paris: Imprimerie Nationale.
Piattelli, D. (1971). "Ricerche intorno alle relazioni politiche tra Roma e l'EΘNOS TΩN IOUDAIΩN dal 161 a.C. al 4 a.C." *Bulletino dell'Istituto di Diritto Romano* 74: 219-340.
Picard, G. C. (1957). *Les trophées romains: Contribution à l'histoire de la religion et de l'art triomphal de Rome*. Bibliothèque des Écoles Françaises d'Athènes et de Rome 187. Paris: de Boccard.
Pickard-Cambridge, A. (1968). *The Dramatic Festivals of Athens*, 2nd edn. Oxford: Clarendon.
Pitcher, L. V. (2012). "Appian." Pp. 219-33 in *Space in Ancient Greek Literature*, ed. I. J. F. de Jong. Mnemosyne Suppl. 339. Leiden: Brill.
Pleket, H. W. (1973). "Some Aspects of the History of the Athletic Guilds." *ZPE* 10: 197-227.
Pleket, H. W. (1975). "Games, Prizes, Athletes and Ideology: Some Aspects of the History of Sport in the Greco-Roman World." *Stadion* 1: 49-89.
Poland, F. (1934). "Technitai." *PW* 5.A.2: 2473-558.
Price, S. R. F. (1984). *Rituals and Power: The Roman Imperial Cult in Asia Minor*. Cambridge: Cambridge University Press.
Raban, A. and K. G. Holum (1996). *Caesarea Maritima: A Retrospective after Two Millennia*. Documenta et Monumenta Orientis Antiqui 21. Leiden: Brill.
Rabello, A. M. (1981). "Divorce of Jews in the Roman Empire." *JLA* 4: 79-102.
Rabello, A. M. (1982). "Divorce in Josephus" (Hebrew). Pp. 149-64 in *Josephus Flavius: Historian of Eretz-Israel in the Hellenistic-Roman Period*, ed. U. Rappaport. Jerusalem: Yad Ben-Zvi.
Rajak, T. (1998). "The *Against Apion* and the Continuities in Josephus' Political Thought." Pp. 222-46 in *Understanding Josephus: Seven Perspectives*, ed. S. Mason. JSPSup 32. Sheffield: Sheffield Academic Press.
Rajak, T. (2001). *The Jewish Dialogue with Greece and Rome: Studies in Cultural and Social Interaction*. AGJU 48. Leiden: Brill.
Ramage, E. S. (2001). "The *bellum iustum* in Caesar's *De bello Gallico*." *Athenaeum* 89: 145-70.
Reich, R. and Y. Billig (2000a). "A Group of Theatre Seats Discovered near the South-Western Corner of the Temple Mount." *IEJ* 50: 175-84.
Reich, R. and Y. Billig (2000b). "A Group of Theater Seats from Jerusalem." Pp. 349-53 in *Ancient Jerusalem Revealed*, ed. H. Geva, 2nd edn. Jerusalem: Israel Exploration Society.
Reinhold, M. (1933). *Marcus Agrippa: A Biography*. Geneva, N.Y.: Humphrey.
Retsö, J. (2003). *The Arabs in Antiquity: Their History from the Assyrians to the Umayyads*. London: Routledge.
Rey-Coquais, J.-P. (1978). "Syrie romaine, de Pompée à Dioclétien." *JRS* 68: 44-73.
Ribichini, S. (1999). "Gad." *DDD* 339-41, 2nd ed.
Richards, G. C. and R. J. H. Shutt (1937). "Critical Notes on Josephus' *Antiquities*." *CQ* 31: 170-77.
Richards, G. C. and R. J. H. Shutt (1939). "Critical Notes on Josephus' *Antiquities*, II." *CQ* 33: 180-83.
Richardson, P. (1996). *Herod: King of the Jews and Friend of the Romans*. Studies on Personalities of the New Testament. Columbia, S.C.: University of South Carolina Press.
Richardson, P. (2004). *Building Jewish in the Roman Near East*. JSJSup 92. Waco, Tex.: Baylor University Press.
Riedweg, C. (2007). *Pythagoras: Leben, Lehre, Nachwirkung: Eine Einführung*, revised edn. Munich: Beck.
Rijksbaron, A. (2001). *Over bepaalde personen*. Amsterdam: Vossiuspers UvA.
Rijksbaron, A. (2002). *The Syntax and Semantics of the Verb in Classical Greek: An Introduction*, 3rd edn. Amsterdam: Gieben.
Ritmeyer, L. (2006). *The Quest: Revealing the Temple Mount in Jerusalem*. Jerusalem: Carta.
Robert, L. (1940). *Les gladiateurs dans l'Orient grec*. Bibliothèque de l'École des Hautes Études: Sciences Historiques et Philologiques 278. Paris: Champion.
Roddaz, J.-M. (1984). *Marcus Agrippa*. Bibliothèque des Écoles Françaises d'Athènes et de Rome 253. Rome: École Française de Rome.
Roll, I. (1983). "The Roman Road System in Judaea." Pp. 136-61 in *The Jerusalem Cathedra: Studies in the History, Archaeology, Geography and Ethnography of the Land of Israel*, vol. 3, ed. L. I. Levine. Jerusalem: Yad Ben-Zvi.
Roller, D. W. (1998). *The Building Program of Herod the Great*. Berkeley, Calif.: University of California Press.
Ronconi, A. (1966). "Exitus illustrium virorum." *RAC* 6: 1258-68.

Ronen, I. (1988). "Formation of Jewish Nationalism among the Idumaeans." Pp. 214-39 in *Jews, Idumaeans, and Ancient Arabs: Relations of the Jews in Eretz-Israel with the Nations of the Frontier and the Desert during the Hellenistic and Roman Era (332 BCE–70 CE)*, ed. A. Kasher. TSAJ 18. Tübingen: Mohr Siebeck.

Rood, T. C. B. (1998). *Thucydides: Narrative and Explanation*. Oxford Classical Monographs. Oxford: Clarendon.

Rood, T. C. B. (2007). "Herodotus." Pp. 115-30 in *Time in Ancient Greek Literature*, ed. I. J. F. de Jong and R. Nünlist. Mnemosyne Suppl. 291. Leiden: Brill.

Roth, J. P. (1999). *The Logistics of the Roman Army at War (264 B.C.-A.D. 235)*. Columbia Studies in the Classical Tradition 23. Leiden: Brill.

Runnalls, D. R. (1971). *Hebrew and Greek Sources in the Speeches of Josephus' Jewish War*. Ph.D. diss., Toronto.

Runnalls, D. R. (1997). "The Rhetoric of Josephus." Pp. 737-54 in *Handbook of Classical Rhetoric in the Hellenistic Period, 330 B.C.-A.D. 400*, ed. S. E. Porter. Leiden: Brill.

Safrai, S. (1976). "The Temple." Pp. 865-907 in *The Jewish People in the First Century: Historical Geography, Political History, Social, Cultural and Religious Life and Institutions*, vol. 2, ed. S. Safrai et al. CRINT 1.2. Assen: Van Gorcum.

Sanders, E. P. (1994). *Judaism: Practice and Belief, 63 BCE-66 CE*, revised edn. London: SCM.

Sandmel, S. (1967). *Herod: Profile of a Tyrant*. Philadelphia, Pa.: Lippincott.

Satlow, M. L. (2001). *Jewish Marriage in Antiquity*. Princeton, N.J.: Princeton University Press.

Sauvaget, J. (1939). "Remarques sur les monuments Omeyyades, I: Châteaux de Syrie." *JA* 231: 1-59.

Schäfer, P. (1997). *Judeophobia: Attitudes toward the Jews in the Ancient World*. Cambridge, Mass.: Harvard University Press.

Schalit, A. (1968). *A Complete Concordance to Flavius Josephus*, suppl. 1: *Namenwörterbuch zu Flavius Josephus*, ed. K. H. Rengstorf. Leiden: Brill.

Schalit, A. (2001). *König Herodes: Der Mann und sein Werk*, 2nd edn. SJ 4. Berlin: de Gruyter.

Schick, C. (1887). "Herod's Amphitheatre." *PEQ* 19: 161-66.

Schlatter, A. (1913). *Die hebräischen Namen bei Josephus*. BFCT 17.3-4. Gütersloh: Bertelsmann.

Schmitt, J. (1921). *Freiwilliger Opfertod bei Euripides: Ein Beitrag zu seiner dramatischen Technik*. Religionsgeschichtliche Versuche und Vorarbeiten 17.2. Giessen: Töpelmann.

Scholtissek, K. (2004). "'Eine grössere Liebe als diese hat niemand, als wenn einer sein Leben hingibt für seine Freunde' (Joh 15,13): Die hellenistische Freundschaftsethik und das Johannesevangelium." Pp. 413-39 in *Kontexte des Johannesevangeliums: Das vierte Evangelium in religions- und traditionsgeschichtlicher Perspektive*, ed. J. Frey and U. Schnelle. WUNT II.175. Tübingen: Mohr Siebeck.

Schottky, M. (1989). *Media Atropatene und Gross-Armenien in hellenistischer Zeit*. Habelts Dissertationsdrucke: Reihe Alte Geschichte 27. Bonn: Habelt.

Schottky, M. (2000). "Phraates IV." *DNP* 9: 960.

Schreckenberg, H. (1967-69). "Einige Vermutungen zum Josephustext." *Theokratia* 1: 64-75.

Schreckenberg, H. (1977). *Rezeptionsgeschichtliche und textkritische Untersuchungen zu Flavius Josephus*. ALGHJ 10. Leiden: Brill.

Schremer, A. (1998). "Divorce in Papyrus Ṣe'elim 13 Once Again: A Reply to Tal Ilan." *HTR* 91: 193-202.

Schröder, B. (1996). *Die 'väterlichen Gesetze': Flavius Josephus als Vermittler von Halachah an Griechen und Römer*. TSAJ 53. Tübingen: Mohr Siebeck.

Schürer, E. (1901-09). *Geschichte des jüdischen Volkes im Zeitalter Jesu Christi*, 3rd and 4th edns. 3 vols. Leipzig: Hinrich.

Schwartz, D. R. (1990). *Agrippa I: The Last King of Judaea*. TSAJ 23. Tübingen: Mohr Siebeck.

Schwartz, D. R. (1994). "Josephus on Hyrcanus II." Pp. 210-32 in *Josephus and the History of the Greco-Roman Period: Essays in Memory of Morton Smith*, ed. F. Parente and J. Sievers. StPB 41. Leiden: Brill.

Schwartz, D. R. (1996). "Temple or City: What Did Hellenistic Jews See in Jerusalem?" Pp. 114-27 in *The Centrality of Jerusalem: Historical Perspectives*, ed. M. Poorthuis and C. Safrai. Kampen: Kok Pharos.

Schwartz, D. R. (2013). *Reading the First Century: On Reading Josephus and Studying Jewish History of the First Century*. WUNT I.300. Tübingen: Mohr Siebeck.

Schwartz, E. (1907). "Zur Chronologie des Paulus." PP. 262-99 in Nachrichten von der königlichen Gesellschaft der Wissenschaften zu Göttingen: Phil.-hist. Kl. Berlin: Weidmann.

Schwemer, A. M. (1995-96). *Studien zu den frühjüdischen Prophetenlegenden* Vitae Prophetarum. 2 vols. TSAJ 49-50. Tübingen: Mohr Siebeck.

Schwenn, F. (1915). *Die Menschenopfer bei den Griechen und Römern*. Religionsgeschichtliche Versuche und Vorarbeiten 15.3. Giessen: Töpelmann.

Scolnic, B. E. (1999). *Chronology and Papponymy: A List of the Judean High Priests of the Persian Period*. South Florida Studies in the History of Judaism 206. Atlanta, Ga.: Scholars Press.

Sevenster, J. N. (1975). *The Roots of Pagan Anti-Semitism in the Ancient World*. NovTSup 41. Leiden: Brill.

Shahar, Y. (2004). *Josephus Geographicus: The Classical Context of Geography in Josephus*. TSAJ 98. Tübingen: Mohr Siebeck.

Shatzman, I. (1991). *The Armies of the Hasmonaeans and Herod: From Hellenistic to Roman Frameworks*. TSAJ 25. Tübingen: Mohr Siebeck.

Shaw, B. D. (1993). "Tyrants, Bandits and Kings: Personal Power in Josephus." *JJS* 44: 176-204.

Shaw, B. D. (1995). "Josephus: Roman Power and Responses to It." *Athenaeum* 83: 357-90.

Shemesh, A. (2009). *Halakhah in the Making: The Development of Jewish Law from Qumran to the Rabbis*. Taubman Lectures in Jewish Studies 6. Berkeley, Calif.: University of California Press.

Sievers, J. (1989). "The Role of Women in the Hasmonean Dynasty." Pp. 132-46 in *Josephus, the Bible, and History*, ed. L. H. Feldman and G. Hata. Leiden: Brill.

Sievers, J. (1990). *The Hasmoneans and Their Supporters: From Mattathias to the Death of John Hyrcanus I*. South Florida Studies in the History of Judaism 6. Atlanta, Ga.: Scholars Press.

Sievers, J. (1997). "Who were the Pharisees?" Pp. 137-55 in *Hillel and Jesus: Comparative Studies of Two Major Religious Leaders*, ed. J. H. Charlesworth and L. L. Johns. Minneapolis, Minn.: Fortress.

Sievers, J. (2007). "The Ancient Lists of Contents of Josephus' *Antiquities*." Pp. 271-92 in *Studies in Josephus and the Varieties of Ancient Judaism: Louis H. Feldman Jubilee Volume*, ed. S. J. D. Cohen and J. J. Schwartz. AGJU 67. Leiden: Brill.

Sievers, J. (2009). "Herod, Josephus, and Laqueur: A Reconsideration." Pp. 83-112 in *Herod and Augustus*, ed. D. M. Jacobson and N. Kokkinos. ISJ Studies in Judaica 6. Leiden: Brill.

Simons, J. (1952). *Jerusalem in the Old Testament: Researches and Theories*. Studia Francisci Scholten Memoriae Dicata 1. Leiden: Brill.

Slater, D. A. (1912). "Was the Fourth Eclogue Written to Celebrate the Marriage of Octavia to Mark Antony?: A Literary Parallel." *Classical Review* 26: 114-19.

Smallwood, E. M. (1976). *The Jews under Roman Rule: From Pompey to Diocletian*. SJLA 20. Leiden: Brill.

Smith, M. (1987). "The Occult in Josephus." Pp. 236-56 in *Josephus, Judaism, and Christianity*, ed. L. H. Feldman and G. Hata. Leiden: Brill.

Smith, M. (1999). "The Gentiles in Judaism, 125 BCE–CE 66." *CHJ* 3: 192-249.

Sorek, S. (2010). *Remembered for Good: A Jewish Benefaction System in Ancient Palestine*. Sheffield: Sheffield Phoenix Press.

Spiess, F. (1881). *Das Jerusalem des Josephus: Ein Beitrag zur Topographie der heiligen Stadt*. Berlin: Habel.

Stählin, G. (1974). "φιλέω." *TDNT* 9: 113-71.

Stein, A. (1915). *Untersuchungen zur Geschichte und Verwaltung Ägyptens unter römischer Herrschaft*. Stuttgart: Metzler.

Stern, M. (1974a). "The Jewish Diaspora." Pp. 117-83 in *The Jewish People in the First Century: Historical Geography, Political History, Social, Cultural and Religious Life and Institutions*, vol. 1, ed. S. Safrai et al. CRINT 1.1. Assen: Van Gorcum.

Stern, M. (1974b). "The Reign of Herod and the Herodian Dynasty." Pp. 216-307 in *The Jewish People in the First Century: Historical Geography, Political History, Social, Cultural and Religious Life and Institutions*, vol. 1, ed. S. Safrai et al. CRINT 1.1. Assen: Van Gorcum.

Stern, M. (1974c). "The Province of Judaea." Pp. 308-76 in *The Jewish People in the First Century: Historical Geography, Political History, Social, Cultural and Religious Life and Institutions*, vol. 1, ed. S. Safrai et al. CRINT 1.1. Assen: Van Gorcum.

Stern, M. (1974-84). *Greek and Latin Authors on Jews and Judaism*. 3 vols. Publications of the Israel Academy of Sciences and Humanities: Section of Humanities. Jerusalem: Israel Academy of Sciences and Humanities.

Stern, M. (1976a). "Aspects of Jewish Society: The Priesthood and other Classes." Pp. 561-630 in *The Jewish People in the First Century: Historical Geography, Political History, Social, Cultural and Religious Life and Institutions*, vol. 2, ed. S. Safrai et al. CRINT 1.2. Assen: Van Gorcum.

Stern, M. (1976b). "The Jews in Greek and Latin Literature." Pp. 1101-59 in *The Jewish People in the First Century: Historical Geography, Political History, Social, Cultural and Religious Life and Institutions*, vol. 2, ed. S. Safrai et al. CRINT 1.2. Assen: Van Gorcum.

Stern, M. (1982). "Social and Political Realignments in Herodian Judaea." Pp. 40-62 in *The Jerusalem Cathedra: Studies in the History, Archaeology, Geography and Ethnography of the Land of Israel*, vol. 2, ed. L. I. Levine.

Jerusalem: Yad Ben-Zvi.

Sullivan, R. D. (1977). "The Dynasty of Judaea in the First Century." *ANRW* II.8: 296-354.

Sullivan, R. D. (1980). "The Dynasty of Cappadocia." *ANRW* II.7.2: 1125-68.

Sydenham, E. A. (1952). *The Coinage of the Roman Republic*. London: Spink.

Syme, R. (1939). *The Roman Revolution*. Oxford: Clarendon.

Taylor, J. (2004). *Pythagoreans and Essenes: Structural Parallels*. Collection de la *REJ* 32. Paris: Peeters.

Taylor, J. E. (1993). *Christians and the Holy Places: The Myth of Jewish-Christian Origins*. Oxford: Clarendon.

Teasdale, A. (1996-97). "Herod the Great's Building Program." *BYU Studies* 36.3: 85-98.

Thackeray, H. S. J. and R. Marcus (1930-55). *A Lexicon to Josephus*. 4 vols. Publications of the Alexander Kohut Memorial Foundation. Paris: Geuthner.

Thesleff, H. (1965). *The Pythagorean Texts of the Hellenistic Period*. Acta Academiae Aboensis: Series A: Humaniora 30.1. Åbo: Åbo Akademi.

Too, Y. L. (2001). *Education in Greek and Roman Antiquity*. Leiden: Brill.

Trebilco, P. R. (1991). *Jewish Communities in Asia Minor*. SNTSMS 69. Cambridge: Cambridge University Press.

Treu, K. (1972). "Freundschaft." *RAC* 8: 418-34.

Tromp, J. (1996). "Jeruzalem als heilige stad in het jodendom van de Perzische, Hellenistische en Romeinse periode." Pp. 74-93 in *Jeruzalem als heilige stad: Religieuze voorstelling en geloofspraktijk*, ed. K. D. Jenner and G. A. Wiegers. Leidse studiën van de godsdienst 1. Kampen: Kok Pharos.

Tsafrir, Y., L. Di Segni, and J. Green (1994). *Tabula Imperii Romani: Iudaea-Palaestina: Eretz Israel in the Hellenistic, Roman and Byzantine periods: Maps and Gazetteer*. Publications of the Israel Academy of Sciences and Humanities: Section of Humanities. Jerusalem: Israel Academy of Sciences and Humanities.

Udoh, F. E. (2005). *To Caesar What Is Caesar's: Tribute, Taxes, and Imperial Administration in Early Roman Palestine (63 BCE–70 CE)*. BJS 343. Providence, R.I.: Brown Judaic Studies.

van Bruggen, J. (1978). "The Year of the Death of Herod the Great (Τελευτήσαντος δὲ τοῦ Ἡρῴδου ..., Matthew ii 19)." Pp. 1-15 in *Miscellanea Neotestamentica: Studia ad Novum Testamentum praesertim pertinentia a Sociis Sodalicii Batavi c.n. studiosorum Novi Testamenti conventus anno MCMLXXVI quintum lustrum feliciter complentis suscepta*, vol. 2, ed. T. Baarda, A. F. J. Klijn, and W. C. van Unnik. NovTSup 48. Leiden: Brill.

van der Horst, P. W. (1991). *Ancient Jewish Epitaphs: An Introductory Survey of a Millennium of Jewish Funerary Epigraphy (300 BCE–700 CE)*. CBET 2. Kampen: Kok Pharos.

van Groningen, B. A. (1967). *Short Manual of Greek Palaeography*, 4th edn. Leiden: Sijthoff.

van Henten, J. W. (1993). "Antiochus IV as a Typhonic Figure in Daniel 7." Pp. 223-43 in *The Book of Daniel in the Light of New Findings*, ed. A. S. van der Woude. BETL 106. Louvain: Peeters.

van Henten, J. W. (1997). *The Maccabean Martyrs as Saviours of the Jewish People: A Study of 2 and 4 Maccabees*. JSJSup 57. Leiden: Brill.

van Henten, J. W. (1999). "Roma." *DDD* 710-11, 2nd ed.

van Henten, J. W. (2000). "Nero Redivivus Demolished: The Coherence of the Nero Traditions in the Sibylline Oracles." *JSP* 21: 3-17.

van Henten, J. W. (2001). "The Honorary Decree for Simon the Maccabee (1 Macc 14:25-49) in Its Hellenistic Context." Pp. 116-45 in *Hellenism in the Land of Israel*, ed. J. J. Collins and G. E. Sterling. Christianity and Judaism in Antiquity 13. Notre Dame, Ind.: University of Notre Dame Press.

van Henten, J. W. (2003). "Moses as Heavenly Messenger in *Assumptio Mosis* 10:2 and Qumran passages." *JJS* 54: 216-27.

van Henten, J. W. (2005a). "Cleopatra in Josephus: From Herod's Rival to the Wise Ruler's Opposite." Pp. 113-32 in *The Wisdom of Egypt: Jewish, Early Christian, and Gnostic Essays in Honour of Gerard P. Luttikhuizen*, ed. A. Hilhorst and G. H. van Kooten. AGJU 59. Leiden: Brill.

van Henten, J. W. (2005b). "Commonplaces in Herod's Commander Speech in Josephus' *A.J.* 15.127-146." Pp. 183-206 in *Josephus and Jewish History in Flavian Rome and Beyond*, ed. G. Lembi and J. Sievers. JSJSup 104. Leiden: Brill.

van Henten, J. W. (2007a). "Noble Death in Josephus: Just Rhetoric?" Pp. 195-218 in *Making History: Josephus and Historical Method*, ed. Z. Rodgers. JSJSup 110. Leiden: Brill.

van Henten, J. W. (2007b). "Royal Ideology: 1 and 2 Maccabees and Egypt." Pp. 265-82 in *Jewish Perspectives on Hellenistic Rulers*, ed. T. Rajak, S. Pearce, J. Aitken, and J. M. Dines. Hellenistic Culture and Society 50. Berkeley, Calif.: University of California Press.

van Henten, J. W. (2008a). "Matthew 2:16 and Josephus' Portrayals of Herod." Pp. 101-22 in *Jesus, Paul, and Early Christianity: Studies in Honour of Henk Jan de Jonge*, ed. R. Buitenwerf, H. W. Hollander, and J. Tromp. NTSup

130. Leiden: Brill.

van Henten, J. W. (2008b). "The Panegyris in Jerusalem: Responses to Herod's Initiative (Josephus, *Antiquities* 15.268-291)." Pp. 151-73 in *Empsychoi Logoi—Religious Innovations in Antiquity: Studies in Honour of Pieter Willem van der Horst*, ed. A. Houtman, A. F. de Jong, and M. W. Misset-van de Weg. AGJU 73. Leiden: Brill.

van Henten, J. W. (2009). "Martyrdom, Jesus Passion and Barbarism." *BibInt* 17: 239-64.

van Henten, J. W. (2010). "Blaming the Women: Women at Herod's Court in Josephus's *Jewish Antiquities* 15.23-231." Pp. 153-175 in *Women and Gender in Ancient Religions: Interdisciplinary Approaches*, ed. S. P. Ahearne-Kroll, P. A. Holloway, and J. A. Kelhoffer. WUNT II.263. Tübingen: Mohr Siebeck.

van Henten, J. W. (2011a). "Barbarism and the Word Group βάρβαρος Etcetera in the Septuagint." Pp. 87-100 in *Septuagint Vocabulary: Pre-History, Usage, Reception*, ed. J. Joosten and E. Bons. SBLSCS 58. Atlanta, Ga.: SBL.

van Henten, J. W. (2011b). "Constructing Herod as a Tyrant: Assessing Josephus' Parallel Passages." Pp. 193-216 in *Flavius Josephus: Interpretation and History*, ed. J. Pastor, P. Stern, and M. Mor. JSJSup 146. Leiden: Brill.

van Henten, J. W. (2011c). "'Knowing Everything' in the Gospel of John and in Josephus: The Case of Manaemus." *NedTT* 65: 195-211.

van Henten, J.W. (2011d). "Rebellion under Herod the Great and Archelaus: Prominent Motifs and Narrative Function." Pp. 241-70 in *The Jewish Revolt against Rome: Interdisciplinary Perspectives*, ed. M. Popović. JSJSup 154. Leiden: Brill.

van Henten, J. W. and F. Avemarie (2002). *Martyrdom and Noble Death: Selected Texts from Graeco-Roman, Jewish, and Christian Antiquity*. The Context of Early Christianity. London: Routledge.

van Henten, J. W. and L. Huitink (2007). "Josephus." Pp. 213-30 in *Time in Ancient Greek Literature*, ed. I. J. F. de Jong and R. Nünlist. Mnemosyne Suppl. 291. Leiden: Brill.

van Henten, J. W. and L. Huitink (2009). "The Publication of Flavius Josephus' Works and Their Audiences." *Zutot* 6: 49-60.

van Henten, J. W. and L. Huitink (2012). "Josephus." Pp. 199-218 in *Space in Ancient Greek Literature*, ed. I. J. F. de Jong. Mnemosyne Suppl. 339. Leiden: Brill.

van Henten, J. W. and S. Joubert (1996). "Two A-Typical Jewish Families in the Greco-Roman Period." *Neot* 30: 121-40.

van Unnik, W. C. (1979). "A Greek Characteristic of Prophecy in the Fourth Gospel." Pp. 211-29 in *Text and Interpretation: Studies in the New Testament Presented to Matthew Black*, ed. E. Best and R. McL. Wilson. Cambridge: Cambridge University Press.

Vermes, G. and M. D. Goodman (1989). *The Essenes according to the Classical Sources*. Oxford Centre Textbooks 1. Sheffield: JSOT.

Versnel, H. S. (1970). *Triumphus: An Inquiry into the Origin, Development and Meaning of the Roman Triumph*. Leiden: Brill.

Versnel, H. S. (1981). "Self-Sacrifice, Compensation and the Anonymous Gods." Pp. 135-94 in *Le sacrifice dans l'antiquité*, ed. O. Reverdin and B. Grange. Entretiens sur l'antiquité classique 27. Geneva: Hardt.

Villalba i Varneda, P. (1986). *The Historical Method of Flavius Josephus*. ALGHJ 19. Leiden: Brill.

Villeneuve, F. and Z. al-Muheisen (2003). "Dharih and Tannur: Sanctuaries of Central Nabataea." Pp. 83-100 in *Petra Rediscovered: Lost City of the Nabataeans*, ed. G. Markoe. London: Thames & Hudson.

Vogel, M. (2002). *Herodes: König der Juden, Freund der Römer*. Biblische Gestalten 5. Leipzig: Evangelische Verlagsanstalt.

von Destinon, J. (1882). *Die Quellen des Flavius Josephus, I: Die Quellen der Archäologie Buch XII-XVII = Jüd. Krieg Buch I*. Kiel: Lipsius & Tischer.

Vössing, K. (2004). *Mensa regia: Das Bankett beim hellenistischen König und beim römischen Kaiser*. Beiträge zur Altertumskunde 193. Munich: Saur.

Wacholder, B. Z. (1973). "The Calendar of Sabbatical Cycles during the Second Temple and the Early Rabbinic Period." *HUCA* 44: 153-96.

Wagenvoort, H. (1980). *Pietas: Selected Studies in Roman Religion*. Studies in Greek and Roman Religion 1. Leiden: Brill.

Wakker, G. C. (1994). *Conditions and Conditionals: An Investigation of Ancient Greek*. Amsterdam Studies in Classical Philology 3. Amsterdam: Gieben.

Wakker, G. C. (1997). "Emphasis and Affirmation: Some Aspects of *mén* in Tragedy." Pp. 209-31 in *New Approaches to Greek Particles*, ed. A. Rijksbaron. Amsterdam Studies in Classical Philology 7. Amsterdam: Gieben.

Walker, S. and P. Higgs, eds. (2001). *Cleopatra of Egypt: From History to Myth*. London: British Museum Press.

Walton, F. R. (1955). "The Messenger of God in Hecataeus of Abdera." *HTR* 48: 255-57.

Warszawski, A. and A. Peretz (1992). "Building the Temple Mount: Organization and Execution" (Hebrew). *Cathedra* 66: 3-46.

Weiler, I. (1974). *Der Agon im Mythos: Zur Einstellung der Griechen zum Wettkampf.* Impulse der Forschung 16. Darmstadt: Wissenschaftliche Buchgesellschaft.

Wellhausen, J. (1914). *Israelitische und jüdische Geschichte*, 7th edn. Berlin: Reimer.

White, J. L. (1986). *Light from Ancient Letters*. Foundations and Facets: New Testament. Philadelphia, Pa.: Fortress.

Wilkinson, J. (1975). "The Way from Jerusalem to Jericho." *BA* 38: 10-24.

Willrich, H. (1929). *Das Haus des Herodes zwischen Jerusalem und Rom*. Bibliothek der klassischen Altertumswissenschaftern 6. Heidelberg: Winter.

Wilson Jones, M. (1989). "Designing the Roman Corinthian Order." *Journal of Roman Archaeology* 2: 35-69.

Wilson Jones, M. (1991). "Designing the Roman Corinthian Capital." *Proceedings of the British School at Rome* 59: 89-150.

Windisch, H. (1964). "Βάρβαρος." *TDNT* 1: 546-53.

Winston, D. (1979). *The Wisdom of Solomon: A New Translation with Introduction and Commentary*. AB 43. Garden City, N.Y.: Doubleday.

Wiseman, T. P. (1991). *Flavius Josephus: Death of an Emperor*. Exeter Studies in History 30. Exeter: University of Exeter Press.

Woelcke, K. (1911). "Beiträge zur Geschichte des Tropaions." *BJ* 120: 127-235.

Wyke, M. (2009). "Meretrix regina: Augustan Cleopatras." Pp. 334-80 in *Augustus*, ed. J. Edmondson. Edinburgh Readings on the Ancient World. Edinburgh: Edinburgh University Press.

Yardeni, A. (1997). "Aramaic and Hebrew Documentary Texts." Pp. 7-129 in *Aramaic, Hebrew and Greek Documentary Texts from Nahal Hever and Other Sites: With an Appendix Containing Alleged Qumran Tests*, ed. H. M. Cotton and A. Yardeni. DJD 27. Oxford: Clarendon.

Zachos, K. L. (2003). "The *tropaeum* of the Sea-Battle of Actium at Nicopolis: Interim Report." *Journal of Roman Archaeology* 16: 64-92.

Zanker, P. (1988). *The Power of Images in the Age of Augustus*. Ann Arbor, Mich.: University of Michigan Press.

Ziegler, K.-H. (1964). *Die Beziehungen zwischen Rom und dem Partherreich: Ein Beitrag zur Geschichte des Völkerrechts*. Wiesbaden: Steiner.

Ziehen, L. (1934). "Theoroi." *PW* 5.A.2: 2239-44.

Zuckermann, B. (1866). *A Treatise on the Sabbatical Cycle and the Jubilee: A Contribution to the Archaeology and Chronology of the Time Anterior and Subsequent to the Captivity, Accompanied by a Table of Sabbatical Years*. London: Chronological Institute.

BIBLIOGRAPHY OF PRIMARY SOURCES

Editions mentioned in Abbreviations are not listed below.

Achilles Tatius. Ed. S. Gaselee. LCL 45. London: Heinemann, 1917.
Adamantius, *Physiognomonica*. Ed. R. Foerster, *Scriptores physiognomonici Graeci et Latini*, 1:297-426. Teubner. Leipzig: Teubner, 1893.
Aelian, *De natura animalium*. Ed. A. F. Scholfield, *Aelian: On the Characteristics of Animals*. 3 vols. LCL 446, 448-449. London: Heinemann, 1958-59.
Aelius Aristides, *Ad Platonem pro quattuor viris*. Ed. W. Dindorf, *Aristides*, 2:156-414. Leipzig: Reimer, 1829.
Aelius Aristides, *Ad Platonem pro rhetorica*. Ed. W. Dindorf, *Aristides*, 2:1-155. Leipzig: Reimer, 1829.
Aelius Aristides, *Adversus Demosthenem de immunitate*. Ed. W. Dindorf, *Aristides*, 2:609-41. Leipzig: Reimer, 1829.
Aelius Aristides, *Ars rhetorica*. Ed. L. Spengel, *Rhetores Graeci*, 2:459-554. Teubner. Leipzig: Teubner, 1854.
Aelius Aristides, *De concordia ad civitates Asiaticas*. Ed. W. Dindorf, *Aristides*, 1:768-96. Leipzig: Reimer, 1829.
Aelius Aristides, *De urbe Roma*. Ed. W. Dindorf, *Aristides*, 1:321-70. Leipzig: Reimer, 1829.
Aelius Aristides, *In Iovem*. Ed. W. Dindorf, *Aristides*, 1:1-11. Leipzig: Reimer, 1829.
Aelius Aristides, *In regem*. Ed. W. Dindorf, *Aristides*, 1:98-112. Leipzig: Reimer, 1829.
Aelius Aristides, *Legatio ad Achillem*. Ed. W. Dindorf, *Aristides*, 2:584-608. Leipzig: Reimer, 1829.
Aelius Aristides, *Orationes Leuctricae*. Ed. W. Dindorf, *Aristides*, 1:611-710. Leipzig: Reimer, 1829.
Aelius Aristides, *Panegyrica in laudem Cyzici*. Ed. W. Dindorf, *Aristides*, 1:382-400. Leipzig: Reimer, 1829.
Aelius Aristides, *Sacri sermones*. Ed. W. Dindorf, *Aristides*, 1:445-551. Leipzig: Reimer, 1829.
Aeschines, *Epistulae*. Ed. V. Martin and G. de Budé, *Eschine: Discours*, 2:123-43. Budé. Paris: Les Belles Lettres, 1927.
Aeschines, *In Timarchum*. Ed. V. Martin and G. de Budé, *Eschine: Discours*, 1:20-86. Budé. Paris: Les Belles Lettres, 1927.
Aeschylus. Ed. H. W. Smyth and H. Lloyd-Jones. 2 vols. LCL 145-146. London: Heinemann, 1922-26.
Aeschylus, *Fragmenta*. Ed. H. J. Mette, *Die Fragmente der Tragödien des Aischylos*, 1-255. Deutsche Akademie der Wissenschaften zu Berlin: Schriften der Sektion für Altertumswissenschaft 15. Berlin: Akademie Verlag, 1959.
Aesop. Ed. A. Hausrath and H. Hunger, *Fabulae Aesopicae soluta oratione conscriptae*, 1.1:1-210; 1.2:1-190. 2 vols. Corpus Fabularum Aesopicarum 1-1.1. Leipzig: Teubner, 1959-70, 2nd edn.
Agatharchides, *De mari Erythraeo*. Ed. K. Müller, *Geographi Graeci minores*, 1:111-94. Bibliotheca Graeca. Paris: Didot, 1855.
Alexander of Aphrodisias, *In Aristotelis Topicorum libros octo commentaria*. Ed. M. Wallies, *Alexandri Aphrodisiensis in Aristotelis Topicorum libros octo commentaria*, 1-591. Commentaria in Aristotelem Graeca 2.2. Berlin: Reimer, 1891.
Anaximenes of Lampsacus. Ed. M. Fuhrmann, *Anaximenis ars rhetorica quae vulgo fertur Aristotelis ad Alexandrum*, 1-97. Teubner. Leipzig: Teubner, 1966.
Andocides, *De reditu*. Ed. K. J. Maidment, *Minor Attic Orators*, 1:462-80. LCL 308. London: Heinemann, 1941.
Antiphon, *De caede Herodis*. Ed. K. J. Maidment, *Minor Attic Orators*, 1:160-230. LCL 308. London: Heinemann, 1941.
Aphthonius. Ed. H. Rabe, *Aphthonii progymnasmata*, 1-51. Rhetores Graeci 10. Leipzig: Teubner, 1926.
Apollonius of Rhodes, *Argonautica*. Ed. W. H. Race, *Apollonius Rhodius: Argonautica*. LCL 1. Cambridge, Mass.: Harvard University Press, 2008.
Appian, *Bella civilia* and *Historia romana*. Ed. H. White, *Appian: Roman History (containing* The Civil Wars*)*. 4 vols. LCL 2-5. London: Heinemann, 1912-13.
Aristophanes. Ed. J. Henderson. 5 vols. LCL 178-180, 488, 502. Cambridge, Mass.: Harvard University Press, 1998-2007.
Aristotle. Ed. H. Rackham et al. 23 vols. LCL 73, 193, 199, 228, 255, 264, 271, 285, 287-288, 307, 316-317, 323, 325, 338, 366, 391, 397, 400, 437-439. London: Heinemann; Cambridge, Mass.: Harvard University Press, 1926-2011.
Aristotle, *Fragmenta*. Ed. V. Rose, *Aristotelis qui ferebantur librorum fragmenta*, 23-425. Teubner. Leipzig: Teubner, 1886.
Arrian. Ed. P. A. Brunt. 2 vols. LCL 236, 269. Cambridge, Mass.: Harvard University Press, 1976-83, 2nd edn.

Aspasius. Ed. G. Heylbut, *Aspasii in Ethica Nicomachea quae supersunt commentaria*, 1-186. Commentaria in Aristotelem Graeca 19.1. Berlin: Reimer, 1889.

Athanasius, *De synodis Arimini in Italia et Seleuciae in Isauria*. Ed. H.-G. Opitz, *Athanasius Werke*, 2.1:231-78. Berlin: De Gruyter, 1940.

Athanasius, *Vita Antonii*. Ed. P. Migne, *Patrologia Graeca*, 26:835-978. Paris: Migne, 1887.

Athenaeus. Ed. C. B. Gulick. 7 vols. LCL 204, 208, 224, 235, 274, 327, 345. London: Heinemann, 1927-41. 2nd edn. of vols. 1-5: *The Learned Banqueters*, by S. D. Olson. Cambridge, Mass.: Harvard University Press, 2006-09.

Basil of Caesarea, *Homiliae super Psalmos*. Ed. P. Migne, *Patrologia Graeca*, 29:207-494. Paris: Migne, 1857.

Calpurnius Siculus. Ed. J. W. Duff and A. M. Duff, *Minor Latin Poets*, 1:218-85. LCL 284. London: Heinemann, 1935, 2nd edn.

Cassius Dio. Ed. E. Cary (on the basis of the version of Herbert Baldwin Foster). 9 vols. LCL 32, 37, 53, 66, 82-83, 175-177. London: Heinemann, 1914-27.

Cassius Dio. Ed. U. P. Boissevain, H. Smilda, and W. Nawijn, *Cassii Dionis Cocceiani Historiarum Romanarum quae supersunt*. 5 vols. Berlin: Weidmann, 1895-1931.

Chariton. Ed. G. P. Goold. LCL 481. Cambridge, Mass.: Harvard University Press, 1995.

Chronicon Alexandrinum seu paschale. Ed. P. Migne, *Patrologia Graeca*, 92:67-1028. Paris: Migne, 1865.

Chronicon paschale. Ed. L. A. Dindorf, *Chronicon paschale*, 1:3-737. CSHB. Bonn: Weber, 1832.

Clement of Alexandria, *Eclogae propheticae*. Ed. O. Stählin, L. Früchtel, and U. Treu, *Clemens Alexandrinus*, 3:137-55. GCS 17. Berlin: Akademie Verlag, 1970, 2nd edn.

Clement of Alexandria, *Exhortatio ad Graecos*. Ed. C. Mondésert, *Clément d'Alexandrie: Le protreptique*. SC 2. Paris: Cerf, 1949, 2nd edn.

Clement of Alexandria, *Exhortation to the Heathen*. Trans. W. Wilson, *The Ante-Nicene Fathers, Translations of The Writings of the Fathers down to A.D. 325*, 2:171-206. Ed. A. Roberts, J. Donaldson, and A. C. Coxe. Buffalo, N.Y.: Christian Literature Publishing, 1885.

Clement of Alexandria, *Paedagogus*. Ed. M. Harl, H.-I. Marrou, C. Matray, and C. Mondésert, *Clément d'Alexandrie: Le pédagogue*. 3 vols. SC 70, 108, 158. Paris: Cerf, 1960-70.

Clement of Alexandria, *Stromata*. Ed. O. Stählin, L. Früchtel, and U. Treu, *Clemens Alexandrinus*, 2:3-518; 3:3-102. GCS 15(52) and 17. Berlin: Akademie Verlag, 2:1960, 3rd edn.; 3:1970, 2nd edn.

Cicero. Ed. H. Caplan, L. H. G. Greenwood, H. M. Hubbell, E. W. Sutton, H. Rackham, J. H. Freese, H. G. Hodge, C. Macdonald, N. H. Watts, R. Gardner, W. C. A. Ker, C. W. Keyes, J. E. King, W. A. Falconer, W. Miller, and D. R. Schackleton Bailey. 29 vols. in 30. LCL 7-8, 30, 40, 97, 141, 154, 158, 189, 198, 205, 213, 216, 221, 230, 240, 252, 268, 293, 309, 324, 342, 348-349, 386, 403, 447, 462, 491, 507. London: Heinemann; Cambridge, Mass.: Harvard University Press, 1913-2010. 2nd edn. of vols. 5, 13-14, 17-18:1931-65.

Constantine Porphyrogenitus, *De legationibus Romanorum ad Gentes*. Ed. C. G. de Boor, *Excerpta historica iussu imp. Constantini Porphyrogeniti confecta*, 1.1:1-227; 1.2: 229-599. Berlin: Weidmann, 1903.

Constantine Porphyrogenitus, *De virtutibus et vitiis*. Ed. T. Büttner-Wobst and A. G. Roos, *Excerpta historica iussu imp. Constantini Porphyrogeniti confecta*, 2.1:1-361; 2.2:1-407. Berlin: Weidmann, 2.1:1906, 2.2:1910.

Cornutus. Ed. K. Lang, *Cornuti theologiae Graecae compendium*, 1-76. Teubner. Leipzig: Teubner, 1881.

Damascius, *Vita Isidori*. Ed. C. Zintzen, *Damascii Vitae Isidori reliquiae*, 2-316. Bibliotheca Graeca et Latina 1. Hildesheim: Olms, 1967.

Demosthenes. Ed. J. H. Vince et al. 7 vols. LCL 155, 238, 299, 318, 346, 351, 374. London: Heinemann, 1926-40.

Didymus the Blind, *Fragmenta in Psalmos*. Ed. E. Mühlenberg, *Psalmenkommentare aus der Katenenüberlieferung*, 1:121-375; 2:3-367. PTS 15-16. Berlin: De Gruyter, 1:1975, 2:1977.

Didymus the Blind, *In Genesim*. Ed. P. Nautin and L. Doutreleau, *Didyme l'Aveugle: Sur la Genèse*. 2 vols. SC 233, 244. Paris: Cerf, 1976-78.

Dinarch. Ed. N. C. Conomis, *Dinarchi orationes cum fragmentis*. Teubner. Leipzig: Teubner, 1975.

Dio Chrysostom. Ed. J. W. Cohoon and H. L. Crosby. 5 vols. LCL 257, 339, 358, 376, 385. London: Heinemann, 1932-51.

Diodorus. Ed. C. H. Oldfather, C. L. Sherman, C. B. Welles, R. M. Geer, and F. R. Walton. 12 vols. LCL 279, 303, 340, 375, 377, 384, 389, 390, 399, 409, 422-423. London: Heinemann, 1933-67.

Diogenes Laertius. Ed. R. D. Hicks. 2 vols. LCL 184-185. London: Heinemann, 1925.

Dionysius of Halicarnassus, *Antiquitates romanae*. Ed. E. Cary (on the basis of the version of E. Spelman), *Dionysius of Halicarnassus: Roman Antiquities*. 7 vols. LCL 319, 347, 357, 364, 372, 378, 388. London: Heinemann, 1937-50.

Dionysius of Halicarnassus, *Ars rhetorica*. Ed. H. Usener and L. Radermacher, *Dionysii Halicarnasei quae exstant*, 6:255-387. Teubner. Leipzig: Teubner, 1929.

Dionysius of Halicarnassus, *De compositione verborum*. Ed. H. Usener and L. Radermacher, *Dionysii Halicarnasei quae exstant*, 6:3-143. Teubner. Leipzig: Teubner, 1929.

Dionysius of Halicarnassus, *De Demosthene*. Ed. H. Usener and L. Radermacher, *Dionysii Halicarnasei quae exstant*, 5:127-252. Teubner. Leipzig: Teubner, 1899.

Dionysius of Halicarnassus, *Epistula ad Pompeium Geminum*. Ed. H. Usener and L. Radermacher, *Dionysii Halicarnasei quae exstant*, 6:221-48. Teubner. Leipzig: Teubner, 1929.

Dionysius Periegetes. Ed. K. Müller, *Geographi Graeci minores*, 2:104-76. Bibliotheca Graeca. Paris: Didot, 1861.

Epictetus. Ed. W. A. Oldfather. 2 vols. LCL 131, 218. London: Heinemann, 1925-28.

Epiphanius, *Adversus haereses*. Ed. K. Holl, *Epiphanius*, 1:153-464; 2:1-523; 3:1-526. GCS 25, 31, 37. Leipzig: Hinrichs, 1:1915; 2:1922; 3:1933.

Erotianus. Ed. E. Nachmanson, *Erotiani vocum Hippocraticarum collectio cum fragmentis*, 99-122. Collectio Scriptorum Veterum Upsaliensis. Göteborg: Eranos, 1918.

Eunapius, *Fragmenta*. Ed. L. A. Dindorf, *Historici Graeci minores*, 1:205-74. Teubner. Leipzig: Teubner, 1870.

Euripides. Ed. A. S. Way et al. 8 vols. LCL 9-12, 484, 495, 504, 506. London: Heinemann; Cambridge, Mass.: Harvard University Press, 1912-2008.

Euripides, *Fragmenta*. Ed. A. Nauck, *Tragicorum Graecorum fragmenta*, vol. 1. Leipzig: Teubner, 1889.

Euripides, *Fragmenta*. Ed. R. Kannicht, *Tragicorum Graecorum fragmenta*, vol. 5. Göttingen: Vandenhoeck & Rupprecht, 2004.

Eusebius, *Chronicon*. Ed. A. Schoene, *Eusebi Chronicorum libri duo*, 1:2-286; 2:4-190. Berlin: Weidmann, 1:1875; 2:1866.

Eusebius, *Commentarius in Isaiam*. Ed. J. Ziegler, *Eusebius Werke*, 9:3-411. GCS 56. Berlin: Akademie Verlag, 1975.

Eusebius, *Commentarius in Psalmos*. Ed. P. Migne, *Patrologia Graeca*, 23:11-1396. Paris: Migne, 1857.

Eusebius, *Demonstratio evangelica*. Ed. I. A. Heikel, *Eusebius Werke*, 6:1-492. GCS 23. Leipzig: Hinrichs, 1913.

Eusebius, *Generalis elementaria introductio*. Ed. T. Gaisford, *Eusebii Pamphili episcopi Caesariensis Eclogae propheticae*, 1-236. Oxford: Oxford University Press, 1842.

Eusebius, *Historia ecclesiastica*. Ed. G. Bardy, *Eusèbe de Césarée: Histoire ecclésiastique*. 3 vols. SC 31, 41, 55. Paris: Cerf, 1952-58.

Eusebius, *Onomasticon*. Ed. E. Klostermann, *Eusebius Werke*, 3.1:2-176. GCS 11.1. Leipzig: Hinrichs, 1904.

Eusebius, *Passio sanctorum decem martyrum Aegyptiorum*. Ed. P. Migne, *Patrologia Graeca*, 20:1533-36. Paris: Migne, 1857.

Eusebius, *Praeparatio evangelica*. Ed. K. Mras, *Eusebius Werke*, 8.1:3-613; 8.2:3-426. GCS 43.1-2. Berlin: Akademie Verlag, 8.1: 1954; 8.2: 1956.

Eusebius, *Vita Constantini*. Ed. F. Winkelmann, *Eusebius Werke*, 1.1:3-151. GCS 63. Berlin: Akademie Verlag, 1975.

Eustathius of Thessalonica, *Commentarii ad Homeri Odysseam*. Ed. G. Stallbaum, *Eustathii archiepiscopi Thessalonicensis commentarii ad Homeri Odysseam*, 1:1-443; 2:1-334. Leipzig: Weigel, 1:1825; 2:1826.

Eutecnius. Ed. I. Gualandri, *Eutecnii paraphrasis in Nicandri* Theriaca, 21-70. Testi e documenti per lo studio dell'antichità 25. Milan: Istituto Editoriale Cisalpino, 1968.

Eutropius. Ed. J. Hellegouarc'h. Budé. Paris: Belles Lettres, 1999.

Florus. Ed. E. S. Forster. LCL 231. London: Heinemann, 1929.

Galen, *Ad Glauconem de methodo medendi*. Ed. K. G. Kühn, *Claudii Galeni opera omnia*, 11:1-146. Leipzig: Knobloch, 1826.

Galen, *De alimentorum facultatibus*. Ed. K. G. Kühn, *Claudii Galeni opera omnia*, 6:453-748. Leipzig: Knobloch, 1823.

Galen, *De atra bile*. Ed. K. G. Kühn, *Claudii Galeni opera omnia*, 5:104-48. Leipzig: Knobloch, 1823.

Galen, *De difficultate respirationis*. Ed. K. G. Kühn, *Claudii Galeni opera omnia*, 7:753-960. Leipzig: Knobloch, 1824.

Galen, *De methodo medendi*. Ed. K. G. Kühn, *Claudii Galeni opera omnia*, 10:1-1021. Leipzig: Knobloch, 1825.

Galen, *De placitis Hippocratis et Platonis libri IX*. Ed. K. G. Kühn, *Claudii Galeni opera omnia*, 5:181-805. Leipzig: Knobloch, 1823.

Galen, *De praesagitione ex pulsibus*. Ed. K. G. Kühn, *Claudii Galeni opera omnia*, 9:205-430. Leipzig: Knobloch, 1825.

Galen, *De propriorum animi cuiuslibet affectuum dignotione et curatione*. Ed. K. G. Kühn, *Claudii Galeni opera omnia*, 5:1-57. Leipzig: Knobloch, 1823.

Galen, *De sanitate tuenda*. Ed. K. G. Kühn, *Claudii Galeni opera omnia*, 6:1-452. Leipzig: Knobloch, 1823.

Galen, *De temperamentis*. Ed. K. G. Kühn, *Claudii Galeni opera omnia*, 1:509-694. Leipzig: Knobloch, 1821.

Galen, *De usu partium corporis humani*. Ed. K. G. Kühn, *Claudii Galeni opera omnia*, 3:1-939; 4:1-366. Leipzig: Knobloch, 1822.

Galen, *In Hippocratis aphorismos commentarii VII*. Ed. K. G. Kühn, *Claudii Galeni opera omnia*, 17b:345-887; 18a:1-195. Leipzig: Knobloch, 1829.

Galen, *In Hippocratis librum VI epidemiarum commentarii VI*. Ed. K. G. Kühn, *Claudii Galeni opera omnia*, 17a:793-1009; 17b:1-344. Leipzig: Knobloch, 17a:1828; 17b:1829.

Galen, *Protrepticus*. Ed. K. G. Kühn, *Claudii Galeni opera omnia*, 1:1-39. Leipzig: Knobloch, 1821.

George Hamartolus, *Chronicon*. Ed. C. G. de Boor, *Georgii Monachi Chronicon*. 2 vols. Teubner. Leipzig: Teubner, 1904 (repr. [corr. by Peter Wirth] Stuttgart: Teubner, 1978).

George Hamartolus, *Chronicon breve*. Ed. P. Migne, *Patrologia Graeca*, 110:41-1286. Paris: Migne, 1863.

George Syncellus. Ed. W. Dindorf, *Georgius Syncellus et Nicephorus Cp.*, 1:1-734. CSHB. Bonn: Weber, 1829.

Gorgias, *Fragmenta*. Ed. H. Diels and W. Kranz, *Die Fragmente der Vorsokratiker*, 2:279-306. Berlin: Weidmann, 2:1952, 6th edn.

Gregory of Nazianzus, *Funebris oratio in patrem (Oratio 18)*. Ed. P. Migne, *Patrologia Graeca*, 35:985-1044. Paris: Migne, 1886.

Gregory of Nazianzus, *In laudem Athanasii (Oratio 21)*. Ed. P. Migne, *Patrologia Graeca*, 35:1081-128. Paris: Migne, 1886.

Gregory of Nyssa, *Apologia in Hexaemeron*. Ed. P. Migne, *Patrologia Graeca*, 44:61-124. Paris: Migne, 1863.

Gregory of Nyssa, *Contra Eunomium*. Ed. W. Jaeger, *Gregorii Nysseni opera*, 1:3-409; 2:3-311. Leiden: Brill, 1960.

Gregory of Nyssa, *De hominis opificio*. Ed. P. Migne, *Patrologia Graeca*, 44:123-256. Paris: Migne, 1863.

Gregory of Nyssa, *De vita Mosis*. Ed. J. Daniélou, *Gregoire de Nysse: La vie de Moïse*. SC 1ter. Paris: Cerf, 1968, 3rd edn.

Gregory of Nyssa, *Epistulae*. Ed. G. Pasquali, *Gregorii Nysseni opera*, 8.2:3-95. Leiden: Brill, 1959, 2nd edn.

Gregory of Nyssa, *In Canticum canticorum*. Ed. H. Langerbeck, *Gregorii Nysseni opera*, 6:3-469. Leiden: Brill, 1960.

Gregory of Nyssa, *In inscriptiones Psalmorum*. Ed. J. McDonough, *Gregorii Nysseni opera*, 5:24-175. Leiden: Brill, 1962.

Gregory of Nyssa, *In sanctum pascha*. Ed. E. Gebhardt, *Gregorii Nysseni opera*, 9:245-70. Leiden: Brill, 1967.

Gregory of Nyssa, *Oratio consolatoria in Pulcheriam*. Ed. A. Spira, *Gregorii Nysseni opera*, 9:461-72. Leiden: Brill, 1967.

Gregory of Nyssa, *Vita sanctae Macrinae*. Ed. P. Maraval, *Gregoire de Nysse: Vie de sainte Macrine*. SC 178. Paris: Cerf, 1971.

Heliodorus. Ed. R. M. Rattenbury, T. W. Lumb, and J. Maillon. 3 vols. Budé. Paris: Les Belles Lettres, 1960, 2nd edn.

Hermogenes, *De inventione*. Ed. H. Rabe, *Hermogenes opera*, 93-212. Teubner. Leipzig: Teubner, 1913.

Hermogenes, *De statibus*. Ed. H. Rabe, *Hermogenes opera*, 28-92. Teubner. Leipzig: Teubner, 1913.

Herodian. Ed. C. R. Whittaker. 2 vols. LCL 454-455. London: Heinemann, 1969-70.

Herodotus. Ed. A. D. Godley. 4 vols. LCL 117-120. London: Heinemann, 1920-25. 2nd edn. of vols. 1-2:1926-38.

Heron, *Dioptra*. Ed. H. Schöne, *Heronis Alexandrini opera quae supersunt omnia*, 3:188-314. Teubner. Leipzig: Teubner, 1903.

Heron, *Pneumatica*. Ed. W. Schmidt, *Heronis Alexandrini opera quae supersunt omnia*, 1:2-332. Teubner. Leipzig: Teubner, 1899.

Hesiod, *Fragmenta astronomica*. Ed. H. Diels and W. Kranz, *Die Fragmente der Vorsokratiker*, 1:38-40. Berlin: Weidmann, 1951, 6th edn.

Hippocrates, *De articulis reponendis*. Ed. É. Littré, *Œuvres complètes d'Hippocrate*, 4:78-326. Paris: Baillière, 1844.

Hippocrates, *Epistulae*. Ed. É. Littré, *Œuvres complètes d'Hippocrate*, 9:312-428. Paris: Baillière, 1861.

Hippolytus, *Refutatio omnium haeresium*. Ed. M. Marcovich, *Hippolytus: Refutatio omnium haeresium*, 53-417. PTS 25. Berlin: De Gruyter, 1986.

Historia Augusta. Ed. D. Magie. 3 vols. LCL 139-140, 263. London: Heinemann, 1921-32.

Homer. Ed. A. T. Murray, rev. W. F. Wyatt. 4 vols. LCL 104-105, 170-171. Cambridge, Mass.: Harvard University Press, 1995-99, 2nd edn.

Horace. Ed. C. E. Bennett and H. R. Fairclough. 2 vols. LCL 33, 194. London: Heinemann, 1914-26.

Hyperides, *Oratio pro Euxenippo*. Ed. J. O. Burtt, *Minor Attic Orators*, 2:466-92. LCL 395. London: Heinemann, 1954.

Isaeus. Ed. E. S. Forster. LCL 202. London: Heinemann, 1927.

Isocrates. Ed. G. Norlin and L. Van Hook. 3 vols. LCL 209, 229, 373. London: Heinemann, 1928-45.

John Chrysostom, *Ad Stagirium a daemone vexatum*. Ed. P. Migne, *Patrologia Graeca*, 47:423-94. Paris: Migne, 1863.

John Chrysostom, *Adversus oppugnatores vitae monasticae*. Ed. P. Migne, *Patrologia Graeca*, 47:319-86. Paris: Migne, 1863.

John Chrysostom, *Commentarius in Isaiam*. Ed. J. Dumortier, *Jean Chrysostome: Commentaire sur Isaïe*. SC 304. Paris: Cerf, 1983.

John Chrysostom, *De Babyla contra Iulianum et gentiles*. Ed. M. A. Schatkin, C. Blanc, B. Grillet, and J.-N. Guinot, *Discours sur Babylas; suivie de Homélie sur Babylas*, 90-274. SC 362. Paris: Cerf, 1990.

John Chrysostom, *De Davide et Saule*. Ed. P. Migne, *Patrologia Graeca*, 54:675-708. Paris: Migne, 1862.

John Chrysostom, *De fato et providentia*. Ed. P. Migne, *Patrologia Graeca*, 50:749-74. Paris: Migne, 1862.

John Chrysostom, *De meretrici*. Ed. R. Abicht, "Quellennachweise zum Codex Suprasliensis," *Archiv für slavische Philologie* 16 (1894): 140-53.

John Chrysostom, *Eclogae I-XLVIII ex diversis homiliis*. Ed. P. Migne, *Patrologia Graeca*, 63:567-902. Paris: Migne, 1862.

John Chrysostom, *Expositiones in Psalmos*. Ed. P. Migne, *Patrologia Graeca*, 55:35-784. Paris: Migne, 1862.

John Chrysostom, *Fragmenta in Jeremiam*. Ed. P. Migne, *Patrologia Graeca*, 64:739-1038. Paris: Migne, 1862.

John Chrysostom, *Homiliae in epistulam II ad Corinthios*. Ed. P. Migne, *Patrologia Graeca*, 61:381-610. Paris: Migne, 1862.

John Chrysostom, *Homiliae in epistulam ad Ephesios*. Ed. P. Migne, *Patrologia Graeca*, 62:9-176. Paris: Migne, 1862.

John Chrysostom, *Homiliae in epistulam ad Galatas*. Ed. P. Migne, *Patrologia Graeca*, 61:611-82. Paris: Migne, 1862.

John Chrysostom, *Homiliae in epistulam ad Romanos*. Ed. P. Migne, *Patrologia Graeca*, 60:391-682. Paris: Migne, 1862.

John Chrysostom, *Homiliae in epistulam II ad Timotheum*. Ed. P. Migne, *Patrologia Graeca*, 62:599-662. Paris: Migne, 1862.

John Chrysostom, *Homiliae in Genesim*. Ed. P. Migne, *Patrologia Graeca*, 53:21-386; 54:385-630. Paris: Migne, 1862.

John Chrysostom, *Homiliae in Joannem*. Ed. P. Migne, *Patrologia Graeca*, 59:23-482. Paris: Migne, 1862.

John Chrysostom, *Homiliae in Matthaeum*. Ed. P. Migne, *Patrologia Graeca*, 58:471-794. Paris: Migne, 1862.

John Chrysostom, *In illud: Vidi Dominum*. Ed. J. Dumortier. SC 277. Paris: Cerf, 1981.

John of Damascus, *Vita Barlaam et Joasaph*. Ed. G. R. Woodward and H. Mattingly. LCL 34. London: Heinemann, 1914.

John Philoponus, *De aeternitate mundi contra Proclum*. Ed. H. Rabe, *Ioannes Philoponus: De aeternitate mundi contra Proclum*, 1-646. Teubner. Leipzig: Teubner, 1899.

Josephus. Ed. S. Haverkamp, *Flavii Josephi quae reperiri potuerunt: Opera omnia Graece et Latine*. 2 vols. Amsterdam: Wetstenios, 1726.

Josephus. Ed. T. Reinach et al., *Œuvres complètes de Flavius Josèphe traduites en français sous la direction de Théodore Reinach*. Publications de la Société des Études Juives. 7 vols. Paris: Leroux, 1900-32.

Josephus. Ed. H. St. J. Thackeray, R. Marcus, A. Wikgren, and L. H. Feldman. 10 vols. LCL 186, 203, 210, 242, 281, 326, 365, 410, 433, 456. London: Heinemann, 1926-65.

Julian, *Adversus cynicos indoctos*. Ed. G. Rochefort, *L'empereur Julien: Oeuvres complètes*, 2.1:144-73. Budé. Paris: Les Belles Lettres, 1963.

Julian, *De regno*. Ed. J. Bidez, *L'empereur Julien: Oeuvres complètes*, 1.1:116-80. Budé. Paris: Les Belles Lettres, 1932.

Julian, *In Eusebiae laudem*. Ed. J. Bidez, *L'empereur Julien: Oeuvres complètes*, 1.1:73-105. Budé. Paris: Les Belles Lettres, 1932.

Justin, *Apologia*. Ed. E. J. Goodspeed, *Die ältesten Apologeten*, 26-89. Göttingen: Vandenhoeck & Rupprecht, 1915.

Justin, *Dialogus cum Tryphone*. Ed. E. J. Goodspeed, *Die ältesten Apologeten*, 90-265. Göttingen: Vandenhoeck & Rupprecht, 1915.

Justin, *Epitoma historiarum Philippicarum Pompeii Trogi*. Ed. M.-P. Arnaud-Lindet, *Abrégé des Histoires philippiques de Trogue Pompée*. Corpus Scriptorum Latinorum, 2003.

Libanius, *Declamationes*. Ed. R. Foerster, *Libanii opera*, 5:13-564; 6:7-658; 7:7-736. Teubner. Leipzig: Teubner, 5:1909; 6:1911; 7:1913.

Libanius, *Epistulae*. Ed. R. Foerster, *Libanii opera*, 10:1-758; 11:1-562. Teubner. Leipzig: Teubner, 10:1921; 11:1922.

Libanius, *Orationes*. Ed. R. Foerster, *Libanii opera*, 1.1:79-320; 1.2:354-535; 2:9-572; 3:4-487; 4:6-498. Teubner. Leipzig: Teubner, 1:1903; 2:1904; 3:1906; 4:1908.

Libanius, *Progymnasmata*. Ed. R. Foerster, *Libanii opera*, 8:24-571. Teubner. Leipzig: Teubner, 1915.

Livy. Ed. B. O. Foster, F. G. Moore, E. T. Sage, A. C. Schlesinger, and R. M. Geer. 14 vols. LCL 114, 133, 172, 191, 233, 295, 301, 313, 332, 355, 367, 381, 396, 404. London: Heinemann, 1919-59. 2nd edn. of vols. 9, 14:1936-67.

Lucan. Ed. J. D. Duff. LCL 220. London: Heinemann, 1928.

Lucian. Ed. A. M. Harmon, K. Kilburn, and M. D. MacLeod. 7 vols. LCL 14, 54, 130, 162, 302, 430-431. London: Heinemann, 1913-61.

Lycurgus of Athens. Ed. J. O. Burtt, *Minor Attic Orators*, 2:14-132. LCL 395. London: Heinemann, 1954.

Lysias. Ed. W. R. M. Lamb. LCL 244. London: Heinemann, 1930.

Marcus Aurelius. Ed. C. R. Haines. LCL 58. London: Heinemann, 1916.

Menander, *Fragmenta*. Ed. T. Kock, *Comicorum Atticorum fragmenta*, 3:3-271. Leipzig: Teubner, 1888.

Menander, *Misumenus*. Ed. F. H. Sandbach, *Menandri reliquiae selectae*, 181, 183-94. OCT. Oxford: Clarendon Press, 1972.

Michael Attaliates, *Historia*. Ed. I. Bekker, *Michaelis Attaliotae historia*, 3-322. CSHB. Bonn: Weber, 1853.

Michael Psellus, *Chronographia*. Ed. É. Renauld, *Michel Psellos: Chronographie ou Histoire d'un siècle de Byzance (976-1077)*. 2 vols. Budé. Paris: Les Belles Lettres, 1:1926; 2:1928.

Nicephorus Gregoras, *Historia romana*. Ed. L. Schopen and I. Bekker, *Nicephori Gregorae Byzantina historia*, 1:3-568; 2:571-1146; 3:3-567. CSHB. Bonn: Weber, 1:1829; 2:1830; 3:1855.

Nonnus, *Dionysiaca*. Ed. W. H. D. Rouse, H. J. Rose, and L. R. Lind, *Nonnos: Dionysiaca*. 3 vols. LCL 344, 354, 356. London: Heinemann, 1940.

Olympiodorus the Younger, *In Platonis Alcibiadem commentarii*. Ed. L. G. Westerink, *Olympiodorus: Commentary on the First Alcibiades of Plato*, 1-144. Amsterdam: Hakkert, 1956.

Onosander. Ed. the Illinois Greek Club, *Aeneas Tacticus; Asclepiodotus; Onasander*, 368-526. LCL 156. London: Heinemann, 1923.

Oppian of Corycus. Ed. A. W. Mair, *Oppian; Colluthus; Tryphiodorus*, 200-514. LCL 219. London: Heinemann, 1928.

Origen, *Commentarium in evangelium Matthaei*. Books 10-17: Ed. E. Klostermann, *Origenes Werke*, 10.1:69-304; 10.2:305-703. GCS 40.1-40.2. Leipzig: Teubner, 10.1:1935; 10.2:1937.

Origen, *Expositio in Proverbia*. Ed. P. Migne, *Patrologia Graeca*, 17:161-252. Paris: Migne, 1857.

Orosius. Ed. M.-P. Arnaud-Lindet. 3 vols. Budé. Paris: Belles Lettres, 1990-91.

Parthenius of Nicaea. Ed. G. Thornley, J. M. Edmonds, and S. Gaselee, *Daphnis and Chloe by Longus; The Love Romances of Parthenius and Other Fragments*, 256-346. LCL 69. London: Heinemann, 1916.

Pausanias. Ed. W. H. S. Jones, H. A. Ormerod, and R. E. Wycherley. 5 vols. LCL 93, 188, 272, 297-298. London: Heinemann, 1918-35.

Philo. Ed. F. H. Colson, G. H. Whitaker, R. Marcus, and J. W. Earp. 12 vols. LCL 226-227, 247, 261, 275, 289, 320, 341, 363, 379-380, 401. London: Heinemann, 1929-62.

Philo of Byblos, *De diversis verborum significationibus*. Ed. V. Palmieri, *De diversis verborum significationibus*, 125-231. Speculum 8. Napoli: D'Auria, 1988.

Philodamus. Ed. J. U. Powell, *Collectanea Alexandrina*, 165-69. Oxford: Clarendon Press, 1925.

Philodemus, *De musica*. Ed. J. Kemke, *Philodemi De musica librorum quae exstant*, 1-111. Teubner. Leipzig: Teubner, 1884.

Philostratus. Ed. C. P. Jones et al. 6 vols. LCL 16-17, 134, 256, 383, 458. London: Heinemann; Cambridge, Mass.: Harvard University Press, 1921-2006.

Photius, *Bibliotheca*. Ed. R. Henry and J. Schamp, *Photius: Bibliothèque*. 9 vols. Budé. Paris: Belles Lettres, 1959-91.

Plato. Ed. H. N. Fowler, W. R. M. Lamb, et al. 12 vols. LCL 36, 123, 164-167, 187, 192, 201, 234, 237, 276. London: Heinemann, 1914-35.

Plato, *Definitiones*. Ed. J. Burnet, *Platonis opera*, 5:III.364a-406a. OCT. Oxford: Clarendon Press, 1907.

Pliny the Elder. Ed. H. Rackham, W. H. S. Jones, and D. E. Eichholz. 10 vols. LCL 330, 352-353, 370-371, 392-393, 394, 418-419. London: Heinemann, 1938-63. 2nd edn. of vols. 1, 3-4:1949-83.

Plutarch, *Fragmenta*. Ed. F. H. Sandbach, *Plutarchi moralia*, 7:13-138. Teubner. Leipzig: Teubner, 1967.

Plutarch, *Lives*. Edited and translated by B. Perrin and J. W. Cohoon, *Plutarch's Lives in eleven volumes*. 11 vols. LCL 46-47, 65, 80, 87, 98-103. London: Heinemann, 1914-26.

Plutarch, *Moralia*. Edited and translated by F. C. Babbitt, W. C. Helmbold, P. H. De Lacy, B. Einarson, L. Pearson, F. H. Sandbach, P. A. Clement, H. B. Hoffleit, E. L. Minar, H. N. Fowler, and H. Cherniss, *Plutarch's Moralia in sixteen volumes*. 16 vols. in 17. LCL 197, 222, 245, 305-306, 321, 337, 405-406, 424-429, 470. London: Heinemann, 1927-76. Index by E. N. O'Neil. LCL 499. Cambridge, Mass.: Harvard University Press, 2004.

Polyaenus. Ed. E. Woelfflin and J. Melber, *Polyaeni strategematon libri octo*, 2-425. Teubner. Leipzig: Teubner, 1887.

Polybius. Ed. W. R. Paton. 6 vols. LCL 128, 137-138, 159-161. London: Heinemann, 1922-27.

Procopius. Ed. H. B. Dewing and G. Downey. 7 vols. LCL 48, 81, 107, 173, 217, 290, 343. London: Heinemann, 1914-40.

Propertius. Ed. G. P. Goold. LCL 18. Cambridge, Mass.: Harvard University Press, 1990.

Pseudo-Apollodorus. Ed. R. Wagner, *Apollodori Bibliotheca; Pediasimi libellus de duodecim Herculis laboribus*, 5-169. Mythographi Graeci 1. Leipzig: Teubner, 1894.

Pseudo-Callisthenes. Ed. W. Kroll, *Historia Alexandri Magni (Pseudo-Callisthenes)*. Vol. 1: Recensio vetusta. Berlin: Weidmann, 1926.

Pseudo-Callisthenes. Ed. H. van Thiel, *Leben und Taten Alexanders von Makedonien: Der griechische Alexanderroman nach der Handschrift L*, 1-167. Texte zur Forschung 13. Darmstadt: Wissenschaftliche Buchgesellschaft, 1974.

Pseudo-Clement, *Homiliae*. Ed. B. Rehm, J. Irmsher, and F. Paschke, *Die Pseudoklementinen*, 1:23-281. GCS 42. Berlin: Akademie Verlag, 1969, 2nd edn.

Pseudo-Galen, *Definitiones medicae*. Ed. K. G. Kühn, *Claudii Galeni opera omnia*, 19:346-462. Leipzig: Knobloch, 1830.

Pseudo-Galen, *Introductio seu medicus*. Ed. K. G. Kühn, *Claudii Galeni opera omnia*, 14:674-797. Leipzig: Knobloch, 1827.

Pseudo-Ignatius, *Epistulae*. Ed. F. X. Funk and F. Diekamp, *Patres apostolici*, 2:83-268. Tübingen: Laupp, 1913, 3rd edn.

Pseudo-Justin, *Oratio ad gentiles*. Ed. J. K. T. von Otto, *S. Iustini philosophi et martyris: Opera quae feruntur omnia*, 2:2-18. Corpus Apologetarum Christianorum Saeculi Secundi 3. Jena: Mauke, 1879, 3rd edn.

Pseudo-Justin, *Quaestiones et responsiones ad orthodoxos*. Ed. J. K. T. von Otto, *S. Iustini philosophi et martyris: Opera quae feruntur omnia*, 3.2:2-246. Corpus apologetarum Christianorum Saeculi Secundi 5. Jena: Mauke, 1881, 3rd edn.

Pseudo-Lucian. Ed. M. D. MacLeod, *Lucian*, vol. 8. LCL 432. London: Heinemann, 1967.

Pseudo-Plutarch, *De Homero*. Ed. J. F. Kindstrand, *Plutarchi De Homero*, 1-117. Teubner. Leipzig: Teubner, 1990.

Pseudo-Seneca, *Octavia*. Ed. J. F. Miller, *Seneca*, 9:410-88. LCL 78. London: Heinemann, 1917.

Pseudo-Socrates, *Epistulae*. Ed. R. Hercher, *Epistolographi Graeci*, 609-35. Bibliotheca Graeca. Paris: Didot, 1873.

Sappho. Ed. E. Lobel and D. L. Page, *Poetarum Lesbiorum fragmenta*, 2-110. Oxford: Clarendon Press, 1968, corr. 1st edn.

Seneca the Younger, *Ad Lucilium epistulae morales*. Ed. R. M. Gummere, *Seneca: Ad Lucilium epistulae morales*. 3 vols. LCL 75-77. London: Heinemann, 1917-25.

Seneca the Younger, *De malo belli civilis*. Ed. F. Bücheler and A. Riese, *Anthologia Latina sive Poesis Latinae supplementum*, 1.1:340-41. Teubner. Leipzig: Teubner, 1894.

Sextus Empiricus. Ed. R. G. Bury. 4 vols. LCL 273, 291, 311, 382. London: Heinemann, 1933-49.

Simplicius, *Commentarius in Epicteti enchiridion*. Ed. F. Dübner, *Theophrasti Characteres*, 1-138. Bibliotheca Graeca. Paris: Didot, 1842.

Socrates of Constantinople. Ed. P. Périchon and P. Maraval. 4 vols. SC 477, 493, 505, 506. Paris: Cerf, 2004-07.

Sopater, *Quaestionum divisio*. Ed. C. Walz, *Rhetores Graeci*, 8:2-385. Stuttgart: Cotta, 1835.

Sophocles. Ed. H. Lloyd-Jones. 3 vols. LCL 20-21, 483. Cambridge, Mass.: Harvard University Press, 1994-96.

Sophocles, *Scholia in Sophoclis Oedipum tyrannum*. Ed. P. N. Papageorgius, *Scholia in Sophoclis tragoedias vetera: E codice Laurentiano denuo collato: Edidit commentario critico instruxit, indices adiecit*, 161-212. Teubner. Leipzig: Teubner, 1888.

Sozomen. Ed. A.-J. Festugière, B. Grillet, et al. 4 vols. SC 306, 418, 495, 516. Paris: Cerf, 1983-2008.

Statius. Ed. D. R. Schackleton Bailey. 3 vols. LCL 206-207, 498. Cambridge, Mass.: Harvard University Press, 2003.

Stobaeus. Ed. C. Wachsmuth and O. Hense, *Ioannis Stobaei Anthologii*. 5 vols. Berlin: Weidmann, 1884-1912.

Strabo. Ed. H. L. Jones (based in part upon the unfinished version of J. R. S. Sterrett). 8 vols. LCL 49-50, 182, 196, 211, 223, 241, 267. London: Heinemann, 1917-32. 2nd edn. of vol. 8:1935.

Suda. Ed. A. Adler, *Suidae lexicon: Edidit Ada Adler*. Lexicographi Graeci 1. 5 vols. Leipzig: Teubner, 1928-38.

Suetonius. Ed. J. C. Rolfe. 2 vols. LCL 31, 38. Cambridge, Mass.: Harvard University Press, 1:1997, 3rd edn.; 2:1998, 2nd edn.

Synesius, *Catastases*. Ed. N. Terzaghi, *Synesii Cyrenensis opuscula*, 283-93. Scriptores Graeci et Latini. Rome: Polygraphica, 1944.

Synesius, *Epistulae*. Ed. R. Hercher, *Epistolographi Graeci*, 638-739. Bibliotheca Graeca. Paris: Didot, 1873.

Tacitus. Ed. C. H. Moore, J. Jackson, et al. 5 vols. LCL 35, 111, 249, 312, 322. London: Heinemann, 1914-37.

Theocritus. Ed. J. M. Edmonds, *The Greek Bucolic Poets*, 8-361. LCL 28. London: Heinemann, 1912.

Theodoretus, *Historia ecclesiastica*. Ed. L. Parmentier and G. C. Hansen, *Theodoret: Kirchengeschichte*, 1-349. GCS

Neue Folge 5. Berlin: Akademie Verlag, 1998, 3rd edn.

Theodoretus, *Interpretatio in Danielem*. Ed. P. Migne, *Patrologia Graeca*, 81:1255-546. Paris: Migne, 1864.

Theodoretus, *Interpretatio in XIV epistulas sancti Pauli*. Ed. P. Migne, *Patrologia Graeca*, 82:35-878. Paris: Migne, 1864.

Theodoretus, *Interpretatio in XII prophetas minores*. Ed. P. Migne, *Patrologia Graeca*, 81:1545-988. Paris: Migne, 1864.

Theodoretus, *Quaestiones in libros Regnorum et Paralipomenon*. Ed. P. Migne, *Patrologia Graeca*, 80:529-858. Paris: Migne, 1864.

Theognis. Ed. D. Young (after E. Diehl), *Theognis*, 1-83. Teubner. Leipzig: Teubner, 1971, 2nd edn.

Theophylact Simocatta. Ed. C. G. de Boor, *Theophylacti Simocattae historiae*, 20-314. Teubner. Leipzig: Teubner, 1887 (repr. [corr. Peter by Wirth] Stuttgart: 1972).

Theophrastus, *Characteres*. Ed. J. S. Rusten and I. C. Cunningham, *Theophrastus: Characters; Herodas: Mimes; Sophron and Other Mime Fragments*, 48-142. LCL 225. Cambridge, Mass.: Harvard University Press, 2002, 3rd edn.

Thucydides. Ed. C. F. Smith. 4 vols. LCL 108-110, 169. London: Heinemann, 1919-23.

Velleius Paterculus. Ed. F. W. Shipley. LCL 152. London: Heinemann, 1924.

Virgil. Ed. H. R. Fairclough and G. P. Goold. 2 vols. LCL 63-64. Cambridge, Mass.: Harvard University Press, 1999-2000, 2nd rev. edn.

Vitruvius. Ed. I. D. Rowland and T. N. Howe, *Vitruvius: Ten Books on Architecture*. Cambridge: Cambridge University Press, 1999.

Xenophon. Ed. C. L. Brownson, W. Miller, et al. 7 vols. LCL 51-52, 88-90, 168, 183. London: Heinemann, 1914-25.

Xenophon of Ephesus. Ed. J. Henderson, *Longus: Daphnis and Chloe; Xenophon of Ephesus: Anthia and Habrocomes*, 212-364. LCL 69. Cambridge, Mass.: Harvard University Press, 2009.

Acts of Apollonius. Ed. E. T. Klette, *Der Process und die Acta S. Apollonii*, 92-131. TUGAL 15.2. Leipzig: Hinrichs, 1897.

Acts of Euplus. Ed. H. Musurillo, *The Acts of the Christian Martyrs*, 310-12. OECT. Oxford: Clarendon, 1972.

Assumption of Moses. Ed. J. Tromp, *The Assumption of Moses: A Critical Edition with Commentary*. SVTP 10. Leiden: Brill, 1993.

Jubilees, the Book of. Trans. R. H. Charles, *The Apocrypha and Pseudepigrapha of the Old Testament in English: With Introductions and Critical and Explanatory Notes to the Several Books*, 2:1-82. Oxford: Clarendon, 1913.

Letter of Aristeas. Trans. J. H. Charlesworth, *The Old Testament Pseudepigrapha*, 2:7-34. London: Darton, 1985.

Martyrdom of Polycarp. Ed. B. D. Ehrman, *The Apostolic Fathers*, 1:366-400. LCL 24. Cambridge, Mass.: Harvard University Press, 2003.

Sibylline Oracles. Trans. J. H. Charlesworth, *The Old Testament Pseudepigrapha*, 1:317-472. London: Darton, 1983.

Babylonian Talmud. Ed. I. Epstein et al. (a.o. Joseph Rabbinowitz), *Hebrew-English Edition of the Babylonian Talmud: Translated into English with Notes, Glossary and Indices*. 30 vols. London: Soncino, 1960-90.

Jerusalem Talmud. Trans. J. Neusner, T. Zahavy, et al, *The Talmud of the Land of Israel: A Preliminary Translation and Explanation*. 35 vols. Chicago, Ill.: University of Chicago Press, 1982-95.

Mishnah. Trans. H. Danby, *The Mishnah: Translated from the Hebrew with Introduction and Brief Explanatory Notes*. Oxford: Clarendon, 1933.

Tosefta. Trans. J. Neusner, *The Tosefta: Translated from the Hebrew, with a New Introduction*. 2 vols. Peabody, Mass.: Hendrickson, 2002.

'Abot de Rabbi Nathan. Trans. J. Neusner, *The Fathers according to Rabbi Nathan: An analytical translation and explanation*. BJS 114. Atlanta, Ga.: Scholars Press, 1986.

Lamentations Rabbah. Trans. A. Cohen, ed. H. Freedman and M. Simon, *The Midrash Rabbah*, 4:1-245. London: Soncino, 1977.

Sifra to Leviticus. Trans. J. Neusner, *Sifra: An Analytical Translation*. 3 vols. BJS 138-140. Atlanta, Ga.: Scholars Press, 1988.

Sifre to Numbers. Ed. S. Horovitz, *Sifre 'al sefer be-midbar we-sifre zuṭa*. Leipzig: Fock, 1917.

FGH   Die Fragmente der griechischen Historiker. Ed. F. Jacoby, C. W. Fornara, G. Schepens, J. Radicke, et al. 4 vols. Berlin: Weidmann; Leiden: Brill, 1923-99.

5/6Ḥev 7. Ed. A. Yardeni, *Textbook of Aramaic, Hebrew and Nabataean Documentary Texts from the Judaean Desert and Related Material*, 2:45-49. Jerusalem: Hebrew University of Jerusalem, 2000.

XḤev/Se 13 and 64. Ed. H. M. Cotton and A. Yardeni, *Aramaic, Hebrew and Greek Documentary Texts from Naḥal Ḥever and Other Sites: With an Appendix Containing Alleged Qumran Texts (The Seiyâl Collection II)*, 65-70, 203-23. DJD 27. Oxford: Clarendon, 1997.

Qumran texts. Ed. F. García Martínez and E. J. C. Tigchelaar, *The Dead Sea Scrolls Study Edition*. 2 vols. Leiden: Brill, 1997-98.

BGU   Aegyptische Urkunden aus den Königlichen (/Staatlichen) Museen zu Berlin: Griechische Urkunden. 19 vols. in 20. Berlin: Weidmann, 1895-2005.

CIA   Corpus inscriptionum Atticarum consilio et auctoritate Academiae Litterarum Regiae Bourssicae editum. Ed. A. Kirchhoff, U. Köhler, and W. Dittenberger. 4 vols. Berlin: Reimer, 1873-97.

CIG   Corpus inscriptionum Graecarum. Ed. P. A. Böckh, J. Franz, E. Curtius, A. Kirchhoff, and H. Röhl. 5 vols. Berlin: Reimer, 1828-77.

CIIP   Corpus Inscriptionum Iudaeae/Palaestinae. Ed. H. M. Cotton, J. Price, et al. 2 vols. in 3. Berlin: de Gruyter, 2010-12.

CIJ   Corpus inscriptionum Judaicarum: Recueil des inscriptions juives qui vont du IIIe siècle avant Jésus-Christ au VIIe siècle de notre ère. Ed. J.-B. Frey. 2 vols. Rome: Pontifical Institute of Christian Archaeology, 1936-52.

IG   Inscriptiones Graecae. Ed. Academia Scientiarum Berolinensis et Brandenburgensis. 15 vols. in 49. Berlin: de Gruyter, 1873-2003.

IGR   Inscriptiones Graecae ad res Romanas pertinentes. Ed. R. Cagnat, J.-F. Toutain, P. Jouguet, and G. Lafaye. 3 vols. Paris: Leroux, 1906-27.

IJO   Inscriptiones Judaicae Orientis. Ed. D. Noy, A. Panayotov, H. Bloedhorn, and W. Ameling. 3 vols. TSAJ 99, 101-102. Tübingen: Mohr Siebeck, 2004.

ILS   Inscriptiones Latinae selectae. Ed. H. Dessau. 3 vols. in 5. Berlin: Weidmann, 1892-1916.

Inscr. It.   Inscriptiones Italiae Academiae Italicae Consociatae ediderunt. Ed. G. Corradi, P. Barocelli, A. Degrassi, et al. 13 vols. Rome: Libreria dello Stato, Istituto Poligrafico e Zecca dello Stato, 1931-86.

JIGRE   Jewish Inscriptions of Graeco-Roman Egypt, with an Index of the Jewish inscriptions of Egypt and Cyrenaica. Ed. W. Horbury and D. Noy. Cambridge: Cambridge University Press, 1992.

OGIS   Orientis Graeci inscriptiones selectae: Supplementum Sylloges inscriptionum Graecarum. Ed. W. Dittenberger. 2 vols. Leipzig: Hirzel, 1903-05.

Res gest. divi Aug.   Res gestae divi Augusti. Ed. F. W. Shipley. LCL 152. London: Heinemann, 1924.

SB   Sammelbuch griechischer Urkunden aus Ägypten. Ed. F. Preisigke, F. Bilabel, E. Kiessling, H.-A. Rupprecht, et al. 27 vols. in 45. Wiesbaden: Harrassowitz; Heidelberg: Selbstverlag des Verfassers; Berlin: de Gruyter; Strasburg: Trübner, 1915-2012.

SEG   Supplementum epigraphicum Graecum. Ed. A. Chaniotis, T. Corsten, R. S. Stroud, R. A. Tybout, et al. Leiden: Brill, 1923-.

SIG   Sylloge inscriptionum Graecarum. Ed. W. Dittenberger and F. Hiller von Gaertringen. 4 vols. in 5. Leipzig: Hirzel, 1915-24, 3rd edn.

BMC   Catalogue of the Greek Coins in the British Museum. Ed. R. S. Poole, B. V. Head, P. Gardner, W. Wroth, G. F. Hill, and E. S. G. Robinson. 29 vols. London: British Museum, 1873-1927.

INDEX OF ANCIENT TEXTS

This index includes passages from the Hebrew Bible, the Septuagint, the New Testament as well as other early Jewish and Christian passages and documentary evidence. References are first to footnote numbers and then, if relevant, to pages of the summary and the excursus.

JOSEPHUS, T. FLAVIUS

Jewish War		1.132	621	1.238	107
1.1	769, 1315, 2903	1.133	1917	1.239	1465
1.3	3054	1.134	1105	1.241	132, 134, 138, 569, 964
1.4	40	1.138	1893	1.242	28
1.5	171	1.144	1963	1.243	43, 142, 167, 358, 738,
1.5-6	731	1.147	1995		1158, 1163, 1404
1.6	3054	1.151	2903	1.244	2514, 2661
1.9	2609-2610, 3054	1.153	56, 61, 1064	1.245	170, 1433
1.11	2617	1.154	1947	1.245-247	994
1.16	2617	1.155-157	440	1.248	517
1.18	2548	1.156	51, 2237	1.248-249	1069
1.19	1, 1642, 2872	1.157-158	133	1.248-273	60
1.23	110	1.158	134	1.249	60, 1434
1.25-26	3054	1.159	596, 619	1.252	464
1.27	2609, 2699	1.160	134	1.254	62
1.34	1192, 1810	1.160-168	133	1.254-255	62
1.36	2872	1.162	28	1.256-260	62
1.38	2747	1.166	1957	1.259	106
1.39	2126	1.169-170	61	1.261	397, 1434
1.40	1521	1.171	171, 172	1.263	181, 2460
1.41-45	66	1.173	1200	1.264	731, 1932
1.43	66	1.175	1218, 1223	1.265	2166, 2177
1.44	66, 2630	1.175-178	133	1.268	731
1.47	644	1.176	134	1.269	68, 735, 796, 1069, 1071
1.48	2747	1.181	51, 757, 1095, 1097	1.269-270	56
1.50	184	1.183	2402	1.270	92, 171, 1070
1.51	525	1.185	42, 47	1.271-272	1020
1.58	65	1.187	2209	1.272	1441
1.60	35	1.192	1192	1.273	63, 1069, 1071
1.63	1651	1.194	56, 1065	1.274	107, 596
1.64	51, 1944	1.199	141	1.278	596, 952
1.75	1938, 2874	1.202	40	1.280	1121
1.77	1383, 1768, 2433	1.203	77	1.281	939, 2460
1.78	2604	1.203-215	2	1.281-285	9, 49, 1137, 1194, 2627
1.78-80	2625, 2673	1.204	1474, 2390	1.282	51, 420, 2627
1.80	1950, 2756	1.204-205	28	1.283-285	1195
1.84	2756	1.205	2745	1.284	51, 205, 2751
1.85	184	1.208	1815, 2433	1.285	3058
1.87	51, 2212	1.209	11, 185	1.286	1932
1.95	1658	1.210	18	1.287	2075
1.99	1975	1.210-211	18, 80	1.288	397, 1867
1.101	623, 921	1.210-213	77	1.290	146
1.103	534	1.211	80	1.292-294	2460
1.107	130	1.212	464	1.293	16, 205
1.109	56, 77, 609, 1058, 1084	1.213	1379	1.294	1932
1.111	373, 609	1.214	464	1.299	1218
1.115	534	1.215	108	1.300	671
1.118	28, 1381, 1938, 2209, 2874	1.220-222	599, 757	1.302	1240, 1379
		1.220-237	255	1.303	40
1.119	2212	1.223	255	1.304	670, 1218
1.120	609, 1060	1.224	40	1.308	1105
1.120-122	1063	1.225	51, 1729	1.309	397
1.121	741	1.226	255, 1434	1.311	64
1.123	1192	1.229	1379	1.318	1893
1.127	534	1.234	77	1.320	40, 51, 464

INDEX OF ANCIENT TEXTS

1.327	1	1.380-381	858	1.404-406	2214, 2528
1.328	462, 1200	1.380-385	602, 703, 846	1.405	2526, 2533
1.329	1111	1.381	852, 860, 861, 863-865	1.406	2535
1.335	172, 629	1.381-382	865, 914	1.407	1793, 2136, 2212, 2226
1.337	2300	1.382	866-868, 871, 873	1.408	1791, 2235-2237, 2240-2242, 2785
1.340-341	51	1.383	793, 875-877, 880, 882-885, 887, 889, 891, 895, 897, 898, 912	1.408-415	2235
1.343	36			1.408-416	2212
1.344	134, 138, 1379			1.409	2254, 2255, 2257, 2259, 2265
1.347	629, 1491	1.383-384	881, 888		
1.349	887	1.384	892, 895, 897, 902-906, 911, 914, 920, 2430	1.410	2245
1.351-352	1710				
1.353	2874	1.385	922, 923, 925, 926	1.411	380, 1925, 2248, 2271-2274, 2977
1.353-357	1	1.386	740, 932, 939, 1090, 1150, 2750, 2935		
1.354-359	1725			1.412	2272, 2275, 2277, 2279-2285, 2522, 2853
1.355	2466	1.386-387	937, 939, 944, 1089, 1102		
1.356	107, 1711			1.413	2246, 2267, 2272, 2286, 2288, 2290-2296, 2299, 2301-2303, 2312
1.356-357	1725	1.386-397	28, 606		
1.357	37, 42, 53, 2867	1.387	640, 931, 1123, 1125, 1127-1129, 1133, 2574		
1.357-358	41			1.414	1995, 2214, 2226, 2304, 2305, 2308, 2312, 2313, 2317, 2785
1.358	10-12, 16, 25, 26, 28, 30, 33, 40, 1711, 1725, 1727	1.387-389	2936		
		1.388	208, 613, 618, 939, 1136-1140, 1142, 1143, 1149, 1150		
1.359	500, 502, 503, 506, 522, 936, 1163, 2104			1.414-415	1762, 1793
				1.415	1760, 1761, 1764, 1776, 1777, 1784, 2272, 2326-2329, 2331
1.359-360	547	1.388-390	1133, 1134, 1173		
1.359-361	158, 501, 505	1.389	1138, 1152, 1158		
1.359-362	182	1.389-390	28, 541, 1163	1.417-421	1932
1.359-363	28	1.390	1133, 1151, 1152, 1166, 1172, 2750	1.416	1381, 2212
1.360	503			1.417-418	2164
1.361	423, 440, 501, 527, 529, 530, 537	1.391	1181, 1186, 1191, 1193, 1197, 1209, 1385	1.418	2809
				1.419	1791, 2164, 2169, 2171, 2173, 2307, 2690
1.361-362	536	1.391-392	1185, 1193		
1.362	363, 534, 535, 541, 577, 592, 595, 598	1.392	392, 1188-1190, 1195	1.419-420	2171
		1.392-393	1196	1.419-421	2163, 2166, 2182
1.362-363	532	1.393	107, 1167, 1184, 1196, 1200, 1202, 1204	1.420	2173-2177
1.363	582			1.421	2179, 2185
1.364	606	1.394	1214, 1216, 1217, 1219, 1222, 1224, 1238	1.422	260, 1955, 2182, 2312
1.365	158, 182, 547, 616, 617, 643			1.422-423	1763
		1.394-395	1221, 1224, 1226	1.422-425	25, 2002, 2199
1.366	619, 620, 622-624, 658	1.395	1218, 1223, 1225, 1227-1229, 1238	1.423	107
1.366-367	625			1.425	107, 2857, 3003
1.366-385	624	1.395-397	1217, 1236, 1357, 1366, 1376, 2226, 2406, 2445	1.426-427	1760, 1761, 1774
1.367	628, 629, 643-645, 652, 665	1.396		1.427	2690
			306, 1375, 1376	1.427-428	2543
1.367-368	650	1.396-397	1372-1374	1.428	2242
1.368	655, 658, 663	1.397		1.429	1787
1.368-369	543, 666	1.398	606, 2347, 2348, 2350, 2351, 2353, 2355-2357, 2359-2362	1.429-430	1636
1.369	643, 665, 670, 676, 827, 1144			1.430	1485
				1.431	1563
1.370	678-680, 682-686	1.398-399	2359, 2393, 2503	1.431-673	125
1.371	686, 692	1.398-400	2349	1.432	134, 2340, 2530
1.372	697, 698, 705, 708, 801	1.399	2364, 2366, 2397, 2442, 2503	1.433-434	77
1.373	668, 695, 714, 716, 725, 727, 739, 763, 785, 789, 805, 809, 811, 813			1.434	71, 88
		1.400	2202, 2242, 2491, 2496, 2499, 2504, 2511, 2512, 2650, 2750	1.435	70, 1541, 1618, 2335, 2335, 2337
				1.436	1324, 1342, 1350
1.373-374	790			1.437	137, 207, 228, 263, 271, 272, 279, 285, 295, 302, 303, 306, 313, 1374, 1401, 1428, 1429, 1541, 1547, 1548, 1554, 1890
1.373-379	703, 704, 712, 725, 767, 786	1.401	1763, 1932, 1938, 1939, 1944, 2678, 2680, 2688, 2811, 2809, 2934		
1.374	711, 809				
1.374-376	718	1.401-428	1760		
1.375	629, 643, 735, 798	1.402	1937, 2125-2127, 2135, 2136, 2226, 2522, 2523	1.437-438	1411
1.376	640, 706, 711, 715, 776			1.438	321, 1339, 1427, 1547, 1554
1.377	811, 823	1.403	27, 1379, 1791, 1932, 1941, 1944, 1971, 1974, 1975, 1980-1985, 1990-1993, 1999, 2212, 2690		
1.377-378	813			1.438-439	455
1.378	640, 692, 770, 771, 789, 843			1.438-440	462, 519
		1.404	2523, 2524, 2526, 2537, 2539	1.439	151
1.379	711, 785, 872, 1485			1.439-440	151
1.380	327, 792, 847, 849, 850-854	1.404-405	2535	1.440	462, 463, 521, 643

INDEX OF ANCIENT TEXTS

1.441	366, 389, 395, 396, 449, 488, 1113, 1115, p.165	1.552	2891	2.5-7	1818, 2221
1.441-443	368, 494, p.166, 167	1.554	260, 422, 2209	2.7	2613
1.441-444	1572	1.556	1019, 1476	2.8	40
1.442	396, 454, 523, 2520, p.165	1.561	199	2.11	2921
		1.562	2143, 2144	2.25	179, 2475
1.443	396, 449, 453, 454, 463, 464, 468, 470, 493, 496, 1344, 1461 p.165, 166	1.565	464	2.26	1867, 2629
		1.566	449, 1654	2.29	170, 1491, 2629
		1.567	746	2.37	1965
		1.570	449	2.38	1098
1.443-444	1350	1.571	373, 464	2.44	1764, 1765, 1787
1.444	1556, 1568, 1570	1.573	449, 2137, 2143, 2144	2.47	623, 874
1.445	2335, 2337	1.574	859	2.54	77
1.445-449	207	1.576	2613	2.55	397, 1630
1.446	449	1.577	1461	2.57	139
1.448	2197	1.578	373	2.62	670
1.449	70, 1314, 1710	1.581-583	1441	2.65	170
1.454	231, 2344	1.583	156, 1436	2.68	275, 1465
1.456	107, 231	1.584	199	2.69	27
1.457	2224	1.584-586	1461	2.76	275, 1465
1.458	70, 1249, 2344	1.586	1926, 2517	2.77	1630
1.460	475	1.588	2137	2.81	2475
1.463	100, 269	1.589	2562	2.84	965
1.465	231, 475, 1249	1.590-594	1461	2.84-86	1926
1.466	2756	1.592	1441	2.85	179, 1461
1.468	70, 207, 1314, 1890	1.593	392, 1441	2.86	12, 965
1.470	380	1.598	2756	2.87	2753
1.473	475, 1098	1.598-599	1461	2.90	909, 1812
1.475	366, 941	1.599	2143, 2144	2.93	179, 2475
1.475-476	1314	1.600	2137	2.95	598, 2345
1.475-480	449	1.602	640	2.97	1380, 1378
1.476	207, 2735	1.602-603	2335	2.100	107
1.477	139	1.604	230	2.102	2645
1.479	1060	1.606	1461	2.106	1463
1.480	565	1.609	392	2.106-107	2342
1.483	101, 107, 125, 135, 366, 449, 2517	1.612	199	2.112-113	2625
		1.613	2212	2.113	110, 171, 1730, 2602, 2604
1.483-484	1119	1.614	1658		
1.484	464	1.616	2022	2.116	2668
1.485	27, 1461	1.617	327	2.118	2604
1.486	1640, 1653, 1654	1.622	125	2.119	30, 2604
1.488	125, 1460	1.623	746	2.119-161	2602
1.489	541, 1449, 1461	1.627	1108	2.119-166	2602, 2608, 2609, 2611
1.492	160, 1678, 1890, 2562	1.630	154	2.120	331, 1530, 2604
1.492-497	2562	1.633	925	2.122	2604
1.493	199	1.633-634	271	2.128	2962
1.494	1924	1.632	205	2.135	1108
1.495	154	1.635	1461	2.136	915
1.496	1461	1.641-644	449	2.137	2605
1.507	464	1.646	107, 449, 2613	2.137-138	2605
1.511	231, 2087	1.646-647	125	2.138	331
1.511-512	107	1.648-655	1818, 2221	2.139	766, 2642, 2673
1.513	231, 1917	1.650	1833	2.139-142	2603
1.515	118, 936	1.654	1019, 1474	2.151	65, 2605
1.516	125	1.654-655	464	2.151-158	2629
1.522	70, 207, 1314	1.655	125	2.153	2629, 2631
1.526	154, 464	1.656-659	2653	2.155	2604
1.527	234	1.660	449	2.156	2608
1.527-529	1461	1.662	1630	2.157	2433
1.529	2099	1.665	2630	2.159	2625
1.530	107, 108, 125	1.666	1764	2.160	1651, 2604
1.532	110, 1734	1.669	2164	2.162	30
1.534	449	1.670-673	315	2.168	2498, 2535
1.535	1690	1.672	1374	2.169-174	1750, 1753, 1818, 1833
1.538	199, 1019, 1474-1475	1.673	340, 2164	2.169-177	1612
1.539	360	2	2909	2.170	170, 1833
1.544	193, 2404	2.1-3	2696	2.172	1764, 2326
1.545	1805	2.3	735, 796	2.175-176	170
1.551	2562	2.5	40	2.176	2501

357

2.178-220	2891	2.487	700	3.385	1898
2.183	358, 2453, 2453	2.490	1556, 1764	3.399-405	2633
2.184-203	1612, 1750, 1818	2.492	1764	3.403	2756
2.188	1951	2.503	1221	3.414	397
2.190	2175	2.505	670	3.431	670
2.192	1951	2.515	264	3.435-437	315, 318
2.197	75	2.530	2126	3.440	2932
2.200-201	1861	2.533	397	3.445	2493
2.206-215	97	2.538	108	3.451	594
2.210	2699	2.596-571	2196	3.457	594
2.212	2756	2.572	2196	3.459	108
2.215	121, 2353	2.572-574	2196	3.470	1953
2.220	1751, 2896, 2909	2.580	915, 1802	3.471	629
2.224	2921	2.582	767	3.472	713
2.224-225	40, 172	2.594	156	3.472-484	711, 789
2.226	2235	2.595	1951	3.480	741, 838
2.231	1893	2.598	2071	3.484	327, 789
2.232	1951	2.604	2373	3.504	392
2.233	741	2.607	108	3.507	1846
2.243	1837	2.616	349	3.509	2526
2.249	197	2.631	667, 1180	3.509-514	2535
2.255	1870, 2154	2.650	1521	3.513-514	2526
2.259	156, 172, 2753	3	767, 2909	3.518	1658
2.264	327	3.1	392, 637	3.536	1550
2.265	170	3.23	1481	4.5	2951
2.266	2877	3.26	1881	4.33	594
2.267	347	3.28	3043	4.39-48	711
2.279	1751	3.34	859	4.45	2864
2.281	1411	3.35	1958	4.54	1951
2.283	156	3.36	27, 1957	4.56	1975
2.284	397	3.39	1951	4.79-80	2479
2.304	1993	3.46	1959	4.86	695
2.318	156	3.47	1960	4.90	191
2.320	741	3.55	2178	4.96	210
2.323	1312	3.56	2493	4.102	1751
2.342	629	3.57	2535, 3017	4.113	108
2.346	1720, 2753	3.59	1951	4.115	1988
2.346-401	789, 2753	3.95	1988	4.123	1718
2.349	2753	3.102	915	4.124	575
2.355-356	2753	3.103	3016	4.127	2629
2.359	659	3.120	1953	4.132	347
2.360	1152	3.130	706	4.151	2684
2.365	2962	3.137	1470	4.152	1847
2.382	2493	3.142	706	4.162	930
2.388	108	3.151	629	4.162-192	711
2.388-391	789	3.153	327	4.163-192	789
2.390-391	784	3.156	1600	4.179	2104
2.393	1810	3.174	1975	4.182	1751, 2849, 3015
2.399	767	3.184-185	2765	4.190-191	789
2.412-413	2860	3.202	724	4.204	3008
2.424	2126	3.212	915	4.213	551, 1734
2.426	2126	3.232	2791	4.222	1964
2.433	2622	3.239	327	4.223	2853
2.437	2622	3.262	2956	4.224	574
2.439	1606	3.289	1658	4.231	110
2.440	2622	3.294	1898	4.260	909
2.443	1513	3.302	623, 874	4.263	292
2.446-449	2622	3.308	170	4.281	1651, 1663
2.458	1960	3.321	2092	4.287	823, 1521
2.459	1957	3.346	1830	4.292	460
2.466	2699	3.355	2756	4.320	639, 691
2.474	2756	3.361	768	4.329	1915
2.475	64	3.361-382	66	4.330	338
2.476	915, 1098	3.362	66, 915	4.335	1837
2.478	686	3.363	909, 911	4.338	1411
2.483	2699	3.369-379	66	4.348	1810, 2666
2.484	851	3.378	915	4.368	1768
2.485	629	3.380	64	4.385	417

INDEX OF ANCIENT TEXTS

4.386	1814	5.208	2788, 2796	6.94	1611
4.388	909	5.208-209	2796	6.99-100	784
4.415	1337, 2661	5.210	2804, 2805	6.99-110	711
4.434	758	5.211	2796	6.103-104	2627
4.440	397	5.212	2799, 2857	6.123	741
4.442	2840	5.213-214	2799	6.124	458, 3013
4.455	1951	5.215	2781	6.125-126	3015
4.468-481	539	5.220-221	2789	6.126	3016
4.469	538	5.227	3009, 3023	6.149	397
4.476-485	984	5.230	1770	6.150	3008
4.480-481	984	5.231-236	2876	6.166	2812
4.496	2609-2610	5.238-246	1938	6.176	1563, 1917
4.503	2620	5.238-247	1763	6.186	1903
4.529	1658	5.239	2306	6.186-187	64
4.550	397	5.242	2283	6.200	154
4.570	397	5.244	2921	6.229	397
4.604	975	5.245	1605, 1606, 2126	6.239	909
4.608-610	1223	5.252	2126	6.246	1953
4.612	2293	5.258	1953	6.278	2831
4.633	397	5.260	2126	6.280	64, 493
5.10	2617	5.275	2831	6.300	2124
5.11	2126	5.283	1144	6.302	1463
5.36	2784	5.291	668	6.311	2834
5.36-37	2781	5.325	1503	6.318	493
5.47	2118	5.332	909	6.325	2126
5.70	2832	5.335	2946	6.328	713
5.72	1513	5.349	1220	6.337	659
5.79	417	5.356	2126	6.343	659
5.52	1953	5.362-419	789	6.345	659
5.136	2876	5.367-369	789	6.353	909
5.140	2941	5.368	915	6.363	2126
5.141	2832	5.376-378	789	6.367	1922
5.142-145	2126	5.376-419	711	6.374	2126
5.145	295	5.380	784	6.413	2945
5.152	233	5.382	784	6.418	38, 1804
5.154	392	5.382-386	3075	6.419	2012
5.156	1988	5.383	2010	6.421	1572
5.161	1995	5.386	784	6.434	38
5.162	1606, 1910, 2203	5.389	784	6.436	1
5.163	2786	5.401-414	784	6.439	2627
5.163-171	1606	5.403-404	784	6.615	1218
5.175	2125	5.408-409	1	7.9	670
5.176-181	400, 1605, 2125, 2128	5.413	1328	7.26	2126
5.177	2127, 2283	5.419	1144	7.36	38
5.178	2130	5.427	2012	7.49	629
5.179	2129	5.438	77	7.50	1751
5.183	2125	5.445	590, 2126	7.59	2360
5.184	2820	5.458	64	7.62	2265
5.184-185	2814	5.460	397	7.65	110
5.184-214	1763	5.461	2433	7.71	108, 2264
5.186	2316	5.467-468	295	7.74	1390
5.187	3010	5.472	637	7.108	176, 561
5.189	1285	5.484	2932	7.118	38, 1536, 1995
5.190	2785, 2786, 2811, 2814, 2856	5.489	629	7.132-133	2505
		5.491	460	7.133	2505
5.190-192	2812	5.512-518	2006	7.136	2217, 2239, 2807
5.192	2849	5.536	108	7.138	38
5.193	3013	5.547	637	7.146	1721
5.194	3013-3014	5.558	392	7.147	38
5.195-198	3017	5.563	2536	7.148	1814
5.196	2854, 3017	5.567	31	7.151	2217
5.197	2847	6.2	1572	7.153-154	38
5.199	3021	6.33-53	711	7.154	38, 1805
5.200	2919, 3018, 3028	6.40	1576	7.157	32
5.201	3021	6.57	1192	7.175	1995
5.201-206	3018	6.58	2756	7.189	2173, 3020
5.202	3018	6.74	623, 874	7.192	851
5.207	2781, 3009, 3026	6.81	915	7.212	668

359

7.216	2215	1.7	1285	2.85	2544
7.218	1611	1.9	2239, 2674	2.87	1418
7.231	1902	1.11	2674	2.93-193	2116
7.234	96	1.13	110, 171, 2195	2.95	2048
7.253	215	1.14	824	2.97	2544
7.260	2366	1.15	2672	2.109	477
7.261	2154	1.20	2672, 3045	2.120	191, 1108
7.264	1758	1.28	1690	2.124	1108
7.267	1758	1.33	2558	2.128	1366
7.269	1790	1.41	765	2.129	2651
7.270	2629	1.45	523	2.133	739
7.273	1915	1.56	176	2.136	108
7.274	2087	1.59	724	2.138	1398
7.277	1218	1.89	1067	2.154	2652
7.279	1418	1.93	769, 2864, 3071	2.162	473
7.285	1099	1.107	769, 1022	2.163	1166
7.286	2785	1.111	1211	2.173	1098
7.286-294	1099	1.112	824, 1669	2.201-204	2558
7.293	2822	1.114	830	2.202	1705
7.297	1988	1.135	215	2.209	824
7.299	2831	1.160	2609	2.210	140
7.300	629, 1932, 3071	1.162	139	2.220	746
7.301	84	1.164	1576	2.223	824
7.318-319	789	1.175	623	2.231	139
7.322	708	1.177	2530	2.237	376
7.323	713	1.178	786	2.262	103
7.323-336	789, 840, 3077	1.181	1218	2.263	731
7.323-388	711	1.186	1647	2.280	376, 1658
7.327	824	1.203	215	2.283	824, 1748
7.327-332	789	1.229	763	2.291	1211
7.330	768, 1902	1.236	1192	2.313-314	1572
7.330-336	96	1.239	3071	2.333	830
7.334	64	1.242-252	2155	2.344	1576
7.336	64	1.247	156	2.346	1272
7.341	64	1.248	100	2.348	830
7.341-388	789	1.255	824	3.1-38	2034
7.343	919	1.258	2803	3.5	696
7.352	768, 1902	1.265	2340	3.7	1005
7.355	767	1.274	1495	3.11	376
7.358	824, 1902	1.277	2340	3.16-17	824
7.358-359	96, 789	1.285	1368	3.23	1637, 2034
7.358	768	1.286	1467	3.32	1067
7.359	392	1.313	786	3.43	170
7.363	2098	1.317	2756	3.43-46	711
7.365	1928	1.319	1477	3.45	763
7.369	1528	1.330	379	3.45-46	784
7.372	64, 1596	1.337	461	3.46	1211
7.376	2001	1.337-338	2155	3.50	1220
7.380	768, 1902	1.442	454	3.53	380
7.382	768, 1902	1.443	454, 496	3.72	1035
7.386	64	2.9-200	1398	3.75	2697
7.386-387	836	2.11	219	3.78	541
7.387	768, 1902	2.39-61	156	3.83	52, 2765
7.383	52	2.41	139, 461, 523	3.84	1754
7.389-401	2478	2.42	84	3.91	1818, 2221
7.419	1550	2.45	84	3.91-92	1628
7.423	75	2.48	1398	3.95	1067
7.428	1790	2.50	1398	3.102	1036
7.448	1023	2.51-52	156	3.103	340
7.451	2013, 2266	2.56	1398	3.108	1136
7.451-453	2013	2.57	1192	3.109-110	2981
7.453	1528	2.59	474, 1398	3.124	2802
7.454-455	3054	2.62	523	3.154	2800
		2.63-79	1434	3.159-187	274, 2876
Jewish Antiquities		2.64	1434	3.178	274, 1587
1-10	2678	2.66	1434	3.179-187	1611
1.2	356	2.69	1398, 2140	3.183	2026
1.5-12	2823	2.83	1207	3.188	1366

INDEX OF ANCIENT TEXTS

3.188-192	272	5.107	824	6.265	2642		
3.189	713	5.115	1713	6.282	668		
3.204-207	272	5.137	140	6.292	191		
3.206	1136	5.166	1503	6.296	1398		
3.210	1528	5.171	1126, 3075	6.298	52		
3.214-218	274	5.177	1221	6.316	724		
3.226	3050	5.178	1946	6.343-344	2690		
3.230	3054	5.185	1187	6.347	1191		
3.260	2220	5.189	576, 988	6.349	667		
3.267	823	5.191	523	6.361	1595		
3.271	463	5.194	1289	6.368	623		
3.274	156, 766	5.197	2681	6.370	493, 917		
3.275	541	5.199	1366	6.371	1322		
3.281	35	5.200	830	6.377	837		
3.219	2867	5.213	1211	6.378	1055		
3.294	2259	5.221	52	7.5	140		
3.299	217	5.226	830	7.13	623, 874		
3.307	956	5.256	822, 1130, 1132	7.24	2584		
3.315	824	5.257	2620	7.43	80		
3.321	2092	5.274	1529, 2813	7.43	1495		
4	392	5.276	139	7.44	191, 392, 397		
4.6	840	5.277	463	7.66	2126, 2775		
4.8	1192	5.292	477, 1965	7.79	724		
4.10	234	5.306	2099	7.110	1021		
4.11-62	170	5.307	541	7.114-115	1263		
4.35	1491	5.328	51	7.130	522		
4.41	100	5.329	373	7.157	1207		
4.48	1333	5.339	2154	7.163	1291		
4.54	3075	5.350	1285, 2106	7.170	1427		
4.62	54	5.359	1192	7.186	456, 1241		
4.68	1220	5.360	1313	7.196	974		
4.83	360	5.375	2238	7.213	1091		
4.84	308	6.5	31	7.228-230	66		
4.100	52	6.9	909	7.229	66		
4.107	176	6.20	713	7.234	2022		
4.110	824	6.26	725	7.258	874		
4.115	2962	6.28	2637	7.278	1468		
4.129	139	6.33	2433	7.284	700		
4.131	100	6.35	140, 1752	7.289	1398		
4.134	475, 523	6.48	120, 1421	7.293	1021		
4.135	369	6.63	114, 1530	7.300	140		
4.177-193	704, 711	6.82	1231	7.301	52		
4.187	108	6.86	2724	7.328	1098		
4.204	2699	6.89	3075	7.338	1087		
4.208	496	6.101	273	7.341	1087		
4.209	264, 265	6.116	668	7.343-344	1594		
4.220	1737	6.129	2504	7.344	523		
4.253	1685, 1687	6.158	139	7.350	1639		
4.262	1241	6.160	139	7.356	1087		
4.264	843, 1413	6.162-165	2633	7.373	830		
4.273	381	6.166	2016	7.374	1087, 2720		
4.288	763	6.167	139	7.380	1464		
4.295	3075	6.170	662	7.384	1087		
4.296-297	786	6.172	1464	7.388	2415		
4.299	661	6.187	840, 1922, 2699	7.390	635, 1529		
4.311	215	6.192	2867	7.391	960		
4.464	496	6.197	1289	7.394	26, 51		
5.11	1928	6.203	1768	8.2	1060		
5.13	473	6.204	1654	8.4	824		
5.21	1067	6.209	84	8.13	746		
5.38	376	6.220	1272	8.20	1087		
5.44	1740	6.233	1208	8.49	1129, 1463, 2962		
5.58	140	6.236	541	8.50	1315		
5.66	623	6.244	2867	8.55	1022		
5.68	2236	6.245	1272	8.56	3054		
5.82	1708	6.251	2699	8.57	1231		
5.83	1951	6.255	1098	8.57-123	2728		
5.90	1751	6.263	960	8.64	2785		

361

8.64-65	2727, 2729	10.92	833	11.278	108
8.97	1285, 2847, 2848	10.94	114	11.280	1366
8.98	2811, 2856	10.96	724	11.303	75, 1608
8.100	264	10.97-102	71	11.304	1884, 2738
8.101-102	340	10.100	71	11.304-347	2738
8.112	473, 1576	10.102	71	11.312	217, 859
8.115	2010	10.115	1915	11.322	84
8.119	1211, 2684	10.126	496	11.323	40
8.123	264	10.150	215	11.326-339	2738
8.139	2785	10.151	2606	11.327	724
8.174	538	10.161	724	11.340	75
8.183	2801	10.186	139	11.343	35
8.184	139	10.190	540, 1460	11.388	73
8.193	381	10.196	1683	12.11	1060
8.205	1280	10.216	972, 2371	12.17	118
8.209	460	10.223	1018	12.65	2580
8.211	198	10.229	71	12.75	1988
8.219	1468	10.229-230	69	12.77	2809
8.223	767, 1093	10.242	2371	12.94	1191
8.225-235	2625	10.250	2433	12.96	2133
8.226	2530	10.252	115	12.98	2133
8.227	713, 2699	10.258	724	12.136	75
8.234	1463, 2625	10.260	724	12.141	2849
8.266	2574	10.266	2690	12.145	2849, 3015
8.269	2651	11-20	2678	12.148	121, 1026
8.270	1922	11.1	2725	12.149	73
8.279	671	11.1-320	2723	12.154	1654
8.279-280	840, 1377, 3077	11.6	1837	12.156	397
8.280	767, 786	11.11	2872	12.158	67
8.282	784	11.13	2727, 2735	12.162	461
8.293	786	11.21	1060	12.206	107, 108, 1505
8.295	767	11.22	73	12.222	731
8.297	1211	11.27	156	12.230	2785
8.300	1087	11.31	2630, 2735	12.233	1960
8.307	1023	11.35	1777	12.234-361	224
8.309	1098	11.67	629	12.236	324
8.339	1464	11.74	73	12.237	225
8.349	3071	11.77	264	12.238-239	226
8.378	217	11.93	2777	12.239	1684
8.383	623, 874	11.94	1021	12.248	607
9.2	2634	11.98	1021	12.256	1037
9.16	725, 2642	11.99	2727, 2736	12.261	108, 1365
9.28	215	11.104	1021	12.263	2485
9.38	671	11.122	73	12.264	1365
9.58	909	11.123	75	12.265	2872
9.59	1181	11.132-133	73	12.265-14.491	2872
9.96	1304	11.133	3053	12.273	909
9.112	67	11.154	264	12.290-291	786
9.122-124	1922	11.159	209, 1434	12.300	725
9.123	1528	11.161	670	12.307	286, 840
9.141	59	11.169	713	12.312	859
9.155	3033	11.173	1352	12.318	2799
9.165	217	11.174	140	12.321	207
9.168	1928	11.184	75, 1608	12.327	1291
9.208	3054	11.188	1813	12.339	781
9.213	2262	11.191	1460	12.348	1951, 2254
9.229	2622	11.195	461	12.357	75, 375
9.231	140	11.197	139	12.373-374	66
9.265	1411	11.208	1021	12.378	36
9.270	473, 3050	11.223	360	12.387	366
9.272	1181	11.233	360	12.395	724
9.248	1464	11.234	360, 2806	12.403	724
10.5	1021, 1639	11.244	1366	12.409	623, 786, 917
10.11	360	11.248	1021	12.412	75
10.16	1001	11.154	1366	12.417	75
10.42	1056	11.260	209, 1460	12.419	2747
10.55	1021	11.261	366	12.434	310
10.59	1639	11.270	75	12.694-695	36

INDEX OF ANCIENT TEXTS

13.1	75	13.373	3013	14.117-118	75
13.5	2725	13.392	534	14.121	51, 1095, 1097
13.8	447	13.393	621	14.123	2402
13.14	1672	13.396	517	14.125	47, 1428
13.28	12	13.397	1960	14.126	130
13.43	644	13.407	1043	14.127	1043
13.43-46	126	13.407-408	77	14.131	1043, 1218
13.46	264, 265	13.408	56, 1058	14.137	56, 398, 1065
13.47	109	13.410	1318	14.138	2339
13.48	75	13.411	1371	14.138-139	45
13.53	2704	13.417	1105	14.140	5
13.57	2215	13.418	534	14.141	1043
13.60	217	13.427	2353	14.143-144	56, 61
13.62	215	13.431	662	14.146	15, 16
13.63	2690	13.433		14.151	1065
13.77	140	14	40	14.153	1778
13.84	360	14.4	56, 607, 1060, 1062	14.157	40, 61, 295
13.85	118	14.4-8	1063	14.158	2, 77
13.93	725	14.6-7	61, 1059	14.158-184	2
13.107	349	14.7	210	14.159	1474, 2154, 2390
13.115	1907	14.8	1043, 1642	14.159-160	28
13.130	1706	14.9	51	14.163-167	14
13.318-319	1110	14.10	1642	14.165	2, 14, 77, 395, 1043,
13.119	960	14.11	61		1083, 1716, 1827, 2154,
13.127	75, 121	14.12	114		2447
13.135	234	14.13	77, 261, 960, 961, 1083,	14.167	14, 1019, 1474
13.143	75		1084, 1533	14.167-168	14
13.146	118	14.14-19	1037	14.168	80
13.166	75	14.16	1043	14.168-177	18
13.171-173	2602	14.22	2009	14.168-178	14, 80, 1019, 1474
13.172	2604	14.25	266	14.169	11
13.173	1166	14.29	397, 534	14.170	80
13.176	447	14.34-36	45, 1793, 2804	14.171	14
13.187	114	14.35	45	14.172	14, 18, 61
13.195	456, 1241	14.36	2804	14.172-174	18
13.211	2984	14.37	1043	14.172-176	18, 19
13.214	108	14.39	42	14.173	83
13.220	360	14.41	61, 1059	14.173-174	18
13.228	1023	14.42	61	14.174	21, 23
13.231	661	14.47	621	14.175	14, 18, 1019
13.236	607, 1241	14.49	1105	14.176	1
13.241	264	14.54	538, 539	14.177	14, 80, 83, 1210
13.251	1796	14.57	2832	14.179-180	77
13.255-258	1651	14.60	84	14.180	464
13.256	215	14.61	2832	14.182	80
13.282	1368, 3071	14.63	767	14.190-195	56
13.284-287	45	14.66	607	14.191-192	1065
13.286	45	14.66-68	45	14.194	1065
13.295	1463	14.71	859	14.196	75
13.300	2625	14.73	47, 56, 61, 1064	14.197	1065
13.304	264, 265	14.75	35, 36	14.198	1108
13.307	2874	14.76	1382	14.199-200	1065
13.308	25	14.77-79	133	14.202-210	2030
13.311	2604, 2673	14.80	1043	14.204	2704
13.311-313	2625, 2673	14.81	749, 1161	14.205	1382
13.313	1950	14.82-89	133	14.210	1801
13.318	1687	14.86	397	14.211	1065
13.319	45, 503, 960	14.88	1380, 1957	14.212	75, 2751
13.320	130	14.89	2566	14.216	1651
13.321	3071	14.90-91	61	14.219	1108
13.329	1280	14.97	61, 1059	14.221	1108
13.330	397	14.98-102	133	14.226	1065
13.335	114	14.99	1043	14.248	75
13.345	45	14.100	170	14.253	108, 1505
13.353	397, 629	14.104	45	14.257	108
13.357	51, 1381, 2212	14.111	45	14.260	849
13.364	551	14.111-118	45	14.276	1043
13.372	264, 1427	14.114	75	14.277	255

14.280	51	14.431	1971	15.7	26, 41		
14.281	114, 255, 1434	14.436	464	15.7-8	395		
14.297-300	5	14.438	1860	15.8	1, 11, 37, 40, 44-48, 50, 53, 55, 58, 233, 949, 959, 1387, 1895, 1934, 1966, 2056, 2098
14.300	138, 1618, 2155	14.442	51		
14.303	28	14.444	295		
14.304	909	14.445	1210, 2226		
14.306	75	14.446	634	15.8-10	45
14.314	1065	14.447	1	15.8-11	p. 3
14.315	81	14.448	59	15.9	42, 45, 48, 133
14.320	75	14.450	40	15.9-10	42, 45, 1022
14.324	142, 167, 1163	14.455	51	15.10	41, 50, 55
14.324-325	43	14.465	36, 51	15.11	20, 59, 61, 89, 176, 518, 588, 945, 1042, 1047, 1058, 1062, 1071, 1746, 2341
14.326	2514	14.467	138, 215		
14.326-327	28	14.468-488	1, 4, 1709		
14.327	233	14.469	9, 51, 53, 949		
14.327-329	994	14.471	669, 1710	15.11-21	1047, 1072, 1074
14.330	60, 517	14.474	870	15.11-22	123
14.330-369	5, 60	14.475	35, 1710	15.12	62, 74, 227, 278, 1071, 2511
14.331-332	1069	14.476	1710		
14.333	60, 1434	14.477	273	15.12-17	945
14.337-342	62	14.481	5, 37, 2166, 2874	15.12-21	1004
14.352-358	1932	14.482-491	1725	15.12-22	56, p.3
14.377	1121	14.484	2466	15.13	60, 63
14.378	1121	14.484-486	1711	15.14	71, 83, 128, 216, 629, 1525
14.339	60	14.485-486	1725		
14.340	62, 68, 1069	14.486	107	15.14-20	69
14.342-348	62	14.487	36, 607	15.15	39, 85, 89, 90, 98, 961, 1058, 1084, 1608, 2706
14.344	505, 1160	14.488	37		
14.345	106, 664	14.489	11, 53	15.16	77, 79, 82, 83, 91, 99, 103, 104, 1047, 1048, 1074, 1075, 1652, 2075
14.346	693	14.489-490	40, 949		
14.352	1111	14.489-491	1719, 2574		
14.355-360	2166	14.490	28, 42	15.17	11, 74, 86, 94, 111, 117, 961, 1049, 1070, 1152, 1599
14.358	1099	14.491	11, 125		
14.361	1099, 1658	15	129, 130, 142, 150, 157, 299, 571, 608, 1528		
14.365	68, 1069, 1071			15.17-18	81
14.365-366	56	15-16	392	15.18	77, 78, 79, 88, 945, 1074
14.366	92, 1070	15.1	6, 7, 12, 30, 37, 93, 112, 949, 1069, 1709, 2166, 2866		
14.367	1478			15.18-19	68, 126
14.367-369	64, 1020			15.18-20	279
14.370	596, 599	15.1-2	41, 126, 279, 973, 1707	15.18-21	951, 945, 951
14.379	1069, 1071	15.1-4	12, 24, p.3, 4	15.19	28, 77, 81, 1143, 1505, 2745
14.379-389	5, 9, 28, 49, 1192, 2627	15.1-7	41		
14.381-382	28	15.1-11	1725	15.20	58, 99, 122, 173, 262, 943, 945, 949, 951, 1088, 1490, 1609, 2087, 2593
14.382	51, 1195	15.1-17.99	2		
15.383	2935	15.2	12, 41, 78, 95, 355, 356, 399, 459, 629, 678, 1093, 1644, 1652, 1711, 1727, 1929, 2056, 2088, 2215, 2256, 2574, 2583, 2601, 2630, 3036		
14.384	2751			15.20-21	1037, 1075
14.385	51			15.21	113, 116, 230, 285, 329, 362, 979, 1028, 1075, 1215, 2595
14.385-386	1195				
14.388-389	1195				
14.389	607, 3058				
14.390	5, 1099	15.2-3	6, 2596, 2601	15.22	189, 181, 195, 215, 218, 221, 311, 318, 395, 967, 1008, 1240, 1249, 1359, 1433, 1541, 2141, 2161
14.393	988	15.3	11, 14, 16, 1019, 2601		
14.394	146	15.3-4	12, 18, 2339		
14.394-401	5	15.4	14, 18, 30, 82, 83, 96, 104, 3077		
14.396-397	1099, 2256			15.23	47, 126, 130, 141, 148-150, 157, 162, 175, 176, 188, 201, 203, 206, 275, 276, 336, 375, 378, 452, 937, 962, 964, 1103, 1114, 1239, 1274, 1394, 1496, 1502, 1536, 1634, 2156, p.3
14.397-389	1137	15.5	1, 24, 25, 34, 48, 107, 179, 195, 198, 253, 365, 418, 429, 501, 526, 553, 576, 611, 612, 939, 936, 1137, 1143, 1200, 1202, 1218, 1370, 1629, 1639, 1671, 1935, 2056, 2209, 2226, 2471, 2510, 2934-2936		
14.400	1099				
14.403	11				
14.403-404	53				
14.404	456				
14.409	671				
14.413	1099				
14.418	397			15.23-24	127, 208, 221, 244, 354, 414, 1413, 1746
14.419	1105				
14.423	380	15.5-7	24, 32, 1725, p.3	15.23-28	130, 374
14.427	2191	15.6	12, 21, 41, 249, 1290, 1724, 2056	15.23-38	161, 949
14.429	64			15.23-41	140
14.430	51	15.6-7	33, 2152	15.23-49	123, p.3

INDEX OF ANCIENT TEXTS

15.24	165, 174, 176, 183, 181, 182, 195, 201, 205, 245, 348, 350, 352, 356, 358, 401, 462, 496, 500, 526, 566, 595, 967, 968, 1008, 1242, 1246, 1309, 1664, 1665, 2547	15.43	400, 1693, 1824, 1937, 1964, 2125, 2152, 2561		1253, 1290, 1292, 1339, 1399, 1541, 1547, 1617, 2518, p.165, 166
		15.44	207, 208, 241, 328, 414, 977, 1206, 1342, 1364, 1400, 1406, 1413, 1517, 1547, 2191	15.65-66	398, p.166
				15.65-67	1471
				15.65-73	453
		15.45	206, 348, 363, 414, 432, 968, 1136, 1664	15.65-87	368, 494, 495, 1393, p.3
15.25	130, 139, 336, 1536, 1995, 2150			15.66	368, 375, 373, 381, 394, 471, 1114, 1423, 1544
15.25-27	165	15.45-46	130, 143, 161, 352, 949		
15.25-28	228	15.45-48	267	15.66-67	139, 269
15.25-29	276	15.46	31, 1242	15.67	139, 368, 373, 1332, 1497, p.165
15.25-31	145	15.47	130, 277, 411, 1980		
15.26	140, 411	15.48	158, 260, 432, 547, 1201, 1233, 1497, 1531, 1533, 1899, 2110, 2194, 2203	15.68	184, 369, 384, 394, 412, 471, 475, 523, 1100, 1257, 1423, 1558, 1567, 2587
15.26-27	496				
15.26-28	412				
15.26-33	1393			15.68-69	p.165
		15.49	114, 173, 258, 267, 270, 284, 329	15.68-70	1104, 1544
15.27	130, 146, 150, 153, 161, 165, 246, 354, 549, 2116	15.49-56	48	15.69	130, 240, 368, 391, 392, 397, 461, 481, 496, 1115, 1251, 1252, 1255, 1257, 1266, 1400, 1408, 1547, 2518, 2585, p.165, 166
15.28	149, 154, 352, 354, 363, 412, 431, 1664	15.50	271, 282, 283, 954, 1345, 1443, 2183, 2554		
15.28-29	145	15.50-56	204, 262, 263, 1023, 1429, 1890, p.3		
15.29	136, 137, 140, 141, 168, 195, 275, 309, 336, 354, 543, 549, 558, 2138	15.51	137, 195, 272, 280, 309, 336, 357, 1274, 1536-1538, 1611, 1613, 1614, 1646, 1713, 1995	15.70	369, 481, 493, 1242, 1302, 1423, 1510, 1541, 1547, p.165
15.30	40, 160, 270, 277, 499, 943, 959, 963, 1491, 1730, 1965, 1966, 2432, 2439, 2370				
		15.51-52	974	15.70-71	392
		15.52	272, 317, 318, 974	15.71	235, 392, 417, 409, 446, 462, 497, 1465, 1897, 1937, 2125, 2146, 2616
15.31	29, 118, 130, 143, 195, 221, 244, 354, 384, 429, 931, 936, 1104, 1242, 1249, 1262, 1282, 1360	15.53	130, 270, 296, 301, 304, 949, 1429, 1541, 1566		
		15.54	1421	15.71-73	1730
		15.55	125, 270, 290, 291, 306, 320, 949, 1242, 1429, 1545	15.71-74	p.165
15.31-32	496			15.72	130, 408, 411, 444, 445, 1242, 1303
15.31-34	180, 1603				
15.32	202, 270, 330, 363, 411, 432, 459, 547, 609, 968, 1008, 1137, 1619, 1722, 2123, 2168, 2414	15.56	129, 137, 1242	15.72-73	1399, 1503
		15.57	318, 401, 2927	15.73	70, 130, 202, 412, 459, 949, 967, 1008, 1314, 1393, 1525, 2137
		15.57-65	1494		
		15.57-87	p.3		
15.32-38	180	15.58	130, 200, 301, 313, 329, 1429	15.74	359, 2574
15.33	156, 170, 2682			15.74-79	416, p.165, 166
15.34	129, 228, 354, 1496, 1734, 1889, 2694	15.58-59	344	15.74-80	1303
		15.58-60	1242	15.74-87	396
15.35	240, 242, 279, 328, 411, 496, 549, 1106, 1242, 1316, 1346, 1414, 1487, 1680, 2189	15.59	323, 330, 344, 349, 979, 2096, 2557, 2739	15.75	28, 142, 431, 523, 547, 1241, 1664, 2209, 2545
		15.59-60	240	15.75-76	526
		15.60	354, 1242, 1405, 1407, 1497, 1564	15.75-79	182, 416
15.35-38	180, 1413			15.76	182, 2226
15.36	131, 208, 244, 967, 1313, 1314	15.62	206, 329, 363, 414, 962, 968, 976, 979, 1496, 1534, p.165	15.77	114, 157, 158, 421, 441, 442, 547, 617, 643, 1027, 1490, 2049, 2226, 2473, p.165
15.37	241, 243, 1314, 1331, 1406, 1496, 1617, 1872				
		15.62-63	130, 143, 432, 459		
15.38	180, 328	15.62-65	1429	15.77-79	1666
15.39	51, 73, 569, 2159	15.62-73	416, 459	15.78	1170, 2137
15.39-40	228	15.62-87	p.164, 165	15.79	416, 432, 439, 498, 503, 520, 536, 626, 756
15.39-41	141	15.63	325, 421, 431, 442, 547, 965		
15.40	125, 229, 311, 372, 965, 1476, 2611				
		15.63-64	p.166	15.80	130, 496, 1198, 1218, 1339, 1342, 1386, 1432, p.165, 166
15.40-41	127, 12	15.63-65	28		
15.41	223, 264, 271, 309, 354	15.63-80	1206		
15.42	125, 130, 161, 202, 213, 242, 279, 328, 330, 411, 459, 949, 959, 962, 963, 1008, 1050, 1091, 1316, 1340, 1346, 1359, 1414, 1441, 1495, 1682, 2189, 2434	15.64	349, 364, 418, 448, 488, 560, 979, 2453, p.3, 165	15.80-81	469, 1303, 1413, 1432, p.165
		15.64-80	1255	15.81	366, 449, 484, 1106, 1241, 1339, 1344, 1345, 1401, 1410, 1411, 1414, 1426, 1479, 1502, 1517, 1656, 1686, p.165
		15.65	158, 377, 386, 390, 397, 421, 453, 461, 463, 481, 493, 547, 595, 990, 1096, 1100, 1102, 1109, 1115, 1242, 1248, 1251-		
				15.81-87	1348, 1345, p.165, 166
15.42-43	496			15.82	269, 368, 370, 470, 476,

	492, 1247, 1284, 1306, 1318, 1324, 1343, 1345, 1350, 1394, 1433, 1471, 1485, 1514, 1541, 1558, 1826, 2555	15.102	549		845, 868
		15.103	107, 575, 577, 2209, 2521, 2618, 2926	15.130	615, 730, 732, 760, 769, 788, 803, 831, 900
		15.104	536, 584, 589	15.130-137	727
		15.104-160	p. 3	15.130-143	712
15.82-83	1544	15.105	580, 581, 590	15.130-145	711, 712, 718
15.82-84	p.165, 166	15.106	259, 603, 597, 599, 744, 1666, 2030	15.131	809, 939, 1203, 1355, 2750, 2934
15.82-87	455, 461				
15.83	369, 473, 464, 491, 1264, 1348, 1363, 1423, 1568	15.106-107	535, 537, 592, 745, 1126, 2422	15.131-134	727, 736
		15.106-108	2412	15.132	5, 28, 657, 730, 736, 753, 848
15.84	381, 461, 1541	15.106-160	593	15.132-134	746
15.85	207, 493, 1242, 1248, 1251, 1252, 1547, 2518	15.107	501, 521, 537, 592, 601, 602, 616, 673, 729, 757, 897, 968, 2411	15.133	758, 759
				15.133-134	740
15.85-86	1405			15.133-135	828, 842
15.85-87	396, 454, 1541, p.165, 166	15.107-108	615, 751, 968, 1004	15.134	730, 733, 767, 916
		15.108	593, 603, 614, 617, 3056	15.134-135	767
15.86	1468, 1472			15.135	717, 720, 735, 755, 767, 778, 796, 803, 831, 873, 1087, 2707
15.87	130, 385, 411, 464, 879, 949, 991, 1230, 1242, 1265, 1348, 1473, 1544, 1571, 1630, 1655, 1680, 2192, p.165, 166	15.108-110	1139		
		15.108-160	602		
		15.109	184, 604, 607, 677, 933, 934, 1137, 1775, 1944, 2348, 2506, p.3	15.135-136	722
				15.136	692, 727, 729, 731, 767, 777, 788, 803, 831, 899, 900, 2608, 2864, 3077
15.88	397, 501, 502, 512, 514, 515, 522, 527, 533, 548, 565, 557, 1163, 1404, 2073, 2138	15.110	182, 605, 622, 617, 618, 643, 692, 730, 737, 1190		
				15.136-137	690, 770, 782, 844
		15.111	536, 609, 617, 623-625, 652, 661, 874, 2071, 2345	15.137	767, 789, 398, 3077
				15.138	711, 767, 770, 772, 783, 797, 790, 822, 831, 841, 844, 871, 3077
15.88-93	33				
15.88-103	182, 497, 501, 1019, p.3	15.111-119	791, 802		
15.88-160	498	15.111-160	624, 2412, 2413	15.139	695, 706, 735, 783, 1517
15.89	509, 734, 1053, 1160, 1402, 1535	15.112	440, 849, 2071, 2312		
		15.112-119	792	15.139-140	646, 657, 784
15.89-90	439	15.113	633	15.140	711, 726, 729, 730, 767, 784, 785, 804, 812, 841, 900
15.89-91	500, 503, 514, 542, 738, 1398	15.114	629, 634, 665		
		15.115	650, 793, 821, 878, 1517		
15.90	439, 503, 504, 2467			15.140-142	735
15.91	503, 514, 734, 1404	15.115-117	643, 795	15.140-144	827
15.92	158, 440, 442, 519, 529, 536, 645, 1110, 2350	15.116	643, 659, 795	15.141	784, 817, 841
		15.116-118	810	15.142	711, 725, 801, 810, 821, 818, 1910, 2927
15.92-93	547, 617, 643	15.117	660, 663, 796		
15.92-95	501	15.117-118	816	15.142-143	784
15.92-96	440	15.117-119	643	15.143	726, 809, 841, 848, 2614
15.93	165, 485, 502, 546, 565, 557, 1163, 1264, 1404	15.118	663, 885, 2358		
		15.119	633, 699, 1320, 1820, 1879	15.143-144	815
15.93-94	558			15.144	767, 810, 822
15.94-95	432	15.120	600, 609, 676, 821	15.144-146	712, 732, 770, 788, 822, 839, 840, 3077
15.94-96	611	15.121	397, 606, 671, 683, 688, 704, 934, 2215, p.3		
15.95	519, 1216, 2254			15.145	741, 822, 825, 829
15.95-96	440, 1666	15.121-122	702, 810, 811	15.145-146	767
15.96	348, 448, 498, 515, 529, 537, 545, 578, 581, 592, 596, 598, 619, 645, 744, 1380, 2422, 2746	15.122	688, 810, 832, 847	15.146	634, 690, 711, 712, 715, 767, 822, 839, 1413
		15.122-126	849		
		15.123	815, 819, 2614	15.147	711, 914
		15.123-124	820	15.147-148	725
15.96-103	363, 535, 1158	15.123-125	923	15.147-159	602
15.97	156, 158, 166, 512, 523, 554, 557, 558, 564, 572, 1307, 1566	15.124	722, 770, 771, 778, 782, 892, 899, 900	15.147-160	703, 846, 1037, 2864, 2868
				15.148	854, 914, 2071
		15.124-126	847		
15.97-98	421, 433	15.125	716, 1592	15.149	854, 857, 870
15.98	29, 113, 541, 556	15.126	629, 640, 706, 712, 718, 719, 794, 848, 1158	15.150	726, 859, 865, 873, 885, 886, 1756
15.98-101	1474				
15.98-103	541, 1019	15.126-159	646	15.150-151	217, 914
15.99	549, 555, 1609	15.127	711, 721, 797, 841, 928	15.151	602, 623, 659, 793, 875, 881
15.100	29, 1041, 1431, 1485, 2482	15.127-128	712		
		15.127-129	712	15.152	496, 641, 866
15.100-103	555	15.127-146	703, 704, 712, 2695, p.3	15.153	726, 885, 895, 901
15.101	142, 165, 541, 563, 560, 1163, 1274, 1539, 1713, 2481, 2579	15.128	640, 710, 714, 725, 767, 809, 2591	15.155	770, 888, 901
				15.156	347, 729, 893, 905, 913, 1925, 2430
		15.129	712, 721, 727, 767, 800,		

INDEX OF ANCIENT TEXTS

15.157	918	15.175	84, 119	15.192-198	930
15.158	758, 821, 1145, 1636, 1880	15.175-176	119, 1037	15.193	437, 1133, 1135, 1143, 1168, 1183, 1192, 1980, 2114, 2449, 2470, 2509, 2747, 2750
15.159	925, 1517, 2057, 2089, 2413	15.176	125, 995, 1004, 1428		
		15.177	261, 465, 468, 946, 960, 1004, 1008, 1037, 1050, 1053, 1082, 1085, 1087, 1533, 2643		
15.160	715			15.194	667, 1170, 1209, 1385, 2207, 2229, 2449, 2470, 2509, p.165
15.161	28, 1021, 1120, 1356, p.3				
		15.177-178	960, 961		
15.161-163	948, 971, 1047, 1088, p.165	15.178	1055, 1402, 1428, 1429, 1932	15.195	1150, 1370
				15.195-196	1385, p.165
15.161-193	929	15.178-181	1076	15.196	107, 1213, 1300, 1370, 1386, 1497, 2113, p.165
15.161-201	p.3	15.179	75, 1059, 1061, 1087		
15.161-263	p.164, 167	15.179-182	307, 1044, 1055	15.197	741, 838, 1167, 1268
15.162	740, 940, 981, 1090, 1135, 2935	15.180	1042, 1059, 1068	15.198	1123, 1198, 1213, 1217, 1385, 1701, p.165
		15.181	56		
		15.181-182	1087	15.198-201	p.165
15.162-163	944, 957, 1208, p.165, 166	15.182	77, 261, 706, 958, 960, 1040, 1053, 1080, 1087, 1533, 2643	15.199	422, 997, 1213, 1220, 1237, 1370, 1385, 1387, 1798, 2209, 2521, 2809, p.165
15.163	171, 963, 1088, 1267, 1592				
		15.183	114, 130, 740, 939, 963, 967, 1037, 1088, 1093, 1114, 1120, 1135, 1278, 1300, 1935, p.165	15.199-200	1218, 1234
15.163-173	1021			15.199-201	448, 1386, 2441
15.164	173, 269, 594, 1037, 1088, 1249, 1274, 1537, 1713, 2518			15.200	1229, 1235, 1385, 2209
				15.201	999, 1357, 1358, 1387, 1798, 2110, 2194, 2209, 2449, p.165
15.164-179	12	15.183-184	184		
15.164-182	115, 937, 945, 1088, p.3, 165	15.183-186	1239		
		15.183-187	368, 1730	15.202	125, 130, 195, 1213, 1239, 1359, 1392, 1503, 1530, p.164
15.165	77, 261, 426, 937, 962, 1008, 1037, 1040, 1051, 1053, 1081, 1083, 1085, 2643	15.183-198	1088		
		15.183-201	28	15.202-203	18, 1104, 1401
		15.184	450, 1102, 1117, 1119, 1617, 2515, p.165, 166	15.202-207	p.166
				15.202-208	1295
15.165-173	946, 1037	15.184-185	1241, 1339, 1413, 2711, p.166	15.202-215	1393
15.165-176	1634			15.202-231	p.3
15.165-178	88, 1428, 2412	15.184-186	1102, 1622	15.202-236	494
15.165-182	1242	15.184-201	1255	15.202-239	1239, 1530
15.166	130, 132, 171, 347, 937, 943, 955, 962, 976, 977, 1036, 1037, 1050, 1094, 1114, 1208, 1278, 1496, 1502, 1533, 1578, 1603, 1634	15.185	130, 198, 517, 1113, 1114, 1243, 1244, 1258, 1260, 1361, 1364, 1393, 1401, 1466, 1469, 1486, 1680, 1733, 2561, p.167	15.202-251	322
				15.202-252	1239
				15.203	140, 1309, 1401, 1429
				15.204	422, 461, 1111, 1242, 1270, 1324, 1401, 1541, 2518, p.165, 166, 167
		15.185-186	494, 1541		
		15.185-187	1261, p.3		
15.166-168	1242	15.186	1037, 1102, p.3, 165, 166		
15.167	277, 963, 982, 983, 1037			15.204-205	1111, 1245
		15.187	1125, 1184, 1214, 1236, 1274, 1301, 1358, 1385, 1497, 1517, 1537	15.204-208	1257
15.167-168	348, 392			15.205	176, 487, 522, 576, 988, 1109, 1113, 1271, 1449, 1469
15.167-170	130, 949, 955				
15.168	240, 347, 448, 936, 962, 988, 998, 999, 1006, 1007, 1010, 1017, 1019, 1029, 1032, 1087, 1496, 1534, 1643, 1990, 2792, 2850, 2989	15.187-193	1120		
		15.187-194	420	15.205-207	1267, 1288, p.165
		15.187-196	2936, p.165	15.205-208	1466
		15.187-197	p.166	15.206	198, 859, 1990, 1537
		15.187-198	1299, 1417, 1793	15.207	370, 461, 1289, 1304, 1324
		15.187-201	28, 606, 2118		
15.169	130, 217, 366, 859, 981	15.188	1739, p.165	15.208	32, 1298, 1310, 1326, 1350, 1351, 1401, 1541, p.165, 166
15.168-169	1630	15.188-189	1168		
15.169-170	1720	15.189	184, 613, 939, 1157, 1162, 2414, 2935		
15.170	256, 981, 997, 1013, 1305			15.209	461, 1324, 1541, 1544, 1560, p.165
		15.189-190	1172, 2049		
15.171	217, 997, 1005	15.189-191	1134	15.210	70, 140, 201, 207, 462, 926, 1284, 1297, 1309, 1321, 1350, 1351, 1401, 1405, 1525, p.165
15.171-173	1029	15.189-192	1133, 1173		
15.172	596, 1019, 1036, 1037	15.189-193	1186		
15.172-182	204	15.190	108, 915, 934, 939, 1135, 1152, 1214, 1236, 1357		
15.173	12, 29, 125, 980, 1002, 1029, 1031, 1039, 1474, 1475, 1804			15.210-211	1250, 1295, 1541
				15.210-212	p.165
15.174	541, 704, 925, 979, 996, 1002, 1037, 1039, 1040, 1044, 1054, 1428, 1429	15.191	541, 1138, 1158	15.211	231, 461, 464, 470, 1324, 1329, 1342, 1394, 1465
		15.191-192	541, 564, 557, 1162, 2196		
		15.192	505, 564, 1305	15.211-212	321, 1321, 1335, 1348, 1352, 1389, 1485, 1556
15.174-176	946, 1037, 1077	15.192-193	1134		
15.174-178	179				

15.212	207, 373, 1326, 1345	15.235-239	1314	15.262-263	1704
15.213	198, 234, 454, 463, 859, 1106, 1410, 1413, 1414, 1465, 1479, 1487, 1626, 1680, p.165	15.235-254	2562	15.262-264	1747
		15.236	70, 207, 494, 1314, 1530, 1545, 1861	15.263	1705, 1728, 1748
				15.264	110, 171, 184, 1728, 1735, 1744, 1745, 2619
		15.236-237	396		
15.214	461, 464, p.165	15.237	139, 276, 503, 1493, 1541, 1547, 1606	15.264-265	1682
15.215	306			15.265	1133
15.215-218	606, 1236, 1417	15.237-238	457, 1401, p.165	15.266	1713
15.216	1366, 2556	15.237-239	1395, 1634	15.267	1750, 1769, 1814, 1822, 1857, 1911, 1930, 2098, 2210, 2227, 2549, 2550, 2581, 2642, 2692, 2731, 2740, p.3
15.217	306, 536, 1236, 1358, 1360, 1473, 1601, 1944, 1949, 2119, 2406, 2445, p.165	15.238	207, 292, 434, 461, 1307, 1324, 1405, 1428, 1539, 1562		
		15.238-239	1516	15.267-268	1810, 1822, 1849, 1864, 2098, 2051, 2674, 2720
15.218	125, 240, 461, 1216, 1299, 1324, 1476, 2188, p.165	15.239	1476, 1545		
		15.240	215, 1307, 1568	15.267-276	1750, 1753
		15.240-242	1555, 1584	15.267-291	1749, 1932, 2007, 2114, 2550, p.4
15.219	331, 382, 512, 1401, 1409, 1416, 1547, 1555	15.240-246	565, 1338, 1555, 1564, p.3		
15.220	24, 459, 843, 1339, 1342, 1401, 1547, 1626	15.241	289, 1808	15.268	338, 1764, 1765, 1767, 1770, 1787, 1788, 1793, 1814, 1882, 1936, 2209, 2225, 2324, 2326, 2809, 2961
		15.242	546, 1350, 1422, 1559, 1565		
15.221	1417, 1420, 1479, 1528				
15.222	313, 369, 370, 1541, 1547, p.165	15.243	965, 1362, 1555, 1563, 1576, 1579, 2007, 2017		
		15.244	1555, 1576, 1593	15.268-269	1791
15.222-223	1458, 1569	15.245-246	1555	15.268-274	338
15.222-231	1422	15.246	1580, 1631, 1944, 2012, 2018, 2135, 2212, 2561	15.269	1766, 1767, 1777, 1782, 1800, 1806, 1837, 1894
15.223	140, 449, 449, 562, 1309, 1401, 1438, 1439, 1443, 1447, 1450, 1454, 1459, 1478, 1514, p.165				
		15.247	130, 400, 1602, 1605, 1622, 1634, 2125	15.269-270	143
				15.269-271	1763
15.223-224	462	15.247-248	1616, 1938	15.270	1773, 1776, 1777, 1783, 1789
15.223-225	p.165, 166	15.247-249	130, 949		
15.223-231	1106	15.247-251	1602, p.3	15.271	107, 217, 859, 1764, 1768, 1771, 1776, 1792, 1793, 1814, 1954, 1974, 2083, 2207
15.223-239	396	15.247-252	131		
15.224	1436, 1448, 1451-1453, 1455, 1514	15.247-266	1749, p.3		
		15.248	113, 400		
15.225	1422, 1436, 1504, p.165	15.249	84, 130, 1619, 1627	15.272	1757, 1763, 1817, 1842, 2861, 2863
15.226	1464, 1468, 1926	15.250	1632		
15.227	1465, 1489, 1504, p.165, 166	15.250-251	130	15.272-290	222
		15.251	125, 204, 915, 1639, 2013, 2085	15.273	997, 1805, 1812
15.228	486, 1109, 1113, 1469, 1473, 1481, p.165, 166			15.274	16, 338, 1565, 1753, 1767, 1812, 1814, 1819, 1825, 1858, 1864, 1882, 2098, 2253, 2551, 2692
		15.252	981, 1634, 1638, 1639, 1647, 1658, 1697, 1745, 2152		
15.229	179, 454, 464, 1436, 1481, 1485, 1488, 1501, 1634, p.165, 166				
		15.252-266	1602, p.3	15.275	1751, 1753, 1862, 2581, 2692
15.229-230	p.165	15.253	1639, 1640, 1663, 1674, 1732		
15.229-231	1019			15.276	151, 667, 1180, 1796, 1816, 1825, 1831, 1833, 1834, 1839, 1840, 1844, 1861, 1848, 1856, 1879, 1809, 2221, 2310
15.229-236	125, 1634	15.253-258	1641		
15.229-247	1336	15.253-266	1640, 1644		
15.230	562, 1431, 1477	15.254	78, 449, 536, 1060, 1557, 1640, 1644, 1648, 1653, 1663, 1680, 1681, 1700, 2211		
15.230-231	1355				
15.231	114, 170, 198, 449, 1332, 1461, 1896, 1914, p. 164, 165			15.276-278	1794
				15.276-279	1796, 1815
		15.254-255	1751	15.277	236, 462, 1751, 1763, 1816, 1818, 1822, 1834-1836, 1839, 1840, 1863, 2153, 2216, 2436
15.231-237	204, 1290	15.255	1679, 2504		
15.232	130, 859, 1509, 2288	15.256	1644, 1668, 1741, 2603		
15.232-234	200	15.256-258	144		
15.232-235	1603, p.165, 166	15.257	1729	15.277-278	1842
15.232-236	1494	15.258	230, 1339, 1661, 1733, 2616	15.277-279	1756, 1838
15.232-239	p.3			15.278-279	1835
15.233	107, 108, 1476, 1512, 1518, 1604, 2288	15.259	371, 1640	15.279	1796, 1797, 1816, 1818, 1823, 1831, 1851, 1854, 2221
		15.260	981, 1380, 1641, 1645, 1702, 1703, 1743, 1964, 2152		
15.233-234	1499, 1634				
15.233-235	1524			15.280	1846, 1918, 2701
15.234	1518, 1520, 1564, 2481	15.260-266	1602, p.3	15.280-288	2103, 2570, 2592
15.234-236	1497, 1512	15.261	2984	15.280-290	1750, 1753
15.235	462, 485, 1250	15.261-264	1745	15.280-291	1753, 1850
15.235-236	1499	15.261-265	1699	15.281	1821, 1828, 1853, 1887, 1903, 2098, 2551
15.235-237	240	15.262	1715, 1721, 1725, 2086		

INDEX OF ANCIENT TEXTS

15.282	1886, 1906	15.308	2065, 2109, 2112		2312, 2328, 2540
15.282-284	2573	15.309	2053, 2076	15.339-341	2242
15.282-290	1854	15.309-310	2057	15.340	2305
15.283	208, 1901, 1927, 2105	15.310	2095	15.341	1763, 1764, 2234, 2687
15.284	936, 1763, 1868, 1869, 1892	15.311	2081, 2084, 2093	15.342	1950, 2135, 2235
		15.311-312	2087	15.342-343	2332, 2510, p.4
15.284-285	1763	15.311-314	2104, 2201	15.342-364	2330, 2332
15.285	426, 1881, 1919, 1923, 1969	15.312	1635, 1791, 2101, 2107	15.343	27, 2353, 2357, 2359, 2389, 2403, 2423, 2434, 2494, 2499, 2503
		15.313	925		
15.285-290	1876	15.314	2051		
15.286	41, 170, 1491, 2098	15.315	330, 909, 2065, 2112, 2115	15.343-344	2363, 2417, 2421
15.287	1126, 1794, 1902, 1912			15.343-349	2330, 2449, p.4
15.288	1886, 2098, 2550, 2551	15.316	260, 1194, 1285, 2055, 2064, 2065	15.343-364	p.4
15.289	1923, 2592			15.344	519, 2345, 2362, 2388, 2393, 2394, 2397, 2418, 2448, 2449, 2495, 2499
15.290	347, 562	15.317	2424		
15.291	40, 1047, 1936, 1960, 1969, 1979, 1997, 2188, 2190, 2191, 2577, 2585, 2701, 2702, 2932, p.4	15.317-325	2117, p.4		
		15.318	1937, 2117, 2125, 2177, 2209, 2270, 2400, 2404, 2522, 2860, 2941	15.344-348	28, 2349, 2389, 2503
				15.345	661, 2386, 2393
				15.346	2378
15.291-298	1932, 2196, 3069	15.319	461, 2147, 2157, 2164	15.346-347	2369
15.292	410, 1093, 1607, 1897, 1933, 1945, 1948, 1950, 1981, 1998, 2004, 2026, 2135, 2190, 2191, 2197, 2313, 2337, 2343, 2577, 2683, 2702, 2873, 2874, 2878, 2899, 2932, 2933	15.319-322	167, 2117, 2137, 2163	15.346-348	2353, 2367
		15.320	2137	15.347	2391
		15.321	395, 1716, 1827, 1964, 2162	15.348	2366, 2385, 2389, 2398
				15.349	1250, 2350, 2405, 2408, 2417, 2420, 2449
		15.322	2141, 2142, 2177		
		15.323	184, 2169	15.350	2124, 2136, 2209, 2403, 2407, 2409, 2508, 2511
		15.323-325	2003, 2117, 2163, 2232, 2711, p.4		
15.292-293	1947, 1970, 2032, 2333			15.350-353	2443, p.4
15.292-298	1929, 1936, 1969, 2164, 2212, 2232, 2233, 2235, p.4	15.324	2171, 2176, 2177, 2180, 2185, 2235, 2282, 2307, 2702, 2951, 3003	15.350-359	2400
				15.351	1513, 2209, 2419, 2428, 2434, 2435, 2437, 2439, 2446, 2450, 2456, 2472
15.293	1383, 1936, 1942, 1950, 1998, 2235, 2237, 2793	15.325	1893, 2185, 2297, 2404		
		15.326	170, 2206, 2439, 2556, 2564	15.351-353	2437
15.293-295	17			15.352	2334, 2439, 2350, 2354
15.294	852, 1968, 1971, 1983, 2517, 2711	15.326-327	2558	15.353	170, 231, 1280, 2427, 2339
		15.326-328	260		
15.294-295	620	15.326-330	2188	15.353-354	395
15.295	1420, 1936, 1941, 1965, 1969, 1979, 1997, 2190, 2557, 2577, 2702, 2932, p.4	15.326-341	2188, p.4	15.353-359	2443
		15.327	107, 330, 2032, 2178, 2223, 2228	15.354	2406, 2408, 2434, 2437, 2462, 2456, 2457, 2472, 2541, 2567, 2679
		15.327-328	2196		
15.296	27, 1791, 1943, 1944, 1952, 1953, 1968, 1997, 2000, 2135, 2235, 2702, 2932, 2998	15.328	422, 1751, 1793, 2032, 2200, 2226, 2227	15.354-359	2524
				15.354-360	2443
		15.328-329	2188, p.4	15.354-364	2332, p.4
		15.328-330	2000, 2002	15.354-379	2679
15.296-298	1939, 2003, 2032, 2522, 2710	15.329	2222	15.355	358
		15.330	2000, 2253, 2690	15.356	260, 859, 2410, 2447, 2467, 2477
15.297	1956, 1985, 1999	15.331	1950, 2236, 2254, 2304, 2306		
15.298	1975, 1997, 2199, 2230, 2231, 2690, 2702, 2932			15.357	2212, 2442, 2447, 2457, 2462, 2485
		15.331-332	2243		
15.299	464, 1576, 2009, 2023, 2033, 2117	15.331-341	1950, 2003, 2188, 2212, 2226, 2233, 2235, 2332, 2522, p.4	15.358	1461, 1491, 2191, 2442, 2453, 2472, 2485, 2492
				15.359	2350
15.299-304	p.4			15.360	2350, 2503, 2525
15.299-316	2005, 2124, 2193, 2424, 2703, p.4	15.332	2234, 2264, 2330, 2331, 2338, 2985	15.360-361	2202
				15.361	1299, 1305, 1657, 2404, 2749, 2750
15.300	2020, 2023, 2033, 2037, 2062, 2561	15.333	2247, 2254, 2257, 2259		
		15.334	380, 2127, 2249, 2257, 2977, 2978	15.362	2516, 2517
15.301	325, 1572, 2029, 2023, 2025, 2030, 2111			15.363	2498, 2523, 2530
		15.335	2272, 2978	15.363-364	2209, 2214, 2225, 2442, 2527, 2539, 2713
15.302	1075, 2031, 2033	15.334-336	2246		
15.303	630, 2039, 2048, 2101, 2542	15.334-338	2243	15.364	2524, 2526, 2584
		15.336	2285, 2522		
15.305	2097, 2366	15.337	2267, 2290, 2293, 2296, 2338, 2560	15.365	140, 1909, 2577, 2581, 2679, 2701, 2746, p.4
15.305-307	2052				
15.305-316	2006, 2036, 2116, p.4	15.338	2309	15.365-366	12
15.306-307	2051	15.338-339	2299	15.365-371	p.4
15.307	217, 1729, 2005, 2043, 2058, 2087, 2102, 2120	15.339	275, 1823, 2171, 2210, 2214, 2225, 2299, 2308,	15.366	330, 2292, 2577
				15.366-367	1890

369

15.367	11	15.396	2234, 2678, 2856, 2865, 3037	16.1-5	1751
15.368	2599, 2603, 2692, 2742			16.4	11, 395, 965, 1865, 2032, 2152
15.368-369	12, 2589	15.396-400	2817		
15.369	114, 2586, 2600, 2603	15.397	2678, 2822, 2844	16.6	397, 2337
15.370	14, 17, 18, 19, 116, 2339, 2603	15.397-401	2678	16.7	270, 276, 277
		15.398	2843, 2845, 2853, 2952, 2958	16.8	449, 449
15.371	2463, 2602, 2621			16.10	544
15.372	220, 575, 2602, 2603, 2671, 2673, 2675	15.398-400	2824	16.11	1423, 1654, 2334
		15.399	2693	16.12	1358
15.372-379	p.4	15.400	2848, 2850, 2852, 3008, 3010, 3027	16.12-15	2209, 2404, 3042
15.373	2615, 2622, 2628, 2632, 2635, 2638, 2644, 2656, 2658, 2660, 2675, 2676, 3045, 3077			16.13	176, 1814, 2012, 2234, 2253
		15.401	2810, 2814, 2822, 2874, 2953, 3027, 3028	16.16	107, 1122
		15.402	3008, 3034	16.18	107
15.373-378	23, 2603, 2707, 2742, 2755	15.402-417	2678	16.18-19	2199
		15.403	1939, 2678, 2774, 2878, 2929, 2931, 2953, 3063	16.19	1975, 2705
15.374	11, 1801, 2622, 2626, 2638, 2656, 2673, 2707, 3045, 3077			16.20	2403
		15.403-408	2678	16.21	381, 2209
		15.403-409	1939, p.4	16.22	1153, 1155, 1304, 2209, 2226
15.375	1259, 2650	15.404	2866, 2888, 2899, 2915, 2920, 2922, 2924, 2930, 2953		
15.375-376	193, 2007, 2632, 2673, 2731			16.24	2234, 2745
				16.24-25	205
15.376	1902, 2504, 2646, 2659	15.404-409	2878, 2926-2928	16.24-26	2199
15.377	1299, 2622, 2626	15.405	2875, 2880, 2899, 2895, 2901, 2907, 2912, 2913, 2915, 2927	16.25	260
15.378	2613, 2622, 2657, 2662			16.26	2404
15.379	1497, 2603, 2617, 2742, 2755			16.27	629, 1133
		15.405-406	2911	16.30	1205
15.380	191, 1992, 2680, 2684, 2704, 2722, 2732, 2757, 2770, 2813, 2862, 2938, 2961, 3008, 3030, 3037, 3039, 3040, 3042, 3057, 3078	15.406	2869, 2874, 2880, 2888, 2913, 2915, 2916, 3063	16.35	1751
				16.36	1810
		15.407	2884, 2913, 2924, 2927	16.40	1565
		15.408	2904, 2915	16.41	1229
		15.409	575, 939, 1684, 1938, 2627, 2678, 2702, 2747, 2866, 2869, 2874, 2877, 3063	16.43	1751
				16.47	661
15.380-400	p.4			16.48	2585
15.380-409	1938			16.51	2226, 2585
15.380-425	2678, 2684, 3037	15.410	2254, 2678, 2685, 2821, 2959, 2963, 3011, 3019	16.54	2087
15.381	194, 2718, 2741, 2757, 2763, 2770, 2777, 2835, 2851			16.56	75
		15.410-420	p.4	16.59	1692
		15.411	2789, 2822, 2832, 2945, 2959, 2985	16.60	2209, 2704
15.381-387	2678			16.61	288, 473, 2227
15.382	713, 2704, 2705, 2715, 2757	15.411-416	2678, 2789, 2812, 3037	16.62	1019
		15.412	2985	16.63	2704
15.382-387	p.4	15.413	2271, 2986, 2988, 2989	16.64	2504, 2543
15.383	2703, 2710, 2743, 2755	15.413-415	2971	16.66	125, 1496
15.383-387	2698	15.414	1701, 2250, 2996, 3006	16.66-74	449
15.384	75, 2715, 2731, 2740, 2754, 2961	15.415	2963	16.68-69	270
		15.416	2759, 2974, 2983, 3006, 3008	16.69	468, 1133, 1485
15.385	2730, 2733, 2734, 2735, 2780, 2978			16.70	1503
		15.417	2685, 2849, 2938, 3023, 3026	16.71	270
15.385-386	2740			16.72	1250, 1412, 2652
15.385-388	2693	15.417-419	1833, 2678, 3009, 3065	16.73	1409
15.386	2693, 2753, 2754	15.418	3023, 3025, 3026, 3028, 3065	16.75	125, 335, 462, 468, 1240, 1420
15.387	2509, 2707, 2729				
15.388	1319, 2678, 2685, 2741, 2767, 2768, 2770, 3043, 3046	15.418-419	3023, 3035	16.75-77	125
		15.419	2856, 3017, 3021, 3035, 3052	16.76-77	1391, 2504
				16.77	1299
15.389	2761	15.420	2678, 2680, 2759, 2866, 2938, 3017, 3042	16.78	11, 270, 462, 2613
15.389-390	2678			16.81	667, 1180
15.390	2875, 3042	15.421	2678, 2680, 3057, 3072, 3078	16.82	230
15.390-403	p.4			16.84	125, 174, 359
15.391	2775, 2784, 2798, 2978	15.421-423	2678, 2790, 2940	16.85	1250
15.391-395	2678, 3064	15.421-425	p.3, 4	16.88	1250
15.391-421	2769	15.422	1136, 3042, 3044, 3055	16.89	956, 1343
15.391-425	2678	15.423	2688	16.90	464, 2412
15.392	2693, 2741, 2820, 2978	15.424	40, 2678, 2869, 3018	16.91	1358
15.393	2808, 2811, 2955, 2956, 3037	15.425	773, 2678, 3045, 3071	16.92	1060, 2344
		16	2334	16.94	186, 191
15.394	2838, 2858	16.1	1751, 1810, 1858, 1947	16.96	426, 1405

INDEX OF ANCIENT TEXTS

16.97	997, 1654	16.201-205	449	16.303	1262, 2613
16.98	108, 700	16.203	1328	16.304	116
16.101	573	16.206	1264	16.305	118, 119, 1250
16.104	1211	16.207	463	16.308	1343
16.108	199	16.208	319, 462	16.309	107, 231
16.115	2032, 3042	16.209	125	16.311	2627
16.119	230	16.210	84	16.313	1774
16.122	1536	16.212	108	16.314	1220, 2119
16.125	1485	16.213	257, 1899	16.315	199, 292, 493, 1461
16.128	107, 231, 2177	16.214	1695	16.317-318	1461
16.129	2226, 2344	16.216	484	16.319	1685, 2218
16.130	859	16.219	1250	16.320	1461
16.131	231	16.220	2119	16.321	1313
16.132	107, 2696	16.221	2086	16.323-324	84
16.134	24	16.222	1559	16.327	2049
16.135	40, 1696	16.223	230	16.337	1935
16.136	607, 2117, 2329, 3056	16.224	596, 1164	16.342	140
16.136-141	1760, 2326, 2331	16.225	1663, 1751	16.343	3056
16.137	1778, 1779, 1801	16.226	449	16.346	936
16.137-138	1762, 1793	16.227	1264	16.347	2364
16.137-141	1764	16.229	125, 1433	16.352	1805
16.138	1762, 1791, 2207, 2209, 2891	16.230	667, 1180, 1434	16.353	602
		16.230-231	1460	16.353-355	1953
16.140	205, 1770, 1792, 1808	16.233	2655	16.355	107
16.140-141	1791	16.234	277	16.356	1250, 1355, 1474
16.141	1925	16.235	1457, 1924	16.356-357	1019
16.142	1770, 1982	16.236	160, 199, 1890	16.356-394	1634
16.143-144	2702	16.237	32, 1307	16.357	1019
16.146	205	16.238	936, 1503	16.358	443
16.146-149	2199, 2745	16.244	84, 551, 1654	16.359	24, 943, 1485
16.148	3003	16.246-253	1461	16.361	1019, 1474, 1893
16.149	1761, 1774	16.247	634	16.361-369	179
16.150	205	16.248	269, 1250, 1581	16.363	395, 462
16.150-151	1391	16.250	2030, 2516	16.366	464
16.150-159	2462	16.252	347, 562, 1925	16.367	230
16.151	2032, 2459	16.254-255	562	16.368	1713
16.153	1568, 2203, 2461	16.255	1113, 2482	16.373	2553
16.154	1200, 2253	16.256	1461	16.375	166
16.156-159	1391	16.257	114	16.376	193
16.156	1875, 2460	16.259	462	16.379	493, 1913
16.157	988, 1495, 2209, 2226	16.259-260	1588	16.379-394	2192
16.158	75	16.261	462	16.382	634
16.159	205, 2460	16.262	464, 562, 1485, 1894	16.385	462
16.160	24	16.263	562	16.386	1458
16.161	32, 661	16.264	1075, 2055	16.388-391	1461
16.163	1814	16.265	462	16.389	494, 1291
16.164	1221	16.267	456, 1241	16.392	2762
16.165	101, 2538	16.269	107, 1658	16.393	179, 1477
16.166	938	16.271	2520	16.394	1037, 2562
16.169	1822	16.272	2108	16.395-404	1751
16.179-181	26	16.276	1241, 1388	16.399	207, 1480, 2579
16.180	24, 1113	16.277	1739, 1932	16.400	2758
16.182	2253	16.279	1250, 3056	16.402	1133, 1739
16.183	2705	16.280	1740	16.404	193
16.183-187	1751	16.282	3056	17.2	233, 1436
16.184	997, 1541, 2104	16.283	602	17.10	1654
16.185	965, 1239, 1479	16.284-285	1932	17.12	1654
16.187	1279, 2872	16.285	602, 2353, 2364	17.13	634
16.188	859, 1698, 2007	16.291	2627	17.20	11
16.188-189	125	16.293	1369	17.20-21	2335
16.192	70, 207, 1314	16.294	667, 1180	17.23	2702
16.193	207, 449, 700	16.295	413	17.24	73, 2492
16.194	373	16.296	2108	17.24-28	620
16.195	174, 1250	16.298	1875	17.25	2353, 2497
16.197	462, 1264, 2057	16.299	32	17.26	73, 2364, 2385
16.198	373	16.300	125, 1240, 1359	17.29-30	634
16.199	1066	16.301	107, 330, 2739	17.32	2585
16.199-200	464	16.302	1307	17.33	988

371

17.34	373	17.161-167	179	18.9	170
17.38	449	17.162	75, 2872	18.9-25	2602
17.41	52	17.163	2104	18.11	2602, 2609, 2611
17.43	2625	17.164	395, 1482	18.12	2605
17.44	349, 634	17.168	965, 1585, 2653	18.19-22	2602, 2611
17.46	29, 1019, 1476	17.171	634	18.26	606, 2413
17.49	634	17.173	107	18.28	2498, 2535
17.50	464	17.173-179	1638	18.31	449
17.53	107	17.175	449, 1832	18.34	2160
17.54	634	17.176	1935	18.39-42	68
17.55	2119	17.180	1463, 1751, 2285	18.40	139, 373
17.56-57	1461	17.181	634, 1751	18.46	2962
17.59-77	1454	17.184	401, 1630	18.47	208, 1169, 1313
17.60	634	17.186	451	18.49	664
17.64	1343	17.189	449, 2498	18.50	2605
17.64-65	1461	17.189-190	598	18.54	330
17.66	2562	17.191	464, 1634	18.55	2220
17.66-67	395, 1926	17.192	11, 94, 1634	18.55-59	1750, 1753, 1818, 1833
17.67	2519	17.195	1231	18.55-62	1612
17.69	464, 1441, 1461	17.196-199	315	18.58	1881
17.75	634	17.197	2801	18.59	65
17.77	1461	17.198	25, 1374	18.66	1398
17.78	2141, 2161	17.199	340, 1564, 2164, p.4	18.67	1556
17.79	397, 1461	17.200	285	18.69	523
17.80	2335	17.200-205	2696	18.72	373
17.81	2200, 2685	17.201	473	18.73	1398
17.83	464	17.202	2343	18.74	523
17.86	1484	17.206	397, 1468	18.79	2217
17.87	2212, 2226	17.207	2613	18.85	248
17.90	551	17.219-223	2343	18.88	2883
17.92	1746	17.220	449, 449	18.90	2885-2889
17.93	449, 551, 1019, 1461	17.229	179	18.91	1939
17.94-95	125, 2504	17.238	2013	18.91-92	2878
17.95	1060	17.246	1230	18.92	40, 939, 1939, 2934, 2935
17.100-102	634	17.247	1588		
17.104	1420	17.254	266, 629	18.92-95	2928
17.105-106	1461	17.255	1764, 1765, 1787, 2822	18.93	2875, 2879, 2916, 2918, 2919
17.106	334	17.258	623, 874		
17.107	634	17.259	2685, 3038	18.93-94	2880, 2889, 2924
17.108	1166	17.264	397, 2625	18.93-95	2921
17.109	1420	17.270	1630	18.94	2920, 2922, 2923
17.116	634	17.284	210	18.95	2885
17.118	634	17.287	1465	18.109	397
17.118-121	1461	17.289	27	18.112	1489
17.123	1249	17.292	1630	18.119	830
17.124	634	17.301	29, 179, 629, 2475	18.121	1822
17.129-130	634	17.304	222, 965, 1513, 1865	18.123	629
17.131	1454	17.304-310	2709	18.143	2335
17.132	1454	17.304-314	395, 1766	18.147	1333
17.137-140	449	17.305	13, 26	18.179	1477
17.142	125, 368, 449	17.305-308	26	18.180	1398
17.143	2285	17.307	26, 2475, 2709	18.188	988
17.146	598, 2510	17.318	179, 598	18.194	2891
17.147	27, 449	17.319	2345	18.202	140
17.148	238, 395, 1924, 2557	17.320	1380, 2452	18.246	305
17.148-164	222, 1749, 1751, 1818, 1866, 2221	17.327	972	18.247-252	2454
		17.321-323	598	18.259	3018
17.149	634, 1509	17.327	1505	18.261-288	1612
17.150-151	2007	17.330	75, 277	18.261-309	1750, 1818
17.151	156, 2221	17.332	2342	18.274	1191
17.152-153	634	17.342-344	2202	18.291-292	1200
17.155	2007	17.344	451, 2413	18.294	988
17.156-164	2192	17.346	2604	18.302	451
17.158	634	17.346-347	171	18.310-313	73
17.159	11, 772	17.347	1635	18.310-379	73
17.160	1913	17.352	371, 383, 1399	18.312-313	1611
17.160-164	1019, 1474	17.355	2202, 2413	18.333	2438
17.161	1763, 1764	18.6	864	18.339	988

INDEX OF ANCIENT TEXTS

18.349	373	20.31	367	115	1951, 1957
18.351	373	20.34	73	117-118	1957
18.352	1333	20.48	590	122	2433
18.359	741	20.51-53	2116	126	1951
18.371	686	20.61	120	128	2220
18.372-377	72	20.64	972	130	1708
18.377-378	73	20.70	1830	136	2756
18.378	1608	20.74	1023	137-138	64
18.379	73	20.78	596	141	2799
19-20	2905	20.83	667, 1180	143	473
19.7	2983	20.86	628	153	1893
19.12-13	1477	20.97	2897	180	2404
19.14	2634	20.101	2116	184	172
19.14-188	1884	20.106-107	172	189	114
19.19	1481	20.109	233, 667, 1180	192	2404
19.24	397	20.117	40, 42	194	1477
19.34	1489	20.120	629	198	1751
19.38	1868	20.133	40, 629	200	2885
19.58	1230	20.134-136	2909	204	487, 2404
19.65	2152	20.139	1662	207	1951
19.66	988	20.149	463, 505	214	628
19.91	233	20.160	266	223	1639
19.95	1884	20.164	1870	224	1675
19.112	487	20.165	2946	225	1482
19.138	2042	20.176	52	227	956
19.158	397	20.179	2160	244	109
19.160	1477	20.182	1187	246	1988, 2874
19.184	1505	20.200	1477	253	653
19.185	2983	20.205	576	259	109, 1467
19.216	3011	20.211	1763	264	1522
19.219	52	20.219	2709, 2771, 3042, 3057	273	1187
19.221	667	20.220-221	2856	277	2327
19.223	1463	20.221	2814, 2832	284	1477
19.225	81, 94	20.228	2778	289	667
19.226	2279	20.235	226	290	837
19.269	1492	20.237	310	293	1870
19.278	75	20.239	1023	318	1951
19.284	75	20.242	1059, 1062	327	623
19.294	2919	20.244	56, 61, 1059, 1064, 1065, 1125	342	1021
19.295	360			345	2672
19.297	2142, 2143	20.245	1067, 1069	358	1021
19.309	75			367	1847
19.314	141	*Life*		371	667
19.317	700	1	569	376	1240
19.323	1843	2	70	387	113
19.328	52	10-12	2602	388	2756
19.329	1763	11	190	391	233, 1696
19.335	1766	17	52, 172	395	628
19.335-336	1763, 1764	21	2622	414	1187
19.343-352	2891	22	767	415	1686
19.356	2491	23	172	422	170
19.360	397	31	2691	423	2671
19.361	2913	32	573	425	1805
19.360-362	2909	36	171, 233, 1730	427	1837
19.363	2909	43	52		
19.363-366	2896	46	1658	*Against Apion*	
20	2909	52	52	1.1	2672
20.1	2893, 2913	56	172	1.5	662
20.2	2897	61	1656	1.11	2670
20.6	2898, 2902	62	2906	1.14	2607
20.6-14	2907, 2913, 2928	65	2220	1.16	2717
20.7	40, 629, 2888, 2890, 2907, 2917	65-67	1818	1.17	1022
		70	233	1.37	772
20.8	2907	75	1675	1.42	772, 1912
20.9	2906, 2909, 2911	83	1893, 2651	1.42-43	1612, 1912
20.11-14	2913	87	110, 233	1.43	1804
20.12	2909, 2912, 2913	96	1658	1.44	1022
20.14	2913	102	1463	1.56	1021

374   INDEX OF ANCIENT TEXTS

1.58	769	1.313	629	2.157	1129
1.60	1758	1.317	1751	2.168	2607
1.61	769	1.318	735, 796, 1412	2.170	2642
1.67	2937	2.3	52	2.175	275, 772
1.91	1822	2.8	667, 1180	2.184	1752, 2707
1.99	52	2.10	1751, 2254	2.190	2532
1.138	1118	2.14	2607	2.190-191	1818, 2221
1.146	1595	2.15	1022	2.193	2684
1.160	347	2.17	607	2.199	156, 1328
1.162	2607, 2979	2.21	1946	2.199-204	156
1.164	2607	2.23	1946	2.205	315
1.165	3071	2.35	275	2.207	758
1.179	3	2.40	859	2.210	2623
1.180	1463	2.46	191	2.213-214	1813
1.183	2239	2.48	2867	2.218	1698
1.184-185	607	2.56-61	142, 504	2.218-220	1612
1.189	1463	2.57	505	2.218-235	1912
1.190-193	1612, 1912	2.57-58	507	2.225-235	1612
1.198	3009	2.58	503, 506, 508, 522, 2467	2.230	2064
1.199	1178, 2217	2.59	1150, 1166	2.234	541, 1471
1.202	1463	2.59-60	503	2.237	1822
1.208	1026	2.60	2116	2.239	1837
1.212	1758	2.83-84	45	2.241	1867
1.216	1893, 2239	2.84	45	2.263	1805
1.220	2672	2.102-104	3009, 3023	2.265	1805
1.221	1893	2.102-109	1611	2.271	1813
1.234	1070, 1180	2.103	3023	2.278	1503
1.237	1026	2.104	3023	2.286	52
1.243	667	2.124	392	2.291	2642
1.250	3071	2.136	52, 2672	2.293	2720
1.253	1070	2.144	1055	2.293-294	1912
1.257	1458	2.145	1752	2.294	2192
1.273	1070	2.146	1612, 1912, 2642		
1.307	2831	2.147	2672		

HEBREW BIBLE / OLD TESTAMENT

Genesis		21:12-14	1628	15:1-18	3023
4:19	2137	21:19	1628	16:4	2876
7:4	1067	22:31	1922	18:3	1753
9:5-6	1628	23:11	35	19:18	759
12:10-20	1576	23:16	264	20:10	455
13:18	1647	23:24	1648	21:17-18	92
24:4	2137	24:12	772	22:18-30	3050
25:1	2137	24:18	1067	23	1611
25:15	1110	26:32	2802	23:41-43	264
34	461, 2155	28	274, 2876	24:17	1628
34:16	2137	29:15-18	3033	25:4-7	35
37:12-36	1859	29:18	3033		
39	156, 461	29:1-37	272, 273	*Numbers*	
40:1-41:13	1434	29:43-46	272, 273	4:3	141
41	2544	31:18	772	4:23	141
41:53-47:27	2116	34:1-2	772	4:30	141
42:1-5	2048	34:22	264	4:35	141
				4:39	141
Exodus		*Leviticus*		4:43	141
1:8-14	2558	1	3033, 3052	4:47	141
10:1-20	2010	1-9	273	8:24	141
12:29-33	1572	1:4	3033	16	170, 1491
14:23	1576	1:5	3050	16:31-32	2782
15	696	1:9	3033	19	129
15:22-17:8	2234	1:13	3033	25	475
20:2-3	1648	1:17	3033	35:16-34	1628
20:3	1823	7:12-18	3050	35:30	1019
20:4-6	1818, 2221	8-9	272		
20:13	1628	8:3-5	280	*Deuteronomy*	
20:14	455	9:3-24	280	1:16-17	1019

INDEX OF ANCIENT TEXTS

5:7	1823	9:11-14	2860	10:44	2137
5:8-10	1818, 2221	10:1-10	2860		
5:17	1628	12:18-19	1093	*Nehemia*	
5:28	455	12:25-13:10	2625	2:8	2854, 2874
6:13	1648	14:11	1922	7:2	2854
13:7	759	15:6	767	10:38	2919
16:16-17	1611	19:13	2069		
17:2-8	1019	21:23-24	1922	*Esther*	
19:11-13	1628			1	461, 1813
19:15-21	1019	*2 Kings*		6:13	29
20	789	9:10	1922	8:14	2874
20:2-4	847	9:30-37	1922		
21:15	1329	9:37	1922	*Psalms*	
22:20-30	455	15:17-22	2622	22:22	3050
23:10-11	3023	24:1-17	71	35:14	759
24	1687	25:27-30	69	44:2	3076
24:1	1685, 1687	25:28	71	46:4-7	784
24:1-4	1687, 1690			78:3	3076
24:3	1685	*1 Chronicles*		80:8-19	2804
24:3-4	1687	5:19	1110	113-118	2725
24:4	1691	23:3	141		
32:19	466	23:24	141	*Ecclesiastes*	
		23:27	141	1:3	2962
Joshua		24:7	2872	1:9	2962
17:16	1951	27:33	29	1:13	2962
		31:17	141	1:14	2962
Judges				2:3	2962
6:33	1951	*2 Chronicles*		2:11	2962
7	786	2-7	2723, 2728	3:1	2962
11:30-31	847	3:4	2729	8:14	2962
20:26	847	6	2010	8:16	2962
		7:1-5	3050	11:2	2962
Ruth		7:3-5	3051		
1:4	2137	7:5	3050	*Isaiah*	
		7:8-10	3061	7:14	784
1 Samuel		7:19	2225	8:9-10	784
2:25	763	9:29	2625	50:1	1685
3-4	2106	11:21	2137		
6:12-23	1426	13:8	2625	*Jeremiah*	
7:8	847	13:21	2137	2:21	2804
9-10	2824	20:5-22	847	3:8	1685
14:6	786	30:1	3061	19	2632
15:1-9	822	30:13	3061	19:10	2632
16:11-13	2633	30:15	3061	52:31-34	69
17:45-47	840	30:23	3061	52:32	71
17:47	789	36:9-10	71		
18:17	789	36:19	2874	*Ezekiel*	
20:8	759	36:22-23	2725	16:38-40	455
21:9	2867			17:5-10	2804
25	1398	*Ezra*		45:2	2850
28:18	822	1	2723, 2725	47:16	2345
		3:1-5	3060	47:18	2345
		3:2-6	3050		
2 Samuel		3:7	2725	*Daniel*	
3	2584	3:8	141	1:8	1460
16:16-17	759	4:3	2725	3	1753
20:16	1398	4:1-5	2723	4	1580, 2371
		4:6	2723	4:15-16	1580
1 Kings		4:24	2723	4:23	1580
5-8	2723	5:1-2	2723	4:25	1580
5:2	2091	5:13-17	2725	4:25-26	1580
5:25	2091	6	2736	4:31	1580
6:2	2727	6:1-15	2723	4:32-33	1580
7:13-46	2860	6:2	2874	4:34-37	1580
8	2010	6:3	2727, 2729	6	1753
8:62-64	3050, 3051	6:3-4	2736	6:17	2917
8:63	3050	6:3-5	2725	7:8	224
8:65	3051	6:15	2723	7:11	224

INDEX OF ANCIENT TEXTS

7:20-21	224	*Micah*		*Zechariah*	
7:24-26	224	4:4	2744	1:1	2723
8:2	2874			1:7	2723
8:9-12	224	*Haggai*		8:4-5	2744
8:23-25	224	1:1	2723		
11:21-45	224	1:15	2723		
		2:1	2723		
Hosea		2:10	2723		
1:5	1951				

SEPTUAGINT (INCLUDING APOCRYPHA)

Genesis LXX		*Psalms LXX*		*1 Maccabees*	
26:5	2225	43:2	3076	1	224
		44:7-8	2641	2:15-28	2872
Exodus LXX		44:8	2641	3:18	786
29	272	77:3	3076	3:44	847
29:28	273	113:1	731-732	3:46	847
		118:128	766	3:47	847
Leviticus LXX		118:163	766	4:42	3051
8-9	272			4:52-56	3051
		Proverbs LXX		4:53	3050
Deuteronomy LXX		8:13	766	4:59	3061
24:1	1685	12:21	1667	6:1-4	508
24:3	1685	15:9	2641	8:17-32	2747
24:4	1691	28:16	766	10:15-21	126
				10:20	29
2 Samuel LXX		*Isaiah LXX*		11:7	528
12:3	2080	8:8	784	11:32	121
		33:15	766	12:30	528
1 Kings LXX		61:8	2641	13:29	1796
3:14	2225			14:4	2744
8:57	784	*Zechariah LXX*		14:4-15	2745
8:58	2225	1:13	710	14:8-12	2744
8:62-64	3050			14:25-49	2745, 2871
8:65	3061	*Baruch*		14:29	2702
9:6	2225	2:27	2643	14:32-34	2745
11:11	2225			14:33-34	2702
11:38	2225	*Bel and the Dragon*		14:35	2871
		5	1844	14:36	2702
1 Chronicles LXX				14:38	2871
6:34	340	*Ben Sira/Jesus Sirach*		14:41	2871
29:17	2641	38:16-17	313	14:41-42	2871
		45:7-13	2876	14:47	1505
2 Chronicles LXX		50:2	2849	14:49	2919
32:8	784	50:50-11	2876		
				2 Maccabees	
1 Esdras		*Epistle of Jeremiah*		1:9	3061
1:1-22	3050	3	1844	1:13-16	508
1:5	1364	7-15	1844	1:18	3061
1:12	1364	39	1844	2:13	1021, 2860
4:54	2773	45	1844	2:21	731
5:4	1364	50	1844	2:24	2617
5:44	2773	54-56	1844	2:30	2617
5:44-45	2773	57-58	1844	2:32	2617
6:24-25	2736	70-71	1844	3:1	2744
6:25	2727			3:2	2860
8:28	1364	*Judith*		3:6	2919
9:36	1686	3:9	1951	3:15	2773
		3:10	1957	3:30	3043
2 Esdras		5:17	766	4	225
7:11	2225	9:11	786	4:7-5:10	225
11:7	2225	12:10	289	4:7-9:29	224
19:13-14	2225	12:10-13:10	289	4:8	225
		13:1	289	4:18	1761
Job LXX		13:11	784	4:23-24	226
22:26	1913			4:23-5:15	226

INDEX OF ANCIENT TEXTS

4:25	731	8:23	635	14:5	234
5:6	1796	9:2	508	14:37	915
5:17	2860	9:5	2489	14:37-46	2479
5:22	731	10:1	3051	14:42	1525
6:12-16	827	10:1-8	3051, 3061	14:37-46	121
6:19	65	10:3	3050	15:2	731
6:23	1146	10:5-6	3061		
6:23A	1650	10:8	75	*Tobit*	
6:23-28	1079	11:7	635	7:12-13	2155
7:2	65	11:13	639		
7:18	827, 1492	11:25	75	*Wisdom of Solomon*	
7:25	2662	11:27	75	1:1	2640
7:30	772	11:29	226	2:19	2643
7:32-33	827	12:42	1130	8:7	2641
8:2-4	847	13:1-8	226	12:18	2643
8:17	1650	13:9	731		

OLD TESTAMENT PSEUDEPIGRAPHA

Letter of Aristeas		7.12	3048	11.22	2624
	3048	7.13	3048	12.8	29
42	2860			13.25	2624
51-82	2860	*4 Maccabees*		15.9	2624
187	120	1.1	2624	16.1	50
		1.8	2624	16.10	150
Assumption of Moses		1.10	2624	16.24	65
11.14	775	1.18	2641	17.7	50
11.17	775	3.18	2624	17.9-10	1650
12.6	775	4.15-17.24	224	17.10	50
		5.23	2041	17.23	50
Jubilees		5.34	331, 1530		
1.27	772	6.5	2662	*Sibylline Oracles*	
1.29	772	6.7	2639	3.27-38	1844
2.1	772	6.9-11	2662	3.586-590	1844
		7	150	3.601-607	1844
3 Maccabees		8.4	1525	4.51	2007
	3048	8.7	1650	5.107-110	2467
1.14	154	9.1	65	5.150-151	2467
3.15	2643	9.6	50	5.226	2467

PHILO

De Abrahamo		*De congressu eruditionis gratia*		*In Flaccum*	
62	1072	79-80	1530	40	894
136	1572	122	2626	146	657
De aeternitate mundi		*De vita contemplativa*		*De fuga et inventione*	
33	943	12	2709	33	474
				49	2163
De agricultura		*De decalogo*		114	796
22	779	16	1218	154	474
60	2623	112	779		
169	2826	119	2641	*De gigantibus*	
		172	387	31	3074
De cherubim					
32	2623	*Quod deterius potiori insidari soleat*		*Quis rerum divinarum heres sit*	
48	176	14	2205	97	2008
106	2022	73	2748	228	1747
		113	1218	301	1747
De confusione linguarum					
13	741, 838	*De ebrietate*		*Hypothetica*	
22	1572	25	2022	1	2602
69	1178	71	1482	198	2602
163	3074	199	779		

INDEX OF ANCIENT TEXTS

De Iosepho
4	457
6	1881
12	1859
40	84, 474
69	2458
142	2969
148	1747

Legum allegoriae
1.103	3074
3.102	2437
3.156	541

Legatio ad Gaium
62	640
109	741, 838
157	2860
203-337	1750
212	3015
262	1041
299-305	1750, 1818
313	1748
317-319	2860

De vita Mosis
1.4	2001
1.59	2624
1.85	2826
1.134	1482
1.168	1669
1.236	1572
2.109-126	2876
2.135	2876
2.136	2083
2.189	2709
2.190	2625
2.247	594
2.255	2278

De mutatione nominum
60	796
222	940

De opificio mundi
13	2748
17	2213
63	2278

71	2969
88	2748

De plantatione
38	2709
92	2657
123	2437

De posteritate Caini
79	3074

De praemiis et poenis
115	943

Quod omnis probus liber sit
53	2458
63	1179
75	2602, 2624
88-91	2613
91	2624
113	1179
121-124	1179
142	24
143	1179

De providentia
2.26	1091

Quaestiones et solutiones in Genesin
1.41	345
2.41	943
3.18	2826
4.52	1040
4.169	2491
4.191a	2001
4.198	886
4.202	176
4.206	2574

De sacrificiis Abelis et Caini
35	2437

De sobrietate
18	2826
23	1329

De somniis
1.68	1227

1.75	2437
1.111-112	1155
1.124	474
1.141-142	772
2.2	2625
2.99	357
2.140	457
2.150	98

De specialibus legibus
1.38	2969
1.62	2488
1.70	387
1.75	746
1.97	3044
1.120	3044
1.132	2064
1.144	3044
1.149	331
1.152	1505
1.229	3044
1.267	2809
1.327	2458
2.93	2438
2.158	1218
2.163	75
2.195	1530
2.208	2574
2.249	943
3.6	940
3.23	915
3.27	1627
3.42	2192
3.51	474
3.66	1040
3.166	741, 838
4.101	2458
4.169	2001
4.147	2641

De virtutibus
3	640
32	65
183	943
212	75

DEAD SEA SCROLLS

1QM
8.6	847
16.4-5	847
17.10	847
18.6	847
19.12	847

1QS
5.8	2603

1Q22
iv.1	775

2Q21
1	775

4Q242
	1580

4Q285
	847

4Q368
1	775

4Q374
7	775

4Q377
2.ii	772

4Q378
26	775

4Q393
3	775

4Q504
1.ii.7-11	775

5/6Ḥev
7	1699

XḤev/Se
13	1687
64	1699

INDEX OF ANCIENT TEXTS 379

EARLY CHRISTIAN WRITINGS

New Testament

Matthew
1:20	839
1:23	384
2	1890
2:3	2555
2:5-6	1890
2:7	1890
2:16	1890
2:8	1890
2:1-18	1738
5:31	1685, 1686
13:55	2775
14:6	3059
16:26	1708
21:43	2804
22:16	11
26:12	340

Mark
1:6	2069
1:13	2371
3:6	11
6:3	2775
6:21	3059
10:12	1687
12:3	11
14:8	340
15:2	2627
15:9	2627
15:12	2627
15:18	2627
15:26	2627
16:1	340
14:54	409
15:16	409

Luke
1:32	155
2:24	3027
6:27	1148
7:12	31
16:7	2091
16:18	1686
23:8-9	2662
23:56-24:1	340

John
2:20	3042
7:51	1019
8:5	455
18:12	2921
19:39	340
19:40	340

Acts
2:14	2699
3:2	3021
3:10	3021
3:11	2814
5:12	2814
7:53	772
8:31	779
12:19-23	2891
12:31	2921
17:30	765
21:26-29	3015
25:21	2473

1 Corinthians
| 6:8 | 757 |

2 Corinthians
| 1:8 | 713 |

Galatians
| 3:19 | 772 |

2 Timothy
| 4:7 | 758 |

Hebrews
1:4-2:16	772
7:9	2748
13:18	1146

James
| 3:13 | 1146 |

1 Peter
| 3:15 | 2469 |

Revelation
| 20:4 | 42 |
| 21:18 | 2275 |

Extra-canonical early Christian writings

Acts of Apollonius
| 27 | 2623 |

Acts of Euplus
| 2:1 | 50 |

Martyrdom of Polycarp
| 13.1 | 1005 |

MISHNA, TALMUD, AND RELATED LITERATURE

Mishna and Tosefta

m. 'Abot
	3074
1.2	1611
1.10-11	14
1.12-15	14

m. Baba Batra
| 2.9 | 30 |

m. Ḥagigah
| 1.1 | 1611 |

m. Kelim
1.6-8	3009
1.6-9	3023
1.8	3024

m. Middot
1.4-5	3018
2.1	2850, 2851, 3010
2.2	2954
2.3	2849, 3010, 3018, 3021
2.5	3021, 3024
2.5-6	2856
2.6	3027, 3028
3.7	2796
3.8	2804, 2805
4.1	2796
4.6	2781
4.7	2788

m. Parah
| 3.5 | 129 |

m. Roš Haššanah
| 1.1 | 36 |

m. Šabbat
| 8.1 | 340 |
| 23.5 | 340 |

m. Sanhedrin
| 4.1-5.5 | 1019 |
| 11.1 | 1037 |

m. Šeqalim
| 6.3 | 3027 |
| 6.5-6 | 2911 |

m. Ta'anit
| 3.8 | 2009 |

t. 'Arakin
| 2:1 | 3027 |

t. Zebaḥim
| 11.6 | 141 |

t. Soṭah
| 13.5 | 3071 |

Babylonian and Jerusalem Talmuds

y. Berakot
| 9.7 | 2631 |

y. Ta'anit
| 4.8 | 2633 |

b. Baba Batra
| 3b-4a | 1699, p.164 |

b. Berakot			b. Ta'anit			Lamentations Rabbah	
61b	2662		23a	2009, 3073		1.5	249
						2.4	2633
b. Giṭṭin			**Midrashim**				
56b	249					Sifra to Leviticus	
			'Abot de Rabbi Nathan			18:3	1753
b. Ḥullin				3074			
24ab	141		A 4.1.2	249		Sifre to Numbers	
			B 6	249		Ed. Horovitz 101	772
b. Sanhedrin							
48b	340						

INSCRIPTIONS AND COINS

BGU			IG			Res gestae divi Augusti	
2 no. 423	151		II² no. 3440	2510		11	2521
			II² no. 3441	2510		13	1796
CIA						26	2122
II no. 467	1823		IGR			27	588, 589
			IV no. 861	1764		32	2337
CIG							
4523	2350		ILS			SB	
			94	2503		8232	3059
CIIP			848	2503		8299	3059
2	3015						
			Inscr. It.			SEG	
CIJ			13 no. 1 II.	38		8 no. 253b	981
88	121					8 no. 463	3059
93	121		JIGRE			8 no. 784	3059
319	121		33	2160			
400	3015					SIG	
494	121		OGIS			II no. 521	1823
508-510	121		90	3059		II no. 996	2275
535	121		229	1972		III 3 no. 274	2514
537	121		414	2057, 2510			
694	1650		415	925, 2312		BMC	
1246	2143		417	2057		20.281	2350
1510	2160		427	2510			
			598	3015			

INDEX OF ANCIENT PERSONS AND PLACES

Unqualified reference numbers after each entry indicate the relevant footnote numbers in this volume. For the appearance of these names in Josephus' own text, there was no need to duplicate existing and readily accessible resources: in Greek, the *Namenwörterbuch zu Flavius Josephus* by Abraham Schalit (Brill 1968); in English, Louis H. Feldman's General Index in the final volume of the Loeb Classical Library edition (or Henry St. John Thackeray's for the LCL *War* volumes); and various digital search tools now available in English and Greek.

Numbers in parentheses after names that are borne by more than one person are those of Feldman's General Index. Since not all of the names included in the General Index are discussed in this volume on *Antiquties* 15, the numbers may not be consecutive here. They are used nonetheless to facilitate comparison with that standard reference work and to avoid the creation of a different enumeration (for each volume of Josephus).

Aaron—272, 273, 280, 308, 1366
Abiah—840
Abilene—2499
Abiram—170, 1491
Abishag—1594
Abner—122, 2584
Abraham—1072, 1218, 1647, 2137, 2155, 3071
Abram, see Abraham—
Absalom—974
Achiab—1629, 1630
Achilles—257, 368, 463, 480, 503
Achitophel—66
Achyrius—1650
Acrabetene—1105
Acropolis (at Athens)—1994, 2186, 2693
Actium (battle of)—28, 142, 146, 164, 306, 389, 423, 502, 541, 580, 590, 606, 608, 609, 617, 619, 646, 676-678, 846, 925, 927, 929, 931, 934, 937, 939, 948, 949, 952, 971, 1037, 1045, 1047, 1089, 1137, 1150, 1152, 1166, 1188, 1190, 1214, 1236, 1267, 1356, 1357, 1417, 1760, 1775, 1796, 1936, 1938, 1953, 2311, 2312, 2348, 2350, 2470, 2755, 2936, p.3
Ada—1695
Adah—2137
Adiabene (kingdom of)—120, 367, 2116
Admetus—2962
Adora—1651
Adriatic Sea—2402
Aelius Gallus, Gaius Aelius Gallus (prefect of Egypt)—2047, 2117, 2118, 2120, 2121, 2122, 2424
Aeneas—2311
Aesopus (servant of Alexandra II)—251
Agamemnon—368
Agraulos—2479
Agrippa, Marcus Vipsanius Agrippa (1)—28, 36, 260, 288, 1021, 1122, 1155, 1358, 1381, 1662, 1766, 2124, 2136, 2209, 2212, 2226, 2270, 2359, 2400, 2401, 2403, 2404, 2407-2409, 2428, 2443, 2444, 2446, 2447, 2456, 2472, 2473, 2476, 2508, 2509, 2510, 2511, 2512, 2522, 2704, 2750, 2896, 3042
Agrippa I (2)—97, 1763, 1766, 1792, 2142, 2335, 2891-2893, 2901, 2909, 2913
Agrippa II (3)—789, 2494, 2498, 2753, 2781, 2782, 2906, 2909, 2910, 2912
Agrippa Postumus, see Postumus—2508
Agrippeion, see Agrippias/ Agrippeum—2212
Agrippeum (room)—2136
Agrippias/Agrippeum (city)—1381, 2212, 2712
Ahasverus—1813
Alabanda—2311
Albans—767
Albinus, Lucceius Albinus (governor of Judea)—2503, 2771, 3057
Alcestis—2962
Alexander (the Great) (1)—882, 996, 1379, 1953, 2203, 2647, 2657, 2738
Alexander Janneus (king of Judea) (4)—56, 621, 1058, 1059, 1099, 1377, 1378, 1380, 1383, 1793, 1960, 2256, 2627, 3013, 3015, 3071
Alexander II (son of Aristobulus II) (5)—47, 130, 133-135, 1428
Alexander IV (son of Herod and Mariamme I) (8)—125, 179, 207, 231, 270, 383, 443, 462, 475, 562, 1019, 1037, 1211, 1241, 1314, 1399, 1409, 1474, 1476, 1480, 1485, 1618, 1634, 1890, 1899, 1908, 1925, 2197, 2332, 2334, 2337, 2339, 2516, 2562, 2645, 2891, p.4
Alexander Balas (2)—126
Alexander (brother of Philo)—3018
Alexander (the prophet)—1676
Alexandra I (queen Salome-Alexandra) (1)—48, 56, 61, 130, 373, 1055, 1058-1062
Alexandra II (daughter of Hyrcanus II) (2)—29, 48, 123, 125, 127, 130, 131-133, 135, 140, 141, 142, 143, 144, 150, 151, 153, 157, 168, 176, 179-183, 185, 188, 192, 193, 195, 198- 209, 213, 221, 222, 227, 228, 230, 233, 235, 237, 240, 241, 244, 245, 247, 249, 253, 258, 259, 260, 276, 285, 287, 296, 301, 313, 320-322, 328-330, 333, 343, 344, 347, 348, 352, 363, 384, 387, 392, 395, 402, 405, 411, 412, 414, 416, 444, 450, 452, 459, 462, 494, 496, 547, 571, 937, 949, 955, 957, 962, 963, 965, 967, 968, 970, 973, 974, 976, 977, 979, 983, 984, 995, 1008, 1037, 1050, 1055, 1058-1062, 1094, 1106, 1114, 1201, 1206, 1208, 1239, 1241, 1242, 1245, 1246, 1257, 1266, 1274, 1278, 1279, 1303, 1309, 1314, 1339, 1342, 1361, 1364, 1393, 1399-1401, 1405, 1407, 1408, 1410, 1421, 1430, 1450, 1469, 1476, 1487, 1493, 1494-1496, 1498, 1499, 1501-1504, 1506-1509, 1512, 1517, 1518, 1520, 1525, 1528, 1534, 1537, 1547, 1564, 1602, 1603, 1605, 1617-1620, 1622, 1626, 1627, 1629, 1630, 1632-1634, 1639, 1664, 1693, 1700, 1746, 1899, 1935, 2191, 2192, 2447, 2481, 2556, 2557, p.3, 4, 165-167
Alexandra III (sister of Antigonus II) (3)—130, 1111
Alexandria (Egypt)—45, 142, 389, 503, 515, 581, 582, 583, 1150, 1357, 1367, 1764, 2047, 2051, 2116, 2121, 2142, 2293, 2305
Alexandrium (fortress)—9, 494, 1105, 1114, 1239, 1241, 1243, 1245, 1361, 1401, 1430, 1486, 1495, 2234, 2711, p. 3, 166
Alexas (friend of Mark Antony)—1167, 1202, 1204, 1268
Alibame—1695
Amanus Mountains—498
Amareus—1699
Amaxia—537
Ambracian Gulf—606
Ammonites—770
Amphitres—1884
Amyntas (king of Galatia)—28, 1183
Ananel (High Priest)—126-129, 141, 195, 215, 218, 222, 223, 311, 2141, 2159, 2161, 2613
Ananus I (High Priest) (1)—2161

INDEX OF ANCIENT PERSONS AND PLACES

Ananus II (High Priest) (4)—639, 711, 789
Ancyra—2311, 2312
Annas, see Ananus I
Anthedon—1380, 1381, 2212
Antigonus Monophthalmus—2804
Antigonus I (son of John Hyrcanus) (3)—2625
Antigonus II (son of Aristobulus II) (4)—5, 9, 11, 12, 21, 30, 37, 38, 40, 42, 44, 45, 47, 48, 50, 53, 54, 58, 62, 68, 74, 92, 93, 130, 133, 517, 949, 1069, 1070, 1074, 1652, 1704, 1705, 1707, 1714, 1716, 1719, 1720, 1721, 1727, 1731, 1746, 1747, 1796, 2166, 2625, 2647, p.3, 4
Anti-Lebanon—440, 517, 1110
Antinous—2480
Antioch (on the Orontes)—42, 43, 47, 498, 515, 1188, 1216, 1387, 1801, 2236, 2497, 2492, 2520, 2857, 3003
Antiochia Pisidia—1764
Antiochus III (the Great, Seleucid king) (3)—356, 2526, 2657
Antiochus IV (Epiphanes, Seleucid king) (4)—65, 66, 224, 225, 508, 1610, 1754, 1801, 2467, 2489, 2872
Antiochus V (Eupator, Seleucid king) (5)—2849
Antiochus VII (Sidetes, Seleucid king) (7)—1796
Antiochus IX (Cyzicenus, Seleucid king) (9)—3071
Antiochus IV (king of Commagene) (15)—1662, 2872
Antipas, Herod Antipas (Herod the tetrarch, son of Herod and Malthace) (3)—305, 830, 1642, 2057, 2335, 2453, 2662, 2891, 3059
Antipater (the Idumaean, father of Herod) (3)—2, 5, 14, 58, 61, 74, 255, 366, 398, 459, 599, 757, 939, 1037, 1043, 1082, 1085, 1095, 1218, 1434, 1630, 1642, 2154, 2209, 2642
Antipater (son of Herod and Doris) (4)—125, 179, 260, 334, 368, 1618, 1695, 1746, 2049, 2137, 2197, 2200, 2209, 2516, 2519, 2562, 2585, 2629
Antipater (Samaritan) (8)—1461
Antipater (surnamed Gadia, friend of Herod) (7)—1642, 1697, 1743
Antipatris—1982, 2712, 2795
Antonia (daughter of Marc Antony)—1398, 2883
Antonia (fortress in Jerusalem)—1605, 1607, 1897, 1936, 1938, 1939, 1945, 1998, 2678, 2683, 2702, 2809, 2812, 2834, 2869, 2874, 2878, 2879, 2880, 2898, 2899, 2915, 2921, 2924, 2929, 2931, 2932, 2933, 2934, p. 4, 210, 308, 311, 324, p.4
Antony, Marc Antony (Marcus Antonius)—1, 13, 25, 28, 37, 38, 40, 42- 44, 47, 48, 57, 60, 68, 81, 99, 107, 108, 142, 144-147, 149, 151, 154-161, 164-168, 170, 173, 178, 182, 185, 205, 228, 277, 352-356, 358, 359, 361, 368, 362, 364, 365, 373, 374, 389, 396, 398, 412, 416, 419, 423, 424, 427, 432, 435, 436, 440, 441, 446, 448, 463, 479, 481, 494, 499, 501, 502, 507, 512, 514, 515, 517, 519, 520, 522, 523, 526-529, 532, 534, 536, 537, 541, 543, 545-547, 549, 557, 558, 560, 563-565, 568, 579, 581-583, 585, 586, 592, 595, 597, 599, 604-606, 608, 611, 613, 614, 616-618, 646, 650, 736, 738, 740, 749, 742, 743, 745, 746, 925, 936, 937, 939, 944, 947, 990, 991, 994, 1027, 1090, 1096, 1100, 1102, 1110, 1133, 1134, 1135, 1137, 1138, 1143, 1147, 1149, 1150, 1152, 1157-1159, 1162-1164, 1166, 1167, 1168, 1170-1174, 1176, 1183, 1186, 1188, 1190, 1195, 1198, 1200, 1202, 1206, 1216, 1218, 1236, 1242, 1248, 1251, 1255, 1257, 1264, 1268, 1290, 1303, 1339, 1343, 1345, 1350, 1357, 1367, 1375, 1379, 1380, 1382, 1393, 1386, 1401, 1404, 1417, 1429, 1432, 1433, 1491, 1497, 1545, 1542, 1551, 1554, 1607, 1617, 1619, 1654, 1666, 1668, 1709, 1730, 1935, 1936, 1938, 2047, 2049, 2114, 2118, 2146, 2202, 2209, 2226, 2254, 2445, 2453, 2471, 2481, 2510, 2514, 2518, 2520, 2545, 2750, 2883, 2934, 2935, 2936, 3058, 3070, p.xiii, 3, 165, 166
Apamea—534
Aphrodisias—911, 1777
Apion (Egyptian sailor)—151
Apollo—29, 155, 507, 1884, 2755
Apollonia—2400
Apollonius (Seleucid official)—1365, 3012
Aqiva (Rabbi)—2631, 2633, 2662
Ara Pacis—1796, 2804
Arabia (region)—158, 529, 536, 537, 592, 596, 597, 617, 619, 621, 625, 652, 671, 922, 923, 969, 1380, 2164, 2345, 2424
Arabia Felix—2122
Arabian Desert—1580
Arabian Peninsula—2121, 2122
Arabs, see Nabateans
Archelaus (King of Cappadocia) (1)—28, 207, 586, 1183, 1384, 1949
Archelaus (son of Herod and Malthace) (2)—210, 223, 285, 1125, 1378, 1618, 2202, 2235, 2344, 2413, 2625, 2629, 2671, 2672, 2879, 2899
Archidamus (king of Sparta)—736, 767
Aretas IV (king of Nabatea)—1037
Argos—2034, 2312, 2479
Ariarathes IV (king of Cappadocia)—2337
Ariarathes V (king of Cappadocia)—2337
Aristobulus I (eldest son of John Hyrcanus) (2)—503, 960, 1110, 2625
Aristobulus II (son of Alexander Jannaeus and Alexandra I) (3)—5, 61, 133, 134, 227, 278, 1063, 1707, 1793, 2627, 2804
Aristobulus III (brother of Mariamme I and son of Alexandra II, called Jonathan in War) (4)—40, 48, 125, 126, 127, 129, 130, 135, 137, 140, 141, 148, 150, 154, 155, 159, 161, 162, 163, 168, 170, 173, 177, 178, 180, 193, 195, 201, 204, 221, 222, 223, 228, 246, 247, 258, 262-264, 267, 269-272, 275-280, 282, 283, 290-292, 294, 296, 297, 301-303, 306, 307, 309, 310, 313, 317, 318, 320, 321, 332, 336, 338-340, 341, 343, 344, 354, 357, 358, 362, 369, 398, 412, 423, 547, 949, 974, 979, 1023, 1104, 1206, 1242, 1274, 1282, 1314, 1374, 1411, 1421, 1429, 1491, 1494, 1495, 1497, 1537, 1539, 1541, 1547, 1564, 1611, 1619, 1634, 1646, 1746, 1890, 2150, 2453, 2554, 3070, p. 3, 4, 166
Aristobulus IV (son of Herod and Mariamme I) (5)—125, 179, 207, 231, 270, 443, 462, 475, 562, 1019, 1037, 1211, 1241, 1314, 1409, 1474, 1476, 1480, 1485, 1618, 1634, 1908, 2197, 2332, 2334, 2337, 2339, 2562, 2891, p.4
Aristogeiton—1884
Aristomedes—2034
Aristotle—711, 712, 839, 1530, 2178
Armenia—72, 448, 501, 515, 532, 536, 579, 580, 581, 582, 583, 584, 585, 586, 588, 589, 590
Armenia inferior—532
Armenia maior—532
Arsinoe (sister of Cleopatra VII)—142, 507
Artabanus (king of Parthia)—120
Artabanus (adviser of Xerxes)—786
Artabazes/Artavasdes II (king of Armenia)—448, 532, 580, 581, 582, 583, 584, 588, 589
Artashes, see Artaxias II
Artaxes, see Artaxias II
Artaxias II (king of Armenia)—581, 584, 585, 588, 589
Artaxerxes (king of Persia)—461, 1021
Artemis—507
Artemis Leucophryene—507, 1992
Asa—2642
Ascalon—135, 1021
Asia Minor—57, 142, 507, 532, 1123, 1777, 1807, 1953, 2236, 2254, 2311, 2543, 2804
Asinius, see Pollio
Asochis, Plain of—1951
Ashtaroth—2345
Assyrian lowland—72
Aste/Vashti—461
Astyages (king of Media)—2804
Athena—1992
Athenio (general of Cleopatra)—643,

INDEX OF ANCIENT PERSONS AND PLACES

644, 645, 646, 647, 650, 652, 654, 655, 657, 659, 665, 686, 727, 735, 784, 795, 798, 804, 810
Athens—38, 315, 725, 736, 767, 786, 790, 804, 1794, 2057, 2311, 2521, 2624, 2693, 2789
Athronges (shepherd, pretender to Judean throne)—210, 1802
Atia (Octavian's mother)—608
Attica—2479
Atossa (mother of Xerxes)—140
Augusteum at Pula—2522
Augustus (see Octavian)
Auranitis/Hauran—2332, 2337, 2345, 2347, 2349, 2350, 2353, 2357, 2363, 2359, 2395, 2389, 2397, 2411, 2413, 2417, 2418, 2421, 2423, 2425, 2426, 2427, 2434, 2443, 2449, 2494, p.4
Avtalyon (sage)—14
Baal—1647
Ba'al Shamim—2312
Baaras-Baaru—2173, 3020
Baasha (king of Israel)—1087, 2642
Baba, see Sons of Baba
Baba ben Butha—1699
Babatha—1699
Babi—1699
Babylon—57, 69, 71, 72, 85, 218, 1004, 1067, 1580, 1837, 2725, 2733, 2753, p. 4, 17, 23, 291
Babylonia—71, 72, 73, 74, 76, 125, 216, 1608, p. 14, 34
Bacchus—2804
Balaam—2962
Baneas, see Panias
Baq'a Quarter—1765
Bar Kokhba—2633
Barclay's Gate—2939, 2943
Baris (fortress)—1938, 1939, 2874, 2931
Barzaphanes—60, 62
Bashan—2345
Basilica Porcia (in Rome)—2789
Bassus, Publius Ventidius Bassus—38
Batanea—27, 1953, 2332, 2337, 2345, 2347, 2349, 2350, 2353, 2357, 2359, 2363, 2389, 2395, 2397, 2417, 2423, 2443, 2449, 2494, 2499, 2702, 2909, p.4
Bathsheba, see Beethsabe/Bathsheba
Bathybius—1884
Bathyllus (freedman)—1461
Beautiful Gate—3018, 3021
Beersheva—2795
Beethsabe/Bathsheba—522
Beirut, see Berytus
Berenice (daughter of Salome and wife of Aristobulus IV) (?)—2891
Berenice (daughter of Agrippa I and Cyprus)—2891
Berossus—1595
Berytus (Beirut)—1019, 1764, 1766, 1792, 2312
Bethel—2620, 2625
Beth-Shean, see Scythopolis
Beth-Zechariah (Battle of)—66

Beth-Zur—639, 2178
Bir Eyub—1763
Bithynia—2311, 2312, 2337
Black Sea—532
Boethus (ancestor of High Priests)—2141, 2142, 2143, 2161
Bostra—520, 625, 652, 2353, 2357
Brasidas (Spartan commander)—635, 718, 731, 815, 1992
Briseis—369
Britain—2913
Brundisium (Treaty of)—164, 608
Caesar, Gaius Julius Caesar (1)—5, 28, 56, 57, 61, 80, 121, 142, 191, 356, 541, 583, 608, 1042, 1059, 1065, 1382, 1417, 1552, 1801, 2030, 2704
Caesarea Maritima—1229, 1378, 1383, 1753, 1761, 1762, 1763, 1764, 1770, 1774, 1777, 1784, 1818, 1823, 1930, 1948-1950, 1995, 1998, 2003, 2098, 2127, 2135, 2171, 2188, 2196, 2212, 2214, 2215, 2225, 2231-2236, 2240-2242, 2245, 2246, 2253, 2254, 2256, 2285, 2293, 2291, 2304, 2305, 2311, 2314, 2324, 2326, 2328, 2329-2333, 2337, 2338, 2442, 2521-2523, 2540, 2553, 2687, 2710, 2712, 2785, 2877, 2891, 2921, 2985, p.xxiv, 4
Caesarea Philippi—1823, 2312, 2498, 2522
Caesarion—583, 2337
Caldus Caelius—64
Caligula, see Gaius Caligula
Calistus (freedman of Gaius Caligula)—2152
Calpurnius, Lucius Calpurnius—1764
Cambyses I (king of Persia)—508, 2467, 2804
Cana—625-627, 1753
Canaan—1753, 2048
Canata—624-626, 652, 663, 849, 2312
Canatha—625, 626, 652, 925, 2312
Caninius Gallus, see Gallus
Cannae (battle of)—789, 813
Capitol (the Capitol, Rome)—512
Cappadocia—28, 207, 586, 1183, 1384, 1944, 1949, 2337
Carrhae (battle of)—57
Cassius, Gaius Longinus Cassius (1)—599, 1121, 2752, 2893
Cato the Younger—121
Catullus—2013
Caucasian Mountains—532
Caesareum (room)—2136
Celadus (freedman)—2342
Cerameicus (district in Athens)—2789
Chaereas—480, 1492
Chalcis (kingdom)—130, 158, 440, 517, 518, 529, 536, 645, 1110, 1111, 2311, 2350, 2909, 2910
Charax Spasini—73
Cherea—2697
Chersiphron—507
Chios (island)—2705
Cicero, Marcus Tullius Cicero—121, 712, 767, 2617

Cilicia—142, 536, 1949
Cilicia Aspera (Rough Cilicia)—586
City of David—2126, 2794, 2946, 2949
Claudius (emperor)—97, 587, 2503, 2891, 2905, 2906, 2909, 2912, 2913, 2915
Cleanthes—1530
Cleopatra VII (Queen of Egypt) (6)—28, 33, 43, 142-146, 156-158, 165-167, 182, 185, 205, 206, 245, 247, 248, 259, 306, 348, 350, 352, 355, 356, 358, 359, 363, 368, 389, 416, 418, 421, 424, 427, 432, 433, 435, 439-441, 497-503, 505-507, 512, 514, 515, 519-522, 526-529, 534-537, 539, 541-543, 545-551, 554-558, 560, 563-566, 568, 570, 576, 577, 580, 582, 583, 592, 593, 595-597, 599, 606, 608, 611, 614, 616, 617, 622, 643, 645, 646, 650, 686, 734, 737-739, 743-747, 749, 750, 752, 760, 798, 925, 939, 968, 979, 1004, 1019, 1134, 1138, 1150, 1158-1160, 1163, 1166, 1188, 1216, 1226, 1236, 1264, 1274, 1307, 1332, 1357, 1367, 1375, 1379, 1380, 1382, 1398, 1402, 1404, 1417, 1474, 1490, 1497, 1535, 1539, 1545, 1568, 1609, 1619, 1634, 1644, 1653, 1661, 1664-1668, 1671, 1679, 1729, 1741, 1899, 1932, 2047, 2116, 2209, 2254, 2337, 2350, 2422, 2445, 2453, 2467, 2481, p.3, 165
Cluvius—1884
Coele-Syria—440, 498, 520, 528, 536, 626, 2503, 2804
Collatinus—767
Coponius Gate—2941
Corinth—13
Cornelius Gallus, Gaius Cornelius Gallus—1150
Costobar—144, 230, 536, 1380, 1602, 1634, 1639-1641, 1644-1647, 1653, 1654, 1658, 1661, 1663-1665, 1670-1672, 1675, 1676, 1678-1681, 1687, 1694, 1695, 1699, 1700, 1702, 1724, 1725, 1729, 1730, 1732, 1733, 1735, 1741 1745, 1749, 1750, 2192, p.3
Cottius I (prefect of the Cottian Alps)—2503
Cottius II (king of the Cottian Alps)—2503
Court of Israel—2854, 2856, 3017, 3018, 3021, 3024, 3025, 3027, 3028, 3035
Court of the Men, see Court of Israel
Court of the Priests—2854, 2856, 3017, 3024, 3025, 3027-3029, 3035
Court of the Women—2854, 2858, 2919, 3017, 3018, 3023, 3024, 3021, 3028, 3035, 3065
Crassus, Marcus Licinius Crassus (governor of Syria)—57, 448
Creon—1675
Croesus—911, 1563
Croton—2607
Ctesiphon—72, 73

Cumanus, Ventidius Cumanus (governor of Judea)—2909
Cutheans—2723
Cyprus (island)—xv, 536, 2116
Cyprus (mother of Herod the Great)—450, 455, 459, 463, 757, 1095, 1106, 1339-1342, 1398, 1410, 1414, 1416, 1423, 1426, 1476, 1479, 1487, 1551, 1626, 1654, 1680, 1681, 2909, p.3, 166
Cyprus Fortress—2702
Cyrus II (king of Persia)—2723, 2725, 2733, 2735, 2736
Dalmatia—2400
Dan (region)—2535
Damascus—440, 517, 534, 645, 1763, 2073, 2236, 2312, 2332, 2353, 2355, 2356, 2359, 2361, 2526, p.4
Daniel—139, 1580, 2690, 2737
Darius (unspecified)—2723, 2736
Darius I (king of Persia, son of Hystaspes) (2)—771, 1777, 2630, 2723, 2734-2736, 2804, 2917
Dathan—170, 1491
David—139, 522, 770, 1263, 1426, 1594, 1654, 1758, 2238, 2415, 2584, 2625, 2627, 2633, 2705, 2725, 2775, 2794, 2867
Dead Sea (see Lake Asphaltitis)
Decapolis—440, 498, 520, 621, 625, 626, 849, 1377, 1378, 2071, 2073, 2406, 2445, 2514
Deiotarus Philadelphus (king of Paphlagonia)—1949
Delfi—2311
Delilah—2099
Dellius, Quintus Dellius—140, 146-149, 153-156, 159, 160, 161, 168, 178, 228, 246, 412, 1393
Delos—2057
Demaratus—786
Demetrius I (Seleucid king) (3)—2704
Demetrius II (Seleucid king) (4)—1706
Demos—2311
Der'a—520, 652
Dinah—461, 2154
Diogenes of Sinope (Cynic philosopher)—1179
Dion—621, 625
Dioscuri—1996, 2317
Diospolis—621, 624, 625
Dome of the Rock (the al-Haram ash-Sharif)—3010
Domitian (emperor)—1676, 2467
Donnus (king of the Cottian Alps)—2503
Dora/Dor—2254, 2256, 2257
Doris (wife of Herod the Great)—2155, 2197
Dositheus—256, 366, 981, 988-990, 992, 994, 995, 998, 1007, 1013, 1017, 1037, 1305, 1423, 1450, 1473, 1630, 1643, 1697, 1720, 1745
Double Gate—2954
Drusilla (daughter of Agrippa I)—1662
Drusus the Elder (Nero Claudius Drusus, Octavian's adoptive son) (1)—2285, 2883
Drusus the Younger (Drusus Julius Caesar, Tiberius' son) (2)—2335, 2891
Drusus Tower (in harbor of Caesarea Maritima)—2283, 2284, 2522
Dura-Europos—76
Dushara—106
Edomites—1645, 1647
Ein Gedi—27
Elaiussa (island)—537
Eleazar (self-sacrifice at Jotapata/Yodfat)—2791
Eleazar (martyr)—65, 1079
Eleazar Avaran—66
Eleazar ben Yair—96, 708, 711, 767, 768, 789, 836, 840, 919, 1902
Electra—918
Eleutherus (river in northern Syria)—440, 528, 529, 536, 1216, 1375
Eli—2154
Elijah—2069
Elthemus (Nabatean commander)—861, 865
el-Harithiyye, see Gaba
El-Mezra'—663
El-Qanawat—625
Emmor—2155
Eophren—3071
Ephesus—507, 2312
Ephraim (tribe)—3061
Epidamnus—2299
Epiphanes (son of Antiochus of Commagene)—1662
Epirus—2402
Eretz Israel, see Israel
Esau—1695
Esebonitis—1953, 1960, 1971, 1984, 2196
Essaioi—2602, 2621
Essenes—30, 331, 1179, 1530, 1651, 2602-2605, 2607, 2609, 2611, 2613, 2615, 2617, 2619, 2624, 2625, 2629, 2631, 2642, 2671, 2673, 2675, 2677, p.x, xi, 4
Esther—1021, 1132, 1460
Ethiopia—768, 2045
Euctemon—151
Euphrates—72, 73, 76, 498, 515, 532, 534, 1048, 2236
Eurybiades—1419
Euxine Sea—2262
Evil-Merodach/Amel-Marduk (Babylonian king)—69, 71
Ezekias (chief-brigand)—2, 14, 1474, 2154, 2390, p.xiii
Ezra—2723, 2736, 3053

Fadus, Cuspius Fadus, governor of Judea—2888, 2896-2902, 2907, 2913, 2917
Fayum—151
Fortuna—1642
Fourth Philosophy—30
Fuel Gate—3018
Gaba—1953, 1957, 1958, 1971, 1984, 2711
Gabala—2254
Gabinius (governor of Syria)—61, 142, 1218, 1308, 1986, 2566
Gad (deity)—1642
Gadara—1377, 1378, 2406, 2442, 2445, 2449, 2452, 2467, 2472, 2486, 2520, 2521
Gadia (surname of Antipater, Herod's father)—1642
Gadia (surname of Antipater, Herod's friend)—1642
Gaius, Gaius Caligula (emperor) (1)—1612, 1657, 1750, 1818, 1861, 1884, 2152, 2453, 2891
Gaius, Gaius Vipsanius Agrippa (son of Marcus Agrippa and Julia) (?)—2508
Gaius Marius—121
Galatia—28, 30, 1183, 2311, 2312
Galilean (the Galilean)—1108, 2622
Galilee—2, 9, 598, 1365, 1378, 1474, 1951, 1958, 2191, 2192, 2196, 2236, 2494, 2499, 2711, 3059, p.ix, xiii
Gallus, Lucius Caninius Gallus—36
Gamala/Gamla—xi, 2254, 2479, 2480, 2951
Gate of the Chain—2941
Gate of the First Born—3018
Gate of Light—3018
Gate of the Sacrifice—3018
Gaulanitis (Golan)—517, 2499, 2909
Gaul (region)—2337
Gaza—529, 536, 1378, 1380, 1381, 1639, 1640, 1645, 1653, 1658, 1681, 1700, 2212, 2236, 2254
Gellius, see Dellius
Germans—64, 1374
Glaphyra—207, 208, 383, 1264, 1314, 1399, 1568, 1899, 2668, 2672, 2735
God—14, 21, 23, 66, 96, 106, 155, 210, 389, 503, 508, 639, 727, 728, 732, 739, 763, 765-767, 770, 772, 773, 784, 786, 788, 789, 814, 820, 822, 824, 825, 827, 828, 830, 831, 834, 835, 839, 840, 847, 1056, 1067, 1087, 1152, 1210, 1211, 1563, 1576, 1580, 1599, 1611, 1642, 1648, 1663, 1747, 1754, 1758, 1823, 1829, 1844, 1847, 1861, 1909, 1912, 1928, 1992, 2007, 2009, 2033, 2083, 2106, 2217, 2225, 2310, 2312, 2467, 2489, 2625, 2635, 2638, 2642, 2643, 2645, 2647, 2651, 2653, 2657, 2667, 2669, 2672, 2673, 2675, 2678, 2684, 2707, 2720, 2724, 2725, 2740, 2742, 2743, 2755, 2765, 2782, 2804, 2807, 2813, 2826, 2867, 3033, 3042-3045, 3047, 3048, 3051, 3052, 3077, 3078, p.4
Goliath—840, 2867
Greece—140, 606, 759, 767, 786, 858, 1123, 1249
Gulf of Arta, see Ambracian Gulf
Gylippus (Syracusan commander)—736

INDEX OF ANCIENT PERSONS AND PLACES

Haddu/Hadad—1647
Haggai—2725
Hanamel, see Ananel
Hannibal—728, 789, 804, 813
Harmodius—1884
Hashmon—2872
Hasmoneans—5, 11, 27, 44, 70, 125, 127, 223, 276, 277, 286, 306, 450, 453, 1525, 1746, 1939, 2824, 2878, 3010
Hauran, see Auranitis
Hauran Mountains—625
Hedjaz—520
Helena (queen of Adiabene)—2116
Heliodorus—232, 317, 830, 1003, 1568, 2759, 3043, 3044
Heliopolis—2254
Heliopolis-Baalbek—2350
Hellas—722
Hellespont—2403
Hera—507, 2311, 2312
Heracles—150, 2299
Herod I (the Great) (1)—1, 2, 4-6, 8-14, 16-18, 21-29, 31-33, 35-37, 40-43, 47-51, 53, 55, 58, 60, 61, 64, 68, 72, 77, 78, 80-83, 86, 88, 94, 96, 99, 101-109, 112-114, 116-127, 130, 131, 135, 138, 139, 141, 142, 149-151, 156-158, 160, 161, 167, 168, 170, 173, 176, 178-183, 186, 188, 191-193, 195-197, 199, 200, 202, 205, 209, 213, 219-224, 229-231, 233, 235-238, 246, 247, 253, 255, 256, 258-260, 262, 263, 267-270, 276, 277, 282-288, 292, 294, 296, 297, 301, 303, 305-308, 312, 315, 319-321, 328-333, 335, 338, 340, 343, 344, 352, 353, 355, 356, 358, 359, 361-363, 365, 366, 368-371, 373, 374, 377, 378, 381, 386, 388, 389, 391, 392, 395-400, 402, 404, 406, 409, 411, 413, 414, 416, 419-421, 423, 424, 427, 433, 435, 440, 443, 446, 448-450, 453, 454, 459, 461-464, 468-472, 475, 479-481, 484, 488, 491, 493, 494, 496, 498, 499, 501, 512, 519, 523, 535-537, 539, 541, 542, 544, 545, 547-551, 553-560, 562-565, 567, 568, 570-572, 576, 577, 590, 592, 593, 595, 597-599, 601-606, 610, 611, 613-620, 622, 624, 625, 628, 629, 633-635, 640, 643, 646, 650, 652, 657, 658, 665, 668, 669, 671, 672, 676, 678, 686, 687, 690, 692, 693, 696, 699, 703-706, 708-714, 716-723, 725, 727, 728, 731, 732, 734-736, 739, 740, 743, 745-747, 749, 751-753, 755, 757, 759, 760, 766, 767, 768-773, 782-791, 795, 796, 798, 801-805, 808, 811, 814-816, 818-822, 824, 826-831, 834, 836, 839-849, 852, 854, 858, 859, 861-865, 871, 873, 889, 892, 897-900, 923, 925, 926, 929-931, 936, 937, 939, 943-949, 951, 952-955, 957, 962, 965, 971, 973, 979-981, 989-991, 995, 997-998, 1002, 1004, 1008, 1010, 1013, 1015, 1019-1021, 1023, 1025, 1027, 1028, 1033, 1036, 1037, 1039-1041, 1043, 1044, 1047, 1054, 1055, 1062, 1070, 1071, 1074, 1075, 1077, 1079, 1087, 1088, 1091, 1095-1098, 1100, 1102-1107, 1111, 1113-1115, 1118-1123, 1125, 1127, 1129, 1133-1135, 1137, 1138, 1141, 1143, 1146, 1147, 1149, 1150-1153, 1155, 1157, 1158, 1162, 1164, 1166-1168, 1170-1173, 1176, 1179, 1181-1184, 1186, 1190, 1191, 1194-1198, 1200-1202, 1204-1206, 1208, 1210, 1211, 1213, 1215-1221, 1224, 1226, 1229-1231, 1233, 1234, 1236-1242, 1244, 1245, 1247-1253, 1255, 1257, 1264, 1266-1268, 1271, 1273, 1274, 1276, 1279, 1280, 1282, 1284, 1288, 1290, 1292, 1295, 1296, 1298-1301, 1303-1307, 1313, 1315-1321, 1324, 1326, 1329, 1331, 1334-1336, 1338-1340, 1342, 1343, 1345, 1346, 1348, 1350, 1352, 1355, 1358-1360, 1364-1367, 1369, 1370, 1372-1374, 1377-1383, 1385-1396, 1399-1402, 1406-1411, 1415-1417, 1419, 1420, 1422-1424, 1428, 1429, 1431-1434, 1436-1438, 1441-1443, 1448, 1451, 1452, 1454, 1455, 1457, 1459-1461, 1464-1466, 1468, 1469, 1471, 1473-1477, 1479-1482, 1484, 1485, 1487, 1488, 1491, 1492, 1495, 1497, 1498, 1501-1505, 1513, 1514, 1517, 1525, 1528, 1530, 1531, 1533, 1536, 1541, 1542, 1544, 1545, 1547, 1548, 1551, 1552, 1554-1559, 1561-1566, 1568-1572, 1574, 1575, 1578-1582, 1584, 1585, 1587, 1589, 1593-1595, 1599, 1600-1603, 1605-1607, 1609, 1617-1620, 1622, 1626, 1627, 1629, 1630, 1632-1636, 1638-1640, 1642, 1644, 1645, 1647, 1652-1654, 1657, 1658, 1661, 1664, 1666, 1668, 1670, 1671, 1678, 1679, 1681, 1682, 1685, 1686, 1693, 1695, 1699-1702, 1704, 1705, 1707, 1709-1721, 1725, 1727, 1729, 1730, 1733, 1736, 1738, 1740, 1742, 1745-1753, 1757, 1760, 1762-1764, 1766, 1767, 1769-1772, 1774-1777, 1779, 1782, 1784, 1787, 1790-1794, 1796, 1798, 1801, 1804-1806, 1810, 1812-1816, 1818, 1821, 1823, 1826-1829, 1831-1833, 1835-1840, 1842-1844, 1845, 1847, 1850, 1853, 1854, 1858, 1861-1863, 1865, 1866, 1868, 1869, 1876, 1881, 1882, 1884, 1885, 1887, 1890, 1892, 1894-1900, 1908-1913, 1916, 1917, 1923-1926, 1928-1930, 1932-1942, 1944, 1946, 1950, 1952-1955, 1957, 1958, 1960, 1965, 1966, 1969, 1971-1975, 1977, 1980, 1982-1985, 1994, 1996, 1997, 1999, 2000-2007, 2009, 2012, 2018, 2021, 2028, 2030, 2032, 2033, 2036, 2043, 2044, 2048-2058, 2060, 2064, 2065, 2070, 2071, 2073-2076, 2079, 2081, 2084, 2086, 2087, 2089, 2093, 2095, 2096, 2098, 2099, 2101, 2103-2105, 2108, 2110, 2112-2114, 2116-2119, 2124-2127, 2135-2138, 2141, 2143-2149, 2152, 2154-2156, 2158-2162, 2163-2167, 2171, 2177, 2178, 2185, 2188-2197, 2199, 2200, 2202, 2203, 2208-2210, 2212-2215, 2221-2229, 2231, 2232, 2234-2236, 2238, 2241, 2242, 2250, 2253, 2256, 2257, 2270, 2285, 2289, 2309, 2312, 2313, 2323, 2324, 2326, 2327, 2329, 2332-2335, 2337, 2339, 2341-2347, 2349, 2350, 2364, 2366, 2388, 2390, 2393, 2395-2398, 2400, 2403, 2404, 2406-2410, 2412, 2413, 2417, 2418, 2423, 2425, 2427-2430, 2433, 2434, 2436, 2437, 2439-2447, 2449, 2450, 2452, 2453, 2456, 2457, 2459-2462, 2465-2472, 2476, 2477, 2481-2483, 2485, 2486, 2488, 2494, 2498-2500, 2503, 2504, 2509-2511, 2513-2522, 2524, 2526, 2540, 2541-2546, 2549-2551, 2553-2558, 2561, 2562, 2564, 2566, 2567, 2570, 2573, 2574, 2576-2578, 2581-2585, 2587, 2592, 2594-2597, 2599-2603, 2613-2615, 2619, 2622, 2624-2627, 2630-2636, 2642, 2645-2648, 2650, 2651, 2653, 2654, 2656-2660, 2662, 2664, 2665, 2667-2669, 2671, 2673, 2674, 2678-2681, 2683, 2684, 2689, 2690, 2692, 2693, 2695, 2696, 2698-2705, 2707-2710, 2713, 2714, 2717, 2720, 2722, 2723, 2727-2729, 2731, 2740-2743, 2745-2747, 2750, 2751, 2753, 2755, 2757, 2760, 2762, 2763, 2766, 2768-2771, 2774, 2775, 2777, 2781, 2782, 2785, 2789, 2801, 2804, 2809, 2812-2814, 2818, 2819, 2821, 2824, 2829, 2856, 2857, 2860, 2861, 2864, 2866, 2868, 2871, 2877-2880, 2886, 2891, 2899, 2915, 2919, 2921, 2927, 2729, 2730, 2932, 2934-2936, 2940, 2941, 2944, 2949, 2954, 2961, 2962, 2985, 2994, 3003, 3034, 3035, 3037-3040, 3042, 3045-3047, 3050, 3056, 3058-3060, 3065, 3066, 3069, 3070, 3073, 3077, p.xiii, xiv, 3, 4, 164-166
Herod III (son of Herod I and Mariamme II) (3)—1618, 2137, 2144
Herod IV (son of Herod I and Cleopatra) (4)—1618
Herod Antipas, see Antipas
Herodians—11, 29, 450
Herodias—305, 2453
Herodion, see Herodium
Herodium (fortress)—xi, 9, 2002, 2003, 2117, 2164, 2166, 2178, 2179, 2182-2185, 2221, 2228, 2232, 2234, 2235, 2282, 2297, 2307, 2702, 2710, 2711, 2951, 3003, p.3, 4
Herodotus—60, 72, 704, 731, 771, 786, 911, 1020, 1563, 1740, 1859

Heshbon (Eshbun)—852, 1960
Hezekiah (chief-brigand), see Ezekias
Hezekiah (king of Judah)—2697, 3050, 3061
Hierosolyma, see Jerusalem
Hillel (sage)—14
Hinnom Valley—1763, 2952
Hippias (Athenian commander)—287
Hippicus (fiend of Herod)—1606, 1910
Hippicus Tower— (search also Hyppicus)—1606, 1910, 2125, 2786, 2940
Hippus—1378
Hiram (king of Tyre)—2860
Holophernes—289
Holy of Holies—3009, 3015
Homer—371, 1147, p.ix
Honi the Circle-Drawer—2009
Horvat Omrit—2522, 2526
House of the Hearth—3018
Hula Valley—2497, 2499
Huldah Gates—2954
Hyrcania—2234, 2566, 2567
Hyrcanus I (2), see John Hyrcanus
Hyrcanus II (son of Alexander Jannaeus and Alexandra I, High Priest) (3)—5, 9, 14, 18, 20, 21, 56-62, 69, 71, 74, 76-81, 86, 88, 89, 92, 94, 98-100, 102-105, 108, 113-123, 125, 129, 130, 132-134, 140, 173, 177, 179, 204, 227, 256, 261, 262, 278, 307, 329, 465, 517, 929, 936, 937, 944-947, 949, 951, 952, 955, 957, 960, 961, 964, 970, 973, 974, 979-981, 983, 984, 988, 995, 998, 1002, 1004, 1007, 1008, 1010, 1013, 1015, 1017, 1019-1022, 1028, 1029-1031, 1033, 1037, 1039, 1040, 1042-1049, 1053-1055, 1057-1060, 1062-1065, 1067-1072, 1074-1077, 1079, 1082, 1083, 1085, 1087, 1088, 1094, 1125, 1215, 1242, 1274, 1402, 1411, 1428, 1429, 1450, 1474, 1475, 1495, 1496, 1505, 1533, 1547, 1609, 1634, 1652, 1699, 1713, 1720, 1746, 1801, 1815, 1932, 2155, 2412, 2511, 2643, p.3, 4, 165
Hyrcanus (the Tobiad) (1)—324, 2785
Hystaspes/Hydaspes—2630, 2735
Idumea—9, 11, 106, 440, 981, 1365, 1378, 1380, 1541, 1639, 1640-1642, 1645, 1646, 1648, 1650, 1651, 1658, 1663, 1665, 1670, 1671, 1674, 1677, 1681, 1699, 1700, 1732, 2211, 2494
Immanuel—784
Inachus—2402
Indates (Parthian commander)—1796
Ilios (Troy)—2404
Io—2402
Ion—1147
Ionia—2704
Ionian Gulf—2299
Isaac—2155, 2795
Ishmael (son of Phabi, High Priest)—2160
Ishmael (son of Phabi, High Priest, not identical with previous one)—2160
Island of the Blessed—1984
Israel—75, 732, 772, 775, 1067, 1223, 1648, 1823, 2106, 2489, 2622, 2673, 2720, 2724, 2740, 2744, 2804, 3017, 3050, 3051, 3061, 3073
Italy—151, 389, 789, 2051, 2199, 2249, 2402, 2607, 2883
Iturea—498, 517, 1110, 1365, 2350
Izates—120
Jacob—732, 2048, 2155, 2205
Jadon/Iddo (prophet)—2625
Jaffa Gate—1606
Jamnia—9
Jason (High Priest)—225, 226, 1796
Jebel Fureidis—2164
Jebel Hauran—2345
Jehoiachin (king of Juda)—69, 71, 2627, 3050
Jehoiachin-Jechoniah, see Jehoiachin
Jehoshaphat (king of Juda)—2642
Jehu—1922
Jephtha—2620
Jeremiah—1615, 2632
Jericho—27, 235, 285-287, 293, 296, 302, 309, 339, 440, 535-539, 592, 598, 611, 986, 1063, 1375, 1421, 1638, 1666, 1763, 1764, 1890, 2127, 2136, 2192, 2702, 2746, 2795, p.3
Jeroboam (king of Israel)—460, 767, 2625
Jerusalem—1, 3-9, 11, 12, 16, 17, 21, 24, 25, 28, 32, 35, 36, 59, 62, 66, 80, 88, 92, 99, 116, 117, 121, 129, 138, 178, 235, 247, 249, 264, 268, 318, 338, 400, 404, 406, 531, 535, 571, 678, 847, 986, 1021, 1032, 1210, 1378, 1379, 1491, 1603, 1605, 1606, 1611, 1651-1653, 1700, 1707-1711, 1721, 1725, 1749, 1750, 1752-1754, 1760, 1762-1765, 1771, 1779, 1793, 1796, 1801, 1804, 1805, 1810, 1818, 1823, 1833, 1837, 1838, 1861, 1882, 1894, 1897, 1910, 1918, 1929, 1930, 1932, 1933, 1936-1938, 1942, 1945-1947, 2001, 2006, 2007, 2010, 2069, 2117, 2124, 2125, 2136, 2141, 2143, 2146, 2155, 2164, 2166, 2177, 2210, 2220, 2221, 2224, 2231, 2234, 2235, 2250, 2254, 2270, 2324, 2329, 2404, 2436, 2440, 2460, 2466, 2520, 2522, 2536, 2549, 2559, 2568, 2570, 2592, 2660, 2665, 2678, 2680, 2699, 2702, 2705, 2710, 2722, 2724, 2738, 2771, 2775, 2785, 2793, 2795, 2809, 2814, 2831, 2833, 2856, 2861, 2907, 2922, 2924, 2940, 2952, 3008, 3027, 3042, 3053, 3058, p.xiii, 3, 4
Jerusalemites—16, 1708, 1750, 1753, 1918, 1929, 2116, 2216, 2678, 2886, 2890, 2898, 3043, 3045, p.4
Jeshua (High Priest)—2160, 2723, 3050, 3061
Jesus (of Nazareth)—340, 1687, 1738, 2371, 2662, 2775, 2804, p.xi, xiii
Jesus (son of Phabi, High Priest)—2160
Jesus/Jason, see Jason
Jethro—2624
Jews—10, 14, 23, 26, 27, 31, 35, 39, 40, 43-45, 47, 48, 50, 56, 61, 66, 71-76, 80, 85, 88, 89, 99, 106, 108, 112, 117, 121, 127, 128, 147, 151, 155, 156, 170, 172, 179, 181, 190, 216, 222, 224, 228, 249, 251, 264, 266, 268, 276, 277, 282, 285, 331, 340, 341, 368, 371, 405, 503, 620, 624, 629, 632, 637, 639, 643, 650, 654, 658-660, 686, 698, 699, 704, 706, 715, 725, 727, 731, 732, 752, 771, 772, 784, 786, 788, 814, 816, 818-820, 822, 827, 830, 831, 843, 848, 862, 923, 1005, 1037, 1049, 1055, 1058, 1066, 1067, 1080, 1085, 1125, 1179, 1210, 1382, 1443, 1474, 1476, 1491, 1517, 1593, 1608, 1611, 1612, 1638, 1641, 1642, 1651, 1662, 1663, 1687-1690, 1751-1754, 1760, 1763, 1769, 1791, 1793, 1796, 1801, 1805, 1806, 1812, 1813, 1815, 1818, 1819, 1821, 1823, 1825, 1826, 1827, 1837, 1847, 1861, 1866, 1882, 1894, 1912, 1928-1930, 1944, 2076, 2087, 2095, 2097, 2104, 2116, 2119, 2154, 2160, 2192, 2211, 2222, 2224, 2227, 2235, 2447, 2460, 2462, 2494, 2550, 2592, 2602, 2608, 2617, 2619, 2627, 2635, 2642, 2658, 2674, 2678, 2692, 2699, 2704, 2706, 2720, 2737, 2745, 2747, 2804, 2823, 2834, 2864, 2871, 2899, 2903, 2904, 2907, 2909, 2915, 2917, 2927, 2962, 3008, 3010, 3015, 3016, 3048, 3051, 3053, 3070, p.xi, xiii, 3, 4
Jezebel—1922
Joab—122
John the Baptist—830, 2069, 2642
John Hyrcanus—1379, 1649-1651, 1939, 1986, 2211, 2625, 2635, 2872, 3071
John of Giscala—1675
Jonathan (son of Saul) (1)—1263
Jonathan the Hasmonean (4)—126, 1099, 2849
Joppa—5, 9, 250, 536, 1378, 1382, 2254, 2256, 2257, 2702
Jordan—9, 74, 76, 440, 626, 731, 847, 849, 1959, 1960, 2071, 2084, 2498, 2517, 2524, 2526, 2528, 2530, 2533, 2535, 2537
Jordan Valley—27, 293, 852, 984, 1105, 195
Joseph (patriarch) (1)—108, 139, 156, 461, 477, 1108, 1398, 1434, 1859, 2116, 2140, 2669
Joseph (brother of Herod) (8)—1095, 1630
Joseph (Herod I's administrator) (7)—1109, 1113-1115, 1245, 1248, 1251, 1260, 1361, 1469, 1622, 1748, p.165-167
Joseph (Herod I's uncle/brother-in-law) (6)—366, 368, 373, 377, 384, 385,

INDEX OF ANCIENT PERSONS AND PLACES

387, 389, 391, 396, 402, 411, 453, 454, 455, 463, 468, 488, 494, 496, 990, 991, 995, 998, 1096, 1100, 1102, 1104, 1106, 1242, 1252, 1255, 1257, 1290, 1339, 1344-1346, 1393, 1398, 1399, 1408, 1414, 1432, 1433, 1472, 1473, 1479, 1485, 1502, 1547, 1571, 1630, 1653, 1655, 1656, 1680, 1686, p.3, 165-167
Joseph (father of Jesus)—2775
Joseph (the Tobiad) (3)—461
Josephus (Flavius Josephus)—passim
Josiah (king of Judah)—2642
Josias/Josiah—2625
Jotapata/Yodfat—66, 318, 1912, 2791
Jotham (king of Judah)—2642
Juba—2503
Juba I (king of Numidia)—2503
Juba II (king of Numidia and Mauretania)—1949, 2122, 2337, 2503
Judah (tribe)—1928, 2642, 2702, 2872, 3061, p.xiii
Judas (the Essene) (6)—2604, 2625, 2673
Judas the Maccabee (4)—840, 2001, 2747, 2849, 2872
Judas Maccabaeus, see Judas the Maccabee
Judea—5, 6, 9, 26, 27, 35, 40, 44, 47, 50, 60, 61, 69, 71, 75, 78, 91, 99, 112, 133, 147, 154, 157, 158, 167, 170, 173, 178, 184, 224, 259, 352, 355, 356, 363, 411, 432, 440, 441, 459, 498, 501, 517, 521, 535, 541, 560, 598, 611, 619, 621, 671, 678, 679, 732, 737, 743, 744, 746, 749, 849, 888, 949, 945, 973, 1019, 1037, 1042, 1044, 1047, 1048, 1072, 1066, 1125, 1137, 1183, 1213, 1215, 1268, 1365, 1377-1380, 1382, 1383, 1466, 1580, 1608, 1645, 1665, 1670, 1681, 1722, 1769, 1771, 1772, 1796, 1813, 1818, 1822, 1833, 1915, 1933, 1947, 2084, 2166, 2202, 2215, 2221-2223, 2256, 2434, 2514, 2602, 2699, 2725, 2726, 2737, 2744, 2753, 2804, 2823, 2883, 2891, 2896, 2897, 2901, 2913, 2921, 3050, 3061, p.ix, xi, xiii
Judean Desert—1687, 2566
Judith—289
Julia (daughter of Octavian and Scribonia)—2400, 2404, 2409, 2508
Julia (wife of Octavian)—2510
Julianus (centurion)—1802
Julias—2909
Julius Africanus—64
Julius Caesar, see Caesar
Jupiter—155, 2311
Jupiter Capitolinus—1793, 2804
Justus of Tiberias—64, 1696
Kafarsaba—1982
Kenat—625
Keturah—2137
Khirbet Dharih—986
Khirbet Mird—2566

Khirbet Tannur—986
Kidron Valley—2832, 2932, 2952, 2958
Korah—170, 1491
Korakesion—537
Kore—1996
Koze, see Qos
Laban—2155
Lake Asphaltitis (Dead Sea)—1010
Lake Gennesaret, see Sea of Galilee
Lake Hula—2497
Lake Phiala (Birket er-Ram)—2535
Lake Serbonitis—1223
Lake Tana—2045
Lamech—2137
Laodicea (Syria)—359, 418, 448, 515, 2182
Laodicea (on the Lycus, Asia Minor)—1764
Lebanon—440, 517, 1110, 1111
Lebo-hamath—3051
Lecythus—1992
Leodamas of Milete—1884
Leontopolis—2161, 2690, 2724
Lepidus, Paulus Aemilius Lepidus—13, 164, 608
Lesbos (island)—2403
Lesser Armenia—532, 586
Leto—507
Leuce Come—2122
Libya—2668
Livia (wife of Octavian)—2312
Lod—621
Longinus, see Cassius Longinus
Longus (Roman soldier)—1903
Lower-Herodium—2179, 2185
Luceria—2883
Lucina—155
Lucius (son of Marcus Agrippa and Julia)—2508
Lucius Mummius—1766
Lucius Pulcher—1766
Lugdunum—2312
Lutatius Catulus, Quintus Lutatius Catulus—121
Lycia—2311
Lycus (river)—1764, 1796
Lydia—911
Lysanias (king of Chalcis)—158, 517-519, 2350, 2351, 2499, 2891
Lysimachus (friend of Herod)—1641, 1697, 1745
Maccabees—2624, 2785, 2872
Machaerus—1959
Madian—139
Magi—2804
Magnesia on the Meander—507
Magnesia on the Sipylus—1972
Malichus I (king of Nabatea)—158, 423, 501, 519, 521, 537, 592, 596, 598, 599, 601, 603, 615-617, 751, 925, 968, 970, 981-984, 995, 1002, 1004, 1006, 1008, 1009, 1015, 1017, 1019, 1029-1031, 1033, 1037, 1450, 1495, 2412, 2430
Malichus (murderer of Antipater)—1434, 2192

Mamre—1647
Manaemus—23, 193, 1211, 1259, 1909, 2602, 2603, 2613, 2617, 2620, 2622, 2624-2627, 2631-2633, 2626, 2627, 2633, 2635-2637, 2639-2642, 2644, 2645, 2647, 2650, 2651, 2653, 2654, 2656, 2658-2660, 2662, 2663, 2665, 2667-2669, 2671-2676, 2707, 2743, 2755, 3056, p.4
Manasse (tribe)—3061
Mandane (daughter of Astyages, king of Persia)—2804
Manlius Capitolinus, Marcus Manlius Capitolinus—121
Manoah—139
Marcius—767
Marcus Julius Alexander—2891
Marcus Terentius Varro, see Varro
Mardonius—767, 786
Mariamme I (wife of Herod I) (2)—58, 125, 135, 138, 139, 149, 150, 157, 158, 167, 176, 179, 188, 195, 201, 204, 207, 221, 222, 230, 231, 247, 260, 270, 276, 313, 321, 322, 347, 368-370, 373-375, 378, 381, 382, 384, 387-389, 391, 392, 395-397, 402, 405, 412, 444, 449, 450, 453-455, 457, 459, 461-463, 468, 469, 471, 472, 479-481, 486, 491, 493, 494, 496, 503, 562, 566, 567, 571, 990, 991, 1019, 1102-1104, 1106, 1111, 1113, 1114, 1239, 1241, 1242, 1245-1248, 1251, 1253, 1255, 1257, 1264, 1266, 1270, 1271, 1274, 1278, 1279, 1282, 1284, 1289, 1290, 1292, 1295, 1298, 1299, 1303, 1304, 1306, 1307, 1309, 1313-1315, 1317, 1321, 1324, 1326, 1331, 1332, 1335, 1338-1342, 1345, 1348-1352, 1355, 1359-1361, 1364, 1366, 1388, 1393-1396, 1398-1402, 1404-1406, 1408-1412, 1414-1416, 1421-1423, 1426, 1428-1430, 1432, 1433, 1436, 1441, 1442, 1450, 1453, 1458-1460, 1462, 1465, 1466, 1468, 1469, 1471, 1473-1476, 1479-1481, 1485-1488, 1491, 1493-1495, 1498, 1499, 1501-1507, 1512-1514, 1517, 1518, 1521-1525, 1527, 1528, 1530-1537, 1539, 1541, 1542, 1544, 1545, 1547, 1556-1565, 1568-1571, 1578, 1603, 1606, 1618, 1626, 1634, 1713, 1719, 1733, 1746, 1861, 1896, 1910, 1914, 1926, 2007, 2137, 2150, 2155, 2156, 2192, 2334, 2447, 2481, 2562, 2891, p.3, 164-167
Mariamme II (wife of Herod I) (3)—167, 2117, 2137, 2144, 2148, 2156, 2158, 2162-2164, 2447
Mariamme Tower—1910, 2125, 2940
Marissa—981, 1021, 1651, 1699
Mars Ultor—2804
Marsaba—2566
Masada—5, 96, 711, 767, 768, 836, 919, 986, 1099, 1102, 1241, 1902, 1932, 2003, 2166, 2478, 2711, 2785, p.xi, 166

Mathias (the son of Margalothus)—179
Mattathias (father of the five Maccabean brothers)—2620, 2872
Mecaenas—2400
Media—448
Mediterranean Sea—498, 520, 2299, 2402
Melchizedek—1218
Menahem (king of Israel)—2622
Menahem (son of Judas the Galilean)—2622
Menelaus (High Priest)—226, 731
Menippus (Spartan envoy)—1859
Mennaeus (ruler of Chalcis)—517
Menoeceus—2479
Mephibosheth (son of Jonathan)—1263
Mesada—1099
Mesopotamia—532, 3053
Messenia—1540, 1941
Metagenes—507
Michal (wife of David)—1426, 1654
Michalitsi Hill (Nicopolis)—606
Milete—507, 1884
Misenum (Italy)—151
Moab—520, 1960
Modein—1796
Monicas (first ruler of Chalcis)—517
Mordecai—108
Moses—139, 155, 704, 711, 772, 773, 775, 1067, 2034, 2624, 2692, 2697, 2765, 3071
Mount Carmel—1951, 1957, 2236, 2254
Mount Casius—1223
Mount Gerizim—1379, 2724
Mount Hermon—1110, 2499, 2528
Mount Ophel (search also Ophel)—1765, 2946
Mount Scopus—2794, 3021
Mount Sinai—2697, 2765, 3071
Mrs. Potiphar—156, 461, 1398, 2140
Musa—68
Mylasa (Asia Minor)—1807
Myos Hormos—2891
Mytilene—2403, 2407, 2443
Nabatea—158, 433, 501, 536, 597, 598, 617, 1647, 2084
Nabateans—423, 520, 521, 596, 598, 601, 602, 605, 614, 617, 619, 622, 624, 625, 632, 642, 646, 650, 652, 655-658, 671, 676, 686, 687, 690, 692, 699, 703, 722, 723, 725, 727-739, 746, 752, 753, 755, 757-760, 763, 766, 767, 770, 768, 778, 784, 789, 791, 792, 798, 802-805, 810, 813, 817, 818, 820, 828, 834, 839, 843, 844, 846, 849, 855, 858, 862, 863, 869, 873, 889, 892, 894, 897, 899-901, 911, 918, 923, 925, 927, 1004, 1139, 1188, 1369, 1925, 2038, 2089, 2345, 2354, 2411, 2412, 2413, 2418, 2419, 2424, 2425, 2427, 2428, 2430, 2434, 2437, 2439, 2614, 2707, 2864, p.3
Nablus—252
Nabonidus (king of Babylonia)—1580

Naples—151
Naupactus (battle of)—786
Nebuchadnezzar—71, 1580, 2371
Nabuchodonosor—1595
Negev Desert—520, 1223
Nehardea—73
Nehemiah—1021, 1434, 2737, 2854
Neptunus—606
Neoptolemus—32
Nero (emperor)—508, 587, 1764, 2285, 2467, 2494, 2709, 2784, 2881, 2909
Neronias—2499
Nicanor Gate—3018, 3021, 3024, 3065
Nicea (city in Bithynia)—2312
Nicias (Athenian commander)—786, 806
Nicolaus of Damascus—42, 48, 116, 142, 306, 392, 494, 704, 925, 1239, 1479, 1530, 1541, 1688, 2004, 2006, 2404, 2462, 2503, 2622, 2690, 2775
Nicomedes II (king of Bithynia)—2337
Nicomedia (city in Bithynia)—2311, 2312
Nicomedia (royal house of)—1434
Nicopolis—606, 2312, 2755
Nike—1823, 2217, 2312
Nile—2045, 2480
Nile Delta—577, 1223
Nisibis—73
North-Africa—608
Octavia (wife of Mark Antony)—43, 155, 606
Octavian—13, 28, 29, 45, 48, 57, 68, 108, 142, 143, 146, 155, 164, 179, 260, 305, 368, 423, 427, 443, 448, 494, 502, 507, 529, 536, 541, 557, 564, 588, 605, 606, 608, 613, 617, 925, 931, 933, 939, 947, 948, 971, 1021, 1037, 1087-1089, 1102, 1118-1120, 1123, 1125, 1127, 1129, 1133, 1134, 1146, 1149-1151, 1158, 1164, 1167, 1170, 1173, 1174, 1176, 1179, 1181-1183, 1185, 1186, 1188-1191, 1193, 1195-1197, 1199, 1200, 1202, 1204, 1205, 1208, 1211, 1213-1216, 1218-1221, 1229, 1230, 1234-1239, 1255, 1267, 1268, 1273, 1280, 1291, 1295, 1298-1300, 1305, 1339, 1355-1358, 1359, 1366, 1367, 1369, 1370, 1372, 1376, 1378, 1379, 1383-1387, 1393, 1417, 1466, 1506, 1528, 1541, 1542, 1545, 1552, 1554, 1601, 1617, 1701, 1730, 1750, 1757, 1760, 1762, 1775, 1791, 1793, 1795, 1796, 1798, 1823, 1846, 1866, 1930, 1938, 1944, 1953, 1992, 1994, 1995, 2007, 2047, 2049, 2099, 2110, 2118, 2119, 2122, 2124, 2135, 2136, 2171, 2194, 2199, 2200, 2202, 2209, 2210, 2212, 2214, 2216, 2225, 2226, 2235, 2242, 2285, 2305, 2308, 2309, 2311-2313, 2329, 2332, 2337, 2339, 2341-2344, 2347, 2349, 2350, 2359, 2361, 2362, 2364, 2365, 2389, 2396-2398, 2400, 2401, 2404, 2406, 2408, 2417, 2418, 2423, 2425, 2427, 2434, 2441-2443, 2445, 2449, 2469-2471, 2475, 2477, 2485, 2486, 2492-2494, 2499, 2503, 2506, 2508-2513, 2517, 2518, 2520-2522, 2524, 2537, 2540, 2575, 2584, 2629, 2635, 2657, 2665, 2680, 2702, 2709, 2713, 2747, 2750, 2751, 2804, 2861, 2883, 2884, 2934, 2936, p.3, 4, 165, 166
C. Octavius (Octavian's father)—608
Odeum (Athens)—1794
Odysseus—371, 2311
Ogyges—1647
Old City (of Jerusalem)—1606
Olympia—2693
Oman—2122
Onias (founder of Jewish temple at Leontopolis)—2690
Onias III (High Priest)—225, 226, 2160, 2690, 2744, 2860
Ophel, see Mount Ophel
Ophellius—106
Ormiza—263
Orodes (king of Parthia)—60, 68
Orontes (river in Syria)—43, 534, 1387, 2492, 2497
Orthosia—528
Ortygia—507
Pacorus (Parthian prince)—60
Pacorus (Parthian cup-bearer and commander)—62, 1434
Pagondas (Beotian commander)—789
Palatine Hill—2755
Palestine—498, 529, 1384, 2009, 2027, 2045, 2068, 2069, 2079, 2254, 2312, 2738, 2886
Palmyra—2236, 2804
Pan—2526
Paneas—2214, 2312, 2332, 2350, 2395, 2442, 2498, 2499, 2521, 2522, 2524-2526, 2530, 2535, 2537, 2540, 2713, p.4
Paneas (battle of)—1665
Paneion-Baneas, see Paneas
Pappus (commander of Antigonus II)—2647
Parthia—63, 68, 448, 532, 536, 581, 583, 1071
Paul (the Apostle)—2473
Peleus—32
Pella—1959
Peloponnesus—718
Pelusium—577, 1223, 1367
Penelope—371
Perdiccas—1379
Perea—9, 598, 1365, 1378, 1959, 2084, 2517, 2519, p.xiii
Pergamum—2200, 2311, 2312
Pericles—342, 1794
Persians—731, 767, 2738
Petra—520, 984, 986, 1010, 1032, 1794
Petronius, Publius Petronius (legate of Syria)—1861, 2913
Petronius, Publius Petronius (prefect of Egypt, sometimes identified as Gaius Petronius)—2005, 2047, 2049-2053, 2090, 2120

INDEX OF ANCIENT PERSONS AND PLACES

Phabeis, see Phiabi
Phabi, see Phiabi
Pharaoh—1434, 1544, 1576
Pharisees—12, 14, 30, 2597-2601, 2605, 2608
Phasael (brother of Herod I)—5, 43, 62-66, 106, 1020, 1071, 1095, 1606, 1910, 2125, 2478, 2514, 2702
Phasael Tower—1606, 2125, 2702, 2809, 2940
Phasaelis—2712
Pheidias—2712
Pheroras (brother of Herod I)—101, 108, 135, 257, 373, 462, 1095, 1096, 1101, 1105, 1119, 1264, 1436, 1441, 1454, 1463, 1476, 1622, 1640, 1695, 1899, 2057, 2513, 2514, 2515, 2516, 2517, 2519, 2562, p.165
Phiabi (ancestor of High Priests)—2160, 2161
Philadelphia (Egypt)—151, 849, 852, 1959
Philadelphia (city of Decapolis)—849
Philip (king of Macedonia) (1)—1884, 2034, 2738
Philip (tetrarch, son of Herod I and Cleopatra) (6)—2335, 2345, 2498, 2522, 2886, 2891, 2909
Philippion (son of Ptolemy King of Chalcis)—130
Philo of Alexandria—3018
Philopater (king of Cilicia)—1949
Phoabes, see Phiabi—
Phobes, see Phiabi—
Phoenicia—440, 498, 529, 1216, 2236, 2253-2255
Phoenicians—1771, 2256
Phormio (Athenian Commander)—786
Photius—308, 1036, 1046, 2909
Phraaspa (Parthian city)—68
Phraatakes—68
Phraates III (king of Parthia)—60
Phraates IV (king of Parthia)—57, 68, 139, 448, 585, 588, 2337, 2341
Pillars of Heracles, see Strait of Gibraltar
Plain of Asochis (Beit Netofa Valley)—1951
Plain of Massyas (Bekaa Valley)—440, 517, 2255
Plain of Sharon—1982, 2236
Plutarch—1599
Pollio (sage)—11, 12, 14, 16-19, 21-23, 96, 116, 1019, 2596, 2601, p.4
Pollio (host of Herod's sons in Rome, possibly C. Asinius Pollio or P. Vedius Pollio)—2339, 2341, 2342
Polemon (king of Pontus and the Bosporus)—28, 1183, 1949
Polybius—1599
Polycarp (martyr)—1005
Polycharmus, Claudius Tiberius Polycharmus—1650
Pompey—43, 47, 56, 61, 133, 440, 498, 534, 621, 1042, 1059, 1064, 1065, 1125, 1218, 1377-1380, 1382, 1383, 1793, 1938, 1963, 2256, 2804
Pontic Mountains—532
Pontius Pilate (governor of Judea)—2883
Pontus—28, 1183, 1944
Pool of Siloam—2949
Postumus, Marcus Vipsanius Agrippa Postumus (son of Marcus Agrippa and Julia)—2508
Priene—2530
Proteros—993
Prusias II (king of Bithynia)—2337
Ptolemaic kingdom—1665, 2738
Ptolemais (Acco)—1216, 1220, 1387, 1951, 2209, 2521
Ptolemy I Soter (king of Egypt) (1)—528
Ptolemy II Philadelphus (king of Egypt) (2)—1216, 2133, 2642, 2809
Ptolemy III Euergetes (king of Egypt) (3)—2867
Ptolemy IV Philopator (king of Egypt) (4)—2643, 3015
Ptolemy V Epiphanes (king of Egypt) (5)—2526, 3059
Ptolemy XI Auletes (king of Egypt) (9)—142
Ptolemy XIV (brother of Cleopatra VII)—506
Ptolemy (king of Chalcis)—130, 440, 1111, 2350
Ptolemy (son of Mennaeus)—517
Ptolemy Caesarion, see Caesarion
Publius Posthumus—722
Pula—2522
Pydna—2337
Pylos (fortress)—1941
Pyrrhus—1542
Pythagoras—2604, 2607, 2608, 3071
Pythius (the Lydian)—2804
Pythodoris of Pontus—1944
Qarn Sartaba—1105
Qasr el-Mushetta—1099
Qos—1640, 1647, 1648, 1651, 1663
Queen of Sheba—2860
Quintus Didius—1188, 1190
Qumran—141, 1580, 1687, 2602, 2622
Rahab—1928
Ramat el-Khalil—1647
Raphia—1223
Razis—121, 915, 2479
Rebecca—2155
Red Sea—520, 1188, 1576, 2121, 2122, 2236, 2424
Rehoboam (king of Judah)—767, 1093
Remoria—2236
Rhodes—167, 613, 939, 1121, 1123, 1124, 1190, 1234, 1239, 1301, 1370, 1417, 1793, 3012
Rhome—2311
Robinson's Arch—1763, 2939, 2945, 2947, 2949
Roma (deity)—1823, 2235, 2311, 2312, 2441, 2442, 2540
Romans—8, 11, 13, 28, 29, 42, 49, 57, 64, 68, 108, 112, 133, 142, 398, 402, 531, 532, 588, 609, 614, 639, 693, 722, 767, 789, 947, 1157, 1158, 1183, 1194, 1196, 1390, 1596, 1599, 1653, 1707, 1710, 1711, 1761, 1796, 1804, 1902, 1935, 1953, 2005, 2030, 2057, 2116, 2196, 2200, 2202, 2235, 2299, 2312, 2396, 2450, 2480, 2627, 2643, 2699, 2742, 2747, 2751, 2879, 2880, 2888, 2898-2900, 2907, 2917, 2920, 2922, 2924, 2953, 3016, 3058, 3060, p.xiii
Rome—5, 13, 28, 29, 36, 38, 51, 99, 133, 170, 182, 249, 502, 526, 581, 583, 589, 609, 767, 1121, 1123, 1158, 1162, 1388, 1610, 1760, 1766, 1793, 1796, 1801, 1932, 2030, 2047, 2050, 2196, 2199, 2311, 2312, 2332, 2335, 2337, 2344, 2339, 2398, 2400, 2449, 2479, 2505, 2510, 2520, 2521, 2548, 2747, 2749, 2789, 2804, 2807, 2891, 2907-2910, 2912, 2913, 3042, 3058, p.ix-xi, xiii, 3, 4
Romulus—2311
Royal Portico (in Athens)—2789
Royal Portico (in Jerusalem)—2678, 2789, 2811, 2812, 2814, 2945, 2955, 2956, 2962, 2963, 2967, 2971, 2978, 2985, 2997, 2999, 3006, 3037
Sabbion—252, 253, 255, 277
Sadducees—30
Salome (sister of Herod) (1)—56, 230, 366, 449, 450, 453-455, 457, 459, 462, 463, 469, 484, 493, 496, 1106, 1113, 1115, 1239, 1264, 1339, 1340-1342, 1345, 1398, 1399, 1410-1412, 1414, 1416, 1422, 1423, 1426, 1432, 1435, 1439, 1441, 1447-1449, 1451-1453, 1455, 1464, 1476, 1479, 1485, 1487, 1488, 1491, 1496, 1498, 1502, 1507, 1520, 1551, 1559, 1626, 1640, 1653, 1654, 1656, 1663, 1680, 1681, 1686-1688, 1690, 1693-1695, 1703, 1743, p.3, 165, 166
Salome-Alexandra, see Alexandra I
Salassi—2359
Salkhad—520, 652
Samaias (sage)—11, 12, 14-19, 21-23, 116, 1019, 2596, 2601, p.4
Samaria (region)—9, 138, 1105, 1365, 1378-1380, 1580, 1603, 1941, 1944, 1951, 1982, 2236, 2723, 2891, 2921
Samaria-Sebaste (city)—138, 536, 1379, 1380, 1580, 1593, 1601, 1631, 1634, 1763, 1823, 1930, 1936, 1939, 1941, 1943-1948, 1950, 1953, 1956, 1957, 1970-1972, 1974, 1977, 1982-1987, 1990, 1994-1997, 1999, 2000, 2003, 2004, 2032, 2135, 2197, 2198, 2212, 2231-2233, 2235, 2253, 2312, 2332, 2333, 2337, 2343, 2442, 2522, 2540, 2690, 2702, 2710, 2712, 2795, 2921
Samarian wilderness—1580
Samos (island)—1123, 2521, 2607
Samosata—2254
Samson—477, 2099

Samuel—120, 139, 2106, 2633
Sanabasarus/Sheshbazzar—2777
Sappho—155
Sarah—1576
Saramallas—106
Scaurus, Marcus Aemilius Scaurus—1766
Scipio, Publius Cornelius Scipio Africanus—804
Scipio, Publius Scipio—804
Scipio, Quintus Caecilius Metellus Pius Scipio Nasica (governor of Syria)—47, 1428
Scythopolis—1928, 1951, 2071, 2236
Sea of Galilee—440, 517, 621, 625, 1377, 1378, 2071, 2345, 2406, 2445, 2497
Sebaste, see Samaria-Sebaste
Sebastus—2212
Second Temple—156, 1996, 2722, 2723, 2727, 2729-2731, 2736, 2739-2742, 2753, 2762, 2768, 2777, 2813, 3050, 3061
Seleucia (on the Tigris)—72, 73, 528
Seleucus IV (Seleucid king) (4)—225
Seneca (the Elder)—1
Seneca (the Younger)—502, 1522, 2116
Sextus Caesar—80
Shemaya/Shammai (sage)—14
Shimon Bothon—2143
Si'a—925, 2312
Sibyls—2673
Sicarii—1870, 2154
Sicily—736
Sidon—531, 1763, 2312
Sikimon/Shechem—461
Simon (royal slave)—139
Simon (the son of Boethus, High Priest)—2137, 2141-2143, 2158, 2161, 2162
Simon (the Essene)—2604, 2625
Simon the Hasmonean—108, 1382, 1505, 2702, 2744, 2745, 2871, 2872, 2984
Simon the Just (High Priest)—2849, 3010, 3015
Simon bar Giora—2620
Sinai Desert—520, 1223
Smyrna—2275, 2311
Soada/Suweida—625
Socrates—167, 1147, 1462, 1492, 1522, 1530, 1867, 1913, 2103
Soemus—176, 368, 1109, 1111, 1113, 1114, 1245, 1255, 1257, 1258, 1260, 1261, 1266, 1267, 1271, 1280, 1284, 1288-1290, 1304, 1361, 1364-1366, 1466, 1469, 1471, 1473, 1554, 1622, 1748, p.165, 166
Solomon—2238, 2641, 2642, 2723, 2727-2729, 2753, 2778, 2801, 2814, 2823, 2826, 2828, 2829, 2856, 3050, 3051
Solomon's Pools—2184
Solomon's Portico—2814, 2856
Solomon's Temple—2727, 2729, 2781, 2785, 2824, 2841, 2847, 2848, 2850, 2856
Solon—911, 2433
Sons of Baba—1602, 1644, 1645, 1653, 1679, 1695, 1699, 1702, 1704, 1705, 1712-1716, 1719, 1720, 1727, 1730, 1731, 1735, 1738, 1741, 1745-1748, 1750, 2192, 2619, p.3
Sophists—503, 2624
Sosius, Gaius Sosius—1, 4-6, 16, 37, 38, 1491, 1709, 1725, 1796, 2466
Sossius, see Sosius
South Arabia—1380, 2424
Southern Hauran—520, 619
Spain—2337, 2400, 2453
Stobi (city in Macedonia)—1650
Strabo of Amaseia—45, 48, 2119, 2120, 2122
Strait of Gibraltar—2299
Straton (king of Sidon)—1383
Straton's Tower—1383, 1949, 1950, 2135, 2212, 2235, 2237, 2257, 2625
Sumuis/Shimei (the son of Gera)—2415
Susa—2804
Syllaeus—230, 413, 603, 1559, 2119, 2121
Sychem/Sychemmes—2155
Syria (region)—1771, 2071, 2073, 2081, 2084, 2329, 2390, 2442, 2443, 2514
Syria (province)—2360, 2442, 2443, 2452, 2500, 2503, 2520, 2514, 2543, 2665, 2804, 2883, 2884, 2886, 2893, 2895, 2913, 2914
Syrians—72, 106, 440, 2038, 2074, 2077, 2745
Tacitus—1, 35, 2311, 2804
Tarentum—1542
Tarichea—2909,
Tarsus—142, 146, 167
Taurus Mountains—498
Tayma—1580
Teiresias—1675
Tell el-Yehudiye, see Leontopolis
Tell Hesban, see Heshbon/Esbun
Tell Megiddo—1957
Tell Sush, see Gaba
Tellus (Athenian)—911
Temple (of Jerusalem)—14, 141, 264, 273, 531, 847, 1019, 1605-1607, 1610-1612, 1651, 1701, 1710, 1750, 1753, 1754, 1762-1764, 1818, 1833, 1861, 1936, 1938, 1939, 2010, 2126, 2124, 2136, 2221, 2234, 2238, 2250, 2536, 2678, 2680, 2683-2685, 2688-2690, 2693, 2695, 2698, 2702, 2709, 2718, 2720, 2722-2724, 2727-2731, 2736-2742, 2753, 2754, 2757, 2760-2762, 2767-2769, 2771, 2773, 2777, 2778, 2781, 2785-2787, 2794, 2796, 2808-2814, 2817-2822, 2824, 2826, 2831, 2832, 2834, 2835, 2838, 2839, 2841, 2844, 2845, 2847-2851, 2855-2857, 2860, 2862, 2864, 2865, 2869, 2878, 2888, 2889, 2919, 2929, 2932, 2937, 2938, 2940, 2941, 2943-1946, 2950, 2951, 2953, 2954, 2961, 2976, 2978, 2989, 2999, 3005, 3006, 3008-3010, 3013 3017, 3023, 3026, 3028, 3037-3040, 3042, 3043, 3046, 3047, 3050, 3051, 3057, 3058, 3060-3062, 3071, 3073, 3078, p.xiii, xxxv, xxxvi, 3, 4
Temple of Apollo (Rome)—29, 2755
Temple Mount—400, 1606, 1937, 1939, 2678, 2794, 2818, 2819, 2821, 2826, 2844, 2845, 2855, 2940, 2943, 3028
Teutoburg Forest (battle of)—64
Thebans—882
Thebes—1675, 2479
Themistocles—1794
Thermopylae (battle of)—786
Three Sages (the Three Sages)—1738, 1890
Thucydides—96, 704, 725, 767, 1859, 2617, 2746, 2751
Tiberias—2909
Tiberius (Tiberius Claudius Nero, emperor)—587, 588, 2285, 2879, 2881, 2882
Tiberius Julius Alexander (procurator of Judea)—2896
Ticinus—804
Tigranes II ("the Great", King of Armenia)—532, 580, 1218
Tigranes III (King of Armenia)—588, 589
Tigris—72, 73
Timagenes—960
Tiridates—68
Tiro (soldier of Herod)—1953
Titus—38, 711, 789, 1804, 3013, 3016
Tobiads—324
Trachonitis/Trachon—27, 1953, 2332, 2337, 2345, 2347, 2349, 2350, 2353, 2356, 2357, 2359, 2361, 2363, 2364, 2369, 2370, 2375, 2385, 2387, 2389, 2395-2398, 2417, 2423, 2443, 2446, 2449, 2494, 2495, 2499, 2909, p.4
Transjordan—1771
Triple Gate—2954
Tripoli—528
Tryphon—2630
Tullus—767
Turin—1794
Turnus Rufus—2631
Tyche—1642, 2308
Tyre—81, 106, 531, 994, 2312, 2526, 2860
Tyropoeon Valley—1765, 2126, 2941, 2947-2949, 2959
Ulatha (region)—2350, 2395, 2497, 2499, 2525
Umm Qais—1377
Upper City (of Jerusalem)—1606, 1763, 2125, 2126, 2187, 2794, 2941
Urtas—2184
Uzziah—1802
Valley of the Cheesemakers, see Tyropoeon Valley

INDEX OF ANCIENT PERSONS AND PLACES

Valley of Esdraelon—1951, 2236
Valley of Jizreel—1951
Valley of Megiddo—1951
Varro, Marcus Terentius Varro (governor of Syria)—2359-2362, 2364, 2366, 2393, 2446
Varus, Publius Quintilius Varus—64, 1454
Vedius, P. Vedius Pollio, see Pollio
Ventidius, Publius Ventidius Bassus, see Bassus
Vespasian—711, 1390, 2633, 2807
Vibius Marsus (governor of Syria)—2893
Virgil—155
Vitellius, Lucius Vitellius—1822, 2880, 2883, 2884, 2886, 2888, 2889, 2901, 2902, 2907, 2912, 2913, 2915
Vitellius, Publius Vitellius—2883
Wadi al-Far'a—1580
Wadi of Egypt—3051
Wadi Hasa—986
Wadi Qelt—286
Wadi Yasul—1763
Warren's Gate—2939, 2943
Water Gate—3018
Women's Gate—3027
Wilson's Arch—2786, 2939, 2941, 2943
Xerxes I (king of Persia)—140, 767, 786, 858, 1434, 1794, 2723
Yarmuk (river)—1377, 2445
Yahweh—1647
Yehoyarib—2872
Yemen—2122
Yohanan ben Zakkai (Rabbi)—249
Zama (battle of)—804
Zealots—711, 789
Zechariah—66, 2725
Zedekiah (king of Judah)—2804
Zenodorus—2332, 2349-2352, 2356, 2361, 2364, 2388, 2393-2399, 2408, 2413, 2417, 2418, 2420, 2421, 2425, 2443, 2448-2450, 2488, 2489, 2491, 2492, 2494, 2503, 2524, p.4
Zerubbabel—2723, 3050, 3061
Zeus—507, 1823, 2311, 2312, 2615
Zillah—2137
Zoara—986
Zipporah—2624

Simons, J. 985, 1939, 2680, 2684, 2727, 2789, 2810, 2814, 2824, 2829, 2830, 2849, 2854, 2860, 2864, 2867, 2944, 3040
Slater, D. A. 155
Smallwood, E. M. 597, 925, 1528, 1653, 1654, 1823, 1854, 1938, 2124, 2337, 2339, 2350, 2440, 2510, 2680, 2891, 3042
Smith, M. 342, 718, 725, 789, 806, 827, 1753, 1859, 1912, 1966, 2005, 2299, 2625,
Spiess, F. 3021
Stählin, G. 29
Stein, A. 2047
Stern, M. 9, 16, 42, 45, 48, 53, 72, 73, 99, 106, 178, 256, 359, 404, 536, 597, 990, 1183, 1197, 1365, 1473, 2030, 2143, 2160, 2236, 2329, 2348, 2452
Sukenik, E. L. 1930
Sullivan, R. D. 80, 586, 587
Sydenham, E. A. 582
Syme, R. 28, 48
Taylor, J. 2607
Taylor, J. E. 2136, 2312, 2522
Teasdale, A. 1939
Thackeray, H. S. J. 212, 600, 894, 911, 919, 1066, 1498, 1596, 1686, 1829, 1912, 2791, 2814
Thesleff, H. 2607
Trebilco, P. R. 1611
Treu, K. 759, 1145
Tromp, J. 1833
Tsafrir, Y. 286, 621, 984, 1099, 1105, 1216, 1223, 1378, 1380-1383, 1944
Udoh, F. E. 28, 26, 531, 591, 592, 610, 1067, 1140, 1379, 1932, 2030, 2051, 2236, 2502, 2503, 2517, 2542, 2543, 2683, 2709
van Beek, D. 3013-3015
van Bruggen, J. 36
van der Horst, P. W. 121
van Groningen, B. A. 1046, 1286
van Henten, J. W. 6, 11, 28, 33, 40, 50, 64, 65-67, 112, 121, 125, 142, 155, 167, 189, 199, 219, 224, 230, 246, 268, 324, 395, 397, 450, 464, 468, 469, 503, 504, 508, 512, 558, 559, 590, 607, 630, 639, 703, 704, 710, 711, 731, 732, 743, 772, 827, 911, 965, 1021, 1037, 1055, 1079, 1150, 1166, 1211, 1391, 1398, 1404, 1407, 1474, 1505, 1522, 1525, 1612, 1638, 1639, 1650, 1665, 1716, 1738, 1749, 1750, 1757, 1758, 1760, 1796, 1823, 1827, 1838, 1861, 1865, 1890, 1894, 1895, 1913, 1926, 1932, 1966, 2093, 2117, 2154, 2311, 2439, 2447, 2467, 2478, 2479, 2541, 2555, 2557, 2562, 2590, 2617, 2624, 2631, 2639, 2641, 2662, 2678, 2679, 2681, 2695, 2702, 2723, 2787, 2864, 2871, 2872, 3059, 3070, 3077
van Unnik, W. C. 2645
Vermes, G. 5, 12, 14, 36, 56, 57, 60, 61, 73, 76, 127, 129, 133, 134, 138, 141, 144, 214, 223-225, 255, 264, 273, 301, 356, 494, 519, 534, 536, 538, 599, 678, 1037, 1043, 1059, 1095, 1110, 1377, 1378, 1380-1383, 1528, 1551, 1651, 1665, 1763, 1944, 1957, 1958, 1960, 2004-2006, 2030, 2047, 2122, 2124, 2137, 2143, 2160, 2161, 2178, 2256, 2329, 2337, 2345, 2348, 2350, 2353, 2359, 2403, 2440, 2441, 2486, 2498, 2499, 2503, 2514, 2526, 2541, 2566, 2602, 2680, 2738, 2872, 2876, 2880, 2883, 2891, 2893, 2909, 2913, 2921, 3015, 3023, 3027, 3040, 3058, 3059
Versnel, H. S. 38, 2480
Villalba i Varneda, P. 704, 712, 789, 839, 2672
Villeneuve, F. 986
Vogel, M. 949, 1576, 1630, 1654, 1932, 2137, 2160, 2309, 2352, 2409, 2680, p.165
von Destinon, J. 494, 945, p.167
von Reibnitz, B. 1145
von Steuben, H. 2199
Vössing, K. 119, 120, 429, 1434
Wacholder, B. Z. 36
Wagenvoort, H. 1087
Wakker, G. C. 761, 804, 808, 824, 910, 995
Walker, S. 534
Walton, F. R. 772
Weber, D. 520
Wes, M. A. 211, 282, 332, 403, 540, 645, 671, 695, 2814
Weiler, I. 1775
Wellhausen, J. 402, 1045
White, J. L. 142, 143, 151, 522, 1001
Wikgren, A. 11, 19, 25, 36, 54, 72, 81, 97, 111, 116, 146, 211, 239, 258, 282, 290, 308, 342, 360, 366, 380, 403, 405, 407, 440, 507, 510, 540, 582, 588, 600, 606, 611, 621, 641, 645, 657, 671, 678, 695, 772, 847, 857, 861, 878, 908, 921, 945, 1037, 1045, 1046, 1066, 1108, 1175, 1190, 1202, 1280, 1287, 1296, 1334, 1337, 1362, 1397, 1428, 1440, 1441, 1539, 1557, 1563, 1576, 1577, 1591, 1642, 1654, 1663, 1685, 1746, 1772, 1817, 1829, 1870, 1957, 1975, 2043, 2092, 2134, 2186, 2240, 2275, 2339, 2395, 2441, 2503, 2675, 2683, 2729, 2776, 2779, 2784, 2800, 2803, 2814, 2815, 2816, 2824, 2833, 2941, 3000, 3005, 3035, 3042, 3044
Wilkinson, J. 2795
Willrich, H. 301, 1805, 2339
Wilson Jones, M. 2983
Windisch, H. 731
Winston, D. 2641
Wiseman, T. P. 1884
Wittenburg, A. 251
Woelcke, K. 1796, 1823
Wyke, M. 543
Yardeni, A. 1687
Zachos, K. L. 1796
Zanker, P. 1158
Zayadine, F. 1763
Zeisel, W. 371
Ziegler, K.-H. 57, 60, 71, 448, 508,
Ziehen, L. 1771
Zuckermann, B. 36